THE OXFORD HANDBOOK OF

THE THEORY OF INTERNATIONAL LAW

THE OXFORD HANDBOOK OF

THE THEORY OF INTERNATIONAL LAW

Edited by

ANNE ORFORD

and

FLORIAN HOFFMANN

with

MARTIN CLARK

OXFORD
UNIVERSITY PRESS

UNIVERSITY PRESS

Great Clarendon Street, Oxford, OX2 6DP,
United Kingdom

Oxford University Press is a department of the University of Oxford.
It furthers the University's objective of excellence in research, scholarship,
and education by publishing worldwide. Oxford is a registered trade mark of
Oxford University Press in the UK and in certain other countries

© The several contributors 2016

The moral rights of the authors have been asserted

First Edition published in 2016

Impression: 1

Published in the United States of America by Oxford University Press
198 Madison Avenue, New York, NY 10016, United States of America

British Library Cataloguing in Publication Data
Data available

Library of Congress Control Number: 2016939860

ISBN 978-0-19-870195-8

Printed and bound by
CPI Group (UK) Ltd, Croydon, CR0 4YY

In memory of Hendrik Meyeringh (1946–2012)
and William Orford (1930–2015)

Acknowledgements

The publication of this *Handbook* would not have been possible without many people and their institutional backers who contributed to this project.

In the first place, thanks are due to Oxford University Press and the editors who commissioned and accompanied this *Handbook*, namely John Louth, Merel Alstein, and Emma Endean.

We are grateful to our assistant (student) editors who undertook painstaking copy-editing and proofing work: from Melbourne Law School Kasia Pawlikowski and Anna Saunders, and from the Willy Brandt School Ana Andrun, Thomas Crenshaw, Nripdeep Kaur, Raphael Zimmermann Robiatti, Heidi Ross, and Karen Simbulan. We also thank Hamish Robertson-Orford who carefully prepared the Notes on Contributors at very short notice.

Our heartfelt thanks go to the *Handbook's* Assistant Editor, Martin Clark, who is currently completing an MPhil at Melbourne Law School and soon to begin doctoral studies at the London School of Economics. Martin has made an outstanding contribution to the editing of this *Handbook*, copy-editing and critically engaging with all of the essays, carrying out his responsibilities with efficiency, intellectual curiosity, humour, and diplomacy, and overseeing the work of the student editors with care and generosity.

We held two authors' workshops in Amsterdam and Melbourne to discuss draft chapters, and are very grateful to the sponsors of those workshops: in Amsterdam, Vrije Universiteit Amsterdam (thanks to the support of Wouter Werner and Geoff Gordon), the European Society of International Law, Oxford University Press, and Melbourne Law School; and in Melbourne, the Institute for International Law and the Humanities (thanks to the support of Dianne Otto), the Sydney Centre for International Law (thanks to the support of Fleur Johns), and Melbourne Law School.

We gratefully acknowledge the funding for editorial assistance on this project provided by an Australian Research Council Discovery Grant (Project ID: DP0770640).

We owe a debt to both of our families, who have patiently supported our work on this project over the past few years, from shifting home bases in Melbourne, Lund, Erfurt, and Rio de Janeiro.

Finally, we thank all the contributors for their commitment to this project and the creativity they brought to their scholarship. It has been a privilege and a pleasure to work with these chapters and their authors.

Anne Orford and Florian Hoffmann

Melbourne & Rio de Janeiro, August 2015

Contents

....

PART II APPROACHES

PART III REGIMES AND DOCTRINES

PART IV DEBATES

TABLE OF CASES

INTERNATIONAL COURTS AND TRIBUNALS

Arbitration Commission of the Peace Conference on Yugoslavia

Eritrea-Ethiopia Claims Commission

European Court of Human Rights (ECtHR)

International Arbitral Tribunals

International Centre for Settlement of Investment Disputes (ICSID)

International Court of Justice (ICJ)

International Criminal Court (ICC)

International Criminal Tribunal for the former Yugoslavia (ICTY)

Permanent Court of International Justice (PCIJ)

World Trade Organization (WTO)

NATIONAL JURISDICTIONS

Australia

Canada

Germany

Israel

Netherlands

United Kingdom

United States

TABLE OF LEGISLATION

INTERNATIONAL INSTRUMENTS

INTERNATIONAL LAW COMMISSION
ARTICLES

European Union Regulations

National Legislation

France

United Kingdom

United States

Notes on Contributors

Antony Anghie is Samuel D Thurman Professor of Law at the University of Utah.

Jason Beckett is Assistant Professor of Law at the American University in Cairo.

Samantha Besson is Professor of Public International Law and European Law and Co-Director of the European Law Institute at the University of Fribourg.

Martin Clark is Research Fellow and MPhil Candidate at Melbourne Law School, and MPhil/PhD Candidate at the London School of Economics and Political Science.

Matthew Craven is Professor of International Law and Director of the Centre for the Study of Colonialism, Empire, and International Law at SOAS, University of London.

Dan Danielsen is Professor of Law and Associate Dean for Academic Affairs at Northeastern University.

Jean d'Aspremont is Professor of Public International Law and Co-Director of the Manchester International Law Centre at the University of Manchester, and Professor of International Legal Theory at the University of Amsterdam.

Megan Donaldson is Junior Research Fellow in the History of International Law at King's College, Cambridge.

Filipe Dos Reis is Research Associate in International Relations at the University of Erfurt.

Mónica García-Salmones Rovira is Research Fellow and Lecturer in International Law at the University of Helsinki.

Ben Golder is Senior Lecturer in Law at the University of New South Wales.

Peter Goodrich is Professor of Law at the Benjamin N Cardozo School of Law.

Geoff Gordon is Assistant Professor of Law at Vrije Universiteit Amsterdam.

Florian Hoffmann is Professor of Law and Director of the Willy Brandt School of Public Policy at the University of Erfurt.

Robert Howse is Lloyd C Nelson Professor of International Law at New York University.

Stephen Humphreys is Associate Professor of Law at the London School of Economics and Political Science.

Fleur Johns is Professor of Law at the University of New South Wales.

Emmanuelle Tourme-Jouannet is Professor of Law at Sciences Po, Paris.

Daniel Joyce is Lecturer in Law at the University of New South Wales.

Oliver Jütersonke is Head of Research for the Centre on Conflict, Development and Peacebuilding (CCDP) at the Graduate Institute of International and Development Studies in Geneva and Research Associate at the Zurich University Centre for Ethics.

Jörg Kammerhofer is Senior Research Fellow and Senior Lecturer in Law at the University of Freiburg.

Oliver Kessler is Professor of International Relations at the University of Erfurt.

Benedict Kingsbury is Murry and Ida Becker Professor of Law and Director of the Institute for International Law and Justice at New York University.

Jan Klabbers is Academy Professor (Martti Ahtisaari Chair) at the University of Helsinki, and Visiting Research Professor at Erasmus School of Law, Rotterdam.

Robert Knox is Lecturer in Law at the University of Liverpool.

Outi Korhonen is Professor of International Law at the University of Turku.

Martti Koskenniemi is Academy Professor of Law and Director of the Erik Castrén Institute of International Law and Human Rights at the University of Helsinki, Hauser Visiting Professor at New York University, and Professorial Fellow at the University of Melbourne.

Dino Kritsiotis is Professor of Public International Law and Head of the International Humanitarian Law Unit, Human Rights Law Centre, University of Nottingham.

Randall Lesaffer is Professor of Legal History at Tilburg Law School and Part-Time Professor of International and European Legal History at the University of Leuven.

Lauri Mälksoo is Professor of International Law at the University of Tartu.

Frédéric Mégret is Associate Professor of Law and William Dawson Scholar at McGill University.

Horatia Muir Watt is Professor of Law at Sciences Po, Paris.

Vasuki Nesiah is Associate Professor of Law at New York University

Gregor Noll is Professor of International Law at Lund University.

Sarah Nouwen is University Senior Lecturer in Law at the University of Cambridge.

Anne Orford is Redmond Barry Distinguished Professor, Michael D Kirby Chair of International Law, and ARC Kathleen Fitzpatrick Laureate Fellow at the University of Melbourne, and Raoul Wallenberg Visiting Chair of International Human Rights and Humanitarian Law at the Raoul Wallenberg Institute and Lund University.

Yoriko Otomo is Lecturer of Law at SOAS, University of London.

Dianne Otto is Francine V McNiff Chair in Human Rights Law and Former Director of the Institute for International Law and the Humanities at the University of Melbourne.

Umut Özsu is Associate Professor of Law at the University of Manitoba.

Rose Parfitt is a Lecturer in Law at Kent Law School and an ARC Discovery Early Career Researcher at Melbourne Law School.

Reut Paz is Senior Fellow at the Justus Liebig-University Giessen.

Anne Peters is Professor of Law and Managing Director at the Max Planck Institute for Comparative Public Law and International Law, Heidelberg.

Kerry Rittich is Professor of Law, Women and Gender Studies, and Public Policy and Governance and Associate Dean of the JD Program at the University of Toronto.

Teemu Ruskola is Professor of Law at Emory University, Atlanta.

Hengameh Saberi is Assistant Professor of Law at Osgoode Hall Law School.

Toni Selkälä is a Doctoral Candidate at the University of Turku.

Gerry Simpson is Professor of Law at the London School of Economics and Political Science.

Thomas Skouteris is Associate Professor of Law at the American University in Cairo.

Chantal Thomas is Professor of Law and Director of the Clarke Initiative for Law and Development in the Middle East and North Africa at Cornell Law School.

Rodrigo Vallejo is Visiting Research Scholar at the Institute for International Law and Justice, New York University.

Martine Julia van Ittersum is Senior Lecturer in History at the University of Dundee.

Jochen von Bernstorff is Chair of Constitutional Law, Public International Law and Human Rights Law at the University of Tübingen.

Wouter Werner is Professor of Law at Vrije Universiteit Amsterdam.

Deborah Whitehall is Lecturer in Law at Monash University.

INTRODUCTION

THEORIZING INTERNATIONAL LAW

ANNE ORFORD

AND FLORIAN HOFFMANN

1 THE PRACTICE OF THEORIZING ABOUT INTERNATIONAL LAW

THEORIZING is an inherent part of the practice of international law. The aim of this *Handbook* is to provide readers with a sense of the diverse projects that have been understood or characterized as exercises in theorizing about international law over the past centuries, explore which aspects of international law have seemed important to theorize about at different times and places, and analyse the uses to which different theories of international law have been put. What do international lawyers think of as theory, and how does it relate to past and present practices of the discipline or the profession? What is the proper relation between theories of international law and other domains of theorizing, such as philosophy, sociology, or history? Should the practice of international law be measured against theories, values, standards, or ideals derived from outside the discipline, or against the values embedded in professional practices, vocabularies, or rhetoric?

Theorizing about international law has of course taken many different forms. During periods in which international law has been at its most precarious, theories of international law have attempted to demonstrate that laws governing the conduct of sovereigns exist at all. At other times, the theory of international law has been concerned with the attempt to connect emerging forms of international legal practice to a philosophical or historical tradition from which international law is said to originate, or to develop a method for interpreting or systematizing international law. The relation of international law to the modern state has been the focus of much theoretical work, both by those seeking to challenge the state's role as the privileged subject of international law or by those seeking to argue that recognition of its importance and status have been lost. And at moments when the varied projects of international law have been at their most politically contested,[1] international legal theory has been concerned to provide accounts of the underlying justifications for rules of international law, the reasons why international law is or should be binding upon states or other actors, and the relation of international law to values such as justice, peace, dignity, or equality.

Theoretical interest in questions about the concept, nature, function, legitimacy, and orientation of international law has grown markedly over the past decades. Work on the theory of international law is one of the most dynamic and fast-developing fields in contemporary international legal scholarship. Established international law journals now regularly include theoretically focused articles, while new journals have been established to meet the growing demand for venues in which such scholarship can be published. Major societies of international law have active theory interest groups. In addition, there has been a renaissance in publishing in the field of international legal theory. Much of the most exciting new research in international law has been concerned with exploring foundational concepts and questions; developing new intellectual histories of the discipline; thinking in innovative ways about the relation between the theory, history, and practice of international law; or providing fresh interpretations of key figures and traditions in the field.

To some extent the current state of international legal theory should not come as a surprise. As a form of law conceived to represent, constitute, and govern the modern system of territorially based nation-states, international law has always been seen both as a function of the powers that be and as governing those powers

---

[1] On the projects of international law, see J Crawford and M Koskenniemi, 'Introduction' in J Crawford and M Koskenniemi (eds), *The Cambridge Companion to International Law* (CUP Cambridge 2012) 1–21, at 14–15 (noting that 'Unlike other legal disciplines, international law usually involves a commitment on the part of those who have recourse to it. It is seen as more than just a neutral arbiter between disputing states or other actors but as bearing in itself some blueprint for improving the world, or those aspects of the world where it operates…Christianity, civilisation, modernity, peace, development, self-determination—these are some notions that have been regarded as the gift brought to the world with the expansion of international law's more technical rules and institutions…Because of international law's strong ideological pull, its operation cannot be understood without examining what projects it invites its practitioners to participate in'); A Orford, 'Constituting Order' in *The Cambridge Companion to International Law* (n 1) 271–89, at 272 (noting that international law has been embraced 'as a vehicle for wide-ranging public projects designed to reorder the world, from dividing up Africa at the end of the nineteenth century, to ending the scourge of war, managing decolonisation, humanising warfare and liberalising trade in the twentieth century').

from an independent vantage point. As a result, international law has long been a methodologically unique and theoretically engaged field of law. It articulates a horizontal, rather than vertical, normativity in which there is no universal sovereign. Its traditional sources bind it to the reality of inter-state relations, yet it is also meant to constrain and configure those relations. Dispute resolution in international law inevitably also raises questions about the grounds of jurisdiction and the particular normativity that is to apply in a given situation.

Indeed, despite claims that international law is inherently a practical rather than a theoretical discipline, the practice of international law draws international lawyers into contemplation of some of the core concerns of politics and philosophy, such as the nature and limits of sovereignty, the basis of obligation in international affairs, the concept of responsibility, the relationship of international and domestic order, the rights of war and peace, and the place of the individual in modern political communities. Prior to the nineteenth century, those who are now characterized as the founding fathers of international law tended to be general scholars in the humanist or scholastic traditions, who drew upon a wide array of vocabularies and methods to deduce the law of nations.[2] Theory was at the heart of their practice.

As the profession of international law became more clearly established during the nineteenth and early twentieth centuries, the kinds of theoretical work typically undertaken by international lawyers shifted from the 'grand theory' approach which seeks to understand the role of law in international relations or to grasp the essential nature of international law, to the more technical forms of theorizing involved in applying an increasingly canonical body of well-established rules, principles, and concepts to the conduct of states and other international actors. The positivist and dogmatic traditions that were increasingly felt to be appropriate for an age of democratic states insisted that international law was no longer something that could be assembled from equity, natural law, local custom, judicial precedent, or moral standards by a group of erudite men.[3] Yet those positivist and dogmatic traditions would nonetheless depend for their legitimacy upon their association with (theoretically informed) foundational commitments to scientific reason and the realization of world peace and economic interdependence through law.[4]

---

[2] See further R Lesaffer, 'Roman Law and the Intellectual History of International Law' in this *Handbook*; M Koskenniemi, 'Transformations of Natural Law: Germany 1648–1815' in this *Handbook*; MJ van Ittersum, 'Hugo Grotius: The Making of a Founding Father of International Law' in this *Handbook*; E Tourme-Jouannet, 'The Critique of Classical Thought during the Interwar Period: Vattel and Van Vollenhoven' in this *Handbook*.

[3] A Carty, *Philosophy of International Law* (Edinburgh University Press Edinburgh 2007) at 2. On positivism and its relationship to democracy, see N Lacey, *A Life of HLA Hart: The Nightmare and the Noble Dream* (OUP Oxford 2004) at 5–6, 225.

[4] See further M García-Salmones, 'Early Twentieth Century Positivism Revisited' in this *Handbook*; J Kammerhofer, 'International Legal Positivism' in this *Handbook*; A Orford, 'Scientific Reason and the Discipline of International Law' (2014) 25 *European Journal of International Law* 369–85.

In the aftermath of the Second World War, however, the discipline of inter-national law began to be dominated by a more avowedly anti-theoretical ethos. That ethos registered across a range of positions, including a pragmatic American tradition that focused on problem-solving as the *telos* of law,[5] an empiricist British tradition that prided itself on rejecting any grand-level or systemic abstractions for an approach based on observation and deduction,[6] and more generally what came to be called the mainstream approach to legal analysis and interpretation that treated law as an objective phenomenon distinct from politics or morality and that starkly reduced the reflective space for theorizing. Within those traditions, the role for theory was at best as an aid to the interpretation and systematization of a body of rules, with questions about the historical pedigree, normative founda-tions, political implications, or practical consequences of those rules largely being treated as outside the remit of the international lawyer.

Of course, there were always international law scholars who resisted the strong separation of theory and practice, and who continued to reflect upon the nature and relevance of their discipline and its relationship to other forms of law and social transformation. We might think, for example, of the world order theory and policy-oriented vision of international law championed by Myres McDougal and Harold Lasswell at Yale,[7] the transformative work of early post-independence scholars such as RP Anand and TO Elias,[8] or the reflective work of legal advi-sors to foreign offices or international organizations theorizing about their prac-tice or the character of international law more generally.[9] In the United States (US), legal scholars struggled to articulate a vision of international law that was capable of responding to the transformations that were taking place in the com-position and conditions of international society due to the potent combination

[5] See further H Saberi, 'Yale's Policy Science and International Law: Between Legal Formalism and Policy Conceptualism' in this *Handbook*. For an exploration of the theoretical foundations of American pragmatism as it operates in the human rights field, see F Hoffmann, 'Human Rights, the Self and the Other: Reflections on a Pragmatic Theory of Human Rights' in A Orford (ed), *International Law and Its Others* (CUP Cambridge 2006) 221–44; B Golder, 'Theorizing Human Rights' in this *Handbook*.

[6] See the discussion in C Warbrick, 'The Theory of International Law: Is There an English Contribution?' in P Allott et al., *Theory and International Law: An Introduction* (British Institute of International and Comparative Law London 1991) 49–71.

[7] See 'Yale's Policy Science and International Law' (n 5).

[8] RP Anand, 'Rôle of the "New" Asian–African Countries in the Present International Legal Order' (1962) 56 *American Journal of International Law* 383–406; RP Anand, *New States and International Law* (Vikas New Delhi 1972); TO Elias, *Africa and the Development of International Law* (AW Sitjhoff Leiden 1972). See further A Anghie, 'Imperialism and International Legal Theory' in this *Handbook*.

[9] For example O Schachter, 'The Relation of Law, Politics and Action in the United Nations' (1963) 109 *Recueil des Cours* 165–256; R St J MacDonald, 'The Role of the Legal Adviser of Ministries of Foreign Affairs' (1977) 156 *Recueil des Cours* 377–484; P Allott, 'Language, Method and the Nature of International Law' (1971) 45 *British Year Book of International Law* 79–135; P Allott, 'Making the New International Law: Law of the Sea as Law of the Future' (1985) 11 *International Journal* 442–60.

of decolonization, the Cold War, and the emerging self-perception of the US and the USSR as superpowers with moral missions.[10] The Francophone world saw the emergence of an internal debate within positivism, in which the statist tradition of voluntarism was challenged by a universalist conception of international law as a coherent system.[11] Positivist certainties about the autonomy and inherent justice of international law were in turn critiqued by scholars associated with the *École de Reims* as well as Third World advocates for a new international economic order, both of whom accused international law of being Eurocentric and productive of inequality.[12] In Germany, an influential account of international law as oscillating between bilateralism and community interest was developed in the work of Bruno Simma and his colleagues over a number of decades,[13] while a group of Frankfurt school-inspired German and US scholars who would subsequently go on to produce critical analyses of globalization, law and development, and other transnational forms of legal ordering were beginning a fruitful dialogue.[14]

---

[10] See, from a wide literature, A A Fatouros, 'International Law and the Third World' (1964) 50 *Virginia Law Rev* 783–823; W Friedmann, 'United States Policy and the Crisis of International Law' (1965) 59 *American Journal of International Law* 857–71; R Falk, 'Law, Lawyers, and the Conduct of American Foreign Relations' (1969) 78 *Yale Law Journal* 919–34; PC Jessup, 'Non-Universal International Law' (1973) 12 *Columbia Journal Transnational Law* 415–29. For a more detailed discussion of this literature, see A Orford, 'Moral Internationalism and the Responsibility to Protect' (2013) 24 *European Journal of International Law* 83–108.

[11] For discussions of these debates within French positivism, see E Jouannet, 'Regards sur un siècle de doctrine française du droit international' (2000) 46 *Annuaire Français de Droit International* 1–57; P-M Dupuy, 'L'unité de l'ordre juridique international: cours général de droit international public' (2002) 297 *Recueil des Cours* 1–489.

[12] See eg C Chaumont, 'Cours général de droit international public' (1970) 129 *Recueil des Cours* 333–528; M Bedjaoui, *Towards a New International Economic Order* (Holmes & Meier New York 1979); M Bennouna, *Droit international du développement. Tiers-monde et interpellation du droit international* (Berger-Levrault Paris 1983); M Flory et al., (eds), *La formation des normes en droit international du développement* (CNRS Paris 1984). For an engagement with these critiques, see A Pellet, 'Contre la tyrannie de la ligne droite: aspects de la formation des normes en droit international de l'économie et du développement' (1992) 19 *Thesaurus Acroasium* 291–355.

[13] See B Simma, *Das Reziprozitätselement im Zustandekommen völkerrechtlicher Verträge* (Duncker & Humblot Berlin 1972); A Verdross and B Simma, *Universelles Völkerrecht: Theorie und Praxis* (3rd edn Duncker & Humblot Berlin 1984); B Simma, 'International Crimes: Injury and Countermeasures' in JHH Weiler, A Cassese, and M Spinedi (eds), *International Crimes of State* (De Gruyter Berlin 1989) 283–316; B Simma, 'From Bilateralism to Community Interest in International Law' (1994) 250 *Recueil des Cours* 217–384. For a comparison of the account developed by Simma to that developed in Martti Koskenniemi's *From Apology to Utopia*, see A Carty, 'Critical International Law: Recent Trends in the Theory of International Law' (1991) 2 *European Journal of International Law* 1–27, at 12 (suggesting that the difference between Simma and Koskenniemi 'is one of attitude to, rather than appreciation of, the nature of the phenomenon').

[14] See the papers from the milestone 1986 Bremen conference published in C Joerges and D Trubek (eds), *Critical Legal Theory: An American–German Debate* (Nomos Baden-Baden 1989), and the reflections on the trajectories that led to that event in C Joerges, DM Trubek, and P Zumbansen, '"Critical Legal Thought: An American–German Debate" An Introduction at the Occasion of Its Republication in the *German Law Journal* 25 Years Later' (2011) 12 *German Law Journal* 1–33.

Nonetheless, by the late twentieth century the continued dominance of a disciplinary divide between theory and practice had begun to seem increasingly constraining. Theoretical concerns were raised in mainstream scholarship with a new insistence. The perceived fragmentation of the canonical corpus of international law into distinct legal regimes, operating in an increasingly autonomous and partially incompatible fashion, triggered a new theoretical interest in the systematic and universal character of international law. Constitutionalist thinkers sought to identify emerging normative standards in the field generally, as well as within different regimes such as international trade law, international human rights law, international humanitarian law, and international criminal law. The normative entrepreneurialism and transnational activities of non-state actors fostered a new theoretical engagement with questions about the concept of sovereignty, the proper subjects of international law, and the recognized sources from which international law derived. The perennial problem of compliance continued to inspire theoretical reflection on the nature of statehood, normativity, and legal governance. Institutional and political developments following the end of the Cold War led to a revival of interest in cosmopolitanism. Many scholars in law and the humanities embraced a cosmopolitan vision of the future of international law in answer to the sense of crisis precipitated by events such as the war on terror, climate change, and the global financial crisis. They have envisaged new forms of international law capable of representing a common humanity.

In addition, a new genre of critical scholarship that emerged in the post-Cold War period began to enliven and provoke impassioned debates about the proper relation between theory and practice in international law. A series of ground-breaking texts were published in English in the late 1980s and early 1990s, giving a new energy to theoretical work in the field. They included *The Decay of International Law* by Anthony Carty, *International Legal Structures* by David Kennedy, *From Apology to Utopia* by Martti Koskenniemi, *Eunomia* by Philip Allott, 'Feminist Approaches to International Law' by Hilary Charlesworth, Christine Chinkin, and Shelley Wright, and *International Law and World Order* by BS Chimni.[15] Each of those texts registered a disenchantment with contemporary representations or self-understandings of international law, and a willingness to draw overtly on ideas and influences from 'outside' the field as a means for disciplinary renewal

---

[15] A Carty, *The Decay of International Law? A Reappraisal of the Limits of Legal Imagination in International Affairs* (Manchester University Press Manchester 1986); D Kennedy, *International Legal Structures* (Nomos Baden-Baden 1987); M Koskenniemi, *From Apology to Utopia: The Structure of International Legal Argument* (Finnish Lawyers' Publishing Helsinki 1989); P Allott, *Eunomia* (OUP Oxford 1990); H Charlesworth, C Chinkin, and S Wright, 'Feminist Approaches to International Law' (1991) 85 *American Journal of International Law* 613–45; BS Chimni, *International Law and World Order: A Critique of Contemporary Approaches* (Sage New York 1993). On the contributions of feminist and Marxist theorizing, see further D Otto, 'Feminist Approaches to International Law' in this *Handbook* and R Knox, 'Marxist Approaches to International Law' in this *Handbook*.

and innovation. Each of those texts resisted the idea that international law was in some strong sense self-contained and distinct from morality, politics, economics, or culture. And each of those texts stood apart from, and indeed in opposition to, the policy-oriented or ideologically committed theories of earlier reformist scholarship in international law. They inspired a new generation of scholars and scholarship overtly concerned with critically theorizing about international law with a view to its transformation.

2 THE CHALLENGES OF THE TURN TO THEORY

While the rapid growth of new theoretical scholarship enriched and enlivened the field of international law, it also brought with it new challenges, most notably in the realm of methodology where questions concerning disciplinary integrity and epistemic authority have loomed large. This *Handbook* offers a response to four of the challenges caused by the rapid expansion in the production of theory.

The first such challenge involves the relation of theory and practice. Some scholars have responded to the 'turn to theory' in international law by calling for a more systematic approach to theorizing, ideally to be undertaken by specialists trained in jurisprudence or philosophy. While the idea of a more specialized and less amateurish approach to theorizing may seem appealing, the danger that this represents for international law (as for other disciplines) is that the vital sense of an inherent interrelationship between the history, theory, and practice of the discipline is lost. A similar tendency to separate history, theory, and practice marked the professionalization of many fields during the twentieth century, amongst them the hard sciences, economics, and even history.[16] Examples include the failed attempts in the US to create a philosophy of science that would be in active collaboration with scientists and the practice of science after the Second World War,[17] the abandonment by mainstream economic thinking of a commitment to reflecting critically upon the relation between its history, concepts, and practice,[18] or the tendency for

[16] See A Orford, 'International Law and the Limits of History' in W Werner, A Galan, and M de Hoon (eds), *The Law of International Lawyers: Reading Martti Koskenniemi* (CUP Cambridge forthcoming).

[17] GA Reisch, *How the Cold War Transformed Philosophy of Science: To the Icy Slopes of Logic* (CUP Cambridge 2005).

[18] See further the arguments in K Tribe, *Land, Labour and Economic Discourse* (Routledge London 1978); GM Hodgson, *How Economics Forgot History* (Routledge London 2001); L Magnusson, *The Tradition of Free Trade* (Routledge London 2004).

historians to forget the historically contingent and deeply political nature of the myths and methods at the heart of their practice.[19] As those examples illustrate, once the history and philosophy of a discipline are abstracted and treated as distinct from its practice, a politically engaged vision of that practice is much harder to realize. Work in each sphere—history, theory, and practice—can proliferate endlessly, with an increasing number of highly technical studies being produced but with a decreasing sense of their relevance for political engagement in the world. The *Handbook* thus seeks to resist the tendency for international legal theory to become a new self-enclosed area of specialization.

A second and related challenge results from the question of what the proper methodological approach to theorizing about international law should be. Here the chapters of this *Handbook* articulate a set of interrelated concerns. Some authors see international law theorizing as amateurish, prone to haphazard borrowing and to attributing epistemic authority to concepts and debates forged outside of its own practice without reflection on their specific disciplinary trajectories or, indeed, on the methodological challenges of such theory transplantation.[20] Other authors implicitly or explicitly reject the assumption that theorists of international law should simply follow the protocols, methods, values, and questions developed in other disciplines, and instead model the ways in which theorists of international law might address and comprehend legal practice as a source of values and epistemic standards.[21] Those authors suggest that it is neither inevitable nor desirable that a turn to theory or engagement in interdisciplinary work by international law scholars should lead to the displacement of the concepts, methods, practices, and experiential life of the discipline itself. While the measure or meaning of international law can of course be understood in part through such interdisciplinary encounters, for many of the *Handbook* authors this is seen to require a commitment to the integration of history, theory, and practice.

A third challenge that may arise from the development of a more specialized approach to theorizing in a normatively oriented field such as international law is that the resulting theories may come to be treated as embodying timeless truths. That tendency is intensified in legal scholarship, where lawyers often treat theorists in the way we have been trained to treat other generators of norms, such as judges or legislatures.[22] The pronouncements of philosophers are thus deployed as

---

[19] C Fasolt, *The Limits of History* (University of Chicago Press Chicago 2004).

[20] See S Besson, 'Moral Philosophy and International Law' in this *Handbook*; 'International Legal Positivism' (n 4); D Danielsen, 'International Law and Economics: Letting Go of the "Normal" in Pursuit of an Ever-Elusive Real' in this *Handbook*.

[21] See eg D Kritsiotis, 'Theorizing International Law on Force and Intervention' in this *Handbook*; S Nouwen, 'International Criminal Law: Theory All Over the Place' in this *Handbook*; F Johns, 'Theorizing the Corporation in International Law' in this *Handbook*; K Rittich, 'Theorizing International Law and Development' in this *Handbook*.

[22] P Schlag, 'A Brief Survey of Deconstruction' (2005) 27 *Cardozo Law Review* 741–52.

authority for the meaning and demands of justice universally, and yet embedded in theoretical pronouncements about justice or power or resistance are particular unarticulated assumptions about the political situation in which justice or power or resistance are understood to be operating.[23] For lawyers seeking to take responsibility for engaging with the practice of the discipline and for its present politics, it is useful to grasp the practice of theorizing as itself historically situated and existing in relation to particular concrete situations.

A final related challenge that has come with the rapid expansion of theoretical work in international law is the difficulty it poses for those seeking to engage with that work for the first time. A central feature of contemporary international law theory remains its methodological plurality. International legal theorists have largely favoured methodological *bricolage*, drawing on a range of disciplines and vocabularies in order to construct specific arguments rather than to build grand theory. This has been intensified by the global nature of international legal scholarship, with different thematic concerns and jurisprudential trends often taking hold in different countries. In addition, the globalized marketplace of ideas often— and paradoxically—produces centralization: one way for consumers to address the proliferation of commodities is to make choices based on brands. Something similar seems to function in the world of legal theory, where the globalization of international law scholarship and the creation of highly networked global communities seems to have reduced rather than pluralized the field. One or two scholars, and even in some cases one or two articles or axioms, are treated as standing in for 'critical approaches' or 'philosophical approaches' or even the theory of international law in general. Providing an opening to the richness and diversity of the field is thus an important spur to the writing of this *Handbook*.

3 Ways of Theorizing International Law

The aim of this *Handbook* is then to provide a much-needed map of the different traditions and approaches that shape contemporary international legal theory and a guide to the main themes and debates that have driven theoretical work in the field. The authors take quite different approaches to their task: some offer a systemization, others an intellectual or contextualist history, others a critical or normative

---

[23] A Orford, 'In Praise of Description' (2012) 25 *Leiden Journal of International Law* 609–25.

evaluation, and still others a performance of an approach or style. Their chapters are arranged in four parts, organized around the themes of histories (Part I), approaches (Part II), doctrines and regimes (Part III), and debates (Part IV).

The underlying aim of Part I (Histories) is to create a methodological awareness of the historical dimension of international legal theory. The chapters introduce some of the key theories and thinkers that have been treated as providing the foundations of international legal theory, and explore the ways in which international legal theory has developed within broader intellectual and political contexts. History figures in these chapters in a variety of ways. First, the nature of the relation between theory and history, or the 'turn to history' as a theoretical move, is foregrounded. The historical consciousness and temporal concepts of progress, development, or civilization embedded within international law are explored as central to the self-constitution of the discipline,[24] and as bound up with its projects of imperial expansion and modernist reform.[25]

In addition, the chapters in this Part take seriously what seems at first a banal observation—that international law and the theory of international law are different in different times and places. All the chapters in this Part pay close attention to the interventions that particular theories make and the context in which they were first presented. A number of the authors draw our attention to aspects of that context that have since been forgotten and that serve as a reminder of the initial potency of theories or texts that has been diminished over time.[26] Theory appears here, in the words of Deborah Whitehall, as 'a call to action put to the international legal order' at moments of great opportunity. Other chapters are interested in exploring what happens when the work of a theorist is taken up in another time and place, seeking to provide historical correction to received readings or posing questions about the grounds on which we approve of some uses of theory or readings of theorists and not others.[27] Overall the chapters in Part I offer a sweeping overview of what counts as 'theory' (and what, for that matter, counts as 'international' or 'law') in different historical situations. The resulting analyses suggest strongly that theorizing about international law is not a linear process, but rather that concepts, values, and ideals that seem to have exhausted their potential

---

[24] M Craven, 'Theorizing the Turn to History in International Law' in this *Handbook*.

[25] U Özsu, 'The Ottoman Empire, the Origins of Extraterritoriality, and International Legal Theory' in this *Handbook*; T Ruskola, 'China in the Age of the World Picture' in this *Handbook*; 'Imperialism and International Legal Theory' (n 8).

[26] 'Roman Law and the Intellectual History of International Law' (n 2); 'Transformations of Natural Law' (n 2); 'Early Twentieth-Century Positivism Revisited' (n 4); J von Bernstorff, 'Hans Kelsen and the Return of Universalism' in this *Handbook*; D Whitehall, 'Hannah Arendt and International Law' in this *Handbook*.

[27] See eg 'Hugo Grotius: The Making of a Founding Father of International Law' (n 2); 'The Critique of Classical Thought during the Interwar Period' (n 2); R Howse, 'Schmitt, Schmitteanism and Contemporary International Legal Theory' in this *Handbook*.

may suddenly reappear, generations later, to do quite different work in quite different settings.[28]

In a broader sense, history also figures in these chapters as a spur to the discussion of questions about method—questions such as the status attributed to historical reconstruction and historiographic method in contemporary international law theorizing more generally, whether there is a 'correct' use of a theorist or a theory, and what constitutes the context within which we might make sense of a particular theoretical contribution. Indeed, many of the themes and modes of inquiry that recur in discussions throughout the *Handbook* have roots in historiography, such as the question of origins, of revisionism, of disciplinary mythologizing, and the role of iconic and intellectual father— and mother—figures in creating invented traditions for the field. In that sense, Part I introduces the more general approach that is taken up throughout the *Handbook*, in offering a genealogy of theory that is both historical and critical.

The chapters comprising Part II (Approaches) reflect some of the different ways in which a general taxonomy of the theory field can be envisaged. To thematize 'approaches' means to engage with disciplinary identities, whether by constructing more or less coherent historical narratives, or by producing semantic unity through differentiation, notably through the pinpointing of dichotomies or contrasts deemed to be constitutive of theoretical discourse. This Part does not purport to offer an encyclopaedic overview of all the different modes in which international legal theory is undertaken today, but rather produces something resembling a 'tag-cloud' of key recurring terms that inform contemporary theorizing. As it turns out, this cloud is not an indiscriminate assemblage of concepts, but reveals a range of different ways of categorizing approaches.

There is, in the first place, a recurrent engagement with the traditional mode of classification, notably by reference to a limited set of master narratives or 'schools of thought' deemed to have shaped the theory landscape. Despite, or indeed because of, the discipline-wide familiarity (or overfamiliarity) of these 'schools',[29] no uniform picture emerges, but rather a kaleidoscopic image of partly overlapping, partly contrasting vocabularies employed to articulate the concept of international law. Hence, the commonly recognized jurisprudential grand *écoles* of positivism,[30] natural law,[31] and realism[32] turn out to be but shards from history that provide starting and breaking points for much more complex and differentiated narratives about what law in the international sphere is and how it works.

---

[28] See eg L Mälksoo, 'International Legal Theory in Russia: A Civilizational Perspective' in this *Handbook*.

[29] See further D Joyce, 'Liberal Internationalism' in this *Handbook*.

[30] 'International Legal Positivism' (n 4).

[31] G Gordon, 'Natural Law in International Legal Theory: Linear and Dialectical Presentations' in this *Handbook*.

[32] O Jütersonke, 'Realist Approaches to International Law' in this *Handbook*.

They are complemented by a dichotomy that defines not just legal theorizing but Western political thought itself, notably liberalism and Marxism,[33] and the distinct approaches to the ontology (agency-orientation versus structuralism) and epistemology (historicism versus historical materialism) of international law they represent—with liberalism being the constitutive master narrative of the international legal project as it has been known so far. There are further currents that either provide the discursive 'conditions of possibility' for these grand 'schools', such as the universe of humanist thought and the 'semiogenesis' of international legality,[34] or that graft new vocabularies onto the older schemes and reinterpret their dichotomies, such as those of the Yale,[35] Global Administrative Law,[36] Law and Economic Analysis,[37] or Feminist Theory 'schools'.[38] Lastly, there is an engagement with some of the significant others of these 'schools', most notably with international law's disciplinary nemesis, international relations,[39] and with normative political philosophy,[40] its constant if uneasy companion.

In all, the styles and outlooks of this Part reflect the spirit of the times. An increasingly erudite if decidedly 'small-caps' ideology-critique largely based on historical mapping rather than on original argument defines the tone of contemporary theorizing. There is a somewhat resigned recognition of an ever increasing complexity and theoretical diversity, an honest attempt to shed light on the blind spots of one's own perspective, a commitment to non-parochialism, an all pervasive endeavour to link theory to practice, and a search for ways to practice theory. Yet, what arguably makes this approach to approaches distinct from the stylized disinterestedness of other disciplinary frameworks such as (some of) international relations or political science is the passionate quest, recurrent in many a chapter in this Part, for the possibility of positive change or—put simply—a 'better world'. That quest is well captured by Dianne Otto, who does not shy away from naming her fundamental motivation as the search for a 'more egalitarian, inclusive, peaceful, just and redistributive international order'.[41]

Part III (Doctrines and Regimes) provides an overview of theoretical discussions relating to core doctrines and areas of contemporary international law, exploring the role of theory in relation to canonical subjects of general international law, such as sources, statehood, state responsibility, and jurisdiction, as well as theories relating to

---

[33] 'Liberal Internationalism' (n 29) and 'Marxist Approaches to International Law' (n 15).

[34] See P Goodrich, 'The International Signs Law' in this *Handbook*.

[35] See 'Yale's Policy Science and International Law' (n 5).

[36] See B Kingsbury, M Donaldson, and R Vallejo, 'Global Administrative Law and Deliberative Democracy' in this *Handbook*.

[37] See 'International Law and Economics' (n 20).

[38] See 'Feminist Approaches to International Law' (n 15).

[39] See F dos Reis and O Kessler, 'Constructivism and the Politics of International Law' in this *Handbook*.

[40] 'Moral Philosophy and International Law' (n 20).

[41] 'Feminist Approaches to International Law' (n 15).

significant specialized regimes, such as international criminal law, international humanitarian law, international human rights law, international environmental law, and international trade law. These chapters give a sense of how lawyers theorize on the run, in response to particular problems or doctrinal dead-ends, and yet in doing so often come back to shared themes or conceptual dilemmas.[42] Many of the regimes explored here are organized around their own invented traditions,[43] in which historical figures, events, and texts are invoked to situate current disciplinary practices within a longer progress narrative. A number of these chapters thus engage with or seek to resist these invented traditions, offering new accounts of the ways in which scholars have drawn on past texts, events, and concepts to consolidate particular theories and traditions that persist through time.[44]

Many of the chapters in this Part comment on the lack of 'overt' theorizing that takes place in relation to specialized doctrines or regimes, and yet find, in the words of Sarah Nouwen, that theory is nonetheless 'all over the place'. Fields that appear to be practitioner-driven and problem-focused, such as law and development,[45] international humanitarian law,[46] or international criminal law,[47] turn out in fact to be premised upon unarticulated theories, while some fields are so dependent upon the theories that structure their operations, such as functionalism in the case of international organizations,[48] pragmatism in the case of human rights,[49] or romanticism born of imperialism in the case of international environmental law,[50] that their foundational premises go unexamined. Core questions about the nature of legal obligation and the status accorded to different subjects drive theorizing across these chapters, informing debates about the contemporary sources of international law,[51] which actors are bound by legal obligations or held to exercise responsibility in particular fields,[52] the criteria according to which the subjects of international law should be recognized,[53] and the relation between public and

---

[42] J Klabbers, 'Theorizing International Organizations' in this *Handbook*; 'Theorizing the Corporation in International Law' (n 21); C Thomas, 'Transnational Migration, Globalization, and Governance: Theorizing a Crisis' in this *Handbook*.

[43] On the role of invented traditions in legitimizing contemporary practices and institutions more generally, see E Hobsbawm and T Ranger (eds), *The Invention of Tradition* (CUP Cambridge 1983).

[44] A Orford, 'Theorizing Free Trade' in this *Handbook*; S Humphreys and Y Otomo, 'Theorizing International Environmental Law' in this *Handbook*; 'Theorizing the Corporation in International Law' (n 21); V Nesiah, 'Theories of Transitional Justice: Cashing in the Blue Chips' in this *Handbook*.

[45] 'Theorizing International Law and Development' (n 21).

[46] F Mégret, 'Theorizing the Laws of War' in this *Handbook*.

[47] 'International Criminal Law: Theory All Over the Place' (n 21).

[48] 'Theorizing International Organizations' (n 42).   [49] 'Theorizing Human Rights' (n 5).

[50] 'Theorizing International Environmental Law' (n 44).

[51] J d'Aspremont, 'Towards a New Theory of Sources in International Law' in this *Handbook*.

[52] G Noll, 'Theorizing Jurisdiction' in this *Handbook*; O Korhonen and T Selkälä, 'Theorizing Responsibility' in this *Handbook*.

[53] G Simpson, 'Something to Do with States' in this *Handbook*; R Parfitt, 'Theorizing Recognition and International Personality' in this *Handbook*.

private actors and domains.[54] A number of the chapters register the ways in which the contemporary crisis of the state has driven a rethinking of the very nature and grounds of international law, whether that be a result of the crisis of the security state in Britain and the US which can no longer rely upon the secrecy of its military and intelligence operations,[55] or the crisis of the neoliberal state form which has been constituted in part through the increasingly undemocratic project of global economic integration.[56] A key theme that recurs throughout this Part is the vital connection between practical innovation, theoretical elaboration, and social transformation, both in relation to the political instrumentalization of theory in practice and in the search for a critical practice of international law in its different articulations.

Part IV (Debates) presents some of the most existential and essential questions informing the discipline's current state and likely future. Those debates represent a set of cross-cutting concerns that arise out of a number of broad phenomena with which all contemporary students and practitioners of international law are confronted. What makes them into debates is the fact that they are both ongoing and unsettled: they are, to apply a Kuhnian metaphor, in that 'revolutionary' state in which old epistemic certainties have been diluted but new certainties have yet to become hegemonic. It is that precious state in which no one is right but everyone can claim to be, and it is for this reason that they reveal much about the deeper state(s) of contemporary international law theory.

Three key themes emerge from the chapters in this section. First, a number of specific issues appear as catalysts for wider engagements with some of the open questions of the discipline. These relate to the modes by which international law is deemed to function or to fail to function, and to the desirable or undesirable outcomes of international legal process. They include religion as one of the conceptual staging grounds of the international legal project,[57] sovereign equality and democracy as perennial utopias of an imaginary international society,[58] and (Third World) poverty as, potentially, part of the very genetic programming of international law.[59] There are also concepts that seek to articulate and problematize particular movements or dynamics within international law as a whole, notably its much-worried-about fragmentation,[60] and the question of its directionality as epitomized in the idea of progress.[61]

---

[54] H Muir Watt, 'Theorizing Private International Law' in this *Handbook*; 'Theorizing the Corporation in International Law' (n 21).

[55] 'Theorizing International Law on Force and Intervention' (n 21). See also *Philosophy of International Law* (n 3) 14–18.

[56] 'Theorizing Free Trade' (n 44); 'Transnational Migration, Globalization, and Governance' (n 42).

[57] R Paz, 'Religion, Secularism, and International Law' in this *Handbook*.

[58] T Skouteris, 'The Idea of Progress' in this *Handbook*; A Peters, 'Fragmentation and Constitutionalization' in this *Handbook*.

[59] J Beckett, 'Creating Poverty' in this *Handbook*.

[60] 'Fragmentation and Constitutionalization' (n 58).   [61] 'The Idea of Progress' (n 58).

Second, there are a variety of 'isms' which have been coined to denote both frameworks of thought and militant stances towards them, and which function as 'essentially contested concepts' of the theory of international law. They are often applied with critical intent and, therefore, tend to generate forceful reactions by the recipients of the label. Two of the arguably most contentious 'isms' concern international 'humanitarianism' as the motivation behind much of the recent expansion of international legality,[62] and 'managerialism', a term used both to denote the technocratization and de-politicization of international legal practice and the attitude attributed to the legal mainstream.[63] On a more structural level, there is 'liberalism' as the system of thought out of which modern international law has emerged,[64] as well as 'legalism',[65] and 'constitutionalism',[66] which denote attendant programs that underwrite many aspects of contemporary international legal doctrine.

Third, there are a set of overarching or meta-themes which come up in virtually all chapters in this section—and, in fact, in this *Handbook*—and which represent the deepest and most existential layer of questions surrounding the international legal project. They address issues of ontology and epistemology not just of (international) law but of the social sciences and, indeed, knowledge as such. As a result, they are rarely discussed openly within legal texts, though they provide fundamental clues to understanding the different positions, theoretical frameworks, and practical attitudes within international legal discourse. One concerns the differential identity of law vis-à-vis other epistemes, most importantly politics, but also the social and the economic. Closely related to this is the question of autonomy: that is, the extent to which international law is deemed to be autonomous and thus clearly distinct from other social systems, or, conversely, whether it is deemed to be merely epiphenomenal in relation to these other systems, a mere function of, say, politics or the economy. There is also the persistent tension between diversity and unity, be it in relation to individuals and states or different laws and institutions. On a yet more abstract level there lurks the spectre of ideology and its critique, which engages questions of (false) consciousness and emancipation, and which is, perhaps, the most protracted debate in which the different sides of the theoretical spectrum are involved. Finally, there seems to be a sense of and engagement with crisis, be it of specific theories, of the state of theorizing, of the profession, of international law in general and the international rule of law in particular, of modernity, or of 'the world as we know it'. It is quite

---

[62] 'Religion, Secularism, and International Law' (n 57); 'Creating Poverty' (n 59).

[63] F Hoffmann, 'International Legalism and International Politics' in this *Handbook*; 'Fragmentation and Constitutionalization' (n 58).

[64] See 'Liberal Internationalism' (n 29).

[65] 'International Legalism and International Politics' (n 63).

[66] 'Fragmentation and Constitutionalization' (n 58).

all-pervasive though not generally pessimistic in tone, speaking rather of a critical consciousness, of counterdisciplinary thinking, of contextualization and complexification, and of a critical professional ethos.

4 CONCLUSION

There are, finally, a number of themes that reappear across all four Parts of the *Handbook*. On the one hand, there are some iconic names (or totems) that function as a form of historical deep structure that few theorists, whether apologetic or critical, are able or willing to ignore. On the other hand, there are certain key concepts around which much theoretical engagement with international law is constructed. In terms of the former, the position of conceptual demiurge is still occupied by Kant, who seems to provide the horizon for many contemporary re-interpretations of international law as a normative or political project. This Kantian predominance says more about the state of contemporary theorizing—whether in its focus on the hegemony of liberalism or on ways to reconstruct critical reason within a globalized international reality—than about the actual Kantian legacy. Accordingly, concepts such as cosmopolitanism, democracy, justice, legitimacy, the rule of law, and the state loom large throughout the *Handbook*, with different Kantian interpretations being used both in justification of mainstream liberal international law and as a critical vocabulary engendering alternative visions.[67]

Other figures recurrently appear, though more eclectically, including Hobbes, and the echelons of classical international law from the Salamancans to Vattel, Grotius, and Pufendorf. Marx, and his international legal interpreter Pashukanis, enters as an irritation on the sidelines, as does a stylized and (almost) personalized nineteenth century, alongside the well-known twentieth century debates and debaters, notably Lauterpacht and Morgenthau, Kelsen and Hart, Schmitt, Arendt, and McDougal. Interestingly, those figures function more as signposts along the road of legal ideas than as authoritative providers of vocabularies and agendas, which may well be in keeping with the general trend to iconoclasm in the contemporary period. Hence, the issues that recur may owe their pedigree, problem-set, or imaginary to the (canonical) icons, but their use transcends and partly contradicts their historical legacy. Some of these key concepts speak to the perennial question of (re-)describing the empirical substances of international

---

[67] On the cosmopolitan legacy, see W Werner and G Gordon, 'Kant, Cosmopolitanism, and International Law' in this *Handbook*.

law, such as the rule of law, sovereignty, jurisdiction, statehood, responsibility, society, the (Third) world, global values, inter-state power, professional ethos, or governance. Others thematize perspectives and intellectual matrices, often in dichotomous pairs, that structure international legal theorizing, such as the dualities between idealism and pragmatism/realism, classical and modern, moderate and radical, and public and private.

In the end, this *Handbook* does not aim to project an artificial sense of coherence onto the diverse field of international legal theory or to construct a new canonical set of authors and doctrines. Instead, we hope it conveys a sense of the theory of international law as a wide-ranging tradition that is dynamic, pluralist, and politically engaged. By historically situating the thinkers, approaches, debates, methods, experiments, critiques, or problems that have shaped theorizing about international law, the chapters show that theorizing is itself a political intervention. In so doing, these chapters make clearer the stakes—whether political, analytical, institutional, or communicative—involved in taking up the theories we use to think about and through international law.

PART I

HISTORIES

CHAPTER 1

THEORIZING THE TURN TO HISTORY IN INTERNATIONAL LAW

MATTHEW CRAVEN

The historical trait should not be founded on a philosophy of history, but dismantled, beginning with the things it produced.[1]

1 INTRODUCTION

IT is a commonplace that the past two decades have been marked by a resurgence of interest in the history of international law.[2] Whether or not this may warrant the grandiose title of a 'turn to history', it is a departure which might prompt a certain level of theoretical reflection: why this sudden interest in the historical at the expense of other forms of analytical or critical endeavours? What might the causes be? What

---

[1] M Foucault, 'Nietzsche, Genealogy, History' in P Rabinow (ed), *The Foucault Reader* (Pantheon Books New York 1984) 76–100, at 93.

[2] See eg M Koskenniemi, 'Why History of International Law Today?' (2004) 4 *Rechtsgeschichte* 61–6, at 61; A Kemmerer, 'The Turning Aside: On International Law and its History' in RA Miller and RM Bratspies (eds), *Progress in International Law* (Martinus Nijhoff Leiden 2008) 71–93, at 71; T Skouteris, 'Engaging History in International Law' in J Beneyto and D Kennedy (eds), *New Approaches to International Law* (TMC Asser Press The Hague 2012) 99–122, at 103; G Galindo, 'Martti Koskenniemi and the Historiographical Turn in International Law' (2005) 16 *European Journal of International Law* 539–59, at 539.

theoretical or intellectual frames have opened up that were not otherwise available? How might it relate to the themes, interests, or preoccupations of mainstream international legal thought up until that time? Whilst these are undoubtedly interesting and important questions, they pose, in turn, two more general questions as to the relationship between theory and history in international legal discourse. One of these, of course, concerns the theoretical and methodological conditions underpinning the representation of something as the past of international law: what is the relationship between the text and the past? How might one understand the act of 'representation'? What kind of international law is being represented? If such questions are concerned with placing 'history' within the ambit of theory, it is also clear that one must attend to the historical (and spatial!) specificity of the theoretical and methodological analytics through which that history is enunciated or disclosed.[3] What serves as 'history' at any one moment—including its boundaries and conditions—also has its historical place.

With such thoughts in mind, I want to try to do two things in this chapter. In the first place, I intend to look back beyond the immediate causes and explanations of the recent turn to history, and focus instead upon their more general conditions of possibility: what was required in order for the productive representation of the past of international law as 'history' to be a meaningful activity? This might appear a somewhat abstruse question were it not for the fact that one may specify with considerable precision the moment at which the law of nations was to acquire an historical hue, requiring its discourse and practice to be organized in temporal terms, and its past 'found' or 'uncovered'. The significance of this, I argue, is not merely confined to an acknowledgement that publicists and jurists suddenly became interested in the past in a way that wasn't apparent before, but that this historical consciousness fundamentally reshaped the conceptualization of what was to become known as 'international law', and placed at centre-stage the problem of historical method. In the second place, and following from this, I want to suggest that not only did the emergence of this historical consciousness have specifiable theoretical and practical dimensions, but that it would become, as Foucault puts it, a 'privileged and dangerous' site, both providing theoretical sustenance to the discipline, and a space for critical engagement. I will conclude with certain reflections upon problems of method associated with contemporary critical international legal history.

2 Turning to History

1795. Robert Plummer Ward, a British author and politician publishes, with encouragement from Lord Stowell,[4] what he proclaims to be the first history of

---

[3] M De Certeau, *The Writing of History* (Columbia University Press New York 1988) at 20.

[4] Then a judge at the Consistory Court and Advocate-General, later additionally appointed judge at the High Court of Admiralty.

the law of nations ever written: *An Enquiry into the Foundation and History of the Law of Nations.*[5] His claim may be doubted, given the earlier accounts provided by Ompteda in 1785[6] and Moser in 1764,[7] as well as, in the same year, by de Martens.[8] But there is little doubt that there was something inaugural about this late eighteenth-century moment in the sense that from that time onwards all international lawyers were compelled to conceive of their subject matter as 'being in time' and as possessed of 'a history'. Not only would the historical account become an important literary genre in the nineteenth century (from Wheaton through to Nys),[9] but every general textbook on the subject of international law would, almost by compulsion, begin with an historical account of one form or another. And to a large extent, this remains the model to this day.

Ward's account itself is revealing enough in terms of the consequences of this turn to history. He makes clear in the preface to the book, that it had not been his original intention to write a book on the history of the law of nations, but rather a treatise on diplomatic law—an account of sovereignty and of the rights and privileges of ambassadors.[10] Having collected the relevant materials, he tells us, he was then prompted to ask himself as to the conditions 'under which we conceive ourselves bound to obey a law, *independent* of those resources which the law itself provides for its own enforcement'.[11] And at this point, the limits of his original project soon became clear. The received answer to this question, as he understood it, was to be found in the Law of Nature, the content of which was to be found in the universal injunctions of 'heart and natural conscience'. Yet, to him, this was unsatisfactory:

[w]hen I considered how difficult it was *for the whole of mankind* to arrive at the *same* ideas of moral good, from the prejudices of education and habit, in the different stages of society in which they might be; more particularly when I recollected the great difference of opinion there was among very learned men, of the same nations and ages, and who had the same sort of education concerning the Law of Nature itself; I was still more staggered in my belief that *all* the world were bound to obey the ramified and definite scheme of duties called the Law of Nations.[12]

He continued by observing that:

although I myself could make out the obligation of the Law of Nations as laid down in the *European* Codes, and that others of the same class of nations, and the same religion with

---

[5] R Ward, *An Enquiry into the Foundation and History of the Law of Nations in Europe* (Butterworth London 1795).

[6] D Ompteda, *Literatur des gesamtennatürlichen und positive Völkerrechts* (Scientia Verlag 1785).

[7] F Moser, *Beyträge zu dem Staats und Völker-Recht und der Geschichte* (JC Gebhard Frankfurt 1764).

[8] GF de Martens, *Summary of the Law of Nations* (W Cobbett trans) (Thomas Bradford Philadelphia 1795).

[9] H Wheaton, *History of the Law of Nations in Europe and America* (Gould Banks New York 1842); E Nys, *Les origines du droit international* (Castaigne Brussels 1893).

[10] *An Enquiry* (n 5) iii–iv.   [11] Ibid 5.   [12] Ibid 8–9.

myself, could, and were bound to do so too; yet that the law was not obligatory upon persons who had never been called upon to decide upon its ramifications; who might widely differ as to its application, and even as to its general and fundamental principles. The history of mankind confirmed to me that there was such a difference in almost all its extent; that men had the most opposite opinions of their duties towards one another, if not in the great outline and first principles of those duties, yet most certainly in the application of them; and that this was occasioned by the varieties of religion and the moral systems which governed them, operated upon also by important local circumstances which are often of such consequence in their direction.[13]

It was, thus, no longer plausible for him to write a treatise on diplomatic law of universal application. Rather, his attention was drawn towards writing a 'history of the people of Europe', not in the 'old' sense as he puts it of enquiring into their general manners, customs, politics, arts, or feats of arms, but in order to discern the maxims which governed their intercourse with one another. It was to be a history, in other words, of a distinctively European law of nations.

Leaving aside, for a moment, the operative conditions under which this historicised account of the law of nations was to emerge, three general features of Ward's enquiry stand out. In the first place, it is notable that his turn to history did not arrive as a consequence of his scepticism towards the universal claims of natural right, but rather the other way round. It was, in part at least, historical enquiry that had led Ward to a position of incredulity in respect of the universal pretensions of natural law (his thesis, as he put it, was 'proved by history').[14] The natural law he encountered was not in its own right alien to him (nor indeed irrelevant), but it was his experience of his own historical subjectivity that led him to the realization that its prescriptions could not be understood as the *ratio scripta* of a singular divine being or of a universal rational consciousness. Rather they appeared to him as moral and religious injunctions specified by time and place, engendered in particular through education and moral learning. If 'being in time', however, was an existential condition that gave expression to Ward's sense of his own 'European' identity (an 'occidental prejudice' as Nietzsche put it),[15] it was also the mode through which that self-knowledge could be both unearthed and transmitted. The search for the 'origins' or 'foundations' of the law of nations thus would not only reveal its point of justification and temporal dispersion, but would also provide active content of what it meant (for Ward) to be a 'modern' European in the late eighteenth century. History, in other words, was not just shaped by, but a means of making intelligible, the social or national contexts within which it was to be produced.

In the second place, and as a consequence of this, Ward's understanding of his own historical condition was one that had not only temporal, but also decisively

---

[13] *An Enquiry* (n 5) 11–12.   [14] Ibid 15.
[15] F Nietzsche, 'On the Uses and Disadvantages of History for Life' in *Untimely Meditations* (D Breazeale ed RJ Hollingdale trans) (CUP Cambridge 1997) 57–124, at 66.

spatial, connotations. If his experience of history was one that positioned at its cen-tre, the place of human agency in the propagation and dissemination of religious, moral and legal insight (and which, furthermore, understood human agency to be the active product of that process), it was one that had as its complement a spa-tial differentiation between the cultural field within which this was to take place (Europe), and that which demarcated the space in which different religious, moral, or legal insights might hold (non-Europe). Yet the temporal and spatial articu-lations were related in a more fundamental way. These were not separate modes of analysis, but were analytically of the same register—the distinction between Europe and non-Europe being of the same character as the distinction between the present of Europe and its own past. As he was to put it, they are all 'foreign countries'.

In the third place, Ward was conscious that the writing of history was ultimately an interpretive activity governed by the 'bent of mind' of the historian in bring-ing understanding to bear on what might otherwise be a 'dry series of events'. '[H]istory may be compared' he suggests, continuing his spatial theme, 'to a vast and diversified country, which gives very different sorts of pleasure to different travellers, or to the same traveller if he visits it at different times'.[16] Thus, from the same facts, he suggests 'one has drawn a history of man; another, of the progress of society; a third, of the effects of climate; a fourth, of military achievements; a fifth, of laws in general; a sixth, of the laws of a particular state'.[17] The 'past' for Ward, in other words, was a vast, heterogeneous, field of experience within which one could identify a range of different historical lineaments dependent upon the field of study with which one is engaged. And his particular project was one of bringing into view a history proper to the law of nations itself, with its own temporality, chronol-ogy, and moments of continuity and change. If, for Ward, this was a chronology that began in Rome and ended with Grotius[18] (after which not much happened, apparently), it was a chronology conditioned by an ongoing process of discipli-nary dispersion (in which 'law' was to be differentiated from politics, economics, sociology, anthropology, and so on), the 'truth' of which would be disclosed in the identification of each discipline's own peculiar moment(s) of origin.

The historical consciousness that Ward brought to bear in his account may thus be thought to have three key features: a critique of universal metaphysics in favour of an emphasis upon the spatial and temporal conditions of social and cultural production (of law, ethics, faith, and so on); a belief that each of these orders of knowledge—the temporal and the spatial—were of the same analytical character; and a belief in the specificity of international legal history as a disciplinary sub-field. Yet, if these are the main methodological assumptions that might be said to inform the content of his work, they are also assumptions that have a bearing upon

---

[16] *An Enquiry* (n 5) xx.   [17] Ibid 19.   [18] Ibid 47.

how that work itself might be received or understood. For, if the history he was to narrate was a history of a contingent historical consciousness, it was one that necessarily posed the same questions of itself: what made it possible for Ward to write this history? What was available to him, in terms of received forms of knowledge or understanding, that made the writing of a history of the law of nations both plausible and necessary? My contention, here, is that Ward was working in a social and intellectual environment in which 'history', as a field of knowledge and a form of social and political consciousness, was not only actively changing shape, but organizing itself around new temporal categories of considerable significance.

3   THE *NEUZEIT* OF MODERNITY

In the most obvious sense, the emergence of a new historical medium within the discourse of international law in the early nineteenth century may be seen to align with two, specifically European, historiographical developments. On the one side was the emergence of a critical, source-based, methodology that had its roots in the long-standing analytics of erudition (concerned with examining the veracity of sources), diplomatics (the textual examination of documents), paleology (an analysis of antiquities), and philology (concerned with placing a text within its historical and cultural context), and which was to become the hallmark of early nineteenth-century 'professional' historiography.[19] On the other side was the emergence of linear, progressive, histories, that were to mark, in particular, the stadial theories of the Scottish enlightenment[20] and which supplanted the repetitive, cyclical, or providential Biblical chronology that characterized historiography until that time.[21]

In Koselleck's terms, these historiographical developments were key characteristics of what he called the 'new time' (*Neuzeit*) of modernity that was to emerge

---

[19] See L Ranke, *Theory and Practice of History* (G Iggers ed) (Routledge London 2010); J Michelet, *Histoire de France* (GH Smith trans) (Appleton New York 1847).

[20] A Ferguson, *An Essay on the History of Civil Society* (5th edn T Cadell London 1782 [1767]); J Millar, *Historical View of the English Government* (MS Phillips and DR Smith eds) (4 vols Liberty Fund Indianapolis 2006 [1787]). See also N de Condorcet, *Outlines of an Historical View of the Progress of the Human Mind* (M Carey Philadelphia 1796 [1795]).

[21] See GG Iggers, QE Wang, and S Mukherjee, *A Global History of Modern Historiography* (Pearson Longman Harlow 2008) at 22. As Foucault puts it, the classical conception of history (whether in the form of a Stoic cosmic chronology or a Christian Providentialism) was one that viewed the past as a 'vast historical stream, uniform in all its points, drawing within it in one and the same current, in one and the same fall or ascension, or cycle, all men, and with them things and animals, every living or inert being, even the unmoved aspects of the earth': M Foucault, *The Order of Things* (Routledge London 1989) at 401.

within Europe in the 'saddle period' of the late eighteenth century, the critical features of which being fourfold: 1) it was a conception in which 'history no longer takes place in time, but rather through time'; 2) in which the future was seen to be radically 'open' rather than cyclical or repetitive; 3) in which the diversity of the world could be brought together under the umbrella of a singular chronology (its 'non-simultaneous' simultaneity); and 4) in which 'the doctrine of the subjective position, of *historical perspective* gained cogency'.[22]

Each of these characteristics of Koselleck's analysis had particular consequences for the construction of international legal knowledge over the ensuing century or more. In its first and most immediate sense, a consciousness of history moving through time was a development that had obvious significance for purposes of the identification and characterization of the sources of international law. The natural lawyers who came to be represented, by Ward and his successors, as representatives of the discursive 'tradition' of international law, had worked with a remarkably limited sense of temporal specificity. Grotius, for example, had argued that:

History in relation to our subject is useful in two ways: it supplies both illustrations and judgements. The illustrations have greater weight in proportion as they are taken from better times and better peoples; thus we have preferred ancient examples, Greek and Roman, to the rest. And judgements are not to be slighted, especially when they are in agreement with one another; for by such statements the existence of the law of nature, as we have said, is in a measure proved, and by no other means, in fact, is it possible to establish the law of nations.[23]

For Grotius, in other words, history was a flat, limitless, field of insight that imposed no order, in its own right, over the marshalling of relevant sources of authority. No sense of temporal proximity operated here as a way of estimating the value of judgement and/or illustration—if anything, authority seemed to be associated with temporal distance (towards the 'better' times of Rome) or with the repetitive reoccurrence of the same (as a means by which 'common agreement' might be discerned).[24] If, in the ensuing century, one may note the subtle appearance of various historical and temporal themes (for example in Pufendorf's account of the development of natural sociability)[25] even as late as Vattel, who wrote very self-consciously about his own 'modern' times, there is

[22] R Koselleck, *The Practice of Conceptual History: Timing History, Spacing Concepts* (Stanford University Press Stanford 2002) at 165–9.

[23] H Grotius, *De Jure Belli ac Pacis* (FW Kelsey trans) (Clarendon Press Oxford 1925 [1625]) at 26.

[24] Ibid xii and 1–2.

[25] For a discussion see I Hont, 'The Language of Sociability and Commerce: Samuel Pufendorf and the Theoretical Foundations of the "Four Stages" Theory' in A Pagden (ed), *The Languages of Political Theory in Early Modern Europe* (CUP Cambridge 1987) 253–76.

no meter, other than judgement of necessity or nature, that separates the opinions of Justinian or Cicero from those of Wolff.[26]

For the jurists of the nineteenth century, the formerly atemporal field of knowledge and reason was to acquire an historical topography of its own. As de Martens was to put it in 1795, whereas Grotius had formerly relied much on the insights of the poets and orators of Rome,

> [the] political situation of Europe is so much changed, since the fifth century in particular, the introduction of the Christian Religion, and of the hierarchical system and all its important consequences, the invention of gunpowder, the discovery of America and the passage to the East Indies, the ever-increasing taste for pomp and luxury, the jealous ambition of powerful states, the multiplication of all sorts of alliances, and the introduction of the custom of sending Ambassadors in ordinary, have had such an influence in forming our present law of nations, that, in general, it is necessary to go no further back than the middle centuries of the Christian Era . . . It is, then, in the history of Europe (and of the states of which it is composed) during the last centuries, that we must look for the existing law of nations.[27]

Immediately, this was to focus attention on the customs and practices of European states, upon the 'positive' or 'voluntary' law of nations as exemplified in treaties and diplomatic exchanges, rather than upon the rationalist discourse of the natural law. But it was also to reshape the way in which the literary tradition of natural law itself was to be received. The figures of Grotius, Pufendorf, Vattel, and so on would acquire a new vital resonance: no longer would they simply be the most prominent, or wise, advocates of a universal metaphysics (and represent, in that sense, a textual, literary tradition of judgement and opinion), but they would become representatives of a definitively historical tradition of thought and practice located in both time and place. As figures, they would begin to appear from behind the veil of their work—as advisors, philosophers, teachers, advocates—engaged in specified diplomatic, legal, and political activity, arguing with greater or lesser distinction as to the nature or content of the law of nations.[28] Their work, furthermore, would no longer be valued merely in terms of its precision, rigour, or exhaustive character, but by the extent to which it spoke to a contemporary moral or political consciousness that was aware of its own historical place. The historicist alignment of judgement and social context that informed this was to add a new evaluative element to all the standard themes: the enslavement of enemies,

---

[26] E de Vattel, *The Law of Nations* (Butler Northampton 1805 [1758]) at xiv ('I have taken the greatest part of my examples from modern history, as most interesting, and to avoid repeating those which Grotius, Pufendorf, and their commentators, have accumulated').

[27] *Summary of the Law of Nations* (n 6) 6.

[28] See eg O Nippold, 'Introduction' (FJ Hemelt trans) in C Wolff, *Jus Gentium Methodo Scientifica* (JH Drake trans) (Clarendon Press Oxford 1934 [1749]) xi–lii, at xxvii ('If we would realize the significance of Wolff to his own age, and perhaps beyond that even to our own, we must needs pay attention above all else to the course of his life. Only from the coign of vantage which a knowledge

claims to territory by way of papal grant, or the pursuit of 'just wars' were questions that could no longer be answered simply in terms of ideas of abstract justice, but in terms that recognized both the historical relativity of ethical judgement and the changing character of the social and political field within which they were to operate.

In the second place, if international law was to discover its new tradition, so also was it to discover new temporal categories. The 'present' would emerge, no longer being a 'moment of profound forgetfulness',[29] but as the measure by which the past was to be revealed and analysed. Categories of legal knowledge would gain or lose significance for the commentator now critically aware of their own surroundings. New questions would appear ('recognition', 'intervention', control over the use of weaponry) and old ones be displaced (for example, marriage, procreation, education, or filial duty). New distinctions would also emerge—between 'international' and 'national',[30] between public and private, between law and political economy. Only now would it become plausible to talk about legal change, or evaluate arguments by reference to the contemporary needs or interests of states or societies. The future, furthermore, would also appear to be radically open: a temporal category towards which energies might be invested (towards liberty, justice, and perpetual peace, and away from despotism, absolutism, and war) and around which intellectual and practical projects, programmes, and policies might gain their measure and purpose.[31] If the theme of 'self-perfection' that had run through the work of both Wolff and Vattel, had already opened out the idea of a *telos* of social and political organization (the procuring of the necessities of life, of peace, security, and well-being), it was in the nineteenth century that identifiable nascent 'futures'—civilization, secularism, humanitarianism, and internationalism—were to become the organizing categories of international legal thought, and provide the conditions for thinking about international law in terms of its infinite progress, development, or fruition.

Thirdly, if ideas of law and justice were temporally conditioned, so also, as Ward had intuited, were they spatially determined. Just as the 'present' of international

---

of his biography supplies can we fully appreciate what we owe to this man or obtain the cultural and historical background upon which the scenes of the work of this philosopher are projected, and against which the figure of Wolff is thrown in extraordinary relief.').

[29] M Foucault, *Society Must be Defended* (D Macey trans) (Picador New York 2003) at 228.

[30] See eg J de Louter, 'Introduction' in C Bynkershoek, *Quaestionum Juris Publici Libri Duo* (T Frank trans) (Clarendon Press Oxford 1930 [1737]) xi–xlvi, at xl–xli ('he disdains the important demarcation between international and national public law and freely intermingles questions of real international relations with those which only concern the constitution of his own country and are ruled by national laws and customs').

[31] K Marx, 'The Eighteenth Brumaire of Louis Bonaparte (1852)' in RC Tucker (ed), *The Marx-Engels Reader* (2nd edn WW Norton and Co New York 1978) 594–617, at 597 ('The social revolution of the nineteenth century cannot draw its poetry from the past, but only from the future').

law, was to be discovered through an analytic that evoked and distinguished past or future, so also did the 'worldliness' of abstract historical knowledge necessarily bring into view the diverse conditions and experiences of people in different parts of the globe.[32] As Koselleck puts it:

With the opening up of the world, the most different but coexisting cultural levels were brought into view spatially and, by way of synchronic comparison, were diachronically classified. World history became for the first time empirically redeemable; however, it was only interpretable to the extent that the most differentiated levels of development, decelerations and accelerations of temporal courses in various countries, social strata, classes, or areas were at the same time necessarily reduced to a common denominator.[33]

If the subsequent nineteenth century treatises organized themselves around the theme of the emergence of a European society of nation states, they typically did so by way of bringing the differentiated temporalities of a non-European world within a unified historical frame through their assimilation into European civilization's pre-modern past. Just as the conditions of savage existence elsewhere in the world, as Locke had already intimated, provided immediate access to the historic underpinnings of civilized European society, so also were nineteenth-century jurists to recognize the conditions of savage or barbaric existence elsewhere as being open to the possibility of maturation and change, and to the acquisition of legal subjectivity (of their 'entry into history' as Hegel was to put it). This, of course, was to lend itself to a new rationality of imperial rule—the production of civilization through beneficent colonization, and to the organization of legal knowledge around those categories (from the conduct of warfare through to territorial title and statehood).[34] It was also to survive in the diachronic organization of economic thought and practice that we now encounter in the term 'development' or 'developing state'.[35]

Finally, if, as Koselleck notes, the *Neuzeit* was to focus attention upon perspective and standpoint—upon, amongst other things, the social and intellectual framework that undergirded the production of the literature of history itself—not only would history be always organized around the present (requiring it to be persistently rewritten), but it would also be indefinitely plural. The differentiated temporalities that marked the geographic orientation of worldly knowledge, were therefore matched by a simultaneous disciplinary dispersion.

---

[32] D Chakrabarty, *Provincializing Europe* (Princeton University Press Princeton 2000) at 7 ('Historicism...posited historical time as a measure of the cultural distance (at least in institutional development) that was assumed to exist between the West and the non-West').

[33] *The Practice of Conceptual History* (n 22) 166.

[34] See A Anghie, *Imperialism, Sovereignty and the Making of International Law* (CUP Cambridge 2005).

[35] S Pahuja, *Decolonising International Law: Development, Economic Growth and the Politics of Universality* (CUP Cambridge 2011).

If nature had its own rhythm, production its phases of development, capital its modes of accumulation, prices their own laws of fluctuation and change, and languages a chronology associated with their own particular coherence,[36] so also would the law of nations have its own history, and one that would be distinct, as Ward noted, from political, economic, social, or cultural history. International legal history, thus, was always to be understood in terms of its own generative specificity, with its own moments of inauguration and change, departures and dispersals. The pursuit of its 'origin' would become an important prerequisite: as being that which enabled its capture as a unified and continuous historical phenomenon, and which disclosed, at the same moment, its fundamental essence.

This was, by no means, to resolve itself in a uniform historiography, but was to bring to the forefront two dynamics. In the first place, it would be conditioned by the simultaneous excision of things impure (politics, ethics, sociology, anthropology, economics, and so on), and their reintroduction in the field of legal knowledge as background conditions. History, in other words, would always be written by reference to a sense of law's boundaries, or of its specificity *in relation to* other fields of knowledge and practice:[37] doctrinal accounts in relation to ethics; institutional or realist accounts in relation to politics; comparative accounts in relation to anthropology or sociology.

In the second place, the harmony that had formerly characterized the relationship between the voluntary and natural law of nations was broken apart, and a situated ethics of international law was to be placed in a condition of permanent struggle against the 'realism' of historical knowledge. As Hayden White explains, historiography was to function at this time as the very paradigm of realistic discourse, 'constituting an image of a current social praxis as the criterion of plausibility by reference to which any given institution, activity, thought, or even a life can be endowed with the aspect of "reality"'.[38] History operated in nineteenth-century Europe, in other words, in precisely the same way as 'God' or 'Nature' had in earlier centuries. From here, and as a consequence, doctrine would be opposed to practice, realism pitched against idealism, the apologetic against the utopian, policy against law, the law 'as it is' as opposed to 'as it should be'. And these oppositions would all be internalized within a legal discourse that endeavoured to both situate itself within the field of power so described, but yet also to transcend it.

---

[36] *The Order of Things* (n 21) 401.
[37] P Allott, 'International Law and the Idea of History' (1999) 1 *Journal of the History of International Law* 1–21, at 1.
[38] H White, *The Content of the Form* (Johns Hopkins University Press Baltimore 1987) at 101.

4 The Historiography of 'Modern' International Law

If, in an immediate sense, the turn to history at the end of the eighteenth century opened the ground for the articulation of a European international law, built upon the (historically conditioned) customs and practices of European nation states,[39] and invested with a teleology that took as its object the advancement of freedom, humanity, peace, and prosperity, it was a consciousness containing, within itself, the conditions of its own critique. For the very object that international lawyers took as their task—the creation of a system of rules and institutions of universal character—was confronted, at every moment, by the apparent particularity of its own historical emergence. If this was not immediately apparent for those engaged in writing the histories of the seamless 'expansion' of international law in the nineteenth and twentieth centuries, or indeed for those concerned with the elaboration of analytical or policy-oriented discourses that operated within historically disinterested fields of enquiry, it was to become very much more so for those either mourning the dissolution of the European nomos,[40] or engaging with the processes of decolonization.[41]

For the new generation 'Third World' scholars of the 1960s such as Anand, Elias, Bedjaoui, Umozurike, and Alexandrowicz the problem was how to put at centre-stage the concerns and interests of the non-European world in conditions under which it had effectively been written out of the discipline's own history. The response was diverse. For some, it was to be achieved through the (re)discovery of lost traditions—of those Asian or African systems of international law that pre-existed colonial rule and interacted with it.[42] For others, it was to be achieved by way of a critique of the ideology of nineteenth century 'doctrinal positivism' which had apparently 'shrunk' the world of international law, ignoring in the process, the empirical practices (treaties, agreements, diplomatic exchanges) that had marked

---

[39] As Wheaton was to observe, the *jus gentium* was 'a particular law, applicable to a distinct set or family of nations, varying at different times with the change in religion, manners, government, and other institutions': H Wheaton, *Elements of International Law* (Fellowes London 1836) at 44–5.

[40] C Schmitt, *The Nomos of the Earth* (GL Ulmen trans) (Telos Press New York 2003).

[41] See eg RP Anand, *New States and International Law* (Vikas Delhi 1972); CH Alexandrowicz, *The European–African Confrontation: A Study in Treaty Making* (AW Sitjhoff Leiden 1973); TO Elias, *Africa and the Development of International Law* (Martinus Nijhoff Dordrecht 1988). See generally A Becker Lorca, 'Eurocentrism in the History of International Law' in A Peters and B Fassbender (eds), *The Oxford Handbook of the History of International Law* (OUP Oxford 2012) 1034–57, at 1042–50.

[42] See eg *Africa and the Development of International Law* (n 41); RP Anand (ed), *Asian States and the Development of Universal International Law* (Vikas Delhi 1972). See further S Sinha, *Legal Polycentricity and International Law* (Carolina Academic Press Chapel Hill 1996).

the relationship between the European and non-European worlds.[43] Others still embraced the European narrative, confident in the promise of a functionalist analytics that envisaged that changes in the structure of international law would simply ensue as a consequence of the changing shape and character of international society.[44] All embraced in one form or another, however, a belief in the possibility of the articulation of a universal history of international law 'in the wake of Empire' so to speak,[45] whilst maintaining at the same time, the same formal commitments to positive law built upon custom and practice, to the idea of progress, or of law 'responding' to the common needs and interests of nation states. If the terms of this new historiography, thus, were to provide new content to the history of international law, they did so largely by leaving intact the methodological precepts that had shaped the work of those such as Ward. Europe still remained, in that sense, the 'silent referent' of historical knowledge.[46]

In more recent years, the problem of *how* to write the history of international law in a way that does not simply subsume the non-European periphery into an essentially European narrative of progress has been a point of constant attention. And in the process, such histories have gained new inflections. Some, such as Anghie and Becker have sought to reinscribe the periphery within an account of mainstream legal thought and practice, either by identifying it as the unspoken 'referent' of doctrinal argument (in which the 'standard of civilization' is seen to invest itself as a trope within the deep structure of legal doctrine),[47] or by bringing to light the critical contribution of scholars from the periphery in appropriating and reformulating key features of the discipline.[48] Others, by contrast, have sought to displace entirely the centrality of European international law by emphasizing the distinctiveness of contrasting world views—in Onuma's terms, the Islamocentric and Sinocentric—in such a way as to problematize any simple account of the 'expansion' of international law, or of its attainment of a condition of universality.[49]

---

[43] CH Alexandrowicz, 'The Afro-Asian World and the Law of Nations (Historical Aspects)' (1968) 123 *Recueil des Cours* 117–214; CH Alexandrowicz, 'Empirical and Doctrinal Positivism in International Law' (1975) 47 *British Yearbook of International Law* 286–9.

[44] See eg RP Anand, 'The Influence of History on the Literature of International Law' in R St J MacDonald and D Johnston (eds), *The Structure and Process of International Law: Essays in Legal Philosophy, Doctrine and Theory* (Martinus Nijhoff The Hague 1983) 341–80, at 341.

[45] N Berman, 'In the Wake of Empire' (1999) 14 *American University International Law Review* 1515–69.

[46] *Provincializing Europe* (n 32) 28, also quoted in M Koskenniemi, 'Histories of International Law: Dealing with Eurocentrism' (2011) 19 *Rechtsgeschichte* 152–76, at 156.

[47] *Imperialism, Sovereignty and the Making of International Law* (n 34).

[48] A Becker Lorca, 'Universal International Law: Nineteenth-Century Histories of Imposition and Appropriation' (2010) 51 *Harvard International Law Journal* 475–552, at 475.

[49] Y Onuma, 'When Was the Law of International Society Born?—An Enquiry of the History of International Law from an Intercivilizational Perspective' (2000) 2 *Journal of the History of International Law* 1–66.

If the main target of such accounts has been the displacement or avoidance of certain facets of the received historical method—denying, for example, the possibility of describing the history of international law in terms of its triumphal, 'progressive', expansion from core to periphery—they have, at the same moment, maintained fealty to the idea that there is a specifiable history of international law whose 'origins' may be traced back to the nineteenth century and beyond, and that the central task is one of redescribing that history in a way that inserts the excluded 'other' back into that story. Whilst, in other words, such counter-histories take on, as Nietzsche described it, a 'critical' as opposed to a 'monumental' cast,[50] they do so nevertheless by leaving intact its basic structure. The problem here is not so much a lack of determination as to what the content of international legal history might be[51]—whether, for example, it is a history of doctrine or practice, a history of structures or processes, a history attentive to the non-European as well as the European experience[52]—but that the question of content, in this case, is not independent of the historical method by which that content is made legible or meaningful. If I am right in observing that international law was to acquire its specifiable and discrete (disciplinary) content through the articulation of historical accounts of its emergence, then it would seem to follow that international law is not simply something that one can examine through the lens of history as if it were some historical artefact existing independently of the means chosen by which it is to be represented, but a field of practice whose meaning and significance is constantly organized around, and through the medium of, a discourse that links present to past. As such, the specification of its origins must always be treated as an act of intervention rather than one of discovery—even if, as we shall see, it is an act which has its own conditions.

In a critique of what he takes to be certain dominant assumptions of mainstream accounts (specifically, those written in progressive, objective, or functionalist terms), Skouteris draws attention to the essentially discursive character of international legal history and to its reducible priority of authorial agency in the 'production' of the past. He forefronts, in the process, two ideas. The first is that the past itself is never available to the legal historian 'as actual events', but only in the form of mediated representations of those events, whether as official records, the work of commentators, or in some other residual or artifactual form. 'History

---

[50] Nietzsche identified three species of history—the monumental, antiquarian, and critical—which served 'the living man' in three different respects: 'to him as a being who acts and strives, as a being who preserves and reveres, [or] as a being who suffers and seeks deliverance': 'On the Uses and Disadvantages of History for Life' (n 15) 67.

[51] Carty observes acutely that 'the reason international legal history is almost impossible to write is that there is no consensus on what international law is': A Carty, 'Doctrine versus State Practice' in *The Oxford Handbook of the History of International Law* (n 41) 972–96, at 974.

[52] For the varieties of history, see M Koskenniemi, 'A History of International Law Histories' in *The Oxford Handbook of the History of International Law* (n 41) 943–71.

and the past' as he puts it, 'are two different things'.[53] The second, and related, observation is that any work of historical reconstruction will always involve acts of selection and arrangement—decisions both as to what is to be represented (state practice, judicial decisions, and so on), and as to how those past events, once reconstructed, will be organized and related to one another.[54] In a positive sense, this draws attention to what Hayden White calls the 'content of the form': bringing into view the (ideological) role of aesthetic structure or narrative organization in the generation of historical meaning.[55] At the same time, however, Skouteris notes that the further one emphasizes the constructed character of history, and the centrality of the historian in its production, the more it 'seems to dissolve any possible ground for assessing the historical past' and undermines 'the possibility of performing much of the work that any jurist is expected to perform in her everyday tasks'.[56] In cutting away the ground from any representation of the past that seeks to 'unveil' meaning or normative insight from the mere fact of its own disclosure, so also, he fears, it seems to cut away the grounds for any kind of historical critique.

Skouteris' concerns, here, as to the unavailability of a straightforward representative account of history may, in some measure, misconstrue the way in which the past is conceptualized within international legal argument. If what is of concern is the way in which ideas and events from the past may be redeployed to new purpose in the present,[57] then the problem may not be that of getting the history straight so much as understanding the conditions under which certain kinds of history appear to make themselves available in contemporary settings. The past, it might be said, only answers the questions we pose of it, but the kinds of questions we might ask, or the styles of analysis we might deploy, are not themselves limitless.

In Foucault's terms, this is to recommend undertaking an analysis of what he calls the 'contemporary limits of the necessary'. What is needed for that purpose, he suggests, is an 'historical investigation into the events that have led us to constitute ourselves and to recognise ourselves as subjects of what we are doing, thinking, saying'.[58] This may be seen to open out two new avenues of thought. In the first

---

[53] 'Engaging History in International Law' (n 2) 112. See also R Koselleck, *Futures Past: On the Semantics of Historical Time* (K Tribe trans) (Columbia University Press New York 2004 [1979]) at 111 ('the facticity of events established *ex post* is never identical with the totality of past circumstances thought of as formerly real. Every event historically established and presented lives on the fiction of actuality: reality itself is past and gone.').

[54] 'Engaging History in International Law' (n 2) 113–14.

[55] See generally *The Content of the Form* (n 38).

[56] 'Engaging History in International Law' (n 2) 118.

[57] For an elegant statement of this point see A Orford, 'On International Legal Method' (2013) 1 *London Review of International Law* 166–76. See also A Orford, 'The Past as Law or History: The Relevance of Imperialism for Modern International Law' (NYU Institute for International Law and Justice, Working Paper No 2012/2), subsequently published in M Toufayan, E Tourme-Jouannet, and H Ruiz Fabri (eds), *International Law and New Approaches to the Third World* (Société de Législation Comparée Paris 2013) 97–118.

[58] M Foucault, 'What is Enlightenment?' in *The Foucault Reader* (n 1) 32–50, at 46.

place, it is to give recognition to the idea that the authorial jurist who claims to exercise sovereignty over the literary patterning of the past of international law, is itself a subject inserted within an (historical and) intellectual context. If this works upon Marx's intuition that we make our own history, but not in conditions of our own choosing, the answer is not merely to strip away all superstition about the past (that is, subject it to a critique of ideology), but to identify and specify the historic conditions that both 'produce' the field of professional expertise that enables international lawyers to imagine themselves as interlocutors within a specifiable discourse and practice, and which also serve to delimit the boundaries of what it is possible to say or think in that context. This may be such as to push historiography in the direction of accounts that both situate the emergence of disciplinary expertise within broader social, economic, cultural, and political fields at the same time as orienting it towards broader questions of structure (the conditioning place, for example, of class and capital).

In the second place, and in a similar sense, it pushes attention towards thinking about the contemporary world of international law, not in terms of a specified set of actors and agencies, powers, and competences, that are already firmly grasped as historically 'given', but as things that are constantly in the condition of being ushered into existence, reinforced, and affirmed. If, as Lang points out, one may understand the regulatory activities of institutions such as the World Trade Organization as contributing to, and shaping, our social, political, and economic knowledge of the world (within which it then seeks to insert itself),[59] so also may one understand the regimes of authority that structure international legal doctrine (states, governments, institutions, and so on) as simply that—claims to authority, knowledge, and truth that pattern behaviour through the repeated injunction that we should act 'as if' they were somehow more than that. History written in this guise is history conscious always of its own productive role in making the world appear.

5 CONCLUSION

The problem I have been trying to put at centre stage in the course of this chapter is one that folds back upon itself: how is one to provide an (historical) account of

---

[59] A Lang, 'The Legal Construction of Economic Rationalities' (2013) 40 *Journal of Law and Society* 155–71.

the emergence of the category of the historical within international law without already presuming its existence? The result, in a sense, is a partial and imperfect performance of that which I am seeking to describe, but it is a performance nevertheless concerned with elucidating the consequences of a very simple idea: everything has a time and place. As I have sketched it out, the consequences of that insight may be thought to have taken two forms, or to have operated in two phases. In the first of these the agenda was to place international law itself within the frame of history—to historicize its normative conditions, to identify its origins, and to map out its emergence and evolution over time. If, initially, this was to gesture towards the dispersion of things in space (to a differentiated geographical legal knowledge) it was nevertheless reintegrated by means of its incorporation within a singular chronology. Development, progress, evolution were the principal watchwords of this spatio-temporal conglomerate. In the second phase, historical knowledge itself has become the point of focus, in which the grounds and conditions for speaking about the past of international law have themselves opened up to examination through the lens of time and place. Here, historical knowledge is insistently contemporary and ideologically laden, capable of producing insight and critique, but nevertheless posing always the problem of how to grasp itself in its own historical conditions. If the history of international law today is unavoidably a history of the present, one task may be to understand the patterns of deployment and consumption, attending to the blind-spots and biases in contemporary accounts, and yet another and perhaps more arduous task may be to understand the (historic) conditions that delimit the parameters of what may or may not be rendered as the past of international law today.

CHAPTER 2

....

ROMAN LAW AND THE INTELLECTUAL HISTORY OF INTERNATIONAL LAW

....

RANDALL LESAFFER

1 Introduction

....

THE pivotal role of Roman law is well established in the historiography of the civil law tradition. Compared to this, its role in the intellectual history of international law is a marginal subject. It has rather drawn scholarly attention as an object of theoretical contention than of substantial scrutiny. Debates turn around two questions: one pertains to the continuity between ancient Roman and modern public international law and the other to the significance of the medieval and early-modern jurisprudence of Roman *private* law for the development of public international law.

The traditional understanding by international lawyers of the history of their field, which was articulated around 1900, has cast a long shadow over the subject. This articulation coincided with the heyday of the sovereign state, positivism, and European imperialism. It is both state- and Eurocentric.[1] Under the traditional

---

[1] M Koskenniemi, 'Histories of International Law: Dealing with Eurocentrism' (2011) 19

narrative, international law's history only truly began with the emergence of the sovereign state. Its intellectual history started with the first systematic expositions of international law as an autonomous body of law regulating relations between states. By and large, writers of the nineteenth century referred to Hugo Grotius (1583–1645) as the starting point for this history.[2] Around 1900, different scholars began to revaluate the significance of contributions from the sixteenth century, in particular from the Spanish neo-scholastics and a few jurists.[3] Since the middle of the twentieth century, the accepted account is that the Spanish neo-scholastics and the humanists stood at the inception of international law as an intellectual field, casting anything which came earlier into the shadows. This view has a deep impact on the debate about the contribution of Roman law to the intellectual history of international law, in both its dimensions.

First, since the nineteenth century, scholars have debated whether there is enough continuity between the 'international law' of the Romans—and by extension that of the whole of Antiquity—and modern international law to include the former in the history of the latter. Many international lawyers of the nineteenth and early twentieth centuries held to the view that the normative systems of international relations of the ancients were altogether too primitive and different to be considered 'international law'. Among the various arguments which have been forwarded for this, two stand out. The first argument is that the great civilizations of Antiquity, and most of all the Roman, were imperialist, leaving no room for equality between states, which was considered a precondition for any international law. The second argument holds that the normative system of the ancients with regards to external relations was embedded in religion. By consequence, it was unilateral and not based on consent.[4] These explanations tie in with state-centric and positivist understandings of international law. After the Second World War,

---

Rechtsgeschichte 152–76; Y Onuma, 'Eurocentrism in the History of International Law' in Y Onuma (ed), *A Normative Approach to War: Peace, War, and Justice in Hugo Grotius* (OUP Oxford 1993) 371–86.

[2] See eg DHL von Ompteda, *Literatur des gesammten natürlichen und positiven Völkerrechts* (2 vols Regensburg JL Montags & Erben 1785 reprinted Scientia Aalen 1963); R Ward, *An Enquiry into the Foundation and History of the Law of Nations in Europe, from the Greeks and the Romans to the Age of Grotius* (2 vols Butterworth London 1795 reprinted Lawbook Exchange Clark 2005).

[3] James Brown Scott (1866–1943) was instrumental in promoting the Spanish neo-scholastics, in particular the theologians Francisco de Vitoria (c 1480–1546) and Francisco Suárez (1548–1617). His *Classics of International Law* (38 vols Carnegie Endowment for International Peace 1911–1950) did much to create a classical text canon of the law of nations. The series included works by the jurists Pierino Belli (1502–1575), Baltasar Ayala (1548–1584), and Alberico Gentili (1552–1608).

[4] C Focarelli, 'The Early Doctrine of International Law as a Bridge from Antiquity to Modernity and Diplomatic Inviolability in 16th- and 17th-Century Practice' in R Lesaffer (ed), *The Twelve Years Truce (1609): Peace, Truce, War and Law in the Low Countries at the Turn of the 17th Century* (Martinus Nijhoff Leiden 2014) 210–32. See also A Nussbaum, 'The Significance of Roman Law in the History of International Law' (1952) 100 *University of Pennsylvania Law Review* 678–89, at 678–81.

several historians of international law challenged and introduced a more relative definition of 'international law', expanding it to all forms of law regulating relations between independent polities, regardless of its religious foundations. This has allowed the indication of the existence of some form of 'international' law for different periods of Antiquity.[5] In most recent times, the view has been forwarded that even hegemony and empire did not signal the end of Roman 'international law'. The Roman Empire had to contend at all times with at least one equal empire, first the Parthian (until 224 CE) and then the Sassanid.[6] Also, the Roman Empire dealt with its 'barbarian' neighbours as well as client states using the rules and procedures of 'international law'.[7]

The acknowledgement of the existence of Roman 'international law' does not, however, exhaust the debate on its relevance for modern international law. The question remains whether Roman international law forms a relevant part of modern international law's history. While there is no support for the idea that Roman and modern international law are parts of one evolving system, there is growing consent that certain customs, institutions, and doctrines of the Romans are at the root of their modern variants. In some cases, one can speak of a continuous process—as for *amicitia*[8] or *bellum justum*[9]—while in other cases, medieval and humanist rediscoveries of Roman law were more instrumental—as with *occupatio* or *uti possidetis*.[10]

Secondly, nineteenth-century international lawyers were very aware—more so than their present-day successors—that medieval Roman as well as canon lawyers discussed subjects of 'international law', but with few exceptions they took a negative view of the work of these medieval scholars. Their reasons varied, but the common denominator was that they considered it proof of the lack of autonomy

---

[5] DJ Bederman, *International Law in Antiquity* (CUP Cambridge 2001); W Preiser, 'Die Epochen der antiken Völkerrechtsgeschichte' (1956) 11 *Juristenzeitung* 737–44; K-H Ziegler, 'Conclusion and Publication of International Treaties in Antiquity' (1995) 29 *Israel Law Review* 233–49.

[6] K-H Ziegler, *Die Beziehungen zwischen Rom und die Partherreich: Ein Beitrag zur Geschichte des Völkerrechts* (Steiner Wiesbaden 1964); B Dignas and E Winter, *Rome and Persia in Late Antiquity: Neighbours and Rivals* (CUP Cambridge 2007).

[7] N Grotkamp, *Völkerrecht im Prinzipat: Möglichkeit und Verbreitung* (Nomos Baden 2009); D Nörr, *Imperium und Polis in der hohen Prinzipatszeit* (2nd edn Beck Munich 1969); R Schulz, *Die Entwicklung des römischen Völkerrecht im vierten und fünften Jahrhundert* (Steiner Stuttgart 1993).

[8] B Paradisi, 'L'amicizia internazionale nell storia antica' and 'L'amicizia internazionale nell' alto medio evo' in *Civitas Maxima: Studi di storia del diritto internazionale* (Olschki Florence 1974) vol 1, 296–338 and 339–97.

[9] SC Neff, *War and the Law of Nations: A General History* (CUP Cambridge 2005) at 34–8 and 46–9.

[10] R Lesaffer, 'Argument from Roman Law in Current International Law: *Occupatio* and Acquisitve Prescription' (2005) 16 *European Journal of International Law* 25–58, at 38–56; L Winkel, 'The Peace Treaties of Westphalia as an Instance of the Reception of Roman Law' in R Lesaffer (ed), *Peace Treaties and International Law in European History: From the End of the Middle Ages to World War I* (CUP Cambridge 2004) 222–37, at 222–4.

of international law.[11] Over the twentieth century, as positivist and state-centred readings of the history of international law receded, scholars took a more neutral view of the role of medieval jurisprudence but the subject in general was met with blanket neglect. The view that the intellectual history of international law really took off in the sixteenth century still holds sway. Studies of medieval Roman and canonistic jurisprudence on matters of international relations remain extremely rare.[12]

The main thrust of this chapter is to correct the existing imbalance in current scholarship that largely ignores or at least underestimates the influence of Roman law on the development of international law. This is done by offering a survey of the historical interactions between Roman law and international law, drawing from general insights into the intellectual history of law in Europe that have remained remarkably absent from the grand narrative of the history of international law. The focus will be on the periods in which these interactions were most pronounced. Next to Roman Antiquity these are the Late Middle Ages (eleventh to fifteenth centuries) and the Early Modern Age (sixteenth to eighteenth centuries).

2 ROMAN ANTIQUITY (SEVENTH CENTURY BCE–SIXTH CENTURY CE)

The oldest traces of Roman 'public international law', in the sense of law regulating relations with other polities, are to be found in the context of the *jus fetiale*. This refers to the rites of the fetial priests used among others to bind the Roman people to treaties with a foreign people or to declare war.[13] The *jus fetiale* offers an example of the fact that among ancient civilizations the norms and procedures regulating foreign relations were binding because of religious sanction—the invocation of a curse of the gods on the Roman people. It was a body of procedures and underlying norms that dealt with, among other things, foreign relations. It was not of international but Roman origin. This did not impede it from forming an effective ground

---

[11] R Lesaffer, 'Roman Law and the Early Historiography of International Law: Ward, Wheaton, Hosack and Walker' in T Marauhn and H Steiger (eds), *Universality and Continuity in International Law* (Eleven International The Hague 2011) 149–84.

[12] Such exceptions are P Haggenmacher, *Grotius et la doctrine de la guerre juste* (PUF Paris 1983); J Muldoon, 'Medieval Canon Law and the Formation of International Law' (1995) 112 *Zeitschrift der Savigny-Stiftung für Rechtsgeschichte, kanonistische Abteilung* 64–82.

[13] Livy, *The History of Rome*, 1.24.4 and 1.32.6. See also A Watson, *International Law in Archaic Rome: War and Religion* (Johns Hopkins University Press Baltimore 1993).

on which to vest binding relations. There is historical evidence of the Romans making treaties whereby both parties invoked their own gods.[14]

As the Romans expanded their power over Italy and the Mediterranean between the fourth and the first century BCE, a greater body of institutions and norms about matters of war and peace, trade, seafaring, and diplomacy developed. Far from only imposing their own customs and ideas, the Romans adopted and adapted those of other peoples such as the Greeks and Carthaginians. The Roman version of 'public international law' extended far beyond the restricted and religion-based *jus fetiale*.[15] As these peoples had in turn been inspired by the 'international law' of the great civilizations of the Ancient Near East, such as the Egyptians, Assyrians, and older Mesopotamian empires, one may speak of a measure of continuity between pre-classical, Greek and Roman 'international law'.[16]

Little of the Roman practice and doctrine of international law has found its way into the compilation of Roman law of the Emperor Justinian (529–65).[17] The main title in the *Digest* covering matters of war and peace is D 49.15 *De captivis et de postliminio redemptis ab hostibus*.[18] Far more informative to modern scholars have been historical texts—such as those by Polybius (c 200–118 BCE) and Livy (59 BCE –17 CE)—as well as rhetorical and philosophical works—chiefly by Cicero (106–43 BCE). It is important to note that much of the latter textual canon was unknown to the medieval jurists so they had only the information from the *Digest* and the other parts of Justinian's compilation to go on. Major historical and rhetorical sources would only be rediscovered and studied by the humanists.

Let us now briefly look at the material substance of Roman international law. Roman legal practices and doctrines in relation to foreign affairs covered all of the major subjects which would constitute 'international law' until deep into the nineteenth century: war and peace, treaties, diplomacy, and (maritime) trade.[19]

The term *jus belli ac pacis* which Grotius would later use to refer to the laws of war and peace-making in the sense of *jus ad bellum*, *jus in bello*, and *just post bellum* came from a speech by Cicero.[20] The Romans knew a rudimentary *jus ad bellum* in their concept of *bellum justum et pium*. Under the *jus fetiale* a war had to be formally declared upon the enemy after the Romans sought redress for the wrong the enemy had allegedly committed. War was an enforcement action after injury,

---

[14] 'Conclusion and Publication of International Treaties in Antiquity' (n 5) 234–9.

[15] ES Gruen, *The Hellenistic World and the Coming of Rome* (University of California Press Berkeley 1984) chs 1–5.

[16] R Ago, 'The First International Communities in the Mediterranean World' (1982) 53 *British Yearbook of International Law* 213–32.

[17] All translations from the *Digest* are from A Watson (ed), *The Digest of Justinian* (2 vols revised edn University of Pennsylvania Press Philadelphia 1998).

[18] See also *Codex Justiniani* 8.50.

[19] For a survey, K-H Ziegler, *Völkerrechtsgeschichte: Ein Studienbuch* (2nd edn Beck Munich 2007) at 35–61.

[20] Cicero, *Pro Balbo*, 6.15.

as it would be in the medieval just war doctrine.[21] Cicero mentioned two just causes for war: defence and avenging a wrong.[22] Roman practice indeed shows that the Romans argued that their wars were defensive or reactions against a prior wrong-doing by the enemy.[23] Roman law distinguished war between public enemies, who had a right to equal treatment under the laws of war, from violence between non-public enemies; such as robbers and pirates.[24] In relation to *jus in bello*, the right to *postliminium* stands out. Through its place in the *Digest* (D 49.15), it became one of the Roman conceptions of the laws of war and peace which was most discussed in medieval and early-modern jurisprudence.[25] The Romans recognized the binding character of treaties during wartime. Main wartime treaties included armistices (*indutiae*),[26] safe conducts, and exchanges of prisoners.[27] There were two major forms of ending wars (*just post bellum*): peace treaties and surrender (*deditio*).[28]

The Roman practice of treaty-making was similar to that of the Ancient Near East or the Ancient Greeks. Treaties were oral agreements which were confirmed by oath and invocations of the wrath of the gods in case of violation. Treaties were commonly written down and published, but this was not constitutive of their binding character. This procedure would remain standard until deep into the Middle Ages. The Roman term for a public treaty made according to this procedure was *foedus*. As the Roman network of foreign relations expanded territorially, it became unpractical to have the treaties confirmed by *fetiales*. Their role in the making of treaties was assumed by magistrates—and later the emperor—while the ritual character of the procedure lessened.[29] Next to *foedus*, the Romans used more informal ways of making treaties. There was the *sponsio* whereby magistrates who had not been mandated by the people or senate made a treaty through the mutual exchange of promises. The people or senate retained the right to reject the treaty afterwards.

---

[21] *War and the Law of Nations* (n 9) 34–8 and 45–68; J von Elbe, 'The Evolution of the Concept of Just War in International Law' (1939) 33 *American Journal of International Law* 665–88, at 666–7.

[22] Cicero, *De re publica*, 3.35a.

[23] *International Law in Antiquity* (n 5) 207–41; WV Harris, *War and Imperialism in Republican Rome 327–70 BC* (Clarendon Press Oxford 1979) 175–254.

[24] *Digest* (n 17) 49.15.24.

[25] Ibid 49.15.5 for prisoners of war; 49.15.19 for property; 41.1.5.7 for the basis of Roman right of booty (*jus praedae*). See also *International Law in Antiquity* (n 5) 242–60; J Plescia, 'The Roman "Ius Belli"' (1989–1990) 92–3 *Bullettino dell'istituto di diritto romano Vittorio Scialoja* 497–523.

[26] *Digest* (n 17) 49.15.19.1.

[27] K-H Ziegler, 'Kriegsverträge im antiken römischen Recht' (1985) 102 *Zeitschrift der Savigny-Stiftung für Rechtsgeschichte, romanistische Abteilung* 40–90.

[28] C Baldus, '*Vestigia pacis*: The Roman Peace Treaty: Structure or Event' in *Peace Treaties and International Law in European History* (n 10) 103–46; K-H Ziegler, 'Friedensverträge im römischen Altertum' (1989) 27 *Archiv des Völkerrechts* 45–62; 'Kriegsverträge im antiken römischen Recht' (n 27) 51–6, 67–70, 79–86.

[29] A Nussbaum, 'Forms and Observance of Treaties in the Middle Ages and the Early 16th Century' in GA Lipsky (ed), *Law and Politics in the World Community: Essays on Hans Kelsen's Pure Theory and Related Problems in International Law* (University of California Press Berkeley 1953) 191–8; 'Conclusion and Publication of International Treaties in Antiquity' (n 5).

Furthermore, the Romans applied the concept of good faith (*bona fides*)—which had been inspired by its Greek analogue (πίστις)—to treaties.[30] Two important types of relationships, next to peace and alliance, were *amicitia* and *hospitium*. *Amicitia* (friendship) entails a mutual recognition of equality and is the precondition on which to vest peaceful relations. It lays down the foundations for further legal relations between peoples. It can either be established through treaty or in a more informal way.[31] *Hospitium* (guest friendship) is a treaty whereby two polities promise legal protection to one another's subjects. As such, it is the basis for trade.[32] Finally, the Romans knew the principle of the inviolability of diplomats.[33]

But the major contribution Roman law made to the intellectual history of international law is probably through the introduction of the term *jus gentium* and its multiple meanings. Originally, *jus gentium* (law of nations) did not refer to relations between polities. It was the law the Roman magistrates applied to foreigners. In this respect, it was a kind of 'universal' private law, albeit of Roman making. It was a set of *formulae*—written documents allowing a case to be taken to court—which were introduced by the magistrate who had jurisdiction over foreigners in Rome, the *praetor peregrinus* (from 242 BCE). Although its development was as casuistic as that of the *jus civile*, it had a higher level of abstraction than the latter as the *praetor peregrinus* had to span differences between the legal cultures involved.[34]

With time, Roman orators and jurists made three semantic moves with *jus gentium*. First, a close association was made between *jus gentium* and *jus naturale*. The Romans adopted the notion of humanity as a universal community and natural law as a universal law innate in (human) nature from Greek Stoic philosophy. Cicero, who played a significant role in transferring Greek philosophical ideas into the Roman literary tradition, associated *jus gentium* with natural law.[35] The association was reiterated by Gaius (second century CE) in a text also quoted in the *Digest*.[36] It highlighted the universal as well as foundational dimension of *jus gentium*. Whereas in fact it was the product of inductive generalization from Roman and foreign legal

---

[30] D Nörr, *Die Fides im römischen Völkenrecht* (Muller Heidelberg 1991); 'Conclusion and Publication of International Treaties in Antiquity' (n 5); *Völkerrechtsgeschichte* (n 19) 39–40.

[31] PJ Burton, *Friendship and Empire: Roman Diplomacy and Imperialism in the Middle Republic (353–146 BC)* (CUP Cambridge 2011); A Heuss, 'Die völkerrechtlichen Grundlagen der römischen Assenpolitik in republikanischer Zeit' (1933) 13 *Klio Beiheft* 1–59, at 46; B Paradisi, 'L'amitié internationale: les phases critiques de son ancienne histoire' (1951) 78 *Recueil des Cours* 325–78.

[32] *International Law in Antiquity* (n 5) 120–36; K-H Ziegler, 'Regeln für den Handelsverkehr in Staatsverträgen des Altertums' (2002) 70 *Legal History Review* 55–67.

[33] *Digest* (n 17) 50.7.18; *International Law in Antiquity* (n 5) 88–119; TRS Broughton, 'Mistreatment of Foreign Legates and the Fetial Priests: Three Roman Cases' (1987) 41 *Phoenix* 50–62.

[34] M Kaser, *Ius gentium* (Böhlau Köln 1993).

[35] Cicero, *De officiis* 3.23: 'The same thing is established not only in nature, that is in the law of nations…'. Translation from Cicero, *On Duties* (MT Griffin and EM Atkins eds and trans) (CUP Cambridge 1991) at 108.

[36] *Digest* (n 17) 1.1.9 (Gaius 1.1): '…By contrast, that law which natural reason has established among all human beings is among all observed in equal measure and is called *jus gentium*, as being the law which all nations observe.'

systems, the Ciceronian move laid the foundation for later conceptions of *jus gentium* as the legal expression of immutable and universal principles.

Secondly, the classical jurist Ulpian (*d* 223/224) defined natural law as the law common to all animals, while *jus gentium* was the law common to all men. Ulpian did not state that *jus gentium* was the natural law of mankind, but many have understood it to be so.[37]

Thirdly, in the *Digest* a definition of *jus gentium* is to be found that encompasses both the original meaning of universal private law as that of a law of foreign relations. In D 1.1.5 the post-classical jurist Hermogenian (lived *c* 300) defined *jus gentium* as the law whereby '…wars were introduced, nations differentiated, kingdoms founded, properties individuated, estate boundaries settled, buildings put up, and commerce established, including contracts of buying and selling and letting and hiring (except for certain contractual elements established through *jus civile*).' The definition of Saint Isidorus, Bishop of Seville (*d* 636) in his *Etymologiae* only included aspects of foreign relations, except for one (mixed marriages).[38]

With these steps, Roman jurisprudence bequeathed to the Middle Ages a concept of *jus gentium* that spanned two meanings: that of a universal law, which might well apply to individuals as to polities; and that of a law applicable to relations between polities. It also bequeathed a strong association between *jus gentium* and *jus naturale*.[39]

3 THE LATE MIDDLE AGES (ELEVENTH TO FIFTEENTH CENTURIES)

Late-medieval jurists did not perceive of *jus gentium* as an autonomous body of law governing relations between independent political entities. Neither did they make it into an autonomous academic discipline with its own literature. But this did not prevent them from writing extensively, and with a great deal of sophistication,

---

[37] *Digest* (n 17) 1.1.1.3–4, see 4: '*Jus gentium*, the law of nations, is that which all human peoples observe. That it is not co-extensive with natural law can be grasped easily, since the latter is common to all animals whereas *jus gentium* is common only to human beings among themselves.'

[38] Isidorus, *Etymologiae*, 5.6: 'The law of nations concerns the occupation of territory, building, fortification, wars, captivities, enslavements, the right of return, treaties of peace, truces, the pledge not to molest embassies, the prohibition of marriages between different races. And it is called the "law of nations" because nearly all nations use it.' Translation from Isidorus, *The Etymologies of Isidore of Seville* (SA Barney et al., eds and trans) (CUP Cambridge 2006) at 118.

[39] K Tuori, 'The Reception of Ancient Legal Thought in Early Modern International Law' in B Fassbender and A Peters (eds), *The Oxford Handbook of the History of International Law* (OUP Oxford 2012) 1012–33, at 1016–8.

on issues relating to war, peace, treaties, diplomacy, and trade between polities and thus making a significant contribution to the intellectual development of international law.

The rediscovery of a full copy of the *Digest* in the third quarter of the eleventh century marked the beginning of medieval jurisprudence. By the end of the century, Roman law was taught on the basis of Justinian's compilation—known since the sixteenth century as the *Corpus Juris Civilis*—at the emerging university of Bologna. By the end of the twelfth century, university teaching of the *jus civile* had spread over Italy, France, Spain, and England. Between the fourteenth and sixteenth centuries it spread to the centre, north, and east of Europe.

But the study of Roman law was only one branch of the learned law of the Late Middle Ages. The Gregorian Reform of the mid-eleventh century and the ensuing rise of the papal monarchy led to the growth of canon law into an extensive and sophisticated body of law. It became the subject of study at university schools of canon law. Around 1140, an authoritative collection of canon law was made by Gratian, the *Decretum Gratiani*. It quickly became the standard source for the discipline. In 1234, Pope Gregory IX (r 1227–1241) promulgated the *Liber Extra*, a codification of canon law from after the *Decretum*, at one and the same time stamping his authority on Gratian's work. Together with the *Liber Sextus* (1298) and two smaller collections from the fourteenth century, these texts constituted the authoritative sources of canon law. The collection was later named the *Corpus Juris Canonici*. As opposed to Roman law, which was not directly applicable law in most places in Europe, canon law was the applicable law of the Church. Through its hierarchical network of courts and the wide jurisdiction it claimed in matters such as family or contract law, it had a huge impact on the legal development of Europe. As canon law had adopted much from Roman law, it was an important factor in the reception of Roman law as well.[40]

Roman and canon law form the twin branches of the late-medieval jurisprudence of the Latin West, the *jus commune*. The civilians and canonists were scholastics as much as the theologians were, and they made a significant contribution to the development of scholastic theory and methodology. The foundational tenet of scholasticism was that truth as revealed by God was laid down in authoritative texts. This was a vast and expanding collection of texts including the Bible, the writings of the Church Fathers, the works of some ancient philosophers such as Plato and Aristotle, and the two *corpora* of Roman and canon law. The authority of the texts was absolute. One should be capable of extracting from the totality of the sources an objective, immutable, and consistent truth. Translated to the world of law this implied that the study of the Justinian and/or canon law texts should

---

[40] J Brundage, *Medieval Canon Law* (Longmans London 1995) 44–56; RH Helmholz, *The Spirit of Classical Canon Law* (University of Georgia Press Athens 1996) 1–32.

lead to the discovery of a law which was complete, consistent, timeless, universal, and which provided a just solution to any legal problem. Scholastic logic—dialectics—was the sophisticated tool the medieval scholars developed to bridge the gap between the idealism of their claims and the reality of the texts.[41]

Legal historians distinguish two major, subsequent 'schools' in the study of Roman law in the Middle Ages. First came the glossators. Their endeavours culminated in the *Glossa Ordinaria* by Accursius (*c* 1182–1263). After these came the commentators, who would dominate most European law schools until the seventeenth century. For canonists, a parallel distinction is made between decretists and decretalists with the promulgation of the *Liber Extra* as the dividing line. It is hard to pinpoint the differences between the glossators and commentators, but in general terms medieval jurisprudence can be understood in terms of an incremental shift from text to content. Whereas the first generations of civilians were mostly concerned with understanding and explaining the authoritative text itself, the later generations took more distance from the texts in their search for the ideal law they hoped to extract from them. This is best illustrated by referring to the main genres of literary production of the two schools. The glossators wrote their explanations down in the form of *glossae*. These were accumulating layers of (mostly marginal) notes in which they offered textual or content explanations, pointed at parallel locations, and reasoned away contradictions. The commentaries of the later civilians were longer discussions on larger fragments of the *Corpus Juris Civilis*, allowing for more systematization and above all, freedom. This enhanced autonomy was even more evident with treatises, which were expositions on a certain topic whereby the author could order his sources freely. Treatises started to emerge from the fourteenth century onwards but only truly broke through in the sixteenth century. The shift from text to content also caused the civilians to expand their canon of texts. They addressed legal questions by applying different sources to the matter, spanning Roman law, canon law but also *jura propria*. Furthermore, the medieval civilians were increasingly involved with practice. Professors of the *jus civile* were frequently asked to render a legal advice in current disputes. Leading commentators such as Bartolus of Saxoferrato (1314–1357) and Baldus de Ubaldis (1327–1400) wrote numerous *consilia*.[42]

Medieval civilians as well as canonists wrote extensively about matters of war and peace, diplomacy, and trade. They developed sophisticated doctrines on these subjects. For the most parts, these writings are not to be found in self-standing texts, but were fully part and parcel of their writings on law in general. Much of the relevant medieval scholarship therefore needs to be extracted from the glosses

---

[41] W Ullmann, *Medieval Foundations of Renaissance Humanism* (Cornell University Press Ithaca 1977) at 14–29.

[42] R Lesaffer, *European Legal History: A Cultural and Political Perspective* (CUP Cambridge 2009) at 252–65.

and commentaries of both civilians and canonists all throughout their works. Furthermore, numerous *consilia* by the commentators are relevant. These could involve *consilia* written for the purpose of a case before a feudal, royal, or imperial court. But it could also pertain to diplomatic disputes, which were not brought into court.[43] Canon law even had a more direct connection to practice as ecclesiastical courts—with the papal *Rota Romana* at the apex of the hierarchy—held jurisdiction over major issues of diplomacy such as the violation of treaties confirmed by oath and claims to the justice of war.[44]

From the fourteenth century onwards, a limited number of treatises on relevant subjects were produced. Most notably among these are the treatise on reprisals by Bartolus,[45] the treatises on war, reprisals and duels by Giovanni da Legnano[46] as well as the treatises by the fifteenth-century Italian canon lawyer Martinus Garatus Laudensis on diplomacy and treaties.[47] The great collection of fifteenth and sixteenth century canon law treatises *Tractatus Universi Juris* contains some additional tracts on war and peace as well as diplomacy.[48] From the fifteenth century, there are more treatises on diplomacy and diplomatic law.[49]

Medieval civilians and canonists discussed matters of war, peace, trade, and diplomacy in their glosses and commentaries at those places where they found a *sedes materiae*, literally 'a seat of the matter' in the authoritative text. As has already been indicated, the Justinianic collection held relatively little information on the Roman 'international law'. The main titles from the *Digest* were D 1.1 *De justitia et jure*, D 49.15 which dealt with prisoners of war, *postliminium* and treaties,[50] D 49.16 *De re militari* which covered matters of military discipline and

---

[43] Jurisprudence also had its influence on diplomatic practice felt through the role of jurists in that practice—as ministers or diplomats—as well as through the use of public notaries to make diplomatic instruments such as treaties. Important collections on notarial practice such as the *Speculum judiciale* (c 1290) of Gulielmus Durantis (c 1237–1296) contained examples of diplomatic instruments: *Speculum juris* (Basel Frobenii 1574, reprinted Aalen Scientia 1975) 4.1 *De treuga et pace*.

[44] *The Spirit of Classical Canon Law* (n 40) 126–7; R Lesaffer, 'Peace Treaties from Lodi to Westphalia' in *Peace Treaties and International Law in European History* (n 10) 9–41, at 22–6.

[45] See Bartolus, 'Tractatus Represaliarum' in *Consilia, questiones, et tractatus [...]* (Venetiis per Batistam de Tortis 1529 reprinted Il Cigno Galileo Galilei Rome 1996) at 115vb–120va.

[46] Giovanni da Legnano, *Tractatus De Bello, De Represaliis et De Duello* (TE Holland ed) (2 vols OUP Oxford 1917 [1477]).

[47] Martinus Garatus Laudensis, *De legatis et legationibus tractatus varii* (VE Grabar ed) (C Mattiesen Dorpat 1905 [1625]); Martinus Garatus Laudensis, *Tractatus de confederatione, pace et conventionibus principum* in *Peace Treaties and International Law in European History* (n 10) 412–47.

[48] *Tractatus Universi Juris* (Venetiis apud Franciscum Zilettum 1584–1586) vol 16 (*De dignitate et potestate seculari*) (with treatises by Garatus and Belli but also with treatises on war by Johannes Lupus and Franciscus Arias, all known to Grotius) but also vols 10–12 (with treatises on truce and peace by Octavianus Volpellius and Nicolaus Moronus).

[49] See B Behrens, 'Treatises on the Ambassador Written in the Fifteenth and Early Sixteenth Centuries' 51 (1936) *English Historical Review* 616–27.

[50] See also *Codex Justiniani* 8.50.

jus in bello,[51] as well as D 50.7 *De legationibus*, on diplomats. To this a few texts on feudal law, the *Libri feudorum*, which had made their way into the medieval version of the Justinianic codification, can be added. This allowed commentators to expand on matters of political organization and public authority. As relevant was the addition of the *Pax Constantiae* of 1183 between Emperor Frederick I (r 1155–1190) and the Lombard League, which elicited writings on peace-making and peace treaties.[52] The main locations in the *Corpus Juris Canonici* were Gratian on just war[53] and the title *De treuga et pace* from the *Liber Extra*.[54]

This all in all limited basis did not prevent medieval jurists from dealing extensively with international relations; quite the contrary. Civilians, as well as canonists, did not have to restrict themselves to Roman 'international law' texts to apply to matters of war, peace, trade, and diplomacy. The whole range of authoritative texts could be brought to bear on these subjects. The civilians applied a multitude of texts and doctrines from Roman law which in origin bore no relation to these matters. Many of these stemmed from Roman private law. The main examples of these 'transplants' include the use of contract law in relation to treaties,[55] property law in relation to territory and boundaries (*jus finium*)[56] as well as *jus in bello* and *jus praedae*,[57] the law of delict and criminal law in relation to the use of force, Roman private arbitration in the context of arbitration between princes and polities,[58]

[51] See also Ibid 12.35. For a more complete survey of relevant passages in the Justinianic texts, see A Wijffels, 'Early-Modern Scholarship on International Law' in A Orakhelashvili (ed), *Research Handbook on the Theory and History of International Law* (Edward Elgar Cheltenham 2011) 23–60, at 29–32 and see especially K-H Ziegler, 'Die römische Grundlagen des europäischen Völkerrechts' (1972) 4 *Ius Commune* 1–27.

[52] Odofredus (d 1265) and Baldus de Ubaldis wrote extensive commentaries on the *Pax Constantiae*. See also Baldus on LF 2.27 *De pace tenenda, et eius violatoribus* from the *Libri feudorum* as well as *Consilium* 2.195 in Baldus, *Consilia* (Venice 1575 reprinted Bottega d'Erasmo Turin 1970); R Lesaffer, 'Gentili's *ius post bellum* and Early Modern Peace Treaties' in B Kingsbury and B Straumann (eds), *The Roman Foundations of the Law of Nations: Alberico Gentili and the Justice of Empire* (OUP Oxford 2010) 210–40, at 216–7; K-H Ziegler, 'The Influence of Medieval Roman Law on Peace Treaties' in *Peace Treaties and International Law in European History* (n 10) 147–61.

[53] *Decretum Gratiani* 23 q 2 c 2, referring to Isidorus, *Etymologiae* 18.1.2/3. On just war in medieval theology and canon law, see J Barnes, 'The Just War' in N Kretzman et al., (eds), *The Cambridge History of Later Medieval Philosophy* (CUP Cambridge 1982) 750–84; *Grotius et la doctrine de la guerre juste* (n 12) 51–444; *War and the Law of Nations* (n 9) 45–82; FH Russell, *The Just War in the Middle Ages* (CUP Cambridge 1975).

[54] *Liber Extra* (1234) X.1.34. For more canon law texts, see J Muldoon, 'The Contribution of Medieval Canon Lawyers to the Formation of International Law' (1972) 28 *Traditio* 483–97.

[55] R Lesaffer, 'The Medieval Canon Law of Contract and Early Modern Treaty Law' (2000) 2 *Journal of the History of International Law* 78–98.

[56] P Marchetti, *De iure finium: Diritto e confini tra tardo Medioevo ed età moderna* (Giuffrè Milan 2001).

[57] *Digest* (n 17) 43.16 (*De vi et de vi armata*) and *Codex Justiniani* 8.4.

[58] K-H Ziegler, 'Arbiter, arbitrato und amicabilis compositor' (1967) 84 *Zeitschrift der Savigny-Stiftung für Rechtsgeschichte, romanistische Abteilung* 376–81.

as well as the use of the contract of *mandatum* for diplomats.[59] But there is also a manifold of less obvious examples, such as from succession law.[60]

To the medieval jurists this came naturally. In fact, they would not have thought of this in terms of 'transplants', and this is for two reasons. First, although the concepts of public and private law were known and operated, they did not define distinct spheres of law yet. Neither was there a strict separation between the international and domestic legal orders. Public authority was not yet monopolized by one level of government. The order of the Latin West was one of a hierarchical continuum of polities and jurisdictions, ranging from the pope and emperor at the top over kingdoms, principalities, feudal lordships and city-states to a myriad of local authorities at the base. These all stood in some hierarchical relation to one another, having original authority or jurisdiction for some matters and being a subject power for others. The authority to engage in war, peace, and diplomacy was, by consequence, diffused over a great variety of entities and the dividing line between what constituted 'public' and 'private' was not clear. While this certainly troubled medieval jurists, the question whether a certain use of force was an instance of public war or private violence was not always easy to answer. Some jurists did refer to the law applicable to international relations as *jus gentium* but that was not the full or exclusive meaning of the term. Its primary meaning was that of a universal law and the distinction between universal private law and public international law was collapsed in it as it was in reality.[61]

Secondly, the medieval jurists did not conceive of a separate jurisprudence of international law, as they did not conceive of their field as fragmented in any way. The law to be found in the authoritative sources of Roman and canon law was not only timeless and universal; it was also 'whole'. It was permeated by one objective, absolute truth, ultimately vested in divine revelation. Principles and rules which applied to one subject were necessarily valid for others. This concept of 'totality'[62] went beyond the law. It stretched to any other field of study, most significantly theology.

In relation to international law as to any other aspect of the law, civil and canon law were more than just two pillars of the *jus commune*. They operated in close conjunction. Many medieval jurists had been exposed to the two branches of the learned law as students and many scholars drew from both textual canons in dealing with concrete issues. It is actually in the interplay between Roman law and canon law (and theology) that medieval jurisprudence was at its most creative and

---

[59] DE Queller, *The Office of the Ambassador in the Middle Ages* (Princeton University Press Princeton 1967).

[60] See the use of *Digest* 24.3.38 by Martinus Garatus Laudensis in *Tractatus de confederatione, pace et conventionibus principum* (n 47) 425 q xxix.

[61] SC Neff, 'A Short History of International Law' in MD Evans (ed), *International Law* (2nd edn OUP Oxford 2006) 3–31, at 6–7.

[62] *Medieval Foundations* (n 41) 14–19.

made its most valuable contributions to the civil law tradition and the jurisprudence of international law. To this, two remarks may be added. First, even when they were dealing with similar questions, Roman lawyers on one side and theologians and canon lawyers on the other had different focuses. The primary concern of theologians and canon lawyers in raising legal questions was what man's behaviour would do to his eternal life. Whether his actions constituted sins or not. In this respect, their law applied in the forum of conscience (*forum internum*) and was first and foremost centred on general rules of morality. Canon law was at the same time the law applicable and enforceable in ecclesiastical courts and thus also pertained to the *forum externum*, providing sanctions in the here and now. In consequence, it was also a detailed and sophisticated technical body of law. The primary focus of Roman lawyers was on the here and now, on the legal effects and sanctioning of human behaviour by other humans. Secondly, in very general terms, one could say that in the interplay between canon and Roman law, the former brought in the general (moral) principles and the latter the technical elements. The formulation of the principles of *pacta sunt servanda* and the general liability for compensation of wrongful damages offer important examples of this.[63]

4 The Early Modern Age (Sixteenth to Eighteenth Centuries)

The first half of the sixteenth century saw the collapse of the medieval legal order of the Latin West. The Reformation made what had been the foundation of its unity into the fault line of its fracture. By the middle of the century, approximately half of Europe rejected the authority of the pope, the ecclesiastical courts, and canon law, thus tumbling one of two pillars on which the order of Europe rested. By the end of the century, canon law had also ceased to play a major role in international relations within the Catholic world. The conquests in the Americas caused the need, at least in the eyes of many, for an international law which was not based on Roman or canon law. The emergence of powerful composite monarchies led to the final destruction of the universal claims of the emperor and the pope in secular, and sometimes even spiritual, matters. Together with the influence of humanism, this led to a gradual 'nationalization' of civilian jurisprudence.[64]

---

[63] W Decock, *Theologians and Contract Law: The Moral Transformation of the Ius Commune (ca 1500–1650)* (Martinus Nijhoff Leiden 2013) at 105–61; J Gordley, *The Philosophical Origins of Modern Contract Law* (OUP Oxford 1991).
[64] See *European Legal History* (n 42) 303–8.

The ensuing crisis of international order of the West would endure until a new legal order was articulated in the second half of the seventeenth century, *after* the Peace of Westphalia (1648), that of the *jus publicum Europaeum*. It fostered intellectual dynamism in the field of international relations and is one of the explanations behind the birth of the law of nations as an autonomous discipline. The collapse of the authority of canon law and the gradual fragmentation of Roman jurisprudence along state-lines forced scholars to look for an alternative locus of authority for the legal organization of international relations. This was to be natural law.

Modern literature has defined two major schools of thought to classify the writers of the law of nations of the sixteenth and early seventeenth centuries: neo-scholastics and humanists. While these are defendable categories, it is not always evident to what school a certain author belongs. Moreover, one should be careful not to overstate the homogeneity within each school or the differences between them. The distinction is sometimes understood as one between theologians and canon lawyers on the one hand and civilians on the other. While the picture from real life is again far more complex than that, it can be held that humanism had a significant impact on the civilian jurisprudence of the law of nations.[65]

In the early sixteenth century, humanism gained a foothold at different law faculties, most famously at Bourges in France. However, humanism did not overhaul the dominant position of the commentators at most European law schools and neither did it lead, even among humanist jurists themselves, to a complete break with scholasticism, regardless of the severe criticism by humanists of it. All in all, there were very few radically consequential humanists among the jurists. On the other hand, humanism had a profound influence on civilian jurisprudence, also in relation to the law of nations. By the middle of the seventeenth century, a reformed paradigm of civilian jurisprudence was in place, which drew on both scholastic and humanist traditions.[66]

The influence of humanism on civilian jurisprudence was fourfold. First, the humanists looked at the authoritative textual canon through the lens of a different paradigm than the scholastics. To them the authoritative sources stemming from Antiquity were not the repository of a revealed, absolute, universal, and timeless truth but the synthetic products of an historic civilization. They were worthy of study because the Greek and Roman cultures were considered the historical high-points of human achievement. Their authority degraded from absolute to relative, from indisputable to that of an example to be emulated. In this respect, the humanist demarche was first and foremost a historical one. The primary endeavour of humanism was to create an historically correct reconstruction of the text and its authentic meaning. However, with few exceptions, even the more radical humanists among

---

[65] *The Roman Foundations of the Law of Nations* (n 52); R Tuck, *The Rights of War and Peace: Political Thought and the International Order from Grotius to Kant* (OUP Oxford 1999).

[66] 'Early-Modern Scholarship on International Law' (n 51) 35–51.

the civilians did not stop there. The historical paradigm did not prevent them from applying Roman law to current issues, much in the same way the commentators had. But, with time, later in the sixteenth century, they started to do so with more critical distance than their medieval predecessors. One took inspiration from Roman law not because it held a claim to absolute authority, but because a certain rule was the best example available. By the mid-seventeenth century, the criterion of evaluation forwarded would be accordance to reason and rational natural law. In this way, humanism helped pave the way for the Modern School of Natural Law with Grotius as the foremost transitional figure. However, until deep into the eighteenth century if not later, a self-evident association between Roman law and natural reason survived. This was helped along by the fact that a claim to rationality implied a claim to universality. Against local and national laws, Roman law could still play a trump card even if the 'universal' character of civilian jurisprudence withered.[67]

Secondly, humanism expanded the classical textual canon of the civilians. In addition to the *Corpus Juris Civilis* and the canonistic, theological, and philosophical sources of medieval scholarship, civilians also drew on newly discovered ancient historical, rhetorical, and philosophical texts. Among others, the works of Polybius, Livy, Seneca (*c* 4 BCE–65 CE), Tacitus (*c* 56–117), and above all Cicero were brought to bear on the law of nations.

Thirdly, as the authority of Roman law became relative, humanism gave a new stimulus to widening the scope of legal argument and looking at other law systems, primarily *jura propria* and emerging national laws. In this respect, humanists contributed to the 'nationalization' of civilian jurisprudence, thereby undercutting the universal authority of Roman law.

Fourthly, humanism fostered the systematization of law. The replacing of the complex 'system' of the *Digest* with that of the more transparent *Institutes* allowed for a more rational ordering of the law and marked a new step in the emancipation from the sources. Moreover, treatises became a far more significant genre than before. From the second half of the sixteenth century, a growing number of autonomous treatises on aspects of the law of nations appeared.[68] The treatises of Belli,[69] Ayala,[70] and Gentili[71] are the best-known examples of these. Grotius, who was an accomplished humanist man of letters, may be counted with them.

---

[67] 'Early-Modern Scholarship on International Law' (n 51) 51.

[68] DR Kelley, 'Civil Science in the Renaissance: Jurisprudence in the French Manner' (1981) 3 *Journal of the History of Ideas* 261–76; *European Legal History* (n 42) 350–9; P Stein, 'Legal Humanism and Legal Science' (1986) 54 *Legal History Review* 297–306; J Witte, *Law and Protestantism: The Legal Teachings of the Lutheran Reformation* (CUP Cambridge 2002).

[69] P Belli, *De re militari et bello tractatus* (HC Nutting trans) (2 vols Clarendon Press Oxford 1936 [1563]).

[70] B Ayala, *De iure et officiis bellicis et disciplina militari libri III* (J Westlake ed JP Bate trans) (2 vols Carnegie Institute Washington DC 1912 [1582]).

[71] Mainly A Gentili, *De iure belli libri III* (JC Rolfe trans) (2 vols Clarendon Press Oxford 1933 [1598/1612]).

These treatises are among the first attempts to treat with the laws of war and peace-making in a systematic as well as a comprehensive way. They marked the emancipation of *jus gentium* in the sense of the law regulating relations between independent polities as an autonomous discipline.[72] Recent scholarship—particularly from the angle of the history of political philosophy—has by and large explained humanist jurisprudence in terms of a direct discovery of and interaction with ancient historical, rhetorical, and philosophical sources, almost completely ignoring the mediating role of medieval scholarship.[73] Some scholars who restored the humanists' entanglement with the Justinianic codification into the discussion have done this without giving acknowledgement to the fact that the humanists stood in an almost 500-year old tradition of studying Roman law and have written about this in terms of an original discovery of Roman law rather than a *rediscovery* through a different looking glass.[74]

The early-modern jurisprudents of international law related with Roman law in two different ways. First, as has been underscored in recent scholarship, they expanded their knowledge about Roman 'international law' thanks to the new discovery of ancient Roman historical, rhetorical, and philosophical sources. Secondly, they continued the dialogue with Roman law which had started in the eleventh century, albeit from a partially different perspective. The expansion of the textual canon by the humanists surely changed their views on ancient Roman law, but it did not prevent them from building on the work of their medieval predecessors, much as they might criticise them. From the humanist perspective, the writings of the medieval jurists were just another source of arguments to bring into the discussion and they would measure them critically as they would even the *Corpus Juris* itself. This also applies to Grotius whose work is full of references to medieval civilians and canonists and who underwrites many of their positions.[75]

[72] More so than most of the neo-scholastic theologians such as Suárez who embedded their reflections into general theological works. Vitoria's famous *Relectiones de Indis* and *De jure belli* could qualify as autonomous expositions but not as comprehensive expositions of the laws of war and peace-making: F de Vitoria, *De Indis et de iure belli relectiones* (Carnegie Institute Washington DC 1917 [1539/1696]). See also F de Vitoria, *Political Writings* (A Pagden and J Lawrence eds) (CUP Cambridge 1991); F Suárez, *Selections from Three Works* (2 vols Clarendon Press Oxford 1944).

[73] *The Rights of War and Peace* (n 65).

[74] DJ Bederman, 'Reception of the Classical Tradition in International Law: Grotius' *De jure belli ac pacis*' (1996) 10 *Emory International Law Review* 1–50; B Straumann, *Hugo Grotius und die Antike: Römisches Recht und römische Ethik im frühneuzeitlichen Naturrecht* (Nomos Baden 2007); B Straumann, 'The *Corpus iuris* as a Source of Law between Sovereigns in Alberico Gentili's Thought' in *The Roman Foundations of the Law of Nations* (n 52) 101–23. For sources with more recognition of medieval jurisprudence, see L Benton and B Straumann, 'Acquiring Empire by Law: From Roman Doctrine to Modern European Practice' (2010) 28 *Law and History Review* 1–38; 'Reception of Ancient Legal Thought' (n 39). In a similar vein, the dependence of the neo-scholastics on medieval canonistic jurisprudence has been significantly underplayed. For an affirmation of the role of canon law, see 'Medieval Canon Law and the Formation of International Law' (n 12) 67–76.

[75] For the critical edition, see H Grotius, *De jure belli ac pacis libri tres* (R Feenstra and CE Persenaire eds) (Scientia Aalen 1993). See also *Grotius et la doctrine de la guerre juste* (n 12).

The combining of these two approaches to Roman law as well as the increasingly relative approach to the authorities and the framework of systematization granted these early jurisprudents of the law of nations the flexibility to rise to the challenges of their day and age and adapt medieval doctrines to them. These challenges included the achievement of external sovereignty as well as the gradual monopolization of external relations by the main princes of Europe, the more encompassing nature of warfare, religious strife, maritime and imperial expansion. In answering these, the sixteenth and early seventeenth century jurisprudents of the law of nations continued to draw on medieval jurisprudence.[76]

One of the primary contributions of the sixteenth and early seventeenth century jurists was their conceptual disentanglement of the two meanings of *jus gentium*. Richard Zouch (*c* 1590–1661) famously restored the Roman term of *jus fetiale* for 'public international law'.[77]

The disentanglement was carried out at the conceptual level but it was certainly not wholly achieved in material terms. The work of Grotius is generally considered to form the synthesis and culmination point of sixteenth-century scholarship, both of neo-scholastics and humanists, as well as the transition point to the classical writers of the seventeenth and eighteenth centuries.[78] Grotius laid out with great clarity the duality of the law of nations which would become one of the hallmarks of the jurisprudence of the classical law of nations: that of the distinction and interplay between natural and positive law. Grotius distinguished two bodies of *jus gentium*: the primary law of nations, which was natural law as applied to polities and the secondary or voluntary—positive—law of nations. The first applied in the forum of conscience (*forum internum*); the second generated legal effects in the here and now (*forum externum*).[79]

The Dutch humanist marked the transition from a direct appeal to the authority of Roman law to an indirect appeal through the mediation of natural law. After Grotius and until deep into the nineteenth century, mainstream doctrine remained dualist. Although some authors—who have often been classified as positivists—such as Samuel Rachel (1628–1691),[80] Johann Wolfgang Textor (1638–1701)[81] or

---

[76] R Lesaffer, 'The Classical Law of Nations (1500–1800)' in *Research Handbook on the Theory and History of International Law* (n 51) 408–40; *Völkerrechtsgeschichte* (n 19) 117–68.

[77] R Zouch, *Iuris et iudicii fecialis, sive iuris inter gentes, et quaestionum de eodem explicatio* (JL Brierly trans) (2 vols Carnegie Institute Washington DC 1911 [1650]).

[78] H Bull, B Kingsbury, and A Roberts (eds), *Hugo Grotius and International Relations* (Clarendon Press Oxford 1990); *Grotius et la doctrine de la guerre juste* (n 12); *A Normative Approach to War* (n 1); *The Rights of War and Peace* (n 65) 78–108.

[79] H Grotius, *De jure belli ac pacis* (FW Kelsey trans) (2 vols Carnegie Institute Washington DC 1913 [1625/1646]) 1.3.4.1, 3.3.4–5 and 3.3.12–13.

[80] S Rachel, *De jure naturae et gentium dissertationum* (JP Bate trans) (2 vols Carnegie Institute Washington DC 1916 [1676]).

[81] JW Textor, *Synopsis juris gentium* (JP Bate trans) (2 vols Carnegie Institute Washington DC 1916 [1680]).

Cornelius van Bynkershoek (1673–1743)[82]—focused on positive law, they did not reject the foundational role of natural law.[83] As Grotius had done, most authors distinguished between a primary natural law, which was applicable to human beings, and a secondary natural law (or primary law of nations), which was derived from it and was applicable to states.[84] Through this, a basis for the entanglement between private and international law was retained.

By the mid-seventeenth century, mainstream doctrine had fixed the locus for the universal validity of the law of nations in natural law. But for many of the writers of the period, primary natural law as applicable to individuals provided the broader context for the law of nations. The great treatises of the naturalists of the seventeenth and eighteenth centuries, starting with Grotius, did not restrict themselves yet to *jus gentium* as the law applicable to the relations between polities, but encompassed lavish discussions on private law.[85] And even when writers did restrict themselves to the law of nations properly speaking, private (Roman) law references and analogies continued to loom large. In fact, much of the medieval and sixteenth-century civilian and canonist doctrines were recycled into the law of nations under the hood of natural law. Examples of this are just war, the principle of *pacta sunt servanda* or the doctrine of the right of sovereigns to punish grave violations of natural law such as cannibalism or incest.[86] The locus of their authority had changed from Roman or canon law to natural law, but the doctrines themselves were not surrendered. This was far more apparent for Roman law, which still had a spontaneous association with being universal and thus constituting more of a treasure trove for the discovery of natural law principles than it was for canon law. Nevertheless, through the intertwining of Roman and canon law during the fourteenth and fifteenth centuries—as in relation to treaties and *jus ad bellum*—the historical impact of canon law was assured. In some instances, new or renewed analogies to Roman law were made, as with the development of the doctrines of *occupatio* and *uti possidetis* for the legitimation of colonial expansion.[87]

---

[82] C van Bynkershoek, *Quaestionum juris publici libri duo* (T Frank trans) (2 vols Clarendon Press Oxford 1930 [1737]).

[83] For the nineteenth century, see C Sylvest, 'International Law in Nineteenth-Century Britain' (2004) 75 *British Yearbook of International Law* 9–69.

[84] See also E Jouannet, *Emer de Vattel et l'émergence doctrinale du droit international classique* (Pédone Paris 1998); E Jouannet, *The Liberal-Welfarist Law of Nations: A History of International Law* (CUP Cambridge 2012) at 11–106; M Koskenniemi, *From Apology to Utopia: The Structure of International Legal Argument* (CUP Cambridge 2005) at 71–122; A Orakhelashvili, 'The Origins of Consensual Positivism—Pufendorf, Wolff and Vattel' in *Research Handbook on the Theory and History of International Law* (n 51) 93–110.

[85] The main examples include the works of Samuel Pufendorf (1632–1694) and Christian Wolff (1679–1754). See S Pufendorf, *De jure naturae et gentium libri octo* (CH Oldfather and WA Oldfather trans) (2 vols Clarendon Press Oxford 1934 [1688]); C Wolff, *Jus naturae methodo scientifica pertractatum* (8 vols Hildesheim Olms 1968–72 [1740–48]); C Wolff, *Jus gentium methodo scientifica pertractatum* (JH Drake trans) (2 vols Clarendon Press Oxford 1934 [1749]).

[86] *The Rights of War and Peace* (n 65) 34–40 and 81–9.

[87] A Pagden, *Lords of All the World: Ideologies of Empire in Spain, Britain and France c 1500–c 1800* (Yale University Press New Haven 1995).

The classical writers of the law of nations of the seventeenth and eighteenth centuries also continued the process of systematization that the commentators had started and the humanists had brought up to speed. Against the backdrop of the claims to universality and rationality which were made for natural law, medieval and later doctrines were brought to a higher level of abstraction and generality, then to be flexibly adapted to relations between states when applied in the context of the law of nations.[88]

5 THE MODERN AND POST-MODERN AGES (NINETEENTH TO TWENTIETH CENTURIES)

In 1927, Hersch Lauterpacht (1897–1960) published his *Private Law Sources and Analogies of International Law*.[89] Lauterpacht listed numerous instances of the use or transfer of private law into public international law. He readily associated private law and Roman law, even mixing the terms at times. Lauterpacht saw three different points of impact of Roman private law upon public international law. First, there was the historical role of civilian jurisprudence in the formation of international law during the Early Modern Age. Secondly, Roman law still had an indirect impact as it was an important historical source for—primarily but not exclusively—the municipal systems of the countries of the civil law tradition. Because Roman law was their common root, it was convenient shorthand for articulating the 'general principles of law as recognised by civilised nations' which the *Statute of the Permanent Court of International Justice* had named as one of the sources of international law.[90] Thirdly, Roman law remained, even up until Lauterpacht's day, a direct source for private law analogies because it was still considered *ratio scripta*. The latter was particularly valid for common lawyers in whose system of private law Roman law had been less incorporated and in whose minds it had better retained its position as an articulation of natural law or general principles.

---

[88] As with the doctrine of *occupatio* which now, contrary to what had been the case under Roman *jus civile*, became generally applicable to land. See 'Acquiring Empire by Law' (n 74) 12–8; 'Argument from Roman Law in Current International Law' (n 10) 40–4.

[89] H Lauterpacht, *Private Law Sources and Analogies of International Law (with Special Reference to International Arbitration)* (Longmans & Green London 1927).

[90] *Statute of the Permanent Court of International Justice* (1921) art 38(3). See also *Statute of the International Court of Justice* (1945) art 38(1)(c).

Lauterpacht's empirical study of nineteenth-century adaptations and analogies of (Roman) private law has not yet been surpassed and makes a convincing argument that the transfer from private law to international law did not come to an end in the eighteenth century. One might argue that the rejection of natural law by late nineteenth-century and early twentieth-century positivists as a material source of law forced them to transfer doctrines from the world of natural law to that of positive law.[91] But Lauterpacht's interest was not historical, nor did his work lead to a renewed interest in the historical impact of Roman private law on international law. Lauterpacht construed his book as a defence for the use of private law analogies as a way of articulating 'general principles of law'.[92] In this he was to be disappointed by later twentieth century practice, most assuredly in relation to Roman law. A perusal of the jurisprudence of the International Court of Justice shows no new direct appeals to Roman law to introduce new doctrines of international law or new interpretations thereof.[93] Roman law has now ceased to play a role in the formation of international law. It can, finally, be relegated to history.

---

[91] Such as the doctrine of self-defence: see *War and the Law of Nations* (n 9) 241–6.

[92] 'Argument from Roman Law in Current International Law' (n 10) 26–38.

[93] H Thirlway, *The Law and Procedure of the International Court of Justice: Fifty Years of Jurisprudence* (OUP Oxford 2013) vol 1, at 232–46 and vol 2, at 1201–5.

CHAPTER 3

TRANSFORMATIONS OF NATURAL LAW

GERMANY 1648–1815

MARTTI KOSKENNIEMI

1 INTRODUCTION

ALONGSIDE professional jurists and diplomats, also political thinkers, philosophers, reformers, and visionaries of all sorts regularly engage with international law. Its materials lend themselves as much to abstract contemplation about the human condition as to demonstrations of technical skill. But jurists, too, oscillate between routine interpretations of technical rules and abstract debates about the frame in which the rules receive meaning. Are the most important legal problems about how best to apply the existing system? Or should the system—the 'frame'—be rethought in some way? An examination of whether jurists have been more inclined to engage in the routines of legal work or debates about the frame tells us much about the law's relationship with the surrounding world. To illustrate this, I will examine the transformation of ideas about international power that took place in the idiom of natural law between 1648 and 1815, a key period of early Western modernity. Although my focus will be limited to Germany, similar developments took place across Western Europe at the time. That the debate was waged in a *legal* idiom has to do with the special role played by university jurists in the Holy Roman Empire (of the German nation). Pressed in part by external events and in part by developments in the relations between the empire's constituent units, jurists switched between abstract justification of the imperial structure and deliberating the technical merits of alternative legislative policies. 'Natural law' and 'positivism' operated side by side, one concerning itself with the inherited frame, the other with the routines of centralized government and policy. These debates had an immediate relevance to how German jurists conceived *jus gentium* (the law of nations) and why they would finally discuss it under the title of 'public law of Europe'.[1] The transformations of natural law in the period 1648–1815 not only consolidated a familiar division of labour between intellectual disciplines but also constructed and delimited the ways in which what is settled in the international world and what is open for political contestation was to be conceived up to our day.

2 FRAME: THE NATURAL REASON OF STATEHOOD

The religious wars of the sixteenth century shook the ideological foundations of European societies. In the realm of the 'Holy Roman Empire of the German Nation', the Peace of Westphalia (1648) intensified confessional oppositions by demanding territorial separation on a religious basis. The devastations had given rise to a popular scepticism, further exacerbated by the advances of the natural sciences. Might it not be possible to understand human society, too, by a vocabulary that would be free from connotations of religious dogma, one that would address invariable, purely empirical aspects of human nature? Already the Dutchman Hugo Grotius had found in humans a certain 'Inclination to live with those of his own Kind, not in any manner whatever, but peaceably', combining it with a complex view of subjective right ('Faculty') that would support a natural law that was 'so unalterable, that God himself cannot change it'.[2] A few years later, Thomas Hobbes in England developed a view of natural law that was simply about the mechanical control of human fears and desires: 'Therefore, before the names of Just and Unjust can have place, there must be some coercive power, to compel men equally to the

---

[1] See further M Koskenniemi, 'Between Coordination and Constitution: International Law as a German Discipline' (2011) 15 *Redescriptions: Yearbook of Political Thought, Conceptual History and Feminist Theory* 45–70. All translations are by the author unless otherwise noted.

[2] H Grotius, *On the Law of War and Peace* (Liberty Fund Indianapolis 2006 [1625]) bk I ('The Preliminary Discourse') § VI (79–80), ch I § IV (138), ch I § X (155).

performance of their Covenants, by the terror of some punishment, greater than the benefit they expect by the breach of their Covenant'.[3]

Engaging with both Grotius and Hobbes, the Saxon Samuel Pufendorf (1632–94) agreed that whatever directives for behaviour existed, they were artificial, human creations.[4] They were not arbitrary for that reason, however, but emerged from the application of reason to empirical data. The idea behind Pufendorf's 'geometrical method' was to break present society down into its anthropologically basic elements and then explain its complexity by recomposing it from the elements thus received.[5] The most basic datum we knew about human beings was their self-love, connected with an intense drive for self-preservation in the conditions of pathetic weakness. For such creatures, reason dictated one overriding rule: it commanded sociability:

Man, then, is an animal with an intense concern for his own preservation, needy by himself, incapable of protection without the help of his fellows, and very well fitted for the mutual provision of benefits.[6]

There was nothing locally specific about these features; the conclusion that humans had to behave sociably had the same universality as the laws of geometry. The state of nature was not, as Hobbes had suggested, a state of constant violence or fear, however. On the contrary, the ability to reason pushed humans to develop 'positive' institutions of all kinds, even before states were in place, including property and contractual networks for the purchase of things needed for sustenance.[7] But these institutions remained precarious as long as there was 'no one who can by authority compel the offender to perform his part of the agreement or make restitution'.[8] The natural history of society peaked in the decision by primitive communities to set up a political state, decide its constitutional form, and subordinate themselves to its ruler.[9] In this way, the state could be received from an argument about self-love, weakness and the ability to reason. Nature itself would explain the necessity

---

[3] T Hobbes, *Leviathan* (CB Macpherson ed) (Penguin New York 1968 [1651]) pt I ch 15 (202).

[4] Although, as he says, some of these precepts are so plain that we can easily mistake them for being innate: S Pufendorf, *On the Duty of Man and Citizen* (J Tully ed) (CUP Cambridge 1991) at 37.

[5] The term '*mos geometricus*' signified either a method that strived for clarity and systemic coherence in general, or precisely the analytical-composite approach expounded above. See H Denzer, *Moralphilosphie und Naturrecht bei Samuel Pufendorf* (Beck Munich 1972) at 35–58, 282–3, and 279–96.

[6] *On the Duty of Man and Citizen* (n 4) 35.

[7] 'Since men's natural state includes the use of reason we cannot, or should not, separate it from any obligation pointed at thereby': S Pufendorf, *On the Law of Nature and of Nations* (Lichfield Oxford 1710) bk II ch 2 § 9 (147). For an extensive discussion of Pufendorf's 'natural private law', valid already in the state of nature, see S Goyard-Fabre, *Pufendorf et le droit naturel* (PUF Paris 1994) at 125–57.

[8] *On the Duty of Man and Citizen* (n 4) 118.

[9] For the famous 'two agreements and a decree' structure of the state-building process, see *On the Law of Nature and of Nations* (n 7) bk VII ch 2 §§ 7–11.

to have positive laws and taxes and a powerful sovereign to maintain peace so that self-love could be directed to productive work and commerce.[10]

Pufendorf's empirical natural law explained and justified the supreme power (*Landeshoheit*) of German territorial rulers, directing them to reasonable objectives; the security and welfare of the community above all. In fact, Pufendorf defined 'law' itself 'as a decree by a superior to an inferior, accompanied by a sanction and an unconditional duty of the subject to obey'.[11] The ruler needed absolute power to rule efficiently. But this did not mean he could rule as he wished. 'The safety of the people is the supreme law', Pufendorf wrote, and he engaged in extensive discussions on good laws and just punishments.[12] The whole point of a *scientific* account of statehood was to bind the ruler to the principles that science (or its representatives) would produce. Between the utopia of scholastic justice and the apology of arbitrary will lay, for Pufendorf, the *social rationality of natural law* as a composite of techniques of peace, security, and welfare. If these were lost, then social power was lost; the link between protection and obedience was broken and the authority of the sovereign would lapse.[13] This, experience told him, nobody had reason to want.

Pufendorf's significance to the law of nations has often been limited to what he had to say about war and treaties in the last three chapters of *De jure naturae et gentium*. However, much more important is the view that among nations, the same principles of sociability would apply as among individuals in the state of nature. Treaties, for example, were like any laws based on the will of the sovereign—not an 'arbitrary' will but one that would support and enforce antecedent social norms, the imperatives of security and welfare. They were binding as they 'define the terms of reciprocal performance of some duty already enjoined by natural law, and those which go beyond the duties of natural law, or at least put in a specific form what seems indefinite in natural law'.[14] That is to say, treaties were binding as long as they were useful, while those that had become 'pernicious' had to be repudiated immediately, for 'no state is obligated more to anyone than to its own citizens'.[15] Under the law of nations the search for *salus populi* became the foundation of foreign policy.[16]

The just causes of engaging in war come down to the preservation and protection of our lives and property against unjust attack, or the collection of what is due to us from others but has been denied, or the procurement of reparations for wrong inflicted and of assurance for the future.[17]

---

[10] *On the Law of Nature and of Nations* (n 7) bk II ch 3 § 16 (210–13).

[11] Ibid bk I ch 6 § 14 (104–8).

[12] Ibid bk VII ch 9 § 3 (1118); *On the Duty of Man and Citizen* (n 4) 151–7.

[13] I Hunter, *Rival Enlightenments: Civil and Metaphysical Philosophy in Early Modern Germany* (CUP Cambridge 2001) at 156 and 158–63.

[14] *On the Duty of Man and Citizen* (n 4) bk II ch 17 § 1 (173).

[15] *On the Law of Nature and of Nations* (n 7) bk VIII ch 6 § 14 (260).

[16] J Brückner, *Staatswissenschaften, Kameralismus und Naturrecht: Ein Beitrag zur Geschichte des politischen Wissenschaft im Deutschland des späten 17 und frühen 18 Jahrhunderts* (Beck Munich 1977) at 171.

[17] *On the Duty of Man and Citizen* (n 4) bk II ch 16 § 2 (168).

The argument from self-love and weakness gave a ready portrait of Europe as a set of egoistic but interdependent sovereignties whose interest was to cooperate, not to fight. War was justified only by a direct injury to oneself, and not by some putative violation of an abstract norm.[18]

Pufendorf's analysis was situated in post-war Germany where efficient authority had broken down and could not be restored by traditional religious or political approaches. The justification of statehood was received from an 'empirical' argument: the observation that human beings were self-loving and weak, and thus in need of a strong hand to guide them. If natural law justified absolutist statehood, it was accompanied by a science of government in which positive law was understood as part of the routines of statecraft, directed towards the realization of the interest of the whole.[19] In a widely read analysis of the constitutional problems of the Holy Roman Empire, Pufendorf had focused on the absence of a single, easily locatable sovereignty in the imperial realm. The overlapping powers of the emperor and the territorial princes emerged from disparate agreements, capitulations and de facto practices. The analysis was altogether geared in a pragmatic direction—how best to realize the interests of each imperial unit?[20] This, he argued, required thinking of Germany as a 'system of states' where the powers of each should be coordinated for the maximum benefit of all, an arrangement also in the general European interest.[21] In a further work, *Introduction to the History of the Great Empires and States of Contemporary Europe* (1682–5), he instructed young men looking for a court position in the arts of government. By making the distinction between 'imaginary' and 'real' interests, Pufendorf aimed to develop a natural law into a scientific statecraft that would enable the deduction of the 'reason of state' from the nation's history and resources.[22]

3 ROUTINES: OPERATING THE STATE-MACHINE

The Pufendorfian frame revolutionized the thinking not only of law but of statecraft and morality and turned *jus naturae et gentium* into the predominant vocabulary

---

[18] *On the Law of Nature and of Nations* (n 7) bk VIII ch 6 § 2.

[19] See further *Pufendorf et le droit naturel* (n 7) 101.

[20] S Pufendorf, *The Present State of Germany* (MJ Seidl ed) (Liberty Fund Indianapolis 2007) ch VII §§ 8–10.

[21] Ibid ch VIII § 3.

[22] S Pufendorf, *Commetarii de rebus Suecicis ab expeditione Gustavi-Adolphi usque ad abdicationem Christinae* (Ribbius Utrecht 1686); S Pufendorf, *Einleitung zu der Historie der*

of eighteenth-century German political thought.[23] The leading early enlightenment German intellectual, jurist, and Rector of the University of Halle, Christian
Thomasius (1655–1728), further developed natural law into a frame for utilitarian
politics that was to operate with the causality of human behaviour, dominated
by the will.[24] Will, again, depended on 'effects' that consisted of reactions to the
external world, dictated by the search for pleasure and the avoidance of pain.
In social life, it was impossible to reach these objectives without cooperation.[25]
Even as the 'wise' may know the precepts of natural law and thus learn to cooperate
spontaneously, this was not the case with ordinary subjects who had to be guided
to the good path. There would be close collaboration between the university and
the ruler. The professor was to give counsel on natural law, on the basis of which
the prince would legislate so as to bring about the security and happiness of his
people.[26]

In his mature *Fundamenta juris naturae et gentium* (1705), Thomasius laid out his
famous threefold distinction between the norms of '*honestum*' (personal morality),
'*decorum*' (social morality/politics) and '*justum*' (positive law), thus demarcating
sharply between 'internal' and 'external' norms, only the latter of which were the
proper field of legal intervention.[27] If the counsel given by the jurist under natural
law had the character of *honestum*, it was up to the prince to decide what was called
for by *decorum* or *justum*, only the latter of which embodied a superior–inferior
relationship. What would this make of the law of nations? Efforts to argue that
there was an analogous (superior–inferior) relationship between 'moral' and 'barbaric' nations led nowhere; who could tell which nations belong in which group?
The whole distinction was an anachronistic leftover from Greek and Roman times.
Moreover, there was no legislator in the international world, and never had nations
come together to set up a common law. But even if they had done this, the force
of their agreement would still be based on natural and not positive law—that is to

---

vornähmsten Reiche und Staaten von Europa, vorinnen des Königreichs Schweden (Knoch Frankfurt
1709); S Pufendorf, *An Introduction to the History of the Principal Kingdoms and States of Europe*
(Knapton London 1728). See further A Dufour, 'Pufendorf' in JH Burns and M Goldie (eds), *The
Cambridge History of Political Thought: 1450–1700* (CUP Cambridge 1991) 561–88, at 584–5.

[23] It was not only the most general part of the law—a jurisprudence—but 'an overarching vocab-
ulary of all discourses about human beings, including history, law, morality and theology': H-E
Bödeker and I Hont, 'Naturrecht, Politische Ökonomie und geschichte der Menschheit. Der
Diskurs über die Gesellschaft in frühen Neuzeit' in O Dann and D Klippel (eds), *Naturrecht—
Frühaufklärung—Revolution* (Meiner Hamburg 1995) at 82.

[24] C Thomasius, *Grundlehren des Natur und Völkerrechts* (F Grunert ed) (Olms Hildesheim 2003
[1709]) bk I ch 1 § 37.

[25] Ibid bk I ch 2 §§ 44–57 (67–9).

[26] Ibid bk I ch 4 §§ 51–7 (85). For Thomasius' conception of the 'wise' (*Die Weise*) and the 'stupid'
(*Die Narren*) see at §§ 1–50 (76–84).

[27] See ibid. For a useful comparison of the three sets of norms—*honestum, iustum, decorum*—see
further F Grunert, *Normbegründung und politische Legitimität: Zur Recht und Staatsphilosophie der
deutschen Frühaufklärung* (Niemeyer Tübingen 2000) at 217–25.

say, it would remain mere counsel.[28] This was not to say that there were no rules on diplomacy, treaty-making, or war. Each was part of the external public law of the state and the jurisdiction of the monarch, to be used for peace and happiness. Instead of ascending to the level of *justum* they were part of *decorum*, aspects of politics and habitual behaviour.[29] This did not deny their reality, only their enforce-ability as positive law. The law of nations was best understood as a set of spontane-ous cultural practices that were very important for the prince and public officials to know. A good politician, Thomasius used to argue, was also a good jurist, and the other way around.[30]

One of Thomasius' most interesting followers was Hieronymus Gundling (1671–1729), a sharp-witted and opinionated lecturer who had no time for metaphysical speculations. The point of the study of *ius naturale et gentium* was utility, he argued, the attainment of 'external peace' brought about by laws understood as commands by a superior supported by sanctions.[31] Like Pufendorf, Gundling received natural rights and duties from the hypothesis of a state of nature where individuals had originally been free and equal and entitled to do whatever they willed. To secure the enjoyment of the fruit of their labour, they had created the institutions of prop-erty and sovereignty, moving from the 'absolute' to a 'hypothetical' state of nature between primitive communities. In due course, families had joined together to form political states to better secure their peace—'when one draws the sword, then all will draw it'.[32] But the widest application of the 'hypothetical state of nature' concerned the basic institutions of international commerce, diplomacy, and war among European nations.[33] This law consisted of contextual derivations of what was needed to preserve peace. For example, diplomatic immunities were received from the fact that submitting ambassadors to the jurisdiction of the receiving states would undermine their ability to maintain peaceful relations.[34] Causing damage violated rights and rights-violation disturbed the peace. However inconvenient it was, in the absence of organized enforcement natural rights were ultimately vin-dicated by war.[35]

As law became intellectual derivations for peace-keeping, it coalesced with wise policy. But Gundling was deeply sceptical about the ability of statesmen to learn

---

[28] *Grundlehren* (n 24) bk I ch 5 § 76 (107).

[29] Ibid bk I ch 5 § 70 and generally §§ 65–81 (105–8).

[30] N Hammerstein, *Jus und Historie: Ein Beitrag zur Geschichte des historischen Denkens an deutschen Universitäten im späten 17 und im 18 Jahrhundert* (Vandenhoeck & Ruprecht Göttingen 1972) 62–71. See also N Hammerstein, 'Thomasius und die Rechtsgelehrsamkeit' in N Hammerstein (ed), *Geschichte als Arsenal: Ausgewählte Aufsätze zu recht, Hof und Universitäten der Frühen Neuzeit* (Wellstein Göttingen 2010) 245–68.

[31] See eg NH Gundling, *Ausführlicher Discours über die Natur und Völcker-Recht* (2nd edn Springs Frankfurt 1734) ch II §§ 18–19 (55).

[32] Ibid ch XXXIV §§ 18–36 (418 and generally 412–21).   [33] Ibid ch I §§ 40–2 (26).

[34] Ibid ch I §§ 69–73 (35).   [35] Ibid ch VI §§ 1–4 (96–7).

this properly. All humans were creatures of passion, and nobody more so than those who ruled the state. Despite the advice they may receive from their natural law counsellors, rulers will prefer to run after short-term benefits rather than wait for the realization of long-term interests.[36] Nations could therefore never trust each other but must be alert towards betrayals, breaches of treaties, and efforts to seize territory. To prevent this, natural law dictated the maintenance of the balance of power. Grotius, Gundling wrote, had allowed preventive action only if there was positive evidence of impending aggression. This was much too strict. Had anyone ever heard of a ruler who would have refrained from attempting conquest whenever he was convinced of his superior power? The balance could often be kept only by striking first; after all, '[o]ne cannot rule the world with *Pater nosters* or destroy one's enemies by *Ave Marias*'.[37]

Gundling collected the widest range of considerations to create a natural law with a realistic grasp on the operations of the state-machine: 'Nobody should think that acting in accordance with the laws is sufficient. Such a person still lacks that which is most important'.[38] As counsellors jurists needed state-wisdom ('*Staats-Klugheit*'): a clear view of the *interests* of their state and those of its neighbours. To enable princes to make such assessments, Gundling produced a work entitled *The Present Situation of European States* (1712, second edition 1733) as the first German study of comparative state-science that would extend beyond public law and into all aspects of the relations between neighbouring states.[39] This would include a description of the history, people, land, property, and climate of each state and the presentation would conclude in a statement of each state's 'State-interest'.[40] Gundling did not endorse a *monarchia universalis*, but not because he would not have valued the peace that it might bring. No prince would agree to give up his *jura majestica* for such a purpose and once it were established, it would sooner or later collapse in a general rebellion.[41] And so the work proceeded with a description of the principal European states— their history, territory, and resources, their industry and commerce, the character of the people and the patterns of rule, key institutions, the economy and the military resources plus, at the end, their 'interest' in the European state-system.

During the course of the eighteenth century, the natural law of nations came to encompass a comprehensive study of the government of early modern (absolutist) states. The universities of Halle and Göttingen produced an unparalleled stream of scholars and studies of public law and the law of nations that were historically and

---

[36] NH Gundling, *Einleitung zu wahren Staatklugheit, aus desselben mündlichen Vortrag* (Frankfurt und Leipzig, Springs 1751) ch VII (252).

[37] NH Gundling, *Erörterung der Frage: ob wegen der anwächsenden Macht der Nachbarn man Degen entblössen könne?* (Frankfurt 1757) §§ 4–6, 8 and 24 (4–6 and 19).

[38] *Einleitung zu wahren Staatklugheit* (n 36) ch I (22).

[39] NH Gundling, *Ausführliche Discours über den jetzigen Zustand Der Europäishecn Staaten. Vol I: Von dem Nutzen und Noth-wendigkeiten der Staaten-Notiz überhaupt* (Frankfurt 1733) at 2.

[40] Ibid 8. For an overview of the sources, see at 9–20, 23–4.   [41] Ibid 23–4.

empirically oriented and aimed to assist European rulers to bring about the security and welfare of their regimes.[42] The most famous eighteenth-century naturalist, Christian Wolff (1679–1754) even proposed a coherent system of natural norms to help the prince to bring about the 'perfection' of his nation. This perfection, he assumed, could be attained by drawing deductive inferences from metaphysical axioms at a high level of abstraction. The eight volumes of his *Jus naturae* (1740–8) extended into a general theory of property and contract, of private and public law, and concluded in the *Law of Nations* (1749) where Wolff extrapolated the rights and duties of states from the assumption that they existed like so many individuals in a state of nature. The most famous aspect of this construction was the view of states forming together a 'supreme state' (*Civitas maxima*) that had 'a kind of sovereignty' over individual states.[43] The natural law in this supreme state was either 'necessary'—the unchanging natural law that also applied between individuals— or 'voluntary'—derived from the consent of its members as a kind of 'fictitious' government of the world.[44]

Wolff's most well-known follower, the Swiss Emer de Vattel (1714–67), transposed Wolff's abstractions into the most widely used textbook of the law of nations in the late eighteenth century. The three-volume *Droit des gens* (1758) was a faithful elaboration on German natural law and went into much detail on the duties that public authorities had towards the security and welfare of their nations. The first book dealt with internal government, agriculture, commerce, education, and welfare. Public authorities, conceived as the nation's representatives, should 'apply to the business of providing for all the wants of the people, and producing a happy plenty of all necessaries of life with its conveniences, and innocent and laudable enjoyments'.[45] Through expounding the 'nation's duties to itself' Vattel aimed to reach the 'duty to humanity', politically realized in a specific territorial context. For it followed from the interdependence of nations that the security and happiness of one depended on the security and happiness of others and vice versa: '[a nation's] duties towards others depend very much on its duties to itself'.[46] If the duties of humanity were only imperfect and unenforceable (because there was no political organization of humanity), and the only perfect obligations were those that reflected the relationship between public authorities and the nation, then a law of nations with perfect, enforceable obligations must reflect the rights and obligations that governments had towards their citizens. This is why the only logical

---

[42] See *Jus und Historie* (n 30).

[43] C Wolff, *Jus gentium methodo scienitifica pertractatum* (JH Drake trans) (Clarendon Press Oxford 1934) prolegomena §§ 9–20 (13–17).

[44] Ibid prolegomena §§ 16, 19 (16–17).

[45] E de Vattel, *The Law of Nations* (B Kapossy and R Whatmore eds) (Liberty Fund Indianapolis 2008 [1758]) bk I ch 6 § 72 (126).

[46] Ibid bk I ch 2 § 13 (85).

place for Vattel to start was the elaboration of the duties that public authorities have towards the nation, to make Book One a treatise on good government.[47]

The second book dealt with the duties of the nation to others and the third with war. The duties of a nation to others consisted largely of derivations from the 'voluntary law of nations' that governed the most varied types of contacts from commercial to territorial and treaty relations, transmitting to the reader a sense of the contingencies of the environment in which states operated and the perspective from which public authorities should react to them. They, as Ian Hunter has pointed out, developed a 'diplomatic casuistry' of an almost endless 'array of "cases", "circumstances", and "occasions", in relation to which an open-ended series of "exemptions to…and moderations of the rigour of the necessary law" will be determined in accordance with national judgment and national interest'.[48] That professional diplomats found Vattel useful must have related to his appreciation of the difficulty of their task. That task required taking seriously an account of the differences that persisted among European nations, their size, resources, history, religion, and so on, as well as the variety of governmental tasks that befell authorities in different countries. Their policy—that is to say, the pursuit of their happiness and security—needed to be carefully measured by reference to their particular situation: 'such and such regulation, such or such practice, though salutary to one state, is often pernicious to another'.[49]

Vattel's law of nations opened a pragmatic, sociologically oriented study of how to act for the good of the nation, in view of its being part of a 'state-system'. It called for prudential statecraft. Again, however, it was unclear if public authorities could be trusted in this respect—they were notoriously gripped by 'disorderly passions, and private and mistaken interests'.[50] Moreover, nations were jealous of each other so that what had been originally constructed as an instrument of security and happiness—political statehood—was also a source of danger. How to check that danger, how to see to it that public authorities would not become a threat to the security of their neighbours required careful management of the balance of power that Vattel regarded as the legal basis of the European states-system. In principle, war was allowed only in case of actual or threatening injury to oneself.[51] Owing to the difficulty to make that determination, however, it was best to accept that if the belligerent parties were at least *claiming* to act in self-defence, then (although only one could be right), they should both be seen to act lawfully. And did 'threat' mean concrete military preparations (the

---

[47] See also S Beaulac, 'Emer Vattel and the Externalization of Sovereignty' (2003) 5 *Journal of the History of International Law* 237–92, at 256–9.

[48] I Hunter, 'Vattel's Law of Nations: Diplomatic Casuistry for the Protestant Nation' (2010) 31 *Grotiana* 108–40, at 125.

[49] *Law of Nations* (n 45) bk I ch 3 § 25 (91).   [50] Ibid bk II ch 1 § 16 (269).

[51] Ibid bk II ch 1 § 7 (265) and bk III ch 3 § 26 (483–4).

concentration of troops on the frontier, say) or did it extend also to the growth of the prosperity of a neighbour suspected of harbouring expansive designs? Vattel did not believe a clear answer could be given to such questions: 'men are under a necessity of regulating their conduct in most cases by probability'.[52] As for rulers who had 'already given proofs of imperious pride and insatiable ambition' the answer was clear. The decision to go to war against Louis XIV in the Spanish succession case had been undoubtedly right. History showed that growth of power often did indicate an aggressive purpose; it was rare for a state that had developed the capacity for victory to remain passive. Even a guarantee from neighbours would not always suffice; the security of the nation had to remain the predominant concern.[53]

******

Written at the outset of the Seven Years' War (1756–1763), Vattel's *Droit des gens* summarized a century of teaching on the law of nations that looked for an exit from the recurrent cycles of violence in Europe by emphasizing the shared civilization and value of a political system where public authorities were assigned to work for the happiness and perfection of their nations. From Pufendorf to Vattel, those authorities adopted the Ciceronian precept according to which there was no essential contradiction between *honestum* and *utile*—the good and the useful—and assumed that by turning the attention of each nation to its own welfare and security, the welfare and security of everyone else would also be enhanced.[54] Such an optimistic view enabled leaving aside the frame—the further justification of European statehood—and instead concentrating on the basic techniques whereby a well-ordered polity would govern its internal and external affairs. From contemplating the state of nature or the histories whereby present states had emerged from it, the attention of *jus naturae et gentium* turned to the practical operation of the state-machines. What European jurists, diplomats, and men of affairs needed in the middle of the eighteenth century were technical instructions on how to make their nations prosper in security and friendly competition. This required believing that natural law would enable the operation of a progressive system of interests that, Carl Becker once ironically remarked, resembled the 'heavenly city' of medieval theologians to which eighteenth-century thinkers looked '[w]ith eyes uplifted, contemplating and admiring so excellent a system, they were excited and animated to correspond with the general harmony'.[55]

---

[52] *Law of Nations* (n 45) bk III ch 3 § 44 (493).   [53] Ibid.

[54] E de Vattel, 'Dialogue of Prince and His Counsellor' in *Mélanges de literature, de morale et de politique* (B Kapossy and R Whatmore eds) (Liberty Fund Indianapolis 2008) at 87.

[55] C Becker, *The Heavenly City of the Eighteenth-Century Philosophers* (2nd edn Yale University Press New Haven 2003) at 63.

4 TRANSFORMATION OF NATURAL LAW I: INTO ECONOMICS

Natural law was rooted in eighteenth-century German politics as a justification of the post-Westphalian territorial settlement. Recourse to the state of nature produced a historical explanation for the state as an instrument of the security and welfare of those households whose heads had, in exchange, subordinated themselves to its superior power. This prompted teachers of *jus naturae et gentium* to develop their science into an empirical state-technique (*Staatskunst*) and a quasi-Machiavellian state-wisdom (*Staats-klugheit*) that elaborated the technical means of what would be needed to realize the interests of what, towards the end of the century, came increasingly to be articulated as 'civil society'.[56] Another follower of Wolff with a keen interest in this process was JHG Justi (1717–1771) who moved between courts in Austria and Germany giving administrative advice and publishing a large number of volumes whose topics ranged from the management of the royal *Kammer* to upholding good order (*Gute Policey*), the nature of statehood and the 'chimera of the balance of power'.[57] In his 'political metaphysic', Justi adopted the Wolffian frame of statehood as an instrument of social 'perfection'. With the help of the metaphor of the state as a 'machine', he presented government as the technical production of the happiness of civil society.[58] Justi had imbibed the view of state power as above all economic wealth and wealth-creation as a matter of private initiative and industriousness. He even argued that one of the objectives of statehood was 'freedom', by which he meant both the state's independence from outside powers and the citizen's economic liberty, both conceived as aspects of governmental policy.[59] In the 1770s and 1780s, the translations of the French Physiocrats and Adam Smith began to circulate in Germany. At this time, Justi concluded that it was no longer possible to rule the state only by lawyers—one needed 'universal cameralists', men who would be knowledgeable about the operation of the private economy and the resources of

---

[56] M Riedl, 'Gesellschaft, bürgerliche' in O Brunner, W Conze, and R Koselleck (eds), *Geschichtliche Grundbegriffe* (2 vols JG Cotta Stuttgart 1975) vol 1, at 748–71.

[57] For biographies, see U Adam, *The Political Economy of JHG Justi* (Lang Oxford 2006) at 23–54; M Obert, *Die naturrechtliche 'politische Metaphysik' des Johann Heinrich Gottlob von Justi (1717–1771)* (Lang Frankfurt 1992) at 7–23; K Tribe, *Governing Economy: The Reformation of German Economic Discourse 1750–1840* (CUP Cambridge 1988) at 56–61.

[58] JHG Justi, *Natur und Wesen der Staaten als die Quelle aller Regierungswissenschaften und Gesetze* (Mitau Steidel 1771 [1760]) ch 3 §§ 30–44 (61–95). See also EP Nokkala, 'The Machine of State in Germany—The Case of Johann Heinrich Gottlob von Justi (1717–1771)' (2009) 5 *Contributions to the History of Concepts* 71–93.

[59] See eg JHG Justi, *Der Grundriss einer guten Regierung* (Garve Frankfurt 1759) Einleitung §§ 32 and 34 (20–2); *Staatswissenschaften* (n 16) 233.

the state as a whole.[60] Justi's writings had already defined the political power of a state as a combination of the wealth of private families and efficient statecraft, taking seriously the existence of a realm of private commercial exchanges that operated best without excessive interference by public power.[61] Unlike many of the older generation of naturalists, Justi regarded commerce in luxury as welcome because it would contribute to the emergence of a wealthy merchant class that would then be emulated by the rest of the population. Indeed it was one of the objectives of the state 'to have rich and powerful merchants'.[62] He advocated the removal of monopolies, guilds, and other restrictive provisions in all other cases apart from protecting the initial operations of large investments. He was, however, critical of trade companies and the associated monopolies and celebrated the dismantling of the Danish West India Company in 1764.[63]

The central metaphor for dealing with international relations in the eighteenth century was the balance of power. Owing to the way it connoted a concrete, almost physical process, it fitted well with naturalist ideas about ruling the state-machine. At this time, jurists were conscious that the power of the state meant not only its military resources but above all its economic wealth, in part a function of domestic production, in part of external trade. In the course of the Seven Years' War, Justi attacked the proposal by the French minister Jean-Henri Maubert de Gouveste that the balance of power ought also to be extended to balance of *trade*, to be regulated as part of European public law. In the *Chimera of the Balance of Power in Commerce and Shipping* (1759), Justi emphasized the impossibility, irrationality, and injustice of the proposal. True, the argument from 'balance of trade' was a logical extension of the view that state power was above all commercial power. But it flew in the face of the realization that it was the nature of commerce to be free. Every nation tried to export as much of its excess product as it could and to buy what it needed from whomsoever was willing to sell at the lowest price.[64] Success in international commerce depended on the industry and skilfulness ('*Arbeitsamkeit und Geschicklihckeit*') of the population and growth of power followed naturally from the expansion of commerce. It would be unnatural and ridiculous to try to limit the way nations traded to pursue their happiness.[65] The effort by the French minister to rally European nations against England under the principle of the balance was, Justi argued, merely a hypocritical effort to dress France's military interests in the garb of a principle of European law.

Interest in empirical statecraft, *cameralism, Policey*, and, ultimately, *oeconomia*, arose quite logically from a basic turn undertaken in German and more generally

---

[60] *Governing Economy* (n 57) 67.   [61] *The Political Economy of JHG Justi* (n 57) 194–9.

[62] JHG Justi, 'Abhandlung von denen Manufakturen und Fabriken I-II (1758/61)', cited in *The Political Economy of JHG Justi* (n 57) 199.

[63] *The Political Economy of JHG Justi* (n 57) at 208.

[64] JHG Justi, *Die Chimäre des Gleichgewichts der Handlung und Schiffahrt* (Altona 1759) at 11–21.

[65] Ibid 27. See further *The Political Economy of JHG Justi* (n 57) 82–92.

European legal and political thought in the eighteenth century.[66] Because natural law in Germany was above all a university discipline, the turn was immediately manifested in the struggle of the faculties, a constant of German academic life. As long as natural law was taught at the philosophy faculty, its expansion into such other areas would be encouraged by rethinking the relations between Aristotelian ethics, politics, and *oeconomia* within practical philosophy. In the law faculty, however, *cameralism* and *Policey* remained cantoned in the theory of statehood and the international world mediated by the natural law tradition. But the prevalence of jurists as experts of statecraft could not last forever.[67] In the last years of the eighteenth century Immanuel Kant's teaching began to penetrate German natural law. This meant a significant turn to individual rights ('*Menschenrechte*') and an effort to redefine the teleology of statecraft as being above all about the security of civil society, the protection of property, and seeing to the functioning of the economic market.[68] With this, the basic ingredients were in place for the shift of attention from *Staatswirtschaft* to *Nationalökonomie*:

... the principles that Smith advanced were integrated with the redefinition of social order that arose from the reform of Natural Law, a reform which also implicated a separation of the State and civil society.[69]

The expansion of the focus of governmental science from the state to the operation of the economy as a whole created the demand for novel kinds of governmental expertise—a call met by the creation of the first faculty of public economy at the University of Tübingen in 1817.[70] In a sense, when natural lawyers realized what they needed to become in order to fulfil the promise they had made to their clients, the rulers, and the governmental decision-makers, they understood that they needed to become economists.

5 Transformation of Natural Law II: Into Philosophy

Neither the Wolffian abstractions nor the empirical-utilitarian turn in natural law took place without criticisms. In the *Critique of Pure Reason* (1781/1787) and

---

[66] I have sketched the way it took place in France in M Koskenniemi, 'The Public Law of Europe: Reflections on a French 18th Century Debate' in H Lindemann et al., (eds), *Erzählungen von Konstitutionalismus* (Nomos Baden-Baden 2012) 55–63.

[67] *Staatswissenschaften* (n 16) 288–9.

[68] See especially W von Humboldt, 'Über die Sorgfalt der Staaten für die Sicherheit gegen auswärtige Feinde' (1797) 20 *Berlinische Monatsschrift* 346–54.

[69] *Governing Economy* (n 57) 175.   [70] Ibid 177–9.

later works on law and morality, Immanuel Kant (1724–1804) attacked both in a way that gradually made it impossible to continue natural law in the traditional vein. Against the rationalists, Kant argued that pure, abstract reason failed to grasp its own situatedness in the world and either left its axioms hanging in the air or defended them in a circular manner. These abstract systems produced nothing that was not put into them from the outside; yet they had no way of dealing with that outside—the 'thing in itself'—to which they therefore had a profoundly *uncritical* attitude.[71] The theory of the *Civitas Maxima* illustrated precisely the kind of *Weltfremd* utopia into which purely logical reasoning would lead; an incident of the hubris of pure reason. But the world's problems cannot be resolved by it. Any attempt to do this would first produce absolutism and then tyranny—'a soulless despotism [that], after crushing the germs of goodness, will finally lapse into anarchy'.[72] It will have to remain up to humans themselves to *choose* the way they are governed. Hence, as Kant stressed, the failure of reason to meet its own demands was ultimately 'fortunate... for the practical interests of humanity'.[73]

But civil philosophers who regarded the task of reason as being merely to align itself with the conditions of empirical existence fared no better in Kant's eyes,[74] or, as he put it in *Perpetual Peace*, their 'philosophically or diplomatically formulated codes do not and cannot have the slightest *legal* force'.[75] It was not only that there existed no way of constraining states. The very idea of drawing norms out of empirical facts—whether the Hobbesian fact of innate hostility or the Grotians' sociability—was fundamentally misconceived. The principles on which civil philosophy built its view of natural law were indeed derived from the 'close scrutiny of the nature and character of man', human history and action.[76] But the resulting notions of 'self-love', 'human animal', 'will', and 'happiness' were *too firmly* embedded in a view of humans responding mechanistically to natural inclinations, activated in response to external stimuli. In the debates over the nature and direction of the enlightenment in Germany, Kant's aim was to vindicate the view of the human being as 'more than a machine'.[77] The key question for Kant was not at all

---

[71] On what Kant calls the 'antinomy of pure reason', see I Kant, *Critique of Pure Reason* (P Guyer and AW Wood trans and eds) (CUP Cambridge 1998 [1781/1787]) at 466–95 [A420/B448]–[A460/B488].

[72] I Kant, 'Perpetual Peace: A Philosophical Sketch' in *Kant: Political Writings* (H Reiss ed HB Nisbet trans) (2nd edn CUP Cambridge 1991) 93–115, at 113. This is Kant's most extreme characterization of a world state. In other places, he shows much more sympathy to it. For example, in the 'Second Definitive Article', he regards it as a thesis necessitated by the same reason that compels humans to join in a state—but unrealizable owing to this being 'not the will of nations': at 105.

[73] *Critique of Pure Reason* (n 71) 342 [A463/B491].

[74] Ibid 345–7 [A469/B497]–[A473/B501].

[75] 'Perpetual Peace' (n 72) 103 (emphasis in original).

[76] *On the Duty of Man and Citizen* (n 4) bk I ch 3.

[77] I Kant, 'What is Enlightenment?' in *Kant: Political Writings* (n 72) 54–60, at 60.

'how to be happy but how we should become worthy of happiness'—a distinction that humans may not always honour, but that they routinely made.[78] In assimilating human beings as parts of (passive) nature, the civil philosophers left no room for human society as distinct from nature, a realm in which legality would uphold everyone's freedom.

Having demolished both available forms of natural law as intellectual enterprises Kant developed his own view of international law that was published in 1795 as the philosophical sketch of *Perpetual Peace*. Here, as is well known, Kant differentiated between three types of law. First, he maintained that the constitution of every state should become 'republican'. This was necessary because freedom could only become a reality where a lawful constitution regulated the rights of citizens vis-à-vis each other. Second, he argued that international law should take the form of a 'federation of free states' that would rule themselves under laws and a jointly agreed federal constitution. And finally, he canvassed the presence of a 'cosmopolitan law' that would entitle individuals to move about freely in the world under conditions of universal 'hospitality'.[79] The proposal was drafted in a gradualist fashion and was accompanied by a series of preliminary actions that, Kant suggested, ought to be carried out as preconditions for stable peace. It also included proposals about the relations of politics and morality and the role of philosophers in government: 'The maxims of the philosophers on the conditions under which public peace is possible shall be consulted by states which are armed for war'.[80] But the ultimate success of policy would nevertheless depend on the moral regeneration of the ruling class.[81]

Although *Perpetual Peace* was received with some interest in Germany and France, it had no actual effect on European diplomacy or the development of the law of nations during or after the French revolution, the context of its publication. Despite its gradualist nature, it was rejected even by sympathetic admirers as perhaps attractive in theory but unworkable in practice, a figment of a scholar's imagination. Some, such as the 'popular philosopher' Christian Garve (1742–1798), argued that it was a mistake to suppose that statesmen could or should operate with principles derived from private morality. They were responsible for the fate of large populations and could not be expected to be overly concerned for the purity of their souls.[82] Others, such as Friedrich

---

[78] I Kant, 'On the Common Saying: "This May Be True in Theory But It Does Not Apply in Practice"' in *Kant: Political Writings* (n 72) 61–92, at 64 and 68–72.

[79] 'Perpetual Peace' (n 72) 105–8.

[80] Ibid (n 72) 115 ('Second Supplement: Secret Article of Perpetual Peace').

[81] I Kant, 'Perpetual Peace: Appendix I: On the Disagreement between Morals and Politics in relation to Perpetual Peace' in *Kant: Political Writings* (n 72) 116–25.

[82] C Garve, *Abhandlung über die Verbindung der Moral mit dem Politik oder einige Betrachtungen über die Frage in wiefern es möglich sei die Moral des Privatlebens bei der Regierung der Staaten zu beobachten* (Korn Breslau 1788).

Gentz, doubted the ability of nature to provide lessons for politicians and rejected the view that a federation could be maintained on purely reasonable grounds and without overwhelming force. Like most commentators, Gentz accepted that despite its precarious nature, there was no alternative to the balance of power.[83]

In the stream of post-Kantian texts on the law of nature and of nations, none would have a similar influence to those of Thomasius or Wolff. A typical work in the new genre of 'rights of humanity' was the 1792 volume by the Erlangen philosopher Johann Heinrich Abicht (1762–1816) that deduced a full conception of law from the 'absolute' and 'conditional' rights of human persons that was emptied of references to both contemporary practice and history. Autonomy was essential and it was realized in society by *Selbstverpflichtung*—voluntary submission to laws designed to make possible social life among free persons.[84] Abicht's law of nations was based on the 'general rights of each people' ('*allgemeine Rechte eines Volks*').[85] Like Gundling, Abicht extrapolated the rules of the law of nations from what he thought was desirable among individuals in the natural state. But he had none of the latter's' sensitivity to the dilemmas of politics and his discussion remained an abstract celebration of the rights of diplomacy and treaty-making with wholly unrealistic views on just war as enforcement.[86] The proposal for a permanent court of nations to develop the law and to decide disputes on the basis of criteria 'derived from the rights of humanity' may well have fitted a jurisprudence class but had not the slightest chance of becoming reality.[87]

Natural law teaching continued in German law faculties even after Kant's devastating critiques but was henceforth largely integrated with 'legal philosophy'. It did provide a platform to debate propositions such as those by Fichte on the closed commercial state or Hegel on world history being the world tribunal. But these were less intended for the use of diplomats than parts of a novel genre of social philosophy whose major interest resided in reflecting about conditions of human freedom that were quite distant from the daily politics of statehood. As idealist philosophy, natural law would continue to exist as a respectable aspect of legal education that, however, would no longer claim to offer young jurists an opening to positions in government or diplomacy.[88]

---

[83] F Gentz, *De la paix perpetuelle* (MB Aoun trans) (CNRS Paris 1997 [1800]) at 66–70.

[84] JH Abicht, *Neues System eines aus der Menschheit entwickelten Naturrechts* (Erben Beyrouth 1792) at 31–3.

[85] Ibid 525.   [86] Ibid 541.   [87] Ibid 550.

[88] D Klippel, 'Naturrecht als politische Theorie. Zur politischen Bedeutung des deutschen Naturrechts im 18 und 19 Jahrhundert' in HE Bödeker and U Hermann (eds), *Aufklärung als Politisierung—Politisierung der Aufklärung* (Meiner Hamburg 1987) 267–93, at 277–82.

6 TRANSFORMATION OF NATURAL LAW III: INTO DIPLOMACY

Following Pufendorf, eighteenth-century German jurists assumed that the principal field for the practical application of natural law were relations between nations. Sovereigns lived in a state of nature and the rules governing their relationships emerged from what was taught by wise statecraft contemplating the attainment of state purpose (*Staatszweck*). This did not mean that they would have viewed the international world as one of endless war. In a competitive and sometimes dangerous world it was possible to agree on reasonable principles that operated for the benefit of all. Division of labour in production and commercial exchanges was one such technique, the balance of power another. Natural law gave articulation to both as mechanisms, indeed almost automatons, that would bring about the desired harmony between *utile* and *honestum*. In the routines of statecraft, this would take place through the turn to economics; as thinking about the frame, it would support a philosophical orientation towards the needs and rights of the individual subject.

The transformation of natural law into economics and idealistic philosophy did not, however, undermine the historical practices of European treaty-making or diplomacy, or the view that this world, too, formed a 'system' in need of its experts. In the 100-page Introduction to his *Droit public de l'Europe* (1758)—a collection of treaties from the Peace of Westphalia onwards—Abbé de Mably put forward a 'science of negotiations', a proposal taken up by the last important representative of the Göttingen school, Georg Friedrich von Martens (1756–1821), as the heart of his effort to turn the law of nations into a ('positivist') science of European diplomacy. For his first lectures, Martens published his own textbook of international law, the *Primae liniae juris gentium Europaearum Practici in usum auditorum adumbratae* (1785), thereafter reproduced in one German and three French editions during his lifetime.[89] The work was written as a handbook on the practices of European diplomacy, to be used in connection with teaching future state officials the workings of European public law. Its notion of law was that of a technical craft that

---

[89] GF von Martens, *Primae liniae juris gentium Europaearum Practici in usum auditorum adumbratae* (Dieterich Göttingen 1785). The German version came out in 1796 as *Einleitung in das positive europäische Völkerrecht auf Verträge und Herkommen gegründet* (Dieterich Göttingen 1796). The French versions came out as *Précis du droit des gens moderne de l'Europe fondé sur les traités et l'usage* (Dieterich Gottingue 1789, 1801, 1821). Below, most references are to the 1801 edition. After his death two additional French versions came out and the book was translated also into English at the request of the United States government (1795). For details, see W Habenicht, *Georg Friedrich von Martens: Eine Biografische und völkerrechtliche Studie* (Vandenhoeck & Ruprecht Göttingen 1934) at 58–9.

the more advanced students were expected to learn during the practical exercises that Martens held twice a week, once in French and once in German. After King George III had sent his sons to study with von Martens, the fame of his courses spread so that they became a kind of Europe-wide diplomatic academy. Martens' most significant work is nevertheless the *Recueil de Traités*,[90] which remained the most expansive collection of treaties, declarations, and other international acts until the publication of the League of Nations Treaty Series.[91]

With Martens, a new conception of the law of nations saw the light of day. This consisted of a formalization of the practices of European diplomacy, understood as the operation of a legal system—'European public law'. Martens transposed the technique his predecessors had used to project public law as the point of unity within a fragmented Europe of quarrelling sovereigns. It now became possible to imagine European diplomacy as the management of a legal system consisting of treaties and customary forms of behaviour. True, no single treaty operated as a European constitution—and as Martens presciently noted, there will probably never be one. But the practices of European nations still converged such that it was possible to speak of what he called a practical and a positive European international law.[92] Kant's *Weltbürgerrecht*, Martens wrote, belonged to philosophy instead of law.[93]

In the domestic sphere, natural law had provided a justification for statehood and the legislative sovereignty of the monarch. 'Positivism' had arisen out of natural law and looked back to it when questions regarding the legitimacy and binding force of domestic laws were posed. The constitutions of the nineteenth century and the civil law codifications (such as the French *Code Civil* of 1804 or the Austrian *ABGB* of 1811) were all inspired by naturalist ideas about statehood, property, contract, family, and other aspects of bourgeois society. If the nineteenth century was—in a huge simplification—a century of positivism, this meant the *naturalization* of those institutions among Europe's elites. There was no longer any need to ask for their pedigree or justification. With Martens, the legitimacy of Europe's division into separate states, the colonization of the non-European world, the manners of professional diplomacy, and the occasional resort to war as

---

[90] GF von Martens, *Recueil des principaux traités d'Alliance, de Paix, de Trêve, de neutralité, de commerce, de limites, d'éxchange etc. conclus par les puissances de l'Europe tant entre elles qu'avec les Puissances et États dans d'autres parties du monde depuis 1761 jusqu'à présent* (Dieterich Gottingue 1791).

[91] The first three volumes came out in 1791 and covered the years from 1761 onwards. In 1801 the *Recueil* was extended to seven volumes with another four to succeed the following year. In 1817 Martens began his *Nouveau Recueil* with yet another four volumes. After his death, the *Recueil* was edited by several German lawyers so that the third series covered the years 1908–44 and consisted of forty-one volumes. The total number of volumes in five series rose to 126: 'Georg Friedrich von Martens: Eine Biografische' (n 89) 62–6. See also F von Martiz, 'Der Recueil Martens' (1921) 40 *Archiv des öffentlichen Rechts* 22–72.

[92] *Précis du droit des gens moderne de l'Europe* (n 89) 9.   [93] Ibid 14.

an instrument of policy, were likewise accepted as aspects of European normality and the juristic everyday. This is why Martens' *Précis du droit des gens modern de l'Europe* no longer opened with a philosophical or historical discussion of the law's background (or 'frame') but went *in medias res*, beginning with a discussion and even enumeration of European states. This was the *a priori* from which the rest of the chapters emerged, justified by nothing else than a passage in the preface according to which it had 'appeared *natural* to examine more closely what are the proper...and the common relations under which the powers of Europe may be considered as a whole'.[94] The law was an effect of European statehood, the will, nature, or interest of the European states:

C'est en rassemblant les principes . . . surtout des grandes Puissances de l'Europe, soit en vertu des conventions particulières, expresses ou tacites, uniformes ou ressemblantes, soit en vertu des usages du même genre qu'on forme par abstraction une théorie du droit des gens de l'Europe général, positif, moderne et pratique.[95]

The rest of the book proceeded with a seemingly endless series of classifications, divisions, and subdivisions. The law was divided into natural and positive, public and civil law. Public law was again subdivided into universal and particular, necessary and voluntary. With these divisions, a series of combinations was attained whereby the whole of the European legal landscape could be grasped: states with full sovereignty and states with less than full sovereignty; unitary and composed states; maritime powers and continental powers; states classified by reference to geographical location, size, and rank and differing by way of type of constitution: monarchy, aristocracy, and democracy, each subdivided further into species.[96] This same technique is followed throughout. Negotiations were classified by method, official envoys by rank and function. The law of territory is discussed by classifying the rules on land and sea, rivers and lakes. Types of diplomatic correspondence were classified by addressee; treaties divided into private and public, conditional and unconditional, and then into a long list of their objects, effects and conditions of validity.[97]

Debates about the just war were, for Martens, unfruitful and unnecessary. War had no intrinsic normative status. It was simply a fact and a process, one of the 'voyes de fait' on a par with—though defined by its opposition to—peace.[98] What mattered was the synchronic arrangement of opposing elements: each received meaning from its negation of the other, not from any moral meaning that 'peace' or 'war' might possess. The task of the jurist was to describe and systematize—and thus to order—the relationships that the categories described. Martens followed

---

[94] *Précis du droit des gens moderne de l'Europe* (n 89) ch VIII (emphasis added).
[95] Ibid 11–12.   [96] Ibid 52–9.   [97] Ibid 81–91.
[98] Although war was endemic in the post-Utrecht period (1713), it was low in destructiveness and normally did not involve civilians.

an eighteenth-century natural history paradigm. One had first to collect the raw data—the flower from the forest, the native from the Orient, the treaty from the conference. One then had to analyse it into its basic elements and classify according-ingly. 'Positivism' here meant taking as 'natural' the presence of a bourgeois Europe of States as the frame against which jurists would carry out their activities, interpreting and systematizing treaties and practices into a legal mirror-image of European diplomacy. The law would be impeccably 'scientific' and hence a reliable assistant to the policy-maker.

7 CONCLUSION

The effort to imagine a law that would be applicable everywhere is as old as legal thinking itself. In Roman law, it peaked in Stoic ideas about law of nature—*jus naturae*—whose binding force lay in the universality of human nature. Alongside that philosophically inspired idea, Romans also developed the law of nations—*jus gentium*—in part to address institutions that, even as they could not be said to be 'natural' in this sense, were nevertheless practiced across the world.[99] The idea of *jus naturae* was in due course Christianized to address laws dealing with immutable aspects of human nature as derived from creation. Again, its high level of abstrac-tion suggested to theologians that there was need for more practical law that would address actually existing human institutions. This was the law of nations that, as Aquinas wrote in the *Summa theologiae* was 'natural to man in a sense, in so far as he is rational, because it is derived from natural law in the manner of a conclusion not greatly removed from its first principles'.[100] In Rome, as well as in the Christian tradition, the relations between natural law and the law of nations were complex and fluid—to the extent in fact that Francisco de Vitoria, the founder of the influ-ential 'School of Salamanca' in sixteenth-century Spain held the whole question of classification to be unimportant.[101] From the Romans to the *Secunda scholastica*, writers read into it such institutions as sovereignty, diplomacy, commerce, and the rules of war. These, it was assumed, were part of human nature, not in an absolute way, but as adaptations of immutable principles into the circumstances of social

[99] The best exposé of pre-Grotian ideas of *jus gentium* is in P Haggenmacher, *Grotius et la doc-trine de la guerre juste* (PUF Paris 1983) at 311–58.

[100] T Aquinas, '*Summa theologiae* IaIIae 95 *articulus 4*' in *Aquinas: Political Writings* (RW Dyson ed and trans) (CUP Cambridge 2002) 133–6, at 136.

[101] F de Vitoria, *Comentarios a la Secunda secundae de Santo Tomás* (Vicente Beltrán de Heredia Salamanca 1934/52) bk III Q62 A1 (79).

life. Even positive law was 'natural' inasmuch as it came about as a response to challenges of government given by the world as it was.

The German tradition of *jus naturae et gentium* continued the effort to find laws that would be universally applicable. It was prompted to do so by the advances of the natural sciences. If only one were able to turn law into a technique of government like operating a machine, then law's authority would be that of a science of social life. But this search was undermined by a doubt about what it meant for a law to be 'natural'. Was it that which worked empirically—or that which philosophy suggested corresponded to perfection of human communities? Would it be what Europeans had been accustomed to doing—or the principles through which they viewed what they were doing? The search for the 'natural' meant different things to different people. Something could be regarded as 'natural' because it was eternal and universal, the search for 'happiness', for example. But something could equally well be termed 'natural' if it was specific as, for example, in 'it is natural for Europeans'.[102] In their search for a truly scientific law—the quintessentially German effort at *Wissenschaft*—jurists of the nineteenth century began thus to elaborate on both the logical form of legal concepts and the historical experiences of actual communities. But despite the internecine methodological struggles between legal orientations, rationalism and historicism have turned out to be not so much opposites as complementary aspects of an effort to create a governmental science whose ultimate justification would be given by the nature of human society itself.

The three transformations surveyed in this chapter suggest the presence of three competing vocabularies about how the world ought to be governed. Should economics or philosophy rule us? Or should we be governed in the way we have always been governed? It is surely no accident that legal imagination remains saturated by ideas that crystallized in the course of the European enlightenment, and that international law's specific debt to German academic jurists from the period 1648–1815 is so great. As long as international law shares the ambition of Western science—at least since the religious wars in the sixteenth century—the temptation has been to think about the most urgent problems of human society in terms of jurisdictional delimitation between different authorities that might somehow correspond to what is 'natural' for society. The 'natural' however is not only indeterminate, to be filled with whatever qualities that we are inclined to feel as 'normal' and decent. Whenever the normative is articulated in the vocabulary of 'nature', it will be accompanied by the familiar Enlightenment effort to elaborate techniques and means of measurement, standards and criteria that we associate with 'natural'

---

[102] On the conflict between universal nature and specific natures, see L Daston, *The Morality of Natural Orders: The Tanner Lectures on Human Values* (Princeton University Press Princeton 2002) at 380–92.

sciences and for which the 'human' appears above all as material to be moulded, experimented with, and objectified for the purpose of being better governed.

* * * * * *

When I entered law school in the 1970s, I learned that natural law is dead. What a mistake. The 'positivist' routines of international law, whether formalist or anti-formalist, sociological, institutional, oriented to process or substance, harked back to larger ideas about the 'frame' that presupposed that there were aspects of our collective experience that were 'natural', and thus no longer to be questioned but instead taken as the solid frame on which our routines were to be based. This seemed fine as long as the routines seemed to work, institutionalization was dense, and practices well embedded. But it continued like that even when this was no longer the case, in the aftermath of 1989, the Iraq wars, the debt explosion, massive poverty, terrorism, environmental degradation. A sense of crisis seems only to have intensified the search for the 'natural'. The rise of racism and xenophobia across the developed world is one illustration, but so is faith in the market. And are not the rise of human rights and international criminal law, too, inspired by an effort to find a foothold in what in a complex world would still be incontestably, naturally 'good' and 'evil'? The one lesson we can take from the history of *jus naturae et gentium* in Germany 1648–1815 is, however, that 'nature' is 'culture', its appearance a result of organized efforts by well-placed technicians to manage present problems. But if 'nature' is 'culture', then there is no distance between routines and frames, and no need to believe that present problems—such as global violence and exploitation—result from some very basic fact about our existence that can only be dealt with by some worldwide governance technology. The struggle of the faculties in Germany—between theology, law, economics, diplomacy—involved varying responses to large questions about the human predicament. The outcome of that struggle still continues to determine what we find problematic in the world, what we find natural, and whose routines we invite to rule us. There is no reason to think that the struggle is over. On the contrary, the 'fragmentation' of the legal and social world today questions the self-evidence of these inherited frames, suggesting that no 'nature' is culturally hegemonic. It is not self-evident which of the competing vocabularies should rule us tomorrow. But if international law is to be among them, it had better learn from its failure to become a natural science.

CHAPTER 4

HUGO GROTIUS

THE MAKING OF A FOUNDING
FATHER OF INTERNATIONAL LAW

MARTINE JULIA VAN ITTERSUM*

1 INTRODUCTION

THE Dutch jurist Hugo Grotius (1583–1645) became known as the 'father of international law' in the nineteenth and twentieth centuries. It is hard to avoid this origins
myth in a town like The Hague, with its various international courts and centres
for the study of international law.[1] The Peace Palace in The Hague and its library

* This essay chapter was first given as a public lecture at Harvard University in November 2011,
when I served as Erasmus Lecturer on the History and Civilization of The Netherlands and Flanders.
I dedicate this essay chapter to the memory of Mark Kishlansky, Frank Baird Jr. Professor of History
at Harvard University and my academic adviser from 1992 until 2002. When I delivered the Erasmus
Lecture, he was in the audience and clearly enjoyed himself, laughing out loud at the thought of
the organist of the New Church of Delft playing 'Yankee Doodle Dandy' to commemorate Hugo
Grotius. The Leverhulme Trust, the Netherland-America Foundation, the Carnegie Trust for the
Universities of Scotland, the Caledonian Research Fund, and the Royal Society of Edinburgh have
financially supported my research and writing. I have also benefitted from various visiting fellow-
ships at Huygens ING in The Hague, in 2009–10, and the summers of 2011 and 2013. I should like
to thank both Ms Ingrid Kost, former Head of Special Collections at the Peace Palace Library, and
Mr Jeroen Vervliet, Peace Palace Library Director, for supporting my research on Grotius for many
years now. They are not afraid of critical appraisals of the patron saint of the Peace Palace

[1] A Eyffinger, *The Hague: International Centre of Justice and Peace* (Jongbloed Law Booksellers
The Hague 2003); A Eyffinger, *Dreaming the Ideal, Living the Attainable: TMC Asser (1838–1913),
Founder of The Hague Tradition* (TMC Asser Press The Hague 2011).

were conceived right from the start as a temple of international law and a shrine for its alleged founding father. PC Molhuysen (1870–1944) and Jacob Ter Meulen (1884–1962), the two most important Directors of the Peace Palace Library (PPL) in the first fifty years of its existence, created the Library's famous Grotiana collection, the biggest collection of Grotius' printed works in the world.[2] Molhuysen also initiated the monumental, seventeen-volume edition of Grotius' correspondence, while Ter Meulen compiled a bibliography of all of Grotius' printed works, still considered authoritative.[3] The tradition remains unbroken today: in 2011, the PPL acquired a first edition of Grotius' magnum opus, *De Jure Belli ac Pacis* (1625), for the sizeable sum of €100,000.[4] Nor is there any sign of the International Court of Justice (ICJ) losing interest in Grotius. His work was cited most recently in a dispute between Singapore and Malaysia over the island of Pedra Branca.[5] ICJ judges routinely receive presentation copies of new editions of Grotius' work. The late Robert Feenstra, the greatest Dutch legal historian of the second half of the twentieth century, offered the ICJ President copies of his 1993 edition of *De Jure Belli ac Pacis* and 2009 edition of *Mare Liberum*, for example.[6] Moreover, Grotius is lionized in countless publications of international lawyers, philosophers, international relations specialists, and legal historians, who invariably present him as a great humanitarian, a prince of peace, and secularizer of international law.[7]

[2] *Briefwisseling van Hugo Grotius* (PC Molhuysen et al., eds) (17 vols Nijhoff The Hague 1928–2001) <http://grotius.huygens.knaw.nl/years> [accessed 19 February 2016]; A Eyffinger, *The Grotius Collection at the Peace Palace: A Concise Catalogue* (Van Gorcum Assen 1983); *The World of Hugo Grotius (1583–1645): Proceedings of the International Colloquium Organized by the Grotius Committee of the Royal Netherlands Academy of Arts and Sciences, Rotterdam, 6–9 April 1983* (APA–Holland University Press Amsterdam 1984).

[3] J Ter Meulen, *Concise Bibliography of Hugo Grotius* (AW Sijthoff Leiden 1925); *Grotius-tentoonstelling te 's-Gravenhage, 13–28 juni 1925* (EA van Beresteyn ed) (Sijthoff Leiden 1925); J Ter Meulen and PJJ Diermanse, *Bibliographie des écrits imprimés de Hugo Grotius* (Martinus Nijhoff The Hague 1950); J Ter Meulen and PJJ Diermanse, *Bibliographie des écrits sur Hugo Grotius imprimés au XVIIe siècle* (Martinus Nijhoff The Hague 1961).

[4] H Nellen, *Grotius's Memory Honoured: On the Acquisition of the First Edition of* De iure belli ac pacis *by the Peace Palace Library* (Peace Palace Library The Hague 2012).

[5] *Sovereignty over Pedra Branca/Pulau Batu Puteh, Middle Rocks and South Ledge (Malaysia v Singapore)* (Judgment) [2008] ICJ Rep 12, at 33, available online at <http://www.icj-cij.org/docket/files/130/14492.pdf> [accessed 19 February 2016].

[6] A Eyffinger, *The International Court of Justice, 1946–1996* (Kluwer Law International The Hague 1995); H Grotius, *De iure belli ac pacis libri tres in quibus ius naturae & gentium: item iuris publici praecipua explicantur* (BJA de Kanter-van Hettinga Tromp ed) (EJ Brill Leiden 1939; 2nd expanded edn with notes by R Feenstra and CA Persenaire Scientia Verlag Aalen 1993); H Grotius, *Mare Liberum, 1609–2009: Original Latin Text and Modern English Translation* (R Feenstra ed and trans) (Brill Leiden 2009). A report on the 'Mare Liberum 1609–2009' conference at the PPL on 11 December 2009, including pictures of Professor Feenstra presenting his *Mare Liberum* edition to the ICJ President, can be found on 'The Hague Justice Portal' <http://www.haguejusticeportal.net/index.php?id=11313> [accessed 19 February 2016].

[7] J Dunn and I Harris (eds), *Grotius* (2 vols Edward Elgar Cheltenham 1997). This is an anthology of classic twentieth century publications on Grotius as 'secularizer', 'humanitarian', 'father of international law', and so on. See also H Bull, B Kingsbury, and A Roberts (eds), *Hugo Grotius and*

I take issue with what I call the 'Grotius Delusion'. My aim is to explain how the origins myth came into being and whose interests have been served by it. It was a combination of Dutch nationalism and the rise of modern international law that turned Grotius into a 'founding father', with a little help, it should be said, from the American delegates at the 1899 Hague Peace Conference. It is based on a highly selective reading of *De Jure Belli ac Pacis* and completely ignores the larger historical context of Grotius' work, particularly his hands-on involvement in Western imperialism and colonialism. I start with a short overview of Grotius' life, briefly discuss his public image in The Netherlands in the early modern period, and then examine how it changed as a consequence of the rise of international law in the nineteenth century. I end with a discussion of recent historical research on Grotius, which aims to properly contextualize his life and work, rather than to focus on just one aspect of it and use that to justify modern-day arrangements for the resolution of conflicts between states.

2 GROTIUS' LIFE AND TIMES

Hugo de Groot, known to the English-speaking world by the Latinized name of Grotius, was born into a prominent *regent* (that is, patrician) family in Delft on Easter Day 1583. Just two years earlier, the Dutch States General had abjured Philip II of Spain and Portugal as the ruler of the Low Countries and de facto created a new state, the Dutch Republic. Grotius started his professional life as a private solicitor, at the tender age of sixteen. In 1604, the directors of the Dutch East India Company or VOC asked him to write a defence of the Company's privateering campaign in Asian waters, aggressively attacking the Portuguese *Estado da India*. Grotius was happy to oblige, and completed his *De Indis* in 1607–8.[8] This treatise of 163 folios remained in manuscript, only to appear in print in the nineteenth century, as *De Jure Praedae/On the Law of Prize and Booty*.[9] At the Directors' request, Grotius did publish chapter twelve of *De Indis* separately in 1609 as *Mare Liberum/The Free Sea* 'or…the Right Which the Hollanders Ought to Have to the Indian Trade'. He continued to support the VOC in word and deed for the rest of

---

International Relations (Clarendon Press Oxford 1990) and P Allott, 'Language, Method and the Nature of International Law' (1971) 45 *British Yearbook of International Law* 79–135.

  [8] H Grotius, *Commentary on the Law of Prize and Booty* (GL Williams trans MJ van Ittersum ed) (Liberty Fund Indianapolis 2006).
  [9] Ibid.

his life, negotiating on the Company's behalf with the English East India Company in 1613 and 1615, for example.[10]

Thanks to the patronage of Johan van Oldenbarnevelt, de facto political leader of the Dutch Republic and a friend of Grotius' father, he was quickly appointed to a number of high-level political positions at the provincial and federal level. He became Advocate-Fiscal (public prosecutor) of Holland in December 1607 and Pensionary (chief legal adviser) of the town of Rotterdam in June 1613. In the latter capacity, Grotius joined the Rotterdam delegation in the States of Holland. In May 1617, he became a member of the Holland delegation in the Dutch States General, the federal government of the Dutch Republic. By all accounts, it was a meteoric political career. Grotius would undoubtedly have succeeded Oldenbarnevelt as political leader of the Dutch Republic had it not been for religious troubles that brought the rebel state to the brink of collapse during the Twelve Years' Truce (1609–1621). Orthodox Calvinists squared off against the so-called 'Remonstrants', followers of the Leiden theologian Arminius. Although Arminius' followers were a minority in the Dutch Reformed Church, they enjoyed the support of the States of Holland, in particular of Oldenbarnevelt and Grotius. The theological bickering developed into a major political crisis that endangered the existence of the Dutch Republic. Prince Maurice of Orange, commander-in-chief of the country's naval and military forces and Stadtholder (governor) of six of its seven provinces, could not stand idly by. In August 1618, he sought to break the political deadlock by means of a regime change, which landed Grotius in prison for almost three years. In view of his close association with Oldenbarnevelt—executed in May 1619—he was lucky to escape with his life.[11]

Yet Grotius' political career was far from over. In March 1621, he escaped from Loevestein Castle in a book trunk. He headed south to Paris, where he lived as an exile for many years and received a pension from the French Crown. As a *quid pro quo*, he dedicated *De Jure Belli ac Pacis* (1625) to Louis XIII of France. Cardinal De Richelieu was eager to tap Grotius' in-depth knowledge of Dutch overseas expansion and commercial governance, and sought to involve him in the establishment of a French East India Company. Yet Grotius was unwilling to burn his bridges behind him. For a long time he believed that he would be reinstated as Pensionary of

---

[10] MJ van Ittersum, *Profit and Principle: Hugo Grotius, Natural Rights Theories and the Rise of Dutch Power in the East Indies, 1595–1615* (Brill Leiden 2006); *Commentary on the Law of Prize and Booty* (n 8); H Grotius, *The Free Sea* (D Armitage ed R Hakluyt trans) (Liberty Fund Indianapolis 2004).

[11] Henk Nellen, *Hugo de Groot: Een leven in strijd om de vrede, 1583–1645* (Uitgeverij Balans 2007) 25–257; HJM Nellen, *Hugo Grotius: A Lifelong Struggle for Peace in Church and State, 1583–1645* (JC Grayson trans) (Brill Leiden 2015) 14–302; *De Hollandse jaren van Hugo de Groot (1583–1621)* (HJM Nellen and J Trapman eds) (Verloren Hilversum 1996); J den Tex, *Oldenbarnevelt* (RB Powell trans) (2 vols CUP Cambridge 1973).

Rotterdam once Prince Maurice's younger brother and heir, Prince Frederic Henry, had established himself in power. Grotius returned to Holland in October 1631 in order to force a breakthrough in the negotiations about his possible rehabilitation. His ostentatious visits to Rotterdam and Amsterdam badly backfired, however. In April 1632, the States of Holland exiled him once more and put a price of 2,000 guilders on his head. The definitive breach with his homeland came after two unhappy years in Hamburg. Grotius accepted the offer of the Swedish chancellor Axel Oxenstierna to become the resident Swedish ambassador in Paris. In the context of the Thirty Years' War, this was an important and sensitive position: after the death of King Gustavus Adolphus, the Swedish armies in Germany were essentially kept afloat with French subsidies. It was Grotius' job to maintain good relations with the French ally, particularly Cardinal de Richelieu. He discharged this task for nearly ten years, albeit with uneven success, due to French opposition to his appointment. He was finally recalled by the Swedish government in January 1645 and arrived in Stockholm five months later. He refused to become one of Queen Christina's privy councillors, however, and took the first ship back to France. After a storm-ridden voyage across the Baltic, his ship was wrecked off the Pomeranian coast in August 1645. Although Grotius safely reached the shore, he died at an inn in Rostock, aged 62. He was buried in the family crypt in the New Church in Delft.[12]

3 GROTIUS' *NACHLEBEN* IN THE LOW COUNTRIES

Grotius' star waxed and waned in the Dutch Republic and its successor state, the Kingdom of The Netherlands, for over four centuries. The Remonstrants, who remain a religious minority in The Netherlands, have claimed Grotius as a 'martyr for toleration'. Grotius' descendants sympathized with their cause. At the turn of the eighteenth century, two Remonstrant divines gained unprecedented access to Grotius' papers and wrote a 300-page biography of their hero, still considered authoritative today. They focused on Grotius' attempts to resolve the religious crises of his age, at the expense of other aspects of his life and work, such as his advocacy of VOC interests. [13]

---

[12] *Hugo de Groot* (n 11) 226–62, 271–7, 317–31, 364–405, 445–51, 470–5, 532–50, 580–92; *Hugo Grotius* (n 11) 302–30, 380–97, 443–99, 548–56, 563–70, 580–7, 661–83, 720–36; MJ van Ittersum, 'The Long Goodbye: Hugo Grotius and the Justification of Dutch Expansion Overseas (1604–1645)' (2010) 36 *History of European Ideas* 386–411.

[13] H Grotius, *Meletius, sive, De iis quae inter Christianos conveniunt epistola* (GHM Posthumus Meyjes ed and trans) (Brill Leiden 1997) 6–7; H Nellen, 'Confidentiality and Indiscretion: The Intricacies of Publishing Grotius' Correspondence Posthumously' in HTM van Vliet (ed),

In the later eighteenth century, Grotius became the darling of the Dutch Patriots, the political opponents of William V of Orange. The Dutch Patriots sought to reform the government of the Dutch Republic along democratic lines and reduce the power of the Stadtholder or abolish the office entirely. For them, Grotius was a noble defender of republican government and freedom, who had fallen victim to the power-hungry Princes of Orange. The only complicating factor was that Grotius' descendants in Rotterdam had meanwhile become clients of the Stadtholder! As a result of Prussian intervention, the Patriot Revolution was crushed in 1787. However, exiled Patriots would return to positions of power in The Netherlands in 1795, in the wake of the French Revolutionary Armies. They brought their idealized image of Grotius with them. As a 'martyr for freedom', he became part of the ideological pedigree of the Batavian Republic, a sister republic of the French Republic.[14]

Grotius' newfound popularity did not survive Napoleon's fall in 1813. The establishment of the new Kingdom of The Netherlands discouraged any talk of the republican heroes of yore. The political elite of The Netherlands, both former Orangists and Patriots, wished to portray itself as being united in the service of King William I, the eldest son of the last Stadtholder. The disestablishment of the Dutch Reformed Church in 1851 also ended the Remonstrant crusade for equal rights. Consequently, there was less need to appeal to Grotius' alleged legacy of toleration. At the same time, Grotius' descendants lost control of his material legacy: thirty-odd volumes of manuscripts—family heirlooms for over two centuries—were auctioned in The Hague in November 1864. The main buyers were the Swedish Government, the Remonstrant Church in Rotterdam, the Municipal Archives of Rotterdam, the Dutch National Archives, Leiden University Library, and Johan Pieter Cornets de Groot van Kraayenburg (1808–1878), a scion of the cadet branch of the family. The Dutch government made no attempt to buy or preserve this unique collection of manuscripts. This lack of interest in Grotius and his material legacy would change dramatically as a result of the rise of international law in the late nineteenth century, which turned Grotius into a Dutch national hero as well as a father of international law. [15]

Produktion und Kontext: Beiträge der Internationalen Fachtagung der Arbeitsgemeinschaft für germanistische Edition im Constantijn Huygens Instituut, Den Haag, 4. bis 7. März 1998 (Max Niemeyer Verlag Tübingen 1998) 135–44; C Brandt and A van Cattenburgh, *Historie van het Leven des Heeren Huig de Groot* (2 vols Van Braan and Linden Dordrecht 1727).

   [14] MJ van Ittersum, 'Confronting Grotius' Legacy in an Age of Revolution: The Cornets de Groot Family in Rotterdam, 1748–1798' (2012) 127 *English Historical Review* 1367–403.

   [15] *Catalogue de Manuscrits Autographes de Hugo Grotius* (WJM van Eysinga and LJ Noordhoff eds) (2nd edn Martinus Nijhoff The Hague 1952); LJ Noordhoff, *Beschrijving van het zich in Nederland bevindende en nog onbeschreven gedeelte der papieren afkomstig van Huig de Groot, welke in 1864 te 's-Gravenhage zijn geveild* (Noordhoff Groningen 1953) 7–14. On JP Cornets de Groot van Kraaijenburg, see Parlementair Documentatie Centrum, 'Jhr JP Cornets de Groot van Kraaijenburg' <http://www.parlementairdocumentatiecentrum.nl/id/vg09llj55bt3> [accessed 19 February 2016].

A reburial of sorts took place in the vestry of the New Church in Delft on 18 October 1889. The gentlemen present, all wearing full dress, were the Keeper of the Royal Crypt, the burgomaster and aldermen of Delft, and JAWL Cornets de Groot van Kraayenburg (1862–1923), grandson and heir of JP Cornets de Groot van Kraayenburg. In a short ceremony, Grotius' remains were transferred into a new leaden casket, which, in turn, was put into a 'beautifully carved' oak coffin, sealed with a ribbon of yellow, black and red—the armorial colours of the Cornets de Groot lineage. Grotius' coffin had also been opened a century earlier, at the time of the burial of his great-great grandson, the Rotterdam burgomaster Hugo Cornets de Groot. At that point, a small copper plaque had been affixed to Grotius' coffin, bearing the inscription: '*het gebeente van HdG*'. ('the remains of H[ugo] d[e] G[root]'). The ceremony in May 1777 had been a private family affair. By contrast, the reburial in October 1889 was a minor media event, reported in several local and national newspapers. It followed hard on the heels of the unveiling of the Grotius statue in the Delft market square three years earlier, and a commemoration in the New Church in April 1883 of the tercentenary of Grotius' birth. The man and the myth were fast becoming public property. Dutch nationalism, American enthusiasm, and the rise of modern international law were the three most important factors in the making of Grotius' modern image.[16]

4 THE 1899 HAGUE PEACE CONFERENCE

The 1899 peace conference in The Hague sealed Grotius' twentieth-century reputation as 'father of international law'. In August 1898, the Russian Tsar invited other European governments to join him in what he called 'the maintenance of general peace and a possible reduction of the excessive armaments which weigh upon all nations'.[17] The Russian government's deteriorating financial position and the growth of German military and naval power were important considerations for the young ruler. Initially, his diplomatic initiative met with strong reservations in Western Europe. The one exception was the Dutch government, which responded enthusiastically to the tsar's proposals.

In January 1899, the Russian Foreign Secretary asked his Dutch counterpart to host the proposed peace conference in The Hague. Four months later, the delegates

---

[16] Royal Library, The Hague, Cornets de Groot Archive, CdG 17 fols 60–1, 122–5, 130–1.
[17] As cited by B Tuchman, *The Proud Tower: A Portrait of the World Before the War, 1890–1914* (Macmillan London 1966) at 239.

of twenty-five countries, including China, Japan, Thailand, Persia, Turkey, Mexico, and the US met at the conference venue, the royal palace *Huis Ten Bosch* (House in the Woods). Expectations were low. The head of the American delegation, Andrew Dickson White—American ambassador in Berlin and founding president of Cornell University—noted: 'probably, since the world began, never has so large a body come together in a spirit of more hopeless scepticism as to any good result'. Yet a strong sense of historical mission and a spirit of teamwork and collegiality resulted in an unexpected breakthrough in late July: the establishment of the Permanent Court of Arbitration (PCA), which still exists today. White was convinced that the Grotius commemoration in Delft on 4 July 1899, organized by the American delegation, had materially contributed to this success.[18]

That is probably too simplistic an explanation for the establishment of the PCA. According to Arthur Eyffinger, the conference delegates were aided in their deliberations by a busy social schedule, which allowed them to exchange ideas and opinions 'off the record'.[19] Dutch government authorities and foreign embassies in The Hague organized a seemingly endless round of lunches, teas, receptions, dinners, concerts, balls, and excursions—on average one social event every other day. White came up with the brilliant idea to organize a Grotius commemoration, a real propaganda coup for the young American republic. It became an iconic event—not least because of American self-publicity—which firmly tied Grotius' legacy to modern international law and confirmed Dutch–American friendship, embedding the history of both countries in the seductive narrative of the progress of Western civilization.[20]

What made the celebration of Dutch history and culture so attractive to White? In her book *Holland Mania* (1998), Annette Stott examines the fetishism for all things Dutch among the urban elites of the United States (US) during the Gilded Age. Americans who claimed pre-Revolutionary Dutch descent organized themselves in exclusive ethnic associations, such as the Holland Society of New York, founded in 1885.[21] Wealthy industrialists became serious collectors of the artwork of the Dutch Golden Age. The fishing villages of Volendam and Marken, just north of Amsterdam, became open-air museums, largely thanks to American tourism. Houses, furniture, and clothing were adapted to what foreign visitors, fresh from a visit to the Rijksmuseum in Amsterdam, imagined the Dutch Golden Age to have been like. Yet Americans were not just attracted to the aesthetics of seventeenth-century Dutch paintings. There was an ideological component as well. John

---

[18] A Eyffinger, *The 1899 Hague Peace Conference: The Parliament of Man, the Federation of the World* (Martinus Nijhoff Leiden 1999) at 15–40, 70–202; C De Armond Davis, *The United States and the First Hague Peace Conference* (Cornell University Press Ithaca 1962) at 90.

[19] *The 1899 Hague Peace Conference* (n 18) 318–33.   [20] Ibid 313–16, 415–19.

[21] See A Stott, *Holland Mania: The Unknown Dutch Period in American Art & Culture* (Overlook Press Woodstock 1998).

Lothrop Motley (1814–1877), a Boston Brahmin and Harvard graduate, became the first American historian to do archival research on Dutch history.[22] It resulted in two very influential publications: *The Rise of the Dutch Republic* (1855) and *History of the United Netherlands* (1861).[23] Thanks to Motley, Americans could celebrate the Dutch as a kindred people. The Dutch had thrown off the yoke of royal government in 1581, established a highly successful Protestant republic—but one tolerant of other religions—and, not coincidentally, created a global trading empire. In October 1903, the Dutch-born Edward Bok (1863–1930) confidently announced to the millions of readers of *Ladies' Home Journal* that Holland, not England, was 'the mother of America'.[24] The notion that all truly American characteristics and ideals originated in Holland was an important incentive for White to organize the Grotius commemoration in Delft on Independence Day 1899.[25]

5 A DUTCH-AMERICAN PARTY

We can follow the preparations for the Grotius commemoration in White's *Autobiography* (1905).[26] Following a tourist trip to Delft in late May 1899, he confided to his journal: 'of all books ever written—not claiming divine inspiration—the great work of Grotius on "War and Peace" has been of most benefit to mankind'. He wrote privately to John Hay (1838–1905), the American Secretary of State, asking permission for the American delegation to 'lay a wreath of silver and gold upon the tomb of Grotius at Delft'. When he received a positive reply from Washington DC on 19 June, he immediately telegraphed his specifications for the wreath to the American embassy in Berlin. The next day, he approached the head of the Dutch delegation at the peace conference, APC van Karnebeek (1836–1925), who responded enthusiastically to the American plans. He suggested that the Dutch

---

[22] MA Peterson, 'A Brahmin Goes Dutch: John Lothrop Motley and the Lessons of Dutch History in Nineteenth-Century Boston' in JD Goodfriend, B Schmidt, and A Stott (eds), *Going Dutch: The Dutch Presence in America, 1609–2009* (Brill Leiden 2008) 109–34.

[23] JL Motley, *The Rise of the Dutch Republic* (3 vols Harper New York 1855–61); JL Motley, *History of the United Netherlands* (4 vols Harper New York 1861–8).

[24] Quoted in *Holland Mania* (n 21) 9.

[25] NT Minty, 'Great Expectations: The Golden Age Redeems The Gilded Era' in *Going Dutch* (n 22) 215–35; DP Weller, 'Old Masters in the New World: The Hudson–Fulton Exhibition of 1909 and Its Legacy' in *Going Dutch* (n 22) 237–68; L Vookles, 'Return in Glory: The Holland Society Visits "The Fatherland"' in R Panetta (ed), *Dutch New York: The Roots of Hudson Valley Culture* (Fordham University Press New York 2009) 257–97; R Panetta, 'The Hudson–Fulton Celebration of 1909' in *Dutch New York* (n 25) 301–38.

[26] AD White, *Autobiography of Andrew Dickson White* (Century New York 1905).

Foreign Secretary (and Honorary President of the peace conference) be involved as well. WH de Beaufort (1845–1918) was 'devoted to the memory of Grotius'. He had delivered a long panegyric on the occasion of the unveiling of the Grotius statue in Delft in September 1886, for example. The American delegation duly visited de Beaufort to hammer out the logistics of the 1899 Grotius commemoration: a solemn ceremony in the New Church at 11am, followed by a luncheon for invited guests in the Delft City Hall. On 2 July, the military attaché of the American embassy in Berlin arrived in The Hague with the 'Grotius wreath', made by Court jeweller Eugene Marcus. It displayed the arms of the Netherlands and the US, along with the following inscription:

To the Memory of Hugo Grotius;
In Reverence and Gratitude,
From the United States of America;
On the Occasion of the International Peace Conference of The Hague.
July 4th, 1899.

White noted in his journal that the wreath was 'a superb piece of work', attracting 'most favorable attention'. Everything was ready for the *grand finale* two days later.[27]

The Grotius commemoration was widely reported by Dutch newspapers. It featured in three *New York Times* articles as well. At 10.15am, the organist of the New Church started playing a series of national songs, including 'Yankee Doodle Dandy'. According to *New York Times* reporter Mrs Hanken-Parker, carriage after carriage rolled up to the door of the church, dislodging 'gayly dressed ladies and profusely decorated men'. The entire Dutch government arrived to participate in the ceremony, as did most of the peace conference delegates, and nearly all ambassadors resident in The Hague. In addition, the pews filled with faculty members from Dutch universities, Leiden in particular, and a large crowd of American tourists. At 11am, an occasional choir of approximately 150 singers performed Mendelssohn's 'How Lovely are the Messengers that Bring Us Good Tidings of Peace'. At the request of the American delegation, Van Karnebeek opened the proceedings. Following a second musical interlude, White rose to deliver his laudation.[28]

[27] AD White, *Autobiography* (2 vols Macmillan London 1905) vol 2, at 274, 291, 316, 317–18, 320, 322–6; *The 1899 Hague Peace Conference* (n 18) 165–9, 196–202, 324–31; J Woltring, 'Karnebeek, jhr, Abraham Pieter Cornelis van (1836–1925)' <http://www.historici.nl/Onderzoek/Projecten/BWN/lemmata/bwn1/karnebeekapc> [accessed 19 February 2016]; H van der Hoeven, 'Beaufort, Willem Hendrik de (1845–1918)' in *Biografisch Woordenboek van Nederland* <http://www.historici.nl/Onderzoek/Projecten/BWN/lemmata/bwn1/beaufort> [accessed 19 February 2016]. For Dutch newspaper reports on the unveiling of the Grotius statue in Delft on 25 September 1886, see Royal Library, The Hague, Cornets de Groot Archive CdG 17 fols 64–6, 69–70, 77.
[28] Royal Library, The Hague, Cornets de Groot Archive, CdG 17 fols 50, 51–2, 97, 99, 100, 109–10; M Hanken-Parker, 'A Tribute to Hugo de Groot' (30 July 1899) *New York Times*; *The 1899 Hague Peace Conference* (n 18) 326–7.

By honouring the writer of *De Jure Belli ac Pacis*, so White informed his audience, the US did not just express her own gratitude, but also spoke on behalf of 'every part of Europe, of all the great powers of Asia, [and] of the sister republics of North and South America'. Significantly, White failed to mention Africa. According to the prominent international lawyers of the day, a certain degree of 'civilization' was required for statehood. It explains White's assertion that 'the sisterhood of nations' included countries 'yet unborn' in Grotius' time (the US) and countries 'now civilized... which Grotius knew only as barbarous'—probably a reference to the peace conference delegates from the Ottoman Empire, Russia, Persia, China, and Japan. What was on full display in White's speech was, of course, the Whig interpretation of history—a story of 'continuous progress', underpinned by Protestantism, tolerance, freedom, and democracy. When the Pilgrim Fathers sailed from Delftshaven in 1620, they had allegedly taken Dutch notions of religious toleration to the New World—Grotius' notions, of course. In no other country, so White noted, had his teachings penetrated more deeply than in the US. Its inhabitants had been thoroughly imbued with 'those feelings of mercy and humanity which Grotius, more than any other, brought into the modern world'. Indeed, the concept of arbitration between states could be found in a single sentence in *De Jure Belli ac Pacis* (bk 2, ch 23): 'But especially are Christian kings and states bound to try this way of avoiding war'.[29] In White's view, Grotius' reasoning informed the Geneva Arbitration of 1872 that had settled the Alabama Claims, ensuring friendly relations between the US and United Kingdom (UK). (For the assistance given to the Confederate cause, the UK paid the US $15.5 million in damages.) White concluded his laudation with Grotius' supposed words of encouragement to the peace conference delegates:

From this tomb of Grotius I seem to hear a voice which says to us as the delegates of the Nations: 'Go on with your mighty work. . . . Go on with the work of strengthening peace and humanizing war: give greater scope and strength to provisions which will make war less cruel: perfect those laws of war which diminish the unmerited sufferings of populations: and, above all, give the world at least a beginning of an effective, practicable scheme of arbitration.'[30]

He then affixed the wreath to Grotius' tomb. It is still there today.[31]

---

[29] H Butterfield, *The Whig Interpretation of History* (Bell London 1931); H Grotius, *De Jure Belli ac Pacis Libri Tres* (FW Kelsey trans) (2 vols Clarendon Press Oxford 1925) vol 2, bk II, ch 23, at 563 'De Causis Dubiis'.

[30] Royal Library, The Hague, Cornets de Groot archives, CdG 17 fols 50–2; M Hanken-Parker, 'Homage to Hugo Grotius' (5 July 1899) *New York Times*; M Hanken-Parker, 'The Hugo Grotius Celebration' (2 September 1899) *New York Times*; *The 1899 Hague Peace Conference* (n 18) 328–9; M Koskenniemi, *The Gentle Civilizer of Nations: The Rise and Fall of International Law 1870–1960* (CUP Cambridge 2001).

[31] On 4 July 2012, the tenth anniversary of the International Criminal Court was celebrated in the New Church in Delft by the International Criminal Court Student Network and the Department of

De Beaufort was entrusted with the pleasurable task of thanking the American delegation and government. In his speech, he emphasized the historical links between the US and The Netherlands. The Dutch had been the first European settlers in the Hudson Valley, and the first to recognize American independence, thanks to a salute fired from Fort Orange at St Eustatius—a Dutch possession in the Caribbean—in November 1776. De Beaufort expressed the hope that the wreath affixed to Grotius' tomb would be 'an everlasting emblem' of the friendly relations between the two countries. Tobias MC Asser (1838–1913), professor of private international law at the University of Amsterdam, spoke in his capacity as president of the *Institut de Droit International*. Asser congratulated the American delegation on the tribute paid to 'the father of our science'. The American delegate Seth Low (1850–1916), President of Columbia University, concluded the proceedings. He also emphasized the historical links between the US and The Netherlands. In his view, the Dutch had taught Americans 'to separate Church and State', and continued to inspire 'devotion to learning, to religious liberty, and to individual and national freedom'. High praise indeed, but was it true? We will return to that question later on in this chapter.[32]

The audience left the New Church to the tune of 'Star Spangled Banner'. Three hundred and fifty invited guests walked across the market square to the Delft City Hall, where they enjoyed a historically themed luncheon, including '*filets de soie à la Grotius*' and '*poulardes à la Washington*'. The American delegates and Dutch authorities raised many a glass to each other. In her *New York Times* article, Hanken-Parker accentuated the connections between the Dutch past and American present. The Delft city councillor who toasted White in garbled English was considered a perfect resemblance of Peter Stuyvesant (1611–1672), the last director-general of Dutch New York. Still, it remained an Independence Day celebration. Hanken-Parker noted that the US ambassador in The Netherlands, Stanford Nevell, had gone from table to table in the Delft City Hall in order to touch the glass of every American visitor, saying quietly: 'we are all over here to-day, but in our hearts we are with the rest of them in our own land; so here's "to home"'.[33]

Philosophy and Religion at Central Michigan University. Professor Hope Elizabeth May of Central Michigan University arranged for a special cleaning of the 1899 sterling silver wreath, which had oxidized quite badly. It is now back at Grotius' tomb in all its splendour. I would like to thank Professor May and Professor Andrew Blom for sharing this information with me.

[32] Royal Library, The Hague, Cornets de Groot Archive, CdG 17 fols 50–2; 'A Tribute to Hugo de Groot' (n 28); *Autobiography* (n 26) vol 2, at 327–8; *The 1899 Hague Peace Conference* (n 18) 199–200, 327, 330.

[33] See sources cited in n 30. Stanford Newell was a member of the Republican Party and practised law in St Paul Minnesota for many years. In 1897, he was appointed Envoy Extraordinary and Minister Plenipotentiary to the Netherlands. In 1899 he was part of the US Delegation to the Hague Peace Conference. He resigned as US ambassador to The Netherlands in 1905.

6 How to Interpret the Grotius Commemoration of 4 July 1899

I have elaborated on the events in Delft in July 1899 in order to highlight the three factors at play in the creation of Grotius as 'father of international law':

1. The conceptualization of the Dutch past by American historians and government officials.

2. The importance of the Dutch Golden Age for Dutch nation-building in the nineteenth and twentieth centuries.

3. The role played by the *Institut de Droit International* and the rise of modern international law more generally

Let me explain this at greater length. It was back to the future for White and Hanken-Parker. The Dutch Golden Age was *the* precursor of the nineteenth-century American present. Allegedly, the Dutch had exported to Colonial New York religious toleration, a thirst for liberty, republicanism, democracy, and so on—everything that was quintessential American according to Gilded Age politicians and intellectuals. In 1872, Motley had joined King William III of The Netherlands in celebrating the third centennial of the Sea Beggar's capture of Brill. Arguably, it was this intense American interest in the Dutch Golden Age that contributed to a new taxonomy of historical figures and events. The sixteenth-century Dutch Revolt became a 'War of Independence', for example. Grotius the alleged champion of freedom and toleration fitted right in with this story of historical progress, culminating, of course, in the birth of the United States of America.[34]

Grotius was part of other, equally powerful historical narratives as well. He became a Dutch national hero at the end of the nineteenth century. The Grotius commemorations of April 1883 and September 1886 had been presented in Dutch newspapers as important manifestations of national unity. The Kingdom of The Netherlands had moved beyond the religious and political infighting characteristic of the Dutch Republic—or so the story went. Dutchmen of all faiths could now come together in Delft to celebrate Grotius' alleged legacy of religious toleration. There were no more Republicans and Orangists: descendants of the *regent* families loyally served the new monarchy. The House of Orange was above party politics, and actively sought to nurture national unity and reconciliation. When, in 1878, the Dutch branch of the Association for the Reform and Codification of International Law first broached the idea of rendering 'national homage' to Grotius, it found

---

[34] D Armitage, *The Declaration of Independence: A Global History* (Harvard University Press Cambridge MA 2007); R Ensel, 'Baudrillard in Brielle. De historische cultuur van de Tachtigjarige Oorlog' (2008) 121 *Tijdschrift voor geschiedenis* 40–55.

an enthusiastic supporter in Prince Alexander (1851–84), the third son of King William III of The Netherlands. The ruling elite of the Kingdom of the Netherlands was determined, then, to incorporate all the great statesmen of the Dutch Golden Age into the national canon—Oldenbarnevelt, Grotius, and the De Witt brothers as well as the Stadtholders.[35]

In the 1890s, it suited Dutch politicians very well that Grotius was not just a Dutch national hero, but also fast becoming a 'father of international law'. They have paid homage to Grotius as a symbol of the country's civilizing mission ever since. In the first half of the nineteenth century, the ruling elite of the Kingdom of The Netherlands faced the awkward question whether a small, truncated country stood any chance of survival in a continent dominated by big nation-states. The Liberal ascendancy in the second half of the nineteenth century brought a solution of sorts: even as a second- or third-rank power in Europe, Dutch politicians told themselves, the Kingdom did have a manifest destiny in international politics. Its overarching moral purpose was to reduce armed conflict in Europe and, to a lesser extent, around the world. This particular brand of Dutch nationalism has been inextricably intertwined with the rise of modern international law and the establishment of international courts in The Hague. Peaceful conflict resolution is in the interests of small powers. The Dutch could not compete in the European arms races that preceded the First World War and the Second World War, for instance. But it is always nice to tell yourself that you occupy the moral high ground. Grotius has proven an ideal mascot for the Dutch government and legal profession. To give just one example, the Dutch Prime Minister Jan Peter Balkenende could not resist referring to him at the inaugural session of the International Criminal Court in The Hague on 11 March 2003. In Balkende's view, the International Criminal Court (ICC) was a realization of Grotian ideals. Allegedly, the author of *De Jure Belli ac Pacis* had sought to create

a system of international law, with clear agreements and procedures for countries to comply with. He believed that a system of this kind was necessary for international justice and stability. Today, ladies and gentlemen, nearly four centuries later, we move a step closer to that ideal.[36]

[35] Royal Library, The Hague, Cornets de Groot Archive, CdG 17 fols 144–7, 150–2; NCF Van Sas, *De metamorfose van Nederland: Van oude orde naar moderniteit, 1750–1900* (Amsterdam University Press Amsterdam 2005); W Vroom, *Het wonderlid van Jan de Wit en andere vaderlandse relieken* (Sun Nijmegen 1997); J ThM Bank, *Het roemrijk vaderland: Cultureel nationalisme in de negentiende eeuw* (SDU The Hague 1990).

[36] Balkende's speech is available on the website of the Coalition for the ICC, see Coalition for the International Criminal Court, 'Welcome by the Prime Minister of the Kingdom of the Netherlands, Dr Jan Peter Balkenende, at the Inaugural Session of the International Criminal Court, The Hague, 11 March 2003' <http://www.iccnow.org/documents/NetherlandsPM11March03.pdf>. On Dutch foreign policy in the Interbellum period, particularly regarding the League of Nations, see R van Diepen, *Voor Volkenbond en vrede: Nederland en het streven naar een nieuwe wereldorde 1919–1946* (Bert Bakker Amsterdam 1999).

The Dutch government, then, continues to affirm Grotius' alleged importance as 'father of international law'. Two myths are feeding off each other: Dutch nationalism/internationalism and the self-understanding of modern international law as a narrative of historical progress—allegedly, we are moving closer to the ideal of 'international justice and stability'.[37]

Why did international lawyers select Grotius as their 'founding father' in the late nineteenth century? As noted earlier, Asser spoke at the Grotius commemoration in July 1899 in his capacity as President of the *Institut de Droit International*. As Martti Koskenniemi shows, international lawyers at the time aspired to be the legal conscience of the *civilized* world. The history of international law was conceived of as a morality tale, played out in European history:

> . . . a story of individual lawyers acting like so many chivalrous knights, defending the oppressed against the oppressors, peace against war, carrying the torch of civilization (from Greece and Rome) through dark ages to the present. It was not kings or diplomats, but writers and scientists who finally woke up '*das schlummerende Rechtsbewusstsein der civilisierten Welt*'.[38]

It explains what made Grotius such an attractive historical figure. He was a burgher of Delft and a properly married man, who had sired eight children with his wife of thirty-seven years, Maria van Reigersberch. His private life conformed to the ideals of the upper bourgeoisie in nineteenth-century Western Europe, the class into which most international lawyers were born. But there was more. Grotius was a Protestant who appeared to have embraced religious toleration—not exactly common in seventeenth-century Europe. Had he not defended the Remonstrants, victims of religious hatred, from the nasty orthodox Calvinists? Surely, it was his moral and intellectual superiority that allowed him to prevail over adversity—three years of captivity at Loevestein Castle, followed by twenty-four years of exile. Had he not sought to humanize war and further the cause of peace in *De Jure Belli ac Pacis*? If true, this added up to a perfect 'founding father', from the perspective of international lawyers in the late nineteenth century, of course. Recent research portrays Grotius in a rather different light, however.

In 2007, Henk Nellen published the most authoritative biography of Grotius to date: *Hugo de Groot: Een leven in strijd om de vrede, 1583–1645*. The English translation appeared in 2015, entitled *Hugo Grotius: A Lifelong Struggle for Peace in Church and State, 1583–1645*. Nellen has also completed the modern, seventeen-volume edition of Grotius' correspondence, comprising nearly 7,500 documents.[39] What do these letters tell us? We are confronted with a man who apparently cared

---

[37] See generally *Gentle Civilizer of Nations* (n 30).

[38] Ibid 78. In this passage, Koskenniemi cites JC Bluntschli, *Das moderne Völkerrecht der civilisierten Staaten als Rechtsbuch dargestellt* (3rd edn Beck Nördlingen 1878) at 18. On the same page, Bluntschli calls Grotius the spiritual father (*geistige Vater*) of modern international law.

[39] See nn 2 and 11.

more for the unity of the Christian churches than anything remotely resembling 'a system of international law'. Grotius considered it his God-given task to heal the religious divisions of Christendom. He tried to apply sophisticated philological techniques to Biblical exegesis in a vain attempt to arrive at a set of core doctrines shared by all Christians. Grotius attached far less importance to issuing new and improved editions of *De Jure Belli ac Pacis* (1631, 1642, and 1646) than to publishing his Annotations on the Old and New Testament (1641, 1644, and 1646). These massive biblical commentaries, running into thousands of pages, were a lifelong project for Grotius, undertaken out of gratitude for the divine assistance that he thought he had received in escaping from Loevestein Castle.[40]

Grotius' doomed efforts to unite the Christian churches have little in common with modern notions of religious toleration and non-discrimination. Separation of church and state was inconceivable to Grotius. He admired the Anglican Church precisely because it was a state church, run by bishops appointed by a monarch, rather than by unruly Calvinist ministers. As a dyed-in-the-wool Erastian, he believed that the secular authorities should have the final say in the appointment of clergymen, in church government, and even in matters of doctrine. The Remonstrants said amen to all of this. They had little choice during the Twelve Years' Truce: a minority in the Dutch Reformed Church, they were totally dependent on the secular authorities for protection against the majority of orthodox Calvinists. Initially, Grotius presented himself as an impartial mediator between the two camps. Yet his claims rang increasingly hollow as the religious and political crisis deepened, resulting in the Stadtholder's *coup d'état* of August 1618. None of this has anything to do with the separation of church and state that is the norm in the Western world today, let alone with a principled toleration of a diversity of beliefs, religious or otherwise.[41]

On the basis of his dramatic life story, could it not be argued, however, that Grotius triumphed over adversity thanks to his moral and intellectual superiority? Modern research paints a rather different picture. Grotius was no hapless victim of the political calamity of August 1618, but made choices of his own, which ultimately proved to be the wrong ones. By claiming the moral high ground and refusing to contemplate compromises of any sort, he did not just cause problems for himself, but also for his direct relatives. Grotius' political record is the subject of his *Verantwoordingh van de Wettelijcke Regieringh van Holland ende West-Vrieslandt/Justification of the Rightful Government of Holland and West-Friesland* (1622). If we may believe this pamphlet, Grotius had simply followed the orders of

---

[40] *Hugo de Groot* (n 11) 348–54, 251–62, 429–38, 487–98, 506–31; *Hugo Grotius* (n 11) 422–9, 302–15, 529–40, 602–18, 629–60.

[41] *Hugo de Groot* (n 11) 109–251, 339–53, 419–38, 451–54; *Hugo Grotius* (n 11) 124–293, 409–29, 517–40, 556–9. See also *Hugo Grotius, Theologian: Essays in Honour of GHM Posthumus Meyjes* (HJM Nellen and E Rabbie eds) (Brill Leiden 1994).

Oldenbarnevelt and the Rotterdam town government, and been an honest broker between factions. These claims were half-truths at best. In reality, Grotius had been a party man: he had coordinated the political activities of Remonstrant-dominated town governments in Holland. As Pensionary of Rotterdam, he had belonged to Oldenbarnevelt's inner circle of political advisers. As one of the most powerful men in the Dutch Republic during the Twelve Years' Truce, he had played for high stakes and lost. That does not make him a martyr. Moreover, when Prince Frederic Henry of Orange became Stadtholder in 1625, there was a real chance of political rehabilitation. If Grotius had asked for a pardon, he would have been allowed to return home. That was the sticking point, of course. Grotius' sense of honour deterred him from requesting one. Exile was a choice of sorts on his part. That, together with his endless polemics with orthodox Calvinists, served to damage the career prospects of his family members in Holland. It cost his younger brother Willem de Groot a prestigious appointment as Pensionary of Delft, for example. Grotius' direct relatives were the real victims of the high drama of his life.[42]

Then there is the little issue, often overlooked, of Grotius' commitment to Dutch imperialism. Supposedly, the manuscript of *De Jure Praedae*—written at the behest of the VOC directors—is only important in so far as it prepares the way for the true magnum opus, *De Jure Belli ac Pacis*. Moreover, international lawyers in the late nineteenth century believed that European colonial empires brought much-needed civilization to benighted natives. Even when evidence became available of ethnic cleansing in, for example, Africa, members of the *Institut de Droit International* persisted in defending the colonial policies of their own national governments. The evils of Western imperialism and colonialism remained a blind spot in modern international law until the Second World War at least. No wonder that its practitioners could not see the darker sides of Grotius either.

Recently, a lot of work has been done on the interrelationship between the rise of international law and European overseas expansion. I only need to point to Antony Anghie's ground-breaking *Imperialism, Sovereignty and the Making of International Law*.[43] The work of David Armitage at Harvard University,[44] Lauren Benton at Vanderbilt University,[45] Peter Borschberg at the National University of Singapore,[46]

---

[42] *Hugo de Groot* (n 11) 109–262, 317–23, 360–1, 364–79, 457–70, 474–5, 480–3; *Hugo Grotius* (n 11) 124–312, 380–7, 437–62, 563–80, 586–7, 594–8.

[43] A Anghie, *Imperialism, Sovereignty and the Making of International Law* (CUP Cambridge 2005); *Gentle Civilizer of Nations* (n 30) ch 2.

[44] D Armitage, *Foundations of Modern International Thought* (CUP Cambridge 2013).

[45] L Benton, *Law and Colonial Cultures: Legal Regimes in World History, 1400–1900* (CUP Cambridge 2002); L Benton, *A Search for Sovereignty: Law and Geography in European Empires, 1400–1900* (CUP Cambridge 2010).

[46] P Borschberg, *The Singapore and Melaka Straits: Violence, Security and Diplomacy in the 17th Century* (NUS Press Singapore 2010); P Borschberg, *Hugo Grotius, the Portuguese, and Free Trade in the East Indies* (NUS Press Singapore 2011).

and John Cairns at the University of Edinburgh,[47] to name a few, is aimed at recovering the imperial contexts of early modern natural law and natural rights theories. My own research shows that Grotius was at the beck and call of the VOC directors in the period 1604–15, and that, even as an exile in Paris, he continued to support Dutch expansion overseas. Both Richelieu and Oxenstierna valued his expertise in commercial governance. In December 1626, the States of Holland met to discuss the very real danger of Grotius divulging to foreign governments his vast knowledge of 'the fisheries and navigation of these provinces, and particularly of VOC policy'. In the end, Grotius decided against selling-out to Richelieu. As Swedish Ambassador in Paris, he had no qualms about sending Oxenstierna regular updates on Dutch exploits in the East and West Indies, however. He obtained his information from his relatives in Holland. Both Willem de Groot and Grotius' second son, Pieter de Groot, served as VOC lawyers, for example. As a *quid pro quo*, he continued to offer policy suggestions and legal advice to the VOC. All through his life and career, Dutch imperialism and colonialism remained a cause close to his heart.[48]

7 GROTIUS THE ANTI-HERO

To conclude, Grotius as a founding father of international law is a historical construct, now well past its sell-by date. It would be far more appropriate to call him the godfather of Dutch imperialism, for example. The commemoration of 1899 was an American initiative that tied in beautifully with, first, the creation of a national canon for the Kingdom of The Netherlands and, secondly, the self-understanding of international lawyers of the time. Grotius became the proverbial knight on a white horse, who assisted the oppressed (the Remonstrants), triumphed over adversity (imprisonment at Loevestein Castle), and supposedly sought to humanize war in *De Jure Belli ac Pacis*. The establishment of international courts in The Hague has been a great boon for the Dutch government in the twentieth and twenty-first centuries. Internationalism is a wonderful *raison d'être* for small countries unable or unwilling to compete militarily in a big, bad world of oversized nation-states. No wonder that the Dutch government keeps propping up Grotius as the patron saint of the Peace Palace. It is surprising, however, that the judges of the various

---

[47] J Cairns, 'After Somerset: The Scottish Experience' (2012) 33 *Journal of Legal History* 291–312; J Cairns, 'Stoicism, Slavery, and Law: Grotian Jurisprudence and Its Reception' (2001–02) 22/23 *Grotiana* 197–232.

[48] 'The Long Goodbye' (n 12) passim and 395, quoting the States of Holland minutes, 21 December 1626. See also above nn 10 and 47.

international courts have mounted so few challenges to the Grotius Delusion. An increasing number of them have not been born and raised in the West. Perhaps they are too polite to speak out against their hosts?

Recent research has shown Grotius' legacy to the modern world to be far more complex, and far more interesting, than imagined by many international lawyers, both then and now. Nellen rightly emphasizes Grotius' abiding interest in the reconciliation of the Christian churches and in applying sophisticated philological techniques to biblical exegesis. Thanks to the modern edition of Grotius' correspondence, we have a much better sense of Grotius' political responsibilities during the Twelve Years' Truce and his central role in the Republic of Letters. His letters also reveal the options open to him after his escape from Loevestein Castle in March 1621. He could have become involved in Richelieu's colonial projects, for example. Or he could have made the concessions necessary for obtaining a pardon from Prince Frederic Henry. If he was a martyr for the cause, he made that choice himself. Finally, his extant working papers in the Dutch National Archives and Leiden University Library are proof that his natural rights and natural law theories were conceived for the sole purpose of justifying Dutch expansion overseas. We can now fit Grotius into the recent critique of modern international law as an ideology that at best ignored, or at worst fully supported, the dirty business of Western imperialism and colonialism.

CHAPTER 5

THE CRITIQUE OF CLASSICAL THOUGHT DURING THE INTERWAR PERIOD

VATTEL AND VAN VOLLENHOVEN

EMMANUELLE TOURME-JOUANNET

1 INTRODUCTION

THE continuous movement of international law has become particularly disquieting today in light of the multiple crises through which the contemporary world is passing. Faced with the problem of the deep instability of the international legal system, the theorist has to accompany and enlighten the choices of practice, taking into account the conditions under which an international law that is compatible with the exigencies of our time can be understood and enabled. These exigencies are linked to the defence of certain humanistic values such as peace, justice, and human rights. In other words, one can propose as an objective the finding of an international law that is broadly able to respond to some of these aspirations. However, this can only be done properly on two conditions that are frequently concealed. On one hand, it is necessary to adopt a synchronic—that is, as it were, sociological—approach, one without contempt for the facts but which also integrates them into theoretical reflection. This means that it is necessary to consider, prior to any such reflection, the reality of an international society divided into sovereign nations but, likewise, the effects, apparently contradicting the former, of an ever more globalized society. On the other hand it seems particularly interesting to engage in the diachronic analysis of the historian, on the assumption that an historical approach is an essential complement to the examination of the intellectual preconditions of the intelligibility of contemporary international law.

Evidently, it is not possible to fulfil such a programme in the ambit of this chapter. Yet some points of reflection on the second condition may be submitted. Several years of work on the history of international law convinces me that the knowledge of the past of international law is fundamental to its understanding. However, this turn to history does not only respond to the ordinary need for a reflection on the embeddedness of the structures of the present in a history which conditions but does not determine them; its importance goes beyond this trivial observation because it connects to one of today's central issues: the problematic and chaotic evolution of modern international law. The current doctrinal discussion focuses on the question of the past when it comes to querying the inter-state structure of the contemporary system.

One of the most recurring questions is if, on account of the persistence or non-persistence of this inter-state structure, contemporary international law is a direct extension of classical law (*droit classique*), where does—or where must—international law differ from classical law in a definite way? This question reaches far beyond the circle of historians to the entire community of international lawyers. The question carries with it fundamental issues. It is not merely of historical interest; it also brings with it a decisive theoretical reflection. On one side are those who would simply uphold classical international law, on the other side are those who would develop a radically different contemporary international law. The status of sovereignty remains at the heart of these discussions and one may stylize the positions thus: either one conceives of the current system of international law as centred on the respect of the sovereign freedom of states, whatever subsidiary purposes are now assigned to it, or one considers that the system is now oriented towards human rights and international justice. The logic of the coexistence of sovereign states stands against the logic of cooperation and justice, and the logic of states and their political interests is replaced by that of the individual and the fundamental values of humanity. Or, to put this another way, humanity is held to be in opposition to sovereignty, and justice to stability. The basic idea remains that these two approaches are antithetical. A legal system which attempts to integrate them would not only be unstable but also deeply unsustainable and destined to implode in the long term.

Some might argue that, at least from a doctrinal point of view, this question actually heeds from the middle of the twentieth century, insofar as classical international thought had seemed settled in the aftermath of the two world wars. It is precisely this point which is of interest for this chapter. No one can ignore the virulent criticism that charged the international order of 1918 with illegitimacy and set out to replace it with a new international law able to carry and realize the humanistic aspirations of the international community as a whole. However, this critique, as legitimate as it was in its desire for peace and justice, was formulated during the tumultuous period between the two wars and often promulgated a caricatured image of classical international law, which resulted in a range of prejudices related to the events in question. Even if one cannot deny the validity of some of the objections raised at that time and which are, no doubt, still relevant, this work of doctrinal deconstruction has, unfortunately, partially obscured the reality of classical thought and the role it could have played in post-war international law. As it is, the misunderstanding of classical thought was conveyed by a host of publicists, be it in a polemical, exaggerated, sincere, or passionate fashion, to the effect that the actual classical conception of (international) law has become obscured and it is no longer known how much modern law is still influenced by it, in what manner, and in relation to which specific points. As a consequence, today's debate is narrowed to classical or contemporary, conservative, or reformist positions. This refusal of traditional theories that characterizes our epoch has encouraged contemporary thought to emancipate itself from established certainties, but, in doing so, has deprived contemporary international lawyers of reliable historical references which would allow them to confront the present with lessons of the past.

For all these reasons, it is not surprising that the two positions are frequently put in question as they both tend to block the central demand for a real analysis of the actual link that connects contemporary law to classical international thought. Instead, a careful reinterpretation of the theories of the past should be seen as offering an essential moment of reflection, allowing a distancing from the platitudes conveyed by interwar authors and paving the way for a doctrinal representation of classical and contemporary international law that is more accurate and that can better serve the whole of the international community.

To this end, a starting point might be to approach the larger theme by initially restricting ourselves to the thought of certain selected authors. One could, for instance, compare the conceptions of international law of two prominent international jurists who are oddly linked across the centuries by one's critique of the other. In 1919, the Dutch jurist Cornelis Van Vollenhoven published a small work in which he issued a fierce critique of classical (legal) thought, which, according to him, was embodied by the eighteenth-century jurist, Emer de Vattel.[1] This was by

---

[1] C Van Vollenhoven, *Les trois phases du droit des gens* (Martinus Nijhoff The Hague 1919).

no means an arbitrary choice and was, no doubt, due to the particular place held, and the singular influence exerted by, this (French-speaking) Swiss jurist. Indeed, the classical conception of international law was never expounded more clearly than in Vattel's 1758 work, *Le droit des gens, ou principes de la loi naturelle, appliqués à la conduit et aux affaires des Nations et des Souverains.*[2] Although revised over time, Vattel's work contains the founding principles of the model of classical international law up until the First World War. Hence, by studying Vattel's and Van Vollenhoven's doctrines, of which the latter offers a distorted reflection of the former, it is possible to contribute to elucidating the concerns, weaknesses, and current incarnations of that classical model. It is, thus, of interest to return to Van Vollenhoven's work and to assess both the way classical thought embodied by Vattel was (mis)understood (Section 2) and confront this critique with a less polemical analysis of his work (Section 3).

2 (MIS)UNDERSTANDING VATTEL

Although his *oeuvre* exerted an extraordinary influence on both theory and practice in earlier centuries, Vattel is relatively unknown today. It is, *a fortiori*, not surprising that this also applies to the critique of Vattel. In picking up the thread of that critique, one may turn to Van Vollenhoven's work, which is exemplary for the internationalist thinking of the interwar period. In certain ways, Van Vollenhoven's work is perhaps more representative of that thinking than the great systems developed at the same time by Hans Kelsen and Georges Scelle. Although the doctrinal rigidity and persuasive force of these two great authors has been undeniable and enduring, the extent to which they represent the intellectual milieu at the time is less certain, and should not be assumed. Moreover, at the time, Van Vollenhoven was just as well recognized among international lawyers as Scelle and Kelsen were, both for his activities as minister plenipotentiary of the Dutch government to the United States, and for his continued advocacy of a complete overhaul of international law. His book, *Trois phases du droit des gens*, appeared at the end of the First World War and had a decisive and lasting impact, as is attested in the works of several renowned international lawyers such as G Gidel, Louis Le Fur, Albert Pillet, G Seals, Alfred Verdross, W Van der Vlugt, and later Eelco Van Kleffens and C Rousseau, all of whom condemned Vattel's 'deleterious system' by referring to Van Vollenhoven's

---

[2] E de Vattel, *Le droit des gens, ou principes de la loi naturelle, appliqués à la conduit et aux affaires des Nations et des Souverains* (Carnegie Institution Washington DC 1916 [1758]).

critique.[3] Indeed, the interest in rediscovering Van Vollenhoven's book lies not only in the impact it may have had on the international legal doctrine of its time, but also in its typically anti-Vattelian orientation. To limit ourselves to the essentials, we will look at the central elements of Van Vollenhoven's position by, first, identifying the principal elements of his unapologetic critique of Vattel, and then, second, by resituating that critique in the context of his thought.

2.1 Van Vollenhoven's Critique of Vattel's Doctrine

Van Vollenhoven shares the critique of classical thought that would later be developed by Scelle and Kelsen, but he envisages a rather different remedy for its main weakness. The central idea in Van Vollenhoven's analysis is that the history of the law of nations is divided into three phases corresponding to different models for international law: the first law of nations originated alongside the modern nation-state in the sixteenth century and was represented by authors such as George Zouche and Cornelius Van Bynkershoek; it was a narrowly defined, incomplete, and often

---

[3] G Gidel, 'Droits et devoirs des Nations: La théorie classique des droits fondamentaux des États' (1925) 5 *Recueil des Cours* 537–97, at 585: 'Vattel mérite la condamnation dont l'a frappé Van Vollenhoven'; L Le Fur, 'La théorie du droit naturel depuis le XVIIIème siècle et la doctrine moderne' (1928) 18 *Recueil des Cours* 259–439, at 331: 'on comprend, en voyant toutes ses compromissions, que Van Vollenhoven ait pu parler de "trahison"…'; A Pillet, *La Guerre et le Droit: Leçons données à l'Université de Louvain en 1921* (A Uystpruyst-Dieudonné Louvain 1922) at 33: 'sous la plume de Vattel le droit international, soit de la paix, soit de la guerre, devient une pure affaire de consentement personnel…En réalité, à partir de cette époque, toute base rationnelle du droit international et en particulier toute base du droit de la guerre a fait défaut chez les auteurs'; EN van Kleffens, 'Sovereignty in International Law: Five Lectures' (1953) 82 *Recueil des Cours* 1–130, at 68: 'Vattel, whom my learned compatriot van Vollenhoven has utterly condemned in a small book which is still well worth reading….'; A Verdross, 'Le fondement du droit international' (1927) 16 *Recueil des Cours* 251–319, at 310, makes similar reference to Van Vollenhoven for his statement: 'La conception de la souveraineté absolue de l'État n'a pénétré dans la science du droit des gens proprement dite qu'avec l'oeuvre de Vattel'; W Van der Vlugt, 'L'Oeuvre de Grotius et son influence sur le développement du droit international' (1925) 7 *Recueil des Cours* 395–506, at 467, also relies on the authority of Van Vollenhoven for his statement that Vattel 'a été un homme aux vues étroites, dénué de sens logique, se perdant à tout moment dans les contradictions…'; G Scelle, *Manuel de droit international public* (2nd edn Monchrestien Paris) also makes reference to Van Vollenhoven in saying that Vattel is the 'prince des positivistes'; C Rousseau, *Principes généraux du droit international public* (Pedone Paris 1944) vol 1, at 22–3. See also W Schücking and H Wehberg, *Die Satzung des Völkerbundes* (F Vahlen Berlin 1921) at 52; PP Remec, *The Position of the Individual in International Law According to Grotius and Vattel* (Martinus Nijhoff The Hague 1960) at 239; M Sibert, *Traité de droit international public: Le droit de la paix* (Dalloz Paris 1951) vol 1, at 12; H Fortuin, 'Grotius and the Netherlands in the Twentieth Century' (1970) 1 *Netherlands Yearbook of International Law* 72–81, at 78; EBF Midgley, *The Natural Law Tradition and the Theory of International Relations* (Paul Elek London 1975); B Vitanyi, 'L'interprétation des traités dans la théorie du droit naturel' (1980) 84 *Revue Générale de Droit International Public* 535–86, at 552; AN Mandelstam, 'La protection internationale des droits de l'homme' (1933) 38 *Recueil des Cours* 125–229, at 173–5.

cruel and inequitable law, but it would, at least, admit to its own brutality.[4] The second law of nations was born in 1758 with Vattel's work and would regulate international conduct until the First World War. This second law of nations—the classical international law—was a real 'monstrosity', responsible for the decay of international relations in the nineteenth century and the trauma of the First World War.[5] The third law of nations was that to which the author aspired: replacing Vattel's law and restoring a moral code of conduct among states with just punishment against those who dare deliberately violate it. This third law which, in the author's words, was 'at the door' after three hundred years, corresponded to Grotius' *On the Laws of War and Peace* which, having acquired considerable fame as of its publication in 1625, had neither been understood nor ever applied.[6]

To deconstruct Vattel's classical international law and make room for a new law of nations, Van Vollenhoven critiques what he considers to be the former's most prejudicial and dangerous aspects. Several objections are made against the Vattelian framework, the common thread of which is the denunciation of state sovereignty. First, as its sole concern was to preserve the sovereign freedom of each state, it effectively renounced any idea of a penal law of nations based on an objective application of the duties of states. The implementation of the law of nations here depended solely on the personal appraisal of individual states. Each state must assess its own obligations under the law of nations. If it fails to do so, it cannot reproach another state that has violated the law of nations with respect to it.[7] The law of war was thereby profoundly modified. It exclusively concerned what Van Vollenhoven terms armed disputes among sovereign states which, to his chagrin, had erased the idea of just war for two full centuries.[8] In his view, perhaps the worst aspect was that this egotist and individualist conception of law lay hidden behind the formal screen of the law of nations, obscuring hypocritically the absolute and unlimited character of each state's sovereignty. Vattel is here taken as espousing a naturalist legal system based on assistance to others, but lacking the bindingness of a positive legal regime, so that obligations only serve to safeguard each state. The result is that the solidarity implied in natural law effectively shields an omnipotent state sovereignty. Vattel's doctrine thus wrought conceptual havoc with the classical understanding of the law of nations and provided the illusion of being a code of conduct among states when, in truth, it was just a particularly apt instrument for the furtherance of imperialist policies and the thirst for conquest on the part of European sovereigns.[9] This, then, produced the charge, often repeated by later authors, that Vattel had achieved the triumph of both positivism in international law and the absolute nature of state sovereignty. As such he at once dug the grave of natural law, of the solidarity between sovereign powers, and of the ancient law

---

[4] *Les trois phases* (n 1) 4ff.   [5] Ibid 23ff.   [6] Ibid 60ff.   [7] Ibid 30–1.
[8] Ibid 29.   [9] Ibid 31.

of just war. And so Van Vollenhoven concludes, without discomfiture or much nuance, that the Vatellian law of nations directly led to the catastrophe of 1914–18.

Having thus exposed classical doctrine in these terms, one easily understands that Van Vollenhoven calls for the permanent abandonment of Vattel's inter-state, unjust, and sovereigntist law in favour of a Grotian law deemed just, remedial, and humanist. In fact there is, for the Dutch jurist, not an actual choice between two laws of nations, but rather an absolute necessity applying to all members of the international community. The First World War had just pulled away Vattel's 'rotten floor' by showing what horrors and consequences classical inter-state law could lead to in its acceptance of the free play of individual state sovereignties and their right to wage war.[10] From Van Vollenhoven's perspective, therefore, it is also clear that one cannot simply denounce this or that feature of the classical doctrine of international law, but must advocate its complete and permanent rejection.

2.2 The Return to Grotius' Law of Nations

The indictment of Vattelian thought naturally drives Van Vollenhoven to propose an entirely different conception for the law of nations, one which would remedy the two main weaknesses of the classical system: relativism and positivism. This being said, it is quite difficult to reconstruct the legal system envisaged by Van Vollenhoven because he did not develop it clearly in his 1919 book. Intended to stir up sentiment and to occasion a redemptive jolt in favour of a return to a Grotian law of nations, the work remains nonetheless incomplete and offers only visions and fragmented solutions. His new law of nations can only be gauged from some general ideas. In essence, it states that the time of Grotius must arrive, involving the putting into practice of *On the Laws of War and Peace* of 1625. As strange and anachronistic as this idea may seem coming from a twentieth-century author, it is not, in fact, the material rules of the sixteenth century that Van Vollenhoven wishes to rehabilitate. Instead he wants to transpose the general system of law developed by Grotius and the spirit in which it was developed. Hence, from the imposing 1625 work Van Vollenhoven discerns what he takes to be two closely related ideas which are bound to undermine the pillars of the classical conception. There is, first and foremost, the aim of abolishing the individual, subjective right of war of the classical period in favour of a 'penal law' against offending countries, which was invented by Grotius but never applied.[11] Then there is the need to restore the authority of natural law in order to establish a set of binding rules imposed over the sovereign will of states. This is, of course, the very natural law which Grotius, according to Van Vollenhoven, ardently defended, but which was then abandoned

---

[10] *Les trois phases* (n 1) 40ff, 58–9.   [11] Ibid 17–18.

by his successors, most notably by Vattel.[12] The conscience of humanity would, however, awake with the end of the First World War to revalue this old law which embodied an international morality to which all states would submit themselves.

Without even going into a more precise diagnosis of Vattel here, one might well question the validity and effectiveness of this double rehabilitation in favour of just war and natural law. Yet, Van Vollenhoven rushes to sweep aside any possible objections, arguing that their restoration would augur in a virtuous cycle of peace and justice extending to all categories of states. In the first place, aggressive states would no longer be allowed to dictate their interests and imperialist policies as they could be collectively punished by others for the wars they waged. Wars of aggression would definitively be banned as would any attempt to trigger a conflict for a cause that was not deemed legitimate under natural law. In the second place, alliances with neighbouring states or friends would not be possible with a view to supporting such wars; indeed, the old European balance of power based on a network of offensive and defensive alliances had to be abolished.[13] No convention-based alliance should be able to stand against the obligations that natural law imposes upon states. Lastly and paradoxically, neutral states would finally be required to engage themselves in enforcing these constraints. Neutrality in the face of belligerent states was an 'abomination' engendered by the Vattelian system, even though Grotius had advocated, to the contrary, the necessity of supporting those whose cause was just.[14] The 'neutral's moral obligation' was to commit itself to the side who was involved in the 'punishment' of culprit states.[15]

However, although Van Vollenhoven is firmly convinced of the need to return to the Grotian system, he is well aware that the doctrine of his Dutch predecessor needs to be rearranged in order to be usefully transposed into the inter-state relations of the twentieth century. Quoting Van Bynkershoek, he points out the dangers of an incautious application of the doctrine of just war. The difficulty lay in execution: in a decentralized inter-state society, each state was able to rely on a just cause for war without any other being able to question it. An objective test for such a just cause—just, that is, according to natural law and international morality, and which alone could authorize any commencement of hostilities—was still lacking. Recognizing the impossibility of squaring this circle in the current state of international relations, Van Vollenhoven offers three additions to the Grotian law of nations: an independent tribunal to decide on the justness of the cause, an impartial and effective system of arbitration between states, and, finally, the development of an objective criterion to determine exactly what kind of war was permitted.[16]

The addition of these complements is interesting for several reasons and needs to be elaborated. It reveals the pragmatic vision of international relations that this grand jurist held, as well as his willingness to take into account inter-state society

---

[12] *Les trois phases* (n 1) 26.   [13] Ibid 62.   [14] Ibid 60–1.
[15] Ibid 61.   [16] Ibid 73–4.

as an insurmountable reality. Indeed, he refrains from challenging the very concept of state sovereignty. The idea is solely to limit its effects and omnipotence.
This is why he proposes the establishment of a 'league of peoples', allowing him to
introduce these complements and not a world state in which he does not believe.[17]
In doing so, he puts a clear distance between himself and authors such as Scelle or
Kelsen, whose later theoretical arguments in large measure aimed to demonstrate
the uselessness or even danger of the notion of sovereignty, with the objective of
achieving a true institutionalized federalism in the case of the former and a world
state in the case of the latter.[18] In addition, Van Vollenhoven does not attempt to
hide the main difficulty of the application of the just war doctrine in a decentralized world, where the subjective interpretations of states oppose each other. In the
end, though this is not quite certain. In alluding to the programme of Aristide
Briand he seems to lean towards an almost complete ban and end to war.[19] He is,
thus, not aiming at a real implementation of the doctrine of just war, but at an abolition of the individual right to make war, with the only legitimate armed actions
being the collective punishment of those who violate this prohibition. In brief, to
Van Vollenhoven it is lawful and right to wage war against war, if it is done in an
impartial and reasoned manner. The concept of collective security is here present
in all but name. He thereby reflects the transitory inter-war spirit in which internationalists become conscious of the need to end all wars and to substitute the
individual right of war with impartial and collective military action. Yet, he does
not entirely commit himself to this spirit, hesitating, as it were, between a return to
the old system of just war and the entire abolition of the law of war.

This last aspect also illustrates how, in his particular context, Van Vollenhoven's
one and only concern is the law of war and not the law of peace. It is, thus, not
surprising that he builds on the work of his predecessor, who similarly wrote in his
1625 work about his concern for limiting the blood-stained wars of his time. Grotius
wrote in the wake of the Thirty Years' War, just as Van Vollenhoven wrote after the
First World War. With centuries between them, both were fully aware of the difficulties of legally regulating the use of armed force and the difficulties of legally
limiting its effects for the sake of peace, justice, and humanity. However, it should
not be forgotten that the same concern is displayed by Vattel in the eighteenth century when the Swiss jurist sought to humanize the *jus in bello* and to regulate the
jus ad bellum. In other words, all three authors have, over the space of three different centuries, shared the same desire for peace, the development of international
law, and the limitation of the right of war. What, then, happened in the context
of the twentieth century that Vattel could be presented by Van Vollenhoven as

---

[17] *Les trois phases* (n 1) 78.
[18] G Scelle, *Cours de droit international public* (Domat-Monchrestien Paris 1948) at 27; H Kelsen,
Théorie pure du droit (H Thévenaz trans) (de la Baconnière Neuchâtel 1953 [1934]) at 181.
[19] *Les trois phases* (n 1) 75.

the antithesis of Grotius? The main reason for this reversal is Van Vollenhoven's need to defend a point of view that seeks to break completely with the present; therefore, he presents the theoretical base of classical international law in a most exaggerated and negative way. This was not done in bad faith but rather because the Dutch jurist, traumatized by the war like everyone at that time, amplified the weaknesses of a doctrine in order to substitute it with another. The vast majority of international lawyers were inspired by this vigorous and striking critique aimed at the development of a different international law on the basis of what they took to be the ruins of classical thinking, and a war later, the *Charter of the United Nations* would appear to them as the first complete example of this new spirit.

However, one needs to return to Vattel's own work to understand this change and to reconstruct a more faithful account of classical thought. The need for such reinterpretation, as limited and subjective as it might be, can hardly be overstated. The classical view of international law that Van Vollenhoven was pleased to decry on the basis of contemporary internationalism was never discussed with any degree of profundity, and nor was the validity of his critical analysis. This is evidently just a case in point among several, and it might well seem insignificant in light of the overall development of internationalism. Yet, Van Vollenhoven's critique still has exemplary value as a result of the impact it has had; indeed, everyone remains, perhaps, an unconscious prisoner of the distortion it inflicts on classical thought.

3 A Less Polemical Analysis of Vattel

Already the reduction of classical doctrine to the thought of a single author is a grave mistake, committed, probably deliberately, by Van Vollenhoven in order to stir up his audience. This simplistic if convenient shortcut is wrong. Most of the excesses charged against Vattel are incorrect, and, in fact, could more appropriately have been levied against predecessors and contemporaries of the Swiss jurist. While it will not be possible to elaborate on this point in more than broad strokes, the particular logic of Vattelian doctrine needs to be explored in order to confront Van Vollenhoven's critique.

3.1 The Logic of Vattel's Doctrine

The essence of Vattel's doctrine, inspired by his master Christian Wolff, consists of the reconstruction of the law of nations as a law of states, based on a strict inter-state conception of international society. What is striking about Vattel, and what, arguably, explains his enormous success afterwards, is not the inconsistency or confusion of his thought, as Van Vollenhoven claimed, but, on the contrary, the articulation, for the first time, of a realist vision of international relations in which states are taken to act primarily on account of their security and that of their population. It is much less his positivism, which, in any case, has to be seen in a nuanced way, than his inter-state orientation which singles him out. However, it would be wrong to assume that Vattel was the only one who opted for such a system, or that he abandoned the idea of cooperation and natural justice. In his 1758 work, *Le droit des gens*, he provides a formula for the law of nations which is, in fact, an ideal synthesis of two currents worked out by Wolff in opposition to Grotius and Pufendorf. Indeed, far from being the antithesis of Grotian doctrine, Vattel's work is, in many areas, a direct heir to Grotius' thought, and Vattel but concretizes and refines the broad strokes of his illustrious predecessor.

It is Vattel's indisputable merit to have theorized with exceptional clarity the classical vision of the law of nations which, unlike the old *jus gentium*, came to acquire a strictly international meaning. And despite the many significant developments that have ultimately contributed to his doctrine, it is characterized by two fundamental aspects that extend through the years up to Van Vollenhoven: the idea that the positive law of nations is based on the concept of state sovereignty and the idea that just war must be abandoned. Several factors help in understanding both points of view and lead to a clarification that will be of interest later on. In the first place, there is Vattel's definitive theorization of the notion of international personality. This is an absolutely essential point for the development of an inter-state law and for the establishment of rules which, today, are indispensable for the continuity of statehood and the imputation of the acts of its representatives to the state. This legal conceptualization goes back to Vattel, who distinguishes himself from his predecessors by denouncing the older theory of patrimonial statehood in a precise and rigorous way, leading to a complete conception of state personality and legal subjectivity around which he will articulate all the rights and duties contained in the law of nations.[20] In a second step, Vattel substitutes the old *jus gentium* with the emerging classical conception of international law, based on a realist observation of European society of his time which reveals to him the decentralized nature of international society. From then on, Vattel sets out to conceive of a law of nations based on the sovereignty of states. He develops the idea that, in law, sovereign states are at once free and equal, and that it is on this dual legal basis that international law must be founded.[21] The third consideration is decisive and deals with Vattel's concern for limiting and humanizing war. Referring directly

---

[20] *Le droit des gens* (n 2) vol 1, bk 1, ch V, §69 (69–70).
[21] Ibid vol 1, bk 1, ch XIII, §172 (163–4).

to Grotius, he advocates the abandonment of the theory of just war in favour of a formalized theory of bilateral warfare.

This last option may appear surprising and call for further inquiry, as on the basis of the same concern for the limitation of war and equally invoking Grotius, Van Vollenhoven will, two centuries later, promote a return to the just war doctrine. Hence, starting from the same observation and the same reference point, the two authors draw diametrically opposed conclusions. Moreover, as was already touched upon, Van Vollenhoven also rejects two aspects he considers to be characteristic of the Vattelian law of nations: Vattel's theory of sovereignty and the abandonment of natural law. It is in relation to these three key critical points— notably natural law, the theory of sovereignty, and the right to wage war—that the pertinence of his interpretation must be assessed.

3.2 Critical Review of Van Vollenhoven's Objections

To begin with the abandonment of natural law, Vattel cannot, as was already shown in the previous section, be held responsible for the drift to positivism, which is already present in the majority of his predecessors.[22] It was the earlier turns to subjectivism, individualism, and voluntarism which had begun to undermine the old natural law from within. Indeed, it is intriguing to see Van Vollenhoven invoke Grotius against Vattel with a view to restoring the authority of natural law in inter-state relations, when Grotius really considered the law of nations to be positive and not natural law. And it is, of course, true that Grotius wanted to subject the princes of Europe to the authority of natural law while admitting that natural law often gives way, at least with regard to the relations between sovereign powers, to the positive law of nations.[23] Therefore, if the primacy of the positive law of nations over natural law is found in Vattel's work, it is only on account of a stream of thought already initiated by Grotius himself.

However, one must not jump to conclusions too rapidly and relativize the emergence of this common positivism, which Vattel only rewrites. Despite the apparent primacy of the positive law of nations, Vattel always simultaneously maintains the existence of a natural law that also applies to inter-state relations. The Vattelian law of nations is divided into two general branches, a natural and a positive law.[24] And

---

[22] See H Muir-Watt, 'Droit naturel et souveraineté de l'État dans le doctrine de Vattel' (1987) 32 *Archives de philosophie du droit* 71–85; E Jouannet, *Emer de Vattel et l'émergence doctrinale du droit international classique* (Pedone Paris 1998) at 144ff.

[23] See 'Droit naturel et souveraineté de l'État dans le doctrine de Vattel' (n 22); *Emer de Vattel et l'émergence doctrinale du droit international classique* (n 22) 144ff.

[24] H Grotius, *Le droit de la guerre et la paix* (J Barbeyrac trans) (2 vols reprint University of Caen Press Caen 1984 [1625]) bk I, ch III, § iv (113–14).

while it is true that, in this conception, positive law can often neutralize the effects of natural law, it remains clear that the most fundamental obligations of states retain the character of natural law. They are, in other words, fixed and immutable and, in the main, include the self-preservation of states and respect for the sovereignty of others. And this natural law remains, for Vattel, a genuine law and not just a simple international morality. Vattel is perfectly clear about this distinction.

To be sure, against Pufendorf and his followers, Vattel admits the existence of a voluntary and arbitrary positive law. But unlike the Grotian jurists, he does not limit the law of nations only to positive law. The Wolffian current—with which Vattel directly associates himself—presents itself as, first and foremost, a reaction to breakaway positivists, with the same desire held by Pufendorf and his followers to anchor the law of nations in the immutable foundation of human nature and thus avoid including the escalations and contradictions of customs and particular agreements in the positive law. To reduce the law of nations to positive law, as was done by Grotius and (especially) by his followers, is, according to Vattel, like 'espousing a conception that is not only wrong but degrading for humanity… there certainly is a natural law of nations since natural law does not oblige states and human beings united in political society any less than it obliges individuals'.[25] Moreover, the Vattelian law of nations acquires real autonomy on account of its applicability to states, as opposed to individuals, whereas for Pufendorf and his successors natural law remains materially identical to the (natural) law applied to individuals. One sees in Vattel, who closely follows Wolff here, the emergence of a homogenous and autonomous system of natural and voluntary norms with a specifically international functionality, notably to regulate the conduct of sovereign nations.

In truth, things are not quite as simple as this initial reading of Vattel might suggest, for it seems that the branch of the law of nations that specifies the fundamental rights and obligations of states is positive, not natural law. Vattel repeatedly declares that this is a voluntary law distinct from natural law as applicable to states.[26] It takes primacy over natural law on account of the primacy he allocates to the obligations assumed by states vis-à-vis one another over the obligations imposed by natural law. The primacy given to such a voluntary law is not, however, surprising for long, even if it has misled many a commentator. If one looks at the foundation of the so-called voluntary law, one realizes that it is much closer to natural than to positive law. Vattel considers voluntary law to be a result of presumed consent among nations (positive in nature), which is, however, imposed by natural law (hence, naturalist in nature). It is, in fact, as he states in the preface to this work, on account of the natural liberty of states, but also of their common good, that a voluntary law of nations arises which incorporates the necessary modifications

---

[25] *Le droit des gens* (n 2) vol 1, vii.   [26] Ibid 15.

of a natural law (of nations) adapted to the mutual agreements among states.[27] Indeed, it is as a result of this naturalist derivation of the voluntary law of nations that, unlike in Grotius' positive law, the common voluntary law of nations cannot, according to Vattel, merely rest on the tacit consent of some 'civilized' nations but on the necessary presumption of consent by all. Hence, while the voluntary law of nations, itself conceived as immutable and necessary, might deviate from the rigour of the natural law, it cannot be considered mutable, contingent, or reversible. In short, contrary to what the terms suggest, Vattel clearly affirms a naturalist and not a positivist basis for the validity of his voluntary law of nations, because the concept of presumed consent is merely declaratory and auxiliary, but not constitutive of its binding force; and if Vattel prefers to refer to it as 'voluntary' this is to distinguish it from the original natural law, even if he ultimately recognizes that the terms are quite the same.[28]

This is also why state sovereignty is far from absolute in Vattel. Although it occupies a decisive place in his legal system, it is not taken to amount to the unlimited freedom of states. It is the freedom for each state to do what it deems necessary for its preservation or improvement, but within the limits of the precept of not harming others. The voluntary law of nations is, like conventional or customary law, or, indeed, natural law, a law that governs the respectful conduct of states vis-à-vis each other. It is a code of good conduct for states, and aims at the stabilization of international relations by legally preserving state sovereignty against mutual attack or violation.

Van Vollenhoven's critique of the positivism of Vattel's law of nations, is, hence, particularly unfounded and has generated a distorted view of classical international law as the gravedigger of natural law and as the promoter of absolute sovereignty. This is to misunderstand the essential part of Vattel's doctrine which remains favourable to natural law and falsely attributes to Grotius the paternity of an entirely different law of nations. This is all the more interesting as there is an

---

[27] *Le droit des gens* (n 2) xx.

[28] Ibid xxi. That said, if, in the same way, one wanted to locate the historical moment in which positivist international law triumphs, one would surely have to envisage two other epochs that have contributed significantly to positivism's consolidation: the era of the great voluntarist dualists at the start of the twentieth century, and those after the Second World War when objectivism substituted itself for the last vestiges of naturalism. In other words, dating the consecration of positivism from Vattel is a serious error of interpretation since this positivism did not totally impose itself until much later. It is also equally due to Vattel's natural law continuing to play a role in and serving as a reference for relations between states. Vattel's law of nations was conceived in conformity with the Europe of the eighteenth century, although it was nevertheless a universal law intended to be applied to all sovereign states. That last point, however, is what will bring the internationalists of the nineteenth century to restrict the circle of sovereign states that can be considered 'civilized', or, said differently, to make international law a regional law limited to European and American states and to justify in this way the great period of colonization.

aspect in Vattel's doctrine that actually leads to a strengthening of the commitment of states to international law.

In an apparently paradoxical way, Vattel emphasizes the role and the importance of the freedom of states and at the same time advocates that mutual respect lies at the basis of his notorious voluntary law because the obligations it lays upon states are taken as based solely on the respect of the sovereignty of each rather than on the assistance rendered to others. In other words, Vattel's voluntary law appears much more individualistic or egocentric than the naturalist conception of its validity actually suggests. The ultimate explanation of this individualist definition of obligation under the voluntary law is simply the primordial and fundamental character of state sovereignty. Vattel, hence, merely proposes that the society of states, which forms the basis of his law, has no centralized power like that which characterizes domestic societies—an observation that has, today, of course, become trivial. In the language of the period, states form among themselves a non-hierarchical state of nature. If this vision of a state of nature among sovereign powers is shared by all natural law thinkers, it is, in Vattel, much more clearly presented and conceptualized insofar as it relies on his complete mastery over the concept of a sovereign state and his resolutely internationalist approach to the issue.

That Vattel, thus, possesses what amounts to a rather modern notion of state sovereignty is a direct consequence of his theory of state personality, in which, as already noted, the state in its entirety is considered as a moral person so that it, and not the reigning prince, is the titulary of sovereignty. On the basis of these conceptual advances towards a viable system, he rejects the idea, imagined by his master Wolff, of a global republic which would impose the law upon its composite states.[29] Indeed, on account of their sovereignty and the absence of such a world state it is an inescapable fact that it is the liberty and equality of states through which the rule of natural and voluntary law must be deduced. Every other premise, such as the existence of a hypothetical world state, is, according to Vattel, not only illusionary but potentially dangerous.

Three reasons explain why Vattel does not retain the *Civitas Maxima* solution which Wolff envisioned, but instead, proposed a law based on a natural state of liberty and equality among states.[30] First, state sovereignty provides a sort of self-sufficiency that individuals do not possess. Second, states are not individuals and so maintain relations of a different sort, characterized by a higher level of caution and prudence. They do not need to be conjoined in a world political community to regulate their differences or to establish peaceful relations. Third, the preservation of sovereign independence is absolutely necessary if a state desired to govern itself an appropriate way, for it can be harmful for the states' citizens if it abandons its responsibilities towards them in favour of a greater entity. In other words, if

---

[29] *Le droit des gens* (n 2) xvii.   [30] Ibid xviii–xix.

the problem of individual submission to law is partly solved by entry into civil society and acceptance of a binding common power, this is different for nations on account of their sovereignty. The absence of a global authority results in an inevitable situation of organized anarchy, moved by sovereign states that remain perfectly free and independent. This, then, is why Vattel sets out to build an international legal system which, by superimposing voluntary law over natural law, limits binding obligations to those that assure a simple coexistence among states.[31] Natural law exists, but it merely binds the conscience of heads of state. It does not prohibit sovereign states from contracting, for instance by treaty, real legal obligations of aid and assistance vis-à-vis other states, yet such conventional obligations can only be contingent and temporary.

To be sure, Vattel has, thereby, contributed to the primacy of an individualist conception of the law of nations, which would later be so bitterly lamented by Van Vollenhoven. However, in doing so Vattel only reproduces a movement of thought initiated long before him, notably by Grotius and also and especially by Wolff, in which the effects of natural law are gradually neutralized by positive law, even if Vattel's doctrine is not, as Van Vollenhoven suggests, the starting point, but rather the result of a doctrinal evolution within the naturalist current that can be traced back to Grotius himself. This evolution does not, as was seen, conspire to liquidate natural law, but to render as the only external constraint on states those obligations that respect the sovereignty, and thus liberty, of each. In essence, this amounts to the establishment of a liberal legal system on the level of inter-state relations, formal and not substantive, emanating from classical natural law and the law of nations but remaining naturalist in tone because it derives from a voluntary law that is not quite positive.

This is why Van Vollenhoven's third critical argument concerning Vattel takes on a special dimension as it raises a final serious objection to Vattelian doctrine: to him, the individual right of each state to wage war without consideration of the justice of its cause amounts to the abandonment of natural law jointly with just war theory. This is at the core of Van Vollenhoven's critique as it concerns the law of war and must, therefore, be looked at in greater depth in terms of its relevance and scope. In his theory of state sovereignty, Vattel establishes the principle that the law of nations is applied subjectively and abstractly, a construction that has evident consequences for the conception of the law of war. The question that arises, as it arose for all his predecessors, is how to administer the old doctrine of just war while taking into account the new account of state sovereignty. Since Grotius, most authors had understood perfectly well that the emergence of the (modern) state and of European society—of which they were aware without articulating it explicitly—required a modification of the terms of the problem of war and of the

---

[31] *Le droit des gens* (n 2) xvii.

unilateral application of just war. Hence, Van Vollenhoven's critique of Vattel is again mistaken, as it was Grotius who first proposed to abandon the doctrine of just war. Yet, Van Vollenhoven's misreading of the intellectual linkage between Grotius and Vattel in relation to the implementation of just war also obscures the reasons why Grotius and Vattel opted, in their respective times, to modify this doctrine.

To reconstruct the terms of this long-standing debate, one needs initially to go back to Grotius' *On the Laws of War and Peace* before returning to Vattel's *Le droit de gens*. It is a well-known fact that in Grotius' 1625 work he expounded two systems for the laws of war.[32] First, he thematized the doctrine of just war as it was developed by thinkers, jurists, commentators, and canonists as of the late Middle Ages and, in particular, within the ambit of scholasticism. However, while he shared in the latter's ideal of justice, he was troubled by the difficulties this system created when applied to the sovereign princes of Europe. The most serious of these difficulties was, for Grotius, the necessary involvement of third parties.[33] For these, he argued, were ever more frequently dragged into the deadly conflicts that tore Europe apart under the obligation of assisting belligerents fighting a just cause. Yet, in the absence of an objective determination of a right and just cause by a supreme authority, third parties were led to fight for others without being certain of the justness of their cause, which might, in actual fact, be gravely harmful. Moreover, third-party intervention merely extended and amplified a conflict, as each such state deemed on account of its own welfare which of the two belligerents' cause was just.[34] In other words, Grotius demonstrates an awareness of the intractable situation which arises from the application of a law that is meant objectively to bind all, but that does not dispose a legitimate authority to interpret it. The danger implied in such a doctrine in the unstable times of Grotius was, of course, unacceptable to someone bent on limiting and eliminating conflict. He, thus, undertook a complete about turn and proposed to abandon just war according to natural law in favour of the conscience of the sovereign princes so as to superimpose the principle of the abstract and bilateral application of a positive law of nations.[35] With this, he also discarded the basis for a true right to neutrality.

Moreover, it is striking that from the seventeenth century onwards, and, hence, well before Vattel, Grotius had already privileged the problem of peace over the realization of justness. In virtue of the positive law of nations that prevails over natural law, he fashioned a regime of impunity which aimed to prevent third parties from intervening by force with a view to punishing the belligerent considered

---

[32] For remarkable works on this point, see P Haggenmacher, *Grotius et la doctrine de la guerre juste* (PUF Paris 1983) at 568; P Haggenmacher, 'Mutations du concept de "guerre juste" de Grotius à Kant' (1987) 11 *Cahiers de philosophie politique et juridique de l université de Caen* 106–25.

[33] *Le droit de la guerre et la paix* (n 24) bk III, ch IV, § iv (769).   [34] Ibid.

[35] Ibid bk III, ch I (713ff).

to have acted unjustly; more precisely, he abandoned the unilateral application of the just war principle in favour of a regime in which justness was determined internally by sovereign powers so as to uphold the abstract and bilateral terms of the law of nations. The solution was to consider the effects of war as legitimate—and, thus, licit—with regard to both sides, and, therefore, to apply the rules of the *jus in bello* to the two belligerents. Thereby, the question of a possible third-party intervention was effectively neutralized through the allocation of equal status to all belligerent states and a strictly formal recognition of the perfect equality of their rights.[36]

The rejection of the just war doctrine can, hence, be primarily attributed to Grotius. It is then taken up and developed by many natural lawyers but especially by Wolff, who, under Hobbes' influence, systematizes this legal regime. Vattel thus merely completes this movement, though he formulates the issues in terms that are more appropriate and internationalist. It is, thus, unsurprising to find the implications of his division of natural and voluntary law in the law of war, with both being applied distinctly in accordance with their respective purpose. The duality goes back to Grotius but it resonates in Vattel who, essentially, clarifies and updates it. It remains, as was seen, still very much associated with the natural law tradition. He begins by thoroughly developing the doctrine of just war, which, according to the 'natural' law of nations, must prevail among states. This means that the law of war is conditioned on the existence of a just cause, a key concept in the classical doctrine by which a state may only legitimately use force on account of a right held by it.[37] From this follows the unilateral application of the *jus in bello* where the only legitimate authority pertains to the just belligerent.[38] The implementation of this unilateral regime on the basis of a just material cause demonstrates well the manner in which Vattel incorporates into classical theory the conditions of implementation and enforcement of the law of nations, especially in relation to the law of war. This, however, is bound to remain a pure reflection of Grotius. It is neutralized, in the same manner, in favour of a voluntary legal regime based on the simple equality and reciprocity among sovereign states.

Yet, in what amounts to a sort of revenge, Vattel places much greater emphasis on the specific characteristics of international society to justify such a decision. It brings up-to-date the inherent relativism of the international society of his time, which was based on the principles of freedom and equality among states.[39] It thereby underlines the perverse and dangerous implications of applying objective law in a system designed to be entirely decentralized and non-hierarchical, that is, in his terms, one which is in a state of nature where states are free, independent, and equal. In the absence of a common power, a condition that necessarily follows from such independence and equality, the law is applied spontaneously and in a

---

[36] *Le droit de la guerre et la paix* (n 24) bk I, ch III, § iv (113–14) and bk III, ch III (750ff).
[37] *Le droit des gens* (n 2) vol 2, bk III, ch III (20ff).   [38] Ibid bk III, ch XI (158ff).
[39] Ibid bk III, ch XII (163–4).

decentralized manner; it rests upon the personal responsibility of each state. This results in the impossibility of a meaningful and effective application of the law on the basis of the material justice of either party, and it is, therefore, inevitable that conflicts degenerate, as everyone may claim to be within their rights, taking advantage of all legitimate means and deliberately excluding their respective opponent.[40]

Two other factors reinforce the inevitable escalation of conflict as a result of the just war doctrine. First, and going back to Grotius' argument, Vattel purports to show that in the absence of any indisputable, objective interpretation of natural law, or its uniform acceptance by the parties, the issue of third party intervention is highly problematic because the latter would be obliged to take part in a conflict in order to support the party whose cause was deemed just, even though none of the belligerents could, in fact, pass such objective judgement. The adverse effects of a subjective intervention by a third party in an ongoing conflict are, thus, redoubled and are only bound to further intensify it. Furthermore, in such circumstances, the outcome of a conflict is difficult to conceive, as the determination of the conditions for its termination follows the same principle as with that of the just cause, notably a subjective assessment of the cause and application of a unilateral regime.[41]

The two last predicaments completely undermine the edifice of the doctrine of just war, which is, henceforth, replaced by the individual right to wage war. However, to Vattel, this neither amounts to a license to do as one pleases nor to sovereignty being an absolute concept. According to him, war can be waged under three conditions only: by sovereign states, in order to remedy a wrong committed by another state in violation of international law, and in order to halt the violation of fundamental rights of a state to self-preservation or the protection of their possessions.[42] The right to wage war remains, thus, severely limited and a war of aggression is excluded entirely from it.

This, then, is where one can behold the actual scope of Vattel's doctrine. It is natural law itself which ordains the abandonment of the natural law-based obligation upon the moral conscience of the sovereign, and which, instead, holds to be coercive only the fundamental obligations of self-preservation and the perfection of voluntary law. It is also natural law which militates for the abandonment of just war theory as the penal law of states in favour of a limited subjective right of war. This rearrangement of the earlier doctrine is significant and easy to spot, but not so easily understood if one does not also study the fundamental issues that underlie it. The final objective for what would become classical international legal doctrine is, indeed, not the legitimation of power politics and the personal interests of each sovereign state; it is not about magnifying sovereignty, in the sense of the freedom to do as one pleases or the unbridled license to declare war. It is, quite to the contrary, a recurrent concern for peace and stability in international relations which,

---

[40] *Le droit des gens* (n 24) bk III, ch VII, § 106 (81).   [41] Ibid.
[42] Ibid bk III, ch III (20ff).

as Vattel never ceases to repeat, cannot be obtained in international law in the same way as in domestic law, as domestic and international society are profoundly different. The only way to maintain peace in the state of nature of international society is to neutralize the old idea of material justice. Rendering the obligations of natural law, in particular those regarding humanitarian concerns and assistance to others, directly coercive is not only entirely illusory in light of the fact of state sovereignty, but also rather dangerous in terms of maintaining a necessary balance among sovereign nations.[43] Experience shows that most nations are only concerned with defending their own interests and that if one of them decides to help another, it may well unwittingly strengthen an enemy or evil nation. Moreover, for Vattel, the humanitarian cause must be applied in a measured and careful way so as to avoid a treacherous drift that could result in the possible destabilization of the European balance of power in favour of a few avaricious and imperialist nations—thus Vattel's defence of the principle of equilibrium as a mechanism capable of maintaining peace among sovereign states while maintaining their independence and avoiding their aggrandizement at the expense of others.[44]

It is this well-known principle of equilibrium that Van Vollenhoven would later severely critique in favour of a league of nations between all states with a collective right to punish those who violate their obligations under international law. In addition, Van Vollenhoven is clearly not only concerned with the establishment of a system of peace that finally works, but he is also eager to reinstate the concept of international justice to its due (and noble) place. More specifically, he wants to restore its true meaning—which is ultimately why he engages in all the deconstructive work, notably to recover what he deems its lost meaning—because he believes that such justice is a prerequisite for the establishment of a true and lasting peace among states. This idea proved to be attractive and generated many a contemporary echo; being seen by many as inaugurating a potential return to a Grotian conception of international law, it fell on fertile ground during the interwar period. However, even if the real role of Grotius is more than doubtful in this respect, it is still possible to discern here two visions of Grotius over two historical periods and by two distinct authors. On the one hand, a fairer view takes Vattel's vision to be that of a liberal and peaceful man who above all wished to maintain stability among states by means of a formal legal system of coexistence that respected the sovereign freedom of each state. It follows as a consequence of this that the regime governing war would have to eschew the idea of a just cause in order to avoid the errors to which its application leads. On the other hand, Van Vollenhoven's vision is that of a moral, material, and natural justice that implies the re-establishment of a penal law among states and the right to just war. Hence, whereas Vattel's conception involves the establishment of a negative minimum of inter-state coexistence

---

[43] *Le droit des gens* (n 24) bk II, ch I, § 17 (268).   [44] Ibid.

as well as a belief in formal and negative justice that privileges freedom above everything else, Van Vollenhoven's design is entirely based on the need for an international society defined by solidarity and altruism which enforces a positive material justice.

4 CONCLUSION

There is a gap here which truly separates the conceptions of these two authors and which explains why one wished to differentiate himself from the other. Yet, one would be falling into the trap of previous interpretations if one ignores what unites them. For their differences should not obscure the fact that both authors are motivated by the desire to conceive of a system of peace that is compatible with sovereignty, while limiting the deadly effects of war. Van Vollenhoven thus shares with Vattel the need to maintain the concept of state sovereignty by refraining from any idea of institutional federalism. Moreover, one might add, Vattel's classical law of nations is but an antithetical logic of justice and humanity. It remains oriented towards the achievement of a certain justice among states, even if the latter is merely formal and liberal. It is a law that would allow states to pursue their own development and, thereby, the welfare of their citizens. Indeed, self-preservation and sovereignty through law is, to Vattel, the route towards the development of civil society. The human being is not left out here, but it is merely assumed that the conditions for her development can only be conceived of from within the state. Is this not precisely what Immanuel Kant concludes shortly after Vattel's *Droit des gens*, in his *Perpetual Peace* published in 1795? Set between the naturalist spirit to enforce ethics and the need to reflect the realities of his time, Vattel crafted a measured legal model that is far from its subsequent description by Van Vollenhoven.

All of these elements of convergence are effectively ignored by Van Vollenhoven in 1919. In his desire to build a new legal system, the Dutch jurist not only distorts the content of Vattel's doctrine but also the underlying reasons for its original development. Van Vollenhoven's interwar critique thus introduced a double error. The first error is historical and concerns an ignorant and superficial reading of traditional international law. But the second error, of a theoretical kind and more serious than the first, consists of the fact that the dissemination of this interpretation has blocked out the ability to learn from the past. The issue of just war is a particularly salient example of this truncated debate, as it is now again brought up by some as a ground for intervention, while the precise reasons for why the concept had been abandoned more than three centuries ago seem to have been forgotten. In order not to fall into this misunderstanding, one needs to return to examine these doctrines in the context of their times. This is not, of course, akin to advocating a return to Vattel's classical law without considering the objections raised by Van Vollenhoven against it. Rather than discarding the legitimate criticisms made during the interwar period, they need to be integrated into a broader reflection about what those criticisms have given us. To the extent that those criticisms rest on false assumptions about the fundamental bases of classical thought, they should not be relied upon. Otherwise one would not comprehend the international law of the past, not understand the international law of the present, and so could not envisage correctly the international law of the future.

CHAPTER 6

....

THE OTTOMAN EMPIRE, THE ORIGINS OF EXTRATERRITORIALITY, AND INTERNATIONAL LEGAL THEORY

....

UMUT ÖZSU

1 INTRODUCTION

....

IN September 1844, Caleb Cushing, lawyer, diplomat, and eventually attorney general, sat down to pen a letter to Secretary of State John C Calhoun. As commissioner to China, Cushing had been tasked with negotiating an agreement that would provide American merchants with access to Chinese goods and markets. His mission had yielded the landmark Treaty of Wang Hiya, an agreement that would 'open' China to American capital, in much the same way as the 1842 Treaty of Nanjing and 1843 Treaty of the Bogue had opened it to British capital by establishing 'treaty ports' in which British nationals enjoyed extraterritorial protection.[1]

---

[1] For the texts see Treaty of Peace, Amity and Commerce between China and the United States (signed 3 July 1844) 97 CTS 105; Treaty between China and Great Britain (signed 29 August 1842) 93

Evidently satisfied with his accomplishment, Cushing now took the opportunity to gloss the treaty with some rather slapdash commentary. Residual attachments to Vattelian universalism notwithstanding, the law of nations, he informed Washington, was not in actuality 'the law of *all* nations', but rather 'the international law of *Christendom*', a complex body of rules and principles governing relations between states that shared a common commitment to 'superior civilization'.[2] Indeed, he argued, there was a fundamental dichotomy between 'the States of Christendom', which were 'bound together by treaties', and 'Mohammedan or Pagan States', whose inhabitants knew little more than 'sanguinary barbarism' and 'phrenzied bigotry' in respect to foreigners.[3] The most visible expression of this dichotomy was the fact that Christian states routinely insisted on the right to exercise extraterritorial jurisdiction over their nationals in non-Christian states (even as they restricted such jurisdiction between themselves in line with the normative ascension of territorial sovereignty within Europe).

According to Cushing, while it would be senseless 'to deny to China a high degree of civilization', that civilization was no less 'different' than that of the Ottoman Empire and its dependencies.[4] As a result, much the same protection mandated for American merchants who operated in North Africa was required for those who would ply their trade in China. If China was to be rendered amenable to imperialist policy through a series of 'unequal treaties', this was due to reliance upon roughly the same kind of extraterritorial jurisdiction that underpinned the centuries-old tradition of Ottoman capitulations, which provided non-Muslim foreigners with privileges of residence and safe passage, a variety of tax exemptions and low customs duties, and partial if not complete immunity from the jurisdiction of Ottoman courts.

Factually dubious and politically problematic though it was,[5] Cushing's memorandum was emblematic of a large body of nineteenth- and early twentieth-century texts deploying the Ottoman Empire as the exemplar of what many contemporaneous lawyers and diplomats were wont to characterize as 'semi-civilized' states. For

CTS 465; Supplementary Treaty between China and Great Britain (signed 8 October 1843) 95 CTS 323. For analysis see GW Keeton, *The Development of Extraterritoriality in China* (Longmans, Green & Co London 1928) vol 2, at 277–81.

[2] 'Cushing to Calhoun, 29 September 1844' reproduced in 'Message from the President of the United States, Communicating an Abstract of the Treaty between the United States of America and the Chinese Empire' in *Public Documents Printed by Order of the Senate of the United States, Second Session of the Twenty-Eighth Congress* (Gales & Seaton Washington 1845) vol 2, no 58 at 1–14, 5 and 7 (emphasis in original).

[3] Ibid 12.   [4] Ibid 11.

[5] For a recent appraisal see T Ruskola, *Legal Orientalism: China, the United States, and Modern Law* (Harvard University Press Cambridge MA 2013) at 132–7. But see also EP Scully, *Bargaining with the State from Afar: American Citizenship in Treaty Port China 1844–1942* (Columbia University Press New York 2001) at 24–6. The assumptions that underlie Cushing's memorandum continue to animate international legal thought. For related analysis of the contemporary 'war on terror', see eg J Desautels-Stein, 'The Canon Reloaded: Equality and Exclusion in the History of International Legal Thought' (copy on file with author).

Cushing, as for so many others, the global dissemination of extraterritoriality—its circulation as an effective technology for administering relations between Europeans and non-Europeans under conditions that departed from formal colonialism—was intimately associated with a host of perceived similarities between sovereign but politically and economically weak extra-European states.

Despite their obvious and irreducible differences, the Ottoman Empire and a host of other states, including China, Japan, Korea, Morocco, Muscat, Persia, Siam, and Zanzibar, were understood by a great many European and American jurists to fall somewhere between two ideal-typical poles—that of the territorially and juris-dictionally integrated European state, 'civilized' and fully entitled to safeguard its sovereignty, and that of the 'stateless' extra-European nation, 'savage' and requir-ing administration in the hands of one or another enlightened power. Populating an intermediate category, these states were deemed to be sufficiently 'civilized' to engage with the West on something approaching an equal basis, or at least with greater power and legitimacy than was accorded to 'uncivilized' peoples, but not 'civilized' enough to forego extraterritoriality, this being understood as an excep-tional mechanism best suited to circumstances in which existing laws were held inapplicable to Western subjects.

It was no accident that Cushing claimed in this connection a certain conceptual and chronological primacy for the Ottoman capitulations. Regardless of whether he was actually justified in assuming that the Treaty of Wang Hiya belonged to the same class of instruments as the Ottoman capitulations, his own experience was confirmation enough that the latter were capable of serving as rough-and-ready models for the treaties that Euro-American powers were busy negotiating throughout the extra-European world. Extraterritoriality had proven expedient in the case of the Ottoman Empire, and it would reinforce American efforts to pen-etrate Chinese markets without absorption into the sphere of Chinese law.

Emerging in the Byzantine borderlands, consolidating itself as a multi-confessional empire projecting power along multiple continental axes, struggling to preserve its sovereignty after entering a period of relative weakness, and eventu-ally unravelling in the face of imperialist rivalry and institutional inertia, the legal status of the Ottoman state was understood differently at different junctures. This chapter argues that it was partly through engagement with the Ottoman Empire, particularly its tradition of extraterritorial consular jurisdiction, that nineteenth-century European and American jurists came to view China, Japan, and a number of other states as 'semi-civilized', setting them against 'civilized' states on the one hand and 'savage' peoples on the other. Not unlike the way in which the early Ottoman state bore the institutional and ideological markings of the unstable frontier region in which it arose,[6] its status was understood by such jurists to be of

---

[6] See C Kafadar, *Between Two Worlds: The Construction of the Ottoman State* (University of California Press Berkeley 1995).

a broadly intermediate modality, falling short of Western standards of 'civilization' while defying assimilation into 'savagery' pure and simple.

Underscoring extraterritoriality's centrality for the consolidation of a legal discourse of 'civilization' has significant implications. International legal history is no longer written with an eye solely to Euro-American experiences, but even those strands of theoretically informed legal scholarship that repudiate Eurocentrism tend to prioritize the colonized 'periphery', focusing on the implications of the encounter between 'civilized' Europeans and 'uncivilized' non-Europeans for the shifting doctrinal architecture of recognition and sovereignty.[7] Though invaluable as a corrective, this framework of analysis frequently loses sight of the crucial importance to international law of developments associated with what, following world-systems theory, may be characterized as the 'semi-periphery'.[8] Influenced by powerful centres of economic production but possessing traditions and institutions equipped to counter formal colonialism, semi-peripheral states' engagement with international law generally manifested a significant degree of agency. Nowhere was this clearer than in the case of the Ottoman Empire, a powerful state that made a point of modifying its profile for different audiences.[9] And in no respect was this instability brought home with greater lucidity than in debates concerning the character and consequences of the capitulations—a set of instruments that, for all their resonance with currently fashionable indicators and informal agreements, remain severely under-examined.[10]

[7] For the classic articulation see A Anghie, *Imperialism, Sovereignty and the Making of International Law* (CUP Cambridge 2005).

[8] A number of attempts have been made to address such blind spots: see eg RS Horowitz, 'International Law and State Transformation in China, Siam, and the Ottoman Empire during the Nineteenth Century' (2004) 15 *Journal of World History* 445–86; L Obregón, 'Completing Civilization: Creole Consciousness and International Law in Nineteenth-Century Latin America' in A Orford (ed), *International Law and Its Others* (CUP Cambridge 2006) 247–64; T Kayaoğlu, *Legal Imperialism: Sovereignty and Extraterritoriality in Japan, the Ottoman Empire, and China* (CUP Cambridge 2010); A Becker Lorca, *Mestizo International Law: A Global Intellectual History, 1842–1933* (CUP Cambridge 2014); L Mälksoo, *Russian Approaches to International Law* (OUP Oxford 2015). Still, considerably more work is needed before one can speak of a comprehensive body of literature.

[9] See D Kołodziejcyzk, 'Khan, Caliph, Tsar and Imperator: The Multiple Identities of the Ottoman Sultan' in PF Bang and D Kołodziejcyzk (eds), *Universal Empire: A Comparative Approach to Imperial Culture and Representation in Eurasian History* (CUP Cambridge 2012) 175–93, at 177 and 192–3.

[10] Though often noted, such similarities are rarely subject to serious scrutiny. For notable exceptions, see M Craven, 'What Happened to Unequal Treaties? The Continuities of Informal Empire' (2005) 74 *Nordic Journal of International Law* 335–82; DP Fidler, 'A Kinder, Gentler System of Capitulations? International Law, Structural Adjustment Policies, and the Standard of Liberal, Globalized Civilization' (2000) 35 *Texas International Law Journal* 387–413, at 408ff; AA Shalakany, 'Arbitration and the Third World: A Plea for Reassessing Bias under the Specter of Neoliberalism' (2000) 41 *Harvard International Law Journal* 419–68, at 431–3.

2 Topoi of Extraterritoriality

International lawyers have often underscored the fact that the Ottoman Empire was the first non-Western state to gain nominal admission to the nineteenth-century 'family of nations'. Turkey was extended the 'advantages' of Europe's public law and political system pursuant to a notoriously imprecise provision in the 1856 Treaty of Paris,[11] concluded only two years after it had taken out the first in a series of loans that would eventually drive it to bankruptcy and compel it to surrender control over tax revenue to European creditors.[12] Though controversial, this move permitted Ottoman authorities to position themselves as representatives of the first extra-European state to subscribe to the body of international humanitarian law that emerged in the late nineteenth and early twentieth centuries. Turkey joined the Red Cross movement in 1868, the first non-Christian state to do so, and also became a party to the 1899 Hague Convention. This was part and parcel of a complex, protracted process of appropriating European legal thought in which new codes were promulgated, a law faculty offering training in both public and private international law was established,[13] an enlarged and augmented foreign ministry was reinforced with European counsellors,[14] and popular European treatises like Henri Bonfils' *Manuel de droit international public* appeared in Ottoman translation.[15]

Of course, putative inclusion within the European state system did not bring any sudden appreciation of Turkey's claim to sovereign equality. The mechanisms of minority protection that emerged in the latter half of the nineteenth century had as their principal objective the task of managing the disintegration of Ottoman authority in the Balkans, and were not thought to be applicable

[11] General Treaty for the Re-Establishment of Peace (signed 30 March 1856) 114 CTS 409, art 7. For legal analysis see especially H McKinnon Wood, 'The Treaty of Paris and Turkey's Status in International Law' (1943) 37 *American Journal of International Law* 262–74. See also MS Palabıyık, 'The Emergence of the Idea of "International Law" in the Ottoman Empire Before the Treaty of Paris (1856)' (2014) 50 *Middle Eastern Studies* 233–51.

[12] On the Ottoman Public Debt Administration, established in 1881 by European bondholders, see especially DC Blaisdell, *European Financial Control in the Ottoman Empire: A Study of the Establishment, Activities, and Significance of the Administration of the Ottoman Public Debt* (Columbia University Press New York 1929). See further R Owen, *The Middle East in the World Economy 1800–1914* (Methuen London 1981) at 191–200.

[13] F Çoker, '"Dârülfünûn-i Osmani" ve "Mekteb-i Hukuk"' (1994) 121 *Tarih ve Toplum* 26–7.

[14] S Kuneralp and E Öktem (eds), *Chambre des conseillers légistes de la Sublime Porte: Rapports, avis et consultations sur la condition juridique des ressortissants étrangers, le statut des communautés non musulmanes et les relations internationales de l'Empire ottoman (1864–1912)* (Les éditions Isis Istanbul 2012) at 9–10.

[15] See H Bonfils, *Hukuk-i Umumiye-yi Düvel* (P Fauchille ed, A Selâhattin and M Cemil trans) (Matbaa-i Jirayir-Keteon İstanbul 1325 [1907–8]).

to the Western states responsible for instituting them as conditions of state-hood in Europe's southeastern periphery.[16] The 1878 Treaty of Berlin, the most ambitious attempt to institute a minority-protection regime prior to 1919, required newly 'liberated' Balkan states to extend civil and political guarantees to their minorities—guarantees that were never demanded of the great powers themselves.[17]

Similarly, it was largely in response to the inter-communal strife and heavy-handed government suppression that marked the empire's long nineteenth century—far and away its 'longest century'[18]—that European powers began to have recourse to what came to be termed 'humanitarian intervention'.[19] In addition to constituting Greece as an independent kingdom in the 1830s, European powers undertook an armed intervention in Lebanon in the early 1860s, reshaped the Balkans after the Russo–Turkish War of 1877–78, and used both force and diplo-macy to fix the status of Crete in the late 1890s, styling most of their actions as necessary for the sake of 'humanity'.[20] Despite (or perhaps because of) its nomi-nal inclusion in the European state system, with all the associated guarantees of integrity and independence, the Ottoman Empire served as a laboratory for 'excep-tional' modes of interference, many of which would later come to be exported to other states and regions.

---

[16] On this see U Özsu, *Formalizing Displacement: International Law and Population Transfers* (OUP Oxford 2015) ch 1.

[17] Treaty for the Settlement of Affairs in the East (signed 13 July 1878) 153 CTS 171. For analysis see especially C Fink, *Defending the Rights of Others: The Great Powers, the Jews, and International Minority Protection, 1878–1938* (CUP Cambridge 2004) especially ch 1. Note that minority protection also boasted deep roots in the Ottoman *millet* system, which ensured that members of non-Muslim communities were afforded a measure of legal autonomy. The system was modified in the mid-nineteenth century, when reforms introduced a general right of equality applicable to all Ottoman subjects. See generally B Braude and B Lewis (eds), *Christians and Jews in the Ottoman Empire: The Functioning of a Plural Society* (2 vols Holmes & Meier New York 1982).

[18] I borrow the expression from İ Ortaylı, *İmparatorluğun En Uzun Yüzyılı* (Hil Yayın İstanbul 1983).

[19] See eg G Rolin-Jaequemyns, 'Note sur la théorie du droit d'intervention à propos d'une lettre de M le professeur Arntz' (1876) 8 *Revue de droit international et de législation comparée* 673–82; E Engelhardt, *Le droit d'intervention et la Turquie: étude historique* (A Cotillon & Cie Paris 1880); A Rougier, 'La théorie de l'intervention d'humanité' (1910) 17 *Revue générale de droit international public* 468–526.

[20] For a comprehensive treatment see D Rodogno, *Against Massacre: Humanitarian Interventions in the Ottoman Empire 1815–1914* (Princeton University Press Princeton 2012). But see also W Smiley, 'War without War: The Battle of Navarino, the Ottoman Empire, and the Pacific Blockade' (2016) 18 *Journal of the History of International Law* 42–69. This was integral to the Concert of Europe's use or threat of force in the name of inter-state equilibrium, a tendency frequently displayed in the creation and dissolution of states on Europe's southeastern periphery. Cf TE Holland, *Lectures on International Law* (TA Walker and WL Walker ed) (Sweet & Maxwell London 1933) at 105. See further E Augusti, *Questioni d'Oriente: Europa e Impero ottomano nel Diritto internazionale dell'Ottocento* (Edizioni Scientifiche Italiane Napoli 2013).

Extraterritoriality, the 'legal fiction' that lay at the basis of consular jurisdiction, showcased and reinforced this curiously unstable legal status. Finding a home in a category of instruments known to the early Ottomans as *ahdnameler* ('letters of promise') and to non-Muslim sovereigns as 'capitulations' (from the *capitula*, or 'chapters', into which they tended to be divided), extraterritorial jurisdiction had initially served as an illustration of Ottoman power rather than its limitations, the sultans having made it available as a means of solidifying political alliances and streamlining commercial relations. By the nineteenth century, though, the kind of consular jurisdiction afforded by these 'gracious concessions' had come to be regarded by many jurists and policy-makers, both Western and Ottoman, as an anomaly—a throwback to a pre-modern era in which national statehood was largely unknown and territorial models of jurisdiction enjoyed only limited influence. Ottoman claims that the capitulations were unilateral privileges were contested by a large number of Western authorities, who grew increasingly fond of the argument that the capitulations, however anomalous, ought to be understood as treaties imposing binding legal obligations upon both parties, not least because the concessions they made available had frequently come to be incorporated into treaties *sensu stricto*.[21] The capitulations ought to have been abolished as a result of the 1856 Treaty of Paris. Even European negotiators at the Congress of Paris had admitted that the capitulations 'circonscrivent l'autorité de la Porte dans des limites regrettables'.[22] Far from resulting in their abolition, though, the Paris settlement was quickly followed by the increased formalization and entrenchment of the capitulations. The argument that the capitulations were understood most appropriately as binding treaties provided Western authorities with considerable leverage in this regard, and eventually came to exert a certain degree of influence over even Ottoman officials, who sometimes felt a need to bolster their traditional conception of the capitulatory regime with ancillary arguments.[23]

[21] For more on this transformation see U Özsu, 'Ottoman Empire' in B Fassbender and A Peters (eds), *The Oxford Handbook of the History of International Law* (OUP Oxford 2012) 429–48. For broader analyses of the Ottoman capitulations see N Sousa, *The Capitulatory Régime of Turkey: Its History, Origin, and Nature* (Johns Hopkins Press Baltimore 1933); H İnalcık, 'Imtiyāzāt' in B Lewis et al., (eds), *The Encyclopaedia of Islam: New Edition* (Brill Leiden 1971) vol 3, at 1179–89; MH van den Boogert and K Fleet (eds), 'The Ottoman Capitulations: Text and Context' (2003) 22 *Oriente Moderno* 575–727; MH van den Boogert, *The Capitulations and the Ottoman Legal System: Qadis, Consuls, and Beratlıs in the 18th Century* (Brill Leiden 2005); E Eldem, 'Capitulations and Western Trade' in SN Faroqhi (ed), *The Cambridge History of Turkey* (CUP Cambridge 2006) vol 3, at 283–335.
[22] 'Protocole no 14—séance du 25 mars 1856' in *Protocols of Conferences Held at Paris relative to the General Treaty of Peace* (Harrison & Sons London 1856) 52–6, at 54.
[23] See eg 'Avant-projet de protocole pour le règlement des conflits capitulaires en matière judiciaire presénté à Nedjmeddîn Bey, ministre de la justice, le 23 février 1911' reproduced in L Ostrorόg, *Pour la réforme de la justice ottomane* (Pedone Paris 1912) 323–32, at 332 (speaking of the need to revise 'anciens traités'). On this tendency, see SS Liu, *Extraterritoriality: Its Rise and Its Decline* (Columbia University Press New York 1925) at 179–80.

3 EXCEPTIONAL JURISPRUDENCE

The peculiarity of the Ottoman capitulations—the uncertainty surrounding their form and function—was a subject of debate in cases brought before the mixed courts that proliferated in the nineteenth century, especially in Egypt, for the purpose of adjudicating disputes between Western and Ottoman subjects.[24] Consider, for instance, the ruminations of an Alexandrian tribunal presiding over an action brought by bond-bidders operating under German protection.[25] As with many such cases, the dispute turned on the question of whether the plaintiffs' suit received support from the capitulations. The plaintiffs argued that 'foreigners, when living in an Ottoman country, are to enjoy the privilege of absolute extraterritoriality and are hence freed from all subjection to the local laws and the local sovereignty'.[26] This argument received little sympathy from the tribunal. Explaining that it was 'manifestly exaggerated', violating the 'most certain principles of the law of nations', the tribunal emphasized that 'each independent state, whether belonging to Christendom or to countries outside of Christendom, is "necessarily" the seat of a real sovereignty, the essence of which is to be "territorial"'.[27] Indeed, it noted, one need only be reminded of the fact that 'the capitulations of the Porte originally had no other character than that of voluntary grants' in order to recognize as much.[28] A capitulatory text might be read broadly or narrowly, loosely or restrictively, as suggesting informal arrangements for inter-state coordination or as entailing strictly binding obligations. Depending on the context and circumstances, a given reading might augment or attenuate a party's sovereign power.

Even more instructive are the numerous debates regarding the question of how and where to try and sentence foreign criminal defendants. A good illustration of this is the 'Joris case', the cause of something of a minor scandal. In 1905 Edouard Joris, a Belgian subject living in Istanbul and sympathetic to various radical and anarchist causes, confessed to participating in an attempted assassination of Sultan Abdülhamid II. The bomb he had prepared had not succeeded in killing the sultan,

---

[24] The classic study is JY Brinton, *The Mixed Courts of Egypt* (Yale University Press New Haven 1930). Formally an Ottoman province until 1914 but effectively autonomous or under European administration after the early nineteenth century, Egypt was an especially complex site for the operationalization of capitulatory privileges: see eg A Benoit, *Étude sur les capitulations entre l'Empire ottoman et la France et sur la réforme judiciaire en Égypte* (A Rousseau Paris 1890) chs 5–7. For recent and more general consideration of Egypt as an 'experimental' zone, see also AM Genell, 'Empire by Law: Ottoman Sovereignty and the British Occupation of Egypt, 1882–1923' (PhD dissertation Columbia University 2013); W Hanley, 'International Lawyers without Public International Law: The Case of Late Ottoman Egypt' (2016) 18 *Journal of the History of International Law* 98–119.

[25] *Sursock Brothers v The Egyptian Government*, reproduced in EA van Dyck, *Capitulations of the Ottoman Empire since the Year 1150* (Government Printing Office Washington 1881) pt 2, at 36–44.

[26] Ibid 39.   [27] Ibid.   [28] Ibid.

but it had led to the death of twenty-six and the injury of nearly sixty others. The Ottoman authorities moved quickly, apprehending Joris and instituting proceedings in the Ottoman courts, where he was tried and sentenced to death. However, Belgian officials rejected this sentence, arguing that Joris should never have been tried in an Ottoman court. Crucially, the Belgians relied upon the French text of their 1838 treaty with the empire.[29] The relevant provision was worded vaguely, but its constituent clauses appeared to assign jurisdiction over the prosecution of Belgian nationals accused of crimes against Ottoman nationals to Belgian consular officials.[30] And so there ensued a classic legal dispute—one with profound theoretical implications for international law. How best to interpret the 1838 treaty? To what extent could the relevant (capitulatory) clauses be enforced, if they could be enforced at all? Whose version of the treaty text—the Belgian or the Ottoman—was to be held authoritative? Had subsequent developments, including developments pertaining to customary international law, altered relations between the two states?

Unsurprisingly, the case attracted significant scholarly attraction. Gabriel Noradounghian, an Ottoman lawyer of Armenian heritage who occupied various posts in the Ottoman civil service before rising to the rank of foreign minister during the Balkan Wars of 1912–13, was sufficiently impressed by the threat of protracted Belgian pressure to pen an extended analysis of the case. Experienced in diplomacy and editor of a widely consulted Ottoman compendium of treaties and other instruments,[31] Noradounghian sought to demonstrate that Brussels' position stemmed from textual and interpretational errors relating to the French version of the treaty.[32] For Noradounghian, the fact that Belgium seemed to have acquiesced in Ottoman assertions of jurisdiction only bolstered this argument, as did a variety of developments since 1838 that appeared to indicate that the treaty was not entirely reflective of actual legal practice.[33] This position garnered a robust reaction from Albéric Rolin, a prominent Belgian jurist deeply involved in the activities of the Institut de droit international. Committed to defending Belgian interests, Rolin dismissed Noradounghian's interpretation of the treaty, stressing, among other things, that consular officials retained the right to judge and carry out sentences against Belgian nationals even if it were true that Ottoman authorities were

---

[29] See Treaty of Amity, Commerce and Navigation between Belgium and Turkey (signed 3 August 1838) 88 CTS 59.

[30] For a brief summary, see 'The Joris Case and the Turkish Capitulations' (1907) 1 *American Journal of International Law* 485.

[31] See G Noradounghian (ed), *Recueil d'actes internationaux de l'Empire ottoman* (4 vols Librairie Cotillon F Pichon Paris 1897–1903).

[32] G Noradounghian, 'Le traité turco–belge de 1838 et la compétence en matière pénale des autorités ottomanes envers les étrangers' (1906) 8 *Revue de droit international et de législation comparée* 119–35, at 120–3.

[33] Ibid 126ff.

empowered to arrest them.[34] For his part, Nicolas Politis, who would go on to serve as foreign minister of Greece before establishing himself as a leading legal scholar of the interwar period, underscored the Ottoman legal system's deficiencies while adopting a more sympathetic stance with respect to the Ottoman position.[35]

Of course, as each of these commentators was aware, even outright attempts to abrogate capitulatory privileges were insufficient to loosen their hold. Western authorities regularly pointed to the fact that they had come to be entrenched in treaty law, as well as the fact that the attribution of most-favoured-nation status precluded denial of consular jurisdiction to one power so long as it remained effective in the case of other powers. That Ottoman authorities ultimately succumbed to pressure and released Joris goes some way to confirming their relative weakness in the face of efforts to interpret capitulatory pledges in expansive terms.[36]

4 THE CIRCULATION OF 'SEMI-CIVILIZATION'

For many nineteenth- and early twentieth-century lawyers, the fact that the Ottoman Empire continued to offer wide-ranging capitulatory privileges was capable of being explained only by accepting the proposition that it was a 'semi-civilized' state, one with a weaker claim to sovereignty and lower 'standard' of justice than fully 'civilized' states. While some were willing to entertain the notion that consular jurisdiction derived from a delegation of power by the 'oriental Sovereign',[37] most underscored what they regarded as Turkey's insufficiently developed legal system when presenting reforms as necessary for the abolition of the capitulations. Nothing short of comprehensive legal and administrative reforms—reforms that would codify existing laws and customs, facilitate the training of a professional bar and bench, impose constraints upon discretionary decision-making, and eradicate

[34] A Rolin, 'L'affaire Joris: étude sur la capitulation' (1906) 8 *Revue de droit international et de législation comparée* 363–82.

[35] N Politis, 'Les capitulations et la justice répressive ottomane à propos de l'affaire Joris' (1906) 2 *Revue de droit international privé et de droit pénal international* 659–83.

[36] For analysis of the debate see W Hanley, 'The Prosecution and Extradition of Edouard Joris' in H de Smaele, H Alloul, and E Eldem (eds), *The Assassination Attempt on Sultan Abdülhamid II (1905): Rethinking European-Ottoman Entanglements* (Palgrave Macmillan New York forthcoming) (copy on file with author).

[37] See eg FT Piggott, *Exterritoriality: The Law Relating to Consular Jurisdiction and to Residence in Oriental Countries* (revised edn Kelly & Walsh Hong Kong 1907) at 5–6 and 8.

or at least minimize corruption and adjudicative delay—would permit Turkey to secure acceptance as a properly modern polity adhering to the rule of law.

Unsurprisingly, this invited all manner of comparisons—some justified, others spurious—between Turkey and other 'semi-civilized' states. Arguably the sharpest example is that offered by James Lorimer, who famously sought to disaggregate 'humanity' into 'three concentric zones or spheres'.[38] For Lorimer, the core of 'humanity' consisted of fully 'civilized' European states, while its outermost periphery was comprised of 'savage' extra-European peoples. Between the two, though, in a kind of intermediate 'zone', were what Lorimer termed 'barbarous' states—first and foremost 'Turkey in Europe and Asia', followed closely by China, Japan, Siam, Persia, and the 'separate States of Central Asia'.[39] Lorimer stressed that the jurisdiction and competence of local courts in 'barbarous' states needed to be restricted, and that European powers had little choice but to maintain a structurally independent judiciary applying a normatively independent body of law.[40] Turkey, which 'occupie[d] a wholly anomalous position' in international law, was the most illustrative of these states, understood alternately as independent (but weak) sovereigns and quasi-independent semi-sovereigns.[41]

Lorimer's work is a particularly well-known illustration of the late nineteenth-century tendency to grade differential levels of legal 'civilization'. But his opinions about the 'semi-civilized' (or 'barbarous') were by no means unique. Franz von Liszt relied upon a nearly identical tripartite model of world order in his 1898 treatise, *Das Völkerrecht*.[42] And on the occasion of the Institut de droit international's consideration of the question of the '[a]pplication aux nations orientales du droit des gens coutumier de l'Europe',[43] Travers Twiss, the organization's vice-president at the time, argued that '[l]es habitants de l'empire ottoman, les Persans, les Chinois, les Japonais doivent être distingués des populations payennes et demi-sauvages', since, when all was said and done, 'les rapports internationaux avec tel peuple de l'Orient diffèrent nécessairement selon le degré de civilisation qui le distingue de ses voisins'.[44] Others at the meeting went even further, with Friedrich Martens arguing that any solution to the problem of consular jurisdiction in Turkey would need to be applied to similarly situated 'peuples orientaux', and NJ Saripolos, an

---

[38] J Lorimer, *The Institutes of the Law of Nations: A Treatise of the Jural Relations of Separate Political Communities* (2 vols W Blackwood & Sons Edinburgh 1883) vol 1, at 101. Subscribing to an insufficiently historicized analysis, the author of the most widely cited study of the question mistakenly presents Lorimer's scheme as indifferent to the 'standard of civilization': GW Gong, *The Standard of 'Civilization' in International Society* (Clarendon Press Oxford 1984) at 31 and also 49.

[39] *Institutes of the Law of Nations* (n 38) 102.   [40] Ibid 217–8.   [41] Ibid 218.

[42] F von Liszt, *Das Völkerrecht, systematisch dargestellt* (O Haering Berlin 1898) at 1–4.

[43] 'Quatrième commission d'étude' (1879–80) 3–4 *Annuaire de l'Institut de droit international* 298–311, at 298.

[44] Ibid 301. See further T Twiss, *On Consular Jurisdiction in the Levant, and the Status of Foreigners in the Ottoman Law Courts* (W Clowes & Sons London 1880).

Athens-based member of the Institut, insisting on the Ottoman Empire's centrality for all questions of extraterritoriality.[45]

Similarly, an influential 1906 American report on consular jurisdiction devoted at least as many pages to the Ottoman capitulations and mixed courts of Egypt as it did to extraterritoriality in coastal China and the Shanghai International Settlement, drawing numerous comparisons in the process between the legal instruments in effect in west and east Asia.[46] Observing that '[t]he conception of sovereignty as territorial is relatively modern' and that 'extraterritoriality is a surviving form of the earlier prevailing conception that it was the duty of a sovereign to protect', the report's author made a point of underscoring the fact that the maintenance of extraterritorial jurisdiction in 'oriental states'—an expression he applied with equal force to 'near' and 'far' East alike—had long been justified on the basis of their common status as '"non-Christian," "semi-civilized," and "barbarous"' polities.[47]

Diplomatic officials frequently leaned upon similar assumptions. When a British minister to China found himself confronted with procedural questions pertaining to the operation of the mixed court in Shanghai, he first requested a memorandum on whether any lessons might be drawn from British experiences in the eastern Mediterranean. Displeased with the memorandum, prepared by a British official who had been dispatched to Shanghai after serving as a consular judge in Istanbul and who was convinced that Turkey's legal order was more advanced than that of China, the minister insisted that any difficulties resulting from the institution of a mixed court in China 'must have been encountered and overcome in Turkey long before there was any knowledge of French or a Code Napoléon'.[48] However strong the countervailing evidence, it was simply obvious, the minister averred, that the British would be confronted in China with the same kinds of problems as they had in the Ottoman Empire.

Interestingly, arguments mobilized to suppress capitulatory regimes resembled each other across a range of 'semi-civilized' states. In the first decades of the twentieth century, the controversial doctrine of *rebus sic stantibus* proved to be of particular importance in this regard. When, for instance, Chinese representatives presented themselves before the Paris Peace Conference, they argued that 'the reasons for the introduction of consular jurisdiction into China ha[d] ceased to exist'

---

[45] 'Quatrième commission d'étude' (n 43) 308–10. For analysis of this and related debates, see M Koskenniemi, *The Gentle Civilizer of Nations: The Rise and Fall of International Law 1870–1960* (CUP Cambridge 2001) at 132–4; J Pitts, 'Boundaries of Victorian International Law' in D Bell (ed), *Victorian Visions of Global Order: Empire and International Relations in Nineteenth-Century Political Thought* (CUP Cambridge 2007) 67–88, especially at 71–6.

[46] FE Hinckley, *American Consular Jurisdiction in the Orient* (WH Lowdermilk & Co Washington 1906).

[47] Ibid 17 and 195.

[48] R Alcock quoted in PK Cassel, *Grounds of Judgment: Extraterritoriality and Imperial Power in Nineteenth-Century China and Japan* (OUP Oxford 2012) at 70 (emphasis added).

by pointing to the fact that a constitution had been adopted, new legal codes had been drafted, the existing system of courts had been overhauled, and a professionally trained bar and bench was being developed.[49] Though largely ignored in 1919, such arguments resurfaced during the *Denunciation of the Treaty of 2 November 1865* case, considered by the Permanent Court of International Justice roughly a decade later.[50] In order to justify its unilateral abrogation of an 1865 treaty with Belgium that had provided for extraterritorial jurisdiction, China invoked article 19 of the League Covenant, which spoke of the reconsideration of treaties that had proven to be inapplicable,[51] and argued that 'no nation mindful of its destiny and conscious of its self-respect, can be fettered forever by treaties which shackle its free and natural development and which are repugnant to the best traditions of international intercourse'.[52] The legal proceedings—in which China did not participate directly—came to an end when Belgium withdrew its application and declared that it was prepared to conclude a new treaty.[53]

This argument was strikingly similar to that developed by contemporaneous Turkish authorities, most famously at the outset of the First World War, when they sought to abrogate the capitulations partly on the grounds that they had outlived their purpose,[54] and during the 1922–23 Conference of Lausanne, the final outcome of which was a definitive peace settlement with Turkey in which the capitulatory regime was abolished. In the latter case, Turkish negotiators held firm to the longstanding Ottoman claim that the capitulations were 'essentially unilateral acts'.[55] However, as a secondary claim, they also maintained that the circumstances under

---

[49] Chinese Delegation to the Peace Conference, *Questions for Readjustment Submitted by China to the Peace Conference* (Vaugirard Paris 1919) at 15. This position received support from contemporaneous Chinese writing: see eg MTZ Tyau, *The Legal Obligations Arising out of Treaty Relations between China and Other States* (Commercial Press Shanghai 1917) at 211. Note, though, that there were other views on the matter: see eg VKW Koo, *The Status of Aliens in China* (Columbia University Press New York 1912) at 350–6.

[50] *Denunciation of the Treaty of November 2nd, 1865, between China and Belgium (Belgium v China)* PCIJ Rep Series A Nos 8, 14, 16, 18 (1927–9).

[51] Covenant of the League of Nations Adopted by the Peace Conference at Plenary Session (adopted 28 April 1919) (1919) 13 *American Journal of International Law Supplement* 128–40, at 136.

[52] 'Statement of the Chinese Government Explaining the Termination of the Sino-Belgian Treaty of November 2nd, 1865' in *Denunciation of the Treaty of November 2nd, 1865, between China and Belgium (Belgium v China)* PCIJ Rep Series C No 16-I (1928) 271–6, at 275.

[53] This move was followed by initiatives on the part of other treaty powers: J Escarra, *La Chine et le droit international* (Pedone Paris 1931) at 20, 41ff.

[54] 'Ottoman Circular Announcing the Abrogation of the Capitulations, 9 September 1914' reproduced in JC Hurewitz (ed), *Diplomacy in the Near and Middle East: A Documentary Record: 1535–1956* (Octagon New York 1972) vol 2, at 2–3. The French original is reproduced in (1914) 21 *Revue générale de droit international public* 488.

[55] 'Memorandum Read by the Turkish Delegate at the Meeting of December 2, 1922, of the Commission on the Régime of Foreigners' in *Lausanne Conference on Near Eastern Affairs (1922–1923): Records of Proceedings and Draft Terms of Peace* (Cmd 1814) (His Majesty's Stationery Office London 1923) 471–80, at 478.

which they had arisen were no longer operative, such that *rebus sic stantibus* displaced the otherwise general rule of *pacta sunt servanda*.[56] To quell any lingering doubts, Turkish delegates further stressed the need to situate the capitulations within their historical contexts. In their view, such contextualization yielded the conclusion that the capitulations were dependent upon an obsolete model of personal law, one that ran directly contrary to modern conceptions of statehood and sovereignty.[57]

This position proved sufficiently compelling to carry the day, with the Allies agreeing to do away with extraterritorial jurisdiction. However, as if to confirm that representatives of 'semi-civilized' states relied upon common patterns of argumentation, delegates from Japan—a state that had shed the moniker of 'semi-civilization' and acquired great-power status after sloughing off its unequal treaties in the 1890s—voiced discomfort at the move, explaining that it had taken decades for Japan to enact legal reforms of the sort required to justify the abolition of extra-territoriality.[58] Even so, other states followed suit in the years to come, with Siam's experience during the 1920s demonstrating that *rebus* arguments tended to enjoy particular traction when linked to participation in multilateral organizations like the League of Nations.[59] If the origins of extraterritoriality owed much to the Ottoman Empire, so too did the arguments through which it was to be abolished—a point well appreciated by intrepid jurists throughout the semi-periphery.[60]

5 CONCLUSION

That the Ottoman Empire was ostensibly incapable of assimilation into European 'civilization' but was clearly able and willing to enter into legal relations with 'civilized' states always presented European and American international lawyers with a number of theoretical challenges. On the one hand, it seemed necessary, as a matter

---

[56] Ibid 478–9.   [57] Ibid.

[58] 'Minutes of the Commission on the Régime of Foreigners, 2 December 1922' in *Lausanne Conference* (n 55) 470. Ironically, Ottoman intellectuals had long followed developments in Japan, being impressed by its rapid modernization and success in war against Russia: C Aydın, *The Politics of Anti-Westernism in Asia: Visions of World Order in Pan-Islamic and Pan-Asian Thought* (Columbia University Press New York 2007) ch 4.

[59] S Hell, *Siam and the League of Nations: Modernisation, Sovereignty and Multilateral Diplomacy, 1920–1940* (River Books Bangkok 2010) especially at 35–7, 42–3, and 240.

[60] See eg Y Tchen, *De la disparition de la juridiction consulaire dans certains pays d'Orient* (Les presses modernes Paris 1931) vol 1, at 9–22 and 171–2 (emphasizing the Ottoman origins of consular jurisdiction and noting that states subject to capitulatory systems had long mounted similar arguments).

of legal logic no less than political prudence, to accord a measure of legal personality to any entity with which a treaty, or treaty-like arrangement, had been struck. Failure to do so would cast doubt on the validity or enforceability of the instrument in question, corroborating fears that the capitulations were at best informal arrangements, the sultan's promise being 'by no means an absolute or unqualified one'.[61] It would also amount to an overt repudiation of sovereign equality—a move that would prove difficult given the vehemence with which Ottoman officials underscored their state's independence.

On the other hand, Western jurists were frequently committed to the proposition that states could and should be distinguished along 'civilizational' lines—an express principle, or at least default presumption, in many legal treatises of the period, particularly from the mid-nineteenth century onwards. As such, they often sought to restrict the type and degree of recognition that was to be extended to semi-peripheral states like Turkey. This had significant implications for treaty-making. States believed to merit no more than what Lorimer termed 'partial political recognition' were often deemed incapable of conducting diplomatic intercourse in accordance with intra-European norms, and this, in turn, suggested that instruments somewhat different from intra-European treaties would be most appropriate under such circumstances.[62] Balancing these two commitments was always a delicate matter, and made for a considerable degree of inconsistency.[63]

It would be misleading to suggest that the Ottoman capitulatory regime constitutes the universal 'paradigm' of extraterritoriality, so as to assign a secondary or derivative status to the capitulatory-style systems that were installed in China, Japan, and elsewhere. Yet, it would be difficult to deny that it was in great part through commercial and diplomatic relations with the Ottoman Empire that extraterritoriality came to acquire the status of a norm for states that were thought to fall somewhat short of the 'standard of civilization'. For all their differences, both textual and contextual, the Ottoman capitulations and the 'unequal treaties' into which China, Japan, and other states entered shared a host of important features, chief among them the institution of complex schemes of extraterritorial consular jurisdiction, the attempt to justify the conservation and augmentation of such jurisdiction on the ground that indigenous laws were inapplicable to Western subjects, and close collaboration with local merchant classes which often came to be viewed with suspicion and resentment. In this sense, the Ottoman Empire offers a glimpse into the processes through which a select group of states underwent transformation in pursuit of the legal 'modernity' of national statehood, with all the accompanying promises of economic liberation and political independence.

---

[61] T Baty, *The Canons of International Law* (J Murray London 1930) at 376.
[62] *Institutes of the Law of Nations* (n 38) 101–2.
[63] Cf 'What Happened to Unequal Treaties?' (n 10) 352ff.

CHAPTER 7

....

CHINA IN THE AGE
OF THE WORLD PICTURE

....

TEEMU RUSKOLA*

1 INTRODUCTION

....

SINCE the end of the Cold War and the roughly contemporaneous massacre by the Chinese government of its own citizens on Tiananmen Square in Beijing on the night of 4 June 1989, China has come to be seen as the leading human rights violator in the East.[1] Its trade practices have become an object of ever-more intense inquiry in the field of international economic law as well, especially since its accession to the World Trade Organization in 2001. But even though China looms large today in the minds of international lawyers as a significant problem that demands their full attention, it is rarely, if ever, approached as a *theoretical* question that might have more general implications. Most scholars approach the topic from the vantage point of the North Atlantic, with China figuring at best as an example—or,

* I would like to thank the editors and Martin Clark for their expert guidance. The chapter was completed while I was a member at the Institute for Advanced Study in Princeton, NJ, supported by a fellowship from the American Council of Learned Societies. I am grateful to both IAS and ACLS. Marcia Tucker of the IAS Historical Studies-Social Science Library provided invaluable assistance. I have received comments on earlier drafts from several individuals. I am especially grateful to David Eng, Nicola di Cosmo, Martti Koskenniemi, and Joan Scott.

[1] On the history and politics of China's troubled relationship to law, see T Ruskola, *Legal Orientalism: China, the United States, and Modern Law* (Harvard University Press Cambridge MA 2013).

more frequently, a counter-example—that illustrates a more central point about the history and character of the international legal order.

This chapter insists on placing China at the centre of international legal theory. Stated most broadly, it asks: How did the multiethnic Qing Empire (1644–1911) on the eastern edge of the Eurasian landmass become 'China', a sovereign nation-state in a world of other, formally equal nation-states? In framing the question, this chapter approaches international law as a foundational aspect of the political ontology of the modern world—one that depends on and sustains a particular metaphysical conception of the world, with associated notions of political time and space. In this light, I analyze the law of nations at its origin as the constitution of Europe: a set of constitutive norms that governed the relationship among the so-called 'Family of Nations', sometimes characterized as the *ius publicum Europaeum*, or the public law of Europe.[2] As this historically specific legal order has become globalized by means of colonialism, it has become effectively the constitution of the world.

Where is China in the world made by modern international law? The Eurocentrism of mainstream scholarship aside, there is a growing literature on the colonial origins of international law. Much of it is concerned with the juridical implications of the 'discovery' of the New World.[3] While the discipline conventionally dates the birth of modern international law from the Peace of Westphalia in 1648, signalling the end of religious civil wars in Europe, the new critical literature views 1492 as a foundational moment. As Carl Schmitt (albeit an older critic from the right) states evocatively in *The* Nomos *of the Earth*, a contemporary analogue to the cosmographic shock entailed by Europe's collision with the Americas would be discovering another planet with life.[4] In a truly unprecedented encounter, how *should* we organize our relationship legally with newly discovered worlds and beings? The answers to the profound questions posed by the New World took centuries to emerge—indeed, they are still not settled, as the status of indigenous peoples remains contested—but what grew out of this colonial episode was modern international law, a transnational political and cultural form that imagines and organizes differences among peoples in a particular way.

A focus on the Americas in this literature is obviously not unwarranted, yet the implications of the history of the New World cannot be extended globally without modification. The chief legal justifications for European domination that emerged from the collision with the Americas worked reasonably well in other places so

---

[2] The phrase *ius publicum Europaeum* dates back to at least the seventeenth century, although today it is probably best known from Carl Schmitt's appropriation of the term. See C Schmitt, *The* Nomos *of the Earth in the International Law of the* Jus Publicum Europaeum (GL Ulmen trans) (Telos Press New York 2003 [1950]).

[3] Most notably A Anghie, *Imperialism, Sovereignty and the Making of International Law* (CUP Cambridge 2005). See also LC Green and OP Dickason, *The Law of Nations and the New World* (University of Alberta Press Edmonton 1993).

[4] *The* Nomos *of the Earth* (n 2) 39.

long as Europeans were dealing with peoples they could characterize to their own satisfaction as 'barbarians' or 'savages' (say, the inhabitants of Africa) or peoples whose political existence could be denied altogether (say, the indigenous peoples of Australia whose land was deemed uninhabited *terra nullius*). Yet ancient Oriental civilizations such as China were more difficult to dismiss. Chinese culture was evidently very different from Europe's, but it had all the markers of a 'high' civilization even as defined by Europeans themselves, thus causing a catachresis in crude binaries of civilized-versus-savage and sovereign-versus-colonizable. If indeed 'in the beginning all the world was America', as John Locke famously observed, and the end goal of civilization was for all the world to become Europe, China occupied an unstable middle ground that resisted assimilation into either 'America' or 'Europe'.[5]

The Orient (to avoid anachronistic use of the term 'Asia') therefore demands a theoretical account of its own, no less than America, and so does China as the dominant Oriental civilization on the eastern end of Eurasia. Importantly, with the significant exception of Hong Kong, China was in fact never colonized formally. With the aid of postcolonial theory, this *non-occurrence* must be analysed as a major *event* in the development of international law. How and why was China not-colonized? To account for China fully, we must ultimately consider its place in the world as a matter of both the politics of sovereignty and the geopolitics of knowledge.

In the remainder of this chapter I contrast the now global international law of European origin with the historically Confucian world of East Asia, structured around Chinese cultural and political hegemony. Both traditions pretended to universality while each in fact embodied a particular set of imperial norms—Eurocentric in one case, Sinocentric in the other. Set against this comparative frame, the chapter considers a few key episodes in the historic encounter between these two imperial formations. Throughout, I analyse the Sino-Western encounter not as a clash of civilizations in geographic space and in historical time, but as the collision of *different conceptions* of space and time. What was at stake in that epistemological collision was the constitution of the international legal order and, ultimately, the modern world.

2 LAW IN THE AGE OF THE WORLD PICTURE

International lawyers' disinterest in China as a theoretical problem in its own right reflects in part a disciplinary division of labour between international law and

---

[5] J Locke, *Two Treatises of Government* (P Laslett ed) (revised edn CUP Cambridge 1988 [1690]) bk 2, ch 5, s 49. For a more extensive analysis of China as a 'queer' subject of international law, see T Ruskola, 'Raping Like a State' (2010) 57 *UCLA Law Review* 1477–536.

comparative law. At least according to some conventional wisdom, international lawyers tend to focus on the universal and the supranational, while comparativists prefer to focus on the particular and the local.[6] From that perspective, providing a theoretical and analytic examination of China's history and constitution belongs in the province of comparative law. Nevertheless, this chapter maintains that a truly comparative investigation of China must account for it also in terms of international law: it must consider *China itself* as a legal subject on the international stage. From the opposite point of view, no examination of China's international legal status is intelligible on its own terms, without the mediation of a comparative analysis.

Trained as a comparativist and hence a relative latecomer to international law, I came to appreciate the connection between the two fields by way of a somewhat unexpected analogy, upon reading Douglas Crimp's *On the Museum's Ruins*.[7] Analysing his career trajectory as an art critic, Crimp observes that his scholarly focus has moved from studying discrete works of art to investigating the ways in which museums are organized to display the objects they house, thereby constituting their institutional frame. The relationship between international law and comparative law is in significant ways not unlike that between museums and their collections. Just as the museum is a kind of representational and institutional matrix that constitutes certain objects *as art*, the global inter-state legal order constitutes certain communities *as states*. Indeed, much as art critics are called upon to critique the objects inside museums, comparativists are called upon to examine the national legal systems that international law frames for their study.

As the analogy suggests, a conventional opposition between the study of 'universal' international law and the analysis of 'particular' national legal systems is untenable. In a perhaps obvious but no less profound sense, international law and comparative law constitute each other's condition of possibility. Universal norms can never be considered only in the abstract: they must always be ultimately translated into and understood in the particular idiom of some local actors somewhere on Earth. Without the mediation of comparative law, international law would be literally unintelligible. At the same time, comparative lawyers' descriptions of the particular and the local are, by definition, exercises of translation, and translatability in turn assumes the possibility of communication across local differences. Both conceptually as well as practically, the universal and particular form part of a single dialectic.

---

[6] For a critical analysis of this disciplinary difference, see D Kennedy, 'The Disciplines of International Law and Policy' (1999) 12 *Leiden Journal of International Law* 9–133. Evidently comparative legal study has a long and varied history. What I am referring to here is a particular, albeit dominant, nationalist tradition that dates to the late nineteenth century.

[7] D Crimp, *On the Museum's Ruins* (MIT Press Cambridge MA 1993).

In an important sense, international law and comparative law are thus part of a joint cultural, political, and epistemological project that has transformed the entire planet into a juridical formation consisting of nation-states. This enterprise nationalizes and ultimately 'privatizes' culture by consigning it to the domestic sphere of each state while leaving international law in an ostensibly acultural or supracultural space. Within this schema, comparative law and international law are fully in cooperation in displacing what are often political differences onto the site of culture. Moreover, in this dialectic of universality and particularity, there is little, if any, room for radical political or cultural difference—the kind of difference that is not readily recouped within a larger state-based logic. This international/comparative law complex is in fact part of a style of political and conceptual organization that Timothy Mitchell has called, in a different context, 'The World as an Exhibition': the world as a kind of art gallery—or a living museum.[8] International law provides the structure for displaying the pictures at this global exhibition, where comparativists (and other area studies experts) specialize in curating individual pieces of art within prefabricated national frames.[9]

This is evidently a highly particular way of conceptualizing our telluric existence. In an essay by the same title, Martin Heidegger characterizes modernity as 'The Age of the World Picture'.[10] According to Heidegger, modernity is defined by two key events: the emergence of 'man' as subject and the emergence of the 'world' as object. The simultaneous subjectification of the modern individual and objectification of the world splinters the primordial connection between the two. There is a separate world 'out there' to which man subsequently has a relationship, rather than always already being in the world and intended toward it (as Heidegger elaborates further in *Being and Time*). This view is clearly distinct from such earlier cosmological schemata as the notion of a Great Chain of Being, for example—a metaphor that links both man and the world ontologically with God.

Yet Heidegger does not simply claim that an older worldview changes into a new one. What distinguishes the modern 'world picture' (*Weltbild*) is the fact that the world itself becomes something that can be conceived and grasped *as a picture*. Moreover, Heidegger's observation is not only philosophical but implies a political element as well. 'The fundamental event of modernity is the *conquest* of the world as picture', he states.[11] The idea of conquest is more than an idle metaphor insofar as modernity was accompanied—indeed constituted—by the West's colonial conquest of the rest of the world. That conquest in turn was justified and ratified by the

---

[8] T Mitchell, 'The World as Exhibition' (1989) 31 *Comparative Studies in Society and History* 217–30.

[9] The argument here draws on T Ruskola, 'Where Is Asia? When Is Asia? Theorizing Comparative Law and International Law' (2010) 44 *UC Davis Law Review* 879–96.

[10] M Heidegger, 'The Age of the World Picture' in *The Question Concerning Technology and Other Essays* (W Lovitt trans) (Garland Publishing New York 1977 [1938]) 115–54.

[11] Ibid 134 (emphasis added).

emerging regime of modern international law. The world picture is thus also a legal picture—a portrait of a legal world.

Historically, it is hardly a coincidence that both international law and comparative law became professionalized in their modern form in the late nineteenth century, at the height of Western imperialism. This era was also the period of World Fairs and of the institutionalization of the modern museum, as well as that of the zoo. Despite their differences, as cultural forms all these institutions followed a similar logic. They displayed diversity and difference in an objectified, inert form for the visual enjoyment of Western viewers, and they did so by bringing the world to the West.[12]

In a truly global view, international law is thus best thought of not merely as a body of rules governing inter-state relations but as a grid of intelligibility that makes the modern world itself possible. In Heideggerian terminology, international law is a discourse of *worlding*. The modern system of sovereign nation-states both depends upon and provides the ground for objective cartographic depictions of the world—in contrast, say, to medieval cosmographic maps, which sought to depict not only the visible world of the *hic et nunc* but worlds within worlds, multiple incommensurable realms of time and space.

Viewed from the perspective of the modern world picture, the Sino-Western historical encounter becomes visible as a clash between different worldviews, different kinds of political and legal cosmologies—not merely an encounter in space and time, but an encounter between different kinds of space and time, underwriting distinctive notions of sovereignty. In the following sections, I will seek to avoid the analytically questionable division of labour between comparative law and international law—part of a larger regime of organization of knowledge that separates (particular) 'area studies' from the (universal) 'disciplines'—by approaching China's place in the world through the lens of what might be called 'comparative international law'.[13] Rather than assuming a single, universal international law, I will analyse two distinctive normative inter-state orders and study them in relation to one another.

Despite the formal symmetry of this comparative framework, it bears noting the obvious: it is the European tradition of inter-state relations that governs the world in which we live. Therefore the comparison below focuses on it first, before turning to China. Stated differently, insofar as this chapter is a map of China's place in law's world, its Eurocentric structure reflects the subject matter it investigates.

---

[12] See eg T Bennett, *The Birth of the Museum: History, Theory, Politics* (Routledge London 1995); RW Rydell, *All the World's a Fair* (University of Chicago Press Chicago 1984); N Rothfels, *Savages and Beasts: The Birth of the Modern Zoo* (Johns Hopkins University Press Baltimore 2002).

[13] It is notable that both international lawyers and comparative lawyers have called for a rearrangement of the two disciplines. See, respectively, M Koskenniemi, 'The Case for Comparative International Law' (2009) 20 *Finnish Yearbook of International Law* 1–8 and BN Mamlyuk and U Mattei, 'Comparative International Law' (2011) 36 *Brooklyn Journal of International Law* 385–452.

3 EUROCENTRIC SOVEREIGNTY

Beginning, then, with the European tradition of international law, what are the forms of time and space in which it dwells? As Heidegger observes in his essay on 'The Age of the World Picture', according to Newtonian metaphysics nature is a self-contained system of units of mass that are in motion. Their motion takes place in time and space. In nature, every point in time is equal to every other, just as every point in space is equal to all others.[14]

In general terms, modern conceptions of political time and space reflect these naturalistic notions. Benedict Anderson analyses famously the transition from the eschatological time of religion to the secular time of history.[15] Borrowing from Walter Benjamin, he describes secular time as homogeneous and empty, marked by the clock and the calendar. It corresponds to what Heidegger calls 'the vulgar interpretation of time': time as an infinite, irreversible succession of 'pure nows' constantly passing away.[16] Henry Ford characterized this notion perhaps most memorably: 'History is just one damn thing after another'.[17] In this conception, just as individual organisms move calendrically through time, so nations too move steadily down a never-ending stream of history. In principle, all nations—young as well as old—enjoy the same rights and must obey the same duties.

Drawing on Anderson, we may characterize law's space in analogous terms: it too is abstract, empty, and homogeneous. To be sure, the surface of the earth is crosscut by politically determined borders, but within its territory each state claims exclusive jurisdiction. Whether one is occupying a square inch of snow in the middle of an uninhabited expanse along the United States–Canadian border in North Dakota or standing on the steps of the Capitol in Washington, DC, legally one is just as much in the United States of America. Cartographic representations of the world confirm this visually. On political maps, different countries may be marked by different colours, but all states are coloured uniformly monochrome, never bleeding into one another.[18]

These objectified views of time and space are key universalizing categories of the modern world. Together, they provide the home of the privileged subject that

[14] 'Age of the World Picture' (n 10) 61.

[15] B Anderson, *Imagined Communities: Reflections on the Origins and Spread of Nationalism* (revised edn Verso London 1991) at 23–5.

[16] M Heidegger, *Being and Time* (J Stambaugh trans) (State University of New York Press Albany 1996 [1953]) at 390–1.

[17] For an attribution of the statement to Ford, see A Ryan, *On Politics: A History of Political Thought* (Liveright New York 2012).

[18] In Richard Ford's terms, this reflects a modern 'synthetic' (in contrast to 'organic') notion of jurisdictional space. RT Ford, 'Law's Territory (A History of Jurisdiction)' (1999) 97 *Michigan Law Review* 843–930.

occupies it, the individual, whose freedom in turn has become the chief, even sole, universal value to have emerged in the wake of the Death of God and the birth of liberalism. In this particular political soteriology the state exists ultimately to establish and protect individual rights that serve to guarantee personal freedom. Modern standardized conceptions of space and time thus create not only equivalences across histories and territories—thereby facilitating exchange and the spread of capitalist economic relations throughout the planet—but they also support the globalization of equally standardized and homogeneous conceptions of individual subjectivity and state-based sovereignty. Indeed, both the individual and the state take an essentially isomorphic legal form: the state's legal subjectivity is premised on the fiction that it, too, is a person ('an international legal person'), and legal relations among states are modelled on those that govern interactions among individuals in their private capacity (the so-called private law analogy of international law). In this view, public international law is a purely formal framework set up by sovereign states to regulate themselves, much like the modern state justifies itself on the fiction of a social contract, as a system of self-government by free individuals.[19]

4 SINOCENTRIC SOVEREIGNTY

If such is the basic legal architecture of the modern world, what, finally, are some of the historic conceptions of political space and time by which China has organized its relations with the outside world?

In the standard US and European historiography, the encounter between China and the West that culminated in the Opium War (1839–42) is depicted as a tragic cultural 'misunderstanding' by the Chinese.[20] According to this view, East Asian diplomacy was structured historically in a ritual hierarchy that centred on China, with lesser states paying symbolic and material tribute to the proverbial 'Middle Kingdom'. (Rendered literally, the term we translate as 'China'—*Zhongguo* 中國— means 'the central state'.) In this imperial cosmology, there was only one true sovereign, the Son of Heaven, whose dominion consisted of 'All Under Heaven' (*Tianxia* 天下). To be sure, he was fully aware of the existence of lesser rulers

[19] For a classic elaboration, see H Lauterpacht, *Private Law Sources and Analogies of International Law (with Special Reference to International Arbitration)* (Longmans, Green & Co London 1926).

[20] For representative accounts, see eg JK Fairbank, *The Great Chinese Revolution 1800–1985* (Harper & Row New York 1986) and A Peyrefitte, *L'Empire immobile, ou le choc des mondes* (Fayard Paris 1989).

around him, such as the monarchs of Korea and Vietnam. However, in addressing them he routinely referred to them in patronizing terms as his younger brothers or cousins. Essentially because of its cultural chauvinism, China was unable to appreciate the norm of sovereign equality and adjust voluntarily to the liberal free trade regime among modern states under the aegis of international law. In this conventional telling, the Opium War may have been tragic but it was inevitable because of China's refusal to submit to modernity.

There is an entire cottage industry of Cold War studies of a so-called 'Chinese world order'.[21] Collectively, they depict a regional state system in which China was indeed in the middle, or at least purported to be. In the imperial ideology that supported that order, political space was graduated and uneven, radiating from a centre and decreasing toward peripheries. Its unevenness reflected the varying capacity of 'barbarians' at China's edges to become 'civilized' (ie, Sinicized): insofar as they were capable of civilization, they too could be embraced within the universal sovereignty of the Middle Kingdom. Such deference to the norms of Chinese civilization was precisely what provided external legitimacy to the Confucian polities of Korea and Vietnam, for example.[22]

This imperial conception of political space as graduated, uneven, and discontinuous—rather than abstract, empty, and homogeneous—was matched by a profoundly teleological notion of time that had no room for isomorphic nation-states moving in tandem along an endless highway of history. In the orthodox Confucian view, the arc of history bends backward, toward a long-lost Golden Age that Confucius himself sought to recover on the basis of the classic works of Chinese antiquity. A ruler's task was to reverse the decay caused by time and return the world to the state of harmony of a bygone era when peace and virtue reigned.[23]

In the end, modern students of the Chinese world order view Sinocentrism as a cultural delusion at best, or else a cynical justification for naked imperial ambition. When China would not yield before the universal values of free trade (by refusing to expand its trade with Europeans beyond the city of Canton) and sovereign equality (by insisting that European diplomatic envoys perform the ritual kowtow that was required of all tributaries appearing before the Qing emperor), a clash became inevitable. China was finally 'opened' for greater trade access in the Opium War. The war concluded with the Treaty of Nanjing (1842), which

---

[21] The seminal work is the edited volume by JK Fairbank, *The Chinese World Order: Traditional China's Foreign Relations* (Harvard University Press Cambridge MA 1968), elaborated on by an entire generation of Fairbank's students.

[22] On Chinese conceptions of political and cultural space, see generally the chapters in Part One of J Harley and D Woodward (eds), *Cartography in the Traditional East Asian and Southeast Asian Societies* (University of Chicago Press Chicago 1994).

[23] On Chinese conceptions of political and historical time, see generally J Huang and J Henderson, *Notions of Time in Chinese Historical Thinking* (Chinese University of Hong Kong Press Hong Kong 2006).

also marked the beginning of China's slow integration into the Euro-American regime of international law. Notably, the British were not satisfied with trade access alone but insisted on the right of extraterritorial jurisdiction as well, justified by the theory that Chinese law was too 'arbitrary' and 'despotic' to be applicable to Anglo-Saxons.[24]

Drawing on recent critiques of the conventional narrative, it seems more fruitful to analyse this history as a collision between two different imperial formations, with distinctive conceptions of political space and time: Western inter-state law based on a Eurocentric worldview, on the one hand, and East Asian tributary ritual based on a Sinocentric worldview, on the other.[25] Such a reframing allows us to consider the encounter between two spatio-temporal orders in terms of comparative international law as well, for it provides an occasion to re-interpret the regime of Sinocentric tributary ritual as a kind of East Asian 'inter-state law' and nineteenth-century international law as a kind of 'political ritual'. Both regimes classified and organized states and peoples according to civilizational criteria, albeit with distinctive discursive justifications—Confucian and liberal, broadly construed.

From this comparative perspective, let us consider again China's historic exclusion from full membership in the 'Family of Nations'. This exclusion was justified in part by China's refusal to observe European rituals of formal equality, such as protocols for receiving diplomatic representatives (and insisting on its own diplomatic practices, including the kowtow). Rather than analogizing states to abstract individuals, China's diplomatic practices with its neighbours were ideally patterned on the model of Confucian kinship relations: *zhong-wai yi-jia* 中外一家 ('the central and outer [states] all form one family'). Ironically, because of an ideological preference for organizing inter-state relations on the basis of a kind of 'family law analogy', rather than one grounded in private law, China was found ineligible for membership in the (other) Family of Nations. By the mid-1800s, China's problem was evidently not that it was guilty of a primitive category mistake—conflating politics and family—but simply belonging to the *wrong* political family. Rather than liberal and chauvinist, the worldviews that clashed were Eurocentric and Sinocentric, each based on its own political and cosmological outlook.

Importantly, what I have described thus far are certain *ideologies* of time and space. They were part of an idealized and self-congratulatory worldview. The so-called tributary system, structured around ritual exchange that is said to have formed its core, was in reality far from systematic, despite the structural-functionalist

---

[24] On the history of extraterritorial jurisdiction in China, see Ruskola (n 1).

[25] This critical reframing draws, most notably, on J Hevia, *Cherishing Men from Afar: Qing Guest Ritual and the Macartney Embassy of 1793* (Duke University Press Durham 1995) and L Liu, *The Clash of Empires: The Invention of China in Modern World Making* (Harvard University Press Cambridge MA 2004).

connotations of the designation.[26] It represented only one—albeit rhetorically privileged—element in a larger political and symbolic order that was highly plural in its constitution.[27] For example, outside their conventional self-representations, Qing emperors presented themselves to Tibetans as Buddhist *cakravartins* ('wheel-turning kings'). A large repertoire of multiethnic political strategies, ranging from orthodox Confucianism to Manchu shamanism, allowed multiple forms of sovereignty to be encompassed within the empire, housing not only Buddhist Tibetans but also numerous indigenous peoples in the southern borderlands, Mongols and Turkic Uighurs in Central Asia, and so on. Equally significantly, numerous times over the course of its history the imperial state entered into treaties with its neighbours on the basis of political equality as well, and in certain cases it even acknowledged formally their superiority.[28]

Similar qualifications apply to the above outline of Western international law and its conceptions of sovereignty. Historically law's conception of time in the West has hardly been empty and homogeneous. Rather, it has been one of progress, whether expressly or implicitly.[29] As every colonist knows, not every point in time is in fact as good as any other: today is better than yesterday. Historically, insofar as some peoples still lived 'in yesterday', they obviously could not enjoy equality with Europe—at least not today. In this Eurocentric view of history, China has often stood for the epitome of Asiatic stagnation, waiting perpetually 'at the threshold of World's History', to borrow Hegel's phrase.[30] Likewise, despite its formally neutral conception of political space, historically international law too has been structured around a centre—Europe—and the source of its sovereignty has been *its* civilization.[31]

[26] While there are classical Chinese terms that can be usefully translated as 'tribute' (for example *gong* 貢), the term 'tributary system' itself is not a Chinese one. Rather, it refers to an analytic framework constructed by Western scholars. Significantly, this framework is congruent with the socialist periodization of pre-1911 China as 'feudal', and it plays a major role in much of PRC scholarship on international legal history as well. See eg Wang T 王铁崖, 'Zhongguo yu Guojifa: Lishi yu Xiandai 中国国际法: 历史与现代 [China and International Law: Historical and Contemporary Perspectives]' [1991] *Zhongguo Guojifa Niankan* 中国国际法年刊 [China Yearbook of International Law] 1–115.

[27] This is one the key insights in the growing body of critical scholarship by new Qing historians. See eg PK Crossley, *A Translucent Mirror: History and Identity in Qing Imperial Ideology* (University of California Press Berkeley 1999); MC Elliott, *The Manchu Way: The Eight Banners and Ethnic Identity in Late Imperial China* (Stanford University Press Stanford 2001); JA Millward, *Beyond the Pass: Economy, Ethnicity and Empire in Qing Xinjiang, 1759–1864* (Stanford University Press Stanford 1998); ES Rawski, *The Last Emperors: A Social History of Qing Imperial Institutions* (University of California Press Berkeley 1998).

[28] See eg M Rossabi (ed), *China Among Equals* (University of California Press Berkeley 1983).

[29] See generally RA Miller and RM Bratspies (eds), *Progress in International Law* (Martinus Nijhoff Leiden 2008); T Skouteris, *The Notion of Progress in International Law Discourse* (TMC Asser Press The Hague 2010).

[30] GWF Hegel, *The Philosophy of History* (J Sibree trans) (Dover New York 1956 [1837]) at 99.

[31] See eg M Koskenniemi, *The Gentle Civilizer of Nations: The Rise and Fall of International Law 1870–1960* (CUP Cambridge 2001) ch 2.

If there was a fundamental 'misunderstanding' by the Chinese, then, it was not that they were constitutionally incapable of comprehending the idea of formal equality—they simply declined that idea as inapplicable to diplomacy—but rather their refusal to recognize that it was *Europe*, not China, that was the true centre of civilization, and hence the true source of sovereignty as well.

5 THE DISENCHANTMENT OF SINOCENTRIC SOVEREIGNTY

Through the twinned processes of imperialism and globalization, international law has delegitimated competing conceptions of political time and space, as it has brought the extra-European peoples into 'world history' (the time of Europe) and into the 'world system' (a global spatial ordering with Europe at its centre).[32] China too has been inscribed in the modern world picture, one member among others in a system of nation-states organized under the aegis of international law. In the process it has secularized its imperial past on the basis of equivalence with other national histories. It no longer insists on being the Middle Kingdom, but instead has taken its seat in the United Nations, next to other member states. (There is hardly a better illustration of 'the world as an exhibition' than the phalanx of colourful flags of identical size waving along First Avenue in New York, outside the General Assembly of the United Nations.) But just how did the cosmologically unique Middle Kingdom become an 'international legal person' with the proper name 'China'? That is, what are some of the concrete ways in which international law has proceeded as a pedagogical project, interpellating China and the rest of the world into the spatio-temporal project of modernity? Below I offer a few episodes by way of illustration.

In the historiography of Sino-British diplomatic relations, no event plays a larger symbolic role than the kowtow controversy surrounding Lord Macartney's 1793 embassy to China—the first British diplomatic mission to succeed in reaching Beijing and obtaining an audience with the Son of Heaven.[33] Charged by King George III

---

[32] For classic analyses of the uneven organization of global time and space, see ER Wolf, *Europe and the People without History* (University of California Press Berkeley 1982) and I Wallerstein, *World-Systems Analysis* (Duke University Press Durham 2004).

[33] For a first-hand account by Macartney himself, see G Macartney, *An Embassy to China, Being the Journal Kept by Lord Macartney During His Embassy to the Emperor Ch'ien-lung 1793–1794* (JL Cranmer-Byng ed) (Longmans London 1962).

with negotiating a trade treaty and thereby placing the relationship between the two countries on a proper legal basis, Macartney was expected by Chinese officials to follow the ordinary protocol upon presentation to the Qing emperor, including performing a series of ritual prostrations. The vast Euro-American literature on the embassy focuses largely on the extended negotiations over the scandal of sovereign equality that this demand entailed, with Macartney insisting that he could not show greater deference to an Oriental monarch than his own, before whom he only kneeled.

Rather than the famous kowtow controversy, I focus here on a less examined aspect of the ultimately unsuccessful embassy. When Macartney arrived in China, he carried with him numerous gifts which were calculated to humble the haughty Chinese sovereign and to showcase commodities the British hoped to introduce to the Chinese market. Alas, the emperor was not impressed. In keeping with tributary logic, he treated the gifts as acknowledgements of his ultimate rulership over All Under Heaven. In his famously condescending reply to George III, the Qianlong emperor stated flatly, 'we have never valued ingenious articles, nor do we have the slightest need of your Country's manufactures'.[34]

Although Macartney's offerings did not produce immediate diplomatic or commercial results, it is important to take note of the larger political symbolism of a number of gifts that were especially highlighted upon their presentation. In his diary, Macartney observed that in preparing for the imperial audience, Sir George Staunton—the secretary of the mission—chose specifically to wear a gown decorated with the insignia for his honorary law degree from Oxford, thus indicating that their mission was a distinctly *legal* one.[35] As to the gifts themselves, a model warship occupied pride of place among them. That this less than tactful present was meant to intimidate is obvious. What is notable is the ship's name, *Sovereignty*, evidently suggesting to the emperor that the Mandate of Heaven was not necessarily the sole, or most effective, source of sovereignty, and that warships too enjoyed a special legal status in inter-state relations.[36]

Equally significantly, Macartney took great delight in presenting to the emperor several globes, with further pedagogical and geopolitical implications: in these material representations of the earth, the putative Middle Kingdom was clearly not in the centre in any meaningful sense. Other gifts provided an even more extensive education in the Western scientific worldview. They included a number of telescopes, allowing one to glimpse the cosmos, and even an entire planetarium made in Germany, designated by the manufacturer literally as a *Weltmaschine*—'a

[34] JD Spence, *The Search for Modern China* (WW Norton New York 1990) at 122.
[35] *An Embassy to China* (n 33) 67–8.   [36] *Cherishing Men from Afar* (n 25) 178.

world machine'.[37] Finally, in addition to offering representations of terrestrial as well as cosmic space, Macartney presented the emperor with the gift of time, in the form of numerous clocks. Although the ornate timepieces varied in size, from the minute to the huge, they all measured the passage of homogeneous empty time according to standardized Western units. Collectively, these presents reflected in a strikingly literal way fundamental assumptions about the nature of law, sovereignty, space, and time, and the normative conception of the world to which they give rise.

The British were not alone in wishing to educate China about the world and its place in it. Consider WAP Martin, the American protestant missionary who directed, under official Chinese supervision, the first Chinese translation of a full-length international law text—the sixth edition of the *Elements of International Law* by Henry Wheaton, a leading mid-nineteenth century treatise by a former US diplomat and reporter of the US Supreme Court.[38] Wheaton's rather anodyne title was rendered into Chinese as *Wanguo Gongfa* 萬國工法, or 'The Public Law of the Myriad States'.[39] The Chinese version was in fact loosely paraphrastic rather than a direct translation. Apart from taking various liberties in rendering the bulk of Wheaton's text, Martin made two critical additions. First, he wrote an introduction summarizing the history of the law of nations and European political history more generally, thereby situating his subject matter squarely in the historical time of Europe. Second, he introduced a vital visual element that likewise did not exist in the original. That is, he inserted on the very first page of his translation a map of the Western and Eastern hemispheres laid next to each other (see Figure 7.1). Again, this conveyed unmistakably that this was the worldview—literally 'the world picture'—that supported the project of international law.

Evidently neither Macartney nor Martin alone can be said to have 'introduced' international law into China. However, they can be usefully analysed as two discrete episodes in a much longer and diffuse process, military as well as socio-cultural, that ultimately resulted in the disenchantment of China's imperial sovereignty.

---

[37] Ibid 77 and M Berg, 'Britain, Industry and Perceptions of China: Matthew Boulton, "Useful Knowledge" and the Macartney Embassy to China 1792–94' (2006) 1 *Journal of Global History* 279–88. To be sure, the planetarium, originally made by a German pietist priest, embodied religious elements as well, even after it had been modified by English artisans in London: in addition to being an astronomical model, it incorporated a clock set to display the coming of the apocalypse. S Schaffer, 'Instruments as cargo in the China trade,' *History of Science* (2006) 44: 217.

[38] H Wheaton, *Elements of International Law* (WB Lawrence ed) (6th edn Little Brown Boston 1855 [1836]).

[39] H Wheaton, *Wanguo Gongfa* 萬國工法 (WAP Martin trans) (Tongwenguan Beijing 1864). For background and a critical analysis of the translation, see *The Clash of Empires* (n 25) 108–39.

西半球

地球全圖

葡牙荷蘭意大里土耳其等國、一曰亞非利加、内有
埃及巴巴里等國、在西
半球者、一曰北亞美利
加、内有美利堅墨西哥
等國、一曰南亞美利加
内有巴西秘魯智利等
國、五洲之外、汪洋大海、
島嶼甚夥、然天下邦國、
雖以萬計、而人民實本
於一脈、惟一大主宰造其端、佑其生理其事焉、

東半球

地球全圖

地之為物也、體圓如球、直徑約三萬里、周圍九萬里
有奇、其運行也、旋轉如
輪、一轉為一晝夜、環日
一周、即為一年、内分東
西兩半球、其陸地分五
大洲、在東半球者、一曰
亞細亞、内有中華日本
緬甸印度西藏波斯猶
太等國、一曰歐羅巴内
有英吉利法郎西俄羅斯奧地利普魯斯西班牙葡

Figure 7.1

6 CHINA IN BIBLICAL TIME AND SPACE

This leaves us with a rather bleak view of law's world and China's place in it. If international law is in fact a key element of the political ontology of the modern world, was the colonization of Chinese conceptions of space and time inevitable? Stated differently, is international law necessarily imperial in its constitution?

By way of contrast to the collisions that took place in the eighteenth and nineteenth centuries, let us go further back in time, to the arrival of Jesuit missionaries in China in the late sixteenth and early seventeenth centuries. This was the first meaningful encounter between China and Europe. It also took place at a point of transition in Western political ontology, before the modern separation of religious and secular notions of sovereignty. In the waning days of the medieval worldview (to generalize grossly) the Pope still claimed jurisdiction over heathens everywhere. In the biblical worldview, God had universal jurisdiction based on the simple fact that He had created the world. As the vicar of Christ on earth, the Pope in turn in the late fifteenth century notoriously made a 'donation' of the newly discovered lands in the Western hemisphere to Spain while assigning the rest to Portugal. In fact, the Pope subsequently regretted his generosity. In order to get around the religious monopoly he had granted, he came up with a series of legalistic arguments and started sending Jesuits to China in his own account as well.[40]

As the first Jesuits arrived in China with the Divine Law of the Ten Commandments, they in fact encountered China as a genuine ontological problem—not merely something to be classified in an exhibit or a museum catalogue, or a reluctant student to be educated in the ways of the West. In terms of space, the Jesuits were fairly confident of China's physical location. The Italian Jesuit Matteo Ricci presented the Chinese with a splendid *mappamondo*. The convention of the genre was still to place Jerusalem at the centre of the map, although Ricci did make the critical concession of placing the Middle Kingdom where it belonged—in the middle.[41] The greater problem was where to locate the Chinese in time. The concept of world history did not exist yet; rather, the task was to determine how the Chinese past aligned with biblical events.

Unfortunately, the year from which the Chinese calculated their origins corresponded to year 2357 BC. This precipitated a major chronological crisis. The dominant Vulgate version of the Bible dated the creation of the world at 4004 BC and the Flood at 2349 BC. By this accounting, Chinese civilization would have originated eight years before the Flood. This was biblically impossible, since it would have been

---

[40] See DF Lach and EJ van Kley, *Asia in the Making of Europe* (University of Chicago Press Chicago 1993) vol 3, bk 1, at 132.

[41] See LM Jensen, *Manufacturing Confucianism: Chinese Traditions and Universal Civilization* (Duke University Press Durham 1997) at 37.

wiped out by the Flood. At the end of the resulting chronopolitical controversy, the Jesuits in China were given permission to use the Septuagint version instead. It dated the Flood at 2957 BC, some six hundred years earlier than the Vulgate. This simple but crucial adjustment made Chinese civilization safely post-diluvian and, therefore, possible. Equally significantly, chronological modifications were made in Europe as well to take account of China's place in the Creation.[42]

This encounter between China and biblical law was distinctly different from China's encounter with nineteenth-century international law. Most notably, with the transition from religious to secular sovereignty completed, the latter encounter was managed by modern nation-states. While the Jesuits adjusted their view of the world to make room for China in it, the British demanded that China adjust to European norms, with the goal of turning it into a (junior) participant in the modern world economy. Rather than insisting that the Chinese existed on a separate but parallel track, one that was destined eventually to converge with the path of progress opened up by the Christian states of Europe, the Jesuits believed that Europeans and the Chinese shared a common origin—not only a possible *telos* located behind an ever-receding horizon.

Among other things, this meant that since Noah was the only survivor of the Flood, the Chinese counted among his descendants, part of an original though lost unity, rather than a group of beings radically outside of Christendom. Indeed, according to the Bible the separation of humanity into scattered groups speaking mutually unintelligible languages was a calamity, not a political fact to be codified normatively by turning the world into a multicultural gallery of national differences. Such diversity was God's retribution for the construction of the Tower of Babel. Moreover, as Jesuits transmitted more information to Europe about the Chinese language, the new knowledge eventually threw into disarray even the traditional divisions among European languages. Ultimately it incited the great seventeenth-century search for what was believed to be a long-lost Universal Language that had been shared by all of humanity. The key to this language, many believed, was to be found in Chinese—the so-called *clavis Sinica*.[43] All of this reflected a belief in universally shared logical, theological, and linguistic structures, of which China was seen as an integral part.

In analysing the contrast between two European *Weltanschauungen* and their responses to China at different historical conjunctures, in important ways the early modern one seems more respectful of China. In the final analysis, however, it succeeds in preserving the dignity of China only at the cost of assimilating it into

[42] See EJ van Kley, 'Europe's "Discovery" of China and the Writing of World History' (1971) 76 *American Historical Review* 358–85; DE Mungello, *The Great Encounter of China and the West, 1500–1800* (Rowman & Littlefield Lanham, MD 1999) at 66–7.

[43] See DE Mungello, *Curious Land: Jesuit Accommodation and the Origins of Sinology* (University of Hawaii Press Honolulu 1985) at 174–246.

its own cosmology, albeit with spatio-temporal adjustments. In conceptual terms, this logic of sameness is no less of an epistemological imperialism than the logic of difference that defines the later encounter. The most vital distinction between these two forms of imperial knowledge, it seems, is that the former had to proceed by persuasion alone, while the latter was able to make the world conform to its categories—using law, warships, telescopes, maps, and clocks to realize and export its worldview.

7 International Law at the End of the Day

Where, then, does this leave China in law's world? Indisputably one of the crowning achievements of modern international law has been its success in turning the erstwhile Qing Empire into one nation-state among others. However, even in today's postcolonial world in which previously colonized lands and peoples have been (mostly) emancipated, the very conceptions of political space and time that justified their conquest in the first place have not been decolonized.[44] As a result, while Chinese sovereignty may have assumed a modern legal form, it remains a troubled concept, as 'the short, tight skin of the nation' has been stretched 'over the gigantic body of the empire', to borrow Benedict Anderson's evocative phrase.[45] Even after centuries of colonialism/globalization, numerous communities in China and elsewhere remain territorially unmoored and historically out of sync with international legal standards. Beyond the question of Tibet, which has its own political cosmology embedded in Buddhism, and the Muslim communities of Central Asia, China has contested imperial borders in Indochina and unresolved disputes over islands most notably in the East and South China Seas.

In the end, other places and times remain, in China and elsewhere. Indeed, we ought not to be too hasty in offering definitive conclusions about the status of international law (or anything else) at the proverbial 'end of the day'. For so long as the world keeps on turning, the day never ends. When it is day-time in Asia, it is night-time in America, and vice versa, with Europe in between.

---

[44] See S Pahuja, *Decolonising International Law: Development, Economic Growth and the Politics of Universality* (CUP Cambridge 2011); M Craven, *The Decolonization of International Law: State Succession and the Law of Treaties* (OUP Oxford 2009).
[45] *Imagined Communities* (n 15) 88.

CHAPTER 8

IMPERIALISM AND INTERNATIONAL LEGAL THEORY

ANTONY ANGHIE

1 THEORIZING INTERNATIONAL LAW

THE questions of what it means to 'theorize' and what the proper object, purpose, and scope of theory consist of remain open and controversial. A great deal depends however on the answers to these questions, for they broadly determine what sort of scholarship is legitimate, and indeed, encouraged, recognized, and rewarded. One approach to the issue of what it means to 'theorize' international law is to examine the works of the great scholars who are understood to constitute the canon of the discipline; jurists such as Francisco de Vitoria, Hugo Grotius, and Emer de Vattel. Broadly, each of these scholars developed a new jurisprudence that sought to explain the character of international law (usually with reference to how it could be seen as universally binding) and then proceeded to outline a vision of international order and justice that could be constructed on such foundations. Thus Grotius wrote at a time when a system of international law based on religious authority alone appeared divisive and destructive, and his great achievement was to construct an international order based on natural law. Similarly, Vattel sought to combine natural and positive law in his jurisprudence. These scholars usually

saw themselves as responding to new developments, whether political or intellectual, which demanded an innovative jurisprudence designed to further the cause
of international justice.

International legal theory could be broadly seen, then, as exploring certain fundamental questions of political order—hence the connection which is now being
developed, with various other disciplines such as intellectual history[1] and political
theory[2]—and the role of law in creating such an order. In addition, these great
works have both addressed and generated a series of questions which have acquired
the status of the 'classic' or enduring questions that all of the most eminent scholars of the discipline have engaged with: what is the character of international law?
Is international law really law? What is the role of international law in the global
community?

In this chapter, I will examine the issue of how imperialism has impinged on
theorizing about international law in different historical periods. Some of the most
central concerns of international legal theorizing cannot be properly explored without taking imperialism into account. Questions regarding the binding nature and
universality of international law, and the subjects of international law, for instance,
are presented with special challenges by the imperial encounter. At the same time,
imperialism is a distinctive experience that has generated new questions and concepts that have been and need to be further explored in order to acquire a better
grasp of the operation of international law and its effects on the world. My basic
argument here is that we are faced by a fundamental paradox: although imperialism has been crucial to the development of international law, it has not really been
a central concern of the theory of international law for much of the last century.
This has been, I would argue, because of a broad tendency to view 'colonial questions' as pragmatic or political issues that did not implicate the great theoretical
concerns of the time, or else to characterize imperialism in a manner that easily
enabled its assimilation into these concerns. These tendencies have also been furthered by a particular and limited understanding of the meaning of 'imperialism'.[3]
I trace then, the ways in which the imperial experience led certain scholars—many
but certainly not all from the non-European world—to ask fundamental questions

[1] See R Tuck, *The Rights of War and Peace: Political Thought and the International Order from Grotius to Kant* (OUP Oxford 1999); D Armitage, *Foundations of Modern International Thought* (CUP Cambridge 2013).

[2] See J Tully, *Public Philosophy in a New Key* (CUP Cambridge 2008) vol 2 (*Imperialism and Civic Freedom*).

[3] Needless to say, imperialism is a complex and contested term. Michael Doyle provides insightful definitions of the terms imperialism and Empire, while suggesting their relationship. Empire is
'a relationship, formal or informal, in which one state controls the effective political sovereignty of
another political society. It can be achieved by force, by political collaboration, by economic, social
or cultural dependence. Imperialism is simply the process or policy of maintaining an empire':
M Doyle, *Empires* (Cornell University Press Ithaca 1986).

about the character and operation of international law. I also demonstrate how these inquiries were largely marginalized and dismissed by the mainstream discipline, particularly in the 1960s and 1970s when the scholars attempting to create a New International Economic Order made the issue of imperialism crucial to their vision of international law and how it needed to be reformed. In more recent times, imperialism has played a more prominent role in theorizing about international law and this has resulted from what I term a shift from 'history' to 'ontology'. I then trace some of the lines of analysis that have followed from this, some of the broad questions and issues that might be the subject of further theorizing in relation to imperialism and international law, and whether the topic of imperialism is of any continuing analytic significance.

2 THE IMPERIALISM OF THEORY

It is evident that imperialism was a central concern of the most eminent scholars of international law such as Vitoria and Grotius.[4] The great scholars of the nineteenth century—John Westlake, James Lorimer, Johann Kaspar Bluntschli—were similarly preoccupied by questions of imperialism and international law.[5] This is understandable, because European imperialism reached its height during this period. International lawyers were eager to make their own contribution to the management of colonial relations, and this involved grappling with questions of the personality of non-European entities, the relationship between law and 'civilization' and the universality of the norms they associated with international law. Indeed, it is astonishing to note how many of these scholars lent their support for the civilizing mission that was fundamental to colonial expansion.[6]

Despite this, by the early twentieth century, colonial questions were seen as largely incidental to the great questions of international law, the central one being: 'how is it possible to establish a legal order among equal and sovereign states?' This analytic framework inevitably prevents any proper examination of

---

[4] F de Vitoria, *De Indis et De Jure Belli Relectiones* (E Nys ed J Pawley Bate trans) (Carnegie Institution Washington DC 1917 [1548]); H Grotius, *De Jure Belli ac Pacis Libri Tres* (FW Kelsey trans) (Clarendon Press Oxford 1925 [1625]).

[5] J Westlake, *The Collected Papers of John Westlake* (L Oppenheim ed) (OUP Oxford 1914) at 139ff; J Lorimer, *Institutes of the Law of Nations: A Treatise of the Jural Relations of Separate Political Communities* (2 vols W Blackwood & Sons Edinburgh 1883–4); JK Bluntschli, *The Theory of the State* (DE Ritchie, PE Matheson, and R Lodge trans) (3rd edn Clarendon Press Oxford 1895 [1875]).

[6] M Koskenniemi, *The Gentle Civilizer of Nations: The Rise and Fall of International Law 1870–1960* (CUP Cambridge 2001).

the experience of colonized peoples who were, by definition, lacking in sovereignty. The more pertinent question for peoples of the Third World is: 'how was
it decided that non-European societies were lacking in sovereignty in the first
place?' Further, prominent scholars such as Sir Hersch Lauterpacht wrote extensively on colonial issues, but not in a way that impinged on the great theoretical
questions of the discipline.[7] By the nineteenth century, the major question was
whether international law was properly law and whether it could further international order.[8] Colonial problems, however, were largely perceived as practical,
administrative problems.

For the peoples and scholars of the colonized world, of course, imperialism was
the central feature of the international law that was continuously deployed against
them by European states to further their own interests. The non-European vision
of international law, therefore, was fundamentally different from that embraced by
European lawyers and states. In her important work on Chinese international law,
Xue Hanqin points to how the work of the eminent scholar Wang Tieya focused in
particular on 'those unequal treaties that China was forced to conclude one after
another with colonial powers during that time, and illustrated how history and
culture of a country had impact on the attitude and position of that country in
international law'.[9] Recent scholarship on important and path-breaking scholars
such as Alejandro Álvarez and Japanese scholars gives some sense of the specific
issues that preoccupied non-European scholars as they grappled to understand
how international law operated and affected their own states and then to use it
effectively themselves.[10] Put simply, the work of these scholars effectively pointed
out that imperialism generates a new epistemology and a new set of questions when

[7] See eg H Lauterpacht, 'International Law and Colonial Questions, 1870–1914' in E Lauterpacht
(ed), *International Law, Being the Collected Papers of Sir Hersch Lauterpacht* (CUP Cambridge 1970)
vol 2, 95–144, at 101–9; H Lauterpacht, 'The Mandate under International Law in the Covenant of the
League of Nations' in *International Law* (n 7) vol 3, 29–84.

[8] The other work that insisted that imperialism was a central aspect of international law was Carl
Schmitt's work, published in 1950 in German with its curious combination of brilliant insight and
unnerving political vision: see C Schmitt, *The* Nomos *of the Earth in the International Law of the* Jus
Publicum Europaeum (GL Ulmen trans) (Telos Press New York 2003 [1950]).

[9] X Hanqin, 'Chinese Contemporary Perspectives on International Law: History, Culture and
International Law' (2012) 355 *Recueil des Cours* 47–233, at 52. Judge Xue further points out that China
was forced through these treaties to pay reparations for various conflicts, including the Opium Wars
and the Boxer Rebellion. In relation to the latter, China was required to pay 450 million tael, which
was more than forty times the cost of the Alaska purchase: see at 52. See also T Ruskola, 'China in
the Age of the World Picture' in this *Handbook*.

[10] The problem these scholars faced was that they would be marginalized within the discipline,
whose analytic framework was essentially imperial, unless they themselves adopted that framework even when examining the realities of their own country, which were very different. This
could have led to scholars from these countries in some ways replicating these imperial analytic
frameworks even more emphatically to demonstrate their own skill and to win admission to
the inner worlds of scholarship and prestige. For a powerful and poignant account of this predicament, see O Yasuaki, '"Japanese International Law" in the Prewar Period—Perspectives on

it is viewed from the perspective of those who have been the object of imperialism. How is international law, its operations and character, experienced and understood by peoples who have been systematically disadvantaged by its applications? What new insights into the fundamental issues regarding international justice, the binding nature of international law, legitimacy and universality do we receive as a result of considering their work?

These contrasts, crudely put, between Western and non-Western scholars may be understood in basic terms. Western scholars of the nineteenth and much of the twentieth century encountered the fundamental problem that international law lacked power and binding authority. This chasm between law and power was precisely the basis of John Austin's famous critique of the discipline and his dismissal of it as not being law properly so called.[11] In the case of the colonial encounter, however, especially in the nineteenth century when European might was ascendant, international law was expressly allied with power. Thus many nineteenth-century scholars who found it difficult to defend their discipline jurisprudentially and practically could lend their services to colonial expansion; in this very different context, power sought law to legitimize itself in justifying conquest and dispossession.

3   DECOLONIZATION AND THE CHALLENGE TO INTERNATIONAL LAW

Decolonization and the efforts of the new states and scholars to present a different vision of international law raised a number of new questions and challenges. As Mohammed Bedjaoui asserted, international law 'consisted of a set of rules with a geographical basis (it was a European law), a religious–ethical inspiration (it was a Christian law), an economic motivation (it was a mercantilist law) and political aims (it was an imperialist law)'.[12] How then could such an international law accommodate new states which had very different cultures and traditions? Even more pointedly, could international law be used to negate the exploitation and subordination which it had previously effected? Was international law a neutral set of principles that could be deployed to fashion a new international

the Teaching and Research of International Law in Prewar Japan' (1986) 29 *Japanese Annual of International Law* 23–47.

[11] J Austin, *The Province of Jurisprudence Determined* (Weidenfeld and Nicolson London 1954 [1832]) at 201ff; J Austin, *Lectures on Jurisprudence or the Philosophy of Positive Law* (5th edn John Murray London 1885 [1863]) vol 1, at 182.

[12] M Bedjaoui, *Towards a New International Economic Order* (Holmes and Meier New York 1979) at 50.

system? New debates and controversies emerged in international law as a result of these questions.

Scholars focused on the Third World predicament took up similar themes and concerns in the concerted drive towards decolonization and its aftermath. Many established international law scholars were concerned about the possibility that the admission of 'new states' would undermine an avowedly European international law. In response, the works of scholars such as CH Alexandrowicz,[13] RP Anand,[14] and TO Elias[15] attempted to demonstrate that international law was not foreign to non-European states; and this resulted in a rich literature regarding the role of international law in the encounters between Europe and Asia, and Europe and Africa, and the manner in which this affected the development of international law. It also raised in a new way the question of the distinctive character of modern international law, given that many ancient systems of states that emerged in Africa and Asia, for instance, had developed various sets of rules and practices about issues such as treaties, the conduct of warfare, and diplomatic immunities.

The Third World was confronted by a number of issues: was international law decisively and unalterably Western? Could the new states make their own contributions to this body of law? Could the new states further their own interests using international law? These questions were not merely of academic interest: they were part of the large Third World project that followed the Bandung Conference, of consolidating Third World sovereignty, furthering the cause of international peace in a time of intense Cold War tensions, and bringing about development in Third World countries. The African–Asian Legal Consultative Organization was created at this time for the explicit goal of furthering international law in a way that benefited Third World countries. The most ambitious of these initiatives—the effort to create a New International Economic Order—attempted to identify and negate the continuing effects of imperialism on the international legal system. Mohammed Bedjaoui's classic work, *Towards a New International Economic Order*, remains the most systematic effort to provide a jurisprudential foundation for this initiative. Bedjaoui's ambition, stated in his introduction, was to 'determine the most suitable methods and modern means of ensuring that international law becomes an efficient instrument of progress in the service of that new order [the New International Economic Order]'.[16] Bedjaoui and his colleagues—such as Georges Abi-Saab, Anand, and Elias—challenged the conventional approach to the discipline by placing the predicament of the peoples of the new states, their poverty, and their disempowerment at the centre of these efforts. This vision of international

---

[13] CH Alexandrowicz, *An Introduction to the History of the Law of Nations in the East Indies* (Clarendon Press Oxford 1967).

[14] RP Anand, *New States and International Law* (Vikas New Delhi 1972).

[15] TO Elias, *Africa and the Development of International Law* (AW Sitjhoff Leiden 1972).

[16] *Towards a New International Economic Order* (n 12) 16. The project is ongoing: see E Tourme-Jouannet, *What is a Fair International Society?: International Law between Development and Recognition* (Hart Oxford 2013).

law, although extremely illuminating and insightful was not, of course, shared by the vast majority of international law scholars.

This Third World initiative failed for many different complex socio-political reasons, amongst them the oil crisis, the policies of the United States (US), and the failure of socialism in Third World states. At the legal level, it was defeated by the prevalence of conservative arguments about the sources of international law (particularly, that General Assembly Resolutions did not count for law-making purposes). And somehow the weakening Third World position seemed to affect the plausibility and credibility of the arguments developed to support the campaign. Many Third World scholars themselves had a sanguine view of international law, believing it could be reformed despite its capitalist and imperial character. These hopes proved largely unfounded. The enduring and important questions raised about international law by the Third World were largely disregarded after the collapse of the New International Economic Order and the emergence and dominance of neoliberal economic policy.

By the time the last major volume on Third World concerns appeared in the 1980s,[17] it was in many ways an addendum, an account of the vision that had now failed. Scholars wrote important works on the relationship between colonialism and international law,[18] but their broader implications were not appreciated. By the 1980s then, imperialism had essentially disappeared as a concern for scholars engaged in the theory of international law. Underlying this situation was a particularly narrow vision which equated imperialism with official colonialism; seen from this perspective, decolonization ended the imperial problem, which was no sooner articulated by Third World scholars than resolved by the emergence of colonized entities as sovereign states. Third World scholars, however, persisted in arguing that formal colonialism was succeeded by neo-colonialism, with its legal doctrines and institutions. The crucial point, then, is that different interpretations of the nature and operation of 'imperialism' lead to very different analytic frameworks and visions.

4 TOWARDS THE PRESENT

In an important recent essay, Jennifer Pitts argues that '[p]olitical theory has come slowly and late to the study of Empire, relative to other disciplines'.[19] This seems

---

[17] FE Snyder and S Sathirathai (eds), *Third World Attitudes toward International Law: An Introduction* (Martinus Nijhoff Boston 1987).

[18] See eg GW Gong, *The Standard of 'Civilization' in International Society* (OUP New York 1984).

[19] J Pitts, 'Political Theory of Empire and Imperialism' (2010) 13 *Annual Review of Political Science* 211–35, at 212.

paradoxical for several reasons. In the first place, the great political theorists claimed that their works were universally applicable and thus were valid for all societies, including non-European societies. Despite such claims, no account was given of imperialism, one of the defining experiences for those societies. Indeed, the European societies that were the focus of these studies could not be properly understood without taking into account their growing imperial character. Secondly, many of the classic theorists—Grotius, John Locke, and JS Mill—had explicitly dealt with colonial themes.[20] Indeed, their professional lives involved dealing in a practical way with colonial administration. Like political theory, international law, especially after what was seen as the successful refutation of the New International Economic Order, appeared impervious to the implications of imperialism for the discipline.[21]

This situation seems all the more ironic given that international law, like political theory, sought to provide a set of rules that would ensure universal order. Disciplines such as anthropology had already conducted searching inquiries into the relationship between their own discipline and imperialism. Further, the pioneering work of Edward Said and other post-colonial scholars had emerged in the 1970s.[22] Post-colonial scholarship had raised a number of fundamental questions that were later to serve as powerful analytical tools in reconceptualizing the relationship between imperialism and international law. First, rather than seeing imperialism as peripheral to modernity, post-colonial scholars asserted not only that the West was created out of the wealth derived from the colonies—a fairly standard argument—but that various disciplines such as anthropology and history had played a crucial role in facilitating the colonial project. Secondly, and even more challengingly, postcolonial scholars argued that the disciplines themselves—the very categories and structures of thought—were shaped by imperialism. In other words, whereas the traditional view treated the disciplines as neutral analytic tools that could be used to address any subject, these scholars argued that the analytic tools themselves were constructed by imperialism and therefore, when

[20] See eg H Grotius, *The Free Sea* (R Hakluyt trans D Armitage ed) (Liberty Fund Indianapolis 2004 [1609]); J Locke, *Two Treatises of Government* (P Laslett ed) (revised edn CUP Cambridge 1988 [1689]). See also US Mehta, *Liberalism and Empire: A Study in Nineteenth-Century British Liberal Thought* (University of Chicago Press Chicago 1999).

[21] I would add that the discipline of international relations seems similarly backward in its engagement with colonialism. See P Darby (ed), *Postcolonizing the International: Working to Change the Way We Are* (University of Hawaii Press Honolulu 2006); BG Jones (ed), *Decolonizing International Relations* (Rowman and Littlefield Lanham 2006); SN Grovogui, *Beyond Eurocentrism and Anarchy: Memories of International Order and Institutions* (Palgrave Macmillan New York 2006); S Krishnan, *Globalization and Postcolonialism: Hegemony and Resistance in the Twenty-First Century* (Rowman and Littlefield Lanham 2009).

[22] For a good overview of post-colonial scholarship and various debates, see B Moore-Gilbert, *Postcolonial Theory: Contexts, Practices, Politics* (Verso New York 1997).

applied, could be seen as producing biased outcomes. Thirdly, post-colonial scholars, and especially those among them who became identified with the subaltern
studies school project within it,[23] raised probing questions about how the most
disadvantaged—the subaltern—can represent him or herself, this in a situation
where even nationalist histories documenting decolonization were presented from
an elitist perspective. One of the central tasks of these scholars was to locate subaltern consciousness and the politics it engendered.[24] The crucial point that subaltern studies scholars made—and which, despite recent controversies, remains an
important one[25]—is that even the nationalist project that was supposed to bring
about liberation of Third World peoples enacted its own exclusions, and marginalized the most disadvantaged.[26] Related to this was the concern to understand how
history—or international law—could be rewritten or rethought from the perspective of these people. Fourthly, the fresh understanding of the character and operation of the disciplines of history that emerged from these inquiries could be used to
rethink continuities between earlier imperial histories and techniques of management and control, and contemporary developments.

These ideas, when transferred and adapted to international law, became the basis
of a new attempt to rethink the relationship between international law and imperialism. Although imperialism had virtually vanished as an important issue for
international law in the 1980s, the significant work done by scholars such as David
Kennedy, Martti Koskenniemi, Hilary Charlesworth, and Christine Chinkin had
created a new interest in developing critical and new approaches to international
law.[27] Much of this critical scholarship drew upon insights from post-structural,
post-modern, and feminist theory. The insights of critical race theory were especially
important because race had played such a significant role in the colonial encounter.

It was in this context that the Third World Approaches to International Law
(TWAIL) project emerged as a means of drawing on the resources developed by
this critical scholarship and indeed, the encouragement provided by critical scholars, while continuing and renewing the project of earlier Third World scholars
such as Anand by using the new insights offered by post-colonial scholarship.

---

[23] See eg R Guha (ed), *A Subaltern Studies Reader 1986–1995* (University of Minnesota Press
Minneapolis 1997).

[24] P Chatterjee, *Empire and Nation: Selected Essays* (Columbia University Press New York 2010) at 291.

[25] See V Chibber, *Postcolonial Theory and the Specter of Capitalism* (Verso New York 2013);
V Chaturvedi (ed), *Mapping Subaltern Studies and the Postcolonial* (Verso New York 2000).

[26] For a superb examination of some of these themes, see D Otto, 'Subalternity and International
Law: The Problems of Global Community and the Incommensurability of Difference' (1996) 5 *Social &
Legal Studies* 337–64.

[27] See eg D Kennedy, 'A New Stream of International Law Scholarship' (1988) 7 *Wisconsin
International Law Journal* 1–49; M Koskenniemi, 'The Politics of International Law' (1990) 1 *European
Journal of International Law* 4–32; H Charlesworth, C Chinkin, and S Wright, 'Feminist Approaches
to International Law' (1991) 85 *American Journal of International Law* 613–45.

The aspirations of TWAIL may be simply stated and reflect the concerns of earlier Third World scholars: of viewing international law from the position of the objects of colonialism; of developing the conceptual tools that could provide an account of imperialism that corresponded with the experiences of those who were its victims; and of formulating alternative visions of justice that might contribute to thinking about global order. This could not be easily achieved by simply reproducing, unchallenged, the vocabularies and frameworks that had been used by the supposedly neutral languages of history, social science, and law. TWAIL is in many respects a political project as much as an intellectual approach.[28] In this sense it is entirely traditional: earlier scholars based their arguments precisely on the belief that international law's central concern is the achievement of justice—a vision of justice expanded to take into account the experiences of Third World peoples. Here I attempt to focus on some of the central concerns and analytical tools that TWAIL has developed and which, I claim, make important contributions to international legal theory.

5 Colonial Continuities

The replication of colonial relations in a supposedly post-colonial world is an enduring theme of much of this scholarship. James Gathii's analysis of the relationship between war and commerce is animated by his attempt 'to identify the extent to which the legacy of colonial disempowerment has continued into the era of decolonization in the relationship between war and commerce in international law'.[29] Recent scholarship has illuminated the effects of colonialism on the development of major areas of international law, including human rights law,[30] international humanitarian law,[31] international investment law,[32] and the law of

---

[28] See JT Gathii, 'TWAIL: A Brief History of Its Origins, Its Decentralized Network, and a Tentative Bibliography' (2011) 3 *Trade Law and Development* 26–64; M Fakhri, 'Introduction—Questioning TWAIL's Agenda' (2012) 14 *Oregon Review of International Law* 1–16.

[29] JT Gathii, *War, Commerce, and International Law* (OUP New York 2010) at xxxi.

[30] MW Mutua, 'Savages, Victims, and Saviors: The Metaphor of Human Rights' (2001) 42 *Harvard International Law Journal* 201–45; B Ibhawoh, *Imperialism and Human Rights: Colonial Discourses of Rights and Liberties in African History* (State University of New York Press Albany 2007); JM Barreto (ed), *Human Rights from a Third World Perspective: Critique, History and International Law* (Cambridge Scholars Newcastle upon Tyne 2012).

[31] F Mégret, 'From "Savages" to "Unlawful Combatants": A Postcolonial Look at International Humanitarian Law's "Other"' in A Orford (ed), *International Law and Its Others* (CUP Cambridge 2006) 265–318.

[32] See IT Odumosu, 'The Law and Politics of Engaging Resistance in Investment Dispute Settlement' (2007) 26 *Penn State International Law Review* 251–87; K Miles, *The Origins of International Investment Law: Empire, Environment and the Safeguarding of Capital* (CUP Cambridge 2011).

international institutions[33] as well as the recent spate of attempts to reconstruct 'post-conflict societies'.[34]

An understanding of these continuities demonstrated the pervasive and enduring impact of imperialism on international law.[35] Imperialism then, is central to international law. Further, imperialism is not simply of historical importance—it was through imperialism that a European international law became universally applicable—but it is also of ontological or epistemological importance. That is, imperialism is a crucial element of the discipline's very character and operation. I have argued that the central doctrines and categories of international law, including, most importantly, the fundamental doctrine of sovereignty, have been shaped by the colonial encounter and that, furthermore, its subsequent operations continue the task of excluding certain societies and empowering others.[36] The 'civilizing mission' that reached its height in the nineteenth century continued to operate well beyond that, and many of the most important projects of contemporary international law reproduce the essential structure of this mission by positing some 'uncivilized' entity that must be transformed by international law and institutions to ensure the progress of civilization. Thus the civilizing mission is not simply an historical phenomenon but an ongoing dynamic that is arguably deeply entrenched as an aspect of international law and is thus an appropriate object of theorizing.[37] A more complex issue arises as to whether particular international legal doctrines which can be identified as having originated in the colonial encounter are for that reason alone inherently colonial in their application and evolution. Can colonial origins be transcended?

This concern about colonial replication, and the manner in which international legal doctrines and indeed institutions could operate to the detriment of Third World peoples was especially important for an ongoing critical scrutiny of the many developments that completely transformed international economic relations in an era of intensified globalization. Historians of Empire have been quick to point out that imperialism was an earlier form of globalization.[38] The creation of the World Trade Organization and the expansion of the activities of the International Monetary Fund and the World Bank had a profound impact

---

[33] A Orford, *International Authority and the Responsibility to Protect* (CUP Cambridge 2011).

[34] R Wilde, *International Territorial Administration: How Trusteeship and the Civilizing Mission Never Went Away* (OUP Oxford 2008).

[35] For an important recent examination of this theme see A Orford, 'The Past as Law or History? The Relevance of Imperialism for Modern International Law' (*Institute for International Law and Justice*, New York University Law School, International Law and Justice Working Paper No 2012/2), subsequently published in M Toufayan, E Tourme-Jouannet, and H Ruiz Fabri (eds), *International Law and New Approaches to the Third World* (Société de Législation Comparée Paris 2013) 97–118.

[36] A Anghie, *Imperialism, Sovereignty and the Making of International Law* (CUP Cambridge 2005).

[37] See L Obregón, 'The Civilized and the Uncivilized' in B Fassbender and A Peters (eds), *The Oxford Handbook of the History of International Law* (OUP Oxford) 917–43.

[38] See eg M Hardt and A Negri, *Empire* (Harvard University Press Cambridge MA 2000); AG Hopkins, *Globalization in World History* (Pimlico London 2002).

on peoples in developing countries, as did the decisive emergence of intellectual property and foreign investment regimes. Again, the basic analytic tools of understanding historical antecedents and the manner in which they entrenched enduring biases against the poorest people assisted in understanding the emergence of a 'Global Imperial State'.[39]

Similarly, this scholarship has emphasized the issue of viewing international law from the perspective of the most disadvantaged; and in this respect is connected with other theoretical traditions which have a similar concern, including feminism and indigenous peoples. Important recent work has stressed the significance of new social movements, actors whose presence and predicament has never been properly addressed in international law and whose attempts to create an international law capable of furthering their own interests is an ongoing project.[40] The focus on these subjects is especially important for at least two reasons. First, it provides a way of understanding the operations of international law on the most disadvantaged even while it raises the question of how they might use international law for their own purposes, as agents of international law rather than merely objects. Secondly, TWAIL scholarship on globalization suggests the need to understand not only divisions between rich and poor countries but between rich and poor people.

The value of these contributions to theorizing international law and its operations took on an entirely new significance as a result of the 9/11 attacks and the 'war on terror'. These events resulted in US policies—broadly supported by the United Kingdom—that included detention with no prospect of trial, the torture of suspects, the launching of counter-insurgencies and the invasion of non-European states that were all too familiar to anyone remotely familiar with imperial history. International legal arguments attempting to justify these practices and calling for the revision of the laws of war and international human rights law because of the new situation relied on the very traditional structure of the civilizing mission. Certain states were 'outlaw states' and needed to be sanctioned by war, and certain people were 'terrorists' and therefore disqualified from the protection of the law. These justifications of violence, together with arguments that new legal frameworks were needed to deal with an unprecedented situation may be found in the work of Vitoria in the sixteenth century.[41] It should not be forgotten that theorizing about Empire often includes theorizing about how to perfect Empire. Even more strikingly, the 9/11 attacks led to prominent scholars such as Michael Ignatieff and

---

[39] BS Chimni, 'International Institutions Today: An Imperial Global State in the Making' (2004) 15 *European Journal of International Law* 1–37.

[40] See B Rajagopal, *International Law from Below: Development, Social Movements and Third World Resistance* (CUP Cambridge 2011); O Onazi, 'Towards a Subaltern Theory of Human Rights' (2009) 9(2) *Global Jurist* 1–25; U Baxi, *The Future of Human Rights* (OUP New Delhi 2006); K Khoday and U Natarajan, 'Fairness and International Environmental Law from Below: Social Movement and Legal Transformation in India' (2012) 25 *Leiden Journal of International Law* 415–41.

[41] *Imperialism, Sovereignty and the Making of International Law* (n 36); M Feichtinger, S Malinowski, and C Richards, 'Transformative Invasions: Western Post 9/11 Counterinsurgency and the Lessons of Colonialism' (2012) 3 *Humanity* 35–63.

Niall Ferguson calling explicitly for the resurrection of Empire.[42] Further, in fighting these new wars, military experts drew directly on the experiences of colonial wars: the French in Algeria, the British in Kenya and Malaya, and even further back, the British in Iraq and the US in the Philippines.

Empire and imperialism thus became once more an important topic for scholarly examination by international lawyers, political scientists, and political theorists. It is clear, however, that different critiques were advanced based on divergent understandings of the key concept of 'imperialism'.[43] And while international lawyers who have been previously impervious or indifferent to the relationship between imperialism and international law have focused on the topic, responses are varied. It is clear for instance, that some scholars see TWAIL perspectives, not always accurately comprehended, as misguided challenges to the discipline, and somewhat defensively insist on the virtues of international law—as though TWAIL completely denounced it.[44] Nevertheless, it is at least heartening that the issue of 'Eurocentrism' of international law is a major and inescapable feature of contemporary studies of the history and theory of the discipline.[45]

6 IMPERIALISM AND THE FUTURE

What is the future of this tradition of theorizing, if it could be called a tradition? After all, the conceptual framework depends on a clear distinction between the colonizer and the colonized, and a few 'Third World' countries such as Brazil, China, and India are now regarded as global powers. This ascent of certain states led World Bank Group President Robert Zoellick famously to proclaim that the old conceptual frameworks founded on distinctions between First and Third Worlds were outdated.[46] Further commentators and diplomats from the putative

---

[42] M Ignatieff, *Empire Lite: Nation-Building in Bosnia, Kosovo and Afghanistan* (Random House London 2003); N Ferguson, *Empire: The Rise and Fall of the British World Order and the Lessons for Global Power* (Basic Books New York 2003).

[43] A Rasulov, 'Writing about Empire: Remarks on the Logic of a Discourse' (2010) 23 *Leiden Journal of International Law* 449–71.

[44] See eg B Fassbender and A Peters, 'Introduction: Towards a Global History of International Law' in *The Oxford Handbook of the History of International Law* (n 37) 1–24, at 4.

[45] For important overviews, see JT Gathii, 'International Law and Eurocentricity' (1998) 9 *European Journal of International Law* 184–211; M Koskenniemi, 'Histories of International Law: Dealing with Eurocentrism' (2011) *Rechtsgeschichte* 152–76; A Becker Lorca, 'Eurocentrism in the History of International Law' in *The Oxford Handbook of the History of International Law* (n 37) 1034–57.

[46] World Bank, 'Old Concept of "Third World" Outdated, Zoellick Says' (14 April 2010) <http://go.worldbank.org/KVZoGQP7Fo> [accessed 21 February 2016].

'Third World' itself, now enjoying a newly won confidence and assurance, have questioned the utility and descriptive accuracy of the term 'Third World'. As a result of developments such as this, what sort of resonance and validity does the term 'imperialism' suggest? Does it serve any useful analytical purpose?

First, for many TWAIL scholars the category of 'Third World' had always been problematic: but this in itself does not impede the development of a conceptual framework that provides powerful insights. As far as TWAIL scholars are concerned, the term 'Third World' referred not only to a particular geographical or politico-legal entity—those countries that had experienced colonization—but also, more broadly, to what might be termed an 'experience'—that of the most disadvantaged, 'The Wretched of the Earth'—whether they be minorities or peasants or indigenous peoples.[47] Some of these groups are victims of the imperialism of the post-colonial state itself. Indeed, correspondingly, it could be argued that there is a 'Third World' in the supposed First World. Legal instruments devised for the 'war on terror' are applied not only in distant countries but within the Western world itself, profoundly undermining their own venerable institutions and norms. Similarly, austerity measures now commonplace in the West resemble those experienced in the Third World, even if created under very different circumstances. It is both ironic and telling that Western governments themselves are concerned about the operations of international investment regimes and instruments that they have deployed in the past against developing countries. It is too general to claim that all these developments can be somehow attributed to 'imperialism' however broadly defined. But the relationship between imperialism and modern versions of capitalism requires further exploration. The subjects and objects of imperialism are continuously shifting, just as imperialism takes very different forms—and always has.

Secondly, while the 'First World'/'Third World' scheme may no longer apply in contemporary international economic relations, events such as the recent Iraq war and ongoing controversies about the work of the International Criminal Court and the Responsibility to Protect[48] all give rise to claims that colonial structures are being reproduced, that a supposedly neutral and universal international law is being used to discipline non-European states. In essence, very ancient, classic forms of imperialism may co-exist with developments in international law which seem far removed from those earlier systems. It is not the case that there is linear progress in all the areas of international relations or that clear demarcations can be made between imperial and post-imperial times. Furthermore, Empire is still a vivid reality for certain groups, such as minorities and indigenous peoples who continue their struggles against what they view as an imperial post-colonial state. Finally, many of the states that are proclaimed to have transcended their Third World status are not

---

[47] See F Fanon, *The Wretched of the Earth* (C Farrington trans) (Grove Press New York 1963).
[48] *International Authority and the Responsibility to Protect* (n 33).

so ready to forget their own histories. The ongoing deadlock about climate change, for instance, stems from a recognizably 'Third World' argument that Third World states are unwilling to impede their own development to remedy a situation caused by rich countries.[49] The ongoing disputes about agriculture in the international trade regime which threaten to unravel the Doha 'development' round of negotiations can surely be traced back to the economic divisions created by colonialism and the efforts of 'Third World' countries to undo its continuing operations. Further, as far as these countries are concerned, international law is still predominantly Western, and the question posed in the late nineteenth century remains that of whether non-European societies can make their own contributions to the discipline.[50]

Thirdly, the emergence of certain Third World states, notably Brazil, India, and China, as global economic powers does not of itself suggest the complete redundancy of imperialism as an analytical tool for examining current developments in political economy. Historians have pointed out that imperialism was a forerunner of contemporary globalization. Scholars such as BS Chimni have argued that globalization reproduces imperial relations, that what we witness now is an 'imperial state in the making',[51] and that the urgent task for international lawyers today is to examine the relationship between capitalism and imperialism.[52] For critical scholars, it was through imperialism that capitalism extended its reach, and the particular legal doctrines and technologies that were used for this purpose continue. It is for this reason that the examination of the colonial origins of international foreign investment law and trade law continue to be illuminating.[53]

Finally, the historian John Darwin argues that 'empire...has been the default mode of political organization throughout most of history. Imperial power has usually been the rule of the road'.[54] Sovereign states emerged as a response against Empire, the basic principle that 'all sovereign states are equal' being a fundamental

---

[49] K Mickelson, 'Leading Towards a Level Playing Field, Repaying Ecological Debt, or Making Environmental Space: Three Stories about International Environmental Cooperation' (2005) 43 *Osgoode Hall Law Journal* 135–71.

[50] This is a general theme that reverberates from the writings of the great Latin American jurists, Andrés Bello and Alejandro Álvarez, to the present: see for instance the contributions of Hisashi Owada and Xue Hanqin in the first issue of the *Asian Journal of International Law*. 'There is today an acute need for the nations of Asia, as well as academics and practitioners working in or on Asia, to have their voices heard on these important issues [of international law, including peace and security, trade and investment, human rights and the environment]': H Owada, 'Asia and International Law: The Inaugural Address of the First President of the Asian Society of International Law, Singapore, 7 April 2007' (2011) 1 *Asian Journal of International Law* 3–11, at 3.

[51] 'International Institutions Today: An Imperial Global State in the Making' (n 39).

[52] BS Chimni, 'Capitalism, Imperialism, and International Law in the Twenty-First Century' (2012) 14 *Oregon Review of International Law* 17–45.

[53] D Alessandrini, *Developing Countries and the Multilateral Trade Regime: The Failure and Promise of the WTO's Development Mission* (Hart Oxford 2010).

[54] J Darwin, *After Tamerlane: The Global History of Empire since 1405* (Bloomsbury Press New York 2008) at 23.

premise of the Westphalian system. And yet, Empire persisted precisely through the policies of these sovereign states—whether Britain or Spain or France—and what we have witnessed more recently is the tendency of powerful sovereign states to establish Empires in one form or another, even if not of the formal sort that existed in the nineteenth century. The current actions of Russia in the Crimea simply tend to confirm this. We might be returning once more to an international system—and international law—driven by rivalries between Great Powers, imperial states intent on protecting their territory, 'spheres of influence', and economic interests. I have focused here on the relationship between colonizers and the colonized, but we could also see even recent developments in international law as being shaped by the powerful presence of rivalries between imperial powers; an important and classic theme. All this may occur even as scholars point to the emergence of new forms of 'de-territorialized Empire'.[55] And, of course, rising countries such as Russia and China have a complex imperial history and it remains to be seen how this may affect their foreign policy.

Imperialism, then, is an ancient form of rule that, over the centuries, has operated through ideological, social, political, and legal means. It has developed a formidable arsenal of technologies of governance. Indeed, new mechanisms of governance, such as international institutions, often reproduce and serve the logic of Empire and the 'civilizing mission', whether through the Mandate System of the League of Nations,[56] the United Nations itself,[57] or the International Financial Institutions. Not only do new technologies of governance reproduce colonial relations, but very old forms of management, suppression, and control persist. The colonial state, the entity established by colonial powers in their overseas possessions in Africa and Asia, was the most developed, explicit, and classic means of entrenching and realizing colonial rule. It is now evident that the 'post-colonial' state itself replicates many of the same features of its predecessor in terms of managing and extracting value from populations and exploiting the resources available—often destroying the environment in the process. In this case, however, it is not colonial but local elites that benefit; elites that are part of a larger global network.[58] And they, like their imperial predecessors, engage in a form of 'divide and rule', usually by exacerbating and manipulating ethnic tensions that are prevalent in many post-colonial societies. Ironically then, it is the supposed post-colonial society which is a site at which imperial relations are reproduced, this time in relation to indigenous

[55] See *Empire* (n 38); JE Alvarez, 'Meador Lecture Series 2007–2008: Empire: Contemporary Foreign Investment Law: An "Empire of Law" or the "Law of Empire"?' (2009) 60 *Alabama Law Review* 943–75; E Meiksins Wood, *Empire of Capital* (Verso London 2003).

[56] *Imperialism, Sovereignty and the Making of International Law* (n 36) 115–96.

[57] M Mazower, *No Enchanted Palace: The End of Empire and the Ideological Origins of the United Nations* (Princeton University Press Princeton 2009).

[58] See BS Chimni, 'Prolegomena to a Class Approach to International Law' (2010) 21 *European Journal of International Law* 57–82.

peoples and minorities, among other groups.[59] The further and larger point is that imperialism may operate in various domains which require further investigation.[60]

Empire, then, is a very ancient form of governance and in the course of its evolution, it has devised numerous very complex ways of establishing and furthering itself. The presence of Empire is enduring and powerful, and a set of analytical tools that would make us alert to its presence and its operations will surely be useful. The validity or otherwise of these tools can only be ascertained by their ability to illuminate and explain.

7 Conclusions

Imperialism has been a central aspect of international law, and focusing on the experiences of those peoples who have been subjected to it provide important insights into the nature and character of international law. Scholars engaged in this project have been attempting over many decades to formulate a language, a conceptual vocabulary, which is adequate to provide an account of these experiences. The task of developing such a vocabulary and corresponding analytic tools is ongoing and inherently incomplete. Nevertheless, it is a rejoinder to the classic Western debates and issues that have governed theorizing about international law for much of the past century that have largely ignored, assimilated, or dismissed these experiences.

It is astonishing in retrospect that the lived realities of the experiences of the vast majority of mankind, the peoples of the Third World, have been so effortlessly overlooked by Western theories which have presented themselves as universal theories regarding government, society, and the individual. It is only recently that the counter-argument has been made, that the experiences of the colonized may suggest something enduring and essential about international law itself.

Important questions remain whether the analytics of imperialism continue to offer any useful insights in a changing international environment. If nothing else, however, the questions and insights that the project of theorizing imperialism have raised about the epistemology of international law and about the techniques by which the discipline suppresses and disempowers certain actors could provide an important means of assessing future developments in international law.

---

[59] See A Bhatia, 'The South of the North: Building on Critical Approaches to International Law with Lessons from the Fourth World' (2012) 14 *Oregon Review of International Law* 131–77.

[60] L Eslava and S Pahuja, 'Between Resistance and Reform: TWAIL and the Universality of International Law' (2011) 3 *Trade Law and Development* 103–31.

CHAPTER 9

EARLY TWENTIETH-CENTURY POSITIVISM REVISITED

MÓNICA GARCÍA-SALMONES ROVIRA

1 INTRODUCTION

BY the beginning of the twentieth century, the age of positivism's moment of greatest creativity had already passed.[1] A new political, legal, and academic culture would nevertheless thrive on the task of translating the important messages of nineteenth-century positivism. The intellectual analysis of previously collected facts, and the '*Verdinglichung*' (reification) of man—peculiar to Nietzsche's philosophy and to other positivists—that replaces government by men with the administration of men were two of the most characteristic activities inherited from that prolific period.[2] This chapter explores the integration of those two elements

---

[1] For a discussion of the nineteenth century as the heyday of positivism, see J Schumpeter, *Economic Doctrine and Method: An Historical Sketch* (R Aris trans) (OUP New York 1954). For a statement, however, to the effect that there is no clear and 'closed' legal positivist doctrine (as to its content and origins) in nineteenth-century positivism, see D Tripp, *Der Einfluss des naturwissenschaftlichen, philosophischen und historischen Positivismus auf die deutsche Rechtslehre im 19 Jahrhundert* (Duncker & Humblot Berlin 1983) at 21.

[2] On Nietzsche's positivism, see generally H Röttges, *Nietzsche und die Dialektik der Aufklärung* (De Gruyter Berlin 1972) at 20. On the positivism of Comte and Saint Simon which applies the

in international law and describes two concrete and highly original outcomes of that process within the multifaceted aspects of early twentieth-century positivism: British international legal positivism, with its move from politics to law; and the transformation of political territory into administrative jurisdictions through the incursions into international law made by Austrian administrative lawyers.[3]

This text *revisits* early twentieth-century positivism in the choice of the types of positivism to be analysed. Much literature exploring the positivism of that period has focused on the approach taken by John Austin (1790–1859), Georg Jellinek (1851–1931), and Heinrich Triepel (1868–1946). These authors stand for three of the main features in the debate of the relationship of positivism and international law. Austin earned the enduring title of 'denier' of international law when he called it 'positive morality', establishing a positivist tradition that 'denies' the nature of law to the norms referring to the interaction of states.[4] Defining the core of international law as resting on the will of the state, Jellinek contributed to the positivist argument with his idea of the *Selbstbeschränkung* or autolimitation of states' will when they produced the international legal order.[5] Finally, Triepel's theory of law revolved also around the notion of a law-creating will (of the state). But it was distinctive. In his case, Triepel highlighted the dualism formed by national law and international law, which was thus practically reduced to treaty law.[6] Scholarship has often stressed the relative neglect of these early developers of positivist doctrines in the project of twentieth-century international law rather than their influence. Moreover, considering the three features of positivism mentioned above, 'denial', 'voluntarism', and 'dualism', for the most part authors have emphasized the restraining effect of positivism on the progress of international law.[7] In order

discourse of natural sciences to the study of man and society, and hopes 'to replace the government of men with the administration of things', see A Supiot, *Homo Juridicus. On the Anthropological Function of Law* (S Brown trans) (Verso London 2007) at 55.

   [3] I am here repeating and elaborating arguments I have put forward in M García-Salmones Rovira, *The Project of Positivism in International Law* (OUP Oxford 2013) in which some of these points are made verbatim.

   [4] J Austin, *The Province of Jurisprudence Determined* (Murray London 1832) at 131–2.

   [5] G Jellinek, *Die Lehre von den Staatenverbindung* (Verlag von O Haering Berlin 1882) at 94, 99.

   [6] H Triepel, *Völkerrecht und Landesrecht* (Verlag von CL Hirschfeld Leipzig 1899).

   [7] A classic review of late nineteenth-century and early twentieth-century positivism that highlights the role of those authors in U Scheuner, 'Naturrechtliche Strömungen in heutigen Völkerrecht' (1950) 13 *Zeitschrift für ausländisches öffentliches Recht und Völkerrecht* 557–614, especially at 569–83. See, at 575, Scheuner's somewhat dismissive appraisal of Oppenheim: 'In Great Britain the positivist attempts of the analytical school and later those by (German-influenced) L Oppenheim, exerted a strong but not lasting influence' (translation mine). Other studies of that period's positivism focusing on Jellinek, and/or Triepel and/or Austin include the following: WG Grewe, *The Epochs of International Law* (M Byers trans) (De Gruyter Berlin 2000) 513–22; J von Bernstorff, *The Public International Law Theory of Hans Kelsen: Believing in Universal Law* (T Dunlap trans) (CUP Cambridge 2010); M Koskenniemi, 'The Legacy of the Nineteenth Century' in D Armstrong (ed), *Routledge Handbook of International Law* (Routledge New York 2009) 141–53; P Capps, 'Methodological Legal Positivism in Law and International Law' in KE Himma (ed), *Law, Morality and Legal Positivism* (Franz Steiner Verlag Stuttgart 2004) 9–19. But see B Kingsbury, 'Legal

to suggest an alternative vision, one that pays particular attention to the enduring impact of positivism on the discipline's later thriving, it is in addition worth 'visiting' such distinguished authors as Lassa Oppenheim, as well as less well known but equally 'splendid' authors such as Ernst Radnitzky (1862–1939) or Leo Strisower (1857–1931), the thirty-second president of the *Institut de Droit International*.[8]

Unlike the positivism of German public lawyers of the previous century, such as Georg von Martens, early twentieth-century positivist international law was truly oblivious to the natural law order inherited from a classic period.[9] Indeed, the vocabulary of natural law was dropped from the language of respectable international lawyers of the time, if not openly then at least in a subtle manner.[10] However, the more pragmatic demands made on the new international law by growing economic interdependence, the strengthening of markets, and the growth of commerce and other forms of intercourse between states called for a working international law, which led to a renewed search for a reliable foundation for the international legal order.[11] In that sense, just as nineteenth-century positivism cannot be placed in opposition to a rejected naturalism, early twentieth-century positivism cannot be thought of in the absence of its naturalist counterpart, the newly devised community of interests.[12] On the one hand, the most advanced texts of

Positivism as Normative Politics: International Society, Balance of Power and Lassa Oppenheim's Positive International Law' (2002) 13 *European Journal of International Law* 401–36. See also von Bernstorff's analysis of Jellinek's 'proto-constitutionalism' and its lasting impact in modern international law in J von Bernstorff, 'Georg Jellinek and the Origins of Liberal Constitutionalism in International Law' (2012) 4 *Goettingen Journal of International Law* 659–75, and Koskenniemi describing the role of the community of interests, cultural developments, and international administration in Jellinek's work in M Koskenniemi, *The Gentle Civilizer of Nations: The Rise and Fall of International Law 1870–1960* (CUP Cambridge 2001) at 206.

[8] On the tradition of *visiting* positivists, see the story in HLA Hart, 'Kelsen Visited' (1963) 10 *UCLA Law Review* 709–28. For the compliment of 'splendid' to Radnitzky by Strisower, see L Strisower, *Die vermögensrechtlichen Massregeln gegen Österreicher in den feindlichen Staaten, ihre internationalrechtliche Wirkung und Zurückweisung* (Universitäts–Buchhandlung Wien 1915) at 29. For the list of presidents of the *Institute de Droit International* see Institut de Droit International, 'Historique' <http://www.idi-iil.org/idiF/navig_historique.html> [accessed 21 February 2016].

[9] On von Martens, see M Koskenniemi, 'Into Positivism: Georg Friedrich von Martens (1756–1821) and Modern International Law' (2008) 15 *Constellations* 189–207.

[10] See eg L Renault, *Introduction a l'étude du droit international* (Larose Paris 1879). For an enumeration of exceptions to that trend of renouncing natural law well into the twentieth century, especially on the question of sources, see *Epochs of International Law* (n 7) 509–12. Grewe mentions for instance John Westlake, predecessor of Oppenheim at the Whewell chair, who in his *International Law* declared that 'custom and reason are the two sources of international law'.

[11] The appearance of those pragmatic demands for instance in the case of the British Empire is discussed in M Lobban, 'English Approaches to International Law in the Nineteenth Century' in M Craven, M Fitzmaurice, and M Vogiatzi (eds), *Time, History and International Law* (Martinus Nijhoff The Hague 2007) 65–90, at 78–88.

[12] I employ here Kennedy's definition of naturalism: 'naturalism refers to theories of international law which locate the binding force of international norms in some source outside sovereignty, which precedes the sovereign, or can be implied from the nature of a community of sovereigns'. D Kennedy, 'International Law and the Nineteenth Century: History of an Illusion' (1996) 65 *Nordic Journal of*

the period contain urgent calls for the codification of norms and for the compilation and analysis of legal cases, which would have a lasting influence in shaping
the discipline of international law.[13] On the other hand, the truly novel element
of twentieth-century positivism is its celebration of the family of nations founded
on the primarily economic interests shared by states. If common interests failed,
one could always seek orientation on the basis of the painful activity of recording existing norms; whereas in times of pragmatic optimism, such as the period
under examination in this chapter, one simply needed to assume the existence of
the mandatory force of international norms on the basis of their communitarian
foundations.[14]

Of course, early twentieth-century positivists did not equate optimism and
community with political naïveté. One feature of the positivism of this period
which cannot be stressed enough is its assessment that there was a lack of solidarity among individuals and, by analogy, among states. While one can ascertain
their important sociological connotations, the notion of 'society'—in the sense of
originating in sociability—was scarcely to be found in the positivist texts to which
I refer.[15] Instead, those texts are characterized by nominalism, that is to say, by the
denial of an existing universal capable of giving access to the foundation of all
humanity,[16] as opposed to the more sociological politics of Georg Jellinek.[17] For
that reason, the lack of solidarity in early twentieth-century positivism was not
only the Darwinist principle of struggle and survival that had gradually permeated the intellectual landscape as a whole, but also a sceptical refusal to deal with
the meaning of entities such as men or states, which were considered to be factual,
empirical—in a word, historical.

Therefore, the conviction that the consent of states was of central importance
in producing law, which became of paramount relevance in early twentieth-
century positivism, arose from a general scepticism towards solidarity and the
firm rejection of natural law.[18] As we shall see later in the chapter, in that period

---

International Law 385–420, at 398. On the unfruitfulness of a sharp distinction between naturalism
and positivism, see 'Into Positivism' (n 9).

[13] L Oppenheim, 'The Science of International Law: Its Task and Method' (1908) 2 *American
Journal of International Law* 313–56.

[14] '[N]o State which is a member of the Family of Nations can at some time or another declare that
it will in future no longer submit to a certain recognised rule of the Law of Nations': L Oppenheim,
International Law: A Treatise (1st edn 2 vols Longmans, Green & Co London 1905–6) vol 1, at 18.

[15] See Lassa Oppenheim's definition of society: 'ubi societas ibi jus, where there is a community
of interests there must be law': L Oppenheim, *The League of Nations and Its Problems* (Longmans,
Green & Co London 1919) at 8.

[16] See this definition in *Nietzsche und die Dialektik der Aufklärung* (n 2) 49.

[17] Jellinek is nevertheless an eclectic author, who endorsed simultaneously the principles of
human sociability and human struggle of interests in G Jellinek, *System der subjektiven öffentlichen
Rechte* (JCB Mohr Tübingen 1905 reproduced Scientia Aalen 1979) at 49–50, 65.

[18] '[W]e know now-a-days that it is impossible to find a law which has its roots in human reason
only and is above legislation and customary law': 'The Science of International Law' (n 13) 329.

lawyers specializing in administrative law spontaneously engaged with international matters. Their approach to respond to that lack of solidarity, adopted the form of attempts to craft a system in which states could, as often as possible, avoid occasions during which explicit interaction as political powers occurred. In fact, due to the incommensurability of states' wills,[19] it was infeasible to subordinate the will of a state to power, and proposals to concentrate on the aspects of states as administrators arose partly on that basis.[20]

Given these sociological and philosophical premises, it is unsurprising that the early positivists of the twentieth century also 'visited' the school of *realpolitik* and many of their theories revolved around the question of the balance of power. In so doing, they became the avant-garde of international relations theorists, having realist inclinations and a pluralist outlook on the world.[21] However, the future world economy was not included among the issues that early twentieth-century positivists considered to be plural. Perhaps, due to their empiricism, they envisaged the world economy as 'the fact of capitalism'.[22]

In the new international law devised on the basis of this type of early twentieth-century positivism, states were less politico-territorial entities than holders of commercial and economic interests. Political interests gave rise to friction and distrust, and were to be set aside from law; whereas only the economic interests protected by international law were instruments of union and progress for the international

---

[19] 'Incommensurability is the absence of a common measure': J Raz, *Engaging Reason: On the Theory of Value and Action* (OUP Oxford 2002) at 46.

[20] Jellinek, interestingly, offers two reasons for a state to bind itself through a treaty: 'firstly', it can do so 'as administrator of the common interests of its people', and 'secondly', in order 'to affirm, consolidate or expand its position towards *third* powers, or also to *protect itself*, to *preserve or to save itself*, finally also to *strengthen itself* from within': *Die Lehre von den Staatenverbindung* (n 5) 105–6 (emphasis added).

[21] B Kingsbury, 'A Grotian Tradition of Theory and Practice? Grotius, Law and Moral Skepticism in the Thought of Hedley Bull' (1997) 17 *Quinnipac Law Review* 3–33, at 19, 33. For an excellent account of the English school of International relations that reveals the striking similarities with early twentieth-century positivism, see P Wilson, 'The English School's Approach to International Law' in C Navari (ed), *Theorising International Society: English School Methods* (Palgrave Macmillan New York 2009) 167–88. That the principle of balance of power was not generally proposed by international lawyers is shown by John Westlake. He expressed his anxiety in his review of the first volume of Oppenheim's *International Law* in 1905: 'The first [moral] is that it is so certain that an over-powerful state would try to disobey the law that a law of nations can exist only if there is a balance of power between the members of the family of nations. We are not so pessimistic, and in any case we could not admit that an attack on a state, made with no other justification than an opinion that its relative power ought to be diminished is allowed by any rule considered by civilized states to be legally binding': J Westlake, 'Book Review: *International Law: Vol I, Peace* by L Oppenheim, LLD' (1905) 21 *Law Quarterly Review* 432–4, at 434.

[22] See for instance this standpoint in F von Wieser, *Recht und Macht, Sechs Vorträge* (Duncker & Humblot Leipzig 1910), that received a positive review by Hans Kelsen: H Kelsen, 'Buchbesprechung: Friedrich Freiherr von Wieser, *Recht und Macht. Sechs Vorträge*, Leipzig 1910' in *Werke* (M Jestaedt ed) (5 vols Mohr Siebeck Tübingen 2007–11) vol 1, at 581–4.

order.[23] That very progress would facilitate states' consent to the submission of vital interests to international arbitration and judicial decision in the future, once obsolete moral positions had changed.[24] In particular, Austrian international lawyers focused decisively on a view of states as administrative units rather than on one revolving around the political potential of international communities.

Finally, despite positivist rhetoric about morality—visible, for instance, in Lassa Oppenheim's foundation of international law in a series of 'morals', the seventh and last of which highlighted the fact that the progressive development of international law depended both on the growth of international economic interests and on a high standard of public morality—early twentieth-century positivists were reluctant to produce *concrete* expressions of morality.[25] Indeed, they discharged lawyers from giving ethical judgements, on the basis of which an attempt could have been made to influence law in one way or another.[26] Certainly, this attitude was the result of articulating a normative vision of international law in which law apolitically reports on the reality of the world. In this manner, partly due to their scientism and partly due to their sole focus on interests, they chose to remain silent on the most pressing moral question facing the international order of the day—the exploitation and territorial deprivation of indigenous populations in the colonies.[27]

In order then to revisit these aspects of the positivist legacy, the first part of the chapter, which is German- and British-oriented, focuses on Lassa Oppenheim's groundbreaking work on the legal theory of international law at the beginning of the twentieth century. Oppenheim's recognition of the economic interdependence of nations was one important factor in his success in establishing the international economic system as the supporting framework of his Family of Nations and as the underlying theory of his international law. As Kingsbury states, Oppenheim followed the European tradition of a modular structure of legally similar units, 'sovereign states', that gave his theory political vitality and intellectual credibility.[28] But

---

[23] Therefore they were careful not to subordinate higher interests to commerce. This point is made by Benedict Kingsbury, who refers to higher interests with regard to wartime commerce: 'Legal Positivism as Normative Politics' (n 7) 428. An example of this is in *The League of Nations and Its Problems* (n 15) 48–55 ('Appendix: Correspondence with the Foreign Office Respecting the Interpretation of Article 23 (h) of the Hague Regulations Concerning Warfare').

[24] L Oppenheim, *The Future of International Law* (JP Bate trans) (OUP Oxford 1921) at 14.

[25] 'For, looked upon from a certain standpoint, International Law is, just like Municipal law, a product of moral and economic factors': L Oppenheim, *International Law, A Treatise* (RF Roxburgh ed) (3rd edn OUP Oxford 1919) at 97.

[26] See the scientific manifesto in 'The Science of International Law' (n 13). For a review of scientism see T Todorov, 'Totalitarianism: Between Religion and Science' (2001) 2 *Totalitarian Movements and Political Religions* 28–42, at 33.

[27] For an analysis of this question, see *The Project of Positivism in International Law* (n 3). But see the interesting approach taken by Radnitzky to the question of the equality of natives and citizens with the home country in E Radnitzky, 'Die rechtliche Natur des Staatsgebietes' (1906) 20 *Archiv fur öffentliches Recht* 313–55.

[28] 'Legal Positivism as Normative Politics' (n 7) 413.

Oppenheim's new international law went deeper than merely the commendatory function of being a provider of unity and progress to an assumed economic common interest. Together with his insistence that the law was only those norms that states had consented to and no more, he envisaged a constitution for international society that went far beyond the fact that its members were states. He claimed that those states had something *constitutive* in common, their interests, which, in a deeper sense, as constitutional principles, were also law.

Having looked at Oppenheim's theory of common interests, the second part of the chapter charts the complex legal theoretical transition embedded in the change of philosophical position as regards the understanding of universalism. This involved a move from the transcendent realist philosophy of an earlier era to the immanent philosophy of the Austrian positivists at the beginning of the century—a philosophy which, championed by Kelsen, would later become extremely influential. The new principles of 'law as a medium' and 'territory as a competence' were formulated by the Austrian lawyers on the basis of a new understanding of international law as an *administrative order*. Those principles rejected the political element embedded in the earlier legal-philosophical conception of territorial sovereignty as the sphere of a legal-political order.[29] The new positivist law was objective and immanent-realist. In a nutshell, this meant that it was devoid of any reference to transcendence (good, right, truth) or any ethical principle of sociability. As a consequence, the principles of 'law as a medium' and 'territory as a competence' were compatible with the politico-philosophical position which held that the reality of the world was composed by interests.

2 Lassa Oppenheim and the Future of International Law

Lassa Oppenheim was born in 1858 in Windecken, near Frankfurt am Main. After several years of teaching in Freiburg and Basel, and having produced five monographs on criminal law, he moved to London in 1895, becoming a British citizen in 1900. He taught first at the London School of Economics, and became holder of the Whewell Chair of International Law at the University of Cambridge in 1908. In 1905–6 Oppenheim published his *International Law* in two volumes and by the middle of the twentieth century he was regarded as the author of 'by common

---

[29] In the influential theory by Karl Viktor Fricker: KV Fricker, *Vom Staatsgebiet* (Ludwig Friedrich Fues Tübingen 1867).

consent the outstanding and most frequently employed systematic treatise on the subject in the English-speaking countries'.[30] In that book, and in subsequent publications, he developed a wholly original theory and one of the most powerful expressions of early twentieth-century international legal positivism.

Oppenheim's advancement of international society in paradoxical combination with the principle of balance of power is said to have raised the enduring appeal of his legal work. Beneath a rigorous positivism and political realism, it bred a powerful political project of liberal cosmopolitanism. Contrary to what one might have thought, legal positivism was best suited to serve this particular political project, which has found a permanent audience in the international legal community.[31] Positivism was best adapted to this project because, despite its purported scientific neutrality, it in fact acknowledged through law the existence of centres of influence and fixed the production of positive norms according to the logic of those power axes, also through the establishment of same-minded international institutions. Moreover, due to its insistence on separating religious or ethical considerations from positive law, positivism could achieve this without the check and control of any morality beyond the consent of the 'authorities' capable of producing law, that is to say, the Western states that had passed the test for membership of the Family of Nations.

Another reason for Oppenheim's success is the systematic approach underlying the legal theory of his works. Although he was sober in the articulation of his methodology 'as he wrote so little about it', he worked indefatigably in the establishment and search for a system and a science of international law.[32]

The theories imported from Germany were invisible in Oppenheim's work because they were the basic tools with which he constructed his international law, functioning as it were, like the foundations of the edifice, and giving his apparently simple theory its particular depth. Oppenheim's paradigmatic concept in this regard is the 'Family of Nations bound by common interests'.[33]

---

[30] A Nussbaum, *A Concise History of the Law of Nations* (Macmillan New York 1947) at 277. See also J Crawford, 'Public International Law in Twentieth-Century England' in J Beatson and R Zimmermann (eds), *Jurists Uprooted: German-Speaking Émigré Lawyers in Twentieth-Century Britain* (OUP Oxford 2004) 681–708, at 697.

[31] See generally Kingsbury's analysis, that in Oppenheim's understanding positivism was best suited to this project because it provided certainty, predictability, stability, and clarity in the formulation of rules, and in the separation of morality and law it guaranteed the avoidance of disagreement, while at the same time it expanded independent ethical agents through legal institutions and professions such as that of judges. Due to the centrality of states' consent in the theory, Oppenheim's positivism also obtained the authority needed for continuing the production of a working system of international law: 'Legal Positivism as Normative Politics' (n 7) 422–5.

[32] M Schmoeckel, 'The Internationalist as a Scientist and Herald: Lassa Oppenheim' (2000) 11 *European Journal of International Law* 699–712, at 701.

[33] Karl Binding (1841–1920), Franz von Liszt (1851–1919), and Heinrich Triepel are names that can be connected both biographically and through their intellectual influence on Oppenheim, but it is impossible to articulate that connection here due to space constraints.

On the other hand the raw materials that he employed to construct his theory of international law were unmistakably British. From Britain originated the legal and cultural matter of the theory and specifically its moral philosophy. Reading Oppenheim's international law, the fact that he named Francis Hutcheson as the English counterpart to Pufendorf makes sense.[34] Hutcheson, who was an accomplished philosopher in his own right, is also credited with having influenced Adam Smith in his 'general direction of liberalism'.[35] Oppenheim was *totally original* in constructing a new system of international law with a British stamp. In his international law it is apparent that he possessed a privileged knowledge of English jurisprudence, of some of its leading intellectual figures, of its political history, and of the reality of the legal and political relations of a commercial empire.[36] To the extent that he was thoroughly permeated by the large academic and political tradition of the British Empire, he was able to think using its legal matter.

His pragmatic approach to the effect that international law had to be found in state practice and in the consent of states as manifested in treaties was in the best nineteenth-century Anglo-American jurisprudential tradition. The Whewell Professor illustrated this point clearly in his treatment of the relationship between international law and municipal law in his famous 1908 piece on 'The Science of International Law'.[37] His discussion was not on an abstract level, but dealt with the important contribution of municipal case law.

On the one hand, he emphasized the role of case law in order to study the sources of international law and ultimately as a way to develop the science of international law. In order to allow the growth of a body of international case law, he also would propose some years later, together with the creation of the International Court of Justice, the importance of an International Court of Appeal.[38] On the other hand, subjecting the work of the courts to the national legislator reinforced his general statist approach.

But Oppenheim's novelty lay mainly in his thinking about what sort of interests would unite the Family of Nations and, together with a magnificent capacity to describe the law, the articulation of those thoughts in his *International Law*. First,

---

[34] The other of the 'English Naturalists' mentioned is Thomas Rutherford: *International Law* (n 14) 83.

[35] E Cannan, 'Introduction' in A Smith, *An Inquiry into the Nature and Causes of the Wealth of Nations* (E Cannan ed) (2 vols Methuen & Co London 1904 [1776]) xiii–xlviii, at xli.

[36] See *The Project of Positivism in International Law* (n 3) 43–110.

[37] 'The Science of International Law' (n 13). The article is still mentioned today as a key work on the method of international law: see eg O Corten, *Méthodologie du droit international public* (Editions de l'Universite de Bruxelles Bruxelles 2009) at 238.

[38] *The League of Nations and Its Problems* (n 15), 64–5. When Schmoeckel remarks on Oppenheim's 'dislike of cases', he might be referring to the scarcity of cases in his exposition of doctrine: M Schmoeckel, 'The Story of a Success: Lassa Oppenheim and His "International Law"' in M Stolleis and M Yanagihara (eds), *East Asian and European Perspectives on International Law* (Nomos Baden-Baden 2004) 57–138, at 103.

there were religious ideas that wound 'a band' around the civilized states, which were for the greater part Christian states. Also science and art were by their nature international and could, to a great extent, 'create a constant exchange of ideas and opinions between the subjects'. But, since not even the most powerful empire could produce everything its subjects needed, the production of agriculture and industry called for exchange. That is why international trade constituted an 'unequalled factor' that promoted the intercourse of states. International trade was the cause of navigation on the high seas and on the rivers. Trade, as a *creator*, would 'call into existence' the networks of railways covering the continents, and the international means of communication. Those 'manifold interests', which caused a constant intercourse between states were the reason for the existence of ambassadors and consuls. Despite the fact that individual states enjoyed sovereignty and independence, there was something stronger than all the powerful factors causing disunity: 'namely, the common interests'.[39] Thus, 'without the pressure exercised upon the States by their interests' the legally binding rules would have never come into existence.[40]

In each of his texts Oppenheim would make clear that it was by 'the growth, the strengthening and the deepening of international economic and other interests, and of international morality' that the Family of Nations and international law would progress.[41] After all, there were 'eternal and economic factors working in its favour'.[42] No doubt, 'the economic and other interests of states' had promoted arbitration among states and were succeeding in the setting up of international courts.[43]

But the interests binding modern states together were 'primarily' of an economic nature.[44] The more spiritual notions of art, science, and religion were international ideas, but he would not base the development of his theory upon them. For instance, when he describes the range of dominion of the Law of Nations, he ponders how the Law of Nations was a product of Christian civilization, pointing out that formerly no intercourse existed between Christian on one side and Mohammedan and Buddhist states on the other. But since the beginning of the nineteenth century, matters had started to change. Economic interests had emerged

[39] See the cautious use of the notion of 'common interest' in J Westlake, *The Collected Papers of John Westlake on Public International Law* (L Oppenheim ed) (CUP Cambridge 1914) at 125.

[40] *International Law* (n 14) 10, 11, 12, 17.

[41] He never specifies what the other interests are, but rather refers to the growth of means of communication like telegraph, railway, and so on: *The League of Nations and Its Problems* (n 15) 33.

[42] Fifteen years later with regard to the same tendency to internationalism, Kelsen referred to forces instead of interests: 'there are strong forces working in that direction': H Kelsen, *Das Problem der Souveränität* (JCB Mohr Paul Siebeck Tübingen 1920) at 320.

[43] *The Future of International Law* (n 24) 5.

[44] 'Economic interests, primarily, but many others also, prevent individual states from allowing the international community of states to remain unorganized any longer': ibid 66.

in relationships between people of different religions. Although there was still 'a deep gulf between Christian civilisation and others, *many interests*, which knit Christian States together knit likewise some non Christian and Christian States'.[45]

The nub of the issue here is not that his openness towards non-Christian States was wrong or misplaced. Never, after all, had Europe avoided intercourse with those capable of helping it to prosperity.[46] At the outset, conceiving a law that would work as a tool to allocate interests could be thought of as economistic but unproblematic: simply a choice. The questionable aspect, however, arises when things other than interests are at stake. Not only today, but also in Oppenheim's time, non-economic international questions were pressing. Ethical problems in the colonization enterprise and the animosity developing between European industrial countries required the legal point of view, but also that it would reach beyond the solely economic perspective. To those pressing problems this economic law was of necessity blind. It was in this manner that the focus on economic interest was an important step in foreclosing further discussion on the theory of international law, which during this period concentrated mainly on commercial exchange and various forms of economic exploitation. 'Interests' claimed monopoly over normativity, interests being at the centre of the theory and the measure of the ethical value of the legal enterprise. The outcome in practice is that other important considerations such as the promotion of real equality among states have no place in a legal discourse devoted to interests.

In his accurate assessment of the growing political import of economic relations among nations he was soon joined by others, like the Swiss international lawyer Max Huber. Throughout Huber's in-depth, sociological study of the evolving nature of international society into 'internationalism', *Beiträge zur Kenntnis der soziologischen Grundlagen de Völkerrechts und der Staatengesellschaft* ('Contributions to the Knowledge of the Sociological Foundations of International Law and the "Société des Nations"'), Huber highlighted—like Oppenheim had done before— the growing unification of international economy and the necessity of fostering morality (*Völkermoral*) as key factors for internationalism.[47] The sophistication of *Beiträge* is missing in Oppenheim's exposition. However, the scope of Huber's work has evident limits in contrast with Oppenheim's grand science of international law. Firmly rooted in the tradition of interests, Huber's sociological foundation of international law was also a manifestation of early twentieth-century positivism,

---

[45] *International Law* (n 14) 31 (emphasis added).

[46] See, the portrait of the sixteenth-century city-state of Venice as a worldly place, in which the foreign (Turkish, Greek, Jewish, and Germanic communities) were ambiguously both welcomed and segregated: F Johns, 'Global Governance: An Heretical History Play' (2004) 4 *Global Jurist Advances* 1–49.

[47] M Huber, 'Beiträge zur Kenntnis der soziologischen Grundlagen de Völkerrechts und der Staatengesellschaft' (1910) 4 *Das öffentliche Recht der Gegenwart* 56–134.

combining an inclination to pacifism with a realist (psychological) reaffirmation of the state, very similar to that of Oppenheim.[48]

3 THE IMMANENT UNIVERSALISM OF THE AUSTRIANS

We may now move to Vienna, the capital of an empire torn apart by both internal and external forces, and take a grip on the original view of universalism that the Austrians lawyers, who were both positivists and philosophers, were producing.[49]

On the one hand, nominalist immanence fleshed out the philosophy of many Austrian lawyers, and more generally, scientists.[50] On the other hand, they combined this philosophical position with a strong standpoint in favour of universalism for the future international law. The former tendency to nominalism was characteristically present in the revision of the Spinozean *homo sui juris* undertaken by renowned Austrian administrative lawyer Adolf Menzel, whose other titles include that of first advisor of Hans Kelsen's *Habilitation, Hauptprobleme der Staatsrechtslehre*, in 1911, in which the germ of the Pure Theory was sown,[51] and that of having formulated, with success, the proposal that legislation and in particular administrative legislation, rather than criminal or civil law ought to

---

[48] 'So strongly as the collective interests, might develop as well as great society interests that would guarantee their respect (might be), one would not be able to escape the fact that the direct and actual centers of action, would be not the community, but its parts, the independent states': see n 47. For a comment, see J Klabbers, 'The Sociological Jurisprudence of Max Huber: An Introduction' (1992) 43 *Austrian Journal of Public International Law* 197–213.

[49] On the pulling apart of the Austrian Empire, see for instance, CE Schorske, 'Politics and Patricide in Freud's Interpretation of Dreams' in CE Schorske (ed), *Fin de Siècle Vienna, Politics and Culture* (Knopf New York 1980) 181–207.

[50] The name of Sigmund Freud, for instance, comes to mind.

[51] A Menzel, *Homo Sui juris. Eine Studie zur Staatslehre Spinozas* (Alfred Hölder Vienna 1904). Kelsen's habilitation was published as H Kelsen, *Hauptprobleme der Staatsrechtslehre entwickelt aus der Lehre vom Rechtsatze* (JCB Mohr Paul Siebeck Tübingen 1911). See Weinberger's comment that 'I would even venture to claim that already in the *Hauptprobleme* all his essential attitudes are present at least in embryo': O Weinberger, 'Introduction' in H Kelsen, *Essays in Legal and Moral Philosophy* (O Weinberger ed P Heath trans) (D Reidel Dordrecht 1973) ix–xxviii, at x. On Menzel as advisor of Kelsen, see C Jabloner, 'Kelsen and His Circle: The Viennese Years' (1998) 9 *European Journal of International Law* 368–85, at 373. Menzel shared with Kelsen important biographical notes. He was also Jewish with origins in Bohemia, studied in Prague and later moved to Vienna and, converted to Catholicism, like Kelsen did before he became Lutheran: W Brauneder, 'Menzel, Adolf' in *Neue Deutsche Biographie* (1994) s 104f <http://www.deutsche-biographie.de/pnd116886129.html> [accessed 22 February 2016].

regulate cartels.[52] In that matter Menzel's novelty was his emphasis on the need for legal thought and legal scholarship for resolving problems originating in other domains, such as the economy.[53]

In his work on Spinoza Menzel described how the philosopher had famously highlighted the limitations imposed on the state by human nature in situations where the state wished to motivate an individual's inner will but found it impossible to offer sufficient reward or threat in exchange.[54] But the Austrian thought that Spinoza's employment of the notion of human nature went beyond the strictly empirical, and thus anticipated, without warrant, a certain meta-principle. The truth was that the question of motivation of the will was a historical one, and that '[n]o certain conclusions can be drawn from the general nature of man'.[55] In sum, despite producing an essentially sound doctrine when he defined law as motivation of the will, the Dutch philosopher's method had been *ungeschichtlich*.[56]

Probably the best embodiment of immanent universalism in the early twentieth-century positivism of Austrian legal theory is the work of Leo Strisower. Strisower was a private international law expert who had an increasing interest in public international law. He was also involved in Hans Kelsen's academic career, as his teacher in legal philosophy and as the supervisor of his dissertation. He published, in 1919, the following definition of law:

Law is an order of behaviours; the space, whose filling through law can be thought, and whose emptiness demands special consideration; it is the space of the human behaviours; that a certain fact [*Tatbestand*] has no legal consequences is from the beginning irrelevant.[57]

As is apparent, for Strisower, law was not an order of real space—rather, law was a space in its own right. Moreover, law was an order of behaviours, and this constituted a medium. This was a composition of the world, or at least of the legal world, with an immanent character. This order of behaviours was not based on a

---

[52] Cartels are firms' agreements that aim to reduce competition. Menzel discussed this issue in 1894, in the authoritative *Verein für Sozialpolitik*, and he published his ideas some years later in A Menzel, *Die Kartelle und die Rechtsordnung* (Duncker & Humblot Berlin 1902). See for instance in the contemporaneous literature the point that Menzel 'has brought the question of the legal regulation (of cartels) to the forefront': F Baumgarten and A Meszlény, *Kartelle und Trust. Ihre Stellung im Wirtschafts und Rechtssystem der wichtigsten Kulturstaaten* (Verlag von Otto Liebmann Berlin 1906).

[53] See this point in Gerber who asked next, 'Why then did these new ideas about the use of law emerge in turn-of-the century Austria?' His answer points to the fact that an elite of educated men were looking for new solutions to the attacks suffered by a class representing the values of economic freedom and competition, and that 'liberal ideas (often supported by Jewish traditions) also contributed to strong belief in the value and efficacy of law': DJ Gerber, *Law and Competition in Twentieth Century Europe: Protecting Prometheus* (Clarendon Press Oxford 1998) at 56, 63.

[54] B de Spinoza, *Theologisch-politischer Traktat* (W Bartuschat ed and trans) (Meiner Verlag Hamburg 2012). For a classic expression of that argument, see C Schmitt, *Der Leviathan in der Staatslehre des Thomas Hobbes. Sinn und Fehlschlag eines Symbols* (Klett-Cotta Stuttgart 2003 [1938]).

[55] *Homo sui juris* (n 51) 88   [56] Ibid 89.

[57] L Strisower, *Der Krieg und die Völkerrechtsordnung* (Manz Wien 1919) at 17.

transcendent principle, the good, the right, or truth, but was an immanent principle of positive organization and compulsion (*Zwang*).

Strisower maintained that 'modern international law...does not leave any remaining space devoid of law' ('*Das moderne Völkerrecht lässt,...keinen rechtsleeren Raum übrig*').[58] He even argued that at the moment, in 1919, the globe was entirely covered by law—that there was no legal vacuum. Although he did not dwell at length on the question of territory, Strisower, in a manner not very different to Kelsen's at a later date, also mulled over the idea of an international legal order regulating behaviours across the globe.

It had been yet another Austrian who provided a ground-breaking contribution instrumental to integrating the question of the legal nature of territory in an immanent and universalist theory of law. Ernst Radnitzky produced a comprehensive overview of existing scholarship dealing with the question within international and constitutional legal theory, 'The Legal Nature of the Territory of the State', and in the process he developed his own position on the question.[59] The contribution by Radnitzky to the understanding of the juridical status of territory in relation to the state might arguably be considered the link between the German theory of territorial sovereignty and Kelsen's normativity theory.[60] Still, Radnitzky considered Carl Viktor Fricker, the originator of the German theory, undoubtedly the authority on the question of territory and public law and his own theory revolved around Fricker's attempt to avoid the reductionism of taking international law to be merely 'higher private law'.[61]

Unlike Fricker, in 'The Legal Nature' Radnitzky based the foundation of public law upon the concept of power and not on that of politics. Further, he genuinely

---

[58] *Der Krieg und die Völkerrechtsordnung* (n 57) 62. The opposite view by the German-Balt and ultra-positivist Carl Bergbohm (1849–1927): 'Never has a positive law considered it necessary and meaningful to regulate the totality of the possible legal materials in its personal and spatial territory, but it rather leaves an amount of that to the side': C Bergbohm, *Jurisprudenz und Rechtsphilosophie* (Duncker & Humblot Leipzig 1892) at 375–6. Strisower specifically mentioned Bergbohm: 'It is at least unclear' whether Bergsbohm's legal empty space 'is understood in the same manner': *Der Krieg und die Völkerrechtsordnung* (n 57) 15. On Bergbohm, see L Mälksoo, 'The Science of International Law and the Concept of Politics: The Arguments and Lives of the International Law Professors at the University of Dorpat/Iur'ev/Tartu 1855–1985' (2005) 76 *British Year Book of International Law* 383–502.

[59] E Radnitzky, 'Die rechtliche Natur des Staatsgebietes' (1906) 20 *Archiv für öffentliches Recht* 313–55.

[60] See the German theory in *Vom Staatsgebiet* (n 29) and later in KV Fricker, 'Gebiet und Gebietshoheit' in K Bücher (ed), *Festgabe für Albert Schäffle* (H Laupp'chen Buchhandlung Tübingen 1901). On the connections between Radnitzky and the Vienna School, see eg B Conforti, 'The Theory of Competence in Verdross' (1995) 6 *European Journal of International Law* 70–7. On the normativity theory of Kelsen, see eg H Kelsen, '"Foreword" to the Second Printing of *Main Problems in the Theory of Public Law*' in SL Paulson and BL Paulson (eds), *Normativity and Norms: Critical Perspectives on Kelsenian Themes* (Clarendon Press Oxford 1998) 3–22. See also SL Paulson, 'Introduction' in *Normativity and Norms: Critical Perspectives to Kelsenian Themes* xxiii–liii.

[61] *Vom Staatsgebiet* (n 29) 6.

observed the world as a big complex of administrative departments or jurisdictions. In a word, Radnitzky transformed the conception of territorial sovereignty into a specific notion of jurisdiction whose historical and conceptual origins could be traced to Austrian administrative law.

Faced with the theory that viewed territory as an object of the state—the theory of property of Paul Heilborn and many others—and, on the other hand, that which described territory as a feature of the state—Fricker's position—Radnitzky chose to refuse both.[62] The first theory could not explain the fact that a state without territory was not a state, because no private law analogy would correspond to that situation. This proved that the theory of property of the territory was not an expression of public law. Radnitzky denied the second theory the quality of law at all, because Fricker's claim that territory was 'a moment in the being of the state' belonged to an 'intellectual region' and 'world of concepts' inaccessible to jurists.[63] To jurists who practised an immanent philosophy, that is.

In Radnitzky's view, the right theory of territory ought rather to originate in the notion of competence. The provenance of the in-depth treatment of the question that the state was the source of competences could be traced back to Albert Hänel (1833–1919).[64] In the description of the relationship between sovereign and non-sovereign states in the *Reich*, Hänel famously dwelt at length on the concept of 'competence-competence' to describe the former's constitutional authority to decide over its own competences.[65] To the material competence to which Hänel exclusively referred, Radnitzky added the principle that in order to be able 'to command', a state not only had to know 'what' to command, but also 'to whom' and 'where'. That is to say, the state had together with a material, a 'personal and a local (*örtliche*) competence'.[66] In this manner Radnitzky was in fact equating territorial sovereignty with an expression of 'local competence'.[67] In a similar manner to the case of the state possessing a 'competence-competence' over material questions, a sovereign state also possessed an unlimited legal power, which was not law, but

---

[62] P Heilborn, *Das System des Völkerrechts* (Springer Berlin 1896) 1–35. Fricker defined the territory as 'a characterization for a moment in the being of the state, its spatial impenetrability': *Vom Staatsgebiet* (n 29) 17.

[63] 'Die rechtliche Natur des Staatsgebietes' (n 59) 338.

[64] A Hänel, *Deutsches Staatsrecht* (Duncker & Humblot Leipzig 1892) at 771–830. See also 'Die rechtliche Natur des Staatsgebietes' (n 59) 339.

[65] Hänel referred to it as originating in the linguistic usages produced within the context of the North German Confederation (*Norddeutscher Bund*): *Deutsches Staatsrecht* (n 64) 772. Stolleis describes the development of the notion of 'competence-competence' as the coronation of Hänel's scientific work: M Stolleis, *Geschichte des Öffentlichen Rechts in Deutschland* (4 vols Beck Munich 1988–2012) vol 2, at 358. Stolleis also mentions Hänel as the support, with Gierke, for German 'anti-positivism' of the 1920s: vol 3, at 171–2.

[66] 'Die rechtliche Natur des Staatsgebietes' (n 59) 339.

[67] 'Die örtliche Kompetenz aber ist gleichbedeutend mit dem Ausdrucke: Gebietshoheit': 'Die rechtliche Natur des Staatsgebietes' (n 59) 340.

local competence over its territory. The actual limitation of physical power was an altogether different question, since states, despite their unlimited legal power did not generally have the real capacity to make conquests and increase their territory. The private law analogy was—again—at hand, also for Radnitzky: was it not the same situation that the poorest of the people also have the legal capacity to buy diamonds, shares, and real state but not the money to do so?[68]

The distinction between Hänel's and Radnitzky's use of competence is important from the point of view of the context in which they developed it. Hänel was disentangling the nineteenth century evolution from *Bundestaat* to *Reich* in which an increasing political centralization of competences—from federal states to *empire*— had taken place in the territories of Germany.[69] In turn, as is apparent in his text, Radnitzky had in mind the activity of the Austrian administration for which the factor of political dependence or independence and the political point of view was not a central issue. Therefore, when Radnitzky's notion of 'local competence' was translated into the language of international law, it carried with it the sense of a concept without political tension, and was based on a history with administrative pedigree.

It was the use of the concept of 'legal power' (*Rechtsmacht*) that allowed Radnitzky to think in these terms. For this he made a double reversal. First, *Rechtsmacht* contained an interesting subjectivized version of 'the territory' as 'a reflex' of a legal quality or feature of the state, namely the 'local competence'. It further embodied an objectivized version of the will of the state, the objectivization of which was achieved by describing the state powers as competences similar to those of an administrative department.[70] These competences formed the state's jurisdiction, which amounted to the scope of the state's sovereignty.

In the context of the efforts to develop a valid and universal theory of international law at the beginning of the twentieth century, the interest in the objectivization of the will of the state, that is the retreat from sovereignty or personal competence, and the coming to the front of the local competence, was twofold. First, it made it possible to refuse to subject the state's will to another will, thus avoiding the relationship of dominant to subordinate will among states.[71] Second, it sanctioned the notion of a community of states which then became a place in which states stay side by side, but did not need to interrelate to each other, as 'will holders', except through the mediation of law.[72]

---

[68] 'Die rechtliche Natur des Staatsgebietes' (n 59) 345.

[69] *Deutsches Staatsrecht* (n 64) 771–830.

[70] 'Die rechtliche Natur des Staatsgebietes' (n 59) 340.

[71] G Deleuze, *Nietzsche and Philosophy* (H Tomlinson trans) (Columbia University Press New York 1983) at 8. As Nietzsche explained, 'Wille kann natürlich nur auf Wille wirken': F Nietzsche, *Jenseits von Gut und Böse* (Alfred Kröner Verlag Leipzig 1930) at 48.

[72] See *Der Krieg und die Völkerrechtsordnung* (n 57) 90.

From the perspective of international law, Radnitzky's argument had far-reaching ramifications. Significantly, the objectivity of the viewpoint for international law was obtained through drawing an analogy with the administration:

The microcosm that corresponds to the macrocosm 'state' is then, neither the individual nor the person of the private law, but the agency [*Amt*] endowed with imperium for a certain jurisdiction [*Sprengel*].[73]

The states stayed in the international community not only as law-makers but importantly also as appliers of international norms in the same sense that an administrative agency applied norms within the state.[74]

In the same vein, Radnitzky explained that the grave conflicts of competences (between states) that had in them the possibility of war were analogous to a situation within the state. This analogy, corresponding to the international conflict, was not the classic one between individuals, but of conflicts of competences between state organs which were often resolved by judicial decision. The most serious conflict of competences within the state was the conflict over the constitution (*Verfassungskonflikt*) that took place directly between the organs of the state. In both cases, the similarity lay in the possibility of a violent solution, either war or revolution. Making reference to the *Hague Conventions*, Radnitzky discovered that in the same way as the peace conventions distinguished between political and judicial conflicts, in which the former had no superior organ capable of handing down a binding judgment, the potentially revolutionary conflict of competences between the organs of the state lacked a binding mechanism to resolve the conflict.

Constructing theory using the administration and concepts originating in administrative law helped Radnitzky to objectivize the international legal realm. Taken as a model for the state's external activity the administration showed a marked tendency to depoliticize that very activity of the state. Most importantly it contributed to a universalist development of law, at once downgrading the role of states as political actors and having recourse neither to universal principles of natural law, such as reason, nor to transcendental principles such as the good, right, or just.

To anyone familiar with the work of Hans Kelsen, those two principles of 'law as a medium' and 'territory as a competence' closely resemble the building blocks that sustain the international legal theory of 'the legal expert of the century'.[75] Kelsen

---

[73] 'Die rechtliche Natur des Staatsgebietes' (n 59) 352. *Sprengel* is a term used in Austria to define the jurisdiction of a court, of an administration, or of a parish over a certain territory.

[74] And that was so, because 'to define the territory of the state as the sphere of local competence, also clarifies that the states adopt a position in today's international community that in many respects comes close to that of the states' organs [*Organe*] within the state': ibid 353. This is what Lauterpacht would later defend in H Lauterpacht, *Recognition in International Law* (CUP Cambridge 1948).

[75] 'This expression has almost become standard': see 'Kelsen and His Circle: The Viennese Years' (n 51) 371. Kelsen is routinely referred to as the 'jurist of the twentieth century': RA Métall, *Hans Kelsen Vida y Obra* (J Esquivel trans) (Instituto de Investigaciones Jurídicas México 1976) at v;

expressed them famously in two important principles: first through the assertion that the international legal order, and *any* valid legal order, constitutes a (coercive) order of human behaviours, and secondly through his choice for the superiority of international law.[76] This is the reason why the administrative style, and not the political discussion, would form the background theme of Kelsen's legal theory.

4 Economic Early Twentieth-Century Positivism: Concluding Thoughts

The ideal of avoiding political disagreement peculiar to early twentieth-century legal positivism, which in Oppenheim takes the single political form of liberal cosmopolitanism, arose in Austria with singular force due to the nominalism practised by some of its most theoretically oriented lawyers. In parallel with the turn to foundational administrative legal principles, nominalism generated in Austrian legal thought the method of de-substantialization of form, of seeking the purity that had its origins within economic circles.[77] In the world of 'what is' there is no 'substance' or principle able to claim scientific or ontological authority over (an)other reality. Something that Austrian scepticism denounced often with irony, that 'substance' was merely a mask for 'interests' and therefore subjective, was celebrated as the community of interests by Oppenheim's and other's pragmatic optimism.[78]

Roscoe Pound referring to Kelsen as 'unquestionably the leading jurist of the time' quoted in Leo Gross, 'Hans Kelsen: October 11, 1881–April 15, 1973' (1973) *American Journal of International Law* 491–501, at 494; see generally SL Paulson and M Stolleis (eds), *Hans Kelsen, Staatsrechtsleher und Rechtstheoretiker des 20. Jahrhunderts* (Mohr Siebeck Tübingen 2005).

[76] 'As a "norm", the law is the specific meaning of an act of will directed at a definite human behaviour': H Kelsen, 'On the Pure Theory of Law' (1966) 1 *Israel Law Review* 1–7, at 1. 'The States, it is true, remain competent, even under international law, to regulate in principle all matters which can be regulated by an order limited in its territorial sphere; but they retain this competence only insofar as international law does not regulate a particular subject matter. The fact that a subject matter is regulated by international law has the effect that it can no longer be regulated arbitrarily by national law': H Kelsen, *General Theory of Law and State* (A Wedberg trans) (Harvard University Press Cambridge MA 1946) at 350–1.

[77] Exemplary in the work of Menger, founder of the Austrian School of Economics: see C Menger, *Untersuchungen über die Methode der Sozialwissenschaften und der Politischen Oekonomie insbesondere* (Duncker & Humblot Leipzig 1883).

[78] The irony of Austrian scepticism is perhaps most visible in Kelsen's work. For example: 'When already the single human being experiences his particular interest naively as "right" [*Recht*], with how much more impetus does every interest-group want to be able to call on "justice" in order to impose its demands.': H Kelsen, *Die philosophischen Grundlagen der Naturrechtslehre und des Rechtspositivismus* (Pan Verlag Rolf Heise Charlottenburg 1928) at 77.

But the process of devaluation of reality which law had to regulate, was the same in both expressions of the positivism analysed in this chapter. In short, the matter for law was composed by the often exclusively economic interests of states. Perhaps the most striking feature of early twentieth-century positivism is that, far from remaining in oblivion, its tendencies to avoid the complexities of politics and its focus on economic themes would be persistently reinterpreted and integrated in international legal theory.

CHAPTER 10

....

HANS KELSEN
AND THE RETURN
OF UNIVERSALISM

....

JOCHEN VON BERNSTORFF

1 INTRODUCTION

....

HANS Kelsen (1881–1973) was a Viennese law professor in between the two world wars, who is seen by many, in particular on the European continent, as one of the most outstanding, if not the most outstanding, jurist of the twentieth century. He was an international lawyer, a legal theorist, and eminent scholar of constitutional law. His extremely successful academic career, in the period before, between, and after the two world wars, took him from Vienna, Cologne, and Geneva, to Harvard and Berkeley. Nearly all his moves and his emigration, however, were involuntary and came in response to life-threatening perils, persecution, or political defamation, all of them had to do with anti-Semitic bias.

Kelsen was a radical modernist thinker, social democrat, and liberal cosmopolitan. His vigorous defence of democracy and a cosmopolitan international legal order made him subject to harsh criticism of mainstream German scholars, most of whom were contemptuous of Weimar democracy and the League of Nations. His writings on international law include numerous articles: a monograph entitled *The Problem of Sovereignty*, a general textbook, Hague Lectures, and a Commentary on the *Charter of the United Nations*.[1] Among Kelsen's students were outstanding international lawyers, namely Alfred Verdross (1890–1980), Josef L Kunz (1890–1970), Hans Morgenthau (1904–80), and also Hersch Lauterpacht (1897–1960).

In the following contribution, I will first attempt to illustrate the deep structure of the Kelsenian approach to international law from an intellectual history perspective (Section 2). This will include the political, doctrinal, and philosophical context in which Kelsen developed his fundamental critique of the then-prevailing German international law theory. As a second step, I attempt to illustrate the subversive and revolutionary force of Kelsen's critical methodology with a couple of examples (Section 3). By way of conclusion I will add a few words on how German international legal scholarship dealt with Kelsen's legacy after the Second World War (Section 4).

2 THE CONTEXTUAL DEEP-STRUCTURE OF THE KELSENIAN APPROACH TO INTERNATIONAL LAW

To anticipate the findings of this particular interpretation of Kelsen's international legal theory, let me say at this point that the reconstructed doctrine of international law can be adequately grasped only if we place it within the tension-filled relationship between the two crucial goals that Kelsen had as a theorist of international law: first, establishing a non-political scientific method for the field of international law, and second, promoting the political project—which originated in the interwar period—of a thoroughly legalized and institutionalized world order. Kelsen's approach to international law was characterized by the constant effort to advance these two prima facie conflicting goals through his writings on international law.[2]

Kelsen saw himself as the founder of a method of jurisprudence that was critical of ideology, the so-called 'Pure Theory of Law'. This new jurisprudential methodology was to allow jurists to engage with law as a subject of study in a non-political, and thus purely 'scientific', way. In addition, as a political individual, Kelsen

---

[1] H Kelsen, *Das Problem der Souveränität und die Theorie des Völkerrechts. Beitrag zu einer reinen Rechtslehre* (2nd edn JCB Mohr Tübingen 1928) at 87; H Kelsen, *Principles of International Law* (Rinehart New York 1952); H Kelsen, *The Law of the United Nations* (Stevens London 1950).

[2] I have developed this thesis more extensively in J von Bernstorff, *The Public International Law Theory of Hans Kelsen: Believing in International Law* (T Dunlap trans) (CUP Cambridge 2010).

developed during the interwar period—probably influenced by his experiences in the First World War—into a committed internationalist, who saw the creation of an institutionalized legal community of states as the only path toward a more peaceful world order. Subsequently, Kelsen, as a legal scholar, found himself confronted with the problem of not being able to openly pursue his own political preferences for the 'cosmopolitan project' of an institutionalized rule of law in international relations, but was compelled to also make the non-political method the postulated yardstick of his own legal-theoretical works when dealing with the legal material. Kelsen's solution was a methodologically guided critique of those theoretical and doctrinal constructs that stood in the way of his own political program, which he had developed at the end of the First World War. The explanatory approach laid out in this chapter, thus, reconstructs the inner connection between Kelsen's legal methodology and the cosmopolitan project underlying his fundamental critique of the *fin de siècle* mainstream German international legal scholarship. Kelsen's way of working, which seems largely 'destructive' toward the traditional doctrine of international law, can therefore be understood and explained as a strategy for uniting two scholarly goals which seem at first glance contradictory.

2.1 The Quest for Objectivity

The central project of the Pure Theory of Law was the creation of an 'objective' legal scholarship. In 1928, Kelsen described the state of German public law scholarship this way:

The discipline becomes a mere ideology of politics. . . . In a society convulsed by world war and world revolution, it is more important than ever to the contending groups and classes to produce usable ideologies that allow those still in power to effectively defend their interests. That which accords with their subjective interest seeks to be presented as what is objectively right. And so the science of the state and the law must serve that purpose. It provides the 'objectivity' that no politics is able to generate on its own.[3]

The 'liberation' from political 'bondage' postulated in the Pure Theory of Law with such Enlightenment pathos is a struggle for the inherent autonomy of legal scholarship on the basis of a new scientific foundation. Already from the time of his *habilitation* in 1911, Hans Kelsen had been searching for a more 'scientific' method of jurisprudence. At the beginning of the twentieth century, Georg Jellinek's (1851–1911) theory of public law was the measure of all things in German-language legal scholarship. Jellinek, the first dean of the Heidelberg law faculty who was of Jewish background, had retained the Hegel-inspired assumption of the will of the sovereign

---

[3] H Kelsen, 'Juristischer Formalismus und Reine Rechtslehre' (1929) 58 *Juristische Wochenschrift* 1723–6.

state as the law's ground of validity, but had enriched his theory of public law with sociological and psychological elements. His work symbolized the transition to a modern broadening of perspectives in German legal scholarship toward the integration of insights from the new neighbouring disciplines, such as, for instance, the emerging field of sociology. In Heidelberg, Kelsen, as a visiting researcher, attended Jellinek's seminar and felt repelled by the devoted band of disciples he felt Jellinek had gathered around himself. By now obsessed with the idea of putting legal positivism on a more objective scientific basis, he worked out a theoretical approach that turned against Jellinek's theoretical approach in two ways.[4] First, it completely displaced the Hegelian notion of will and the personification of the state as a subject capable of an exercise of will. Second, it radically rejected Jellinek's broadening to include sociological and psychological questions, which Kelsen wanted to purge entirely from the subject matter of jurisprudence. By applying contemporary neo-Kantian epistemological insights to jurisprudence, Kelsen became, with his project of the 'Pure Theory of Law' (1934) the *Alleszermalmer* ('universal destroyer')[5] of the traditional methodology in German-language jurisprudence.[6]

This modern revolt arose before and during the First World War, in the collapse of the old Viennese world, which was marked by the rise of the masses, nationalism, and anti-Semitism.[7] Moreover, the 'kakanian'[8] multiethnic state, whose unity had been secured, not least through an efficient, thoroughly juridical administrative structure, was beginning to break apart. During the increasingly ideological usurpation of the societal discourse, Kelsen called for a scientific—that is, non-political—approach to the law. The project of the Pure Theory of Law, which was initially directed against the premises of the preceding German voluntaristic positivism ('*Staatswillenspositivismus*'), can thus be understood as a scholarly reaction to the centrifugal forces of the ideologized *Zeitgeist*.

The foundation of Kelsen's theory of international law was the 1920 monograph *Das Problem der Souveränität und die Theorie des Völkerrechts [The Problem of*

---

[4] This is what Kelsen had to say in his autobiographical sketch: 'I was completely intoxicated by the feeling of embarking on a new path in my discipline.': H Kelsen, 'Autobiography' in *Hans Kelsen Werke* (M Jestaedt ed) (3 vols Mohr Siebeck Tübingen 2007) vol 1, 29–91, at 41.

[5] As Theodor Adorno and Max Horkheimer said of Kant: see TW Adorno and M Horkheimer, *Dialektik der Aufklärung: Philosophische Fragmente* (Suhrkamp Frankfurt am Main 1998 [1947]) at 100.

[6] The most compact and lucid recent account of the methodological orientation of the Vienna School from the perspective of the history of public law, along with extensive references, can be found in M Stolleis, *A History of Public Law in Germany 1914–1945* (T Dunlap trans) (OUP Oxford 2004) at 151–60. For a comprehensive analysis and interpretation of Kelsen's doctrine of international law, see H Dreier, *Rechtslehre, Staatssoziologie und Demokratietherie bei Hans Kelsen* (Nomos Baden-Baden 1986).

[7] On this, see CE Schorske, *Fin-de-Siècle Vienna: Politics and Culture* (Knopf New York 1979) at 116–80.

[8] As Robert Musil famously depicted the dual Austrian monarchy being both imperial and royal in nature (in German *kaiserlich* and *königlich*, abbreviated 'k & k'); R Musil, *The Man Without Qualities* (S Wilkins trans) (Vintage New York 1996) vol 1.

Sovereignty and the Theory of International Law]. This book, which, according to Kelsen himself, was largely already completed during the First World War, was the second important monographic publication after Kelsen's *habilitation* thesis of 1911, *Hauptprobleme der Staatsrechtslehre* [*Chief Problems in the Theory of Public Law*].[9] The critical thrust of the 1920 monograph was directed against the main traditional approaches to international law theory by German-speaking theorists, from Adolf Lasson (1832–1917) to Jellinek, from Heinrich Triepel (1868–1946) to Erich Kaufmann (1880–1972). In its constructive aspect, this monograph, with its emphasis on the primacy of international law, connected with the theory of international law developed by Karl von Kaltenborn-Stachau (1817–66) in the mid-nineteenth century. As an important contribution to the development of the Pure Theory of Law, Kelsen's monograph had a lasting impact on the conception of international law by the three Viennese students and companions, Verdross, Kunz, and Lauterpacht.

2.2 The Cosmopolitan Project

The first two decades of the twentieth century were a historical phase in which the pacifist–liberal currents in Europe and the United States (US) regarded the inadequate development of the international legal system as the chief reason behind the outbreak of the war. If we shift our view to the broader environment of international legal theory, it is apparent that Kelsen and his pupils, like a number of other authors of the interwar period, saw themselves as part of a modernization movement in international law. This international movement for a new law of nations arose during the First World War and reached its climax in the 1920s. The shared enthusiasm for a changed, more peaceful world order prompted legal scholars in various countries, coming from different methodological backgrounds, to try and prepare, in scholarly manner, the road to what they called 'a new international law'. As part of this movement, one could mention, in addition to the authors of the Vienna School, Lammasch (1853–1920), Nippold (1853–1920), Krabbe (1857–1932), and Duguit (1859–1928) from the pre-war generation, and for the younger generation, Scelle (1878–1961), Politis (1872–1942), Álvarez (1868–1960), JL Brierly (1881–1955), and Lauterpacht.[10] During the First World War, Kelsen had been an active office-holder of the declining Habsburg monarchy, and unlike the Austrian

---

[9] H Kelsen, *Hauptprobleme der Staatsrechtslehre entwickelt aus der Lehre vom Rechtssatze* (Mohr Tübingen 1911).

[10] James W Garner, in his Hague Academy lectures of 1931, sought to provide an overview of the reform movement in the 1920s: JW Garner, 'Le développement et les tendances récentes du droit international' (1931) 35 *Recueil des Cours* 605–720.

pacifist, politician, and legal scholar Lammasch, he had refrained from publishing pacifist or cosmopolitan writings during the war.[11] But the publication of his monograph *Das Problem der Souveränität und die Theorie des Völkerrechts* [*The Problem of Sovereignty*] in 1920 quickly made him into a pacesetter in international law theory within the renewal movement during the interwar period.

Driven by a spirit of enlightenment and cosmopolitan pacifism, these thinkers set out to destroy what they felt were the detrimental tenets of classic international law theory. At the centre of the critical analyses stood the concept of state sovereignty and its place within the international legal order. Although methods and results diverged strongly, what characterized the representatives of this movement was a shared claim to modernization, understood as a project of demystification of international legal theory. The dynamic of this movement sprang from the reaction against classical international law, which was portrayed as the product of European pre-war nationalism.

For example, Brierly, in his inaugural lecture in 1924, emphasized that 'the world regards international law today as in need for rehabilitation'.[12] In light of this criticism, the theoretical landscape of international law in the nineteenth century seemed dominated by mystically transfigured notions of sovereignty. From this perspective, the traditional doctrines of international law, with their 'subjective' orientation focused on the 'will' of the individual state, had contributed to the rupture of civilization represented by the First World War.[13] For the reformers, it was not only international politics, but also international legal scholarship infected by the dogma of sovereignty that bore responsibility for the inadequate elaboration of the Hague order.[14] It was the League of Nations that initially served as a screen onto which the hopes for a more peaceful world order through new forms of collective security, arbitration, and adjudication were projected.

Kelsen also saw in a reform of the international legal system—including a strong world organization and compulsory adjudication—the key to a more peaceful

---

[11] This probably had something to do with his involvement at the ministerial level of the Austrian war department during the First World War, a position that was beneficial to his career. On this, see G Oberkofler and E Rabofsky, *Hans Kelsen im Kriegseinsatz der k.u.k. Wehrmacht. Eine kritische Würdigung seiner militärtheoretischen Angebote* (P Lang Frankfurt am Main 1988) at 13.

[12] JL Brierly, *The Basis of Obligation and Other Papers* (Clarendon Press Oxford 1958) at 68. On Brierly, see C Landauer, 'JL Brierly and the Modernization of Transnational Law' (1993) 25 *Vanderbilt Journal of Transnational Law* 881–918. On the cultural–historical rupture of 1914, see M Stolleis, *Der lange Abschied vom 19. Jahrhundert. Vortrag gehalten vor der Juristischen Gesellschaft zu Berlin am 22. Januar 1997* (de Gruyter Berlin 1997).

[13] The criticism focused above all on Jellinek's doctrine of self-obligation: JL Brierly, 'Le fondement du caractère obligatoire du droit international public' (1928) 23 *Recueil des Cours* 463–589, at 482–4; H Lauterpacht, *The Function of Law in the International Community* (OUP Oxford 1933) at 409–12.

[14] N Politis, 'Le problème des limitations de la souveraineté et la théorie de l'abus des droits dans les rapports internationaux' (1925) 6 *Recueil des Cours* 1–121, at 5–27.

world. His self-conception as it related to international law was thus fed from two central, basic beliefs that were not hard to find within the liberal, German-speaking bourgeoisie in Central Europe, which—not necessarily but often—had a Jewish background. First, the unrestrained faith in the specific validity and pacifying force of the legal form, also applicable in international relations; second, the belief in social progress through scientific, that is, 'objective' understanding. The Pure Theory of Law regarded the supposedly ideologized jurisprudence of international law as an obstacle to the further development of the international legal system.[15] Kelsen shared this mindset with his closest student of international law, Kunz, and with Lauterpacht, who had studied with Kelsen in Vienna before emigrating to the United Kingdom (UK).[16]

The belief in progress through 'objective' scientific understanding, on the one hand, and in the power of the pacifying medium of the law, on the other, is a cultural phenomenon of a vanished epoch of European jurisprudence in the late nineteenth and early twentieth centuries. Emerging out of the gradual demise of the Habsburg Empire, it found its most radical champion in Kelsen. In his short autobiography, Kelsen himself had depicted the Pure Theory of Law as a being decisively coined by the pre-First World War Austrian context.[17] After all, it had been the force of the law that had been perceived as holding together the multiethnic empire, bound to replace the missing 'homogenous' society in the absence of common cultural foundations.

2.3 The Methodological Toolkit

According to Kelsen, the quest for the epistemological Archimedean point outside of politicization and subjectivity could succeed only through the formalization of jurisprudential concepts. The legal form had to be purified—it had to be empty. Expelling the political could succeed only in a conceptual world that is subject to its own distinct, objectifiable laws. The latter entailed the basic principles of the unity and specificity of scientific cognition, logical coherence, and a systematic internal structure free of contradictions.

---

[15] According to Michael Hardt and Antonio Negri, this cosmopolitan impetus of the 'Pure Theory', Kelsen's quest for world government through law, made him the chief theorist of an 'imperial' global legal order: M Hardt and A Negri, *Empire* (Harvard University Press Cambridge MA 2001) at 3–22.

[16] On the relationship between Lauterpacht and Kelsen, see M Koskenniemi 'Lauterpacht: The Victorian Tradition in International Law' (1997) 2 *European Journal of International Law* 215–63, at 218–25; A Carty 'The Continuing Influence of Kelsen on the General Perception of the Discipline of International Law' (1998) 9 *European Journal of International Law* 344–54, at 352–4. On Kelsen's relationship to JL Kunz, see *The Public International Law Theory of Hans Kelsen* (n 2) 4ff and 283–5.

[17] See *Werke* (n 4).

These basic structures or postulates of Kelsenian thinking, already evident in his doctoral dissertation on Dante Alighieri in 1905,[18] had only later been methodologically secured by the Neo-Kantian transcendental argument.

In the late nineteenth century during Kelsen's studies Hegel was unfashionable—and Neo-Kantianism or, to be more precise, various versions of Neo-Kantianism, were in vogue. Inspired by Neo-Kantian epistemology, the first general point of attack for Kelsen was what he regarded as the lack of a stringent methodological distinction between *Sein* ('Is') and *Sollen* ('Ought'), which made a scientific construction of public law impossible.[19] The concept of a strict and constitutive separation of scientific methodologies, the beginnings of which were already evident in Jellinek,[20] was radicalized by Kelsen, drawing on Georg Simmel (1858–1918), Wilhelm Windelband (1848–1915), and Heinrich Rickert (1863–1936).[21] Kelsen regarded the multidimensional analysis of law, which was characteristic of Jellinek, as epistemologically inadmissible. Kelsen particularly found the use of insights from sociology and psychology in interpreting legal norms an unacceptable jumble of different methods. According to Kelsen's strict separation-thesis, one could not derive from the 'Is-statements' of sociology any conclusions that were relevant for jurisprudence as a science of normative 'Ought'. The principle difference in the explanatory *Denkform* ('form of thinking') of the 'Is' and the normative *Denkform* of the 'Ought' revealed, in Kelsen's words, two 'separate worlds' that were irreconcilable.[22]

And yet, while insisting on the separation between these divergent methodologies, there was no question for Kelsen that there could be a mutual enrichment of 'Is-sciences' ('*Seinswissenschaften*') like sociology, and legal scholarship:[23]

Nor let it be said that the jurist may not also undertake sociological, psychological, or historical studies. On the contrary! These are necessary; except that the jurist must always remain aware that as a sociologist, psychologist, or historian he is pursuing a very different path from the one that leads him to his specifically juridical insights. He must never incorporate the results of his explanatory examination into his construction of normative concepts.[24]

---

[18] On this, see *The Public International Law Theory of Hans Kelsen* (n 2) 78–82.

[19] On the methodological dualism in his early work, see SL Paulson, 'Kelsen's Earliest Legal Theory: Critical Constructivism' in SL Paulson and BL Paulson (eds), *Normativity and Norms: Critical Perspectives on Kelsenian Themes* (OUP Oxford 1998) 23–44, at 23; C Heidemann, *Die Norm als Tatsache. Zur Normentheorie Hans Kelsens* (Nomos Baden-Baden 1997) at 24–8.

[20] On Jellinek's rejection of methodological syncretism, see G Jellinek, *System der subjektiven öffentlichen Rechte* (Mohr Tübingen 1919) at 17.

[21] 'Kelsen's Earliest Legal Theory: Critical Constructivism' (n 19) 29ff.

[22] *Hauptprobleme der Staatsrechtslehre, entwickelt aus der Lehre vom Rechtssatz* (2nd edn Mohr Tübingen 1923) at 8. On this, see GH von Wright, 'Is and Ought' in *Normativity and Norms* (n 19) 365–82, at 365–7.

[23] H Kelsen, 'Zur Soziologie des Rechts. Kritische Betrachtungen' (1912) 34 *Archiv für Sozialwissenschaft und Sozialpolitik* 601–14 at 602.

[24] *Hauptprobleme* (n 22) 42; H Kelsen, 'Law, State, and Justice in the Pure Theory of Law' (1958) 57 *Yale Law Journal* 377–90, at 383. For a more comprehensive discussion of this problem, see *Rechtslehre, Staatssoziologie und Demokratietheorie* (n 6) 136–40.

Legal 'science' was to be established as an autonomous, purely normative discipline.[25] For Kelsen, the Pure Theory of Law was a 'theory of positive law' in that its aim was to eliminate from the subject matter theories of substantive justice, morality, and ethical considerations.[26] By distancing itself from natural law thinking, as well as from the methodologically 'syncretistic' blending of Is and Ought, the Pure Theory of Law attempted to create the cognitive preconditions for the autonomous existence of a fully contingent legal medium. Traditional legal doctrine constantly endangered this autonomy by creating ideological distortions and unreflected discursive representations of the law and its institutions.[27] According to Kelsen, legal positivism in this sense had to secure the autonomy of the law, since 'only the positivistic understanding of the law creates the prerequisite for the existence of an autonomous legal order and legal 'science', while the natural law perspective allows the law, finally and ultimately, to be absorbed into reason, morality, and nature, and legal scholarship into ethics, politics, or even natural sciences'.[28]

In international law, this process of autonomization proved especially difficult in that, contrary to the modern constitutional state, most of its norms were of a customary law-nature. In addition, compared to state law, its link to philosophical natural law continued to be very close. As a reaction to the renewed, fundamental challenge to legal character of international law during the First World War, the 1920s had witnessed a renaissance of natural law theories in international legal scholarship.[29] Following the First World War, which contemporaries experienced as a civilizational rupture on a world-historical scale,[30] a growing longing for eternal values, metaphysics, and a substantive foundation of the law had made itself felt. The old positivist law of nations had been unable to prevent neither the outbreak of the war nor the large-scale violations of the laws of war. Once again, the objective principle was sought out in the Christian doctrine of natural law, which in German *fin de siècle* jurisprudence was believed to have been overcome by the 'juristic method'. Under the impact of the gas-poisoned trenches, catholic natural law had been rediscovered in Germany, first by Cathrein (1845–1931),

---

[25] On the doctrine of the *Rechtssatz*, see H Kelsen, *Allgemeine Staatslehre* (Springer Berlin 1925) at 51.

[26] H Kelsen, *Reine Rechtslehre* (Deuticke Leipzig 1934) at 1; H Kelsen, *Introduction to the Problems of Legal Theory* (BL Paulson and SL Paulson trans) (OUP Oxford 1992) at 7.

[27] On the 'idea of the autonomy of jurisprudence', see A Baratta, 'Rechtspositivismus und Gesetzespositivismus: Gedanken zu einer "naturrechtlichen" Apologie des Rechtspositivismus' (1968) 54 *Archiv für Rechts- und Staatsphilosophie* 325–50, at 337.

[28] *Das Problem der Souveränität* (n 1) 87.

[29] Josef Kohler, for example, saw the reason for the incompleteness of international law in the fact that it still lacked the shared basis of a natural law, from which every law had to proceed: J Kohler, *Grundlagen des Völkerrechts* (Enke Stuttgart 1918).

[30] On this, see Stolleis: 'The world "after", after the "storms of steel", was hardly recognizable as an offshoot of the world "before". In that sense, 1914 remains an enormous rupture. It marked the first great explosion of aggression in the era of nationalism.': *Der lange Abschied* (n 12) 22.

Mausbach (1861–1931), and Schilling (1874–1956) and later by Kelsen's own pupil, Alfred Verdross,[31] and in France by Louis le Fur (1870–1943).[32] Kelsen and Kunz also rejected these newer natural law approaches with the goal of ensuring the 'purity of the science of international law'.[33]

The dichotomy of Is/Ought, and the specifically jurisprudential Ought-category they worked out allowed Kelsen and his students henceforth to castigate both sociological and ethical, as well as moral ascriptions and deductions, in the *legal* analysis of the law as methodologically inappropriate. As they saw it, this was the only way for the law to become a medium of contingent norm-creation on the international level, and, in general, the only way to enable a sober and, if necessary, critical assessment of the state of development of the law and its repercussions on society.

2.4 The Critique of German Staatswillenspositivismus and the Grundnorm of International Law

Starting from his strict separation of Is and Ought, Kelsen had—already in his 'constructivist' phase—criticized the 'dogma of the will' in jurisprudence as the result of a blending of psychological and sociological Is-considerations and normative Ought-considerations.[34] In fact, from a strict normative perspective, the 'will' of the (assumed) personified state ('*willensfähige Staatspersönlichkeit*') was nothing other than the central point of imputation for all acts of the organs of the particular state.[35] In this way, Kelsen had tried, already in his *habilitation* thesis, to replace the 'state as a legal person of will' with the concept of formal imputation.[36] Kelsen developed this approach further in *The Problem of Sovereignty* and the *Theory of International Law* and arrived at the assumption of the complete identity

[31] In 1918, immediately following the end of the war, the Jesuit Viktor Cathrein tried to revive the Christian roots of international law. The theologians Josef Mausbach and Otto Schilling, in their own monographs, drawing on the Spanish late scholastics, endorsed this view. See V Cathrein, *Die Grundlage des Völkerrechts* (Herder Freiburg 1918); J Mausbach, *Naturrecht und Völkerrecht* (Herder Freiburg 1918); O Schilling, *Das Völkerrecht nach Thomas von Aquin* (Herder Freiburg 1918). See also A Verdross, *Die Verfassung der Völkerrechtsgemeinschaft* (Springer Wien 1926).

[32] In France, Louis Le Fur established a natural law theory of international law: see L Le Fur, 'La théorie du droit naturel depuis le XVIIème siècle et la doctrine moderne' (1927) 18 *Recueil des Cours* 259–439.

[33] On natural law in the doctrine of international law, see JL Kunz, *Völkerrechtswissenschaft und Reine Rechtslehre* (F Deuticke Leipzig 1923) at 72–4.

[34] *Hauptprobleme* (n 22) 162ff. See also *Die Norm als Tatsache* (n 19) 35.

[35] *Hauptprobleme* (n 22) 189. On the notion of imputation and its origins in nineteenth-century German legal thought, see 'Kelsen's Earliest Legal Theory: Critical Constructivism' (n 19) 33ff.

[36] 'Kelsen's Earliest Legal Theory: Critical Constructivism' (n 19) 33. Paulson calls this early phase of Kelsen's legal theory the constructivist phase. On this phase, see also *Die Norm als Tatsache* (n 19) 23–33.

of state and law. The 'identity thesis' became the pivotal point in the sought-after revision of the conceptual apparatus of international law.

The provocative assumption that the state and the law were congruent terms for the legal scholar was based on two different strands of justification, though Kelsen often intertwined them in *The Problem of Sovereignty* and the *Theory of International Law*. The first strand is the demand for a strict separation between Is and Ought and the various ought categories described earlier, according to which the state can be represented in jurisprudence not as a causal-construct, but exclusively as a normative legal order.[37] The second strand is Kelsen's theory or critique of 'juristic fictions' ('*Juristische Fiktionen*'), which was already part of Kelsen's critical methodology in his previous works. According to this theory, the notion of the state as a 'person' and 'bearer' of the law was a 'personifying fiction' ('*personifikative Fiktion*') used by the prevailing doctrine.[38] With reference to Vaihinger's '*Die Philosophie des Als-Ob*',[39] Kelsen recognized in the jurisprudential use of the concept of the '*willensfähige Staatsperson*' a doubling or 'hypostatization'.[40] The real function of the legal person as a unifying point of imputation of norms became in traditional legal scholarship a living, human-like figure, a state organism. The latter was mythically transfigured and endowed with primal omnipotence:

Legal thinking is a thoroughly personifying one and—to the extent that it hypostatizes the persons it creates—can be compared to mythological thinking, which, anthropomorphically, suspects a dryad behind every tree, a spring god behind every spring, Apollo behind the sun, thus doubling nature as an object of cognition.[41]

The construction of the legal person, an achievement of nineteenth-century legal thought, was reduced by Kelsen down to its normative core. In Kelsen's eyes, this was merely a metaphor for the unity of a system of legal norms.[42] The notion of a dualism of state and law, according to which the 'unbounded Leviathan' had to be tamed by the law, was to be abolished by the identity thesis.[43] Kelsen saw the identity thesis as a fundamental break with the existing voluntaristic foundations of the science of the state and international law, as represented above all by Jellinek's *Allgemeine Staatslehre*.[44] He was the first author who attempted to break with this tradition of German *Staatswillenspositivismus* in international law on explicit 'positivist' premises. For him, in the debate over the 'source' or the 'validity ground' of international law, neither an argumentative strategy based solely on

[37] *Hauptprobleme* (n 22) 16.

[38] *Das Problem der Souveränität* (n 1) 18; H Kelsen, 'Theorie der Juristischen Fiktionen' in HR Klecatsky (ed), *Die Wiener Rechtstheoretische Schule* (2 vols Europa Verlag Vienna 1968) vol 2, 1215–41.

[39] H Vaihinger, *Die Philosophie des Als-Ob* (2nd edn Reuther & Reichard Berlin 1913).

[40] *Das Problem der Souveränität* (n 1) 18.   [41] Ibid.

[42] M Baldus, *Die Einheit der Rechtsordnung* (Duncker & Humblot Berlin 1995) at 158.

[43] Horst Dreier speaks of a 'profanization' of the state: *Rechtslehre, Staatssoziologie und Demokratietheorie* (n 6) 208–13.

[44] On this see the discussion in *The Public International Law Theory of Hans Kelsen* (n 2) 44–73.

natural law or socio-biological or psychological assumptions, nor one based solely on positivism and consensus were sustainable by themselves. The doctrine of the a priori '*droit objectif*' (Scelle) or of Christian natural law (Verdross) were too vague; to become concrete, they had to resort after all to 'declaratory' positive law through a kind of metaphysical doubling. The doctrine of the consensus of the sovereign will of the states, for its part, required extra-positivistic standards to establish an objectivized, binding nature of international law vis-à-vis the will of individual states.[45] To that end, it had developed the constructs of an 'objective international law' derived from the nature of the community of states (Jellinek), the doctrine of the 'common will' (Triepel), and the 'tacit' or 'common consent' arising from silence (Lassa Oppenheim (1851–1919)). Kelsen had thus attacked both the natural law and the consensus foundations of international law at their respective Achilles' heels: the lack of concreteness for natural law, and the absence of a binding normative nature in the voluntaristic-consensual theories. He developed the first in depth structural critique of the semantic cage which this tradition had erected:

The theory of international law, in particular, vacillates back and forth uncertainly between the antipodes of a state-individualistic and a human-universalistic perspective, between the subjectivism of the primacy of the legal order of the state and the objectivism of the primacy of international law . . .[46]

Instead, in a radicalized neo-Kantian version of positivism, international law for Kelsen was valid because international lawyers assumed it to be valid. This hypothesis underlying international legal discourse is embodied in Kelsen's notion of the hypothetical *Grundnorm*, replacing the circular move between the sovereign will and the objective and binding law above the state. Through the hypothetical formulation of the Basic Norm, he sought to capture this paradox in the abstract idea of an—intellectually presupposed—binding nature of the law. Through the hypothetical articulation of the Basic Norm, international legal scholarship was to be freed from the need for an ultimate extra-legal foundation of the law. In his eyes, the hypothetical Basic Norm, as a placeholder[47] for the idea of a specifically legal validity, secured the 'objectivity' of the scholarly understanding of the law.[48]

---

[45] For a fundamental language-analytical study of the various argumentative strategies concerning the 'basis of obligation,' see M Koskenniemi, *From Apology to Utopia: The Structure of International Legal Argument* (reissue CUP Cambridge 2005) at 268.

[46] *Das Problem der Souveränität* (n 1) 319–20.

[47] See the precise explanation of this in J Raz, 'Kelsen's Theory of the Basic Norm' in *Normativity and Norms* (n 19) 47–68, at 67: 'He [Kelsen] is able to maintain that the science of law is value-free by claiming for it a special point of view, that of the legal man, and contending that legal science adopts this point of view; that it presupposes its basic norm in a special, professional, and uncommitted sense of presupposing. There is, after all, no legal sense of normativity, but there is a specifically legal way in which normativity can be considered.'

[48] Alf Ross speaks in this context of Kelsen as a 'quasi-positivist': A Ross, 'Validity and the Conflict between Legal Positivism and Natural Law' in *Normativity and Norms* (n 19) 147–63, at 159–61.

Very much in the spirit of the interwar movement to modernize international law, the monumental 'dogma' of the sovereign will of the individual state was thus emphatically knocked off its pedestal by Kelsen and his students: its foundational role was being rejected. Kelsen's transcendental system of formal concepts, together with the assumption of the primacy of international law, created an international law without substantive state sovereignty; its place was taken by a legal cosmos which, hierarchical and structured through delegation, elevated international law philosophically above the state. Kelsen, in his construction of this monist legal universe, interestingly relied on Christian Wolff's (1679–1754) concept of *civitas maxima* (through Kaltenborn) and not on Kant's essay on eternal peace. I assume this was because Kant still retained a strong notion of substantial state sovereignty, which Kelsen did not want to endorse—sovereignty instead is relegated in the Pure Theory to nothing more than the formal attribute of the highest level of norms in a given legal system.

From the perspective of legal scholarship, universal law encompassed all legal norms as parts of a unified legal system. The norms of international law and national law were grounded in a unified theoretical conception of the law. Moreover, this conception reduced law to its 'pure' form, which, from the perspective of legal science, could take on any possible content. Freed from their a priori ethical and political limitations, international law and national law could be employed as a medium of potentially unlimited social change. The horizon was opened up—everything was possible. This included the realization of world state structures as a possible goal of international politics. International law can look and operate like national law—it can, for instance, directly empower or obligate individuals. Thus it can also take the form of national penal or administrative law. There is no categorical distinction between national and international law. The dualism of national and international law is being replaced by a continuum of various systemically connected emanations of the law, be they what we used to call international, regional, transnational, national or local. Kelsen's use of the word 'universal' can thus be understood in a twofold sense: 'universal' stands for both the unity of international law and national law, and the contingent content of the medium of law as a 'form' that could be used in any conceivable way.

3 THE LIMITS OF OBJECTIVITY

Kelsen's Neo-Kantian formalization of jurisprudence does not contain its own theory of interpretation. For Kelsen, the process of the interpretation of a norm by the legal practitioner and the legal theorist defied complete objectification. When it came to the realm of the application of the law, the Pure Theory of Law dispensed entirely with its own substantive theory of interpretation. Instead, such a theory was completely absorbed into the doctrine of the hierarchical structure of the legal system ('*Stufenbaulehre*'). According to the 'dynamic' variant of this theory, norm-application was considered a dynamic intellectual process moving from a higher to a lower norm in the hierarchical structure of the legal system. Applying a norm to a specific case creates an individualized lower norm through the reference to the text of a 'higher' norm. Kelsen describes this 'intellectual activity' of legally authorized courts and public officials as the act of 'authentic' interpretation.[49] In this process, the higher norm only to a limited extent predetermined the content of the new lower norm. Norm application by authorized organs, such as courts or public officials thus involved an act of interpretation. The input by the higher level of norm-production created merely the semantic 'framework' that had to be respected by the lower norm. This act of interpretation by law-applying organs, which chose one of the possible readings within the outer semantic limits, was conceptualized as a creative act, as individualized legislation. As a theoretical consequence of this assumption, Kelsen erased the conceptual difference between adjudication and legislation.[50] Moreover, for Kelsen there was no 'scientific' method by which only one of the several readings of a norm could be identified as the 'correct' one. There was no 'objectively correct' interpretation of norms.[51] With interpretation came an unavoidable intrusion of subjectivity, politics, values, and idiosyncratic preferences. While exposing the dilemma of interpretation, Kelsen stopped short of contributing to its methodological containment. Instead, he completely removed methodological questions regarding the act of interpretation from the Pure Theory's realm of cognition.[52]

The lack of compulsory jurisdiction in most areas of international law, however, renders this problem particularly acute in international law. The pure theory of international law has no real answers to the question of the interpretation of norms by those who apply the law. The reappearance of the 'political' in the application of the law that Kelsen accepted as unavoidable is another way of describing the central conundrum of the law, which Jacques Derrida described as the '*Heimsuchung*

---

[49] *Reine Rechtslehre* (n 26) 90; *Problems of Legal Theory* (n 26) 77.

[50] Through his realistic doctrine of the dynamic application of the law as interpretation, Kelsen comes closer to the communicative paradigm of later legal theories, like those of Jürgen Habermas, Pierre Bourdieu, and Niklas Luhmann, than all other contemporary legal theories.

[51] *Reine Rechtslehre* (n 26) 96; *Problems of Legal Theory* (n 26) 81. This has important repercussions for the notion of democratic legitimacy. See for international adjudication: A von Bogdandy and I Venzke, 'Zur Herrschaft internationaler Gerichte: Eine Untersuchung internationaler öffentlicher Gewalt und ihrer demokratischen Rechtfertigung' (2010) 70 *Heidelberg Law Journal* 1–49.

[52] On this and the critique, see *The Public International Law Theory of Hans Kelsen* (n 2) 191–220.

durch das Unentscheidbare' and Niklas Luhmann as the '*Entscheidung des Unentscheidbaren*'.[53] Despite Kelsen's illuminating theoretical equation of adjudication and legislation, it remains problematic within this context that the Pure Theory of Law, as a theory of law, promotes the civilizational function of a specific judicial rationality without being able to explain its application in legal practice.

The issue of interpretation arises, however, not only in the area of the application of the law, but also on the level of international legal scholarship. To the question of the angle from which the legal scholar should interpret the monist legal system created by Kelsen, the latter has a particular answer, one that grants an unexpected amount of room to the 'political' with regard to the structure of the legal system. According to Kelsen, the makeup of the hierarchically structured legal system depends fundamentally on a basic interpretational decision that is prior to legal 'science', meaning it is 'political' in Kelsen's understanding. The question here is whether the monistic legal cosmos is constructed on the foundation of the primacy of national law or the primacy of international law. If state law is given primacy, it forms the highest level of norms, and international law is conceived as a subordinated system of norms derived from the respective national constitution. By contrast, if international law is given primacy, the state legal systems are subordinated sub-systems of international law and are coordinated by it. For Kelsen, the primacy question is based on a fundamental political decision that cannot be answered by legal 'science'.[54] Looking at international law, the structure of the created transcendental world of scientific legal cognition itself depends, according to Kelsen, on a fundamental 'political' value-decision by the jurist.

Kelsen was thus trying to describe the political dimension of every form of international legal scholarship—that is, the question inherent in any discourse on international law, namely whether a norm is interpreted from the standpoint of a supraordinated system of international law, or from the perspective of the sovereign individual state to which any binding norm must be traced back—by way of the so-called 'choice hypothesis'. Traditional doctrine according to Kelsen made the mistake of constant and unreflected changes between state-centred and universalizing perspectives on international law ('*Wechsel des Erkenntnisstandpunktes*'). On the primacy question, he called for a single and coherent decision by the respective international lawyer on the chosen vantage point. If one considers that the doctrine of the primacy of state law entails, according to Kelsen, a denial of international law as an autonomous legal system, it becomes clear that Kelsen's construct of international law is subject to the provision of a fundamental political decision. One reason why Kunz and Verdross openly dissented from the 'choice

---

[53] J Derrida, *Gesetzeskraft. Der mystische Grund der Autorität* (Suhrkamp Frankfurt am Main 1991) at 49; N Luhmann, *Das Recht der Gesellschaft* (Suhrkamp Frankfurt am Main 1993) at 317.

[54] H Kelsen, *Rechtsgeschichte gegen Rechtsphilosophie? Eine Erwiderung* (Springer Vienna 1928) at 317.

hypothesis' was that central aspects of their shared cosmopolitan project—such as direct rights and obligations of the individual under international law and the post-sovereign empowerment of international organizations—depended on how this choice was made.[55]

However, Kelsen's formalized and deductive conceptual apparatus described earlier, that is, the claim to unity of cognition and hierarchical system-building, forced him to acknowledge that both primacy assumptions were inherently consistent. In a paradoxical way, Kelsen's formal understanding of legal scholarship, which sought to expel the political from the realm of legal cognition, generated in the choice hypothesis the far-reaching theoretical concession that legal cognition in international law, at its core, was also subjective and political in character.[56] In order to rescue his claim to objectivity, Kelsen demanded the jurist's transparent decision on whether the norms of international law should be interpreted on the basis of the primacy of state law or that of international law. To him, a 'science' of international law was still possible, in spite of a fundamental political decision on the part of the jurist about the posited total construct. Scientific objectivity thus—in a more abstract sense—lay in making political preferences transparent and pursuing a strict deductive construction of the system on this basis.

4 THE RECEPTION OF KELSEN'S INTERNATIONAL LAW THEORY IN GERMAN INTERNATIONAL LAW SCHOLARSHIP AFTER THE WAR

The 'objective' science postulated by Kelsen, which was to be achieved through the constructive uncoupling of the abstract concepts from the current content of

---

[55] On the quarrel over the *Wahlhypothese*, see *The Public International Law Theory of Hans Kelsen* (n 2) 104–7.

[56] It would take until 1989 before Martti Koskenniemi, following David Kennedy, was able to explain and comprehensively describe for contemporary doctrine what Kelsen had called an unreflected permanent change between the two epistemological standpoints ('*Wechsel des Erkenntnisstandpunktes*') in international law with the help of the linguistic distinction between 'ascending' (apology) and 'descending' (utopia) arguments in international legal discourse: see generally *From Apology to Utopia* (n 45); D Kennedy, 'Theses about International Law Discourse' (1980) 23 *German Yearbook of International Law* 353–91. On Koskenniemi and Kelsen, see J von Bernstorff, 'Sisyphus was an International Lawyer: On M Koskenniemi's *"From Apology to Utopia"* and the Place of Law in International Politics' (2006) 12 *German Law Journal* 1015–35.

the norms, already offered contemporary critics a twofold point of attack under the slogan of a 'radical-logicistic metaphysics'.[57] Because of their distance to current law, the concepts generated by Kelsen's approach seemed to have little usefulness not only for those who applied the law, but also from the perspective of many mainstream legal scholars.[58] Moreover, the cosmopolitan project behind the central critical assumptions of the Pure Theory, which had resonated with the international reform movement, was not well received in the increasingly nationalist atmosphere in German international law scholarship in the late interwar period.

Kelsen emigrated in 1934 due to anti-Semitic persecution in Germany. Kunz and Lauterpacht had already left Austria before the war to pursue their careers in the UK (Lauterpacht) and the US. Kelsen, like Kunz, also eventually ended up in the US, where he continued to publish on international law during and after the Second World War. Verdross, having been suspended for a semester in 1938 as the new Nazi rulers vetted him carefully, remained a full professor at Vienna University during the 1930s and 1940s.[59]

Kelsen's work on international law, which he expanded upon during his emigration in Geneva at the *Institut universitaire de hautes études internationales* and later at the University of Berkeley, culminated in his commentary on the *Charter of the United Nations* and his *Principles of International Law*. Kunz worked in the US as the editor of the *American Journal of International Law* and taught at the University of Toledo. With the predominance of Anglo-American pragmatism in the field of international law, the audience for Kelsen's writings shrank increasingly after the Second World War. The renewed Renaissance of natural law[60] and the 'realistic' current that began in international legal jurisprudence in the fifties also did little to boost the acceptance of Kelsen's theory of international law. At the beginning of the 1960s, the optimism of the 1920s had given way to a deep scepticism about the potential and value of law in international relations.

---

[57] A contemporary example of this critique is E Kaufmann, *Rechtsidee und Recht* (Schwarz Göttingen 1960) at 198.

[58] Moreover, as Erich Kaufmann and Wilhelm Jöckel noted early on, they were not truly 'pure' in the sense of the Kantian categories. Both authors had pointed out that Kelsen's *Rechtsformbegriffe* were not transcendental legal concepts in the sense of pure legal categories, but merely highly abstracted 'general empirical concepts' of jurisprudence, which were by no means situated before any kind of experience. *Rechtsidee und Recht* (n 57) 193; W Jöckel, *Hans Kelsens rechtstheoretische Methode. Darstellung und Kritik ihrer rundlagen und hauptsächlichsten Ergebnisse* (Mohr Tübingen 1930 reprint Scientia Aalen 1977) at 162.

[59] For short biographical sketches of Kelsen, Kunz, and Verdross, see *The Public International Law Theory of Hans Kelsen* (n 2) 272–85.

[60] The term 'natural law' is used with a variety of meanings: first, as ontological natural law of the Scholastic tradition; second, in the sense of the 'rational' natural law of the Enlightenment; and third, by way of negative demarcation against legal positivism to describe an extra-judicial justification of norms. Unless specified, the term is used here with the first meaning.

In addition, Kelsen's own draft for a new world organization institutionalizing the international rule of law in the post-war era, published in 1944, was not considered during the negotiations in San Francisco. Kelsen's two central projects thus proved impossible to implement. Both the attempt to introduce a 'scientific' method of international law on the basis of the Pure Theory of Law, and the political project of a thoroughly legalized global order had to be regarded by Kelsen and Kunz as failures for the time being during the crisis of the United Nations in the Cold War era. In the 1950s and 1960s, it was Kelsen's more practical oriented UN Charter commentary, which became his most influential and most frequently cited international law publication. In the commentary, Kelsen, in an attempt to produce a non-political legal analysis, offers his readers all possible and often divergent interpretations of the respective Charter provisions, without giving preference to one of these interpretations; leaving this 'political' choice to those actors who apply the provisions in practice. The commentary seems to have been used frequently in the diplomatic practice of the UN, in particular by states intending to challenge orthodox interpretations of the Charter by the three major Western powers.

Until the 1990s, his general theory of international law, however, was basically ignored in the post-war mainstream German international law literature. Instead, the German post-war international law scene was being dominated by the legacy of Verdross, one of Kelsen's closest students at the beginning of his career. Verdross turned to natural law in the neo-scholastic tradition in the 1920s, whereas Kelsen continued to insist on a radical separation of law and morality, which in his view turned the Pure Theory of Law into a 'radically realistic legal theory'.[61] Verdross instead developed a unique blend of doctrinal constructivism and neo-scholastic speculation about an international community, based on common moral values of a constitutional nature (including, of course, the notion of international *jus cogens*). It became the dominating German approach to the post-war field of international law. It would therefore be mistaken to equate Kelsen's international legal theory with mainstream German international legal scholarship either before or after the Second World War.

The personal relationship between Verdross and Kelsen was heavily burdened by an incident which had taken place in 1934. Kelsen, because of his Jewish background, was forced by the publisher to relinquish his position as Editor in Chief of the *Zeitschrift für Öffentliches Recht*. The *Zeitschrift für Öffentliches Recht* was the journal of the Kelsen-school, founded by Kelsen himself, who had involved Verdross as a second editor in the interwar period. When the publisher offered Verdross to take over as the new Editor in Chief, Kelsen expected Verdross to decline in protest. Verdross, however, accepted the offer and henceforth appeared as Editor in Chief of the journal without Kelsen's participation. Their relationship seems to have never fully recovered afterwards.

---

[61] *Reine Rechtslehre* (n 26) 17; *Problems of Legal Theory* (n 26) 18.

5 Kelsen's Contribution to International Legal Theory: The Empty Universal Legal Form

Kelsen's contribution to international law has not been forgotten. It combined a critical distance vis-à-vis the concrete emanations of the law and of legal scholarship with an unrestrained faith in the possibilities of the legal medium in international relations. Kelsen's radicalized nineteenth-century belief in scientific objectivity and his cosmopolitan convictions led him to discover and deconstruct the fundamental paradoxes of modern state-based international legal discourse. But does his sovereignty-critique and his defence of the primacy of international law thesis as one possible option to construct the hierarchical monist legal universe make him a chief theorist of Allied interwar dominance over Germany (Carl Schmitt) or of a current 'imperial' global legal order (Hardt and Negri)?[62] Yes and no. Yes if these claims are meant to express that Kelsen and his school were the first to detect and explain how international law could be used to implement political projects through novel institutions and laws connecting the international and the national level; inter alia by directly empowering and holding to account private actors through international law in a monist legal system. And no, if 'chief theorist of an imperial global order' is meant to say that the Pure Theory *qua* theory promoted a specific imperialist (economic) project.[63] Kelsen himself always maintained that both the primacy of international law-perspective and the primacy of domestic law-perspective were scholarly valid and defendable perspectives.

---

[62] M Hardt and A Negri, *Empire* (Harvard University Press Cambridge MA 2001), ch. 1.1.

[63] This is the allegation made by Mónica García-Salmones Rovira in *The Project of Positivism in International Law* (OUP Oxford 2013) 120ff. In this interesting monograph, which contains a very helpful analysis of Oppenheim's international legal project, Kelsen, who in his autobiography expressed that he since the First World War had supported socialist redistribution of wealth to the great masses, and who had not published a single line defending any concrete international economic project during his entire academic career, is characterized as a precursor of European 'neo-liberal' thought and as a towering figure of what is called 'economic positivism'. This interpretation seems to result from a problematic equation of Oppenheim's and Kelsen's approaches to international law and from contemporary (interwar German) stereotypes of 'liberal' legal scholarship. After the Second World War Kelsen, who had to emigrate three times because of anti-Semitic threats and persecution, had also been made responsible in German post-Second World War scholarship for having—as a positivist—prepared a theoretical ground for obedience to murderous Nazi laws; an equally problematic claim due to the fact that the Pure Theory takes no normative stance with regard to individual obedience or resistance to the law in force. Moreover, in the 1930s Nazi scholars and judges explicitly used (Darwinist) natural law and thus explicit anti-positivist approaches to reinterpret the law in force in line with Nazi ideology and preferences. On Nazi natural law, see M Stolleis, *The Law under the Swastika: Studies on Legal History in Nazi Germany* (University of Chicago Press Chicago 1998) 87ff.

Moreover, the anti-ideological metaphor of the 'empty universal legal form' is not particularly well suited to defend from a scholarly perspective a particular economic project. The affirmative dimensions of Kelsen's Pure Theory, which can only be indirectly deduced from Kelsen's deconstruction of sovereignty, thus find a strong theoretical counter-balance in the Pure Theory itself. It is not only that, according to Kelsen, the legal scholar is supposed to lay open his or her own political (cosmopolitan or national) preferences when analysing international law, but also and more importantly that the Pure Theory creates a reflexive distance vis-à-vis the current contents of the international legal order. There is no inevitability or essentialism as to the content of international legal structures. Rules and principles could be entirely different. Imagining international law's 'foundation' or its 'constitution' as being empty thus creates a transformative potential. Vacating the constitutional space in order to fill it with new anti-hegemonic substance now becomes an intelligible project.

CHAPTER 11

....

SCHMITT, SCHMITTEANISM AND CONTEMPORARY INTERNATIONAL LEGAL THEORY

....

ROBERT HOWSE

1 INTRODUCTION

....

CARL Schmitt (1888–1985), Hitler's chief legal official in the 1930s, when he was crushing the rule of law in Germany, an international law apologist for Nazi aggression, the extent of whose post-war repentance is suggested by his vicious anti-semitic rants well into the 1960s: why should such a man have a prominent place in contemporary debates and discourses about international law?[1] Each year,

---

[1] In this chapter, I have drawn freely from earlier writing on Schmitt, including R Howse, *Leo Strauss: Man of Peace* (CUP New York 2014) ch 2; R Howse and R Teitel, 'Does Humanity-Law Require (or Imply) a Progressive Theory of History? (And Other Questions for Martti Koskenniemi)' (2013) 27 *Temple International and Comparative Law Journal* 377–97. Thanks to Ruti Teitel and Sam Moyn for helpful comments on a draft.

when I teach Schmitt's *Concept of the Political* in my seminar on the history and theory of international law at New York University, I pose this question to the students. It isn't rhetorical. My own answer is that we need to study Schmitt himself to understand and assess the use and abuse of his ideas in contemporary international legal discourse. Some will say it doesn't matter: we can freely borrow the slogans, arguments, concepts of a thinker without being caught in the purposes, motives, and ultimate grounds of that thinker's views. This is the explicit position of one of the scholars with whom I shall engage in this essay, Paul Kahn.[2] On the other end of the spectrum, and close to my own position, is Martti Koskenniemi, who, while deploying Schmitt also in a manner that I shall criticize, nevertheless does so on the basis of a critical consciousness of, or deep engagement with, Schmitt as a thinker. Certainly, detached from context or Schmitt's comprehensive worldview, notions such as the exception, the friend/enemy distinction, false universalism (the invocation of humanity to serve one's own interests and exclude the other), seem vivid, evocative, and applicable to a range of international legal controversies; the so-called 'war' on terror being an obvious example, which in some way Schmitt seems to have anticipated in his *Theory of the Partisan*.[3] Schmitt, in his most theoretical writing, tended to the view that all arguments and concepts have only a polemical or situational meaning rather than a permanent or essential one; so there is a sense in which the casual or opportunistic invocation of Schmitt is itself in a Schmittean spirit.

This chapter proceeds in three sections. In the first section, I provide an overview of the Schmittean concepts and arguments that have gained the most purchase in contemporary international legal discourse, primarily international legal theory. I am not here interested in engaging with interpretative controversies about specific works of Schmitt; however, in the interests of disclosure, I do take the view, contrary to the approach of Heinrich Meier,[4] for example, that Schmitt's position is not a theological, in the sense of a religiously grounded, one, but is based on atheistic or nihilistic premises. When Schmitt refers to 'political theology' he intends the *secularization* of theological categories. In Section 2, I critically engage with a select group of scholars who have deployed Schmitt in contemporary international legal theory. These are: Martti Koskenniemi, Eric Posner, and Adrian Vermeule, Paul Kahn, and Nehal Bhuta. The selection is simply based on the prominent place that Schmitt has had in the recent writing of this group, and also with a view to

---

[2] P Kahn, *Political Theology: Four New Chapters on the Concept of Sovereignty* (Columbia University Press New York 2012).

[3] C Schmitt, *The Theory of the Partisan: Intermediate Commentary on the Concept of the Political* (GL Ulmen trans) (Telos Press New York 2007).

[4] See H Meier, *Carl Schmitt and Leo Strauss: The Hidden Dialogue* (JH Lomax trans) (University of Chicago Press Chicago 1995). For a discussion of my differences with Meier, see *Leo Strauss: Man of Peace* (n 1) 25.

avoiding a parochially 'American' or parochially 'European' emphasis. In the third and final part, the conclusion, I offer some observations about what the use of Schmitt in contemporary international legal theory may tell us about the state of the discipline, its fault lines, and anxieties.

2 CARL SCHMITT, LIBERALISM, AND INTERNATIONAL LAW

Schmitt wrote extensively on conceptual and doctrinal questions of international law.[5] The works in question range from early attacks on the Versailles treaty, the criminalization of war and the League of Nations, to justifying German expansion into Eastern Europe through the concept of *Grossraum*, to opposing the Nuremberg trials and then, during the Cold War, reviving the concept of *Grossraum* to propose an alternative international legal order to that of supposed 'American' moralistic universalism (*Nomos der Erde*),[6] to arguing against the treatment of 'partisans' (or terrorists) as common criminals rather than warriors of a kind (*Theory of the Partisan*). Schmitt also wrote treatises on international law. With the partial exception of *Nomos der Erde* and *Theory of the Partisan*, however, it is not Schmitt's writings dedicated to international law or international order that have filtered into contemporary international legal theory, but concepts and arguments from his most famous works of political theory—*Political Theology*[7] and *The Concept of the Political*.[8] This makes sense, as whatever theoretical bite the works on international law have really depends, if sometimes only indirectly, on the more basic intellectual moves in these two seminal works. The works in question, it must be borne in mind, are primarily attacks on liberal constitutionalism in the Weimar Republic, as well as liberalism and the rule of law as such, and only secondarily or derivatively concerned with international order. This may be why international legal theorists have tended to gloss over many of the argumentative steps in these

---

[5] These writings are comprehensively and lucidly addressed in C Jouin, *Le retour de la guerre juste: Droit international, epistemologie et ideologie chez Carl Schmitt* (Vrin/EHES Paris 2013).

[6] C Schmitt, *The* Nomos *of the Earth* in the International Law of the *Jus Publicum Europaeum* (GL Ulmen trans) (Telos Press New York 2003 [1950]).

[7] C Schmitt, *Political Theology: Four Chapters on the Concept of Sovereignty* (G Schwab trans) (University of Chicago Press Chicago 2005 [1922]). All further references are to this edition.

[8] C Schmitt, *The Concept of the Political* (G Schwab trans) (University of Chicago Press Chicago 2007 [1927]). All further references are to this edition.

writings and (as I shall try to show in the next section) have ended up deploying Schmittean concepts in rather tortured and obfuscating ways. At the same time, one reason why these writings have had such an attraction for international legal theorists has arguably been the rise of constitutionalist discourse in international law and legal theory.

Together, *Political Theology* and *The Concept of the Political* disclose the fundamentally legal-political orientation of Schmitt's thought. These works operate as polemics against liberalism as a philosophy or ideology, but Schmitt also gives clues as to the weaknesses or vulnerabilities of Weimar liberal democracy, which can be used by the enemies of liberalism in an actual legal-political project of its destruction (in which Schmitt himself was actively engaged as a public lawyer through a series of interpretations aimed at breaking open the Weimar constitution to make it vulnerable to the consolidation of power in the hands of a single man).[9]

Political Theology begins with an articulation of the familiar Schmittian doctrine of the 'exception'. Schmitt seeks to shatter the liberal ideal of the submission of political power to the rule of law by positing a situation where the very survival of the *Rechtstaat* itself would depend on the suspension of all legal norms. Schmitt rejects the answer of liberal jurisprudence to this dilemma—limited or circumscribed emergency powers—in the following terms:

If measures undertaken in an exception could be circumscribed by mutual control, by imposing a time limit, or finally, as in liberal constitutional procedure governing a state of siege, the question of sovereignty would then be considered less significant but would certainly not be eliminated.[10]

Schmitt thus basically admits that in almost all circumstances, albeit not necessarily all, the liberal approach to emergencies will be adequate to protect both the rule of law and the state's survival.

This leads to the revelation that the real ground of Schmitt's position is not a conservative or a realist attack on liberal legalism, but rather the desire for 'a philosophy of concrete life'. 'The exception is more interesting than the rule...In the exception the power of real life breaks through the crust of a mechanism that has become torpid by repetition.'[11] It is in the case of the exception, where the survival of the state is at stake and dependent on decisions that cannot be normalized through the application of emergency provisions contained in an *ex ante* legal framework, that the foundation of the entire political order on acts of decision or will out of nothingness becomes apparent.

---

[9] See D Dyzenhaus, *Legality and Legitimacy: Carl Schmitt, Hans Kelsen and Herman Heller in Weimar* (OUP New York 1997) at 70–85.
[10] *Political Theology* (n 7) 13–15.   [11] Ibid 15.

Schmitt's nihilism is *political* nihilism. He could come closer to Hitler than the other thinkers identified by Leo Strauss (1899–1973) in 'German Nihilism' (which include Ernst Junger (1895–1998) and Martin Heidegger (1889–1976))[12] because his form of nihilism could legitimate destruction not simply as the clearing away of a rotten decadent civilization but as the characteristic form of political *founding*.[13] In *Political Theology*, Schmitt cleverly turns on its head Hans Kelsen's (1881–1973) systematic liberal philosophy of law: Kelsen posits a *Grundnorm*—the norm that cannot be justified by any other norm of the system itself, as the system's necessary logical foundation, a conceptual requirement of its completeness. For Schmitt, this presupposition of Kelsen's, a kind of neo-Kantian regulative ideal, reveals that any legal system, any political order is ultimately based on a 'decision [that] emanates from nothingness.'[14]

In the chapter that bears the title of the work as a whole, 'Political Theology', we can grasp the significance of Strauss' stress on the atheistic character of German nihilism. Schmitt writes: 'conceptions of transcendence will no longer be credible to most people'.[15] *Political* nihilism is possible because, as the historical development of the West shows, theological concepts that may have underpinned politics in earlier times of belief can be translated into immanent, secular categories. As Schmitt maintains in the next and last chapter of *Political Theology* man's 'evil', which justifies traditionally his submission to rule, the demand of obedience, must not be thought of any longer in terms of the fall or loss of innocence but rather through the Nietzschean notion of 'mutual penetration of opposites'.[16] What has been known as 'evil', greediness, and striving for power, is connected to the goodness or at least superiority of a certain class of men. For man's evil requires that to live together men need to be subject to control from above, and in a godless world this control requires a class of men strong and resolute enough to dominate, whose 'evil' is vitality and power, and thus, in fact something admirable, unlike evil understood as weakness. But in a godless world what will give these men the *authority* to impose 'an absolute decision created out of nothingness'?[17] In an age lacking in transcendence, the 'absolute decision created out of nothingness' must somehow be ratified by 'the will of the people' (or at least premised on the unity of the people under the leader).

In *The Concept of the Political*, Schmitt attempts to solve this difficulty of political nihilism. He proposes the friend/enemy distinction as the core of the

[12] L Strauss, 'German Nihilism' (1999) 26 *Interpretation* 353–78.

[13] See Y Sherratt, *Hitler's Philosophers* (Yale University Press New Haven 2013) at 103: Schmitt 'enshrined Hitler's tyranny in law. He relegated democracy to a burnt memory, and like a dark phoenix from its ashes, he allowed tyranny to rise: authoritative, powerful and legitimate'.

[14] *Political Theology* (n 7) 31–2. See the discussion in J-F Kervégan, *Que faire de Carl Schmitt?* (Gallimard Paris 2011) at 132–5.

[15] *Political Theology* (n 7) 50.   [16] Ibid 61.   [17] Ibid 66.

political. Who is a friend and who is an enemy is completely mutable, dependent on a concrete situation, and cannot be traced to any subsisting opposition whether moral, aesthetic, economic, or religious. Thus, the friend/enemy distinction provides a democratic criterion for the decision—preserving the collective existence or way of life of an entire people against a mortal enemy—but at the same time a criterion beyond discussion, because it does not refer to any normative benchmarks outside the concrete situation in which the decision about the enemy is taken by the *Führer*. Schmitt emphasizes that the friend/enemy decision does not simply apply to the case of hostilities or actual war, but to the possibility of war. This conforms to Strauss' analysis of German nihilism: it is not actual fighting that is loved by the nihilists, but the atmosphere of intensity and seriousness produced by a society living in the permanent shadow of the possibility of a war to defend its existence and way of life against a mortal enemy.

Because, according to Schmitt, the decision about the enemy is always existential and concrete, it precludes the idea of a war fought for justice, that is, in the name of a universal principle. This becomes the basis for Schmitt's attack against liberalism (or the concrete 'enemy' that hides behind the ideology of liberalism), which, according to Schmitt seeks a final war to end all wars, a war in the name of a universal humanitarian ideology that would replace the political itself, the opposition of peoples and nations, with a world state. 'What remains is neither politics nor state, but culture, civilization, economics, morality, law, art, entertainment, etc.'[18]

But what is it that allows one to expect that the liberal 'enemy' will not be victorious—thereby creating a concrete and permanent situation where the political, and Schmitt's analysis of it, are irrelevant? The final part of the *Concept of the Political* answers this question through a presentation of man's 'innocent' evil in a manner quite similar to that of *Political Theology*. Evil becomes 'dangerousness', which as 'brutality', 'vitality', and so forth is admirable, serving to maintain the will of the strong to dominate the weak. It is because one can expect that there will always be men with a will to dominate that the apparent end of the political through the victory of the liberal 'enemy' will not really result in a collapse into chaotic conflict, where ordinary men destroy each other in the struggle for survival and gain. Thus, Schmitt's discussion of 'evil' and 'dangerousness' is preceded by the question of 'upon whom will fall the frightening power implied in a world-embracing economic and technical organization'.[19] According to Schmitt, every 'order' must be a concrete one where someone or some ruling group is in charge, on the top, making decisions that can be imposed without question, at least in principle.

---

[18] *Concept of the Political* (n 8) 53.   [19] Ibid 57.

3 Carl Schmitt and Contemporary International Legal Theory: Four Illustrations

3.1 Martti Koskenniemi

Of all the contemporary international legal theorists I have read who deploy Schmitt, it is Martti Koskenniemi who engages with Schmitt's thought most systematically and critically, including not only *Political Theology* and *Concept of the Political* but also *Nomos der Erde*. Koskenniemi suggests: 'The idea would be to think *with* and *against* Schmitt in the interests of today's politics.'[20] Among Koskenniemi's most important insights is that Schmitt should not be read as attacking universalism as such when he attacks the liberal universalism of (Anglo-American) international law. He is not in favour of the state as such; preserving a world of sovereign states at potential war with one another is not an end in itself. Rather, Schmitt's concern is with defending an alternative anti-liberal universal position, which he never really articulates, but which Koskenniemi (wrongly in my view) assumes is religious or theological. Rather, I tend to agree with Strauss, who similarly sees that behind Schmitt's attack there is a universal normative position to which Schmitt does not own up, but views that position as a political atheism of the right, an aristocratic politics of human 'seriousness', which maintains the intensity and dignity of human life through the preservation of the world of conflict and sacrifice, blood and belonging, as against the liberal utopia of 'culture, civilization, economics, morality, law, art, entertainment, etc'.[21] In any case, as Koskenniemi has pointed out, it is Hans Morgenthau (1904–80) who, deeply influenced by Schmitt as a young scholar, turned Schmitt's ideas in the direction of a defence of power politics between states of a 'realist' character, without the anti-liberal orientation of Schmitt's underlying values. One question then is whether it would be ultimately more relevant for contemporary international legal theory to grapple with Morgenthau's position rather than Schmitt's.

Be that as it may, it is the very distinction between false and true universalism that gets Koskenniemi into difficulties when he invokes Schmitt in his own critique of liberal legal internationalism. Koskenniemi does not subscribe to what Schmitt saw as the true universalism, and thus he deploys Schmitt without the perspective from which *liberal* legal universalism is to be judged as false. As a result, Schmitt's

---

[20] M Koskenniemi, 'International Law as Political Theology: How to Read *Nomos der Erde*?' (2004) 11 *Constellations* 492–511, at 494 (emphasis in original).

[21] See L Strauss, 'Notes on Carl Schmitt, *The Concept of the Political* (1932)' (JH Lomax trans) in *Concept of the Political* (n 8) 97–122.

view of human seriousness reduces to the claim that invoking universal values in the name of humanity as a whole is essentially a strategy of particular powers, or particular kinds of interests, which seek hegemony or dominance by masking what benefits them as what is good or right universally.

If the idea is that norms that claim universal force can and are invoked by actors with particular ends as a justification for the exercise of power to achieve those ends, then it is well-worn if not trite. David Luban notes:

Anyone who voluntarily has recourse to the institutions of the law has ulterior motives: nobody has ever filed a lawsuit out of disinterested curiosity in the answer to a legal question. In everyday litigation, we hardly think it is noteworthy or morally condemnable to learn that a plaintiff has a self-interested motive for the suit.[22]

What gives the rhetoric of Schmitt and Koskenniemi its punch is the implication or assumption that use or abuse of the universal claim in the service of domination undermines the normative logic of the universal claim itself or leads to a result that even those who are supportive of the universal claim would admit is unambiguously undesirable. This is the, so to speak, 'internal' critique of international legal order as the order of universal humanity, that is, one that does not depend on Schmitt's underlying anti-liberal counter-perspective.

For Schmitt, the universal humanity claim is, fundamentally, a specious claim for a peaceful human community where violence is everywhere eliminated. This apparently utopian goal is, according to Schmitt, a cover for an imperial project to eliminate all 'enemies' (real and potential belligerents). Schmitt says this could even entail total war, on the grounds that a war to end all war can justify any horror in light of its utopian goal and the notion of its being fought on behalf of 'humanity' itself. Thus, Schmitt is saying that the result of invoking humanity is the greatest inhumanity (the contradiction of the normative logic itself as well as a result that seems unambiguously horrible, war that is inhuman without limits).[23] But, fundamental to the humanity-orientation in legal internationalism is a *rejection* of war without limits, precisely in the name of values of humanity.

Echoing Schmitt's invocation of Pierre-Joseph Proudhon's (1809–65) statement that 'whoever invokes humanity wants to cheat', Koskenniemi refers to 'the ease with which such purportedly universal terms [as humanity] may be used for dubious purposes'.[24] Whatever one thinks of humanitarian intervention-type justifications for the Iraq war raised by a handful of pundits such as Michael Ignatieff, is there any evidence that they actually in any way *enabled* the Bush Administration to execute what Koskenniemi sees as this part of an imperial project? Elsewhere,

---

[22] D Luban, 'Carl Schmitt and the Critique of Lawfare' (2010) 43 *Case Western Reserve Journal of International Law* 457–71, at 462.

[23] *Concept of the Political* (n 8) 54–5.

[24] M Koskenniemi, 'Book Review: Ruti Teitel, *Humanity's Law*' (2012) 26 *Ethics & International Affairs* 395–8.

Koskenniemi distinguishes 'false' universalism from the true 'universalism' reflected in the critique of the Iraq war based on an asserted consensus about it violating international law.[25] In the same essay, Koskenniemi concedes that universalism can be a source of resistance to hegemonic and oppressive power as well as a means of exercising it. The danger of false universalism now has to be weighed against the promise of true or benign universalism. Well, the universalism of humanity-based liberal legal internationalism has played a significant role in the opposition to the abuses of the war on terror.[26]

What is more real, given the data we have, humanity law's negative potential 'to be used for dubious purposes' or its capacity to thwart some of the worst harms done in the pursuit of dubious purposes? Koskenniemi supported the bombing of Serbia in 1999 as 'formally illegal and morally necessary.'[27] He simply prefers to see benign humanitarian intervention as a Schmittean exception to the law than to integrate it into legal normativity through the relativization of sovereignty in the name of humanity. What Koskenniemi seems most concerned with is disparaging a kind of simple moralism detectable in certain human rights advocates, undoing their purported pretension to purity and messianism. This is hardly a substitute for weighing the results on the ground, positive and negative, of humanity-based liberal legal internationalism.

3.2 Eric Posner and Adrian Vermeule

In *The Executive Unbound*,[28] Eric Posner and Adrian Vermeule argue that Schmitt should replace James Madison as the key thinker of the American constitutional republic. Deploying Schmitt's notion of the 'exception' they argue that the existence of emergencies or unforeseen situations renders meaningful legal restraint of executive action impractical and indeed undesirable. In general, and ironically, Posner and Vermeule end up proving the case of liberal responders to Schmitt such as David Dyzenhaus because what they show is that, depending upon the kind of emergency, judicial review and legal restraint may be weakened or be extremely deferential. Thus, in fact, contra Schmitt, a liberal constitutional order need not be destroyed by the problem of emergency or the exception. Rather, it adapts. Certainly having to address the exception does not place the decider beyond

---

[25] See M Koskenniemi, 'What Should International Lawyers Learn from Karl Marx?' in S Marks (ed), *International Law on the Left: Re-Examining Marxist Legacies* (CUP Cambridge 2008) 30–52.

[26] See R Teitel, *Humanity's Law* (OUP New York 2011) at 105–38.

[27] M Koskenniemi, '"The Lady Doth Protest Too Much": Kosovo, and the Turn to Ethics in International Law' (2002) 65 *Modern Law Review* 159–75, at 162.

[28] EA Posner and A Vermeule, *The Executive Unbound: After the Madison Republic* (OUP New York 2011).

normative judgement altogether. Indeed, as Posner and Vermeule illustrate, the degree of deference that is afforded to the executive by the courts and by Congress is based on explicit normative arguments and trade-offs. The law does not simply surrender to the decision, as Schmitt suggests it must. When it comes to international law, this pattern is repeated. Posner and Vermeule seem to think they are making a Schmittean move when they note, for instance, that human rights treaties 'permit certain derogations in emergencies' but in fact this goes against Schmitt because it indicates that the problem of the emergency is capable of being addressed infra-legally. Similarly, inspired by Schmitt's scepticism about liberal human rights, Posner and Vermeule claim that 'states face no penalty for violating the treaties, which they do frequently, sometimes without any real justification, but more commonly on the basis of tendentious interpretations, most famously the Sharia-based interpretations of some Muslim countries'.[29] Posner and Vermeule assume there is an objective content to human rights norms that allows them to make a confident judgement (in any event, one without any empirical basis) that the norms are violated frequently; not only that, this content is sufficiently fixed for it to be transparent that some 'interpretations' of the treaties are 'tendentious'. This should be contrasted with the Schmittean view correctly articulated by Koskenniemi of 'legal indeterminacy' where the meaning of rights is unstable, and it is a matter of each political position reading its own normative preferences into the law. Finally, Posner and Vermeule point to the typical case as that of attempting to justify oneself based on *interpretation* of the law; if there were no penalty of any kind for violation, as they also claim, why bother justifying? Justification implies the un-Schmittean view that the sovereign decision is beyond any possibility of judgement or justification against a higher or external legal norm.

Where Posner and Vermeule do copy Schmitt is in their normative attack on 'global liberal legalism'. They say that someone has to be in charge of putting global liberal legalism into operation. This directly echoes Schmitt's question: 'upon whom will fall the frightening power implied in a world-embracing economic and technical organization?' One only has to think about the question posed this way quickly to come to the conclusion that the range of political, legal, and institutional actors in the world community today are not, as Posner and Vermeule go on to detail, up to the task of exercising the frightening power in question. But note the Schmittean assumption that never gets challenged or justified; namely that the only imaginable kind of normative order is one where power is exercised hierarchically, from a sovereign controlling authority downward. Ruti Teitel and I have argued that the emerging international legal order is one that is in many respects decentralized, where there are multiple points of interpretation, decision and authority that engage with one another; this is a genuine order in that legal

---

[29] *The Executive Unbound* (n 28) 158.

norms provide a basis for stabilizing expectations, for cooperation, and for delib-eration about differences. It is an order that is real even if incomplete, and inter-dependent with other legal orders.[30] As Leo Strauss suggested, there is a sense in which Schmitt was trapped within the Weimar liberal positivist categories against which he polemicized.[31] Schmitt's arch-enemy Hans Kelsen, with his idea of the legal system, could not imagine that legality could have the requisite validity while taking such a messy open-ended form. Common to both Kelsen's positivist con-cept of a legal system (a hierarchically organized machine that fully determines all outcomes juridically) and to Schmitt's notion of the sovereign decision is in fact an assumption that normativity must intrinsically be unified, closed and fully deter-mined. One would have thought that one productive result of Anglo-American legal scholars engaging with this vision of a legal system would be a questioning of its naturalness or inevitability given the character of the common law and its characteristic method of developing norms.

3.3 Paul Kahn

In *Political Theology: Four New Chapters on the Concept of Sovereignty*,[32] Paul Kahn, who is the director of the Schell Human Rights Center at Yale Law School, deploys Schmitt against contemporary liberal theory, especially of the Rawlsian sort, which he argues, cannot deal with that which is beyond reason in political life. It has no place for categories or phenomena such as 'sacrifice', which seem to harken back to the morality of pre-liberal or even anti-liberal societies, and have religious overtones, even though for Kahn these notions are essential to concrete political life, including in liberal democracies, which after all exist in a world where war has certainly not been abolished. According to Kahn, '[t]ogether international and domestic law are to subject the entire domain of the political to juridifica-tion. Reflecting this project of universal juridification, we increasingly find asser-tions that the very idea of sovereign power is anachronistic'.[33] Kahn opposes to this

---

[30] 'Does Humanity-Law Require (or Imply) a Progressive Theory of History?' (n 1). See also R Teitel and R Howse, 'Cross Judging: Tribunalization in a Fragmented but Interconnected Global Order' (2009) 41 *New York University Journal of International Law & Politics* 959–90.

[31] 'Notes on Carl Schmitt, *The Concept of the Political* (1932)' (n 21) 100–22. For analysis, see *Leo Strauss: Man of Peace* (n 1) 40–4. See also Strauss' direct response to Kelsen, raising the possibility of a normative legal order that 'cannot be fully codified juridically in an unambiguous manner' but nevertheless guided by a set of 'unambiguous directives' that in a never fully determined way inform the necessarily incomplete and unsystematic web of positive laws and multiple interpretations of those laws: L Strauss, 'Foreword to a Planned Book on Hobbes (1931)' in *Hobbes' Critique of Religion and Related Writings* (G Bartlett and S Minkov trans and eds) (University of Chicago Press Chicago 2011) 137–50, at 140.

[32] *Political Theology* (n 2).   [33] Ibid 45–6.

attempted juridification, which he sees as purporting to exclude real politics, what he considers the Schmittean view that

[n]orms are constrained from above and below: they neither create nor apply themselves. They cannot preclude the exception, and they cannot sustain themselves. A state must will itself into being (there must be order brought out of chaos) but it must also will its contin-ued existence (there must be judgments). A philosophy of law in the light of the sovereign function must be a philosophy of the will.[34]

Further, 'the *Universal Declaration of Human Rights*...expresses just norms but has no power to create political order. Every norm depends for its practical exist-ence upon a decision. It must be taken up as the object of the will of some indi-vidual or group.'[35]

But is the view that Kahn presents here really Schmittean or one that liberal theory denies? Kant, for example, never claimed that juridification, even the reali-zation of the republican federation of *Perpetual Peace* would be achieved through the agency of moral principles or legal norms alone; his theory of history posits that a transnational juridical order will come about through non-moral and to some extent immoral means; violence, commerce, empire. But Kahn does have a point, even if it is not really a Schmittean one. International lawyers and legal scholars, it seems to me, are even today haunted by the anxiety created through a certain kind of doubt or questioning as to whether international law is really law at all. We, thus, can tend to overemphasize international law as a formal positive legal order, whose norms, or at least core norms, correspond to compelling moral intuitions. International law somehow is feared not to have the mantle of genuine legality if it is not placed beyond political struggle and contestation. Admitting or even celebrating the extent to which international law is the on-going product of such struggle and contestation risks the old attack that international law is 'just' politics dressed up in lawyers' language. Kahn may actually be helpful in overcom-ing this fear, because in fact his book is a powerful reminder that *all* legal norms, whether domestic or international, depend on political struggle, political decision-making, and human judgement, which have an inherent extra-legal and perhaps even extra-rational element. Works like those of Ryan Goodman and Derek Jinks on the socialization of international law or Beth Simmons' *Mobilizing for Human Rights* provide some elements of a response to Kahn's concern,[36] as does arguably my work with Teitel on 'beyond compliance', stressing that the real-world effects of international law come through it shaping and being shaped by political meaning.[37]

---

[34] *Political Theology* (n 2) 65.   [35] Ibid 52.

[36] R Goodman and D Jinks, 'Measuring Human Rights Treaties' (2003) 14 *European Journal of International Law* 171–83; B Simmons, *Mobilizing for Human Rights: International Law and Domestic Politics* (CUP Cambridge 2009), both discussed in R Howse and R Teitel, 'Beyond Compliance: Rethinking Why International Law Really Matters' (2010) 1 *Global Policy* 127–36.

[37] 'Beyond Compliance' (n 36).

Kahn seems to be on more genuinely Schmittean ground where he attacks liberalism for being unable to account for the experience of sacrifice, of killing, and being killed as essential to political life.[38] Yet, as we already noted, Schmitt attacked liberal internationalists for inviting a *war* to end all wars, fought in the name of liberal universal values, of 'humanity'. Thus, for Schmitt, liberalism seems to have no difficultly contemplating sacrifice for the sake of liberal ideals. Indeed, he warns that the sacrifice in such a war might be enormous. Where Schmitt's anti-liberalism kicks in is in his view that the goal of a pacified society or world is a degraded or wrong human ideal; the possibility of struggle to the death for the way of life of one's own nation is what gives political life, indeed human life, its desirable seriousness and intensity.

Kahn questions whether a sovereign nation will ever, and, I sense, should ever yield to external—that is, international—legal norms where its survival is at stake. Kahn thinks this is intuitively obvious, but if that is so, then why would states and their militaries accept to have their hands tied by the laws of war, where, indeed, survival is often at stake, making a necessity a legal, not simply a political judgement? But does international law really contemplate the possibility of a hard conflict where a state is likely to risk its survival if it yields to legal norms? The need to avoid exactly such a conflict accounts for the hemming and hawing of the International Court of Justice (ICJ) in the *Nuclear Weapons* reference, where the Court (to the dismay of many) declined to hold that the use of nuclear weapons is per se in violation of international law.[39] Kahn simply assumes Schmitt is right that situations where collective survival is at stake are inherently incapable of being addressed within a legal normative framework.

In his assessment of the project of European integration, Kahn notes:

Schmitt believed that a world in which potential enemies are feared is not one that can be fully ordered by law. Thus, the European project of creating a transnational order of law without exception required that no national community view any other within the European Union as a potential enemy. Out of this comes the idea of European citizenship, as well as the limits on the potential extension of that idea.[40]

What Kahn does not realize is that his own description of the European Union (EU) is at odds with Schmitteanism. For the ordering by law to which Kahn refers does not obviate a genuine *politics* within the EU and between and within its member states. Many differences are resolved or managed *politically*, but not in the shadow of violent conflict as the ultimate issue of those differences. The EU, thus, allows us to think the possibility of a post-Schmittean politics, or at least to

---

[38] *Political Theology* (n 2) 25–8.
[39] *Legality of the Threat or Use of Nuclear Weapons* (Advisory Opinion) [1996] ICJ Rep 226.
[40] *Political Theology* (n 2) 11.

question Schmitt's and indeed Kahn's assumption that pacification means depo-liticization and that war or its possibility are at the heart of an authentically politi-cal experience.

Kahn also makes the Schmittean argument that political changes such as revolution, secession, or the founding of a new regime cannot be encom-passed within normative frameworks, but must be understood as decisions or acts of will that constitute a complete break with prior norms and cannot be judged against any constant law. He is aware of the Canadian Supreme Court's *Quebec Secession* decision, and the Court's challenge to that Schmittean approach: even an act such as secession, which is a break in the polity itself can be guided by some continuous legitimate political principles that have a certain force from shared constitutional experience and their relation to universal norms. But Kahn then points out that there is no guarantee that Quebec's secession would follow the normative pathway set out by the Court. This seems to confuse (and indeed such confusions, sometimes intentional, abound in Schmitt himself) the normative and the empirical question. The Court recognized that it could not police effectively how the political actors in the secession process were constrained by the norms that the Court had identified.[41] But this does not mean that the norms would be ineffective or meaningless in shaping the behaviour of the political actors, and in providing a basis for the assessment of the relative legitimacy of their positions and deci-sions in political bargaining. Kahn's position is also powerfully challenged by the existence of what is generally called, after Teitel's seminal work of that name,[42] transitional justice: the space between an old and a new legal order is imagined other than as a complete normative gap or vacuum, but as itself regulated by norms that are appropriate in situations of political transition. Indeed, transitional justice as a real world phenomenon shows that Schmitt's notion that there is no effective normativity, except that emanating from sov-ereign decision, is highly dubious.

---

[41] *Reference re Secession of Quebec* [1998] 2 SCR 217. For an articulation of the kind of approach that the Court would eventually adopt in this case as anti-Schmittean, see R Howse and A Malkin, 'Canadians Are a Sovereign People: How the Supreme Court Should Approach the Reference on Quebec Secession' (1997) 76 *Canadian Bar Review* 186–227. See also the dis-cussion of the decision in R Howse and R Teitel, 'Humanity Bounded and Unbounded: The Regulation of External Self-Determination under International Law' (2013) 7 *Law & Ethics of Human Rights* 155–84.

[42] R Teitel, *Transitional Justice* (OUP New York 2000). Teitel's work engaged critically with a field that had started to emerge in the 1990s: see further CS Nino, *Radical Evil on Trial* (Yale University Press New Haven 1998); NJ Kritz, *Transitional Justice: How Emerging Democracies Reckon with Former Regimes* (United States Institute of Peace Washington DC 1995); R Teitel, *How Are the New Democracies of the Southern Cone Dealing with the Legacy of Past Human Rights Abuses?* (Council on Foreign Relations New York 1990).

3.4 Nehal Bhuta

All of Koskenniemi, Posner and Vermeule, and Kahn are preoccupied with what might be called 'existential' or foundational questions about the reality or essence of international legal normativity. As I have suggested, they may apply Schmitt in un-Schmittean ways and misidentify certain arguments as Schmittean because of a surface affinity with Schmitt's critique of elements of liberalism. But Schmitt is an interlocutor, of sorts, in their own theorizing. Yet, there is another way that Schmitt has also filtered into international legal scholarship, notably as a set of constructs that can be added on to workmanlike doctrinal scholarship in order to increase its theoretical octane. There is a pressure on international legal scholars to be theoretical or conceptual (if they are not empirical) that comes from the prevailing norms in the American or Anglo-North American legal academy. Bringing into the picture a dense, difficult, and controversial thinker like Schmitt signals somehow that one is being 'theoretical'. I think the kind of engagements of Koskenniemi, Posner and Vermeule, and Kahn with Schmitt described in the previous sections are, whatever my criticisms, useful as opportunities to consider fault lines in international law and its relation to politics as well as providing possibilities to challenge some core assumptions of the Schmittean position, even if they do not themselves take up these possibilities. I am much less persuaded of the use of Schmittean constructs as a means of ordering contemporary doctrine or classifying contemporary doctrinal disputes. The best illustration of that approach I have found so far is the work of Nehal Bhuta. One reason that Bhuta is a useful example is that he deploys Schmitt in articles that deal with a quite diverse range of doctrinal and policy questions in international law, including targeted killing, rights of religious expression, *ius post bellum*, and the law of occupation. The question is: what actual work is Schmitt doing in these pieces? Let us take the most recent one first. In 'Two Concepts of Religious Freedom in the European Court of Human Rights', Bhuta claims that

The conceptualization of the right [of freedom of conscience] was embedded in a political ethos defined by a polemical opposition to two alternative possibilities: implicitly, a formal liberal ideal of freedom of conscience that sets clear and calculable limits to state interference on individual *autonomy*; and, explicitly, a radical materialist secularism identified with the Communist bloc. Even as Christian democratic thought embraced rights, it did so on an understanding that rights formed an important part of the imbuement of the state with a *moral-cultural political substance* that overcame the weaknesses of liberal forms in the face of aggressive nonliberal antagonists. This ethos, I would suggest, is a 'militant' one, wittingly or unwittingly absorbing a key lesson of Schmitt—that a political order is necessarily a concrete value order shaped in antagonism to other active political visions.[43]

---

[43] N Bhuta, 'Two Concepts of Religious Freedom in the European Court of Human Rights' (2014) 113 *South Atlantic Quarterly* 9–35, at 19–20 (emphasis in original).

This statement by Bhuta is followed by a lengthy parsing of the European Court of Human Rights case law on freedom of religious expression: the headscarf cases and the *Lautsi* case on the display of crucifixes in Italian classrooms.[44] Bhuta does not actually provide any account of the post-war development of human rights in European political and legal discourse in 'the face of aggressive nonliberal antagonists'. But of course, even if it were true that as a historical fact, human rights discourse and jurisprudence in post-war Europe did develop in relation to such antagonists, this would not demonstrate the truth of the Schmittean proposition cited by Bhuta that a political order is *necessarily* shaped by antagonism with enemies or opponents holding contrary political visions. It would simply be one data point. On the contrary, what invoking Schmitt seems to do is to provide some relief to Bhuta from having to prove the larger historical thesis; for *if* we take Schmitt on authority that concrete political orders are always shaped that way, Bhuta's specific thesis is at least plausible. (Bhuta also has an argument about the development of conceptions of religious freedom or tolerance at earlier points in European history; here the work is done by citing Samuel Moyn rather than Carl Schmitt, but this argument (largely) disappears also once the case analysis starts up.)

In his 'States of Exception: Regulating Targeted Killing in a Global Civil War'[45] Bhuta makes an allusion to Schmitt in the very title. Bhuta takes up the highly topical question of whether and to what extent the laws of war, international human rights law, or other legal frameworks ought to apply to drone attacks and other targeted killings of persons who are not clearly state actors. I was actually quite excited when Bhuta began the article by invoking Schmitt's *Theory of the Partisan*, which does seem to destabilize, quite presciently, the boundaries between combatants, enemies, and common criminals. Here it might seem quite interesting to see how Schmitt's analysis might be a departure point for a retheorizing of the legal framework applicable to 'terrorists', and responding to terrorists through targeted killings. But Bhuta quickly tells us that in fact, today's 'terrorists' are not Schmitt's partisans, because they are not rooted territorially but operate on a free-flowing transnational basis. Regardless of how accurate that is as a characterization of the terrorists to whose apparent threats targeted killings are a response, Bhuta's reading of *Theory of the Partisan* is inaccurate, since Schmitt explicitly indicates that the issue he is addressing relates also to 'cosmopirates' and 'cosmopartisans' and he imagines a future where the partisan will shed his telluric nature and go global or

---

[44] See *Şahin v Turkey* (ECtHR, Application No 44774/98, 10 November 2005); *Dahlab v Switzerland* (ECtHR, Application No 42393/98, 15 February 2001); *Lautsi v Italy* (ECtHR, Application No 30814/06, 3 December 2009); *Lautsi v Italy* (ECtHR Grand Chamber, Application No 30814/06, 18 March 2011).

[45] N Bhuta, 'States of Exception: Regulating Targeted Killing in a "Global Civil War"' in P Alston and E Macdonald (eds), *Human Rights, Intervention, and the Use of Force* (OUP Oxford 2010) 243–74.

cosmic.[46] But Bhuta's reading allows him to call up Schmitt as an opening act and then dismiss him. Once Schmitt is dismissed Bhuta can go on to conduct a lengthy tour through contemporary international human rights and humanitarian law doctrine of which the upshot reads like what any number of think tank or foreign ministry memos probably do, 'there are no clear conceptual–logical bases to decide which of these frameworks is properly applied to the targeted killing of terrorist suspects, and thus that transparent political and policy choices must be made'.[47] It is less than clear whether Bhuta endorses the full Schmittean implication of this inconclusive conclusion; since the decision as to which normative frameworks apply is apparently a decision out of nothingness as 'there are no clear conceptual–logical bases' for it, perhaps the decisions about targeted killings themselves cannot be constrained at all by international legal normativity.

Bhuta's 'New Modes and Orders: The Difficulties of a Jus Post Bellum of Constitutional Transformation'[48] contains forty-two references to Schmitt throughout the text. Yet all of these references come down to a single point, namely that post-bellum nation-building cannot proceed through the application of abstract norms or models of constitutionalism, but requires 'order-creating power', the creation or recreation of the will of people to live together as a single polity. I would fully agree with that; yet Bhuta does not draw the full conclusion that is needed to really characterize this insight as Schmittean, namely that this creation or recreation requires the imposition of concrete order from the top down, by the strongest, most capable of domination, man or group of men who are available. Ultimately, Bhuta's attack on the notion that international legal norms embed certain liberal democratic conceptions of constitutionalism serves not to support the 'sovereignty' of 'peoples' but to defend the status quo of what he calls 'diplomatic bricolage' in state-building by institutions such as the Security Council—as if there could be nothing in between the fantasy of creating a new polity wholly from abstract norms of liberal democratic orientation, on the one hand, and the unprincipled and unstable compromises denoted by 'diplomatic bricolage', on the other. Again as suggested in the discussion of Kahn earlier, this middle ground could be thought of precisely as the site of transitional justice. Seeing the sleight-of-hand applied so crudely here by Bhuta gives us an opportunity to question the typically Schmittean move of going from the recognition that legal norms may be *underdetermined* and *underdetermining* to their abandonment to normatively unstructured compromise and accommodation.

Bhuta's invocation of Schmitt sets up an expectation of theoretical radicalism or conceptually driven critique. But then the analysis ends up in an almost complete

---

[46] *The Theory of the Partisan* (n 3) 80. The partisan can be imagined according to Schmitt as operating far beyond traditional territorial configurations of power, even to the point of ultimately perhaps fighting in and for outer space!

[47] 'States of Exception' (n 45) 246.

[48] N Bhuta, 'New Modes and Orders: The Difficulties of a Jus Post Bellum of Constitutional Transformation' (2010) 60 *University of Toronto Law Journal* 799–854.

stand-pat type position; there is no point in trying to imagine things done much differently than they are. None of Bhuta's conclusions would put the noses of diplomats, judges, UN officials, and old-fashioned international law luminaries out of joint. If there is critique it is only of those who dare to dream.

4 CONCLUSION

I first engaged in scholarly consideration of Carl Schmitt's political theory as a scholar of constitutional law and political theory, before my research turned in the direction of the theory of international law. What is most striking to me is that (with the partial exception of Martti Koskenniemi), despite the fact that Schmitt did write extensively about international law, Schmitt is brought into international legal theory as a kind of authority for truths about politics that liberal legal internationalists have somehow suppressed or denied, but without critical examination of the basis for those truths and the extent to which they are really Schmittean (or indeed valid points against liberal international legal conceptions) except when combined with Schmitt's full and radical attack both on liberalism and legality. None of the scholars examined are prepared to embrace that full and radical attack, because as Koskenniemi admits clearly and Kahn more obscurely, or mutedly, doing so would imply adopting and defending a fascist, atavistic authoritarian, or right-wing nihilist stance as a counter-conception of liberal internationalism. But, to my mind, confronting Schmitt with the living reality of international law today has a real intellectual value; once we assume that we need to question Schmitt in light of that living reality, rather than smothering that reality in Schmittean propositions that are taken as articles of faith, then a valuable questioning of Schmitt's binaries becomes possible. For the living reality of contemporary international law does put into question whether there must be either authoritative hierarchy or normative chaos—either fully determined and determining legal normative outcomes or the decision out of nothingness The sense that international law's complex relation to the political is ill-captured by continental positivism on the one hand or Anglo-American human rights moralism, on the other, does not automatically justify bringing in Schmitt. Leo Strauss, Hannah Arendt,[49] and Judith Shklar,[50] to

---

[49] See eg DJ Luban, 'Hannah Arendt as a Theorist of International Criminal Law' (2011) 11 *International Criminal Law Review* 621–41. See also D Whitehall, 'Hannah Arendt and International Law' in this *Handbook*.

[50] See eg S Moyn, 'Judith Shklar on the Philosophy of International Criminal Law' (2014) 14 *International Criminal Law Review* 717–37.

give three examples, are thinkers whose (different) perspectives are rooted in the experience of twentieth-century political extremes, and all of whom address the danger of different kinds of liberal legalism obscuring the force and meaningfulness of the political and the nature of human judgement, but who, unlike Schmitt, are not caught within liberal/anti-liberal polemics. That such polemics in our own time tend to confine or channel debates about international law in its relation to politics, is an explanation as to why Schmitt is so easily invoked, but also a reason for caution in doing so, and for expanding the sources of our reflections in the history of political and legal theory.

CHAPTER 12

HANNAH ARENDT AND INTERNATIONAL LAW

DEBORAH WHITEHALL

THIS chapter reconsiders the arc of Hannah Arendt's writings about international law. Rather than evincing a haphazard or ambivalent narrative by a peripheral figure, her scattered remarks arguably present a careful pattern of demands upon international law, announced at the discipline's key formative turns, for the resolution of the Jewish Question or rather, the series of issues problematizing Jewishness as uncertainty about citizenship, nation, and race from the eighteenth century onwards.[1] The timing and context of Arendt's attention to this question as a political theorist is important. Arendt was a German-Jewish émigré who survived twentieth-century totalitarianism and observed the unfolding of a new international law after each of the world wars. Her experience of Jewish exile and diaspora gave her a sense of the problem, the urge to understand its depths, and what might be needed in its place. International law is an important site for her attention even where law is adjuvant or ancillary to the broader sweep of her analytical project.

---

[1] The term, the 'Jewish Question', is not a twentieth-century invention. In the mid-nineteenth century, Karl Marx famously identified the Jewish Question with the call for political emancipation by Jews as Jews, and for the preceding generation of Jews in the eighteenth century, the term denoted a claim for social recognition: K Marx, 'On the Jewish Question' in J O'Malley (ed), *Marx: Early Political Writings* (CUP Cambridge 1994) 28–56; S Benhabib, *The Reluctant Modernism of Hannah Arendt* (Rowman and Littlefield Lanham 2003 [2000]) at 36–8. Subsequent iterations of the Jewish Question include the Zionist call for a Jewish Palestine and the tragic anti-Semitic programmes of Nazi Germany to excise Jews from the European nation-state. For an exposition of the varying viewpoints that underpin and complicate the Jewish Question and the significance of the concept within Arendt's broader political theory see the now classic text, RJ Bernstein, *Hannah Arendt and the Jewish Question* (Polity Cambridge 1996) at xi-xii.

Arendt repeatedly returns to international law expecting answers as a political thinker for the working out of tensions within the idea of nation for the sake of humankind and the plural life of politics.

1 INTRODUCTION

Hannah Arendt (1906–75) appears in international legal theory with accelerating frequency despite, or perhaps because of, her different standpoint as a political theorist.[2] The rediscovery of her writings by international lawyers following the centennial anniversary of her birth pitches her as an interlocutor for meeting and extending disciplinary debates from the outside.[3] Her writings on totalitarianism, imperialism, statelessness, minorities, refugees, human rights, non-violence, geno-cide, freedom, human plurality, and revolution confirm points of thematic coales-cence with the contemporary concerns of organizing globally. Shared projects or thematic cross-overs do not, alone, make a case for putting the reciprocity between her politics and international law above other, more obvious disciplinary alliances with history, political theory, sociology, and philosophy. Indeed, Arendt's scat-tered comments about international law never cohere as an argument about global law but rather alchemize meaning from law for politics. This point is significant.

---

[2] Texts exemplifying the recent surge of interest in Arendt by international legal scholars or by schol-ars interested in international law include, for example, S Benhabib, 'International Law and Human Plurality in the Shadow of Totalitarianism: Hannah Arendt and Raphael Lemkin' (2009) 16 *Constellations* 331–50; L Bilsky, 'When Actor and Spectator Meet in the Courtroom: Reflections on Hannah Arendt's Concept of Judgement' (1996) 8 *History and Memory* 137–73; D Luban, 'Hannah Arendt as a Theorist of International Criminal Law' (2011) 11 *International Criminal Law Review* 621–41; A Kemmerer, 'Kelsen, Schmitt, Arendt, and the Possibilities of Constitutionalization in (International) Law' (2010) 23 *Leiden Journal of International Law* 717–22; A Kesby, *The Right to Have Rights: Citizenship, Humanity, and International Law* (OUP Oxford 2012); J Klabbers, 'Possible Islands of Predictability: The Legal Thought of Hannah Arendt' (2007) 20 *Leiden Journal of International Law* 1–23; M Goldoni and C McCorkindale (eds), *Hannah Arendt and the Law* (Hart Oxford 2012).

[3] The basis for Arendt's reputation as a political theorist is her prolific stream of essays and mono-graphs written from her exile from Germany in the early 1930s until her death in 1975: H Arendt, *The Origins of Totalitarianism* (Harcourt New York 1976 [1950]); H Arendt, *The Human Condition* (Chicago University Press Chicago 1998 [1958]); H Arendt, *Eichmann in Jerusalem: A Report on the Banality of Evil* (Penguin New York 2006 [1963]); H Arendt, *On Revolution* (Penguin New York 2006 [1963]); H Arendt, 'On Violence' in *Crises of the Republic* (Harcourt Brace New York 1972) 103–98; H Arendt, *The Jewish Writings* (Schocken Books New York 2007). Recent edited collections suggestive of the popularity of Arendt's broader political consciousness amongst political theorists include: S Benhabib (ed), *Politics in Dark Times: Encounters with Hannah Arendt* (CUP New York 2010); R Berkowitz, T Keenan, and J Katz (eds), *Thinking in Dark Times: Hannah Arendt on Ethics and Politics* (Fordham University Press New York 2010).

Even where Arendt speaks about emergent principles of international criminal law or human rights, she gives international lawyers scant normative direction about what their discipline does, or should do, or should look like.[4] International legal scholars learn from a political investigation that encounters the initiatives (or silences) of global governance as specific, separate events without expectation of a script, sequel, or cross-referencing over time. Indeed, the apparent lack of continuity follows from Arendt's habit of problematizing situations or events rather than locating historical sequences within a conceptual trajectory or identifying political data as the product of a specific system of power. Jonathan Schell says her thinking 'seems to "crystalize" (the word is hers) around events' but never produces 'systematically ordered reflection'.[5] Margaret Canovan similarly describes Arendt's methods as anti-systematic.[6] Consistent with this methodology, Arendt does not directly articulate a framing narrative that might resolve the puzzle of her encounter with international law. International legal writing about Arendt says relatively little about the broader cartographic problem or else emphasizes her approach as haphazard or segmented, contingent on instabilities within her thinking. This is not to say that Arendt's interest in international law is discontinuous. Rather, it leaves open the possibility that Arendt's thinking organizes around a problem or a question rather than a set response or outcome.

Reading the encounter between Arendt and international law as a story within a story makes palpable the grid where her politics intersects, illuminates, and makes demands of international law. It also responds to the commonly expressed interest of international lawyers to know her political theory for their discipline. In an early essay by an international lawyer about Arendt, Jan Klabbers calls for a 'reconstruction' of her 'sketchy thinking' about the discipline and scopes the likely field of engagement as including human rights and international criminal law.[7] These remain clear intersections between Arendt and international legal writing, though there is a tendency to analyse each, and their author's broader seam of writing, disjunctively.[8] Arendt's immediate reading audience did the same. Her fame

---

[4] Cf theorists of domestic constitutional law engage more directly with Arendt's engagement with legal concepts, eg, M Wilkinson, 'Between Freedom and Law: Hannah Arendt on the Promise of Modern Revolution and the Burden of "The Tradition"' in *Hannah Arendt and the Law* (n 2) 35–62.

[5] J Schell, 'Introduction' in *On Revolution* (n 3) xi–xxix, at xii.

[6] M Canovan, *Hannah Arendt: A Reinterpretation of Her Political Thought* (CUP Cambridge 1992) at 5.

[7] 'Possible Islands of Predictability' (n 2) 2.

[8] The habit of compartmentalizing Arendt's writing into discreet legal or thematic threads in part reflects the diverse relevance of Arendt's writing for legal thought and further, the disciplinary practice of lawyers in finding and communicating meaning through patterns of organization. Compartmentalization informs the organization of the essays in *Hannah Arendt and the Law* (n 2) as well as the focused discussions by international lawyers on particular seams in Arendt's writing and the corresponding issues for international law (for example, on human rights, genocide, or global constitutionalism: see sources cited in n 2).

(and then, her infamy) hinged on the reception of her monograph, *The Origins of Totalitarianism* (1951), including its radical history of rightlessness, and the subsequent publication in the *New Yorker* of her controversial report on the Jerusalem trial of Adolf Eichmann, a prominent member of the Third Reich's Schutzstaffel who was instrumental in organizing the transportation of Jews to the notorious death camps (1963).

Seyla Benhabib takes up Klabber's invitation to piece together a fuller reconstruction of *Origins* and *Eichmann* in Arendt's thinking.[9] Benhabib does not, however, discover a basis for synthesizing differences but instead extracts evidence of a 'transformation' over time. She suggests that discreet passages in the two tracts represent 'book-ends marking the evolution of Arendt's thought from scepticism towards international law and human rights in the 1950s toward a cautious confirmation of their role in shaping politics among nations in the 1960s'.[10] The relevant passages support Benhabib's discovery of tactical fluidity in how Arendt receives (and expects) international law as a possible answer for present-day political tragedy.[11]

My response to the task of reconstruction is different. The question that interests me is whether there might also be a framing narrative implicit in Arendt's approach to international law that relates her apparently disjointed remarks to the progressive deepening of her analytical project. That is, where Benhabib emphasizes a disaggregated encounter between Arendt and international law, this chapter suggests an alternative reading that highlights continuity and narrative cohesion. Benhabib's sophisticated, though disjunctive, study leaves aside key passages in Arendt's broader writings and consequently de-prioritizes an important subtext that pins her subject's varied remarks about international law together. What appears to Benhabib as inconsistencies in Arendt's thinking figure, to this reader,

---

[9] 'International Law and Human Plurality in the Shadow of Totalitarianism' (n 2). Benhabib reads Arendt's commentary about international law from the perspective of political theory not law. Nevertheless, her voice carries considerable weight for international legal theory given her longstanding reputation as an Arendt scholar who investigates her subject's response to genocide, human rights, citizenship, and equality: see eg S Benhabib, *The Rights of Others: Aliens, Residents, and Citizens* (CUP Cambridge 2004) 49–69 ('"The Right to Have Rights": Hannah Arendt and the Contradictions of the Nation-State'); S Benhabib, *The Reluctant Modernism of Hannah Arendt* (new edn Rowman & Littlefield Lanham 2003); S Benhabib, 'Introduction' in *Politics in Dark Times* (n 3) 1–14.

[10] 'International Law and Human Plurality in the Shadow of Totalitarianism' (n 2) 333 and 338. Other commentators also emphasize Arendt's changing attitudes or her uncertainty about the effectiveness of the emergent system of international human rights. See eg S Besson, 'The Right to Have Rights: From Human Rights to Citizens' Rights and Back' in *Hannah Arendt and the Law* (n 2) 335–55, at 339–40; S Power, 'The Lesson of Hannah Arendt' *New York Review of Books* (29 April 2004) <http://www.nybooks.com/articles/archives/2004/apr/29/the-lesson-of-hannah-arendt/> [accessed 22 February 2016].

[11] Benhabib refers to passages in *Origins* (n 3) 292 and in *Eichmann* (n 3) 277–9 to support her argument about the shifts in Arendt's attitude towards international law over time: 'International Law and Human Plurality in the Shadow of Totalitarianism' (n 2) 332–3.

as isolated lines in contexts preoccupied with the political dilemmas of stateless-ness and the role of the nation in post-genocide organizations.[12] Could apparent disjunctions be symptomatic of Arendt's analytic methods, a tendency to prob-lematize individual events or situations, rather than a failure to think or address those issues systematically? Do narrative twists cohere to a pattern of problemati-zation not about global governance per se, but about the political events to which international law responds and sometimes fails to resolve?

Judith Butler offers inspiration for one kind of synthesis by reading Arendt's critique of Zionism entirely through her experience of Jewish exile and diaspora.[13] The details are familiar. Arendt entered France in 1933 as a stateless non-person, remained until the Nazi occupation in 1940, and afterwards found refuge in the United States where she became a citizen in 1951.[14] The Jewish Question became the coordinating theme in her thinking from the moment of her physical exile onwards. In a key passage in *Origins*, Arendt identifies the pre-war refugee question or the puzzle of statelessness as 'primarily a Jewish problem' that captured the full complexity of the 'Jewish Question' for Jews, and its apparent 'insolubility' for all sides.[15] The Jewish Question now referred to greater dangers than the nineteenth-century calls for political emancipation or the eighteenth-century claim by the Jewish parvenu for social recognition.[16] From Arendt's mid-twentieth-century per-spective, disenfranchisement clarified that the Jewish Question was now a political predicament that called for an urgent and radical solution for which there were several prominent responses.[17] For Zionists, the Jewish Question signified the need for recognition of a people through the foundation of the Jewish state; and for anti-Semites, it required its final solution through the extermination of European Jewry. Arendt sympathized with neither position as both gave up legal equality for the homogeneity of the nation-state.[18]

Her contribution departs from narratives that characterize Jews as either a pariah people or a chosen people. She speaks from the vantage of the secular Jew to ask not what the world ought to do about her people but rather what can

---

[12] Benhabib also situates Arendt's remarks about international law in the broader setting of her discussion of anti-Semitism, political plurality, nationalism, genocide, statelessness, rightlessness and equality, but does not identify these themes as part of a linking narrative: 'International Law and Human Plurality in the Shadow of Totalitarianism' (n 2) 334–8 and 342–4.

[13] J Butler, *Parting Ways: Jewishness and the Critique of Zionism* (Columbia University Press New York 2012). See also J Butler, 'The Charge of Anti-Semitism: Jews, Israel, and the Risks of Public Critique' in *Precarious Life: The Powers of Mourning and Violence* (Verso London 2004) 101–27.

[14] RJ Bernstein, 'Hannah Arendt on the Stateless' (2005) 11 *Parallax* 46–60, at 47; E Young-Bruehl, *Hannah Arendt: For Love of the World* (Yale University Press New Haven 2004 [1982]) 115–63.

[15] *Origins* (n 3) 289–90.

[16] See eg H Arendt, 'The Enlightenment and the Jewish Question (1932)' in *The Jewish Writings* (n 3) 3–18; H Arendt, 'Berlin Salon (1932)' in *Essays in Understanding: 1930–1954: Formation, Exile, and Totalitarianism* (Schocken Books New York 1994) 57–65.

[17] *Origins* (n 3) 56.   [18] Ibid 290.

we do to understand the past and move beyond Jewish suffering as our ontological condition? She says '[t]he human sense of reality demands that men actualize the sheer passive givenness of their being, not in order to change it but in
order to make articulate and call into full existence what otherwise they would
have to suffer passively anyhow'.[19] Arendt's engagement with politics, history,
and international law, arguably represents a new means for *actualizing* Jewish
identity, and through actualization, of resisting historical patterns of suffering
and grief. The Jewish Question and its provocation for dilemmas concerning
the nation 'run like red threads through the whole' of Arendt's writing about
international law.[20]

Butler's specific intervention in framing a narrative of this kind is part of a broader
study of the critique of Zionism by Jewish writers, including Arendt. She rejects the
proposition that any opposition to Israel or Zionism is necessarily counter-Jewish or
anti- Semitic even as it questions the existing line 'as the defining horizon of the ethical'.[21]
The 'ethical self-departure' describes the manoeuvre by Jewish writers against the
hegemonic control of Zionism over the category of Jewishness and further, against the
subjugation of the Palestinian nation by the Jewish state of Israel.[22] Butler describes
an ethical practice that derives from an existing knowledge order or tradition but
which demands its translation, and as a result the interruption and reformation of
the original category. Ethical translation is a 'relational practice that responds to an
obligation that originates outside the subject' and further, is 'the act by which place is
established for those who are "not-me", comporting me beyond a sovereign claim in
the direction of a challenge to selfhood that I receive from elsewhere'.[23] The paradox
of ethical translation is its Jewish route towards a new paradigm of justice that is also
counter-hegemonic in its rejection of the familiar form. For Arendt, her response to
the problem of statelessness orders her counter-Zionist politics as an ethical translation of the Jewish claim to nation. If she sometimes speaks against Israel, her voice is
not for Palestine or another national cause, nor could it be against the Jewish people
or the idea of nation itself. Rather, her position arises from her situation as a Jew and
expresses empathy for the predicament of 'being nothing but human', of homelessness on an unprecedented scale, of rootlessness to an unprecedented depth, and asks
the question, how might a political community rally against the repetition of historical dramas that so placed the Jewish people?[24]

Arendt's responses to international law derive from complications associated
with what Butler names the counter-hegemonic 'translation' of Jewish suffering.

---

[19] *Human Condition* (n 3) 208.

[20] Arendt describes her method in *Origins* (n 3) in terms of using the fundamental concepts of
totalitarianism to structure her study 'which run like red threads through the whole': H Arendt,
'A Reply to Eric Vogelin' in *Essays in Understanding* (n 16) 401–8, at 403. Other writers similarly
identify *The Jewish Question* as a connective theme for understanding Arendt's broader body of
writing: eg, *Jewish Question* (n 1).

[21] *Parting Ways* (n 13) 2.   [22] Ibid 4–5.   [23] Ibid 9.   [24] See eg *Origins* (n 3) vii.

Butler's particularization of Arendt's critique of Zionism provides inspiration for a study of the counter-hegemonic, or counter-sovereign claims that Arendt made of international law and for understanding these as claims made on behalf of the Jewish nation. Arendt repeatedly asks what international law and international institutions can do to account for the past and secure the future. The question involves persistent negotiation and renegotiation of the demands and limits of nation that characterize the task of ethical translation. Herein lies a double tension that complicates what Arendt asks of international law. First, statelessness in the twentieth century realized the nation as the site of danger and belonging. Arendt's ardent anti-nationalism is never anti-nation but rather figures nationalism as the root cause of discrimination directed at minorities and which in the extreme example, justified their superfluity and liquidation. Second, statelessness recast the claim for belonging and nation as a plea for pluralization. The unsolved difficulty for Arendt was how to revise the idea of universal entitlement to make space for an idea of plurality that protects the whole of humanity but avoids the chance for constriction implicit in abstract standards.

Reading Arendt's response to international law as a series of demands arising out of her problematization of the Jewish Question is implicit in the opening lines of *Origins*. She observes that European histories of anti-Semitism, imperialism and totalitarianism 'have demonstrated that human dignity needs a new guarantee which can only be found in a new political principle, in a new law on earth, whose validity this time must comprehend the whole of humanity while its power must remain strictly limited, rooted in and controlled by newly defined territorial entities'.[25] Here, Arendt arguably makes demands of the existing frame of interconnected states and its development through emergent institutions and principles, as a stateless person and a Jew, for a new rule to answer the perplexities of nation. The full course of her encounter with international law reflects four categories of demand that take up, in different contexts, the problems of national recognition and justice for Jews: the protection of the Jewish nation; the protection of minorities; international human rights; and the early evolution of crimes against humanity.

2 THE JEWISH QUESTION

A series of essays written by Arendt in the 1930s and 1940s, later published as *The Jewish Writings*, analyse the interwar and then post-war interventions of the

---

[25] *Origins* (n 3) ix.

international community in relation to the formation of the Jewish State. Attention to the activities of the League of Nations and United Nations (UN) make these essays an important historical record of the participation of Jews in brokering an international resolution for Jewish sovereignty in the Middle East. The essays are also significant insofar as Arendt clarifies the paradigm for her subsequent thinking about the dilemmas of nation. Put in Butler's terms, the essays reflect the broader project of ethical translation of Jewish suffering that complicate Arendt's position as a Jewish activist. Though Arendt repeatedly backs Jewish claims for nation, her analysis resists the Zionist call for hegemony over Palestine and is critical of using international law as a means of obtaining leverage for Israeli sovereignty. The important nuance of her position is that she does not reject the prospects for a solution for the Jewish Question through international law. Indeed, it is arguable that she conceives international law as the only practical means for achieving lasting peace between rival nations in the Middle East. Despite operational deficiencies and a pattern of bias toward powerful states, international law offers a stabilizing structure for political processes from which freedom and justice emerge. That is, Arendt comes to international law claiming and expecting the resolution of the Jewish Question on certain terms: by processes that allow for the authentic recognition and inclusion of Jewish interests; for institutional transparency; and by taking equal responsibility for the national entitlements of both Jews and Arabs.

Arendt repeatedly speaks for the possibilities of nation by demanding full representation of Jewish interests in international peace negotiations and in wartime preparations. She puts the claim for inclusion as a secular Jew and frames her discursive entry into legal debates in representative terms, repeatedly calling for Jewish solidarity and identifying her position with the collective pronouns, 'we', 'our past', and 'us'. Speaking from the vantage of nation was Arendt's strategy for Jewish inclusion in institutional decision-making in the absence of a motherland with legal status as a state, as well as a technique for critical engagement with her community.[26] She says:

> Justice for a people . . . can only mean national justice. One of the inalienable human rights of Jews is the right to live and if need be to die as a Jew. A human being can defend himself only as the person he is attacked as. A Jew can preserve his human dignity only if he can be human as a Jew.[27]

History proved that the lack of a nation-state left Jews vulnerable to violent strategies of discrimination, exile, and extermination as well as pre-empting marginality in international legal processes even where the aim was benevolent or protective.

---

[26] Arendt identifies the Jewish Question as one of national homelessness and argues for national emancipation and belonging: H Arendt, 'A Way Toward the Reconciliation of Peoples (1942)' in *The Jewish Writings* (n 3) 258–63, at 261; H Arendt, 'The Assets of Personality (1945)' in *The Jewish Writings* (n 3) 402–4, at 402.

[27] 'A Way Toward the Reconciliation of Peoples (1942)' (n 26) 261.

The conundrum of representation reflects the problem of legal status and was apparent in the peace conferences following the Armistice in 1918, wartime negotiations in the early 1940s and at Dumbarton Oaks, and the post-war conference in San Francisco.

In the first cases, two Jewish delegations attended negotiations for the Minority Treaties that followed the 1919 Paris Peace Conference, the Zionist political limb, the *Jewish Agency*, and the Comité des Délégations Juives that represented the religious and cultural interests of European Jewry who identified as citizens of existing (already emancipated) states and as a religious minority within those states. Neither group made proposals on behalf of the Jewish nation but deferred to the League as the juridical and political guarantor of their fragmented claims. Arendt faults the organization of the delegations on the basis that each 'spoke and acted without actually being rooted in the Jewish people' and consequently, each permitted political negotiations to proceed in the absence of a carefully delineated 'Jewish political cause'. The timing of mismanagement was crucial because it meant that Jews missed a pre-totalitarian opportunity to participate in the resolution of the Jewish Question as a political question. Instead of focusing on the politics of diaspora or the absence of a homeland, which Arendt identifies as the root cause for dispossession, the minority treaties 'depoliticized' the Jewish Question by interpreting it as a call for cultural and religious freedom.[28]

In the 1940s, Arendt returned to the lack of political preparedness by Jews for peace. The source of the problem again belonged, in equal parts, to the Jewish councils and groups who refused to combine politically and to the exclusivity of wartime and post-war negotiations led by the allied powers. In the 1944 essay, 'Days of Change', Arendt cautions Jews about the prospects for freedom and justice through war or peace in the absence of a recognizable national status and an audible national voice. She says '[i]t would be foolish to believe that peace will be easier for us than a war in which, right to the end, we fought as allies but were never recognized as one of the Allied nations'.[29] Later, Arendt joins the problem of fragmentation to her demand for political inclusion, blaming Jews as much as the international community for the failure of the Jewish people to influence the post-war legal and institutional landscape in their national interest. In the days prior to the San Francisco Conference, Arendt estimates 'Jewish chances' as one of 'sparse prospects' and 'divided representation' where old habits of deference to existing structures of power and internal dissension continue to prevail. The problem she envisages relates to the restricted status of Jewish groups as 'advisors' to the American delegation (not independent participants) as much as the fragmentation of Jewish interests caused by an 'intra-Jewish spat' that ensured 'in defiance of all

---

[28] H Arendt, 'The Minority Question (1940)' in *The Jewish Writings* (n 3) 125–33, at 125–6.
[29] H Arendt, 'Days of Change (28 July 1944)' in *The Jewish Writings* (n 3) 214–17, at 214.

the rules of arithmetic, *two Jewish advisers are less than one*'.[30] Full national participation is necessary for freedom and justice because 'we—not as individuals, not as American adherents of the Jewish religion, but as a people—have special interests and demands that we must represent one way or another'; political solidarity is necessary for the effectiveness of participation; and a refusal to compromise to powerful states is necessary if Jews are to 'relearn the language of freedom and justice' for themselves as a people and not 'live on their knees', worshipping power and hopeful of the gifts of international philanthropy.[31]

Arendt uses the same split-tone—for and against Jewish organization and for and against the structural promise of international law—in respect of the failed wartime proposal for a Jewish army.[32] Although she elsewhere counts violence as pre-political, Jewish resistance dedicated to 'fighting for peace, for *our* peace' presented the only viable alternative to the 'passive' and 'valueless' death of submitting to certain deportation and physical annihilation or trusting the goodwill of the allied powers.[33] The Warsaw uprising exemplified the dignity of acting as a nation and the impossibility of success without international collaboration. Arendt was certain that the international order would remain incomplete and Jewish annihilation an ever-present threat until there was a formal place at the table for 'the pariah' amongst the world's people.[34]

The contradictory aspect of Arendt's hopes for Jewish freedom through international law also characterizes her response to the formalization of Jewish sovereignty in Israel. Here, questions of national entitlement for Jews produced the Arab Question or the Palestine Question, complicating the Jewish claim for nation and the coordination of those claims by the international community.[35] Arendt strongly opposes the imperialist ambitions motivating international support for the Zionist claims to territory from 1917 onwards, led by Britain as the relevant colonial power in Palestine and subsequently by the League and the UN.[36]

---

[30] H Arendt, 'Jewish Chances: Sparse Prospects, Divided Representation (20 April 1945)' in *The Jewish Writings* (n 3) 238–40.

[31] H Arendt, 'Jewish Politics (1942)' in *The Jewish Writings* (n 3) 241–3, at 243.

[32] Ibid; H Arendt, 'From Army to Brigade (6 October 1944)' in *The Jewish Writings* (n 3) 227–9, at 227; 'A Way Toward the Reconciliation of Peoples (1942)' (n 26) 263.

[33] See 'On Violence' (n 3) and 'Days of Change' (n 29) 217.

[34] 'A Way Toward the Reconciliation of Peoples' (n 26) 263.

[35] Arendt's *The Jewish Writings* (n 3) critically assesses the evolution of Jewish sovereignty in the Middle East in three distinct phases across three decades, according to: (i) the Balfour Declaration made by the British foreign secretary Arthur Balfour to the British Jewish community in November 1917 proposing support for the establishment of a Jewish 'national home' in Palestine; (ii) arrangements made by the League for British administration of Palestine for the purposes of securing a national home for Jews under the British *Mandate for Palestine* (Cmd Paper 1785, December 1922) which took effect between 1922 and 1948; and (iii) the formal recognition of the State of Israel by the UN from May 1948 after the end of the British Mandate (14 May 1948) and the failure to implement the international proposal for the peaceful partition of Palestine envisaged by the UN: 'Future Government of Palestine' GA Res 181 UN Doc A/RES 181(II) (29 November 1947).

[36] H Arendt, 'The Balfour Declaration and the Palestine Mandate (19 May 1944)' in *The Jewish Writings* (n 3) 204–6.

She considered that Zionism ought not be the beneficiary (or agent) of projects to revitalize the strategic and financial goals of empire in the Middle East: first by the old colonial master (Britain) and then by the new (the US).[37] Arendt's central complaint, however, relates to the ethical (mis)use of international law to prioritize Zionist claims at the expense of Palestinian sovereignty. She envisages a role for international institutions in encouraging a 'good peace' through negotiation and compromise between the two nations rather than the imposition of a 'programme'.

Specifically, she identified as the mistake of the international community its willingness to give away the sovereign rights of Palestine without the authority of its indigenous population.[38] The formalization of the pledge through arrangements for the international administration of Palestine and the eventual formation of Israel wrongly served Jewish nationalism—as an 'illusionist, utopian, and unpolitical element'—but not Arendt's long-held ambition for the Jewish nation.[39] The refinement of her complaint as counter-Zionist not counter-Jewish is significant in understanding her position as a demand made of the international legal order. She says '[a] home my neighbour doesn't recognise and respect is not a home' and the problem of Jewish sovereignty 'could not...be resolved by any declarations of distant powers or by any legalistic interpretations of international agreements'.[40] The point is not to dismiss the relevance of international law but rather to ask more of institutions and rules in pivotal constitutive moments of global governance. An international programme for peace was (and arguably remains) 'hopelessly inadequate' where the world community does not encourage collaborative resolution or else imposes a settlement that reflects a Pax America or Pax Britannica.[41] Nor does Arendt reject the validity of the Jewish national claim in particularizing her requirements for peace. Rather, she interrupts the Zionist proposition that the

---

[37] H Arendt, 'Achieving Agreement between Peoples in the Near East—A Basis for Jewish Politics (16 March 1945)' in *The Jewish Writings* (n 3) 235–8, at 236.

[38] 'The Balfour Declaration and the Palestine Mandate' (n 36) 204.

[39] 'Achieving Agreement between Peoples in the Near East' (n 37) 235. Identifying sovereign rule as un-political is consistent with Arendt's plural theory of politics. Here, the meeting of divergent voices through collaborative action is constitutive of the political (as the space for politics and freedom) and the individual subjects who meet together: see eg *Human Condition* (n 3) 175–247.

[40] 'Achieving Agreement between Peoples in the Near East' (n 37) 235.

[41] Arendt repeatedly returns to the question of a Jewish Palestine and proposes, in line with the postwar proposals by the UN mediator in Palestine (Count Folke Bernadotte), a bi-national confederation as the only practical alternative to international control which could secure 'political implementation' and 'guarantee permanent cooperation, and not national sovereignty' and offer 'a solution in which the true interests of both peoples might be safeguarded': H Arendt, 'The Failure of Reason: The Mission of Bernadotte (1948)' in *The Jewish Writings* (n 3) 408–13, at 409 and 413. See also H Arendt, 'Can the Jewish–Arab Question be Solved? (17 and 31 December 1943)' in *The Jewish Writings* (n 3) 193–98, at 194–5; 'The Balfour Declaration and the Palestine Mandate' (n 36) 206; 'Achieving Agreement between Peoples in the Near East' (n 37) 236; H Arendt, 'Peace or Armistice in the Near East? (1950)' in *The Jewish Writings* (n 3) 423–50, at 427–8, 431, 440 and 444.

stateless Jew is the founding category for Jewish sovereignty and reformulates the national claim to emphasize receptivity to the claims of others.[42] Arendt sees the stateless Jew as a radical reason against Jewish sovereignty and a persuasive case for cohabitation between nations in the Middle East.[43] To do otherwise would repeat historical wrongs against the Jews through the dispossession of Arabs.

In *Origins*, Arendt explains the contradiction implicit in the Zionist articulation of the Jewish Question. She highlights the tragic irony where:

> After the war it turned out that the Jewish question, which was considered the only insoluble one, was indeed solved—namely by means of a colonized and then conquered territory—but this solved neither the problem of the minorities nor the stateless. On the contrary, like virtually all other events of our century, the solution of the Jewish question merely produced a new category of refugees, the Arabs, thereby increasing the number of the stateless and rightless by another 700,000 to 800,000 people.[44]

Arendt's indirect reference to the international community's part in encouraging a solution for the Jewish Question through Jewish sovereignty picks up on a history of promises by Britain and then the UN about territorial rights in Palestine. It is the effects of the global initiatives, not the initiatives themselves however, which focus this important passage. The passage problematizes the absence of legal equality for Arabs in Israel and notes the irony whereby the Jewish Question became, in its post-war articulation, a metonym for the Arab Question. When Arendt addresses international law directly she does so not merely to criticize (or affirm) it, but to ask more of it, as a possible solution for the enduring problems of the Jewish nation. She asks international law to take charge of the Jewish Question in a manner that does not compromise Palestine and gives structure to her specifically Jewish claim for legal equality, plurality, and freedom. Here, the Jewish Question, or rather the full breadth of statelessness whether experienced by the Jew or as a consequence of the Jew's dream for national sovereignty, is the invitation for a new international law.

3 Minority Treaties

The Jewish claim to nation also informs Arendt's criticisms of the series of treaties designed to resolve nationalist tensions and protect European minorities in the

---

[42] *Parting Ways* (n 13) 8–9.

[43] Arendt subsequently argues that the absence of a political consciousness that followed from Jewish diaspora and exile led Zionists wrongly to identify the Jews as a chosen people with sovereign entitlements over others: see eg *Origins* (n 3) 243.

[44] Ibid 290.

wake of the First World War.[45] She positions her commentary halfway through *Origins* in the final chapter of her study on nineteenth-century imperialism and immediately before her extended analysis of twentieth-century totalitarianism: the link between two radical iterations of nationalism.[46] Arendt criticizes the agreements (and consequently the post-war vision for national equality through the League) for setting the conditions for the resurgence of German nationalism and exacerbating the vulnerability of European minorities, most notably Jews. The Minority Treaties had the unintended consequence of reinforcing the reciprocity between nation and state and generating a 'law of exception' that affirmed ethnic minorities as an 'exceptional phenomenon' or an 'unfortunate exception' and a 'deviation from the norm' in the territories where they found themselves.[47] Her view restates common responses by international lawyers, both past and present, to the strategies deployed by the League to manage minorities after the First World War.[48]

Arendt's analysis is also strategic for historiographies of international law that emphasize a restructuring of disciplinary priorities away from questions of sovereign obligation toward the resolution of nationalism after Versailles. That is, Arendt critically intervenes in respect of a pivotal moment for the modern reformulation of international law. Nathaniel Berman identifies the turning signalled by the post-Versailles system in terms of a 'modernist renewal of international law' or a 'new international law' that established present-day 'legal techniques' for

[45] The Minority Treaties are the series of bilateral agreements between the Allied and Associated Powers and numerous successor states created as a consequence of the Peace Treaties agreed at the Paris Peace Conference in 1919. Entry into the Treaties was a condition of the diplomatic recognition of the successor states and guaranteed membership in the newly formed League of Nations. The intention of the Treaties was to secure citizenship for all peoples living within the successor states (for example, the rights of German-Jews to be German citizens, or the rights of Polish-Jews to be Polish citizens) and to guarantee their cultural and religious freedoms. For details of the post-WWI settlements, see JR Crawford, *The Creation of States in International Law* (2nd edn OUP Oxford 2007) at 516–18; 'International Law and Human Plurality in the Shadow of Totalitarianism' (n 2) 336–7. For a critique of the failure of the Minority Treaties to facilitate self-determination and its selective application for the benefit of the Great Powers, see A Anghie, 'Nationalism, Development and the Postcolonial State: The Legacies of the League of Nations' (2006) 41 *Texas International Law Journal* 447–64, at 448–51; A Cassese, *Self-Determination of Peoples: A Legal Reappraisal* (CUP Cambridge 1995) at 23–33, especially at 26.

[46] *Origins* (n 3) 267–302 ('The Decline of the Nation State and the End of the Rights of Man').

[47] Ibid 267, 269 and 276. See also *Eichmann* (n 3) 268 where Arendt argues that the Minority Treaties allowed for the discriminatory treatment of the Jews as a minority group under the 1935 Nuremberg Laws.

[48] For example, Antony Anghie argues that international law reproduces 'the dynamic of difference' in which 'the minority is characterized as the 'primitive' that must be managed and controlled in the interests of preserving the modern and universal state': A Anghie, *Imperialism, Sovereignty and the Making of International Law* (CUP Cambridge 2005) at 207 and 115–95. See also BEC Dugdale and WA Bewes, 'The Working of the Minority Treaties' (1926) 5 *Journal of the British Institute of International Affairs* 79–95; *Self-Determination of Peoples* (n 45) 26.

responding to claims for national sovereignty.[49] He identifies the inadequacy of the programme and importantly, for reading Arendt's uptake of the Arab Question in the *Jewish Writings*, the consequent stubbornness of the League's example for prioritizing self-determination and national sovereignty. Not only did the 'new international law' leave Europe more 'unsettled' and more unequal, it established a pattern for the international management of national claims that continues today. For Berman, the partition of Palestine in 1948 and the continuing politics of law in the Middle East is a reminder of the earlier error and its persistence as the organizing standard for contemporary global governance.

Reading Arendt's response to the Minority Treaties alongside her critique of Zionism elucidates the full circle of the nation-state dilemma for Jews. If Arendt is critical of Jewish sovereignty in the Middle East (and the part played by international law in facilitating the ambitions of the Jewish nation) the reason is apparent from the European example. In both cases, international agreements failed to achieve parity between national groups: the earlier example facilitated the subordination of Jews and the second, the sovereign power of Jews over the Palestinian nation. Arendt does not reject a solution for the Jewish Question through international law but rather identifies the failure of particular historical iterations to match intention with action. She insists on the 'inadequacy of the Peace Treaties', the narrow vision of the peace-makers who 'never quite realised the full impact of the war whose peace they had to conclude', and the failed attempt to regulate the nationality problem through the creation and expansion of nation-states.[50] More positively, she identifies the 'real significance' of the post-war restructuring of Europe to be the shared dream by the international community for the survival of the multi-national state where majority and minority nations could cohabitate. The Minority Treaties marked 'something entirely new' insofar as the arrangements gave form to hopes for 'a lasting *modus vivendi*' in which an international body with international legal authority would oversee the protection of minorities.[51]

The initiative backfired because the peace-makers attempted to secure minority rights within the existing frame of the nation-state without renegotiating the structure's sovereign expectations. Arendt explains that the Peace Treaties endorsed the right to self-determination as an unequal entitlement between nations and used the Minority Treaties to carve out a rule of exception for the minor peoples left without a national government or independent territory. She

---

[49] N Berman, *Passion and Ambivalence: Colonialism, Nationalism and International Law* (Martinus Nijhoff Leiden 2012) at 369–77; N Berman, "But the Alternative is Despair": European Nationalism and the Modernist Renewal of International Law' (1995) 106 *Harvard Law Review* 1792–1903. See further references to the 'new international law' established under the management of the League in *Imperialism, Sovereignty and the Making of International Law* (n 48) 123.

[50] *Origins* (n 3) 270.   [51] Ibid 275–6 and 279.

notes that the restructuring arrangements after the First World War charged the League, and not the governments of the succeeding states, with the protection of minorities. Efforts by the League to enforce the new regime were uneven or careful to avoid the disapprobation of the sovereign states.[52] Unsurprisingly, the minor nationalities believed that the absence of national sovereignty (through national territory and independent government) deprived them of human rights and emancipation according to the template for freedom established by the French Revolution. The embittered and interregional aspect of the minorities presented an escalating risk to European security alongside the hardening of nationalist claims by the sovereign powers and the failure of the League to maintain equilibrium between groups.

Arendt identifies the twin-problem to be a direct and explosive consequence of the recognition of 'the minority as a permanent institution' in international law. Recognizing the 'exceptional' status of minor peoples as stateless persons who lived outside the ordinary protections of state law confirmed 'that only nationals could be citizens, only people of the same national origin could enjoy the full protection of legal institutions, that persons of different nationality needed some law of exception until or unless they were completely assimilated and divorced from their origin'.[53] The international intervention allowed for the 'transformation of the state from an instrument of the law into an instrument of the nation' so that 'the supremacy of the will of nation over all legal and "abstract" institutions was universally accepted'.[54] What the Minority Treaties did not protect was the elementary rights of citizenship including the entitlement to live and work in a territory. Superficial entitlements to culture and society included in the arrangements could not inhibit the slide towards mass denationalizations, statelessness, and rightlessness of minorities in the interwar period. For Arendt, this gap in the Minority Treaties explains the genesis of the modern refugee problem insofar as it implicitly affirmed the presumptive logic of the old trinity, state–people–territory, and the secondary status of minor nations without national territory and government.[55]

Nevertheless, her critique of the agreements, published in the year preceding the 1951 Refugees Convention, does not reject the possibility of an international legal solution for the problem of statelessness.[56] Rather, Arendt expresses concern for the inadequacies of a regime that failed to achieve parity between

---

[52] See eg G Zyberi, 'The International Court of Justice and the Right of Peoples and Minorities' in C Tams and J Sloan (eds), *The Development of International Law by the International Court of Justice* (OUP Oxford 2013) 327–52.

[53] *Origins* (n 3) 275.   [54] Ibid. See also at 279.

[55] Arendt's comments about the Minority Treaties also criticize the absence of any international agreement (in the interwar period) for the protection of refugees: ibid 280–81 and 284.

[56] *Convention Relating to the Status of Refugees* (opened for signature 28 July 1951 entered into force 22 April 1954) 189 UNTS 137.

nations within the reformulated state system. The accidental consequence of the international arrangement for minorities was that it left minorities vulnerable to redefinition by the totalitarian imagination. Minor nations were now non-nationals, and under the Nuremberg Laws in Nazi Germany, second-rate citizens without political rights and later, 'alien blood' to be physically liquidated (through forced expulsion or physical extermination) as stateless non-persons. The post-war minority system 'had become a mockery' because it was ineffective against the will of the nation-state and its drive towards denationalization of peoples without the birth-rights attaching to nation. Arendt's critique is arguably a call to action put to the international legal order at the point of greatest opportunity—when the symptoms of instability associated with nationalism and competing claims for territory were the subject of international attention and arrangement.

These criticisms arguably stem from Arendt's personal experience of exile and constitute claims put to international law on behalf of the Jewish people. The Jewishness of Arendt's complaint and her resignation to international law is apparent in the final pages of her critique of the Minority Treaties. She identifies Jews to be 'the *minorité par excellence*' who possess special needs because of their international diaspora and lack of a homeland. Their interregional status meant self-determination in Europe (or anywhere) was impossible without international intervention and legal protection very unlikely in the post-war situation of reinvigorated national and authoritarian ideologies. Arendt explains that the Jewish people were 'the only minority whose interests could be defended only by internationally guaranteed protection'.[57] Though she frequently criticizes the political methods of Jews she nevertheless notes that Jewish groups, by necessity, were a prominent influence on the formulation of the Peace Treaties and the Minority Treaties.[58] Participation represented the only opportunity to be heard in the absence of any alternative basis of power. Arendt distils issues surrounding minority status, statelessness, and the nation-state in the post-war period as the Jewish Question. The League's failure to manage the disintegration of the state system was a failure to renegotiate the Jewish Question as a question of national recognition. Arendt is clear that 'statelessness is primarily a Jewish question' and that this affiliation was a pretext used by governments and the international community for ignoring it. The subsequent uptake of the Jewish Question in the Middle East was equally problematic for it transferred, in Arendt's view, the problem of Jewish statelessness and exile to the Arabs.[59] The creation of the new category of the minority by international law carried with it an extraordinary responsibility of protection. The failure to renegotiate the problem of nation within Europe, and then within the Middle East, pointed to the urgency of the task for the international community.

---

[57] *Origins* (n 3) 289.   [58] Ibid.   [59] Ibid 290.

4 THE RIGHT TO HAVE RIGHTS

The dilemmas of nation reappear in the context of Arendt's study of the emergent categories of rightlessness and statelessness that made visible the right to have rights.[60] Arendt famously coined the latter phrase to describe the right 'to live in a framework where one is judged by one's actions and opinions' and 'belong to some kind of organized community' that became apparent 'when millions of people emerged who had lost and could not regain these rights because of the new global political situation'.[61] A right to have rights refigures the universal entitlement in terms of 'the right of every individual to belong to humanity'.[62] International legal scholars with interests in human rights theory intervene in the ongoing debates that circulate around the phrase.[63] These literatures commonly interpret Arendt's concept as a provocation for thinking about the conditions for meaningful entitlement that arise from citizenship. The right to have rights redescribes the prospects for protection from the sovereign government of a nation-state and not, at least in the historical moment identified by Arendt, by international law.

The emphasis on citizenship, as the relevant standard of belonging and as a derivative of the organizing model of the nation-state, follows from the emphasis and framing of Arendt's analysis. The right to have rights is the circular measure of recognition and protection that is the consequence of belonging to an identifiable political community. Its circularity and, for some, incoherency (one legal theorist

---

[60] The key passages in Arendt's writing about human rights also identify the most frequently cited sections by international lawyers and immediately follow from her study of the Minority Treaties: *Origins* (n 3) 290–302 ('The Perplexities of the Rights of Man').

[61] Ibid 296–7.   [62] Ibid 298.

[63] Examples of writings by theorists of domestic and international law about the 'right to have rights' concept include: 'The Right to Have Rights: From Human Rights to Citizens' Rights and Back' (n 10); H Brunckhorst, 'Are Human Rights Self-Contradictory? Critical Remarks on a Hypothesis by Hannah Arendt' (1996) 3 *Constellations* 190–9; *The Right to Have Rights* (n 2); F Michelman, 'Parsing "A Right to Have Rights"' (1996) 3 *Constellations* 200–8; C Thomas, 'What Does the Emerging International Law of Migration Mean for Sovereignty?' (2013) 14 *Melbourne Journal of International Law* 1–59. Human rights theorists continue to give considerable attention to the concept, see eg, '"The Right to Have Rights": Hannah Arendt and the Contradictions of the Nation-State' (n 9) and the echoes of Arendt's idea and support for it in S Benhabib, 'Claiming Rights across Borders: International Human Rights and Democratic Sovereignty' (2009) 103 *American Political Science Review* 691–704; P Birmingham, *Hannah Arendt and Human Rights: The Predicament of Common Responsibility* (Indiana University Press Bloomington 2006); JL Cohen, 'Rights, Citizenship and the Modern Form of the Social: Dilemmas of Arendtian Republicanism' (1996) 3 *Constellations* 164–89; B Cotter, 'Hannah Arendt and the "Right to Have Rights"' in AF Lang and J Williams (eds), *Hannah Arendt and International Relations: Reading Across the Lines* (Palgrave Macmillan New York 2005) 95–112; JD Ingram, 'What is a "Right to Have Rights"? Three Images of the Politics of Human Rights' (2008) 102 *American Political Science Review* 401–16; S Parekh, *Arendt and the Challenge of Modernity: A Phenomenology of Human Rights* (Routledge New York 2008); J Rancière, 'Who is the Subject of the Rights of Man?' (2004) 103(2/3) *South Atlantic Quarterly* 297–310.

notices the 'right to have rights is itself *ipso nomine* a right' and describes the idea
as the strange entitlement that arises where no rights or legal status in fact exist),
echo the 'perplexities of the rights of man' and achieve a kind of equivalence in
her writing with the dilemmas or perplexities of nation. Specifically, the right to
have rights is a consequence of the paradox expressed by eighteenth-century political rights discourse that insisted on the inalienable 'Rights of Man'. Arendt suggests the promise presented by the '"abstract" human being who seemed to exist
nowhere' was also an invitation to sovereign authorities to delineate who counted
as human and who did not according to national affiliation. The false promise
of 'humanity' became visible in moments of ardent nationalism where the
abstract standard stands only for persons who were members of a people or nation
and, importantly, who also enjoy the protections of sovereign self-government.
Arendt explains:

[t]he whole question of human rights . . . was quickly and inextricably blended with the
question of national emancipation; only the emancipated sovereignty of the people, of
one's own people, seemed able to insure them. As mankind, since the French Revolution,
was conceived in the image of a family of nations, it gradually became self-evident that the
people, and not the individual, was the image of man.[64]

Minorities without prospects for self-determination became the exemplary category for understanding the imperative of the right to have rights, and among
minorities, Jews figured as the representative type of pariah people without a
motherland who depended entirely upon their capacity to join together in 'some
kind of interterritorial solidarity'.[65] Jews also became the exaggerated example of
the flaw in abstract standards. If the nation is the foundation for the right to have
rights, nationalism inspires dangerous choices about who counts as human and
who is superfluous and unworthy of protection.[66]

  Benhabib makes assumptions about Arendt's hesitation toward international
human rights from remarks made in the course of the analysis of the right to have
rights in *Origins*. Not only does Arendt focus her attentions on the promise of civil
rights within the setting of a nation-state, she dismisses the 'many recent attempts
to frame a new bill of human rights' because 'no one seems able to define with any
assurance what these general human rights, as distinguished from the rights of citizens, really are'.[67] Arendt's criticism coalesces with her distrust of collective categories or abstract standards that can accommodate or exclude anyone or everyone.
Benhabib cites a passage where Arendt expresses frustration with the absence of
political expertise driving debates for an international paradigm to protect human

---

  [64] *Origins* (n 3) 291.   [65] Ibid 292.
  [66] For argument that unfolds around the joint problems of the precariousness of life and the delineation by power of lives worth living that is reminiscent of Arendt's critique of the nation-state and the
right to have rights see: *Precarious Life* (n 13).
  [67] *Origins* (n 3) 293.

rights.[68] Arendt's complaint, however, is not merely about the amateurish aspect of the pre-legislative process at the supra-national level. The subtlety of the criticism becomes clear in a further passage juxtaposing the right to have rights with the prospects for universal protection through international law. The passage reads:

This new situation ... would mean ... that the right to have rights ... should be guaranteed by humanity itself. It is by no means certain whether this is possible. For, contrary to the best-intentioned humanitarian attempts to obtain new declarations of human rights from international organizations, it should be understood that this idea transcends the present sphere of international law which still operates in terms of reciprocal agreements and treaties between sovereign states; and for the time being, a sphere that is above nations does not exist.[69]

Here, Arendt introduces a critical ambiguity that arguably recasts her criticism about international law.[70] True to her analytic practice, she problematizes the task that faces 'humanity' through international law, remaining receptive to global offerings, but she does not offer a form or strategy for its completion. What is important is the possibility that 'humanity itself' (previously, a 'new law on earth, whose validity this time must comprehend the whole of humanity') may supply the solution.[71] Her seeming ambivalence about 'whether this is possible' does not extinguish the hopes for a solution beyond the 'present sphere of international law' or in 'a sphere above nations'. Arendt's frustrations with the limitations of global law are temporal or situational. Her confidence in the future promise of international law finds a reason in her residual complaint about the dilemmas of nation.

Although she repeatedly envisages entitlement within the frame of the nation-state and the category of citizen, Arendt expresses an equal loss of faith with nationalist sentiments wherever they appear: whether voiced on behalf of Europe's sovereign nation-states or minority peoples.[72] The passage cited by Benhabib

---

[68] In the relevant passage, Arendt explains 'that all societies formed for the protection of the Rights of Man, all attempts to arrive at a new bill of human rights were sponsored by marginal figures—by a few international jurists without political experience or professional philanthropists supported by the uncertain sentiments of professional idealists. The groups they formed, the declarations they issued, showed an uncanny similarity in language and composition to that of societies for the prevention of cruelty to animals. No statesman, no political figure of any importance could possibly take them seriously; and none of the liberal or radical parties in Europe thought it necessary to incorporate into their program a new declaration of human rights': (n 3) 292.

[69] Ibid 298.

[70] Arendt's methods problematize historical situations by illuminating (rather than proposing alternatives for) the complications implicit in governmental practices and principles. Bridget Cotter, for example, suggests Arendt's 'main value...as a theorist lies in her ability to expose...the contradictions and tensions within and among the principles and practices of Western modernity. She was less focussed on proposing solutions. Instead, she tended to issue warnings against neglect and to encourage vigilance...': 'Hannah Arendt and the "Right to Have Rights"' (n 63) 95.

[71] *Origins* (n 3) ix and text accompanying above n 25.

[72] Benhabib gives considerable attention to these framing issues, including the Jewish Question, statelessness, and the right to have rights in order to explain Arendt's brief comments on international

announces internationalist initiatives to be 'even worse' than the efforts of state-less persons to 'clamor for rights' through a 'fierce, violent group consciousness'.[73] Again, she reminds her readers that the problem of statelessness (which finds equivalence in her writing with the Jewish Question) cannot find its answer through the skewed models of nation that frequently appear in nationalist ide-ologies. Arendt's reservations about international law arise in the context of this contradiction. Her scepticism about the existing model of entitlement (the Rights of Man or the Rights of Citizen) and her desire to supplement it with a plural, republican model of political equality which 'is not given us' but which we might 'produce...through organization' nevertheless raises a further possibility.[74] Her responses to global law at this point are postural, a call to action, and an articula-tion of claim where alternatives have failed. Arendt's asks for two things: a new guarantee by and for humanity, and a solution for the perplexities of nation that produce statelessness or exile from the 'family of nations'.[75]

Arendt's twenty-first-century readers frequently understand the right to have rights to imply separation between domestic and international law as differently oriented projects with differently orientated opportunities for effective protection.[76] Arendt's criticisms of the international and commitment to modalities of belong-ing that attach to territory and the legal status of citizenship point to tensions between legal regimes. Nevertheless, she repeatedly returns to the relationship between the global and the national, indeed explores the ambiguities of each in the context of reflections on the other. Although Arendt clearly suggests that interna-tional law (through the Minority Treaties) played some part in permitting or even facilitating the modern phenomenon of statelessness and is suspicious of collective or group categories (like 'humanity' or 'mankind'), she does not discount the cor-rective capacity of international law. She identifies statelessness as the 'global polit-ical situation' and argues against presently existing deficiencies in international law that exist 'for the time being'.[77] Further, her criticism of international legal developments remarks on the need for 'humanity' to guarantee the rights to its own inclusiveness, a point that might be taken as being reflective of the reciprocity between global law and politics, not their separation.[78] Arendt does not resign her-self, and Benhabib clearly concurs here in her reading of *Eichmann*, to the impos-sibility of locating a solution or a part-solution for the problem of nation within global legal initiatives. My suggestion is that the invitation to international law is

---

law rather than as drawing out the subtleties of those remarks: see 'International Law and Human Plurality in the Shadow of Totalitarianism' (n 2).

[73] *Origins* (n 3) 292.   [74] Ibid 301.   [75] Ibid 291 and 294.

[76] Cf for examples of the interconnectedness of domestic and international rights after Arendt and the role of the idea of the right to have rights as a 'delegitimating gesture' that foregoes placing limits on the conception and place of right-bearing, see eg *The Right to Have Rights* (n 2) 145.

[77] *Origins* (n 3) 297–8.   [78] 'Possible Islands of Predictability' (n 2) 2.

present much earlier and arguably informs her entire oeuvre. In *Origins*, Arendt perceives the idea of 'humanity' and the promise of protection by all humankind to be a critical juncture where the problems of nation become visible and available for renegotiation. It is here that international law has important work to do and finds its enduring challenge.

5 CRIMES AGAINST HUMANITY

International law more clearly attracts Arendt's favour in her 1963 text about the Jerusalem trial of Adolf Eichmann.[79] Benhabib interprets *Eichmann* as a turning point in Arendt's receptivity to the promise of international law where she 'has not only accepted the categories of the *Genocide Convention*' but also provides 'a philosophical condemnation of the crime of genocide in light of her concept of human plurality'.[80] Clearly here, Arendt engages with the idea of international law as a body of principle to a depth not evident in earlier writings. The Epilogue to *Eichmann* develops an extended argument against the quality of justice meted by the application of domestic law within a national forum. The report remains controversial not only for Zionists but for those more generally sympathetic to Jewish histories because Arendt insisted on the mismatch between the 'new and unprecedented' crime of the 'blotting out of whole peoples' and the inadequacy of the relevant juristic principles and processes.[81] Her commentary nevertheless hedges its apparent bias toward international law in several fundamental respects. Arendt's text is a trial report; sympathetic references to international law develop from her concern with the inadequacies of that process, and importantly, her sense of an alternative through international law is conjectural and futural.

First, Arendt's text is foremost a 'trial report' and gathers together details 'on the strictly factual level' and points to 'phenomenon which stared one in the face at the trial'.[82] Her task was not to piece together an argument for or against international law. Instead, she remains the 'trial reporter' and navigates the problems

---

[79] *Eichmann in Jerusalem* originally appeared in the form of five reports published by the *New Yorker* in 1963 following Arendt's coverage of the trial in 1961: see H Arendt, 'Note to Reader' in *Eichmann* (n 3) xxiv. The encounter between Arendt and the juridical models presented by the trial (judgment, crime, responsibility) is the subject of the film in her name: M von Trotta (director and screenplay) and P Katz (screenplay), *Hannah Arendt* (Zeitgeist Films 2012). See further D Whitehall, 'People in Glass Houses: Lessons for International Law from Margarethe von Trotta's *Hannah Arendt*' (2014) 2 *London Review of International Law* 329–53.

[80] 'International Law and Human Plurality in the Shadow of Totalitarianism' (n 2) 332–3.

[81] *Eichmann* (n 3) 255 and 257.   [82] Ibid 280 and 287.

of international law in response to the content of the judgment and the objections to the Court's competence argued by the defence. To the impartial observer, the trial reiterated the problem of retroactive laws in a court of victors earlier faced by the Nuremberg Trials and exacerbated those difficulties by attributing the juridical function to a domestic court and classifying the crime as one 'against the Jewish people' instead of 'against humanity'. Arendt takes up the invitation presented by these observations to examine the problems of justice in Jerusalem by investigations that address a series of international legal questions raised in the course of the trial relating to universal jurisdiction; the meaning of genocide and 'crimes against humanity'; the kidnapping (not extradition) of Eichmann by Israel; the analogy between genocide and piracy; the identification of Israel as *hostis humani generis*; the passive personality-principle; enforced migration; and prominently, the establishment of a permanent international criminal tribunal. There is, however, no sense of international law's correctness or preference. Rather, Arendt's address to international law arises in the context of giving attention to the specific 'problems of legality' that compromised the judgment and that arose from Israel's conviction 'that justice, and nothing else, is the end of law'.[83]

Benhabib gathers a sense of the shift from the 'not yet' of *Origins* to the 'just possible' in *Eichmann* from a passage in the latter text where Arendt assumes the sovereign voice of the judge to rewrite the Court's sentencing remarks. The vocabulary here echoes the legal paradigms for genocide or crimes against humanity pursuant to the 1948 Convention and 'performatively introduces' a normative rationale 'that might distinguish just from unjust law on radically egalitarian grounds'.[84] Specifically, Arendt condemns Eichmann for his part in coordinating a policy that amounted to an ethical and political denial of plural political forms where human beings co-exist or co-habit in a manner that allows for new productions of power through interdependency and relationship. She addresses the accused by clarifying his iniquity:

Let us assume, for the sake of argument, that it was nothing more than misfortune that made you a willing instrument in the organization of mass murder; there still remains the fact that you have carried out, therefore actively supported, a policy of mass murder . . . And just as you supported and carried out a policy of not wanting to share the earth with the Jewish people and the people of a number of other nations—as though you and your superiors had any right to determine who should and who should not inhabit the world— we find that no one, that is, no member of the human race, can be expected to share the earth with you.[85]

---

[83] *Eichmann* (n 3) 265–6.
[84] *Parting Ways* (n 13) 173. See also *Convention on the Prevention and Punishment of the Crime of Genocide* (opened for signature 9 December 1948 entered into force 12 January 1951) 78 UNTS 277.
[85] *Eichmann* (n 3) 279.

Eichmann is, at least superficially, the highpoint of Arendt's support for the innovative categories of post-war international law that legal scholars increasingly link to the Jerusalem trial.[86] Arendt speaks directly against the genocidal act that intends to destroy a whole people (the wish 'to make the entire Jewish people disappear from the face of the earth' that comprises the 'new crime' which is 'against the human status' or 'an attack on human diversity') and names the physical extermination of the Jews as a nation, 'the unprecedented crime of genocide'.[87] If the language of 'genocide' is new to her writing in *Eichmann*, the problem it presents for her is far from novel.

Eichmann arguably extends a trajectory of thinking about international law that was present in Arendt's work decades before its publication. Read in the context of her earlier writings, the text repeats in a new context the earlier claim upon international law to respond to the dilemmas of nation. The second and third qualifications to her openness to an international legal solution in *Eichmann* become visible as part of her search for an alternative paradigm for justice that arises from her frustration with existing models.

One qualification reflects Arendt's sense of the emergent character of the global option. She refers to the 'yet unfinished nature of international law' which leaves the new question of genocide to 'ordinary trial judges to render justice without the help of, or beyond the limitation set upon them through, positive, posited laws'.[88] Arendt's claim is an invitation to develop international laws to address the new crime but does not resolve the form or content of the legal answer. She merely states:

... all trials touching upon 'crimes against humanity' must be judged according to a standard that is today still an 'ideal'. If genocide is an actual possibility of the future, then no people on earth—least of all, of course, the Jewish people, in Israel or elsewhere—can feel reasonably sure of its continued existence without the help and the protection of international law. Success or failure in dealing with the hitherto unprecedented can lie only in the extent to which this dealing may serve as a valid precedent on the road to international penal law. And this demand, addressed to the judges in such trials, does not overshoot the mark and ask for more than can reasonably be expected.[89]

Arendt's comments are not a criticism about international law but rather reflect on the discipline's yet-to-catch-up-to status in relation to 'unprecedented' problems impacting on humankind, globally, as a whole. Here, her voice is one of a political claimant who demands change and looks for it in the obvious location.

The originality and scope of genocide also explains why Arendt turns toward international law as an alternative to justice according to national laws. The

---

[86] See eg L Bilsky, 'The Eichmann Trial: Towards a Jurisprudence of Eyewitness Testimony of Atrocities' (2014) 12 *Journal of International Criminal Law* 27–57; W Schabas, 'The Contribution of the Eichmann Trial to International Law' (2013) 26 *Leiden Journal of International Law* 667–99.
[87] *Eichmann* (n 3) 267–8 and 273.   [88] Ibid 274.   [89] Ibid 273.

procedural deficiencies of the Jerusalem Court, the further qualification to her apparent support for international law, included the failure to give due regard to the unique and universal character of genocide. Casting Eichmann's actions in terms of a 'crime against the Jewish people' missed the 'unprecedented' character of genocide and the conceptual scale of policies to exterminate a people beyond the group itself.[90] If genocide is a crime against humanity, human diversity or the human status, a national court applying domestic law could not fathom its full significance or adequately render judgement upon it. Arendt explains that all the shortcomings of the Jerusalem trial stem from 'current Jewish historical self-understanding' that stubbornly joins centuries of anti-Semitism (and punishment for national discrimination) to genocide.[91] She situates her call for an international tribunal in the alternative to inadequacies of the national process—Israel's insistence that genocide was a question for the law of one nation not all nations; the misunderstanding of genocide as part of a history of wrongs; and the remarkable mistake whereby the gravity of the events were '"minimized" before a tribunal that represents one nation only'.[92] Israel invoked the logic of nation, a modality of thinking that the Nazis used against the Jewish people, to explain its authority to kidnap, indict, try, and hang *Eichmann*. This was a 'show' for the purposes of the fledgling Jewish state and not a 'law-governing proceeding'.[93] Arendt's invitation to international law completes the circle of her complaint against Jewish nationalism first articulated in her counter-Zionist writings and repeats the counter-nationalist sentiment underpinning her broader political commentary.

Reading *Eichmann* as a significant development in Arendt's approach to international law elides the reality of the trial's significance for her thinking through of the problems of nation. The trial was a new (and specifically juridical) context in which Arendt takes up the challenge of understanding her history as a Jewish woman.[94] The irony of Benhabib's interpretation is her recognition of *Eichmann* as Arendt's 'most intensely Jewish work' where 'she identifies herself morally and epistemologically with the Jewish people'.[95] This fact explains Arendt's particular interest in international law. *Eichmann* is a re-articulation of the Jewish Question as a problem that raises the fundamental tension between nation and nationalism. The supra-national character of international law is the basis for Arendt's invitation to the discipline.

---

[90] *Eichmann* (n 3) 267.   [91] Ibid.   [92] Ibid 270.   [93] See *Parting Ways* (n 13) 59.

[94] Arendt's critical methodology derives from her need to understand and move beyond historical traumas experienced by the Jewish People, and of herself as a Jew: H Arendt, 'What Remains? The Language Remains: A Conversation with Günter Gaus' in *Essays in Understanding* (n 16) 1–27, at 12; H Arendt, 'Understanding and Politics (The Difficulties of Understanding)' in *Essays in Understanding* (n 16) 307–27, at 308–11.

[95] S Benhabib, 'Arendt's *Eichmann in Jerusalem*' in D Villa (ed), *The Cambridge Companion to Hannah Arendt* (CUP Cambridge 2000) 65–85, at 65. See also *Parting Ways* (n 13) 176.

6 CONCLUSION

International legal writing about Arendt frequently perceives caveats and turns in her thinking about international law. Her encounter with the discipline admittedly lacks an insider's insights about the complexities of legal doctrine and the limitations of law for navigating political dilemmas. Nevertheless, Arendt is mindful of the reciprocity between politics and law. She repeatedly comes to international law as a site for negotiating tensions between the idea of nation and nationalism that inform her conceptualization of the Jewish Question and of the challenges that impede its resolution. Her invitation to the international is innovative but it is not a cold-call. She speaks for a different kind of international law to the one that others propose or which already intervenes in situations of concern for the Jewish people. Arendt's line of questioning derives from her personal experience of Jewish exile and diaspora and asks for resolution of the enduring problem of group associations. The dilemmas of the national claim present for Arendt the limit and possibility of twentieth-century international law in its unfolding after each world war.

The attention in this chapter to understanding Arendt as making a series of demands on nascent forms of international law draws upon much of the same material cited by alternative readings. International legal writing about Arendt sometimes forgets that her comments about global law are a coincidence of working through the complexities of the Jewish Question. The oversight persists even where examination of themes including totalitarianism, statelessness, rootlessness, citizenship, and human rights diligently footnote Arendt's own history of exile. The difference emphasized here is the way in which the Jewish Question becomes part of the picture. The chapter takes inspiration from Butler's interpretation of Arendt as a thinker who speaks as a Jew against prominent strands within Jewish politics, including the Zionist claim to sovereignty in the Middle East. Butler reminds us that:

[i]n each and every case, there is a question of whether the criticism can be registered publicly as something other than an attack on the Jews or on Jewishness. Depending where we are and to whom we speak, some of these positions can be heard more easily than others... Moreover, in every case we are confronted with the limits on audibility by which the contemporary public sphere is constituted.[96]

How Arendt's multiple meetings with international law are heard depends, of course, on the situation of her reader as well as the content and context of her contribution.

---

[96] *Parting Ways* (n 13) 118–19.

Remembering the historical setting in which she lived and survived as a Jew makes her a nonconformist among Jews, who speaks to and of international law as a new realm for the enduring questions of the Jewish nation. In Arendt's hands, the Jewish Question becomes a synecdoche for a series of encounters between the Jew, as a political claimant, and international law. That is, the Jewish Question becomes the reference for international law in its specific orientation—across time and space—around the problem of Jewish emancipation. The details of the encounter between the Jew and international law are unstable and metamorphose depending on the relevant situation of threat and the international legal response to it. The instability at the heart of the Jewish Question arguably explains what Benhabib characterizes as a transformation or shift in Arendt's thinking about international legal discipline: its function, its pattern of interventions, and her appraisal of its performance. For this reader, Arendt's encounter with international law is not a site of disjunction or discontinuity in her thought. Rather, her reflections about international law illuminate the full complexity of the Jewish Question for her, including its ironies and contradictions, and importantly, its mutability in form and substance. The phrase denotes a burden that begins with the stateless Jew but shifts to include wrongs committed by her as a consequence of her own dream for nation. The 'insolubility' or 'intractability' of the dilemmas of nation for the Jewish people is not something Arendt accepts. She turns to international law as a Jewish woman imploring the international community to champion her case for nation: as a Jew speaking for Jews, and as a Jew speaking against statelessness or rootlessness which bears the different 'curse' of Jewish sovereignty.[97]

---

[97] *Origins* (n 3) 290.

CHAPTER 13

INTERNATIONAL LEGAL THEORY IN RUSSIA: A CIVILIZATIONAL PERSPECTIVE, OR

CAN INDIVIDUALS BE SUBJECTS OF INTERNATIONAL LAW?

LAURI MÄLKSOO[*]

1 INTRODUCTION

THE civilizational approach to international law has become increasingly popular in scholarship. For example, Onuma Yasuaki from Tokyo has used it for critically analysing the Western-centric historiography of international law, the mainstream doctrine of sources of international law, and the predominant concept of human rights.[1] Onuma's core message is that international law, in order to become truly

* Research and writing of this chapter has been supported by grants of the European Research Council and the Estonian Research Council (IUT 20–50). All translations are by the author unless otherwise noted.

[1] O Yasuaki, *A Transcivilizational Perspective on International Law* (Martinus Nijhoff Leiden 2010).

universal, must do much more than in the past, and today take into account the experiences and values of 'other', non-Western civilizations. For example, since China is widely considered to be the rising power in the twenty-first century, scholars and practitioners are increasingly interested in what Chinese approaches to international law are and will be, postulating that these would necessarily be shaped by China's unique history, culture, and civilization.[2]

Yet many in the West encounter the civilizational approach to international law with mixed feelings. 'Civilization' is a notoriously ambiguous concept and, consequently, scholars often do not agree on how many civilizations there are nowadays.[3] In the colonial period and during the time of so-called classical international law, Europe and the West abused the civilizational rhetoric.[4] Moreover, the theory of international law has been traditionally preoccupied with 'states', not 'civilizations'. What does it then mean for international law, particularly in the context of the claim regarding its universality, that different civilizations matter or should matter more? Is focusing on the civilizational differences not the opposite of universality and, thus, a step backwards for international law? Throughout centuries, the intellectual culture of international law in the West has been characterized by a powerful universalist ideal associated with natural law. More than that, to the extent that legal positivism aimed at being scientific and followed the self-perceived ideal of progress, it also contained a universal message. Thus, today's realists might argue that the call for taking other civilizations into account to a greater degree in the context of international law just amounts to a call for the global redistribution of power, this time to the disadvantage of the West.

However, the notion of 'civilization' does not need to be used in order to promote it, but also in order to understand the world better. In this chapter I argue that the concept of 'civilization', although admittedly an ambiguous and problematic one, may be a useful analytical lens for making sense of international legal theory outside the West. Throughout the last centuries, other non-Western civilizations have struggled with the predominance of the West, and have related and referred to it one way or another. We can therefore presume that this dialogue—and often contest—of civilizations and the ways they have been constructed by political leaders and intellectuals has left its marks on international legal theory as well. David Kennedy has pointed out that international law is 'different in different places',[5]

---

[2] See eg X Hanquin, 'Chinese Contemporary Perspectives on International Law: History, Culture and International Law' (2012) 355 *Recueil des Cours* 99–233.

[3] For classic historical and political texts on civilizations, see eg A Toynbee, *A Study of History* (Barnes & Noble New York 1995); SP Huntington, *The Clash of Civilizations and the Remaking of World Order* (Simon & Schuster New York 1996).

[4] See eg M Koskenniemi, *The Gentle Civilizer of Nations: The Rise and Fall of International Law 1870–1960* (CUP Cambridge 2001); A Anghie, *Imperialism, Sovereignty, and the Making of International Law* (CUP Cambridge 2004).

[5] D Kennedy, 'The Disciplines of International Law and Policy' (1999) 12 *Leiden Journal of International Law* 9–133, at 17.

and my starting point here is that, by analogy, international legal theory may also be that.

Specifically, I will in the following focus on international legal theory in Russia and in the Russian language, broadly sketching an international legal theory in the country from the mid-nineteenth century onwards.[6] My claim is not an essentialist one—that Russia 'is' a separate civilization—rather, my starting point is, much more cautiously, that the debate about whether it is a distinct civilization and its stances towards the West have deeply influenced international legal theory in the country. Moreover, certain elements of the theory of international law, such as the relationship between the state and the individual in the context of international law may involve choices that can indeed be called 'civilizational'. For one reason or another, but perhaps also for reasons of cultures, histories, and civilizations differing from each other, scholars outside the West such as in Russia tend to put different emphases in terms of how they construct international law.

2 Russia as Part of 'the' (European) Civilization: International Legal Theory during the Late Tsarist Period

Russia's encounter with international law goes far back in history and is an intriguing subject. Princes of Kiev concluded treaties with Byzantium in at least the tenth century. However, during the Mongol–Tatar Yoke (around 1220–1480), Russia remained separated from the mediaeval European/Catholic *respublica Christiana*.[7] The country was officially included in the European community of nations only as a consequence of the Great Northern War (1700–21) in which Tsar Peter the Great defeated Sweden in the Baltic region. However, during the eighteenth and early nineteenth centuries imperial Russia had a more or less passive attitude to the *ius publicum Europaeum* and rather than developing its own independent scholarship, merely translated several major European treatises of international law.

---

[6] For an extended argument and narrative, see L Mälksoo, *Russian Approaches to International Law* (OUP Oxford 2015).

[7] M de Taube, 'Études sur le développement historique du droit international dans l'Europe orientale' (1926) 11 *Recueil des Cours* 341–535. See further L Mälksoo, 'Russia–Europe' in B Fassbender and A Peters (eds), *The Oxford Handbook on the History of International Law* (OUP Oxford 2012) 764–86.

Original international legal theory in Russia acquired its momentum only in the second half of the nineteenth century. The name of FF Martens (1845–1909), professor of international law at St Petersburg University is well known in the West,[8] as is the fact that Martens was a vocal proponent of the theory that international law applied and could only apply between 'civilized peoples' which in his estimation, at least since Peter the Great, included Russia.[9] What is not so well known in the West is that Russian international legal theory during the late Tsarist period was altogether much more diverse than the overarching doyen figure of Martens as an individual could be. Vladimir Grabar (Hrabar) (1865–1956)[10] and David Levin (1907–90)[11] have analysed and compared the works of other Russian international legal theoreticians of that time, such as NM Korkunov (1853–1904), MN Kapustin (1828–99), PE Kazanskyi (1866–1947), LA Kamarovskyi (1846–1912), VP Danevskyi (1858–98), AS Yaschenko (1877–1934), AN Stoyanov (1830–1907), O Eichelmann (1854–1943), and others. One reason why the works of other Russian legal theoreticians beside Martens have not resonated so much in the West is that these scholars published almost exclusively in the Russian language. Some other Russian internationalists of the late Tsarist era, such as M Taube (1869–1961), B Nolde (1876–1948), and A Mandelstam (1869–1949) became slightly more well known in the West because their post-1917 works written in emigration were published in Western European languages.[12]

Not all international law scholars in Tsarist Russia agreed with the central tenets of the theory of Martens, including his premise that international law was applicable to 'civilized nations' only.[13] Yet if one ought to generalize, the outlook and orientation of international legal theory in late Tsarist Russia appears 'European'. The arguments and disagreements between liberals (Martens) and conservatives (for example, Eichelmann or Kazanskyi) were themselves carried out in a liberal and pluralist fashion. Cosmopolitan ideas were widespread and the doubt about the usefulness of state sovereignty nagged many authors at the time.[14]

---

[8] See VV Pustogarov, *Our Martens: FF Martens, International Lawyer and Architect of Peace* (WE Butler ed and trans) (Kluwer Law International The Hague 2000); the symposium on Martens, 'The European Tradition in International Law: FF Martens' (2014) 25(3) *European Journal of International Law* 811–91.

[9] F von Martens, *Völkerrecht: Das internationale Recht der civilisirten Nationen* (C Bergbohm trans) (2 vols Weidmannsche Buchhandlung Berlin 1883) vol 1.

[10] VE Grabar, *The History of International Law in Russia, 1647–1917: A Bio-Bibliographical Study* (WE Butler ed and trans) (Clarendon Press Oxford 1990).

[11] DB Levin, *Nauka mezhdunarodnoga prava v Rossii v kontse XIX i nachale XX v* (Nauka Moscow 1982).

[12] See also GS Starodubtsev, *Mezhdunarodno-pravovaya nauka rossiiskoi emigratsii* (Kniga i biznes Moscow 2000).

[13] *Nauka mezhdunarodnoga prava v Rossii v kontse XIX i nachale XX v* (n 11) 86.

[14] For a general background of liberal ideas in Russian legal thought at that time, see also A Walicki, *Legal Philosophies of Russian Liberalism* (Clarendon Press Oxford 1987).

In this chapter, I will use the question of whether theorists accepted individuals as subjects of international law (besides states) as a central question for examining how international legal theory has been constructed in Russia throughout different periods. Of course, other similar 'test questions' are conceivable—such as the questions of whether international law is truly law or only negligible positive morality, when was international law born (a popular one in the Russian scholarship), how international law and domestic law of a country relate to each other, among many others. However, there is not enough space to review all such (sub-)debates in Russian scholarship here.

The question of who are the subjects of international law is a central question in the theory of international law. At first glance, it may appear relatively unpractical. Ultimately, however, it has a strong influence on how one sees the whole field including such central principles of international law as state sovereignty and human rights. It is not necessary to give a sophisticated definition of the notion of the subject of international law here, except that, typically, it is used to denote the capacity to have rights and obligations under this particular branch of law.

International law can be constructed either via individuals as cosmopolitan (global) law or via states as inter-state law. The representatives of the English School of International Relations have pointed out that the Grotian and Kantian approaches to the international system and international law differ from each other.[15] It does make a difference whether one constructs international (or cosmopolitan) law primarily through states or individuals. We can speak of a certain *Zeitgeist* in terms of what (and who) have been enlisted as subjects of international law in the scholarship. I would even argue that the question 'are individuals subjects of not?' is not primarily a matter of proof but of what one prefers to believe in; of what one's underlying political philosophy of the world is. The answer reflects one's ideology of international law.

In post-Second World War Europe (on the Western side of the Iron Curtain) and the US, the theoretical position that besides states individuals can also be subjects of international law has gained widespread recognition.[16] Altogether, the debate on 'could individuals also be subjects of international law?' is currently not a source of major excitement among the theoreticians in the West.[17] It is clear that there is no single 'logical' answer to the question whether they can be or not. Pragmatically, the main question that most scholars in the West seem to agree with is how to better protect human rights in the framework of international law. In this sense,

---

[15] H Bull, *The Anarchical Society: A Study of Order in World Politics* (3rd edn Palgrave New York 2002) at 146 (also referring to the work of Martin Wight).

[16] See A Cassese, *International Law* (2nd edn OUP Oxford 2005) at 142–150.

[17] However, see MC Kettemann, *The Future of Individuals in International Law: Lessons from International Internet Law* (Eleven International Publishing The Hague 2013); A Peters, *Jenseits der Menschenrechte. Die Rechtsstellung des Individuums im Völkerrecht* (Mohr Siebeck Tübingen 2014).

there is little disagreement and the emphasis on the importance of the protection of human rights continues to be a quasi-consensus in the West. Nevertheless, it is interesting to note that the more conservative position that questions the wisdom of raising individuals to the status of subjects of international law continues to exist in the West as well.[18] In this sense, the conservative, state-centric—some would say, classical—approach differs from theories of transnational law or global administrative law, for example, which emphasize transnational networks that all, one way or another, focus on private actors.

It is interesting to note that in contemporary Russia the whole debate has a specific weight and character. Whether individuals and other non-state entities could be formally accepted as subjects of international law seems to have become *the* major international legal-theoretical debate. It is also evident that this debate is primarily a proxy for a larger debate whether Russia should follow the Western extensive concept of human rights or should remain faithful to its state-centred tradition of governance. In the following, let us look at the historical trajectory and the context of this debate in Russia.

During the Tsarist period, a number of scholars accepted individuals as subjects of international law and even constructed international law as the cosmopolitan law of the whole of humankind, that is, not just the law between sovereign states (governments). Martens, who has otherwise been extremely favourable of human rights and even defined 'civilization' in his international law of civilized nations via human rights,[19] was in this context not even the most liberal-'progressive' Russian scholar since while he argued with conviction that international law protected the individual, the latter was in his opinion nevertheless not a subject of international law. Along with Martens, Korkunov and Eichelmann considered states to be the only subjects of international law, but Kazanskyi, Kamarovskyi, and Iashchenko included individuals as well.[20]

A specific feature of pre-1917 international law scholarship in Russia was that its representatives were almost entirely expelled or escaped from Bolshevik Russia. Baron Michael Taube, the successor of Martens at the international law chair at St Petersburg University, did not hesitate to call Russia's turn in and after 1917 a civilizational break. In his view other, 'non-European' forces had seized power in Russia since 1917.[21] Post-1917 Bolshevik Russia also experienced the territorial loss of the Baltic provinces of Estonia, Livonia, and Curonia which had been among the

---

[18] See eg JR Crawford, *Brownlie's Principles of Public International Law* (8th edn OUP Oxford 2012) at 121 (considering classifying the individual as the subject of international law as 'unhelpful').

[19] FF Martens, *Sovremennoe mezhdunarodnoe pravo tsivilizovannykh narodov* (2 vols Yuridicheskii Kolledzh MGU Moscow 1996 [1882]) vol 1, at 8–9 (from the foreword of Martens to the first edition in 1882; interestingly, this part was not printed in the German edition, referred to at n 9).

[20] *Nauka mezhdunarodnoga prava v Rossii v kontse XIX i nachale XX v* (n 11) 48.

[21] M von Taube, *Rußland und Westeuropa. Rußlands historische Sonderentwicklung in der europäischen Völkergemeinschaft* (Stilke Berlin 1928) at 3.

traditional hinterlands of the capital's St Petersburg's pro-European elites, including in the field of international law.

3 KEY FEATURES OF INTERNATIONAL LEGAL THEORY IN THE USSR

International legal theory was an important subject matter for the Soviet international law scholarship and a solid number of monographs were published. Marxism-Leninism as an ideology was in itself quite 'theoretical' or philosophical and therefore attempts to apply it directly to the context of international legal theory were persistently made in Soviet scholarship.[22] In this sense, the Soviet approach to theory differed from Anglo-American pragmatism and orientation to the solution of practical problems of the international community or the concrete state. In 1976, Grigory Tunkin (1906–93) wrote in his diary quite programmatically: 'We must show our theory of international law'.[23] Subjectively, Soviet scholars were convinced that in terms of theory of international law the socialist tradition was superior to the Western one. For example, Tunkin wrote in his diary when lecturing in South Korea in 1993:

I think about the Korean professors. Not strong and from where [sic]. Studied in the United States where the science of international law does not shine. Except for English, they do not know other languages. The teaching of international law has only practical, narrowly practical purposes. They understand very little of theory.[24]

The Soviet theory of international law has inspired quite interesting academic commentary in the West. Different Western interpretations have been offered on the merits and weaknesses of international legal theory in the USSR. While the German-Baltic school of *Ostrecht* was highly critical of the Soviet international legal theory and exposed its logical weaknesses and political hypocrisies,[25] Anglo-American scholars of the political left have emphasized its positive features, such as

---

[22] DB Levin, *Mezhdunarodnoe pravo, vneshnyaya politika i diplomatia* (Mezhdunarodnye otnoshenia Moscow 1981); YY Baskin and DI Fel'dman, *Mezhdunarodnoe pravo. Problemy metodologii* (Mezhdunarodnye otnoshenia Moscow 1971).

[23] VG Tunkin, *The Tunkin Diary and Lectures* (WE Butler ed) (Eleven International Publishing The Hague 2012) at 74.

[24] Ibid 137.

[25] See eg T Schweisfurth, *Sozialistisches Völkerrecht? Darstellung—Analyse—Wertung der sowjetmarxistischen Theorie vom Völkerrecht 'neuen Typs'* (Springer Berlin 1979).

the Soviet emancipatory program on self-determination of peoples[26] or the USSR's progressive social legislation which globally influenced the advancement of social and economic rights in the twentieth century.[27]

Yet the main puzzle for Soviet theory of international law was whether after the Bolshevik revolution in Russia international law could be considered universal or whether it had become regionally fragmented along ideological lines. In the early 1920s, Yevgeni A Korovin (1892–1964) had argued that international law was no longer universal and that the Soviets now had their own international law.[28] Later on, this position was rejected in Soviet scholarship (including by Korovin himself) and the existence of universal international law was reaffirmed in principle. Yet at the same time, Soviet scholars continued to promote the concept of 'socialist international law' as a specific and privileged regional form of international law applicable between the USSR and socialist states. For example, it was this concept that was meant to justify the Soviet intervention in Czechoslovakia in 1968. Thus, the affirmation of the universality of international law by later Soviet scholars was at best relative; in reality the Soviet theory made a clear distinction between international law applicable between socialist and capitalist countries, and international law applicable between socialist countries. The claim of the universality of international law may have been merely a tactical one since in reality international law and its central concepts were understood quite differently in the West and the USSR.

Altogether, Soviet approaches to international law followed from Soviet approaches to law and world history more generally. One central tenet was that law as such was merely a political means in the class struggle, both within the state and internationally. Law was not at all autonomous from politics, as it was at least theorized by most legal scholars in the West. Thus, along these lines, observers in the West during the Cold War pointed out that the Soviet doctrine of international law closely followed Moscow's foreign policy. To the extent that Soviet foreign policy changed—from Stalin to Khrushchev, for instance—international legal doctrine changed as well, and instead of the more hostile Korovin, the more conciliatory Tunkin became more prominent. The other central tenet of Soviet approaches to international law was that the Soviets built on Muscovy's tradition of state-centrism. Compared to the Soviet doctrine, elements in Tsarist-era theories of international law—and this is a paradox because Tsarist Russia was not known as a liberal stronghold in Europe—appeared liberal.

As I have already argued, the debate on whether individuals could be subjects of international law is primarily a proxy debate on what is the correct relationship

---

[26] B Bowring, *Law, Rights and Ideology in Russia: Landmarks in the Destiny of a Great Power* (Routledge London 2013) at 81.

[27] J Quigley, *Soviet Legal Innovation and the Law of the Western World* (CUP Cambridge 2012).

[28] EA Korovin, *Das Völkerrecht der Übergangszeit. Grundlagen der völkerrechtlichen Beziehungen der Union der Sowjetrepubliken* (Stilke Berlin 1929) at vii, 7–8. The original Russian edition was published in 1923.

between the principles of state sovereignty and human rights. In the context of subjects of international law, Soviet theoreticians strongly opposed the idea that individuals (or, worse, transnational corporations) could be subjects of international law. For example, David I Fel'dman (1922–94) from Kazan State University argued in 1971 that Western attempts to make individuals subjects of international law were ideologically nourished by rejections of state sovereignty and an erroneous understanding of domestic and international law as being intertwined or even 'one'.[29] In the same work, Fel'dman emphasized: 'Socialist theory of international law rejects the concept of individuals being subjects of international law.'[30] Even in a study dedicated to Immanuel Kant's influence on international legal theory, Fel'dman concluded that Western adherents of natural law theory misrepresented the relationship between state sovereignty and human rights—according to the Soviet theory, human rights were to be protected within the state only and could not pierce the veil of state sovereignty.[31] Fel'dman repeated this position in a later collective monograph written by Kazan University scholars.[32] David B Levin (1907–90) concluded in 1974 that individuals could not be subjects of international law.[33] Levin held that with the help of this theory, Western scholars attempted to undermine state sovereignty and propagated their 'reactionary' idea of the transformation of international law into supranational world law.[34]

The economic and political crisis in the USSR brought along Gorbachev's perestroika and a 'wind of change', including new thinking along humanist lines on what the relationship between the state and the individual should be. During the last years of the perestroika period, the leading Soviet international law scholars published another edition of the prestigious seven-volume course on international law.[35] While in the first volume, the rest of the chapters on the subjects of international law volume was written by NA Ushakov (1918–2001), the younger scholar Rein Müllerson (1944) received the task of writing the section on individuals as potential subjects of international law. What Müllerson wrote in 1989, in the liberal tradition of Martens, must have sounded a little like an ideological earthquake in Soviet international law theory:

Categorical denial of international legal subjectivity of the individual in Soviet international legal literature is to a certain extent connected to the étatist approach to international law and relations, aggrandizement of the role and meaning of the state not only

---

[29] D Fel'dman (ed), *Mezhdunarodnaya pravosub'ektnost'* (Yuridicheskaya literatura Moscow 1971) at 20.

[30] Ibid.

[31] D Fel'dman and Y Y Baskin, *Uchenie Kanta i Gegelya o mezhdunarodnom prave i sovremennost'* (Izdatel'stvo Kazanskogo Universiteta 1977) at 78–9.

[32] D Fel'dman et al., *Metodologia issledovaniya teoreticheskikh problem mezhdunarodnoga prava* (Izdatel'stvo Kazan'skoga Universiteta 1986) at 11.

[33] DB Levin, *Aktual'nye problemy teorii mezhdunarodnoga prava* (Nauka Moscow 1974) at 57.

[34] Ibid 54, 79.

[35] *Kurs mezhdunarodnoga prava v 7 tomakh* (VN Kudryavtsev ed) (Nauka Moscow 1989–93).

inside society but also in the international arena. A new political thinking, placing at the centre of our concerns the human being and demanding the humanization of international relations, recognizes the active role of the individual in the determination and protection of its rights and liberties . . . Consequently, the breadth of international legal subjectivity of the individual expands.[36]

Yet already in the second volume of the course, dedicated to the general principles of international law, Anatoli P Movchan (1928–98) wrote about the principle of the protection of human rights in a way that would have been hardly comprehensible in the West. According to Movchan, human rights were not directly applicable and yet their very existence in international law was very much owed to the efforts of the USSR, and so on.[37] In earlier Soviet literature, too, human rights was treated as merely one of a number of central principles of international law, almost in passing, and in importance very much 'behind' other principles related to state sovereignty and non-intervention.[38] However, the very possibility that individuals could also be recognized as subjects of international law, as indicated by Müllerson, VS Vereshchetin (1932), and some others during the perestroika period,[39] constituted a potential break from Soviet theoretical thinking and in some ways a return to the pre-1917 tradition and debates in Russia.

4 INTERNATIONAL LEGAL THEORY IN POST-SOVIET RUSSIA

During the second biannual conference of the European Society of International Law in Paris in 2006, Professor Yuri M Kolosov (1934–2015) from Moscow's MGIMO University was asked during the question and answer session of his panel what in Russian scholarship of international law had changed since the collapse of the USSR in 1991.[40] Kolosov gave his answer along the lines that if you took

---

[36] R Müllerson in RA Müllerson and GI Tunkin (eds), *Kurs mezhdunarodnoga prava v 7 tomakh* (VN Kudryavtsev ed) (Nauka Moscow 1989) vol 1, at 180.

[37] AP Movchan in II Lukashuk (ed), *Kurs mezhdunarodnoga prava v 7 tomakh* (VN Kudryavtsev ed) (Nauka Moscow 1989) vol 2, at 157.

[38] RL Bobrov, *Osnovnye problemy teorii mezhdunarodnoga prava* (Mezhdunarodnye otnohenia Moscow 1968) at 261–3.

[39] See eg NV Zakharova, 'Individ—sub'ekt mezhdunarodnoga prava' (1989) 11 *Sovetskoe gosudarstvo i pravo* 81–95.

[40] Kolosov's written remarks at this conference are printed in: H Ruiz Fabri, E Jouannet, and V Tomkiewicz (eds), *Select Proceedings of the European Society of International Law* (Hart Oxford 2008) 165–8.

the Marxism-Leninism away from Soviet theory, the main features of international legal theory and doctrine in the Russian Federation remained essentially the same as it was in the USSR: legal positivism and an emphasis on state sovereignty. Positivism as opposed to natural law and state-centrism as opposed to individual-centrism remained the continuous threads from the Tsarist period up until the post-Soviet period. Apparently, this has been connected with the historical strength of statehood in Russia and with the prevalence of the authoritarian model of governance.[41] With some remarkable liberal exceptions during the Tsarist period, the Russian tradition has tended to be Hegelian rather than Kantian. Notwithstanding the views of Martens and some other liberal theoreticians during the Tsarist period, state practice in Russia has certainly been étatist and Hegelian rather than Kantian.

One can see at least as many continuities as breaks in Soviet and Russian international legal theory over the last half-century. After the collapse of the USSR, the Soviet Association of International Law, established in 1957, was named Russian Association of International Law and continues to publish its yearbooks and hold annual meetings in Moscow.[42] In the post-Soviet period, leading Soviet international law scholars such as Evgeny T Usenko (1918–2010), Igor I Lukashuk (1926–2007), and Stanislav V Chernichenko (1935) continued publishing on international legal theory. One difference, however, is that after the collapse of the USSR, some formerly leading Soviet international law scholars (for example the Georgian Levan Aleksidze (1926)[43] and the Estonian Rein Müllerson[44]) ended up living and working outside the 'russkyi mir'. At the same time, some noteworthy younger authors outside Russia such as in the independent Ukraine have published on international legal theory in the Russian language also during the post-Soviet period.[45]

Kolosov's point would indicate that since old ideological divisions have disappeared, an approximation between Western and Russian international legal theory has taken place. Does it then mean that Western mainstream and Russian scholars nowadays share the view that individuals could also be subjects of international law? As I already indicated, in contemporary Russia there is an active debate about the interrelationship between state sovereignty and human rights. In

---

[41] See further R Pipes, *Russia under the Old Regime* (2nd edn Penguin Books London 1993).

[42] See International Law Association Russian Branch, <http://www.ilarb.ru/> [accessed 23 February 2016] and SV Bakhin (ed), *Rossiiskaya Assotsiatsia Mezhdunarodnoga Prava 1957–2007. Biograficheskii slovar'* (St Petersburg State University St Petersburg 2007).

[43] See LA Aleksidze, *Nekotorye voprosy teorii i mezhdunarodnoga prava. Imperativnye normy (jus cogens)* (Tbilisi State University Tbilisi 1982).

[44] R Müllerson, *Sootnoshenie mezhdunarodnoga i natsional'noga prava* (Mezhdunarodnye otnoshenia Moscow 1982).

[45] AA Merezhko, *Nauka politiki mezhdunarodnoga prava: istoki i perspektivy* (Iustinian Kiev 2009); AA Merezhko, *Istoria mezhdunarodno-pravovykh uchenii* (Takson Kiev 2006); AA Merezhko, *Vvedenie v filosofiu mezhdunarodnoga prava* (Iustinian Kiev 2002).

terms of the subject status of individuals, the balance has certainly moved towards the Western position. Yet it has not reached that and it seems that compared to the perestroika era moment of liberal awakening, state-centric conservatives have regained their positions.

During the early days of the independent statehood of the Russian Federation, Vladimir A Kartashkin (1934), currently professor at the Peoples' Friendship University in Moscow, argued in favour of the view that the individual has become subject of international law.[46] Yet this position was soon refuted by Lukashuk, the then Russian member of the International Law Commission (ILC) and the unofficial doyen of the country's scholarly community at the time who argued that recognizing the individual as a subject of international law would not be the best way to protect its interests.[47]

Furthermore, Chernichenko, one of the most prominent international legal theoreticians in post-Soviet Russia, made it one of his main concerns that individuals could not be subjects of international law. His persistent rejection of the possibility that individuals could be (or could become) subjects of international law, besides states, occasionally resembles an ideological crusade (or, as he himself would probably argue, legitimate self-defence in the face of liberal/Western agitation).[48] He connects the doctrinal position that individuals can be subjects of international law with the theory of monism, considers it unfounded and fights against its resurgence in the Russian doctrine, in particular among younger colleagues in legal academia.[49] On the one hand, the scholarly exchange seems highly formalized and ritualized; at the surface, the conversation is merely about the correctness of the theoretical positions, particularly in terms of formal logic. However, in substantive and existential terms, it is as if Chernichenko is trying to say in his writings: 'the individual as a subject of international law is a liberal Western conspiracy, I have seen through it, and I for one will not surrender my original position.' In this way, Chernichenko is also ensuring the continuity of his Soviet-era views which rejected the possibility that the individual could be a subject of international law.[50] In any case, it is the very opposite of what, for example, Thomas M Franck (1931–2009)

---

[46] VA Kartashkin, *Prava cheloveka v mezhdunarodnom i vnutrigosudarstvennom prave* (Institut gosudarstva i prava Moscow 1995) at 100.

[47] II Lukashuk, *Mezhdunarodnoe pravo* (2nd edn Beck Moscow 2001) vol 1, at 27.

[48] SV Chernichenko, *Teoria mezhdunarodnoga prava* (NIMP Moscow 1999) vol 1, at 113ff; SV Chernichenko, 'Eshe raz o mezhdunarodnoi pravosub'ektnosti individov' (2005) 4 *Moskovskii zhurnal mezhdunarodnoga prava* 11–26.

[49] SV Chernichenko, *Ocherki po filosofii i mezhdunarodnomu pravu* (Nauchnayakniga Moscow 2009) at 651; SV Chernichenko, 'Vopros o sootnoshenii mezhdunarodnoga i vnutrigosudarstvennogo prava kak pravovykh sistem (razmyshlenia po povodu nekotorykh knig kolleg)' in SV Bakhin (ed), *Mezhdunarodnye otnoshenia i pravo: vzglyad v XXI vek* (St Petersburg State University Press St Petersburg 2009) 52–89.

[50] SV Chernichenko, *Lichnost' i mezhdunarodnoe pravo* (Mezhdunarodnye otnoshenia Moscow 1974).

tried to do in the 1990s—to empower the human being, also via international law.[51] Similarly, Usenko has emphasized the link between the question of who could be a subject of international law and the question of whether international law and domestic law were different or 'same' fields of law. Western scholars would unnecessarily blur the line between international and domestic law—in reality, according to Usenko, individuals cannot be subjects of international law.[52]

Yet it would not be correct to say that the rejection of individuals as subjects of international law is exclusively a matter of different generations in Russia; all older scholars who matured during the Soviet era rejected this idea after the collapse of the USSR as well. For example, Gennady V Ignatenko (1927–2012) from Yekaterinburg propagated a favourable attitude towards the idea that individuals would be subjects of international law—the question, according to him, was no longer 'whether individuals were subjects but to what extent'.[53] According to Ignatenko's and Oleg I Tiunov's (1937) textbook, the expansion of the subjects of international law was connected with the spread of democratic principles in contemporary society.[54] Since there is a tradition of collective textbooks in Russia and the authors sometimes even overlap with other textbooks, Ignatenko familiarized his Russian readers with the idea of individuals as subjects of international law elsewhere as well.[55]

Furthermore, the textbook compiled at Kazan State University in Tatarstan postulates that individuals can be subjects of international law, albeit in a limited manner.[56] Yet some contemporary Russian textbook authors, such as Pavel Biryukov (1966) from Voronezh State University, are not yet quite sure whether individuals could be counted as subjects of international law.[57] On the other hand, it is interesting to note that the textbooks of Russia's *grandes écoles* of international law in Moscow, MGIMO and Diplomatic Academy, are both lukewarm towards the idea that individuals might be subjects of international law along with states.[58] They adhere to the conservative tradition which constructs international law mainly via the states. Similarly, a textbook compiled by a group of scholars from Moscow and edited by Gennady M Melkov (1932),

[51] TM Franck, *The Empowered Self: Law and Society in the Age of Individualism* (OUP Oxford 1999).

[52] ET Usenko, *Ocherki teorii mezhdunarodnoga prava* (Norma Moscow 2008) at 131–2 and 167–8.

[53] GV Ignatenko and OI Tiunov (eds), *Mezhdunarodnoe pravo* (6th edn Norma Moscow 2013) at 120.

[54] Ibid 66.

[55] See eg GV Ignatenko in VI Kuznetsov and BR Tuzmukhamedov (eds), *Mezhdunarodnoe pravo* (2nd edn Norma Moscow 2007) at 74. For his collected essays, see GV Ignatenko, *Mezhdunarodnoe pravo i vnutrigosudarstvennoe pravo: problemy sopryazhannosti i vzaimodeistvia* (Norma Moscow 2012).

[56] RM Valeev and GI Kurdyukov (eds), *Mezhdunarodnoe pravo* (Statut Moscow 2011) vol 1, at 363.

[57] PN Biryukov, *Mezhdunarodnoe pravo* (5th edn Yurait Moscow 2011) at 126–7.

[58] AN Vylegzhanin (ed), *Mezhdunarodnoe pravo* (Yurait Moscow 2009) at 138; AV Kovalev and SV Chernichenko (eds), *Mezhdunarodnoe pravo* (3rd edn Prospekt Moscow 2008) at 170.

mentions quite thoroughly all conceivable pro and contra arguments in the debate about whether individuals could be subjects of international law, and comes to the conclusion that individuals, transnational corporations, and non-governmental organizations cannot be subjects of international law.[59] In an article in an edited volume, Insur Z Farkhutdinov (1956) comes to the conclusion that only states can be full subjects of international law which is particularly fascinating because he uses private person-driven international economic law as the main example.[60] Elsewhere, Farkhutdinov depicts how globalization and the flow of capital over borders in the form of investments can become a challenge for state sovereignty, and yet state sovereignty must remain the central principle in international law.[61]

The other side of the question of whether individuals could be recognized as subjects of international law is the attitude towards state sovereignty. During the post-Soviet period, the principle of state sovereignty received abundant attention in Russian scholarship. Aleksei A Moiseev (1971), international law scholar from Moscow's Diplomatic Academy, has taken a quite conservative, even absolutist-Hegelian, take on state sovereignty.[62] The problem of state sovereignty has been studied from the angle of political science,[63] conservative philosophy,[64] and even with reference to Orthodox writers and practices, that is, theology.[65] Probably the most influential recent book on sovereignty has been a collection of speeches and essays of politicians and experts, reflecting the thinking of the current political elite around President VV Putin and Prime Minister DA Medvedev.[66] This book, edited by Nikita Garadzha, lays out in a clear political language why the principle of state sovereignty remains a central one for Russia. For example, in his annual speech to the Federal Assembly, President Putin declared in 2002:

All our historical experience testifies: such a country as Russia may live and develop in the existing borders only if it is a powerful state [*derzhava*] . . . I would like to

---

[59] GM Melkov (ed), *Mezhdunarodnoe pravo* (RIOR Moscow 2009) at 136.

[60] IZ Farkhutdinov, 'Mezhdunarodnaya pravosubyektnost' v XXI veke: problemy i tendentsii' in S Bakhin (ed), *Mezhdunarodnye otnoshenia i pravo: vzglyad v XXI vek* (St Petersburg State University St Petersburg 2009) 198–214, at 209–10.

[61] IZ Farkhutdinov, 'Suverenitet gosudarstva i mezhdunarodnoe pravo: vyzovy globalizatsii' in AG Lisitsyn-Svetlanov (ed), *Novye vyzovy i mezhdunarodnoe pravo* (RAN Institut gosudarsvta i prava Moscow 2010) 53–66.

[62] AA Moiseev, *Suverenitet gosudarstva v mezhdunarodnom prave* (Vostok Zapad Moscow 2009).

[63] AL Bredikhin, *Suverenitet kak politiko-pravovoi fenomen* (Infra-M Moscow 2012); MV Ilyin and IV Kudryashova (eds), *Suverenitet. Transformatsia ponjatii i praktik* (MGIMO-Universitet Moscow 2008).

[64] NI Grachev, *Proiskhozhdenie suvereniteta* (Zertsalo-M Moscow 2009); IA Ivannikov, *Istoria politiko-pravovoi mysli o forme Rossiiskogo gosudarstva* (Yurlitinform Moscow 2012).

[65] AV Sitnikov, *Pravoslavie, instituty vlasti i grazhdanskogo obshestva v Rossii* (Aleteia St Petersburg 2012); YE Svechinskaya, *Imperskaya ideologiya v Rossiiskoi gosudarstvenno-pravovoi mysli* (Yurlitinform Moscow 2011).

[66] N Garadzha (ed), *Suverenitet* (Evropa Moscow 2006).

remind you: throughout its history, Russia and its citizens have been carrying out a truly heroic deed. Heroic deeds in the name of the territorial integrity of the country, in the name of stable life within it. Maintenance of the state in a vast space, preservation of the unique community of peoples while keeping strong positions of the country in the world—this is not only enormous work. These are also huge sacrifices and deprivations for our people.[67]

Perhaps then it is fair to conclude and admit that certain civil rights have been part of this deprivation in most historical periods in Russia. President Putin constructs the territorial integrity and historical grandness of Russia as a highest value to which other values, such as, tacitly, human rights and liberty, must subordinate themselves. Individuals and non-governmental organizations (NGOs), on the other hand, may have an undetermined relationship to the territorial integrity of Russia. In the same volume, Vladislav Surkov (1964), the then ideologist of the Putin administration, even complains that at some Russian universities, there are no longer 'teachers' but rather NGO representatives supported by foreign grants.[68] The Russian Federation continues to be, even after the collapse of the USSR, by far the largest country territorially on Earth. That control over land and space would continue to be existentially important for Russia can already deduced from the fact that Russia's economic development largely depends on natural resources that are extracted from its vast territory. Compared to the West, Russia may be a 'peripheral' empire, as Boris Kagarlitski (1958) has argued,[69] but it has been an empire nevertheless.

In this sense, the debate about in which relationship the state and the individual should live—and whether individuals should be recognized as subjects of international law—are not merely theoretical exercises, *Glasperlenspiele*. Indeed, this theoretical debate seems to be a confirmation of the old adage, sometimes attributed to Kant, that nothing is more practical than a good theory. Russia's survival as an independent power and its strength and greatness is the continuous political axiom; everything else, including the direction of international legal theory, seems to follow from this premise. In the contemporary Russian context, the doctrinal position that individuals are 'below' the state, in its effects if not in intentions, ends up justifying why the questionable practices that we can read about almost monthly in newspapers, are not really that bad or in any case not so much the business of international law. The reverse is true as well: those scholars who seem to be dissatisfied with the situation of human rights demand more and

---

[67] VV Putin speech on 18 April 2012, quoted in ibid 21.

[68] *Suverenitet* (n 66) 72. See further L Mälksoo, 'Contemporary Russian Perspectives on Non-State Actors: Fear of the Loss of State Sovereignty' in J d'Aspremont (ed), *Participants in the International Legal System: Multiple Perspectives on Non-State Actors in International Law* (Routledge London 2011) 126–38.

[69] BY Kagarlitski, *Periferiinaya imperia. Rossia i mirosistema* (Librokom Moscow 2012).

more vocally that the individual's status as subject of international law be recognized in the doctrine.[70]

5 The Impact of Civilizational Thinking on Contemporary Russian Theory of International Law

One interesting phenomenon in contemporary Russia is that the rigid Soviet division of 'bourgeois' and 'socialist' authors in scholarship has been transformed into a division between 'native' (that is, Russian; *otechestvennyi*) and 'foreign' or 'Western' international legal theory and doctrine. For example, this conceptual dividing line is still pervasive in most textbooks of international law and appears in a recent monograph on international legal theory by EV Safronova from Belgorod State University.[71] Foreign and Russian authorities on international law and legal theory are clearly distinguishable and the latter are usually given special visibility in the Russian scholarly literature.[72] It is as if Russian scholarship of international legal theory would be trying to solve riddles that are not universal but primarily or at least simultaneously 'Russian'. While it is possible to see in this tendency a certain intellectual parochialism (and sometimes it is, especially when Western authors are quoted through third sources as in Safronova's otherwise interesting treatise), it can also be a hallmark of intellectual cultures in major powers insisting on 'independence', also in a cognitive sense. Such states and academic cultures tend to be self-centric and self-referential; they subjectively feel that intellectually they have already 'got it all' and do not need to refer to or 'borrow' much from the others who, through their otherness, also happen to appear less trustworthy.

Such a phenomenon may have deeper historical, cultural, and even theological roots than contemporary international lawyers themselves might realize. For example, the Moscow scholar of semiotics Boris Uspenski has demonstrated the important role Old Slavonic language historically played in Orthodox thinking in Russia.[73]

---

[70] See TD Matveeva, 'Evoliutsia doktriny mezhdunarodnoi pravosub'ektnosti' [2012] *Rossiiskiy ezhegodnik mezhdunarodnoga prava* 27–42, at 33; TD Matveeva, 'Chelovek i mezhdunarodnoe pravo (k voprosu o mezhdunarodnoi pravo sub'ektnosti individa' [2010] *Rossiiskiy ezhegodnik mezhdunarodnoga prava* 52–67.

[71] EV Safronova, *Mezhdunarodnoe publichnoe pravo. Teoreticheskie problemy* (RIOR Moscow, 2013).

[72] SV Chernichenko, *Teoria mezhdunarodnoga prava* (NIMP Moscow 1999) vol 1, at 12; EV Safronova, *Mezhdunarodnoe publichnoe pravo. Teoreticheskie problemy* (RIOR Moscow 2013) at 4.

[73] B Uspenski, *Vene kultuuri jõujooni. Valik artikleid* (P Lepik trans) (Ilmamaa Tallinn 2013) at 301ff.

Truthful content and correct language could not be separated from each other; the Old Slavonic language served as an icon of Orthodoxy.[74] Other languages were associated with other religious traditions; for example Latin symbolized Catholicism and was at least in sixteenth-century Muscovy seen as dirty, compromised, and heretical.[75] Does the contemporary Russian scholarly practice of neatly distinguishing between the 'native' and the 'foreign' scholars of international law still echo these distant times in Europe, including Eastern Europe, when religion determined right and wrong? Are contemporary international legal theoreticians direct successors of medieval scholars and monks trying to prove the correct way of understanding God?

Oscar Schachter from Columbia University wrote in 1977 that the professional community of international lawyers

. . . though dispersed throughout the world and engaged in diverse occupations, constitutes a kind of invisible college dedicated to a common intellectual enterprise. As in the case of other disciplines, its members are engaged in a continuous process of communication and collaboration.[76]

Schachter's image of the 'invisible college' has proven to be a very popular one. However, based on the Russian self-referential practice (which, however, Russians could object, is not very different from scholarly practices in the field of international law in the US), are international lawyers globally really all in the same college or temple? Perhaps instead there are a number of fragmented colleges, epistemic communities, each speaking a different language or at least a dialect of the same language, and thinking they are 'predominant' while being relatively ignorant about the others? Each of such temples seems to have its own leading authorities and hierarchies and a result is that the way international law is talked about has different accents—or even content—in places like New York and Moscow.

The collapse of Communism in Russia triggered hopes and optimistic predictions that the country would 'return to' Europe—including in relation to legal theory which in the West, and after Germany fully joined the West, is nowadays dominated by liberal thought. This did not happen or happened only insufficiently, and the increasingly visible argument in Russian legal theory for explaining this is the uniqueness of 'civilization'. As the argument goes, Russia has a right to its own viewpoint and interpretation—also in the context of international law—since it is not the same as the West. Authors arguing for this view point out that Russia might be a different civilization after all, and international law should take the uniqueness of civilizations into account.[77] Civilizational method has also become popular

---

[74] *Vene kultuuri jõujooni* (n 73) 310.   [75] Ibid 311–15.

[76] O Schachter, 'The Invisible College of International Lawyers' (1977) 72 *Northwestern University Law Review* 217–26.

[77] See EL Sadykova, 'Mezhtsivilizatsionnyi dialog kak institut sistemy mezhdunarodnykh otnoshenii' in AA Moiseev (ed), *Vestnik Diplomaticheskoi Akademii MID Rossii. Mezhdunarodnoe pravo* (Diplomaticheskaja Akademija Moscow 2013) 248–57.

in the comparative study of politics.[78] One does not necessarily need to look for logical consistency in these new approaches, at least when politicians start solving these riddles—for example Surkov has postulated somewhat puzzlingly that 'Russia civilization belongs to European civilization'.[79] On the one hand, contemporary Russia tries to be European and on the other hand, it rejects the 'false' (too liberal) Europe in the sense that Russia's civilizational rhetoric ultimately becomes a camouflage for the rejection of liberal values and practices in Europe. This connection between arguing for a unique Russian 'civilization' and the rejection of liberal values is very visible in the sophisticated attack on the Western concept of human rights that has recently been undertaken by Patriarch Kirill of the Russian Orthodox Church.[80]

'Civilization' has made it into international legal theoretical analysis in Russia. EV Safronova argues in her recent monograph that the differences between the West and the rest, apparently including contemporary Russia, cannot be simply thought away with reference to opposing geopolitical interests. Safronova argues that civilizational differences explain why some favour state sovereignty to human rights and vice versa:

Values that have primary importance in European and American (Anglo-Saxon) civilization, are far less important for other peoples. Thus many Western ideas such as individualism, liberalism, democracy, separation of Church and state, and so on are not reflected in Orthodox, Muslim, Buddhist and Confucian cultures. The nature of the categories of 'freedom', 'justice' and 'equality' is understood differently. . . . Different civilizations, for example, do not reject human rights or human freedom, but understand and evaluate it differently . . . Unfortunately, current legal standardization takes place based on West European legal culture.[81]

Furthermore, Safronova argues that of all the general principles of international law, the West has been trying to raise the status of the protection of human rights at the cost of other main principles such as state sovereignty, a move which has been particularly visible in the context of humanitarian interventions such as in Kosovo in 1999.[82] In the human rights literature too, theoreticians such as Elena A Lukasheva from the Institute of State and Law of the Russian Academy of Sciences, have attempted to explain differences between the West and Russia through civilizational factors.[83] However, for Lukasheva these factors do not necessarily speak in

---

[78] MV Gorbachev, *Tsivilizatsionnaya metodologia v politicheskoi komparativistike* (Saratovskaya gosudarstvennaya akadeemia prava Saratov 2011).

[79] V Surkov, *Suverenitet—eto politicheskii sinonim konkurentosposobnosti* in *Suverenitet* (n 66) 43f.

[80] See Patriarch Kirill of Moscow, *Freedom and Responsibility. A Search for Harmony, Human Rights and Personal Dignity* (Darton Longman and Todd London 2011).

[81] *Mezhdunarodnoe publichnoe pravo* (n 71) 42–3.   [82] Ibid 115–16.

[83] EA Lukasheva, *Chelovek, pravo, tsivilizatsii: Normativno-tsennostnoe izmerenie* (Norma Moscow 2009).

favour of Russia but rather explain its backwardness compared to the West in the sphere of human rights.[84]

6 Conclusion

The debate about the interrelationship between the state and the individual, of which the question of whether individuals can be subjects of international law forms a part, is not unique to Russia. A similar chapter could probably be written on different views on international law in the US[85] and probably elsewhere in major countries, not to speak of the evolution of international legal theory in a certain country within different time periods. Each time period has to tell where the balancing point between different principles of international law lies.

Yet one thing that has come out of this chapter is that the current 'point of balance' in Russia is somewhere elsewhere than in the West. For historical, ideological, and other reasons, Russia is now having the debate—or rather, a silent and rapid theoretical transition—that the West had after the Second World War. In this sense, there is a certain time-lag between Eastern Europe (Russia) and the West that may even indeed have civilizational dimensions. It is likely that when leaders of major powers and power blocs meet and the argument of 'international law' comes up between them, international law partly means 'different things to different people'. International law scholarship should not overestimate these regional differences or make them out as more significant than they are, but it seems no more viable to think, under the disguise of universality of international law, that the rest of the world understands international law—or must understand it—in the same way as the West. Human history—and the history of international law and international legal thought—can be written as a centripetal search for unity and universality, but simultaneously also as a centrifugal pull of powerful regional and cultural differences. To the extent that the centrifugal forces remain active, international law will have to integrate regional fragmentation, and universal organizations such as the United Nations will continue to represent primarily the lowest common denominator between the states, regions, and 'civilizations' of the world.

---

[84] *Chelovek, pravo, tsivilizatsii* (n 83).

[85] On the history of the US tradition of international law, see MW Janis, *America and the Law of Nations 1776–1939* (OUP Oxford 2010).

PART II

APPROACHES

CHAPTER 14

NATURAL LAW IN INTERNATIONAL LEGAL THEORY

LINEAR AND DIALECTICAL PRESENTATIONS

GEOFF GORDON

1 INTRODUCTION

NATURAL law has a peculiar way of being everywhere and nowhere in the body of international law today. Often taken to be in some way foundational of positive law,[1] and traditionally accepted to declare positive law either void or defective in any given case,[2] its applicability in theory has been widened to the point of near-ubiquity by association with both naturalism, on the one hand, and the

---

[1] See I Hunter, 'Natural Law as Political Philosophy' in DM Clarke and C Wilson (eds), *The Oxford Handbook of Philosophy in Early Modern Europe* (OUP Oxford 2011) 475–99.

[2] Cf P Capps, 'International Legal Positivism and Modern Natural Law' in J d'Aspremont and J Kammerhofer (eds), *International Legal Positivism in a Post-Modern World* (CUP Cambridge 2014) 213–40; P Capps, 'Natural Law and the Law of Nations' in A Orakhelashvili (ed), *Research Handbook on the Theory and History of International Law* (Edward Elgar Cheltenham 2011) 61–92.

rhetoric of justice on the other.[3] Yet it is hardly to be found in practice,[4] and has been described as dead.[5] In addressing such a diffuse and conflicted field, choices are necessary and omissions inevitable. Some will be unconventional. I propose here to tell two stories about natural law in international legal theory, both roughly organized around a meeting point of sorts for the associations with naturalism and justice. This will also function as a brisk overview, drawing on three active periods of natural law scholarship bearing on international law, as well as recent developments.

The first story relates in brief the renewed attention to natural law doctrine as part of historiographical and epistemological inquiries in international law and legal theory, with particular attention to the foundational role of natural law doctrine in a hegemonic project.[6] The second presents still another means of understanding natural law and its ongoing role in international law, namely as a dialectic by which new conceptions and vocabularies of political organization have arisen under varying historical circumstances.[7] The dialectical presentation, however, is not to the exclusion of the linear presentation of consolidating global hegemony, but fits within or alongside it.

This may seem contradictory. But it is emblematic of the unusual role between hegemony and resistance played by international law,[8] and reinforces the

---

[3] See eg M Shaw, *International Law* (6th edn CUP Cambridge 2008) at 53–4.

[4] A notable exception is the jurisprudence of Judge Cançado Trindade: see eg *Application of the International Convention on the Elimination of All Forms of Racial Discrimination (Georgia v Russian Federation)* (Preliminary Objections) [2011] ICJ Rep 70, at 322 (Judge Cançado Trindade, Dissenting Opinion).

[5] M Koskenniemi, 'Miserable Comforters: International Relations as New Natural Law' (2009) 15 *European Journal of International Relations* 395–422, at 403. For the possibility that natural law survived after all, but in a transformed state, see further M Koskenniemi, 'Transformations of Natural Law: Germany 1648–1815' in this *Handbook*.

[6] See eg I de la Rasilla del Moral, 'Francisco de Vitoria's Unexpected Transformations and Reinterpretations for International Law' (2013) 32 *International Community Law Review* 287–318; A Orford, 'The Past as Law or History? The Relevance of Imperialism for Modern International Law' (Institute for International Law and Justice, New York University Law School, International Law and Justice Working Paper No 2012/2), subsequently published in M Toufayan, E Tourme-Jouannet, and H Ruiz Fabri (eds), *International Law and New Approaches to the Third World* (Société de Législation Comparée Paris 2013) 97–118; M Koskenniemi, 'Empire and International Law: The Real Spanish Contribution' (2011) 61 *University of Toronto Law Journal* 1–36; 'Miserable Comforters' (n 5); A Anghie, *Imperialism, Sovereignty and the Making of International Law* (CUP Cambridge 2005); R Lesaffer, 'The Grotian Tradition Revisited: Change and Continuity in the History of International Law' (2002) 73 *British Year Book of International Law* 103–39; W Grewe, *The Epochs of International Law* (M Byers trans and rev) (de Gruyter Berlin 2000 [1984]); D Kennedy, 'Primitive Legal Scholarship' (1986) 27 *Harvard Journal of International Law* 1–98. For a related inquiry focused on the hegemonic term, rather than the historiographical, see M Koskenniemi, 'International Law and Hegemony: A Reconfiguration' (2004) 17 *Cambridge Review of International Affairs* 197–218.

[7] Cf I Hunter, 'The Recovery of Natural Law: Hochstrasser's History of Morality' (2001) 30 *Economy and Society* 354–67, at 355.

[8] Cf M Koskenniemi, 'Law, Teleology and International Relations: An Essay in Counterdisciplinarity' (2011) 26 *International Relations* 3–34; N Krisch, 'International Law in Times of Hegemony: Unequal

foundational character of natural law in international legal theory. Umut Özsu writes of dialectical analysis in international law as potentially 'capable of explaining how international law is hardwired in ways that systemically disempower less resourceful actors while permitting these same actors to wage struggles of emancipation in its name.'[9] The ambition here—applied specifically to natural law, and limited to a brief outline with an eye towards further study—is similar: to demonstrate how natural law continues to inform efforts—both hegemonic and counter-hegemonic—to define a foundation and *telos* for the international system.

In this chapter, I turn first to an overview of three active periods of natural law scholarship bearing on international legal theory. I then trace in brief the role of natural law doctrine as part of a linear consolidation of liberal hegemony internationally from the early modern period forward. Thereafter, I offer the dialectical presentation covering the same timeframe. In closing, I will return to how natural law continues to contribute both to the possibility of new normative programmes internationally, as well as the hegemonic.

2 OVERVIEW

Different instantiations of natural law doctrine are closely bound up with two origin stories of modern international law. First, the doctrine of the neo-scholastics of the Salamanca School contributed to one supposed birth of the modern international system, coincident with the Peace of Westphalia.[10] Second, an adaptation of natural law—the so-called law of nature—established the foundation of Enlightenment liberalism, and the mindset that ultimately produces the label of international law, attributed to Jeremy Bentham.[11] The different doctrinal instantiations reflect different aspirations to the universal, joined to different appreciations of the political. In the following section, I turn first to the period of Vitoria through Grotius, thereafter to a formative period of Enlightenment liberalism,[12]

Power and the Shaping of the International Legal Order' (2005) 16 *European Journal of International Law* 369–408.

  [9] U Özsu, 'The Question of Form: Methodological Notes on Dialectics and International Law' (2010) 23 *Leiden Journal of International Law* 687–707, at 698.

  [10] L Gross, 'The Peace of Westphalia, 1648–1948' (1948) 42 *American Journal of International Law* 20–41.

  [11] M Janis, 'Jeremy Bentham and the Fashioning of "International Law"' (1984) 78 *American Journal of International Law* 405–18.

  [12] The temporal division—neo-scholastics through Grotius, a new period commencing with Hobbes—approximates the schema employed by Richard Tuck in his seminal work, *Natural Rights Theories*, but it bears noting that the nature of the inquiry is not the same, and neither are

and I conclude this section by turning to adaptations of natural law theory made by twentieth-century figures.

2.1 Vitoria through Grotius

Vitoria, working at the University of Salamanca in the early sixteenth century, helped to found what has come to be known as the Salamanca School in a period of disintegrating religious and social cohesion among the peoples of Europe. At the same time, the world was expanding as a function of the exploration and exploitation of the new world, further stretching the viability of norms and bonds that had historically anchored rules of conduct among European peoples. Against these trends, Vitoria operated in an official environment still defined by consolidated political authorities associated with the Holy Roman Empire and the Catholic Church.[13] To provide for normative cohesion across peoples in the face of social disintegration, coupled with competition to subjugate an expanding world, Vitoria adapted the natural law doctrine of Thomas Aquinas together with vestiges of the Roman *jus gentium*.[14] Vitoria's adaptation was significant for the new vision of the political community to which it was joined. His doctrine reflected a normative potential vested in a comprehensive phenomenon of human collectivity, not identified with imperialist authorities, and also distinct from—but inclusive of—new and independent peoples.[15]

Vitoria characterized comprehensive collectivity in terms of interdependence among the people and peoples of the world.[16] The interdependence that he observed flowed from an Aristotelian appreciation of natural social inclinations and a universal capacity to communicate, to the effect that '[n]ature has established a bond of relationship between all men'.[17] The roots in a natural, comprehensive collectivity established an objective foundation for law in the new context of international relations, and reliance on sociability entailed an immanent condition of interconnection by which to comprehend 'the common good of all.'[18] In this way,

---

the conclusions drawn. See R Tuck, *Natural Rights Theories: Their Origin and Development* (CUP Cambridge 1979).

[13] Cf A Orford, 'Jurisdiction without Territory: From the Holy Roman Empire to the Responsibility to Protect' (2009) 30 *Michigan Journal of International Law* 981–1015, at 984–9; AH Snow, 'The Law of Nations' (1912) 6 *American Journal of International Law* 890–900, at 890–2.

[14] 'The Grotian Tradition Revisited' (n 6) 121–5.

[15] F de Vitoria, 'De Indis Noviter Inventis' (J Pawley Bate trans) in JB Scott, *The Spanish Origin of International Law: Francisco de Vitoria and His Law of Nations* (Clarendon Press Oxford 1932 [1532]) appendix A, i–xlvi, at xxxviii.

[16] F de Vitoria, 'De Potestate Civili' (GL Williams trans) in *The Spanish Origin of International Law* (n 15) appendix C, lxxi–xci, at lxxiv–lxxv.

[17] 'De Indis Noviter Inventis' (n 15) xxxviii.   [18] Ibid.

Vitoria envisioned the human community as a discrete collective entity with interests and ends of its own—not to the exclusion of the particular collective such as the state, but in addition to it.[19] The difference was that the subjective authority of the nation-state would yield before the consolidated norms of the world collective within the latter's proper areas of interests or ends.[20] Likewise, the normative order of the natural whole would be objective for flowing from the thing itself, rather than any subjective aspiration to define it.[21] That objective foundation served as a counterforce to rising political independence among discrete national collectives, even as it liberated them from the regimes of Emperor and Pope; it supported a consolidated statement of authority intended to sustain norms of conduct—both natural and positive—across increasingly independent peoples, but without subjecting them to imperial control in the form of any singular potentate.[22]

Following Vitoria, Suárez, also in Salamanca for a time, took further the interdependent underpinning of Vitoria's social vision. He joined Vitoria's statement of natural law to an emphasis on underlying political unity: 'the human race, into howsoever many different peoples and kingdoms it may be divided, always preserves a certain unity'.[23] Unity reinforced universality: 'although a given sovereign state, commonwealth, or the kingdom, may constitute a perfect community in itself, consisting of its own members, nevertheless, each one of these states is also, in a certain sense, and viewed in relation to the human race, a member of that universal society'.[24] Suárez observed the universal society, in turn, to give rise to 'true law', discernible in norms of conduct evidenced by the 'whole world'.[25]

After Suárez, Grotius has also been described as a last member of the Salamanca School,[26] though he has, at the same time, been understood as the starting point for what follows in the period of Enlightenment liberalism.[27] I focus here on commonalities with the Salamanca School. Grotius, like Vitoria and Suárez, subscribed to an idea of a 'society of mankind' or 'human society' encompassing humanity as a whole.[28] He founded that society in both natural and empirical roots. Grotius' world society—and the natural law applicable to it—arose naturally out of the universal capacity for and inclination to sociability and communication, together

---

[19] 'De Indis Noviter Inventis' (n 15) xxxviii.

[20] F de Vitoria, 'De Jure Belli' (J Pawley Bate trans) in *The Spanish Origin of International Law* (n 15) appendix B, xlvii–lxx, at lvi.

[21] 'De Potestate Civili' (n 16) xc.   [22] 'The Grotian Tradition Revisited' (n 6) 125–6.

[23] F Suárez, *A Treatise on Laws and God the Lawgiver* in *Selections from Three Works of Francisco Suárez, SJ* (GL Williams et al., trans) (Clarendon Press Oxford 1944) vol 2, 3–646, at 348.

[24] Ibid 348–9.   [25] Ibid 459.   [26] *The Spanish Origin of International Law* (n 15) 3.

[27] See also MJ van Ittersum, 'Hugo Grotius (1583–1645): The Making of a Founding Father of International Law' in this *Handbook*. For still another influential account, see H Bull, B Kingsbury, and A Roberts (eds), *Hugo Grotius and International Relations* (OUP Oxford 1992).

[28] H Grotius, *Mare Liberum* (JB Scott ed R van Deman Magoffin trans) (Clarendon Press Oxford 1916 [1609]) chs 1, 5, 12.

with the fact of interdependence.[29] He described the natural wellspring of universal norms as follows: 'This Sociability…or this Care of maintaining Society in a Manner conformable to the Light of human Understanding, is the Fountain of Right, properly so called'.[30] In addition, Grotius' natural law included a right to intervene, in the name of human society, in particular cases of injustice.[31] Thereby the natural law affirmed universal rights of human society capable of trumping any particular right vested in smaller social and political collectives.

Notably, however, the Salamanca School's doctrine of interdependence and collective unity included endorsements of commerce and private property under law.[32] The natural unity founded on social inclinations included a universal right among individuals to trade, which established grounds justifying colonial exploitation and the aggrandizement of particular interests vested in colonial powers.[33] The common good was held to include a personal right to private property, comprehended according to tenets associated with commutative, rather than distributive justice.[34] As a consequence, the affirmations of trade and private property implicitly privileged individualism, together with competition and acquisition, in the interrelationships making up the universal collective in theory. That allowance for acquisitive individualism, despite the Salamanca School's driving concern with the possibility of national atomization in a world not defined by emperor or pope, suggests a compromised doctrine, one that aspired to communal objectivity, but was conducive to the competitive subjectivity that ultimately came to define international law established among the colonial powers.

But though elements of the ultimate failure of the Salamanca School's pretension to a harmonious basis in natural law for international norms were present from the start, the political concept underlying the School's application of natural law to international legal theory nonetheless bears appreciating in historical context.[35] It was a concept that altered the dominant political image of the time, the body politic, understood by analogy to the human body as an organic but differentiated whole. The Salamanca School disassociated the unitary body politic from its human instantiation, otherwise understood to be literally vested in the figure of the sovereign, and reconceived it according to a socially-constituted consciousness.[36] The recourse to a socially-constituted consciousness was not new. Dante, for

---

[29] H Grotius, *De Jure Belli ac Pacis Libri Tres* (FW Kelsey trans) (Clarendon Press Oxford 1925 [1625]) Prolegomena, at [23]–[24].

[30] Ibid [7]–[8].   [31] Ibid bk II, ch xxv, § viii, para 2.

[32] F de Vitoria, 'On the American Indians', in A Pagden and J Lawrance (eds), *Vitoria, Political Writings* (CUP Cambridge 1991) 231–92, at 252–4ff.

[33] *Imperialism, Sovereignty and the Making of International Law* (n 6) 13–31.

[34] 'Empire and International Law: The Real Spanish Contribution' (n 6) 15ff.

[35] P Zapatero, 'Legal Imagination in Vitoria: The Power of Ideas' (2009) 11 *Journal of the History of International Law* 221–71.

[36] 'De Potestate Civili' (n 16) lxxiv–lxxv.

example, in *De Monarchia*, citing Aristotle and following the work of Ibn Rushd, relied on the idea of a collective mind belonging to humanity as a whole, as a conceptual support for world empire.[37] Dante, however, still held the collective mind to affirm the authority of a singular figure, namely the emperor. An innovation of the Salamanca School was to diminish the singular figure representing conscious control over the body,[38] as applied to the whole of the human community, allowing thereby a comprehensive consciousness but not a singular head. Herein, again, are roots that will be seen to conduce towards the definitive turning away from Thomist natural law in Enlightenment theory. Nonetheless, the Salamanca School reconceived the nature of the political community to project a markedly different figure of central authority, to allow for new possibilities of political organization and interaction in a changing world, while sustaining its collective coherence.[39] The effect may be understood for its rejection of the hegemonic powers of the time, as well as its contribution to a different hegemonic order, as will be returned to below.

2.2 Enlightenment Liberalism and the Law of Nature

I turn now to the Enlightenment, and the move from natural law to a new law of nature. The Enlightenment, it bears noting, does not refer to a perfectly unified intellectual phenomenon, but is a label encompassing a number of competing political ideas and ambitions in Europe.[40] Those ambitions were, in part, the product of the forces of disintegration against which the Salamanca School had posed its affirmation of an organic and comprehensive collective phenomenon. Thus the Reformation and Counter-Reformation gave rise to a number of competing objectives, in which competing powers of the time largely aimed at monopolizing local and regional controls, coupled to expanding colonial empires.[41] The new political ambitions occurred coincident with the ascendant vocabulary of a new science, as well as a rising sentiment of bourgeois individualism.[42] Thomas Hobbes mastered this new vocabulary and sentiment in the service of one particular political program and in the interests of a particular set

---

[37] D Alighieri, *Monarchy* (P Shaw trans) (CUP Cambridge 1996 [c 1312–13]). For further discussion of Dante's collective mind in a related context, see J Bartelson, *Visions of World Community* (CUP Cambridge 2009) at 48–60.

[38] 'De Potestate Civili' (n 16) lxxv–lxxvii.

[39] See generally 'Legal Imagination in Vitoria' (n 35).

[40] Cf 'Natural Law as Political Philosophy' (n 1); J Israel, *Enlightenment Contested: Philosophy, Modernity and the Emancipation of Man* (OUP Oxford 2006).

[41] Cf I Hunter, 'The Figure of Man and the Territorialisation of Justice in "Enlightenment" Natural Law: Pufendorf and Vattel' (2013) 23 *Intellectual History Review* 289–307; *Imperialism, Sovereignty and the Making of International Law* (n 6).

[42] Cf J Israel, *Radical Enlightenment: Philosophy and the Making of Modernity 1650–1750* (OUP Oxford 2002).

of what might be called clients (namely, William Cavendish and his royalist cohorts); Samuel Pufendorf, influenced also by Hobbes' work, did so with another vision, tied to other interests; so too with Immanuel Kant, so too with Emer de Vattel, etc.[43] Below, however, I will for the most part treat these disparate programs for those characteristics in common that allow them to be treated as a group, noting differences in the text or notes where appropriate.[44]

Against a changed and changing social environment, the common link between the new law of nature and the old natural law was the intent to understand the norms appropriate to human persons and peoples as a function of human nature. But a new methodology was employed, represented by the 'state of nature' thought experiment, giving rise to a distinct political vocabulary.[45] The state of nature, as is well known, posits the situation of humanity under imagined conditions of anarchy. Every member of humanity imagined to be in that situation is understood according to certain uniform attributes, including a primary interest in survival. The only means out of that situation is the social contract, the sum of so many individual, imagined acts of contract. Universal norms were no longer to be founded and understood in terms of the comprehensive collective, and a proper understanding of the body as a whole, but in terms of the individuals comprised by the collective body. Individualism, however, was not identical to diversity. The individual was the individual abstracted. The reflective and analogical method of the Salamanca School thinkers gave way to a deductive method and abstraction. The distinct pretension to universality of Enlightenment liberalism arose from the uniform representation of the individual as a common unit. Individuals were understood as equals, exhibiting a capacity for communication and an inherent self-interest, not necessarily in that order.

I begin with Hobbes. Though he is known as a proponent of or apologist for power and absolutism, and was dismissed for related reasons by Kant,[46] he nonetheless was engaged in founding the authority of the monarch in the imagined authority of the people[47]—and their imagined ability to alienate it. The monarch

---

[43] See eg I Hunter, *Rival Enlightenments: Civil and Metaphysical Philosophy in Early Modern Germany* (CUP Cambridge 2006).

[44] The work of the classical figures canvassed here has given rise to many, sometimes conflicting interpretations and schools of thought. I present here a plausible account, but one that can only be very partial and very condensed. Cf W Werner and G Gordon, 'Kant, Cosmopolitanism, and International Law' in this *Handbook*. For still other accounts, see J d'Aspremont, 'The Foundations of the International Legal Order' (2007) 18 *Finnish Yearbook of International Law* 219–56, at 225–6; R Tuck, 'Hobbes' Moral Philosophy' in T Sorrell (ed), *The Cambridge Companion to Hobbes* (CUP Cambridge 1996) 175–207, at 190–1.

[45] Cf A Pagden, 'Human Rights, Natural Rights, and Europe's Imperial Legacy' (2003) 31 *Political Theory* 171–99, at 180.

[46] I Kant, 'Perpetual Peace: A Philosophical Sketch' in *Kant: Political Writings* (H Reiss ed HB Nisbet trans) (2nd edn CUP Cambridge 1991 [1795]) 93–130.

[47] R Tuck, 'Hobbes and Democracy' in A Brett and J Tully (eds), *Rethinking the Foundations of Modern Political Thought* (CUP Cambridge 2006) 171–90.

was no longer the natural expression of authority for an organic or divinely constituted body politic; rather, the queen or king enjoyed sovereignty—however absolute—by virtue of the supposed will of the people.[48] Imagined acts of contract, effecting mutual acts of alienation, established public authority.[49] Public authority was no longer a natural outgrowth of an organic condition or phenomenon in the world, but an artificial construction, brought into the world by constructive acts of will.[50]

Though the metaphor of the body remains in Hobbes' work, in the figure of the Leviathan, it is a figurative rendering, a product of the many acts of will that it comprises.[51] If the Salamanca School represented an early move away from the corporeal instantiation of the body politic, Hobbes represented a still more definitive shift. While the Spanish School thinkers had diminished identification of the universal body with any one manifestation in the flesh, they still understood the unity of political community everywhere as an organic body. The body of the Leviathan, by contrast, is an artifice, constructed locally out of individual acts of agency.[52] Thereby, Hobbes marked a radical shift in the political terms underpinning the political community: from a unitary entity to so many acts, from the organic body to the negotiated contract.

Hobbes did not initiate the change in political conditions that the Leviathan represented, but he, together with others, consolidated rising sentiment—and channelled its expression going forward, fixing the terms by which change in political community would be understood at that point in time, and establishing the vocabulary by which public authority would be invoked thereafter.[53] Kant, among others, subscribed to roughly democratic change as expressed in the turn to contractual reasoning, though he disavowed Hobbes' absolute monarch, and was at odds with various other imagined products of the social contract.[54] In part, however, Kant's disagreement with Hobbes reflects the degree to which Hobbes captured the expression of political sentiment, insofar as Kant was obliged to communicate appreciably different sentiments according to common terms of reference.

For Kant, unlike for Hobbes, the product of the act of contract represented a necessary step in a world-historical process towards a greater cosmopolitan condition,

---

[48] T Hobbes, *Leviathan* (CB Macpherson ed) (Penguin Classics New York 1985 [1651]) at 223–8.

[49] Ibid 190ff.   [50] Ibid 223–39.

[51] Cf Q Skinner, 'The State' in T Ball, J Farr, and R Hanson (eds), *Political Innovation and Conceptual Change* (CUP Cambridge 1989) 90–131.

[52] Cf Q Skinner, 'The Sovereign State: A Genealogy' in H Kalmo and Q Skinner (eds), *Sovereignty in Fragments: The Past, Present and Future of a Contested Concept* (CUP Cambridge 1979) 26–46, at 34–8.

[53] Cf Q Skinner, 'The Ideological Context of Hobbes' Political Thought' (1966) 9 *Historical Journal* 286–317.

[54] For a salient statement of differences, see 'Miserable Comforters' (n 5). On Kant, cosmopolitanism, and international law more generally, see also W Werner and G Gordon, 'Kant, Cosmopolitanism, and International Law' in this *Handbook*.

a comprehensive Kingdom of Ends.[55] The instrumental logic that defines Hobbes' theory is crucial also to Kant's theory, but is not the whole of it.[56] Though the ordered political community under law must in the first instance be achieved by act of contract, the act of contract establishing the sovereign state was not merely a rational choice, the goal of so many acts of self-interest, but a moral obligation as well.[57] Further, the product of the act of contract was not merely ideational support for a particular community under a particular sovereign, but also knowledge of an outstanding moral obligation yet to be fulfilled, part of an ongoing project for humankind as a whole.[58] In some respects, however, the rational choice had to come first, and the moral knowledge would follow.[59] Conflict would drive people into pacific arrangements, which would lead to the realization of a moral imperative to perfect a just normative order.[60]

The interrelationship of functional and moral motives in Kant's work underscores the degree to which Enlightenment liberal theory was deployed to support new forms of political organization, on the basis of the peculiar adaptation of natural law into the law of nature. Consider a remarkable point in Kant's comparison of international and cosmopolitan right. International right is founded in the appreciation of the self-interest of states; cosmopolitan right is founded on an appreciation of the fundamental conditions of humanity. But international right promises world peace where cosmopolitan right cannot:

nature also unites nations which the concept of cosmopolitan right would not have protected from violence and war, and does so by means of their mutual self-interest. . . . Thus, states find themselves compelled to promote the noble cause of peace, though not exactly from motives of morality.[61]

The vocabulary of self-interest, joined to the rising democratic and bourgeois sensibility realized in terms of the contract, founded and gave definition to the possibility for progressive international politics, when morality was understood not to suffice. Just as the Salamanca School articulated a new political conception in an optimistic effort to capture new historical conditions for a political organization in the world, so too did Kant, together with Hobbes, 'sorry comforter' though the latter turned out to be.

Other sorry comforters included Pufendorf and Vattel, and they were formative in their transposition of Hobbes' contractual premises and method to international legal theory.[62] The elevation of contractual premises constrained the

---

[55] I Kant, 'Idea for a Universal History with a Cosmopolitan Purpose' in *Kant: Political Writings* (n 46) 41–53, at 47–9.

[56] Ibid 45–6.   [57] ibid 44–5.   [58] Ibid 51–3.   [59] Ibid 50–1.   [60] Ibid.

[61] 'Perpetual Peace' (n 46) 114.

[62] See generally 'The Figure of Man and the Territorialisation of Justice in "Enlightenment" Natural Law' (n 41). As Hunter demonstrates, Pufendorf and Vattel had separate agendas, but they were ultimately complementary in elevating the subjective individualism at the core of Hobbes' theory.

binding nature of norms in relations between states, insofar as the absence of a world sovereign indicated the failure to have moved beyond anarchic conditions of original right.[63] This consigned states to the state of nature and the law that inheres in that otherwise imagined state, a condition that admits no magistrate.[64] Absent a magistrate, the laws of nature were pronounced and interpreted by specialists in the esoteric science of morality comprehended according to the dominant rationality of contract.[65]

That science revealed a law of nature that bound sovereigns directly, but, absent the construction of a global leviathan, admitted no systemic possibility for disinterested enforcement, nor a unified basis by which to apprehend the communal good. The Salamanca School's pretension to objective grounds for the authority was boxed into so many subjective commitments. The lack of objective grounds for enforcement likewise entailed for Pufendorf the impossibility of positive international law, allowing instead more or less prudential commitments made among sovereigns in the interests of their respective commonwealths, and backed by the moral sanction of natural law.[66] In a similar but slightly less stark fashion, Vattel divided norms among necessary and voluntary law. The law of nature comprised the former, necessary law in all cases valid, but in a direct and personal way, realizable only subjectively.[67] The voluntary law, by contrast, represented those rules to which sovereigns voluntarily consented among one another. The effect of the work of Pufendorf and Vattel was to coronate subjective individualism in international relations.

Though their embrace of the law of nature came to define the international system of equal and independent sovereigns, such that they have become known for a retrograde character,[68] Pufendorf and Vattel also represented the new possibilities for political organization under the changing historical conditions of political relations at the time.[69] Their contribution may be understood again by contrast

---

[63] Kant simultaneously laments and affirms this in the same passage in which he refers to Hobbes, Pufendorf, and Vattel as sorry comforters, bitterly holding that '[t]he way in which states seek their rights can only be by war, since there is no external tribunal to put their claims to trial.... [and] peace can neither be inaugurated nor secured without a general agreement between the nations': 'Perpetual Peace' (n 46) 103–4.

[64] S Pufendorf, *Of the Law of Nature and Nations: Eight Books* (B Kennett trans) (S Aris London 1729 [1672]) bk V, ch 13, §2.

[65] Ibid bk I. See also 'Miserable Comforters' (n 5) 401; S Hall, 'The Persistent Spectre: Natural Law, International Order and the Limits of Legal Positivism' (2001) 12 *European Journal of International Law* 269–307, at 275.

[66] 'The Persistent Spectre' (n 65) 274.

[67] E de Vattel, *The Law of Nations, or, Principles of the Law of Nature, Applied to the Conduct and Affairs of Nations and Sovereigns* (GG and J Robinson London 1797 [1758]) Preliminaries, § 28.

[68] Cf JL Brierly, *The Law of Nations: An Introduction to the International Law of Peace* (OUP Oxford 1963) at 37.

[69] Cf G Cavaller, 'Vitoria, Grotius, Pufendorf, Wolff, and Vattel: Accomplices of European Colonialism and Exploitation or True Cosmopolitans?' (2008) 10 *Journal of the History of International Law* 181–209.

with the old political imagery of the body. Understanding persons and peoples as parts of a natural body entails understanding the natural delimitations on them that are conjoint with their distinct contributions to that body.[70] One part of the body is stronger than another, one suited for speaking, one suited for listening, etc. With different natural capacities comes different rights and responsibilities: *suum cuique*. By contrast, following the state of nature, the law of nature takes all individuals as equal. The new pretence to equality represented new possibilities for opportunity associated with a rising bourgeois class, the spread of popular and democratic sentiment, and the multiplication of wealth across parts of Europe generated by capitalism and colonialism.[71] Thus the celebratory image of the giant and the dwarf as free and equal, adopted by Vattel and others:

Since men are naturally equal, and a perfect equality prevails in their rights and obligations, as equally proceeding from nature—Nations composed of men, and considered as so many free persons living together in a state of nature, are naturally equal, and inherit from nature the same obligations and rights. Power or weakness does not in this respect produce any difference. A dwarf is as much a man as a giant; a small republic is no less a sovereign state than the most powerful kingdom.[72]

The effect was a sharp move away from conceptual innovations of the Salamanca School, though not necessarily in the direction of retreat. The Salamanca School had reconceived a universal body politic, its guiding consciousness rendered independent of any one, figurative head. The Enlightenment liberals now gave every sovereign a subjective power to channel a guiding consciousness as the empowered head of a self-made body.

2.3 The Contemporary Turn

The end of the nineteenth and the beginning of the twentieth century witnessed a return to the natural law doctrine articulated up through the work of Grotius. Though Grotius had never really fallen out of the mainstream, Vitoria and Suárez, together with others who had not enjoyed the same level of sustained interest, were reclaimed principally by Ernest Nys, Camilo Barcia Trelles, and James Brown Scott, and deployed, in the name of a new international solidarity, against the

---

[70] See eg 'De Potestate Civili' (n 16) lxxiii.

[71] Cf 'Hobbes and Democracy' (n 47) 171. This equality, it bears emphasizing, was largely limited to the states of Europe by virtue of the notorious 'standards of civilization'—the standard itself associated with conflated naturalist and natural law speculation—thereby facilitating subjugation of the non-European world. See B Bowden, 'The Colonial Origins of International Law: European Expansion and the Classical Standard of Civilization' (2005) 7 *Journal of the History of International Law* 1–24.

[72] *The Law of Nations* (n 67) Preliminaries, § 18, largely repeated at bk IV, ch 6, § 78.

reigning individualism and voluntarist positivism of the eighteenth into the nineteenth century.[73] The reclamation was coordinate with a sense of growing closeness and complexity in the interrelationship among states in the international system.[74] The turn back to the Salamanca School was made to address the 'new' conditions of international community, and solidarity was, in name, the adopted political ambition. Still, the return to the Spanish School was not greatly marked by meaningfully new doctrinal development.

The initiation of a new development in natural law doctrine arrives with a succeeding wave of twentieth-century scholars, such as Alfred Verdross and Hersch Lauterpacht. Both were students of Hans Kelsen, but, unlike Kelsen, were not content to critique the positivism of international law strictly from within his sophisticated positivist theory.[75] Each purported to connect an appreciation of positivism to some grounding in natural law, repairing a split between natural and positive law that widens following the work of Pufendorf and Vattel.[76] To a certain extent, this is unremarkable. As Stephen Hall and others point out, the Thomist natural law tradition of the Salamanca School, unlike the school of Enlightenment liberalism, affirms the integrated nature of positive and natural law.[77] But Verdross and Lauterpacht, among others, further began to merge the recovered natural law vocabulary with a sophisticated appreciation of then-dominant terms of positivism and liberalism, to articulate a new political conception for changing circumstances of international relations. They initiated a vocabulary in which the appreciation of agency and autonomous will, still joined to contractual language, could be merged

[73] See E Nys, *Les origines du droit international* (Alfred Castaigne Bruxelles and Thorin & Fils Paris 1894); C Barcia Trelles, 'Fernando Vazquez de Menchaca (1512–1569): L'école espagnole du Droit international du XVIe siècle' (1939) 67 *Recueil des Cours* 430–534; C Barcia Trelles, 'Francisco Suarez (1548–1617) (Les théologiens espagnols du XVIe siècle et l'école moderne du Droit international)' (1933) 43 *Recueil des Cours* 385–553; C Barcia Trelles, 'Francisco de Vitoria et l'École moderne du Droit international' (1927) 17 *Receuil des Cours* 109–342; *The Spanish Origin of International Law* (n 15).

[74] See eg A Snow, 'International Law and Political Science' (1913) 7 *American Journal of International Law* 315–28. That sense has lately been contextualized according to the legacy of competing colonial ambitions in the West. See eg M Koskenniemi, 'Colonization of the "Indies": The Origin of International Law?' in Y Gamarra (ed), *La idea de la América en el pensamiento ius internacionalista del siglo XXI* (Institución Fernando el Católico Zaragoza 2010) 43–63; cf A Pagden, 'The Genesis of "Governance" and Enlightenment Conceptions of the Cosmopolitan World Order' (1998) 50 *International Social Science Journal* 7–15. A non-exhaustive list of other relevant factors includes advancing industrialization and the advance of capitalism on other fronts, as well as ascendant forms of democratic governance, together with the rise of global revolutionary politics. Cf E Hobsbawm, *The Age of Empire: 1875–1914* (Weidenfeld and Nicholson London 1987).

[75] H Lauterpacht, 'Kelsen's Pure Science of Law (1933)' in E Lauterpacht (ed), *International Law, Being the Collected Papers of Hersch Lauterpacht* (CUP Cambridge 1975) vol 2, 404–30.

[76] Concerning the roots of that split, see 'The Figure of Man and the Territorialisation of Justice in "Enlightenment" Natural Law' (n 41) 296.

[77] 'The Persistent Spectre' (n 65) 269–73.

with an appreciation of an organic and unified whole, reminiscent of the old body politic, and representative of progressive ends. Lauterpacht wrote:

An initial hypothesis expressed in the terms of *voluntas civitatis maximae est servanda* would point, as the source of law, to the will of the international society expressing itself in contractual agreements between its constituent members, in their customs, and in the general principles of law which no civilized community can afford to ignore; it would refer to the *civitas maxima* as meaning that super-State of law which States, through the recognition of the binding force of international law *qua* law, have already recognized as existing over and above the national sovereignties.[78]

Iain Scobbie has written that a 'natural law thesis...is the thread which runs through and unifies Lauterpacht's work.'[79] Early in his career, Lauterpacht staked out 'the philosophical bases of international law' in 'the problem of relation of states to humanity'.[80] In his study of Grotius, Lauterpacht referred back to Vitoria and Suárez as laying the 'foundations of the jurisprudential treatment of the problem of the international community as a whole'.[81] In Grotius, however, Lauterpacht found 'a scientific basis—that of the law of nature and of the social nature of man—for the "volitional" law of nations'.[82] Though Lauterpacht operated by reference to Grotius, he was establishing a new position for natural law as a matter of international legal theory. The turn to science underscored that new position, which reflects both classical and Enlightenment natural law theory, but was not identical to either. That new position exhibited empirical rigor, founded in 'the social and political realities of the international community', to rival positivism;[83] it likewise sustained comprehensive political unity while simultaneously facilitating human autonomy. What Lauterpacht aimed to do, through Grotius, 'was to endow international law with unprecedented dignity and authority by making it part not only of a general system of jurisprudence but also of a universal moral code'.[84] To do so was to elevate international law and international community to the proper ends of the natural human condition.[85]

---

[78] H Lauterpacht, *The Function of Law in the International Community* (reissue OUP Oxford 2011 [1933]) at 429–30.

[79] I Scobbie, 'The Theorist as Judge: Hersch Lauterpacht's Concept of the International Judicial Function' (1997) 8 *European Journal of International Law* 264–98, at 266. Josef Kunz also observed the embrace of natural law elements in Lauterpacht's work: JL Kunz, 'Natural Law Thinking in the Modern Science of International Law' (1961) 55 *American Journal of International Law* 951–8, at 955.

[80] H Lauterpacht, 'Spinoza and International Law' (1927) 8 *British Year Book International Law* 89–107, at 91.

[81] H Lauterpacht, 'The Grotian Tradition in International Law' (1946) 23 *British Year Book of International Law* 1–53, at 17.

[82] Ibid 43.

[83] H Lauterpacht, 'The Absence of an International Legislature and the Compulsory Jurisdiction of International Tribunals' (1930) 11 *British Year Book of International Law* 134–57, at 151.

[84] 'The Grotian Tradition' (n 81) 51.   [85] Ibid 24.

Anthony Carty's exploration of Verdross' early, interwar work makes clear Verdross' desire 'to reactivate the cultural power of a sixteenth-century Spanish catholic intellectual tradition', a reaction against Enlightenment individualism, but not an outright rejection of its legacy in positive international law.[86] Carty describes the product as an organic theory of 'the integral association of the part to the Totality, which in turn divides itself into parts'.[87] In this complex relation of part and whole, autonomous actors recognize one another by virtue of 'a notion of potentiality, completed in community'.[88] Pursuing this idea throughout his career, Verdross dedicated a later article to 'Two Arguments for an Empirical Foundation of Natural-Law Norms'.[89] There, he made clear that a re-examination of natural law was critical to an ongoing project of 'laying the foundation to legal philosophy'.[90] He asked: 'how can social norms be ascertained from the Is of human nature'? His answer, in short, was that human nature exhibits a constant substance, but its proper expression will be a contingent one, the product of an independent will applied to uniform ends in historical context.[91] The product was a complex admixture of *telos*, autonomy, and historicity, by which Verdross envisioned a unitary community underlying international law, discerned in conjunction with the norms that arise naturally out of the interactions of individuals everywhere at any given point in time.[92]

Others pursued similar projects. Pieter Kooijmans, later judge of the International Court of Justice (ICJ), turned to what he called 'modern natural law' in his treatise on the doctrine of the legal equality of states, which he fashioned as an inquiry into the foundations of international law.[93] Kooijmans identified modern natural law with a number of contemporaneous scholars—most notably, perhaps, including JL Brierly and Raoul Padirac, as well as Verdross[94]—while noting that some of those included 'themselves denied that they uphold the doctrine of natural law'.[95] Nonetheless, Kooijmans identified a school of thought and distinguished it from both the Salamanca School and the Enlightenment naturalists. The new school of natural law, following Kooijmans, adhered to the Salamanca School pretension

---

[86] A Carty, 'Alfred Verdross and Othmar Spann: German Romantic Nationalism, National Socialism and International Law' (1995) 6 *European Journal of International Law* 78–97, at 94.

[87] Ibid 87.   [88] Ibid 88.

[89] A Verdross, 'Two Arguments for an Empirical Foundation of Natural-Law Norms: An Examination of Johannes Messner's and Victor Kraft's Approaches' (1975) 3 *Syracuse Journal of International Law and Commerce* 151–8, at 151.

[90] Ibid 158.   [91] Ibid 153.   [92] Ibid 155–6.

[93] P Kooijmans, *The Doctrine of the Legal Equality of States: An Inquiry into the Foundations of International Law* (AW Sythoff Leyden 1964) at 192–3.

[94] Others included Wilfried Schaumann, Ernst Sauer, Friedrich Buchholz, Josef Felder, and Friedrich von der Heydte: ibid at 215–38. For a still more comprehensive list of mid-century jurists arguably adopting aspects of natural law jurisprudence, see 'Natural Law Thinking in the Modern Science of International Law' (n 79) 951.

[95] *The Doctrine of the Legal Equality of States* (n 93) 215.

to an objective foundation for law in unitary community, as against the subject-ivity that followed from Enlightenment liberalism, but took the objective founda-tion to be knowable only as a matter of historically-contingent expression.[96] Thus Kooijmans eschewed 'an eternal, unvariable natural law' as 'a misconception of the historical development'.[97] Instead, an appreciation of human agency and change in material conditions over time led to 'a natural law with variable content'.[98]

Consider as well the work of another former judge of the ICJ, Alejandro Álvarez. Though Álvarez described himself as opposed to natural law,[99] his work shows all of the hallmarks of the modern natural law identified by Kooijmans: namely, a set of historically contingent norms arising naturally out of a condition of interdepend-ence, reflecting ineluctable global solidarity in contemporary world relations.[100] He did so, in part, as part of a consistent challenge to the individualist orthodoxy of vol-untarist positivism, which he sustained from (and against) the bench of the World Court itself.[101] In that light, Álvarez is reflective of what Arnulf Becker Lorca has made clear: that the story of the universalist project of international law, though joined to the hegemonic project, includes its exercise by international jurists situ-ated outside of Western centres of expansive powers.[102]

The various links, above, between agency, historicity, and ends represent one of the primary meeting points between naturalism and justice raised at the outset. Natural law doctrine serves as a proxy statement for a comprehensive political community, a natural unity manifest in historically contingent ways, ostensibly

---

[96] *The Doctrine of the Legal Equality of States* (n 93) 192–247.   [97] Ibid 215.

[98] Ibid. The phrase has also been attributed to Rudolf Stammler, an influential neo-Kantian jurist in Germany at the turn of the twentieth century: see R Stammler, *Die Lehre von dem Richtigen Rechte* (J Guttentag Berlin 1902).

[99] *International Status of South-West Africa* (Advisory Opinion) [1950] ICJ Rep 128, at 175 (Judge Álvarez, Dissenting Opinion), 479.

[100] See eg ibid 177.

[101] See G Gordon, 'Innate Cosmopolitan Dialectics at the ICJ: Changing Perceptions of International Community, the Role of the Court, and the Legacy of Judge Álvarez' (2014) 27 *Leiden Journal of International Law* 309–30.

[102] A Becker Lorca, 'Universal International Law: Nineteenth-Century Histories of Imposition and Appropriation' (2010) 51 *Harvard International Law Journal* 475–552, at 547. It must be noted, however, that Becker Lorca focuses on jurists adopting positivist doctrines of the nineteenth cen-tury. Moreover, Becker Lorca demonstrates that nineteenth-century non-European jurists on the whole tended towards positivist doctrine and away from natural law and naturalism. He offers the following explanation, at 489 (citations omitted):

the natural law remnants that carried on to the mid-nineteenth century were particularly detri-mental to the interests of non-European nations. . . . Non-European international lawyers there-fore welcomed positivism's break with the naturalist tradition, for positivism confined law to the rules emanating from sovereign will while displacing detrimental rules deduced from general naturalist principles. . . . For example, only the first attempts to assimilate international law at the beginning of the nineteenth century in China and Japan depended on drawing parallels between international law as natural law and Confucianism. As soon as professional international lawyers took over the legal aspects of the interaction with Western powers, latter generations of Chinese or Japanese intellectuals opted for positivism.

perceived according to the acts and experiences of individuals and collectives in the context of material, social, and cultural conditions at any given point in time. That convergence found its most elaborate—and perhaps still most controversial— exegesis in the work of the New Haven School, which at once hardened the pretension to a scientific vocabulary, while amplifying the apprehension of a natural and unitary social dimension underlying international law.[103] The New Haven School avowedly 'use[d] the expression "world community"...not in a metaphoric or wistfully aspirational sense but as a descriptive term' (noting as well, in that use, overlap with the International Encyclopedia of Social Sciences).[104] The foundation of international norms became a vast, ineluctable social phenomenon: 'international law is part of larger world social process that comprehends all the interpenetrating and inter-stimulating communities on the planet.'[105]

The picture that emerged was the unitary, natural law community of the Salamanca School, but raised to a level of wild complexity meant to convey the same scientific grounding to which Lauterpacht aspired. Consider the New Haven School appraisal of the Salamanca School: 'the early "natural" law approach, though sometimes cognisant of the larger community of humankind, more often adopted partial and unevaluated conceptions of that community and did not develop the notion of interpenetrating community processes embracing all peoples.'[106] All of the foregoing suggests a vocabulary by which a collective whole may be comprehended by reference to the diversity of its constituent parts, rather than their abstracted identity, with the image of the unitary whole arising out of the sum total of acts of agency bearing on interconnectedness in the world—but arising naturally out of those acts, not as a willed or artificial construction.

The twentieth-century development has continued to evolve. Process theories, such as transnational legal process,[107] and other theories adopting the insights of social constructivism,[108] exhibit aspects of the new natural law in their affirmation of norms arising naturally out of ineluctable conditions of interrelationship.[109]

---

[103] See also H Saberi, 'Yale's Policy Science and International Law: Between Legal Formalism and Policy Conceptualism' in this *Handbook*.

[104] M McDougal, WM Reisman, and A Willard, 'The World Community: A Planetary Social Process' (1987) 21 *UC Davis Law Review* 807–972, at 808–9.

[105] Ibid 808.   [106] Ibid 812.

[107] Cf H Koh, 'Why Do Nations Obey International Law?' (1997) 106 *Yale Law Journal* 2599–662.

[108] Cf A Wendt, *Social Theory of International Politics* (CUP Cambridge 1999).

[109] Though these theories carry forward the adaptation of natural law peculiar to international law in the twentieth century, they also cut against the most prominent reformulation of natural law in twentieth-century legal philosophy. That reformulation, a primarily Catholic, neo-Thomist account under the banner of so-called 'new natural law' by figures such as John Finnis and Germain Grisez, ties natural law to practical reasoning, with the express intent to avoid recourse to assertions of what *is* to determine what ought to be: see J Finnis, *Natural Law and Natural Rights* (Clarendon Press Oxford 1980); G Grisez, 'The First Principle of Practical Reason: A Commentary on the *Summa Theologiae*, 1–2, Question 94, Article 2' (1965) 10 *Natural Law Forum* 168–201. This line of thinking has, by comparison with its own successes in general fields of theoretical inquiry not specifically addressed to international law, found relatively limited purchase in international legal theory. But it

Norms are understood as functions of dynamic, intersubjective processes of agency and internalization in which subjects and norms are mutually-implicating and mutually-constituted. One contemporary school of thought bears noting for its express adoption and adaptation of a natural law vocabulary, namely the interactional theory of international law developed by Jutta Brunnée and Stephen Toope.[110] They incorporate the natural law theory of Lon Fuller—though minimizing it as 'weak natural law'[111]—applying it to international law as part of a legitimacy calculus. Fuller provided a test of 'internal morality', in the form of eight criteria, by which to measure law's legitimacy.[112] Brunnée and Toope join that set of universal criteria to an external test concerning a demonstration of 'shared purposes' across actors, which purposes will be 'strongly rooted in specific contexts'.[113] Thus the interactional theory of law proceeds in the mode of natural law thinking in international legal theory established in the twentieth century, affirming norms by observation of historically contingent purposes manifest in the interactions of interconnected actors in the world, provided those norms meet certain minimum universal standards incumbent upon the idea of law in community. I will return to still more contemporary developments later in the chapter following a brief encapsulation of the linear and dialectical stories discernible in the historical narrative thus far.

3 LINEAR AND DIALECTICAL DIMENSIONS

As Koskenniemi has lately demonstrated—in conjunction with similar work by Anghie, Miéville, and others—natural law theory is foundational to discontents of international law and the international system.[114] This historiographical narrative

has contributed to scholarship questioning the capacity of liberal or pluralist conceptions of international law to operate in a perfectly neutral register. See eg RP George, *In Defense of Natural Law* (Clarendon Press Oxford 1999) cf 'The Recovery of Natural Law' (n 7) 355.

[110] J Brunnée and S Toope, *Legitimacy and Legality in International Law: An Interactional Account* (OUP Oxford 2010).

[111] Ibid 29.   [112] Ibid 20–55.

[113] J Brunnée and S Toope, 'International Law and Constructivism: Elements of an Interactional Theory of International Law' (2001) 39 *Columbia Journal of Transnational Law* 19–74, at 71.

[114] 'Colonization of the "Indies"' (n 74); 'Empire and International Law' (n 6); *Imperialism, Sovereignty and the Making of International Law* (n 6); C Miéville, *Between Equal Rights: A Marxist Theory of International Law* (Brill Leiden 2005). See also 'The Colonial Origins of International Law' (n 71) 1; B Buchan, 'The Empire of Political Thought: Civilization, Savagery and Perceptions of Indigenous Government' (2005) 18(2) *History of the Human Sciences* 1–22; RA Williams Jr, *The American Indian in Western Legal Thought: The Discourses of Conquest* (OUP New York 1990).

is by and large a linear one, following a singular facet of natural law doctrine over time for its role in the development of the international system. The narrative demonstrates an identity between contemporary international law and the natural law innovations of Samuel Pufendorf,[115] and, working backwards, observes in the Salamanca School the roots of the liberalism that Pufendorf represents.[116] In this way, the deep roots of a hegemonic enterprise may be seen to extend back to early-modern natural law doctrine.

An extremely brief and partial canvass—much of it already alluded to, and all of it done by reference to other works, including other chapters in this volume—must suffice here, however inadequate, merely to sketch some of the discontents associated with that enterprise. In the first place, in each of the historical periods observed here, natural law served to support new possibilities for sovereign identity and political community arising in the West, which possibilities worked hand in glove with the colonial enterprise.[117] Natural law was fundamental to the notorious standards of civilization, which legitimized the violence of colonial expansion and the maintenance of colonial powers.[118] Major publicists like James Lorimer and John Westlake, among others, relied on conflated naturalist and natural law arguments as a prop and apology for colonialism and a system of European privileges under international law.[119] Anghie's chapter in this volume, reflecting his seminal work, makes clear the connection between international law, from the Salamanca School forward, with the subjugation and exploitation of vast regions of the world by Western powers.[120] The chapters by Özsu and Ruskola in this volume explore the imperial project sanctioned by international law in the areas of the so-called semi-periphery, including the Ottoman Empire and China.[121] Luis Eslava and Sundhya Pahuja, reflecting TWAIL (Third World Approaches to International Law) scholarship and advocacy, though not addressing natural law in particular, have explored the complex and coercive role played by universalist international law in global sites of disempowerment over time.[122] Once the historiographical treatment is allowed, once natural law is understood in a contiguous relationship with the development

---

[115] 'Miserable Comforters' (n 5).   [116] 'Empire and International Law' (n 6).

[117] 'Human Rights, Natural Rights, and Europe's Imperial Legacy' (n 45) 180.

[118] 'The Colonial Origins of International Law' (n 71) 1.

[119] See eg J Lorimer, *The Institutes of Law: A Treatise of the Principles of Jurisprudence as Determined by Nature* (2 vols W Blackwood and Sons Edinburgh 1880); J Westlake, 'The Principles of International Law' in *The Collected Papers of John Westlake on Public International Law* (L Oppenheim ed) (CUP Cambridge 1914) 78–85, at 78–82.

[120] A Anghie, 'Imperialism and International Legal Theory' in this *Handbook; Imperialism, Sovereignty and the Making of International Law* (n 6); A Anghie, 'The Evolution of International Law: Colonial and Postcolonial Realities' (2006) 27 *Third World Quarterly* 739–53.

[121] See U Özsu, 'The Ottoman Empire, the Origins of Extraterritoriality, and International Legal Theory' and T Ruskola, 'China in the Age of the World Picture' in this *Handbook*.

[122] L Eslava and S Pahuja, 'Between Resistance and Reform: TWAIL and the Universality of International Law' (2011) 3 *Trade, Law and Development* 103–30, at 105.

of international law as a whole through the centuries, then it is complicit also in those practices of disempowerment. That disempowerment has facilitated both extreme material inequality in the world today, and ongoing threats to indigenous identities.[123] Likewise, a variety of work grouped under the title of feminist theory explores, among other things, the manifold ways that a combination of naturalism and universalism in international law serves to disempower women in a variety of contexts, including the creation and perpetuation of unequal status across the world,[124] and the construction and maintenance of gender stereotypes with disparate but consistently damaging effects.[125] Finally, mainstream recognition of imperial projects pursued under international law by the US since the 2003 Iraq War have focused on various and blended appeals to rationalism, naturalism, and justice.[126] All of the foregoing studies have contributed to an evolving understanding of emergent patterns of global governance, the latest legacy of the linear presentation, tied to familiar, expansive powers.[127]

Crucial to this linear narrative of natural law underlying a hegemonic enterprise of international law is the development of twin privileges for commutative justice and private property.[128] The two together are productive of elements of Enlightenment theory applied to international law, including presumptions in favour of individualism and subjectivity in the international system, and a coordinate suppression of social justice. The logic of self-interest becomes a logic of rationality, giving rise to a functional vocabulary elevated as the sole vocabulary capable of communicating ends in the international environment.[129] In brief, roots of *dominium* in the Salamanca School develop into liberal individualism,[130] which serves to promote on universal terms a liberal theory of politics that underlies international law and world relations today.[131] The analysis dovetails with depictions of natural law as

---

[123] Cf 'The Empire of Political Thought' (n 114) 1.

[124] See eg H Charlesworth, C Chinkin, and S Wright, 'Feminist Approaches to International Law' (1991) 85 *American Journal of International Law* 613–45. See also D Otto, 'Feminist Approaches to International Law' in this *Handbook*.

[125] A Orford, 'Feminism, Imperialism and the Mission of International Law' (2002) 71 *Nordic Journal of International Law* 275–96.

[126] See eg 'International Law in Times of Hegemony' (n 8) 393; A Paulus, 'The War against Iraq and the Future of International Law: Hegemony or Pluralism?' (2004) 25 *Michigan Journal of International Law* 691–734.

[127] See eg A Anghie, 'Civilization and Commerce: The Concept of Governance in Historical Perspective' (2000) 45 *Villanova Law Review* 887–912, at 891; M Koskenniemi, 'The Fate of Public International Law: Between Technique and Politics' (2007) 70 *Modern Law Review* 1–30.

[128] 'Empire and International Law' (n 6); *Imperialism, Sovereignty and the Making of International Law* (n 6).

[129] 'Miserable Comforters' (n 5).

[130] 'Empire and International Law' (n 6); 'Colonization of the "Indies"' (n 74).

[131] The liberal theory of politics is a theory 'which identifies itself on two assumptions. *First*, it assumes that legal standards emerge from the legal subjects themselves.... *Second*, it assumes that once created, social order will become binding on these same individuals.': M Koskenniemi, *From Apology to Utopia: The Structure of International Legal Argument* (reissue CUP Cambridge 2006)

foundational of the Western colonial project, and, with it, the deep structure of modern international law.[132] International law thereby underwrites the power of individual persons over objects and other people, and consolidates that power in select offices by means of vocabularies of universality and instrumentalism.

The linear narrative describes the successful advance of a hegemonic enterprise in international law and relations, founded in and informed by natural law doctrine. Consequently, it describes natural law in a way that is static, revealing a consistent thread though different periods in the elevation of the individual, the affirmation of the subjective, a compromised moral vocabulary, and a compromised pretension to *telos*. Those factors conduce to a system of law that employs a functional vocabulary, by which particular ends are assimilated into a pretension to universality. Appreciating this historical continuity is crucial to appreciating the consequences of aspects of natural law doctrine operating in combination with a coordinate series of world-historical developments. Despite that continuity, however, natural law has not been one thing at all times. To define natural law as an undifferentiated whole identical with the compromised character of contemporary international law, and according to identical discontents in all periods, would be anachronistic and misleading. Rather, the linear narrative concerns the development of the empire of the liberal international system. The inquiry into natural law is subordinated to a demonstration of the roots of liberal ideology, and an examination of those aspects that have contributed in consistent fashion to an expansive phenomenon that has been developing at least since the early-modern roots of the international system. But it does not represent a comprehensive examination of natural law doctrine per se.

The dialectical story focuses on the aspects of change, and demonstrates how the doctrine has also served to open up new possibilities for political organization, including emancipatory change, in historical and political contexts. The different conceptions of Vitoria and Pufendorf, by this presentation, contribute to nodal points in the dialectic, and we are today at a point of synthesis, which is not identical with either, but reflects elements of both. As noted, each of the first two stages of natural law in international legal theory involved a different conception of the political. The first period fitted within a political theology reliant on analogy to the body,[133] though it reconfigured the appreciation of that body and its guiding consciousness. The second period still more radically reconceived the body politic in terms of contract. Friedrich Kratochwil has appraised the shift as

---

at 21 (emphasis in original). As presented throughout that work, and on the basis of these two fundamental assumptions, the liberal theory of politics simultaneously underwrites and obscures particular exercises of social and political control.

[132] *Imperialism, Sovereignty and the Making of International Law* (n 6).

[133] Cf E Kantorowicz, *The King's Two Bodies: A Study in Mediaeval Political Theology* (Princeton University Press Princeton 1957).

'one of the most far reaching conceptual revolutions'.[134] Each conception, body, and contract, foregrounded different interests and ambitions, opened up new possibilities, and raised new problems.[135] The third, current stage, commenced with the reaction against individualism and the positivist orthodoxy of the eighteenth and nineteenth centuries, turning to the Salamanca School for support, but disfavouring the immutable character of its pretension to universality. As noted, twentieth-century figures sought instead to accommodate classical natural law doctrine with a refined doctrine of legal positivism, a distinct pretension to empirical science, and a basic appreciation of liberal autonomy, as well as the fundamental authority accorded to sovereign states. In light of these diverse and not wholly complementary epistemic and ontological mandates, a natural body politic was held to be discernible on the basis of a comprehensive and accurate observation of social and political reality, more satisfying than the different epistemological foundations on which antiquated natural law doctrines and the formal system of interstate relations and international law purported to rest. That natural reality was understood in terms of the lived, historical reality of relations in the world.

In consequence, the return to a conception of a unified body politic, in keeping with classical natural law doctrine, has been carried forward in conjunction with twinned appeals to a social nature and historical context. The organization of an organic body politic, and the norms appropriate to it, are apprehended in terms of specific, historical acts and practices—the sum of particular exercises of universal (and universally-bounded) aptitudes or inclinations, in combination with changing material conditions. A basic unity underlying a contingent vocabulary emerges, one that is consistently expressive of an immanent condition of interconnectedness, which founds aspirations to a *telos* for the international system across changing manifestations in material contexts. To return for a moment to Kant, the contemporary position approximates his posture with respect to moral theory. To paraphrase: the basic unity—or the moral good—is not hard to appreciate, but its systemic expression will be complex.[136]

Also in keeping with a Kantian theme, the legacy of natural law today suggests a complex account of both autonomy and ends. That legacy can be discerned in diverse work, some of it relatively far from the familiar natural law vocabularies. Recent theoretical works in international law join visions of its future to appeals to some common, constitutive capacities for communication and choice,[137]

---

[134] F Kratochwil, 'Reflections on Theory and Practice' (2003) (European University Institute Working Paper, SPS No 2003/16) at 4.

[135] Ibid.

[136] See I Kant, *Fundamental Principles of the Metaphysics of Morals* (TK Abbott trans) (Prometheus Amherst 1987 [1785]) at 29–31, § 1.

[137] See eg N Onuf, 'The Constitution of International Society' (1994) 5 *European Journal of International Law* 1–19, at 4, 10–13, 18–19.

others to an appreciation of otherwise inchoate global or transnational publics, and emergent global or transnational public goods, reflecting a sense of an ineluctable political phenomenon, as well as some understanding of moral or material ends appropriate to it.[138] These current lines of thought—together with the myriad schools associated variously with social constructivism, process theory, and interactional theory, as touched on earlier—suggest new ways of conceptualizing political organization under changing historical circumstances, establishing new but naturally-occurring grounds for political organization, tied to an appreciation of human nature. Each aims to merge the unity of the Spanish School with the autonomy of the Enlightenment liberals, while each, properly conceived, aims to defy controlling forms of organization otherwise definitive of international and world relations. And each takes further the idea of an organic body politic arising naturally out of individual acts of agency globally.

Notably—if for understandable reasons—a figurative head is once again missing from the foregoing presentations of a renewed, organic body. Whereas the Salamanca School entertained the idea of a social consciousness, however, and Dante even posited the collective mind, the contemporary scholars treated here largely eschew such apparently mystical speculations. But for the same reasons, contemporary theorists must contend with the recent critique raised in the context of managerialism and expertise: the system of international law, so the critique goes, suffers from a failure of normativity, an absence of any guiding consciousness or conscience.[139] At the same time, it bears noting that this absence works together with the post-modern mandate: to cut off the head of the king.[140] In the light of these conflicting pressures, then, I turn at last to an example of recent developments, pointing to possibilities for further inquiry suggestive of ongoing changes in the dialectics of natural law within the international legal theory.

I turn for the purpose to the recent dialogue of sorts between Janne Nijman and Anthony Carty. They each expressly explore a new interpretation of natural law as a counter-hegemonic program. But in doing so, they also confront post-modern theory that has advanced alongside a critique of hegemony. Their confrontations with post-modern theory suggest a still-changing image of mind and body at work in the natural law dialectic. Post-modern theory, as noted, would decapitate the constructed body politic, thereby denying the modern pretension to channel a universal consciousness via the constructed heads of sovereign states represented by

---

[138] See eg N Krisch, 'The Decay of Consent: International Law in an Age of Global Public Goods' (2014) 108 *American Journal of International Law* 1–40. Thomas Franck's community of rules is also applicable here: TM Franck, *The Power of Legitimacy among Nations* (OUP Oxford 1990).

[139] 'The Fate of Public International Law' (n 127); D Kennedy, 'Challenging Expert Rule: The Politics of Global Governance' (2005) 27 *Sydney Law Review* 5–28.

[140] M Foucault, 'Truth and Power' in *Power/Knowledge: Selected Interviews and Other Writings, 1972–1977* (Harvester Press Brighton 1980) 109–33, at 121.

governments.[141] But there arguably remains, once the construction is beheaded, to provide for 'a philosophy that would enable man to re-establish a sense of wholeness by determining or finding "meaning"'.[142]

Rather than behead the king, Nijman and Carty explore a means to redeem the subject. They adopt aspects of post-modern critique, but reject some related conclusions.[143] To this end, they propose alternatives to a vocabulary still limited to terms propounded by Hobbes, making clear their projects fall within a distinct natural law idiom.[144] Nijman provides that her theory may 'be placed in a natural law tradition', though 'contrary to premodern and modern perspectives it does not conceive of natural law as a set of divine or universalistic dictates'.[145] Carty affirms that 'the inspiration of the *ius natural* is that we return to recognize the other as similar, as reflections of the self, images of the self to be found in others because we have a common origin'.[146]

Thus both have turned to natural law to redeem the subject from liberal subjectivity, as well as from the opposed and unsparing critical deconstruction of the subject. For Nijman, this means reconceiving legal personality in such a way as to ground a renewed system of international law oriented towards distributive justice and an affirmation of plurality.[147] For Carty, it means not only defying the imposition of a particularistic language on others, in the guise of universality,[148] but also an escape for international law from 'the prison house of language'[149] reflecting the synchronic nature of modern international legal structures.[150] That synchronic nature corresponds, not coincidentally, with the turn to commutative (as opposed to distributive) justice observed by Koskenniemi—commutative justice reflecting the privileging of an individualism in which the individual is constantly reduced to a counterweight, an abstraction without any personal integrity, a universalized unit existing outside of time and outside of history.[151] To redress this, a substantial appreciation of historical context is critical, but not one that lapses into sheer

---

[141] JE Nijman, 'Paul Ricoeur and International Law: Beyond "The End of the Subject". Towards a Reconceptualization of International Legal Personality' (2007) 20 *Leiden Journal of International Law* 25–64, at 36–7.

[142] Ibid 38.

[143] To borrow the helpful medical analogy used by Florian Hoffmann, they adopt the same diagnosis, but pursue a new remedy: FF Hoffmann, 'Gentle Civilizer Decayed? Moving (Beyond) International Law' (2009) 72 *Modern Law Review* 1016–34.

[144] A Carty, 'New Philosophical Foundations for International Law: From an Order of Fear to One of Respect' (2006) 19 *Cambridge Review of International Affairs* 311–30, at 312.

[145] 'Paul Ricoeur and International Law' (n 141) 33.

[146] 'New Philosophical Foundations' (n 144) 312.

[147] JE Nijman, *The Concept of International Legal Personality: An Inquiry into the History and Theory of International Law* (TMC Asser Press The Hague 2004).

[148] A Carty, 'International Legal Personality and the End of the Subject: Natural Law and Phenomenological Responses to New Approaches to International Law' (2005) 6 *Melbourne Journal of International Law* 534–52, at 545.

[149] Ibid 548.   [150] Cf D Kennedy, *International Legal Structures* (Nomos Baden-Baden 1987).

[151] 'International Legal Personality and the End of the Subject' (n 148) 547ff.

relativism.[152] For the purpose, Nijman and Carty each turn to a Hegelian natural law argument, founded in principles of alterity, and adapted by way of Paul Ricoeur's sense of history and hermeneutics.[153] In short, the 'historical-political community' arises out of a struggle for recognition, productive of an ethos of mutual recognition, as opposed to a struggle for survival, with its ethos of self-preservation.[154] This produces a body that figuratively appears capable of vision.[155] And this new body politic is proposed in opposition to the body always engaged in an internecine struggle for survival, which admitted only an ethos of self-preservation and self-interest.

Following the Hobbesian theory of knowledge, founded in contract, the individual is comprehended in terms of interests and alienation, which conduces to the paranoid condition of international relations and consequent perversions of international law.[156] Nijman and Carty, by contrast, explore the possibility of a theory of international law founded in a vocabulary of alterity, and a political community unified by a definitional association of self and other. Instead of an order that oscillates between fear and security,[157] established according to mutual acts of alienation, they contemplate an order that oscillates between strangeness and respect, established according to mutual acts of recognition. In oscillating between strangeness and respect, of course, there remains the possibility for great mischief. That is a facet of a dialectical presentation: a constant oscillation, each shift triggered by developments associated with the last.[158]

4   CONCLUSION

In closing, two points about why we keep returning to the natural law idiom in international law. First, both the hegemonic and the dialectical presentations

---

[152] 'International Legal Personality and the End of the Subject' (n 148) 536.

[153] 'Paul Ricoeur and International Law' (n 141) 33 and 63.

[154] Ibid 61–3; 'International Legal Personality and the End of the Subject' (n 148) 552.

[155] But Florian Hoffmann offers a tantalizing wrinkle on the vision of Carty's natural law, and Nijman's by extension. Relying on Arendt, he proposes to understand mutual recognition as occurring in a radically restricted temporal space: 'In this space between the us and the (O)ther, human agency is concentrated in the present.': 'Gentle Civilizer Decayed?' (n 143) 1033. The result is 'a revolutionary moment that unfolds in the short space after one and before another law, when humans are radically thrown back to their own communal responsibility and when they have to found authority, rather than rely on someone else's'.: at 1034.

[156] Cf P Allott, *Eunomia: A New Order for a New World* (OUP Oxford 1990) at xii.

[157] Cf B Buchan, 'Liberalism and Fear of Violence' (2001) 4(3) *Critical Review of International Social and Political Philosophy* 27–48.

[158] And in that light, I wish to emphasize that the purpose of this chapter, considering natural law over time, is not to defend any one definition of natural law.

suggest the possibility that international law has never entirely left the broad confines of the natural law paradigm. The diminution of natural law in practice had to do with the reconfiguration of natural law according to the premises of Enlightenment liberalism. That reconfiguration, which reduced the natural law to a platform for the subjective expression of will, served to open new space for political organization by means of the same theoretical construction that continues to define the liberal hegemonic project. Today, there are new configurations that have been developing for nearly a century, which exhibit aspects drawn from each of the prior two major periods; there also already exist possibilities for new inquiries which appear capable of going farther still. The new configurations are all bound up with the perceived entropy of old conceptions and constructions of political organization, and perceptions of a changed global political context.

Secondly, Koskenniemi has suggested that natural law is historically attractive in times of transformation or crisis, when 'basic aspects of the world are questioned'.[159] This would be true for any number of legal systems, where recourse to some ready-made but independent set of legal values offers an escape of sorts from intolerable legal relations under positive law or other regimes. But there is an especial appeal for international law. Natural law—not unlike voluntarist positive law, but differently—presupposes or reflects the community to which it applies and the order which it sustains. At the same time, the international community is a historically unstable construction.[160] Moreover, an international public realm comprehended as an area of competition among state interests, defined wholly in terms of diplomatic practices, has long seemed insufficient. Philip Allott refers to this condition as a pathological 'unsociety'.[161] And the unsociety of sovereign states has been under increasing pressure, socially and politically, since its apex in the nineteenth century, most recently as a function of so-called globalization, and the multiplication of transnational interactions of all sorts. There exists a perceived need for a more thorough and adequate expression under law of political and social interconnectedness in the world and across international boundaries. In this vein, the vocabulary of natural law suggests one means of giving voice to a basis for common, normative relations that go beyond the tenuous and highly mediated relations for which international law, for the most part, currently provides. On that note, however, it bears restating: natural law offers this potential only on the basis of pre-figured community—or, still more precisely, on the basis of pre-figured commonality and pre-determined community. Natural law opens up a new future by constraining it from the outset. For that reason, it cannot offer a full or satisfactory solution to the problems it addresses. Likewise, for that reason, natural

[159] 'Law, Teleology and International Relations' (n 8) 13.
[160] Cf R-J Dupuy, 'Communauté internationale et disparités de développement' (1979) 165 *Recueil des Cours* 9–231.
[161] *Eunomia* (n 156) 243–8.

law is rarely invoked any more with great enthusiasm; more often it is minimized, acknowledged but hardly celebrated. In short, what role it may have is limited. As has been seen, the constraints of natural law—to the extent that they are exploited in any given historical context—inevitably become part of the problem under the changing conditions upon which they work, prompting again and again a return to the dialectic.

Thus natural law retains its relevance for international legal theory today, as one framework by which to comprehend or imagine changing possibilities and norms for a political organization in an international and a world community. But it retains its relevance in both of the two senses charted here, dialectical and hegemonic. The former demonstrates the ongoing capacity of natural law doctrine to articulate alternative normative programs, including programs for changing forms of political organization. The latter helps to train a light on persistent hegemonic aspects of international law as they arise within the vocabulary of new normative programs going forward. In sum, natural law remains a carrier for ideas of new political possibility, even as it must confront the hegemonic character of international law as it has developed and may develop, in part, out of iterations of natural law possibilities.

CHAPTER 15

MARXIST APPROACHES TO INTERNATIONAL LAW

ROBERT KNOX

1 INTRODUCTION

ATTEMPTING to describe the definitive 'Marxist' approach to anything is difficult. The Marxist tradition is a fractious one, filled with splits, disagreements, and denunciations. Frequently the subject of these disagreements is whether the opposing side's position is even 'Marxist'. This fractiousness is due in no small part to the fact that Marxist theory is never simply theory, but instead is conceived of as a *guide to action*.

Whilst this is equally true of Marxist *legal* theory, there is another—seemingly countervailing—problem: the relative lack of attention that Marxists have paid to law. The writings of Marx and Engels have almost no *systematic* engagement with legal questions, instead making only scattered and fragmentary references. This is even truer of international law, which only crystallized in its 'modern' incarnation towards the end of their lives. Of course, Marxism is not simply the words of Marx and Engels, and writers in the Marxist tradition have theorized and analysed law. Yet compared to studies of political economy, aesthetics, or politics, Marxist studies of law have been relatively rare, and international law even more so.

Added to this is a final complication. More than any of the other positions surveyed in this *Handbook*, 'Marxist international legal theory' cannot be considered as a 'separate entity' from Marxist theoretical (and political) commitments *as a whole*. Whereas being a legal positivist does not necessarily commit one to any conscious, coherent, or systematic understanding of historical development, or of the relationship between the economy and society, the same cannot be said of Marxist theory. Marxist international legal theory cannot be understood simply as an 'internal position' to the international legal discipline. Rather, it is the disciplinary application of the wider project of Marxism.

As such, Marxist international legal theory can *only* be understood in relation to a number of other debates. Particularly important are Marxist debates about the relationship between the 'base' and 'superstructure', about the nature and function of the state, and theories of ideology and hegemony. These debates have primarily played out in Marxist 'domestic' legal theory. Equally, insofar as we are dealing with *international* law, it is vital to understand debates as to the dynamics of international capitalism, conducted under the rubric of 'imperialism'.

This chapter will attempt to chart a course through this complex terrain. It will begin by tracing the general contours of Marxist theory, and examine Marx and Engels' work. Following this, it will examine Marxist theories of imperialism and their understanding of international law. It will then look specifically at Marxist international legal theory, before concluding with some political reflections.

2 MARX AND ENGELS

2.1 Base, Superstructure, and Historical Materialism

As Susan Marks notes, '[t]o engage with Marxism is…to engage with the idea that history is to be understood in materialist terms'.[1] It is for this reason that the Marxist method is known as 'historical materialism'. Long and complicated debates surround the precise nature of historical materialism, but the usual starting point is Marx's *Preface to the Critique of Political Economy*. There, Marx argued that 'legal relations as well as forms of state are to be grasped neither from themselves nor from the…general development of the human mind'. Instead, they had 'their roots in the material conditions of life'.[2] These relations—in their totality—constitute '*what are called the social relations, society, and, specifically a society at a*

---

[1] S Marks, 'Introduction' in S Marks (ed), *International Law on the Left: Re-Examining Marxist Legacies* (CUP Cambridge 2008) 1–29, at 2.

[2] K Marx, 'Preface to a Contribution to the Critique of Political Economy' in RC Tucker (ed), *The Marx-Engels Reader* (2nd edn WW Norton and Company New York 1978) 3–6, at 4.

definite stage of historical development.[3] It was on the basis of these social relations that legal, political, and cultural relations arose:

In the social production of their life, men enter into definite relations that are indispensable and independent of their will . . . The sum total of these relations of production constitutes the economic structure of society, the real foundation, on which rises a legal and political superstructure and to which correspond definite forms of social consciousness.[4]

This particular description—which has come to be known as the base (or basis) and superstructure metaphor—has been controversial. Nonetheless, it establishes a basic position for Marxists, who have sought to understand law by seeing it as determined by social relations of production, and to situate it within the context of broader political-economic structures.

Marx and Engels argued that the nature of economic relations 'will naturally vary according to the character of the means of production'.[5] Different levels of the development of the productive forces would lead societies to arrive at 'a definite stage of historical development'.[6] Examples of these included ancient society, feudal society, and bourgeois society. Each of these societies had its own internal economic logic, conditioning how and why production and consumption took place, and the way in which it would reproduce itself. These distinctive logics also give rise to *specific configurations of the superstructure*. Vitally, this did not mean saying that the 'economic structure' would always be the visible, most important element in any society, but rather that the 'economic structure' explained why specific social forms (be they law, politics or religion) 'played the chief part' in particular modes of production.[7]

Marx and Engels did not simply consider economic structures to be static entities governed by 'laws'. Since these structures are *social* relations they are also relationships between groups of people, that is to say between *classes*. Societies following the end of primitive 'communism', have been marked by a division between those engaged in producing social wealth and those who are able to appropriate it. Thus (to simplify grossly): in ancient societies there were slaves and slave-owners; in feudal societies there were peasants, the nascent bourgeoisie, and feudal lords, and under capitalism there are workers and capitalists. In any given mode of production these classes exist in opposition. They constantly engage in low-level struggles and sometimes meet in open warfare over the nature of the mode of production. Hence, Marx and Engels' famous dictum that '[t]he history of all hitherto existing society is the history of class struggles'.[8] It is through the political, cultural, and *legal* superstructure that classes 'become conscious of this conflict and fight it out'.[9]

---

[3] Ibid (emphasis in original).   [4] Ibid 4.

[5] K Marx, 'Wage Labour and Capital' in *The Marx-Engels Reader* (n 2) 203–17, at 207.

[6] Ibid.

[7] K Marx, *Capital: A Critique of Political Economy* (Penguin Books New York 1990 [1867]) at 176.

[8] K Marx and F Engels, 'Manifesto of the Communist Party' in *The Marx-Engels Reader* (n 2) 469–500, at 473.

[9] 'Preface to a Contribution to the Critique of Political' (n 2) 5.

Consequently, there are two avenues through which the 'economic structure' impacts upon the law. On the one hand, the logic of a given mode of production will throw up distinctive social arrangements and social forms, of which law is one. On the other hand, the class struggle will be expressed through, and impact upon, the law.

2.2 The Legal Theory of Marx and Engels

In *The German Ideology* Marx and Engels argued that '[c]ivil law develops simultaneously with private property…out of the disintegration of the natural community'.[10] As modes of production based on communal ownership gave way to individual ownership, it was necessary to regulate such property relations between individuals—such regulation took the form of law. In ancient and feudal times, since private property had not extensively developed, neither did the law.

With the disintegration of the feudal order, through the rise of industry and trade, law was able to develop further. Marx and Engels argued that wherever there was trade 'the highly developed Roman civil law was immediately adopted'.[11] It was only following the revolutions of the bourgeoisie to overthrow the feudal nobility that 'the real development of law' could occur.[12] This development was—with the exception of England—achieved through a refinement of the Roman Civil Codex (to which even England had to turn eventually).

Marx and Engels, then, traced the 'real development in law' to the rise, extension and systematization of private property. However, they were also at pains to argue that property relations were not a result of law. For them, such a position was the result of the juridical illusion that private property was the result of individual will. *Contra* this, they argued that a 'thing' only becomes 'true property in intercourse, and independently of law'. This was because in actual fact ownership and the benefits thereof were rooted in social relationships, not just in abstract legal title. Hence whenever new forms of social intercourse arise the law is 'compelled to admit them among the modes of acquiring property'.[13]

In *The German Ideology* Marx and Engels addressed a relatively narrow set of legal issues, primarily property law. However, in an earlier piece—*On the Jewish Question*—Marx elaborated a similar analysis, but ascribed it a much wider legal significance. In this text, Marx sought to trace the rise of law and the 'rights of man' to the position of organizing principle of society. Drawing on Hegel, he understood 'modern' societies as divided between 'political community', where people act as communal beings, and 'civil society', where people act as private individuals.[14] This

---

[10] K Marx and F Engels, 'The German Ideology' in *The Marx-Engels Reader* (n 2) 146–200, at 188.
[11] Ibid.   [12] Ibid.   [13] Ibid.
[14] K Marx, 'On the Jewish Question' in *The Marx-Engels Reader* (n 2) 26–52, at 34.

was not always the case. Historically, 'civil society had a *directly political* character' because its various aspects—property, the family, and so on—were *political*, taking the forms of lordship, castes, and guilds.[15] Ownership, production, and appropriation were tied directly to political questions of status.

This changed with the rise of modern (capitalist) societies. In capitalist societies there is no longer a direct link between one's customary, status-based position and the appropriation of value; instead this is mediated through *the market*. In such a situation, the interpenetration between 'state' and 'society' is no longer tenable. As a result, the '*formation of the political state*, and the dissolution of civil society into independent *individuals*' were part and parcel of the same historical process.[16] This was where law entered the picture. When civil society had a directly political character, relationships between individuals were mediated through *privilege* and *status*, but once civil society was composed of independent individuals, their relations needed to instead be mediated through *law*.[17]

Consequently, the 'so-called *rights of man*, as distinct from the *rights of the citizen*, are simply the rights of a *member of civil society*, that is of egoistic man, of man separated from other men and from the community'.[18] Here 'liberty' is 'the right to do everything which does not harm others', the 'limits of which were determined by law'. This liberty was the liberty of 'man regarded as an isolated monad, withdrawn into himself'.[19] The 'practical application of the right of liberty'—which is embodied in the law, which itself regulates relationships across society—'is the right of private property'.[20] Moreover, since civil society was the mechanism through which the material basis of society was reproduced, the role of political society was simply to preserve civil society.[21]

Marx and Engels thus drew a structural link between the emergence of capitalism and the dominance of law and legal relations. However, as noted earlier, they also sought to understand the ways in which classes directly instrumentalized law. Marx's *Capital*—whilst sharing many of the insights above—is interesting in this respect, particularly in relation to the question of the working day. In Marx's account, labour-power is a unique commodity because it is able to produce new value. This is because capitalists only need pay workers sufficient money to reproduce their own existence. The difference between wages and the value that workers produce through their labour is known as *surplus value*. Capitalists constantly strive to increase their surplus value and can do so by increasing the length of the working day, or by forcing workers to be more 'productive'.

In Chapter Ten of *Capital*, Marx showed the vital role that law played in capitalist exploitation. Law is the *form* through which the employer and employee meet each other 'as free persons, as independent owners of commodities'.[22] In other words,

---

[15] 'On the Jewish Question' (n 2) 44 (emphasis in original).
[16] Ibid 45–6 (emphasis in original).   [17] Ibid.   [18] Ibid 42 (emphasis in original).
[19] Ibid.   [20] Ibid.   [21] Ibid 43.   [22] *Capital* (n 7) 519.

it is through the *contract* that the labour-capital relationship is constituted. More importantly, '[t]he establishment for a normal working day is the result of centuries of struggle between the capitalist and worker' and this struggle was conducted through legislation.[23] From the fourteenth century to the end of the seventeenth century 'capital tried to impose' a lengthened working day on a nascent working class 'by acts of state power'.[24] Yet from the 1800s, legislation became aimed at shortening the working day. For Marx, this legislation was only able to become effective after it had been 'wrung step by step in the course of a civil war lasting half a century'.[25]

This law became a site of class struggle, where 'the labourers' came together 'as a class, [to] compel the passing of a law, an all-powerful social barrier by which they can be prevented from selling themselves and their families into slavery and death'.[26] This struggle *drew the working class together* as a political subject, weakened the power of the bourgeoisie, and lessened the rate of exploitation. However, there were real limits to this struggle: the law did not end exploitation, but encouraged capitalists to increase the 'productivity' of their workers through mechanization and increased labour discipline.

Law and legislation also played a vital role in 'primitive accumulation'. By primitive accumulation, Marx referred to the process through which the preconditions for capitalism were posited. Here, a key process was the transformation of the feudal populations into proletarians. This could only be accomplished through the abolition of customary land use rights, meaning that people could only gain their subsistence through seeking *employment*. In England this was accomplished through a series of Acts of Parliament dubbed the Enclosure Acts.[27] Furthermore, when these nascent labourers had been turned off the land they were subject to legislation banning begging and vagabondage.[28] The aim of this legislation was to compel these former peasants 'into accepting the discipline necessary for the system of wage labour'.[29] For Marx, therefore, law was an important tool in the hands of the emerging bourgeoisie.

Since primitive accumulation did not just take place at home, but also 'abroad', this was the closest that Marx came to discussing *international* law. Marx noted that the dawn of capitalist production was marked by the 'discovery of gold and silver in America, the extirpation, enslavement and entombment in mines of the indigenous population of that continent, the beginnings of the conquest and plunder of India, and the conversion of Africa into a preserve for the commercial hunting of blackskins'.[30] Since 'the colonies provided a market for the budding manufactures' and 'the treasures captured outside Europe flowed back to the mother country' they enabled European capitalists to establish huge reserves of wealth.[31] Marx did

---

[23] *Capital* (n 7) 382.   [24] Ibid.   [25] Ibid 409.   [26] Ibid 416.   [27] Ibid 886.
[28] Ibid 897.   [29] Ibid 899.   [30] Ibid 915.   [31] Ibid 918.

not mention international law in this context, although he did note that the 'power of the state' was deployed.[32] Despite this, it is clear that these international processes were mediated through international law—for example, colonial expansion was enabled through the law of territorial acquisition and treaties played a central role in guaranteeing trade and navigation.

3 MARXIST THEORIES OF IMPERIALISM

If Marxism entails understanding law as embedded in a specific matrix of economic relations, then understanding international law requires understanding the particularities of the international economy. Marx and Engels had a contradictory understanding of this. On the one hand, they described a world economy characterized by violent, nation-state based conflict, uneven development, and the co-existence of different modes of production. On the other hand, they also held to a more 'diffusionist' account of capitalism, seeing it as spreading relatively evenly from Europe.[33] In such a vision, '[n]ational one-sidedness' had become 'more and more impossible'.[34]

Following Marx and Engels' deaths it became vital to resolve this tension. The deepening and spread of capitalism saw an intensification of colonialism and national rivalries. In order to intervene in this conjuncture, Marxists expanded upon the first aspect described earlier—emphasizing the uneven character of capitalist development and its violent and predatory nature. These questions of *imperialism* became central to the Marxist tradition.

'Classical' Marxist accounts of imperialism begin with Rudolf Hilferding. Hilferding argued that in the late 1800s Marx's predictions as to the concentration of capital had proved correct.[35] As firms went bankrupt and were bought up by others, capitalist industry became increasingly monopolistic. In order to guarantee their stability and profits, firms formed *cartels*, fusing industrial and financial capital together. This development turned capitalists against 'free trade', which would undermine their cartels and they pushed for tariffs. However, tariffs *limited* the potential size of the market and so restricted profits.

The solution to this problem was to first increase the size of the tariff territory through the acquisition of colonies, and second to export *capital*. The latter case

---

[32] *Capital* (n 7) 915.   [33] 'Manifesto of the Communist Party' (n 8) 476.   [34] Ibid 477.
[35] R Hilferding, *Finance Capital: A Study of the Latest Phase of Capitalist Development* (Routledge New York 1981)

no longer simply involved the sale of commodities abroad but rather involved establishing foreign business ventures and directly exploiting foreign labour. This required the large-scale development of and investment in factories, transport infrastructure, and so forth. In both of these instances it was the less-developed capitalist economies which provided the fullest scope for increased profits. This necessarily involved state-led interventions to subdue, develop, and transform these economies. Thus, monopoly capitalism domestically gave rise to the continuous global expansion of capital, which had to violently subdue and transform less-advanced economies; this was imperialism.

Although Hilferding laid the groundwork for a theory of imperialism, he was more concerned with analysing how finance capital operated *domestically*. It was Bukharin and Lenin who drew the strands of his argument together. Essentially, they followed Hilferding, but claimed that the developments he described had given rise to an *international division of labour*, representing a qualitatively distinct stage of capitalism, which was now 'a world system of colonial oppression and...financial strangulation of the overwhelming majority...by a handful of "advanced" countries'.[36]

They further argued that this system gave rise to intense *rivalry* between capitalist states.[37] Because of the exclusionary nature of the tariff system, capitalists *competed* against each other for 'economic territory'. Insofar as these capitalists dominated their respective states, 'economic' competition was also transformed into political and military competition. Thus, for Lenin and Bukharin, imperialism was marked by a struggle *between the advanced capitalist powers* 'for the division and redivision of the world'.[38]

These authors did not engage in many explicit reflections on international law. But given the close connection between international law and the events they analysed, some reflection was inevitable. They all suggested that international law was one of the mechanisms through which the struggle between imperial powers was conducted and through which colonial oppression was enacted. This was especially true in the case of treaties, which were seen as codifying particular balances of forces. Lenin, for instance, argued that the Treaty of Versailles was 'an unparalleled and predatory peace' and that '[t]hrough the Treaty' a situation had arisen 'wherein seven-tenths of the world's population are in a condition of servitude'.[39] He also thought that the international institutions of his time embedded and

---

[36] VI Lenin, *Imperialism, the Highest Stage of Capitalism: A Popular Outline* (Foreign Languages Press Peking 1970) at 5.

[37] NI Bukharin, *Imperialism and World Economy* (Merlin Press London 1972).

[38] Ibid 150.

[39] VI Lenin, 'Speech Delivered at a Conference of Chairmen of Uyezd Volost and Village Executive Committees of Moscow Gubernia October 15, 1920' in MS Levin (ed), *VI Lenin, Collected Works* (Progress Moscow 1966) vol 31, 318–33, at 326.

articulated the rivalries thrown up by imperialism. In particular, he characterized the League of Nations as a 'sheer fraud...an alliance of robbers, each trying
to snatch something from the others'.[40] This was in contrast to Karl Kautsky—one
of Lenin's main political opponents—who thought that the monopoly tendencies
of capitalism were *eliminating rivalries* between states. For Kautsky it was necessary to judge the League according to 'what could be made of it if the Socialists
of the world took the greatest interest in it'. He thought the League 'represent[ed]
the only rational method of putting an end to litigious international questions'.[41]

Lenin's account of the juridical nature of colonialism was in some respects
contradictory. On the one hand, he did not envisage that colonial domination had
to be directly juridical. Since, for him, imperialism was primarily about the logic
of 'economic annexation', the power of finance capital was 'such a decisive force in
all economic and in all international relations' that it subjected 'even states enjoying the fullest political independence'.[42] Consequently, imperialism was not just
composed of colonies but also 'diverse forms of dependent countries which, officially, are politically independent, but in fact, are enmeshed in the net of financial and diplomatic dependence'.[43] These were 'semicolonial' states. However, at
the same time, he clearly thought that the direct juridical relationship between
colonial power and colony was the primary form of imperialism. He argued that
political annexation 'often makes economic annexation easier, cheaper...more
convenient, less troublesome'[44] and stated that the 'semicolonial' states were 'transitional forms'.[45] History has not borne this out and later Marxists have argued that
these forms were in fact *generalized* as 'neo-colonialism'.[46]

Lenin's broader reflections on the role of international law tend to be closer to
the idea that imperialism need not be expressed legally. He argued that '[l]aws
are political measures' which could not 'prohibit economic phenomena'.[47] In
his analysis, the fundamental driving force of imperialism was its economic
logic, which could manifest itself in many different forms, only some of which
were 'legal'. For Lenin, the '*forms* of the struggle' between imperialists 'constantly change in accordance with varying...causes, but the *substance* of the
struggle, its class *content*, positively *cannot* change'.[48] This had important political consequences, since it followed that 'without the revolutionary overthrow
of capitalism, no international arbitration courts, no talk about a reduction of

---

[40] 'Speech Delivered at a Conference of Chairmen of Uyezd Volost and Village Executive
Committees of Moscow Gubernia October 15, 1920' (n 39) 323.

[41] K Kautsky, 'The League of Nations', *Justice* (10 April 1923) 3.

[42] *Imperialism, the Highest Stage of Capitalism* (n 36) 97.   [43] Ibid 101.

[44] VI Lenin, 'A Caricature of Marxism and Imperialist Economism' in *VI Lenin, Collected Works*
(n 39) vol 23, 28–76, at 44.

[45] *Imperialism, the Highest Stage of Capitalism* (n 36) 96.

[46] K Nkrumah, *Neo-Colonialism: The Last Stage of Imperialism* (Panaf London 1971).

[47] 'A Caricature of Marxism and Imperialist Economism' (n 44) 488.

[48] *Imperialism, the Highest Stage of Capitalism* (n 36) 89 (emphasis in original).

armaments, no "democratic" reorganisation of the League of Nations will save mankind from new imperialist wars'.[49]

Although other Marxist theorists of imperialism have different analyses of the precise forces driving imperialism, they tend to share this relatively problematic account of international law. Whilst admirably tracing the way in which law articulated imperialist social relations, the connections established between the two were contingent and conjunctural, without any deeper materialist theory *of* international law. In such a vision, international law figures as something of a passive 'vessel' which sometimes expresses the 'real life' of the international economy, and sometimes is simply ignored or overridden. Although this advanced beyond Marx and Engels' accounts of the world economy, it was also a theoretical step back: as it cannot explain the specificity of *legal* logic and what role this logic plays in capitalist social relations. The criticism of this type of position was the starting point for Evgeny Pashukanis' commodity-form theory.

4 MARXIST INTERNATIONAL LEGAL THEORY

4.1 The Commodity-form Theory

Evgeny Pashukanis is perhaps the most important Marxist legal theorist. Most of the 'revivals' in Marxist legal theory have been centred around the 'rediscovery' of his thought, and he remains a key reference point. Pashukanis was a Bolshevik jurist who came to prominence following the Russian Revolution. He was the main Soviet legal theorist in the 1920s and 1930s, establishing a loyal school and dominating the Soviet legal academy. Although not a Trotskyist, his work increasingly fell out of favour with the Stalin regime and he was executed in 1937.[50]

For Pashukanis, any account of law had to look at what differentiated it from other social forms. Such differentiation could not lie in law's 'function' in regulating social life, since we know that 'collective life exists even among animals', yet 'it never occurs to us to affirm that the relationship of bees or ants is regulated by law'.[51] Instead, the correct starting point was to note that 'under certain conditions the *regulation* of social relationships *assumes a legal character*'[52]—the task was to

---

[49] VI Lenin, 'Conditions of Admission into the Communist International' in *VI Lenin, Collected Works* (n 39) vol 31, 206–11, at 208.

[50] JN Hazard, 'Pashukanis is No Traitor' (1957) 51 *American Journal of International Law* 385–8.

[51] EB Pashukanis, 'The General Theory of Law and Marxism' in P Beirne and R Sharlet (eds), *Pashukanis: Selected Writings on Marxism and Law* (Academic Press London 1980) 37–131, at 58.

[52] Ibid (emphasis in original).

analyse what this 'character' (or form) was and what conditions gave rise to it. As such, accounts which merely sought to 'introduce the element of class struggles'[53] into a positivistic theory of law, simply gave 'a history of economic forms with a more or less weak legal colouring'.[54] This—one might argue—is an apt description of how Marxist theorists of imperialism understood international law.

Following Marx's *On the Jewish Question* (and his scattered musings in *Capital*), Pashukanis argued that the conditions that give rise to the legal form are those of commodity exchange. In order for commodities to be exchanged, their 'guardians must...recognize each other as owners of private property'; this 'juridical relation, whose form is the contract...mirrors the economic relation'.[55] Accordingly, each commodity owner must recognize the other as an equal, in an abstract, formal sense. But since within any exchange there is the possibility of dispute, there needs to be a way to regulate these disputes, and it is here that law arises. For Pashukanis, the legal form is that which regulates disputes between formally equal, abstract individuals.

Since commodity exchange predates capitalism, so too did law;[56] however, it existed in specific *pockets* of social life, intertwined with custom, status, religion, and privilege.[57] As capitalism came to dominate, so too did commodity exchange, and therefore law. However, it was not simply that there was more exchange, and therefore more law. In the logic of *capitalism* (as opposed to exchange generally) 'separate and random acts of exchange turn into a broad systematic circulation of commodities'.[58] In this situation, value ceases to be embodied in specific exchanges and becomes *an abstract category*, since everything must be exchangeable. A similar transformation occurs with law, with the rise of an abstract, universal legal subject.[59]

In his account of international law, Pashukanis combined this commodity-form theory with Lenin's account of imperialism. Pashukanis argued that international law was in fact the *oldest* form of law, since one could trace rudimentary international legal institutions 'to the most ancient periods of class and even pre-class society'.[60] This was because commodity exchange initially took place not between individuals but amongst communities.[61] However, as with domestic law, it was only with capitalism that international law came to full-flower. Firstly, capitalism witnessed the extension and blossoming of commodity exchange internationally. Secondly, the independent sovereign state, generally seen as the central subject of international law, was itself a product of the development of capitalism. This began

---

[53] 'The General Theory of Law and Marxism' (n 51) 41.   [54] Ibid 42.   [55] *Capital* (n 7) 178.
[56] 'The General Theory of Law and Marxism' (n 51) 79.   [57] Ibid 80-1.   [58] Ibid 77.
[59] Ibid 77-8.
[60] EB Pashukanis, 'International Law' in *Pashukanis: Selected Writings on Marxism and Law* (n 51) 168-83, at 175.
[61] Ibid.

with the formation of absolute monarchies, whose economic basis was 'the development of mercantile capital'[62] but it was only with the bourgeois revolutions that this process was fully completed. These developments separated 'state rule from private rule, and transformed political power into a special force and the state into a special subject', a subject 'not to be confused with those persons who…were the bearers of state authority'.[63]

Since these states are *class states* enmeshed in a system of imperialism, their class basis is expressed through international law. Thus, picking up on Lenin's theory of imperialism, Pashukanis argued that rather than a neutral body of global rules, international law is '*the legal form of the struggle of the capitalist states among themselves for domination over the rest of the world*'.[64] Like Lenin, Pashukanis studied the role of particular treaties in structuring and articulating imperialist domination, arguing that a 'treaty obligation is nothing other than a special form of the concretization of economic and political relationships'.[65] Similarly, Pashukanis was attentive to the way in which international law structured the relationship between the advanced capitalist countries and the colonial world. He argued that the 'division of states into civilized and "semi-civilized"'[66] was rooted in the exploitative logic of imperialism, and that international law was 'the totality of forms which the capitalist, bourgeois states apply in their relations with each other, while the remainder of the world is considered as a simple object of their completed transactions'.[67] Finally, he drew attention to the fact that directly juridified colonial domination was not the only mechanism of international capitalist exploitation. Just as 'private law assumes all subjects are formally equal yet simultaneously permits real inequality in property' so too did international law recognize that 'states have equal rights yet in reality they are unequal in their significance and their power'.[68] This is even more the case given the absence of a centralized international state.

This latter proposition is the central starting point of China Miéville's 2005 attempt to apply systematically Pashukanis' insights to the study of international law—*Between Equal Rights*. This book has been at the centre of the contemporary revival in Marxist international legal theory, and—like Pashukanis—has become an obligatory reference point. Miéville argues that a full application of Pashukanis' commodity-form theory is able to illuminate some of the central problems of the international legal discipline. In particular, Pashukanis is able to answer the age-old question of whether international law is 'really' law.

One of the criticisms most frequently levelled at international law is that it cannot really be law because there is no overarching sovereign to enforce it. By insisting that law was to be understood as a relationship between abstract, formally equal subjects, Pashukanis displaced this focus. However, one might still ask, absent

---

[62] 'International Law' (n 60) 173.   [63] Ibid 174.   [64] Ibid 169 (emphasis in original).
[65] Ibid 181.   [66] Ibid 172.   [67] Ibid.   [68] Ibid 178.

some notion of enforcement, can we really talk about law? It is here that Miéville attempts to go beyond Pashukanis. Miéville argues that Pashukanis failed to properly account for the violence at the heart of the commodity-form. Pashukanis—in what Miéville dubs a 'characteristic slip'[69]—argued that '[c]oercion...contradicts the fundamental precondition for dealings between the owners of commodities'.[70] For Miéville, this cannot be true. In order for a commodity 'to be meaningfully mine-not-yours...some forceful capabilities are implied', absent this, it could be taken from me, and there would be no act of exchange.[71] This connection between violence and exchange carries over into the *legal form*, as the violence of allowing something to 'remain mine-not-yours' is also the vindication of legal rights.

It is this argument, for Miéville, that fundamentally cements international law's 'law-ness'. Because coercion is *inherent* in the commodity form—that is, it can operate as between the parties themselves—there is no need for a superordinate overarching 'sovereign' to be present. Rather, 'without superordinate authorities ...the coercive violence of the legal subjects themselves...regulates the legal relation'.[72] Indeed, as Pashukanis himself pointed out, even domestically 'a major portion of civil law relationships' are carried out without any state intervention.[73]

The question of violence is also intrinsically linked to the question of law's content. Miéville follows Martti Koskenniemi in arguing that international law is *indeterminate*. Famously, Koskenniemi holds that the international legal order is structured by a fundamental tension. On the one hand, it is composed of independent, sovereign states which can only be voluntarily bound. This creates principles which take 'state will' as their starting point. On the other hand, this cannot not be a source of *obligation* for states, since international law needs to *bind* states, even when they do not desire to be bound. For Koskenniemi this tension is a symptom of the broader structure of the international legal order itself: one can always proceed from state interest (apology) or world order (utopia). The attendant arguments are both equally legitimate, and mutually opposed, meaning international law can never provide an 'answer' on its own terms.

Miéville accepts this account, although he argues it is idealist, since it locates this contradiction in liberal thought, rather than capitalist social relations.[74] More importantly, Miéville asks how it is, given indeterminacy, that arguments are nonetheless *resolved*. Miéville turns to Marx, who argued—in the context of the Factory Acts—that 'between equal rights, force decides'; that is to say that insofar as there are two equally compelling legal arguments, it will be *force* which chooses between them.[75] Domestically, this is done by the state. However, in the international legal arena '[t]here is no state to act as final arbiter of competing claims' and accordingly

---

[69] C Miéville, *Between Equal Rights: A Marxist Theory of International Law* (Brill Leiden 2005) at 126.

[70] Ibid 143.   [71] Ibid 126.   [72] Ibid 133.   [73] 'International Law' (n 60) 180.

[74] *Between Equal Rights* (n 69) 54.   [75] *Capital* (n 7) 344.

'[t]he means of violence remains in the hands of the very parties disagreeing over the interpretation of law'.[76]

The form that this violence takes is conditioned by the social relations in which it is articulated. Internationally this is *imperialism*, the vision of which Miéville—like Pashukanis—takes from Lenin and Bukharin. Miéville takes this to its logical extreme, arguing that since '[t]he necessity of this unequal violence derives precisely *from*...juridical equality', it follows that 'in its universalised form, predicated on juridical equality...*international law assumes imperialism*'.[77]

As such, there is a *structural* connection between international law and imperialism—firstly, insofar as the international legal form is bound up with the spread of international capitalism, and secondly, because only the violence of imperialism can effectively resolve legal arguments. Thus, whilst relying on classical Marxist theories of imperialism, the commodity-form theory goes beyond their account of international law. International law and imperialism are not simply coincident, but fundamentally connected. However, Miéville goes further than this. He argues that with the full flowering of capitalism internationally, international law becomes *universal*, permeating 'every international incident and the very fabric of the international system'.[78] Thus, rather than simply being structurally connected, international law actually comes to *structure* and constitute the world.[79]

4.2 Ideology Critique

Ideology is one of the tools that Marxists have deployed most frequently to understand law. As previously noted, Marx and Engels' first elaborations of law were in *The German Ideology* and Marx characterized law as an 'ideological form'.[80] Ideology was particularly important during the 'revival' of Marxist legal theory in the 1970s. As Cain and Hunt note, this was part of a wider revival of Marxism—triggered by the translation of Louis Althusser and Antonio Gramsci—which was concerned 'to escape from the conceptual grip of inevitable historical processes, to reassert the analytic independence of structures from their bearers and...to insist on the ability of people to change these structures'.[81]

Of course, in these debates 'ideology' took on a very specific meaning. In its older conceptions, ideology has historically been understood as 'false consciousness'. In this vision, '[i]deology is a process accomplished by the so-called thinker consciously...but with a false consciousness. The real motive forces impelling him

---

[76] *Capital* (n 7) 292.   [77] Ibid 293 (emphasis in original).   [78] Ibid 282.
[79] Ibid 283.   [80] 'Preface to a Contribution to the Critique of Political Economy' (n 2) 5.
[81] ME Cain and A Hunt, *Marx and Engels on Law* (Academic Press London 1979) at ix.

remain unknown to him.'[82] Here, law essentially serves as a 'smokescreen' to cover up the 'real' processes at work in the world—in particular, class and the class struggle. Althusser and Gramsci were seen to move beyond this.[83]

These debates did not have a huge impact upon the international legal field. Here the most important theories of ideology have been those of ideology *critique* drawn from the Frankfurt School, exemplified in the work of Susan Marks. Drawing on John Thompson, Marks defines ideology as how '*meaning serves to establish and sustain relations of domination*'.[84] This conception of ideology is a *critical* one, insofar as 'ideology' is not taken as a neutral description of 'beliefs' or 'worldviews'.[85] It is also not an 'epistemological' position concerned with failures to 'comprehend' reality.

There are manifold ways in which meaning might serve to establish and sustain relations of domination. However, Marks argues that there are a number of key ideological manoeuvres, each with its own 'discursive strategies'. The key moves are 'legitimation', which is 'the process by which authority comes to seem valid and appropriate';[86] 'dissimulation' whereby 'relations of domination are obscured, masked or denied';[87] 'unification' through which social relations are made to seem harmonious and coherent;[88] 'reification' which makes social relations seem as if they are not the product of human relations and therefore appear eternal;[89] and 'naturalization' which makes 'existing social arrangements come to seem obvious and self-evident.'[90] Crucially for Marks, these positions are not caused by ignorance. Although illusion may be involved in any of them, 'it is not a simple case of error or ignorance of social reality'.[91] Instead, whilst we may be aware of exploitation and inequality in the world, we act *as if* we are not. Illusion comes in with the failure to realize the impact of acting in such a way.[92]

As a form of ideology, international law performs all of these manoeuvres. For example, in *The Riddle of All Constitutions* Marks argues that the uneven development of global capitalism has thrown up a system of 'low intensity democracy'. Low intensity democracy 'meets the immediate needs of anti-authoritarian crisis, easing tensions, and restoring order' but 'does so in a manner that forestalls far-reaching structural change.'[93] Marks argues that international law helps stabilize this. Here, international law essentially sets up the criteria through which democracy can be monitored by international organizations, focusing heavily around the idea of elections. In so doing international law engages in naturalization, by

---

[82] F Engels, '[Letter on Historical Materialism] To Franz Mehring' in *The Marx-Engels Reader* (n 2) 765–7, at 766.

[83] A Hunt, 'The Ideology of Law: Advances and Problems in Recent Applications of the Concept of Ideology to the Analysis of Law' (1985) 19 *Law & Society Review* 11–37.

[84] S Marks, *The Riddle of All Constitutions: International Law, Democracy, and the Critique of Ideology* (OUP Oxford 2003) at 10 (emphasis in original).

[85] Ibid 11.   [86] Ibid 19.   [87] Ibid 20.   [88] Ibid.   [89] Ibid 21.
[90] Ibid 22.   [91] Ibid 23.   [92] Ibid.   [93] Ibid 57.

proclaiming low-intensity democracy as the only form of democracy; unification, because it detaches political rights from broader issues and reification because democracy is de-historicized.[94] International law, then, lends a veneer of democratic legitimacy to the intensification of capitalist exploitation.

One can find similar accounts throughout the contemporary Marxist international legal corpus. Tor Krever, for example, has argued that international criminal law abstracts individuals' actions from broader social relations.[95] As such, horrific actions are no longer seen as part of a global system of violence but instead the actions of a few 'rotten apples' with emphasis placed on '*abnormality* of conjunctural violence, rather than with the *normality* of the forces…that lurk beneath'.[96]

Despite the numerous *possible* variations of international legal ideology it is this abstraction that is perhaps the most common manoeuvre. Marks herself has recognized this in her later work. In 'Human Rights and Root Causes', she argues that human rights law tends to eschew broader enquiries into *systemic* causation. Whilst there is a focus on some of the conditions that 'engender and sustain' the problems of the world, very little attention is given to 'the larger framework within which those conditions are systematically reproduced'.[97] This means that the 'practical' focus on human rights is profoundly *depoliticizing*. Thus, one of international law's key roles is the creation of 'false contingency'[98] which draws our attention away from the systemic problems of capitalism.

4.3 International Law and the Third World

Historically, one of the most important sites for the reception of Marxist theories of imperialism was the 'Third World'. Many Third Worldist jurists and activists articulated accounts of international law heavily influenced by Marxism. Mohammed Bedjaoui, for example, argued that international law had 'permitted colonization, the exploitation of man by man, and racial discrimination' and 'facilitated and legalized the enrichment of the affluent countries'.[99] This was because classical international law was 'derived from the laws of the capitalist economy and the liberal political system'.[100] Contemporary international law continued to enable neo-colonial exploitation.[101]

---

[94] *Riddle of All Constitutions* (n 84) 63–7.

[95] T Krever, 'International Criminal Law: An Ideology Critique' (2013) 26 *Leiden Journal of International Law* 701–23, at 720.

[96] Ibid 722.

[97] S Marks, 'Human Rights and Root Causes' (2011) 74 *Modern Law* Review 57–78, at 71.

[98] S Marks, 'False Contingency' (2009) 62 *Current Legal Problems* 1–21.

[99] M Bedjaoui, *Towards A New International Economic Order* (Holmes & Meier New York 1979) at 63.

[100] Ibid 49.   [101] Ibid 37.

For Bedjaoui, the problem was not that law *created* 'unequal relationships'[102] but rather that there was a 'dichotomy between law and reality',[103] where formal legal equality covered up real inequality through a 'laissez-faire and easy-going attitude which...led...to legal non-intervention, which favoured the seizure of the wealth and possessions of weaker peoples'.[104] This was a result of his broader understanding of law as 'a "moment" in the evolution of social and economic acts, stabilizing...the balance achieved between them'.[105] Accordingly, there was no *necessary* relationship between law and imperialism. Although law was conservative, 'if reality changes so as to become more egalitarian, the law inevitably...takes the new material data into account'.[106]

Bedjaoui's approach of rooting legal argument in the changing relationships of imperialism is reflected in contemporary Marxist scholarship. Perhaps the most prominent exponent of this approach is BS Chimni, who argues that 'the juridical is simultaneously the sociological'.[107] According to Chimni, the intimate interconnection between the 'domestic' and 'international' under capitalism means that international relations flow from the *internal organization* of states.[108] Since every state in the global order sits atop a mode of production, '[t]he foreign policy of a state is integrally linked to its domestic policy'.[109]

However, the capitalist mode of production is always global, and so the international economy is not just an agglomeration of national economies. Rather, capitalism produces a world market which 'functions on the basis of an international division of labour', which defines the relationship between domestic economies and the world economy.[110] Consequently, Chimni argues that 'international law and institutions [are] a device which serves sectional global interests'.[111] The dominant classes within the international division of labour seek to realize their interests *through* international law.[112] Therefore, 'any change in the international division of labour' will be reflected in international law.[113]

For Chimni, there have been five 'epochs' of imperialism, each of which fundamentally shaped international law. The first was from 1600–1760, the period of 'old colonialism'. This was characterized by primitive accumulation and mercantilist

---

[102] *Towards a New International Economic Order* (n 99) 112.   [103] Ibid 63.   [104] Ibid 49.

[105] Ibid 106.   [106] Ibid 112.

[107] BS Chimni, *International Law and World Order: A Critique of Contemporary Approaches* (Sage New York 1993) at 218.

[108] BS Chimni, 'Marxism and International Law: A Contemporary Analysis' (1999) *Economic and Political Weekly* 337–49, at 337.

[109] Ibid.   [110] *International Law and World Order* (n 107) 221.

[111] 'Marxism and International Law' (n 108) 338.

[112] Of course, the process is complicated, with class interest not being *directly* translated into international law, because foreign policy is a 'compound expression of several factors: dominant class interests, the compromise with other social classes, national security concerns, cultural anxieties, resistance movements [and so forth]': BS Chimni, 'Prolegomena to a Class Approach to International Law' (2010) 21 *European Journal of International Law* 57–82, at 68.

[113] *International Law and World Order* (n 107) 221.

expansion, as well as the consolidation of territorial 'Westphalian' states. Legally, this period saw the transition from 'feudal international law' to 'bourgeois international law'.

Whereas old colonialism was based on the *backwardness* of European manufacture, and the need to accumulate materials from the colonies, the new colonialism (1760–1875) reversed this. A greater stress was placed upon colonies as *markets*. International law emerged on a firmer basis, more strongly structured around sovereignty. However, with the growing importance of colonies for European development, '[b]ourgeois international law shrank from a universal law of nations to being a Christian law of nations'.[114] In this way the non-European world was opened up to capitalist penetration and exploitation. These tendencies were exacerbated in the period of 'imperialism' (1875–1945), which was marked by the rise of monopoly capitalism. There was a strong push to acquire new colonial territory, particularly in Africa, and international law was key in enabling this. International law became increasingly structured around 'civilization', as opposed to Christianity, a move that 'was inspired partly by the need to accommodate the rise of non-European great powers some of which were not Christian'.[115]

For Chimni, decolonization was a contradictory phenomenon. It achieved progress in liberating the former colonial territories from direct political domination. However, 'the end of colonialism did not signify the end of imperialism but the beginning of...imperialism without colonies'.[116] Thus, 1945–1980 was marked by the rise of *neo-colonialism*, a situation in which 'political independence goes hand in hand with economic dependence'.[117] Whilst international law did for the first time posit the sovereign equality of all states, this coexisted with real inequality *facilitated* through international law. The international law of the neo-colonial period, then, can be characterized as 'bourgeois democratic' because—like liberal democracy—formal equality was juxtaposed with material inequality and exploitation.

This leads to the present period, that of 'globalization'. Chimni argues that from the 1980s, the most important development in capitalism was the rise of a transnational capitalist class. This class is a truly *global* one, with no particular ties to any national economy, and led the drive towards 'globalization'. Transnational capital requires a '*functional unified global economic space*' in which capital is able to have free movement.[118] For Chimni, international institutions have played a vital role in this process. In a role analogous to that of the state in the earlier stages of capitalism, international institutions have removed 'local impediments to the process of capital accumulation'.[119] Thus, the WTO, IMF, and World Bank have

---

[114] *International Law and World Order* (n 107) 231.   [115] Ibid 233.
[116] Ibid 235.   [117] Ibid 250.
[118] BS Chimni, 'International Institutions Today: An Imperial Global State in the Making' (2004) 15 *European Journal of International Law* 1–37, at 9 (emphasis in original).
[119] Ibid 7.

remodelled the economies of peripheral societies along lines that make them much more attractive for transnational capital and reshaped their political life through the discourse of good governance.

The sum total of these relationships means that a *global state* is in the process of formation. The function of this state 'is to realize the interests of transnational capital and powerful states in the international system to the disadvantage of third world states and peoples'.[120] Accordingly, this is a global *imperial* state. It is important to note here that Chimni is not arguing that a global state has *displaced* national states. Rather, he argues that the *structural* role of sovereign states in the international order has been transformed through globalization, leading to international institutions and these states performing the *functions* of a global state. This, he argues, is a step back from the gains made by bourgeois democratic law, and a new global social movement must attempt to democratize the global state.

Chimni's account might be seen as something of a materialist account of international law 'from above', with its focus on changing patterns of capitalist accumulation.[121] Insofar as 'resistance' does appear, it does so briefly in his account of decolonization. In stark contrast to this is Bill Bowring's work. Bowring starts from the proposition that one cannot view law and rights as 'deracinated empty forms'[122] but instead they must be understood as 'the subjects and objects of real struggles in the real world'.[123] Thus, he gives a 'substantive account' of international law, in which it is understood as the product of human struggle.[124] In his vision, international law responds to great historical upheavals (the French, Russian, and anti-colonial revolutions) by embedding their principles.

5 CONCLUSION: SO WHAT? (IS TO BE DONE)?

One of Marx's most famous quotes is his eleventh thesis on Feuerbach, namely that '[t]he philosophers have only *interpreted* the world, in various ways; the point, however, is to *change* it'.[125] Whilst this can be interpreted in a boringly vulgar

---

[120] 'International Institutions Today' (n 118) 1–2.

[121] See also M Neocleous, 'International Law as Primitive Accumulation; Or, the Secret of Systematic Colonization' (2012) 23 *European Journal of International Law* 941–62; A Rasulov, 'Writing About Empire: Remarks on the Logic of a Discourse' (2010) 23 *Leiden Journal of International Law* 449–71.

[122] B Bowring, *Degradation of the International Legal Order: The Rehabilitation of Law and the Possibility of Politics* (Routledge-Cavendish Oxford 2008) at 109.

[123] Ibid 111.   [124] Ibid 112.

[125] K Marx, 'Theses on Feuerbach' in *The Marx-Engels Reader* (n 2) 143–5, at 145.

fashion, it does express an important truth. Lurking in the background of the debates recounted this chapter is the question of what role, if any, law can play in emancipatory social change.[126]

Each of the positions described earlier has its own answer to this question, but we might—for the sake of argument—divide them into two camps: the 'opportunists' and the 'denialists'. In some respects, the former camp is the largest. Marks argues that a virtue of ideology critique is that ideology is never unidirectional. Because ideology is always unstable, it is possible to find 'counter-systemic logics' in international law, by noting the contradiction between the promise and reality of law and insisting that the promise be fulfilled.[127] Similarly, Chimni holds '*contemporary* international law...offers a protective shield...to the less powerful States in the international system'.[128]

Against this, Miéville has trenchantly insisted that '[t]he attempt to replace war and inequality with law...is precisely self-defeating, a world structured around international law cannot but be one of imperialist violence'.[129] This argument has met with a robust response from many of the authors referred to in this chapter. In actual fact, these camps are something of a simplification. Miéville's argument is for the *structural* connection between international law and imperialism, but this does not necessarily have *immediate* consequences for day-to-day practice.

As I have argued elsewhere, this debate—sometimes conducted under the rubric of 'reform or revolution'—needs to be structured by a concept of strategy and tactics.[130] Marxists do not believe that the problems of the world are simply the result of chance occurrences. They instead are undergirded by wider and deeper systems of social relations, with their own logics. In order to resolve these problems we must fundamentally transform our social order. At the same time, in order to transform this social order it is necessary to engage in a number of smaller, more defensive acts, which constitute the day-to-day practice of social movements.

Thus, in a long-term, structural, and *strategic* sense, we wish to overthrow the existing order. But in a short-term, conjunctural, *tactical* sense it is necessary to work within it. The task, then, is to figure out how these interrelate. But this problem cannot be resolved empirically. If the considerations made in this chapter are correct, then what might—in the short term—look like 'emancipation', could in the longer run reinforce relationships of oppression and domination. In order to truly answer these questions, there needs to be a deeper *jurisprudential* theory

---

[126] G Baars, 'Reform or Revolution—Polanyian versus Marxism Perspectives on the Regulation of the Economic' (2011) 62 *Northern Ireland Legal Quarterly* 415–32; R Knox, 'Strategy and Tactics' (2010) 21 *Finnish Yearbook of International Law* 193–229; O Taylor, 'Reclaiming Revolution' (2011) 22 *Finnish Yearbook of International Law* 259–92.

[127] *The Riddle of All Constitutions* (n 84) 144.

[128] BS Chimni, 'Third World Approaches to International Law: A Manifesto' (2006) 8 *International Community Law Review* 3–28, at 26 (emphasis in original).

[129] *Between Equal Rights* (n 69) 319.   [130] 'Strategy and Tactics' (n 126).

about the structural relationship between law and capitalism, and law and imperialism.[131] The great advantage to Pashukanis (and Miéville), no matter what one thinks of their answers to these questions, is that they *actually attempt to do this*. Whilst much of the work noted in this chapter offers gestures in this direction, or contains implicit theoretical perspectives, there is little systematic reflection on these issues. Absent this, whilst impressive strides can be made, the question of the relationship between law and social change on a broader level—what we might dub *the* question of Marxist legal theory—remains unanswered.

---

[131] R Knox, 'What is to be Done (With Critical Legal Theory)?' (2011) 22 *Finnish Yearbook of International Law* 31–50.

CHAPTER 16

REALIST APPROACHES TO INTERNATIONAL LAW

OLIVER JÜTERSONKE

Even realists are human[1]

1 INTRODUCTION

ALREADY in 1931, the legal scholar Max Radin warned that '[a] word like "realism" is so likely to become a mere incantation, a word to bless or ban, that unless progressives and traditionalists, realists and conceptionalists all alike are careful, they may find themselves tripping over their terms to the no small damage to their intelligibility and intellectual integrity'.[2] That risk continues to be omnipresent, and whereas international relations theorists have long come to accept that *political* realism constitutes 'the primary or alternative theory in virtually every major book and article addressing general theories of world politics, particularly in security affairs',[3] international legal scholars are less certain of both their own *legal* realist heritage, as well as of the degree to which they should be engaging

---

[1] M Radin, 'Legal Realism' (1931) 31 *Columbia Law Review* 824–8, at 828.   [2] Ibid 824.
[3] JW Legro and A Moravcsik, 'Is Anybody Still a Realist?' (1999) 24 *International Security* 5–55, at 5.

with their political realist counterparts. This chapter on realist approaches to international law will seek to outline some of the linkages between a genuinely legal realist approach to (international) law and jurisprudence, and the claims of political realists about the role and status of law in the international sphere.

The chapter proceeds in three sections. The first explores realism as an argumentative strategy. What does it mean to be 'realistic', to think about the 'reality' of international rules and institutions, and ultimately to be a (legal or political) 'realist'? Furthermore, what does such an argumentative structure look like in international legal thought? The second section of the chapter then explores the intellectual heritage of what has explicitly been labelled 'legal realism', in both its American and Scandinavian versions. How does a legal realist position fit into the canon of legal theory, and what marks has it left on contemporary international legal thought? Finally, the third section of the chapter seeks to relate the views of political realism about international law to the ways in which international lawyers themselves have sought to include an external position about the reality of international law into their own theories and doctrines.

2 THE REALISTIC POINT OF VIEW

In general terms, realism implies having a sober outlook on a particular set of circumstances, without being influenced by interests or preferences, or misled by ephemera of one sort or another.[4] In scholarly circles, realism has been employed in a variety of disciplines, from the visual arts and literature to various strands of philosophy, including the philosophy of science, epistemology, and ethics.[5] Simply stated, social theory sees realism as consisting of an objective, fact-driven perspective on moral beliefs and judgements (moral realism), a focus on competing societal interests and power struggles (political realism), and the view that the normativity of positive law can be reduced to social facts (legal realism). It is at once an

---

[4] See the discussion in D Bell, 'Introduction: Under an Empty Sky—Realism and Political Theory' in D Bell (ed), *Political Thought and International Relations: Variations on a Realist Theme* (OUP Oxford 2009) 1–25.

[5] The origins of realism are often traced back to the early scholastic period, and to a debate between (Platonic) realists who claim the independent existence of universals or abstract objects, and nominalists who deny the existence of such universals. John of Salisbury's *Metalogicon* thus already talks of the 'Nominalist sect'—see John of Salisbury, *The Metalogicon of John of Salisbury: A Twelfth-Century Defense of the Verbal and Logical Arts of the Trivium* (DD McGarry trans) (University of California Press Berkeley 1955 [1159]) at 96. See also MH Carré, *Realists and Nominalists* (OUP Oxford 1946).

argumentative tactic as well as a label for particular schools of thought, and part of the challenge of using (and making sense of) the term is the way in which people tend to oscillate from one meaning to another without necessarily being aware that they are doing so. As a result, interlocutors may well be talking past one another, making the subsequent debate particularly tedious.

The international realm has been one issue area in which realism has not only reared its head occasionally, but where it has been a constant feature of modern debate. Especially since the interwar period, international legal scholars, particularly those working on public international law, have felt obliged to grapple with the matter, either in terms of a realist (external) perspective *on* international law, or from a realist position *within* international law theory itself. Yet this distinction is often lost, and as Hersch Lauterpacht already lamented, an appeal to realism can simply constitute an (at times objectionable) method of argument in which the speaker lays an exclusive claim to wisdom: 'I am a realist; I am a sound person; I am a practical man; I look to realities; I see things as they are and not as I would like them to be'.[6] Whereas you, the opponent, '[y]ou are a Utopian; you are a dreamer; you see people and events as what you think they ought to be and not as what they are'.[7] We encounter such an argumentative practice on a daily basis, concerning the justifiability of military strikes on Iraq and Syria in 2015 just as much as in debates over the Abyssinia Crisis in Lauterpacht's day. On that level of analysis, we are indeed all realists, and if it is 'nothing else than the method, or temper, or attitude most calculated to realize our desires', to quote Lauterpacht again, '[w]ho but a crank or a fool does not wish to be a realist in that sense?'[8]

Realism, it would seem, is thus a relational concept, in that a claim to being realist defines itself and is evaluated with regard to an opposing conception that is deemed less realistic, that is, idealistic, utopian, formalist, positivist, legalist, or whatever happens to be perceived as the 'other' at that point in the conversation.[9] One is not absolutely and categorically a realist, but more realistic than one's interlocutor—a fact that we wish to make clear in our heated discussions and use as an argumentative device to discredit our opponent. As a rhetorical and reflective practice, the resort to realism does not result in the entrenchment of a particular position, but constitutes a constant oscillation in a debate between opposing extremes—extremes that themselves are hypothetical, and thus unrealistic or idealistic when viewed from the opposing perspective. In philosophy, such dialectics can

---

[6] H Lauterpacht, 'On Realism, Especially in International Relations' in E Lauterpacht (ed), *International Law, Being the Collected Papers of Hersch Lauterpacht. Volume 2: The Law of Peace* (5 vols CUP Cambridge 1975) vol 2, 52–66, at 53.
[7] Ibid.   [8] Ibid 54.
[9] See also BS Chimni, *International Law and World Order: A Critique of Contemporary Approaches* (SAGE Publications New Delhi 1993) at 30.

be related back to Immanuel Kant's distinction between transcendental realism and transcendental idealism in his *Critique of Pure Reason* (1781/87),[10] and in aesthetics and poetry, the terms of the debate were marked by an extensive correspondence on the subject between Friedrich Schiller and Johann Wolfgang von Goethe in the mid-1790s.

In international law, this discursive oscillation has been elegantly captured by Martti Koskenniemi in his analysis of the structure of international legal argument.[11] In their constant concern to demonstrate that their subject matter is distinct from politics, he maintains, international lawyers attempt to show that international law is both normative and concrete.[12] It is normative in that it does not simply entail a description of a particular rule or institution, but also imposes a measure of 'oughtness' onto it, certain requirements or obligations about how things *should* be. But legal abstractions need to be grounded in fact, that is, in the reality of the international sphere. The concreteness of international law thus refers to its responsiveness to changes in the behaviour, will, and interests of states and other authoritative actors, while normativity denotes international law's degree of autonomy from the behaviour of these actors.

The argumentative resort to realism plays a central role in this discursive tussle between normativity and concreteness that lies at the heart of the liberal vision. Without concrete processes, international law would face the charge of being utopian, as it would mean assuming the existence of a natural morality independent of the behaviour, will, and interests of states. This is why international lawyers turn to treaties, customs, and decisions of international institutions—to the 'canvas'[13] of verifiable facts that prevent legal ideas from constituting mere philosophical abstractions. Without a normatively compelling set of rules, however, international law would be unable discursively to establish its independence from state policy, hence opening up the charge of being an apology for power. And so, international legal argument continues its oscillation between idealist aspiration and realist(ic) awareness of the international sphere, between normative abstraction and sociological description. All sides lay claim to a greater dose of realism by either debunking the hypocritical servant of power or unmasking the naïve imagination of the utopian believer in the importance of international legal rules and institutions.

---

[10] I Kant, *Critique of Pure Reason* (P Guyer and AW Wood ed and trans) (CUP Cambridge 1998 [1781/87]).

[11] M Koskenniemi, *From Apology to Utopia: The Structure of International Legal Argument* (re-issue CUP Cambridge 2005).

[12] For a concise overview, see M Koskenniemi, 'International Law in the World of Ideas' in J Crawford and M Koskenniemi (eds), *The Cambridge Companion to International Law* (CUP Cambridge 2012) 47–63, at 60–1.

[13] Ibid 60.

3 LEGAL REALISM

Beyond its use as an argumentative tool, realism—at least in spirit if not always explicitly—rears its head periodically as more of a collective wave in many academic disciplines. 'No science deserves the name', EH Carr observed,

until it has acquired sufficient humility not to consider itself omnipotent, and to distinguish the analysis of what is from aspiration about what should be . . . In both physical and political sciences, the point is soon reached where the initial stage of wishing must be succeeded by a stage of hard and ruthless analysis . . . The impact of thinking upon wishing which, in the development of a science, follows the breakdown of its first visionary projects, and marks the end of its specifically utopian period, is commonly called realism.[14]

International law is no exception to this cyclical movement. Already the early classicists, the likes of Christian Wolff and Emer de Vattel, sought to break away from 'pure' divine and natural law to offer a more realistic appraisal of the justifications for state action.[15] This was reflected in the distinction between two varieties of non-consensual law: the 'necessary' and the 'voluntary' law of nations.[16] The first referred to duties and obligations internal to the state and based on a theological conception of conscience, while the second sought to conceptualize external duties towards international society in a way that captured the reality of inter-state relations characterized by self-interest—thus echoing the Hobbesian perspective that a state's authority rested on its de facto capacity to offer protection to its citizens.[17] But we would have to wait until the twentieth century before the term 'realism' came to be used to denote a particular theoretical position in the field of law.

With hindsight, developments in jurisprudence may be seen as components of ideological responses to social change,[18] and this was particularly evident in the way legal realism emerged in the United States (US). The common law, transported across by the British to their colonies, had to be adapted to the complex circumstances of a heterogeneous system with a multiplicity of jurisdictions subsumed under the constitution of 1787. It then had to be modernized to accommodate the

[14] EH Carr, *The Twenty Years' Crisis, 1919–1939: An Introduction to the Study of International Relations* (M Cox ed) (Palgrave Basingstoke 2001 [1939]) at 9–10.

[15] The classicists' break with natural law is a complex story that cannot be detailed here—suffice it to say that what emerged is the by now familiar differentiation between rationalism and empiricism, between the triumph of scientific reason versus a focus on experience and sense perception. In legal terms, this amounts to debates between legal formalism on the one hand, and various sociological approaches to law that are often equated with (twentieth century) realism, on the other.

[16] *From Apology to Utopia* (n 11) 108–22.

[17] See also A Orford, 'Constituting Order' in J Crawford and M Koskenniemi (eds), *The Cambridge Companion to International Law* (CUP Cambridge 2012) 271–89, at 272–7.

[18] G Edward White, 'From Sociological Jurisprudence to Realism: Jurisprudence and Social Change in Early Twentieth-Century America' (1972) 58 *Virginia Law Review* 999–1028, at 1028.

industrial and technical revolution that commenced in earnest after 1870 and, with an ever-growing amount of new legislation and cases, the sources of law also had to be simplified in order to be practically manageable. The challenges were at the fore-front of a transformation that went from 'classical' legal thought to 'progressivism' and the 'legal realism' of the early 1930s.[19]

Late nineteenth-century US legal reasoning, enshrined in the constitution of 1787 with the words 'a government of law and not of men', was embodied by Christopher C Langdell, appointed dean of Harvard Law School in 1870. According to Langdell, law was a science consisting of principles and doctrines, for which all necessary materials were available in printed books. And just as Rudolf von Jhering had mocked a similar legal conservatism in continental Europe with his famous critique of the 'heaven of legal concepts'[20]—in which lawyers used a 'dialectic-hydraulic interpretation press' to squeeze any desired meaning into a legal text or concept, as well as a 'hair-splitting machine' with which the applicant to this heaven for legal theorists had to divide a single hair into 999,999 equal parts—Langdell's vision was similarly taken to the cleaners by Justice Oliver Wendell Holmes Jr. Law was not about books, Holmes asserted, but about people: in order to know 'the law and nothing else', he argued, 'you must look at it as a bad man, who cares only for the material consequences which such knowledge enables him to predict, not as a good one, who finds his reasons for conduct, whether inside the law or outside of it, in the vaguer sanctions of conscience'. The bad man 'does not care two straws for the axioms or deductions', yet what he does want to know is how the courts will ultimately act: 'The prophecies of what the courts will do in fact, and nothing more pretentious, are what I mean by the law'.[21]

Holmes' approach to law and his so-called 'prediction theory' paved the way for what came to be known as 'sociological jurisprudence':[22] instead of the 'mechanical jurisprudence'[23] of classical legal thought, instead of deductive legal reasoning that

---

[19] As Neil Duxbury points out, however, one needs to be wary of portraying American legal theory as a 'pendulum-swing vision' going from formalism to the legal realist 'revolt' against such formalism, back to the formalism of process jurisprudence and the 'law and economics' movement, before again swinging to the realism of Critical Legal Studies. Such readings tend to over-dramatize distinctions between supposedly opposing theoretical positions and schools of thought. N Duxbury, *Patterns of American Jurisprudence* (Clarendon Press Oxford 1995) at 1–7. For details and further references, see O Jütersonke, *Morgenthau, Law and Realism* (CUP Cambridge 2010) at 106–15.

[20] R von Jhering, *Scherz und Ernst in der Jurisprudenz: Eine Weihnachtsgabe für das juristische Publikum* (Wissenschaftliche Buchgesellschaft Darmstadt 1988 [1885]) at 257 and 262–3.

[21] OW Holmes, 'The Path of the Law' (1897) 10 *Harvard Law Review* 457–78.

[22] While the likes of Pound and Benjamin N Cardozo explicitly drew inspiration from European, and in particular German, sociological approaches to law (notably from the so-called German Free Law Movement or *Freirechtsschule*), the American conception of 'sociological jurisprudence' was markedly different. See A Auburtin, 'Amerikanische Rechtsauffassung und die neueren amerikanischen Theorien der Rechtssoziologie und des Rechtsrealismus' (1933) 3 *Zeitschrift für ausländisches öffentliches Recht und Völkerrecht* 529–67.

[23] R Pound, 'Mechanical Jurisprudence' (1908) 8 *Columbia Law Review* 605–23.

was deemed neutral and thus apolitical, it was time for legal theory and practice to build on insights from the social sciences. Law was not simply a body of rules to be applied, but a means of social control. Holmes had been a member of the Metaphysical Club of pragmatist philosophers with William James and Charles S Peirce,[24] and in this vein, it was now argued that law was all about experience rather than logic, about facts rather than general propositions. This trend was particularly evident in the famous 'Brandeis Brief' submitted by Louis D Brandeis to the US Supreme Court in the case *Muller v Oregon* (1908),[25] over whether maximum hours laws for women were unconstitutional under the *Lochner v New York* (1905) ruling.[26] The Brandeis Brief contained two pages of legal reasoning and ninety-five pages of sociological and economic data on the living conditions of women working in factories.[27]

In the wake of the Great Depression, which had further strengthened the conviction that market processes were social constructs, and that the law was out of sync with a complex social reality, a group of American legal theorists emerged that came to be associated with 'legal realism'. Perhaps its most famous proponents were Karl N Llewellyn, who had a well-known debate about realism with the elderly Roscoe Pound in the early 1930s, and Jerome Frank, whose emphasis on psychoanalysis made many people believe that legal realism could be boiled down to the assertion that a judge's decision depended solely on what he or she had eaten for breakfast.[28] Crucially, it was the law's indeterminacy that was at the core of the legal realist agenda.[29] Laws were seen to regulate social life, and in order to do so effectively, legal realists called for the incorporation of insights from economics, sociology, political science, anthropology, and social psychology.

In a similar vein, and at about the same time as their American counterparts, a group of Scandinavian scholars were also seeking to inject a dose of reality into the dusty shelves of legal formalism. In many ways the counterpart to Holmes, the leading figure in this movement was Axel Hägerström, philosopher at Uppsala University in Sweden. Hägerström maintained that nothing existed outside of space and time—everything else was speculative metaphysics that was ultimately harmful to sound, 'scientific' analysis. What came to be known as Scandinavian

---

[24] See L Menand, *The Metaphysical Club: A Story of Ideas in America* (Farrar, Straus and Giroux New York 2001).

[25] 208 US 412 (1908).   [26] 198 US 45 (1905).

[27] MJ Horwitz, *The Transformation of American Law 1870–1960: The Crisis of Legal Orthodoxy* (OUP New York 1992) at 209.

[28] For the Llewellyn–Pound debate, see KN Llewellyn 'A Realistic Jurisprudence—The Next Step' (1930) 30 *Columbia Law Review* 431–65; R Pound, 'The Call for a Realist Jurisprudence' (1931) 44 *Harvard Law Review* 697–711; KN Llewellyn, 'Some Realism about Realism: A Reply to Dean Pound' (1931) 44 *Harvard Law Review* 1222–64. On Frank, see eg J Frank, *Courts on Trial: Myth and Reality in American Justice* (Princeton University Press Princeton 1949).

[29] See A Altman, 'Legal Realism, Critical Legal Studies, and Dworkin' (1986) 15 *Philosophy and Public Affairs* 205–35.

legal realism is then the output of three of his pupils, all of whom were to hold chairs in law: Anders V Lundstedt and Karl Olivecrona in Sweden, and Alf Ross in Denmark.

While agreeing with their American counterparts that a more realistic juris-prudence involved conceptualizing a 'law in action' based on empirically observ-able facts, the works of these Scandinavian proponents constituted a rather more fundamental—and at times perhaps exceedingly polemical—assault on what they deemed to be the law's dependence on 'supernatural' sources, 'mystico-magical' thinking, and 'imaginative lucubration'.[30] Alf Ross, in particular, set out to elab-orate a realistic jurisprudence that would live up to the name of legal 'science':

The leading idea . . . is to carry, in the field of law, the empirical principles [of logical posi-tivism] to their ultimate conclusions. From this springs the methodological demand that the study of law must follow the traditional patterns of observation and verification which animate all modern empirical science; and the analytical demand that the fundamental legal notions must be interpreted as conceptions of social reality, the behaviour of man in society, and as nothing else.[31]

Echoing Holmes' predictive theory, Ross argued that statements about the law's validity must be interpreted as referring to socio-psychological facts, and moreover that such statements are relatable to the reasoning of future judgments:

Assertions concerning valid law are according to their real content a prediction of future social happenings. The latter are fundamentally indeterminate and do not permit of being unambiguously predicted. Every prediction is at the same time a real factor liable to influ-ence the course of events and to that extent a political act.[32]

According to the Scandinavian legal realists, Holmes and the generation of American legal theorists building on his insights focused too much on a critique of the process of judicial decision-making and did not pay enough attention to the metaphysical foundation of empty standard terms such as 'right', 'duty', and 'own-ership'. These constitute abstract entities that are pernicious to the scientific study of law in that they tend to occlude a complex factual reality—they are, as Ross famously asserted, akin to the notion of 'tû-tû' employed by certain peoples in the South Pacific. Such terms constitute a mediating element with no independent

---

[30] See AL Escorihuela, 'Alf Ross: Towards a Realist Critique and Reconstruction of International Law' (2003) 14 *European Journal of International Law* 703–66. For a more detailed appraisal of Scandinavian legal realism, and in particular of the role of Alf Ross in the history of twentieth-century European international law, see also the other contributions in (2003) 14(4) *European Journal International Law* 653–841.

[31] A Ross, *On Law and Justice* (University of California Press Berkeley 1959) at xi, also cited in 'Alf Ross' (n 30) 711–12.

[32] *On Law and Justice* (n 31) 49, also cited and discussed in H Zahle, 'Legal Doctrine between Empirical and Rhetorical Truth: A Critical Analysis of Alf Ross' Conception of Legal Doctrine' (2003) 14 *European Journal of International Law* 801–15, at 809.

semantic meaning, and as such can be done away with once the law has been given a more scientific basis: '[t]he notion that between purchase and access to recovery something was created that can be designated as ownership is nonsense'.[33]

Overall, legal realism has left an ambiguous legacy. It ranges from the 'cliché' that we are all realists now to the view that legal realism constituted a 'juris-prudential joke', a rule-scepticism that, following HLA Hart's decisive critique in *The Concept of Law*,[34] can easily be dismissed as a historical curiosity[35] and confined to the 'museums of jurisprudential archaeology'.[36] Nonetheless, sub-sequent analysis has highlighted that Hart's critique may have itself missed the point, by misconstruing the legal realists' descriptive theory of adjudication as a type of rule-scepticism on the level of a general theory of law.[37] In any event, Hart is remembered for having countered the realists by asserting that indeterminacy was linguistically a result of the inherent 'open texture' of legal rules, and that most common law and legislation was definitive enough not to face the problem.[38] Ronald Dworkin[39] then went even further by arguing that Hart was too focused on 'rules', and thus missed a variety of other principles and policies (including moral and political appraisals) that judges would draw upon to make determinate decisions in ambiguous cases. This position has in turn been questioned by the Critical Legal Studies movement, whose propo-nents emphasize that substance and procedure cannot be differentiated and that, essentially, legal reasoning is in itself political.[40]

Concretely, the heir of American legal realism is often taken to be Myres McDougal who, together with the political scientist Harold Lasswell, called for a new direction in legal education, one that would constitute 'conscious, efficient, and systematic *training for policy-making*'.[41] A too narrow focus on general doctrines and the formal validity of legal rules, they argued, only nurtured the law's indeterminacy and exac-erbated the artificial distinction between law and policy, between formulations *de*

---

[33] A Ross, 'Tû-tû' (1957) 70 *Harvard Law Review* 812–25, at 820–1, also cited in 'Alf Ross' (n 30) 714.

[34] HLA Hart, *The Concept of Law* (J Raz and PA Bullock eds) (2nd edn OUP Oxford 1994 [1961]) at 124–54.

[35] MS Green, 'Legal Realism as Theory of Law' (2005) 46 *William and Mary Law Review* 1915–2000, at 1917.

[36] F Schauer and VJ Wise, 'Legal Positivism as Legal Information' (1997) 82 *Cornell Law Review* 1080–110, at 1081.

[37] See B Leiter, 'Legal Realism and Legal Positivism Reconsidered' (2001) 111 *Ethics* 278–301, at 279.

[38] Interestingly, on this issue Hart is very close to the position of Alf Ross—a convergence that can also be seen in Hart's distinction between primary and secondary rules, which is close to Ross' terminology of rules of conduct and rules of competence. See K Waaben, 'Alf Ross 1899–1979: A Biographical Sketch' (2003) 14 *European Journal of International Law* 661–74.

[39] R Dworkin, *Taking Rights Seriously* (Harvard University Press Cambridge MA 1977).

[40] See J Hasnas, 'Back to the Future: From Critical Legal Studies Forward to Legal Realism, or How Not to Miss the Point of the Indeterminacy Argument' (1995) 45 *Duke Law Journal* 84–132.

[41] HD Lasswell and MS McDougal, 'Legal Education and Public Policy: Professional Training in the Public Interest' (1943) 52 *Yale Law Review* 203–95, at 206 (emphasis in original).

lege lata and *de lege ferenda*.[42] International law would only be relevant if it did not focus on formal authority, but rather on effective control established through value-dependent policies and processes—and this required the development of a legal 'policy science' based on democratic values and incorporating the methods of the social science into the study of law. As many commentators have pointed out, however, Lasswell and McDougal's policy science ultimately failed to transform the discipline, and may even have been counter-productive in demonstrating the specificity of international law in the face of sustained criticisms by political realists about its relevance. Indeed, the approach encouraged (American) international lawyers to evaluate choices based on a set of liberal-democratic values that, couched in a vocabulary of 'human dignity', were assumed to be universal and shared by a single international community. In so doing, however, the New Havenites risked undermining their own legal realist heritage, and alienated legal internationalists in the US seeking to find a workable basis for 'co-existence' with the Soviet Union.[43]

4 REALISM ABOUT INTERNATIONAL LAW

The Scandinavian trio of Lundstedt, Olivecrona, and Ross had much more to say about international law than did the American legal realists, and their reasoning had a decidedly Kelsenian ring to it. The onus was particularly on the problematic use of central terms such as 'sovereignty', which in their view constituted another one of those metaphysical constructions: international law is defined as the body of legal rules binding upon states in their relations with one another; states are considered territorial entities that are sovereign; and sovereignty means direct subjection to international law.[44] As Escorihuela writes, this constituted 'a circular, and

---

[42] MS McDougal, 'International Law, Power and Policy: A Contemporary Conception' (1953) 82 *Recueil des Cours* 133–259, at 144.

[43] See D Kennedy, 'The Disciplines of International Law and Policy' (1999) 12 *Leiden Journal of International Law* 9–133, at 28, and H Saberi, 'Yale's Policy Science and International Law: Between Legal Formalism and Policy Conceptualism' in this *Handbook*. A useful critique of the New Haven School approach can be found in PR Trimble, 'Review Essay: International Law, World Order, and Critical Legal Studies' (1990) 42 *Stanford Law Review* 811–45. A more contemporary statement of the approach can be seen in WM Reisman, S Wiessner, and AR Willard, 'The New Haven School: A Brief Introduction' (2007) 32 *Yale Journal of International Law* 575–82. A variety of legal scholars have sought to build on insights from the New Havenites in recent decades, including the Transnational Legal Process Movement around the work of Harold Hongju Koh, which, with its focus on how norms shape behaviour, is closely aligned with social constructivism (see n 49 below). See also HH Koh, 'Transnational Legal Process' (1996) 75 *Nebraska Law Review* 181–207.

[44] See A Ross, *A Textbook of International Law* (Longmans, Green & Co London 1947) at 11ff, referred to in 'Alf Ross' (n 30) 715–16.

viciously circular, definition, with the consequent theoretical result of rendering the concept of international law "unmeaning", according to Ross' neologism, that is, tautological, logically useless and finally empty of any independent meaning'.[45]

Another 'tû-tû' concept for Ross was 'territory'. There may be a set of rules stating which area belongs to a specific state as its territory, but that 'this area has the character of "territory"' is per se meaningless. This characterization has meaning only when taken together with another set of rules expressing the legal consequences that are attached to an area's character as territory.[46] In sum, as Lundstedt asserted, '[f]or the whole of mankind there are a few evils worse than this fatal law of nations' based on the idea that sovereign states have the right to rule over their own territory:

It is simply by exalting certain interests of a nation into 'rights', by transforming divers [and] entirely absurd notions of retribution and revenge into something as sublime as *justice*—it is just by means of these manipulations in their idealistic disguise that chauvinism, nationalism, and militarism originate and are kept alive.[47]

In relation to international affairs, Lundstedt's quote highlights the conceptual and argumentative grey zone between 'legal' realism on the one hand, and a broader category of 'political' realism that reached its heyday during and after the Second World War. Indeed, it is a group of mid-twentieth-century political realists (many of whom were disillusioned 'internationalist' jurists of the interwar period) that is commonly identified with this position, and many international law textbooks and core lectures refer to the likes of Hans J Morgenthau and George Kennan (rather than to Llewellyn and Lundstedt) when they tackle the issue of realism from an international law perspective. Charles Chaumont,[48] for instance, talks in this vein of '*l'école réaliste anglo-saxonne*', and also of a '*méthode réaliste*' that is essentially an abandoning of formalism to instead focus on the empirical reality (the 'is') of the international system, of which the juridical 'ought' is an integral part—a perspective that would subsequently be echoed and developed by constructivist approaches to international relations theory.[49] Again, there is a rather complicated story to tell here, one that can only be outlined briefly in the following paragraphs.

---

[45] 'Alf Ross' (n 30) 716.   [46] 'Tû-tû' (n 33) 821.

[47] AV Lundstedt, 'The Responsibility of Legal Science for the Fate of Man and Nations' (1932) 10 *New York University Law Quarterly Review* 326–40, at 335.

[48] C Chaumont, 'Cours général de droit international public' (1970) 129 *Recueil des Cours* 333–528, at 361–2.

[49] For a concise overview of constructivism in the study of world politics, as well as for an attempt to relate it to international legal theory, see J Brunnée and SJ Toope, 'International Law and Constructivism: Elements of an Interactional Theory of International Law' (2000) 39 *Columbia Journal of Transnational Law* 19–74. In the field of international relations, key texts include NG Onuf, *World of Our Making: Rules and Rule in Social Theory and International Relations* (University of South Carolina Press Columbia 1989); F Kratochwil, *Rules, Norms and Decisions: On the Conditions of Practical and Legal Reasoning in International Relations and Domestic Affairs* (CUP Cambridge

To do so, it is worth returning to Hersch Lauterpacht's famous monograph, *The Function of Law in the International Community*,[50] which neatly captures the spirit of the day around what was termed the doctrine of non-justiciable disputes. As Lauterpacht explains, this doctrine of the inherent limitations of the judicial process is 'the work of international lawyers anxious to give legal expression to the State's claim to be independent of law', and its principal function is thus 'to supply a legal cloak for the traditional claim of the sovereign State to remain the ultimate judge of disputed legal rights in its controversies with other states'.[51]

From Vattel onwards, international lawyers had been trying to paper over the tension between insisting on the sovereign prerogatives of states while at the same time claiming the existence of an international legal order that somehow obliges states to have recourse to, and then also abide by, the decision of judicial settlement. Debates began to rage as to whether any dispute was, in effect, a 'legal' dispute, or whether one should distinguish between 'justiciable' and 'non-justiciable', or even 'legal' and 'political' disputes, with the latter encompassing those involving the 'vital interests' of states, interests that were formally acknowledged to be outside of the law's scope.

It was precisely on this topic that a certain Hans Joachim Morgenthau began his career as a scholar of international law in the 1920s. Following the work of the Swiss internationalist Otfried Nippold, he argued that while the common distinction between legal disputes and disputes over conflicts of interests might hold in theory, it was of little use for a practice-oriented analysis. All disputes are obviously related to the interests of the parties involved; of importance is whether the interests are such that international judicial settlement is deemed too risky. 'Legal' and 'political' were not opposing terms, Morgenthau claimed, and legal issues could themselves be of a political or non-political nature. In a formulation that echoes Carl Schmitt's subsequent conceptualizations of 'the political' (written in the context of German public law debates over the infamous article 48 of the Weimar Constitution), Morgenthau argued that the essential characteristic of the political is the degree of intensity with which an object of state action is related to the substantiality, or individuality, of the state itself.[52] Consequently, he proposed to distinguish between 'objective' and 'subjective' limits to judicial settlement, a distinction that could be captured by the concept of 'tensions' (*Spannungen*): a disagreement between states is called a 'dispute' if it can be expressed in legal terms, whereas 'tension' refers to a situation 'involving a discrepancy, asserted by one

---

1989). See also O Kessler and F Dos Reis, 'Constructivism and the Politics of International Law' in this *Handbook*.

[50] H Lauterpacht, *The Function of Law in the International Community* (Clarendon Press Oxford 1933).

[51] Ibid 6–7.

[52] HJ Morgenthau, *Die internationale Rechtspflege, ihr Wesen und ihre Grenzen* (Noske Leipzig 1929) at 58 and 62.

State against another, between the legal situation on the one hand and the actual power relation on the other'.[53]

Via stints in Geneva and Madrid, Morgenthau would eventually emigrate to the US in 1938, where he would become a leading figure of the 'realist school' of international politics.[54] His early works on the doctrine of justiciable disputes are important because they would later constitute the backbone of his popular writings on political realism, notably in his textbook *Politics among Nations: The Struggle for Power and Peace*.[55] There he would repeat the distinction between disputes (that is, legally formulated conflicts) and tensions (or 'unformulated conflicts of power'), as well as his insistence that a balance of power was the basis for international cooperation. It was his disillusionment with the way the dominant doctrine of legal formalism was thinking about 'politics in terms of law'—rather than like the Ancient Greeks, who had still 'thought of law in terms of politics'—that would lead him to develop his critique of what he called a 'decadent legalistic statecraft' operating under the motto of *fiat justitia, pereat mundus*.[56]

As Morgenthau was eager to point out, Lassa Oppenheim had similarly declared a balance of power to be the 'first and principal moral' of the law of nations in his famous textbook *International Law: A Treatise*[57]—a statement that was subsequently deleted in posthumously published editions of Oppenheim's textbook by none other than a certain Hersch Lauterpacht.[58] True to their discipline of international law, the likes of Lauterpacht tried to undermine the realism of the view that there were practical limits to justiciability by arguing that 'it is the refusal of the State to submit the dispute to judicial settlement, and not the intrinsic nature of the controversy, which makes it political'.[59] Morgenthau, however, not having had any luck finding a position in an American law school, would go on to turn his back on the discipline, and instead of continuing his pursuit of a '*théorie realiste du Droit international*',[60] would soon metamorphose his rule-scepticism into a position that took him beyond the realm of international legal theory altogether.

The idea that 'power politics' had to be taken seriously in light of the failure of the Wilsonian experiment was, of course, not a theme that was unique to Morgenthau (another household name of political realism who began as a student of Kelsen is John H Herz), nor one that was not discussed in international law circles. One need only think of the works of other international lawyers of the time, such as

---

[53] *Die internationale Rechtspflege, ihr Wesen und ihre Grenzen* (n 52) 71.
[54] For an in-depth analysis see *Morgenthau, Law and Realism* (n 19).
[55] HJ Morgenthau, *Politics among Nations: The Struggle for Power and Peace* (Knopf New York 1948).
[56] HJ Morgenthau, *Scientific Man vs Power Politics* (University of Chicago Press Chicago 1946) at 98 and 107.
[57] L Oppenheim, *International Law: A Treatise* (2 vols Longmans, Green, and Co London 1905–6).
[58] See *Morgenthau, Law and Realism* (n 19) 68–73. See also MW Janis 'Book Review: The *New Oppenheim* and Its Theory of International Law' (1996) 16 *Oxford Journal of Legal Studies* 329–36.
[59] *The Function of Law* (n 50) 164.
[60] HJ Morgenthau, *Positivisme mal compris et théorie réaliste du Droit international* (Mélanges Altamira Madrid 1936).

Charles de Visscher's *Theory and Reality in Public International Law*,[61] Wolfgang G Friedmann's *Introduction to World Politics*,[62] Gerhart Niemeyer's *Law without Force*,[63] or Georg Schwarzenberger's *Power Politics*.[64] What distinguished these authors and their work from Morgenthau, however, is that their reflections generally remained within the confines of the discipline, and thus did not seek to raise existential questions about the relevance of international law per se. Take Schwarzenberger, for instance: his inductive approach to international law works on the assumption that there are legal 'rules' created through an objective process of law creation; in the international sphere, the scope of these rules may be limited due to the social backdrop of power politics, but this has no bearing on the normativity of the rules as such; law and politics remain separate.[65] For Morgenthau, in contrast, what he termed 'social forces' had a direct significance on the normative study of law, and not merely on the description of the law's environment: these 'sociological, ethical and other factors constantly penetrate into the legal rules, establish new ones, change old ones and so on'.[66] From this perspective, international law is thus not only confined in scope, but is not particularly binding either, as the sanction that is supposed to kick in is not empirically observed.

The disastrous consequences of the legalist internationalism of the interwar period had resulted in a veritable aversion to international law, in both academic and policy circles. As Josef F Kunz, another disciple of Hans Kelsen who emigrated to America, observed in 1950, the pendulum had swung from the 'boundless optimism' of Geneva to the other extreme, 'from overestimation to underestimation of international law, from the emphasis on international law to the emphasis on power, from optimism to pessimism, to the new "realistic" approach'.[67] Soon, international law was dropped as an examination topic for entrance into the US Foreign Service, the Carnegie Endowment ceased its funding of the Hague Academy of International Law, and the Rockefeller Foundation lost interest in the Graduate Institute in Geneva. And Morgenthau's writings, with their focus on the 'will to power' and the critique of the legalistic experiment of international Geneva, played no insignificant part in that development.

So immense has been the influence of this trend that, since then, the history of international legal theory can appropriately be described as an attempt to recover the validity

---

[61] C de Visscher, *Theory and Reality in Public International Law* (Princeton University Press Princeton 1957).

[62] WG Friedmann, *Introduction to World Politics* (Macmillan London 1951).

[63] G Niemeyer, *Law without Force: The Functions of Politics in International Law* (Princeton University Press Princeton 1941).

[64] G Schwarzenberger, *Power Politics: An Introduction to the Study of International Relations and Post-War Planning* (Jonathan Cape London 1941).

[65] See *From Apology to Utopia* (n 11) 191–7.   [66] Ibid 198.

[67] JL Kunz, 'The Swing of the Pendulum: From Overestimation to Underestimation of International Law' (1950) 44 *American Journal of International Law* 135–40, at 138.

of the international legal tradition from it, and to discover, articulate and promote a viable synthesis.[68]

The success of Morgenthau's endeavour to decouple legal formalism from an understanding of the realities of politics is reflected in the fact that much of international legal scholarship has been sidelined by international relations theory ever since—and this despite a series of efforts to bridge the two fields with a combined research agenda.[69] Yet such work, according to David Kennedy, tends to remain at the margins, not least because 'professionals from each field experience their interdisciplinary work as broadening only by remembering an unduly cramped version of their own field, just as they had once separated their fields by seeing an unrealistically narrow version of their counterparts across the disciplinary divide'.[70] As Judith N Shklar already observed in the 1960s, the likes of Morgenthau had ensured that the formalism of juristic thought took root among its professed opponents: the same arguments that legal theoreticians had previously used to separate law from morality were then used by political realists to preserve politics from both law and morality. 'The realistic picture of politics is, in fact, that of legalism gone sour.'[71] Essentially, Morgenthau's legalism critique is significant because it points to the ways in which formal law brings the spectre of universalization onto itself by dint of its own argumentative structure—and therefore also goes some way towards explaining international law's move from formalism to a 'culture of dynamism'[72] that is preoccupied with technical and bureaucratic issues of coordination and effectiveness, and engrossed in the language and methods of political science.

In a sense, the 'political ideology of Geneva' in the 1920s was not very different from the 'political ideology of Washington' that established itself after the war. In both cases, the US took a lead in establishing international law and institutions, but did not always go on to sign the ensuing treaty. It promoted but did not join the League of Nations, and similarly, did not ratify the 1951 *Convention Relating to the Status of Refugees* or the *Convention on the Rights of the Child*.[73] The US declares

---

[68] *International Law and World Order* (n 9) 24.

[69] Notably AM Slaughter Burley, 'International Law and International Relations Theory: A Dual Agenda' (1993) 87 *American Journal of International Law* 205–39.

[70] 'The Disciplines of International Law and Policy' (n 43) 106. Most recently F Kratochwil, *The Status of Law in World Society: Mediations on the Role and Rule of Law* (CUP Cambridge 2014).

[71] JN Shklar, *Legalism: Law, Morals, and Political Trials* (Harvard University Press Cambridge MA 1964) at 126.

[72] M Koskenniemi, *The Gentle Civilizer of Nations: The Rise and Fall of International Law 1870–1960* (CUP Cambridge 2001) at 496.

[73] *Convention Relating to the Status of Refugees* (opened for signature 28 July 1951 entered into force 22 April 1954) 189 UNTS 137; *Convention on the Rights of the Child* (opened for signature 20 November 1989 entered into force 2 September 1990) 1577 UNTS 3. See SV Scott, 'Is There Room for International Law in *Realpolitik*? Accounting for the US "Attitude" towards International Law' (2004) 30 *Review of International Studies* 71–88.

itself a promoter of a certain set of universal values, but its status as hegemon prevents it from accepting to be bound by specific obligations in which these values may result. As Morgenthau aptly expressed it, 'American globalism assumes the existence of one valid legal order whose content is defined by the US and which reflects the content of American foreign policy'.[74] This, perhaps, and despite the elaboration of a considerably more diverse and nuanced palette of international legal thought since,[75] is the crux of the realist legacy: international law is at once both relevant and irrelevant, because it is conveniently conceived of as formal law one day and as an informal regime of like-minded states the next.

5 CONCLUSION

'Anyone who, in these days, chooses to speak of "The Reality of the Law of Nations"', Hersch Lauterpacht began a lecture at Chatham House in 1941, 'lays himself open to the charge of untimely simplicity or even audacity'.[76] In many respects, this assessment continues to be apt today, when the conception of international law offered by the likes of Morgenthau, and the 'legalism' critique it entailed, seems narrow, overly formalist, and ultimately old-fashioned—decidedly twentieth-century remnants of the Cold War that do not sit well with contemporary perspectives on 'global problems' requiring 'global solutions', the vehicle for which is a variety of 'multistakeholder partnerships' that seek to transcend inter-state relations entirely. All this is not to say, of course, that realist perspectives have disappeared from contemporary international legal theory—one need only think of global administrative law, for instance, with its ambition of generating a (realist) sociology of global normativity based on a 'social fact' conception of law.[77] But these newer perspectives that entail realist elements (the legal transnationalism literature is another candidate) do not explicitly identify with 'realism' as a school of thought, which, particularly in its political guise, is generally frowned upon for its supposed lack of finesse and sophistication. Does the path of the realist not

---

[74] HJ Morgenthau, 'Emergent Problems of United States Foreign Policy' in K Deutsch and S Hoffman (eds), *The Relevance of International Law* (Anchor Books Garden City 1971) 69–79, at 71.

[75] Readers are encouraged to refer to the graphical representation of new approaches to international law offered by 'The Disciplines of International Law and Policy' (n 43) 36.

[76] H Lauterpacht, 'The Reality of the Law of Nations (1941)' in *International Law, Being the Collected Papers of Hersch Lauterpacht* (n 6) vol 2, 22–51, at 22.

[77] See eg B Kingsbury, 'The Concept of "Law" in Global Administrative Law' (2009) 20 *European Journal of International Law* 23–57.

over-determine international law's supposed lack of binding force, and ultimately lead to claims about its irrelevance? But if it is true that realist scholars of international relations continue to caricature international law in this way, then it is equally true that much of international law scholarship does something similar with (political) realism.

A straw-man version of realism is offered in which it is asserted that realists believe that international law does not matter. This fiction about realism makes a nice conceptual contrast—a null hypothesis backdrop—for arguments about how international law does matter.[78]

As the previous sections have sought to illustrate, realist approaches to international law go beyond the strict confines of the label 'legal realism' to incorporate an 'external' point of view[79] that seems to coalesce into a 'political realism' emphasizing the primacy of the state, national interests, and an anarchical international system in which these interests are played off one another in so many variations of the 'balance of power' theme. Partly, this has to do with the seemingly constant struggle of international lawyers to show that international law is really law, and not just a sideshow to international politics—or even worse, an overly zealous attempt to formalize lots of gesticulation about something loosely defined as 'international morality'. But perhaps more importantly, it also has something to do with what Koskenniemi has called international law's 'extradisciplinary fixation',[80] namely its internalization of the scientific outlook it inherited from the legal realists.

To come through legal realism is to learn that neither voluntarism *nor* empiricism is tenable, that law is neither an effect of psychology nor of sociology—and that legal competence does involve a 'magic' that makes it independent from those particular forms of expertise.[81]

In order for international law to be concrete, we need to know 'objectively' what the content of the law actually is. Yet, the normativity of the law cannot be based on empirics alone—the 'ought' cannot only be derived from the 'is'—and thus we are back to the oscillation between fact and value that is at the heart of the argumentative tension between apology and utopia in international legal thought.

---

[78] RH Steinberg, 'Overview: Realism in International Law' (2002) 96 *Proceedings of the American Society of International Law* 260–2, at 261.

[79] *The Concept of Law* (n 34) 89.

[80] M Koskenniemi, 'International Law in a Post-Realist Era' (1995) 16 *Australian Year Book of International Law* 1–19, at 1.

[81] M Koskenniemi, 'Introduction: Alf Ross and Life Beyond Realism' (2003) 14 *European Journal of International Law* 653–9, at 657 (emphasis in original).

CHAPTER 17

CONSTRUCTIVISM AND THE POLITICS OF INTERNATIONAL LAW

FILIPE DOS REIS AND OLIVER KESSLER

1 INTRODUCTION

AT first sight, it appears to be an easy task to discuss the relationship between constructivism and international legal theory. Whereas the majority of international relations (IR) theorists were happy to treat international law as epiphenomenal, constructivists always referred to international law extensively in order to challenge IR's foundations in a positivist philosophy of social sciences. One only has to remember that the now classic book by Friedrich Kratochwil, *Rules, Norms and Decisions*, had the subtitle 'On the Conditions of Practical and *Legal* Reasoning in International Relations and Domestic Affairs'.[1] Kratochwil did not simply want to contribute to IR, but also to legal theory and jurisprudence.[2] He even devoted a whole chapter to the concept of law.[3]

---

[1] FV Kratochwil, *Rules, Norms, and Decisions: On the Conditions of Practical and Legal Reasoning in International Relations and Domestic Affairs* (CUP Cambridge 1989) (emphasis added).

[2] Ibid 1.

[3] Ibid 181–211. The same holds true for Onuf's reference to 'rules' and 'rule' or Wendt's three cultures of anarchy. See N Onuf, *World of Our Making: Rules and Rule in Social Theory and International*

Yet the question of how constructivism relates to international law in general and international legal theory (ILT) in particular is somewhat more complicated, simply because there is no agreement on what constructivism actually *is*. Ever since its emergence, it was divided into a 'thin' and 'thick',[4] 'conventional' and 'critical',[5] 'soft' and 'radical',[6] or 'moderate' and 'radical'[7] version. The moderate version circles around the work of Alexander Wendt and has touched upon questions of international law through contributions by, for instance, Christian Reus-Smit, Ian Hurd, Emanuel Adler, Thomas Risse, Martha Finnemore, and Richard Price.[8] The radical version is predominantly represented by the work of Nicholas Onuf and Friedrich Kratochwil.[9] These two strands of constructivism differ fundamentally in their take on 'the politics of law'.

Given the mutually incompatible streams of constructivist theory building, it is neither useful to throw them together under one heading, nor to search for a common ground that would somehow link these literatures in an intelligible and coherent manner. An adequate answer to the question of what constructivism has to offer to ILT thus needs to reflect upon these differences. In this chapter, we argue that the two versions differ in their very understanding of the politics of international law and thus the way they connect to ILT. We show that the moderate version is formed as an attempt to marry sociological institutionalism with (what this version perceives to be) critical theory.[10] This leads moderate constructivists to make visible the force of law through states' compliance and, subsequently, the politics of law involved in their reasons for doing/not

---

Relations (University of South Carolina Press Columbia 1989); A Wendt, *Social Theory of International Politics* (CUP Cambridge 1999).

[4] *Social Theory of International Politics* (n 3).

[5] T Hopf, 'The Promise of Constructivism in International Relations Theory' (1998) 23 *International Security* 171–200.

[6] R Palan, 'A World of Their Making: An Evaluation of the Constructivist Critique in International Relations' (2000) 26 *Review of International Studies* 575–98.

[7] O Kessler, 'Sleeping with the Enemy? On Hayek, Constructivist Thought, and the Current Economic Crisis' (2012) 38 *Review of International Studies* 275–99.

[8] See, for instance, C Reus-Smit, 'Politics and International Legal Obligation' (2003) 9 *European Journal of International Relations* 591–625; C Reus-Smit (ed), *The Politics of International Law* (CUP Cambridge 2004); I Hurd, 'Legitimacy and Authority in International Politics' (1999) 53 *International Organization* 379–408; I Hurd, *After Anarchy: Legitimacy and Power in the United Nations Security Council* (Princeton University Press Princeton 2007); T Risse, '"Let's Argue!": Communicative Action in World Politics' (2000) 54 *International Organization* 1–39; M Finnemore, 'Are Legal Norms Distinctive?' 32 *Journal of International Law and Politics* 699–705; R Price, 'A Genealogy of the Chemical Weapons Taboo' (1995) 49 *International Organization* 73–103.

[9] Please note that the demarcation between moderate and radical constructivism should not be understood as a strict divide but can be understood as an heuristic. There are of course authors whose approaches could be added to both camps.

[10] This, however, is built on an uneasy combination of 'is' and 'ought' and thus on how legal norms actually work.

doing so. Much of the discussion then focuses on how legal norms emerge, and how they get institutionalized and are subsequently followed by states. Primary examples are the literatures on the power of human rights and on the concept of legitimacy. By taking compliance as its central *problématique*, this literature often refers to liberal writers in ILT and shares with them a functional understanding of law.

The radical version differs insofar as it starts with the counterfactual validity of norms: norms cannot be observed by looking at what actors do, but need to be reconstructed by showing how behaviour is *justified*. Validity can only be determined when 'observable' behaviour is put into a 'wider' context through the assemblage of actions and events into a narrative. Hence, for radical constructivists, the force of law is associated with the 'construction' of the legal field itself: the politics of law is linked to the disciplinary or communicative structures and practices (to name different possible trajectories) through which interpretations, justifications, and reconstructions are put in place and made intelligible. Both Kratochwil and Onuf—albeit differently—link 'the politics of law' with the social dimension of law encapsulated in terms of constitutive rules, discourse, field, or social systems. Hence, they take pains to discuss legal theories to highlight the politics of courts, legal interpretation, and legal reasoning. Radical constructivists thus link to ILT through the work of the Critical Legal Studies literature to point at law's internal paradoxes, exclusionary forces, and systemic blind spots. For example, Onuf and Kratochwil—similarly to David Kennedy or Martti Koskenniemi—see law as a practice where practice is understood as a world of artifice (ie, of our making).

To show the difference between the two strands of constructivism, this chapter is structured in three sections. The moderate version is discussed in Section 2. Section 3 deals with the radical constructivist's contribution to ILT. Section 4 points to further questions constructivism could raise in ILT. That section moves the discussion beyond the reconstruction of constructivism itself and advances a constructivist agenda in ILT that focuses on processes of legalization, that is, the drawing of boundaries, ways of sense-making (semiosis), and particular contingency associated with the 'making' of legal facts, cases, and argumentation. The constructivist interest in how international lawyers 'make sense' of their world does not result from an anthropological or ethnographic interest, but from the kind of politics involved. From this perspective, the politics of international law is neither reducible to what states do, nor to the political agenda of international lawyers. Rather, the politics of international law is linked to law being a distinct rationality and discourse with its own rules of formation, spatio-temporal fixes, and modes of exclusions. Highlighting the social dimension of international law, for example, points to the reconfiguration of space-time in law with crucial repercussions for the self-description of law and the kind of expertise to which it gives rise.

2 THE CONTOURS OF CONSTRUCTIVISM

The advent of constructivism has to be seen in the light of IR's regime debate of the late 1970s and early 1980s. Back then, with the image of the United States as the declining hegemon, IR theorists began to wonder about the limits and contours of state cooperation when the hegemon is not able to overcome the imperative of international anarchy anymore. One answer led to regimes in which the 'public good' character of a stable order could be transformed into a 'club' rationality on the basis of shared principles, norms, rules, and procedures. Within regimes, it was said that not the balance of power, but the exchange of information and knowledge would characterize the politics of state cooperation.[11]

With the concepts of rules and norms (re-)entering the vocabulary of IR, the door was opened for constructivists to challenge the positivist regime-approach to rules and norms on their own ground. On the one hand, this focus on rules and norms automatically moves constructivists close to matters of international law. On the other hand, different modes of constructivism instantly emerged with crucial repercussions for how they related to the regimes literature.

Moderate constructivists are content to define constructivism as the study of norms in international life.[12] If one follows the Kelsenian way and understands law as a system of norms, then these constructivists share the lawyers' interest in norm creation, diffusion, and enforcement. The power of law derives from the ability of these legal norms and rules to alter states' behavior. The politics of law becomes visible in the capacity of legal norms to 'cause' and constrain the behaviour of legal persons.

As a consequence, the moderate constructivists' agenda is defined by the attempt to explain when, why, and how states comply with international law. This strand of constructivism engages in a long discussion with rational IR approaches to clarify their critique, build bridges, and produce a research program in the Lakatosian

---

[11] S Krasner, 'Structural Causes and Regime Consequences: Regimes as Intervening Variables' (1982) 36 *International Organization* 185–205; see also R Keohane, *After Hegemony: Cooperation and Discord in the World Political Economy* (Princeton University Press Princeton 1984). For a critique, see F Kratochwil and JG Ruggie, 'International Organization: A State of the Art on an Art of the State' (1986) 40 *International Organization* 753–75.

[12] See A Klotz, *Norms in International Relations: The Struggle Against Apartheid* (Cornell University Press Ithaca 1995); 'A Genealogy of the Chemical Weapons Taboo' (n 8); M Finnemore, 'Norms, Culture, and World Politics: Insights from Sociology's Institutionalism' (1996) 50 *International Organization* 325–47, at 325; PJ Katzenstein (ed), *The Culture of National Security: Norms and Identity in World Politics* (Columbia University Press New York 1996); J Brunnée and S Toope, 'Constructivism and International Law' in J Dunoff and M Pollack (eds), *Interdisciplinary Perspectives on International Law and International Relations: The State of the Art* (CUP Cambridge 2012) 119–45. For a critique see A Wiener, *The Invisible Constitution of Politics: Contested Norms and International Encounters* (CUP Cambridge 2008).

tradition as requested by rationalist IR scholars.[13] How constructivism and rationalism relate to each other has become the primary obsession for moderate constructivists.[14] To pursue this 'new program', moderate constructivists have high hopes for sociological institutionalism. Martha Finnemore, for example, opened a review article on sociological institutionalism, in which she attempts to marry this school of thought with constructivism, with the observation that, on the one hand, '[i]nternational relations scholars have become increasingly interested in norms of behaviour, intersubjective understandings, culture, identity, and other social features of political live';[15] on the other hand, however, the prevailing realist and liberal IR theories[16] were not able to grasp these concepts fully. She therefore proposed that constructivists embrace the sociological institutionalism developed around John W Meyer (the so-called Stanford School) as it 'developed a particularly powerful set of arguments about the role of norms and culture in international life'.[17] The Stanford school could also complement constructivism as it tells 'us what the social structure is':[18] what the Stanford school calls 'world cultural rules' and understands as the foundation of Western modernity à la Max Weber with its emphasis on justice and progress. These rules constitute the actors of IR.[19] Finnemore thus assumed that by marrying 'norms' with sociological institutionalism, constructivism could generate new research questions, in particular regarding the legitimacy of international organizations[20] and human rights.[21]

We can see that the confinement of constructivism as a study of norms, accompanied by the interest in compliance and sociological institutionalism, amounts to translating constructivism into an 'empirically' driven research program to 'test'

---

[13] R Keohane, 'International Institutions: Two Approaches' (1988) 32 *International Studies Quarterly* 379–96. See also M Finnemore and K Sikkink, 'Taking Stock: The Constructivist Research Program in International Relations and Comparative Politics' (2001) 4 *Annual Review of Political Science* 391–416.

[14] See *Social Theory of International Politics* (n 3). For international law see J Brunnée, 'Promoting Compliance with Multilateral Environmental Agreements' in J Brunné, M Doelle, and L Rajamani (eds), *Promoting Compliance in an Evolving Climate Regime* (CUP Cambridge 2012) 38–54, at 43; R Goodman and D Jinks, 'International Law and State Socialization: Conceptual, Empirical, and Normative Challenges' (2005) 54 *Duke Law Journal* 983–98; I Johnstone, *The Power of Deliberation: International Law, Politics and Organizations* (OUP Oxford 2011).

[15] 'Norms, Culture, and World Politics' (n 12) 325.

[16] Keohane called both schools of thought 'rationalistic': see 'International Institutions: Two Approaches' (n 13).

[17] 'Norms, Culture, and World Politics' (n 12) 325.   [18] Ibid 327.

[19] This social structure is 'ontologically primary' and it is thus possible to overcome agent-based fallacies and resulting state-centrism, which are committed by liberal and realist IR theories. At the same time, sociological institutionalists could benefit from IR in order to become more sensitive to politics: ibid 333 and 344.

[20] M Barnett and M Finnemore, *Rules for the World: International Organizations in Global Politics* (Cornell University Press Ithaca 2004); *After Anarchy* (n 8).

[21] T Risse-Kappen, S Ropp, and K Sikkink (eds), *The Power of Human Rights: International Norms and Domestic Change* (CUP New York 1999).

the validity of norms and, hence, to marry the study of norms to positivist 'standards' so as to evaluate the quality of scientific work. Norms are thus framed as independent variables and become an explanatory structure.[22]

The empirical 'value added' of constructivism was soon found: moderate constructivists have pointed out that non-state actors, and in particular so-called 'transnational advocacy networks', facilitate the diffusion and implementation of norms in issue areas such as the environment or human rights.[23] These networks attempt to build links among actors in civil societies, states, and international organizations—both on the domestic as well as the transnational level.[24] By introducing these networks, we can observe a double move away from the statist and static undertone of prevailing IR approaches. First, the 'explanandum became how ideas and identities were formed and who or what did the forming'.[25] And second, these 'transnational advocacy networks' provide the missing link to explain how, why, and when international actors such as states comply with these norms.[26]

This research program was further advanced through the 'norm life cycle model'.[27] To see how moderate constructivists theorize and understand norms, it is useful to discuss this model in detail. The model's purpose is to explain the process from the emergence to the internalization of a norm through three stages. The first stage analyses the emergence of a norm. As norms 'do not appear out of thin air',[28] they are actively created, framed, and promoted by so-called norm entrepreneurs.

[22] J Checkel, 'The Constructive Turn in International Relations Theory' (1998) 50 *World Politics* 324–48, at 328. Probably the most prominent definition in this context is Peter Katzenstein's: PJ Katzenstein, 'Introduction: Alternative Perspectives on National Security' in *The Culture of National Security* (n 12) 1–32, at 5 (emphasis in original):

> The authors [in this volume] use the concept of *norm* to describe collective expectations for the proper behavior of actors . . . In some situations norms operate like rules that define the identity of an actor, thus having 'constitutive effects' that specify what actions will cause relevant others to recognize a particular identity. In other situations norms operate as standards that specify the proper enactment of an already defined identity. In such instances norms have 'regulative' effects that specify standards of proper behavior. Norms thus either define (or constitute) identities or prescribe (or regulate) behavior, or they do both.

[23] Here, authors such as Martha Finnemore, Margaret Keck, Thomas Risse, Stephen C Ropp, Kathryn Sikkink, and others did valuable research.

[24] M Keck and K Sikkink, *Activists beyond Borders: Advocacy Networks in International Politics* (Cornell University Press Ithaca 1998). See also S Khagram, J Riker, and K Sikkink (eds), *Restructuring World Politics: Transnational Social Movements, Networks, and Norms* (University of Minnesota Press Minneapolis 2002).

[25] A Sinclair, *International Relations Theory and International Law: A Critical Approach* (CUP Cambridge 2010) 144.

[26] M Finnemore and K Sikkink, 'International Norm Dynamics and Political Change' (1998) 52 *International Organization* 887–917; T Risse and K Sikkink, 'The Socialization of International Human Rights Norms into Domestic Practices: Introduction' in T Risse, S Ropp, and K Sikkink (eds), *The Power of Human Rights: International Norms and Domestic Change* (CUP Cambridge 1999) 1–38.

[27] 'International Norm Dynamics and Political Change' (n 26).   [28] Ibid 896.

Norm entrepreneurs are motivated by 'altruism, empathy, and ideational commit-ment'[29] and need some kind of platform to organize, such as non-governmental organizations (NGOs) and/or transitional advocacy networks. These platforms col-lect and distribute expertise and help to coordinate behaviour. As norm entrepre-neurs deal with powerful states, they are not able to 'coerce' but need to 'persuade' states.[30] The first states that are persuaded become and act as 'norm leaders'. After a 'critical mass' accepts the norm, a 'tipping point' is reached through which the norm 'cascades'.[31] In this second stage of 'norm cascades', a different dynamic is ob-servable: the main actors are now states and international organizations. Networks start to play a minor role, even though their influence is not to be neglected. Yet, at this stage, states 'socialize' and start to comply 'for reasons that relate to their identities as members of an international society',[32] such as legitimacy, reputa-tion, or esteem. According to Finnemore and Sikkink, norms enter their third and final stage when they are completely 'internalized by actors and achieve a "taken-for-granted" quality that makes conformance with the norm almost automatic'.[33] At this point, norms are enacted through law, bureaucracies, or professional train-ing. When new norms emerge and disperse in the world order, earlier norms then cease to exist.

Finnemore and Sikkink's three-stage 'life cycle' model was further devel-oped into a five-phase 'spiral model' in the influential edited volume *The Power of Human Rights*.[34] In the opening chapter Risse and Sikkink attempt to 'present and develop a theory of stages and mechanisms through which inter-national norms can lead to changes in behavior',[35] or—to put it differently and following Katzenstein[36]—how ideas (individualistic cognitive commitments) become norms (collective behavioural claims on individuals).[37] First, Risse, and Sikkink build on the work on 'transnational advocacy networks'. These networks are crucial in three manners. First, they blame 'norm-violating states' in the international arena and 'remind liberal states of their own identity as promoters of human rights'; secondly, they 'empower and legitimate' domestic non-state actors (especially NGOs); thirdly, they create a 'transnational struc-ture pressuring [the norm-violating] regime'.[38]

This process of internalization and domestic implementation can be under-stood as a 'process of *socialization*'. And the concept of socialization constitutes a

---

[29] 'International Norm Dynamics and Political Change' (n 26) 898.   [30] Ibid.

[31] Ibid 901.   [32] Ibid 902.   [33] Ibid 904.

[34] *The Power of Human Rights* (n 26). For an assessment almost fifteen years later, see the fol-low-up volume, T Risse, S Ropp, and K Sikkink (eds), *The Persistent Power of Human Rights: From Commitment to Compliance* (CUP Cambridge 2013).

[35] 'The Socialization of International Human Rights Norms into Domestic Practices' (n 26) 2.

[36] *The Culture of National Security* (n 12).

[37] 'The Socialization of International Human Rights Norms into Domestic Practices' (n 26) 7.

[38] Ibid 5.

wonderful playground to test various causal mechanisms that link constructivism with broader debates in social theory. For example, norms are internalized due to 'processes of instrumental adaptation and strategic bargaining' (strategic action); 'processes of moral consciousness-raising, argumentation, dialogue, and persuasion';[39] or 'processes of institutionalization and habitualization' (ie, historical and sociological institutionalism).[40]

The subsequent 'theory-building' of socialization is then advanced through the 'spiral model of human rights change'.[41] The spiral model has a similar mechanistic rationale as the norm life cycle model and examines similar issues. According to this model, human rights violating states start, through external pressure from transnational advocacy networks, with human rights talk. By doing this, they are entrapped by a coalition of domestic opposition and international networks—and ultimately obey these norms. The spiral model thus explains how norms are institutionalized, legalized, and habitualized.

Moderate constructivists, with their focus on socialization and norms as causes, link with ILT in specific ways. First—and most obviously—moderate constructivists share the interest in the (liberal) legal question of 'why states comply'.[42] Generally speaking, this question is answered by recourse to the three legal traditions of Hobbes (power), Locke (interest), and Kant (legitimacy). How international law matters thus depends on what kind of 'culture' of the international we find ourselves in.

At the same time, constructivists have reformulated these three traditions by linking them to different *rationalities of action*. These rationalities of action are enacted by sociological institutionalism and March and Olson's distinction between a 'logic of consequence' and a 'logic of appropriateness'.[43] While the 'logic of consequences' represents the rationalistic decision-making on the basis of instrumental rationality, the logic of appropriateness is a perspective that sees human action as

[39] J Habermas, *The Theory of Communicative Action, Volume 1: Reason and the Rationalization of Society* (T McCarthy trans) (Beacon Press Boston 1984); "Let's Argue!" (n 8); N Deitelhoff and H Müller, 'Theoretical Paradise: Empirically Lost? Arguing with Habermas' (2005) 31 *Review of International Studies* 167–79.

[40] See P Hall and R Taylor, 'Political Science and the Three New Institutionalisms' (1996) 44 *Political Studies* 936–57; J March and J Olsen, 'The New Institutionalism: Organizational Factors in Political Life' (1984) 78 *American Political Science Review* 734–49.

[41] 'The Socialization of International Human Rights Norms into Domestic Practices' (n 26). The 'spiral model' draws not only on the 'life cycle' model but also on the 'boomerang pattern' developed in *Activists beyond Borders* (n 24).

[42] HH Koh, 'Why Do Nations Obey International Law?' (1997) 106 *Yale Law Journal* 2599–659, at 2599. See also L Henkin, *How Nations Behave: Law and Foreign Policy* (Columbia University Press New York 1979); A Chayes and AH Chayes, *The New Sovereignty: Compliance with International Regulatory Agreements* (Harvard University Press Cambridge MA 1998); 'Legitimacy and Authority in International Politics' (n 8).

[43] 'The New Institutionalism' (n 40).

driven by rules and norms.[44] Here, rules are followed because they are perceived as natural, rightful, expectable, and legitimate.

The recourse to the logic of appropriateness subsequently opened the door to an engagement with political and social theory, such as Jürgen Habermas' communicative rationality. This approach was subject to a larger debate in Germany in the 1990s. In particular, the so-called ZIB-debate, coined after the journal (*Zeitschrift für Internationale Beziehungen*) in which the debate started, tried to marry Habermasian thought with the regime literature. Moderate constructivists such as Harald Müller or Thomas Risse tried to show that actors in world politics do not only follow a strategic logic of action but often a complementary logic of persuasion or, as it was also called, a 'logic of arguing'.[45] This question was transformed into an empirically driven research program by the early 2000s to inquire into the institutional configurations that would allow for arguing and persuasion to take place.[46] Nicole Deitelhoff, for example, argued that the creation of the permanent International Criminal Court (ICC) in The Hague could be understood from 'the logic of arguing'. The logic of arguing, for instance, explains why the *Rome Statute* was far more progressive than the 'conservative model' proposed by the International Law Commission in 1994 and favoured by the P5.[47] This logic of arguing encompassed non-state actors, in particular transnational advocacy networks, like Amnesty International, which provided valuable legal expertise to small- and medium-sized states. This expertise was put into practice in a number of regional conferences organized by non-state actors together with countries in favour of the court. These conferences, far away from the UN headquarters in New York and the influence of P5, provided an environment for argumentation and persuasion.

A second avenue, by which moderate constructivists link with ILT, is constituted by a common interest in 'legitimacy'. Although legitimacy is still confined to the question 'why states comply',[48] the literature on legitimacy differs in significant ways from the discussion on various logics of action that we just discussed. At this point, it is interesting to note that legitimacy was almost absent from debates in IR (and most of IL as well) until the late 1980s. Its advent in the early 1990s both symbolizes the hope of a new world order after the end of the Cold War and marks one

---

[44] For a critique see O Sending, 'Constitution, Choice and Change: Problems with the "Logic of Appropriateness" and Its Use in Constructivist Theory' (2002) 8 *European Journal of International Relations* 443–70.

[45] H Müller 'Internationale Beziehungen Als Kommunikatives Handeln. Zur Kritik Der Utilitaristischen Handlungstheorie' (1994) 1 *Zeitschrift Für Internationale Beziehungen* 15–44; "Let's Argue!" (n 8); 'Theoretical Paradise: Empirically Lost?' (n 39). For an overview see P Niesen and B Herborth (eds), *Anarchie der kommunikativen Freiheit: Jürgen Habermas und die Theorie der internationalen Politik* (Suhrkamp Frankfurt am Main 2007).

[46] 'Theoretical Paradise: Empirically Lost?' (n 39).

[47] N Deitelhoff, 'The Discursive Process of Legalization: Charting Islands of Persuasion in the ICC Case' (2009) 63 *International Organization* 33–65, at 38.

[48] TM Franck, *The Power of Legitimacy among Nations* (OUP New York 1990).

of the most significant shifts in the international political vocabulary. Previously confined to the analysis of domestic politics, it was soon assigned to the application and performative power of international rules more generally.

For moderate constructivists, the concept of legitimacy provided an avenue to explore the normative dimension of politics which also implies an inquiry into the role law could play for normative progress. For example, Ian Hurd in a well-received article in the journal *International Organization* is interested in the question '[w]hat motivates states to follow international norms, rules, and commitments?'.[49] Hurd explicitly links legitimacy with 'the normative belief by an actor that a rule or institution ought to be obeyed' and he continues that

[i]t is a subjective quality, relational between actor and institution, and defined by the actor's perception of the institution. The actor's perception may come from the substance of the rule or the procedure or source by which it was constituted. Such a perception affects the behaviour because it is internalized by the actor and helps to define how the actor sees its interest.[50]

Legitimacy comes into play when the prevailing utilitarian logics of actions in IR, based on coercion (Hobbes) or self-interest (Locke), have difficulty explaining certain events and situations, such as the fact that great powers respect the norm(s) of sovereignty. Legitimacy thus complements rationalist IR approaches and can provide a 'bridge between rationalistic and constructivist approaches'.[51]

Legitimacy thus provides an avenue to leave behind the confines of inter-state politics, to embrace normative aspirations of world politics, and provide a common research agenda between moderate constructivists and international legal scholars where the concept—similar to IR—enjoys increasing popularity. Here, two approaches stand out and seem of particular interest when it comes to discussing the relationship between ILT and constructivism. This is, on the one hand, the work of Thomas Franck in the late 1980s and early 1990s and, on the other hand, the 'interactional framework' to international law developed by Jutta Brunnée and Stephen Toope.

Franck, similarly to many moderate constructivists, asks why 'powerful states obey powerless rules?'[52] For Franck, they do so in the case of a particular rule because 'they perceive the rule and its institutional penumbra to have a high degree of legitimacy'.[53] He defines legitimacy itself as 'a property of a rule or a rule-making institution which itself exerts a pull toward compliance on those addressed normatively because those addressed believe that the rule or institution has come into being and operates in accordance with generally accepted principles of right

---

[49] 'Legitimacy and Authority in International Politics' (n 8) 379.   [50] Ibid 381.
[51] *After Anarchy* (n 8) 2.
[52] *The Power of Legitimacy among Nations* (n 48) 3. See also *How Nations Behave* (n 42); *The New Sovereignty* (n 42); 'Why Do Nations Obey International Law?' (n 42).
[53] *The Power of Legitimacy among Nations* (n 48) 25.

process'.[54] Franck is thus interested in process rather than substance (such as ideas of global justice would emphasize). As the idea (that nations comply with international law as long as they perceive its rules as legitimate) is not directly observable, Franck starts with the identification of specific properties of rules. He uses these properties to develop indicators that make rules more or less legitimate and thereby generate more or less compliance. These properties are their determinacy (semantic clarity), coherence (consistency with other rules), symbolic validation (authenticity through pedigree and rituals), and adherence (connection to secondary rules).

As a slightly different approach, Brunnée and Toope perceive their 'interactional framework' of international law as explicitly interdisciplinary.[55] In particular, they try to bring various strands of moderate constructivism together with the legal philosophy of Lon Fuller.[56] They are interested in how legal obligation is created and how a distinctive legal legitimacy is produced. According to Brunnée and Toope, the production of legal legitimacy requires the synthesis of three things. First, norms (legal and non-legal) need to be embedded in an underlying set of shared understanding such as collectively held background knowledge, norms or practices. Here, they draw on the work on norm entrepreneurship and socialization, as already discussed above. Second, to distinguish legal from non-legal norms, they draw on a number of criteria of legality promoted by Fuller.[57] According to Fuller, these criteria—such as, for instance, generality, non-retroactivity, congruence and clarity—create fidelity to law among social actors. And finally, while for Fuller, the fulfillment of these criteria is enough, Brunnée and Toope argue that legality can only exist as a practice within what Emanuel Adler calls a 'community of practice'.[58]

3 RADICAL CONSTRUCTIVISM AND THE STUDY OF INTERNATIONAL LAW

The last section discussed how moderate constructivism has entered ILT in recent years. When we look at the more radical version of constructivism, the picture is a different one, in particular in relation to its understanding of the politics

---

[54] *The Power of Legitimacy among Nations* (n 48) 24.

[55] J Brunnée and S Toope, *Legitimacy and Legality in International Law: An Interactional Account* (CUP Cambridge 2010); J Brunnée and S Toope, 'Interactional International Law: An Introduction' (2011) 3 *International Theory* 307–18.

[56] L Fuller, *The Morality of Law* (Yale University Press New Haven 1969).   [57] See ibid.

[58] E Adler, *Communitarian International Relations: The Epistemic Foundations of International Relations* (Routledge London 2005).

of international law and its link to ILT. For radical constructivism, the work of Nicholas Onuf and Friedrich Kratochwil stands out, as both referred, from early on, to international law to advance their projects.[59] For example, in *World of Our Making*, Onuf attempts 'to reconstruct a self-consciously organized field of study, or discipline, called International Relations'.[60] And this act of reconstruction is in turn only possible within a constructivist framework. For Onuf constructivism is a

way of studying social relations—any kind of social relations.... [I]t stands on its own as a system of concepts and propositions. Constructivism is not a theory as such. It does not offer general explanations for what people do, why societies differ, how the world changes.[61]

For Onuf, constructivism is more a meta-theoretical form of reasoning than a substantial theory of politics, although Onuf described his own substantial theory of politics in his early writings as 'Kantian'[62] and later on as 'republican'.[63]

It is crucial that constructivism is put forward as a challenge to IR's core assumption that 'politics' can be attributed to anarchy and hence sovereign states. To start with anarchy, international law can only play an insignificant role given its lack of sanctioning power, which deprives it of much potential force. Yet the constructive view that international relations presuppose concepts of the social, puts international law right at the centre of political analyses. First, international law constitutes a distinct social sphere with its own modes of exclusion, internal hierarchies, and disciplinary structures. Second, and this is what Onuf focuses on, the social is encapsulated in the concept of 'rules'. Hence, in order to understand constructivism, we need a concept of (legal) rules:

[C]onstructivism holds that people make society, and society makes people. This is a continuous, two-way process. In order to study it, we must start in the middle, so to speak, because people and society, always having made each other, are already there and just about to change. To make a virtue of necessity, we will start in the middle, between people and society, by introducing a third element, *rules*, that always links the other two elements. Social rules (the term *rules* includes, but is not restricted to, legal rules) make the process by which people and society constitute each other continuous and reciprocal.[64]

---

[59] Onuf actually introduced the notion 'constructivism' to the academic field of IR: see *World of Our Making* (n 3).

[60] Ibid 1.

[61] N Onuf, 'Constructivism: A User's Manual' in V Kubálková, N Onuf, and P Kowert (eds), *International Relations in a Constructed World* (ME Sharpe Armonk 1998) 58–78, at 58.

[62] N Onuf, 'The Constitution of International Society' (1994) 5 *European Journal of International Law* 1–19, at 2.

[63] N Onuf, *The Republican Legacy in International Thought* (CUP Cambridge 1998); N Onuf and P Onuf, *Nations, Markets, and War: Modern History and the American Civil War* (University of Virginia Press Charlottesville 2006).

[64] 'Constructivism: A User's Manual' (n 61) 59 (emphasis in original). But Onuf's work is not just about rules. Only the first part of his central monograph, *World of Our Making*, is dedicated to the question of rules (chs 1–4). The second part (chs 5–8) is concerned with rule. For Onuf rules and rule are intertwined, as rules produce rule and vice versa: 'By constituting conditions of rule, rules

Rules do not determine social behaviour but provide the conditions of possibility and act as 'sign posts', as Wittgenstein has put it. This allows Onuf to see that through rules agents construct our world;[65] on the other hand, rules can only be made visible through the study of texts and discourses.[66]

For example—and of great importance for his analyses of international law—Onuf follows John Searle's[67] categorization of speech acts,[68] which Onuf links to types of legal practices. For Onuf 'all rules *are* either assertives…or directives…or commissives'.[69] Commissives consist in the declaration of the speaker's commitment to some stated course of action, they typically contain verbs such as 'promise' or 'offer', and they 'fit words to the world'.[70] Directives concern an action the speaker wishes the hearer to perform, they typically involve verbs such as 'ask', 'demand', 'command', 'forbid', 'permit', or 'caution' and they 'fit the world to words'.[71] Assertives are statements declaring a belief, which the speaker wishes the hearer to accept, they appear typically with verbs such as 'state', 'affirm', 'report', 'characterize', 'attribute', 'insist', or 'dissent' and they 'either reflect an existing words-to-world fit or propose a new one'.[72] Or to put it differently, 'all rules are either assertives of the form, I state X counts as Y, or directives of the form, I state that X person (should, must, may) do Y, or commissives of the form, I state that I (can, will, should) do Y'.[73]

These different types of rules then bring Onuf to different practices:[74] first, naming and relating (or designating position) which can be identified with instruction rules; secondly, having and using (or allocating possession and use) which can be related to assertives or conferrals; and finally, enabling, and making unable (or exercising control) which mirrors directives. Of course, in reality these three activities and their related rule types are mixed. Yet, they allow us to do things: instruction rules are principles and they help us to rank and choose between a large

always distribute privilege, and always preferentially': *World of Our Making* (n 3) 128. Here, in questions about the distribution of politics, Onuf situates the realm of politics.

[65] N Onuf, 'Do Rules Say What They Do? From Ordinary Language to International Law' (1985) 2 *Harvard International Law Journal* 384–410, at 396.

[66] This puts Onuf close to the critical legal theory of David Kennedy. In contrast to Kennedy, however, Onuf takes recourse to the ordinary language philosophy of the later Wittgenstein: ibid 391–5.

[67] JR Searle, *Expression and Meaning: Studies in the Theory of Speech Acts* (CUP Cambridge 1979) 30–57.

[68] Speech acts can be one of five types: assertives (or constatives), directives, commissives, expressives, and declarations. Expressives serve to convey an attitude or emotion. For Onuf, they are not rule candidates as they are only related to the speaker and are over when acknowledged by the hearer. The same holds true for declarations, which do not require the acknowledgement of the hearer. Thus, these two are neglected in the later discussion.

[69] 'Do Rules Say What They Do?' (n 65) 401.   [70] *World of Our Making* (n 3) 93.

[71] Ibid.   [72] Ibid.   [73] Ibid 90.

[74] To show this Onuf draws on work undertaken with V Spike Peterson: see N Onuf and VS Peterson, 'Human Rights from an International Regimes Perspective' (1984) 37 *Journal of International Affairs* 329–42.

number of instructions; conferring rules are regulation and help to routinize; and directives are what normally—that is, by legal positivists—is called law because they are formally enacted and subject to enforcement. We can find all three types of speech acts in both the domestic and the international sphere. Nevertheless, there are differences between the domestic and the international order, as the latter lacks the formalization of the former and consists therefore of more self-referential rules. Nonetheless Onuf claims: 'But law they are, whatever damage this does to the positivist conception of proper legal order'[75] and concludes 'that the international legal order, although lacking a constitutional template for extrusion of legal rules, is very much a legal order'.[76]

Kratochwil pursues a slightly different agenda. At first sight, he appears to share the moderate constructivists' agenda as he 'examines the role of norms in international life'. Yet that is as far as the similarity goes. His interest in norms is not motivated by some empirical test of legal validity, but by the view that IR's 'treatment of norms suffers from a variety of epistemological shortcomings'.[77] These shortcomings are rooted in the very definition of IR as the study of anarchy and its sharp distinction between the domestic and international order. In a piece co-authored with John Ruggie in 1986, Kratochwil argues that the regime literature is grounded on problematic theoretical assumptions as 'epistemology fundamentally contradicts ontology'.[78] On the one hand, the concept of regimes, drawing on terms such as 'principles', 'norms', 'rules', or 'expectations', is based on an intersubjective ontology but relies, on the other hand, on a positivist epistemology, which cannot fully grasp intersubjective phenomena. These shortcomings result also from the fact 'that the work on regimes is characterized by an egregious lack of familiarity with legal theory'.[79] What is needed to overcome these 'epistemological anomalies' is a new research program open for intersubjectivity.[80]

Kratochwil blames not only the literature on regimes for having a problematic concept of (international) law, but is also highly critical of many prevailing approaches in ILT. Here, his main concern is that it is not possible to define what 'law' is as

attempts at defining a demarcation between legal and other norms is bound to fail because [sic] it fundamentally misconstrues the problem of arriving at a decision through the utilization of rules and norms. Although judges are bound by the 'law' it can be shown that not all 'legal' rules are characterized by sanction, or form part of a deductive hierarchical

[75] 'Do Rules Say What They Do?' (n 65) 407.   [76] Ibid 410.

[77] Rules, Norms, and Decisions (n 1) 1; F Kratochwil, 'How Do Norms Matter?' in M Byers (ed), The Role of Law in International Politics: Essays in International Relations and International Law (OUP Oxford 2000) 35–68.

[78] 'International Organization' (n 11) 764.

[79] F Kratochwil, 'Thrasymachos Revisited: On the Relevance of Norms and the Study of Law for International Relations' (1984) 37 Journal of International Affairs 343–56, at 344.

[80] Rules, Norms, and Decisions (n 1) 257–62.

system of norms. Consequently, legal rules and norms cannot be conceptualized as possessing one common characteristic, or by being treated merely as institutional rules.[81]

For Kratochwil, such a purely referential model of language, that tries to find a universal and transhistorical fixed definition of law, should be abandoned, as it cannot capture the different meanings of 'law'. He proposes instead to follow the line of the late Ludwig Wittgenstein[82] and look at how 'law' as a concept is 'used' in different contexts. The different uses of the concept can then be better understood as 'family resemblances', which are part of a particular 'language game'. Thereby it is possible to 'spell out some criteria that in *our society* are part of the language game of law'.[83] For example, in our society 'law is a particular branch of practical reasoning'[84] and 'can be conceived as a particular system of communicative action'.[85] Thus, law cannot be reduced to written texts, such as it is done through 'a quick look at statutes, treatises or codes, but it can only be ascertained through the performance of rule application to a controversy and the appraisal of reasons offered in defence of such a decision'.[86]

Nevertheless it is important to notice at this point that not all normative argumentations are legal and that law can be distinguished, although not always sharply, from other often-similar modes of reasoning such as bargaining, debates, or moral and rights-based reasoning. Thus, by 'emphasizing the *style* of reasoning with rules rather than either the intrinsic characteristics of the norms, their membership in a system, or the contribution to an overarching goal, we can give a more realistic account of the legal enterprise'.[87] As legal reasoning is a specific style of reasoning, only a set of specific reasons given can be successful. First, legal argumentation draws primary on sources, *topoi*, the creation of sub-types through further distinction, and analogies. In particular, analogies 'lie at the heart of legal reasoning' as their task is 'to establish similarities among different cases or objects in face of (striking) dissimilarities'.[88] Second, what counts as an analogy or valid legal reasoning is no longer attributable to formal determinations. Instead, it is important to emphasize that legal argumentation is always embedded in a life-world, that is, a set of wider contingent 'historical and sociological background conditions' and 'that law is always part of a political project that connects present via the past to a future "utopia"'.[89] Third, the language game of 'law' is connected to the idea of third-party settlement and official rule-handlers, such as judges, who are authorized to take

---

[81] *Rules, Norms, and Decisions* (n 1) 186.

[82] L Wittgenstein, *Philosophical Investigations* (Macmillan New York 1953).

[83] F Kratochwil, *The Status of Law in World Society: Meditations On the Role and Rule of Law* (CUP Cambridge 2014) at 65.

[84] *Rules, Norms, and Decisions* (n 1) 18.   [85] 'Thrasymachos Revisited' (n 79) 350.

[86] *The Status of Law in World Society* (n 83) 65–6; *Rules, Norms, and Decisions* (n 1) 18.

[87] *Rules, Norms, and Decisions* (n 1) 187 (emphasis in original).   [88] Ibid 223.

[89] F Kratochwil, 'Legal Theory and International Law' in D Armstrong (ed), *Routledge Handbook of International Law* (Routledge London 2009) 35–68, at 56.

binding decisions about what the law 'is'. Nevertheless, a mere institutionalization of third-party procedures and positions is not enough, because this does not, as examples from magic to theology show, entail legal reasoning per se.[90] For Kratochwil, the notion of legal authority is connected to the idea that legal decisions are binding: they are valid even if mistaken and can only be overruled through higher instances. Furthermore, legal authorities are bound by law. This means that although they have discretion to decide, not everything goes. Finally, becoming a lawyer implicates learning a new language and specific technique (*ars legis*).[91] Lawyers frame the world according to a 'jural ontology'[92] and learn what is part of the law and what not—what counts, for instance, as a legal fact and what not. Learning 'such a language and speaking about the world in such a way means to participate in a practice, a shared form of life, as Wittgenstein called it', as it is more about the 'knowing how' as the 'knowing what'.[93]

As a summary, then, we can see that radical constructivism is quite similar to the CLS movement in ILT as it shares many of its interests. The reason that both Onuf and Kratochwil engage with international law, however, has less to do with the identification of the paradoxical and exclusionary forces in international law per se. Rather, they primarily challenge IR's preoccupation with anarchy through which IR is decoupled from social and political theory. In the next section we want to step beyond the mere reconstruction of constructivism and ILT and put constructivism into practice to show what kind of questions it can generate.

4 Constructivism, International Law, and the Challenge of World Society

The previous two sections have outlined how constructivists approach questions of international law and its role in world politics. Moderate constructivists frame the legal force in world politics in terms of compliance where the politics of international law is ultimately linked to the question of 'why do states obey legal norms?'. This question is particularly relevant in legal areas such as human rights or trade law where non-state actors and norm entrepreneurs persuade and argue with states to change the normative framework of world politics. With it comes a

---

[90] *The Status of Law in World Society* (n 83) 65–6.
[91] *Rules, Norms, and Decisions* (n 1) 238; *The Status of Law in World Society* (n 83) 66.
[92] C Stone, 'From a Language Perspective' (1981) 90 *Yale Law Journal* 1149–92.
[93] *The Status of Law in World Society* (n 83) 67.

functionalist understanding of law: law helps to advance a normative agenda in world politics and thus is employed for the normative progress of the global order. The link to ILT is then established through the interest in legitimacy or the margins of global justice.

Radical constructivists link the force of law to law itself. Here, one can think of the juridical field, discursive practices, or the legal system as attempts to conceptualize this self-referentiality of legal operations or legal practices.[94] For radical constructivists, references to the critical legal studies movement proved to be particularly important.[95] For radical constructivists, constructivism is not confined to the study of norms itself, as many believe, but the study of international law as a social system characterized by contingency and not by necessity (as natural systems would propose).

The study of contingency takes different forms in the various strata of international life. International law, like the economy, is characterized by a very specific contingency. How contingency is reproduced and managed changes continuously.[96] The vocabulary of norms, rights, and risks provide different vocabularies to deal with contingency and the modern notion of norms is only one possibility of structuring legal argumentation. The politics of law then is related to the way in which the boundaries of the legal and non-legal are drawn,[97] the complexity and contingency of legal argumentation,[98] and ways of world making by lawyers.[99] The politics of international law is thus not confined to 'states', but to the inclusionary and exclusionary forces of law that constitute law as a distinct social sphere, that is, the way lawyers make sense of their world and how they make legal facts, cases, and arguments.

In this section, we want to point to two questions that we think are of particular interest for a constructivist ILT and that take the changing contours of the global order as a starting point: as the global order changes, the questions are what role international law plays and how its temporal, spatial, and reflexive conditions

---

[94] For an ethnographic approach, see A Riles, *The Network Inside Out* (University of Michigan Press Ann Arbor 2000).

[95] See also A Orford, *International Authority and the Responsibility to Protect* (CUP Cambridge 2011); S Singh, 'The Potential of International Law: Fragmentation and Ethics' (2011) 24 *Leiden Journal of International Law* 23–43.

[96] Thus, constructivists emphasize 'historicity', see F Kratochwil, 'History, Action and Identity: Revisiting the "Second" Great Debate and Assessing Its Importance for Social Theory' (2006) 12 *European Journal of International Relations* 5–29.

[97] F Johns, *Non-Legality in International Law: Unruly Law* (CUP Cambridge 2013).

[98] D Kennedy, *International Legal Structures* (Nomos Baden-Baden 1987); *Rules, Norms, and Decisions* (n 1); M Koskenniemi, *From Apology to Utopia: The Structure of International Legal Argument* (reissue CUP Cambridge 2005).

[99] A Orford, 'Embodying Internationalism: The Making of International Lawyers' (1998) 19 *Australian Year Book of International Law* 1–34; D Kennedy, *Of War and Law* (Princeton University Press Princeton 2006); F Kratochwil, 'Has the Rule of Law Become a Rule of Lawyers? An Inquiry in the Uses and Abuses of an Ancient Topos in Contemporary Debates' in G Palombella and N Walker (eds), *Relocating the Rule of Law* (Hart Oxford 2009) 171–96.

change. To highlight key aspects of our argument, we would like to point to the advent of risk and its consequence for expertise in international law.

4.1 The Acceleration of Legal Practices: From Norms to Risk?

Both international relations and international legal scholars commonly describe legal practices in terms of norms and rules. This is in particular true for constructivist approaches. This vocabulary at the same time determines the temporality (and 'function') of legal practices. For legal proceedings to commence there has to be a perceived violation of an existing norm or the failure to fulfil an obligation. Legal proceedings then usually start by asking whether a particular situation gives rise to a case, what the case is, and what legal institutions have the authority to deal with it (in overall: questions of jurisdiction). The legal proceedings then need to clarify whether the act or omission of an act indeed violated a norm or whether a norm actually existed that regulates that behaviour (raising questions of norm existence vis-à-vis norm enforcement). Subsequent debates then may question how norms relate to each other, where they enter, how they are to be applied, and so on—until they also determine what secondary rules are in place. The function international law then has to play is to translate political disputes into legal claims and thereby help to 'civilize nations'.[100]

With the advent of the war on terror and the various pre-emptive and precautionary practices it brought about, it appears that international law changes its temporality. It has not only to deal with events, acts, and decisions that were located in the past, but it has also to deal with future events. Pre-emption and precaution as principles of legal reasoning inevitably escape the temporality of norms-based reasoning and embrace risk-based approaches. Even though risk and norms are two different ways in which time can be 'bound', the way the present and the future relate to each other is different as risk is more future-oriented. This becomes much clearer when we remind ourselves that one cannot violate risk as one can violate a norm. In contrast, risk requires continuous adaptation of expectation on the basis of new information while norm-based reasoning is counter-factually valid and thus inherently normative.[101]

The emergence of a risk-based rationality in international law is in particular visible in the context of targeted killings.[102] Individuals can be 'non-innocent'

---

[100] M Koskenniemi, 'The Place of Law in Collective Security' (1996) 17 *Michigan Journal of International Law* 455–90, at 489.

[101] Risk and norms thus give rise to different kinds of expectations: cognitive in the case of risk and normative in the case of norms.

[102] This section is based on O Kessler and W Werner, 'Extrajudicial Killing as Risk Management' (2008) 39 *Security Dialogue* 289–308, at 305.

under international law in three ways: either they are responsible for some wrongdoing in the past, or they are said to be individually dangerous, or they are dangerous because they belong to a group (combatant). The first legal category is the most prominent one and follows the law enforcement paradigm with fundamental legal notions and categories in place (due process and so forth). If an individual is killed because he or she is found to be individually dangerous, as in the second category, there are clear standards in place, such as the demand for an independent investigation where the 'legality' of the act is reconstructed *ex post* (with standards given by necessity, proportionality, and so forth). The third category is governed by international humanitarian law (and hence the law of war) with clear rules on how to separate combatants and non-combatants. Also in that case, there are rules and standards in place. Through the invocation of 'risk' as 'danger', we see that established legal categories are blurred with the consequence that states manoeuvre between legal categories because suspected terrorists are said to constitute unlawful combatants or count as 'civilians directly participating in hostilities'. The terrorist remains a 'legitimate' target because he could use force. Hence, we see how the war paradigm of states is supplemented with elements of the law enforcement paradigm, insofar as the law enforcement vocabulary is used without the acceptance of its standards.

4.2 Expertise between Evidence and Intelligence

This change from norms to risk also changes legal expertise.[103] Usually, the issue of expertise is discussed together with the role of scientific knowledge in legal proceedings, raising the question of how law is connected with other sciences. Yet, as David Kennedy has reminded us,[104] international law itself constitutes a field of expertise.[105] In the context of the norm, this expertise is structured around cases. The lawyer is supposed to know the history of legal norms as discussed and (not) applied in legal cases. A good lawyer is also familiar with dissenting opinions, the *travaux préparatoires* of treaties, and maybe background stories about why

---

[103] On international legal expertise in general, see also A Leander and T Aalberts, 'Introduction: The Co-Constitution of Legal Expertise and International Security' (2013) 26 *Leiden Journal of International Law* 783–92.

[104] *Of War and Law* (n 99).

[105] In particular, the realm of warfare is increasingly shaped by international law and in particular the law of force (both *ius ad bellum* and *ius in bello*) as 'this vocabulary—of just war, legitimate targeting, proportionate violence, and prohibited weaponry—has been institutionalized by the military... As such law today shapes the politics, as well as the practices, of warfare': *Of War and Law* (n 99) 7.

certain decisions and judgments were made.[106] The expertise lawyers provide is past-directed and not future-oriented. It is not the task of a lawyer to say what will happen, but to translate present and past events into legal concepts on the basis of evidence. With the advent of risk rationality, this evidence does not derive from the past, but the rationalization of a possible future. As a consequence, this has blurred the distinction between evidence and intelligence. As de Goede and de Graaf have pointed out, in this context, legal cases operate on the pre-mediation of possible futures with the consequence that the legal questions of aim and intent are replaced by a focus on the potential harmfulness of allegedly attempted conduct.[107] Judgments are reached regardless of whether an action has taken place (for example whether a farewell message was distributed that could point to a terrorist act)—or whether it was simply retrieved by intelligence on the home computer. The consequence of risk then is not only that these legal rationalities are blurred and used for political purposes, but that legal proceedings, the fabrication of legal knowledge, and the formulation of legal argumentation are destabilized.

5 Conclusion

This chapter has discussed different constructivist approaches to ILT. It has differentiated between a moderate and a radical version. The moderate version grasps legal force in terms of compliance, which leads it to conceptualize the politics of international law in the 'assemblage' of states and non-state actors in processes of norm creation, dispersion, and implementation. The radical version on the other hand associates the force of law internally with legal operations and the legal system. This links the radical constructivists with social theoretical literatures around the juridical field, legal system, or discourse analysis that are also detectable in the critical legal studies movement. Radical constructivists are interested in norms—but not for their own sake. Rather, they allow us to reconstruct ways of sense-making of specific practices. At the same time, they are counter-factually valid and thus escape a positivist philosophy of science. This is the reason why the politics of indeterminacy, for example, easily links with the radical constructivist literature. Also the recent turn to ethics, the emergence of new managerialism within international law, the 'dark sides' of legalism, or the emergence of international legal expertise are of inherent interest for constructivists.

---

[106] On the disciplinary processes, especially the 'technologies of the self', involved in becoming an international lawyer, see 'Embodying Internationalism' (n 99).

[107] M de Goede and B de Graaf, 'Sentencing Risk: Temporality and Precaution in Terrorism Trials' (2013) 7 *International Political Sociology* 313–31, at 320.

Where radical constructivists differ from critical legal scholars is the path they currently take. Even though both keep true to their interest in 'contingency', they pursue it in different ways. The critical legal studies movement currently undergoes a 'turn to history' where historical inquiries are used to advance a critical agenda in the sense that they undermine the foundations of orthodox legal knowledge. Contingency is thus related to the 'history of the present' and the excluded alternatives and avenues that 'stabilize' our modern presuppositions. Radical constructivists, on the other hand, link contingency to social processes (legal operations, practices, discourses, and so forth). Their analyses thus focus on how transformation of the world order redefines the role and contours of the legal system, discourse, or field and show this through the redefinition, destabilization, and rearrangement of legal categories through changes in legal semantics.

This chapter outlines some of the resulting questions by looking, first, at the advent of risk in international law, how the shift from norms to risk is linked to a different temporality of international law itself, and how this changes the argumentative moves and contours and the function of legal experts. A way ahead for constructivism and ILT is provided by an interest in the changing contours of the global order as, for example, represented in the concept of world society. World society is not an attempt to create a new 'totalizing' approach that encapsulates everything under one grand narrative. Rather, it is a way to take seriously the fact that international law as a social sphere requires a concept of the social that is different from that operating at the national level and which it cannot collapse into concepts like global justice. Thus, the task is to reconstruct the changing role law plays in the current global order while at the same time analysing how international law reproduces and changes its constitutive boundaries through which it makes sense of its world, and allows for career paths, positions, and the performative power of expertise.

CHAPTER 18

THE INTERNATIONAL SIGNS LAW

PETER GOODRICH

Divisa autem omnis vita est in negotium et otium.[1]

1 INTRODUCTION

IN the remarkable 'Epistle Dedicatorie' to his 1652 translation of Selden's *Mare clausum*, Marchamont Nedham reasons that it is by 'his Learned Pen' that the 'eminent Autor', John Selden, has bravely maintained the sea territories of our Britannia.[2] She is indeed portrayed in the frontispiece of the volume as the emblem of both the insular and oceanic public sphere of England—*Angliae reipub.*—to whom Neptune offers homage in the form of treasures and arms. The muse of history, Clio, meanwhile stands on Britannia's outstretched left hand and seeks to place a crown of laurels on her head while simultaneously holding a quill ready to inscribe her glory on the skies (Figure 18.1). 'It is a gallant sight to see Sword and Pen in the victorious Equipage together' and Nedham concludes that: 'The Pen it is which manifests the Right of Things'.[3] And sure enough there follow slightly over 500 pages of archival

---

[1] Aristotle, *Politics*, bk 7 ch 14.
[2] J Selden, *Of the Dominion, or, Ownership of the Sea* (Du Gard London 1652) at fol br.
[3] Ibid fol br–bv.

Figure 18.1 Britannia

Source: Copyright 2015 by the Regents of the University of California,
The Robbins Collection, School of Law, University of California at Berkeley.

proofs, of documents, of statutes, charters, commissions, licenses, letters, prescripts, proclamations, edicts, maps, schemata, pictures, medallions, and coins all destined to prove what the frontispiece already had inscribed, made visible, and shown, namely:

What then should great *Britannia* pleas,
But rule as Ladie o're all seas

It is interesting and indicative that the earlier, Latin edition of the book, published in 1635, did not carry the imperial image of Britannia, but rather a devise that shows a scholarly figure plucking grapes from a vine that encircles the trunk of a leafy tree. The motto is the contraction of an Erasmian adage, *non solus*, not alone, and below the picture, in case the meaning is not clear, is added *iuxta exemplar,* meaning according

Figure 18.2 iuxta exemplar
Source: Copyright 2015 Peter Goodrich

to the example of the Romans (Figure 18.2). The picture of tree and vine is an emblem of amity, of the community of humanistic lawyers, and of the commonality of Latin and of the civil law, the *jus gentium* or 'droict des gens' that governs international relations and human affairs in their universality.[4] It will be the argument of this chapter that, as these brief examples adumbrate, for there to be international law, juridically governed communication, and commerce amidst the babel of cultures, conflicts, and languages, of the early seventeenth-century empires, there first has to be a medium for communicating an initial semiotic of identity and jurisdiction.

2 Laws and Arms

The beginnings of international law, the *nomos* of the earth, as well as the even more exemplary question of the dominion of the seas with which Selden was so

---

[4] A Alciato, *Emblemata* (Bonhomme Lyons 1551) *Amicitia etiam post mortem durans.*

concerned, starts in the law of nature and is expressed in the earliest markings, patterns, rhythms, and signs that delineate human inhabitation and community. The first lawyers, just to borrow from Sir Philip Sidney, were *Vates*, foreseers, poets, prophets, and bards who could apprehend the invisible and future patterns of human community and so brought peoples together.[5] The poet, the creator, proffers a figure of the pre-legal, and embodies and improves upon nature in 'freely ranging onely within the Zodiack of his owne wit'.[6] It is imagination, the idea, the glimpses that the poet grasps of the divine and invisible order of nature that determines the first pattern of community, property, and law:

For what else is the awaking his musicall instruments, the often and free changing of persons, his notable *Prosopopeias*, when he maketh you, as it were, see God comming in his Maiestie, his telling of the Beastes joyfulness, and hills leaping, but a heavenlie poesie, wherein almost hee sheweth himself a passionate lover of that unspeakable and everlasting beautie to be seene by the eyes of the minde, onely cleered by fayth?[7]

Where Sidney sees the poets and in the above lucubration, the psalmists, as the first lawyers, the Anglican *nomikoi*, the learned antiquarians and humanistic legal scholars of the Inns of Court and the other universities viewed the lawyer as inexorably bound at root to an angelological hierarchy, which is to say to nature and divinity.

Take as prosaic a text as Cowell's *Institutiones iuris Anglicani* which was published first in 1605 and which gains a somewhat unfavourable mention in Selden's *Mare clausum*.[8] Citing Bracton, for reasons doubtless politic, rather than Justinian, he opens with the classical definition of legal learning, given in Latin terms as *jurisprudentia est divinarum atque humanarum rerum notitia*.[9] Take this apart. The subtitle of these Anglican *Institutes* which begins nonetheless with *Opus non solum*, intriguingly predicting Selden's motto, *non solus*, then moves immediately to state that it is the *notitia*, the fore-knowledge, the signs of the divine that are the primary object of jurisprudential study. This should be taken seriously and literally, which is to say both visually and unspeakably. The first band of law is a matter of signs, of *notitia dignitatum* and *symbola heroica*, to be sure, but also of musical patterns, itinerant rhythms, and the colours, metals, and other natural figures that signify the divine inscription of law, the *nomos* in nature herself. Thus, and however much law and arms might seem to divide and oppose tribes, communities, and latterly nations, the domain of visible signification is what makes law, the *ius*

---

[5] P Sidney, *An Apologie for Poetrie* (Clarendon Press Oxford 1907 [1595]) at 8.   [6] Ibid 8.

[7] Ibid 6–7.

[8] J Cowell, *Institutiones iuris Anglicani, ad methodum et seriem institutionum imperialium compositæ & digestæ. Opus non solum juris Anglicani romanique in hoc regno studiosis, sed omnibus qui politeian & consuetudines inclyti nostri imperii penitus scire cupiunt, utile & accommodum* (Legat Cambridge 1605). There is an English version of the work, somewhat truncated: J Cowell, *The Institutes of the Lawes of England, Digested into the Method of the Civill or Imperiall Institutions* (Roycroft London 1651).

[9] *Institutiones* (n 8) 1.1.

gentium, possible: the law of nature is what Nature, that is, what God teaches to all animals—*ius naturali est, quod Natura, id est, Deus omnia animalia docuit.* This law of nature, is common to all—*omnibus animalibus commune sit.* Thus, and I will not belabour the point, Sidney's poetic Zodiac within is shared by all, a point which Selden as a humanist and antiquarian fully appreciated even if he challenges the appearance of the same amicable norm at the beginning of book 2 where Cowell, again citing Bracton, notes that water, air, the sea, and the coasts are by the law of nature common to all—*Naturali iure communes sunt omnes.*[10]

Where it is a question of knowledge of things divine and human and specifically of the notes of such things, because their referents may be common but they are unspeakable and invisible in themselves, then the *notitia*, the signs, are all that there is. The first law is that of signification and this gains its initial semi-systematic treatment in Bartolus' *Tractatus de insigniis* of the mid-fourteenth century.

'Rank or office' he states, 'as for example the insignia of proconsuls or legates, or, as we can indeed see today, the insignia of bishops' are proper and limited to their officeholders.[11] Thus, 'just as names are created to identify persons, so insignia and coats of arms are devised for this purpose', and we may add to a more general, because visible, effect.[12] The social order emerges out of nature in the form of licit media and inscriptions, a point that the Inns of Court heraldic systematizers of the mid-sixteenth century were at great pains to promulgate. Bossewell, for instance, in his *Concordes of Armorie*, is incisive on the genealogy of arms and signs. Citing to Isidore of Seville's *Etymologiæ*, he begins with the general proposition *arma generaliter omnium rerum instrumenta sunt*—arms are the instruments of all things.[13] To understand the full implications of this proposition it is necessary to understand that these visual instruments, colours, banners, shields, coat armor, livery, and such like, are a language of honour. These insignia or signs are no ordinary indicators but are expressly *symbola heroica*, and 'it is known that almighty God is the original author of honouring nobility, who, even in the heavens hath made a discrepance of heavenly spirits, giving them several names, as ensigns of honour' and creating nine orders of angels (messengers) as named in the scriptures and as mimicked, according to Gerard Legh, by the nine orders of the Inns of Court.[14]

---

[10] *Institutiones* (n 8) 2.1.3–4. See also *Of the Dominion* (n 2) 391–2 where Selden says Cowell has 'in too careless a manner' and 'unadvisedly' here recycled some 'reliques of Ulpian, or of the School of Imperial Law'.

[11] B da Sassoferrato, *A Grammar of Signs: Bartolo da Sassoferrato's 'Tract on Insignia and Coats of Arms' [Tractatus de insigniis et armis]* (O Cavallar, S Degenring, and J Kirshner eds and trans) (Robbins Collection Berkeley 1995 [1358]) at 109.

[12] Ibid.

[13] J Bossewell, *Workes of Armorie, Devyded into Three Bookes* (Totelli London 1572) at fol Air. Bossewell relies heavily upon G Legh, *The Accedens of Armory* (Totill London 1562).

[14] *Accedens* (n 13) fol 135v. B Chasseneuz, *Catalogus gloriæ mundi* (Vincent Valgriss Venice 1576) provides a most detailed angelology of the orders of honour under the heading, at 62: *Erit de ordine cœlestium corporum et de locis spiritum etiam infernalium. Quinquaginta considerationes habet.*

Honour itself is the representation of virtue and its bearers are nobility, according to John Ferne, a contemporary of Bossewell's, from the Latin *nosco*, to know, meaning he 'is known, through the heroical virtues of his life…*nobilitas* and *notus* mean the same'.[15] As to the virtues that underpin the orders of honour, Bossewell borrows from Cicero's *Offices* and 'declares the definition and efficacie thereof…as the gentle reader maye partely bee satisfied, at the first sighte'.[16] The first virtue, preceding justice, is *Prudence, Sophia* in the Greek, the mother of all virtues depicted by a woman with a snake in her left hand and a shield with a crystal mirror floating under her right hand (Figure 18.3). The snake is the hieroglyph of wisdom and

Figure 18.3 Legh

Source: Copyright 2015 Peter Goodrich

---

[15] J Ferne, *The Blazon of Gentrie* (Winder London 1586) at 4.   [16] *Workes* (n 13) fol 4r.

requires minimal comment beyond allusion to the Biblical relation between the serpentine and the exodus from Eden which here marks the fact that while one hand, here the right hand gives, the left hand retains and conceals. The more dramatic symbol is the shield with its image of the mirror, of which Bossewell comments, citing Solomon in the *Psalms*, 'Like as in water bee shewed the visages of them that beholde it, so unto men that bee prudent, the secretes of mens hartes be openly discovered'.[17] The principle at play is one of a double signification appropriate to a dual law, *utrumque ius* as it used to be called, that had both a spiritual and a positive meaning. The sign, in other words, was an image of something not present, the intelligible marker of an opaque and occluded identity or esoteric knowledge. Thus the beginning of justice and law, the prior virtue of wisdom and the honour that accompanied it was required before any jurisprudence would be possible. As the systematizing herald, lawyer, and ramist John Guillim puts it in 1610,

arms are tokens or resemblances, signifying some act or quality of the bearer . . . but according to their modern . . . and present use, arms may be said to be hieroglyphical or enigmatic symbols or signs, testifying the nobility or gentry, acquired by the virtue and good service performed by their bearers or ancestors, either in martial exploits abroad or by their learning and wisdom.[18]

The crucial point to observe in the initial delineations of these heraldic and symbolic works, what Nicolas Causin in his famous lexicon of symbols termed *scientia imaginum*, is that the order of honour precedes the juridical, and that the visible comes before the verbal.[19] In the beginning, we learn biblically, was the sign. The Solomonic metaphor of an acquatic mirror and the depiction in Bossewell of a looking glass both indicate an order of the visible that precedes the babel of languages and transcends the din of war. We begin with notes, *notitia*, signs that are sewn into liveries and coat armours, that are painted on shields, etched in banners, blazoned on tunics, sculpted in public places, and recorded in the archive of literary and humanistic studies. These are sometimes termed *icunculae*, little icons of presence and of visible legitimacy.[20] By the end of the sixteenth century, as Kantorowicz usefully points out, the classical juxtaposition of arms and laws, and specifically the doctrine of the two swords, in which arms dominated laws, has given way to an art of law in which it is art that precedes and in most instances will

---

[17] *Workes* (n 13) fol 4v.

[18] J Guillim, *A Display of Heraldry Manifesting a More Easie Access to the Knowledge Thereof than Hath Been Hitherto Published by Any, through the Benefit of Method* (Roycroft London 1679 [1610]) at fol 3r.

[19] N Causin, *De Symbolica Aegyptiorum sapientia, in qua symbola, parabola, historiæ selectæ quæ ad omnem emblematum, aenigmatum, hieroglyphicorum cognitionem viam praestant* (Agrippa Cologne 1623) np.

[20] T Philipot, *A Brief Historical Discourse of the Original and Growth of Heraldry, Demonstrating upon What Rational Foundations, that Noble and Heroick Science Is Established* (Holt London 1672) at 7. The work itself is ramist in intention and aims to save the art of signs from the 'mysterious canting' of some of the learned who have never read it.

subjugate arms.[21] What is at issue, as Bossewell emphasizes, is a knowledge of the visual signs of *imperium*, an attention explicitly to the *arcana* of rule which are in the first instance to be understood as the symbolic visual elements of an imaginary, which is to say imagistic, order of signs of honour and of identity and office. These may be used in war or diplomacy but they are first a matter of *literarum studium*, of humanistic and emblematical study, of the notations of the art of universal law.

3 *Lex insulæ*

There is a peculiar and significant feature to the frontispiece image in the English version of *Mare clausum*. It is the figure of Clio, the muse with a quill in hand who waits not only to record Britannia's deeds but also to note, which is to say inscribe and mark her possession of the sea. It is a curious thing and a great obstacle to the early law of the seas that in fact the ocean is trackless and cannot be marked, ploughed, or otherwise confined. Early on, the glossator Baldus noted *possessio dignitatis, probatur per insignia*—possession of a dignity is proved by signs. Selden and Grotius, when they debate the dominion and freedom of the seas start from exactly this problem. How is the pen militant to mark the water? What discernible notes, insignia, or other symbols can be implanted or made such that the dominion, variously described by Baldus as power, jurisdiction, territory, or distraint (*districtus*), could be universally, which is to say extralinguistically, asserted? Insofar as law inscribes the bonds of law, *vinculae iuris*, the possession and property of peoples, the oceans create a peculiar and exemplary problem of being without notation, changing and unmarked. Selden cites St Ambrose on this point: '*Geometrician audivimus, Thalassometram nunquam audivimus...* I have heard of a Geometrican, or one that could measure Land, but never of a Thalassometrician, one that could measure or lay out Bounds in the Sea'.[22] There can be no jurisdiction, which Cormack reminds us, citing Cowell, means power to do justice,[23] if the inscription of the 'right of things' cannot be performed on account of their being nothing to write upon what Ovid terms these unknown waves—*fluctibus ignotis*.[24] If there is aquatic law, then, says Grotius, it is that of

---

[21] E Kantorowicz, 'On Transformations in Apolline Ethics' in *Selected Studies* (Augustin New York 1965) at 399.

[22] *Of the Dominion* (n 2) 5.

[23] B Cormack, *A Power to Do Justice: Jurisdiction, English Literature, and the Rise of Common Law, 1509–1625* (University of Chicago Press Chicago 2007) 5, citing J Cowell, *The Interpreter* (Legate Cambridge 1607) at fol Oo4v ('Jurisdiction').

[24] Ovid, *Metamorphoses*, 1.134.

the winds, blowing from all directions, untamed and thus in emblematic depiction, chaos, freedom for all, from all quarters of the globe, to share in common, as friends—*amicorum omnia sunt communia*.[25]

The sea is inconstant and immeasurable according to the classical lawyers and so something of a test case for the *jus gentium*, and a problem for a trinitarian structure of law that had things, bonds and proprietary relations, as the middle part of all juridical structure. Not even time immemorial will mark the waters, nor impart any visible law to the chaos of oceanic immensity. At sea, there is classically no positive or civil law, but only faith, nothing else but natural legislations, which leads Grotius at the start of *De Iure praedae* to cite Lucretius to the effect that what order there is arrives solely by virtue of 'the figures of nature and its law'—*sed natura species ratioque*.[26] Nature manifests an inner law, reason being the synonym for *ratio* and thence *lex scripta*, if only the eye of faith is capable of reading it as such. There is ironically a hidden, unwritten, undeclared law of nature which only the putatively universal eye of faith can discern or divine. An emblem from the 1593 edition of Broissard's emblems can provide an image of this *ius quaesita alteri*, this invisible law of chaos, of lawlessness (Figure 18.4).

Broissard's emblem 49 shows a shipwreck. The mast of the ship has snapped and a figure climbing the prow of the ship seeks to escape the doomed vessel. On the shore a figure kneels, a broken trowel, its handle in the form of a cross, is witness to the shipwreck, and prays to an image of Christ crucified, emanating light, in the heavens. At the base of the cross is an anchor and the Latin motto states in no uncertain terms that the certitude of hope comes from heaven alone. The explanatory essay indicates that only through the eyes of the mind—*ad quos oculorum mentis*—can divine wisdom, his providence, and safe haven be ascertained.[27] It transpires paradoxically that the emblem can evidence the notes, the inscriptions, the law of the unmarked, of that which cannot be possessed but only shared amongst the community of humanity as such.

Developing out of the heraldic tradition of *impresa* and *notitia*, the emblem book, the invention of a jurist, offers through the new medium of print the widest circulation of images of law in humanistic circles.[28] In the emblem given from

---

[25] Adage 94 in the early editions and subsequently adage 1 in all editions published after 1508. See W Barker (ed), *The Adages of Erasmus* (University of Toronto Press Toronto 2001). I have used Richard Taverner's English edition: R Taverner (ed), *Proverbes or Adagies, Gathered out of the Chiliades of Erasmus* (How London 1569) which indeed treats the adages as common property. For an incisive discussion of this theme, see K Eden, *Friends Hold All Things in Common: Tradition, Intellectual Property, and the Adages of Erasmus* (Yale University Press New Haven 2001).

[26] H Grotius, *De Iure praedae* (MJ van Ittersum ed GL Williams trans) (Liberty Fund Indianapolis 2006 [1606]). S Jones, 'The Poetic Ocean in *Mare Liberum*' in O Ben-Dor (ed), *Law and Art: Justice, Ethics and Aesthetics* (Routledge London 2011) 188–203, offers a most incisive discussion.

[27] JJ Broissard, *Emblematum liber* (de Bry Frankfurt 1593) at 98.

[28] See P Goodrich, *Legal Emblems and the Art of Law: Obiter Depicta as the Vision of Governance* (CUP Cambridge 2014) at 23–48.

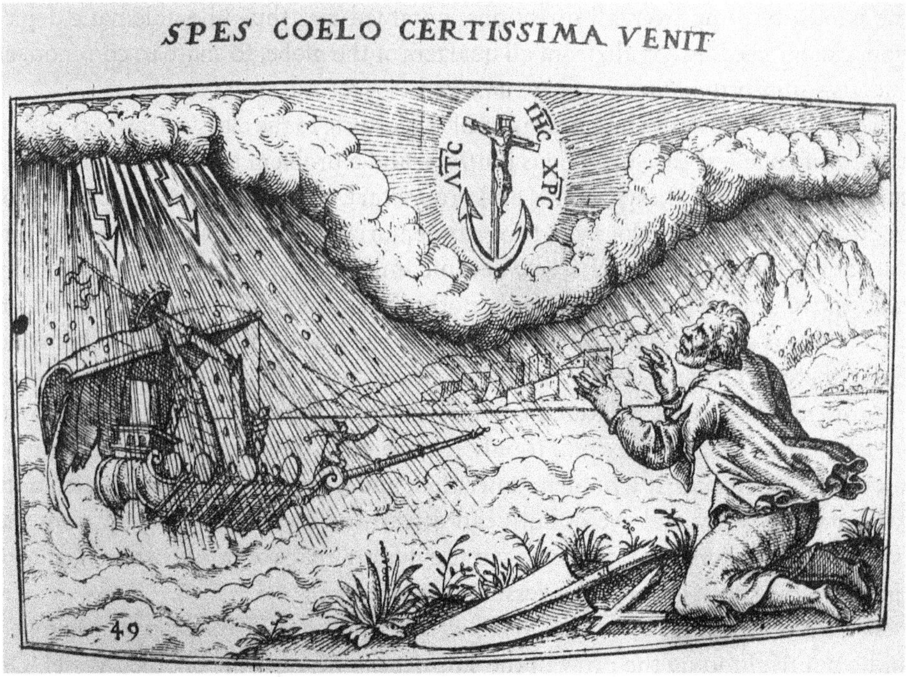

Figure 18.4 Broissard
Source: Copyright 2015 Peter Goodrich

Broissard we can see that the depiction makes one level of meaning evident and accessible. There is a dual order, *duplex ordo*, that rules the world from on high and is manifest below. The clouds in the picture symbolize death and the cross, Greek letters—*graeculæ tenebræ*—and crescendo of rays of light signal the ironically invisible source of power. The figure of the crucifixion is for the lawyers of the period simply a synecdoche, a marker of something greater concealed, a code. As for the world below the heavens, separated by the cord of clouds, it has no visible order. Lightning and hail strike the ship, the seas rise up, and if scrutinized closely one can see that waters around the ship have been depicted as clouds, mimicking the heavenly nimbus and signalling, as if this were not already clear, that the ship is close to death.[29]

The dual order that the emblem signals, the contrast between chaos and salvation, the incomprehensibility of the ocean and the serenity of the heavens, darkness and light, shows the point of origin of the *jus gentium*, the first signs of not simply the necessity but the covert presence of *anima legis*, the spirit of law. Attending

---

[29] The root of this image is in B Aneau, *Picta poesis* (Bonhomme Lyons 1552) at 49: *Sine justitia, confusio.* We find the same image reproduced in the English emblematist G Whitney, *A Choice of Emblemes, and Other Devises* (Plantyn Leiden 1586) at 122.

further to the image, we can see that it is in fact light, specifically Jupiter's spear, the flashes of lightning that do not simply threaten the shipwrecked humanity, but also mark the first and most direct moment of their contact with the inner and unmarked law. It is a very jurisprudential image, and, to borrow from Blumenberg's study of shipwrecks and their spectators, it evidences that what escapes the concept is left to the long-term work of images.[30] Put differently, it is the image that survives, that subtends and propels the order of disposition and administration, of governance rather than of rule. It is thus to the image again that the juridical theology of common law turns when seeking to devise a manner of inscribing a law of the sea that is internationally visible and recognizable as an image of jurisdiction, the insignia of possession, and distraint.

As the term juridical theology suggests, the recourse to images is religious at root and belongs to the legal knowledge of things divine that the Roman lawyers and their Anglican—and some would argue distant—descendants, the practitioners of the *mos britannicus*, start from. The emblematic image is important to an understanding of the genealogy of governance not simply because it is at some levels universally apprehensible, but also because it introduces Roman forms into common law. The image is an envelope and contains not simply an affective force, the *longue-durée* of visual attraction already noted, but also the basic structures of Roman law, not so much the *iconomus* or order of Catholic images but the *œconomus*, the less dramatic and so potentially more insidious pictures of administrative and domestic disposition. The emblematic expresses in visual but also enigmatic form the norms of interior disposition which are in Broissard's emblem also envisioned from the perspective of the land, from that of the faithful viewer, and further, in the background, the repose of the city, of institutions and domicile, œconomy and interiority that is glimpsed viscerally in the terrors of shipwreck, of misadventure that can be calmly viewed from the shores.

If we accept the importance of the image to the juridical, its trajectory from note, to ensign, to emblem, then the inscription of law upon the sea, the proof of ownership and commonality through signs can act as something of a test case for the international signature of law. How can the image, which is enigmatic in the sense of being plural in meaning, bring order to the chaos of the sea. The answer initially returns to the ecclesiastical jurisdiction and the methods of division of the world concocted by the Papacy. The beginning of the argument is the assertion by Grotius that the sea cannot be noted or marked, and is therefore free to all: 'But no man is ignorant that a ship passing the sea leaveth no more right than the way thereof'.[31] There is no pen that can mark the water, no hand that can stay the waves,

---

[30] H Blumenberg, *Shipwreck with Spectator: Paradigm of a Metaphor for Existence* (MIT Press Boston 1997) at 1.

[31] H Grotius, *The Freedom of the Seas* (JB Scott ed R van Deman Magoffin trans) (OUP New York 1916 [1608]) at 34.

no King Cnut who can order the tides to recede, and so any attempt to set limits or mark boundaries is simply an assertion of vanishing signs, a hopeless effort to inscribe by means of imaginary or fantastical lines—*imaginaria linea*. What Grotius here denies, despite his humanism and his poetry, in the name of reason as against astronomy and fantasy, Selden takes up and reorients as a species of image of inner law.

To give each their due, as the *Digest* records that justice requires and art effects had historically necessitated that this due could be given. It had to have bounds and limits, and Selden then notes properly that '*Terminus*, the God of Bounds, was received heretofore among the *Romanes* for the God of Justice'.[32] Starting on land, with its solid bounds and visible shores, with its promontories and peninsulas, headlands, isthmuses, creeks, and islands, Selden argues that at these points of contact between land and sea, the inscription of insignia, and so possession is possible. Once a solid and evident starting point is defined, then, following the example of Pope Alexander VI and his Cardinals, it should be acknowledged that there is the possibility of a possession that 'bee bounded by an imaginarie Line' that attaches at each end to land, from one arctic to the other, in the case in point. As the papal imaginary lines were short-lived and ineffective, Selden moves swiftly to cite the civilians on the primary point of principle. He is expansive and includes Bartolus, then Bodin's *De republica*, Hieronymous de Monte and finally Baldus, all to the point that what can be measured from the land, can be possessed not simply as far as the eye can see, but further, as far as the internal Zodiac, the *anima legis* itself can imagine. The lawyer is now a thalassometrician and, as Cormack has well illustrated, this becomes the art of mapping a 'litoral' if not a literal jurisdiction. Selden draws upon the mariner's art and tools, the rhumb lines, and loxodromes, the compass rose and its striation of the waters so as to generate what Cormack expressly and significantly terms an 'emblem of royal *imperium*'.[33]

The precise manner of this imaginary expansion of the land and of its lines and loxodromes over the seas deserves attention. It is a legal and so cautious strategy insofar as it proceeds *ad similia*, analogizing dominion over the sea to the enclosure and measurement of land. Well over half way through Book II, Selden alights upon a proclamation of James I which directly addresses the safety of 'our Ports, Havens, Roads, Creeks, or other places of our Dominion...and Jurisdiction'.[34] Note immediately the road that is slipped into the otherwise nautical and distinctly extra-terrestrial, *non terra firma*, terms. A map is then called in aid and is shown to set out certain limits to the freedom of the sea which 'Prescribed limits' were 'pointed out by direct lines draw from one point of land or adjacent Island, to the next Point or Island upon the English shore' (Figure 18.5). What is thus cut off from the sea are spaces termed '*Regias Cameras*, The Kings Chambers, and the

---

[32] *Of the Dominion* (n 2) 135.   [33] *A Power to Do Justice* (n 23) 269.
[34] *Of the Dominion* (n 2) 364.

guftioris ufu, dominio ejus, quod circumquaque ad.
jacet, diffufius defignato : ita finus hi ampliffimi fimili

Figure 18.5 Anglia

Ports Roial. Even as in an hous the inner private Rooms, or Chambers, or Closets, which in barbarous Latin are wont to bee termed *Cameræ* are reserved for the Master'.[35] There follows, as if to make this point both visible and irrefragable, a map of England and its islands, promontories, ports, creeks, coves, and the loxodromic lines by means of which the havens, *Cameræ*, and chambers of the sovereign can be drawn, seen, and understood. More than that, there are four compass roses, one in each corner of the map, although the *Scala Leucarum*, the scale of leagues, hides the south-west rose but not its lines and measures. There follows a schema of promontories, *Rumbi*, which is to say points, and leagues. These lines, 'in their full extent, do by these presents make answer, and to the best of our knowledge and understanding, declare, that the said Chambers…of his Majestie, are the whole Sea-Coasts which are intercepted or cut off by a streight line drawn from one point to another, about the Realm of England.'[36] The King, in sum or short, is arbiter and commander of the peace in his own closets. Thus does Selden declare the *lex insulæ*, the law of the Island, by showing it, by indicating an inside and an outside, a *duplex ordo*, friend and enemy, and most importantly, bounds that follow the limits of right and because of that 'were not then in imagination'.[37] What is inscribed on the chart by the 'iron pencil' of the thalassometrician becomes part of the realm, the real, the law.

There are other signs, of course, in Selden's expansive collation of all of the evidences of dominion and right. Britannia seated on a globe, the sea underneath her on a Roman coin from the time of Antoninus Pius, is proof of right made visible by 'brass-coin', by image and insignia, the latter being *Imperator*, and the letters SC standing for the consulship of Stilico.[38] An earlier image, though this can hardly be exhaustive, is taken from Pancirolus' depiction of the *Notitia* of the East and has at the top of the image the effigies of the Princes and the book of instructions, *foelix liber*, and below are three women with diadems on their head representing the three provinces, Asia, *Insulæ* (the Isles), and Hellespont (Figure 18.6). Selden's argument from the picture is that Hellespont cannot represent anything other than the sea itself: 'flowing between; which beeing thus joyned with the Isles to the Proconsulship of Asia, upon one and the same account of Dominion, the Provinces of Asia and Europe became in a civil sens, either continual or contiguous'.[39] It is an argument of serial proximity by which the ownership of territory allows the annexation of adjoining territories and then of adjoining islands and the sea or straits between continent and province, mainland, and island which become by propinquity territories. This is shown in the emblem by the three crowned women and incidentally also by the fact that Asia alone has shoes, whereas the Isles and Hellespont are unshod because their feet may get wet.

---

[35] *Of the Dominion* (n 2) 365.   [36] Ibid 370.   [37] Ibid 372.   [38] Ibid 245.
[39] Ibid 86. G Pancirolus, *Notitia utraque dignitatum, cum Orientis, tum Occidentis ultra arcadia honorique tempora* (Gabiano Lyon 1608) at fols 68v–69r.

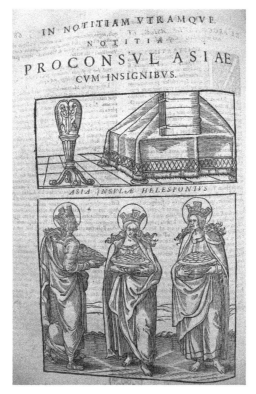

Figure 18.6 Pancirolus 'Asia'
Source: Copyright 2015 Peter Goodrich

4 *ŒCONOMIC* AND EMBLEMATIC IMAGES

It is significant that in the image of Eastern dominion and indeed in subsequent images from the *Notitia utraque, dignitatum, cum orientis, tum occidentis,* the book of instructions drawn up by the *magister scriniorum*, the tome is closed.[40] The image of the written law, of all the records, documents, commissions, promulgations, and scriptural exornations upon which Selden relies so heavily, not to say massively, are firmly shut, the metal clasps of the voluminous volume are closed and by implication this is far from an open book but more an enigma, a hieroglyph, as said, of the laws. The image makes the hieroglyph present, it provides access to an esoteric set of highly indexical signs. The propinquity of territories is matched to the proximity of knowledge and to the power that the images

---

[40] *Fœlix liber injunctus Notariis laterculi*, according to J Selden, *Titles of Honor* (Stansby London 1631) at 325.

provide. Closeness, abutment, and the adjacent are, however, only forms of association and ideally identify an occupied space with the escaping or vanishing objects
in its vicinity. The image is of an enigma, which is to say that it is of a set of indexical and plural referents that only the qualified, those higher in the hierarchy, those
next to the sovereign, closer to things divine and legal, can interpret and relay.

The cenobitically learned Bradin of Cormack illustrates this point by prolong-
ing his gaze on the early maps. The compass rose that we find in quadruple form
in Selden's emblematical map of Anglia (and *Scotia pars*), with a *fleur de lys* atop
the South East rose, is not simply a compass joining 'imaginary lines…to a natural phenomenon', but is also and variously a symbol of the sun, a 'panegyre', a
heavenly globe ruling down on the glorious kingdom, island, and seas of England.
The emblem is also code, however, as Cormack shows by way of reference to John
Speed's *Theatre of the Empire of Great Britaine* (1611), for the quadripartite royal
arms, the heraldic representation of England:

Speed's atlas provides a lesson in the transformation of a mariner's cartographic tool into
a symbol of sovereignty . . . It does so symbolically, and to the extent that, through its imaginary lines extending from a center, it delineates the central logic of early British empire,
a jurisdictional strategy through which contestable space beyond the law could be structured as natural possession.[41]

Our interest is that this strategy of annexation, this bringing into law, is initially
a visual process, an imagistic enterprise and scopic projection of jurisdiction. The
latter term, *juris-dictio*, could indeed be made subordinate here to what the theologians termed *verba visibilia*, the all-important sacramental rituals that have their
origin in the *legis actiones*, the sacraments of law that gain their most prominent
expression in what we might term *visibilia iuris*. It is precisely the visibilities of law
that can transcend the limitations of language and constraints of territory to signal
internally and externally, nationally and internationally, to friend and to foe, the
imaginary occupation, the imperial possession of spaces and of persons, of land
and sea.

The images that the common lawyers relay, and Selden is simply the best known
of exemplars, are only superficially depictions of common law. It is the great and
hitherto unacknowledged paradox of the Anglican *notitia dignitatem* and of the
Inns of Court emblem books that while they might appear at first glance to be
enigmas of common law, they in fact fall into a long tradition of Roman imagery
and classical juristic references. At the level of the image—of pictures addressed *ad
omnia*, to all—the code or lexicon that is apprehended is one that relays a roman
tradition, civilian juristic *exempla* and the emblematical depictions of a continental law. The legal image is a Latin borrowing, as the expression *ius imaginum*,

---

[41] *A Power to Do Justice* (n 23) 274–5. See also J Speed, *Theatre of the Empire of Great Britaine*
(Balsett and Chiswell London 1676 [1611]).

used by English lawyers, makes pretty clear. To speak across the borders of the insular jurisdiction, to address the seas and lands overseas, beyond the Hellespont, and the ultramontane, required recourse to international signs of law, to classical images, that like the banners, flags, coat armour, and ensigns that Bartolus had written about, could convey in simple yet indexical and esoteric form the juridical aura, the corporate personality, the band and bonds that the subject carries with them as representative of England and as party to an international, which is to say a visible and present *ius gentium* or universal law.

The English reception of Roman law comes in many respects most directly in the form of images. The very popular legal emblem books are not simply continental in origin but they also circulate an imagery of the tripartite structure of the universal law, namely persons, things, and actions. There is thus a primary lexicon and figuration of subjects, possessions, and communications that declares without speaking, that precedes presence and structures the preliminaries of interaction. The *emblemata Romanorum* as I am tempted to label them achieve through imagery a transmission and relay that was for political reasons less possible through texts and specifically the great compilations of law, the *corpus iuris canonici* and the accompanying *emblemata Triboniani* as Hotman and other humanist lawyers termed much of the Justinian collection of fragments and other excisions from the sibylline leaves of the classical law.[42] Appropriately enough, the *emblemata Triboniani* are signs of novel insertions, emendations and updatings of the classical texts, modes of reception, and accommodation of classical laws to the custom and use of a contemporary context.

The beauty and appropriateness of the emblem to the juridical cause of depicting jurisdiction and international comity lies first in their detachable character. The emblem, as an inserted image, an engraving added to an extant pattern, a foreign body interposed into a domestic form, is the very mirror of the purpose of the jurist in setting out the laws of the sea and the other aquatic chambers and international closets—*vestibulas*—of the sovereign. The emblem as image and so as sign is a foreign intervention in a double sense. It is an image that appears in the texts of law, and it is a civilian and frequently classical Latin and occasionally Greek reference within the English common law. That much is evident and the English edition of Ripa's *Iconologia* nicely captures this dimension of emblematic insertion in describing these depictions as painted thoughts, as 'Representatives of our Notions; they properly belong to Painters, who by Colours and Shadowing, have invented the admirable Secret to give Body to our Thoughts, thereby to render them visible'.[43] Each has its classical meaning and with it an accompanying doctrine and

---

[42] On which, see V Hayaert, *Mens emblematica et humanisme juridique: le cas du 'Pegma cum narrationibus philosophicis' de Pierre Coustau (1555)* (Groz Geneva 2008) at 111–12 and 144–5 on the emblem as *accommodatio*.

[43] C Ripa, *Iconologia, or Moral Emblems* (Motte London 1709) np.

learning, normative sense and figurative associations, but most importantly they convey a moral code for the 'Public Benefit…[and are] instructive to all sorts of People whatsoever'.[44]

These moveable signs, detachable images, floating signifiers of the jurisdiction of the image form a pan-European substrate of all legal interventions and communications. As the theological displaces into the social, and juridical theology rises from the ashes of Reformation schisms there is a final point to consider with respect to the didactic and properly preparative role of emblematic depictions. The *mos emblematicus* introduces not only novelty—signs of the times—into law but it also expands the range and the levels of juristic presence and social penetration. The emblematists thought in terms of an expanded method of *lectio mixta*, of a plurality of levels of meaning and of disciplines of interpretation designed to accommodate both the movable form and the triplex character of the *emblemata*, but I will suggest that in fact there is a better way of apprehending this novel set of depictions of the licit and illicit, of the rules of law as rules of life.

The insight that the emblem accommodates or rather intrudes so as to modernize and concretize the abstraction and the overwhelming prolixity of legal texts can help to remind the contemporary jurist that the *emblemata* are in fact representations of legal action in its classical sense, namely that of doing what is promised, enacting what is said. The emblems show, in cautionary or didactic form, how the variegated hierarchy of subjects should behave and act. There is an element of interior instruction in this transition from the *litera mortua* of the text to the *anima legis*, the image of its being put into practice. The lawyers, in short, were borrowing the methods of the prior universality, that of the Roman Church, and putting the *iconomic* practice of religious images into *œconomic*, which is to say administrative and governmental effect. The image makes the *duplex ordo* of rule and administration, sovereignty and governance, briefly manifest. What this means is that disposition, rhetorical action, emerges momentarily in the legal institution of life, or at least in one of the more visible dimensions of published law. A final and parting emblem from the German moralizing emblematist Julius Wilhelm Zincgref can make the point that the image not only disseminates law to previously untouched spaces but also that these *interpositae picturae*, mark a subtle but definite shift from a spectacular and distant mode of sovereign rule to a more subtle and pervasive *œconomic* rule.

Emblem 66, *Idem pacis mediusque belli*, as suitable for peace as for war, shows an arm emergent from a cloud holding a sword whose blade is wrapped around by a leafy vine (Figure 18.7).[45] This symbol of a muted blade, of laws and in Zincgref's explanatory essay, arts overcoming arms, dominates the landscape and touches the sky. The discursive account of the emblem begins, as in my epigraph, with the

---

[44] *Iconologia, or Moral Emblems* (n 43).

[45] JW Zincgref, *Emblematum ethico-politicorum centuria* (Merian Heidelberg 1619) at fol r3r.

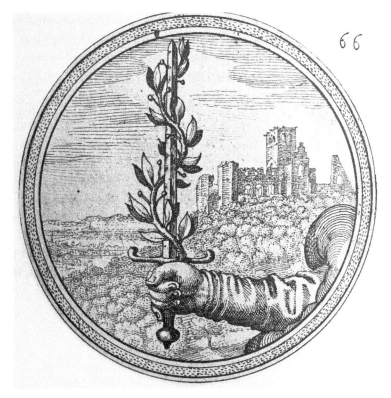

6 6

Figure 18.7 Zincref 'Arma'
Source: Copyright 2015 Peter Goodrich

proposition that all life is divided between *otium* and *negotium*. Where in previous depictions of arms and laws, the sword was usually in the sovereign's right hand and laws, books, and arts, were in the left and were to be enforced, according to the doctrine of two swords, by the sword dominant, the new emblem demotes the sword to a secondary place under the tutelage and subordinate to the literary and legal, to *studium* and art.[46] Law and art, *negotium* and *otium*, divide the realm and smother the sword because 'arms are not the proper mode of dealing with foreigners [*hostes*], but rather it is much better to practice peace by means of arts'.[47] Law itself indeed should ideally give way to art, a point that Zincgref makes by concluding that philosophy belongs to times of leisure and peace (*in otio et quiete*) and is attached inseverably to justice and to truth in all times (*in utroque tempore*). The emblem thus comes as the herald of the new *oeconomic* role of the image and as the

---

[46] G Rollenhagen, *Nucleus Emblematum Selectissimorum* (Passae Cologne 1611) at 32. *Ex utroque Cæsar* is a standard example, and is repeated of course in the English barrister Wither's work: G Wither, *A Collection of Emblemes Ancient and Moderne* (Allot London 1635).
[47] *Emblematum* (n 45) fol r2v.

index of rejuvenation, all of which is much more visible and apparent in the picture than in the Latin text that I have cited from. The fructifying vine, this laurel that surrounds, softens and strangles the sword, dominates the landscape which is itself a scene of nature, of forest and hills with spires in the distant valley below. Two things are striking. First that the ecclesiastical is far from view, it is rather the castle that is closest to the foreground, the secular and juridical has displaced the more usual representations of the divine. Law has entered the secular world as an image. Secondly, the vegetal symbol, the sign of art dominating force is outside the castle and entering the world. It floats between heaven and earth but it is nonetheless and signally *en route*, itinerant, peripatetic, and I will hazard in-between and inter-national. That is the function of the sign, of the order of honour that the symbolic and specifically the emblematic inaugurates in the early modern era. As Zincgref puts it, the *vates*, the foreseers, those that truly inhabit the Zodiac of their own wit as artists must, are inexpert in the use of force, and indeed they cannot be taught (*indocilem*) to fight. Their war is art, their weapons are images, their commerce is leisure.

....

CHAPTER 19

MORAL PHILOSOPHY AND INTERNATIONAL LAW

....

SAMANTHA BESSON*

What we miss is what might have been done.[1]

1 INTRODUCTION

....

THE moral philosophy of international law is a kind of philosophical or theoretical[2] enquiry pertaining to international law. It is normative[3] and consists, more

* Special thanks to Anne Orford and Florian Hoffmann for inviting me to join the project, and for their critical comments and feedback. I would also like to thank my research assistant, Odile Ammann, for her help with the editing and formatting of the chapter. Parts of the second section of the chapter are borrowed from S Besson and J Tasioulas, 'Introduction' in S Besson and J Tasioulas (eds), *The Philosophy of International Law* (OUP Oxford 2010) 1–27.

[1] J Waldron, 'International Law: "A Relatively Small and Unimportant Part" of Jurisprudence?' in LD d'Almeida, J Edwards, and A Dolcetti (ed), *Reading HLA Hart's 'The Concept of Law'* (Hart Oxford 2013) 209–23.

[2] I am using the terms philosophical and theoretical interchangeably in this chapter.

[3] The adjective 'normative' is used to refer to what is based on (moral) values (for example equality, justice, fairness).

specifically, in the 'reasoned moral evaluation of existing international law'[4] that should 'guide the design and reform of international law'.[5] To quote Allen Buchanan, the concern of the moral philosophy of international law 'is with what the law should be',[6] rather than with what it is.

The moral philosophy of international law amounts to more than merely another theoretical approach to international law. It happens to be one of the most established forms of international legal theory to date.[7] It has flourished from the 1970s onwards, and even more since 2000, in reaction to the long absence of international legal philosophy or, at least, to the absence of alternative forms of normative philosophy of international law within international legal theory. Of course, things have started to change: moral philosophy is no longer the only alternative to 'realist' or, more generally, non-normative theorizing about international law. Normative philosophical accounts of international law are gradually emerging from within international legal scholarship, just as they did in domestic law in centuries past.[8]

Accordingly, a chapter on the moral philosophy of international law cannot merely amount to an exposition and discussion, albeit critical, of the main features of this specific approach to international legal theory and its contributions. It also has to pertain to the nature of the philosophy of international law in general and to what its method should be.[9] Hence the apparently equivocal title of the present chapter— 'Moral Philosophy *and* International Law'—signals that a meta-theoretical discussion in international legal theory is very much needed. The time has come indeed to escape the Manichean opposition between 'realism' and 'moralism' that is said to have long plagued international legal theory. In that opposition, moralism has been qualified as the posture of both normative international legal theorists and international moral philosophers alike who endorse normative positions about the law as either already being the law or as having to become the law at any price,[10] thus leaving no place for normative theories of international law that do not conflate law and morality.

The structure of the chapter is two-pronged and reflects these two angles on the topic. First, it offers a critical discussion of the origins, aims, and main contributions of moral philosophies of international law. Secondly, it moves up a level to a

---

[4] See A Buchanan, 'International Law, Philosophy of' in E Craig (ed), *Routledge Encyclopedia of Philosophy* (Routledge London 2006) <https://www.rep.routledge.com/articles/international-law-philosophy-of/v-1/> [accessed 24 February 2016]. See also A Buchanan, *Justice, Legitimacy and Self-Determination: Moral Foundations for International Law* (OUP Oxford 2004) at 15.

[5] See *Justice, Legitimacy and Self-Determination* (n 4) 2.   [6] See ibid 4.

[7] See S Besson and J Tasioulas, 'Introduction' in S Besson and J Tasioulas (eds), *The Philosophy of International Law* (OUP Oxford 2010) 1–27; A Orford, 'In Praise of Description' (2012) 25 *Leiden Journal of International Law* 609–25.

[8] See also 'International Law: "A Relatively Small and Unimportant Part" of Jurisprudence?' (n 1) 222–3.

[9] For an early and brief treatment of the question, see *Justice, Legitimacy and Self-Determination* (n 4) chs 10 and 11.

[10] See eg A Orford, 'Moral Internationalism and the Responsibility to Protect' (2013) 24 *European Journal of International Law* 83–108. See also, albeit in other words, R Kolb, 'Deux arguments nocifs pour le droit international public' (2013) 23 *Revue suisse de droit international et européen* 337–50.

meta-theoretical discussion of international law, and in particular to how international legal theory should best be conceived and conducted. It argues for the development of normative legal philosophies of international law that take the normativity of law and hence its legality more seriously than international legal theorists have so far, but also—and this is key to their future positioning in international legal theoretical debates—than moral philosophers of international law have themselves.

2 MORAL PHILOSOPHY OF INTERNATIONAL LAW

2.1 The Origins

While classical legal philosophers from Hugo Grotius to Hans Kelsen have certainly grappled with normative questions about international law,[11] it is also the case that, until comparatively recently, the post-1960 revival of legal philosophy in Anglo-American scholarship has tended to neglect international law.

This 'poor relation' status is attributable to a variety of causes. In part, it may reflect a commendable intellectual prudence on the part of philosophers of law. For one might reasonably suppose that many of the questions of legal philosophy are best approached in the first instance via their application to municipal state legal systems, which are both more familiar and more highly developed, before advancing to their international counterparts. Of course, one should guard against this prudential policy hardening into the dogma that the philosophical study of international law can shed no independent light on philosophical questions either about law in general or its domestic instantiations. Legal theorists inspired by the jurisprudential work of Herbert Hart, for instance, have now come to realize the cost of such missed opportunities.[12]

However, there are probably less obviously benign causes for the long absence of philosophical treatment of international law. These include the relative insularity of international law as a field within legal studies, widespread scepticism about whether international law is really law, as well the nagging suspicion, shared by

---

[11] See eg H Grotius, *De Jure Belli et Pacis Libri Tres* (FW Kelsey trans) (Clarendon Press Oxford 1925 [1625]); H Kelsen, *The Law of the United Nations: A Critical Analysis of Its Fundamental Problems, with Supplement* (F Praeger New York 1950).

[12] For just such a critique of the mainstream reading of HLA Hart, *The Concept of Law* (J Raz and PA Bulloch eds) (3rd edn OUP Oxford 2012) ch X, see 'International Law: "A Relatively Small and Unimportant Part" of Jurisprudence?' (n 1).

both international lawyers and domestic lawyers, that, with its cumbersome and obscure methods of norm-creation and its frail enforcement mechanisms, international law does not yet constitute a worthwhile subject for normative inquiry and should first establish itself as a legal practice and perhaps as a doctrinal subject before being further theorized.[13] This also explains why outsider-theoretical approaches have been so successful in international law:[14] approaches external to the law appeared more 'scientific' and hence more authoritative. And this in turn may account for why interdisciplinarity has had so much more traction among international legal scholars than in domestic law.[15] Another likely cause for the philosophical neglect of international law is the corrosive influence of the general realist thesis that political morality does not reach beyond the boundaries of the state, or that only a very minimalist morality does, or, more charitably still, that although a richer political morality might eventually come to apply globally, to elaborate on it in the current state of the world is to engage in a utopian endeavour.[16]

As a result, to the extent that international law has been the object of theoretical attention in recent decades, much of it has come from writers drawing on either international relations theory or various approaches inspired by postmodernism.[17] Whatever one's view of the respective merits of these two schools of thought, their prevalence has had the consequence of sidelining the discussion of philosophical questions, particularly those of a normative character. Adherents of both schools tend to be sceptical about the coherence, tractability, interest, or utility of the conceptual questions addressed by philosophers. More importantly, the purportedly scientific, 'value-neutral' method favoured by the great majority of international relations theorists, especially adherents to the dominant 'realist' tradition, and the scepticism about reason endorsed by postmodernists, seem to allow little scope for an intellectually respectable form of normative inquiry. So, from the perspective of

---

[13] On international law scholars' inferiority complex, see J Klabbers, 'The Relative Autonomy of International Law or the Forgotten Politics of Interdisciplinarity' (2004) 1 *Journal of International Law and International Relations* 35–48, at 41.

[14] See eg in the field of economics, politics, or international relations: A-M Slaughter, 'International Law and International Relations Theory: A Dual Agenda' (1993) 87 *American Journal of International Law* 205–39; A Dunoff and M Pollack, *Interdisciplinary Perspectives on International Law and International Relations* (CUP Cambridge 2012); E Posner and A Sykes, *Economic Foundations of International Law* (Harvard University Press Cambridge MA 2013); A van Aaken, 'Behavioral International Law and Economics' (2014) 55 *Harvard International Law Journal* 421–81.

[15] See 'The Relative Autonomy of International Law or the Forgotten Politics of Interdisciplinarity' (n 13).

[16] For a presentation and discussion of those critiques, see Section 2.3 below.

[17] See eg K Abbott, 'Modern International Relations Theory: A Prospectus for International Lawyers' (1989) 14 *Yale Journal of International Law* 335–411; WM Reisman, 'The View from the New Haven School of International Law' (1992) 86 *American Society of International Law Proceedings* 118–25; M Koskenniemi, *From Apology to Utopia: The Structure of International Legal Argument* (revised edn CUP Cambridge 2005).

contemporary legal philosophy, the similarities between these two camps are per-haps at least as important as their differences.

The long marginalization of normative philosophical inquiry into international law is especially regrettable, since the most pressing questions that arise concerning international law today are arguably primarily normative in character. Of course, this is not to say that past[18] and present[19] international relations theorists and inter-national lawyers have not considered normative questions raised by international law. The point is merely that they have not done so philosophically. This explains how the moral philosophy of international law developed in reaction to this dearth of normative accounts of international law *within* international legal theory. First accounts appeared in the 1970s, but most contributions were published post-2000.

Early landmark works on international themes in normative political and/ or moral philosophy were Michael Walzer's *Just and Unjust Wars*,[20] Charles Beitz's *Political Theory and International Relations*,[21] and Henry Shue's *Basic Rights: Subsistence, Affluence, and US Foreign Policy*.[22] Those were then joined by the influential writings of other philosophers and lawyers.[23] Special mention should

---

[18] See eg the early and mid-twentieth-century international lawyers whose focus was the moral foundations of international law: A Verdross, *Die Verfassung der Völkerrechtsgemeinschaft* (Springer Berlin 1926); JL Brierly, *Law of Nations* (Clarendon Press Oxford 1928); H Lauterpacht, *The Function of Law in the International Community* (Clarendon Press Oxford 1933).

[19] See eg RA Falk, *Law in an Emerging Global Village: A Post-Westphalian Perspective* (Transnational Publishers Ardsley 1998); P Allott, *Eunomia: New Order for a New World* (Clarendon Press Oxford 1990). One may also think of critical writings on international law published by fem-inist or 'third world approaches to international law' scholars: see eg H Charlesworth and C Chinkin, *The Boundaries of International Law* (Manchester University Press Manchester 2000); A Anghie, *Imperialism, Sovereignty and the Making of International Law* (CUP Cambridge 2007).

[20] M Walzer, *Just and Unjust Wars: A Moral Argument with Historical Illustrations* (4th revised edn Basic Books New York 2006).

[21] C Beitz, *Political Theory and International Relations* (Princeton University Press Princeton 1979).

[22] H Shue, *Basic Rights: Subsistence, Affluence, and US Foreign Policy* (2nd edn Princeton University Press Princeton 1996).

[23] See eg J Nickel, *Making Sense of Human Rights: Philosophical Reflections on the Universal Declaration of Human Rights* (University of California Press Berkeley 1987); TM Franck, *Fairness in International Law and Institutions* (OUP New York 1995); G Teubner, *Global Law without a State* (Dartmouth Aldershot 1997); W Twining, *Globalisation and Legal Theory* (Northwestern University Press Evanston 2000); O O'Neill, *Bounds of Justice* (CUP Cambridge 2000); TW Pogge, *World Poverty and Human Rights: Cosmopolitan Responsibilities and Reforms* (Polity Press Cambridge 2002); F Tesón, *A Philosophy of International Law* (Westview Press Boulder 1998); MC Nussbaum, *Women and Human Development: The Capabilities Approach* (CUP Cambridge 2000); *Justice, Legitimacy and Self-Determination* (n 4); L May, *Crimes Against Humanity: A Normative Account* (CUP New York 2004); MNS Sellers, *Republican Principles in International Law: The Fundamental Requirements of a Just World Order* (Palgrave Macmillan New York 2006); L May, *War Crimes and Just War* (CUP Cambridge 2007); L May, *Aggression and Crimes Against Peace* (CUP New York 2008); J Griffin, *On Human Rights* (OUP Oxford 2008); W Twining, *General Jurisprudence: Understanding Law from a Global Perspective* (CUP Cambridge 2009); CR Beitz, *The Idea of Human Rights* (OUP Oxford 2009); A Altman and CH Wellman, *A Liberal Theory of International Justice* (OUP Oxford 2011); J McMahan, *Killing in War* (Clarendon Press Oxford 2011); C Fabre, *Cosmopolitan War* (OUP Oxford

be made of two seminal monographs. First of all, and especially important, given his dominant influence on Anglo-American political philosophy, has been the publication in 1999 of John Rawls' final work, *The Law of Peoples*, which has already sparked a voluminous secondary literature.[24] Secondly, Allen Buchanan's *Justice, Legitimacy, and Self-Determination: Moral Foundations for International Law*, which appeared in 2004, is arguably the most systematic and comprehensive discussion of the morality of international law by a contemporary moral philosopher.[25] Unlike its predecessors, Buchanan's theory is not only holistic in coverage, thus providing a rare systematization of the moral regime of international law, but also, unlike John Rawls' theory, it focuses on the institutional and legal dimensions of international law, thereby addressing many of the difficulties facing non-ideal moral theories of international law.

Most work on the moral philosophy of international law appeared after 2000. Since 2006—eight years after the publication of its first, print edition—the online version *Routledge Encyclopedia of Philosophy* has included a lengthy entry on 'International law, Philosophy of'.[26] Since then, various collected volumes have been published with a main or partial emphasis on the moral philosophy of international law. The co-edited volume *The Philosophy of International Law* published in 2010 largely comprised authors who were moral philosophers of international law.[27] A similar project was published in 2012 under the title *Philosophical Foundations of European Law*.[28] Finally, there has been a multitude of recent philosophy journals or special issues entirely or partially devoted to the discussion of topics in the moral philosophy of international law.[29]

Regrettably, one of the side effects of the boom in the moral philosophy of international law has been the reinforcement and entrenchment, somehow, of 'realist' and postmodern approaches to international legal theory within international legal

2012); E Jouannet, *What is a Fair International Society? International Law between Development and Recognition* (Hart Oxford 2013).

[24] J Rawls, *The Law of Peoples with 'The Idea of Public Reason Revisited'* (Harvard University Press Cambridge MA 1999). See eg R Martin and DA Reidy (eds), *Rawls' Law of Peoples: A Realistic Utopia?* (Blackwell Oxford 2006); J Tasioulas, 'From Utopia to Kazanistan: John Rawls and the Law of Peoples' (2002) 22 *Oxford Journal of Legal Studies* 367–96; A Buchanan, 'Rawls' Law of Peoples: Rules for a Vanished Westphalian World' (2000) 110 *Ethics* 697–721; C Beitz, 'Rawls' Law of Peoples' (2000) 110 *Ethics* 669–96; G Brock, 'Recent Work on Rawls' Law of Peoples: Critics versus Defenders' (2010) 47 *American Philosophical Quarterly* 85–101.

[25] *Justice, Legitimacy and Self-Determination* (n 4).

[26] 'International Law, Philosophy of' (n 4).

[27] See generally *The Philosophy of International Law* (n 7).

[28] J Dickson and P Eleftheriadis, *Philosophical Foundations of European Union Law* (OUP Oxford 2012).

[29] See eg *Transnational Legal Theory; Ethics and International Affairs*; and special issues in (2005) 18(4) *Leiden Journal of International Law* (on cosmopolitanism, global justice, and international law); (2002) 13(4) *European Journal of International Law* (on Tom Franck); (2013) 24(1) *European Journal of International Law* (on Michael Walzer).

scholarship itself, at the price of normative legal philosophies of international law. A common view is indeed that if normative approaches can strive outside international law scholarship and theory, then there is no clear need to develop normative approaches to international law from within. As a result, many international lawyers interested in normative theorizing have merely endorsed or joined the moral philosophy of the international law project.[30]

All this has contributed to further entrenchment—rather than alleviation—of the artificial opposition between 'realist' approaches of international law and so-called 'moralist' ones, alluded to in the introduction.[31] True, many international legal scholars pigeonholed into the latter group have gradually distanced themselves from that label,[32] rightly claiming that endorsing a particular moral philosophy of international law does not imply that they negate the distinction between law and morality, the importance of the rule of law, and the existence of content-independent grounds of the legitimacy of international law. This echoes the legal positivist defence articulated by some advanced moral philosophers of international law, such as Buchanan, for fear of being accused of being natural lawyers.[33] However, the need to make such basic distinctions between a normative argument about what the law should be and an argument about what it is, and the corresponding conflation between one's moral philosophy of law and a theory of legal validity show how limited the predominant understanding of the normativity and legality of international law still is both in moral philosophy of international law and in international legal theory.

2.2 The Aim, Scope, and Standards

The main aim of moral philosophers of international law is to contribute to the formulation of moral standards for the evaluation of public international law, both in general and with respect to its main parts. Such standards, they claim, should play a vital role in determining the basis and proper extent of our allegiance to international law and institutions and in guiding their reform.

In short, moral standards are concerned with what human beings, as individuals or groups, owe to other human beings, and perhaps also other beings, in light of the status and interests of the latter, where the breach of the relevant standards typically validates certain characteristic responses: blame, guilt, resentment,

---

[30] See eg SR Ratner, 'Ethics and International Law: Integrating the Global Justice Project(s)' (2013) 5 *International Theory* 1–34; *A Philosophy of International Law* (n 23).

[31] See eg 'Moral Internationalism and the Responsibility to Protect' (n 10).

[32] See eg A Cassese, 'Introduction' in A Cassese (ed), *Realizing Utopia: The Future of International Law* (OUP Oxford 2012) xvii–xxii.

[33] See the critique by Buchanan in *Justice, Legitimacy and Self-Determination* (n 4) 20–1.

punishment, and so on. More concretely, moral standards refer to a rich and diverse repertoire of concepts through which the notion of moral concern has historically been elaborated: obligation, justice, rights, equality, among many others. Morality, therefore, consists of a set of standards which, among other things, places restrictions on our—often self-interested—conduct in order to pay proper tribute to the standing and interests of others.

There are as many kinds of moral philosophy of international law as there are conceptions of morality. They share common traits, however, especially with respect to scope and standards, and this explains how they may be said to belong to the same philosophical tradition.

With respect to scope, unlike other forms of moral (or political) philosophy, the moral philosophy of international law does not (only) pertain to a given domestic community, but takes the discussion further to encompass conduct beyond the state. It may either be about conduct within all political communities and the corresponding transnational moral standards, on the one hand, or about relations among agents that are not members of the same political community and the relevant international moral standards, on the other.[34] Some moral standards, of course, might be of both sorts. For example, human rights norms are typically conceived as applying within all political communities, but their (threatened) breach is also often taken to justify (at least *pro tanto*) some form of preventive or remedial response by other political communities or international agents. The task of a moral philosophy of international law is to elaborate the content and draw out the practical implications of such moral principles for international law.

Importantly, however, the moral philosophy of international law does not approach international relations generally as other forms of moral philosophy of international justice or political morality do. Instead, it focuses on international law and international legal institutions specifically.[35] The breadth of the field becomes clear when one looks at the diversity of areas of international law addressed, and of the general or specific moral questions that arise in those contexts.[36] The fields in international law most routinely addressed by moral philosophers of international law are the laws of war, international humanitarian law, international human rights law, international law on self-determination, international economic law, international criminal law, and international environmental law. In response to the fragmentation of the philosophical treatment of the general transitive moral questions arising across these different fields of international law, a scant few moral philosophers of international law have provided an 'integrated' moral theory of international law.[37] One may distinguish therefore between general and specific moral philosophies of international law.

---

[34] See *Justice, Legitimacy and Self-Determination* (n 4) 17ff.
[35] On this distinction, see ibid 190–1.
[36] See 'International Law, Philosophy of' (n 4) section 1.
[37] See eg *Justice, Legitimacy and Self-Determination* (n 4) 4, 59.

In terms of applicable standards, unlike forms of non-moral normative philosophy of international law, moral philosophies of international law operate by reference to morality only, and hence to normative standards external to the law—even if they are reconstructed by some moral philosophers from the international legal practice itself or even if those moral philosophers take international law as a key element in their social or political epistemology.[38] This is an important distinction as it signals, as I will explain later in this chapter, the fundamental difference between the most law-sensitive moral philosophies of international law and the most morality-related legal theories of international law and in turn how normative legal philosophies of international law may be differentiated from moral philosophies of international law.

For the rest, one may observe the same diversity of substantive and methodological approaches as in domestic moral philosophy.

The substantive debates familiar to moral and political philosophers writing about domestic communities are brought one layer up the ladder into the international sphere. One may mention, for instance, debates between consequentialist and non-consequentialist approaches to morality or between liberal and non-liberal ones. It would be a grave error, however, to assume that a commitment to a normative theory of international law necessarily carries with it some specific ethical-political commitment, such as a liberal cosmopolitanism that insists on the appropriateness of implementing an essentially liberal-democratic political vision through the medium of international law. On the contrary, the appropriateness of doing so is a central question for debate once we have accepted that normative international legal theory is a viable and worthwhile enterprise. Moral or political philosophy does not amount to the more fundamental discipline and it is a mistake, as a result, to think that the moral philosophy of international law cannot inform general moral or political philosophy in return. In fact, as the moral philosophy of international law ripens, the distinction between it and moral and political philosophy *tout court* becomes less clear.[39]

Another set of debates familiar to moral and political philosophers exported into the moral philosophy of international law pertains to method. One of those debates relates to the opposition between ideal and non-ideal moral theorizing. To paraphrase Buchanan, whereas the task of ideal theory is to set the most important moral targets for a better future in international law, non-ideal theory's task is to guide our efforts to approach those ultimate targets, both by setting intermediate moral targets and by helping us to determine which means and processes for achieving them are morally permissible.[40] The latter depends on the former, however, and the former depends on the latter to assess its feasibility and accessibility—both

[38] See generally *Justice, Legitimacy and Self-Determination* (n 4).
[39] See 'International Law, Philosophy of' (n 4) section 5.
[40] *Justice, Legitimacy and Self-Determination* (n 4) 60–1.

of them being conditions of any moral theory. This explains why they cannot be contrasted as a choice. The best moral philosophies of international law should therefore aim at providing both ideal and non-ideal elements.

2.3 The Critiques

Moral philosophy of international law has provoked considerable scepticism as an enterprise. Sometimes this takes the form of denying the very possibility of a normative theory of international law: doubt is cast on the existence of justifiable transnational and international moral standards that might appropriately be reflected in international law. More often, however, it is scepticism about the scope and content of the relevant moral standards: even if it is conceded that some moral standards obtain in the case of international law, they are thought to be severely limited in their coverage and very minimal in their demands. These two brands of scepticism may be referred to, respectively, as radical and moderate.[41]

2.3.1 *Radical Scepticism*

A primary basis for radical scepticism about the project of a moral philosophy of international law consists in scepticism about the objectivity of morality itself. The argument here is that morality (pejoratively described as 'utopianism' or, in international law debates, as 'moralism') presents itself as a set of constraints, discoverable by reason, on the pursuit of self-interest by individuals and states. By contrast, the realist critique of morality reveals all moral principles to be themselves products of circumstances and interests and weapons framed for the furtherance of interests.[42]

Yet even if correct, the corrosive implications of scepticism about moral objectivity extend not just to the normative theory of international law, but to any form of thought involving moral judgement. This is not necessarily an argument against it, but it does show that it is not a problem uniquely afflicting normative theorizing about international matters. Moreover, it places its advocates under special pressure to avoid self-refutation, since they typically do wish to assert the appropriateness of moral judgements in some non-international contexts. In addition, it is far from obvious that either the Marxist or any other brand of realist critique has securely established the advertised conclusion that morality is merely the product of, and perhaps also ideological window-dressing for, underlying interests (or preferences, desires, and so on). Moral scepticism of this sort is highly controversial in

---

[41] See also *Justice, Legitimacy and Self-Determination* (n 4) 29ff.
[42] See eg EH Carr, *The Twenty Years' Crisis 1919–1939: An Introduction to the Study of International Relations* (Palgrave Macmillan 2001 [1939]) at 65.

philosophical circles today. How easy is it to dispute, after all, that the proposition 'slavery is unjust' is plainly true, even as '2+1=3' is plainly true? And why must the best explanation of anyone's belief in the former proposition, unlike their belief in the latter, necessarily exclude appealing to the fact that the proposition in question is true?[43]

Perhaps a more constructive observation is that there are many ways in which morality can be admitted to be 'subjective' without thereby failing to be 'objective' in some significant sense that allows for moral propositions to be straightforwardly true or justified, for belief in true moral propositions to take the form of knowledge, and for changes in moral belief over time to represent genuine cognitive progress or regress. In particular, the objectivist need not embrace the metaphysical claim that moral values, such as justice, are radically mind-independent, like the famed Platonic forms, existing in splendid isolation from human modes of consciousness and concern.

So, a nuanced appreciation of the kind of 'objectivity' requisite to the meaningful pursuit of a normative approach to international law may serve to quell sceptical concerns of the first sort about the prospects for developing a normative theory of international law. And this is just as well, since many of those who press such concerns seem themselves to subscribe to numerous moral propositions.[44]

2.3.2 *Moderate Scepticism*

Other more moderate forms of scepticism about the enterprise of a normative theory of international law concentrate not so much on the nature of morality, but on the putative subject matter—in particular, relations among states—about which such theories seek to make moral judgements. Even if moral reasoning is in principle capable of attaining a respectable degree of objectivity, the argument goes, its remit either does not extend to the case of international law, or else does so only in a highly attenuated form.

One line of argument of this kind turns on regarding the sphere of international law's application, at least in the present and the foreseeable future, as a state of nature.[45] This is because it is a domain in which the key agents—territorial states—exhibit three important features: (i) they are ultimately motivated by the fundamental aim of ensuring their own survival; (ii) they are approximately equal in power, in the sense that no one state (or stable grouping of states) can permanently dominate all the others; and (iii) they are not subject to a sovereign capable of securing peaceful cooperation among states by authoritatively arbitrating conflicts

---

[43] See T Nagel, *The Last Word* (OUP Oxford 1997) ch 6.

[44] See *The Twenty Years' Crisis 1919–1939* (n 42).

[45] See eg K Waltz, *Man, the State, and War: A Theoretical Analysis* (Columbia University Press New York 1959).

among them. In such circumstances, it is contended, it would be deeply irrational for a state to conform its conduct to moral demands; hence, morality is inapplicable to the sphere that international law purports to govern.[46]

There is good cause to resist this sort of sceptical argument, even in its most moderate form.[47] If the international sphere were a state of nature, it is very doubtful that it could sustain any institution meriting the name of 'law'. Yet, it makes good sense to speak of international law governing the relations between sovereign states through norms and institutions enabling cooperation, even in the absence of a global sovereign. More generally, the ultimate or predominant determinant of a state's behaviour cannot be the desire to ensure its survival (or, in another version, to maximize its power). Anyway, it is obviously not the case that compliance with moral standards inevitably imperils a state's chances of survival. Finally, liberal approaches to international relations may emphasize the responsiveness of a state's preferences to the internal character of the state (for example, whether its constitution is democratic) and its society (for example, the extent to which it is pluralistic and accommodating of internal differences).

In response, an advocate of the state of nature analogy might be tempted to stretch the notion of state preference for survival, or power, so that it encompasses all of the seemingly countervailing evidence for the irreducible diversity of states' interests. Doing so, however, would lead to the trivialization of the state of nature argument, rendering it unfalsifiable by any empirical evidence.

Nothing in the foregoing observations is inconsistent with acknowledging a core of authentic insight in the state of nature argument. One way of spelling it out is in terms of feasibility constraints on an acceptable normative theory of international law. These are different from, and in all probability far more limiting than, those that apply in the domestic case.[48] What we may rightly take issue with, however, is the sweepingly negative conclusion that sceptics who appeal to the state of nature analogy seek to draw from this insight.

There are more plausible ways of motivating moderate scepticism about the prospects of a normative theory of international law than simply invoking a state of nature analogy. Another line of thought appeals to the ethical-political significance of an important feature of the international domain: the great diversity that exists in ethical and political concepts among different cultures, and also the considerable divergence in judgements among those who deploy the same concepts.

One way of elaborating this general line of thought is by means of the notion of ethical pluralism. The latter doctrine is wholly compatible with the objectivity of

---

[46] See the general outline of the 'state of nature' argument in *Justice, Legitimacy and Self-Determination* (n 4) 29–30.

[47] For those critiques, see ibid 31–7; *Political Theory and International Relations* (n 21) 185–91.

[48] See *Political Theory and International Relations* (n 21) 187.

ethics, and so is not to be confused with ethical relativism and hence with radical scepticism about value. But, given the profusion of objective ethical values and the diverse number of ways in which their content may be acceptably elaborated and relations between them ordered, proponents of this view are doubtful that a 'global ethic' applicable to all states and suitable for embodiment in international law and institutions will be anything other than minimalist in content.[49] Instead, it will predominantly consist of a limited set of universal norms.

A second line of thought purports to stand aloof from all philosophical controversies, such as those concerning ethical objectivism, and focuses instead on the conditions of a legitimate international law; one that can credibly claim to be binding on all its subjects. John Rawls, for instance, has argued that it is necessary for the principles underlying law, at both the domestic and the international levels, to be justifiable to all of those subject to them. In both cases, the operative form of justification must be in terms of a form of public reason—rather than ordinary, truth-oriented moral reasoning—that is responsive to the fact of reasonable pluralism. In the case of a liberal society, this is a pluralism about conceptions of the good held by individual citizens, who are nonetheless reasonable in that they accept the criterion of reciprocity (they are prepared to cooperate with others on fair terms as free and equal citizens) and the burdens of judgement. In the Rawlsian conception of the international case, however, the justification is directed at political communities, rather than the individuals who compose them, and reasonable pluralism extends to conceptions of justice, not simply conceptions of the good.[50] This means that, for Rawls, decent but non-liberal societies may be counted as members in good standing of the Society of Peoples; they have good standing even in terms of an ideal theory of international justice. This is despite the fact that such societies are not democratic and may engage in various illiberal practices. Rawls' approach also leads to a notoriously truncated list of human rights, certainly as compared with the *Universal Declaration of Human Rights*,[51] and to the inapplicability of principles of distributive justice (including Rawls' famous 'difference principle') to the global sphere: neither the difference principle nor any other principle of distributive justice bears on relations *between* societies, nor is respect for it mandated *within* each society in order to ensure its good standing under the Rawlsian Law of Peoples.

Of course, there is a great deal that needs to be said in assessing the pros and cons of moderate scepticism of the last two varieties. The key point is that moderate scepticism is not really all that sceptical. On the contrary, it presents itself as

---

[49] See eg M Walzer, *Spheres of Justice: A Defense of Pluralism and Equality* (Blackwell Oxford 1993) at 28–30.

[50] *The Law of Peoples with 'The Idea of Public Reason Revisited'* (n 24) 11, 19 (the international case) and 136–7 (the domestic case).

[51] 'Universal Declaration of Human Rights' GA Res 217A(III) (10 December 1948) UN Doc A/810.

a self-consciously moral and critical position *within* the enterprise of articulating a normative theory of international law.

2.4 The Contributions

From the perspective of international law and its scholarship and hence from a meta-theoretical perspective, one may identify three major contributions of general moral philosophies of international law—leaving aside important field-specific contributions as in the laws of war or human rights law context.

2.4.1 *Thinking Normatively about International Law*

The first and main contribution of moral philosophies of international law has been to show that one may think normatively about international law. From the perspective of moral philosophy, this is not particularly worth emphasizing because any social practice may be assessed normatively. For international lawyers, however, who for a long time had difficulty understanding the normativity of international law and how it may or may not differ from that of domestic law, it has been a key contribution to further development inside international legal theory, especially as an argument to eschew the anti-normative stance of 'realists' and postmodern theorists of international law alike.

The criticism one may make, however, is that most moral philosophers of international law to date have contented themselves with a social science understanding of their object. This is surprising, and not only to a lawyer, given that their object is legal and hence, prima facie at least, normative. All the same, most moral philosophers of international law to date have addressed their material (international law and international legal institutions) as morally inert and seen the only normative element in the picture as stemming from the moral standards applied to that institution.[52] This, however, corresponds to an impoverished account of law but also of legal philosophy. One may argue indeed that there is no 'legal normativity' as such, that is, distinct from (moral) normativity, but rather a special (moral) normativity of law due to a special socio-political context that contributes to specifying or even generating norms anew.[53] What this means, in other words, is that the normativity of law is neither pure and distinct from morality, nor merely moral. Of course, this critique affects institutional or non-ideal moral theories of international law less than ideal ones, for their focus is on existing

---

[52] See eg *Political Theory and International Relations* (n 21).
[53] See J Raz, 'The Normativity of Law' (2013, unpublished manuscript on file with author) on the law's 'double moral life'.

institutions and their internal potential for progress and reform.[54] However, the critique still bites because, even in non-ideal moral philosophies of international law, the relevant reasons and their generation are not necessarily attributed to the legal context and its institutions.

2.4.2 *Conceptualizing the Legitimacy of International Law*

A second and more specific contribution of moral theorizing of international law has been to bring to the fore justifications of the legitimate authority or legitimacy of international law that are not strictly legal. Again, from a moral perspective, this has meant revisiting well-trodden paths for domestic legal philosophers.[55] For international lawyers, however, emphasizing how the authority of international law needs a moral justification to bind and not only to coerce, on the one hand, and how consent does not suffice morally to create an obligation, on the other, has been particularly fruitful to discussions pertaining to how best to make international law in particular, but also to how best to organize the relations between domestic and international law.[56]

However, a critical remark is in order. Moral philosophers of international law have focused mostly on content-dependent reasons for the authority of international law, such as global justice or human rights.[57] They have only rarely realized how advanced legal philosophers are in their understanding of the legitimacy of law and in particular of content-independent reasons the law gives for its authority. This neglect partakes of the same lack of understanding of the specific (moral) normativity of international law alluded to before.

2.4.3 *Isolating the Legality of International Law*

A third contribution of the moral philosophy of international law to the theory of international law derives from the other two: it has contributed to isolating and understanding the legality of international law itself. This has, of course, not been intended by most moral philosophers of international law given their often limited understanding of law's social and normative specificities.[58] However, their external take on international practice has indirectly helped international lawyers to

---

[54] See *Justice, Legitimacy and Self-Determination* (n 4) 53ff and especially at 57–9 (on the 'Vanishing Subject Matter Problem' in ideal theories).

[55] See eg J Raz, 'The Problem of Authority: Revisiting the Service Conception' (2006) 90 *Minnesota Law Review* 1003–44.

[56] See eg A Buchanan, 'The Legitimacy of International Law' in *The Philosophy of International Law* (n 7) 79–96; J Tasioulas, 'The Legitimacy of International Law' in *The Philosophy of International Law* (n 7) 97–118; S Besson, 'The Authority of International Law: Lifting the State Veil' (2009) 31 *Sydney Law Review* 343–80.

[57] See eg R Goodin, 'Enfranchising All Affected Interests, and Its Alternatives' (2007) 35 *Philosophy and Public Affairs* 40–68.

[58] See eg *Political Theory and International Relations* (n 21).

consolidate their own internal understanding of that social and normative practice's specificity, that is, its legality.[59] It has also contributed to developing international lawyers' sense of their own discipline. It is to this vindication process I would like to turn now.

3 Towards a Legal Philosophy of International Law

3.1 The Meta-Theoretical Turn

Even though the long absence of normative legal philosophy of international law has been compensated for by resorting to moral philosophizing about international law, there is no reason why this may not change. This raises the more general meta-theoretical question of how best to conduct normative theorizing about international law, and whether and how this may be done within the boundaries of legal philosophy itself.

There are many reasons for a turn to meta-theory for international law. First of all, the international legal order is still relatively young, and this makes a discussion of the nature and role of theorizing international law—and of the relationship of that theorizing to practice—particularly important.[60] Secondly, even though the theory of international law has now become a booming field of scholarship, its meta-theory remains largely underdeveloped. Overall, international lawyers have tended to be very pragmatic about the way they conceive of international law.[61] When they are not, they have turned critical. In fact, to date, discussions of the meta-theory of international law have been pursued almost exclusively by critical legal scholars.[62]

---

[59] See eg M Giudice and K Culver, *Legality's Borders: An Essay in General Jurisprudence* (OUP Oxford 2010). See also L Murphy, *What Makes Law: An Introduction to the Philosophy of Law* (CUP Cambridge 2014) ch 8 ('What Makes Law Law? Law Beyond the State').

[60] See eg W Twining et al., 'The Role of Academics in the Legal System' in P Cane and M Tushnet (eds), *The Oxford Handbook of Legal Studies* (OUP Oxford 2003) 920–49, at 941.

[61] See ibid 944.

[62] See eg M Koskenniemi, 'International Legal Theory and Doctrine' in *Max Planck Encyclopedia of Public International Law* (OUP Oxford 2011); M Koskenniemi, 'The Methodology of International Law' in *Max Planck Encyclopedia of Public International Law* (OUP Oxford 2011); M Koskenniemi, 'Between Commitment and Cynicism: Outline for a Theory of International Law as Practice' in Office of Legal Affairs, *Collection of Essays by Legal Advisers of States, Legal Advisers of International Organizations and Practitioners in the Field of International Law* (United Nations New York 1999) 495–523.

This has led to their views becoming not only mainstream[63] for lack of contestation, but also over-theorized[64] due to over-concentration.

As a result, and since the mid-twentieth century, positions in the field have become starkly contrasted. One may depict the debate as consisting primarily of a binary opposition between pure theoretical approaches to international law that regard legal scholarship as 'science'[65] and non-theoretical approaches to international law that object to the project of a legal science and criticize any theoretical endeavour as falling either into the trap of apology (politics) or utopia (moralism).[66] Any scholarly project that falls between the two has been quickly disparaged as non-'scientific'[67] and, in some cases, as morally activist by the first group, and as either apologetic or utopian by the second. Of course, there has been a wealth of outsider-theoretical approaches to international law that frame their discussions of international law in a theoretical context other than law. As we have seen in the case of moral philosophy of international law, however, neither of those theories has been particularly interested in the law as law and, most importantly, they have clearly situated themselves outside of international legal theory and hence outside its meta-theory as such.[68]

Normative approaches to international law and international legal theory developed within international law have paid a high price for this state of the meta-theory of international law. Arguably, therefore, the most important reason to develop a meta-theory of international law lies in understanding the specific normativity of international law—the very understanding that is missing in moral philosophies of international law as explained in the previous section. So far, indeed, whereas defenders of a purely legal kind of normativity have endorsed a pure theory of international law,[69] others who do not see or are not interested in the normativity of law (for instance because they see consent, power, rationality, or ideology as the main source of motivation behind international law) have endorsed other disciplines to approach international law such as economics, politics, or international relations.[70]

---

[63] See S Singh, 'Appendix 2: International Law as a Technical Discipline: Critical Perspectives on the Narrative Structure of a Theory' in J d'Aspremont, *Formalism and the Sources of International Law: A Theory of the Ascertainment of Legal Rules* (OUP Oxford 2013) 236–61.

[64] See eg A Rasulov, 'New Approaches to International Law: Images of a Genealogy' in JM Beneyto and D Kennedy (eds), *New Approaches to International Law: The European and the American Experiences* (TMC Asser The Hague 2013) 151–91.

[65] See eg *The Law of the United Nations* (n 11); J Kammerhofer, 'Law-Making by Scholarship? The Dark Side of 21st Century International Law "Methodology"' in J Crawford and S Nouwen (eds), *Select Proceedings of the European Society of International Law* (Hart Oxford 2012) 115–26.

[66] See eg 'Between Commitment and Cynicism' (n 62) 496, 500.

[67] On those debates see A Peters, 'There is Nothing More Practical than a Good Theory: An Overview of Contemporary Approaches to International Law' (2001) 44 *German Yearbook of International Law* 25–37; A Peters, 'Realizing Utopia as a Scholarly Endeavour' (2013) 24 *European Journal of International Law* 533–52.

[68] See 'The Relative Autonomy of International Law or the Forgotten Politics of Interdisciplinarity' (n 13).

[69] See eg 'Law-Making by Scholarship?' (n 65).   [70] See eg sources cited in n 14.

This has forced those few theorists of international law interested in legal reasoning and the moral normativity of law into moral philosophy and to be categorized by others as 'international moralists'.

Interestingly, some of those methodological debates have been reopened lately in a broader fashion. That revival has come mostly from international legal scholars trained in the German[71] or American[72] traditions. Another explanation lies in the (counter-)disciplinary 'call to arms' emitted lately by some critical legal scholars and more 'mainstream' international legal scholars.[73] Realizing the predominance of outsider theories of international law at last (even in the guise of interdisciplinarity) and perhaps also the meta-theoretical sterility of critique for the development of international law, international legal scholars have called for a more methodological involvement of international lawyers. Regrettably, for the time being, those debates tell us very little about what law and its 'discipline' should be, except that it should be cultivated to save international law as a profession.[74] Based on both the practical dimension of law and the normativity of the practice of law, one may argue that theory is central to the practice of international law, and that its very centrality to the practice explains a great deal about the kind of theory it should be: a normative legal philosophy of international law.[75]

3.2 A *Legal* Philosophy of International *Law*

Qua participants in a normative practice, lawyers are enacting and applying norms in a given social-political context. Arguably, therefore, normative legal theorizing is required by the normative practice of law. It helps capture what the concept and nature of law amounts to, that is, its 'legality'. As a normative concept, the law encapsulates one or many values of legality, and normative reasoning is thus a necessary part of its application. Legal theory facilitates that normative reasoning in the practice of law, and enables the law-immanent justification and critique that are characteristic of legal practice *qua* normative practice. So, the relationship

---

[71] See eg I Feichtner, 'Realizing Utopia through the Practice of International Law' (2012) 23 *European Journal of International Law* 1143–57; 'Realizing Utopia as a Scholarly Endeavour' (n 67).

[72] See eg 'The Role of Academics in the Legal System' (n 60); SR Ratner and A-M Slaughter (eds), *The Methods of International Law* (American Society of International Law Washington DC 2004); G Shaffer and T Ginsburg, 'The Empirical Turn in International Legal Scholarship' (2012) 106 *American Journal of International Law* 1–46.

[73] See *Formalism and The Sources of International Law* (n 63), by reference to, eg, J Crawford, 'International Law as a Discipline and Profession' (2012) 106 *Proceedings of the American Society of International Law* 471–86; M Koskenniemi, 'Law, Teleology and International Relations: An Essay in Counterdisciplinarity' (2012) 26 *International Relations* 3–34; J Klabbers, 'Counter-Disciplinarity' (2010) 4 *International Political Sociology* 308–11.

[74] See eg 'International Law as a Discipline and Profession' (n 73) 482.

[75] See also S Besson, 'International Legal Theory *qua* Practice of International Law' in J d'Aspremont et al., (eds), *International Law as a Profession* (CUP Cambridge forthcoming 2016).

between legal theory and practice is not (only or centrally) one of 'science' external to its object. Legal theory is internal to legal practice, which needs it in order to be self-reflective and critical. Normative legal theorizing amounts to theorizing about norms albeit in a contextualized and practical fashion: it takes place in a legal context and is therefore distinct from abstract moral theorizing about the law.

Of course, there is a risk of circularity between the theory and practice of law, as a result. That circularity is virtuous, however. Legal theory helps shape the law, but without the practice there would be nothing to theorize and shape in return. It remains distinct from practice, however, to the extent that theory does not enact and enforce legal norms for lack of (practical) authority to do so. Another risk is that of parochialism. If legal theory is part of the practice of law, then the parochial practice of law may influence the universality of the theory. The enquiry behind legal theory may remain universal, however, despite being part of a (parochial) practice to the extent that its reasoning and conclusions are universally valid across legal cultures (even if the concept of law itself is parochial).[76]

The practical role of legal theory has two normative implications for what is a good legal theory. First of all, legal theory should take the practice of law (and hence of theory) seriously. It should situate itself in the legal practice *qua* self-reflective practice, by being a practice-situated theory that is relevant to the justification and critique that are immanent to the practice. Secondly, legal theory should take the normativity of law (and hence of theory) seriously. It should do more than describe the law, as a result, but also more than merely justify or criticize it in order to reform it. This echoes the opposition between ideal and non-ideal accounts of international law, and Buchanan's argument about the need to bridge them and provide both in the same general theory of international law. What his argument missed, however, was how international law itself and international legal theory offer that self-reflective and generative normative framework for which non-ideal moral philosophers of international law are longing.[77]

These dimensions of normative legal theory illuminate how legal philosophy of international law differs from moral philosophy of international law. On the one hand, international legal theory does not approach international law as a distinct moral object. It is situated in the law, and not outside it. On the other, international legal theory takes the special context of the normativity of law seriously. It does not regard it as another form of global social practice to evaluate, and hence as a morally inert institutional reality. Nor does it underestimate the law's own normative context and ability to develop new norms and its own grounds of legitimacy. This also explains in turn why it would be wrong to argue that taking the (moral) normativity of international law seriously may lead to international moralism[78]

---

[76] See J Raz, 'Can There Be a Theory of Law?' in MP Golding and WA Edmundson (eds), *The Blackwell Guide to the Philosophy of Law and Legal Theory* (Blackwell London 2004) 324–42.

[77] See *Justice, Legitimacy and Self-Determination* (n 4) 57–9.

[78] For this critique, see eg 'Moral Internationalism and the Responsibility to Protect' (n 10).

or equate it with international moral activism.[79] Not only are moral philosophers of international law not necessarily moralists, as argued in the first section, but international legal theorists are not moral philosophers of international law. They may draw from the latter's research and engage with them, but their methods and approaches to international law are distinct.

3.3 The Case in Point: The Philosophy of International Human Rights Law

The current boom in moral philosophies of (international law on) human rights provides an interesting case to illustrate this chapter's point. Based on the reasoning I have presented so far, I would like to argue that international human rights law is a normative practice and that its theory is best developed as a legal theory of that practice.[80] This is something current moral philosophies of international law do not have and, arguably, cannot capture adequately about human rights.

First of all, then, international human rights should be approached as a normative practice. It is indeed a relationship of rights and duties between a right-holder and a duty-bearer. More particularly, it ought to be regarded as a normative legal practice: human rights law holds a central position in human rights practice. As such, international human rights should not be conflated with the moral reality of universal moral rights. Of course, the latter may be theorized separately through moral philosophy or together with international human rights law, depending on one's take on the relationship between international human rights and universal moral rights, but certainly not as a morally constraining blueprint to be merely translated and enforced by legal practice.[81] It is crucial indeed to look at how those moral rights are specified and transformed by the legal practice in return.

Secondly, if this holds, then the theory of the normative practice of international human rights law is best developed *qua* normative legal theory of that practice, and not as moral philosophy. Human rights theory is therefore best conceived as a legal theory of legal (and moral) rights. More specifically, it should start from the hard questions in the legal practice of human rights and make the most of the moral justifications, but also of the critiques articulated within that practice itself.[82] To do so, it can make use of the methodological resources of legal theory and

---

[79] For this critique, see eg 'Law-Making by Scholarship?' (n 65).

[80] For a full argument to that extent, see S Besson, 'The Law in Human Rights Theory' (2013) 7 *Zeitschrift für Menschenrechte/Journal for Human Rights* 120–50.

[81] *Contra On Human Rights* (n 23); J Tasioulas, 'Towards a Philosophy of Human Rights' (2012) 65 *Current Legal Problems* 1–30.

[82] See also S Besson, 'Justifications' in D Moeckli, S Shah, and S Sivakumaran (eds), *International Human Rights Law* (2nd edn OUP Oxford 2014) at 34–52.

then contribute to human rights practice itself.[83] Human rights theory should not therefore be conflated with a moral philosophy of moral rights only according to which legal human rights are a mere translation of moral rights (so-called 'ethical' theories of human rights),[84] nor with a political philosophy of a (non-normative) practice of rights only according to which the practice of legal rights is treated as morally irrelevant or inert (so-called 'political' theories of human rights).[85]

Importantly, the legal practice of human rights should not only be the object of human rights theory, but also the context of human rights theory *qua* legal theory of a normative practice and hence *qua* part of that practice of immanent justification and critique. This is not only a key methodological realization for human rights theory, but also a key meta-theoretical realization for human rights theorists themselves, and for human rights research in general. They should understand themselves as situated in the practice, with the responsibilities that come with it. Thinking and writing for lawyers means writing as a lawyer, and the same applies to international human rights law.[86]

4 CONCLUSION

After explaining how the long absence of normative legal philosophy of international law has been compensated for by resorting to moral philosophizing about international law and what the contributions of those philosophers to international legal scholarship have been, this chapter turned to the more general meta-theoretical question of how best to conduct normative theorizing about international law, and whether and how this may be done within the boundaries of legal philosophy itself.

This chapter argued that the time has finally come for recent developments in the field of the moral philosophy of international law to lead to the development of normative theoretical and meta-theoretical research in international law, thus breaking away from the sterile oppositions between 'realist' and so-called 'moralist' approaches to international law. More specifically, the way we do theory of international law should reflect the normativity of the practice of international law

---

[83] See also 'The Law in Human Rights Theory' (n 80).

[84] See eg *On Human Rights* (n 23); 'Towards a Philosophy of Human Rights' (n 81).

[85] See eg *The Law of Peoples* with *'The Idea of Public Reason Revisited'* (n 24); *The Idea of Human Rights* (n 23).

[86] *Contra* eg *On Human Rights* (n 23) ch XI. See eg S Besson, *Human Right as Law* (forthcoming 2016, manuscript on file with author).

and be responsive to the pivotal role of normative reasoning in that practice *qua* self-reflective practice. While moral philosophers of international law and especially some of their non-ideal accounts have opened the way, they have stopped short of fully grasping the normativity of law. What we need now is a normative legal philosophy of international law, one that can take international law seriously, at last.

CHAPTER 20

INTERNATIONAL LEGAL POSITIVISM

JÖRG KAMMERHOFER

So setzest du der ewig regen,
Der heilsam schaffenden Gewalt
Die kalte Teufelsfaust entgegen,
Die sich vergebens tückisch ballt![1]

1 INTRODUCTION

POSITIVISM is as dead as it is all-pervading. No fashion-conscious international lawyer would be caught dead espousing positivism. And yet none can do without constantly—and near-exclusively—referring to 'positive law' in order to make a 'legal point', particularly when one leaves the ivory-tower for the classroom or courtroom.[2] The theoretically inclined class among international legal scholars has long abandoned international legal positivism as anything but a pawn in their grand narratives about

---

[1] 'So, to the actively eternal/Creative force, in cold disdain/You now oppose the fist infernal,/ Whose wicked clench is all in vain!' JW von Goethe, *Faust: A Tragedy* (B Taylor trans) (Ward, Lock, and Co London 1889 [1808]) Scene 3, at 39.

[2] F Hoffmann, 'Teaching General Public International Law' in J Kammerhofer and J d'Aspremont (eds), *International Legal Positivism in a Post-Modern World* (CUP Cambridge 2014) 349–77.

the historical development of international legal theory.[3] This narrative is one of the 'progress' of ideas.[4] 'We' are—our world of ideas is—perceived as being *so* much further developed today than those of Lassa Oppenheim's, Herbert Hart's, or Hans Kelsen's time. The realist, pragmatist, critical, instrumentalist, economist revolution in international legal theory (take your pick) has, some might claim, swept away the old, tired, and discredited positivists, wedded as they are to the majesty of the state, an emperor without clothes. This may be an accurate sociological description of the lack of importance of 'positivism' among theorists of international law today. But theories are resilient. Ideas remain *active* in the public realm, a thought once thought cannot be un-thought.[5] So it is with positivism. Despite everything, certain theorists are still peddling certain emanations of this creed. Equally, some of the ideas that are typically ascribed to 'positivism' form the backbone of black-letter lawyers' arguments about the law—though they are mostly unsupported by a theoretical superstructure.

Much of today's critique reveals the misconceptions *about* positivism more than the shortcomings *of* this approach. Then again it may be unfair to blame critics, as the label 'positivism' has a number of connotations. For example, there is Comtean sociological positivism or the logical positivism of the Vienna Circle. Even if we attach the adjective 'legal' to positivism, there are vast differences between differing traditions or streams of *legal* positivism. (The connection of Alf Ross' version of legal realism to the ideas of the Vienna Circle, on the one hand, and the connection of logical to legal-sociological positivism, on the other, may however give us pause). Lastly, legal positivism as an approach to general legal philosophy often differs from a specifically *international* legal positivism. It may be impossible to construct a coherent set of arguments encompassing all legal positivisms, whether *per genus proximum et differentia specifica* or by way of a 'family resemblance'.

2 Positivism and Formalism

'Legal positivism' has too often been conflated with 'formalism' in traditional Anglo-Saxon jurisprudential discourse as well as in newer critical streams of scholarship. In German discourse there is a similar, if less pervasive, confusion

---

[3] M Koskenniemi, *The Gentle Civilizer of Nations: The Rise and Fall of International Law* (CUP Cambridge 2001); M García-Salmones Rovira, *The Project of Positivism in International Law* (OUP Oxford 2013).

[4] T Skouteris, *The Notion of Progress in International Law Discourse* (TMC Asser The Hague 2010).

[5] P Allott, *Eunomia: New Order for a New World* (OUP Oxford 1990) at 214, 288; earlier: E de Bono, *I am Right, You are Wrong: From This to the New Renaissance, From Rock Logic to Water Logic* (Viking London 1990) at 288.

between legal positivism and the jurisprudence of concepts (*Begriffsjurisprudenz*).[6] While there is a specific sense in which positivism can be called 'formalism', there are at least two debates where this equivocation is not pertinent.

First, positivism is not formalism in the sense of the debate between realism and formalism, as conducted in US legal scholarship.[7] The argument is that positivist approaches contain or are exhausted by the assertion that a legal decision 'can be deduced by logical means from predetermined legal rules'.[8] Not only is this an argument that most positivists, foremost Hart and Kelsen, do not hold or support, despite the persistent straw man, it is also conducted on an entirely different plane. 'Whereas positivism is a theory of law, *formalism is a theory of adjudication*, a theory about how judges actually do decide cases and/or a theory about how they ought to decide them.'[9] While it is debatable whether a theory of law need necessarily contain a theory of adjudication, it is submitted that theories of adjudication neither exhaust theories of law nor that positivism pre-determines one's theory of adjudication to a significant extent.

Second, international legal positivism is also not formalism in the sense of Martti Koskenniemi's 'culture of formalism'.[10] For Koskenniemi 'formalism [is] a culture of resistance to power, a social practice of accountability, openness, and equality'.[11] Koskenniemi suggests that formalism 'seeks to persuade the protagonists...to [justify preferences] by reference to standards that are independent from their particular positions or interests'.[12] This independence is itself instrumental; the formalist view 'refuses to engage with the question of its objectives precisely *in order to* constrain those in powerful positions.'[13] *This* formalism is a political

---

[6] Discussing this particular confusion see eg K Larenz, *Methodenlehre der Rechtswissenschaft* (5th edn Springer Berlin 1983) at 22–3 n 8; W Ott, *Der Rechtspositivismus: Kritische Würdigung auf der Grundlage eines juristischen Pragmatismus* (2nd edn Duncker & Humblot Berlin 1992) at 116.

[7] J d'Aspremont, *Formalism and the Sources of International Law: A Theory of the Ascertainment of Legal Rules* (OUP Oxford 2011) at 18–21. For the intra-US debate, see eg B Leiter, 'Review Essay: Positivism, Formalism, Realism' (1999) 99 *Columbia Law Review* 1138–64; AJ Sebok, 'Misunderstanding Positivism' (1995) 93 *Michigan Law Review* 2054–134; BZ Tamanaha, *Beyond the Formalist–Realist Divide: The Role of Politics in Judging* (Princeton University Press Princeton 2010).

[8] HLA Hart, 'Positivism and the Separation of Law and Morals' (1958) 71 *Harvard Law Review* 593–629, at 602 n 25. See also A Ross, 'Validity and the Conflict between Legal Positivism and Natural Law (1961)' in SL Paulson and B Litschewski Paulson (eds), *Normativity and Norms: Critical Perspectives on Kelsenian Themes* (Clarendon Press Oxford 1998) 147–63, at 150.

[9] 'Positivism, Formalism, Realism' (n 7) 1144 (emphasis added).

[10] See eg *The Gentle Civilizer of Nations* (n 3) 494–509; M Koskenniemi, 'What is International Law For?' in MD Evans (ed), *International Law* (3rd edn OUP Oxford 2010) 32–57, discussed in *Formalism and the Sources of International Law* (n 7) 27–9.

[11] *The Gentle Civilizer of Nations* (n 3) 500.   [12] Ibid 501.

[13] 'What is International Law For?' (n 10) 39 (emphasis added).

force,[14] not an epistemology of law. Koskenniemi believes that '[t]he way back to a Kelsenian formalism, a formalism *sans peur et sans reproche* is no longer open'.[15] Equally, Koskenniemi notes that 'when formalism loses political direction, formalism itself is lost'.[16] But this 'formalism' is a *culture*, not a theory.[17] Koskenniemi is in effect making a sociological argument about the sub-system 'international legal discourse', not describing an approach to the cognition of (international) law.

However, legal positivism *could be* called 'formalism' in a (set of) different sense(s). If law is constructed or perceived primarily in its form as a vessel, or if law-ascertainment is seen in a formal manner (as it is by Jean d'Aspremont),[18] then the specific *content* of the law is not as determinative as it is with non-formalist approaches. Certainly, no theory of law can ignore the content of legal norms[19]— even a Kelsenian structural analysis[20] of the legal order requires the identification of empowerment norms as part of the content of the normative material. Yet, for formalists in this sense the behaviour required—*what* one ought to do—is not determinative of normative status—*that* one ought to do it. This is what Kelsen (pointedly) wanted to express when he wrote that 'any content can be part of the law. No human behaviour on its own, that is, on the basis of its content, can be excluded from potentially forming the content of a legal norm.'[21] Modern streams of positivism that focus on the vessel, rather than the content of the vessel—on the legal *form*—can and have rightly been called formalism. However, particularly with regard to the differences between the Kelsenian and Hartian traditions—the only two jurisprudentially informed schools of international legal positivism at the moment—it is all too easy to attempt an overarching description that does not do justice to either. Hence, an exhaustive explanation of how much and which kind of 'formalism' is held by positivists will not be attempted and Section 4 will discuss one such tradition on its own merits.

---

[14] F Hoffmann, 'An Epilogue on an Epilogue' (2006) 7 *German Law Journal* 1095–102, at 1099: 'a re-description of international legal practice as a professional stance that takes comprehension of the field's epistemological condition as an ethical precept for political responsibility.'

[15] *The Gentle Civilizer of Nations* (n 3) 495.

[16] 'What is International Law For?' (n 10) 49.

[17] *The Gentle Civilizer of Nations* (n 3) 508.

[18] *Formalism and the Sources of International Law* (n 7) 12–13.

[19] H Kelsen, 'Juristischer Formalismus und Reine Rechtslehre' (1929) 58 *Juristische Wochenschrift* 1723–6, at 1723 n 1.

[20] AJ Merkl, 'Prolegomena einer Theorie des rechtlichen Stufenbaues' in A Verdross (ed), *Gesellschaft, Staat und Recht: Festschrift für Hans Kelsen zum 50. Geburtstag* (Springer Vienna 1931) 252–94, at 252.

[21] '...kann jeder beliebige Inhalt Recht sein. Es gibt kein menschliches Verhalten, das als solches, kraft seines Gehalts, ausgeschlossen wäre, Inhalt einer Rechtsnorm zu sein.' H Kelsen, *Reine Rechtslehre* (2nd edn Deuticke Vienna 1960) at 201. All translations, unless otherwise noted, are by the present author.

3 DOES INTERNATIONAL EQUAL 'CLASSICAL' LEGAL POSITIVISM?

Those who have not reflected upon these matters in a deep and sustained manner have developed a narrative of nineteenth- and early twentieth-century international legal scholarship dominated by 'positivists',[22] whereas from the mid-twentieth century we perceive an increasing loosening of the positivist 'strictures' on international law with the resurgence of naturalism and the development of a pragmatist-instrumentalist view of international law.[23] This caricature of a status quo in *fin de siècle* scholarship is sometimes called 'classical' international legal positivism, and names like Anzilotti, Hall, Jellinek, Oppenheim, and Triepel are associated with it. In this narrative, international reality is shaped by the co-existence of sovereign nation states where *par in parem non habet imperium*. Thus, this 'classical' international positivism is unique and distinct from domestic positivism. Its essentialist positions follow from the problem of order amongst sovereigns:[24] states are the original, pre-legal subjects of international law; they are sovereign(s). An order binding them cannot come into being without or against their will, hence all international law must have its origin in the will of states. This combination of state-centrism and voluntarism is but the logical extension of 'sovereigntism'. International legal positivists, this narrative alleges, are those that hold these positions in some form.

The best that can be said about this narrative is that it is not utterly wrong. All the elements discussed can be found in one form or another in 'positivist' writings. Positivism as a scholarly approach to (international) law did come to prominence during the latter half of the nineteenth century. The proportion of non-positivist writings increased after the Second World War. But scratch the surface and the narrative falls apart. The last two decades have seen a surge in scholarship deconstructing that narrative, both by critical scholarship and more traditional (intellectual) historical research.[25] It is not possible in the limited space available to

---

[22] See R Collins, 'Classical Legal Positivism in International Law Revisited' in *International Legal Positivism in a Post-Modern World* (n 2) 23–49; J von Bernstorff, 'German Intellectual Historical Origins of International Legal Positivism' in *International Legal Positivism in a Post-Modern World* (n 2) 50–80.

[23] This could be called the 'generalist textbook narrative', see eg MN Shaw, *International Law* (6th edn CUP Cambridge 2008) 24–31.

[24] 'Classical Legal Positivism in International Law Revisited' (n 22) at 28.

[25] See eg D Kennedy, 'International Law and the Nineteenth Century: History of an Illusion' (1996) 65 *Nordic Journal of International Law* 385–420; *The Gentle Civilizer of Nations* (n 3); A Perreau-Saussine, 'Three Ways of Writing a Treatise on Public International Law: Textbooks and the Nature of Customary International Law' in A Perreau-Saussine and JB Murphy (eds), *The Nature*

describe in detail how recent scholarship has demolished the straw man. One example among the many problematizations, relativizations, and clarifications presented must suffice for the present purpose: the so-called '*Lotus* principle'. This most reviled and (allegedly) most egregiously unthinking expression of early twentieth-century positivism is the idea, taken out of context, that '[r]estrictions upon the independence of States cannot...be presumed.'[26] As recent scholarship has shown,[27] the judgment of the Permanent Court in *Lotus*, even on the point where the famous dictum is taken from, must be read in context and is hardly the expression of the 'extreme positivist school' (JL Brierly)[28] or an 'excessively deferential approach to State consent' (Bruno Simma)[29] that it is alleged to be.

Certainly the words usually cited as the '*Lotus* dictum' find their place in that judgment and there is voluntarism in the majority's argument. But the argument is developed in a much more subtle way than our narrative, this *Schlagwortjurisprudenz*,[30] imagines. If we look at the Permanent Court's argument, rather than simply taking convenient phrases in a predatory manner, we will find that, far from postulating a necessary freedom of states, it actually proceeded on the basis of a wide-ranging 'restriction imposed by international law'—not imposed by its 'very nature'[31]—upon states not to exercise jurisdiction abroad. The law could be different; jurisdiction exercised with respect to acts abroad is regulated in the way discussed only 'under international law as it stands at present',[32] not by necessity. This is 'excessive deference' only to international law, not to the will of states. Equally, the dictum itself can be read in a more nuanced way:

We have a restatement of the very idea of positive law: that only positive law is positive law and that we simply cannot presume law ('restrictions') to be valid if their validity cannot

---

of *Customary Law: Legal, Historical and Philosophical Perspectives* (Cambridge University Press Cambridge 2007) 228–55, at 244–52.

[26] SS '*Lotus*' *(France v Turkey)* (Judgment) PCIJ Rep Series A No 10 (1927) at 18.

[27] See eg O Spiermann, '*Lotus* and the Double Structure of International Legal Argument' in L Boisson de Charzournes and P Sands (eds), *International Law, the International Court of Justice and Nuclear Weapons* (CUP Cambridge 1999) 131–52; J Kammerhofer, 'Gaps, the *Nuclear Weapons* Advisory Opinion and the Structure of International Legal Argument between Theory and Practice' (2010) 80 *The British Yearbook of International Law* 333–60.

[28] JL Brierly, 'The "*Lotus*" Case' (1928) 44 *Law Quarterly Review* 154–63, at 155.

[29] See Judge Simma castigating the Court eighty-three years after the Permanent Court's judgment for allegedly following the *Lotus* dictum in its *Kosovo* advisory opinion: *Accordance with International Law of the Unilateral Declaration of Independence in respect of Kosovo* (Advisory Opinion) [2010] ICJ Rep 403, at 478 (Declaration of Judge Simma).

[30] The 'jurisprudence of key words'. The formulation is taken from M Jestaedt and O Lepsius, 'Der Rechts- und der Demokratietheoretiker Hans Kelsen—Eine Einführung' in M Jestaedt and O Lepsius (eds), *Hans Kelsen: Verteidigung der Demokratie: Abhandlungen zur Demokratietheorie* (Mohr Siebeck Tübingen 2006) vi–xix, at xvii.

[31] *Lotus* (n 26) 18.   [32] Ibid 19.

be proven by regress to its sources. 'Restrictions' are only applicable if they are positive law of the normative system 'international law'. If there is no law, there is no law. No more than this was meant.[33]

The arguments against reading *Lotus* in a simplistic manner only scratch the surface of one argument attributed to the straw man of nineteenth to twentieth-century positivism. That the picture we paint of the twentieth century is an illusion, as David Kennedy observes,[34] is probably true, but it is not the point to be made here. A 'turn to history' must mean taking greater care in using historical arguments, not that legal theory should become or be resolved in legal historiography. This oversimplification and overgeneralization of historical international legal positivism and its arguments is relevant for the present chapter, both because this straw man image of positivism is received so uncritically by positivism's contemporary detractors and because it serves as a guide for today's un(der)-theoretical 'positivist'.

Alexander Orakhelashvili's *The Interpretation of Acts and Rules in Public International Law* discusses the topic on the basis of a positivism that comes close to the straw man described above.[35] This is not the place to comprehensively review Orakhelashvili's work,[36] but a cursory glance may be instructive. 'It is', he writes, 'axiomatic that international law is the body of rules produced by consent and agreement between sovereign States.'[37] For him 'the character of international law' is such that 'State consent is the principal basis of legal obligations'; '[p]ositivism and consensualism are necessary in international law...the legitimacy of which rests on the expression of the will of States which know of no sovereign government over and above them.'[38] True, it is not quite the straw man position, but it is not far from it. Also, at some points 'where positive law reasoning may prove insufficient to provide effective legal regulation',[39] he argues that recourse may be had to 'extra-positivist factors'.[40] This is not an unusual position among 'orthodox generalists' who combine straw man positivism with pragmatic flexibility, in Orakhelashvili's case calling it naturalism (another straw man), in order 'to find amicable, practicable or desirable solutions [in line with generalists'] personal cosmopolitanism or

---

[33] 'Gaps, the *Nuclear Weapons* Advisory Opinion and the Structure of International Legal Argument between Theory and Practice' (n 27) 343. See also '*Lotus* and the Double Structure of International Legal Argument' (n 27) 132–4.

[34] 'International Law and the Nineteenth Century' (n 25).

[35] Mainly in A Orakhelashvili, *The Interpretation of Acts and Rules in Public International Law* (OUP Oxford 2008) at 51–69.

[36] For a critique of some aspects, see J Kammerhofer, 'Book Review: Alexander Orakhelashvili, *The Interpretation of Acts and Rules in Public International Law* (2008)' (2009) 20 *European Journal of International Law* 1282–6.

[37] *The Interpretation of Acts and Rules in Public International Law* (n 35) 285.

[38] Ibid 53.   [39] Ibid 52.   [40] Ibid. See also at 60–9, 96–101.

internationalism.[41] The theoretical oversimplification in this narrative is also illustrated in the following passage:

Positivism is the only possible way of explaining how the bulk of international law is created and operates. Unlike other schools of thought . . . positivism does not refer to values or perceptions. . . . positivism is the basis of international legal reasoning[; this] follows from the fact that States are both principal producers and principal consumers of international law.[42]

These statements are muddled. If positivism were not to refer to values, then it could not describe law, which is value (ought), not pure fact. If it were not to refer to perceptions, it would not be positivism, but speculative reasoning on 'the good' or practical reason. If we knew a priori that states were able to create law, we would not need any legal theory, as theory is necessary to tell us where to look for the 'producers' of law in the first place. As this section has shown, much of the discussion of international legal positivism suffers from a certain disconnect from discussions in general jurisprudence. Anti-intellectualism is rampant in international legal scholarship, as are attendant delusions of nonetheless being able to say something about these theoretical matters.

The point of this chapter is to show how radically different modern, philosophically and jurisprudentially informed forms of international legal positivism are (foremost those inspired by Hart and Kelsen), how little they are touched by the constant attack on the positivist–voluntarist straw man, and how unfair it is to lump them together with unthinking 'positivists'. We should, in the critique, contextualization, and application of international legal positivism, not take its weakest, most inconsistent form, but one that can legitimately make a claim to providing a jurisprudential basis for international law and legal scholarship. Reconstruction of some aspects of one of these schools is the aim of the next section.

4 Neo-Hartian Socio-Psychologico-Linguistic Positivism

Like all texts, the writings of Herbert Hart and Hans Kelsen are embedded in their own historical and cultural context. As (legal-)theoretical texts, they are embedded

---

[41] J Kammerhofer, 'Orthodox Generalists and Political Activists in International Legal Scholarship' in M Happold (ed), *International Law in a Multipolar World* (Routledge Abingdon 2011) 138–57, at 145.

[42] *The Interpretation of Acts and Rules in Public International Law* (n 35) 53.

in their own philosophical tradition and culture. The development of Hart's and Kelsen's theories over time has given rise to its own problems.[43] However, the difference in the underlying philosophical cultures has too often been downplayed or neglected and is the cause for much misunderstanding in the interpretation of Hart's and Kelsen's works on the European continent and in the Anglosphere, respectively.[44] Restrictions of space allow this chapter to attempt a new form of portraying elements of only one such positivist approach—it will be refracted through a looking-glass, a specific 'external point of view'. The Hartian family of positivism will be cast through a 'distorting mirror'. Such a narrative may allow us to see the familiar in a new light and to discover why others may be perplexed by the seemingly obvious. The contention here is that Hart was right to try to focus on distancing his theory from legal realism, because at least some neo-Hartians have rendered it very close to Alf Ross' version of Scandinavian legal realism.[45]

Jurists from Germanophone and many other continental European countries are typically as perplexed by Hart's arguments as Anglophones are by Kelsen's. For many, Hart oscillates confusingly between sociological, psychological, and linguistic jurisprudence, particularly in founding the validity of law.[46] From their perspective, it is unclear whether the (collective) state of mind of officials, their use of words or the sociological 'fact', or a combination of these (and, if so, exactly what combination) either creates or 'founds', in a strong, metaphysical sense, law. Further, it is unclear whether any or all of the above are 'only' epistemic tools to aid our cognition of the law. Hart's style—the professional philosopher being very English and hiding the philosophical background assumptions under a veil of easy rhetoric—makes his arguments difficult to understand for the continental scholar who is used to a much more foundational fare of deep and deeply theoretical argument. But neither a sustained analysis of the continental unease with Anglo-Saxon positivism nor a discussion of the basics of Hart's thoughts on international law will be advanced here—there is neither the space nor is such a *modus operandi* particularly helpful on this level of inquiry.

---

[43] See eg C Heidemann, *Die Norm als Tatsache: Zur Normentheorie Hans Kelsens* (Nomos Baden-Baden 1997); SL Paulson, 'Four Phases in Hans Kelsen's Legal Theory? Reflections on a Periodization' (1998) 18 *Oxford Journal of Legal Studies* 153–66; SL Paulson, 'Arriving at a Defensible Periodization of Hans Kelsen's Legal Theory' (1999) 19 *Oxford Journal of Legal Studies* 351–65; GJ Postema, *Legal Philosophy in the Twentieth Century: The Common Law World* (Springer Dordrecht 2011) at 263.

[44] J Kammerhofer, 'Positivistische Normbegründung' in E Hilgendorf and JC Joerden (eds), *Handbuch Rechtsphilosophie* (Metzler Stuttgart forthcoming 2016) <http://ssrn.com/abstract=2296874> [accessed 24 February 2016].

[45] On Scandinavian legal realism, see further O Jütersonke, 'Realist Approaches to International Law' in this *Handbook*.

[46] See eg H Eckmann, *Rechtspositivismus und sprachanalytische Philosophie: Der Begriff des Rechts in der Rechtstheorie HLA Harts* (Duncker & Humblot Berlin 1969) at 70–1; M Pawlik, *Die Reine Rechtslehre und die Rechtstheorie HLA Harts: Ein kritischer Vergleich* (Duncker & Humblot Berlin 1993) at 15, 64–5, 162–3.

Instead, the 'distorting mirror' argument will be developed for modern international legal positivism of the Hartian mould, with Jean d'Aspremont's *Formalism and the Sources of International Law*—the most important current application of Hartian positivism in this field—as the central example.[47] D'Aspremont's work shows most clearly how neo-Hartian (international) legal positivism connects with Alf Ross' legal realism through the more sociologically inclined interpretations and developments in jurisprudential literature,[48] because it uses a strong social thesis on the basis of 'communitarian semantics'.[49] But there are good reasons why Hart was adamant about distancing his theory from realism, including Ross',[50] more so than from natural law.[51] Hart clearly saw a danger in conflating the two approaches; Ross, in contrast, felt a kinship to Hart more than to Kelsen.[52] It will be argued later in the chapter that Hart might have resisted the 'sociologized' form of his approach in modern international legal positivism, because it is susceptible to a critique of self-destructive reductionism.

4.1 Jean d'Aspremont's Neo-Hartian International Legal Positivism

D'Aspremont sets himself a specific task, namely to describe how international legal rules can be ascertained (identified, cognized) in a formal manner. D'Aspremont's project is to produce an epistemology of international law, rather than a general theory of law or a theory of interpretation.[53] The Hartian 'rule of recognition' provides, as its creator has it, 'conclusive affirmative indication' that a rule belongs in a legal system;[54] it is thus not the formal source of validity, but a tool for cognition.

---

[47] Since the publication of that monograph, d'Aspremont has developed his theory and, among other things, has distanced himself from Tamanaha and drawn closer to Michael Giudice and Stanley Fish: see eg J d'Aspremont, 'Wording in International Law' (2012) 25 *Leiden Journal of International Law* 575–602.

[48] See eg BZ Tamanaha, *A General Jurisprudence of Law and Society* (OUP Oxford 2001); W Twining, *General Jurisprudence: Understanding Law from a Global Perspective* (CUP Cambridge 2009).

[49] *Formalism and the Sources of International Law* (n 7) 195–217.

[50] See eg HLA Hart, 'Scandinavian Realism' [1959] *Cambridge Law Journal* 233–40; HLA Hart, *The Concept of Law* (Clarendon Press Oxford 1961) at 85–8, 243 (on the internal–external aspects of rules).

[51] On the latter relationship, see eg P Capps, 'International Legal Positivism and Modern Natural Law' in J Kammerhofer and J d'Aspremont (eds), *International Legal Positivism in a Post-Modern World* (CUP Cambridge 2014) 213–40.

[52] See eg 'Validity and the Conflict between Legal Positivism and Natural Law' (n 8) 161–3; A Ross, 'Book Review: HLA Hart, *The Concept of Law* (Clarendon Press Oxford 1961)' (1962) 71 *Yale Law Journal* 1185–90.

[53] *Formalism and the Sources of International Law* (n 7) 12, 14–15.

[54] *The Concept of Law* (n 50) 92.

In this respect, there is a certain phenomenal convergence with the Kelsenian *Grundnorm*, but this parallel should not be taken too far.[55] For d'Aspremont, 'Hart believes that the meaning of law, and especially the meaning of the rule of recognition, must be inferred from the social conventions among the law-applying authorities'.[56] This is the social thesis: the 'formal law-ascertainment derived from social practice...inferring the meaning of the standard pedigree of rules derived from the practice of law-applying authorities'.[57] The social practice approach to meaning is at the heart of d'Aspremont's formal (international) law-ascertainment. Hart's own rather dismissive treatment of international law[58] is to be reformed: d'Aspremont seeks to 'demonstrate the relevance of the social thesis for the ascertainment of international legal rules.'[59]

D'Aspremont adopts the interpretations and revisions of Hart's social thesis in parts of the expansive Hartian literature and adapts it to international law. He does so along two avenues of argument: first, the introduction of 'communitarian semantics' and second, an expansion of the concept of 'law-applying authority'. Thus the social (or, rather, socio-linguistic) factor is strengthened vis-à-vis Hart. As to the first component, the identification ('ascertainment') of law happens through formal criteria. The meaning of these criteria can be discovered because they—the non-linguistic jurisprude would say: the words and sentences that we use to describe them—are used in a reasonably similar way by those whose voice matters. In d'Aspremont's words: 'the meaning of law-ascertainment criteria originates in the convergences of the practice of law-applying authorities.'[60] This convergence is not to be mistaken for 'total and absolute agreement', but is rather described as a 'shared feeling of applying the same criteria',[61] just as in ordinary (non-formal) languages. This set of shared understandings—a practice combined with 'a sense by...actors that they are using the same criteria'[62]—is the so-called communitarian semantics.

The second component concerns the *agents* of communitarian semantics. It is well known that Hart narrowed the social facts which constitute the rule of recognition to 'legal officials'.[63] D'Aspremont, however, is unhappy about the possibilities of transposing this concept to international law without modifications.[64] Following Brian Tamanaha, he expands the group of 'law-applying authorities', as

---

[55] Just as the rule of recognition helps us to identify law belonging to a legal system, the *Grundnorm* is the transcendental possibility for the cognition of 'something' as a norm of a particular normative order. *Legal Philosophy in the Twentieth Century* (n 43) 317. For a warning against us going too far even in this shallow analogy, see *Die Reine Rechtslehre und die Rechtstheorie HLA Harts* (n 46) 159–62.

[56] *Formalism and the Sources of International Law* (n 7) 55.   [57] Ibid 15.

[58] *The Concept of Law* (n 50) 208–31.

[59] *Formalism and the Sources of International Law* (n 7) 195.   [60] Ibid 197.

[61] Ibid 201–2.   [62] Ibid 213.   [63] See eg *The Concept of Law* (n 50) 98, 113–14.

[64] *Formalism and the Sources of International Law* (n 7) 203.

he calls them: '[a] "legal" official is whomever, as a matter of social practice, members of the group (including legal officials themselves) identify and treat as "legal" officials.'[65] Because '[i]n the reality of international law', d'Aspremont argues, 'it can hardly be contested that other "social actors" participate in the practice of law-ascertainment', these 'should be taken into account in the determination of the communitarian semantics constitutive of the meaning of law-ascertainment criteria.'[66] In line with the general thrust of Hartian theory, he is adamant that the communitarian semantics are law-*identificatory*, not law-creative. Accordingly, the undisputed law-creators are not necessarily the basis for these practices, nor are those who are not mentioned in article 38 of the *Statute of the International Court of Justice* excluded from delivering the relevant practice, nor does the practice create law.[67] Legal scholars form a special cohort. While they are not practice-generators, they are 'grammarians of formal law-ascertainment',[68] because they analyse that practice, and because their work impacts on the practice of social actors *sensu stricto*.[69]

4.2 Sociological Hartianism Comes Close to Ross' Legal Realism

D'Aspremont's use of a 'socio-legal positivist approach',[70] on the basis of Hartian positivism and forming its extreme sociological wing, is instructive. D'Aspremont, via Tamanaha—though acknowledged by neither author—is arguably closer to Alf Ross' legal realism than is generally assumed. Hart's words—that the *Concept of Law* could be seen 'as an essay in descriptive sociology'[71]—may be unfortunate in their generality,[72] but may nonetheless serve as a programmatic statement for parts of the Hartian tradition. It is observed from time to time that Hart and Ross are surprisingly close.[73] Hart is neither *this* kind of realist nor is his theory a development of Ross' arguments, but to some extent he used Ross as both a positive and negative model in *The Concept of Law*. Thus, if one takes Hartian positivism further along the road of 'non-metaphysicality' and further emphasizes the empirical

---

[65] *A General Jurisprudence of Law and Society* (n 48) 142 (emphasis omitted).
[66] *Formalism and the Sources of International Law* (n 7) 204.   [67] Ibid 204–5.
[68] Ibid 209.   [69] Ibid 209–11.
[70] *A General Jurisprudence of Law and Society* (n 48) 132 (capitalization removed); *Formalism and the Sources of International Law* (n 7) 59–60.
[71] *The Concept of Law* (n 50) vii.
[72] L Green, 'Introduction' in HLA Hart, *The Concept of Law* (J Raz and PA Bullock eds) (3rd edn OUP Oxford 2012 [1961]) xv–lv, at xlv.
[73] See eg S Ratnapala, *Jurisprudence* (CUP Cambridge 2009) at 116; E Pattaro, 'From Hägerström to Ross and Hart' (2009) 22 *Ratio Juris* 532–48; S Eng, 'Lost in the System or Lost in Translation? The Exchanges between Hart and Ross' (2011) 24 *Ratio Juris* 194–246.

elements of the social, psychological, and linguistic factors, as Tamanaha and d'Aspremont do, inevitably the spectre of Rossian realism arises and so do new avenues of critique.

First, sociological Hartianism and Ross are close primarily in their (implicit) theory of scholarship. For one, there is a decidedly anti-metaphysical foundation to their respective enterprises.[74] In other words, scholarly cognition must in some sense be based on 'facts' and be 'empirical': non-factual 'reality' and non-empirical cognition are frowned upon or denied. For the Scandinavian realists this is most clearly argued for in Axel Hägerström's legal works,[75] but Ross does not differ on this point[76] because his theories are founded on the logical positivism of the Vienna Circle.[77] The anti-metaphysical elements in Tamanaha are much less pronounced and it is doubtful whether he has formed a view on the nature of scholarship. Nonetheless his anti-metaphysical sensibility comes through indirectly in several places, as when he criticizes, in his leading monograph *A General Jurisprudence of Law and Society*, 'essentialism' in Hart and privileges conventionalism and the socio-legal method.[78] Tamanaha's anti-intellectualist style of writing hides this, but the 'essences' criticized are easily translated into Hägerström's or Ross' 'metaphysics'.

Second, both traditions aim, in the last instance, at *one* method of cognition for the juridical world, a juridical theory-of-everything. It is no wonder that Hart combined societal, psychological, and linguistic factors, as all these play a role in the construction of law on an empirical, factual account. As Hart himself acknowledges in his postscript to *The Concept of Law*: '[the book] seeks to give an…account of law as a complex social and political institution'[79]—privileging the factual. It is no wonder, then, that Leslie Green's introduction to the third edition of *Concept* opens with the bold statement '[l]aw is a social construction. It is an historically contingent feature of certain societies'[80] and denies the Pure Theory's ideal of autonomous legal scholarship: 'a jurisprudence built only using concepts drawn from the law itself is inadequate to understand *law's nature*…[jurisprudence] is but one

---

[74] Even Hart himself sometimes warned of 'metaphysical obscurities': HLA Hart, 'Problems of the Philosophy of Law' in *Essays in Jurisprudence and Philosophy* (Clarendon Press Oxford 1983) 88–119, at 93.

[75] For an overview of these positions, see J Bjarup, *Skandinavischer Realismus: Hägerström–Lundstedt–Olivecrona–Ross* (Alber Freiburg 1978) at 23–74.

[76] A Ross, *On Law and Justice* (University of California Press Berkley 1959) at ix–xi, 18.

[77] Ibid 40; *Skandinavischer Realismus* (n 75) 76–8; H Zahle, 'Legal Doctrine between Empirical and Rhetorical Truth: A Critical Analysis of Alf Ross' Conception of Legal Doctrine' (2003) 14 *European Journal of International Law* 801–15, at 805.

[78] *A General Jurisprudence of Law and Society* (n 48) at 149–52, 155–70.

[79] HLA Hart, *The Concept of Law* (PA Bullock and J Raz eds) (2nd edn OUP Oxford 1994 [1961]) at 239.

[80] 'Introduction' (n 72) xv.

part of a more general political theory.'[81] Hart, however, acknowledged the normative character of law, that is, its character as counter-factual norm; the sentence
quoted above continues '...law as a complex social and political institution with a
rule-governed (and in that sense "*normative*") aspect.'[82] Whether the normativity
of law is a significant factor in Hart's legal theory is disputed in literature, but it
is submitted here that he knew that to deny the difference between social practice
and the law would make him a legal realist (and thus subject to the criticism levelled, not least by himself, against that approach). Tamanaha, by contrast, seems
unaware of the closeness to Ross (and the attendant *problematique*) and is happy
to proclaim:

The ultimate test [for a legal theory] . . . is whether it enhances our ability to describe, understand, and evaluate legal phenomena *across a variety of contexts*. . . . *this merged approach*
will provide a theoretically sophisticated and empirically informed way to understand law
and its relationship with society.[83]

Similarly, Ross may distinguish between 'the law in action and the norms of law'
and discuss the latter in terms of 'the abstract idea content of directives', but seeks
to reinterpret (in light of the anti-metaphysical foundation of his realism) the 'idea
content' as 'ideology'. Thus the two branches 'are not two independent spheres
of existence, but different sides of one and the same reality'.[84] Equally, the 'doctrinal study of law [scholarly propositions about the valid law in force] can never
be detached from the sociology of law.... [it] must be recognised as an empirical
social science'.[85] In a different publication Ross adds: '[t]o state that a rule or a
system of rules exists is the same as to state the occasion of a complex of social
facts—understanding "social facts" broadly, to include psychological conditions
too.'[86] Thus, legal scholarship is for both approaches in some sense primarily a
sociological enterprise.

Third, the sociological wing of Hartianism, on the one hand, and Rossian
Scandinavian Legal Realism, on the other hand, both envisage legal scholarship
as using three sources: societal developments directly, language (as used in society), and mental states (in society or parts of it). Correspondingly, they intermix
three scholarly methods: empirical or quasi-empirical sociology, linguistics or
the philosophy of language, and collective psychology. As demonstrated in the
previous passage, Ross combines the sociological and psychological aspects, but
to a large degree his form of realism hinges on a philosophy of language as well.
This is evident in section 3 of *On Law and Justice*, where the notion of 'rules

---

[81] 'Introduction' (n 72) (emphasis added).   [82] *The Concept of Law* (n 79) 239 (emphasis added).
[83] See *A General Jurisprudence of Law and Society* (n 48) 134–5 (emphasis added); BZ Tamanaha,
Realistic Socio-Legal Theory: Pragmatism and a Social Theory of Law (Clarendon Press Oxford 1997)
at 152.
[84] *On Law and Justice* (n 76) 19.   [85] Ibid 19, 40.
[86] 'Validity and the Conflict between Legal Positivism and Natural Law' (n 8) 159.

of chess' is analysed in a fashion reminiscent of Hart. All three elements are combined:

The primary rules of chess . . . are directives. Although they are formulated as assertions about the 'ability' or 'power' of the pieces [and so on,] it is clear that they are intended to indicate how the game is to be played. . . . Thus we cannot but adopt an introspective method. . . . 'valid law' means the abstract set of normative ideas which serve as a scheme of interpretation for the phenomena of law in action, which again means that these norms are effectively followed, and followed because they are experienced and felt to be socially binding.[87]

The same three elements are already present in Hart and—with a different emphasis—in the socio-legal approaches.[88] In d'Aspremont's conception of international law, for example, the three elements are conveniently summarized as follows:

[T]he social foundation of formalism in the ascertainment of international legal . . . essentially requires a shared feeling of applying the same criteria. In that sense, formalism in law-ascertainment is no different from ordinary language. . . . Short of any minimal correspondence in meaning, law-applying authorities will never come to share the feeling that they speak the same language and, hence, their practice will not generate any communitarian semantics.[89]

Here we have the search for a way of 'speaking law' (communitarian semantics) that is conditioned by socio-psychological factors. This is slightly different from Ross, but not enough to not be able to call these variants forms of legal realism.[90] In effect the argument shared by Ross and Hartianism is this: since ordinary language is based on social practice, since it is our state of mind that determines language and since language determines the way we think, these three factors are in reality one. What a Kelsenian would call a combination or admixture of methods is, they argue, really one inseparable method, and the only possible method left to a scholarship of law that is not swallowed up by the mire of 'metaphysics'.

4.3 Sociological Hartianism is Less Responsive to Anti-Realist Critique

As mentioned earlier, Hart was acutely aware of the need to incorporate the normative sphere of law into his theory. The normative sphere is different from a

---

[87] *On Law and Justice* (n 76) 14, 15, 18.
[88] See *Realistic Socio-Legal Theory* (n 83); *A General Jurisprudence of Law and Society* (n 47).
[89] *Formalism and the Sources of International Law* (n 7) 201–2.
[90] *A General Jurisprudence of Law and Society* (n 48) 131, calling Hart's theory 'a realistic (though not Legal Realist) approach to law.'

purely factual level; it creates two different standpoints: the predictive and the normative point of view. In his discussion, he is close to Kelsen: 'the normative point of view...stresses certain common *formal* features that both moral and legal duty possess in virtue of their both being aspects of rule-guided conduct.'[91] An important tradition of Hart exegesis stresses this aspect as indispensable. As Gerald Postema writes:

> To say that someone is subject to an obligation is fundamentally different from saying that the person is likely to suffer some consequence ... The concept of obligation is a normative concept; the concept of prediction is an empirical one. They are not only different concepts; they are fundamentally different kinds of concepts, operating in different conceptual domains. .... Any account of the nature of law that fails to take seriously and account for this normative dimension of law is fatally flawed.[92]

However, this point seems to have been forgotten by the time Tamanaha publishes his *A General Jurisprudence of Law and Society*. He seems to focus exclusively on the divide between the internal and external perspectives,[93] which is close but crucially different to the normative/descriptive divide presented earlier.[94] The internal and external perspectives are concerned more with the participant–observer problem in sociology, rather than with the distinction between sociological and other methods of looking at 'the law'. Indeed, Hart's incorporation of the normative/descriptive divide is directed more against legal realists, including Ross,[95] than against Austin. Tamanaha, in keeping with the socio-legal programme of one overarching method of scholarship, claims that 'a legal positivism based on actual social practices should itself be grounded in the social theory of law I set out'.[96] In keeping with this view, the normative is interrogated—*qua* internal perspective—on its merits in taking seriously the internal beliefs and belief-system of participants in 'legal practice'. This in itself negates even the partial autonomy of a normative aspect of rules. His focus on shared belief systems and introspection,[97] rather than pure behaviourism, sounds exactly like Ross: '[w]hat is valid law cannot be ascertained by purely behaviouristic means....behaviour...can only be comprehended and predicted...by means of the hypothesis of a certain ideology which animates the judge and motivates his actions.'[98]

D'Aspremont, for his part, seeks to preserve the normative character of international law, not on essentialist, but rather only on instrumentalist grounds.

---

[91] 'Problems of the Philosophy of Law' (n 74) 93 (emphasis added). See also *The Concept of Law* (n 50) 10–11, 79–83.

[92] *Legal Philosophy in the Twentieth Century* (n 43) 282–3.

[93] See eg *A General Jurisprudence of Law and Society* (n 48) 153–95.

[94] He identifies the two distinctions: ibid 179. See also at 135.

[95] *The Concept of Law* (n 50) 243.   [96] *A General Jurisprudence of Law and Society* (n 48) 152.

[97] *On Law and Justice* (n 76) 15.   [98] Ibid 37.

Normativity helps us in certain respects, for instance, by enhancing international law's legitimacy or efficacy:[99] 'normativity [is not elevated to] a constitutive element of international law'.[100] The 'exclusive internal point of view'[101] to which d'Aspremont refers and the communitarian semantics[102] which he develops, is, then, no different from Tamanaha's social practices—sociology which takes the internal worlds of meaning of participants seriously—except that it has a slightly linguistic twist.[103] Thus the ascertainment of international law, as envisaged by d'Aspremont, ends up being a matter of a sociology of the linguistic socio-psychological practices of international lawyers. Ross' conception of international legal scholarship does not really differ much from this: on a *socio-psychological account* of the conditions under which the…feeling of legal obligation arises', '[t]he sources of International Law are…the general factors (motive components) that determine the concrete content of law in international judicial decisions.'[104]

If this trend towards the socio-psychological is taken in an unreconstructed substantive form, as seems to be the case with Tamanaha more than with d'Aspremont, then, as the latter argues, 'the social thesis makes the question of the validity of the international legal order as a whole utterly vain';[105] 'it is the practice [which] determine[s our] object of studies'.[106] It is no wonder that Tamanaha relies on Eugen Ehrlich's writings,[107] but takes no heed of Kelsen's (contemporary) and powerful critique of Ehrlich's brand of legal sociology.[108] As far as it looks at law *as law*, even a 'descriptive sociology' of law must already have taken the autonomous, specifically normativist viewpoint on board before it even begins its task. Kelsen's critique of Ehrlich applies here:

[T]he separation of this *legal* sociology can only be achieved by using a concept which originates in a categorically different view-point than that of an explicative sociology, [that is] in normativist scholarship's concept of law. Legal sociology cannot determine . . . what law is, as it has to presuppose normativist scholarship's concept of law.[109]

---

[99] *Formalism and the Sources of International Law* (n 7) 29.   [100] Ibid 30.

[101] Ibid 201, citing GP Fletcher, 'Law as Discourse' (1992) 13 *Cardozo Law Review* 1631–7, at 1634.

[102] *Formalism and the Sources of International Law* (n 7) 196.

[103] See also J d'Aspremont, 'Towards a New Theory of Sources in International Law' in this *Handbook* at 557 ('Social practice provides some rough meaning to the words upon which the language of law is based.').

[104] A Ross, *A Text-Book of International Law: General Part* (Longmans, Green and Co London 1947) at 47, 83.

[105] *Formalism and the Sources of International Law* (n 7) 215.

[106] 'Towards a New Theory of Sources in International Law' (n 103) 560–1.

[107] Foremost here is E Ehrlich, *Grundlegung der Soziologie des Rechts* (Duncker & Humblot Munich 1913) in later editions and English translations.

[108] The following paragraphs are adapted from an earlier contribution: J Kammerhofer, 'Hans Kelsen in Today's International Legal Scholarship' in *International Legal Positivism in a Post-Modern World* (n 2) 81–113, at 103–5.

[109] '[D]ie Abgrenzung dieser *Rechts*soziologie muß durch einen Begriff vollzogen werden, dessen Bestimmung von einem ganz anderen Standpunkte aus erfolgt, als der einer explikativen Soziologie

Socio-legal views of law attempting to avoid both the reduction of law to a prediction of future behaviour and the radical denial of 'ought'—taking the internal
perspective, the self-reconstruction of the 'metaphysical concept' of law by legal
officials, at its word—have to provide for a 'transformation' of facts into law. The
solutions fail to provide an account that separates 'is' and 'ought' and, thus, provide
more than an empiricist prediction. In the alternative, such accounts must take the
normative side ('ought') as a given and thus include (in an implicit fashion) the
normativist positivism that Kelsen sought to dissect from the sum total of views
or approaches to 'the law'. It is submitted that Hart was semi-aware of this need
and thus included the normative view on law, but others (Tamanaha in particular)
fail to respond to this problem and thus are stuck within Ehrlich's terms, to which
Kelsen had already responded in 1914.[110]

However, perhaps d'Aspremont, in particular, has a valid point when he disa-
vows 'validity' as 'ought' in his study of the *ascertainment* of international legal
rules.[111] It can be argued that reductionism of the basis, the origin or the nature of
legal rules—as claimed against the socio-legal Hartians noted earlier—is not necessarily implied in the reduction of the *cognition* of law in social factors. In other
words, it is a defensible epistemological presumption that 'the law' as a thought-
object cannot be directly observed and measured by humans; we are reasonably
reduced to deducing its 'existence' via empirical phenomena. We can presume, for
example, that a statute has been created by looking at sheets of paper constituting
the law gazette; or that a judgment has been passed by observing a person dressed
in black banging a little wooden hammer on a table.[112]

Yet this still comes at a cost if we focus on the socio-psycho-linguistic practice of
officials alone without taking into account what the law *says* about which facts are
relevant. If we did not know that we should look for the actions of a certain person
dressed in black (because the law tells us that this is the way judges dress and this is
the table at which judges sit, and so on), we would be lost. Even if we take linguistic
factors into account, what we are studying is not the law, but something only marginally (and, more importantly, only contingently) connected to the law, that is,
the way we talk about the law. This is at best peripheral or penumbral knowledge
and is much less certain than if the thing itself is the object of knowledge. It is a bit

---

ist, nämlich durch den normativen Rechtsbegriff. Was Recht ist,…das kann die Rechtssoziologie
nicht bestimmen; sie muß den normativen Rechtsbegriff voraussetzen.' H Kelsen, 'Eine Grundlegung
der Rechtssoziologie' (1914–1915) 39 *Archiv für Sozialwissenschaft und Sozialpolitik* 839–876 at 875
(3 *HKW* 357) (emphasis removed).

[110] 'Eine Grundlegung der Rechtssoziologie' (n 109) 841 (3 *HKW* 321).

[111] See eg *Formalism and the Sources of International Law* (n 7) 215 (emphasis added): 'It is
argued here, however, that, *as far as the ascertainment of international legal rules is concerned,*
the social thesis makes the question of the validity of the international legal order as a whole
utterly vain.'

[112] In similar terms: *Reine Rechtslehre* (n 21) 1–4.

like arguing that looking at the way we talk about our body is medical science or looking at the way we talk about the weather is meteorology.

5 CONCLUSION

Had there been space in this chapter another 'distorting mirror' might have been held up to Kelsenian traditions and conceptions of legal scholarship and this would have taken another form. In this case, the narrative would have been an attempt to challenge Kelsenian presumptions about the theory of 'legal science'. Most of the critique of Kelsen in the Anglosphere is based on an implicit post-linguistic-turn theory of scholarship. Those brought up in that Anglosphere frequently profess confusion and perplexity upon reading Kelsen's writings.[113] Those hailing from a Germanophone country may find his arguments debatable or objectionable, but seldom do they find it difficult to understand his writings. The contention would have been that this perplexity is due to cultural factors, foremost the implicit assumption of a post-linguistic-turn world-view by Anglophones as a basis for their interpretation of a non-linguistic theorist.

Foremost (and in contrast to the post-Hart and post-realist consensus in the Anglo-Scandinavian tradition) is the Kelsenian commitment to a multiplicity of scholarly methods on an equal footing. As Otto Pfersmann writes, 'Kelsen argues for a concept of pluri-disciplinarity, that is, the strict distinction between disciplines while using multiple disciplines contemporaneously (each according to its own object of cognition and within its own canon of method).'[114] On Kelsen's understanding, as he received it from a Kantian (or, more likely, neo-Kantian) inspiration, cognition has constitutive properties.[115] Differences in the scholarly method used—in a very specific epistemological sense—produce different objects: 'law'

---

[113] First among these Hart himself: HLA Hart, 'Kelsen Visited' (1963) 10 *UCLA Law Review* 709–28.

[114] 'Kelsen [vertritt] ein Konzept der Pluridisziplinarität, das heißt der strikten Unterscheidung und gleichzeitigen Übung mehrerer Disziplinen nach deren jeweils eigener Objektbestimmung und Methodenkanon.': O Pfersman, 'Hans Kelsens Rolle in der gegenwärtigen Rechtswissenschaft' in R Walter, W Ogris, and T Olechowski (eds), *Hans Kelsen: Leben–Werk–Wirksamkeit. Ergebnisse einer Internationalen Tagung, veranstaltet von der Kommission für Rechtsgeschichte Österreichs und dem Hans Kelsen-Institut (19.–21. April 2009)* (Manz Vienna 2009) 367–87, at 378.

[115] *Reine Rechtslehre* (n 21) 74–5. There is some support in Kant's writings for such a view, see eg I Kant, *Kritik der reinen Vernunft* (Hartknoch Riga 1781/87) B 197; O Höffe, *Immanuel Kant* (8th edn CH Beck Munich 2014) at 98 (emphasis added): 'Die Kategorien haben eine (transzendental-)ontologische Bedeutung: *die modi cognitandi entpuppen sich als modi essendi.*' ('Categories have (transcendental-)ontological import: *the modes of cognising turn out to be modes of being.*')

seen from the perspective of a structural analysis of a normative order is not 'law' as societal practice. This piece of pseudo-/pop-/neo-Kantianism is one of the key factors for the culture of misreading Kelsen in the Anglosphere and, on a wider and much 'thinner' conception, for the sense of autonomy of a specifically legal scholarship amongst Germanophone lawyers. The linguistic and realist turns combined with the empiricist and utilitarian/consequentialist tradition in the Anglo-Saxon family of (legal) cultures has meant that the equality, autonomy, and separation/separability of scholarly methods and enterprises (which is so obvious to Kelsen and his heirs) is utterly alien to the Anglo-Saxon tradition. In other words, the foundational concept of one tradition is outside the realm of reasonable arguments for another tradition. However, both sides are caught in the illusion that they are talking about the same thing when they speak of 'legal scholarship'. With a slightly different emphasis, one might also say that not one but two language games are being played here without many people taking notice of it. A communications breakdown ensues.

There are, thus, essential, categorical, and unbridgeable differences between these traditions. (International) legal theory errs in considering Hart and Kelsen close relations. They are close only on the 'surface' of specific legal-philosophical issues (such as the separation of law and morals). Genealogically, they are oceans apart, as their theoretico-philosophical foundations are incomparable and incompatible. To judge Kelsen on Anglo-Saxon jurisprudential terms is as useless as to judge Hart on Germanic terms. Their underlying conceptions of the world are just too different. This is not sufficiently taken into account by most scholars. Legal positivism now has at least two meanings, which proceed from such incommensurable origins as to make a theoretical denotation with the same term impossible. Singular legal positivism is indeed dead. What we have are multiple positivisms that produce different readings of the legal world. The more international legal scholarship advances into the realm of legal theory proper and the less it subsists on shallow jurisprudence, the more it will realize that its natural instinct as diplomacy's daughter towards the all-embracing middle way is not possible. Legal theorizing means making stark choices and provoking incommensurability: clarity comes at the price of fragmentation.

CHAPTER 21

....

YALE'S POLICY SCIENCE AND INTERNATIONAL LAW

BETWEEN LEGAL FORMALISM AND POLICY CONCEPTUALISM

....

HENGAMEH SABERI

1 INTRODUCTION

....

IN 1943, an enduring collaboration between a political scientist and a legal scholar began to develop as policy-oriented jurisprudence.[1] Harold Lasswell and Myres

[1] MS McDougal and HD Lasswell, 'Legal Education and Public Policy: Professional Training in the Public Interest' (1943) 52 *Yale Law Journal* 203–95 (introducing for the first time policy-oriented thinking and education in law). It was Richard Falk who later described the methodology inspired by McDougal and Lasswell as the 'New Haven Approach' and suggested that '[t]he coordination of inquiry around a common methodology, if significant, leads to the development of "a school," an approach to the study or treatment of a subject-matter that is a significant event in the history of the "subject" with the aim to both "acknowledge" and "hasten" such a recognition for the McDougal-Lasswell approach': RA Falk, 'On Treaty Interpretation and the New Haven Approach: Achievements and Prospects' (1968) 8 *Virginia Journal of International Law* 323–55, at 330 n 11. Others have referred to the same phenomenon as 'the Yale Approach' and 'the Yale School of International law'.

McDougal considered the past and contemporaneous record of international law jurisprudence to be inadequate to meet the needs of the post-Second World War world. In their view, international law was historically riddled with the inertia of philosophical properties such as speculative, transcendental, metaphysical, and theological absolutes, 'the ancient philosophical exercise of logical derivation', and a 'quest for the ultimate and absolute meaning of law and justice'.[2] To remedy that, they centred the application of their comprehensive jurisprudence on international law and introduced the New Haven School's (NHS) policy-oriented approach.

Policy-oriented international law aimed to replace the legalism of traditional thinking with the pragmatism of interdisciplinary and social scientific insights. That pragmatism was well captured in two central ideas: contextualism and problem-solving orientation. In a synoptic description, New Haven's jurisprudence views law as a process of authoritative and controlling decisions that are located in various phases of contextual analysis. In any process of legal decision-making, there are parties with claims about values who pose demands on authoritative decision-makers to weigh their claims and counterclaims and to make prescriptions.[3] Legal decision-making requires a three-tier analysis of 'values', 'phase', and 'conditions'. These conceptual categories provide reasonably full access to the values contested; knowledge about participants with a claim over values; and the past, present, and future of value distribution in the world power process.[4] Conditions refer to the particular location of a context within the larger context of world power process,[5] whereas phase analysis considers specific factors that help dissect each individual context.[6]

See G Gottlieb, 'The Conceptual World of the Yale School of International Law' (1968) 21 *World Politics* 108–32. For ease of reference, I will use NHS, an acronym which was first used in 1985 by Michael Reisman, himself a close student of the NHS: WM Reisman, 'Remarks: McDougal's Jurisprudence: Utility, Influence, Controversy' (1985) 79 *American Society of International Law Proceedings* 266–88, at 277.

[2] HD Lasswell and MS McDougal, *Jurisprudence for a Free Society: Studies in Law, Science and Policy* (New Haven Press New Haven 1992) vol 1, at 71, 178.

[3] MS McDougal, 'The Impact of International Law upon National Law: A Policy-Oriented Perspective' in MS McDougal et al., (eds), *Studies in World Public Order* (Yale University Press New Haven 1960) 157–236, at 168.

[4] For one such application to the question of coercion, for instance, see MS McDougal and FP Feliciano, *The International Law of War: Transnational Coercion and World Public Order* (New Haven Press New Haven 1994) at 16–20.

[5] See MS McDougal, HD Lasswell, and JC Miller, *The Interpretation of Agreements and World Public Order: Principles of Content and Procedure* (Yale University Press New Haven 1967) at 34 (identifying some of the factors that affect the authoritative process of interpretation and application of international agreements as follows: changes in the relative strength of contending visions of world public order which commend persuasion or coercion as instruments of social change; changes in the composition of territorial communities affecting the modalities of communication and common perception of meaning; changes in the technology of communication; and changes in strategies of cooperation in shaping and sharing values that may affect expectations about future modalities of such cooperation).

[6] These are participants, perspectives, situations, base value, strategies, outcome, and effect. See MS McDougal, HD Lasswell, and MW Reisman, 'Theories about International Law: Prologue to a Configurative Jurisprudence' (1968) 8 *Virginia Journal of International Law* 188–299, at 198.

Contra traditional rule-oriented adjudication or interpretation, a policy-oriented decision-maker or legal scholar treats each case as an individual context. Yet the guiding star of decision-making, and what makes policy-oriented international law relevant for the future of a democratic world order, is the promotion of the universal values of human dignity. These values, presented as indices of human dignity,[7] remain raw postulates rather than ripe fruits of reasoning. To avoid the metaphysical pitfalls of normative justification that, under the NHS's account, have historically plagued jurisprudence and fuelled endless disputes, the policy-oriented scholars of human dignity neither seek nor offer any normative justification for their preferred value commitments.[8] Considering the Cold War understanding of the values of human dignity that belonged to the free world vis-à-vis totalitarianism, it is not particularly surprising that the application and interpretation of these values happened to correspond with the practice and desires of the leader of the free world, the United States (US).

Despite its masterly design and broad scope, the NHS's policy science received its fair share of criticism at the time and persuaded only a handful of disciples. On the one hand, some scholars were sceptical about the plausibility of scientific objectivity and the impartial application of the NHS's methodology to international legal questions.[9] On this view, New Haven's pseudo-scientism was nothing more than a complex language with a simple objective: the maintenance and legitimation of the US national interest. On the other hand, some scholars reacted to McDougal's broad understanding of the social processes that defined law. These critiques were plainly aimed against the intrusion of power politics and policy into law either in a positivist spirit[10] or in line with the concerns of international relations scholars who opposed the implications of realism.[11] Yet a third group simply

---

[7] These values, which are in fact categories of desired events or preferences, are power (participation in making important decisions—those involving severe deprivations), respect (access to other values on the basis of merit without discrimination on the grounds irrelevant to capacity), enlightenment (access to the knowledge which is the basis of rational choice), wealth (control over economic goods and services), well-being (enjoyment of physical and psychic health), skill (proficiency in the exercise of latent talent), affection (enjoyment of sympathetic human relationships), and rectitude (sharing a sense of community responsibility). See MS McDougal, 'International Law, Power, and Policy: A Contemporary Conception' (1953) 82 *Recueil des Cours* 133–259, at 168.

[8] MS McDougal, 'Perspectives for an International Law of Human Dignity' in *Studies in World Public Order* (n 3) 987–1019, at 993.

[9] See generally L Gross, 'Editorial Comment: Hans Kelsen: October 11, 1886–April 15, 1973' (1973) 67 *American Journal of International Law* 491–511, at 499; OR Young, 'International Law and Social Science: The Contributions of Myres S McDougal' (1972) 66 *American Journal of International Law* 60–76, at 74 ('McDougal has leaned toward a somewhat uncritical acceptance of the views of the American "establishment" on a number of specific issues in the field of international relations').

[10] See eg JL Kunz, *The Changing Law of Nations: Essays on International Law* (Ohio State University Press Columbus 1968) at 169; A D'Amato, '*Studies in World Public Order* by Myres S McDougal and Associates' (1961) 75 *Harvard Law Review* 458–61, at 460.

[11] S Hoffmann, 'Henkin and Falk: Mild Reformist and Mild Revolutionary' (1970) 24 *Journal of International Affairs* 118–26, at 118–20 (accusing the NHS of doing its best to undermine all the elements of law's distinctiveness).

targeted the convoluted style and complex presentation of New Haven's jurisprudence, which rendered it either incomprehensible or impractical.[12] Each strand of scepticism consists of nuanced and specific objections to various theoretical and practice-oriented features of the McDougal–Lasswell project, but policy as legitimation, policy as invasion of power into law, and the policy framework as conceptual 'grandiloquence'[13] in fact comprise the body of resistance against the methodological renewal of New Haven's jurisprudence.

As interpreted by the received wisdom and perpetuated by McDougal himself, this resistance has been attributed to international lawyers' resolute aversion to policy thinking and their strict loyalty to traditional rule-oriented approaches.[14] Under this tale, the cold reception of the NHS by the mainstream discipline reflects a conflict between law and policy—a rivalry between the comfort of law's determinacy and autonomy and the flexibility and uncertainty of policy, in which the policy-oriented heresy lost ground as it faced a hard-headed discipline mostly concerned with formalist legal reasoning and wary of extra-legal social phenomena tainting the image of the rule of law.

This chapter poses a challenge to the conventional narrative about the career of the NHS by arguing that the mainstream discipline's rejection of the policy-oriented methodology was not a rejection of policy thinking as such, but rather an opposition to the conceptualism and formulaic determinism of New Haven's jurisprudence resulting from a peculiar combination of a contextualist methodology and a non-cognitive view of normative values of human dignity. Rather than between law and policy, the tension was between two different perceptions of flexibility and rigidity. This tension resulted from the NHS's dogmatic and erroneous presentation of what they dubbed 'traditional' and 'rule-oriented' approaches as formalist and the mainstream discipline's more

---

[12] See eg H Briggs, 'The Interpretation of Agreements and World Public Order—Principles of Content and Procedure' (1968) 53 *Cornell Law Review* 543–6, at 543 (calling the Lasswell–McDougal language 'dogmatic scientism'); G Fitzmaurice, '*Vae Victis* or Woe to the Negotiators: Your Treaty or Our "Interpretation" of It?' (1971) 65 *American Journal of International Law* 358–73, at 360 ('[T]his book ... is written in a highly esoteric private language,—we do not say jargon, but a kind of juridical code which renders large tracts of it virtually incomprehensible to the uninitiated (or at least to the unpracticed and unversed), short of a word by word "construe," such as we did in school with our Latin unseens').

[13] The word is borrowed from Erwin Griswold who, recognizing the importance of Lasswell's and McDougal's approach to legal education, nevertheless found it to be 'impaired by a certain tendency towards grandiloquence': EN Griswold, 'Intellect and Spirit' (1968) 81 *Harvard Law Review* 292–307, at 297.

[14] McDougal noted:

We got much more attention than we wanted before we wanted it ... We thought we'd have several years to formulate the stuff and write it up before we got too much attention, but we got too much success too quickly to serve intellectual purposes, and then we got the reaction.

'Curriculum Committee Report' (1960) 1–6, cited in L Kalman, *Legal Realism at Yale 1927–1960* (University of North Carolina Press Chapel Hill 1986) at 185.

accurate understanding of the policy-oriented international law as a new mode of formalism. I introduce this new mode of formalism as 'policy conceptualism' to suggest that the story of the NHS's career was not a simple rivalry between law and policy per se, but one between two understandings of an interpretive stance towards 'experience' and 'logic' of a (pseudo-)scientific method. There was hope in the determinative capacity of the interpretative tools facilitated by law on one side, and faith in the predictability of outcomes guaranteed by the democratic policies of human dignity on the other. The real confrontation was between two conceptions of formalism: the formalism of law that the NHS attributed to the international law discipline and was committed to refuting and the formalism of policy—'policy conceptualism'—that the discipline found in the policy-oriented approach and did not countenance.

To be sure, neither side would have admitted in the least to the slightest traces of 'formalism' in their prescribed way of arriving at legal outcomes. And, to be fair, the putative, old legal formalism against which policy science rose did not most accurately describe the spirit of the mainstream international law discipline of the day either. Yet the two opposing perceptions of formalism, one attributed to the law and one resulting from the policy conceptualism of the NHS, were so strong as to erect an insurmountable wall of conflict between the advocates of policy sciences and their interlocutors.

The next two sections will locate policy conceptualism in the epistemic structure of New Haven's policy science (Section 2) and show how that approach was inherited from Lasswell's behaviouralism (Section 3). Section 4 will then recount some of the debates between the NHS and its contemporaneous critics to demonstrate that the discipline's rejection of policy science was a rejection of policy conceptualism and its resulting dogmatism rather than hostility against policy-based reasoning as such. The historical and jurisprudential significance of this counter-narrative will follow in a brief conclusion.

2 CONCEPTUALISM AND EPISTEMIC STRUCTURE OF NEW HAVEN'S JURISPRUDENCE

The principal alternative of the policy-oriented approach to the legal formalism against which it set itself up is contextualism. Context-sensitivity through a comprehensive examination of elements of 'values', 'phase', and 'conditions' in New Haven's jurisprudence embodies the pragmatist promises of policy-consciousness with a normative direction.[15] Yet due to the epistemic structure of New Haven's contextualism and problem-solving methodology, these two fundamental promises of the Yale approach in fact remained unrealized.[16] The unreflective adoption of eight postulates as indices of universal human dignity in principle[17] and subjecting the entire enterprise of contextual inquiry to the superiority of those postulates fatally blunts the true promises of pragmatism. New Haven's jurisprudence, as taught by McDougal and Lasswell and followed by their disciples, operates on an epistemic incongruence between a general contextualist ambition which commands a rigorous examination of all non-evaluative contextual elements on the one hand, and a peculiar exemption of the normative values of human dignity from all inquiry and doubt on the other. The result is twofold: defining those normative commitments in accordance with some parochial standards and misrepresenting them as universal values; and applying those normative commitments to overrule all other contextually verified factors in a manner that legal outcomes are simply over-determined with the highest degree of predictability in any number of legal questions.

In addition to the inherent problems plaguing the contextualist methodology of the NHS that result from its non-cognitive view of the determinative values of human dignity, its very contextualist framework of analysis of the various aspects of social processes of interaction between agents has been presented in multilayered sets of conceptual categories. The over-determining role of the postulates of human dignity only becomes evident at the time of the application of policy-oriented methodology. So when sceptics point to the partiality of policy-oriented jurisprudence towards US foreign policy interests, they consider the rigid determination of legal outcomes in light of human dignity superseding all other contextual elements. They do not, therefore, go beyond the peculiar issues of application to consider the fundamental consequences of an epistemic discriminatory view of the normative and the non-normative. In other words, they focus exclusively on the consequences of the application of the policy-oriented approach and neglect its epistemic structural makeup, which is in fact the cause of the rigid application of the NHS's contextualist framework to legal questions in practice.

While the crucial difference between regarding the over-determining role of the NHS's normative commitments as a mere problem of application or inherent in its epistemic structure is nuanced, the formulaic presentation of contextual categories and conceptual tools delineating what constitutes 'context' in the social processes of law is too bold to escape the first glance of any casual reader of New Haven's

---

[15] See nn 3 and 4.

[16] See H Saberi, 'Love it or Hate It, but for the Right Reasons: Pragmatism and the New Haven School's International Law of Human Dignity' (2012) 35 *Boston College International and Comparative Law Review* 59–144.

[17] See n 7 and accompanying text.

jurisprudence. These complex categories of contextual elements, besides the NHS's generally convoluted style, in fact explain why most of the mainstream international lawyers' engagement with McDougal was limited to the implementation of policy-oriented jurisprudence in the world public order writings. The conceptual categories of contextual elements, on a theoretical height before touching the ground of implementation and actual legal decision-making contestation, seemed too abstract to be interpreted, critically assessed, adopted, or rejected on their face. One would expect that a jurisprudential heresy as intelligent and ambitious as the NHS should have been met by copious critical consideration and theoretical reflection of jurisprudes on the nature of its theoretical teachings. But with very few exceptions, the lion's share of the debate between McDougal or his associates and their critics circled around the doctrinal bearings of a policy-oriented approach for questions of world public order and were recorded mostly in the genre of book reviews.[18] This fact in itself attests to the complexity and abstractness of New Haven's conceptual framework of contextualism, articulated in formula and categories that did not touch a chord in the minds of the mainstream lawyers who, like mainstream political scientists of their time, did not appreciate the method-driven conceptualism of behaviouralism in which such categories had their roots.

So what is introduced here as policy conceptualism is in fact a combination of two essential features of New Haven's jurisprudence: first, the over-determining role of human dignity leading to rigid and defining implications of those values for legal outcomes (manifested in application); and second, the conceptual categorization of contextual elements—elements that eventually are all to be subordinated to human dignity (constituting the complex structure of the contextualist approach of policy-oriented jurisprudence). It was this policy conceptualism that defined the essence of the mainstream discipline's sceptical reaction against the policy-oriented approach. By re-listening to the echoes of the doctrinal dialogue between McDougal and his critics over some of the questions in fashion for international lawyers of the time, one can appreciate that the flame of scepticism was not fanned by a principled opposition to the employment of policy in legal thinking per se, but by the particular method of the application of policy that in structure, application, and outcome was as rigid as (if not more rigid than) a positivism-inspired legal analysis or abuse of deduction.

To appreciate the roots of policy conceptualism, however, it is helpful to first revisit Lasswell's configurative policy science which in principle defined the NHS's configurative approach. Lasswell's strong commitment to the method-driven, scientific approach of behaviouralism, on the one hand, and what eventually came to be a non-reflective commitment to a set of norms signifying human dignity,

---

[18] For a prominent exception, see WL Morison, 'Myres S McDougal and Twentieth-Century Jurisprudence: A Comparative Essay' in WM Reisman and BH Weston (eds), *Toward World Order and Human Dignity: Essays in Honor of Myres S McDougal* (Free Press New York 1976) 3–78, at 3.

on the other, betrays an oscillation between transcendentalism and pragmatism—between the eternal and the temporal, the absolute and the contingent, and the universal and the particular. His normative commitments already estranged him from behaviourists and triggered their criticism, but it did not substantively distinguish his policy conceptualism from behaviouralism's enthusiasm for categories of conceptions, analytical tools, levels of analysis, and precision of applied methods of scientific analysis.

3 CONCEPTUALISM AND BEHAVIOURALISM

Political scientists view behaviouralism as a landmark movement of the 1950s and 1960s which divided the history of their field. Divided about the scope of its impact, many of its proponents, at least in retrospect, thought it fell short of its potential as a revolutionary disciplinary change,[19] while its hostile critics accused it of a hegemonic scientific takeover.[20] As is the case with any transformative movement, sifting through the specious and the genuine in the stock of all that has been attributed to behaviouralism still fuels academic debates. Standing at the opposite end of the spectrum to the disciplinary reform proposals of some of the German émigrés such as Leo Strauss and Hans Morgenthau (who were equally dissatisfied with the state of the study of politics), behaviouralism proposed a systematic change that has received its fair share of censure for propagating ahistorical research.[21] For all the critiques of ahistoricism, however, revisionists have furnished a defence by questioning what 'historical' research in fact means. If 'being historical' for a discipline means conducting original research on the past, they contend, then American politics was no more historical before behaviouralism than it was afterwards.[22]

---

[19] See eg JC Wahlke, '1978 APSA Presidential Address: Pre-Behavioralism in Political Science' (1979) 73 *American Political Science Review* 9–31, cited in R Adcock, 'Interpreting Behavioralism' in R Adcock, M Bevir, and SC Stimson (eds), *Modern Political Science: Anglo-American Exchanges since 1880* (Princeton University Press Princeton 2007) 180–208, at 180–1.

[20] See eg SS Wolin, 'Political Theory as a Vocation' (1969) 63 *American Political Science Review* 1062–82, cited in 'Interpreting Behavioralism' (n 19) 181. Some revisionists also call for moderation when assessing the reach and depth of behaviouralism's impact: see R Adcock and M Bevir, 'The Remaking of Political Theory' in *Modern Political Science* (n 19) 209–33, at 209–10 (challenging specifically the idea that behaviouralism eliminated or took over political theory).

[21] See eg HJ Morgenthau, *Scientific Man vs Power Politics* (University of Chicago Press Chicago 1946); B Crick, 'The Science of Politics in the United States' (1954) 20 *Canadian Journal of Economics and Political Science* 308–20.

[22] 'Interpreting Behavioralism' (n 19) 192.

Whatever differences about the level of impact and the ahistorical trait of be-haviouralism, there is little dispute about the advancement of techniques and importance of research skills promoted by the movement. Reliance on techniques, however, though often associated with quantitative work, should not discount the special place of theory in behaviouralism. For behaviouralism, in fact, propagated a conception of theory that linked self-conscious abstraction with systematic empirical research in the interest of producing analytical frameworks.[23] In a neo-positivist search for universalism, behaviouralism started with macro-level assumptions about political systems or societies and worked with theories at a high level of conceptual abstraction that could systematically be applied to the empirical results it attained through sophisticated quantitative techniques.

Aspiring to liberate theory from particular historical contexts and find a scientific universal language, some of the masterminds of behaviouralism such as Harold Lasswell[24] and David Easton[25] laid the foundation for what the movement adopted as the standards for evaluating a theoretical framework: universality, deductive structure, and instrumental utility for empirical research.[26] This instrumental utility was different from the instrumentalism championed by early twentieth-century American social and political thinkers sympathetic to pragmatism. Utility in short, for behaviouralists, could mean anything but the advancement of a substantive normative ideal. This is where Lasswell, quite dramatically, broke apart from the movement to whose nourishment he had devoted his widely acknowledged prodigious intellectual energy.

Lasswell, it must be noted, took pains to qualify the limits of the universality of theory. Put more accurately, the genius of Lasswell did not neglect the potential risk of reverting to logical abstraction through a behaviouralist-advocated universalism of theory. Lasswell is thought to have taken to AN Whitehead—despite no explicit evidence—and accepted the philosophical idea of 'emergence' in his reference to 'emergent' and the 'manifold of events'.[27] There is more supporting evidence in Lasswell's 'developmental' thinking and general framework of contextual analysis for the presence of a multilayered conception of 'emergence'.[28] 'Emergent evolution'—with its conceptions of existential and functional emergence—maintains that no single theory or explanation could equally apply to the phenomena coming into existence at different points or standing at different levels of organization. The result is pluralism of propositions and non-deducibility—both unpredictability and

---

[23] 'Interpreting Behavioralism' (n 19) 207–8.

[24] See HD Lasswell and A Kaplan, *Power and Society* (Yale University Press New Haven 1950).

[25] See D Easton, *The Political System: An Inquiry into the State of Political Science* (Knopf New York 1953).

[26] 'The Remaking of Political Theory' (n 20) 215.

[27] H Eulau, 'The Maddening Methods of HD Lasswell: Some Philosophical Underpinnings' in A Rogo (ed), *Politics, Personality, and Social Science in the Twentieth Century: Essays in Honor of Harold D Lasswell* (University of Chicago Press Chicago 1969) 15–40, at 21.

[28] 'The Maddening Methods of HD Lasswell' (n 27) 22.

irreducibility—of phenomena.[29] To reconcile 'emergence', which requires an inductive analysis of details, with a theory of the whole, Lasswell states that '[s]ound political analysis is nothing less than correct orientation in the continuum which embraces the past, present, and future. Unless the salient feature of the all-inclusive whole are discerned, details will be incorrectly located'.[30] Then, in case this does not just yet sufficiently stress theory and perception of the whole, a few pages later Lasswell writes '[t]he gradual creation of a sense of wholeness, and of assurance in the discovery of interdetail connections within the all-encompassing totality, also requires new methods of formal exposition'.[31]

Despite a lifetime search for 'new methods of formal exposition', for Lasswell, the choice of the level of analysis and one between an intensive or extensive configurative approach, at least so far as the modern analysis of human relationships is concerned, is a matter of expediency and not principle. It is the level of analysis that in fact determines the appropriate mode of analysis. What might be accurately generalizable on one level of analysis could well be limited in another. It is the responsibility of the behaviouralist scientist to be alert to her 'observational standpoint' and level of analysis at every step in order to determine the scope of the total context and the limits of generalizability in that context.

Perhaps the most developed articulation of the levels of analysis in Lasswell's work comes later and is introduced as the well-known idea of intellectual tasks that travel between different disciplines:

Any problem-solving approach to human affairs poses five intellectual tasks . . . goal, trend, conditions, projection, and alternative. The first question, relating to goal, raises the traditional problem of clarifying the legitimate aims of a body politic. After goals are provisionally clarified, the historical question arises. In the broadest context, the principal issue is whether the trend of events in America or throughout the world community has been toward or away from the realization of preferred events. The next question goes beyond the simple inventories of change and asks which factors condition one another and determine history. When trend and factor knowledge is at hand, it is possible to project the course of future developments on the preliminary assumption that we do not ourselves influence the future. Finally, what policy alternatives promise to bring all preferred goals to optimal fulfillment?[32]

This bold and sophisticated outline of the intellectual tasks of a policy scientist appears to leave no doubt about a masterfully crafted design of a problem-solving oriented approach to social science. Yet upon further probing, some legitimate questions overshadow the appearance of the prima facie unmistakable contextualism assumed in the structure of this approach. It bears emphasis that some of these questions are questions of application, but others are not. They relate rather to the

---

[29] 'The Maddening Methods of HD Lasswell' (n 27) 23.
[30] HD Lasswell, *World Politics and Personal Insecurity* (McGraw-Hill New York 1935) at 4.
[31] Ibid 16.
[32] H Lasswell, *The Future of Political Science* (Atherton Press New York 1963) at 1–2.

very design of the intellectual tasks with which policy scientists of democracy are entrusted. First, goal clarification in policy science remains an intuitive rather than natural or scientific task. That the clarified norms reflect the native properties of their authors would be innocuous if policy science did not give so much credence to objectivity. As it stands now, however, maintaining an 'observational standpoint' is at worst a mirage, and at best a noble dream. Secondly, trend (historical) and condition (scientific) thinking processes are either nothing more than fact-gathering, or, as is more likely given the method-driven nature of policy science, they proceed on the basis of a formulated method of historical and scientific interpretation. If they are the former, the value of their fact-gathering effort depends on the manner in which those facts will be used. If they are the latter, however, they are circumscribed by the restrictions of the projected goals—if there has been progress towards or decline away from the realization of those goals—and accompanying assumptions that not only impact but in fact shape their results. Thirdly, developmental and alternative thinking are similarly influenced by conceptually determinative factors. Projecting the course of future events is true to its problem-solving promise only when it adopts a comprehensive probabilistic approach. Imbued with the optimism of the realization of initially projected goals, it is a jubilant self-fulfilling prophesy. Likewise, policy alternatives are meaningful when the pigeonholes of original normative assumptions and the results of prior historical and scientific tasks have not already so predictably conscribed the ambit of permissible and impermissible policies.

Lasswell's contextualism and problem-solving oriented theory is a response to the limitations of both empiricism and rationalism. Yet both in structure and in application, it relies on a form of deductive reasoning of its own. This deductive scheme is not incidental to policy science, but rather inherent in its larger intellectual progenitor of behaviouralism and the role and epistemic character of its normative commitments. In the first place, suspicious of the insidiously masked analytical categories and hypotheses of the empiricist investigator, Lasswell's policy scientist forthrightly adopts the transparent, analytical categories that (allegedly) contextualize the framework of analysis. That the different categories of intellectual tasks above, for instance, imbricate, instantiate, and substantiate one another is not disputed by policy science—there is, after all, an order of priority in which they are recommended to take place. But that the investigator is advised to checkmark all these categories in any particular context regardless of the subject matter suggests the importance of pursuing a strict method for analysis. This categorical conceptualism is equally true in other elements of context (values, phase, and conditions) so fundamental to New Haven's jurisprudence. The legal scientist has to operate the comprehensive contextual analysis using the recommended categories regardless of whether and how the subject matter lends itself to such an examination.[33]

---

[33] For an illustration in international law, see 'Love it or Hate it' (n 16) 111–12 n 284. See also CM Chaumont, '*Law and Public Order in Space* by McDougal, Lasswell & Vlasic' (1964) 3 *Columbia*

In the second place, in addition to the categorical conceptualism often presented as a 'verbal juggling act' inspired by behaviouralism,[34] the predominant normative values and goals of policy science, both applied as one of the categories of contextual elements and as the defined subject of the first intellectual tasks, in the last analysis, give the contextual and problem-oriented investigation a deductive effect. In a sensible contextualist frame, normative values find a place among all other considerations subject to a balancing act of decision-making to determine their practical implications. But in a system where human dignity, by definition, overrules all the other contextual factors and has the a priori, last determinative word, it is almost a redundancy to state that decisions are deduced from the categorical values of human dignity.[35]

In a like manner, the guiding star function of the goals clarified through the first intellectual task for historical, scientific, developmental, and alternative thinking merely satisfies the analyst that all the categories of the recommended configurative method have been exhausted to forestall the intrusion of unwarranted assumptions or untested hypotheses. But in fact, the cumulative effect of all the prescribed intellectual tasks is a reinforcement of the avowedly clarified (that is, postulated) values of human dignity. The net result of intellectual labour is simply determined by the original postulates. If empiricists' disguised assumptions foist meaning upon the facts (as behaviouralism claims), the clearly articulated normative assumptions of policy science equally determine the results of their investigation. One would surely prefer disclosed assumptions over disguised hypotheses, but that does not substantially change the fact that unjustified assumptions finally determine the results, or the fact that policy science misrepresents a deduction from those assumptions for contextually verified solutions.

Journal of Transnational Law 271–4 (suggesting at 271 that the policy-oriented 'distinctions constantly made between trends, claims, activities, policies, interactions, appraisals, and recommendations, as much as those between participants, objectives, situations, base values, strategies, outcomes, and effects appear not only somewhat repetitive but also relatively artificial, or at the very least not altogether sound'). For an admiring description of New Haven's categorical concepts of contextual analysis and a clear statement of its method-oriented approach, see S Wiessner and AR Willard, 'Policy-Oriented Jurisprudence' (2001) 44 *German Yearbook of International Law* 96–112.

[34] B Moore, *Political Power and Social Theory: Seven Studies* (Harper & Row New York 1962) at 99.

[35] Though 'deduce' is a word that the New Haven masters avoid and only use to scoff at what they refer to as formalism of the rule-oriented approach, Weston, an associate, uses the same word openly to describe the basic modality of policy-oriented interpretation of agreements: 'The overriding "goals" of interpretation which the authors [of the work under review] recommend and from which they *deduce* particular policies to fit exact issues are designed, consistent with the New Haven Approach generally, "to give effect to the goals of a public order of human dignity."': BH Weston, '*The Interpretation of Agreements and World Public Order* by Myres S McDougal, Harold D Lasswell, and James C Miller' (1969) 117 *University of Pennsylvania Law Review* 647–64, at 650 (emphasis added).

With this background in mind, let us now turn to the reaction of international lawyers to the translation of policy science methodology into international law.

4 IN THE SHADOW OF HYPERBOLE: TWO IMAGES OF FORMALISM

That international law in particular took a strong position against policy conceptualism and a deductive method in a post-realist age, when the myth of conceptualism and the certainty of legal outcomes had already been dispelled, should not be startling. Perhaps behaviouralist-inspired theories had less luck persuading lawyers, compared to social scientists, across various disciplines because, in light of the practical nature of legal reasoning, the implications of deduction from policy, functionally similar to deduction from legal principles and different only in content, could more readily be detected and resisted in the process of legal decision-making.

More likely, however, international lawyers from the US were impatient with policy conceptualism because, coming from a tradition that had always countenanced policy considerations in handling problems of international relations, they had a different expectation about the function of policy from what was on offer from the NHS. As it is generally a matter of first impression about the application of policy in legal reasoning, to these lawyers policy implied flexibility, avoiding binary oppositions and textual application of rules, and legal labour that does not aim to furnish highly predictable results. The policy-oriented approach, countering this expectation, starts with postulates of human dignity, which are diametrically contrasted with human indignity, and both represented by a Cold War-inspired polarization, and which establishes a conceptually complex contextual framework that pivots around those postulated normative commitments. In doing so, through a conceptually ingenious process of contextual analysis, the policy-oriented approach eventually deduces the outcomes that would best promote human dignity as defined by the friends of its representatives. This is certainly different from the flexibility that international lawyers have habitually associated with the application of policy in legal decision-making.

To be clear, the claim here is not that the mainstream discipline as a whole articulated a defence against deduction from policy, or defined what that meant, or connected the consequences of the policy-oriented approach to its epistemic structure. The argument simply is that the disciplinary distrust of the policy-oriented approach was not a distrust of policy per se, but a consequence of justified scepticism about rigid outcomes dissonant with a deeply rooted consciousness about policy in international law. This long-rooted consciousness was not systematic, but rather fluid, organic, and natural. Correspondingly, reactions to the 'world public order' writings did not follow a systematic critique of policy deduction, or a theoretical elucidation to that effect. Nor was a discipline ingrained in an unsystematic and organic policy thinking consciousness eventually persuaded by a systematic, configurative theory of the application of policy that in the last analysis robbed its subject—policy—of its natural and familiar function and turned it into its opposite.

The disciplinary reaction to rigidity and policy conceptualism embedded and inherent in policy-oriented jurisprudence is best illustrated by the disagreements between McDougal and associates and the discipline they aimed to reform over a number of important practical questions of international law. Rather than attempting to cast a general theoretical net over the general misgivings of international lawyers about the rigidity of the policy-oriented approach—a theoretical explanation that was scarcely formulated as such by the discipline itself—it is more helpful to listen to the echoes of some of those disagreements to bring the point home. But before turning to that, one last note on the place and function of policy in the NHS's policy-oriented approach to legal decision-making is in order.

4.1 The Analytical Function of Policy in New Haven's Jurisprudence

Although anyone with some degree of allegiance to the NHS's legacy would cringe at the thought of attempting to define law in McDougal's view, it would be helpful to recall his outstanding critiques of the rule-oriented conception of law to make sense of where policy comes into play. First, in McDougal's legal realist-inspired critical account, mainstream international law has perpetuated the descriptive/prescriptive or *de lege lata/de lege ferenda* dualism and thereby ignored, and consequently masked, the inevitable presence of policy in legal decision-making dressed in the language of law.[36] Secondly, the rule-oriented approach takes technical rules to adequately capture the entire intellectual process of decision-making from description of precedent, to prediction of outcomes, and prescription.[37] Thirdly and relatedly, it comfortably ignores the inherent ambiguity of legal language (and language in general) resulting in gaps

---

[36] 'International Law, Power, and Policy' (n 7) 144.   [37] Ibid.

and complementarity of rules which simultaneously drives each individual case to diametrically opposite directions.[38]

Stated most economically, McDougal's diagnosis of what he calls rule-oriented jurisprudential theories of the past and his alternative policy-oriented approach take 'policy' to fulfil two tasks: to furnish teleological reasoning (substance) and to facilitate the performance of a balancing test (process). Policy provides content to fill in the gaps and interpret ambiguities in a manner consistent with the higher-ranked desiderata in the hierarchy of social needs and ideals. In its divisive function of balancing between various desiderata, policy is also associated with enlightenment and a guarantor of rationality as it distinguishes between the subjective and the objective, the past precedent and the future prediction, and the more immediately achievable policy goals and the aspirations that may have to be replaced with alternative objectives.

Both in structure and application, teleological inference in New Haven's jurisprudence is substantiated by categories (conditions, phase, and values) that constitute a contextual inquiry. In practice, however, the value category overrules other contextual categories in implications and in function as a directive for determining outcomes. So the teleological value of the value category exceeds that of other contextual considerations. All the other contextual variables are subject to further inquiry, to empirical verification (be it historical, trend, or scientific thinking), and to a cost–benefit act of balancing. But policy implications of the value category, irrespective of the other variable contextual conditions, remain unchanging and unchangeable in any number of particular cases. So what the promotion of the NHS's normative commitments would bind the decision-maker to ensure is, in the last analysis, freestanding from the other context-specific circumstances, and merely moves between the two poles of human dignity and human indignity.

Likewise, as a balancing tool, the epistemically unjustified choice of the normative values of human dignity restrains the function of policy analysis. To weigh the varying measure of urgency or contribution of different policies in a context-sensitive investigation, not only should the value and significance of each value category in that particular context be assessed against all other contextual elements, but also the specific implications, fluid meaning, and dynamic consequences of each value

---

[38] 'International Law, Power, and Policy' (n 7) 152, 156. See also MS McDougal and RN Gardner, 'The Veto and the *Charter*: An Interpretation for Survival' in *Studies in World Public Order* (n 3) 718–60, at 723–6. For complementarity of rules, see MS McDougal and F Feliciano, *Law and Minimum World Public Order: The Legal Regulation of International Coercion* (Yale University Press New Haven 1961) 56–7; MS McDougal, 'The Ethics of Applying Systems of Authority: The Balanced Opposites of A Legal System' in HD Lasswell and H Cleveland (eds), *The Ethic of Power: The Interplay of Religion, Philosophy, and Politics* (Harper New York 1962) 221–40, at 221–6; MS McDougal, 'Jurisprudence for a Free Society' (1966) 1 *Georgia Law Review* 1–19, at 2–4; MS McDougal, 'Law as a Process of Decision: A Policy Oriented Approach to Legal Study' (1956) 1 *Natural Law Forum* 53–72, at 61–3.

category must be determined in conjunction with, and in recognition of, all those other circumstantial factors. Power, wealth, enlightenment, rectitude, or other values might well imply one thing in one case and another in the next one, depending on all the other interacting agents and elements present in the contextual game.

If one were to take the teleological capacity of policy seriously, one would have to wonder about the potential of other conceivable desiderata, such as security, distribution of resources, and the inclusion of voices from the periphery. Depending on different circumstantial factors in a genuinely contextual analysis, such values might give a different meaning to power, wealth, and enlightenment, not necessarily yielding to the direct interest of McDougal's assigned representative of human dignity.[39] To hold the value category as a whole in an unrivalled position in no need of epistemic justification and then to read the implications of its subcategories categorically in line with the practice and interest of the designated representatives of human dignity eviscerates the notion of balancing from all its essential features but the name.

This rigidly determinative function of policy in legal decision-making resulting from what this chapter has introduced as the NHS's policy conceptualism in effect mirrors what Duncan Kennedy refers to as 'policy formalism' or 'social conceptualism'.[40] Symptomatic of this kind of formalism is 'select[ing] policies arbitrarily, underestimat[ing] the conflicts among them, and offer[ing] no defense of balancing as a rationally determinate procedure'.[41] The NHS avowedly commits itself to a preference for a set of postulated values over others, consistently interprets them in a manner leading to most predictable consequences without considering the slightest possibility of disharmony in implications even among its randomly selected values, and, as suggested above, leaves much to be desired in the way of a meaningful process of balancing.

4.2 International Law and Policy Conceptualism

To understand the reactions of the international law discipline against Yale's policy conceptualism, let us now look at some of the illustrative examples of significant debates dividing the NHS and its opponents.

---

[39] McDougal is said to be concerned for human dignity in developing nations, like all nations, 'but he does not see the developing countries as requiring the separate and urgent attention of the legal process': R Higgins, 'Policy and Impartiality: The Uneasy Relationship in International Law' (1969) 23 *International Organization* 914–31, at 924.

[40] D Kennedy, 'Legal Formalism' in NJ Smelser and PB Baltes (eds), *The International Encyclopedia of the Social and Behavioral Sciences* (Elsevier Amsterdam 2001) vol 13, 8634–8, at 8635, citing KE Klare, 'Judicial Deradicalization of the *Wagner Act* and the Origins of Modern Legal Consciousness, 1937–1941' (1978) 62 *Minnesota Law Review* 265–339.

[41] 'Legal Formalism' (n 40) 8636.

4.2.1 *Interpretation of International Agreements*

The predictable closure epistemically inherent in the NHS is what triggered some of the critiques of McDougal's reliance on 'shared expectations', among other contextual factors, in legal interpretation.[42] The irony was that the NHS set itself the task of jurisprudential renewal, of revolutionizing the history of rule-oriented approaches of the past and their endemic formalism. Shared expectations could be taken to either refer to specific expectations in a particular agreement or to general expectations 'attached to the whole pattern of relationships between parties, including procedures for the interpretation of agreements'.[43] In the former case, it would only be a distorting concept as it dominates all other relevant functions of the process of interpretation, and in the latter, it is too general and vague to function as a useful guiding principle at all. Yet McDougal finds 'shared expectations' to help fill the gaps successfully and bring a kind of closure that in a rule-oriented approach, given the complementarity of rules, would be either an illusion or contrived through an arbitrary assignment of a specific meaning to a rule to justify the adjudicator's preferred outcome.[44]

The outer limit of the subject of 'shared expectations' is, however, undefined, and coming to an agreement on whose 'expectations' to include or exclude remains debateable. A solution, which is McDougal's use of policy, is to proceed on the basis of some postulated specific goals of interpretation, and policing the outer borders of shared expectations with the aim of fostering consensus over human dignity. But the 'very *postulation* of fixed goals for interpretation is bound…to have a distorting and misleading effect, for what is at stake in interpretation is not a means–end form (type) of calculus to design means for reaching fairly stable ends'.[45] Postulating goals and values as final arbitrators between relevant but competing alternatives does not resolve the choice between those alternatives. It instead eliminates the choice altogether.

---

[42] G Gottlieb, 'The Conceptual World of the Yale School of International Law' (1968) 21 *World Politics* 108–32, at 126–7.

[43] Ibid 126.

[44] In the context of the law of war, McDougal describes the problem with complementarity of rules as follows:

> the rules of the law of war, like other legal rules, are commonly formulated in pairs of complementary opposites and are composed of a relatively few basic terms of highly variable reference. The complementarity in form and comprehensiveness of reference of such rules are indispensable to the rational search for and application of policy to a world of acts and events which presents itself to the decision-maker, not in terms of neat symmetrical dichotomies or trichotomies, but in terms of innumerable gradations and alternations from one end of a continuum to the other; the spectrum makes available to a decision-maker not one inevitable doom but multiple alternative choices.

MS McDougal, 'The Processes of Coercion and Decision: General Community Policies' in *Law and Minimum World Public Order* (n 38) 1–96, at 57.

[45] 'The Conceptual World of the Yale School of International Law' (n 42) 127–8 (emphasis altered).

Against McDougal's over-emphasized accusation that lawyers neglect the complementarity and ambiguity of rules, critics responded with various degrees of sophistication. Some in fact did respond in the way that McDougal in his unyielding conviction about their legalism had anticipated—they simply did not appreciate the radical interpretive fact about complementarity or any other linguistic shortcomings of legal rules.[46] Others reacted with more nuance, and used, somewhat vaguely, 'plausible interpretation' as the yardstick to measure law's 'elasticity'.[47] Policy in their view is broader than what McDougal grants— compliance with international law itself is a policy 'by which government elites seek to attain certain goals'.[48] The main problem of McDougal's expectation of legal interpretation, according to another reviewer, is in its emphasis on predictability, secured through technical means and jargon. But in fact an acceptable combination of predictability and flexibility, from the viewpoint of states, is a political question and not a technical one: 'States do not ask how to maximize one, but how to optimize the mixture of both'.[49]

Yet some others, sympathetic to and raised in the NHS, essentially gave some deference to McDougal's indeterminacy thesis but were critical of the extent to which McDougal is willing to go to discredit the capacity of legal language to justifiably determine outcomes. Richard Falk is an example of this group when he writes:

[A]cceptance of McDougal's position virtually severs the link between language and meaning. For if complementary norms are equally plausible under most circumstances, then no predictable impact upon behavior derives from the adoption of a new prohibitive rule. . . . Although legal rules, especially broad principles . . . such as self-defense, are not delineated precisely enough that violative behavior can be identified with confidence, something quite definite is communicated by the rule.[50]

Far from merely taking a familiar, intermediate path and repeating a rule versus standard solution, Falk in fact elsewhere turns his attention to the alternative sort of determinacy that McDougal seeks under the cover of flexibility of policy and the

---

[46] See eg 'Vae Victis or Woe to the Negotiators' (n 12) 373 (summing up the NHS's work on the treaty interpretation as work that, while '[a]iming at order and liberality', uses concepts that 'by their very breadth, open the door to anarchy and abuse').

[47] OJ Lissitzyn, 'Western and Soviet Perspectives on International Law—A Comparison' (1959) 53 *Proceedings of the American Society of International Law* 21–30, at 23.

[48] Ibid. See also R Fisher, 'Law and Policy in International Decisions' (1962) 135 *Science* 658–60, at 659–60 ('[I]n urging deciders to look away from rules to policy, [McDougal] overlooks the fundamental policy of having disputes, differences, and questions of right, professedly and in fact, decided according to rules. . . . To accept his policy-science is all but to ignore the policy of having law').

[49] PH Rohn, '*The Interpretation of Agreements and World Public Order: Principles of Content and Procedure* by Myres S McDougal, Harold D Lasswell, James C Miller' (1969) 63 *American Political Science Review* 540–2, at 542.

[50] RA Falk, 'The Adequacy of Contemporary Theories of International Law: Gaps in Legal Thinking' (1964) 50 *Virginia Journal of International Law* 231–65, at 240–1.

critique of indeterminacy of rules: 'the extent of policy and normative flexibility represents less a jurisprudential "fact"...than a policy chosen because it promotes other policies'.[51] Falk is not concerned with the law's objectivity or preserving some limit of linguistic determinacy—though both of these matter to him to a moderate degree—but rather he attempts to draw attention to the promotion of one kind of determinacy over another at the expense of an exaggerated portrayal of the indeterminacy of rules. What results from the policy-oriented approach to treaty interpretation is not too much flexibility and chaos but in fact too little room for manoeuvre and too little appreciation of the complexity of contextual interpretation.[52] The complexity and limitations of any interpretation are swept away by the *generality of method* advocated by the NHS, which views the 'tasks of treaty interpretation to be homogeneous regardless of the subject matter of agreement and of the arena wherein the interpretative event is located'.[53] Rather than accounting for changing circumstantial factors, there is a great expectation invested in 'genuine shared expectations' of the parties as reinforced or altered in view of the 'general community policies' in the policing process of interpretation to establish the meaning of international agreements. This is just as confining as, if not more than, strict reference to rules for guidance:

Such an orienting formulation, preliminary to the application of 'the method' for consulting context, is at once too abstract and too indefinite to give the interpreter guidance and *too directive* to allow the interpreter and those subject to his interpretation an awareness of 'the openness' of the interpretative situation.[54]

An elaborate discussion of a policy-oriented approach to legal interpretation demands more space. The intention here is merely to illustrate two points: that McDougal chose to underappreciate international lawyers' recognition—albeit a mostly implicit and unarticulated recognition—of the relative degree of determinacy of rules, principles, and standards; and that his own alternative contextualist interpretation was regarded as beset by the same indeterminacies, unless harnessed by a directional normative framework such as human dignity, in the way that it was employed by New Haven's jurisprudence.

---

[51] RA Falk, '*Law and Minimum World Public Order: The Legal Regulation of International Coercion* by Myres S McDougal and Florentino P Feliciano' (1963) 8 *Natural Law Forum* 171–84, at 179.

[52] Falk speaks of the limits of any method of interpretation resulting from

the nature of the agreement process, the imperfections of language as the medium by which agreements are communicated through time and across space, the dynamic character of international public policy that shifts directives to correspond with shifts in the structure and preferences of international society, and the inability of international institutions to induce compliance with their will in relation to certain kinds of disputes about treaty obligations.

RA Falk, 'On Treaty Interpretation and the New Haven Approach: Achievements and Prospects' in *The Status of Law in International Society* (Princeton University Press Princeton 1970) 342–77, at 369.

[53] Ibid.   [54] Ibid 369–70 (emphasis added).

McDougal's directional method of interpretation in essence sought to provide a middle ground between the classic textualist approaches inherited from Vattel and comprehensively codified in the 1935 Harvard Research *Draft Convention on the Law of Treaties*, on the one hand,[55] and the views of those who found original intent to be no more than a fiction and emphasized the judicial creativity of the decision-maker, on the other.[56] The result, however, was a method-driven system of interpretation that replaced the presumed constraints of rules with a formulated articulation of 'shared expectations' and 'community policies' and developed a contextualist framework with a degree of predictability in which there was in fact little need for judicial creativity.

4.2.2 *Complementarity and Ambiguity of Rules*

Another challenge to McDougal's alleged complementarity of legal norms, in the context of the principles of military necessity and of humanity, invites him to justify the polar interaction of these principles with regard to permissible coercion. Against the principle of military necessity which permits necessary and proportionate means and prohibits militarily unnecessary and disproportionate ones, there is the principle of humanity, which under the name of higher values of 'a public order of human dignity' requires 'that the least possible coercion be applied to human beings, and that all authorized control over human beings be oriented towards strategies of persuasion with the widest possible participation in decision, rather than towards strategies of coercion'.[57] The reviewer asks if, given the higher order of the normative system of human dignity, these two principles in fact ought not to be one and the same, that is, that 'economy of force' should be already imbued and ordered by the higher normative framework.[58]

In other words, if the normative commitments to human dignity were to supersede all other considerations, then military utility would already be defined by limits on human behaviour in war and in peace. If this is so, the reviewer asks when

---

[55] 'Harvard Research Convention on the Law of Treaties' (1935) 29 *American Journal of International Law Supplement* 657–1240, at 913–18. On the textualist approach, McDougal and associates write: 'It is the grossest, least defensible exercise of arbitrary formalism to arrogate to one particular set of signs—the text of a document—the role of serving as the exclusive index of the parties' shared expectations. We join with those who condemn textualism of this kind as a violation of the human dignity to choose freely': MS McDougal, HD Lasswell, and JC Miller, *The Interpretation of International Agreements and World Public Order: Principles of Content and Procedure* (Yale University Press New Haven 1967) at xvii.

[56] 'The view we recommend thus rejects the excessive emphases of recent years both upon hierarchy as in Beckett and Fitzmaurice, and upon freedom of decision as in Hyde, Stone, and others. The choice between an ordered hierarchy of rules and the rejection of all rules is one which unnecessarily restricts the available alternatives': 'On Treaty Interpretation' (n 52) 117.

[57] *Law and Minimum World Public Order* (n 38) 72.

[58] WV O'Brien, '*Law and Minimum World Public Order: The Legal Regulations of International Coercion* by Myres S McDougal and Florentino P Feliciano' (1962) 72 *Yale Law Journal* 413–20, at 419.

'a military commander manages to limit his means to the minimal requirements of objective military utility will he not have gone a long way towards ensuring that the basic values of human dignity are disturbed as little as possible?'[59] Both the tone and the intent impelling this reaction give the impression that the focus here is not on a fundamental question about McDougal's position on complementarity in general, but specifically on the merging of humanitarianism into military assessment. At the cost of erring on the side of a close reading, however, the review could also be thought to cavil about McDougal's over-emphasis on complementarity, and cast doubt on the need for balancing, in particular in a system where human dignity, in the final analysis, overrules all the circumstantial factors that could possibly impact the decision-making process.

4.2.3 *Implicit and Explicit Reactions to Policy Conceptualism*

It is the discipline's implicit or explicit reference to what this essay presents as policy conceptualism that McDougal either entirely evades, or distortedly translates into a defence of the rule of law to then abruptly dismiss. This rhetorical game characteristic to McDougal might be more visible in his reactions to some of the more implicit critiques of conceptualism. Those critiques were mostly buried in substantial arguments for what could justifiably be read as amounting to merely a concern for the rule of law. There were enough positivists still around, after all, who had no reservations to expressing rage over what they saw as a disastrous consequence of policy arguments replacing the rule of law.[60] Some may have made a nuanced distinction between national and international law to suggest that, contrary to the former, wherein 'the national interests were being frustrated by a strong and entrenched legal system', the latter is already injuriously subject to conflicting interpretations by nations in light of domestic policies.[61] That nuanced addition aside, many distrusted allowing policy greater importance in the unstable international arena.

Yet, for all the implicit dissatisfaction with conceptualism in the application of the policy-oriented method, many expressed clear discontent with the rigidity inherently embedded in New Haven's jurisprudence and its policy conceptualism. Foreshadowed by Roscoe Pound's idea of comparative study of systems of law as systems and starting from the study of the interactions of individuals in groups or societies and their 'divergent drives, competing desires, conflicting ambitions', and the need for 'social controls' to solve the conflicts thereof,[62] and anticipated by

---

[59] 'Law and Minimum World Public Order' (n 58).

[60] For an example of a positivist-inspired debate with McDougal, see L Gross, 'Voting in the Security Council: Abstention from Voting and Absence from Meetings' (1951) 60 *Yale Law Journal* 209–57. For McDougal's rebuttal, see MS McDougal and RN Gardner 'The Veto and the *Charter*: An Interpretation for Survival' (1951) 60 *Yale Law Journal* 258–92.

[61] 'Law and Policy in International Decisions' (n 48) 659.

[62] R Pound, 'Philosophy of Law and Comparative Law' (1951) 101 *University of Pennsylvania Law Review* 1–19, at 1–2, cited in AR Blackshield, 'The Policy Science Approach to Jurisprudence: A Critique

Karl Llewellyn in 'the overall design of decision-making and authority-applying functions in the context of all social processes', the McDougal–Lasswell apparatus still stands alone for being 'highly abstract' and 'conceptual'.[63] In contradistinction to Llewellyn's—and in fact to legal realism's—idea of studying each 'cluster' of legal phenomena as a *sui generis* category, the McDougal–Lasswell formula seeks to establish an analytical method that equally fits all social phenomena; 'the result is that they automatically assume, without any genuine empirical inquiry, that the formula does fit whatever subject they take up'.[64]

Focusing on the expected contribution of a 'theory', Oran Young writes that the adopted conceptual apparatus from Lasswell

failed to support the development of any theory (or theories) in the formal sense. In fact, it tends to hinder the development of theory severely by introducing excessive numbers of potentially relevant factors while the crucial problem in developing viable formal theories is to construct simple logical models by stripping away as many factors as possible without undermining the predictive accuracy of the resultant propositions.... Much of [the apparatus] is characterized by *a rigid formalism* that frequently makes it difficult to fit observations of the real world into the framework's categorizations with any comfort. The scheme tends to encourage the proliferation of logically possible boxes or categories that sometimes have little substantive content and that often become difficult to manage in analytic terms.[65]

Oriented by a social science perspective, Young is wary of the formulaic structure of policy science and the way its method-driven approach stands apart from the most desirable aspect of a theory: parsimony. So he attributes any success the NHS has had to McDougal's brilliance rather than to Lasswell's framework of analysis,

---

of the Legal and Sociological Concepts of Lasswell and McDougal' (Australian Society of Legal Philosophy, Working Paper No 5, 1964) 17.

    [63] 'The Policy Science Approach to Jurisprudence' (n 62) 61.

    [64] Ibid 18. Even the admirers of the NHS, who believe McDougal's theories have 'a remarkable capacity to stimulate thinking about law and legal processes', 'have a most comprehensive viewpoint', and a conceptual structure which is 'brilliantly successful in achieving comprehensiveness and synthesizing capability' cannot help but wish that he 'had given equal treatment to the problem of identifying other components of the laws of war to that they gave to identifying policy goals': EM Jones, 'Law and Minimum World Public Order: The Legal Regulation of International Coercion by Myres S McDougal and Florentino P Feliciano' (1963) 15 Journal of Legal Education 341–9, at 345, 347. See also 'The Interpretation of Agreements and World Public Order by Myres S McDougal, Harold D Lasswell, and James C Miller' (n 35) 117 (finding, as a close associate of the New Haven School, 'excessive theoretical abstraction' to be a problem plaguing Interpretation of Agreements). For a contrary view, see eg CH Peterson, 'The Public Order of the Oceans by Myres McDougal and William T Burke and Law and Public Order in Space by Myres McDougal, Harold D Lasswell, and Ivan A Vlasic' (1965) 18 Journal of Legal Education 115–18, at 118 ('[I]n international law change from sterile conceptualism has been slow and sporadic. The Public Order books are the first truly major effort in this direction').

    [65] OR Young, 'International Law and Social Science: The Contributions of Myres S McDougal' (1972) 66 American Journal of International Law 60–76, at 68–9 (emphasis added).

as the 'employment of the conceptual apparatus alone is not a sufficient condition for the production of outstanding legal analysis'.[66]

Misgivings about the NHS's conceptual apparatus were not merely because of its complexity, but also because it was viewed largely as superfluous.[67] Richard Posner took an exemplary quote from *Law and Public Order in Space* to suggest that, as realistic and sophisticated as it was, the work was riddled with a set of formal characteristics: 'an elaborate analytic machinery; an appearance of logical or scientific rigorousness and precision; a specialized vocabulary; and great length—for the authors are indefatigable in applying the "various relevant intellectual techniques" to every facet of every problem they take up'.[68] The comprehensive modality is mostly nothing more than 'empty conceptualizing', introducing, for instance, a standard of 'reasonableness' that, while promising to resolve the question of occasional exclusive competence in outer space, is in fact just the beginning and not the end of legal analysis.[69]

It was not only the complex conceptual apparatus of policy science, but also the centrality of a set of values representing human dignity in legal decision-making, that raised dismissive eyebrows and a great deal of suspicion about the return of conceptualism. McDougal saw the novelty of policy sciences as a development of legal realism and its extension from critique to a positive proposal. A colleague at Yale, Grant Gilmore, disagreed and found some resemblance between the New Haven apparatus and Langdellian conceptualism: 'Despite the novelty of its trappings, the work of McDougal and Lasswell, particularly in its insistence that everything can be reduced to a few general principles, can, not unfairly, be taken as a return toward older theories of law'.[70] The NHS evades both natural law and positivism by giving a primary place of importance to 'community interests', 'as the

---

[66] 'International Law and Social Science' (n 65) 69. For a contrary view, see MN Schmitt, 'New Haven Revisited: Law, Policy and the Pursuit of World Order' (1990) 1 *United States Air Force Academy Journal of Legal Studies* 185–204, at 193 ('the value of the New Haven approach is to be found, in great part, in its comprehensive nature').

[67] R Posner, '*Law and Public Order in Space* by Myres S McDougal, Harold D Lasswell, and Ivan A Vlasic' (1964) 77 *Harvard Law Review* 1370–4, at 1370.

[68] Ibid 1371.

[69] Posner continues, ibid:

All the authors really have to say about the problem of national sovereignty in space is that the law of the sea, with its basic rule of freedom, offers a closer analogy than the law of the air, with its rule of sovereignty. While this is a sound observation, it should not require several hundred pages to make, and little is gained by garnishing it with a high-sounding, but on examination almost meaningless, 'rule of reason.'

See also G Vernon Leopold, '*Law and Public Order in Space* by Myer [sic] S McDougal, Harold D Lasswell, and Ivan A Vlasic' (1964) 42 *University of Detroit Law Journal* 238–41, at 238–9 (complaining about 'semantic gymnastics' of McDougal and associates that 'only serve to confuse and obscure their labors' and their use of 'pseudo mathematically' stated propositions that are in fact novel abstractions).

[70] G Gilmore, *The Ages of American Law* (Yale University Press New Haven 1977) at 90.

explanation of the "is", as the criteria for the "ought", and as an answer to the "why" of the law is a substitution of a policy-oriented "community interest" for a restatement "rule".[71] 'Community interest', therefore, is an absolute in and of itself for policy-oriented jurisprudence:

Whether following the policy-oriented absolute is in the interest of the community any more than following 'rules' or, indeed, any other absolute, depends on the evaluation of the community interest in view of the logical conclusion that may inevitably follow from the hypothesis of the policy-oriented jurisprudence.[72]

5 CONCLUSION

Contrary to the received wisdom, the NHS's success in antagonizing the discipline against its policy-oriented heresy was not due to the latter's principled hostility against policy reasoning, but rather to a clear (if not clearly articulated) opposition to New Haven's policy conceptualism. The NHS's apparent partiality for the 'particular' disguised as the 'universal' is not only a question of application, but also results from the very epistemic structure of New Haven's jurisprudence. Both these points have significant jurisprudential and historical implications.

First, the conventional story that inaccurately pits New Haven's policy pragmatism against a unifiedly defiant, formalist international law leaves the NHS with little more than banal academic visibility. The real, but invisible, impact of New Haven's jurisprudence is in presenting a mode of policy reasoning—policy conceptualism—that triggered such an opposition amongst international lawyers who preferred the contextualist possibilities not entirely foreclosed in legal interpretive labour over the over-determinative and formulaic function of human dignity and other conceptual categories of the NHS.

Secondly, another invisible but enduring legacy of the NHS, understood through the present counter-narrative, is a new vista through which to caution against the pitfalls of policy reasoning and to demand the realization of its promises in our own time. International legal theory has a relatively clear sense about the abuse of deduction when found in legal interpretation, but it has little to say about similar defects in policy reasoning. Equally under-theorized are our ideas about the very concept of policy and its place in international legal argumentation.

---

[71] E Ereli, 'The Public Order of the Oceans by Myres S McDougal and William T Burke' (1963) 16 Vanderbilt Law Review 1009–16, at 1016.

[72] Ibid.

Pursued policy objectives might be principled or flexible and their application flexible or principled. So a combination of principled policies and flexible application of those policies or vice-versa might well permeate the words and practice of international lawyers, used simultaneously or selectively—depending on the context—to address international legal problems. And then there is percolation of these conflicting modalities—principled policies and unprincipled applications or the other way around—through different professional roles that international lawyers habitually adopt—what Richard Falk calls 'a kind of odd and unappreciated overlap between…"careerist" or "vocational" concerns of international lawyers and the moral imperatives of good citizenship on matters of world affairs'.[73] We can begin to understand all that complexity only when we acknowledge the fallacy of an inherent association between law and formalism and between policy and anti-formalism. Retelling the story of the NHS is an effort to do just that.

---

[73] RA Falk, 'The Place of Policy in International Law' (1972) 2 *Georgia Journal of International and Comparative Law* 29–34, at 30.

CHAPTER 22

....

INTERNATIONAL LAW AND ECONOMICS

LETTING GO OF THE 'NORMAL' IN PURSUIT OF AN EVER-ELUSIVE REAL

....

DAN DANIELSEN

1 Introduction to the Field

....

SINCE the early 1990s, building on the work of law and economics scholars of the domestic law of the United States from the 1970s and 80s, a body of international law and economics scholarship has emerged comprising a distinct strand of international legal theory.[1] While the volume of international law and economics

[1] For some representative examples of international law and economics scholarship, see W Aceves, 'The Economic Analysis of International Law: Transaction Cost Economics and the Concept of State Practice' (1996) 17 *University of Pennsylvania Journal of International Economic Law* 995–1068; E Benvenisti, 'Collective Action in the Utilization of Fresh Water: The Challenges of International Water Resources Law' (1996) 90 *American Journal of International Law* 384–415; R Cooter, 'Structural Adjudication in the New Law Merchant: A Model of Decentralized Law' (1994) 14 *International Review of Law and Economics* 215–31; J Dunoff and J Trachtman, 'Economic Analysis of International Law: An Introduction and a Caveat' (1999) 24 *Yale Journal of International Law* 1–59 (and see at Appendix B, which contains a selected bibliography of scholarship applying economic approaches

scholarship is considerable, the work to date has been primarily driven by two goals.[2] The first is to demonstrate that a number of issues of traditional concern to international lawyers—such as the sources and legitimacy of international rules, the scope of legitimate jurisdictional authority of states, international institutions and other international actors, the relative merits of national rules, international rules, private ordering and international institutions to address pressing issues of global concern—can best be explained and understood through the application of one or more existing economic choice frameworks mainly associated with 'new institutional' economics such as transaction cost analysis, comparative institutional analysis, game theory, rational choice theory, and public choice theory.[3]

to international legal issues); A Guzman, *How International Law Works: A Rational Choice Theory* (OUP New York 2008); G Hadfield, 'Law for a Flat World: Legal Infrastructure and the New Economy' (USC Center in Law, Economics and Organization, Research Paper No C10-7, 2010); W Mock, 'Game Theory, Signaling and International Legal Relations' (1992) 26 *George Washington Journal of International Law and Economics* 33–60; J Paul, 'New Movements in International Economic Law' (1995) 10 *American University Journal of International Law and Policy* 607–18; E Posner and A Sykes, 'Economic Foundations of the Law of the Sea' (University of Chicago Law School, John M Olin Law and Economics Working Paper No 504, 2009); PB Stephan, 'Barbarians inside the Gate: Public Choice Theory and International Economic Law' (1995) 10 *American University Journal of International Law and Policy* 745–68; PB Stephan, 'Accountability and International Lawmaking: Rules, Rents, and Legitimacy' (1996–97) 17 *Northwestern Journal of International Law and Business* 681–735; A Sykes, 'The Economics of Injury in Antidumping and Countervailing Duty Cases' (1996) 16 *International Review of Law and Economics* 5–26; J Trachtman, *The Economic Structure of International Law* (Harvard University Press Cambridge MA 2008); J Trachtman, 'The Theory of the Firm and the Theory of the International Economic Organization: Toward Comparative Institutional Analysis' (1996–97) 17 *Northwestern Journal of International Law and Business* 470–555. For an early precursor of international law and economic scholarship, see W Röpke, 'Economic Order and International Law' (1954) 86 *Recueil des Cours* 203–73.

² For an extended analysis of international law and economics theory and scholarship, see D Danielsen, 'Economic Approaches to Global Regulation: Expanding the International Law and Economics Paradigm' (2011) 10 *Journal of International Business and Law* 23–90.

³ The term 'new institutional economics' was first coined by Oliver Williamson: O Williamson, *Markets and Hierarchies: Analysis and Antitrust Implications* (Free Press New York 1975). In many ways, 'new institutional economics' comes to have shape as a field in part in relation to its focus on 'institutions' in dynamic economic processes and in part in relation to the methods of institutional economic analysis it leaves behind. As to the analytic focus of the field, Claude Ménard and Mary Shirley offer a useful description: 'For new institutionalists the performance of a market economy depends upon the formal and informal institutions and modes of organization that facilitate private transactions and cooperative behavior. NIE [New Institutional Economics] focuses on how such institutions emerge, operate, and evolve, how they shape different arrangements that support production and exchange, as well as how these arrangements act in turn to change the rules of the game.': C Ménard and M Shelly, 'Introduction' in C Ménard and M Shelly (eds), *Handbook of New Institutional Economics* (Springer Heidelberg 2002) 1–18, at 1–2. One prominent scholar of institutional economics, Thrainn Eggertsson, has suggested the field of 'new institutional economics' may be divided into two distinct sub-schools—a 'neo-institutional school' and a 'new institutional school'—with the former staying closer to the classical rationality assumptions of *homo oeconomicus* and the later advocating more heterogeneous influences in economic decision-making including political, cultural, and psychological influences that challenge more orthodox economic assumptions about the rational basis of choice: see T Eggertsson, *Economic Behavior and Institutions* (CUP Cambridge 1990) at 7–10. International law and economics scholars tend to the 'neo-institutional'

The second goal is to suggest that the actual behaviour of international actors will approximate the behaviour predicted by the economic choice analysis, and therefore this form of analysis can offer policy solutions to complex questions of international regulation and governance—such as when and under what circumstances national regulatory competition will be more effective than other institutional options such as private ordering, informal state cooperation, treaties, harmonized international norms or international institutions at enhancing efficiency or welfare or what system of jurisdictional rules and techniques for resolving jurisdictional conflicts will best preserve legitimate sovereign interests without unduly interfering with economic activity globally.

To a large extent, then, international law and economics scholars have sought to demonstrate the virtues of certain forms of economic modelling techniques for answering questions of institutional arrangement and the limits of jurisdictional authority that have posed challenges central to the discipline of international law. More specifically, international law and economics scholars have focused their analytic attention on determining which institutions should make which rules in the global order and whose rules ought to apply in what circumstances in a global economy lead by private economic actors based on an economic assessment of which institutions or rules will increase efficiency and consequently maximize general welfare.[4] Borrowing traditional conceptions from both international law and neo-classical economics, these scholars describe a world comprised primarily of two types of actors—individuals and states—that are presumed to know their interests and to pursue them through self-interested bargaining. The outcomes of these bargains (private economic transactions or inter-state cooperation, treaties, or bilateral or multilateral institutions) or refusals to bargain (no private economic transaction or state non-cooperation or regulatory competition) are generally thought to be welfare enhancing for the bargainers themselves (as no bargainer would freely enter into or refuse a bargain unless it advanced the

---

end of Eggertsson's typological range—paying little or no attention to political or cultural differences in their analyses of economic behavior of either states or private actors.

[4] See eg 'The Economic Analysis of International Law: Transaction Cost Economics and the Concept of State Practice' (n 1) (seeking to bring together insights from international law, international relations, and economics for the interdisciplinary study of international cooperation); *How International Law Works* (n 1) 23 ('This book is interested in questions relating to compliance with international law and cooperation in international affairs.'); *The Economic Structure of International Law* (n 1) ix (seeking to elaborate a law and economics-based account of the structure of the international legal system 'including the rise, stability and efficiency of custom; compliance with treaty; the establishment of international organizations; the use of dispute settlement in international treaty structures; and host of other topics). Cf LF Damrosch et al., 'The Nature of International Law' in LF Damrosch et al., (eds), *International Law Cases and Materials* (4th edn West St Paul 2001) at 1–55 (providing an introduction to the central concerns of the discipline of international law including the structure and organization of the international political system, sovereignty and the inter-state relations, the binding character of international law, enforcement of and compliance with international law, among others).

bargainer's interest to do so) and, with some caveats, for the aggregate welfare of the globe as a whole. Thus, international law and economics theory reflects a general view that whether the bargainers are individuals in pursuit of economic gains or states in pursuit of power, prestige, or economic benefits for their constituents, the gains from unimpeded bargaining will generally exceed the losses and negative externalities and therefore lead to a net increase in both individual and aggregate welfare.[5]

While asserting that net 'gains from trade' should normally result from free self-interested bargaining whether among states or individuals, international law and economics scholars acknowledge that beneficial bargains sometimes are not concluded and that bargaining is sometimes neither free nor unimpeded. In the case of individuals, the obstacles to welfare-enhancing bargains are usually attributed to high transaction costs that may reduce or overwhelm the benefits of the bargain or to regulation that restricts or impedes beneficial bargains that would otherwise have been made. In the case of states, the obstacles to welfare-enhancing bargains may result from high transaction costs, regulatory interference from international rules (or domestic rules extra-territorially applied), or from interest-group capture that may lead state bargainers to advance the interests of political leaders or powerful organized groups rather that the aggregate interests of their individual constituents. These scholars also acknowledge that bargains between individuals or states that enhance the welfare of the parties may produce adverse externalities or spillover effects that harm third parties. While international law and economics scholars may differ on whether they see these obstacles to or adverse effects from bargaining as pervasive, occasional, or exceptional, these scholars nevertheless generally treat these obstacles and adverse

---

[5] With respect to individuals, see eg 'New Law Merchant' (n 1) (individual businesses and business groups will generate more efficient norms for business transactions than states); S Choi and A Guzman, 'National Laws, International Money: Regulation in a Global Capital Market' (1997) 65 *Fordham Law Review* 1855–908 (allowing issuer choice among national securities law regimes is more likely to lead to efficient global capital markets than extraterritorial application of state securities regimes). With respect to states, see eg *How International Law Works* (n 1) at 17 (citations omitted) ('[T]he book adopts a set of rational choice assumptions. States are assumed to be rational, self-interested, and able to identify and pursue their interests. Those interests are a function of state preferences, which are assumed to be exogenous and fixed. States do not concern themselves with the welfare of other states but instead seek to maximize their own gains or payoffs.'); 'The Firm and International Economic Organization' (n 1) at 473–4.

> The main hypothesis of this paper suggests that states use and design international institutions to maximize the members' net gains (NG), which equals the excess of transaction gains from engaging in intergovernmental transactions (TG), minus the sum of transaction losses from engaging in intergovernmental transactions (TL), and the transaction costs of intergovernmental transactions (including transaction costs of international agreement or of creating and running institutions, TC). Thus, stated mathematically, they maximize the present value of $NG = TG - (TL + TC)$. "Intergovernmental transaction" is a kind of transaction in power, including prescriptive jurisdiction, between states.

effects as 'distortions' from the welfare-enhancing benefits that normally should result from unimpeded, self-interested bargaining.[6]

As one might expect from these background presuppositions and premises, the policy prescriptions international law and economics scholars advance most often seek to facilitate freer bargaining by reducing the perceived distortions identified with their models. While the details of these policy prescriptions are diverse, they tend to evidence certain general preferences and values—decentralized, bottom-up normative frameworks are usually preferred to centralized, 'command-and-control' legal regimes, 'private' forms of international ordering are usually preferred to 'public' ones, and 'national' rule-making is generally preferred to 'international' rule-making.[7] These preferences and values notwithstanding, as with law and economics scholars in national contexts, most international law and economics scholars recognize, at least in theory, that a regime of rules and/or institutions may be justifiable in circumstances where their models suggest that states are likely to over-regulate private economic actors or each other through unnecessary or

---

[6] See eg 'New Law Merchant' (n 1) at 215–6 (suggesting that states will not behave in economically efficient ways when regulating, Cooter states:

Central planning is a way of making law, as well as commodities. To implement a central plan, officials must have the power to allocate resources. To possess this power, the orders issued by planning officials at the top must trump the rights of property and contract enjoyed by people and enterprises at the bottom. Thus, public law crowds out private law. . . . An advanced economy involves the production of too many commodities for anyone to manage or regulate. As the economy develops, the information and incentive constraints tighten upon public policy. These facts suggest that as economies become more complex, efficiency demands more decentralized lawmaking, not less).

PB Stephan, 'The Political Economy of Choice of Law' (2001) 90 *Georgetown Law Journal* 957–70, at 960 (discussing the appropriate framework for determining whether inter-state cooperation is likely to increase or decrease global welfare, Stephan states:

In any particular case, we must ask whether the benefits of a potentially desirable agreement, discounted by the likelihood of a particular institutional structure achieving it, is greater than the costs generated by a potentially undesirable agreement, discounted by the likelihood of that structure producing such an agreement. Rarely is the answer to this question obviously in the affirmative. There are two categories of reasons why international cooperation may produce undesirable outcomes. First, negotiators may give excessive weight to the preferences of private groups with unrepresentative preferences but especially low organizational costs. . . . Second, persons with an interest in the institutions established or promoted by international cooperation may seek the adoption of agreements that expand the competence, discretion and authority of those institutions at the expense of desirable regulatory outcomes).

[7] For representative examples of these 'general preferences and values' at work, see 'Transaction Cost Economics and State Practice' (n 1) (focusing on the role of 'state practice' in facilitating 'endogenous governance structures' and the general positive attributes of such structures, including reduced transaction costs, party-negotiated solutions to problems and changed circumstances, informality, flexibility and adaptability); 'New Law Merchant' (n 1) (focusing on the general superiority of decentralized law-making rather than 'command-and-control' regulations and the potential efficiency gains to be had from deriving business norms from actual business practices); 'Accountability and International Lawmaking' (n 1) (focusing on a general difference in accountability between national and international law-making and inferring a higher likelihood of welfare-reducing rules at the international level justifying a skeptical attitude towards international regulation in general).

illegitimate extra-territorial assertions of regulatory jurisdiction or under-regulate through sub-optimal amounts of inter-state cooperation or regulatory competition. In such limited circumstances, international rules or institutions may be useful to the extent they create incentives that induce states to use their regulatory power to increase rather than reduce global welfare.

If one approaches international law and economics theory from the perspective of the mainstream international lawyer or the neo-classical or new institutional economist, the world view, presuppositions, assumptions, and expectations embedded in international law and economics scholarship would be familiar. To some, the world depicted in international law and economics scholarship made up of public and private, state and individual, interest-based bargaining and a general tendency towards increased total welfare to the extent bargains are freely undertaken and regularly enforced may seem more like a description of the world as it is (or perhaps as it would be if 'distortions' from what would otherwise be welfare-enhancing bargaining could be reduced or eliminated). Moreover, a focus on distortions that may result from sub-optimal institutional arrangements or inefficient jurisdictional rules may seem an appropriate focus for scholars looking to economic theory to provide answers to some important global challenges that have traditionally been preoccupations of international law scholars generally. Doubtless, exploring methods for analysing the relative efficiency of different institutional arrangements for international rule-making and different regimes for allocating jurisdiction and managing legal conflicts among sovereigns seems a useful and potentially important enterprise.

2 CRITIQUES AND LIMITS

Without denying the importance of the issues international law and economics scholars have studied, it remains surprising that many of the significant global issues that international law and economics scholars *do not* address are ones that receive regular research attention from economists and international legal scholars working in other theoretical traditions. For example, issues of poverty, income inequality, economic growth, and the role of law in the distribution of wealth and power globally are generally not addressed, except perhaps indirectly in connection with general assertions that increasing individual welfare gains through legal rules that facilitate unimpeded arm's length bargaining will ordinarily increase global efficiency and welfare in the aggregate. Also avoided are questions regarding the impact of culture, institutional context, or power asymmetries on the behaviour of different public and private actors in the global order. Also absent is an exploration of the role economic actors play in shaping the structure of regulatory institutions and the behaviour of states and international institutions or the effects of this public/private bargaining on individual or general welfare. In short, left behind are much of the struggle, crisis, conflict, and complexity that comprise the global legal and economic order we see all around us and read about in the daily press.

For example, little or no attention is given to issues of distribution—whether of economic resources among private actors or power among public ones. Even retaining the focus on institutional arrangements that have preoccupied international law and economic theorists, one might expect them to theorize and explore questions such as: how regulation at one or another level of the international system might affect the distribution of resources among different constituencies or groups around the world? How might one or another regime of jurisdictional rules or limits shape the ability of different actors to capture a more equitable share of resources in the global economy? What is the role of particular legal arrangements in the production or reduction of income inequality?

In this same vein, international law and economics scholars have given very little attention to the substantive rules that could be expected to result from their proposed policy reforms with respect to the institutional level of rule-making or jurisdictional power of particular regulators or the relative welfare impact of those reforms on various global constituencies. Instead, these scholars tend to predict that the prescribed institutional or jurisdictional reform will generally result in the production of sub-rules with certain characteristics (more flexible, reflective of actual state or business practice, facilitative of regulatory competition or party choice) that will bring about more efficiency or general welfare.[8]

Assuming, as I suspect most lawyers and economists would, that there are numerous possible combinations of institutional arrangements and sub-rules that could theoretically result in a similar increase in aggregate efficiency gains in the global economy, it would be difficult to decide which among them was superior as a theoretical or a policy matter without knowing much more particularly which substantive rules would emerge from which institutional arrangement or jurisdictional regime, the relative net welfare effects from each, and the relative distribution of welfare effects of each on different constituencies.[9] For example, efficiency

---

[8] See sources cited in n 7.

[9] The possibility that different legal rules might be 'efficient' in a particular situation while producing radically different distributional consequences for affected constituencies was recognized in law and economics theory in the early and canonical piece of law and economics scholarship: G Calabresi and D Melamed, 'Property Rules, Liability Rules, and Inalienability: One View of the Cathedral' (1972) 85 *Harvard Law Review* 1089–128. Calabresi and Melamed went on to argue that if multiple, efficient rules were possible, then choosing among them was inherently normative and could not be made on the basis of efficiency criteria alone: at 1118–21.

gains being roughly equal, some might assert a preference for the institutional arrangement and rule combination that leads to the most equitable distribution of those gains. Of course, such a preference is neither a logical implication of the theory itself nor the only imaginable option as a normative matter. An alternative position might favour the institution and sub-rule combination that allocated efficiency gains to the actors best able to redeploy the gains to generate future growth. In other words, in order to justify a particular policy reform based on the welfare effects predicted by a particular international law and economics choice model, the theory would need both an effective method for assessing the cumulative welfare effects of the proposed institutional arrangement and sub-rule combination relative to others and some normative frame for adjudicating better and worse distributional outcomes in the event of more than one efficient combination. Without both of these analytic and the normative components it would be difficult to justify a preference for one arrangement over another either analytically or as a matter of policy.

Also absent from international law and economics theory is any sustained attention to the impact that differences in culture, local institutional context, relative wealth, or bargaining power might have on the ways in which different private and public actors behave or bargain either in individual transactions or in the system as a whole.[10] If the world were a culturally and institutionally homogenous place made up of relatively equal bargainers with regard to wealth and bargaining power, one might perhaps more safely assume that individuals or states would likely make similar decisions and behave in similar ways when faced with similar economic or legal incentives or adversities. In such circumstances, an economic choice model might be devised to describe the most prevalent economic behaviour patterns and predict, based on those 'normal' patterns, the expected welfare effects of particular economic or legal changes. Such an assumption would be much more risky if one were trying to describe or predict the effects of an economic or legal change as it interacts with the numerous and diverse institutional arrangements, legal systems, cultural contexts, and power asymmetries that can be readily observed in the functioning global system.

These issues might be important to the work of international law and economics theorists in a variety of ways. For example, different cultural expectations or understandings about the background institutional, cultural, or power context might shape the way in which local economic actors, institutions, or even states might

---

[10] The possible exception might be the public choice scholars, though their work seems more oriented to articulating general potentialities and tendencies within states than to analysing the particular political structure or institutional orientation of any particular state. See eg 'Barbarians inside the Gate' (n 1) 746 ('Public choice theory seeks to apply certain insights derived from the study of private economic behavior to collective action problems, including the form of concerted activity that constitutes government'); 'Accountability and International Lawmaking' (n 1).

respond to policy reforms or economic or institutional changes elsewhere in the system. Or differences in cultural norms or practices or local institutional arrangements could lead to 'blind spots' that could make it more difficult for particular actors, whether private or public, to recognize the extent to which an economic or institutional change elsewhere in the system could affect them and whether or how they should respond. A third possibility is that cultural expectations or established institutional structures may lead private actors or policy-makers to over- or under-value the benefits (or costs) of a particular economic or institutional change based on familiarity with their own system and/or bias against change.

Just as differences in cultural expectations, norms, and institutions seem likely to shape how individuals or state actors might interpret or react to economic conditions, disparities in wealth might also affect the way poorer or wealthier players experience the impact of adverse or positive effects of a particular institutional change or economic event, leading to over- or under-reactions that deviate from the responses predicted in the 'normal' case. Moreover, differences in bargaining power may lead to suboptimal distributions of the costs and benefits of particular institutional changes or events from the standpoint of maximizing total welfare. In bargains struck in reaction to an institutional change in the global system, powerful players may be able to extract more of the gains from or displace more of the costs to weaker players even if the powerful actually value the gains or suffer the losses less than the weak resulting in lower aggregate welfare gains than might have resulted from the change or event if bargainers were able to achieve deals that reflected their interests absent power asymmetries.

In sum, the basic notion here, which is hardly a controversial one in the social sciences, is that differences in culture, institutional structures or customary practices, or asymmetries in resources or power may shapes an actor's preferences and values, and in turn, the way in which that actor might respond to institutional or economic change. If, as seems likely, this is not infrequently the case, then the predictive usefulness of international law and economics choice models that assume similar reasoning and responses by actors across the global system to similar stimuli would be significantly affected and the policy prescriptions put forward based on those models would be harder to justify on empirical grounds. Moreover, if more than a negligible number of different global actors or constituencies in different contexts make economic choices differently with respect to similar stimuli, how do we decide which choices are 'rational' or 'normal' and which 'deviant' or 'aberrational' in general or with respect to particular institutional or economic changes? It would seem that some implicit cultural or normative choices would be necessary prerequisites both to use the economic choice models for analysis and to permit any policy inferences to be drawn from the analytic results. As we shall see, the limitations of international law and economics choice models articulated here do not eliminate the potential usefulness of these models for analytic or policy purposes. However, these limitations do undermine assertions of value-neutrality and universal applicability as regards both the assumptions that animate the models and the analytic conclusions that might be drawn from them.

Another aspect of the current global legal and economic order that is readily observable at the local, national, and transnational level but largely avoided by international law and economics theory is the ubiquitous phenomenon of bargaining between public and private actors over the content of rules and the structure of regulatory and governance institutions, as well as the role of dynamic adjustments by public and private actors individually and in the aggregate to changes in other parts of the system. Public and private bargaining poses a range of possible issues that one might expect would be of interest to international law and economics scholars even if they retained their focus on questions of increasing the efficiency of international institutional arrangements and jurisdictional rules. For example, if individual economic actors bargain to maximize economic gain and states bargain to maximize political power or prestige or the welfare of some or all of their national constituents, how can we measure the relative efficiency or welfare gains of institutional changes brought about through public/private bargains when the factors the bargainers are economizing or maximizing are not analytically or normatively commensurate?

Public/private bargaining also poses a challenge to the general tendency among international law and economics theorists to prefer private over public ordering and market allocation over regulatory allocation of economic resources in the absence of special circumstances. Since the functioning global order includes 'public' and 'private' bargainers, 'public' and 'private' rule-makers and rules and institutions that are the result of some or all of public/public, private/private or public/private bargaining, it becomes much more difficult to distinguish even as a matter of theory between 'public' rules and 'private' transactions or between 'market' adjustments or 'rule-based' adjustments to economic incentives or institutional reforms. As a consequence, the tendency by international law and economics theorists to assert a general preference for private, market allocations of resources based on establishing a predictable correlation between the analytically indeterminate 'public' or 'private' origins of an institutional or economic change and the positive or negative welfare effects resulting from that change seem speculative at best and, in any event, reliant on norms and premises brought to rather than deriving from their analyses.

A third issue with regard to public/private bargaining arises from the law and economics insight based on the work of RH Coase that private actors will bargain to adjust or ameliorate the adverse economic consequences of legal rules if the transaction costs of doing so do not exceed the benefits to be gained from the bargain.[11] If this insight is correct, it seems equally likely that public authorities would also seek

---

[11] See R Coase, 'The Problem of Social Cost' (1960) 3 *Journal of Law and Economics* 1–69.

to adjust or ameliorate the perceived or anticipated adverse effects of an economic or institutional change elsewhere in the global system by making adjustments in their own rules or institutional practices. Moreover, if the transaction costs of achieving a legislative or institutional change at home might be high, public authorities could be expected to seek to alter the adverse effects of the change by bargaining with other public or private actors in the system, both at home and abroad. In other words, we might imagine public adjustments to include passing new legislation, adopting new administrative rules, altering executive, judicial or administrative enforcement or interpretive practices, or bargaining with other public regulatory entities or private actors to limit, deflect or compensate for the real or anticipated adverse effects of the change elsewhere in the global system.

From these examples, one might expect that international law and economics theory itself would predict both public/private bargaining and other institutional adjustments to ameliorate welfare-reducing adverse effects resulting from an institutional reform (and adjustments to that reform) among public and private actors whenever the adverse effects of the reform and/or adjustments were likely to exceed the costs of ameliorating them. As a consequence, it would seem that modelling such behaviour would require an understanding both of how a reform would affect the initial bargaining behaviour of diverse public and private actors in the system in response to the reform as well as how the impact of original change and ameliorating bargains might themselves be ameliorated or altered through further bargaining and adjustments. Moreover, a decision to exclude any or all of these theoretical predictions and readily observable bargaining and adjustment behaviours by actors in the functioning global economy would itself require a number of analytic and normative choices as to the interests and effects that are or should be included in a simplified analytic model as well as assumptions about the limited impact of the exclusions on the validity or usefulness of the behavioural predictions resulting from the model and any policy prescriptions based on those predictions.

From this brief exploration of the research questions, methods, and policy conclusions international law and economics theorists have generated as well as a range of the important issues and questions they have tended *not* to address, we can see that at least at this stage in its development, international law and economics theory deploys a quite limited range of analytic methods to analyse a quite narrow and particular set of international problems, at least when judged in relation to the much broader range of questions and methods deployed by international legal theorists and economists working in the global context. There may be many possible explanations for particular choices of research questions among a group of scholars working in or toward a theoretical tradition ranging from a kind of path dependence based on the focus or methodological preoccupations of disciplinary forebears to a 'learning by doing' iterative process of research development based on modest expansions from prior work or methods to the idiosyncratic interests or political projects of the scholars doing the work to 'you've got to start somewhere' randomness. In the case of international law and economics theorists, my intuition is that the choice of research topics, analytic methods, and policy prescriptions has been guided and supported, often implicitly, by a shared set of background principles, assumptions, presuppositions, and teleological expectations about the normal unfolding of economic behaviours and processes and the adverse consequences of disruptions to that normal unfolding derived from 'new institutional economics'.[12] In a sense, international law and economic theory seems to rest on a kind of faith— in the truth of the particular economic premises asserted and the correlative truth that actors will (generally? on average? more often than not?) behave in predictable ways in accordance with those economic premises. As a consequence, whether the accounts resulting from international law and economics theory seem analytically compelling comes to depend in large part on the extent to which one shares the often implicit teleological implications of the presuppositions and assumptions that comprise the background 'normal' case against which efficiency and distortions are measured and the often unacknowledged normative values reflected in the choice of research topics studied or in the policy prescriptions advanced.

Earlier in this chapter, I described some of the most common presuppositions, assumptions, and expectations that I have found in much of international law and economics scholarship. To the extent that these choices of assumptions, methods, and expectations are taken up in this scholarship, they are most often explained or justified on the grounds that simplifying models and assumptions are necessary to reach analytic conclusions because the complexity of 'real world' economic life is impossible to capture. This would seem to be particularly the case for theorists trying to analyse legal and economic processes on a global scale. After all, the complexity and diversity of interests, institutional forms, cultural and political practices, and public and private actors operating in the global legal and economic

---

[12] Malcolm Rutherford, the eminent economic historian of institutional economics, describing common critiques of 'new institutional economics' by economists from other strands of institutional economics, states:

> They argue that its theory is often too abstract and formal; that it sometimes adopts an extreme, reductionist, version of individualism; that the individual is seen as an overly rational and overly autonomous being, constrained, but not otherwise influenced by, his institutional and social setting; that orthodox welfare criteria are not appropriate for appraising institutional change, and that a complacent attitude prevails concerning the efficiency characteristics of markets and of institutions that emerge spontaneously. The NIE [New Institutional Economics] is thus portrayed as more formalist, (particularly in its neoclassical and game theoretic manifestations), individualist, reductionist, oriented toward rational choice and economizing models, and generally anti-interventionist. [T]hese labels apply to some more than others, but . . . they are labels that new institutionalists have willingly applied to themselves, in part in order to clearly distinguish themselves from [old institutional economics].

M Rutherford, *Institutions in Economics: The Old and the New Institutionalism* (CUP Cambridge 1996) at 4.

system could never be captured fully in any model or account. In such circumstances, it would seem to be inevitable that a necessary part of any useful analysis of global social phenomena would involve analytic choices and simplifying assumptions based on interests, normative values, and provisional viewpoints. But the inevitable need for *some* analytic choices, assumptions, and normative views to guide social science research at the global level would not say anything about the validity or usefulness of particular choices of research topics, methods, or values. Rather, the validity or usefulness of such choices would (or should) depend on the extent they reflect or predict more accurately (or more convincingly) than alternative methods or accounts aspects of the behaviours, institutional practices, or substantive preferences of actual actors in the functioning global system.

3 Conclusion: A Way Forward?

If I am correct in my intuition that the shared background worldview of 'normal' economic processes has limited the range of research questions engaged, the methods used, and the policy reforms prescribed in international law and economics work, then engaging issues and questions previously left out such as poverty, distributional equity, cultural or institutional difference, the implications of public/private bargaining over rules and institutions to name only a few, will not be simply a matter of applying existing theory to new areas of study. Rather, innovation in international law and economics both at the level of theory and of substantive research will require better methods for identifying and foregrounding the assumptions and normative values that animate the research choices and policy conclusions in both existing and future scholarship on the one hand, and for tracing and comparing the analytic and normative implications of different research choices and values by reference to their usefulness in reflecting or predicting the observable behaviour of actors in the world around us. In short, a new critical practice of self-conscious analytic introspection and normative transparency would be useful to move international law and economic theory beyond its prior limits.

The goal of such a critical practice would be to place into the frame of disciplinary analysis not only the social phenomenon under observation, but also an assessment of the relative merits of the researcher's choice of values, assumptions, and premises based on their usefulness and limits as compared with alternative choices in illuminating the causal complex of processes at play in the social phenomenon being studied. Moreover, to the extent policy inferences or prescriptions are drawn from the research, their ideological persuasiveness or normative legitimacy would be subject to contestation based, in part, on the relative persuasiveness of the values, assumptions, and premises on which the justifying research is based. Implicit in such a disciplinary practice would be an acknowledgement that all accounts of social phenomena are partial, tentative, and conjectural, that the causal 'reality' of any social phenomenon can never be fully known, and that 'theories' are provisional hypotheses proffered to guide research towards the formulation of better hypotheses, not incontrovertible truths to be defended. While the conventions of social science scholarship require scholars to articulate analytic assumptions and to justify them on methodological grounds, certain background understandings and practices can become so common as to 'go without saying'. Moreover, even among scholars that attempt to articulate their analytic assumptions, it is much less common to examine the normative implications of one's choice of analytic assumptions and justify them in normative terms. I have argued thus far that unarticulated (and perhaps unconscious) assumptions and normative commitments have precluded the application of international law and economics theory to some of the most important questions in international law and global political economy—questions of distribution, inequality, and power.

In arguing for a turn in international law and economics theory to theoretical introspection and normative transparency, I build on a long tradition of similar critical interventions in the history of the social sciences in general and economics in particular. In fact, controversies and critical reflections on the costs and benefits of simplifying assumptions and conscious (and sometimes unconscious) analytic or normative biases in social science theory, research methods, and policy conclusions are as old as the disciplines themselves. In the field of economics, this tradition of theoretical introspection has been primarily the province of heterodox institutional economic theorists who have challenged the generalizing and normalizing tendencies of classical and neo-classical economic theory based on an assertion that the analytic conclusions and policy prescriptions these theoretical traditions generate bear little resemblance to the behaviour of economic actors in everyday life that the theories purport to explain or influence.[13]

---

[13] See eg R Coase, *The Firm, the Market, and the Law* (University of Chicago Press Chicago 1990) at 3 (citations omitted) ('The preoccupation of economists with the logic of choice, while it may ultimately rejuvenate the study of law, political science, and sociology, has nonetheless had, in my view, serious adverse effects on economics itself. One result of this divorce of the theory from its subject matter has been that the entities whose decisions economists are engaged in analysing have not been made the subject of study and in consequence lack any substance. The consumer is not a human being but a consistent set of preferences. The firm to an economist, as Slater has said, "is effectively defined as a cost curve and a demand curve, and the theory is simply the logic of optimal pricing and input combination." Exchange takes place without any specification of its institutional setting. We have consumers without humanity, firms without organization, and even exchange without markets.'). For an historical discussion of these debates among various strands of institutional economists, see *Institutions in Economics* (n 12) 27–50.

In the remainder of the chapter, I will draw attention to two such heterodox institutional economists, Thorstein Veblen and Gunnar Myrdal, whose work seems particularly helpful in suggesting how an introspective critical practice of attention to viewpoints and values in research topics, methods, and policy conclusions might expose and open to challenge the normalizing assumptions, premises, and tendencies that seem to pervade and limit innovation in international law and economics theory. In addition, the work of Veblen and Myrdal provides evidence of an established alternative tradition in economic theory dedicated to the importance of including history, cultural diversity, institutional specificity, distributional effects, and power in economic analysis that might suggest methods for bringing these additional variables into international law and economics theory and thereby enabling it to address some of the important issues and questions that currently seem beyond its analytic scope.[14]

The American economist, sociologist, and forebear of 'old' institutional economics, Thorstein Veblen, provides an excellent example of the type of critical intervention I have in mind for international law and economics theory in his challenge to the disciplinary practices of classical economics in an 1898 essay, 'Why Economics is Not an Evolutionary Science'. He states:

The standpoint of the classical economists, in their higher or definitive syntheses and generalizations, may not inaptly be called the standpoint of ceremonial adequacy. The ultimate laws and principles which they formulated were laws of the normal or the natural, according to a pre-conception regarding the ends to which, in the nature of things, all things tend. . . . It is a projection of the accepted ideal of conduct. This ideal of conduct is made to serve as a canon of truth, to the extent that the investigator contents himself with an appeal to its legitimation for premises that run back of the facts with which he is immediately dealing, for the 'controlling principles' that are conceived intangibly to underlie the process discussed, and for the 'tendencies' that run beyond the situation as it lies before him. . . .

With later writers especially, this terminology is no doubt to be commonly taken as a convenient use of metaphor, in which the concept of normality and propensity to an end has reached an extreme attenuation. But it is precisely in this use of figurative terms for the formulation of theory that classical normality still lives its attenuated life in modern economics . . . By their use the theorist is enabled . . . without misgivings, to construct a theory of such an institution as money or wages or land-ownership without descending to a consideration of the living items concerned, except for convenient corroboration of his normalized scheme of symptoms. . . . In all this the agencies or forces causally at work in the economic life process are neatly avoided. The outcome of the method, at its best, is a body of logically consistent propositions concerning the normal relation of things—a system of

---

[14] Some additional institutional economists whose work builds on diverse economic theoretical traditions to bring more complexity, particularity, culture, history, values, ideology, and psychology into institutional economic thought include Clarence Ayers, John Commons, Thrainn Eggertsson, Alexander Field, Avner Grief, Wendall Gordon, Alan Grunchy, Westley Michell, Douglass North, Warren Samuels, A Allan Schmid, and Marc Tool.

economic taxonomy. At its worst, it is a body of maxims for the conduct of business and a polemical discussion of disputed points of policy.[15]

The Nobel prize-winning economist Gunnar Myrdal strikes a similar note regarding the challenges and inevitability of values in economic research and the correlative need to strive to make one's economic assumptions and normative perspectives explicit in the 1968 prologue to his great work of development economics, *Asian Drama: An Inquiry into the Poverty of Nations*. He states:

The problem of objectivity in research cannot be solved simply by attempting to eradicate valuations. . . . On the contrary, every study of a social problem, however limited in scope, is and must be determined by valuations. A 'disinterested' social science has never existed and never will exist. For logical reasons, it is impossible. A view presupposes a viewpoint. Research, like every other rationally pursued activity, must have a direction. The viewpoint and the direction are determined by our interest in the matter. Valuations enter into the choice of approach, the selection of problems, the definition of concepts, and the gathering of data, and are by no means confined to practical or political inferences drawn from theoretical findings. . . .

The value premises that actually and of necessity determines approaches in the social sciences can be hidden. The student himself may be unaware of them. In fact, most writings, particularly in economics, remain in large part ideological. Some two centuries ago, the modern social sciences branched off from the metaphysical philosophies of natural law and utilitarianism. As our heritage from these philosophies, we continue to attempt to 'objectify' and 'neutralize' the valuation viewpoints and the value-loaded concepts used in scientific analysis. . . . Throughout the history of social studies, the hiding of valuations has served to conceal the inquirer's wish to avoid facing real issues. . . . I have seen few efforts in recent years by economists to reform themselves on this score, least of all among those devoting themselves to abstract economic theory. . . .

Efforts to run away from valuations are misdirected and foredoomed to be fruitless and damaging. The valuations are with us, even when they are driven underground, and they guide our work. When kept implicit and unconscious, they allow biases to enter. The only way in which we can strive for objectivity in theoretical analysis is to lift up the valuations into the full light, make them conscious and explicit, and permit them to determine the viewpoints, approaches, and concepts used. In the practical phases of a study the stated value premises should then, together with the data—established by theoretical analysis with the utilization of those same value premises—form the premises for all policy conclusions.[16]

To sum up these insights so far, the argument is not that we can do without theoretical viewpoints, simplifying assumptions or normative values, but rather, that because we can't, we should make every effort to place those viewpoints, assumptions, and values at the centre of our analytic and critical practice as part of the

---

[15] T Veblen, 'Why Economics is Not an Evolutionary Science' (1898) 12 *Quarterly Journal of Economics* 373–97, at 382–4.

[16] G Myrdal, *Asian Drama: An Inquiry into the Poverty of Nations* (3 vols Pantheon New York 1968) vol 1, at 31–3).

social phenomena we study. Moreover, the usefulness of particular viewpoints, assumptions, and values should be a function of the extent to which they bring us closer to the 'real world' we hope to capture or describe, even as we acknowledge that 'reality' is always, to some extent, beyond our capacities for description or comprehension. Myrdal makes these points as follows:

[Science] always begins *a priori* but must constantly strive to find an empirical basis for knowledge and thus become more adequate to the reality under study. This is also the reason why we can never achieve perfection—merely an approximate fitting of theory to facts.[17]

As such, acknowledging and defending our particular theoretical viewpoints and analytic methods, *does not* reduce the validity of our work, but it does require us to justify our choices and our conclusions based on their accuracy in relation to the data or phenomena we are studying and usefulness relative to accounts based on alternative viewpoints and methods. Moreover, our work becomes 'objective' in Myrdal's terms and 'evolutionary' in Veblen's only to the extent we are willing to adjust our accounts and conclusions in recognition of alternatives that seem more accurate or useful at capturing the 'reality' we are studying.

Returning to Veblen, he helpfully connects the critique of the usefulness of a notion of 'normal processes' or 'general tendencies' in economic activity to an expansion of the range of activities that should be included to generate a more dynamic and therefore realistic conception of economics based on cumulative change in culture and institutions. He argues:

The notion of a legitimate trend in a course of events is an extra-evolutionary preconception, and lies outside the scope of an inquiry into the causal sequence in any process. The evolutionary point of view, therefore, leaves no place for a formulation of natural laws in terms of definitive normality, whether in economics or in any other branch of inquiry. Neither does it leave room for that other question of normality[:] What should be the end of the developmental process under discussion?

The economic life history of any community is its life history in so far as it is shaped by men's interest in the material means of life. This economic interest has counted for much in shaping the cultural growth of all communities. Primarily and most obviously, it has guided the formation, the cumulative growth, of that range of conventionalities and methods of life that are currently recognized as economic institutions; but the same interest has also pervaded the community's life and its cultural growth at points where the resulting structural features are not chiefly and most immediately of an economic bearing. . . . The economic interest does not act in isolation, for it is but one of several vaguely isolable interests on which the complex of teleological activity carried out by the individual proceeds. . . . There is, therefore, no neatly isolable range of cultural phenomena that can be rigorously set apart under the head of economic institutions, although a category of 'economic institutions' may be of service as a convenient caption, comprising those institutions in which

---

[17] Ibid 25.

the economic interest most immediately and consistently finds expression, and which most immediately and with the least limitation are of an economic bearing.

From what has been said it appears that an evolutionary economics must be the theory of a process of cultural growth as determined by the economic interest, a theory of a cumulative sequence of economic institutions stated in terms of the process itself.[18]

With these ideas in mind, and in the spirit of Veblen and Myrdal, a productive 'next move' in the development of international law and economics theory could be a more thorough critical investigation of the analytic limits and normative consequences of the predominant predilections, tendencies, and assumptions that have served as the often unstated background 'normal' against and through which international law and economic scholars have characterized the global order and justified calls for policy reform in the name of increased global efficiency and welfare enhancement as well as a critical practice of making such predilections, assumptions, and tendencies as explicit as possible in our work in the future. Doing so could lead to innovation and expansion of international law and economics theory and its focus of study in several ways. First, it could make us more aware of the ways in which our worldviews, habits of mind, and normative predilections shape our research choices and analytic methods as well as our policy conclusions and thereby make us more attentive to trying to incorporate into our theory and scholarship the analytic costs and benefits and normative consequences of the choices we make relative to others we might make. Second, remaining focused on the fact that our work is always an approximation of the social phenomena we study, made up in part of the numerous choices that often unconsciously animate our theory, could perhaps open more space for exploring the possibilities and effects of relaxing or replacing some of those choices and assumptions on our theories and methods. Such experimentation may lead to alternative accounts of the workings of global economic processes that, in turn, lead us to further experimentation on the one hand, and revision of past analytic choices and methods on the other. From these alternative accounts, different theoretical viewpoints, hypotheses, and values might emerge that could suggest new research methods perhaps better suited to taking up some of the many important issues of global concern that have been avoided or excluded from international law and economics analysis thus far.

Bringing these practices of critical introspection and normative transparency to bear in and on international law and economics theory and scholarship will likely result in more limited and tentative analytic conclusions based on the particular assumptions and values employed, more modesty in drawing concrete policy conclusions from theoretical work, more normative justification for preferring one set of assumptions or policy prescriptions over another, and more uncertainty about what we know and what can be known from our analytics about the global legal

---

[18] 'Why Economics is Not an Evolutionary Science' (n 15) 392–3.

and economic order. Yet from the multiplicity of tentative and limited accounts, assumptions, research methods, and conclusions that should emerge from this critical practice (and from the need to develop methods for comparison of the strengths and weaknesses of each in relation to alternative choices and conclusions), we may find ourselves more able to engage with the dynamic complexity and diversity of behaviour we observe in the global economy we see all around us. It would seem, then, that if we seek to get closer to understanding the ever-elusive and ever-changing 'reality' of global legal and economic life, we may need to let go of the notion that the objective of the study of law and economy is the identification of 'general' economic tendencies based on 'normal' economic behaviour and legal rules that shape economic behaviour in accord with such general tendencies across differences in culture, wealth, power, or values.

CHAPTER 23

LIBERAL INTERNATIONALISM

DANIEL JOYCE

1 INTRODUCTION

LIBERAL internationalism is both familiar and slippery as a concept. This chapter aims to offer a frame through which to evaluate the significance of liberal inter-nationalism, but also to consider the ways in which it has become over-familiar, and to explore whether making it strange again might offer some form of re-newal of its critical and normative possibilities. The chapter comprises three sections. The first considers the significance of liberal internationalism as an idea and frame through which to evaluate international law. The second revisits a series of key events that have shaped the development of liberal internation-alism and critical responses to it. The final section engages with and expands upon contemporary efforts at re-appraisal and renewal. By framing the story of liberal internationalism through key debates and events, it is hoped that a bal-anced account of both the strengths and limits of liberal internationalism will emerge. What is offered is far from a progress narrative, but rather a series of engagements with a set of ideas about the structure of international law and its animating principles.

Part of the picture offered is that of liberal internationalism as an attempt to blend international relations and law (especially in the United States (US) context), and politics and constitutionalism (more so in the European context).[1] In Europe constitutionalism is a mechanism for transforming and expanding transnational identity and community, while in the US internationalism has often been configured as a limit to or complication of domestic constitutional order. Liberal internationalism in this vein can be analysed as an argument made to a domestic polity for the practice of international law elsewhere. International law through 'liberal internationalism' comes packaged as the export of 'international rule of law' or as a key ingredient in the 'toolkit' of international norm cultivation and containment. Liberal internationalism is for some the way to interact with others across borders, but it can too often represent an approximation of internal values applied externally. This approach loses some of the normative appeal of liberal internationalism, particularly when it is translated into contemporary practice involving military and other forms of intervention and social manipulation. The resulting justification of questionable means by lofty ends is exemplified by the invasion of Iraq in 2003.

Thus it becomes important to consider how the compound concept of 'liberal internationalism' can be analytically differentiated from either liberalism or internationalism, and to ask whether it has been conceived in an overly restrictive or even parochial fashion, to its detriment. The over-familiarity of the concept reflects the difficulty in separating out the everyday practice and assumptions of international lawyers from a certain form of international legal liberalism.[2] There is also ongoing difficulty in establishing consensus about what 'liberalism' itself might entail, as Jeremy Waldron reflects:

... the history of liberal thought is a history of rival and incompatible schemes for specifying principles of property, principles of justice, principles of right, and principles of public economy, to satisfy these requirements of equality, security, and freedom.[3]

Liberal internationalism has been critiqued both for its perceived utopianism and for its reduction to sharp policy methods and technique, whether in norms surrounding democratic governance and rule of law implementation or in the practice of intervention. Whilst both critiques are powerful, this chapter argues that neither compels abandoning the ideals inherent in the project of realizing a lasting liberal international order. Of particular resonance for the future development of international law are the associations of internationalism with inclusivity and of

---

[1] For an extended analysis of the Transatlantic divide, see G Verdirame, '"The Divided West": International Lawyers in Europe and America' (2007) 18 *European Journal of International Law* 553–80.

[2] M Koskenniemi, *From Apology to Utopia: The Structure of International Legal Argument* (2nd edn CUP Cambridge 2005) at 5, 85, 92–4.

[3] J Waldron, 'Kant's Theory of the State' in I Kant, *Toward Perpetual Peace and Other Writings on Politics, Peace, and History* (P Kleingeld ed and DL Colclasure trans) (Yale University Press New Haven 2006) 179–200, at 189.

liberalism with a culture of tolerance. Nonetheless, it is necessary to take seriously the shortcomings highlighted by critical engagement with the history of liberal internationalism in the twentieth century, and the ways in which such critique points to the potential renewal of liberal internationalism through a certain form of estrangement.

2 SIGNIFICANCE

Why then is liberal internationalism significant? Liberal internationalism as an idea is central to the modern development of international law—at least in its European and North American incarnations. As Martti Koskenniemi has noted, the first generations of international lawyers were less positivists concerned principally with sovereignty, and more 'centrists who tried to balance their moderate nationalism with their liberal internationalism'.[4] Their project of general international law was about developing international institutions and frameworks to enable the coordination of international society for trade, peace, and security, and the civilizing of conflict. Central to such processes was a conception of international society, built on notions of state sovereignty and cooperation, but also along lines of idealism, internationalism, and institutionalism.

Liberal internationalism was in part an accommodation of these conflicting attachments to sovereignty and some notion of an international society. It offered a conception of international society as a collection of liberal democracies. This was an international society built in the image of Western democracy and rule of law conceptions, moving away from earlier eras of aristocratic diplomacy and towards international organization, economic interdependence, and participation.[5] Participation, public opinion, and openness became important elements of the liberal vision of internationalism as practices of diplomacy and international organization shifted in line with political developments from the nineteenth century onwards.[6] Liberal internationalism exists in part as a normative prescription for international society and the kinds of international laws with which it self-regulates. It can also take the form of a fighting creed for international lawyers.

---

[4] M Koskenniemi, *The Gentle Civilizer of Nations: The Rise and Fall of International Law 1870–1960* (CUP Cambridge 2002) at 4.

[5] Ibid 228.

[6] H Nicholson, *Diplomacy* (3rd edn OUP London 1963).

Immanuel Kant is often treated as a founding father of liberal internationalism. For Kant, peace was attainable if democratic nations formed a federation committed to international right and the peaceful settlement of disputes:

For if fortune so determines that a powerful and enlightened people can constitute itself as a republic (which according to its nature necessarily tends toward perpetual peace), then this republic provides a focus point for other states, so that they might join this federative union and thereby secure the condition of peace among states in accordance with the idea of international right and gradually extend this union further and further through several such associations.[7]

This idea has been immensely influential in thinking about the possibility of international law's framework and the place of democracy and multilateral institutional power within it. But it has also been misunderstood. For Kant's vision of perpetual peace also relied on an initial division between liberal and illiberal states and did not guarantee peace between them.[8] A leading contemporary liberal internationalist, Michael Doyle, has argued that Kant's ideas have been supported by subsequent history, and that liberal internationalism has had three main effects, creating 'incentives for a separate peace among liberal states, for aggression against nonliberals, and for complaisance in vital matters of security and economic cooperation'.[9]

In current international legal practice liberal internationalism is implicated in the development of rule of law mechanisms,[10] in the proliferation of international treaties, courts and tribunals, and in both the communicative and governance infrastructure of the international system. Despite their influences, liberal internationalism does not simply equate with cosmopolitanism (for it does not stand for world government) nor with democracy (for international law is in some ways profoundly undemocratic). It also does not guarantee peace, for conflict between liberal and illiberal states is anticipated and to a degree normalized. Nor is it solely individualistic in its conception—though part of its influence can be felt in the development of international human rights frameworks, in the international criminal trial, and of course in the voluntarism of much of international law and the individualistic conception of the state as its foundational building block. However, liberal internationalism has become linked in international legal scholarship with the broad-brush application of 'liberal' values and ideals—often regarding process,

---

[7] I Kant, 'Toward Perpetual Peace: A Philosophical Sketch' in *Toward Perpetual Peace and Other Writings on Politics, Peace, and History* (n 3) 67–109, at 80.

[8] MW Doyle, 'Kant and Liberal Internationalism' in *Toward Perpetual Peace and Other Writings on Politics, Peace, and History* (n 3) 202–42, at 202–4, 206; R Parfitt, 'The Spectre of Sources' (2014) 25 *European Journal of International Law* 297–306, at 301.

[9] 'Kant and Liberal Internationalism' (n 8) 207; cf M Doyle, 'Liberalism and World Politics' (1986) 80 *American Political Science Review* 1151–69.

[10] For a critique of rule of law rhetoric, see C Miéville, *Between Equal Rights: A Marxist Theory of International Law* (Pluto Press London 2005) at 304–19.

participation, and civil and political rights—to questions of international governance and community.

Yet there is also a more expansionist and often belligerent tendency to liberal internationalism. The basis for this is the claim that if liberal internationalism is in part
about a vision for international society, then it also affects our duties to each other.
On this account, we are responsible for what happens beyond our borders, and owe
duties to those with whom we share both thick and thin relations. As discussed later
in the chapter, in the post-9/11 era of security concerns[11] and pre-emptive analysis,
liberal internationalism has taken on a more overtly interventionist intent, though
at times this has been clothed with the continuity of an earlier rhetoric of humanitarianism. For critics, these developments have meant that liberal internationalism
has become a diminished, and even dangerous, tradition in the post-1989 period,
veering towards a certain form of democratic idealism as signalled by the declaration by some of its proponents of the end of history. Liberal internationalists have
in general failed to embrace critical internationalist responses to the illiberalism of
much of international law's historical development. This reflects the ways in which
liberal internationalism has tended to be articulated more in terms of 'liberal states'
as exemplars, rather than in exploring more fully the broader virtues of internationalism. This has led to an over-simplification, and at times parochial self-limitation,
of what liberal internationalism might signify.[12] What is often realized in its place
is a rather thin form of networked and 'connective' power accompanied by the presumptive universalism of market economics.[13] Part of the trouble here too may have
been the political elite's embrace of liberal internationalism (and international law)
as a form of moral messaging and justification for conflict or economic domination
by conservative governments in the post-Cold War period.

Liberal internationalism can have different implications for both international
law and international relations, though it also signals their connection. The early
critics of liberal international law, EH Carr and Hans Morgenthau, who are
discussed in the next section, were also founders of international relations as a
discipline. For international legal theory, liberal internationalism connotes an
interest and engagement with international relations scholarship and ideas of the
network and of participation.[14] For some international relations theorists liberal

---

[11] See further, S Marks, 'What Has Become of the Emerging Right to Democratic Governance?'
(2011) 22 *European Journal of International Law* 507–24, at 513–15.

[12] S Marks, 'The End of History? Reflections on Some International Legal Theses' (1997) 3 *European
Journal of International Law* 449–77.

[13] A-M Slaughter, 'America's Edge: Power in the Networked Century' (2009) 88 *Foreign Affairs*
94–113.

[14] A-M Slaughter Burley, 'International Law and International Relations Theory: A Dual Agenda'
(1993) 87 *American Journal of International Law* 205–39; A-M Slaughter, 'International Law in
a World of Liberal States' (1995) 6 *European Journal of International Law* 503–38; A-M Slaughter,
A New World Order (Princeton University Press Princeton 2004).

internationalism signifies, in part, a commitment to an open, but rule-bounded, international system, where international law has relevance and practical utility.[15] For others such as Robert Keohane, there has been a broader movement to a form of institutional liberalism.[16]

In quite a different register, liberal internationalism is associated with moments or events rich with historical possibility, resonant of political revolution, industrial and technological transformation. For example, appeals to a form of liberal internationalism have been significant elements of movements for social and political change. Recent and powerful examples include the Charter 08 movement in China and the Arab Spring.[17] Important critical scholarship has also illuminated the ways in which neoliberal agendas have degraded liberal institutions and values.[18]

Yet another dimension is the way in which the material aspects of the liberal peace have centred on facilitating trade among nations—exemplified by the WTO framework for trade liberalization.[19] The role of a free market between states is a key concern of liberal internationalism. Economic interdependence is figured as a central goal and mechanism for achieving liberal peace. This has been accompanied by the opening up of markets as part of rule of law development following 1989. As Chimni notes, however, what is '[o]verlooked...is the role played by international economic and political structures and institutions in perpetuating the dependency of third world peoples and in generating conflict within them'.[20]

It is also true that liberal internationalism's critics have sometimes themselves shared liberal and/or functionalist visions of the international order, which have operated in tension with broader possibilities for re-appraisal of 'internationalism', whether liberal, socialist, radical, or conservative. Law and international law have been so implicated in the liberal political project that our efforts at critique to date have tended to illuminate problems of power, indeterminacy, inequality, and hubris, but at the expense of a wider interest in normative concerns. As the next section will show, the turn to origins, history, and narrative within the discipline perhaps offers a more productive means of searching for self-understanding.

---

[15] GJ Ikenberry, 'The Future of the Liberal World Order: Internationalism after America' (2011) 90 *Foreign Affairs* 56–68.

[16] RO Keohane, 'Twenty Years of Institutional Liberalism' (2012) 26 *International Relations* 125–38.

[17] See further 'China's Charter 08' (P Link trans) [2009] 56(1) *New York Review of Books* <http://www.nybooks.com/articles/archives/2009/jan/15/chinas-charter-08/> [accessed 25 February 2016]; A Sa'adah, '"Homeless in Tahrir": From Hope to Anguish in the Middle East' (2015) 47 *International Journal of Middle East Studies* 153–68.

[18] W Brown, 'Neo-Liberalism and the End of Liberal Democracy' (2003) 7(1) *Theory & Event* np.

[19] DZ Cass, *The Constitutionalization of the World Trade Organization: Legitimacy, Democracy, and Community in the International Trading System* (OUP Oxford 2005).

[20] BS Chimni, 'Third World Approaches to International Law: A Manifesto' (2006) 8 *International Community Law Review* 3–27, at 16.

3 EVENTS

Liberal internationalism is often presented in international legal scholarship as a response to historical 'events' and as heralding change and reform, framed through a narrative of progress from war to peace, from division to union, or from anarchy to government. Where there is uncertainty in approaching world government or community, there is a form of transcendence and cosmopolitanism offered in the arc of world history. Indeed Martti Koskenniemi has reflected on the difficulty for international law to exist without some form of guiding progress narrative: international law is 'for' humanity.[21] However, important scholarship regarding 'the event' points to various ways in which events can both produce and foreclose possibility and renewal in international law terms. As Fleur Johns, Richard Joyce, and Sundhya Pahuja reflect: '[c]aught between irruption and containment, events, then, seem to confront international law in a contradictory way'.[22] Consideration of key events can lead to a teleological view of history and international law's development, but can also draw into view the agency and layering of responsibility across the field, its institutions, and participants.

International lawyers need not be constrained by the discipline of chronology or the contextualism of certain forms of historical practice. Rather as Anne Orford writes of international law's relationship to its intellectual history: '[t]he past, far from being gone, is constantly being retrieved as a source or rationalisation of present obligation'.[23] It is in such a fashion that the discipline can reclaim the concept of liberal internationalism, both understanding it in its various contexts, but also redeploying it anew. Liberal internationalism might be understood as both an object for critique and as a rather challenging set of ideas about the kind of international law and community which might yet be possible. How has it then been understood by the discipline thus far, and how might that story be complicated?

As noted earlier, when international lawyers think of liberal internationalists, we often begin by turning to the enduring influence of Immanuel Kant and notions of a perpetual liberal peace.[24] Or else we might consider the late nineteenth-century international law with its emphasis on society and the development of a 'collective (European) conscience' and international sensibility.[25] Also often mentioned is US President Woodrow Wilson, his 'Fourteen Points', and the interwar rise and failure

---

[21] M Koskenniemi, 'Law, Teleology and International Relations: An Essay in Counterdisciplinarity' (2012) 26 *International Relations* 3–34, at 5.

[22] F Johns, R Joyce, and S Pahuja, 'Introduction' in F Johns, R Joyce, and S Pahuja (eds), *Events: The Force of International Law* (Routledge Abingdon 2011) 1–17, at 4.

[23] A Orford, 'On International Legal Method' (2013) 1 *London Review of International Law* 166–97, at 175.

[24] See 'Toward Perpetual Peace' (n 7).   [25] *Gentle Civilizer of Nations* (n 4) 51.

of the League of Nations.[26] Here then 1918 marks a significant event in the familiar history of liberal internationalism, marking a turn to the development of multilateral institutional settings (and also the establishment of the Permanent Court of International Justice in 1922).

But liberal internationalism's historical trajectory is far less certain than its familiar retelling, for key events and texts soon lead both to conflict and critique. The Fourteen Points may represent a renewal of liberal internationalism in the wake of the First World War, with their orientation towards open and public diplomacy, peace, colonial reform, and international organization and treaty-making, but they soon came to be seen by critics in the interwar period as wishful thinking and naïve. For example, EH Carr and Hans Morgenthau saw liberal internationalism as representing a certain kind of institutional idealism based on the false hope of some notion of eventual world government if not perpetual peace. Carr prophetically concluded on the eve of the Second World War:

In theories of international law, utopia tends to predominate over morality to an extent unparalleled in other branches of jurisprudence. Moreover, this tendency is greatest at periods when anarchy is most prevalent in the practice of nations. During the nineteenth century, a comparatively orderly period in international affairs, international jurisprudence took on a realist complexion. Since 1919, natural law has resumed its sway, and theories of international law have become markedly more utopian than at any previous time.[27]

More overt in his realist critique of the liberal internationalism of the interwar years was Hans Morgenthau. Morgenthau was withering in his assessment of the discipline of international law and its liberal internationalist tendencies in between the wars, writing that '[i]nstead of asking whether the devices were adequate to the problems which they were supposed to solve, it was the general attitude of the internationalists to take the appropriateness of the devices for granted and to blame the facts for the failure'.[28] International law was disconnected from events.

The war years also brought changes which would come to vastly expand the reach and practice of international law, with the *Atlantic Charter* (1941) prefiguring the *Charter of the United Nations* (1945). This was a high point for ideas of a New Deal-style welfare state, with supplementary notions of internationalism

---

[26] 'President Woodrow Wilson's Fourteen Points (8 January 1918)' <http://avalon.law.yale.edu/20th_century/wilson14.asp> [accessed 25 February 2016]. For a broader analysis of the League of Nations era, see D Kennedy, 'The Move to Institutions' (1987) 8 *Cardozo Law Review* 841–988; A Mills and T Stephens, 'Challenging the Role of Judges in Slaughter's Liberal Theory of International Law' (2005) 18 *Leiden Journal of International Law* 1–30, at 4–7.

[27] EH Carr, *The Twenty Years' Crisis 1919–1939: An Introduction to the Study of International Relations* (Macmillan London 1939) at 224.

[28] HJ Morgenthau, 'Positivism, Functionalism, and International Law' (1940) 34 *American Journal of International Law* 260–84, at 260; cf HJ Morgenthau, *Politics among Nations: The Struggle for Power and Peace* (Knopf New York 1948).

embodying a commitment to free markets as well as to redistribution, development, aid, and even self-determination. This itself involved pulling back from more
cosmopolitan notions of world government, whilst retaining a focus on institution-
building, reform, rule creation, and the judicial settlement of disputes.[29] Liberal
internationalism was for a time re-animated by the creation of the United Nations
(UN), the international bill of rights, Bretton Woods institutions, and the beginnings of international criminal justice at Nuremburg and Tokyo.

But the age of rights and international institutions was an age of ideological
division and realist statecraft. Liberal internationalism was connected to a
hegemon, the US, and its allies in Europe, while the new order was still rather
statist in character with a commitment to formal sovereign equality, tempered by
the emergence of the individual as a subject of international human rights law.
Its key commitment to international institution-building, treaty-making, and
multilateral mechanisms for international peace and security, financial order,
trade, and development, was supplemented by developing forms of executive and
juridical power.[30] It was also a time of conflict. Though often narrated as a point
of departure, and even an originary moment, Martti Koskenniemi is dismissive
of the significance of 1945 in terms of the development of international theory,
remarking that:

The Second World War did not end in a blueprint for a new international law. There
was little discussion about international law 'ideas'—apart from dismissing them as utterly unreal or counterproductive. A pragmatic spirit accompanied the outbreak of the
Cold War.[31]

Events of the Cold War period were also of significance for the direction and shape
of liberal internationalism. The development of a number of its current limitations
may in fact relate more closely to the ideological stalemate of the Cold War period
accompanied by the threat of nuclear war, the cultural imperialism of various
forms of US and Soviet public diplomacy, and the idea that the international community was divided into liberal and illiberal states or blocs. The legacy of this
period is illustrated in a variety of areas. For example, it can be seen in uncertainty
regarding regulation of the media and the internet, or in the sidelining of the issue
of aggression in international criminal law. It is also evidenced by the ambivalence

---

[29] Some US international law scholars remained interested in (if not world government) the reform and revitalization of the UN, including giving it a greater representative character and enforcement capabilities: see eg LB Sohn and G Clark, *World Peace through World Law* (Harvard University
Press Cambridge MA 1958).

[30] See further G Simpson, *Great Powers and Outlaw States: Unequal Sovereigns in the International
Legal Order* (CUP Cambridge 2004) chs 6 and 9; A Orford, *International Authority and the
Responsibility to Protect* (CUP Cambridge 2011) ch 2.

[31] M Koskenniemi, 'International Law in the World of Ideas' in J Crawford and M Koskenniemi
(eds), *The Cambridge Companion to International Law* (CUP Cambridge 2012) 47–63, at 55.

felt about the work of rule of law mechanisms in development terms and the place of poverty alleviation in international agendas. Further examples include ongoing debates regarding the hierarchy of human rights and of the suitable frame through which to approach questions of peace, security, and intervention.

From this division developed powerful schools of Western international legal theory such as the New Haven approach of Myres McDougal, a variant of liberal internationalism. New Haven set itself objective policy goals backed by a claim to rigour and the explanatory power of social science, but which in key historical responses, such as to the Vietnam War, came to be seen as offering a particularly US-centric and consequently rather limited vision of the possibilities of international law and society.[32] International law was to serve foreign policy interests,[33] but there remained visionary and even idealistic variants of the New Haven school's approach.[34]

While the New Haven school and its fellow travellers within the field focused on the development of policy, with a goal of determining a framework for rational decision-making and efficient institutions, this was also a time of great upheaval and internationalist energy in the form of increasing agitation for reform and for substantive forms of equality within the international system.[35] These movements have been largely left out of the story of liberal internationalism or have been characterized as oppositional to its progress.

Perhaps it is time to question this absence and to reclaim (or reconsider) the internationalism of nonliberal figures such as Marcus Garvey or Ho Chi Minh, whose motivations can also be traced to reforming the otherwise illiberal colonial tendencies within the discipline?[36] And what of possible connections between the culture of liberalism, the emergence of the welfare state, ideas of collective responsibility and the related internationalism involved in efforts to undermine the unjust

---

[32] See further MS McDougal, HD Lasswell, and L Chen, *Human Rights and World Public Order: The Basic Policies of an International Law of Human Dignity* (Yale University Press New Haven 1980); MS McDougal, HD Lasswell, and WM Reisman, 'The World Constitutive Process of Authoritative Decision: Part 1' (1967) 19 *Journal of Legal Education* 253–300; MS McDougal, HD Lasswell, and WM Reisman, 'The World Constitutive Process of Authoritative Decision: Part 2' (1967) 19 *Journal of Legal Education* 403–37; MS McDougal, HD Lasswell, and WM Reisman, 'Theories about International Law: Prologue to a Configurative Jurisprudence' (1968) 8 *Virginia Journal of International Law* 188–299. See also H Saberi, 'Yale's Policy Science and International Law: Between Legal Formalism and Policy Conceptualism' in this *Handbook*.

[33] 'International Law in the World of Ideas' (n 31) 55.

[34] Richard Falk is of interest here. Falk's work is broad in scope, developing in a different direction to McDougal and the New Haven school, returning to questions of democratic world 'governance': see eg RA Falk, *On Humane Governance: Toward a New Global Politics* (Polity Press Cambridge 1995).

[35] S Pahuja, *Decolonising International Law: Development, Economic Growth and the Politics of Universality* (CUP Cambridge 2011).

[36] I am indebted to Rose Parfitt for this provocative insight.

distributive consequences of the international economic order, the broader movement of Third World Approaches to International Law or in more contemporary scholarship focusing on the decolonization of the discipline?[37] Indeed the TWAIL critique offers an important lens through which to consider the darker imperialist origins of international law, whilst pointing to a different kind of international law that might yet still be possible.[38] It is time to view liberal internationalism from a range of perspectives and to unshackle the concept from tired and over-familiar notions of a *Pax Americana*. Liberal internationalism might be more complex than policy-makers or realist critics would have us believe. It is, after all conflictual and hopeful in character, responsive to the Enlightenment project and also to the violence of Empire or reformation. As John Docker has written,

[w]hat is admirable in the cosmopolitanism, internationalism, toleration and interest in difference and plurality in Enlightenment philosophy, dissident thinking about religion, and poetics is indeed in tension with the race-thinking associated with colonialism, empire and imperium . . .[39]

Some thinkers within the liberal tradition have attempted to offer a more self-critical and complex account of international law's progress and failings. Guglielmo Verdirame has, from a distinctively European liberal perspective, hinted at a richer tradition of liberalism in international thought which has been left out of view in the embrace of rather reductive versions of liberal internationalism such as the New Haven approach. In a wide-ranging essay considering the state of law and strategy after Iraq and 9/11, Verdirame highlights the oversimplification of liberalism in critical international legal perspectives whilst offering a critique of the lack of imagination and intellectual rigour with which mainstream Western international lawyers and diplomats have responded to the tectonic shifts of 1989.[40] For Verdirame the end of the Cold War was a lost intellectual opportunity for international law to shift its paradigm, even as regards a meaningful entrenchment of democracy.[41]

---

[37] M Bedjaoui, *Towards a New International Economic Order* (Holmes & Meier New York 1979); A Anghie and BS Chimni, 'Third World Approaches to International Law and Individual Responsibility in Internal Conflict' in SR Ratner and A-M Slaughter (eds), *The Methods of International Law* (American Society of International Law Washington DC 2004) 185–210, at 185–95; 'Third World Approaches to International Law: A Manifesto' (n 20); *Decolonising International Law* (n 35); M Craven, *The Decolonization of International Law: State Succession and the Law of Treaties* (OUP Oxford 2007). Again Richard Falk is of interest here as he connects both with this scholarship and with a US scholarship regarding internationalism, democracy, and peace: see 'International Law and International Relations Theory: A Dual Agenda' (n 14) 211–12.

[38] A Anghie, *Imperialism, Sovereignty and the Making of International Law* (CUP Cambridge 2005).

[39] J Docker, *The Origins of Violence: Religion, History and Genocide* (Pluto Press London 2008) at 215.

[40] G Verdirame, 'The "Sinews of Peace": International Law, Strategy and the Prevention of War' (2006) 77 *British Yearbook of International Law* 83–162.

[41] Ibid 123.

The end of the Cold War in 1989 offered the event of events for many contemporary adherents of liberal internationalism.[42] The collapse of the Soviet Union and the broader strategic ramifications of 1989 brought ideas of a re-unified Europe into closer focus and saw a turn in international legal scholarship towards neo-Kantian conceptions of a liberal peace which were triumphally offered in place of Cold War division.[43] Emblematic of this move, which was accompanied by renewed interest in the insights of international relations scholarship, is the work of Anne-Marie Slaughter who championed an influential approach to international law and relations premised on the centrality of liberal values, law and the transnational operation of a 'community of courts'. Slaughter and others argued for democratic values to be central to arguments for legitimacy within international law and for the recasting of the international system as a 'world of liberal states'.[44]

Other manifestations of liberal internationalism involved reform and revival of the UN as a key actor in a range of activities including rule of law, development, international criminal justice and peacekeeping.[45] There was also the steady proliferation (and increased use) of international courts and tribunals, leading subsequently to questions of institutional hierarchy, of normative conflict and even fragmentation. But liberal internationalism redux offered more than simply additional international organizations, increased executive power and the growth of tribunals. The turn to humanitarianism within the field of human rights[46] was accompanied by an active NGO and civil society sector. Liberal internationalism found new avenues in theories of judicial and civil society networks and was re-energized by the connective possibilities of an information society driven by the internet.

A key debate, catalyzed by the end of the Cold War, concerned the relationship between international law and democracy. Some scholars such as Thomas Franck combined both a theoretical interest in 'fairness' as an organizing liberal principle for international law, with arguments for an 'emerging norm of democratic

---

[42] For an extended analysis of the ongoing impact of ideas of the liberal peace upon the structuring of international law, see R Buchan, *International Law and the Construction of the Liberal Peace* (Hart Oxford 2013).

[43] FR Tesón, 'The Kantian Theory of International Law' (1992) 92 *Columbia Law Review* 53–102.

[44] See A-M Burley, 'Law among Liberal States: Liberal Internationalism and the Act of State Doctrine' (1992) 92 *Columbia Law Review* 1907–96; 'International Law in a World of Liberal States' (n 14). Slaughter has also sought to ground her internationalism in a form of non-utopian and often domestically focused liberalism as a defence against realism: see 'International Law and International Relations Theory: A Dual Agenda' (n 14) 237–9.

[45] This is paralleled by the neoliberal international relations theory with its focus on institutions: see eg 'Twenty Years of Institutional Liberalism' (n 16); A Orford, 'Moral Internationalism and the Responsibility to Protect' (2013) 24 *European Journal of International Law* 83–108, at 98–108.

[46] *International Authority and the Responsibility to Protect* (n 30) 102; A Orford, *Reading Humanitarian Intervention: Human Rights and the Use of Force in International Law* (CUP Cambridge 2003); D Rieff, *A Bed for the Night: Humanitarianism in Crisis* (Simon & Schuster New York 2002); D Kennedy, 'The International Human Rights Movement: Part of the Problem?' (2002) 15 *Harvard Human Rights Journal* 101–25.

governance'.[47] As with liberalism in international law there remained disagreement as to what might constitute 'democracy' and how it might be fostered. Franck's proposal appeared both innovative and rather technical in its emphasis on the forms of democratic governance, such as free and fair elections, at the expense of deeper animating questions regarding the quality of democracy which might be achieved. Similarly historical arguments for the spread of democracy in terms of numbers of liberal states and their achievement of peace often overlooked the divisions within and between them, along with bigger substantive questions regarding the mixed experience of democracy in international law. The most that could be claimed was for a 'separate peace' amongst liberal states.[48] A broader idea of what world peace might look like appeared unrealistic to many.

Susan Mark's critique of the revival of liberal internationalism in the form of the 'democratic norm thesis' points to the ways in which ideology critique can enhance our understanding of the complexity and necessity of democracy. Marks argued for a 'principle of democratic inclusion', recognizing that democracy operates ideologically but also as a transformative and critical ideal within international law.[49] It typifies a critique from which liberal internationalism has, for many, never recovered. The contemporary practice of liberal internationalism reeks of moralism, parochialism, hypocrisy, and imperial ambition—has it lost its analytical and rhetorical power?

4 RENEWAL?

Is liberal internationalism exhausted by the turn of recent events? Are we now overly familiar (and consequently disenchanted) with liberal internationalism, to the point where it has lost some of its critical purchase and perhaps also its coherence? As Raymond Geuss has written:

A particular world-view dominates the contemporary political scene. It is composed of the assumption that societies should be organized as modern states conjoined with a

---

[47] TM Franck, *Fairness in International Law and Institutions* (Clarendon Press Oxford 1995); TM Franck, 'The Emerging Right to Democratic Governance' (1992) 86 *American Journal of International Law* 46–91; 'The End of History?' (n 12) 460–3.

[48] 'Kant and Liberal Internationalism' (n 8) 230.

[49] S Marks, *The Riddle of All Constitutions: International Law, Democracy, and the Critique of Ideology* (OUP Oxford 2000) at 148–51; cf 'What Has Become of the Emerging Right to Democratic Governance?' (n 11).

commitment to a form of liberalism, democracy as a form of government, and a system of individual human rights. This conjunction, in my view, does not make much sense.[50]

This necessitates examination of both the critique of liberal internationalism and the possibility of its renewal. Here it is useful to think of the attempt to resituate debates over participation, democracy, and pluralism in international law within a fresh context of technological revivalism, driven in part by the internationalism of the internet and digital media.[51] The possibility of such transformation should not be discounted—it is important to recognize the exclusion which is formative of every community, but also, as Koskenniemi has urged, to 'negotiate' the exclusion and 'widen its horizon'.[52] For example, Karen Knop has pointed to the ways in which self-determination was an important and critical facet of liberal internationalism for women in the interwar years and beyond.[53]

Let us not forget liberal internationalism's translation into moral internationalism and its contemporary forms of intervention. Even in its milder forms such as 'rule of law' advocacy and implementation, liberal internationalism can be connected to the practice of violence, reflected in China Miéville's haunting conclusion that: '[a] world structured around international law cannot but be one of imperialist violence. The chaotic and bloody world around us *is the rule of law*'.[54] But international law is not merely a proxy for an internationalized rule of law. Failing to separate the rhetoric of diplomacy from the normative intent of law risks losing some of the deeper insights of Kant and others regarding the significance of the development of a richer conception of international society and the goal of perpetual peace.[55] International law is connected with and productive of violence, but it is also a mechanism for peace and sociality across borders.

In her study of the development of the Responsibility to Protect doctrine (R2P) Anne Orford has argued that '[i]n grounding the authority of the state and the international community on the capacity to protect, the concept represents a significant shift in thinking about the lawfulness of authority in the modern world' and thus heralds a major normative shift in thinking about international relations and law.[56] Orford argues that:

[t]he international legal solution to the tension between individual freedom and worldly authority has classically been liberal—it depends upon preservation of a space within

[50] R Geuss, *History and Illusion in Politics* (CUP Cambridge 2001) at 153.

[51] See HR Clinton, 'Remarks on Internet Freedom' (21 January 2010) <http://www.state.gov/secretary/20092013clinton/rm/2010/01/135519.htm> [accessed 25 February 2016]. For a biting critique see E Morozov, *The Net Delusion: How Not to Liberate the World* (Allen Lane London 2011).

[52] *Gentle Civilizer of Nations* (n 4) 517.

[53] K Knop, 'Of the Male Persuasion: The Power of Liberal Internationalism for Women' (1999) *American Society of International Law Proceedings* 177–85, at 177.

[54] *Between Equal Rights* (n 10) 319 (emphasis in original).

[55] For a counter-perspective grounded in a more nuanced account of European liberalism and with equal critical energy, see 'The "Sinews of Peace"' (n 40) 160–2.

[56] *International Authority and the Responsibility to Protect* (n 30) 41.

which autonomous subjects can freely choose to subject themselves to authority and bind themselves to the order that they bring into being.[57]

She suggests that in place of the classically liberal resolution of that tension, we are witnessing a new stress on the notion of authority. Whilst it is not possible to resolve that tension, a reconsideration of liberal internationalism might assist in bringing more fully into view both normative and practical questions relating to the ongoing structuring of the international system. A re-appraisal of the normative potential of liberal internationalism's commitment to a culture of tolerance and inclusivity, might yet herald a response to that development in international legal theoretical terms.

In particular, it may be that the decline of US power will enable further (and different) explorations of ideas regarding the place of international society in our system of international law. The English school of international relations offers a distinctive commitment to international society and a useful departure from US approaches. It also points to the need for liberal internationalism to rise above parochial concerns and state-centrism.[58] The end of the American century has led to much soul-searching within US liberal internationalist scholarship in both international law and international relations. But perhaps the concept's greatest hope for renewal lies in its de-coupling from idealized domestic preferences translated for international audiences elsewhere, and in its re-appraisal as a more inclusive and international method in international law and relations; one that is both practical and yet offers a theory of international society, not merely a justification for dubious means in the name of neoliberal ends.

The defenders of liberal internationalism are taking stock and making their argument for renewal in a variety of ways.[59] G John Ikenberry's recent work has focused on the ways in which a liberal international order may not in fact pass with the fading pre-eminence of US power. His argument rests in part on a broader view of the development of liberal internationalism, dating back at least to the Peace of Westphalia in 1648, and in looking forward to China and other rising powers' perceived self-interest in maintaining the multilateral and open system of international relations and trade.[60] Barriers to entry are, on this account, falling, yet the underlying rules of engagement will remain secure. Ikenberry concludes that:

. . . the liberal international order has sown the seeds of its own discontent, since, paradoxically, the challenges facing it now—the rise of non-Western states and new transnational

---

[57] *International Authority and the Responsibility to Protect* (n 30) 209–10.

[58] See further T Dunne, *Inventing International Society: A History of the English School* (St Martin's Press New York 1998).

[59] For an earlier iteration see S Hoffmann, 'The Crisis of Liberal Internationalism' (1995) 98 *Foreign Policy* 159–77.

[60] For an attempt to factor China into the Kantian peace debate, see MV Suri, 'Conceptualizing China within the Kantian Peace' (2013) 54 *Harvard International Law Journal* 219–58.

threats—are artifacts of its success. But the solutions to these problems—integrating rising powers and tackling problems co-operatively—will lead the order's old guardians and new stakeholders to a new agenda of renewal.[61]

Samuel Moyn has critiqued Ikenberry and liberal internationalism's 'new agenda [which] is to figure out how to encode its values on the world order before the arrival of…the post-American era'.[62] Renewal will have to look further afield.

Liberal internationalism signals progressive as well as more authoritarian prospects for international law and any renewal needs to look further than a revival of Kant's ideas. The ideas and practice of internationalism are much more deeply embedded within the discipline and over a much wider arc of history.[63] The challenge remains whether it can offer a participatory and authoritative frame for understanding the discipline and its potential for evolution. Hope for liberal internationalism's renewal may in part stem from broadening the frame through which it can be viewed and from the 'realisation that there is not one liberal internationalism but several'.[64] Liberal internationalism is not tied to one meaning, one event or series of events, nor even solely to international law. It is a grand political theory that has offered a vocabulary for liberal elites at a time of US hegemony. But it could still offer international law and its constituents an opportunity for greater peaceful interaction and a means to revisit the project of international society.

Rethinking the founding conception of international society offers one way forward. Whilst conceptions of 'internet freedom' or an 'information society' will not bypass earlier critiques of a form of democracy within international law, they may bring new conceptions of the social and new technologies for community-formation (or at least for interaction and communication).[65] But might the flourishing of the internet yet intensify a form of communicative capitalism and threaten to flatten and privatize these transnational mechanisms for renewal and exchange?[66] Even with that potential in mind, international society still represents an ideal worth preserving. As Tim Dunne and Matt McDonald reflect: 'we should look to a humanitarian internationalism in which greater "voice opportunities" exist for those previously silenced and where institutions are measured in terms

---

[61] 'The Future of the Liberal World Order' (n 15) 68; cf GJ Ikenberry, *Liberal Leviathan: The Origins, Crisis, and Transformation of the American World Order* (Princeton University Press Princeton 2011).

[62] S Moyn, 'Soft Sells: On Liberal Internationalism' *The Nation* (3 October 2011) 40–3, at 43.

[63] *Imperialism, Sovereignty and the Making of International Law* (n 38) ch 1; M Koskenniemi, 'Empire and International Law: The Real Spanish Contribution' (2011) 61 *University of Toronto Law Journal* 1–36.

[64] T Dunne and M McDonald, 'The Politics of Liberal Internationalism' (2013) 50 *International Politics* 1–17, at 9.

[65] D Joyce, 'Media Witnesses: Human Rights in an Age of Digital Media' (2013) 8 *Intercultural Human Rights Law Review* 231–80.

[66] J Dean, *Publicity's Secret: How Technoculture Capitalizes on Democracy* (Cornell University Press Ithaca 2002).

of how far they advance global justice'.[67] Perhaps after all, international lawyers can make liberal internationalism strange again and widen its, and our, collective horizons. The enduring significance of the concept lies in its normative framework for social interaction on the international plane and in its connection to ideas of peaceful co-existence.

---

[67] 'The Politics of Liberal Internationalism' (n 64) 14.

CHAPTER 24

....

FEMINIST APPROACHES TO INTERNATIONAL LAW

....

DIANNE OTTO

1 INTRODUCTION

....

THE arrival of 'feminist approaches to international law' is often traced to an article of the same name, co-authored by Hilary Charlesworth, Christine Chinkin, and Shelley Wright, published in the *American Journal of International Law* (*AJIL*) in 1991.[1] Yet feminists have sought to influence the development of international law at least since the early twentieth century, when women's international peace organizations supported the development of international law and the establishment of international institutions as a means to resolve international disputes peacefully.[2] A second originary account, also in wide circulation, is that feminism arrived in international law in the early 1990s by another route, with the global campaign to have women's rights recognized as human rights and, in particular, the demand that violence against women be recognized as a violation of international human rights law.[3] Not only does this second account deny the long history of feminist

[1] H Charlesworth, C Chinkin, and S Wright, 'Feminist Approaches to International Law' (1991) 85 *American Journal of International Law* 613–45.

[2] 'Resolutions Adopted by the International Congress of Women at the Hague, May 1, 1915' in J Addams, EG Balch, and A Hamilton (eds), *Women at the Hague: The International Congress of Women and Its Results* (Macmillan & Company New York 1915) 150–9, at 154–5 (Resolution 11).

[3] See C Bunch, 'Women's Rights as Human Rights: Toward a Re-Vision of Human Rights' (1990) 12 *Human Rights Quarterly* 486–98; C Bunch and N Reilly, *Demanding Accountability: The Global*

engagement, it also reduces feminist aspirations to a narrow, though important, band of issues in international human rights law, betraying the diversity of the doctrinal and substantive areas of feminist interventions in international law. The account of 'feminist approaches' that I tell in this chapter is not one of origins, generations, or progress, but of hope and despair, paradox and conundrum, repetition and conflict, and the importance of history in the present.

Both of the abovementioned arrival stories mark moments of hope in feminist engagement with international law, although they were also the product of despair about the apparent imperviousness of international law to feminist perspectives. By the early 1990s, this despair had many dimensions. It included the continuing lack of women's participation in the international institutions that made and applied the law,[4] the marginalization of 'women's issues' by their location in specialist institutions and legal instruments,[5] the ongoing failure to treat women as fully autonomous rights-bearing subjects of the law,[6] the limited scope of state responsibility,[7] and the inability of 'humanitarian' law to provide robust protections for civilians.[8] There was also growing awareness of the liberal bias and arrogance of many western feminist perspectives,[9] and concern that, where feminist ideas were incorporated into international legal and institutional practices, they were susceptible to serving, rather than challenging, the imperial mission of international law.[10]

The hope that emerged from this surge of discontent led feminist international lawyers in different directions. On the one hand, more critical feminist analyses were forged, for which the *AJIL* article was a beacon. International law's impermeability was understood as structural; as embedded in its normative assumptions and institutional arrangements, which all needed substantial feminist reconstruction. On the other hand, the demand that violence against women be taken seriously as an international legal issue was an effort to break through institutional

Campaign and Vienna Tribunal for Women's Human Rights (Rutgers University Center for Women's Global Leadership New Brunswick and UNIFEM New York 1994).

[4] H Charlesworth, 'Transforming the United Men's Club: Feminist Futures for the United Nations' (1994) 4 *Transnational Law & Contemporary Problems* 421–54.

[5] AC Byrnes, 'The "Other" Human Rights Treaty Body: The Work of the Committee on the Elimination of Discrimination against Women' (1989) 14 *Yale Journal of International Law* 1–67.

[6] HB Holmes, 'A Feminist Analysis of the *Universal Declaration of Human Rights*' in C Gould (ed), *Beyond Domination: New Perspectives on Women and Philosophy* (Rowman & Allanheld Totowa NJ 1983) 250–64.

[7] C Romany, 'Women as *Aliens*: A Feminist Critique of the Public/Private Distinction in International Human Rights Law' (1993) 6 *Harvard Human Rights Journal* 87–125.

[8] J Gardam, 'A Feminist Analysis of Certain Aspects of International Humanitarian Law' (1988) 12 *Australian Yearbook of International Law* 265–78.

[9] IR Gunning, 'Arrogant Perception, World-Travelling and Multicultural Feminism: The Case of Female Genital Surgeries' (1991) 23 *Columbia Human Rights Law Review* 189–248.

[10] CT Mohanty, 'Under Western Eyes: Feminist Scholarship and Colonial Discourses' (1988) 30 *Feminist Review* 61–88.

resistance by building a mass protest movement around the brutal material realities of many women's everyday lives, demanding legal reform and robust accountability mechanisms that, it was hoped, would make an immediate difference in women's lives. Together, the two directions that feminist hope took in the early 1990s illustrate one of the conundrums at the heart of feminist engagements with international law—namely, how to engage critically with the law's gendered languages and practices, while simultaneously seeking to use it to advance women's rights and world peace in the present.

While feminist encounters with international law are always fraught with danger for feminist ideas, the reverse is also true: that law's claims to objectivity, universality, and neutrality, and its privileging of only certain 'lives that matter',[11] are endangered by feminism. In what follows I tell of encounters between feminism and international law in four sections. I start by outlining the diversity of feminist visions for (and against) international law to highlight the dynamism of the field, the contestation between its various political and legal commitments, and the different ways that the feminist subject of law is conceived. I suggest that the field is best understood as a network of circulating ideas about theory, method, and practice, rather than, as it is often described, a series of relatively autonomous and competing strands or generations of feminist thought. Secondly, I canvas the range of critical analyses that feminists have developed in the wake of the *AJIL* article, traces of which can now be found in every sub-discipline of international law. Thirdly, I discuss the trajectories of feminist reform projects in international law, and the contradictory effects of the intuition that a focus on addressing violence against women would provide an effective springboard to broader legal change. I conclude by highlighting the paradoxes of feminist engagement with international law and argue that the practices of critique and reform, and their productive tensions, are essential to resisting the law's colonization of feminist politics and keeping feminist imaginaries of a better world alive. It is in the interstices of hope and despair, conundrum and paradox, that feminists have the best chance of understanding how international law might yet be a means for promoting feminist change.

2 Visions

The term 'feminist', which I have already made liberal use of, needs some initial explanation. Arvonne Fraser describes feminism's 'original meaning' as 'the

---

[11] See J Butler, *Precarious Life: The Powers of Mourning and Violence* (Verso London 2003).

theory of and struggle for equality for women' and their political, economic, and social inclusion.[12] However, for many feminists, the vision of women's inclusion and equality in the existing social and legal order is inadequate. Their ambitions are more transformative, seeking to challenge the masculinist ways of thinking that are embedded in the underlying templates that determine what equality and inclusion look like, discursively and in practice. While feminist visions of international law all imagine a future where sex/gender is a category of analysis that not only matters, but makes a difference, just what difference is hoped for, beyond endangering its masculinist certainties, is influenced by feminism's many genealogies. A well-worn method of representing this multiplicity is to identify various genres of feminist legal scholarship, in terms of their philosophical and political commitments.[13] In international law, these taxonomies usually adopt 'liberal' feminism as their starting point, moving on to describe other genres generationally as, in various ways, responses to the limitations of liberalism like: 'radical' and 'cultural' feminisms which focus on women's subordination (rather than inequality) as the foundational site of oppression; 'Marxist' and 'socialist' feminisms which centre attention on the exploitation of women's economic and reproductive labour; 'critical race' and 'postcolonial' feminisms which position sex/gender as one of multiple intersecting axes of oppression in the larger context of imperial power; and 'poststructural' and 'queer' feminisms which understand the identities and practices associated with gender and sexuality as fluid and multiple, rather than naturally determined and dualistic.[14]

Elements from several of these approaches are likely to be found in most feminist projects in international law; although there is no doubt that radical feminist ideas have been very influential in recent years.[15] This influence has focused attention on women's sexual subordination and victimhood, making many feminists uncomfortable because it has had the paradoxical effect of granting new legitimacy to long-standing protective gender tropes,[16] rather than challenging them. While identifying the dominant strand(s) informing any particular feminist intervention is empowering and critical knowledge, it is often more useful to think of feminist ideas in international law as operating as a network, aspects of which are drawn

---

[12] AS Fraser, 'Becoming Human: The Origins and Development of Women's Human Rights' (1999) 21 *Human Rights Quarterly* 853–906, at 859.

[13] See eg N Lacey, 'Feminist Legal Theory and the Rights of Women' in K Knop (ed), *Gender and Human Rights* (OUP Oxford 2004) 13–56.

[14] See eg H Charlesworth and C Chinkin, *The Boundaries of International Law: A Feminist Analysis* (Manchester University Press Manchester 2000) at 38–48.

[15] J Halley, *Split Decisions: How and Why to Take a Break from Feminism* (Princeton University Press Princeton 2006). Halley refers to these ideas as 'sexual subordination feminism': at 27.

[16] See J Halley et al., 'From the International to the Local in Feminist Legal Responses to Rape, Prostitution/Sex Work, and Sex Trafficking: Four Studies in Contemporary Governance Feminism' (2006) 29 *Harvard Journal of Law & Gender* 335–423.

upon depending on politics, history, context, strategy, and goals, rather than as parallel sets of ideas that function in isolation from or opposition to each other—although they can do this as well, and sometimes with paralyzing effects, as with opposing feminist views about whether prostitution should be regulated as work or criminalized as violence against women.[17] While such internal feminist debates foster the critical self-reflection that is part of the life-blood of feminism, it is important to work against the *stasis* that understanding feminism in terms of competing strands installs. It is more useful, and apt, to think of feminist approaches to international law as a shifting and contested network of ideas and allegiances that, in seeking to make sex/gender a central analytical category, draw on multiple and sometimes competing feminist perspectives and engage with other critical traditions in law. This approach makes visible those less dominant feminist ideas that remain engaged in a variety of ways, providing an abundant reservoir of historical and theoretical knowledge, grounded analyses, and experiential evidence with the power to trouble masculinist certitudes.

My search for more detail about the feminist visions of the future—feminist utopias, if you like—that have informed feminists' engagements with international law has not been very fruitful. While the starting point is usually the desire to change women's disadvantaged position vis-à-vis men around the world, there are many ways that a feminist might go about promoting such change, as I have already indicated. For some, the project is to realize the liberal humanist promises of universality and equality, while for others it is to struggle against neoliberal economic globalization and its deeply gendered inequitable effects. For some, the primary subject of feminist analysis is women, while for others the feminist subject includes women, men, and all other sex/gender identities, and for yet others she is an intersectionally constituted subject located in her specific history, especially her colonial history, and the many other vectors of disadvantage that have an influence on her situation, such as race, caste, indigeneity, sexuality, and economic status. However, even this does not exhaust the possible subjects of feminism, as gender is also an analytical system that attributes value to objects and ideas that have little or no relationship at all with sexed bodies and identities. In this approach, the subject of feminism is the entire discursive framework of international law, and the task is to reveal its reliance on gendered signs to order ways of thinking that legitimate and normalize an inequitable world order and then to radically reconstruct its entire conceptual framework. Doris Buss and Ambreena Manji describe this project as one of 'reading, negotiating and troubling boundaries' of the discipline of international law itself, in order to offer a 'more transgressive account' of its impact and tell a different story about its possibilities.[18]

---

[17] JA Chuang, 'Exploitation Creep and the Unmaking of Human Trafficking Law' (American University WCL Research Paper 2013) at 29–37 (copy on file with author).

[18] D Buss and A Manji, 'Introduction' in D Buss and A Manji (eds), *International Law: Modern Feminist Approaches* (Hart Portland 2005) 1–16, at 5.

What that radical reconstruction would look like, and what kind of world would be constituted and supported by it, relies on imagination and vision.[19] In what ways sex/gender would matter in a reimagined feminist world is an open question. There is no doubt that, for at least the past century, feminists have hoped, in vain, that international law would provide a means of securing international peace and security, and obviate the need for militaries and weapons. Linking this vision with some of the other feminist imaginaries in circulation, the shared vision might be described as a more egalitarian, inclusive, peaceful, just, and redistributive international order, that embraces those ethics and priorities currently belittled and marginalized as 'feminine'. Hilary Charlesworth and Christine Chinkin capture something of this vision when they imagine a feminist re-visioning of the list of *jus cogens* norms (the 'most essential' or peremptory rules of international law that can never be derogated from).[20] They suggest the list, which includes the prohibition of genocide, slavery, murder/disappearances, torture, prolonged arbitrary detention, and systematic racial discrimination, would be expanded to also include the right to peace, to food, to primary health care, to reproductive freedom, and, not least, to be free from systematic gender discrimination[21]—a different world indeed. However, thinking outside the confines of the discipline, while remaining firmly engaged with it, presents many challenges, as does keeping hold of the feminist subject, while continuing to resist her essentialization and domestication in legal texts and practices. Feminist dreams of a different and better future world have a crucial role to play in sustaining hope and fuelling creativity, resilience, persistence, and solidarity in the face of despair and continuing marginalization, and there is clearly a need for more of them.

3 CRITIQUE

Critique, as I use the term here, is a mode of engagement that aims to make visible the conceptual and structural underpinnings of legal discourse, in order to understand how, despite its claims to objectivity and universality, certain structures of inequality come to be naturalized and particular subjects are privileged while others are marginalized or excluded. Feminist structural critiques of international

---

[19] See eg DG Dallmeyer (ed), *Reconceiving Reality: Women and International Law* (American Society of International Law Washington DC 1993).

[20] H Charlesworth and C Chinkin, 'The Gender of *Jus Cogens*' (1993) 15 *Human Rights Quarterly* 63–76.

[21] Ibid 75.

law are located, not always comfortably, in the broader field of critical theories of international law. While drawing on the insights of other critical traditions, like postcolonial and queer theories, feminist critiques also present a challenge to many aspects of the critical tradition. The goal of critique is to open new possibilities for transformative change by scrutinizing international law's foundational claims and thereby revealing its allegiances to certain arrangements of power. Once revealed, the hope is that the underpinnings can be contested and reassembled to make it possible for law—a very different type of law in many critical imaginaries—to be engaged for more emancipatory ends. As Wendy Brown and Janet Halley put it, (left) critique 'facilitates discernment of how the very problem we want to solve is itself produced, and this may help us avoid entrenching or reproducing the problem in our solutions'.[22]

The critique offered by Charlesworth, Chinkin, and Wright in 1991 sought to expose the masculine bias of supposedly neutral international legal rules by examining some of their impacts on women's lives. They argued that international law is a 'thoroughly gendered system'[23] because its normative and institutional structures and practices privilege men and male power while masquerading as universal, making the law unreceptive to the voices and experiences of women.[24] Part of the conceptual scaffolding supporting this gendered operation, to which they draw particular attention, is the liberal distinction between public and private spheres. This distinction restricts the field of international law to what is considered public, working in a number of ways to locate issues of concern to women outside its boundaries.[25] One effect is to insulate matters considered to fall within the domestic jurisdiction of states from the purview of the international. They offer the example of the right to self-determination, where the treatment of women by claimant groups has never been identified as a factor relevant to determining worthy beneficiaries because it is considered an internal (private) issue.[26] Another effect is to consign arrangements within the domestic sphere to the realm of privacy, which serves to reinforce male power in families. Charlesworth, Chinkin, and Wright presage a feminist 'transformation' of international law, which would go beyond seeking to reform the present law and instead promote a fundamental restructuring of the discourse that would render patriarchal dominance unviable.[27]

Postcolonial feminist critiques have a particularly significant role to play in a field of law that has served European as well as masculinist genealogies of power. Charlesworth, Chinkin, and Wright wrestle with the issue of the different experiences of Third World and western women, and the propensity for the latter to

---

[22] W Brown and J Halley, 'Introduction' in W Brown and J Halley (eds), *Left Legalism/Left Critique* (Duke University Press Durham 2002) 1–37, at 27.
[23] 'Feminist Approaches to International Law' (n 1) 615.   [24] Ibid 644.
[25] For further development, see *The Boundaries of International Law: A Feminist Analysis* (n 14).
[26] 'Feminist Approaches to International Law' (n 1) 642–3.   [27] Ibid 644.

dominate, offering as a resolution that feminism must be reoriented so as to 'deal with the problems of the most oppressed women, rather than those of the most privileged'.[28] While this enables them to articulate a unified international feminist goal to achieve 'a rethinking and revision of those [male] structures and principles [of international law] which exclude most women's voices',[29] postcolonial scholars throw into question the extent to which a cohesive feminist project is possible, or even desirable. To start with, Third World feminisms are themselves diverse and marked by the constantly 'shifting ground' of political positions, as Vasuki Nesiah emphasizes in her examination of debates on veiling.[30] Further, postcolonial critiques are concerned with the 'double jeopardy' that colonialism has created for women in the postcolony, which gender analysis, by itself, can only partially explain and address.[31] It follows that an important feminist focus has been to examine the role that international law has played in compounding women's inequality in development initiatives. It has been shown, again and again, that the promotion of the developmental nation-state, in the wake of decolonization, has actually reduced women's access to economic resources, limited their educational opportunities, and increased their work burdens.[32] Neoliberal economic policies are in many respects compounding these problems by, for example, formalizing land ownership as a precondition of access to credit without regard to women's interests in land[33] and promoting women's equality as an instrumental value, necessary for the achievement of economic goals rather than as an end in itself.[34] Clearly, resisting the gendered recolonizing effects of economic liberalization necessitates also challenging the underlying neo-imperial framework of international political economy.

In light of the long history of feminist concern with the peaceful resolution of disputes, it is hardly surprising that the laws relating to the use of force (*jus ad bellum*) and the international humanitarian law rules that apply during armed conflict (*jus in bello*) have been an important focus for critique. Feminist scholars have closely interrogated the many claimed exceptions to the otherwise absolute prohibition of the use of force, critically examining how an exception is justified, whose interests it serves, and the gendered effects that flow from

---

[28] 'Feminist Approaches to International Law' (n 1) 621.   [29] Ibid.

[30] V Nesiah, 'The Ground beneath Her Feet: TWAIL Feminisms' in A Anghie, K Mickelson, and O Okafor (eds), *The Third World and International Order: Law, Politics and Globalization* (Martinus Nijhoff Boston 2003) 133–43.

[31] J Oloka-Onyango and S Tamale, '"The Personal Is Political" or Why Women's Rights Are Indeed Human Rights: An African Perspective on International Feminism' (1995) 17 *Human Rights Quarterly* 691–731.

[32] See eg E Boserup, *Women's Role in Economic Development* (Earthscan London 1970).

[33] A Manji, 'Eliminating Poverty? "Financial Inclusion", Access to Land, and Gender Equality in International Development' (2010) 73 *Modern Law Review* 985–1003.

[34] K Rittich, 'Engendering Development/Marketing Equality' (2003) 67 *Albany Law Review* 575–93.

its enactment, producing deeply unsettling analyses of many of the justifications offered.[35] While the invisibility of gender issues in the legal principles
supporting the use of force in self-determination struggles by colonial peoples
was an early focus,[36] humanitarian intervention in the name of halting widespread human rights abuses has more recently received sustained analysis, as
has its reframing as the responsibility to protect.[37] The critique is that humanitarianism functions as a complement to militarism by enabling the deployment
of normative arguments, including the protection of women's rights, to support
military campaigns.[38] Since 9/11, the expanding official justifications for resort
to pre-emptive force have raised challenging questions about the conditions
under which a feminist might support the use of force, exposing some fundamental differences in feminist perspectives, particularly when armed force is
(ostensibly) justified as necessary to rescue women from widespread violence
and abuse.[39] Relatedly, feminist analysis of international humanitarian law has
exposed its deeply gendered frames of reference, which rely on dualistic gender
stereotypes of heroic (male) combatants and vulnerable (female) civilians who
need military protection.[40] It has been argued that claims of military necessity
and protections provided for predominantly male combatants trump principles
that are meant to provide protection for civilians, such as the principle of distinction (between civilians and combatants),[41] and indeed that the whole body
of law bears little relationship to women's (and men's) diverse experiences of
armed conflict.[42]

Since 1991, feminist work to expose the gendered commitments that underpin
the discipline of international law has touched all its branches and sub-disciplines.
I have only offered a snapshot here, but there is a growing survey literature which

[35] See eg G Heathcote, *The Law on the Use of Force: A Feminist Analysis* (Routledge-Cavendish
London 2011).

[36] See eg C Chinkin, 'A Gendered Perspective to the International Use of Force' (1989) 12 *Australian
Yearbook of International Law* 279–93.

[37] See eg A Orford, *Reading Humanitarian Intervention: Human Rights and the Use of Force in
International Law* (CUP Cambridge 2003).

[38] See V Nesiah, 'From Berlin to Bonn to Baghdad: A Space for Infinite Justice' (2004) 17 *Harvard
Human Rights Journal* 75–98.

[39] See K Engle, '"Calling in the Troops": The Uneasy Relationship among Women's Rights, Human
Rights, and Humanitarian Intervention' (2007) 20 *Harvard Human Rights Journal* 189–226. *Contra*
C MacKinnon, 'Women's September 11th: Rethinking the International Law of Conflict' (2006) 47
Harvard International Law Journal 1–31.

[40] See eg H Kinsella, 'Securing the Civilian: Sex and Gender in the Laws of War' in M Barnett and
R Duvall (eds), *Power in Global Governance* (CUP Cambridge 2005) 249–72.

[41] See J Gardam, 'Women and the Law of Armed Conflict: Why the Silence?' (1997) 46 *International
and Comparative Law Quarterly* 55–80.

[42] See eg JG Gardam and MJ Jarvis, *Women, Armed Conflict, and International Law* (Kluwer Law
International Boston 2001); H Durham and T Gurd (eds), *Listening to the Silences: Women and War*
(Martinus Nijhoff Leiden 2005).

can provide further guidance.[43] Many of international law's foundational commitments have been questioned using the lens of feminist theory and the experience of women's everyday lives. The masculine assumptions embedded in much critical and postcolonial legal scholarship have also been challenged. By making gender an analytical issue of primary importance, blistering challenges to the discipline's claims to universality, objectivity, and neutrality have been launched. Yet despite exposing international law's many allegiances to patriarchal and imperial power, and showing how these allegiances are deeply embedded in its historical development and conceptual building blocks, very little has changed. In a sobering reflection, fifteen years after their 1991 article, Charlesworth, Chinkin, and Wright note an increased visibility of the language of feminism in international law, but that it is often deployed to ends that are of no benefit to women.[44] In a similar vein, Buss and Manji observe 'a sustained feminist presence' in international law that has challenged the idea that it only deals with relations between states, yet they question what impact this has had on women's lives.[45] Even worse, feminist contributions to international law can end up facilitating the same military and imperial projects that they set out to oppose, in the name of advancing women's participation and rights, as Anne Orford has warned.[46] It would seem that feminist critique is not yet robust enough to sufficiently understand how the problems feminists want to solve can be reproduced in their solutions.

4 REFORM

Alongside and sometimes in tension with structural critiques, law reform has always been an important feminist goal. By reform, I mean efforts to engage with international law, on its own terms, to make it more responsive to the concerns of women and/or neglected feminized issues, and to increase its capacity to support social change in gendered relations of power. The paradox of feminist law reform, as usefully explained by Joan Scott, is that while the goal is to eliminate 'sexual difference' as a marker of women's exclusion and/or inferiority, feminism nevertheless

---

[43] See eg D Otto, 'Feminist Approaches' in A Carty (ed), *Oxford Bibliographies Online: International Law* (Oxford University Press New York 2012) <http://www.oxfordbibliographies.com/view/document/obo-9780199796953/obo-9780199796953-0055.xml> [accessed 25 February 2016].

[44] C Chinkin, H Charlesworth, and S Wright, 'Feminist Approaches to International Law: Reflections from Another Century' in *International Law: Modern Feminist Approaches* (n 18) 17–45.

[45] 'Introduction' in *International Law: Modern Feminist Approaches* (n 18) 4.

[46] A Orford, 'Feminism, Imperialism and the Mission of International Law' (2002) 71 *Nordic Journal of International Law* 275–96, at 283.

makes its claims on behalf of 'women' who are discursively produced by sexual difference.[47] That is, feminism ends up reproducing the sexual difference that it sets out to eliminate. This paradox was recognized as long ago as 1788, in the writings of Olympe de Gouges,[48] who authored the 1791 *Declaration of the Rights of Woman and Female Citizen*[49] in protest at the exclusion of women from the *Declaration of the Rights of Man and Citizen*, adopted by the French revolutionary government in 1789. It is played out in contemporary feminist debates about whether law reform efforts should focus on addressing the specificities of women's situations or, alternatively, on seeking their inclusion in universal norms. Either way, the problem of sexual difference, which produces the prototype abstract human individual as male, remains—whether sexual difference is embraced and asserted as a demand for new laws that recognize women's difference or whether it is declared to be irrelevant to the application of universal laws, which ends up ignoring the difference that needs to be recognized and women disappear again in masculine universals. In recent years, feminist reform projects—many of which can be traced back to the new focus on violence against women in the early 1990s—have been particularly prolific in international human rights law and international criminal law. I will examine developments in both of these areas of law before turning to the obstacles they have faced, the dilemmas they raise, and how to account for the limited real life impact they have had for women.

Many of the historical struggles for women's rights adopted the law reform strategy of seeking new law that recognized and responded to women's sexual difference, often also in the hope that this would lead to women's broader political, social, and economic inclusion.[50] This approach enjoyed a revival in 1989, when Charlotte Bunch famously called for a 'transformation' of international human rights law to respond to women's specific experiences of violation and degradation.[51] She identified violence against women as a 'touchstone' that illuminates the failure of universal human rights to problematize the structural relations of male domination.[52] Her call was taken up by many local, regional, and international women's groups and human rights non-governmental organizations, prompting renewed emphasis on female-specific human rights violations. While new attention was also drawn to women's rights to reproductive freedom, to sexual autonomy, to work as sex workers, and to non-discrimination on the basis of sexual orientation and

---

[47] JW Scott, *Only Paradoxes to Offer: French Feminists and the Rights of Man* (Harvard University Press Cambridge MA 1996) at 3.

[48] Ibid 4.

[49] O de Gouges, 'Declaration of the Rights of Woman and Female Citizen' in *Women in Revolutionary Paris 1789–1795* (DG Levy, HB Applewhite, and MD Johnson eds and trans) (University of Illinois Press Urbana 1979) 92–6.

[50] 'Becoming Human' (n 12).

[51] C Bunch, 'Women's Rights as Human Rights: Toward a Re-Vision of Human Rights' (1990) 12 *Human Rights Quarterly* 486–98.

[52] Ibid 490.

gender identity, it was the issue of violence against women that had the most success in producing new law. Several new human rights instruments specifically address-ing violence against women have been adopted, including the General Assembly's *Declaration on the Elimination of Violence against Women*,[53] the Committee on the Elimination of Discrimination against Women's *General Recommendation No 19*[54] that interprets violence against women as a form of sex discrimination prohibited by the *Convention on the Elimination of All Forms of Discrimination against Women*,[55] two regional treaties that focus solely on addressing the issue,[56] and the inclusion of a specific prohibition in a third regional treaty.[57] The Special Rapporteur on Violence against Women, Its Causes and Consequences—a position created by the Commission on Human Rights in 1994—has helped to keep the issue on the main-stream agenda, with now numerous reports on various aspects of the problem and recommendations on how it should be addressed,[58] while the human rights treaty bodies all routinely raise the issue in their concluding observations to states parties' reports.[59] There are few international law reform efforts that can claim such prodi-gious results when measured in terms of formal legal developments.

Simultaneously, many feminist human rights advocates have sought trans-formative outcomes for women by pursuing the strategy of reinterpreting uni-versal norms so that they are inclusive of women. Under the banner of gender mainstreaming, addressing violence against women has also proved to be a pro-ductive touchstone. Feminists argued that domestic violence, when severe and where states have not taken adequate measures to address it, satisfies all the ele-ments of torture, the prohibition of which is not only contained in treaty law but also is considered to have attained *jus cogens* status.[60] Further, being forced to seek unsafe abortions because of the state's failure to provide access to safe abortions is argued to be a violation of the right to life, which requires states to take positive

---

[53] 'Declaration on the Elimination of Violence against Women' GA Res 48/104 (20 December 1993) UN Doc A/RES/48/104.

[54] Committee on the Elimination of Discrimination against Women, 'General Recommendation No 19: Violence against Women' (29 January 1992) UN Doc A/47/38.

[55] *Convention on the Elimination of All Forms of Discrimination against Women* (opened for sig-nature 1 March 1980 entered into force 3 September 1981) 1249 UNTS 13.

[56] *Inter-American Convention on the Prevention, Punishment and Eradication of Violence against Women* (adopted 9 June 1994 entered into force 5 March 1995) 33 ILM 960; *Council of Europe Convention on Preventing and Combating Violence against Women* (opened for signature 11 May 2011 entered into force 1 August 2014) CETS No 210.

[57] *Protocol to the African Charter on Human and Peoples' Rights on the Rights of Women in Africa* (adopted 11 July 2003) AU Doc Assembly/AU/Dec.14(II) at art 20.

[58] See eg R Manjoo, 'Report of the Special Rapporteur on Violence against Women, Its Causes and Consequences' (14 May 2013) UN Doc A/HRC/42/39.

[59] See D Otto, 'Women's Rights' in D Moeckli, S Shah, and S Sivakumaran (eds), *International Human Rights Law* (2nd edn OUP Oxford 2014) 316–32.

[60] See eg R Copelon, 'Recognizing the Egregious in the Everyday: Domestic Violence as Torture' (1994) 25 *Columbia Human Rights Law Review* 291–367.

measures to ensure access to contraception and good-quality maternal health care.[61] The strategy extended to economic, social, and cultural rights highlighting, for example, that several elements of the right to adequate housing, including 'adequacy', 'security of tenure', and 'habitability', were in need of reinterpretation to recognize the impact of domestic violence.[62] All of these proposals, and more, have been taken up by the human rights treaty bodies in their work, and are specifically flagged in the gender mainstreaming general comments that they have adopted.[63] The result is, on one level, profound: women's rights are no longer marginalized in specialist international institutions and legal instruments.

In international criminal law, too, feminist law reform efforts related to addressing violence against women have met with considerable success. Although rape has long been prohibited as a war crime, it has historically been treated as an infringement of family honour rather than as a violation of women's rights and, in practice, has generally been treated as a random—unfortunate, but inevitable—side-effect of armed conflict, rather than as an international crime.[64] As a consequence, international prosecutions have paid little attention to crimes involving sexual violence. However, the widespread sexual violence that occurred in the Balkans and Rwandan conflicts galvanized feminists into action, which resulted in the explicit inclusion of rape as a constituent element of crimes against humanity in the statutes establishing the ad hoc International Criminal Tribunals for the Former Yugoslavia and Rwanda.[65] Building on these formal developments and the jurisprudence and experience of the international criminal tribunals, many other feminist concerns were addressed in the drafting of the *Rome Statute of the International Criminal Court*,[66] which integrated gender issues more broadly into substantive criminal law, as well as into the operations of the Court, and its investigatory, procedural, and evidentiary mechanisms.[67]

---

[61] See F van Leeuwen, 'A Woman's Right to Decide? The United Nations Human Rights Committee, Human Rights of Women, and Matters of Human Reproduction' (2007) 25 *Netherlands Quarterly of Human Rights* 97–116.

[62] G Paglione, 'Domestic Violence and Housing Rights: A Reinterpretation of the Right to Housing' (2006) 28 *Human Rights Quarterly* 120–47.

[63] Human Rights Committee, 'General Comment No 28: Article 3 (The Equality of Rights between Men and Women' (29 March 2000) UN Doc CCPR/C/21/Rev.1/Add.10; Committee on the Elimination of Racial Discrimination, 'General Recommendation No XXV: Gender-Related Dimensions of Racial Discrimination' (26 April 2001) UN Doc HRI/GEN/Rev.5; Committee on Economic, Social and Cultural Rights, 'General Comment No 16: The Equal Right of Men and Women to the Enjoyment of all Economic, Social and Cultural Rights (Art 3 of the *International Covenant on Economic, Social and Cultural Rights)*' (11 August 2005) UN Doc E/C.12/2005/4.

[64] See C Chinkin, 'Rape and Sexual Abuse of Women in International Law' (1994) 3 *European Journal of International Law* 1–17; KD Askin, *War Crimes against Women: Prosecution in International War Crimes Tribunals* (Martinus Nijhoff Leiden 1997).

[65] See R Copelon, 'Gender Crimes as War Crimes: Integrating Crimes against Women into International Criminal Law' (2000) 46 *McGill Law Journal* 217–40.

[66] *Rome Statute of the International Criminal Court* (opened for signature 17 July 1998 entered into force 1 July 2002) 2187 UNTS 90.

[67] See B Bedont and K Hall-Martinez, 'Ending Impunity for Gender Crimes under the International Criminal Court' (1999) 6 *Brown Journal of World Affairs* 65–85.

Yet, while the focus on violence has proved to be very effective in mobilizing women's movements around the world and fostering normative developments, there remains a significant gap between the substantive legal reforms and practices on the ground.[68] As Margaret Bruce predicted in 1971, the realization of equality for women raises 'highly complex problems' that require fundamental change, 'not only in law, but also in social customs and beliefs'.[69] The hope that the focus on gendered violence would provide an entry point to a broader re-visioning of international human rights law remains just that. Instead, the strategy to highlight the specificities of violence against women has had the unintended effect of reinforcing traditional gender stereotypes by casting women, especially poor women and those in the Third World, as helpless victims in need of rescue, which has attracted paternalistic and imperial, rather than rights-based, responses.[70] Ultimately, the masculinity of the universal subject of international human rights law has been re-inscribed, despite the best efforts of feminists to change this.[71] These conservatizing effects help to account for the 'success' of the focus on violence against women, in that it does not (necessarily) challenge conventional gender tropes and can therefore engender support from unlikely bedfellows, including traditionalists of all persuasions. De Gouges' paradox of simultaneously needing to reject and rely on women's sexual difference continues to trap feminists in the repeating cycles of reconstituting women as 'other' to the masculine universal. The emphasis on violence has also distracted from the need to develop rights-based challenges to the global structures that perpetuate women's economic disadvantage.[72]

In the field of international criminal law, the picture is similarly desultory. Despite the formal success of reform efforts, there is very little evidence of changed practices. There have been few successful prosecutions for sexual violence, despite its hypervisibility in those recent conflicts that have been the subject of international prosecutions.[73] While considerable effort has been directed to introducing evidentiary and procedural innovations capable of supporting and protecting victim-witnesses who agree to testify—which some feminists hoped would even reshape stigmatizing

---

[68] A Edwards, *Violence against Women under International Human Rights Law* (CUP Cambridge 2010).

[69] MK Bruce, 'Work of the United Nations Relating to the Status of Women' (1971) 2 *Revue des droits de l'homme* 365–412, at 365–6.

[70] See R Kapur, 'The Tragedy of Victimization Rhetoric: Resurrecting the "Native" Subject in International/Post-Colonial Feminist Legal Politics' (2002) 15 *Harvard Human Rights Journal* 1–37.

[71] See D Otto, 'Disconcerting "Masculinities": Reinventing the Gendered Subject(s) of International Human Rights Law' in *International Law: Modern Feminist Approaches* (n 18) 105–29.

[72] See AM Miller, 'Sexuality, Violence against Women, and Human Rights: Women Make Demands and Ladies Get Protection' (2004) 7 *Health and Human Rights* 16–47.

[73] See S Pritchett, 'Entrenched Hegemony, Efficient Procedure, or Selective Justice: An Inquiry into Charges for Gender-Based Violence at the International Criminal Court' (2008) 17 *Transnational Law & Contemporary Problems* 265–305.

attitudes towards sexual violence in armed conflict[74]—it has become increasingly clear that a progressive legislative framework is not nearly enough.[75] Despite all the procedural innovations, many victims still experience testifying as humiliating and silencing because they are unable to control the telling of their own stories and are made to feel ashamed.[76] Among the unintended consequences of these feminist reforms has been the reinforcement of essentialized notions of ethnic difference by treating rape and sexual violence as constituent elements of genocide and crimes against humanity, which recognizes only certain ethnicized victims of sexual violence.[77] Further, the relentless portrayal of women as powerless victims who lack sexual and political agency has reinforced the same gender stereotypes that help to fuel sexual violence and its weaponization.[78] Thus, again, we see evidence of the paradoxical nature of feminist engagements with international law.

The feminist paradox is that both law reform strategies re-instantiate women's difference from men, albeit in different ways. The call for new law that recognizes women's particular concerns runs the risk of maintaining women in a 'special' protective category that reinforces rather than challenges gender hierarchy, while the strategy to redefine universals to be inclusive of women runs the risk that the specificities of women's experience will again disappear in masculine universals. Thus, feminist 'successes' generally fall well short of feminist aspirations for transformative change in the conceptual and structural framework of the discipline, as well as in the everyday lives of women.

5 THE EXILE OF INCLUSION

Feminist engagements with international law are marked by both hopefulness and despair, by creative advocacy as well as by deepening critique.[79] A vast and diverse

---

[74] See F Ni Aoláin, 'Radical Rules: The Effects of Evidential and Procedural Rules on the Regulation of Sexual Violence in War' (1997) 60 *Albany Law Review* 883–905.

[75] See K Fitzgerald, 'Problems of Prosecution and Adjudication of Rape and Other Sexual Assaults under International Law' (1997) 8 *European Journal of International Law* 638–63.

[76] See MB Dembour and E Haslam, 'Silencing Hearings: Victim-Witnesses at War Crimes Trials' (2004) 15 *European Journal of International Law* 151–77.

[77] See DE Buss, 'Rethinking "Rape as a Weapon of War"' (2009) 17 *Feminist Legal Studies* 145–63.

[78] See eg K Engle, 'Feminism and Its (Dis)contents: Criminalizing Wartime Rape in Bosnia and Herzegovina' (2005) 99 *American Journal of International Law* 778–816; J Halley, 'Rape in Berlin: Reconsidering the Criminalisation of Rape in the International Law of Armed Conflict' (2008) 9 *Melbourne Journal of International Law* 78–124.

[79] D Otto, 'The Exile of Inclusion: Reflections on Gender Issues in International Law over the Last Decade' (2009) 10 *Melbourne Journal of International Law* 11–26.

literature has been fostered, law reform projects are in abundance, and gender mainstreaming has been embraced as a system-wide strategy across the United Nations organs and agencies. In some respects, there is the sense, at last, of inclusion. Yet feminist assessments of the 'success' of this engagement almost invariably exhibit a keen awareness of the attendant complexities, distortions, and unintended consequences that cloud and trouble the feminist project. It would seem that the feminist condition in international law is to be torn between 'resistance' and 'compliance';[80] between the hope that normative developments may yet result in material improvements in women's lives, and despair about the continued re-inscription of masculinist stereotypes and ways of thinking. Is it, as Scott suggests, that feminism struggles within the liberal framework of democratic politics, where individuality has been equated with masculinity, and therefore has 'only paradoxes to offer'?[81]

While it is true that paradoxes abound, there are also other dynamics at work. The long history of feminist labours in international law, like the persistent emancipatory efforts of Third World peoples, has created a 'critical instability' at the heart of the law which gives it a 'dual quality'.[82] All of these efforts have left traces of discontent in the law—described by Sundhya Pahuja as a 'productive restlessness'[83]—which provide footholds for further destabilizations. In its continuous reconstitution, the masculinity of the law, like its allegiance to empire, keeps open the potential for feminist change. This dual quality is one way to understand the rollercoaster of feminist hope and despair. However, there is more. While striving to achieve the maximum justice possible within the existing systems of law and politics, it is also critically important to keep alive visions of justice beyond the law.[84] In this project of imagination and vision, as in critical engagement with law in the present, historical memory is of profound importance. Without it, feminists are deprived of knowledge about the complexities and paradoxes of their struggle, and may mistakenly believe that they are at the beginning of their struggle and fail to see when re-invention is required.

It is always dangerous to challenge dominant forms of power. There are the dangers of marginalization and ostracism, of legitimating laws and institutions that are deeply antagonistic to feminist change, and of making things worse for women. As Chandra Mohanty has said, 'our minds must be as ready to move as capital is,

---

[80] S Kouvo and Z Pearson (eds), *Feminist Perspectives on Contemporary International Law: Between Resistance and Compliance* (Hart Oxford 2011).

[81] *Only Paradoxes to Offer* (n 47) 5.

[82] S Pahuja, *Decolonising International Law: Development, Economic Growth, and the Politics of Universality* (CUP Cambridge 2011) at 255.

[83] Ibid 256.

[84] W Brown, 'Suffering Rights as Paradoxes' (2000) 7 *Constellations* 209–29.

to trace its paths and to imagine alternative destinations'.[85] While feminist critique has often been seen as a drag on feminist legal advocacy and reform—as too abstract and utopian to assist the practical project of improving women's lives—it is important to understand the practices of critique and activism as mutually supportive. Together they work to ensure the survival and dynamism of feminist politics that can resist containment by international law and its institutions and sustain compelling imaginaries of feminist futures. The burgeoning feminist project in international law, with its long history, many genealogies, and confounding conundrums, has barely begun.

---

[85] CT Mohanty, *Feminism without Borders: Decolonising Theory, Practising Solidarity* (Duke University Press Durham 2006) 221–51 ('"Under Western Eyes" Revisited: Feminist Solidarity through Anticapitalist Struggles').

CHAPTER 25

KANT, COSMOPOLITANISM, AND INTERNATIONAL LAW

WOUTER WERNER AND GEOFF GORDON

1 INTRODUCTION

IT speaks to the richness of Immanuel Kant's work that this chapter falls, in this *Handbook*, among the chapters on approaches to international law, rather than among the histories. The work of Kant not only occupies an important place in the history of ideas in international legal theory; his work also constitutes an enduring source of inspiration for widely diverging contemporary approaches to international law. Our principal interest in this chapter is with the way in which Kantian ideas have been adopted and transformed in contemporary international law and international theory. Our aim is *not* to assess whether these approaches have used Kant's work 'correctly' or to defend our own reading of Kantian theory (although offering some defence of how we read Kant is of course unavoidable). Instead, we proceed by reference to four core Kantian ideas incorporated in contemporary cosmopolitan thinking: (i) the categorical imperative; (ii) the roughly contractual notion of a federation of free republics; (iii) the conception of a cosmopolitan right of hospitality; and (iv) the idea of an innate cosmopolitanism. We will discuss each idea separately, first briefly introducing its place in Kantian thought, then setting out how (traces of) the idea can be found in positive international law, and finally how it has been adopted and transformed in international legal scholarship.

First, a brief statement of purpose and method: with a topic such as *Kant, cosmopolitanism, and international law*, making difficult choices in the selection of material is unavoidable. In some respects, our selection will be intentionally unorthodox, in order to bring out under-appreciated aspects of the Kantian cosmopolitan legacy in international law. This will reflect our dissatisfaction with the way in which the term 'cosmopolitanism' has regularly been used in legal and philosophical literature. More often than not, 'cosmopolitanism' is defined as a matter of liberal individual rights and equality between humans. We will refer to this liberal-individualism as liberal cosmopolitanism, in keeping with common usage. The liberal designation, however, applies equally to another form of cosmopolitanism with Kantian roots that we cover here, a state-oriented variety of liberal cosmopolitanism, from which a considerable degree of constitutional theory in international law derives. For the distinction between individual and state-oriented cosmopolitanism, we draw on Gerry Simpson's multiple readings of liberalism, one reading seeing in individual persons the only units of normative value, the other treating states as individuals and the primary units of normative value for purposes of the international legal system.[1] Simpson identifies the latter with the classical posture of international law. Hereafter, we refer to state-oriented cosmopolitanism as contractual cosmopolitanism, to focus on the agency attributed to states individually, and the mode of cosmopolitan practice arising out of the classical posture of international law. Finally, a last form of cosmopolitanism that we cover here represents a special, collectivist perspective behind international law. We refer to it as innate cosmopolitanism. This last form of cosmopolitanism in particular has hardly been recognized as such, even though it appears frequently in international legal argumentation. We intend to shed light on each of these three forms of cosmopolitanism and to discuss the role of Kantian ideas in their articulation.

Our chapter can thus be read in two ways. In one sense it reads like a classical handbook chapter, which introduces the reader to some core topics on Kantian philosophy, cosmopolitanism, and international law. The chapter, in other words, aims to provide an accessible introduction to topics that have been discussed at greater or lesser length in more specialized literature. In another sense, the chapter

---

[1] G Simpson, 'Two Liberalisms' (2001) 12 *European Journal of International Law* 537–71. For reasons particular to an argument he makes, Simpson refers to the two liberalisms as Charter liberalism, reflecting the classical international law emphasis on independent states, and liberal anti-pluralism, reflecting the particular ideological emphasis of normative individualism.

has a more pointed aim: to demonstrate how important it is to acknowledge different forms of cosmopolitanism at work in international law, and to shed new light on the 'forgotten' tradition of innate cosmopolitanism. In this context, our aim is not to advocate one of the forms of cosmopolitanism or to rank them in one way or the other. Instead, we hope that this chapter will contribute to a better understanding of the roles that Kantian cosmopolitan traditions play in how we think about and practise international law today.

2 A Framework for the International

Before we proceed to discussing the more specific ideas developed by and through Kant, it is necessary to set out how all four Kantian ideas operate within a specific framing of the international in Kant's theory. Kant's perception of the international is structured around four basic and interrelated tensions that allow for and yet limit the possibilities of human progress.

The *first* tension is that between free will and moral ends as definitive of the human condition. This tension is projected onto the international system as a tension between subjective rights of collectivities (primarily states) and global justice or order. The combination suggests an international system that must oscillate between particularism and universality, between the subjective claims of discrete collective organizations, be they states or otherwise, and pretensions to a global order in which autonomy is subordinated to the rules of conduct in the community. Moreover, the condition of order cannot be enforced upon states by a world state or hegemon without lapsing into tyranny.[2] In the face of the conflict between free will and order or ends, however, a tentative resolution may be found in the form of reflective judgment, arguably representing a middle course between an exercise of reason and an appreciation of nature or natural order.[3] Translated into the realm of international law, it is through the free will of states that aims of order, justice, and stability have to be achieved.

The *second* tension involves a territorial conception of the globe oscillating between cosmopolitanism and inter-statism. In Kant's work, the globe, by virtue of its very form, ties mankind together. Or as Kant puts it, all people enjoy a 'right

---

[2] I Kant, 'Perpetual Peace: A Philosophical Sketch' in *Kant: Political Writings* (HS Reiss ed HB Nisbet trans) (2nd edn CUP Cambridge 1991) 93–130, at 113.

[3] I Kant, *Critique of Judgment* (JC Meredith trans and N Walker ed) (OUP Oxford 2007 [1790]). See also J Bartelson, 'The Trial of Judgment: A Note on Kant and the Paradoxes of Internationalism' (1995) 39 *International Studies Quarterly* 255–79, at 270–2.

to communal possession of the earth's surface. Since the earth is a globe, they cannot disperse over an infinite area, but must necessarily tolerate one another's company'.[4] At the same time, however, Kant's theory departs from the pragmatic idea that the nation state is the highest level of political organization that is practically desirable. What we call Kant's pragmatism in this case arises out of his rejection of a world state for fear of its despotic potential, and is founded on the idea that 'laws progressively lose their impact as the government increases its range, and a soulless despotism, after crushing the germs of goodness, will finally lapse into anarchy.'[5] The globe, in other words, is not only a space where mankind resides; it is also a space divided-up in territorial units that find themselves in a state of nature, with the possibility of war always looming large. The global space also becomes a site of territorial division and inevitable conflict between groups seeking to leverage the geographical situation into the power to control possible ends of universal order. It is 'the desire of every state (or its ruler) to achieve lasting peace by thus dominating the whole world, if at all possible. But *nature* wills it otherwise';[6] for that reason, 'peace is created and guaranteed by an equilibrium of forces and a most vigorous rivalry'.[7]

But equilibrium is not the endpoint for Kant, and competition and progress are closely linked in his thought. Thus, *third*, Kant exhibits an optimistic sense of progressive history, away from conditions of territorial division, anarchy, and conflict prevailing in the present: conflict is construed as a precursor to harmony. Conflict—including wars, military preparations, and anguish—represents 'the means by which nature drives nations to make initially imperfect attempts' to leave a lawless state of relations, and enter into peaceful, juridical relations.[8] Though conflict is a precursor to harmony, the effect of their relationship is a sharp distinction between the present and future, in which the future both diminishes and amplifies the present: diminishes the appreciation of the present for being a debased condition; but amplifies its significance insofar as present conditions render the future ideal impossible to realize directly. Thereby the present is linked and subordinated to a future ideal, by comparison with which the present is wanting. Consequently, conditions of present conflict can be perceived and even justified as a precondition of future harmony.

The *fourth* tension is a reflection of each of the other three, and is manifest as a tension between pragmatism and idealism in the application of Kant's thought. All of the foregoing dualities inclined Kant towards pragmatism in his construction of the international, whereby conflict among nations is harnessed to contain itself. Kant is clear, however, that the arrangement he proposes for perpetual peace is not identical with his ideal endpoint: the peaceful international federation does

---

[4] 'Perpetual Peace' (n 2) 106.   [5] Ibid 113.   [6] Ibid (emphasis in original).
[7] Ibid 114.
[8] I Kant, 'Idea for a Universal History with a Cosmopolitan Purpose' in *Kant: Political Writings* (n 2) 41–53, at 47.

not represent the comprehensive society of universal laws in which humanity reaches its highest expression.[9] Instead, it represents in Kant's work the best possible arrangement for the near future.[10]

Finally, we note that the framework we describe varies from the express framework in which Kant situated what he called cosmopolitan right. Kant's express framework included *public right*; pertaining to the national collective and the individuals it comprises; *international right*, pertaining across collectives and individuals in collectives; and *cosmopolitan right*, limited to the right of hospitality that states owe to strangers. We will touch on this framework and Kant's description of international and cosmopolitan right in the points below. We have chosen, however, to highlight the four tensions in Kant's construction of the international—between particularism and universality, territorialism and commonality, conflict and progress, and pragmatism and idealism—not only to situate the ideas that we will discuss in the next sections, but also because they speak to contemporary international scholarship as they reflect what Martti Koskenniemi has called the 'sensibilities' of international legal thinking up until our present time.[11] International law also operates within a tension between sovereign right and cosmopolitan order; between the particular and the universal; the globe as a territorially divided world and as a common space for mankind; a constant going back and forth between notions of progress and the conditions of *realpolitik*. Likewise, Kant's series of four tensions establishes in the international an internally oppositional character, reflective of how his work has established a binary framework by which the international system is perceived, caught in a perpetual present between conflict and order, resistance and empire. It is therefore not surprising that Kant still speaks to so many different legal scholars in our time; nor is it surprising that his work has been taken up for so many different projects in international law. Kant's work has been found fundamental to the Western colonial project, but also a site of inspiration for resistance to related expressions of empire.[12] Against these

---

[9] I Kant, 'On the Common Saying: "This May Be True in Theory, But It Does Not Apply in Practice"' in *Kant: Political Writings* (n 2) 61–92, at 90; 'Perpetual Peace' (n 2) 114; I Kant, 'The Metaphysics of Morals' in *Kant: Political Writings* (n 2) 131–75, at 164–75.

[10] But see P Kleingeld, 'Approaching Perpetual Peace: Kant's Defence of a League of States and His Ideal of a World Federation' (2004) 12 *European Journal of Philosophy* 304–25.

[11] M Koskenniemi, *The Gentle Civilizer of Nations, The Rise and Fall of International Law 1870–1960* (CUP Cambridge 2001).

[12] For an example of scholarship finding Kant's work fundamental to the Western colonial project, see W Mignolo, 'The Many Faces of Cosmo-polis: Border Thinking and Critical Cosmopolitanism' (2000) 12 *Public Culture* 721–48. For an example of scholarship finding in Kant's work a site of inspiration for resistance to expressions of empire, see M Koskenniemi, 'Miserable Comforters: International Relations as New Natural Law' (2009) 15 *European Journal of International Relations* 395–422. For an example of both at once, see J Tully, 'The Kantian Idea of Europe: Critical and Cosmopolitan Perspectives' in A Pagden (ed), *The Idea of Europe: From Antiquity to the European Union* (CUP Cambridge 2002) 331–58.

sensibilities, and Kant's framework for the international, we turn now to the four core ideas as they are evident in cosmopolitan scholarship today.

3 The Categorical Imperative and Liberal Cosmopolitanism

For Kant, the categorical imperative functioned as the articulation of what it means to act as a rational, moral being. The categorical imperative differs from a hypothetical imperative, which is conditional in nature (if you want to achieve X, you should do Y). By contrast, the categorical imperative sets out what morality entails, irrespective of particular goals or desires one might have. Kant formulated the categorical imperative in three ways. His primary formulation was the invocation: 'Act only on that maxim whereby thou canst at the same time will that it should become a universal law.'[13] Kant's second formulation is identified as the humanity formula,[14] which holds: 'So act as to treat humanity, whether in thine own person or in that of any other, in every case as an end withal, never as means only.'[15] Kant's third formulation is the autonomy formula, which is predicated 'in the idea of the will of every rational being as a universally legislating will.'[16]

The categorical imperative primarily sets out which obligations follow from the idea of moral agency. Since the categorical imperative deals with the *obligations* of moral agents, one should be cautious about translating it directly into a theory of human *rights*. Having said that, echoes of especially the second formulation of the categorical imperative can be found in contemporary human rights law. Take for example the notion of 'human dignity' that underpins several post 1945 human rights treaties. Expressions of the idea of human dignity appeared, inter alia, in the *Universal Declaration of Human Rights*' recognition 'of the inherent dignity and of the equal and inalienable rights of all members of the human family (as) the foundation of freedom, justice and peace in the world' and in the Preamble of the *International Covenant on Civil and Political Rights* stating that the rights set out in the substantive provisions 'derive from the inherent dignity of the human person'.[17]

---

[13] I Kant, *Fundamental Principles of the Metaphysics of Morals* (TK Abbott trans) (Prometheus Books Amherst NY 1987 [1785]) at 49.

[14] R Johnson, 'Kant's Moral Philosophy' in EN Zalta (ed), *The Stanford Encyclopedia of Philosophy* <http://plato.stanford.edu/archives/sum2012/entries/kant-moral/> [accessed 26 February 2016].

[15] *Fundamental Principles of the Metaphysics of Morals* (n 13) 58.   [16] Ibid 61.

[17] See 'Universal Declaration on Human Rights' (10 December 1948) GA Res 217A(III) UN Doc A/810; *International Covenant on Civil and Political Rights* (opened for signature 16 December 1966 entered into force 23 March 1976) 999 UNTS 171.

Critics have pointed out that the concept of 'human dignity' is a radically underdetermined concept (an 'empty container', as some have put it)[18] that was incorporated into human rights treaties because it made it possible to accommodate conflicting world views.[19] Even if this is correct, however, the idea of human dignity still points to something also alluded to in Kant's categorical imperative: human beings have a value in and of themselves. They always retain something that escapes us; something that cannot be completely addressed in terms of hypothetical imperatives and instrumentalism. Human dignity, undetermined as it is, thereby comes with the obligation to treat human beings also as ends in themselves.

In legal and political thinking, Kant's categorical imperative has been taken up by a wide variety of scholars. One example is the work of John Rawls, whose *A Theory of Justice* ranks among the most influential works in political philosophy of the twentieth century.[20] Rawls updated Kant's categorical imperative to hold that individuals are 'self-originating sources of valid claims'.[21] Proceeding from this basic premise, Rawls reconstructed the social contract thought experiment, by means of his famous original position and veil of ignorance devices. In the imagined original position, there is not yet any collective organization; rather, each prospective member of a collective negotiates its rules from behind a veil of ignorance, which ensures that no one knows what her or his personal attributes and situation outside of the original position may be. Consequently, no one is capable of leveraging or maximizing any personal advantages. Presuming that the negotiation proceeds along rational and reasonable lines, Rawls ended up with two basic principles of justice: (i) the liberty principle, holding that 'each person is to have an equal right to the most extensive basic liberty compatible with a similar liberty for others' and (ii) the difference principle, which allows for socio-economic inequalities only insofar as they benefit the least well-off in society and which requires equal opportunities for social positions in society.[22]

---

[18] R Urueña, *No Citizens Here: Global Subjects and Participation in International Law* (Brill Leiden 2012) at 113.

[19] As McCrudden has put it, 'the significance of human dignity, at the time of the drafting of the *UN Charter* and the *UDHR* (and since then in the drafting of other human rights instruments), was that it supplied a theoretical basis for the human rights movement in the absence of any other basis for consensus': C McCrudden, 'Human Dignity and Judicial Interpretation of Human Rights' (2008) 19 *European Journal of International Law* 655–724, at 677, quoted in ibid 109. For another investigation of dignity and Kant, see M Rosen, *Dignity: Its History and Meaning* (Harvard University Press Cambridge MA 2012).

[20] J Rawls, *A Theory of Justice* (revised edn OUP Oxford 1999 [1971]).

[21] J Rawls, 'Kantian Constructivism in Moral Theory' (1980) 77 *Journal of Philosophy* 515–72 at 543.

[22] *A Theory of Justice* (n 20) 60.

Rawls' defence of the two principles of justice, however, was limited to domestic political societies. He denied that similar principles apply in international (global) relations. In an explanation of his method, which he called Kantian constructivism, Rawls made clear that the thought experiment in *A Theory of Justice* necessarily incorporated assumptions tied to personal experience—which he further situated within a Kantian political and philosophical tradition.[23] Therefore, rather than proposing a single, global negotiation from a comprehensive original position, Rawls posited a second original position for international purposes, one negotiated by peoples, rather than people. The peoples negotiate from behind another veil of ignorance, hiding their material situation, cultural attributes, and so on. Not only was the negotiating unit changed, however, but also the nature of the negotiation: rather than negotiating rules for the international *de novo*, the peoples of the world are asked whether or not they would affirm the rules of international law.[24] By design, the result comes quite close to core provisions of positive international law, such as the prohibition of intervention, the right to self-defence, *pacta sunt servanda*, and the protection of state sovereignty.[25] What is new is a mandate for right policy intended to further liberal-progressive ideals—such as the Kantian aspiration to a stable, federated peace—which Rawls associates with the rules of international law.[26] Curiously, the Kantian tradition is contextualized and delimited as a matter of method—the first original position is localized; a second is necessary to avoid bias towards a Kantian community—but in the product, the Kantian program of a peaceful federation is legitimized as global policy.

Rawls' conception of a law of peoples, however, has come under attack by scholars working within the so-called liberal cosmopolitan tradition. Unlike Rawls, they do not hold that a completely different set of normative requirements applies once we leave the boundaries of the domestic political community. On the contrary, they believe that it is possible to globalize Rawls' update of the normative position of the individual in Kantian ethical theory, and to rethink transnational relations according to the methodology of *A Theory of Justice*.[27] Thus, liberal cosmopolitans today found their ethical doctrine in Rawls' articulation of individuals as self-originating sources of valid claims, a position that goes back to Kant's categorical imperative. In proceeding from the categorical imperative, they reject the

[23] *A Theory of Justice* (n 20) 515.

[24] J Rawls, *The Law of Peoples, with the Idea of Public Reason Revisited* (Harvard University Press Cambridge MA 1999) at 41.

[25] Ibid 35–42.   [26] Ibid 4, 83.

[27] See eg R Pierik and W Werner, 'Cosmopolitanism in Context: An Introduction' in R Pierik and W Werner (eds), *Cosmopolitanism in Context: Perspectives from International Law and Political Theory* (CUP Cambridge 2010) 1–16, at 8–9.

compromise solution of a federated peace. The one Kantian tradition is thereby set in opposition to the other.

Founding their ethical theory principally in the humanity formulation of the categorical imperative, liberal cosmopolitans such as Thomas Pogge, Simon Caney, and Kok-Chor Tan hold individuals to represent the 'primary normative unit', and the 'ultimate unit of concern'.[28] This is normative individualism elevated to the level of cosmopolitan theory. It is characterized by two primary features: universality or all-inclusiveness; and generality. Universality or all-inclusiveness means 'the status of ultimate unit of concern attaches to every living human being equally'.[29] Generality means that individuals are 'the ultimate units of concern for everyone', generating 'obligations binding on all'.[30] All forms of collectivity, from the particular to the global, are understood as pass-throughs for the individuals they comprise: the collective holds no value of its own. International law and institutions must be able to justify their existence in terms of doing justice to the equal worth of all individuals in the world.

Another such thinker is Allen Buchanan, who proposes a comprehensive moral framework for the system of international law.[31] That framework proceeds largely according to standards of human rights, achieved and enforced on the basis of a common obligation to establish and support institutions capable of ensuring baseline standards of well-being in the world.[32] In international legal theory, the work of Fernando Tesón has made perhaps the most outspoken claim to operate within a Kantian tradition of thought.[33] In a controversial and often criticized move, Tesón translates Kant's categorical imperative into a conception of international law in which only states truly representing the people and respecting human rights deserve equal standing in the international community. The criticism of Tesón, however, reflects a broad criticism of liberal cosmopolitanism generally, which goes to its split from Rawls' more cautious treatment of the international (and Kant's before him): the projection of liberal values onto the world in the name of individuals everywhere courts the hegemonic and despotic abuses that Kant himself feared in a consolidated global regime.

---

[28] FR Tesón, 'The Kantian Theory of International Law' (1992) 92 *Columbia Law Review* 53–102, at 54; 'Cosmopolitanism in Context: An Introduction' (n 27) 2.

[29] TW Pogge, 'Cosmopolitanism and Sovereignty' (1992) 103 *Ethics* 48–75, at 49; 'Cosmopolitanism in Context: An Introduction' (n 27) 2.

[30] 'Cosmopolitanism and Sovereignty' (n 29) 49; 'Cosmopolitanism in Context: An Introduction' (n 27) 3.

[31] A Buchanan, *Justice Legitimacy and Self-Determination: Moral Foundations for International Law* (OUP Oxford 2004).

[32] See also ibid; A Buchanan and RO Keohane, 'The Preventive Use of Force: A Cosmopolitan Institutional Proposal' (2004) 18 *Ethics & International Affairs* 1–22.

[33] See eg the rather far-reaching claim by Tesón himself that he presents 'the' Kantian theory of international law: 'The Kantian Theory of International Law' (n 28).

4 THE 'PACIFIC FEDERATION' AND CONTRACTUAL COSMOPOLITANISM

The term 'contractual cosmopolitanism', as we use it, refers to a stream of con-temporary scholarship that holds that states have created cosmopolitan conditions and cosmopolitan institutions through their free will, as expressed in international treaties and other developments of international law. Some scholars have argued that the UN Charter resembles—or is—a world constitution that transcends the sovereignty of its founding members.[34] Others argue that emergent manifesta-tions of hierarchy among norms of international law establish a constitutional framework for the international system. In a complex argument posed against the background of the 2003 Iraq intervention, Jürgen Habermas argued in favour of a reformed United Nations (UN) regime to resuscitate what he called 'the Kantian project' in international affairs, which he identified as the ideal of 'a future global domestic politics'.[35]

It should be noted here that Kant distinguished his idea of a pacific federation from the *cosmopolitan* right of hospitality, in accordance with his distinction be-tween international and cosmopolitan right. The right of hospitality, which we revisit in greater depth in the next section, was derived from a cosmopolitan pre-condition, that 'all nations are *originally* members of a community of the land', in which, by virtue of the shape of the globe, 'everyone has an original right to share'.[36] The pacific federation, by contrast, derives from international right. Kant's conception of international right presumes a state of nature and a right to make war among states as a primary condition of international affairs, prior to any act of will by states to leave that condition. For Kant war is thus a natural, initial con-dition between states, whereas the condition of peace is something that must be attained and maintained. In the absence of a world legislator, the transition from the condition of war to the condition of peace is to be secured by the states them-selves, through their own free will. It is up to states to enter into a legal arrange-ment that subjects them to the law and outlaws war as a possible instrument for their foreign policies. As Garrett Brown points out, the arrangement demonstrates 'the importance of voluntary contractualism behind Kant's federation and the idea that political obligation is grounded by a moral self-commitment and con-comitance to universal principles of law and membership'.[37] The net result of the

---

[34] B Fassbender, 'The United Nations Charter as Constitution of the International Community' (1998) 36 *Columbia Journal of Transnational Law* 529–619, at 537.

[35] J Habermas, *The Divided West* (Polity Cambridge 2006) at 48.

[36] 'The Metaphysics of Morals' (n 9) 172.

[37] GW Brown, 'Kantian Cosmopolitan Law and the Idea of a Cosmopolitan Constitution' (2006) 27 *History of Political Thought* 661–84, at 673.

legal arrangement is not a world state, but rather a common legal framework that respects the independence of states, yet binds all members that have joined in. The treaty establishing a pacific federation is not a treaty that ends a particular war, but one that seeks 'to put an end to all wars forever'.

For Kant, states do not just have the option to join the pacific federation, they are under a moral obligation: states, like individuals, are morally obliged to leave the state of nature, and historically bound to do so. To that end, all states may and should require other states to do the same: 'Every people, for the sake of its own security, thus may and ought to demand from any other, that it shall enter along with it into a constitution...in which the Right of each shall be secured.' The pacific federation is thus a double edged sword: it establishes peace among its members, but underscores that states opting out constitute a danger, one that also imperils moral progress, as they prefer the state of nature over the legal arrangement establishing the pacific condition. In this context, it is worth mentioning Kant's somewhat ambiguous category of the 'unjust' or 'unlawful enemy' (*der ungerechte Feind*): the unjust enemy is the state that refuses to leave the state of nature or frustrates the effectuation of the pacific federation through its acts of will.[38] Against such spoilers of the peace, Kant argues, the rights of states pursuing the pacific federation are 'unlimited in quantity or degree'[39] with respect to neutralizing the threat emanating from the unjust enemy. This includes the formation of collective defence alliances, measures for containment, and regime-change. Kant defines the unjust enemy as the one that betrays the imperative requiring states to create and maintain a condition of perpetual peace. It is 'someone whose publicly expressed will, whether expressed in word or in deed, displays a maxim which would make peace among nations impossible and would lead to a perpetual state of nature if it were made into a general rule'.[40]

The idea of a pacific federation is thus by no means derived from a pre-existing cosmopolitan condition. Nor does it represent the cosmopolitan ideal, a world republic, which Kant rejects for its despotic potential. The pacific federation, by contrast to the cosmopolitan condition, is rooted in a grim conception of the state of nature, a state which we have not yet left behind. And yet Kant's optimistic sense of progressive history not only distinguishes his vision from a Hobbesian condition prevailing among states, but links the product of international right—world federation—with a cosmopolitan condition in the future. The peaceful federation may be a first step towards a flowering of cosmopolitan right that exceeds the narrow allowance for hospitality. In his *Idea for a Universal History*, for example, Kant

---

[38] As Martin Frank has put it, 'Kant's ungerechter Feind ist daher ungerecht, weil er der Pflicht zum Austritt aus dem Naturzustand nicht nachkommen will, oder weil er Maximen vertritt, deren allgemeine Befolgung die Etablierung der Rechtsordnung verunmöglichen': M Frank, 'Kant und der ungerechte Feind' (2011) 59 *Deutsche Zeitschrift für Philosophie* 199–219, at 210.

[39] 'The Metaphysics of Morals' (n 9) 170.   [40] Ibid.

argues that an initial stage of global federation would ultimately be a prelude to a still more comprehensive global constitution;[41] in *Perpetual Peace* he situates the federation of peoples within 'an infinite process of gradual approximation' of a state of global public right;[42] and the ultimate ambition of a comprehensive global constitution is confirmed in the *Critique of Pure Reason* as well.[43] By the same token, Kant's progressive optimism underscores that his concept of a federation of peoples, as a first step, remains a pragmatic one.

Kant's contractual pragmatism has not gone unchallenged as a matter of constitutional theory. Jürgen Habermas has made a notable effort to redeem the ends of an ideal cosmopolitan condition within Kant's construction of the international. Habermas holds that Kant erred in identifying the ideal cosmopolitan future with a world republic, with the thick solidarity and one-dimensional political culture that might entail.[44] Taking a step back to take a step away from thick preconditions associated with a hypothetical world republic, Habermas notes that the modern constitutional state allows only for indirect expression of popular sovereignty, as mediated by divided government and proceduralist models of representative democracy.[45] Accordingly, Habermas proposes to build upon the division and representation of the authority flowing from citizens, conceived now as dual citizens of a state and the world in a federated world constitutional system (distinguished from a strictly contractual federal system among states).[46] In this system, both individuals and states are represented under the political organization of the world constitution.[47] The state is preserved as the primary source and expression of democratic legitimacy, even as its authority is subordinated to the institution of global domestic politics.[48] Habermas proposes that institution to include a supranational capacity vested in something like a reformed UN Security Council, and a transnational forum represented by a reformed UN General Assembly, reconceived as a World Parliament, a bicameral body including representatives of world citizens, on the one side, and, on the other, delegates from democratically elected parliaments.[49]

---

[41] 'Idea for a Universal History with a Cosmopolitan Purpose' (n 8) 50–1. See also P Kleingeld, 'Approaching Perpetual Peace: Kant's Defence of a League of States and his Ideal of a World Federation' (2004) 12 *European Journal of Philosophy* 304–25.

[42] 'Perpetual Peace' (n 2) 130.

[43] I Kant, 'Appendix from "The Critique of Pure Reason": Transcendental Logic II, Dialectic I: Of Ideas in General' in *Kant: Political Writings* (n 2) 191; See also I Kant, *Critique of Pure Reason* (JMD Meiklejohn trans) (Colonial Press New York 1899 [1781/87]); GW Brown, 'State Sovereignty, Federation and Kantian Cosmopolitanism' (2005) 11 *European Journal of International Relations* 495–522, at 512–16.

[44] *The Divided West* (n 35) 122–3.   [45] Ibid 128.   [46] Ibid.

[47] J Habermas, 'The Constitutionalization of International Law and the Legitimation Problems of a Constitution for World Society' (2008) 15 *Constellations* 444–55, at 448–51.

[48] *The Divided West* (n 35) 139–43;

[49] 'The Constitutionalization of International Law' (n 47) 449. See also Habermas' vision for the European Union as a forerunner of the world constitutional arrangement: J Habermas, 'The Crisis of

Habermas' reconstruction of the constitutional potential within the Kantian tradition is devoted to sustaining the cosmopolitan ideal that Kant denied in rejecting the world state, and the idealism that Habermas embraces is manifest in two optimistic aspects of his vision. First and most plainly, it is manifest in the call for large-scale reform of UN institutions to achieve a capable organization for world domestic government, along with the conditions in the world necessary to effectuate that reform.[50] Second, it is manifest in his vision that individuals have the capacity to accommodate within themselves, as citizens and agents of the world and state, separate and potentially conflicting identities and powers, associated with two collective systems of authority that must both support and restrain one another. Habermas attributes the failure of the cosmopolitan ideal in Kant's work to a conceptual flaw flowing from undue weight given to the social contract thought experiment.[51] In place of Kant's pragmatic construction of the international, then, Habermas would rehabilitate its ideal potential.

By contrast, contemporary constitutional theorists in international law purport for the most part to proceed according to more modest claims, remaining largely within the formal terms of international law, and purporting only to describe acts and developments in the international system as it already exists. Likewise, today's constitutional cosmopolitan scholarship—by scholars such as Christian Tomuschat, Bardo Fassbender, and Ernst-Ulrich Petersmann—shares in more traditional manner the contractual underpinnings among states that Kant adopts as a matter of international right.[52] Even those theories of a cosmopolitan constitution that describe an emergent hierarchy of norms—including the work of Erica de Wet, Anne Peters, and Neil Walker—tend to do so in terms that remain within the formal structure of international law, posed for instance as arguments of customary law formation or general principles rising to the level of a source of law under Article 38 of the Statute of the International Court of Justice (ICJ).[53] Likewise, contemporary theories of international constitutionalism also reject pretensions to a unitary world government. As a result, arguments for an emergent constitution today remain in keeping with Kant's ideas for achieving world order by means of a constitutional federation, in terms of a perceived commitment to the

---

the European Union in the Light of a Constitutionalization of International law' (2012) 23 *European Journal of International Law* 335–48.

[50] See eg WE Scheuerman, 'Review Essay: Global Governance without Global Government? Habermas on Postnational Democracy' (2008) 36 *Political Theory* 133–51.

[51] *The Divided West* (n 35) 126–32.

[52] See eg E-U Petersmann, 'How to Constitutionalize International Law and Foreign Policy for the Benefit of Civil Society?' (1999) 20 *Michigan Journal of International Law* 1–30; 'The United Nations Charter* as Constitution of the International Community' (n 34) 537.

[53] See eg A Peters, 'Global Constitutionalism Revisited' (2005) 11 *International Legal Theory* 39–67, at 46; N Walker, 'The Idea of Constitutional Pluralism' (2002) 65 *Modern Law Review* 317–59, at 354–9.

global association organized around certain commonly adopted baseline norms.[54] Also in keeping with Kant's ideas of constitutional federation, the emergent constitutional hierarchy may be seen as an immature or thin manifestation of a cosmopolitan condition likely to thicken over time.[55]

Each of the constitutional theories purports to discern a progression away from something like a state of nature in international relations. But each is subject to healthy skepticism about the reality of any constitution achievement. Moreover, each tends to recognize skepticism directed against the others. Fassbender, for instance, observes a 'sort of Decalogue' in value-oriented constitutionalism,[56] whereas de Wet holds simply, 'it would not be accurate to describe the UN Charter as "the constitution" of the international community'.[57] They are, all together, still subject to the criticism voiced by Koskenniemi, that the absence, at the international level, of the sort of common understandings and common cause enjoyed at the domestic, renders the turn to constitutionalism in international law quixotic or worse.[58]

5 INNATE COSMOPOLITANISM AND COSMOPOLITAN HOSPITALITY

Kant's description of cosmopolitan hospitality, though the focus of considerable work lately, was a narrow category in and of itself.[59] We situate it within the larger context of innate cosmopolitanism, which we draw from throughout Kant's work. Accordingly, we begin with the treatment of innate cosmopolitanism, an underappreciated aspect of the Kantian tradition.

Innate cosmopolitanism arises out of three related strands of thought discernible in Kant's work, each of which has already been touched on earlier in other

---

[54] E de Wet, 'The International Constitutional Order' (2006) 55 *International and Comparative Law Quarterly* 51–76.

[55] See eg A Peters, 'The Merits of Global Constitutionalism' (2009) 16 *Indiana Journal of Global Legal Studies* 397–411.

[56] B Fassbender, 'The Meaning of International Constitutional Law' in N Tsagourias (ed), *Transnational Constitutionalism: International and European Perspectives* (CUP Cambridge 2007) 307–28, at 318.

[57] 'The International Constitutional Order' (n 54) 51, 54.

[58] M Koskenniemi, 'The Fate of Modern International Law: Between Technique and Politics' (2007) 70 *Modern Law Review* 1–30, at 15–16.

[59] For another account of Kant's category of cosmopolitan right, see P Kleingeld, 'Kant's Cosmopolitan Law: World Citizenship for a Global Order' (1998) 2 *Kantian Review* 72–90.

contexts: one recognizes a fundamental interconnection rising to the level of collectivity inherent or immanent in the condition of humanity; another recognizes individuals alongside states and other collectivities as agents in a comprehensive situation of world relations, and the third is the line of thought associating the human condition with a progressive history. These three strands are present across the variety of Kant's work, including *Fundamental Principles of the Metaphysics of Morals, Idea for a Universal History with a Cosmopolitan Purpose, On the Common Saying: 'This May Be True in Theory, But It Does Not Apply in Practice', Perpetual Peace: A Philosophical Sketch*, and *The Metaphysics of Morals*. Thus, to offer examples out of order, 'international right involves not only the relationship between one state and another within a larger whole, but also the relationship between individual persons in one state and individuals in the other or between such individuals and the other state as a whole'.[60] Likewise, 'individuals and states, coexisting in an external relationship of mutual influences, may be regarded as citizens of a universal state of mankind'.[61] Finally, the human race is 'engaged in progressive improvement in relation to the moral end of its existence' in which the universal order joining humanity as a whole becomes manifest.[62] Or, as Kant puts it in his eighth proposition from his *Idea for a Universal History*: 'The history of the human race as a whole can be regarded as the realisation of a hidden plan of nature to bring about an internally – and for this purpose also externally – perfect constitution as the only possible state within which all natural capacities of mankind can be developed completely.'[63]

In keeping with Kant's moral theory, the proper expression of the human will is a function of the rational order as a whole, and the ultimate condition of being human is defined not by reference to the individual, but by the flourishing of an interconnected whole. That interconnected whole represents the sum of the relations in the world of every agent to every other, and includes individuals, states, and other collectives. Thereby, innate cosmopolitan theory finds its Kantian roots in an immanent interconnection of all human agency as part of an ineluctable whole encompassing everyone in the world. This reading of Kant supports a comprehensive vision of world relations: attention shifts from the discrete individual (à la liberal-individual cosmopolitanism), or discrete entity in the world (à la state-oriented contractualism and federation), to the world as a discrete entity. The intended result is a juridical world society, inclusive of nations and individuals alike, under a normative regime properly derived from the unique nature of humanity as a whole, rather than from any one or several particular, subjective wills.

The innate cosmopolitan community corresponds with two related frameworks for community in Kant's work: first, in Kant's framework for a universal society,

---

[60] 'The Metaphysics of Morals' (n 9) 165.   [61] 'Perpetual Peace' (n 2) 98.
[62] 'On the Common Saying' (n 9) 88.
[63] 'Idea for a Universal History with a Cosmopolitan Purpose' (n 8) 50.

encompassing all collectives and individuals alike as moral agents, made clear in his *Metaphysics of Morals*, and second, in the framework discernible in Kant's theory of practical morality, according to which the individual cannot be understood to the exclusion of the greater human community. The moral imperative exists by the special appreciation of the human individual as part of an interpenetrating human collective, one that is mutually constitutive. The nature of this immanent, collective phenomenon gives rise to basic norms appropriate to relations in the world. In this context, innate cosmopolitanism describes a Kantian republicanism that is free of distortions that have been imposed upon it by presuming constraints of democratic consent. With respect to Kant's work as a whole, it is impossible to draw moral norms from individuals outside of a collective social framework; likewise, the conditions of competition and contract among states appear as points in a greater historical framework. The world republican condition, on the other hand, exists always and everywhere as an immanent condition of possibility, and in this sense it is the constitutive condition of Kantian cosmopolitanism. Liberal-individualism and state-oriented contractualism, by contrast, isolate out fragments of the total framework—social, temporal, and geographical—developed across the full body of Kant's work.

Innate cosmopolitanism under law measures the international order, in whole or in part, against the perceived will or ends of the world collective. In comparison with contractual cosmopolitanism, the innate cosmopolitan collective precedes and is not contingent on positive legal terms of any global rapprochement. In comparison with liberal cosmopolitanism, which proceeds by reference to a world of individuals, innate cosmopolitanism proceeds by reference to the individuality of a world whole. Consider the judgment of the International Criminal Tribunal for the former Yugoslavia (ICTY) in the *Kupreškić* case, in which the Court announced a rule of customary law, not on the basis of state practice and *opinio juris*, but on the basis of an exigency attributed to a collective humanity: 'law may emerge through a customary process under the pressure of the demands of humanity or the dictates of public conscience, even where State practice is scant or inconsistent'.[64]

The innate cosmopolitan perspective may also be observed in contemporary theories of international law and relations that found the normativity of the system either in grand sociological explanations, or in some intersubjective phenomenon. Examples of process theory and social constructivism, including transnational legal process theory and the interactional theory of international law, correspond with aspects of innate cosmopolitanism in Kant's work, as do elements of recent inquiries into societal constitutionalism.[65] Such theories tend to join normative

---

[64] *Prosecutor v Kupreškić* (Judgment) (ICTY, Trial Chamber, Case No IT-95-16-Y, 14 January 2000) at [527].

[65] G Teubner and A Beckers, 'Expanding Constitutionalism' (2013) 20 *Indiana Journal of Global Legal Studies* 523–50; G Teubner, *Constitutional Fragments: Societal Constitutionalism and*

and descriptive arguments, drawing norms from patterns perceived in vast social and technical processes. Consequently, innate cosmopolitanism typically recognizes international legal norms and institutions in accordance with observed acts, expectations, and understandings relevant to the world collective, reflective of the actual expression of its contingent nature or will, properly discerned at any given point in time. Put simply: proper legal rules will correspond with historical norms that already characterize the lived reality of the world collective.

The pretension to observe a foundational body of norms in the lived reality of the world collective creates a contradiction for the innate cosmopolitan program. Innate cosmopolitanism can be found in progressive theories of international law, intended to move international law past the anarchic conditions of a system founded in equal and independent sovereign states.[66] But in tying itself to a claim to represent historical reality, innate cosmopolitanism joins itself to status quo conditions in the world. Moreover, it does so by appealing to some special competence in select practitioners to observe norms arising out of extraordinarily complex conditions of interconnectedness in the world. In theory, innate cosmopolitanism suggests the potential to entrench the privileged position of elite actors under status quo conditions.

Perhaps for reasons like this, the immanent condition of universal humanity gave rise, for Kant, only to the relatively narrow category of cosmopolitan right synonymous with the law of hospitality. We turn to it now. Kant described the law of hospitality as a bedrock norm, with elemental but minimal content: minimal because the immanent condition of humanity was not realized in Kant's time, and would only be progressively realized, though perhaps not ever fully realized, as part of a gradual historical approach. Thus a proper cosmopolitan condition might supersede the limited demands of hospitality, for instance in accordance with a more comprehensive cosmopolitan constitutional condition; but in a situation still dominated by the relatively anarchic situation of international right, a bedrock norm of hospitality was the floor below which persons and groups could not justifiably descend in their conduct—but also the maximum that might reasonably be expected under current conditions.

Globalization (OUP Oxford 2012); J Brunnée and S Toope, *Legitimacy and Legality in International Law: An Interactional Account* (CUP Cambridge 2010); HH Koh, 'Why Do Nations Obey International Law?' (1997) 106 *Yale Law Journal* 2599–659.

[66] Consider two very different efforts to move the international legal system past the anarchy of a consent-based arrangement among states. The first being the work of Alejandro Álvarez, both in scholarship and from the bench of the ICJ: see eg A Álvarez, 'The Reconstruction and Codification of International Law' (1947) 1 *International Law Quarterly* 469–81; *International Status of South-West Africa* (Advisory Opinion) [1950] ICJ Rep 128, at 175 (Dissenting Opinion of Judge Álvarez). The second being the work of Myres McDougal and the New Haven School: see eg MS McDougal, WM Reisman, and AR Willard, 'The World Community: A Planetary Social Process' (1987) 21 *UC Davis Law Review* 807–972.

According to Kant, '[h]ospitality means the right of a stranger not to be treated as an enemy when he arrives in the land of another. One may refuse to receive him when this can be done without causing his destruction; but, so long as he peacefully occupies his place, one may not treat him with hostility'. Note that Kant's cosmopolitan right is even more limited than, for example the natural right to travel, proselytize, and trade as put forward by the Spanish School in the sixteenth century. The right to hospitality in Kant's work does not come with an obligation to allow foreigners on the territory, unless refusal of entry would result in their destruction. It does put states under an obligation, however, to treat foreigners that are present on the territory with a minimum of respect. In sum, the limited assignation of cosmopolitan right, then, is a compromised category, posited as a function of a historical perspective that is optimistic with respect to an indefinite future, but, by comparison, pessimistic with respect to a correspondingly indefinite present.

Expanding a right to hospitality under existing political conditions may result in grave injustices, as Kant makes clear in his discussion of colonialism. Kant contrasts his optimism regarding the human race that 'can gradually be brought closer and closer to a constitution establishing world citizenship' with the realities of 'the inhospitable actions of the civilized and especially of the commercial states of our part of the world. The injustice which they show to lands and peoples they visit (which is equivalent to conquering them) is carried by them to terrifying lengths'. Given the greed and injustices brought about by colonial powers, Kant praises China and Japan as having 'wisely refused them entry'. In this sense, Kant's limited allowance for the cosmopolitan right of hospitality mirrors the simultaneous affirmation of present-day historical conditions, alongside progressive aspirations, identified with innate cosmopolitanism today.

Since 1945, Kant's work on hospitality has been extensively discussed in the context of migration and asylum law. It should be noted that the background of such debates is generally quite different from Kant's concern about colonial powers abusing the right of hospitality to foster their commercial and imperial projects. The main concern in contemporary debates on migration and hospitality is most often *not* how to stop rich, powerful countries abusing the peoples and resources in poorer countries; rather it is the treatment of citizens who have migrated from poor, unstable, or unsafe countries to other states. This raises questions about how one should regulate entry at the borders but also, and increasingly, how one should treat people that have already managed to enter and live within a foreign society.[67] This shift in focus partly explains why Kant's limited category of cosmopolitan right has come in for criticism in the past decades. Jacques Derrida, for instance,

---

[67] T Spijkerboer, 'A Distributive Approach to Migration Law: Or the Convergence of Communitarianism, Libertarianism, and the Status Quo' in *Cosmopolitanism in Context* (n 27) 249–74.

finds it to contain internal contradictions—reflected in the double origin of *hostis* as host and enemy, as well as in the conditional nature Kant ascribes to a supposedly unconditional or bedrock norm—which cripple its efficacy or coherence. While this criticism seems to bypass the specific function in a way not totally fair to Kant's idea of hospitality,[68] at the least, the critique underscores how the tension between present conditions and future ends constrains cosmopolitanism in Kant's work.

Considering the radically different context in which it was written, it is remarkable to find that the 1951 *Refugee Convention* contains basic provisions that almost perfectly echo Kant's cosmopolitan right.[69] The Convention upholds the right of states to refuse foreigners entry to their territory, thus reifying the conception of the globe as composed of territorial, sovereign units. At the same time, the *Convention* puts states under an obligation not to return foreigners to places where they have to fear persecution as well as the obligation to respect minimum standards in the treatment of foreigners.

While some contemporary authors regard Kant's notion of hospitality as too limited for current global conditions, others have taken up his idea of a gradual expansion of world citizenship to make sense of transformations in the international legal and political order. A notable example is the work of Seyla Benhabib, whose book *The Rights of Others* takes Kant's cosmopolitan right of hospitality as well as his idea of the possibility of a gradual evolution of citizenship as its starting point.[70] Benhabib's work departs from a basic tension—one that plays out in particular in liberal democracies—between an adherence to universal human rights on the one hand and the acceptance of state sovereignty on the other. While this tension cannot be solved other than through a world state, Benhabib argues that at the very least states should grant (limited) membership to those who reside on the territory of a state and engage in democratic, deliberative processes, through which the boundaries of citizenship are constantly reconsidered and reinvented. Migration and citizenship issues, then, help to remind us that 'the unity of the demos ought not be understood as if it were a harmonious given, but rather as a process of self-constitution, through more or less conscious struggles of inclusion and exclusion'.[71] Benhabib's perspective mirrors the twinned sense of phenomena and future change adopted by process theory and social constructivism—our two

---

[68] J Derrida, 'Hostipitality' (2000) 5 *Angelaki: Journal of the Theoretical Humanities* 3–18, at 15. Brown responds to Derrida's critique by noting that Kant did not propose to achieve the full cosmopolitan condition on the basis of cosmopolitan right—that is, hospitality—alone: GW Brown, 'The Laws of Hospitality, Asylum Seekers and Cosmopolitan Right: A Kantian Response to Jacques Derrida' (2010) 9 *European Journal of Political Theory* 308–27.

[69] *Convention relating to the Status of Refugees* (opened for signature 28 July 1951 entered into force 22 April 1954) 189 UNTS 137.

[70] S Benhabib, *The Rights of Others: Aliens, Residents, and Citizens* (CUP Cambridge 2004).

[71] Ibid 216.

broad examples of contemporary theory with an innate cosmopolitan bent—as well as Kant's tendency to join his progressive optimism to doubts about any final closure or end point for universal society.

6 CONCLUSION

In review, the three strands of Kantian cosmopolitanism—liberal, contractual, and innate—exist in an inconsistent relationship with one another, sometimes complementary, sometimes contradictory. The divergences among the three underscore the scope of cosmopolitan visions today, as well as the breadth of the Kantian traditions that underlie them. Each raises different possibilities for cosmopolitan law and politics; each must respond to different critiques. Nonetheless, they are all bounded by their common heritage.

Consider, in this light, the rapid advance of international criminal law over the last two decades. As forums, the International Criminal Court (ICC), and predecessors such as the ICTY, and the International Criminal Tribunal for Rwanda (ICTR), may be construed as a progressive step forward in the enforcement of human rights. They may equally represent evidence of a thickening constitutional formation in the international system. They also represent the affirmation of a global social and political collective, in the form of the realization of the collective's highest power, to deprive individuals of liberty, as a criminal sanction, in the name of the collective. At the same time, international criminal tribunals and international criminal law are neither solely nor perfectly reflective of liberalism in form and function. Moreover, neither the turn to ad hoc tribunals, nor the adoption of the Rome Statute actually announce a constitution or even a federation. Thirdly, the operation of the ICC is frustrated or made controversial by the failure of any cohesive culture capable of supporting the efficacy or the legitimacy of the institution. And finally, the ICC gives rise to new forms of politics in the name of cosmopolitan values that come with their own mechanisms of exclusion, discipline, and friend–enemy distinctions.[72]

These conflicting conditions demonstrate that Kant's cosmopolitan legacy continues to find new expression in practice and discourse, but that its realization is hardly stable. His legacy is a conflictual one, in part due to conflict built into his construction of the international in the first place. As such, there is an

---

[72] SMH Nouwen and WG Werner, 'Doing Justice to the Political: The International Criminal Court in Uganda and Sudan' (2010) 21 *European Journal of International Law* 941–65.

epistemological dimension to the dilemma, which allows us to conclude where we began. Kant allows a number of ways to envision a cosmopolitan ideal, but few ways to conceive of it in a perpetual, non-ideal present.[73] Instead, our knowledge of present conditions is confined to the familiar dichotomy between self-defeating particularism and hegemonic universalism, conflict, and empire.

---

[73] We note here, however, the provocative argument of Jens Bartelson, who finds in Kant's *The Contest of the Faculties* the possibility of approaching Kantian internationalism in a different temporal mode, potentially capable of escaping the contradictions raised here by means of reconstructing historical signs: see 'The Trial of Judgment: A Note on Kant and the Paradoxes of Internationalism' (n 3) 272–4. See also I Kant, 'The Contest of the Faculties' in *Kant: Political Writings* (n 2) 176–90.

CHAPTER 26

GLOBAL ADMINISTRATIVE LAW AND DELIBERATIVE DEMOCRACY

BENEDICT KINGSBURY,

MEGAN DONALDSON,

AND RODRIGO VALLEJO

1 INTRODUCTION

AN early framing of 'global administrative law' (GAL) provisionally 'bracket[ed] the question of democracy' as too ambitious an ideal for global administration.[1] To many, the bracketing of democracy has appeared analytically unpersuasive and normatively dubious. This chapter is an initial attempt to open the brackets and bring GAL and democracy into conversation. It addresses two separate observations: first, that democracy currently lacks tools to respond to the globalization and diffusion of political authority; and secondly, that GAL is not presently

[1] B Kingsbury, N Krisch, and R Stewart, 'The Emergence of Global Administrative Law' (2005) 68 *Law & Contemporary Problems* 15–61, at 50.

democratic—it has no room for democratic concerns in its emerging norms. The juxtaposition of democracy and GAL yields insights for the way in which each might contribute to the reimagination of global governance.

Section 1 presents the idea of GAL and notes some of its contributions to international legal theory, in particular its applications to ideas of administration, law, and justification. Section 2 explores the way in which GAL's focus on innumerable capillary-level sites of power may open promising terrain for the instantiation of democracy, and particularly deliberative democracy, beyond the state. Section 3 reverses the perspective, and considers how work on GAL can be enhanced by engaging with, and drawing ideas from, work on deliberative democracy. Section 4 briefly notes the rising impact and future potential of democratic striving in the practice of institutional entrepreneurship and GAL lawyering.

2 GLOBAL ADMINISTRATIVE LAW AND ITS CONTRIBUTIONS TO INTERNATIONAL LEGAL THEORY

GAL is the body of law or law-like principles and mechanisms governing the procedural dimensions of an increasingly important global, or at least transnational, 'administration'. As a field of study it has focused on the design of global governance institutions and their interactions with other extra-national and national regulatory bodies, the rules and decisions they produce, and the procedural standards and mechanisms governing their processes, including those relating to transparency, participation, reason-giving, review, and accountability. Unlike other accounts, particularly those tracing a 'constitutionalization' of the world,[2] GAL does not seek to make sense of the entire complex of legal orders and their relation to one another. Rather, it is oriented towards the frayed edges of various orders, the cornucopia of new institutional forms that are springing up and not easily classified within existing categories, and the circulation and metamorphosis of borrowed ideas and principles in the fluid administrative 'space'.[3]

The methodology of GAL is distinctive. GAL scholarship has focused on identifying and mapping global administration and, through an inductive methodology, discerning (and to some extent developing) procedural norms applicable to

---

[2] See eg A Peters, 'Fragmentation and Constitutionalization' in this *Handbook*.
[3] See N Krisch, 'Global Administrative Law and the Constitutional Ambition' in P Dobner and M Loughlin (eds), *The Twilight of Constitutionalism?* (OUP Oxford 2010) 245–66.

it.[4] In a domain of international legal theory increasingly crowded with competing conceptions of the transnational in public law terms,[5] GAL is distinct in its renunciation of any comprehensive vision of order, and of any *a priori* normative foundation. There is nevertheless a normative concern inherent in the GAL project. GAL studies tend to bridge description and prescription. Major elements of GAL are discerned as emergent in institutional practice, and GAL scholarship is to some extent an attempt to systematize and disseminate this practice. The effort in GAL scholarship to typologize, and in some respects encourage adoption of, certain mechanisms, and to name them collectively as GAL, is itself a normative intervention.[6] It also lays bare for more searching normative analysis the realities of governance not captured by more formal doctrinal accounts.

GAL scholarship thus contributes to international legal theory in at least three ways: it draws attention to the rapid expansion and emerging patterns of 'administration'; it offers a fresh angle on debates over the meaning of 'law' in the global context; and it reframes narratives of justification attributed to global decision-making.

2.1 Administration

GAL scholarship has drawn attention to an immense variety of exercises of power by bodies which otherwise have received little or no attention in legal scholarship—the flows of quotidian, often capillary-scale decision-making and rule-making which GAL characterizes as 'administration' in global governance. This 'administration' extends well beyond the conventional field of 'administrative law' within most states. The institutions whose organization and actions are studied range from formal interstate treaty-based institutions,[7] through to less formal

---

[4] For more on the GAL project, see materials gathered at Institute for International Law and Justice, New York University School of Law, 'Global Administrative Law Project' <http://www.iilj. org/GAL> [accessed 26 February 2016].

[5] N Walker, 'Beyond Boundary Disputes and Basic Grids: Mapping the Global Disorder of Normative Orders' (2008) 6 *International Journal of Constitutional Law* 373–96.

[6] S Marks, 'Naming Global Administrative Law' (2005) 37 *New York University Journal of International Law & Politics* 995–1001. See also C Harlow, 'Global Administrative Law: The Quest of Principles and Values' (2006) 17 *European Journal of International Law* 187–214 (warning about possible ideologies underlying the development of GAL, while stressing that a pluralist understanding of global administration structured around the principle of subsidiarity might be preferable); C Bories (ed), *Un droit administratif global?* (Pedone Paris 2012).

[7] Such as the International Monetary Fund, international and regional development banks, the Organisation for Economic Co-operation and Development, the World Trade Organization, the World Health Organization and other UN 'related organizations' or 'specialized agencies', and regional organizations like the Association of Southeast Asian Nations, the Organization of American States, the African Union, and the League of Arab States. On the relationship between the law of international organizations and global administrative law, see eg B Kingsbury and L Casini,

networks of regulators or ministries,[8] to hybrid and wholly private transnational bodies often established under national law,[9] and to the 'distributed administration' whereby one entity's standards are given practical effect by national entities, non-governmental organizations (NGOs), or companies specialized in certification, verification, inspection, or audit.

Making these practical exercises of power the object of study opens up a new terrain in asking exactly where, how, and with what effects power is exercised. The inquiry is bottom-up. It is not initially constrained by the question which often channels and corrals international law inquiry, namely whether there is a formal international legal source for the power. In this perspective, it is immaterial whether the administration occurs in the interstices of formal treaty regimes, or is based in private contracts, or produces norms or decisions that formally are hortatory or non-binding in character, or whether it is conducted entirely by self-constituted bodies of experts, or in negotiations between interested parties.[10] The concept of GAL in a 'global administrative space' provides an optic for understanding phenomena such as the increasing imbrication of global, regional, national and even 'private' regulation, the proliferation of global regimes targeting the conduct of individuals and firms directly, and the growing importance of 'meta-regulation' in the substantive content of international law.

The focus of GAL on this panoply of quotidian exercises of power is accompanied by inquiry as to the motivation, and normative views, of participants in these exercises of power when they choose to (or are compelled to, or choose not to) adopt specific GAL mechanisms in particular forms.[11]

2.2 Law

The contention that there is an extant 'law' of global administration offers new avenues into perennial debates about the definition and nature of 'law' in

---

'Global Administrative Law Dimensions of International Organizations Law' (2009) 6 *International Organizations Law Review* 319–58.

[8] Such as the International Organization of Securities Commissions, the International Competition Network, and the International Network for Environmental Compliance and Enforcement. Networks of this kind are found in dozens of different sectors, from anti-corruption and law enforcement to health and human rights.

[9] Such as the Codex Alimentarius Commission, the Internet Corporation for Assigned Names and Numbers, and the World Anti-Doping Agency.

[10] See S Cassese, 'Administrative Law without the State: The Challenge of Global Regulation' (2005) 37 *New York University Journal of International Law & Politics* 663–94.

[11] E Benvenisti and G Downs, 'Toward Global Checks and Balances' (2009) 20 *Constitutional Political Economy* 366–87 (highlighting special interest motivations for the development of some GAL features); E Benvenisti, *The Law of Global Governance* (Brill The Hague 2014).

transnational governance.[12] Certain GAL-type procedural norms (largely applicable to domestic institutions engaging in administrative activities under, or pursuant to, global regimes) are articulated in treaties, or in customary international law, and are unambiguously a part of the corpus of international law. Others, found for example in the internal rules of procedure of treaty bodies, or articulated in 'general comments' of United Nation (UN) treaty bodies, might in international legal jargon be described (not very helpfully) as 'soft law'. However, some of the most intense generation and refinement of procedural norms is currently occurring within global institutions, both interstate and hybrid/private, as they increasingly modify their practices on consultation, review, and disclosure, and codify these changes in more detailed and formal 'policies', 'guidelines', and the like.[13] These changes may be influenced by domestic constitutional law, or the law of the EU, or be prompted by the way in which domestic law sets procedural thresholds for the global norms or decisions which domestic authorities will enforce.[14]

Over time, this diverse practice may, in conjunction with domestic public law, give rise to broadly cast 'general principles of law', and by that avenue be incorporated within the dominant paradigm of international law, but it does not at present have a clear legal status within that system. Its law-like quality rests on a social fact conception bearing some loose relation to Hartian positivism,[15] an approach which

---

[12] B Kingsbury, 'The Concept of "Law" in Global Administrative Law' (2009) 20 *European Journal of International Law* 23–57; L Murphy, *What Makes Law: An Introduction to the Philosophy of Law* (CUP Cambridge 2014) at 145–82; E Fromageau, 'La théorie des institutions du droit administratif global. Étude des interactions avec le droit international public' (PhD thesis, Université de Genève/Aix-Marseille Université, 2014).

[13] This phenomenon is particularly visible in the increasing formality of transparency commitments, and in the provision or reform of more structured arrangements for review of internal decision-making. See eg M Donaldson and B Kingsbury, 'Power and the Public: The Nature and Effects of Formal Transparency Policies in Global Governance' in A Bianchi and A Peters (eds), *Transparency in International Law* (CUP Cambridge 2013) 502–32; E Suzuki and S Nanwani, 'Responsibility of International Organizations: The Accountability Mechanisms of Multilateral Development Banks' (2006) 27 *Michigan Journal of International Law* 177–225.

[14] See eg R Stewart, 'US Administrative Law: A Model for Global Administrative Law?' (2005) 68(3) *Law & Contemporary Problems* 63–108 (suggesting that GAL will likely develop through iterative and even confrontational 'top-down' and 'bottom-up' approaches); S Cassese, 'Global Standards for National Administrative Procedures' (2005) 68(3) *Law & Contemporary Problems* 109–26 (providing a detailed analysis of some 'top-down approaches' and warning against uncritically transposing conceptions of domestic administrative law to the very different transnational institutional context); N Krisch, 'The Pluralism of Global Administrative Law' (2006) 17 *European Journal of International Law* 247–78 (suggesting a pluralist structure on the grounds that it is not only analytically rigorous, but also normatively preferable); E Benvenisti, 'The Interplay between Actors as a Determinant of the Evolution of Administrative Law in International Institutions' (2005) 68(3) *Law & Contemporary Problems* 319–40 (using a public choice perspective to examine how GAL may be shaped in different institutional settings); and the essays in S Cassese (ed), *Research Handbook on Global Administrative Law* (Elgar Cheltenham 2016).

[15] 'The Concept of "Law" in Global Administrative Law' (n 12).

has been vigorously contested.[16] For scholars willing to accept such an expansive view of 'law', GAL may provide a promising site for the elaboration of a renewed *jus gentium* or 'inter-public' law, in which sovereign states would nevertheless still play a privileged role.[17] In any case, GAL scholarship directs attention to the resonance of (public) law and legal ideas beyond the formal international–national legal order.

2.3 Justification

By making visible much more of the decision-making constitutive of the contemporary transnational order, GAL scholarship invites attention to pressing questions of the justification (or legitimation) of these exercises of power. The orthodox formal account of such exercises of power as delegations by states of their own (democratically or empirically justified) powers will rarely be sufficient. Nor in most cases is transnational power justifiable in any direct way by its advancement of human rights, peace, or the rule of law.[18]

More convincing justifications typically assess inputs, processes, and outputs of global governance institutions. The increasing demands for transparency, participation of affected groups, reason-giving, and rights of recourse or review, all have direct bearing on the inputs to and the processes of power. Such demands may be protective of rights, whether of states, individuals, or collective entities. They may also help produce better outputs, by correcting errors and increasing fidelity to the purposes which a given arrangement was intended to achieve. These GAL procedures have a normative grounding that can be shared even where there exists little consensus on substantive values or on the ultimate ends to be served by the institutions.

The dual life of GAL as both practice and theory—that is as both a mapping of real-world phenomena and an intellectual framing—means that GAL's normativity is complex and layered. The identification of a unified body of practice, and the placing of this practice under the banner of 'law', suggests a certain normative desirability inherent in the idea of GAL. The identification of GAL as lying in the

---

[16] On GAL as merely politics, or as good governance practices of a managerial nature, see M-S Kuo, 'Inter-Public Legality or Post-Public Legitimacy? Global Governance and the Curious Case of Global Administrative Law as a New Paradigm of Law' (2012) 10 *International Journal of Constitutional Law* 1050–75; D Dyzenhaus, 'Accountability and the Concept of (Global) Administrative Law' in H Corder (ed), *Global Administrative Law: Innovation and Development* (Clarendon Press Oxford 2009) 3–31; A Somek, 'Administration without Sovereignty' in *The Twilight of Constitutionalism?* (n 3) 267–87.

[17] See B Kingsbury, 'International Law as Inter-Public Law' in HR Richardson and MS Williams (eds), *Nomos XLIX: Moral Universalism and Pluralism* (New York University Press New York 2009) 167–204.

[18] See D Dyzenhaus, 'The Rule of (Administrative) Law in International Law' (2005) 68(3) *Law & Contemporary Problems* 127–66; K-H Ladeur, 'The Emergence of Global Administrative Law and Transnational Regulation' (2012) 3 *Transnational Legal Theory* 243–67.

procedural qualities of existing institutions, and the consequent focus on purely procedural aspects of administration rather than higher order questions of which institution deals with which problems, may work to legitimate a highly uneven institutional apparatus skewed to the interests of the most powerful.[19] At the same time, the internal coherence of GAL and its ability to offer some grip on the status quo demands that it maintain a certain distance from the momentary fluctuations in how institutions decide upon, and justify, their procedures. The procedural norms at the heart of GAL must be at least connected to and animated by some higher end. Whether deliberative democracy might be relevant to that higher end is the question addressed in the following sections.

3 GAL as a Global Terrain
for Deliberative Democracy?

As global policy-making becomes extensive and demanding in its institutional forms and far-reaching in its effects, it seems increasingly insufficient to theorize the state as the only possible locus of democracy. Citizens of democracies voice dissatisfaction with the enterprise of perfecting democratic control over an ever-shrinking domain in which policy can still be determined or steered chiefly through their national political systems.[20] It may be possible to reimagine and renew democracy in

---

[19] Analytically, it may be difficult to disentangle juridification from more superficial institutional change. Within many international organizations, particularly multilateral development banks, the increasing formalization of internal policies, creation of quasi-independent review bodies, and description of these bodies in terms borrowed from appellate judicial review, gives a quasi-legal veneer even to decision-making that is not fully juridical. In particular, these bodies are called upon to interpret and apply what are often rather loosely drafted texts, and do so without any apparent intention to adhere to norms of interpretation developed in international (or any other) law. This trend is part of a pattern of borrowing the garb of law and legal institutions for purely managerial processes. Conversely, the claim to having some legal quality may actually have the effect of imposing internally felt imperatives of consistency, and normative aspirations that do contribute to a strengthening of procedural norms. See M Donaldson and B Kingsbury, 'Ersatz Normativity or Public Law in Global Governance: The Hard Case of International Prescriptions for National Infrastructure Regulation' (2013) 14 *Chicago Journal of International Law* 1–51.

[20] See eg S Battini, 'The Globalization of Public Law' (2006) 18(1) *European Review of Public Law*, <http://ssrn.com/abstract=895263> [accessed 26 February 2016] (distinguishing between 'control' or 'substitution' of domestic authorities' right to regulate as the forms through which this process is operating); and the contributions to the symposium on global public goods in 'Symposium: Global Public Goods and the Plurality of Legal Orders' (2012) 23 *European Journal of International Law* 643–791. The challenges of governance under contemporary conditions are such that some have claimed it is now impossible to understand the settlement of social choices in democratic terms at all, even within the

these new global conditions: on a national scale, democracy has proven resilient in the face of changing functional demands, and understandings of democracy have evolved greatly with the consolidation of the administrative state, the entrenchment of judicial review, and the proliferation of non-electoral modes of oversight and participation.[21] However, the problem of democracy beyond the state is more urgent and more protean than it appeared in earlier eras.

Arguments for global democratic institutions, indeed for top-down global democracy in any form, are met with staunch normative and positive-political scepticism.[22] We contend that, in promoting the bottom-up scrutiny of very specific institutional exercises of power and related issues of institutional design, GAL opens space for investigation of whether bottom-up pathways and minor pro-democratic quotidian inflections in such institutions might hold greater promise. We argue that GAL shares some of the preoccupations central to normative arguments for democracy, and offers a terrain in which aspects of deliberative democracy, in particular, might take root.[23]

Perhaps most basically, democracy is bound up with a concern with self-government. The resonance of democracy as a political ideal for the age of governance can also lie in the fundamental commitment of many people to non-dominance: democracy facilitates resistance to the domination of the many by the few.[24] This has particular salience in global regulatory governance, with overwhelming majorities of people currently exerting little influence, in part because they lack the bureaucratic and political resources of a responsive state or civil society capable of articulating their position in the global sphere, but also as a result of the fundamental inequities in the contemporary economic order. From this perspective, the levelling and emancipatory impetus of democracy poses a profound challenge to the existing statist order and the system of international law that sustains it.[25]

state: see eg E Rubin, 'Getting Past Democracy' (2001) 149 *University of Pennsylvania Law Review* 711–92; E Rubin, *Beyond Camelot—Rethinking Politics and Law for the Modern State* (Princeton University Press Princeton 2005) ch 4.

[21] J Keane, *The Life and Death of Democracy* (Norton London 2009); F Vibert, *The Rise of the Unelected: Democracy and the New Separation of Powers* (CUP Cambridge 2007).

[22] See eg T Nagel, 'The Problem of Global Justice' (2005) 33 *Philosophy & Public Affairs* 113–47.

[23] For a brief analysis of the different approaches to 'democracy' in global governance, see S Wheatley, 'A Democratic Rule of International Law' (2011) 22 *European Journal of International Law* 525–48, 528. See also J Bohman, *Democracy across Borders: From Demos to Demoi* (MIT Press Cambridge MA 2007) at 3–5; G de Búrca, 'Developing Democracy beyond the State' (2008) 46 *Columbia Journal of Transnational Law* 221–78. For a fine-grained analysis of the way in which different approaches to democracy could inform transnational food governance issues, see B Adamson, 'The New Zealand Food Bill and Global Administrative Law: A Recipe for Democratic Engagement?' (LLM thesis, University of Toronto, 2012).

[24] See eg S Slaughter, 'Transnational Democratization and Republican Citizenship: Towards Critical Republicanism' (2014) 3 *Global Constitutionalism* 310–37.

[25] For one argument about the evolution of the normative core of international law, see B Simma, 'From Bilateralism to Community Interest in International Law' (1994) 250 *Recueil des Cours* 217–384.

Admittedly, 'administration' is at face value an incongruous site in which to look for democratization. However loosely defined, administration is to some extent distanced from fundamental questions about the nature of existing institutions, and about the general direction of the substantive norms being pursued.[26] Yet GAL's focus on the use of procedural norms and mechanisms to secure 'accountability'—that those exercising power can be called to give an account of their actions, and are potentially subject to sanctions when they have fallen short of applicable standards—is one element of operationalizing self-government and non-dominance. Like international law itself, 'accountability' is consistent with a range of more comprehensive normative visions of transnational ordering. Calls for greater accountability of power beyond the state are increasingly framed as a means to overcome the 'problem of disregard' in global governance, seeking to give weight to the interests or the fate or the life-world of individuals and communities affected by such power but improperly undervalued or neglected in its processes.[27]

The realm of 'administration' may thus be important in relation to democratic goals. Moreover, analysing power in global institutions from the quotidian upward, rather than in a constitutionalist vein from the grand institutions and principles downward, helps to identify key issues in the relations between constitution and administration which bear on locating sites where democratic striving may make a difference. The constitutional emphasis on institutional allocation needs to be blended with the GAL focus on institutional workings and on interactions between institutions in the global administrative space. Higher order norms are often inflected or totally offset by lower order 'administrative' norms and decisions in the routine operations of power systems—particularly power systems beyond a single state, where there is little scope for constitutional review. Jurisdictional logic—in which lower-order decision-making takes place within certain predetermined constitutionally set bounds—does not hold nearly as tightly within the global administrative space as it does within robust national legal systems. One corollary of this is that historical and sociological assumptions about how power systems evolve, developed from the experience of these processes during

See also the essays in the first part of A Cassese (ed), *Realizing Utopia: The Future of International Law* (OUP Oxford 2012).

[26] On the potential tensions in practice between campaigns for procedural norms and for more comprehensive and substantive transformations, see R Buchanan, 'Perpetual Peace or Perpetual Process: Global Civil Society and Cosmopolitan Legality at the World Trade Organization' (2003) 16 *Leiden Journal of International Law* 673–99

[27] On the 'problem of disregard' see R Stewart, 'Remedying Disregard in Global Regulatory Governance: Accountability, Participation and Responsiveness' (2014) 108 *American Journal of International Law* 211–70. On permutations of 'accountability' in the global order, see RW Grant and RO Keohane, 'Accountability and Abuses of Power in World Politics' (2005) 99 *American Political Science Review* 29–43.

state consolidation and within the state, may no longer hold. Power beyond the state is today organized in different forms—forms that are perhaps more open to adjustment from the lower reaches.[28]

In a superficial sense, democracy is a spectral presence in GAL even as it is presently characterized: the separation of powers implicit in the notion of a domain of 'administration' recalls a central feature of Western democracies, and notions of 'publicness' are closely allied with a democratic imperative.[29] More substantively, we may even be tempted to see in GAL procedures some features of deliberative democracy.

Deliberative theories of democracy generally regard open and inclusive deliberation as intrinsically enhancing the democratic legitimacy of governing decisions by ensuring procedural conditions that are supposed to make those judgements somehow those of the collective concerned.[30] These theories typically recommend or require deliberation, participation, and publication. Deliberation is understood with varying degrees of stringency, but requires some form of discourse, rather than merely episodic voting or bargaining, in at least certain stages of the process of reaching decisions about norms. Participation in this deliberation is required under conditions of equality. Publication involves some orientation to 'public' reason, most minimally, the publication of reasons put forward by participants, but sometimes also encompassing substantive characteristics ranging from a loose commitment on the part of participants to reason from a notional general interest, rather than self-interest, to some stricter criterion for the arguments which may be put forward.

GAL norms are concerned with transparency, participation, reason-giving, review and reconsideration, and accountability of decision-makers more broadly. The institutionalization of these principles seems likely to facilitate deliberation, and open up processes of decision-making to larger deliberative communities.

---

[28] P Lindseth, *Power and Legitimacy: Reconciling Europe and the Nation-State* (OUP Oxford 2010); P Lindseth, 'Supranational Organizations' in I Hurd, I Johnstone, and JK Cogan (eds), *The Oxford Handbook of International Organizations* (OUP Oxford forthcoming 2017).

[29] See 'The Concept of "Law" in Global Administrative Law' (n 12). By *publicness* we mean the claim made for law that it has been wrought by the whole society, by the public, and the connected claim that law addresses matters of concern to the society as such. See J Waldron, 'Can There Be a Democratic Jurisprudence?' (2009) 58 *Emory Law Journal* 675–712. For further analytical elaboration, see also N Walker, 'On the Necessarily Public Character of Law' in C Michelon et al., (eds), *The Public in Law: Representations of the Political in Legal Discourse* (Ashgate Publishing Farnham 2012) 9–31; D Dyzenhaus, 'The Public Conscience of the Law' (2014) 2 *Netherlands Journal of Legal Philosophy* 115–26.

[30] That said, there remains a major tension in the theorization of deliberative democracy between the moral legitimacy conferred by ideal procedures and the epistemic advantages of deliberation. On the variety of accounts of deliberative democracy, see J Bohman, 'Survey Article: The Coming of Age of Deliberative Democracy' (1998) 6 *Journal of Political Philosophy* 400–25. See also A Bächtiger et al., 'Disentangling Diversity in Deliberative Democracy: Competing Theories, Their Blind Spots and Complementarities' (2010) 18 *Journal of Political Philosophy* 32–63, at 35–53.

Visions of GAL as an instantiation of 'inter-public law' resonate with the notion of public reason by identifying the collective interests being affected even by private governance, moving this governance into institutional sites, and subjecting it to institutional procedures, which require appeals to a general interest rather than purely individual or sectoral interests.

GAL could thus be conceived as fostering in global administration an inter-linked web of deliberative arenas—the prerequisites of deliberative democracy. These arenas force actors to explicate and scrutinize heterogeneous interests (national, sectoral, technical, or self-avowedly public interests), and eventually to transform their preferences as part of the elaboration of shared interpretations. Deliberative arenas require even non-state and private actors to justify their positions in light of public reasons, and to hold decision-makers accountable for the decisions ultimately reached. Ongoing criticism and experimentation sustain the design and redesign of various institutional arrangements with the goal of nurturing deliberative processes to satisfy democratic legitimacy standards and enhance responsiveness. If GAL actually fosters these deliberative arenas, it would join other 'democratic-striving' approaches to governance beyond the state.[31]

4 CHALLENGES FOR GAL FROM DELIBERATIVE DEMOCRACY

While aspiration for democratic-striving in GAL holds promise as a form of critique, GAL as presently theorized lacks certain key elements necessary for its administrative sites to be loci of deliberative democracy. GAL has to date renounced any comprehensive theoretical framework through which to judge practice, and has been traced in a wide range of institutional contexts which transcend distinctions conventionally presumed to be essential for deliberative democracy (for

---

[31] See 'Developing Democracy beyond the State' (n 23). See also J Cohen and CF Sabel, 'Global Democracy?' (2005) 37 *New York University Journal of International Law and Politics* 763–97; T MacDonald and K MacDonald, 'Non-Electoral Accountability in Global Politics: Strengthening Democratic Control within the Global Garment Industry' (2006) 17 *European Journal of International Law* 89–119; and DH Rached, 'Doomed Aspiration of Pure Instrumentality: Global Administrative Law and Accountability' (2014) 3 *Global Constitutionalism* 338–72, at 368. But see M-S Kuo, 'Taming Governance with Legality? Critical Reflections upon Global Administrative Law as Small-C Global Constitutionalism' (2011) 44 *New York University Journal of International Law and Politics* 55–102 (claiming that the GAL approach necessarily entails a technocratic privatization of legitimacy).

example, between public and private authority).[32] Thus, GAL has little to say where there is no (or no agreed upon) pre-existing and defined political community, or no accepted structure of representation.[33] It is these questions which are at stake in the future development of GAL. Despite the affinities between GAL and certain descriptive features of deliberative democracy, there are aspects of GAL which appear to limit the extent to which GAL alone can instantiate any kind of credible deliberative democratic environment. Some of these limitations are inherent in attempts to infuse deliberative democracy into global governance generally; some are particular to GAL.

If progress is to be made, it is useful to ask what ideas about deliberative democracy can offer to the development of GAL. Attention to deliberative democracy in its captious function brings to the fore of the GAL project a series of questions that are not suggested—perhaps not even allowed—by the original framing of GAL. The following sections will introduce these challenges and detail the prospective contributions that attention to deliberative democracy could make to each.

4.1 Subservience to Structure

First, the focus on purely procedural aspects of administration may actually detract from critical examination of 'constitutional' aspects of governance. GAL works within existing institutions, and does not in itself argue for the allocation of particular issues to one institution or type of institution over another.[34] As it develops, GAL might come to preclude questions of major public importance being determined by institutions which are not conducive to some minimal procedural apparatus, including in extreme cases of absolute discretion or purely private, negotiated

---

[32] For an approach to global administration which begins from Habermasian theory, and works from this theory to make sense of practice, see M Goldmann, 'A Matter of Perspective: Global Governance and the Distinction between Public and Private Authority (and Not Law)' (2013) <http://ssrn.com/abstract=2260293> [accessed 26 February 2016]. See also M Kumm, 'The Legitimacy of International Law: A Constitutionalist Framework of Analysis' (2004) 15 *European Journal of International Law* 907–31; A von Bogdandy and I Venzke, *In Whose Name? A Public Law Theory of International Adjudication* (OUP Oxford 2014).

[33] It is also not clear what it would mean to take some variant of deliberative democracy, unbounded by the nation-state, as an end of GAL without envisaging some kind of redistributive program that also transcends the nation-state. Narrowly understood, this is a question about what happens to particular accounts of deliberative democracy if we remove the background assumption of the welfare state guaranteeing basic resources for life. But it also goes more generally to questions about the nature of the deliberation which is structurally possible within current practices and supporting conceptions of global administration.

[34] International law itself also contains few resources from which to argue, for example, that certain new international organizations should be created, or that there should be an international organization at all, rather than, say, an informal network or task force, to deal with a given problem.

decision-making. But for now it has little more to say about foundational, structural questions of the allocation of powers to particular institutions.

This is critical as the current global institutional endowment is highly uneven, and likely to be disproportionately shaped by the interests and concerns of more powerful states (and the most powerful factions within states).[35] Institutional sites of decision-making will hence often be highly skewed to particular constituencies, predetermining the terrain of debate in ways that will not themselves be subject to free debate among equals.[36]

GAL is beginning to offer a way forward in focusing serious analytic and normative attention on hitherto-neglected possibilities which are opened up by the holistic view of a global administrative space: inter-relations between institutions, multi-institutional compensatory approaches to participation and to voice and recognition, and cross-institutional review and checking functions. Concerns for deliberative democracy foster and prioritize examination of these structural questions in ways that accountability or other existing GAL imperatives do not.

4.2 Passive Acquiescence to Substantive Norms

Second, 'administration' typically occurs in the shadow of, or in response to, higher order norms or decisions that will not be open to challenge in the administrative process, at least not in any direct way. This is evident in institutions such as the World Bank, which in relative terms have very sophisticated GAL mechanisms. Affected people and NGOs may access certain of the Bank's documents associated with projects, must be consulted on major projects affecting them pursuant to the 'safeguards' policies, and may make requests for inspection to the Bank's Inspection Panel if they believe the Bank has fallen short of what is required by its own policies. But even if a request for inspection is successful and the Inspection Panel engages in extensive fact-finding, including meeting with the complainants and consulting widely in the country concerned,[37] the question at issue is not an open-ended one. The Inspection Panel is undertaking a narrow forensic inquiry concerning whether or not Bank staff followed internal policies in

---

[35] It is telling that rules of international trade and investment law, which protect primarily commercial interests, are among the sharpest and most detailed GAL norms now in existence. See BS Chimni, 'Co-Option and Resistance: Two Faces of Global Administrative Law' (2005) 37 *New York University Journal of International Law and Politics* 799–827.

[36] See eg 'Developing Democracy beyond the State' (n 23) 235–6. For a broader articulation of this problematic aspect of GAL, see 'Global Administrative Law and the Constitutional Ambition' (n 3) 259–62.

[37] On the Inspection Panel's encounters with project-affected people, see E Brown Weiss, 'On Being Accountable in a Kaleidoscopic World' (2010) 104 *Proceedings of the American Society of International Law* 477–90, at 484.

planning and approving a given project. Although Panel recommendations may stimulate broader reflection by the Board and Bank staff about the project, and provide material for NGOs and project-affected people to campaign for cancellation or redesign, they do themselves answer the substantive question of whether the contested project should (all things considered) go ahead.

Including deliberative democracy as a critical tool accessible to the GAL project could open these substantive issues to debate. It would no longer be sufficient to fulfil procedural norms aimed at accountability and internal rule-following; instead, decisions would have to be justified on broader grounds. Reforms in this direction could draw on explorations within GAL of possibilities for operationalizing *ex ante* deliberation, organized competition, learning, review, and revision, as a means to achieve bottom-up long-term change in normatively attractive directions.

4.3 Struggles to Align Multiple Systems of Law and Concepts of Representation

Third, the landscape of global administration involves a patchwork of institutional sites with potentially divergent structures of representation and participation. Much global administration occurs through and in the shadow of a dense and sophisticated body of international law that is premised on a theoretical edifice of political affiliation and representation (insofar as it foregrounds formal, statist interaction), but which is not in any obvious sense 'democratic'.[38] Even a minimal norm of equality of states is subject to arrangements in many interstate organizations, such as the UN, which privilege some states over others on wholly realist grounds. Global administration also interacts intensively with the national or sub-national public law of particular states, grounded in localized structures of representation which do not adequately capture the rewards and burdens which national decisions may generate beyond the state. GAL has to date not articulated a comprehensive theory of representation, although there are inevitably latent notions of political community and representation at work in the crafting of GAL

---

[38] Despite increasing support for (liberal, electoral) democracy as a substantive norm (for example in the context of civil and political rights, as a criterion of entry into global or regional treaty regimes or institutions, and in the focus on democratization as an objective in development assistance for transitional and post-conflict societies), the prevailing *sources* of international law have not been understood as having any necessary component of actual, rather than formal, popular consent. Constitutional checks on treaty-making are a feature of domestic rather than international law, and violation of constitutional provisions does not necessarily affect the validity of a treaty at international law. Many of the acts and pronouncements that constitute evidence of the existence of customary norms emanate essentially from national executives. On the trajectory of an asserted 'right' to democratic governance, see S Marks, 'What Has Become of the Emerging Right to Democratic Governance?' (2011) 22 *European Journal of International Law* 507–24.

mechanisms (for example, where institutions are granting standing for participation in an anti-formalist way, on the basis of individuals' exposure to concrete effects of particular decisions, or on a crude corporatist basis by allowing a certain number of participants from particular sectors).[39] These approaches might in fact be optimal, but there are obvious dangers as well. In a laissez-faire system better-resourced actors will be more able to dominate administrative processes, and crude corporatism may fall well short of reflecting the parties affected by particular decisions.

Insofar as the present structures and sources of international law are to be preserved, democratic ideals and practices must live alongside more formalist structures of representation through consent and delegation, and emanating from national public law. A GAL project taking deliberative democracy as a touchstone would need to consider how best to bridge, reconcile, or restructure these divergent forms of representation, and compensate for their shortcomings, rather than aiming to build deliberative democracy on a global scale from a tabula rasa.

4.4 The Sprawl of Administration

Finally, the sheer diversity of 'administration' is an obstacle to articulating compelling normative criteria explaining what procedures should be applied at specific sites.[40] Attention to deliberative democracy provides criteria by which to sort through this dizzying diversity. For example, it is regularly argued in GAL that a pronounced deleterious impact on identifiable individuals or classes of individuals requires notice, consultation, and individually triggered review procedures. The grounds for this are that decisions about the application of sanctions, or the determination of refugee status, may have critical and irreversible effects for particular individuals, and decisions about the allocation of resources in natural disasters or post-conflict situations may be matters of life and death for whole communities. Deliberative democracy adds to this interest-based account a public component— the reasons given must be reasons which could reasonably be given by all parties

---

[39] Compare N Walker, 'The Post-National Horizon of Constitutionalism and Public Law: Paradigm Extension or Paradigm Exhaustion?' in C MacAmhlaigh, C Michelon, and N Walker (eds), *After Public Law* (OUP Oxford 2013) 241–63. The absence of strict criteria for representation is not the absence of a normative orientation, but rather a normative orientation in its own right: see eg B Kingsbury, 'First Amendment Liberalism as Global Legal Architecture: Ascriptive Groups and the Problems of the Liberal NGO Model of International Civil Society' (2002) 3 *Chicago Journal of International Law* 183–95.

[40] For some sense of the variation in mechanisms currently applied across different institutions, see the detailed survey of participation mechanisms in S Cassese, 'A Global Due Process of Law?' in G Anthony et al., (eds), *Values in Global Administrative Law* (Hart Oxford 2011) 17–60; 'Remedying Disregard in Global Regulatory Governance' (n 27).

in a setting of public deliberation, and must speak to and fairly address all of the public(s) involved.

5 Democratic Striving in Global Administrative Lawyering

GAL plays a valuable analytical role complementing conventional paradigms of international law by providing some additional grip on the complex realities of global administration and stimulating avenues for awakening, contestation, and reflection upon their ends, forms, and procedures.[41] The program of GAL thus offers an alternative to the impasse between grand narratives of indulgent legitimation and sheer resistance, by 'allying itself with the struggles of those for whom the hope of a better future provides the courage to live in the present'.[42]

The proliferation of procedural protections in global governance is part of a macro-sociological phenomenon, the massive growth across the world in the number of organizations and in sub-specialist expertise and processes expressed through specialized organizational forms and accompanying codes.[43] In individual cases and perhaps structurally, it has identifiable political causes, including pursuit by global beneficiaries of liberal or neoliberal programs, expedient responses to external pressures, window dressing, inter-institutional competition, mimesis, and

---

[41] See eg AC Deshman, 'Horizontal Review between International Organizations: Why, How, and Who Cares about Corporate Regulatory Capture' (2011) 22 *European Journal of International Law* 1089–1113 (using a GAL framework to analyse the dispute between the World Health Organization and the Council of Europe over the former's reaction to the H1N1 pandemic, and to explore the conditions, formats, and procedures under which horizontal review between international organizations might occur); D Richemond-Barak, 'Regulating War: A Taxonomy in Global Administrative Law' (2011) 22 *European Journal of International Law* 1027–69 (using a GAL framework to describe and assess the effectiveness of several regulatory initiatives over private military and security companies).

[42] S Benhabib, *Critique, Norm, and Utopia: A Study of the Foundations of Critical Theory* (Columbia University Press New York 1986) at 15. See 'Doomed Aspiration' (n 31) 372; M Donaldson and B Kingsbury, 'The Global Governance of Public Law' in C MacAmhlaigh, C Michelon, and N Walker (eds), *After Public Law* (OUP Oxford 2013) 264–85, at 285 (concluding that '...the most fruitful engagement with a putative global public law, particularly global administrative law, is one that recognizes its current fluidity, seeing it not as a source of a particular formula for legitimacy or checklist of requirements, but as a field in which these requirements and their foundations are being articulated and contested.').

[43] JW Meyer and P Bromley, 'The Worldwide Expansion of "Organization"' (2013) 31 *Sociological Theory* 366–89; GS Drori, JW Meyer, and H Hwang (eds), *Globalization and Organization: World Society and Organizational Change* (OUP Oxford 2006).

least-cost problem solving. But even if in a particular case the immediate motivations for institutional and procedural reform are wholly strategic, these reforms have effects precisely because the case for greater participation, reason-giving or independent review, for example, is articulated by someone—whether NGOs or states critical of the institution, or staff inside it—as normatively desirable. Highly disparate normative justifications are given by these advocates for procedural change in particular institutions. Some of them are animated by an aspiration aligned to some extent with deliberative democracy—a kind of democratic striving in relation to the specific institution they examine or in relation to the norms of global administration more broadly. This aspiration tinges GAL, not so much in its academic scholarship or its practice as in its advocacy. The activities of institutional entrepreneurship and global administrative lawyering, although by no means explicitly committed to deliberative democratic aims, have in many cases carried within them a modest form of democratic striving with regard to global governance.

In conditions of intensifying globalization and dispersed political authority, deliberative democracy offers one point of departure, a sort of beacon, casting light on what is important, and consequently also on where the dangers for the good governance enterprise in this post-national context lie. Conceived as a regulative ideal, deliberative democracy arguably still provides one meaningful way in which we can make transnational forms of political order at least intelligible from a democratic cosmology, providing an attractive path for their understanding, assessment, and critique, focused not only on procedural or institutional aspects of governance but also the ethos that should be animating them.

PART III

REGIMES AND DOCTRINES

CHAPTER 27

TOWARDS A NEW THEORY OF SOURCES IN INTERNATIONAL LAW

JEAN D'ASPREMONT

1 INTRODUCTION

THE idea of a renewal of the theory of sources can be received with a feeling of idiosyncrasy. Indeed, in twenty-first century thinking about international law the theory of sources has come to be perceived as the aegis ensuring the survival of the *ancien régime* and, thus, the nemesis of change in international law. Said differently, the theory of sources is often seen as a cognitive and argumentative constraint frustrating the new projects that international lawyers want inter-national law to serve in a disaggregated and heterogeneous international society. Once the embodiment of progress, the theory of sources is now thought of as the barrier thereto. Against the backdrop of such disrepute, exploring the possibility of rejuvenating the sources of international law inevitably looks very reactionary.

The feeling of reactionarism that can accompany any inquiry into the possibility of a renewal of the theory of sources is fundamentally and doubly relative. Indeed, it is the result of the specific way in which the mainstream theory of sources has been designed by its architects as much as the way in which such a mainstream construction has been portrayed and received by the subsequent generations of international lawyers. This is why approaching the possibility of a rejuvenation of the theory of sources in terms of temporality is considered vain here. This chapter accordingly approaches the idea of a 'new theory of sources' from another perspective. It looks at how the theory of sources came to be crafted as a platform for the objectivizing of meaning and a bridle to crude politics, and how it failed in that liberal project. Yet, it argues thereafter that this possible failure of the classical theory of sources should not be construed as a failure of the principle of such a theory, but rather the failure of the specific (representation of the) theory of sources as it was inherited from the twentieth century and depicted by its critiques. In making such an argument, this chapter seeks to advocate a specific avenue for reconstructing the theory of sources beyond naïve objectivism. More specifically, it puts forward a social theory of sources that makes it possible to construe the theory of sources as a tradition and a practice rather than as a set of rules that operates mechanically.

This chapter starts by recalling how the rise of the theory of sources in thinking about international law came to epitomize the modern shift from a subject-based perspective to a rule-based perspective as a well as a move away from theories of substantive validity, such a shift having been then understood as a factor of progress (Section 2). It then turns to the growing disrepute that subsequently affected this modern theory of sources, and, more specifically, the reformist or abolitionist attitudes that have been observed in twentieth and twenty-first century international legal scholarship (Section 3). After concurring with the finding of a failure of the objectivization of meaning and the displacement of politics attempted by the theory of sources, the chapter reflects on the possibility of a renewal (Section 4). It ends with a few concluding remarks on the possibility of emancipating the theory of sources from the objectivization of meaning and the displacement of politics (Section 5).

Before embarking on such an argument, one important epistemological caveat must be formulated with a view to contextualizing and relativizing the inquiry made here and upholding its persuasiveness. The reconstruction of the theory of sources is not revolutionary *stricto sensu*. Because it is still grounded in the same ancestral paradigm as the mainstream theory of sources, it does not in itself bring about a paradigm shift.[1] The suggested reconstruction is not a change of the theory but rather a change within the theory. It remains grounded in the same tradition and, as a result, the suggested change to the theory of sources advocated here remains inevitably anchored in continuity.[2] The reconstruction attempted here, however subversive it may be in the eyes of some readers, inevitably perpetuates some ancestral paradigmatic moves observed in international legal thought.

---

[1] On the notion of paradigm shift, see generally T Kuhn, *The Structure of Scientific Revolutions* (4th edn University of Chicago Press Chicago 2012 [1962]).

[2] On the notion of tradition, see A Macintyre, *Whose Justice? Which Rationality?* (Duckworth Press London 1988) at 364.

Whether a radical break away from that tradition and total revolution of international law thinking is possible is, however, another question which does not need to be addressed here.[3]

2 FROM THEORIES OF SUBSTANTIVE VALIDITY TO A RULE-BASED INTERNATIONAL LAW: THE RISE OF THE MODERN THEORY OF SOURCES

The theory of sources was not totally absent from the early thinking about international law. Theories of the substantive validity of rules, such as those found in scholastic theories, allowed for an autonomous concept of sources.[4] Yet the dualism—by virtue of which immanent considerations would trump any formal aspects of validity—at the heart of such theories of substantive validity inevitably demoted sources to a very secondary mechanism. The emergence of a theory of sources properly so-called—that is, a theory whereby a rule would be identified and validated on the basis of its formal pedigree—was further frustrated by the rise of a subject-based approach to international law between the end of the eighteenth century and the beginning of the nineteenth century.[5] It suffices to recall, once again, that the appellation 'international law' was coined and designed in direct reference to its main 'fabricants'.[6] According to this approach, a correlation was established between states as the makers of international law and those rules that could qualify as rules of international law.[7] According to this subject-based approach, 'international law [was] conceived of as *horizontal* law, in which the

---

[3] On the possibility of total critique, see generally RM Unger, *Knowledge and Politics* (Free Press New York 1984).

[4] F de Vitoria, *Political Writings* (A Pagden and J Lawrence eds) (CUP Cambridge 1991); A Gentili, *De Iure Belli Libri Tres* (JC Rolfe trans) (Clarendon Press Oxford 1933 [1598]).

[5] For an historical account of the concept of subject, see the fascinating work of JE Nijman, *The Concept of International Legal Personality: An Inquiry into the History and Theory of International Law* (TMC Asser Press The Hague 2004).

[6] J Bentham, *An Introduction to the Principles of Morals and Legislation* (Kessinger Whitefish, MT 2005 [1781]) at 326.

[7] TJ Lawrence, *The Principles of International Law* (PH Winfield ed) (7th edn Macmillan London 1923) at 1–14; L Oppenheim, *International Law: A Treatise* (RF Roxburgh ed) (3rd edn Longmans, Green & Co London 1920–1) vol 1, at 1. See JL Brierly, *The Law of Nations: An Introduction to the Law of Peace* (H Waldock ed) (6th edn Clarendon Press Oxford 1963 [1930]) at 1 and 41ff.

subjects of the law are also the makers of the law'.[8] As a result thereof, processes leading to the creation of legal rules properly so-called were necessarily involving the subjects of international law.

The simultaneous resilience of (naturalist) scholastic-inspired approaches in the tradition of Hugo Grotius—exemplified by Samuel Pufendorf[9] and subsequently by Christian von Wolff (who borrowed from Aristotelian theory)—continued to impede the design of a theory of sources understood as the exclusive validator of rules. It is only with emancipation from the naturalist models of substantive validity[10] that theories of sources came to impose themselves decisively and be elevated as the linchpin of the system of thought accompanying international law. This, however, did not happen in one day and some of the intermediary stages in the rise of the theory of sources must be briefly recalled.

For the first time, room for the elaboration of a theory of sources was created by those legal scholars of the nineteenth century who elevated the will of the state to the status of the only validator. In particular, under the influence of Vattel and Martens, natural law and reason were demoted to a secondary parameter, thereby creating the possibility for a theory of sources. It is fair to contend that, subject to a few exceptions,[11] the great majority of nineteenth-century international legal scholars—at least according to the image of that period that we have inherited[12]—adhered to a voluntary conception of law that created space for a theory of sources.

The idea that the voluntarists of the nineteenth century paved the way for the emergence of a theory of sources is certainly not without paradox. Indeed, voluntarism is not structurally different from substantive validity.[13] If the will of the state is the validator of rules, there is no autonomous pedigree by virtue of which the rule is identified and validated. In both substantive validity and voluntarism, there is simply no neutralization of the indeterminacy—and the politics—of the will that ought to be determined, whether such a will is that of the state or God or is simply reason. In that sense, the voluntarist scholars of the nineteenth century were still

---

[8] P Allott, 'The True Function of Law in the International Community' (1998) 5 *Indiana Journal of Global Legal Studies* 391–413, at 404 (emphasis in original).

[9] S Pufendorf, *On the Law of Nature and of Nations* (CH Oldfather and WA Oldfather trans) (Clarendon Press Oxford 1934 [1672]).

[10] See eg P Guggenheim, 'Les Origines de la Notion autonome du Droit des Gens' in *Symbolae Verzijl: Présentées au professeur JHW Verzijl à l'occasion de son LXX-ième anniversaire* (Martinus Nijhoff The Hague 1958) 177–89.

[11] See eg J Lorimer, *Principes de droit international* (E Nys trans) (C Muquardt Brussels 1884) at 19–29.

[12] See generally D Kennedy, 'International Law and the Nineteenth Century: History of an Illusion' (1996) 65 *Nordic Journal of International Law* 385–420.

[13] See J d'Aspremont and J Kammerhofer (eds), *International Legal Positivism in a Post-Modern World* (CUP Cambridge 2014).

one step away from inventing the theory of sources as exclusive validator. However, by moving away from the will of God, nature or reason, these scholars prepared the ground for the sophisticated conceptual engineering that led to the design of the theory of sources in the twentieth century.

The great majority of twentieth-century scholars did not shed their predecessors' idea that international law rests on the consent of states.[14] The consensus on the idea that the will of the state is the most obvious material source of law remained unchallenged.[15] The main difference between nineteenth- and twentieth-century international legal scholars, however, lies in the fact that the latter tried to devise formal law-ascertaining criteria with which to capture state consent.[16] This is precisely how twentieth-century scholars came to devise a sophisticated theory of sources[17] according to which international legal rules stemmed from the will of states expressed through one of the formal sources of international law. It was meant to provide an objective platform whereby rules could be ascertained and their meaning determined, thereby supposedly displacing the politics inherent in the determination of state or divine will.[18] The objective ascertainment and meaning that this tool was meant to produce was quickly perceived as progress.[19] According to this construction, such a theory of sources, especially by virtue of the formalism allegedly accompanying it, was also meant to provide predictability in the behaviour of law-applying authorities while simultaneously endowing judicial decisions with a greater legitimacy and authority.[20] This construction became the

[14] D Anzilotti, 'Il diritto internazionale nei giudizi interni (1905)' in Società Italiana per l'Organizzazione Internazionale (ed), *Opere di Dionisio Anzilotti: Scritti di diritto internazionale pubblico* (2 vols Cedam Padova 1956–7) vol 1, 281–539, at 318; *The Principles of International Law* (n 7) 1–14; L Oppenheim, *International Law: A Treatise* (2 vols 1st edn OUP Oxford 1905–6) especially vol 1, at 92; G Schwarzenberger, *International Law as Applied by International Courts and Tribunals: Volume 1 General Principles* (3rd edn Stephens London 1957); P Guggenheim, 'What is Positive International Law?' in GA Lipsky (ed), *Law and Politics in the World Community: Essays on Hans Kelsen's Pure Theory and Related Problems of International Law* (University of California Press Berkeley 1953) 15–30.

[15] One of the first most complete expressions of this formal consensual understanding of international law has been offered by D Anzilotti, *Corso di diritto internazionale: Lezioni tenute nell'Università di Roma nell'anno scolastico 1922–23* (Athenaeum Rome 1923) at 27. For a more recent manifestation of the voluntary nature of international law, see P Weil, 'Towards Relative Normativity in International Law?' (1983) 77 *American Journal of International Law* 413–42.

[16] See the refinement of the theory of consent in OA Elias and CL Lim, *The Paradox of Consensualism in International Law* (Kluwer Law International The Hague 1998).

[17] A Pellet, 'Cours Général: le Droit International entre souveraineté et communauté international' (2007) 2 *Anuário Brasileiro de Direito Internacional* 12–74, especially at 15, 19, and 31.

[18] M Koskenniemi, 'International Law in a Post-Realist Era' (1995) 16 *Australian Yearbook of International Law* 1–19.

[19] T Skouteris, *The Notion of Progress in International Law Discourse* (TMC Asser Press The Hague 2010) especially ch 3.

[20] See EJ Weinrib, 'Legal Formalism: On the Immanent Rationality of Law' (1988) 97 *Yale Law Journal* 949–1016.

theory of sources as we understand it today and still enjoys a strong support among twenty-first century scholars.[21]

While the theory of sources designed in the twentieth century was sophisticated and widely embraced, it was characterized by an extreme theoretical paucity. The architects of the theory of sources as well as the adherents thereto all remained very aloof from debates about its theoretical foundations. Very few scholars ventured into a study of the ontology of the theory of sources.[22] This dominant 'anti-theoretical'[23] posture can probably be explained by the growing self-assurance gained by international legal scholars who, after their branch of law was recognized as equal to other legal disciplines, did not deem it necessary to unravel the foundations of their understanding of international law, including those of the theory of sources.[24] This being said, it is not the object of this chapter to further investigate the reasons why the theory of sources—albeit sophisticated—was made an idol built on clay fleet. What is important here is that the lack of interest paid by international legal scholars to the foundations of the theory of sources has most likely not been alien to the growing challenges to the theory of sources witnessed in the second half of the twentieth century, to which we now turn.

3 From Reformism to Abolitionism: The Fall of the Theory of Sources

This section argues that as early as the middle of the twentieth century, international legal scholars had grown wary of the limitations and conceptual flaws of the theory of sources as it had been conceived. It shows that the discontent towards the theory of sources first manifested itself through reformist projects (Section 3.1) before turning into more radical abolitionist approaches (Section 3.2). It then discusses the rationale of such discontent (Section 3.3).

---

[21] See eg A Orakhelashvili, *The Interpretation of Acts and Rules in Public International Law* (OUP Oxford 2008) at 51–60.

[22] A classical example is R Jennings and A Watts (eds), *Oppenheim's International Law* (2 vols 9th edn Longman London 1992) vol 1.

[23] The expression is Martti Koskenniemi's: see M Koskenniemi, 'Repetition as Reform: Georges Abi-Saab *Cours Général de droit international public*' (1998) 9 *European Journal of International Law* 405–11, at 406.

[24] TO Elias, 'Problems Concerning the Validity of Treaties' (1971) 134 *Recueil des Cours* 333–416, at 341. See K Zemanek, 'The Legal Foundations of the International System' (1997) 266 *Recueil des Cours* 9–335, at 131ff.

3.1 Reformism

The discontent towards the theory of sources is not just a contemporary phenomenon. By the middle of the twentieth century, the theory of sources had already been condemned for its constraints on the 'advancement' of international law. Such discontent was originally only of a reformist character, in that it was first geared towards reform of the theory of sources rather than its abandonment. Indeed, subject to the early challenge by the New Haven School (discussed later) the first form of discontent manifested itself in a search for some 'adjustments' to the drawbacks of classical sources doctrines, and especially their relationship with state consent.[25] Such a quest for adjustments, for instance, gained ground in American scholarship, which at that time was strongly associated with Columbia Law School.[26]

The idea of 'soft law' can probably be construed as another reformist challenge to the theory of sources. The softness thesis postulates that international law is better viewed as a continuum between law and non-law. It mends the traditional theory of sources by conflating legal acts and 'legal facts' ('*faits juridiques*')[27] in the theory of the sources of international law.[28] Accordingly, norms enshrined in soft instruments, such as political declarations, codes of conduct, and gentlemen's agreements, are considered as part of this continuum between law and non-law. In the traditional theory of the sources of international law, norms enshrined in a non-legal instrument (that is, those norms with soft instrumentum) can still have legal effect. For instance, they can partake in the internationalization of the subject matter,[29] provide guidelines for the interpretation of other legal acts,[30] or pave the

---

[25] C Tomuschat, 'Obligations arising for States without or against Their Will' (1993) 241 *Recueil des Cours* 195–374, at 216ff; 'The Legal Foundations of the International System' (n 24) 144ff.

[26] See eg O Schachter, 'International Law in Theory and Practice' (1982) 178 *Recueil des Cours* 9–395, at 60–74.

[27] The term 'legal fact' is probably not the most adequate to translate a concept found in other languages. It however seems better than 'juridical fact'. I have used the former in earlier studies about this distinction: see J d'Aspremont, 'Softness in International Law: A Self-Serving Quest for New Legal Materials' (2008) 19 *European Journal of International Law* 1075–93.

[28] For an early systematization of the distinction between legal acts and legal facts, see D Anzilotti, *Cours de droit international, premier volume: introduction—theories générales* (Sirey Paris 1929). See also M Virally, *La pensée juridique* (LDGJ Paris 1960) at 93; G Abi-Saab, 'Les sources du droit international: essai de déconstruction' in M Rama-Montaldo (ed), *International Law in an Evolving World: Liber Amicorum Eduardo Jiménez de Aréchaga* (Fundación de Culture Universitaria Montevideo 1994) 29–49, at 29, 40.

[29] On this question, see J Verhoeven, 'Non-intervention: affaires intérieures ou "vie privée"?' in *Mélanges en hommage à Michel Virally: Le droit international au service de la paix, de la justice et du développement* (Pedone Paris 1991) 493–500.

[30] See A Aust, 'The Theory and Practice of Informal International Instruments' (1986) 35 *International and Comparative Law Quarterly* 787–812; RJ Dupuy, 'Declaratory Law and Programmatory Law: From Revolutionary Custom to "Soft Law"' in RJ Akkerman, PJ van Krieken, and CO Pannenborg (eds), *Declarations of Principles: A Quest for Universal Peace* (Sitjhoff Leyden 1977) 247–57, at 255.

way for further subsequent practice that may one day be taken into account for the emergence of a norm of customary international law.[31] By virtue of the idea of softness these legal facts are elevated into law.[32] The idea of softness was thus designed to reform the mainstream theory of sources, which was seen as unable to capture all normative phenomena on the international plane and therefore as constraining the progressive development of international law.

3.2 Abolitionism

As early as the middle of the twentieth century, reformist discontent was supplemented by radical abolitionist constructions whereby the theory of sources was discarded as a validator of international legal rules. The first—and probably most—radical form of abolitionism came with the New Haven School which, drawing on the earlier critique by legal realists, advocates a process-based identification of international law that leads to an abandonment of the distinction between law and non-law. The New Haven School builds upon the realist critique of formalism and concurs with its finding that formalism fails to offer a complete description of authoritative international decision-making because international law cannot be reduced to a system of rules.[33] Like legal realism, the New Haven School is premised on the idea that international law is a form of social engineering that could be used as a tool to attain certain societal goals.[34] In particular, the New Haven School perceives law as 'a *flow of decisions* in which community prescriptions are formulated, invoked, and in fact applied'.[35] Because international law is construed as the product of a social process, the New Haven approach minimizes the role played by rules and thus the possible role of the theory of sources. It is an anti-rule-based approach.[36] From the perspective of New Haven, the theory of sources offers little insight into the structures, procedures, and types of decision that take place in the contemporary world community. The New Haven School thus backs away from the

---

[31] This is, for instance, the intention of art 19 of the ILC Articles on Diplomatic Protection on the 'recommended practice' by states: see International Law Commission, 'Draft Articles on Diplomatic Protection' (2006) UN Doc A/61/10 annex 1.

[32] A Boyle and C Chinkin, *The Making of International Law* (OUP Oxford 2007) at 211–29; AT Guzman, 'The Design of International Agreements' (2005) 16 *European Journal of International Law* 579–612.

[33] MS McDougal, 'International Law, Power, and Policy: A Contemporary Conception' (1953) 82 *Recueil des Cours* 133–259 at 162–4; RA Falk, 'Casting the Spell: The New Haven School of International Law' (1995) 104 *Yale Law Journal* 1991–2008.

[34] See the remarks of I Scobbie, 'Wicked Heresies or Legitimate Perspectives?' in M Evans (ed), *International Law* (2nd edn OUP Oxford 2006) 83–112, at 94.

[35] 'International Law, Power, and Policy' (n 33) 181 (emphasis in original).

[36] See MS McDougal, 'Some Basic Theoretical Concepts about International Law: A Policy-Oriented Framework of Inquiry' (1960) 4 *Journal of Conflict Resolution* 337–54.

theory of sources.[37] Hence, law-ascertainment and validation by virtue of a theory of sources become pointless operations.

Another form of abolitionist challenge to the theory of sources has, more recently, been found in the effect- (or impact-) based approaches to international law which have been embraced by a growing number of international legal scholars.[38] For these scholars, what matters is 'whether and how the subjects of norms, rules, and standards come to accept those norms, rules and standards. If they treat them as authoritative, then those norms can be treated as…"law"'.[39] In their view, any normative effort to influence international actors' behaviour, if it materializes in the adoption of an international instrument, should be viewed as part of international law. This effect- (or impact-) based conception of international law—which entails a shift from the perspective of the norm-maker to that of the norm-user—has itself taken various forms. For instance, it has led to conceptions whereby compliance is elevated to the law-ascertaining yardstick.[40] It has also resulted in behaviourist approaches to law where only the 'normative ripples' that norms can produce seem to be crucial.[41] Whatever its actual manifestation, effect- (or impact-) based approaches to law-ascertainment have proliferated throughout contemporary international legal scholarship and have marked a move away from the theory of the sources.

3.3 Rationale for Discontent

One common reason for the reformist and abolitionist projects pertains to the failure of the objectivization of meaning and the displacement of politics that the theory of sources was meant to produce. The idea is that the theory of sources fails in the same way that theories of substantive validity and voluntarism did.[42] As a result, the theory of sources, and especially the formalism that comes with it, was

---

[37] R Higgins, *Problems and Process: International Law and How We Use It* (OUP Oxford 1995) at 8–10.

[38] For a few examples see, JE Alvarez, *International Organizations as Law-Makers* (OUP Oxford 2005); J Brunnée and SJ Toope, 'International Law and Constructivism: Elements of an International Theory of International Law' (2000) 39 *Columbia Journal of Transnational Law* 19–74, at 65.

[39] J Klabbers, 'Law-Making and Constitutionalism' in J Klabbers, A Peters, and G Ulfstein, *The Constitutionalization of International Law* (OUP Oxford 2009) 81–125, at 98.

[40] See eg 'International Law and Constructivism' (n 38) 68.

[41] *International Organizations as Law-Makers* (n 38) x–xi, xiii, 63, 122; ND White, 'Separate but Connected: Inter-Governmental Organizations and International Law' (2008) 5 *International Organizations Law Review* 175–95, especially at 181–6.

[42] See generally I Venzke, 'Post-Modern Perspectives on Orthodox Positivism' in *International Legal Positivism in a Post-Modern World* (n 13) 182–210.

lambasted either as an 'abuse of deduction'[43] or for creating an illusion of objective rationality and content-determinacy in legal reasoning.[44]

Reformism and abolitionism do not only originate in a principled objection to theories of sources for their failure to provide objective meaning and displace politics. Reformism and abolitionism have also been nourished by a more concrete and progressive agenda. For instance, a common driving force behind these challenges to the theory of sources is programmatic.[45] I refer here to international lawyers' use of new or adjusted criteria of law-identification with the hope of contributing to the subsequent emergence of new rules in the *lex lata*. In mind is the identification of rules which, while not strictly speaking legal rules, are seen as constituting an experimentation ground for future legal rules the emergence of which is deemed desirable.[46] This programmatic attitude is widespread in the field of human rights law and environmental law.[47]

The reformist and abolitionist challenges to the theory of sources are also informed by the idea that international law is inherently good and should therefore be expanded. International lawyers tend to consider that any international legal rule is better than no rule at all and that the development of international law should be promoted as such.[48] Any new legal rule is deemed a step away from the anarchical state of nature towards a greater integration of the international community.[49] Accordingly, reforming or abolishing the theory of sources is seen as instrumental in expanding the realm of the international community with a view to ensuring what is seen as progress.[50]

[43] D Kennedy, *The Rise and Fall of Classical Legal Thought* (Beard Washington DC 2006 [1975]) at xviii.

[44] See eg D Kennedy, 'The Disciplines of International Law and Policy' (1999) 12 *Leiden Journal of International Law* 9–133, at 84; D Kennedy, 'When Renewal Repeats: Thinking against the Box' (1999) 32 *New York University Journal of International Law and Politics* 335–500; M Koskenniemi, *From Apology to Utopia: The Structure of International Legal Argument* (reissue CUP Cambridge 2005) at 306.

[45] This argument has also been made in L Blutman, 'In the Trap of a Legal Metaphor: International Soft Law' (2010) 59 *International and Comparative Law Quarterly* 605–24, at 617–18. In the same vein, see WM Reisman, 'Soft Law and Law Jobs' (2011) 2 *Journal of International Dispute Settlement* 25–30, at 25–6.

[46] For an avowed programmatic use of soft law and customary international law, see RJ Dupuy, 'Droit déclaratoire et droit programmatoire: de la coutume sauvage a la "soft law"' in Société française pour le droit international (ed), *L'élaboration du droit international public, Colloque de Toulouse* (Pedone Paris 1975) 132–48.

[47] See eg A Pellet, 'The Normative Dilemma: Will and Consent in International Law-Making' (1989) 12 *Australian Yearbook of International Law* 22–53, at 47.

[48] This was insightfully highlighted by J Klabbers, 'The Undesirability of Soft Law' (1998) 67 *Nordic Journal of International Law* 381–91, at 383.

[49] On the various dimensions of this enthusiasm for the international, see DW Kennedy, 'A New World Order: Yesterday, Today, and Tomorrow' (1994) 4 *Transnational Law & Contemporary Problems* 329–75, at 336.

[50] On the idea of progress see *The Notion of Progress in International Law Discourse* (n 19) ch 3.

The quest for accountability in the international arena has also warranted the challenge outlined earlier. Indeed, to a large extent, the reformist and abolitionist challenges to the theory of sources originate in a preoccupation with the accountability deficit inherent in the exercise of public authority outside traditional channels. In this sense, reform and abolition of the theory of sources are meant to allow a better capture of those exercises of public authority which do not manifest themselves in treaty-making, the adoption of formally binding acts of international organizations, custom-making behaviour, or unilateral promise.

The reformist and abolitionist challenges to the theory of sources can also be explained by international lawyers' quest to stretch the frontiers of their own discipline.[51] As I have argued elsewhere, international lawyers often seek to vindicate international law's expansion by 'legalizing' phenomena outside of international law, notably by truncating, adjusting, or discarding the theory of sources. Moving away from the traditional theory of sources, in this context, has helped scholars find new subject materials and open new avenues for legal research.[52]

Inevitably, advocates and counsel in international judicial proceedings are often inclined to take liberty with the theory of the sources of international law.[53] To them, the theory of sources frustrates creativity.[54] Moving away from the theory of sources grants them leeway to stretch the limits of international law and unearth rules that support the position of the actor that they represent and offers more freedom for creative argumentation before adjudicative bodies. This phenomenon is manifest particularly in cases where applicable rules are scarce.[55] It commonly materializes through the invocation of soft legal rules or the use of a very liberal ascertainment of custom and general principles of law.

Informed by these various rationales, the reformist and abolitionist challenges to the theory of sources have been thriving lately. Although some of these grievances may originate in straw men mysteriously associated with the theory of sources over the years,[56] these objections are too serious—or at least have been taken too seriously—to be discarded. Although the theory of sources originated in astute craftsmanship by early twentieth-century international lawyers and constituted

---

[51] I have expended this argument elsewhere: see 'Softness in International Law' (n 27).

[52] For an illustration of that phenomenon, see eg D Johnston, 'Theory, Consent, and the Law of Treaties: A Cross-Disciplinary Perspective' (1988) 12 *Australian Yearbook of International Law* 109–24.

[53] J-P Cot, 'Appearing "for" or "on behalf of" a State: The Role of Private Counsel before International Tribunals' in N Ando, E McWhinney, and R Wolfrum (eds), *Liber Amicorum Judge Shigeru Oda* (Kluwer Law International The Hague 2002) vol 2, 835–48.

[54] Interestingly, the same argument has been made as far as legal scholars are concerned: see 'International Law and Constructivism' (n 38) 65.

[55] For a recent example, see eg *Pulp Mills on the River Uruguay (Argentina v Uruguay)* (Judgment) [2010] ICJ Rep 14, at 132–42.

[56] See *International Legal Positivism in a Post-Modern World* (n 13).

a remarkable exercise of conceptual engineering, it cannot be denied that it has grown incapable of serving the ambitions that drove its architects. It is against this backdrop that the next section identifies some avenues to rejuvenate the theory of sources.

4 FROM STATIC OBJECTIVISM TO DYNAMIC LINGUISTIC COALESCING: A SOCIAL THEORY OF SOURCES

From a practical point of view, it seems hardly disputable that the theory of sources has the potential to provide international actors with a greater sense of what their freedoms and powers are while also allowing judicial decisions to attain a higher degree of legitimacy and authority.[57] Yet, even if this finding were to be empirically demonstrated, such practical relevance for the theory of sources would not suffice to counter the compelling principled theoretical objections raised against it, recalled earlier.

The renewal of the theory of sources envisaged here is premised on the idea that the theory of sources can be conceived independently from the objectivation of meaning and the displacement of politics, and can remain a useful tool to cognize, critique, reform and, more globally, make sense of international law as a normative practice. In particular, the theory of sources can constitute the dynamic platform necessary for a group of individuals to share at least a way of organizing experience and stipulations of relevance and irrelevance. According to this view, the theory of sources provides the language without which international lawyers cannot constitute an interpretative community capable of meaningfully debating and critiquing international law. This is true even if fixing the vocabulary of that community remains an unattainable horizon.[58] In that sense, the rationale for the theory of sources is the possibility of communication.

The rejuvenation advocated here—which I have already spelled out in greater detail elsewhere[59]—derives the validators prescribed by the theory of sources from the social practice of those authorities who apply them. According to

---

[57] See 'Legal Formalism: On the Immanent Rationality of Law' (n 20).

[58] J d'Aspremont, 'Wording in International Law' (2012) 25 *Leiden Journal of International Law* 575–602.

[59] J d'Aspremont, *Formalism and International Law: A Theory of the Ascertainment of Legal Rules* (OUP Oxford 2011) ch 1.

this conception, the practice of law-applying authorities is what nourishes the theory of sources and allows it to evolve constantly along the lines of the practice of actors—broadly defined—engaged in the practice of law-identification. It is conspicuous that such an understanding of the foundations of the theory of sources is not unheard of, especially in analytical jurisprudence.[60] It is not the place to rehash such jurisprudential debates. First, this has been done extensively in the literature. Second, and more fundamentally, such theories would need to be completely reinvented as they cannot be mechanically applied to international law. Indeed, it seems that the social theory of sources advocated here proves to have less kinship with Hart's social thesis than communitarian theories of knowledge.[61]

This section first explains how the social theory of sources can be dynamic and capture new forms of exercise of public authority at the international level (Section 4.1). It then argues that the social theory of sources externalizes the question of ultimate validity (Section 4.2). Next it contends that the social doctrine of sources allows a move away from voluntarism and state-centrism (Section 4.3). Finally, it argues that the social theory of sources allows one to construe the theory of sources as a practice and a tradition rather than a set of rules (Section 4.4). In making these arguments, this section will seek to demonstrate that the social theory of sources can address some of the most compelling objections that were raised by the reformist and abolitionist projects described earlier, while still being constitutive of an interpretative community of international law.

4.1 A Dynamic Theory of Sources of International Law

According to the social theory of sources, internal social practice makes the emergence of a common language possible despite law's inevitable indeterminacy. Social practice provides some rough meaning to the words upon which the language of law is based. Rules are thus ascertained on the basis of criteria which coalesce by

---

[60] Such a conception echoes Salmond's understanding of legal systems according to which the validity of law is strictly a function of judicial recognition and this recognition is a matter of social fact. For Salmond, the ultimate rule of validation is not derived or postulated but lies in the facts of the unified recognitional practice of courts: see JW Salmond, *Jurisprudence, or the Theory of the Law* (7th edn Sweet and Maxwell London 1924) at 57. The social conception of the theory of sources put forward here, even more manifestly, corresponds with HLA Hart's and his follower's so-called social thesis (or the conventionality thesis). According to Hart's theory, the social thesis purports to provide foundations to law-ascertainment criteria—which, in Hart's theory, are embodied by the rule of recognition. For a detailed outline of Hart's social thesis, see *Formalism and International Law* (n 59) chs 1 and 3.

[61] Cf Section 4.5 below.

virtue of a practice conceived in terms of convergent behaviours and agreements in judgements among law-applying authorities.[62]

Such a theory of sources is inevitably dynamic in that it can accommodate changes in contemporary international rule-making and evolve alongside the practice of international law-applying authorities. It is true that, by definition, the application of a theory of sources produces a static snapshot of rules existing at the moment that cognition of those rules is sought. The static character of this mapping of rules on a given topic at a given moment of time is one of the reasons why one resorts to a theory of sources. The static character of the product of the application of a theory of sources is precisely what allows it to fulfil some of its functions, such as indicating the applicable law in a contentious case before an international tribunal. While the product of the application of the theory of sources is by definition static, the rules of recognition which it prescribes need not be: those rules can evolve with the social practice. In other words, although geared towards a static result, that is, producing a snapshot of existing rules at a given time, the social theory of sources depicted earlier is in itself dynamic because its rules of recognition fluctuate and change along with the practice of law-ascertainment by international law-applying authorities. This means, more specifically, that social practice can produce law-ascertainment criteria beyond the mainstream model conveyed under the banner of art 38 of the Statute of the International Court of Justice (ICJ). In that sense, the social theory of sources makes it possible for the source theory to accommodate new pluralized forms of public authority which currently cannot be apprehended using the mainstream doctrine of sources. From the perspective presented here, it is at least theoretically conceivable that the mainstream model of ascertaining international legal rules can be reconstructed in a way that allows the normative products thereof to fall within the scope of international law. New formal international law-ascertainment criteria could thus be devised which elevate the norms originating in these pluralized exercises of public authority at the international level into rules of international law.

It should be made clear that attributing a social foundation to the theory of sources is certainly not the end of the matter. On the contrary, this is where the debate begins: important normative and conceptual choices must still be made to construct the 'social'. The greatest debate of all probably lies in the determination of those actors entitled to generate the social practice.[63] It is acknowledged that there is a real exercise of power in such a definitional exercise whereby change is

---

[62] HLA Hart, 'Jhering's Heaven of Concepts and Modern Analytical Jurisprudence' in *Essays in Jurisprudence and Philosophy* (Clarendon Press Oxford 1983) 265–77, at 277.

[63] See *Formalism and the Sources of International Law* (n 59) ch 8. For an extensive concept of law-applying authority, see W van der Burg, 'Two Models of Law and Morality' (1999) 3 *Associations* 61–82, at 63–4. See also K Culver and M Giudice, *Legality's Borders: An Essay in General Jurisprudence* (OUP Oxford 2010).

apprehended and constructed.[64] This is, however, an inquiry that ought to be taken on elsewhere. Other aspects for the social theory of sources envisaged here should now be spelled out.

4.2 Moving Away from Voluntarism and State-Centrism

Commentators often equate the mainstream theory of sources that arose in the twentieth century with a conception of sources of law that is exclusively based on the consent of states.[65] Construed in this way, the mainstream theory of sources has been lambasted for assuring the continued authority of the state.[66] There is no doubt that, if conflated with voluntarism, the theory of sources remains inextricably plagued by contradictions and fails to offer a satisfying theory to explain the binding character of international law.[67] According to the argument made here, however, voluntarism is primarily an approach to the authority and legitimacy of international law, which is a different issue from that of the ascertainment of rules.[68] The social theory of sources does not ignore the impact of the theory of sources on the authority and legitimacy of international law, but nor does it seek to explain why international law is binding or why subjects abide by its rules, for these are very different questions.[69]

It is true that, on the basis of the mainstream theory of sources as was developed in the twentieth century, scholars approach the creation of international law from a primarily state-centric perspective. This is due to the fact that mainstream conceptions of the sources of international law remain largely focused upon state consent, something that, as was explained in Section 2, was inherited from the nineteenth century. Yet the current state-centric character of the mainstream theory of sources in international law does not require that, as a matter of principle, any theory of

---

[64] S Fish, *Doing What Comes Naturally: Change, Rhetoric, and the Practice of Theory in Literary and Legal Studies* (Duke University Press Durham 1989) at 23–4.

[65] See eg J Brunnée and SJ Toope, 'An Interactional Theory of International Legal Obligation' (University of Toronto Legal Studies Research Series Working Paper No 08-16, 12 July 2008) at 31–3.

[66] A Carty, 'Conservative and Progressive Visions in French International Legal Doctrine' (2005) 16 *European Journal of International Law* 525–37.

[67] See eg ibid 534; *From Apology to Utopia* (n 44) 303–87.

[68] Using the distinction between the question of the sources of law and the question of the foundations of law, Robert Kolb makes the same argument: see R Kolb, *Réflexions de philosophie du droit international: Problèmes fondamentaux du droit international public: Théorie et Philosophie du droit international* (Bruylant Brussels 2003) at 51. See also S Besson, 'Theorizing the Sources of International Law' in S Besson and J Tasioulas (eds), *The Philosophy of International Law* (OUP Oxford 2010) 163–85, at 166 (for Besson, however, consent is insufficient to ensure the authority and legitimacy of international legal rules).

[69] The conflation of formalism and consensualism has long been rejected by normativist approaches to international law, as is illustrated by Hans Kelsen's work. In the same vein, see also 'Theorizing the Sources of International Law' (n 68) 166.

sources be assimilated with the intent of states.[70] The social theory of sources—as described here—is indifferent to the actual material source of law. In the pluralized contemporary international legal system, it would be entirely conceivable for law to emanate from non-state entities. The social theory of sources that has been sketched here is thus not averse to the theoretical possibility of international legal rules made by non-state entities.

4.3 The Theory of Sources as Tradition and Practice Rather Than a Set of Rules

Another consequence of the abovementioned social theoretical framework is indeed that one can move away from a theory of sources construed as a set of rules.[71] The theory of sources, although it continues to serve as container of the 'rule of recognition', does not necessarily boil down to a set of rules. In this respect, it is worth emphasizing that the concept of the 'rule of recognition' can be highly misleading if it brings one to think that the theory of sources boils down to a set of rules, thereby condemning law-identification interpretation to an infinite regress in which international lawyers continually seek a second order rule to interpret the formal validator (that is, the law-ascertainment criterion).[72] Similarly, one should not be lured by the image conveyed by art 38 of the Statute of the ICJ—which has, wrongly, been elevated into the gospel of the law of sources. In contrast, the social theory of sources presented here allows one to envisage the law-identifiers provided by the sources as a practice and a tradition. This means that, in the end, the social theory of sources probably shares less kinship with the—sometimes unelaborated[73]—Hartian theory of sources than it does with the social theories of knowledge elaborated by philosophers like Stanley Fish,[74] Michael Polanyi,[75] or Alasdair MacIntyre.[76]

First, understanding sources as practice means that it is the practice of the community of professionals that share some formal linguistic signs to determine its

---

[70] For similar criticisms of the association of the source doctrine and consensualism, see GJH van Hoof, *Rethinking the Sources of International Law* (Kluwer Law Deventer 1983) at 289.

[71] I have developed this argument more extensively elsewhere: see J d'Aspremont, 'The Idea of "Rules" in the Sources of International Law' (2013) 84 *British Yearbook of International Law* 103–30.

[72] The concept of rules on which the theory of sources is often articulated creates an infinite need for other rules to guide the interpretation of such source rules. Indeed, the meaning of the law-ascertainment rules is itself dependent on rules that inform their application and which must themselves be interpreted. On this problem, see 'Post-Modern Perspectives on Orthodox Positivism' (n 42).

[73] N MacCormick, 'The Concept of Law and "The Concept of Law"' in RP George (ed), *The Autonomy of Law: Essays on Legal Positivism* (OUP Oxford 1996) 163–94, at 191.

[74] S Fish, 'Fish v Fiss' (1984) 36 *Stanford Law Review* 1325–47.

[75] M Polanyi, *Knowing and Being: Essays* (M Grene ed) (Routledge London 1969).

[76] *Which Rationality? Whose Justice?* (n 2).

object of study, and hence its objects of agreement and disagreement. Such practice is by definition 'not fixed and finite'.[77] It is always in full flux. Determining such criteria becomes a matter of 'understanding', rather than 'listing'.[78] Although dynamic and in flux, the social theory of sources understood as practice is not completely unstable and indeterminate. It is formally 'principled'[79] in that it deploys itself through reference to formal criteria.

Second, the social theory of sources presented here is better understood as a tradition because it undoubtedly presupposes a leap of faith by those actors engaging in law-ascertainment.[80] The theory of sources as a tradition allows one to embed the dynamism of social practice in continuity. Indeed, so construed, the theory of sources is an ongoing process of composition[81] on the occasion of which each actor not only perpetuates the tradition but also 'contributes to the content of the tradition that develops',[82] sometimes without much awareness of the tradition which they perpetuate and adjust at the same time.[83] The theory of sources, as a tradition, is thus continuously adjusted to the needs of the moment.[84] Understanding the theory of sources as a tradition also 'allows for significant degrees of conflict and dissent'[85] while permitting paradigmatic commensurability in the interpretive community of international law.

5 CONCLUDING REMARKS: SOURCES AND THE FANTASY OF A DISPLACEMENT OF POLITICS

If reconstructed along the lines of the social perspective presented here, the theory of sources can be approached with greater modesty. It allows one to

---

[77] 'Fish v Fiss' (n 74) 1329.   [78] Ibid.   [79] *Doing What Comes Naturally* (n 64) 11.

[80] *Which Rationality? Whose Justice?* (n 2) 359. For a similar discussion with a focus on international lawyers, see M Koskenniemi, 'Between Commitment and Cynicism: Outline for a Theory of International Law as Practice' in Office of Legal Affairs (ed), *Collection of Essays by Legal Advisers of States, Legal Advisers of International Organizations and Practitioners in the Field of International Law* (United Nations New York 1999) 495–523.

[81] MT Mitchell, 'Michael Polanyi, Alasdair MacIntyre, and the Role of Tradition' (2006) 19 *Humanitas* 97–125, at 105–6.

[82] Ibid.

[83] M Polanyi, *Science, Faith and Society* (University of Chicago Press Chicago 1964) at 76.

[84] M Polanyi, *Personal Knowledge* (University of Chicago Press Chicago 1958) at 160. On this aspect of Polanyi's theory, see 'Michael Polanyi, Alasdair MacIntyre, and the Role of Tradition' (n 81) 104.

[85] 'Michael Polanyi, Alasdair MacIntyre, and the Role of Tradition' (n 81) 106.

emancipate it from the dreams of objective meaning and a total displacement of politics which traditionally accompany the idea of a theory of sources construed as a set of rules. Indeed, the social theory of sources presented here does not seek to objectivize meaning or to displace politics. It assumes some inevitable methodological and normative choices which are themselves consciously inherited and assumed as practice and tradition. In that sense, politics is not displaced but lies at the heart of the social theory of sources presented in this chapter.

The 'politics' of tradition and practice at the heart of the social theory of sources calls for three concluding remarks. First, as the foregoing has demonstrated, the social theory of sources presented here is, by definition, exclusive of formal content-determination methods. It is alien to theories of adjudicative neutrality and immanent intelligibility of legal arguments. It does not seek to explain the whole phenomenon of law, and certainly not its content or adjudicative truth. In other words, the social theory of sources is reductionist, for it is not about providing the means to establish authoritative interpretations. Second, the social theory of sources depicted in this section is openly premised on a strong conceptual and methodological bias. Making a plea for the preservation of the central role of the theory of sources and grounding it in social practice is certainly not neutral. It manifests a particular choice for a particular take on law. It is not denied that the source theory is accordingly dependent on a particular 'value fact'[86] which boils down to a choice of a particular cognitive approach—in the form of a set of formal law-ascertaining indicators—in order to make sense of law and of its practices. Approaching international law from the standpoint of its social sources corresponds to a formal conception of law zeroed in on law as a product.

Last but not least, the social theory of sources outlined in this chapter leaves many questions unanswered. One of them pertains to the modes of cognizing the consistency of social practice that is necessary for the existence of the social theory of sources put forward here. Indeed, such a practice is not an objectively observable fact: the data is necessarily constructed according to methodological choices.[87] An equally important question left unanswered is the determination of which actors qualify as generating communitarian semantics by their practice. The importance of this question should not be underestimated: altering our understanding of law-applying authority (and thus our definition of those who produce social practice) necessarily affects the type of semantics that inform law-ascertainment criteria prescribed by a social theory of sources. This raises questions pertaining to political choices about who is empowered to generate practice conducive to the emergence of social practice determinative of the validators of the social theory

---

[86] M Greenberg, 'How Facts Make Law' (2004) 10 *Legal Theory* 157–98.

[87] A MacIntyre, 'Epistemological Crises, Dramatic Narrative, and the Philosophy of Science' (1977) 60 *Monist* 453–72.

of sources. As noted earlier, politics are not displaced but lie at the heart of the social theory of sources. Thus, in contrast to its nineteenth- and twentieth-century ancestors described in Section 2, the social theory of sources can only function if it transparently assumes the politics of the (construction of the) social practice that nourishes it. In doing so, it can alleviate some of the objections levelled by the reformists and the abolitionists against earlier theories of sources, while still serving as a condition of possibility of the interpretative community of international law. This proposition is not quite a paradigmatic revolution. Infact, it rests on conceptual moves faithful to the very same paradigmatic framework as the theory it criticizes. Yet, by opening the door to social change from within, its potential contribution is probably unequalled.

CHAPTER 28

SOMETHING TO DO WITH STATES

GERRY SIMPSON

It is universally agreed that...[international law] has something
to do with States[1]

1 INTRODUCTION

IN the fly-leaf of *The Canons of International Law*, there is a photograph of Thomas
Baty in a white linen suit. The only just corporeal Baty seems to merge into the
pale background against which he stands. He is there but not-quite-there: as in-
substantial and ungraspable as the state itself sometimes seems, poised between
materiality and abstraction, and between unity and fragmentation. In this chapter,
I want to suggest that the law of sovereignty and statehood tends to be practiced,
organized, and theorized around two sets of argument (and a sleight of hand),
and that this tendency has produced certain effects on the distribution of political
resources in global politics.

---

[1] T Baty, *The Canons of International Law* (Murray London 1930) at 1. Colin Warbrick provided
the prompt to think about Baty in this way: C Warbrick, 'States and Recognition in International
Law' in MD Evans (ed), *International Law* (2nd edn OUP Oxford 2006) 217–75.

The first argument is structured around the material and immaterial qualities of statehood. This opposition, of course, is a *leitmotif* of many standard accounts of statehood but the effects of this relation of form and substance has produced a jurisprudence of mystery, and this, in turn, has complicated life for would-be sovereigns and especially non-European political communities or states aspiring to join the family of nations. Peter Fitzpatrick has talked about the way in which non-European peoples were 'called to be the same yet repelled as different, bound in an infinite transition which perpetually requires it to attain what is intrinsically denied to it'.[2] This 'infinite transition' is emblematic of the law of sovereignty and is produced partly by the elasticity of the doctrinal ground and partly by the remarkable stability of a very particular and idealized sovereign subject. The result is a sovereignty always just out of reach: a sovereign equality retractable even when statehood itself is acquired. This idea of sovereignty is present in the nineteenth-century obsessions with incomplete sovereignties (Lorimer) or 'families of nations' (Oppenheim), in the post-decolonization distinctions between negative and positive sovereignty (Robert Jackson) and in the early twenty-first-century formulations of 'earned sovereignty', 'conditional sovereignty', and 'sovereign responsibility'.

The second argument rests on an idiom of fragmentation and unity. How stable, conceptually and historically, is the sovereign state? Here, in order to show how, at each juncture, the claim by pre-sovereign political communities to self-determination has been administered or compromised through, alternately, the diffusion of sovereignty (into sub-sovereigns as a way of taming radical claims to self-identity) and the unification of sovereignty around a particular sort of sovereign state (to the exclusion of other forms of political organization), I want to juxtapose an apparent golden age of post-Charter state sovereignty with both a nineteenth-century in which sovereignty seemed to be decentralized or hybrid, and an early twenty-first-century in which sovereignty appears to have become, again, more protean.

The sleight of hand, meanwhile, operates around the relationship between routine statehood and *sui generis* sovereignty.[3] Abnormality here becomes a way of addressing theoretical crises (why 'constitute' here and 'declare' there? Why equal sovereignty here and earned sovereignty there? Why self-determination here and not here? Or extinction there but immortality here?) while at the same time permitting the historically situated, politically contingent deployments of the 'universal' legal norm of sovereignty against some interests and for others.[4]

---

[2] P Fitzpatrick, '"We Know What It is when You Do Not Ask Us": Nationalism as Racism' in P Fitzpatrick (ed), *Nationalism, Racism and the Rule of Law* (Dartmouth Aldershot 1995) 3–26, at 11.

[3] N Berman, 'Sovereignty in Abeyance: Self-Determination and International Law' (1988) 7 *Wisconsin Journal of International Law* 51–105.

[4] '[T]his definition of sovereignty must therefore be associated with the borderline case and not the routine': C Schmitt, *Political Theology: Four Chapters on the Concept of Sovereignty* (G Schwab trans) (MIT Press Cambridge MA 1985) at 5.

2 END STATE

The end is where we start from

(Eliot)[5]

I want to begin, though, with a lengthy, preliminary section in which I ask—taking my prompt from Baty—whether international law might not now have less to do with states than it did in 1930.[6] It can sometimes seem, after all, as if everything *but* the state is on the rise (the rise of corporations, the rise of institutions, the rise of ethnic warfare, the rise of supranationalism). It would be hard to envisage a book about contemporary political life on 'The Rise of the State' (at least not quite yet). Incapacitated at the local level (states, when they are not fragmenting into warring factions, are pleading with multinational corporations to help them build roads) and marginalized at the international level (where the action is private or institutional or sub-national), the state looks distinctly sclerotic and old-hat. To 'theorize' about states, then, might be like theorizing about blacksmithing: quaint, old-fashioned, historical and, now, beside the point. For a long time, it was end-state talk that dominated. And the idea of the death of sovereignty came in the guise of a conceptual challenge to the whole vitality of the state as an organizing principle in human relations.

At a seminar I gave at the University of Nottingham over a decade ago, a book I had just written on unequal sovereigns was described—a little contemptuously I thought—as 'statist'. My interlocutor on that occasion wanted to convey the idea that I had written a twentieth-century book for the twenty-first century. Why arrange states into clever little hierarchies so close to their expiry date? Globalization, by denationalizing and deterritorializing economic governance, had rendered null the whole idea of political independence. Meanwhile, new non-state

---

[5] TS Eliot, 'Little Gidding' in *Four Quartets* (Harcourt Brace and Co New York 1943) 29–39.

[6] A word on the demarcation of topics in this *Handbook*: Rose Parfitt's chapter is ostensibly about legal personality and recognition, mine is on statehood and sovereignty: see R Parfitt, 'Theorizing Recognition and International Personality' in this *Handbook*. Yet, what might this division of tasks signify? Legal personality, in its broader senses, encompasses the derivative personality of individuals, say, under the *Optional Protocol to the International Covenant on Civil and Political Rights* (opened for signature 16 December 1966, entered into force 23 March 1976) 999 UNTS 171, or the personhood of corporations or the rights and duties of international organizations (these matters are taken up in chapters by Fleur Johns and Jan Klabbers, respectively: see F Johns, 'Theorizing the Corporation in International Law' and J Klabbers, 'Theorizing International Organizations' in this *Handbook*). But the idea of 'personality' may be more hospitable, too, to more 'outside the box' work. Sovereignty and statehood are trapped in a philosophical and legal tradition going back at least to Bodin or late-mediaeval Europe, but legal personality seems more fluid, open to 'interventions' (to use one of the words from the Amsterdam conference in this *Handbook*) based on the particularity of institutional innovation: the League of Nations in Ethiopia, the UN in the Congo, NATO and the EU in Kosovo.

actors were everywhere. Individuals could make claims at the international level (human rights), they were guilty of crimes so monstrous that their trials took place at the international level (individual responsibility) and they drew together to influence policy as part of 'civil society' (NGOs) and through the application of commercial muscle (corporations).

States, meanwhile, were creating the conditions for their own withering through the establishment of more and more intrusive institutions (an international criminal court with jurisdiction over citizens or a World Bank increasingly resorting to the imposition of particular economic, and therefore political, programmes on sometimes reluctant sovereigns. These critiques were tied together by a knowing historicism; states had been invented, and now they could be disinvented. This was not simply a descriptive concern. At different points in the history of international law, to be radical and engaged (or utopian)[7] was to be against the state. Human rights law, for example, offered up an ongoing programme of opposition to the state (with its prisons, torturers, and censors). The ecology movement told us that states had failed us (sovereignty threatened us with doom), and states were failing themselves in Somalia, in Bosnia, in the Democratic Republic of the Congo. Even those that did function were either too big (unwieldy, bullying, prone to resisting right-thinking projects of internationalization such as the International Criminal Court or Rio/Kyoto) or too small (by-passed and rendered irrelevant by the sweep of global capital).[8]

Indeed, the symptoms of morbidity were all around and now we have rediscovered (via global warming and *pace* Isocrates) that individual states themselves are far from immortal.[9] Plato's great lost city of Atlantis represents a model here for the dissolution of states in general. *Critias* describes a great polity: superbly organized, highly ordered, aesthetically perfect, and endowed with material advantage. Alas, 'the divine portion in them began to fade...they became unable to bear their prosperity and grew corrupt'.[10] Zeus decides to punish the 'wretched state': 'He summoned all the gods to a meeting in the most awesome of his dwellings...and when the gods had assembled, he said...'.[11] These are the final elliptical words of the *Critias* dialogue. Atlantis is destroyed, cast down to the bottom of the ocean and, at the same time, combines Grotius' two end-states: '[t]he extinction

---

[7] 'I' th' commonwealth would by contrivances execute all things: for no kind of traffic would I admit; no name of magistrate; No occupation; all men idle...no sovereignty': Shakespeare, *The Tempest*, 2.1.23.

[8] This passage adapts G Simpson, 'The Guises of Sovereignty' in T Jacobsen, C Sampford, and R Thakur (eds), *Re-Envisioning Sovereignty: The End of Westphalia?* (Ashgate Aldershot 2008) 59–68.

[9] H Grotius, *Hugo Grotius on the Law of War and Peace: Student Edition* (SC Neff ed) (CUP Cambridge 2001) at 171. The state of Carpatho-Hungary was barely mortal; it lasted for less than a day: N Davies, *Vanished Kingdoms: The History of Half-Forgotten Europe* (Allen Lane London 2011).

[10] Plato, *Timaeus and Critias* (R Waterfield trans) (OUP Oxford 2008) at 121.   [11] Ibid.

of a people …may be brought about in two ways: either by the destruction of the body, or by the destruction of that form or spirit'.[12] We cannot read Plato or Grotius without thinking of say, Nauru, as a representative end state. Could The Maldives or Tuvalu or Nauru and the making and unmaking of states by the international system, represent a possible trajectory for the history and future of statehood itself: imperial outpost, mandate, extraction, trust, independence, tax haven, offshore processing, submersion, extinction? Grotius, after all, begins his discussion of extinction with the 'first type of destruction…the engulfing of peoples by the sea…'.[13]

Yet, international law, it is generally agreed—and in the face of a couple of decades of post-statism—still does have something to do with states. In an immediate sense, in contemporary international law, states, if they are not quite immortal, are hard to kill. There is a considerable presumption in favour of the continuation of a state even when it is experiencing severe decline: 'Extinction is thus, within broad limits, not affected by more or less prolonged anarchy within the State'.[14] This is so even when states stop breathing for a considerable time. Usually, this occurs as a result of annexation during war. The spirit of the state, though, remains at large, tended by a commitment to preservation on the part of other states in the system. The 'illegality' of the absorption counts against the permanence of its effects.[15]

And so, the numbers increase. There are roughly between 194 (the number of United Nation (UN) member states as of 1 October 2013) and 200 (depending on the status of contested cases) of them, and they continue to dominate the way many international lawyers speak, think, and write. And not just international lawyers: popular and professional representations of international diplomacy and war are bound up with states, and what they might do or not do to each other. Whatever we might think about the underlying conditions of international life (political economy, culture, institutionalism), the inclination remains to write of, say, crises, in terms of what the 'United States' might do to 'Syria' or whether the 'Democratic Republic of the Congo' might sue 'Rwanda'. Writing in this mode is a sort of shorthand for a whole series of more complex or less biddable categories of

---

[12] H Grotius, *De Jure Belli ac Pacis Libri Tres* (FW Kelsey trans) (Clarendon Press Oxford 1925 [1625]) bk 2 ch 9, pt 3, s 3, at 312.

[13] Ibid bk 9 ch 4. Or the United Kingdom: John Lanchester recently described the banks as an 'existential threat' to the British polity. What does it mean for international law that all states now seem so vulnerable? A certain sort of pragmatic international law refuses to get excited about this sort of thing. Nauru may slip under the ocean but the state will sail on, the British polity may indeed disintegrate in the face of another financial crash or two but then it will simply represent state failure and not the failure of the state: J Lanchester 'Let's Call It Failure' [2013] 35(1) *London Review of Books* 3–6. See also C Storr, 'End State: Nauru and the Legal Construction of Territory' (Unfinished PhD Thesis, Melbourne Law School 2013–).

[14] JR Crawford, *The Creation of States in International Law* (1st edn OUP Oxford 1979) at 417.

[15] On the other hand, recalling Grotius, where there is total obliteration or 'submersion…over any considerable period of time', then extinction may well follow: see ibid at 417–18.

thought and action. So we remain trapped in states: thinking through them, living in them, seeking protection from them, identifying ourselves with them.

International law seems to have something to do, also, with sovereignty (or sovereign equality, of which, more later). Sometimes sovereignty is posited as the ground of international law ('the society of sovereign states') or an historical origin of international legal order ('Westphalian sovereignty' as the baptismal figure of international law). At other times, or in other places, it is thought of as an obstacle to the creation of a credible or enforceable international juridical order ('state sovereignty versus the ICC' or 'state sovereignty versus human rights' and so on). States, of course, are said to be sovereign or possess sovereignty or enjoy sovereignty. In the *Nicaragua Case* there are references to something called 'sovereign statehood' (the title of a book by Alan James), but sovereign statehood, from a particular perspective, has the appearance of a tautology.[16] In classical international law, states are sovereign and the sovereign is a state. Sovereigns are thought to monopolize plenary power internally (they have no formal internal competitors) and are recognized by other sovereigns as the sole authoritative representative of a territory. But there have been—at times—claims for the sovereignty of organizations like the EU or even the Security Council. Sometimes this is category error; at other times it is prescience. For example, there has been a debate about the 'sovereignty' of the EU for as long as I have been a legal scholar.[17] Still, most people take the view that Europe does not enjoy 'sovereignty' but is some sort of supranational *sui generis* 'entity' (to use an agnostic term of art in these sorts of discussions).

Despite calls to abandon the idioms of sovereignty as 'unhelpful and misleading',[18] this language is likely to remain with us. To conclude this introductory section, then, and to reintroduce the overarching themes—we might consider some different associations at play when sovereignty and statehood are distinguished. First, there is the suggestion that states possess a material existence (a seat at the UN, a territory, a passport control booth) that sovereigns (perhaps those 'in abeyance' or exile) lack. Or, alternatively, sovereignty might be viewed as the inherent thing—the natural right, the immutable fact—while states are the (mere) creations of formal and reversible acts of recognition.[19] Second, and from the perspective of fragmentation and unity, the 'state' might summon an image of solid presence or unified whole, while 'sovereignty' is subject to fissure and instability (in 2003, Iraq's statehood remained intact while its 'sovereignty' yo-yoed between its people(s), its

---

[16] See *The Creation of States in International Law* (n 14); J Crawford, 'Sovereignty as a Legal Value' in J Crawford and M Koskenniemi (eds), *The Cambridge Companion to International Law* (CUP Cambridge 2012) 117–33. See also *Military and Paramilitary Activities in and against Nicaragua (Nicaragua v United States)* (Merits) [1986] ICJ Rep 14.

[17] See eg N MacCormick, 'Beyond the Sovereign State' (1993) 56 *Modern Law Review* 1–18.

[18] *The Creation of States in International Law* (n 14) 421.

[19] See also 'Theorizing Recognition and International Personality' (n 6); M Craven, 'Statehood, Self-Determination, and Recognition' in *International Law* (n 1) 203–51.

state organs and the Coalition Provisional Authority). Or, sovereignty might be the surviving essence while the state dissipates and fails (as in Somali 'sovereignty'). From the perspective of normality and abnormality, statehood might seem like the normal end-state of political organization (think of the way self-determination was equated with independence in the Declaration on the Granting of Independence to Colonial Countries and Peoples of 1960)[20] while sovereignty is dispersed (in organizations or non-state entities or inchoate states like Kosovo), or states might appear abnormal (the organization of community into statehood being a 500 year blip) while sovereignty is always with us so that in this way we might associate states with birth, sovereigns with death. The state is immortal but the sovereignty of the people (or particular configurations of people) or the Monarch is subject to the laws of space, decay, and time. Or, alternatively, sovereignty might mark the birth of organized political life, while the configuration of that sovereign as state is a portent of its eventual demise.[21]

3 MATERIAL/ABSTRACT

Between the idea / And the reality...

(TS Eliot)[22]

Questions of the state and sovereignty have often rotated around the formal and deformalized aspects of authority, control, and power over a particular territory. In the doctrine on the acquisition of territorial sovereignty, arbitrators, scholars, and lawyers have struggled to reconcile the requirements of formal title (through purchase, cession, treaty) with the facts on the ground (the effectiveness of the relevant authority, the intensity of the control). This carries over into more contemporary concerns about the extent of a state's sovereignty over a disputed territory.

In *Rasul v Bush*, for example, the United States (US) Supreme Court considered whether Guantanamo Bay was part of Cuban sovereign territory (and therefore not, generally, subject to federal jurisdiction) or fell under effective and long-term US control and authority (and therefore capable of conferring on federal district

---

[20] 'Declaration on the Granting of Independence to Colonial Countries and Peoples' (14 December 1960) GA Res 1514(XV) UN Doc A/RES/1514(XV).

[21] Wendy Brown makes an argument along these lines in relation to walls, 'reappear[ing] at the moment of political sovereignty's dissipation...Thus would the walling of the nation-state be the death rattle of landed nation-state sovereignty': W Brown, *Walled States, Waning Sovereignty* (Zone Books Cambridge MA 2010) at 43–4.

[22] TS Eliot, 'The Hollow Men (1925)' in *Poems 1909–1925* (Faber & Faber London) 123–8.

courts the jurisdiction to hear *habeas* claims).[23] The majority judges, emphasizing the effectiveness and permanence of American control over the airbase, found that the *habeas* claims of Rasul et al., could be entertained by US federal courts. As Justice Stevens put it in a piece of reasoning typical of this tendency:

[T]he reach of the writ depended not on formal notions of territorial sovereignty, but rather on the practical question of 'the exact extent and nature of the jurisdiction or dominion exercised in fact by the Crown'.[24]

Justice Kennedy, in a more discursive separate opinion, characterizes Guantanamo Bay as US territory 'in every practical respect'; the indefinite lease, he goes on to say, suggestively, has 'produced a place that belongs to the United States'.[25] Justice Scalia, aggressively dissenting, refused to countenance these references to effectiveness and practicality. For him, the lease conferring on Cuba 'ultimate sovereignty' was sufficiently clear to dispose of the matter there and then.[26]

This, of course, replicates the familiar debates between 'declarativists' and 'constitutivists' in relation to statehood itself. Are states facts in the way that chairs might be regarded as facts? Are they facts in the way a treaty is a fact?[27] Or are they inter-subjective persons, whose existence is wholly dependent on the will of other persons in the relevant community? International lawyers have gone back and forth *ad nauseum* on this question. Sometimes this masquerades as a dispute between a political and a juridical approach to sovereignty. But it is never quite clear where the law and politics of this dispute lie. The declaratory theory of statehood emphasizes 'facts' (the presence of territory or a permanent population) or the political realities on the ground (the effectiveness of governmental control). In this sense, it can seem to defer entirely to politics (the politics of brute strength or facticity). But this approach depends on the translation of these facts into legally cognizable categories through the application of norms (the *Montevideo Convention*, say, with its list of tangible criteria for the establishment of statehood).[28] The extra-textual adaptation and amendment of the *Convention* to incorporate other criteria for statehood (the requirement that new states not be brought into being through an illegal use of force or through the 'effectiveness' of a racist government) has further enhanced the impression that facts are subject to normative constraint or construction, and open to the play of political preference. The constitutive view, meanwhile, seems to give rein to a more formal, less substantive practice of recognition whereby sovereigns come into existence through an official act of inter-subjective recognition

---

[23] *Rasul v Bush*, 542 US 466 (2004).

[24] Ibid 482 (Stevens J) (footnote omitted), quoting *Ex parte Mwenya* [1960] 1 QB 241, 303 (Lord Evershed MR).

[25] *Rasul v Bush*, 542 US 466 (2004) 487 (Kennedy J).   [26] Ibid 501 (Scalia J).

[27] These are the questions that begin James Crawford's defining work on the subject.

[28] *Montevideo Convention on the Rights and Duties of States* (signed 26 December 1933) 165 LNTS 19.

regardless of any facts or 'political realities'. But the constitutive approach is also criticized for being excessively 'political'.[29] If acts of uncontrolled recognition bring states into being then there seems to be little room for law: 'full international personality is not a concession of grace on the part of existing states'.[30]

In the end, most international lawyers try to bring the two approaches into some sort of alignment. Lauterpacht's *Recognition in International Law*—attempting to bring 'idea and reality' into harmony—delivers the *locus classicus* here (though not classical enough to have its central claims widely adopted). The state, fully formed and exercising rights to which it is entitled, is a product of declaration and law in one sphere, and recognition and diplomacy in another. The inter-state system can neither bear too much reality (this is 'the arbitrariness of policy') nor too great a reliance on elusive legal form (this is 'the disintegrating element of uncertainty and controversy').[31] But the *via media* is not a complete success either, surely. Lauterpacht adopts Hall's reasoning:

Theoretically, a politically organized community enters of right…into the family of states…so soon as it is able to show that it possesses the marks of a state. The commencement of a state dates nevertheless from its recognition by other powers…[32]

Sovereigns are, as it were, born three times: first as organic self-identifying communities, second as rights-bearing proto-states, third as unencumbered subjects of international law. In the third section of this chapter I look at the movement from self-determination to proto-statehood (and the points in between). In the remainder of this section, I turn to the transition from proto-state to unencumbered self (and back).

These debates about the material and abstract qualities of statehood feed into the more (obviously) doctrinal question of recognition. It would be an ultra-declarativist who felt brave enough to talk about statehood without reference to some theory or practice of recognition. Most of us, most of the time, think recognition (at least some of the time) belongs with statehood.[33] Oppenheim's first edition of 1905 puts it pretty bluntly: 'a state is, and becomes, an international person through recognition only, and exclusively'.[34]

---

[29] For a discussion of the political consequences and historical roots of these approaches, see 'Theorizing Recognition and International Personality' (n 6).

[30] H Lauterpacht, *Recognition in International Law* (CUP Cambridge 1947) at 76.

[31] So, eg, the question of China's statehood was raised during the Manchurian crisis. No doubt things were confused within China at this point. The writ of the central government hardly extended beyond Peking. But, very few legal counsel were prepared to say that China no longer existed. Perhaps inevitably, the Legal Adviser to the Japanese Government took a more robust line on extinction: see T Baty 'Can an Anarchy Be a State?' (1934) 28 *American Journal of International Law* 444–55. See also T Ruskola, 'China in the Age of the World Picture' in this *Handbook*.

[32] WE Hall, *International Law* (OUP Oxford 1880) at 73.

[33] For other places in international law in which recognition is important see, eg, the recognition of belligerents and governments (and facts), and the non-recognition of unlawful situations.

[34] L Oppenheim, *International Law* (2 vols OUP Oxford 1905–6) vol 1, at 109.

But what is a state before it is an international person? Some nineteenth-century writers argued that a mere state was not a member of the family of nations (for example, Oppenheim). The family of nations was open only to states possessing certain abstract qualities recognizable only to other family members. Recognition then operates as a way of controlling membership of the core. This was the 'standard of civilization', a norm never quite defined because it was incapable of definition. It operated as elusive cultural marker rather than achievable legal standard. Montaigne saw the meaning of these cultural markers best, 300 years before Oppenheim, when he described speaking to a native who saw all men as 'halves' and could not comprehend why the destitute halves put up with poverty while their wealthy halves were 'fully bloated'. One of the natives was a commander and led a highly organized mass of men. After battle he was accorded the privilege of 'having paths cut for him through the thickets in forests'.[35] Montaigne was impressed: 'Not at all bad, that. Ah! But they wear no breeches...'.[36]

States that failed to wear breeches or come up to standard—John Westlake had said that they lacked 'good breeding'—became more susceptible to intervention, discipline, and general loss of status.[37] These are the 'abnormal' cases. James Lorimer is a key figure here. Indeed, he even uses the language of abnormality as a way of ordering the *Institutes*, his book-length apology or justification for a series of recessive taxonomies of statehood.[38] His tripartite distinction—civilized states, barbarians (the Ottomans), and savages (everywhere else)—is familiar enough. And this tripartite scheme goes back to Pufendorf who wants to draw a distinction between those entirely outside the system (towards whom 'it will be necessary for other men to show them no more mercy than they do birds of prey') and the marginal cases who are 'so partial [a very Lorimer word] as to be just in the Observation of compacts with [only] some particular Allies...their Credit, it is evident, must very much sink, but it would be too severe to deny them every degree of esteem', as well as forward to Rawls with his ordering of states into liberal, decent, and outlaw.[39]

[35] M de Montaigne, 'Of Cannibals' in *Essays* (JM Cohen trans) (Penguin London 1958 [1580]) 105–18.

[36] Ibid.

[37] J Westlake, *Chapters on the Principles of International Law* (OUP Oxford 1894) at 6.

[38] J Lorimer, *The Institutes of the Law of Nations: A Treatise of the Jural Relations of Separate Political Communities* (2 vols W Blackwood and Sons Edinburgh 1883–4).

[39] S Pufendorf, *The Law of Nature and Nations* (CH Oldfather and WA Oldfather trans) (Clarendon Press Oxford 1925 [1688]) bk 8 ch 4 s 5, at 802, quoted in R Tuck, *The Rights of War and Peace: Political Thought and the International Order from Grotius to Kant* (OUP Oxford 1999) at 161–2; J Rawls, *The Law of Peoples, with The Idea of Public Reason Revisited* (Harvard University Press Cambridge MA 2001). Civilization is still there as an organizing principle of international law as late as 1947: in order to be a state, 'the inhabitants of the territory must have attained a degree of civilisation': CC Hyde, *International Law Chiefly as Interpreted and Applied by the United States* (2nd edn Little Brown

Lorimer's big idea was that uncivilized states (China, Japan, even the US) hovered around the margins of civilization, lacked a reciprocating will and so could not enter into full relations with the civilized core. So, to quote Wheaton, a near contemporary across the Atlantic 'the public law...has always been and still is, limited to the civilized and Christian peoples of Europe and to those of European origin'.[40] The effects (or source) of this were found in the capitulations created under the unequal treaties between European powers and the uncivilized margins (textualizing the idea that European citizens in China required protection from barbarian local law) and the unequal sovereignty of Siam, the Ottomans, Japan, and China (states that in most other respects seemed wholly sovereign). Lorimer's classifications are astonishingly ornate but perhaps not as odd as they seem on first blush. *Nonage*, of course, as we have seen, becomes a familiar idea in the mandates and in the trusteeship doctrine. The idea that some states are 'crazy or sinister', as Martin Wight puts it,[41] is reflected in Lorimer's ideas of about the *imbecility* of states. This comes in two forms: either congenital (because of some racial defect) or political (because of the nature of a particular political orientation). Communism and nihilism are given as examples. We get a sense of empire's confusions about the stability of these terms in *Heart of Darkness* where Empire begins with project and ends in hallucination. Marlow experiences these Lorimeresque categories as precarious and absurd.[42] Africans are first described as enemies by one of the other administrators but Marlow can't quite believe in this designation: 'he called them enemies!', Marlow exclaims. Later he conjures with possible definitions (natives,[43] enemies,[44] criminals[45]) but concludes that they are merely 'unhappy savages' (indeed, they are so demoralized that they don't even find him appetizing (at 60)). In the end, they become obscure to him: 'not enemies, not criminals, not

---

Boston 1947) at 23, quoted in *The Creation of States in International Law* (n 14) 73. Foucault uses the same terms but describes them differently:

> The savage is basically a savage who lives in a state of savagery together with other savages...The barbarian, in contrast, is someone who can be understood, characterized, and defined only in relation to a civilisation, and by the fact that he exists outside it....And the barbarian's relationship with that speck of civilisation—which the barbarian despises, and which he wants—is one of hostility and permanent warfare.

M Foucault, '*Society Must Be Defended*': *Lectures at the Collège de France* (D Macy trans M Bertani and A Fontana eds) (Picador New York 1997 [1975–6]) at 195. On enemies of mankind, see R Yamato, *The Constitution of the Outlaw of Humanity* (2012, unpublished manuscript on file with the author).

[40] H Wheaton, *Elements of International Law* (GG Wilson ed) (reproduction of 2nd edn RH Dana ed Clarendon Press Oxford 1936 [1866]) at 15.

[41] M Wight, *Power Politics* (H Bull and C Holbraad eds) (revised edn Bloomsbury Academic London 2002).

[42] J Conrad, *Heart of Darkness* (Penguin London 2007 [1899]).

[43] To be exploited or cared for.   [44] To be fought by firing into the continent.

[45] To be punished then rehabilitated: 'The philanthropic desire to give some of the criminals something to do' (at 24).

earthly...phantoms' (at 24), they are 'incomplete, evanescent...' (at 65).[46] Marlow ends up exasperated 'What would be the next definition I would hear?' (at 84). One gets the same feeling reading the international law of the period.[47]

Of course, Lorimer's central distinction (if not his endless classifications) was a fairly standard nineteenth-century view; Hegel, for example, knew that any equality between states (what he calls 'autonomy') was merely a formality.[48] And it doesn't seem to be generated by Lorimer's apparent naturalism. As many people have pointed out, 'positivism' too was implicated with its distinction between civilized and uncivilized states and its belief that actual existence or capacity was somehow anterior to recognition in international law (for example, Anghie). Uncivilized states sat beyond international law. Relations in these cases were a matter of something other than law. James Crawford, in a footnote, compares two editions of Oppenheim: 'Lauterpacht omits the sentence: "It is discretion and not International Law, according to which the members of the Family of Nations deal with such States as still remain outside that family".'[49] Omitting this sentence has been the distinctively twentieth-century project of modernizing international law, and yet, the discretion remains.

And so the abstractions of 'Christianity' 'civilization', 'family membership', and 'savagery' became the substance of 'effectiveness', 'territory', and 'statehood'. International society was opened up to hitherto under-civilized peoples (the Japanese, the Koreans, the Thais), and this was followed, as we shall see in the next section, by a radical expansion in the membership of the family of nations. The move from abstraction to material reality promised emancipation, and it would be odd not to register that in some respects international law *was* formally de-racialized. After all, Japan became a 'Great Power' at Versailles, China (or a version of China) became one in 1945. But familiar hierarchies were quickly restaged. Colonial peoples were catalogued in A, B, and C mandates in an arrangement that recalls Pufendorf and Lorimer; new European states were subject to the regulatory effects of minority treaties (a form of administration not deemed necessary in the case of the core European states with their minorities); and the post-war era explosion of new sovereigns was managed through a system of, what one scholar

---

[46] In the end, the Westerners, too, turn out to be 'phantoms'.

[47] This section is drawn from a forthcoming article in the *European Journal of International Law*, G Simpson, 'James Lorimer and the Character of Sovereigns: *The Institutes* as 21st Century Treatise' (manuscript on file with the author).

[48] For a discussion of the Hegelian provenance of international legal personality see 'Theorizing Recognition and International Personality' (n 6). For a discussion of the way in which sovereignty was both territorial (and thus excluded nomadic peoples and pirates) and social (and thus excluded incompletely socialized territorial states and civilizations), see A Anghie, 'Finding the Peripheries: Sovereignty and Colonialism in Nineteenth Century International Law' (1999) 40 *Harvard International Law Journal* (1999) 1–80, at 25–34.

[49] *The Creation of States in International Law* (n 14) 13.

called, 'negative sovereignty'.[50] These new states were not quite fully members of society. These were quasi-sovereigns or conditional sovereigns. They fell short of the standard set by the archetypal European sovereign.[51] And now, in a later move, we see the way in which the abstractions of good governance, earned sovereignty, and responsibility to protect are again disciplining peripheral but materially effective states. The contemporary version of the standard of civilization has bled into other areas of international norm development from the responsibility to protect (after all, Tony Blair called outlaws 'irresponsible states') to the idea of a failed and therefore permeable state to the concept of crimes against humanity, with the claims of humanity used as a way of wedging open the sovereignty of malefactors.[52]

These shifts back and forth between materiality and abstraction, shifts linked together by social and juridical practices of recognition, have managed and consolidated a tenacious division between states that were put on earth by God and others that are here quite by chance.[53] But this distinction reflects an even deeper and more salient division in world politics: that between poor and rich states.[54] International lawyers still speak of sovereign equality but in the face of both sharp material differences and the formal mechanics of privilege this was to risk absurdity. An international law founded on 'sovereign equality' and an international legal practice of making distinctions, might be understood, then, as a way of both reinforcing *and* not talking about a persistent state of affairs. Statehood moves back and forth between the two poles of functional requirement and grand passion,

---

[50] See 'Theorizing Recognition and International Personality' (n 6). See also RH Jackson, *Quasi-States: Sovereignty, International Relations and the Third World* (CUP Cambridge 1993).

[51] This early-twentieth-century story is told in 'Theorizing Recognition and International Personality' (n 6).

[52] On the persistence of these 'imperial legal practices' see A Anghie, 'Rethinking Sovereignty in International Law' (2009) 5 *Annual Review of Law and Social Science* 291–310; J Bartelson, 'Three Concepts of Recognition' (2013) 5 *International Theory* 107–29.

[53] I am paraphrasing Mikhail Gorbachev. At times, international law has enacted this distinction through an under-articulated theory about abnormality and normality that lies in the background of most discussions of statehood. It often seems as if there are normal cases where there is the routine application of legal norms alongside strongly constrained acts of recognition, and then there are the cases we actually study. For example, in the case of self-determination, there are states arising out of the process of decolonization and therefore not subject to the usual rules about government or independence. They become states because it is morally imperative that they achieve independence. But the process, a serious departure from the existing practice, and outcome, the creation of quasi-sovereigns and the liberation of a billion people from imperial rule, does not seem to tell us much in general about statehood and sovereignty. There are states established after the liquidation of pseudo-empires, in Yugoslavia or the Soviet Union, but the formation of these states is atypical because of special historical circumstances (Lithuania) or the presence of nuclear weapons (Ukraine) or the, perhaps, brutal behaviour of the parent state (Bosnia) or because Europeans have imposed special settlements in these areas. No matter where we look, then, there is the spectre of the *sui generis*: Bangladesh is a geographical quirk, Eritrea an entity with prior treaty rights to autonomy, Kosovo a special case.

[54] I am not suggesting that this distinction maps exactly on to the division of rich and poor human beings though there is substantial overlap.

between states as things-in-the-world conforming to some juristic template and recognizable to and by each other, and states as political projects worth defending, dying for, living one's life in. This resembles the relationship between formal sovereignty and substantive sovereignty; or the relationship between a legal order committed to defending sovereignty in the abstract and an order committed to defending substantive conceptions of the good pursued by some sovereigns.

4 FRAGMENTATION/UNITY

...neither division nor unity...

(Eliot)[55]

Most atlases contain two maps of the world. In one, the world is depicted through its rivers, mountains, tectonic plates, and oceans. As a child, I rarely consulted this map. The imagery seemed too messy, the earth too disorganized; it wasn't clear where anything was. In the other map, the world is arranged around territorially sovereign states. Each parcel of territory is demarcated and, often, the borders possessed an almost geometric neatness.[56] This was the world of states, each allocated its own colour but functionally identical—there was very little on the map that suggested doubt or prevarication. But it turned out that this map of sovereignties represented a world idealized through sovereign statehood. There was, most of all, an absence of a sense that sovereignty was contestable or that this contest has been staged partly as a relationship between the idea of sovereignty as a unified, secular, field (sovereigns as stable, unitary, equal) and sovereignty as a way of organizing political space hierarchically (sovereigns as partial, whole, or incomplete, or super-sovereign, or aspirant).

There are two great divides, then, in the law and politics of sovereignty. The first is between sovereign equals and unequal sovereigns (see the earlier discussion). The second is between sovereigns and would-be sovereigns. In this section I want to talk about the transition from non-sovereignty to sovereignty, and the way in which this transition has been managed through a combination of fragmentation (the sub-division of sovereignty) and unity (the refusal to countenance non-sovereign expressions of political community).

[55] TS Eliot, *Ash Wednesday: Six Poems* (Faber & Faber London 1930).
[56] See also K Knop, 'Statehood: Territory, People, Government' in *The Cambridge Companion to International Law* (n 16) 95–116, at 95.

By the middle of the last century, the centralized territorially sovereign state had become the paradigm form of political organization. The idea of territorially discrete, uniform sovereigns has been around since at least Westphalia but it enjoyed a peak of sorts in the 1960s when many 'peoples' became sovereign through acts of self-determination. This latter principle was the portal through which communities stepped in order to acquire the magic of sovereignty. But the principle of self-determination, as I will discuss in a moment, was also a regulative norm, governing, neutralizing, preventing, and forestalling acts of self-realization and discouraging (many) peoples from choosing to form their own state and (often) refusing to recognize non-state formations *as such*. This marks a contrast with two other periods, bookending the Charter era, when, what we might think of (anachronistically, in the earlier case) as, self-determination was managed through the fragmentation of sovereignty.

The late nineteenth and early twentieth century was a period in which sovereignty was reformulated (Leopold's privatization of sovereignty in the Congo), dispersed (the Ottoman experiments in local sovereignties), graded (the civilized/uncivilized distinction), divided (the Turkish suzerainty over Bosnia, Bulgaria's complicated status under the Treaty of Berlin (1878)),[57] and dispersed in all sorts of plural ways. Nineteenth century-textbooks on international law describe a highly variegated sovereignty. John Westlake, for example, devotes nearly half of his *Chapters on the Principles of International Law* (1894) to the different manifestations of sovereignty in the international legal order, teasing out the distinctions between semi-sovereigns, protectorates, vassals, and so on.[58] These sub-categories were established largely as a way of organizing relations among the large European powers (the disposition of European territories often depended on a treaty of some sort amongst those powers) but they also acted to control and govern the expression of sovereign desire.[59] In this way, early claims to self-determination (not yet on the scene as a legal norm) were sublimated in a series of pseudo-sovereignties.[60] These nineteenth-century models of sub-sovereignty were deployed in the administration of the colonial project and by the early twentieth century, the fragments of sovereignty were necessary to shore up the ruins of empire. And so, at Versailles, the claims to unitary statehood on the part of Syrians or Macedonians were either redirected (minority rights guarantees) or displaced into forms of indirect colonial administration (mandate, trusteeship). In this way, self-determination was defanged and empire was reformulated.

---

[57] *Treaty for the Settlement of Affairs in the East* (signed 13 July 1878) 153 CTS 171.

[58] See *Chapters on the Principles of International Law* (n 37).

[59] Or to facilitate exchange between sovereigns. In this way, sovereignty was recognized in order that it be alienated: see 'Three Concepts of Recognition' (n 52) 122–3.

[60] L Benton, *A Search for Sovereignty: Law and Geography in European Empires, 1400–1900* (CUP Cambridge 2009).

It was not until the heights of the decolonization period were reached that sovereign statehood settled into a position of market dominance. At this point Europe had not yet taken off as an alternative quasi-supranational model, at the UN conference in San Francisco the idea of distinguishing states formally on the basis of material capacity or ideological predilection had been rejected, and experiments in sovereignty (Danzig, the mandates, the trusts) were deeply unpopular and, in many instances, tainted.[61]

What happened next was decolonization through self-determination. At one time, this was one of the most fashionable subjects in international law. If the *Oxford Handbook* had been produced twenty years ago it would surely have featured in the chapter listing. Indeed, I wrote my first ever paper at law school on self-determination. I had read Kurt Vonnegut's essay on the 1967 Biafran secession, war, and famine more or less just as I encountered international law for the first time.[62] Vonnegut describes appalling atrocities committed by the Nigerian military but he ends his essay by asking us not to hate the Nigerian state. I was enraged by his polemic, and felt that international law must have a relevant repertoire of solutions or responses, or at least a language of regret.

I discovered that there was a principle with (apparently) direct application to the Biafran case. The right to self-determination already had generated a substantial normative literature, and there had been two periods of transformative state-creating during which the principle of self-determination seemed to have played a constitutive role. In 1919, the remnants of the dissolved Austro-Hungarian and Ottoman Empires were reorganized (in the Hapsburg case) into new nation-states (for example, Yugoslavia and Czechoslovakia, to name two that themselves disintegrated in the face of later self-determination claims) and (in the Ottoman case) into mandates to be held in trust by the victorious Great Powers (for example, Syria and Iraq, to name two currently undergoing processes of dissolution as a result of fresh Great Power intervention and internal claims to self-rule).[63]

By 1960, the second of these ideas had itself been expanded and deepened to accommodate or promote the decolonization of much of Africa and Asia. In both these periods, 'statehood' was posited as the answer to a number of recurring problems: state failure, claims to national self-government, European empire and racism, territorial demarcation, and so on. Statehood was, by far, the preferred outcome of national liberation struggle. In 1960 at the General Assembly meeting in New York, two resolutions were passed within twenty-four hours of one another,

---

[61] *Conditions of Admission of a State to Membership in the United Nations* (Advisory Opinion) [1948] ICJ Rep 57.

[62] K Vonnegut, 'Biafra: A People Betrayed' in *Wampeters, Foma and Granfalloons (Opinions)* (Delacorte Press New York 1974) 141–60.

[63] For a discussion of this history as a series of refurbishments of the constitutive doctrine see 'Theorizing Recognition and International Personality' (n 6).

both of which articulated a change in the essential character of the principle. In the *Declaration on the Granting of Independence to Colonial Countries and Peoples*, the 'Magna Carta'[64] of decolonization, the pattern of meticulous preparation for independence, favoured by the Charter and central to the mandate scheme, was abandoned in favour of 'a speedy *and unconditional* end to colonialism'.[65] In Principle 3 of the *Declaration*, it was stated that, 'inadequacy of political, economic, social or educational preparedness should never serve as a pretext for delaying independence'. The next day, UN General Assembly *Resolution 1541(XV)*, with its references to free association and even integration gestured back to the nineteenth century but it was made very clear that full independence and statehood were the preferred results of a process of decolonization.[66] Effectiveness no longer mattered; what mattered were anti-colonial results. The paradox in all of this, of course, was that acts of self-determination were restricted to already existing colonial administrative borders. Decolonization set the European imperial project in international legal stone.

Accordingly, self-determination during this period was defined as the right held by the majority within a colonially defined territory to external independence from colonial domination by metropolitan powers alien to the continent or pseudo-European colonial rule. It applied neither to ethnic groups within these territories nor to majorities who were being oppressed by indigenous 'alien' elites. Neither secession nor democratic representation were regarded as part of this novel right of self-determination. Resolving self-determination into full statehood was more important than any expression of self-determination on the part of a people. And so, Biafra was unlucky to be the wrong sort of ethnically and territorial identifiable nation (that is, one that was part neither of a dead state-empire (say, an Austro-Hungary) nor a demoralized metropolitan colonizer (say, a Portugal).

A post-*Charter* solution to the problem of self-determination offered the possibility of a return to the more fluid forms of sovereignty found in the nineteenth century. I have written elsewhere about these multiple or plural sovereignties: metaphysical sovereignty, extraterritorial sovereignty, deferred sovereignty, internationalized sovereignty, incipient sovereignty, and deterritorialized sovereignty.[67] The most obvious institutional manifestation of this is found in 'state-building', repeating such exercises at Versailles (the mandates) and Potsdam (the Control Council in Germany), where the 'international community' governs a

---

[64]   See eg H Gros Espiell, *The Right to Self-Determination: Implementation of United Nations Resolutions* (United Nations New York 1980) at 8.

[65]   'Declaration on the Granting of Independence to Colonial Countries and Peoples' (14 December 1960) GA Res 1514(XV) UN Doc A/RES/1514(XV).

[66]   'Principles which Should Guide Members in Determining Whether or Not an Obligation Exists to Transmit the Information Called for under Article 73(e) of the *Charter*' (15 December 1960) GA Res 1541(XV) UN Doc A/RES/1541(XV).

[67]   See generally 'The Guises of Sovereignty (n 8).

particular territory as its people prepare either for independence or are punished for the wrong-doing of the state or as part of the interminable deferral of political claims. In the end, these renewed forms may indeed represent 'the creation of an international juridico-political space that, without doing away with every reference to sovereignty, never stops innovating and inventing new distributions and forms of sharing, new divisions of sovereignty'[68] or they may simply be a return to a nineteenth-century model of controlling the appetites of non-state peoples.

All of this presents a particular problem for peoples seeking self-realization of some sort. They find themselves trapped in a legal discourse that switches back and forth between unity (a model of statehood that was sometimes culturally alien or organized around unified colonial boundaries (this was *uti possidetis juris*) or administered by unfamiliar, often repressive, elites) and fragmentation (novel formations of quasi-sovereignty as a method of colonial control and then. later, limited forms of autonomy, devolution, federalism when statehood was sought).[69] In the end, this movement often helped defuse revolutionary desire, tame rebellious instinct or, more latterly, merely changed the arrangements of extraction.

This operated at a conceptual level where the international law of self-determination has been largely about reconfiguring state boundaries rather than political community; at the level of nationalist politics where the practice of self-determination seems to have often found itself on the wrong side of progressive futures (Biafra, Croatia, and so on); and in the relationship between political economy and representation where self-determination (from neo-colonialism through development to neo-liberalism) sometimes seems to be beside the point. Self-determination—organized around a schism between normality and abnormality—has been reduced to a principle that will accommodate the birth of states (of highly specialized form) in 'extraordinary circumstances' (dissolution of states, end of European empire) but in other cases simply offers false hope of authentic self-rule.

...

In the end, then, international lawyers perhaps ought to understand their work on statehood and self-determination as being connected to a relationship between, on one hand, the historical situatedness of sovereignty and empire, the advantages (or disadvantages) it has bestowed on people, the damage it has done (and averted) in international society, and the fact that we might like some states and dislike others, and, on the other, the formal-egalitarian legal ideal of treating statehood and

---

[68] J Derrida, *Rogues: Two Essays on Reason* (P-A Brault and M Naas trans) (Stanford University Press Stanford 2005) at 87.

[69] The formations are novel but the idea of novel formations is not: 'Every new age and every new epoch in the coexistence of peoples, empires, and countries, of rulers and power formations of every sort, is founded on new spatial divisions, new enclosures, and new spatial orders of the earth': C Schmitt, *The Nomos of the Earth in the International Law of the Jus Publicum Europaeum* (GL Ulmen trans) (Telos Press New York 2003) at 79.

sovereignty agnostically as international legal concepts capable of being under-stood, isolated, and applied as such. This might in the end simply be part of a broader relationship between sovereignty's diplomatic, tactical face and its legal-rational-universal face. But I have argued here that this relationship is constituted by a deeper structure of argument in which sovereignty is managed through the dialectics of form and function, and unity and fragmentation.

CHAPTER 29

....

THEORIZING RECOGNITION AND INTERNATIONAL PERSONALITY

....

ROSE PARFITT

1 INTRODUCTION

....

THE term international personality refers to 'the capacity to be the bearer of rights and duties under international law'.[1] The history of this concept is often traced back to the efforts of an influential group of European international lawyers in the second half of the nineteenth century to construct a 'positivist' system of international law based on state consent.[2] For this reason, international personality tends to be understood as a formalized, more technical version of the 'troubled' and 'unhelpful' concept of sovereignty developed by scholars working in the natural law tradition.[3] In contrast to this older understanding of sovereignty as

---

[1] J Crawford, *The Creation of States in International Law* (2nd edn OUP Oxford 2006) at 32.
[2] M Craven, 'Statehood, Self-Determination and Recognition' in MD Evans (ed), *International Law* (3rd edn OUP Oxford 2010) 203–51, at 215–17.
[3] *Creation of States* (n 1) 32.

'something intrinsic, carrying with it certain natural rights', Craven, for example, argues that the notion of international personality assumes 'the existence of a systemic order that attributed a range of competences to certain designated actors'.[4] However, since only states can possess 'full' international personality under the positivist doctrine of international law, including rights to sovereign equality, self-defence, non-intervention, and territorial integrity, only states can do the attributing—whether directly, by means of 'constitutive' recognition, or indirectly through the formulation of rules of designation. Given the circular nature of this argument, the concept of international personality has come to be seen by Craven and others as emblematic of international law's normative indeterminacy no less than the 'unhelpful' concept of sovereignty it sought to reformulate.[5]

Nonetheless, the language of international personality has made it possible for many non-state entities to be endowed with international rights and duties,[6] including international organizations, peoples, individuals, multinational corporations, indigenous groups and, according to some scholars, even cities and animals.[7] This chapter does not aim, however, to provide either a taxonomy of international personality[8] or a history of recognition.[9] Instead, it will examine the way in which the legal effect of recognition on international personality has been theorized. It will therefore distance itself slightly from the indeterminacy thesis. Bringing some of the most prominent theories of the relationship between recognition and international personality into conversation with some of their most recent and radical alternatives, it will ask why colonial patterns of inequality persist, in spite of the globalization of international personality in the process of decolonization. Is it possible that orthodox theories of this relationship have 'determined' these patterns in some way? The focus will therefore be on *international* recognition (that is, interstate recognition, as opposed to recognition of governments and belligerents),[10]

---

[4] 'Statehood, Self-Determination and Recognition' (n 2) 215.

[5] M Koskenniemi, *From Apology to Utopia: The Structure of International Legal Argument* (reissue CUP Cambridge 2005) at 224–302; 'Statehood, Self-Determination and Recognition' (n 2) 217–20.

[6] *Creation of States* (n 1) 28.

[7] For an excellent collection see F Johns (ed), *International Legal Personality* (Ashgate Farnham 2010). Additionally, on corporate personality, see eg JE Alvarez, 'Are Corporations "Subjects" of International Law?' (2001) 9 *Santa Clara Journal of International Law* 1–36; on indigenous personality, see eg B Kingsbury, 'Reconciling Five Competing Conceptual Structures of Indigenous Peoples' Claims in International and Comparative Law' (2001) 34 *New York University Journal of International Law and Politics* 189–250; and on animals, see eg Y Otomo and E Mussawir (eds), *Law and the Question of the Animal: A Critical Jurisprudence* (Routledge London 2013).

[8] See eg *International Legal Personality* (n 7).

[9] See eg M Fabry, *Recognizing States: International Society and the Establishment of New States since 1779* (OUP Oxford 2010).

[10] On which see eg H Lauterpacht, *Recognition in International Law* (CUP Cambridge 1947) at 87–174 (governments) and 175–328 (belligerents); T-C Chen, *The International Law of Recognition, with Special Reference to Practice in Great Britain and the United States* (LC Green ed) (Praeger New York 1951) at 97–130 (governments) and 303–407 (belligerents); BR Roth, *Governmental Illegitimacy in International Law* (OUP Oxford 1999) chs 5–7 (governments).

and on the personality of entities which identify (whether actually or potentially) as *territorial* (such as states, colonies, 'mandates', and indigenous peoples).[11]

The chapter begins with a theoretical history of the relationship between recognition and personality, starting with an examination of the work of GWF Hegel, before moving to the contemporary debate and its politics.

2 THE DOCTRINES OF RECOGNITION AND INTERNATIONAL PERSONALITY IN HISTORICAL PERSPECTIVE

The impact of Hegel's philosophy of recognition and its role in the construction of individual 'self-consciousness' continues to reverberate throughout the social sciences.[12] Yet Hegel's insistence that the relationship between individual recognition and 'personality' (one of the terms he used to signify fully realized 'self-consciousness')[13] found its parallel in the relationship between *state* recognition and the constitution of the 'personality of the state'[14] has received relatively little attention, given how fundamental this idea has been to international legal theorizing on this topic.

For Hegel, true self-consciousness or personality could be constituted only in and through its acknowledgement by another formally equal self-consciousness/ personality. Such recognition, in turn, could only take place in the aftermath of a 'life-and-death struggle' between two as-yet-unrealized 'consciousnesses', each of which, being unrealized, he saw as being split between two conflicting 'wills'—that of the Master (the 'will to independence') and Bondsman (the 'will to dependence').[15] Hegel's point was to demonstrate that independence is in fact conditioned on dependence—that society and individuality are mutually constitutive. The ultimate form of society was, in his view, the European nation-state, characterized as a form of collective individual which likewise required the recognition of other states in order to obtain *international* personality.[16] However, the function of recognition in the international context was paradoxical in that the nation-state,

---

[11] See also *Creation of States* (n 1) 30.

[12] GWF Hegel, *Phenomenology of Spirit* (AV Miller trans) (OUP Oxford 1977 [1807]) at 111–38.

[13] GWF Hegel, *Elements of the Philosophy of Right* (HB Nisbet trans) (CUP Cambridge 1991 [1835]) at 67–9.

[14] Ibid 317 and 366–7.   [15] *Phenomenology of Spirit* (n 12) 111.

[16] *Philosophy of Right* (n 13) 366–7.

being 'the absolute power on earth',[17] was 'consequently a sovereign and independent entity in relation to others', meaning that 'the power of its sovereign' must be a 'purely *internal* matter'.[18] The relationship between independence and dependence therefore remains unresolved in the international context, meaning that international law must 'always...be tainted with contingency'.[19]

Personality in Hegel's scheme was not, however, available to the 'uncivilized' individual or collective. Notoriously, he declared that 'the African', for example, was incapable of distinguishing 'between himself as an individual and his essential universality', and was therefore unable to participate in the necessarily reciprocal process of recognition.[20] It followed from the same logic, in his view, that 'civilized nations' (that is, Western European states) were entitled to 'treat as barbarians other nations which are less advanced than they are'.[21]

Hegel's writings were published in the first decades of the nineteenth century, and quickly made an impact on the thinking of contemporary international lawyers.[22] Prior to the late eighteenth century, the question of the relationship between recognition and sovereignty had maintained a residual connection to the status of individual monarchs—actual living 'persons'—and was therefore treated by jurists working in the natural law tradition as a strictly internal matter, beyond the scope of the 'law of nations'.[23] 'External legality followed from internal legality',[24] such that one sovereign's recognition of another had no function beyond the formal, at best evidentiary one of 'declaring' the latter's existence. It followed from the same inside-out logic that *non*-recognition would be 'tortious'.[25]

Several jurists continued to insist upon the declaratory theory of recognition throughout the nineteenth century, such as De Martens, for whom it followed from the principle of sovereign equality that '*[u]n État naît et existe par lui-même*' and therefore that '*en principe, la raiconnaissance est la constatation formelle d'un fait accompli*'.[26] However, a number of factors came together to give Hegel's theory a

---

[17] Ibid.   [18] Ibid 366–7.   [19] Ibid 368.

[20] GWF Hegel, *Lectures on the Philosophy of World History* (HB Nisbet trans) (CUP Cambridge 1975 [1837]) at 177.

[21] *Philosophy of Right* (n 13) 376.

[22] See A von Bogdandy and S Dellavalle, 'George Wilhelm Friedrich Hegel (1770–1831)' in A Peters and B Fassbender (eds), *The Oxford Handbook of the History of International Law* (OUP Oxford 2012) 1127–31.

[23] See Q Skinner, 'From the State of Princes to the Person of the State' in Q Skinner, *Visions of Politics*, Vol. II (CUP Cambridge 2004) at 368-413; G Gordon, 'Natural Law in International Legal Theory: Linear and Dialectical Presentations' in this *Handbook*.

[24] A Orford, *International Authority and the Responsibility to Protect* (CUP Cambridge 2011) at 162. See also CH Alexandrowicz, 'The Theory of Recognition *in Fieri*' (1958) 34 *British Yearbook of International Law* 176–98.

[25] 'The Theory of Recognition *in Fieri*' (n 24) 180.

[26] FF de Martens, *Traité de Droit International* (A Léo trans) (A Chevalier-Marescq Paris 1883) vol 1, at 359.

special traction, encouraging the constitutive theory to become predominant from the 1860s, particularly in Britain and North America. One such factor concerned the revolutions of the seventeenth and eighteenth centuries, which led to the emergence of many new states in the Americas and elsewhere.[27] Another, relatedly, was the gradual transformation of the 'international' from an inter-dynastic into an inter-state jurisdictional space.[28] Reflecting on these developments, advocates of the constitutive position insisted—on exactly the same grounds of sovereign equality—that existing international persons should be entitled to decide whether or not to accept the new rights and duties associated with an additional member of the 'family of nations'.[29] Wheaton, for example, was one of the first to articulate a constitutive theory of recognition, in the second edition of his *Elements of International Law* (1863).[30] Wheaton's argument—that while the 'internal sovereignty of a State' did *not* 'depend on its recognition by other States', a state's 'external sovereignty' *would* 'require recognition by other States in order to render it perfect and complete'[31]—was taken directly from Hegel's *Elements of the Philosophy of Right*.[32]

A third factor leading to predominance of the constitutive position concerned the acceleration of European imperialism. Hegel's philosophy, which posited recognition by those considering themselves to be 'self-conscious' as the condition for the attainment by (O)thers of personality, allowed the concept of civilization (already possessed of a long international legal history[33]) to be fused with that of international personality, such that international rights and duties could be cast as something that only 'civilized' states could possess. What civilization meant in international legal terms was left unclear,[34] but idealized notions of European behaviour and institutions were certainly invoked.[35] The standard 'test' came to be whether a state's 'government was sufficiently stable to undertake binding commitments under international law and whether it was able and willing to protect

---

[27] *International Authority* (n 24) 162.

[28] 'Statehood, Self-Determination and Recognition' (n 2) 210.

[29] See *From Apology to Utopia* (n 5) 273.

[30] H Wheaton, *Elements of International Law* (WB Lawrence ed) (2nd edn Sampson Low London 1863).

[31] Ibid 36–9.

[32] See 'The Theory of Recognition *in Fieri*' (n 24) 195; *Creation of States* (n 1) 8.

[33] A Anghie, 'Imperialism and International Legal Theory' in this *Handbook*; A Anghie, *Imperialism, Sovereignty and the Making of International Law* (CUP Cambridge 2005) at 13–31; JL Beard, *The Political Economy of Desire: International Law, Development and the Nation State* (Routledge-Cavendish Oxford 2006).

[34] M Koskenniemi, *The Gentle Civilizer of Nations: The Rise and Fall of International Law 1870–1960* (CUP Cambridge 2001) at 101.

[35] See eg L Oppenheim, *International Law: A Treatise* (2 vols Longmans, Green & Co London 1905–6) vol 1, at 33; W Hall, *A Treatise on International Law* (3rd edn Clarendon Press Oxford 1890) at 42; J Lorimer, *The Institutes of the Law of Nations: A Treatise of the Jural Relations of Separate Political Communities* (2 vols W Blackwood and Sons Edinburgh 1883–4) at 117 and 155.

adequately the life, liberty and property of foreigners'.[36] In this context, the quality of relativity attached to the constitutive theory of recognition gave it an advantage over its declaratory rival in allowing it to cope with supposedly anomalous entities like the Chinese, Japanese, and Ottoman Empires—entities which met the criteria for statehood, yet which European states were reluctant to treat on a basis of equality. Westlake, for instance, asserted that such entities had been *partially* recognized, and that it was possible to '[admit] outside states to parts of [international] law without necessarily admitting them to the whole of it'.[37]

However, while its Eurocentric and indeed racist implications were overt, we should be wary of attributing international law's complicity with colonialism exclusively to the so-called 'standard of civilization'. For statehood (or the 'standard of statehood', as we might call it) was (and remains) just as exclusionary in its effects.[38] Although this exclusivity affected 'wandering tribes' *within* Europe as much as without,[39] the territorial state, its juridical personification and hence the very concept of international law itself are the combined product of a specifically European history, as Schmitt was later to argue.[40] For better (in his view) or worse, it was '[o]nly through the personalization of European territorial states' that 'a jurisprudence of interstate *jus inter gentes* [could] arise'.[41] The decision of the 'professional' international lawyers of the late nineteenth century to adopt the terminology of 'personhood', from Klüber to Bluntschli to Oppenheim, should therefore be understood as a decisive normative move,[42] with its roots in the 'allegorical tendency' of 'Renaissance individualism', which made it 'customary for European jurists to think of a personification of political powers'.[43]

In 1918, however, Europeans suddenly found themselves faced with the idea that 'barbarians' could be German[44] and that 'Africans' could be their vanquishers.[45]

---

[36] G Schwarzenberger, 'The Standard of Civilization in International Law' (1955) 8 *Current Legal Problems* 212–34, at 220.

[37] U Özsu, 'The Ottoman Empire, the Origins of Extraterritoriality, and International Legal Theory' and T Ruskola, 'China in the Age of the World Picture' in this *Handbook*; J Westlake, *The Collected Papers of John Westlake on Public International Law* (L Oppenheim ed) (CUP Cambridge 1914) at 82. See also *A Treatise on International Law* (n 35) 43–4; *Institutes of the Law of Nations* (n 35) 216–19; *International Law: A Treatise* (n 35) 33.

[38] G Simpson, 'Something to Do with States' in this *Handbook*.

[39] Oppenheim gives the examples of 'Jews and Poles': *International Law: A Treatise* (n 35) 100.

[40] C Schmitt, *The Nomos of the Earth in the International Law of the* Jus Publicum Europaeum (GL Ulmen trans) (Telos Press New York 2006 [1950]) at 144.

[41] Ibid 147.

[42] JL Klüber, *Droit des Gens Moderne de L'Europe* (JP Aillaud Paris 1831) vol 1, at 32; JC Bluntschli, *The Theory of the State* (DG Ritchie trans) (3rd edn Clarendon Press Oxford 1895) at 22; *International Law: A Treatise* (n 35) 99.

[43] *The Nomos of the Earth* (n 40) 144–5. See generally *From Apology to Utopia* (n 5).

[44] 'Reply of the Allied and Associated Powers to the Observations of the German Delegation on the Conditions of Peace' (1919) 6 *International Conciliation* 1341–1426.

[45] See eg WEB DuBois, 'Worlds of Color' (1925) 3 *Foreign Affairs* 423–44; M Garvey, *The Tragedy of White Injustice* (Haskell House New York 1927).

During the ensuing conceptual crisis, those attempting to make sense of recognition and personality entered enthusiastically into the interwar spirit of modernist experimentalism described by Berman.[46] Once again, international lawyers fell into two camps.

Broadly speaking, those supportive of the League of Nations system sought to emphasize the lawful (as opposed to 'contingent') nature of the newly institutionalized international legal system through the development of a set of innovative approaches to recognition. Building on a logic developed in the previous century, when the less-than-full personalities of several protectorates, such as Morocco, were constituted via multilateral treaties among the 'great powers',[47] one such approach interpreted accession to the Covenant (open, in theory, to colonies and to the British dominions as well as to states) as a form of collective constitutive recognition.[48] Under article 2(1), all entrants into the League, whatever their status, were required to meet the condition of being 'fully self-governing'. Counter-intuitively, in other words, full self-government was deemed to be compatible with colonial rule—as long as the metropole in question was itself deemed to be 'self-governing'. As this indicates, self-government under the League served a similar constitutive function to the nineteenth-century standard of civilization.[49] A second innovation concerned the new 'national states'/'national minorities' regime constructed in Central and Eastern Europe, where the minorities commitments of these new states were interpreted as being 'coeval' with their 'sovereignty',[50] both of them having been constituted simultaneously in the minorities treaties concluded between these nascent states and the Allies at the end of the War. A third innovation was made by jurists associated with solidarist movement, who insisted that international personality was vested in the individual, rather than the state.[51] Nonetheless, as in Hegel, 'primitive' (that is, non-European) individuals tended to be cast even by this group of scholars as unready for this privilege.[52] Fourthly, with the inauguration of the mandates system a new, tripartite form of subjectivity was devised for the former colonies of the defeated Central powers which fell, at least in principle, somewhere between the non-personality of the colony and the full personality of the sovereign state.[53]

[46] N Berman, *Passion and Ambivalence: Colonialism, Nationalism, and International Law* (Martinus Nijhoff Leiden 2012).

[47] *Creation of States* (n 1) 294–9.

[48] See eg LM Friedlander, 'The Admission of New States to the League of Nations' (1928) 9 *British Yearbook of International Law* 84–100.

[49] For a discussion in the context of the Ethiopian Empire's accession, see R Parfitt, 'Empire des Nègres Blancs: The Hybridity of International Personality and the Abyssinia Crisis of 1935–36' (2011) 24 *Leiden Journal of International Law* 849–72.

[50] *Passion and Ambivalence* (n 46) 168.

[51] G Scelle, *Précis de droit des gens* (2 vols Sirey Paris 1932) vol 1, at 7–14.

[52] Ibid 143.

[53] *Covenant of the League of Nations* (signed 28 June 1919 entered into force 10 January 1920) [1919] UKTS 4.

In the second camp fell those, associated in particular with the rise of fascism, who considered the League system irrelevant, if not toxic. For such jurists, the contingency inherent in the relationship between recognition and international personality represented an advantage rather than a limitation. After all, the philosophy of fascism had no interest in subordinating the state to the individual or nation via principles like self-government or solidarity. On the contrary, as the *Manifesto of Fascist Intellectuals* declared (in overtly Hegelian terms), fascism advocated the sacrifice of the individual to an idea—'fatherland' (*Patria*)—from which 'his reason to live, his liberty and every one of his rights' were derived. The (European) state should therefore be understood as a 'process' of continual 'historical self-realization', through which 'the tradition...of civilization, far from remaining a dead memory of the past, assumes the form of a personality [*personalità*] conscious of the end it strives to realize'.[54]

In the nearly seventy years that have passed since the collapse of the League and the defeat of fascism, the imperialistic logic and indeed the hubris of interwar modernism, whether in its pro- or anti-League manifestations, has been roundly defeated—or so it would seem. The first and most important step towards this supposed victory for equality was the conclusion of the *Montevideo Convention on the Rights and Duties of States* in 1933—a direct attempt led by the Latin American states to check that hubris. In referring to '[t]he state as a person of international law', the Convention famously elided the 'objective' concept of statehood with the 'subjective' concept of international personality before proclaiming that '[t]he political existence of the state is independent of recognition by the other states'.[55] Crucially, in this new iteration of the declaratory theory of recognition, 'external legality' followed not from 'internal legality' but rather from the 'fact' of statehood, as defined by the four supposedly objective criteria.

According to the mainstream perspective, the passage of the four 'Montevideo' criteria into customary international law marked the beginning of the end both for the constitutive theory and for the so-called 'standard of civilization' upon which it relied.[56] Already in 1947, Lauterpacht could declare that '[m]odern international law knows of no distinction, for the purposes of recognition, between civilized and uncivilized States'.[57] Yet to nomadic and other un-state-like peoples it was clear that juridical objectivity remains in the eye of the beholder. Indeed, the subjective, if not directly constitutive character of the post-1933 standard of statehood has

---

[54] 'Manifesto degli intelletuali fascisti' *Il Mondo* (21 April 1925) (my translation).

[55] *Montevideo Convention on the Rights and Duties of States* (signed 26 December 1933 entered into force 26 December 1934) 165 LNTS 19.

[56] See eg JL Brierly, *The Law of Nations: An Introduction to the International Law of Peace* (5th edn Clarendon Press Oxford 1955) at 129 and 132; A Cassese, *International Law* (2nd edn OUP Oxford 2005) at 74. See further See A Becker Lorca, *Mestizo International Law: A Global Intellectual History 1842-1933* (CUP Cambridge 2015) at 305–52.

[57] *Recognition in International Law* (n 10) 31.

become all the more obvious since decolonization (on the basis of the expressly anti-conditional 'right of peoples to self-determination',[58] coupled, however, with the principle of *uti possidetis juris*) and the eventual collapse of Communism. Kelsen's point that 'in the province of law there are no absolute, directly evident facts, facts "in themselves", but only facts established by the competent authority in a procedure prescribed by the legal order' therefore remains as pertinent today as it was in 1941.[59] For if states are the only 'competent authority' available to establish the 'fact' of international personality, then it runs counter to the principle of sovereign equality that recognition—whether on the basis of a standard of civilization or 'only' one of statehood—could be anything but constitutive. Given the Eurocentric tendencies of both 'standards', one could, indeed, ask whether it is possible to make any meaningful distinction between the constitutive and declaratory theories of recognition at all.

In spite of these problems, the declaratory approach has remained predominant in mainstream theorizing on recognition throughout the post-1945 period,[60] and the compromise attempted by Lauterpacht—the argument that recognition was 'declaratory of facts' but 'constitutive of rights'—did not make the transition to orthodoxy.[61] Those who acknowledge the difficulty of separating the declaratory and constitutive theories have tended to follow Crawford into the ambivalent position of rejecting the constitutive approach, with the qualification that 'this does not mean that recognition does not have important legal and political effects', including effects that are 'properly speaking constitutive'.[62] This is clear, for example, from the response to the recognition practice associated with the collapse of Communism in Eastern Europe.[63] The Badinter Commission set up in 1991 to arbitrate the process of Yugoslavia's 'dissolution' insisted (in three of its ten *Opinions*) that recognition was 'purely declaratory' in its impact.[64] In the meantime, however, the European Commission (EC) states (under the auspices of which the

---

[58] 'Inadequacy of political, economic, social or educational preparedness should never serve as a pretext for delaying independence': 'Declaration on the Granting of Independence to Colonial Countries and Peoples' GA Res 1514 (XV) (14 December 1960) UN Doc A/RES/1514, at para 3. On the relationship between self-determination and statehood, see *Creation of States* (n 1) 128–38.

[59] H Kelsen, 'Recognition in International Law' (1941) 35 *American Journal of International Law* 605–17. See also *From Apology to Utopia* (n 5) 274.

[60] From a selection of widely used textbooks in English, French, and Russian, see eg *International Law* (n 56) 73–4; P Daillier and A Pellet, *Droit international public* (7th edn LGDJ Paris 2002) at 556–7; VP Panov et al., *Mezhdunarodnoe pravo* (Rior Moscow 2009) at 113.

[61] H Lauterpacht, 'Recognition of States in International Law' (1944) 53 *Yale Law Journal* 385–458; *Recognition in International Law* (n 10) 6.

[62] *Creation of States* (n 1) 27.

[63] See generally J Klabbers et al., (eds), *State Practice Regarding State Succession and Issues of Recognition: The Pilot Project of the Council of Europe* (Kluwer Law International The Hague 1999).

[64] Arbitration Commission of the Peace Conference on Yugoslavia, *Opinion No 1* (29 November 1991) 92 ILR 162, 163; *Opinion No 8* (4 July 1992) 92 ILR 199, 200; *Opinion No 10* (4 July 1992) 92 ILR 206, 207.

Commission had been established) declared 'their readiness to recognize' whichever of the emerging republics had 'constituted themselves on a democratic basis'
and accepted 'international obligations... with regard to the rule of law, democracy
and human rights'.[65] This return by the EC to a conditional form of recognition
on the basis of what could very plausibly be construed as an updated standard of
'civilization' was coupled with an apparent downgrading of the importance of the
criteria for statehood (as under the League). Bosnia-Herzegovina, for example, was
recognized in the midst of a civil war, before the four criteria had been met,[66] and
was admitted to the United Nations (UN) (open only to states)[67] less than four
months later.[68] In this situation, as Hillgruber argues, recognition 'did not serve
merely as a refutable assumption that the criteria [for statehood] had been met',
but 'actually... as a substitute for these features, which were obviously missing'.[69]

Thanks to this and other examples of recognition practice in the post-Cold
War period, some mainstream theorists have begun to move towards a partial
acceptance of the constitutive theory—although there is, naturally enough, some
reluctance to refer explicitly to a new standard of civilization.[70] Structurally,
however, the three criteria (as employed by the EC) of democracy, human rights,
and the 'rule of law' do appear to have begun to fulfil the same function. Indeed,
not only does this new 'standard' appear to be capable of compensating for certain of the criteria for statehood when these are deemed to have been met inadequately; it is also powerful enough, it seems, to revoke or downgrade aspects
of the rights of existing international persons if these have been violated to a
significant degree.[71]

The next section will look more closely at the way in which these developments
are starting to be theorized. It will begin with a brief examination of three mainstream approaches, all advocating the use of recognition to constitute and maintain forms of international personality that meet this new triple standard, before
moving on to examine a broader set of concerns regarding recognition and personality that are emerging from the critical response to these mainstream approaches.

---

[65] 'Guidelines on the Recognition of New States in Eastern Europe and in the Soviet Union
(16 December 1991)' (1991) 61 British Yearbook of International Law 559–60.

[66] See R Wilde, International Territorial Administration: How Trusteeship and the Civilizing
Mission Never Went Away (OUP Oxford 2008) at 138–41.

[67] Charter of the United Nations (signed 26 June 1945) art 4(1).

[68] International Territorial Administration (n 66) 226–8.

[69] C Hillgruber, 'The Admission of New States to the International Community' (1998) 9 European
Journal of International Law 491–509, at 493. The International Court of Justice avoided pronouncing
on these developments in 2008. See Accordance with International Law of the Unilateral Declaration
of Independence in Respect of Kosovo (Advisory Opinion) [2010] ICJ Rep 403.

[70] See eg J Vidmar, Democratic Statehood in International Law: The Emergence of New States in
Post-Cold War Practice (Hart Oxford 2013).

[71] See G Simpson, Great Powers and Outlaw States: Unequal Sovereigns in the International Legal
Order (CUP Cambridge 2004).

3 CONTEMPORARY THEORIES OF RECOGNITION AND INTERNATIONAL PERSONALITY

Mainstream theoretical readings of the relationship between recognition and personality have tended to focus on constructing and disciplining what Nijman, in her intellectual history of international legal personality ('ILP'), calls 'well-functioning' states.[72] Like the interwar solidarists, Nijman seeks to return 'ILP' to what she sees as its 'original' conceptualization as something vested not in the state, but in the individual. The 'well-functioning state', she argues, 'has full ILP, but only derived from its citizens'.[73] Citing Hannah Arendt, Nijman argues that '[c]itizenship is a defining element of man's *humanity*'.[74] Thus,

[i]f a state does not live up to the demands of human rights law and thus fails to perform its primary function as a political community, another community, namely the international community, has to fill the void. ILP will then flow back to its initial source: the individual subject.[75]

This perspective, of course, resonates closely with the 'responsibility to protect' concept recently taken up with some enthusiasm at the UN.[76] Under the rubric of 'R2P', states which fail to meet the new tripartite standard (democracy, human rights, the 'rule of law') can be singled out for intrusive projects of 'reconstruction' (as in post-invasion Iraq, Afghanistan, and Mali) or—if the transgression is serious enough to meet the bar of genocide, ethnic cleansing, war crimes, and/or crimes against humanity—for forcible intervention (as in Libya in 2011).[77] Nijman's argument also resonates, in the opposite direction, with the 'earned sovereignty' approach, proponents of which celebrate the trend towards requiring separatist 'substate entities' (such as Kosovo, Palestine, and South Sudan) to 'earn' their 'sovereignty' by meeting an institutional standard based explicitly on 'the rule of law, democracy and human rights'.[78] The 'consent of the international community in the form of international recognition' is considered necessary to confirm the 'final status' of the new 'sovereign'.[79]

---

[72] JE Nijman, *The Concept of International Legal Personality: An Inquiry into the History and Theory of International Law* (TMC Asser Press The Hague 2004).

[73] Ibid 468.   [74] Ibid 461–2 (emphasis in original).   [75] Ibid 471.

[76] See eg Secretary-General, 'Responsibility to Protect: Timely and Decisive Response' (25 July 2012) UN Docs A/66/874–S/2012/578. For a critique, see *International Authority* (n 24).

[77] On Libya, see Security Council, 'Resolution 1970' (26 February 2011) UN Doc S/RES/1970.

[78] MP Scharf, 'Earned Sovereignty: Juridical Underpinnings' (2003) 31 *Denver Journal of International Law and Policy* 373–86, at 384–5.

[79] PR Williams and FJ Pecci, 'Earned Sovereignty: Bridging the Gap between Sovereignty and Self-Determination' (2004) 40 *Stanford Journal of International Law* 1–40, at 9. See also C Drew,

Yet the idea, implicit in all three of these new approaches, that '[t]o be a legal person' (in Nijman's sense of being the citizen of what she calls a 'well-functioning' state) 'is a necessity for living a humane life'[80] has worrying implications. After all, it was Hegel who first asserted that the 'highest duty' of individuals was 'to be members of the state'—by which, as we have seen, he meant the 'civilized' state. Having traced the meaning of the term 'civilization' from that of white/European to 'self-governing' to 'rule of law', democracy and human rights-respecting, the question arises as to what should happen, as a matter of international law, when the legitimacy of a supposedly 'well-functioning' state is rejected by the individuals over which it claims jurisdiction. Are such individuals (identifying, perhaps, with groups as diverse as ETA, the Naxalites, Islamic State, the Tamil Tigers, and the IRA) then less than 'human'? Hegel's answer would certainly have been in the affirmative, and this new orthodoxy appears to tend in a similar direction.

Scholars associated with the Third World Approaches to International Law (TWAIL) movement[81] have been particularly alert to the implications of these new theoretical developments in the field of recognition and personality.[82] In their view, both the *process* through which international personality has been transferred to the 'Third World' and the 'racialized' *form* it has taken there have repeatedly belied the promise of liberation which 'independence' held out. Regarding process, Anghie gestures towards Fanon's critique of Hegel's recognition 'dialectic' to point out that the doctrine of constitutive recognition presented non-European peoples with 'the fundamental contradiction of having to comply with authoritative European standards in order to win recognition and assert them'.[83] Regarding form, Anghie argues that it was *only* in the course of restricting 'native personality' to the capacity to cede land to Europeans,[84] or negating it entirely via the doctrine of *terra nullius*,[85] that positivist jurisprudence was able to develop a coherent concept of 'full' sovereignty/international personality. Mutua makes a similar argument in relation to Africa's 'juridical states' which he describes as 'timebombs ready to explode'.[86]

'The Meaning of Self-Determination: "The Stealing of the Sahara" Redux?' in K Arts and PP Leite (eds), *International Law and the Question of Western Sahara* (IPJET Leiden 2007) 87–105, at 95.

[80] *The Concept of International Legal Personality* (n 72) 467.

[81] See JT Gathii, 'TWAIL: A Brief History of Its Origins, Its Decentralized Network, and a Tentative Bibliography' (2011) 3 *Trade Law and Development* 26–64.

[82] *Imperialism, Sovereignty and the Making of International* Law (n 33); BS Chimni, 'International Institutions Today: An Imperial Global State in the Making' (2004) 15 *European Journal of International Law* 1–37; MW Mutua, 'Why Redraw the Map of Africa? A Moral and Legal Inquiry' (1995) 16 *Michigan Journal of International Law* 1113–76.

[83] *Imperialism, Sovereignty and the Making of International* Law (n 33) 107–8. See F Fanon, *Black Skin, White Masks* (R Philcox trans) (Grove Press New York 2008 [1952]).

[84] *Imperialism, Sovereignty and the Making of International Law* (n 33) 77–81.

[85] Ibid 83–4.   [86] 'Why Redraw the Map of Africa?' (n 82) 1114.

Feminist and queer theorists of international law, meanwhile, have been among the most willing to confront the anthropomorphic terminology of 'recognition' and 'personality', focusing in particular on the image of the body.[87] Charlesworth and Chinkin, for example, draw on Naffine's description of the individual legal subject as a 'bounded, heterosexual male body' against which bodies without 'clear definition' are recognized as 'deviant and undeserving'[88] to argue that the state ('full' international person) likewise has no 'natural' points of entry. Violation of the right of non-intervention therefore becomes the clearest possible breach of international law.[89] Yet many states, not to mention indigenous peoples and other non-state groups, have been unable to claim this kind of 'bounded' international personality, and have been constructed instead as having 'permeable, negotiable, penetrable, vulnerable boundaries in the same way that women's bodies have been constructed in criminal law'.[90] This distinction lends itself to an analogy 'between the position of Third World states and that of women'.[91] As Ruskola points out, however, to assume that because 'full' international persons are gendered male then 'colonized and conquered' entities must be 'gendered female' is 'a *non sequitur*', for international personality, like gender, 'is neither a fixed attribute nor a logical conclusion, but a relational identity'.[92] Ruskola notes that even though the Chinese Empire, for example, had been an object of veneration for centuries before it was forcibly 'opened' to European trade, it came to be understood as 'hypercivilized', as 'degenerating into senile old age', which meant '[a]s an international person, it could therefore be dismissed as indolent and hopelessly effete'.[93] In this way,

[i]n China casual imperial penetrations were anticipated primarily to arouse a desire to assume a more manly posture [by 'opening up' its economy to free trade]...In contrast, rhetorically Europe's full-scale continental rape of Africa suggested a desire to *discipline*, rather than arouse, Africa's excessive, sexualized, and ungovernable hypermasculinity by means of brutal, calculated mass violence.[94]

Unlike the critiques outlined so far, Marxist theorizing in this area does not see recognition as a mechanism for constituting certain 'classes' of international person as juridically unequal.[95] On the contrary, sovereign equality is an assumption to be

---

[87] See D Otto, 'Feminist Approaches to International Law' in this *Handbook*.

[88] N Naffine, 'The Body Bag' in N Naffine and R Owens (eds), *Sexing the Subject of Law* (Law Book Sydney 1997) 79–93, at 85, quoted in H Charlesworth and C Chinkin *The Boundaries of International Law: A Feminist Analysis* (Manchester University Press Manchester 2000) at 129.

[89] *Boundaries of International* Law (n 88) 129–30.   [90] Ibid.

[91] H Charlesworth, C Chinkin, and S Wright, 'Feminist Approaches to International Law' (1991) 85 *American Journal of International Law* 613–45, at 618. See also K Knop, 'Re/Statements: Feminism and State Sovereignty in International Law' (1993) 3 *Transnational Law & Contemporary Problems* 293–344.

[92] T Ruskola, 'Raping Like a State' (2010) 57 *UCLA Law Review* 1477–1536, at 1495.

[93] Ibid 1496.   [94] Ibid 1498–9 (emphasis in original).

[95] See R Knox, 'Marxist Approaches to International Law' in this *Handbook*.

taken seriously. Pashukanis, for example, pointed out that the function of formal equality in the international legal realm, as in domestic law, was to disguise and hence to perpetuate the vast material disparities upon which the capitalist system thrives. '[M]odern international law' is therefore 'the legal form of the struggle of the capitalist states among themselves for domination over the rest of the world'.[96] Building on this, Miéville suggests that the 'classical' imperialism of the nineteenth century, characterized by widespread formal *inequality*, was actually an 'interruption' to the logic of the expansion of sovereign equality and 'free trade imperialism', beginning in the eighteenth century.[97] No wonder, he argues, that decolonization has had so little impact on the global distribution of power and wealth—since 'formal sovereign independence not only does not preclude domination, but can, through recognition, *be the very institution by which domination is exercised*'.[98]

A number of theoretical attempts have been also made to tackle the question of why—in spite of its questionable material benefits—statehood (and the 'full' range of rights and duties it implies) continues to be desired as the ultimate form of collective emancipation, from Scotland to Palestine to Mindanao.[99] In response to this question, Otomo has turned to feminist psychoanalytic theory to argue that the state form allows international legal subjects (self-constructed as male) deliberately to forget the constitutive (maternal) role of recognition in the constitution of subjectivity, and instead to see themselves as *self*-constituting—always-already possessed of international personality. The 'encounter between sovereign states' is thus 'mediated by a specular identification with the Sun/Father/God, whose imagined gaze empowers the sovereign speaking subject[s] to *recognise themselves* under the rubric of a masculine subjectivity'.[100] A two-pronged attempt to respond to the question of the state as an object of collective desire has also been made by the author of this chapter. I have drawn, in the first place, on Bakhtin's concept of the dialogic to suggest that international personality, as constituted through recognition, might usefully be understood as hybrid: half-international legal Self; half-disciplinary Other. This can work against 'peripheral' international persons, but in certain contexts can also be mobilized for strategic purposes.[101] In the second place, my work in this area is indebted to the thinking of two Marxist theorists, Louis

---

[96] E Pashukanis, 'International Law' in P Beirne and R Sharlet (eds) *Selected Writings on Marxism and Law* (PB Maggs trans) (Academic Press London 1980) 168–82, at 172.

[97] C Miéville, *Between Equal Rights: A Marxist Theory of International Law* (Brill Leiden 2005) at 238.

[98] Ibid (emphasis in original).

[99] See S Pahuja, 'Decolonization and the Eventness of International Law' in F Johns, R Joyce, and S Pahuja (eds), *Events: The Force of International Law* (Routledge Abingdon 2011) 91–105.

[100] Y Otomo, 'Of Mimicry and Madness: Speculations on the State' (2008) 28 *Australian Feminist Law Journal* 53–76, at 65 (emphasis added).

[101] See '*Empire des Nègres Blancs*' (n 49).

Althusseur and Bernard Edelman, and argues that interpellation (self-recognition) is just as important as external recognition to the process of 'international legal reproduction' (as I have called it). Interpellation is here understood as a double process, in which the reproduction of 'free and equal' individual subjectivity and 'sovereign' international subjectivity are harnessed together in the service of the expansion of the global 'free' market.[102] Nonetheless, and however the 'mimetic desire' for recognition is characterized, Ruskola's point—that 'Western incursions' into Imperial China 'did not constitute a violation of pre-existing sovereignty... but in fact the creation of a sovereignty on the Western model as something to be violated'—remains fundamental.[103]

There remains to be examined an important set of demands for recognition and international personality which tend not to focus on statehood: those made by minorities and indigenous peoples. These demands often centre on the protection of cultures and identities.[104] In this context, Tourme-Jouannet has argued that a new 'international law of recognition' has emerged in the post-Cold War era in response to the demand of such groups for 'a right to legal protection for their cultures and, for some, a claim for reparation of historical wrongs inflicted by colonization that bruised and spurned their identities'.[105] Tourme-Jouannet cites numerous multilateral protections for cultural diversity,[106] as well as declarations on minority and indigenous rights[107] and reparations for 'historical crimes'[108] to argue that 'a legal status of difference has emerged alongside the legal status of equality in international law'.[109]

Such a position is not without its critics, however.[110] For example, theorists of indigenous personality have, like Anghie, picked up Fanon's point that post-colonial

---

[102] R Parfitt, *International Personality on the Periphery: History, International Law and the 'Abyssinia Crisis'* (book manuscript currently under review).

[103] 'Raping Like a State' (n 92) 1531–2.

[104] See eg C Taylor, 'The Politics of Recognition' in A Gutmann (ed), *Multiculturalism: Examining the Politics of Recognition* (Princeton University Press Princeton 1994) 25–73; A Honneth, *The Struggle for Recognition: The Moral Grammar of Social Conflicts* (J Anderson trans) (Polity Press Cambridge 1995); P Markell, *Bound by Recognition* (Princeton University Press Princeton 2003).

[105] E Tourme-Jouannet, *What is a Fair International Society? International Law between Development and Recognition* (Hart Oxford 2013). See also E Tourme-Jouannet, 'The International Law of Recognition' (2013) 24 *European Journal of International Law* 667–90, at 668–9.

[106] *Convention on the Protection and Promotion of the Diversity of Cultural Expressions* (opened for signature 20 October 2005 entered into force 18 March 2007) 2440 UNTS 311.

[107] 'United Nations Declaration on the Rights of Indigenous Peoples' (13 September 2007) GA Res 61/295 UN Doc A/RES/61/295 annex 1.

[108] 'Declaration of the World Conference against Racism, Racial Discrimination, Xenophobia and Related Intolerance' (Durban, 8 September 2001) ('Durban Declaration and Programme of Action').

[109] *What is a Fair International Society?* (n 105) 125–201.

[110] See eg Jean d'Aspremont's response: J d'Aspremont, 'The International Law or Recognition: A Reply to Emmanuelle Tourme-Jouannet' (2013) 24 *European Journal of International Law* 691–9, and Tourme-Jouannet's rejoinder: E Tourme-Jouannet, 'The International Law of Recognition: A Rejoinder to Jean D'Aspremont' (2013) 24 *European Journal of International Law* 701–5.

recognition simply does not fit into (and is thus excluded from) the reciprocal Hegelian template.[111] Moreover, as Bhandar points out, essentialization is not the only risk that comes with restricting indigenous rights to those which can be contained within the parameters of 'culture'. For such recognition legitimizes a territorial dispossession based on racist ideas (also imported from Hegel) about the relationship between property and legal subjectivity.[112] This, Bhandar argues, has created a 'fundamental paradox' at the heart of indigenous personality, resulting from the insistence of the courts of settler states from Canada to Australia that evidence of continuous occupation dating from the 'pre-sovereignty' period must be demonstrated by indigenous land claimants.[113] Indigenous land rights are therefore recognized only if 'defined in relation to Anglo-European norms of private property ownership and colonial sovereign power'[114]—norms that are by definition alien to the culture whose 'authenticity' they are called upon to prove. Thus, although Western property norms have been 'transformed with the ascendance of intangible and intellectual forms in an era of global capitalism', the 'dialectic of recognition' remains 'firmly embedded in a nineteenth century, modern conceptualization of the subject and property relations', such that aboriginal personality remains bound 'to the old tombstones of the triumvirate: culture, nation, land'.[115] Ultimately, then, Tourme-Jouannet's position is vulnerable to the argument that the identification of indigenous subjectivity with indigenous 'culture' has allowed indigenous rights to be recognized only when these do not undermine the 'foundations' of the settler state—foundations which, from the indigenous perspective, are illegitimate.

4 CONCLUSION

In emphasizing the zigzagging theoretical trajectory both of doctrine and critique regarding the relationship between recognition and international personality, and the material effects of this trajectory on disadvantaged peoples, states, and other entities, I have attempted to impart some of my own sense of the negative impact

---

[111] GS Couthard, 'Subjects of Empire: Indigenous Peoples and the "Politics of Recognition" in Canada' (2007) 6 *Contemporary Political Theory* 437–60, at 443–5; B Bhandar, 'Plasticity and Post-Colonial Recognition: "Owning, Knowing and Being"' (2011) 22 *Law and Critique* 227–49, at 227–8.

[112] 'Plasticity and Post-Colonial Recognition' (n 111) 229.

[113] See (in Australia) *Members of the Yorta Yorta Aboriginal Community v Victoria* (2002) 214 CLR 422; (in Canada) *R v Powley* [2003] 2 SCR 207.

[114] 'Plasticity and Post-Colonial Recognition' (n 111) 236.   [115] Ibid 236–7.

that mainstream doctrines of recognition and international personality have had, and continue to have, on relations of domination globally.

As mentioned in the introduction, the oscillation of recognition doctrine between the 'constitutive' and the 'declaratory' positions, and the incapacity of the concept of international personality to resolve the 'sovereignty paradox', have led many scholars to the conclusion that these concepts, like international legal doctrine more generally, are normatively indeterminate. However, as many of the critics featured in Section 2 point out, when it comes to international legal subjectivity, the short straw seems always to be drawn by the Other—whether characterized by race, gender, sexual orientation, class, culture, or any other supposed marker of dialectical inferiority. The extent to which orthodox theories of recognition and personality have, as I have argued, played a role in *determining* global inequalities would seem to be connected, at least to some extent, with the resilience of Hegelian thinking in this area of international legal theory.

Hegel asserted, very simply but very effectively, that while all individuals are equally capable of being recognized and obtaining personality, some entities we might *think* of as individuals actually do not meet this more intuitive benchmark. It is therefore arguable that the problem lies not only with the doctrine of recognition and (international) personality, but also with the theoretical underpinnings of more fundamental, ostensibly 'factual' or 'objective' concepts like individuality, humanity and, in the international legal context, statehood. The task of collapsing the dichotomies on which these concepts rest—between subject and object, law and fact, constitution and declaration, and ultimately Self and Other—will be the next challenge for theorizing in this area.

CHAPTER 30

THEORIZING JURISDICTION

GREGOR NOLL

1 INTRODUCTION

JURISDICTION is a composite term referring to that which is right (*jus*) and that which is said (*dicere*). It is decisive for any consideration of jurisdiction whether one chooses to subordinate *jus* to *dicere*, or *dicere* to *jus*. As the law is always anterior to a pronouncement of justice based on it, the choice of subordination decides whether one lets the past rule over the present, or the present rule over the past. Does the law trump the decision, or does the decision trump the law? In Christian metaphysics, the temporal choice is exacerbated and stands between the past and the future. Jurisdiction is determined, primarily, by (past) creation and, ultimately, by (future) deliverance. The question is then how much weight is accorded to creation and to deliverance respectively. While international law is commonly taken to be a 'secular' order today, this polarity still undergirds its doctrines of jurisdiction. But it does so in rather muted ways.

In writings on international law, jurisdiction is a term used to delimit and legitimize the exercise of one state's power against that of others. It is also used to delimit and legitimize the exercise of institutional power, as that of a court or tribunal, against the power of states. Specialist literatures on subject matters such as international criminal law, international economic law, and international human rights law discuss where exactly those limits are, or should be. There are few, if any, attempts to think the fundamentals of jurisdiction.

The practice of international law confirms that jurisdictional questions are prior to questions of material justice. 'Do I have a mandate to deal with this case?' This is what a judge or a state representative would need to think before applying international law to the facts in a concrete situation. In court judgments, issues of jurisdiction and of justice are often separated and dealt with consecutively.[1] Jurisdictional questions are termed as 'preliminary', and considered quite literally *before* passing across the boundary of material justice. The very term 'material justice' tells us how much of a challenge the concept of jurisdiction is to secular legal scholarship. If justice rendered by a court is termed 'material', would not issues of jurisdiction be metaphysical? What share of worldly events is a state or a court entitled to rule on? What are the extensions, conditions, and limitations of this entitlement? By whom was it conferred, when, and how?

I think that jurisdiction is about attachment played out in a triangle. This triangle links the *creator* of jurisdictional entitlement to its *holder* and to the *share of the world* to which it relates. To exemplify, the *share of the world* might be a human being, a company, a territory, or a particular deed subjected to jurisdiction. The *holder* of jurisdictional entitlement is a state or a court. The *creator* of jurisdictional entitlement might be a worldly entity such as a number of states (endowing a human rights court with jurisdiction). Or a less tangible entity might be set as the creator (endowing the sovereign state with worldly jurisdiction).

The triangle of attachments leads me to two questions. First, how is a share of the world attached to a holder of jurisdictional authority so as to 'fall under' its jurisdiction? Second, how is the holder of jurisdictional entitlement attached to its creator? I am going to seek answers in general international law writings first (Section 2). A line of cases decided by the European Court of Human Rights (ECtHR) helps me to articulate an understanding of the term 'jurisdiction' additional to and different from the account given by general international law writings (Section 3). In Section 4, I shall emphasize the connection of jurisdiction to the past by considering the concept of *kerygma* in Christian theological tradition. Section 5, in turn, reflects the connection of jurisdiction with the future, drawing in particular on the redemptive role of human rights law. In Section 6, I find that both connections render the content of jurisdiction too unstable, and pursue the possibility of a new and secular reading of the concept. To that end, I draw on a particular text by the

---

[1] In *Nicaragua*, one of the most famous cases adjudicated by the International Court of Justice, the Court first presented an extensive reasoning on its jurisdiction and the admissibility of the case before pronouncing itself on the substantive 'merits' of the case. Its jurisdiction reasoning came in a separate 107-page judgment, while the judgment on the merits comprised 277 pages. Seventeen months passed between the two judgments: *Military and Paramilitary Activities in and against Nicaragua (Nicaragua v United States)* (Jurisdiction and Admissibility) [1984] ICJ Rep 392; *Military and Paramilitary Activities in and against Nicaragua (Nicaragua v United States)* (Merits) [1986] ICJ Rep 14.

British philosopher Simon Critchley, which I see pointing the way towards a contemporary understanding of jurisdictional normativity.

2 JURISDICTION IN PUBLIC INTERNATIONAL LAW

What answers to the questions posed in the introduction do jurisdictional doctrines of contemporary public international law provide?

The first question was how a share of the world is attached to a holder of jurisdictional authority so as to 'fall under' its jurisdiction. The answer given by international law is extremely concrete. International lawyers who care to begin their exploration of jurisdiction on the conceptual level tend to stipulate a definition. Here is one fairly representative example: 'Under public international law, jurisdiction refers to the authority of a state to make law applicable to persons or things and to enforce law through judicial and nonjudicial means'.[2]

From there on, authors proceed to distinctions of various kinds with little, if any, explanation of their rationale. One set of distinctions branches out into 'territorial' and 'extraterritorial' jurisdiction,[3] another features the enumeration of jurisdictional 'categories'. Echoing the subdivision into three branches of domestic government, authors distinguish between prescriptive jurisdiction and enforcement jurisdiction, and at times also judicative jurisdiction.[4] Jurisdictional claims articulated in criminal law are categorized as 'principles' based on territory (the territorial principle), personal attachment to the state (the nationality, passive, and active personality principles), security interests (the protective principle), or the universal rejection of a particular conduct (the principle of universality). To quite some extent, these 'principles' reflect the three constituent elements of the state as defined in international law (territory, population, and capacity to enter into

---

[2] American Law Institute, *Restatement, Fourth, The Foreign Relations Law of the United States—Jurisdiction, Preliminary Draft No 1* (12 September 2013) at 1.

[3] This distinction is usefully discussed in C Ryngaert, *Jurisdiction in International Law* (OUP Oxford 2008) at 6–8, with further references.

[4] Terminology varies somewhat without necessarily signifying substantial differences. The term 'legislative jurisdiction' is used synonymously to 'prescriptive jurisdiction'; 'executive jurisdiction' is used synonymously to 'enforcement jurisdiction', and 'adjudicative jurisdiction' is used synonymously to 'judicative jurisdiction'. An exhaustive discussion of the extent to which the two-pronged and the three-pronged categorization finds support with courts and writers can be found in *Restatement, Fourth, The Foreign Relations Law of the United States* (n 2) 6–8.

relations with other states). If anything, state authority is principal in those claims of jurisdiction.

What authors call 'principles' or 'categories' are, I think, but secondary phenomena that resist inclusion into one and the same organizational model and that trespass the boundaries of public international law into both private international law and a domestic law of jurisdiction. They offer a language to articulate delimitations, overlaps, competing claims, and white spots of jurisdictional exercise of state power, neither less nor more.

'The law of jurisdiction is about *entitlements* to act', wrote Rosalyn Higgins, the former president of the International Court of Justice, in a scholarly monograph.[5] As states are equally sovereign, they appear to form an irreducible plurality. For that reason, the story of jurisdiction needs to be told in the plural form of 'entitlements'. International legal terminology simply confirms the assumption that shares of the world are attached to a jurisdictional authority *in multiple ways* and moulds these plural attachments into 'categories' and 'principles'. These are not necessarily internally coherent in practice. The absence of a central arbiter provides for conflicts amongst states and perpetual discussion amongst commentators. We are left asking the prior question *how* this attachment is brought about; or, what principle governs the 'principles'.

3 JURISDICTION IN HUMAN RIGHTS LAW

Adding to the confusion, the term 'jurisdiction' may denote something quite different from the 'entitlements' that we looked into earlier.[6] A human rights treaty obliges a state bound by it only to protect those individuals within the jurisdiction of that state.[7] Hence, the law of human rights uses 'jurisdiction' as an aggregate

---

[5] R Higgins, *Problems and Process: International Law and How We Use It* (Clarendon Press Oxford 1994) at 146 (emphasis in original).

[6] Marko Milanovic makes the point that the term 'jurisdiction' has a plurality of meanings in international law, and that the meaning of human rights law jurisdiction cannot be reduced to an international law meaning of the term: see M Milanovic, *Extraterritorial Application of Human Rights Treaties: Law, Principles and Policies* (Oxford University Press Oxford 2011) ch 2.

[7] See eg *International Covenant on Civil and Political Rights* (opened for signature 16 December 1966 entered into force 23 March 1976) 999 UNTS 171 art 2 (emphasis added): 'Each State Party to the present *Covenant* undertakes to respect and to ensure to all individuals within its territory and subject to its *jurisdiction* [the rights in the *Convention*]'; *Optional Protocol to the International Covenant on Civil and Political Rights* (opened for signature 16 December 1966 entered into force 23 March 1976) 999 UNTS 302 art 1 (emphasis added): 'A State Party to the *Covenant* that becomes

term, operating at a different level than the permissive 'principles' and 'categories' driving jurisdictional sub-practices in the inter-state law of jurisdiction.

Asking when a person is 'within the jurisdiction of a state' means to ask a question distinct from whether a state 'may claim' jurisdiction under any of the inter-state jurisdictional categories. In human rights cases, respondent states have an interest in *limiting* the scope of the jurisdiction concept so as to break the link between state conduct and the violation of a particular human right. By contrast, a state drawing on any of the permissive jurisdictional 'principles' is typically interested in *enlarging* their scope so as to affirm the lawfulness of its conduct. In arguing with a permissive concept of jurisdiction, state conduct is usually linked to a branch of government or a form of attachment between state and individual set out in criminal law. The human rights question of being within *the* jurisdiction of a state operates at an abstract and cumulative level, where the state and its exercise of power are analysed in their totality.

That totalizing level appears to be more adequate when considering my second question. In comparison to the patchwork of permissive jurisdictional principles, jurisdiction in human rights law would seem to provide a better starting point to consider how the holder of jurisdictional entitlement is attached to its creator. Courts and doctrinal writers do not pursue that question at greater depth. 'It is as if legal thought cannot, or can no longer, articulate the terms of its own existence',

a party to the present *Protocol* recognizes the competence of the Committee to receive and consider communications from individuals subject to its *jurisdiction* who claim to be victims of violations by that State Party...'; *Convention against Torture and Other Cruel, Inhuman or Degrading Treatment and Punishment* (opened for signature 10 December 1984 entered into force 26 June 1987) 1465 UNTS 85 art 2.1 (emphasis added): 'Each State Party shall take effective legislative, administrative, judicial or other measures to prevent acts of torture in any territory under its *jurisdiction.*'; *Convention on the Rights of the Child* (opened for signature 20 November 1989 entered into force 2 September 1990) 1577 UNTS 3 art 2.1 (emphasis added): 'States Parties shall respect and ensure the rights set forth in the present *Convention* to each child within their *jurisdiction...*'; *American Convention on Human Rights* (opened for signature 22 November 1969 entered into force 18 July 1978) 1144 UNTS 123 art 1 (emphasis added): 'The States Parties to this *Convention* undertake to respect the rights and freedoms recognized herein and to ensure to all persons subject to their *jurisdiction* [the *Convention* rights].'; *European Convention on Human Rights and Fundamental Freedoms* (signed 4 November 1950) CETS No 5 art 1 (emphasis added): 'The High Contracting Parties shall secure to everyone within their *jurisdiction* the rights and freedoms defined in...this *Convention.*' To be sure, the *African Charter on Human and People's Rights* (opened for signature 27 June 1981 entered into force 21 October 1986) does not contain a jurisdictional provision: 'The Member States of the Organization of African Unity parties to the present *Charter* shall recognize the rights, duties and freedoms enshrined in this Chapter and shall undertake to adopt legislative or other measures to give effect to them.': art 1. Neither does art 2 of the *International Covenant on Economic, Social and Cultural Rights (ICESCR)* (opened for signature 16 December 1966 entered into force 3 January 1976) 993 UNTS 3 allude to jurisdiction, but its *Optional Protocol* does in its art 2: *Optional Protocol to the International Covenant on Economic, Social and Cultural Rights* (10 December 2008) UN Doc A/RES/63/117, art 2.

as Shaunnagh Dorsett and Shaun McVeigh note in their important contribution to jurisdictional literature.[8]

When pressed to interpret the term 'jurisdiction' inscribed in art 1 of the *European Convention on Human Rights and Fundamental Freedoms* (*ECHR*), the ECtHR cast it as a 'threshold criterion'[9] for the responsibility of a particular state for adapting its conduct to the content of Convention rights. Higgins' dictum that jurisdiction is about entitlements to act needs to be complemented. Jurisdiction in human rights law is about the responsibility incurred when states do act. In human rights law, the term 'jurisdiction' performs the function of attributability in the general international law of state responsibility.[10]

Let us stay with the ECtHR. After all, it is one of the most important international mechanisms in the human rights field due to its power to bind governments and its massive production of judgments. In a meandering line of cases, the ECtHR has tried to delineate the contours of 'jurisdiction' for the purposes of human rights law. Who is responsible for human rights compliance in an occupied territory or during military action in foreign territory (for example, the cases of *Louizidou, Cyprus, Bankovic, Issa, Al-Skeini,* and *Jaloud*)?[11] Under whose jurisdiction is an area that is controlled by rebels who enjoy the support of a foreign power (*Ilascu* and *Catan*)?[12] These are some of the challenges the Court has faced over the years.

In its 2011 Grand Chamber Judgment in *Al-Skeini*, the ECtHR gave an extensive account of this case law so far. To start with, jurisdiction is 'presumed to be exercised normally throughout the State's territory'.[13] The Court thinks the 'territorial principle' to be the default mode of exercising jurisdiction, providing the first and dominant category in its inventory of case law. The second category is 'State agent authority and control' and is organized around personality. The Court subdivides this category into three: 'acts of diplomatic or consular agents on foreign territory'; the 'extraterritorial exercise of public functions in another state that consented to it, invited it or acquiesced into it'; and the 'full and effective control over

---

[8] S Dorsett and S McVeigh, 'Questions of Jurisdiction' in S McVeigh (ed), *Jurisprudence of Jurisdiction* (Routledge-Cavendish Abingdon 2007) 3–18, at 3.

[9] *Al-Skeini v United Kingdom* (2011) 53 EHRR 18, at [130].

[10] For a state to be responsible for a wrongful act, a form of attachment between act and state needs to be constructed. That form is termed 'attributability', and its conditions are set out in International Law Commission, 'Responsibility of States for Internationally Wrongful Acts' (28 January 2002) UN Doc A/RES/56/83, annex 1, ch 2.

[11] *Loizidou v Turkey* (1995) 20 EHRR 99; *Cyprus v Turkey* (2002) 35 EHRR 30; *Bankovic v Belgium* (2007) 44 EHRR SE5; *Issa v Turkey* (2004) 41 EHRR 567; *Al-Skeini* (n 9); *Jaloud v The Netherlands* (ECtHR, Application No 47708/08, 6 December 2011).

[12] *Ilascu v Moldova and Russia* (2004) 40 EHRR 1030; *Catan v Moldova and Russia* (2013) 57 EHRR 4.

[13] *Al-Skeini* (n 9) at [130]. The enumeration of categories that I sketch in the following is at [131]–[142].

an individual'. The third category provides for situations where jurisdiction presupposes 'effective control over an area'.[14] In the requirement that control be 'full
and effective' or 'effective' outright so as to constitute jurisdiction, the power to
exclude or supplant other, potentially competing powers, appears to be decisive.

Yet is there a common understanding behind the superficially neat subdivision into 'normal' territorial jurisdiction and 'exceptional' extraterritorial jurisdiction? The 2004 Grand Chamber judgment in *Ilascu v Moldova and Russia*
suggests quite the opposite. At issue was a human rights violation alleged to have
taken place in an area of the Republic of Moldova controlled by Russian-backed
rebels. Were the claimants under the jurisdiction of Moldova or of Russia? Both,
claimed a feeble majority, applying the territorial principle and its extraterritorial exception in parallel. Nonetheless, the Court majority came to the conclusion that Moldova was not responsible for the violations of human rights in its
rebel-controlled area (while Russia was). As the Moldovan government lacked
authority in that part of its territory where the violations took place, the Court
thought that the 'factual situation reduces the scope of that jurisdiction in that
the undertaking given by the State under Article 1 must be considered by the
Court only in the light of the Contracting State's positive obligations towards
persons within its territory'.[15]

By hinging its interpretation of 'jurisdiction' onto the territoriality principle in
earlier judgments, the Court had painted itself into a corner. Its majority was now
presenting quite amazing verbal constructs to justify that Moldova's jurisdiction
could be both engaged and factually disabled at the same time. It is unsurprising
that there was a massive disagreement on this course within the Court: of its
seventeen judges, eleven backed an array of five dissenting opinions. The question
how the impugned conduct might or might not fall within Moldova's jurisdiction
played a dominant role in all of these.

Pace *Ilascu*, jurisdiction in human rights law is best understood as a binary concept, in analogy to the function played by attributability norms in the law of state responsibility. Either one is within the jurisdiction of a state, or one is not. Either an act
is attributable to an actor, or it is not. Why did the *Ilascu* Court insist that one could be
within the jurisdiction of a state, and, at the same time outside its 'scope'?

As I see it, two ideas affect the reasoning of the ECtHR in its jurisdiction cases.
One is unity in law: the idea that a single concept of jurisdiction applies to all of
international law, including human rights law, and that this concept is rooted in
territory. This idea makes us read the concept of jurisdiction in human rights law

---

[14] In addition to these three categories, the court adds a fourth on the 'Convention Legal Space'.
This is, however, not an additional and clearly delimited group of cases in which jurisdiction is
deemed to be exercised, but perhaps more of an attempt by the ECtHR to row back from an unfortunate expression used in *Bankovic* (2007) 44 EHRR SE5.

[15] *Ilascu* (n 12) at [333].

through the 'territorial principle' found in general international law.[16] But as that principle is only one facet of jurisdiction in general international law, albeit an important one, the idea of unity through law only reaches so far. The other idea is unity in fact. The concept of jurisdiction should be understood in the light of states' factual power. Wherever a state exercises this power, be it within or outside the confines of legal entitlements, it exercises human rights jurisdiction.[17] For those subscribing to this idea, jurisdiction in human rights law does not have to be conceptually coherent with jurisdiction in general international law. The point of the former is to condition and mitigate any exercise of power anywhere in the world through the law of human rights. It is a redemptive strategy, and it derives its normative force from the image of a good life to be attained in the future.

Would not the actual exercise of state power alone have been sufficient to bring about the same outcomes in the line of cases on jurisdiction? Why are arguments from territory so important? The answer is that each of the two ideas affecting ECtHR judgments represents a specific heritage in legitimizing the exercise of power. First, in Western and westernized contexts, territoriality comes with one of the strongest conceivable mandates by the divine. God 'said unto' the male and female he had just created: 'Be fruitful, and multiply, and replenish the earth, and subdue it: and have dominion over the fish of the sea, and over the fowl of the air, and over every living thing that moveth upon the earth' (Genesis 1:28). This mandate is known as *dominium terrae* and it is no less than the first *juris dictio*, the speaking of justice by the first instantiation of power and justice itself.

The second idea draws its legitimacy not from past creation, but from future redemption. While the first is invested in law, the second is invested in justice. In Section 5 below, I will explain in more detail how it works and why it is so important.

4 THE CONCEPT OF JURISDICTION AND *KERYGMA*

In the introduction, I suggested that jurisdiction always faces us with a hierarchical choice. Are we going to subordinate speech (*dicere*) to the law (*jus*), or,

---

[16] In 2004, the ECtHR said as much in *Ilascu* (n 12) at [312]. Yet in 2011, the linkage between 'jurisdiction' in art 1 of the ECHR and the meaning of the term in public international law was conspicuously absent from the lengthy recapitulation of earlier case law (*Al-Skeini* (n 9) at [131]–[132]). It is too early to conclude on what this obliteration means.

[17] 'To my mind, "jurisdiction" means actual authority' stated Judge Loucaides in his partly dissenting opinion in *Ilascu* (n 12) at [1], then developing this understanding at some length.

inversely, law to speech? As I have to depart from somewhere, here is my choice for the moment. *Jus* is adverbial in its relation to *dicere*,[18] which makes the act of speaking central. *Juris dicere* is speaking to someone that which is right. The element of speech is, I think, material. The meaning of *dicere* needs to be considered first, so as to understand what *jus* it is capable of engendering.

At this juncture, and perhaps out of a reasonable historical reflex, some have turned to sources in Roman law to construe *dicere* and its adverbial *jus*.[19] I will follow a different path. The problem of jurisdiction poses itself in an international legal order founded on Christian structures. For that reason, I shall consider how the concept of jurisdiction might be tethered to one particular Christian tradition of thought and then turn to the possibility of reading it in a secular way.

Jurisdiction as a concept, I suggest, has a precursor in the Greek term *kerygma*, literally the voicing of a sound by humans or animals. The German Jesuit theologian and philosopher Erich Przywara (1889–1972) identifies the Greek term *kerygma* as a 'primordial word' for Christianity, central for developing a philosophy of revelation.[20] How, one might ask, are revelation and jurisdiction related to each other? The Christian tradition originates quite literally with the word 'being with God' and, more radically, 'being God' (John 1:1). The speaking of that which is right is one mode of revealing the creator's will. Revelation is the word, the *logos* of jurisdiction, being uttered and materializing in the world.

Kerygma establishes a relation between the creator and the world analogous to that established between the law and the world through jurisdiction. Justice is the point at which *kerygma* and jurisdiction intersect. Both are about justice: spiritual justice in the former case, and, we tend to think, worldly justice in the latter case. I shall first consider the formal aspect of *kerygma*, to then move on to the material aspect of justice as expressed in the concept of justification.

In developing the formal role of *kerygma*, Przywara bundles three aspects: the convoking herald, the message proclaimed, and the realm implied by convocation. A state convoking a people, a military convoking an army, or a sacred authority convoking the faithful to sacrificial service are examples Przywara offers.[21] He terms the convoking person a 'herald', a term he further explicates in the German original as '*Heeres-Waltender*', which would be a person who is in charge of an army. The etymological ties between the verb *walten* and the noun *Gewalt*,

---

[18] E Benveniste, *Indo-European Language and Society* (Faber and Faber London 1973) 391, referred to in 'Questions of Jurisdiction' (n 8) 3.

[19] Peter Goodrich offers examples of this approach among contemporary authors, concurrently warning of the historical idiosyncrasies to which it delivers us: P Goodrich, 'Disciplines and Jurisdictions: An Historical Note' (2010) 48(2) *English Language Notes* 153–61.

[20] E Przywara, 'Christliche Urworte: Kerygma, Mysterium, Kairos, Oikonomia' in *Analogia Entis: Metaphysik: Ur-Struktur und All-Rhythmus* (Johannes Verlag Einsiedeln 1962) 495–508, at 495 and 489–501.

[21] Ibid 499.

denoting power as well as violence, reverberate strongly with Przywara's associ-ation of *kerygma* with the military.[22] I do not think this association is merely a metaphorical one. In the world, the *kerygma* of the herald and the jurisdiction of the *judex* always imply representation of a higher power, a power ultimately rooted in a supreme spiritual violence.[23]

This reading is fortified once we involve the writings of the Christian Apostle Paul in it. By means of a violent divine intervention, Paul had been called to the service of what then was a religious splinter group within Judaism. *Kerygma* was a decisive experience for him, and he would be acutely aware of the dan-gers that lie in the neglect of jurisdictional borders between the spiritual and the worldly. In a letter to one of the emerging Christian congregations threat-ened by Roman authorities, Paul explains why the faithful should submit to worldly authority:

Let every soul be subject unto the higher powers. For there is no power but of God: the powers that be are ordained of God. Whosoever therefore resisteth the power, resisteth the ordinance of God: and they that resist shall receive to themselves damnation. For rulers are not a terror to good works, but to the evil. Wilt thou then not be afraid of the power? do that which is good, and thou shalt have praise of the same.[24]

A believer cannot evade jurisdiction by resisting the call of worldly powers. What is more, resisters 'shall receive to themselves' the judgment. This confirms that the sounding of the herald always requires the re-sounding of those addressed, even by those whose answer is disobedience.[25]

Przywara emphasizes that the kerygmatic message implies a realm. At the time of the Gospel, the Roman Empire was an evident point of reference. *Euangelion* is the term with which Przywara denotes the message of the Roman Caesar into the entirety of the Roman realm, 'independently whether it is a message of punish-ment or grace'.[26] *Euangelion* is the worldly form *kerygma* takes, and *kerygma* points to the spiritual realm which exists alongside the worldly realm of the *euangelion*. *Euangelion* then is a medium in the revelation of the creator's *logos*, just as the *dic-tio juris* is a medium in the revelation of the law.

---

[22] The *Oxford English Dictionary* adds another dimension. The first item under the entry on 'herald' is an officer having 'the special duty to make royal or state proclamations' or who bears 'sov-ereign messages between princes or sovereign powers'.

[23] G Agamben, *Homo Sacer: Sovereign Power and Bare Life* (D Heller-Roazen trans) (Stanford University Press Stanford 1998) at 30–8.

[24] Romans 13:1–3, King James Version. The original Greek term for 'power' is *exusia*, translated by Luther with the tellingly ambiguous *Gewalt*.

[25] Other translations operate with the term 'judgement' instead of 'damnation': see eg the New International Version of Romans 13:2. The German translation of FE Schlachter, *Die Bibel* (Bible Society of Geneva Geneva 2000) graphically suggests that resisters extend damnation on themselves (*ziehen sich selbst die Verurteilung zu*), which implies an active participation by the subject of juris-diction in the process of damnation.

[26] 'Christliche Urworte: Kerygma, Mysterium, Kairos, Oikonomia' (n 20) 499.

Beyond extreme instantiation through *kerygma* and jurisdiction, beyond abstract literality in biblical or legal *logos*, the creator as much as the law remains largely inaccessible. Worldly speech is therefore so important. Przywara considers the overwhelming emphasis Calvinism puts on both sermon and a congregation's response to it as 'the absolute form' of kerygmatic Christianity. Hence, *kerygma* would be as much the sounding of the herald, on behalf of the creator, as the re-sounding of those called by the herald. Herein, the triangular relationship of creator, holder of jurisdictional authority, and share of the world emerges.

With the reference to Calvinism, Przywara emphasizes the particular importance *kerygma* had for the Reformation, a process whose onset would see empires displaced by states, and ecclesiastical jurisdiction reduced to a shadow of its former self. Those diminutions, with the possibility of universal empire giving way to the sovereign equality of states, created persevering confusion, because there was no longer one imperial messenger, but a plurality of messengers, all endowed with equal standing. While contemporary international law has no difficulty with affirming a purely domestic exercise of jurisdiction, it obviously lacks an independent criterion that would resolve conflicts of jurisdiction in the pluriverse of sovereign and equal states.

Reverting to my quote of Paul's 'Letter to the Romans' (13:1) earlier, the plural form of 'higher powers' would seem to be compatible with the pluriverse of sovereign states as long as it is clear which of these powers is the relevant one in any given moment and matter. Yet the permissive nature of inter-state jurisdiction remains so obviously unable to achieve this *ex ante*. As to 'power', Przywara helpfully explains the original Greek term *exusia* as a being (*usia*) that goes beyond itself (*ex*) to constitute a realm of being (*Seinsbereich*).[27] This suggests a power forever reaching out into the domain of other powers, rather than an order where powers and their jurisdictions are clearly and neatly separated.

The movement of reaching out contradicts any idea of a law of jurisdiction as a stable order. Considered from this perspective, the international law of jurisdiction can only be captured descriptively, trailing and depicting which state momentarily dominates in any given issue. So the 'entitlements' that Rosalyn Higgins alludes to are really self-entitlements. Once a state has successfully established its 'higher powers' in a particular territory, over a particular person, or in a particular person, it appears as legitimized by the higher spiritual power of the creator who 'ordained it'. Self-founding 'entitlements' and a univocality underwritten by the creator are indeed coupled, it would seem.

[27] E Przywara, 'Christ und Obrigkeit' in E Przywara et al., (eds), *Christ und Obrigkeit: Ein Dialog* (Glock und Lutz Nürnberg 1962) 7–27, at 13.

5 DEVELOPMENTS FROM EARLY MODERN INTERNATIONAL LAW

Yet is it really that easy? I think that reading would cede too much power to the state as holder of jurisdictional authority, always trailed by the ever-serviceable creator of that authority. I would like to show that this reading is not necessarily drawing on Christian metaphysics at large, but on a particular Protestant metaphysics. This consideration will help me, so I hope, to set apart the international law concept of jurisdiction prevailing in 'entitlements' from a concept of jurisdiction particular to human rights law.

Here is what I suggest. The jurisdiction of human rights law is thought to be fundamentally different than the jurisdiction of 'entitlements'. The former gives greater weight to redemption, and therewith to the future, the *telos* or end of worldly time. Jurisdiction as inter-state 'entitlements', by contrast, emphasizes creation, emergence, and legitimation by the creator—a creator who, at the beginning of times, endowed kings with spiritual power in the world.

Let me start with the impact that the Reformation had on international law. It dramatically reconfigured the relationship between creator and holder of jurisdictional power by supplanting the spiritual rule of the pope in the world with the spiritual rule of the sovereign in the world, or, rather, the reformist world of nation-states. When kings became, or made themselves into, the highest authority of reformed churches, the separation of the worldly and spiritual realms was altered decisively. If sovereigns were also spiritual authorities then the problem of coordinating their jurisdictions would not merely be a worldly one, to be decided by worldly strength and force: it would be a spiritual problem too, providing for a structural inter-reformationist conflict. As a relapse into religious feud by worldly sovereigns would be incompatible with the idea of Westphalia, the remaining option would be to freeze this latent conflict and wilfully to ignore its spiritual dimension. This would explain why rules on state responsibility allow for the possibility of shared responsibility without determining a hierarchy amongst co-responsible states.[28] These rules simply circumvent the open question of *exusia*. It would explain, too, why a permissive-descriptive approach of 'entitlements' should be attractive to contemporary textbook authors. The concreteness of existing institutions, such as the division of power, or of territory and population, must be incredibly appealing to a cornered legal doctrine. After all, the post-reformation

---

[28] 'Responsibility of States for Internationally Wrongful Acts' (n 10) arts 16 and 17. See also International Law Commission, 'Draft Articles on Responsibility of International Organizations' (9 December 2011) UN Doc A/66/100 ch IV, reflecting norms on the responsibility of an international organization in connection with the act of a state or another international organization.

stalemate has denied authors any possibility to organize jurisdiction according to a first principle or an ultimate *telos*.

What, then, of human rights? Those are the flip side of the entitlement coin, yet not in the facile sense that state powers boosted by reformation come with boosted responsibility. The Reformation froze inter-state international law in a stalemate of spiritually equal sovereigns. Yet it opened the possibility for these sovereigns to extend their jurisdiction to matters of faith formerly reserved to the ecclesiastical domain. Concretely, this made the religious obligation of *agape* into a matter of law.[29] The question of what humans 'in truth'[30] owe to other humans would now be channelled through the state, and come under its jurisdiction.

The second question I seek to answer here is how the holder of jurisdictional authority is attached to its creator. At this point, this question is subverted by the radical change to worldly authority experienced with the Reformation. With the introduction of human rights through the revolutionary declarations of the seventeenth century, the legitimizing significance of creation declined, while that of redemption grew. First, the French Declaration's reference to a 'Supreme Being' changes the temporal source of legitimacy from the past of creation to the present of 'Being'. Second, human rights instruments declare what it means to be human by listing the rights inalienably human, and therewith the essence of being human. In that, they also perform a revelation of what it means that Christ is 'wholly man' (*totus homo*). Third, human rights instruments are rife with eschatological references. For example, the Preamble to the *Universal Declaration of Human Rights* envisages 'the advent of a world in which human beings shall enjoy freedom of speech and belief and freedom from fear and want has been proclaimed as the highest aspiration of the common people'. It proclaims an end, rather than restores a beginning.

Is human rights jurisdiction being constructed so differently that there is a total disconnect from the inter-state jurisdiction of 'entitlements'? Not so. I suggested earlier that the move of spiritual authority into worldly sovereigns also fettered

---

[29] Once Paul has invited the faithful to submit to the higher powers, to pay tributes, and to render dues, he adds the imperative to love the other: 'Owe no man any thing, but to love one another: for he that loveth another hath fulfilled the law': (Romans 13:8, King James Version). The command of *agape* is echoed in the language of 'respect, protect, fulfil' said to explain the nature of state's obligations under human rights law: see A Eide, 'Realization of Social and Economic Rights and the Minimum Threshold Approach' (1989) 10 *Human Rights Law Journal* 36–51. Eide's language has found its way into the work of the Committee on Economic, Social and Cultural Rights, advising states on the implementation of the obligations under the *ICESCR*. See Committee on Economic, Social and Cultural Rights, 'General Comment 12: The Right to Adequate Food (Article 11)' (12 May 1999) UN Doc E/C.12/1999/5, at para 15.

[30] W Hamacher, 'The Right Not to Use Rights: Human Rights and the Structure of Judgments' in H de Vries and LE Sullivan (eds), *Political Theologies: Public Religions in a Post-Secular World* (Fordham University Press New York 2006) 671–90, at 671.

that authority to worldly institutions and their delimitation. Hence, the question of *agape* is subjected, through its juridification, to territorial borders, and to the limits of state institutions. While the obligation of *agape* was universal, the jurisdiction of human rights law can be no more than pluriversal.

6 JURISDICTION AS THE CALL OF CONSCIENCE

Today, the concept of jurisdiction seems to be too much tied to the past or too much tied to the future. The past looms large in the creationist form of jurisdiction that emphasizes the significance of territory. And the future exercises its pull through a messianic form of human rights jurisdiction pre-empting redemption. Both forms of jurisdiction presuppose a worldly power that is utterly unstable: *exusia*, the being which always goes beyond itself in its striving towards universality.[31] So we have two forms of jurisdiction that are inherently unstable. As we saw in a line of ECtHR cases, they compete with each other. This competition multiplies their internal instabilities.

Too much past, too much future: is there no living in the present? Since jurisdiction in international law has lost a stable metaphysical base, it is more cacophony than calling. So, after the death of God, let us start all over again. Are we capable of discerning a calling beyond that cacophony, a calling that evokes faith in its justness? What would it mean, in concrete terms, to listen for such a calling?

First and foremost, it means a methodological shift. My attention has so far been directed to the *speaking* of that which is just. Now, in the absence of unequivocal speech, it turns to the *listening* for that which is just. I go beyond the traditional emphasis of the perspective of the speaker, the monarch and ultimately the creator and redeemer. To organize jurisdiction as *listening* is to organize it from the perspective of the person who subjects herself to that jurisdiction in good faith. That person is always a human being of flesh and blood living in this world in a particular moment: a secular listener. If the old metaphysics no longer evince faith, the point for starting anew is necessarily secular.

Second, it means a shift from the strength of the imagined judex, creator, and redeemer to the weakness of the listening subject. This brings us back, and forcefully so, to Paul, who so far only appeared as the author of a short passage in his Letter

---

[31] 'Christ und Obrigkeit' (n 27) 13.

to the Romans, where he affirmed that those who have been called should continue to submit themselves to worldly jurisdiction. Now, who is that Paul? A Jew literally struck off his horse by a calling. And a violent persecutor of the very Christian movement whose apostle he then became by virtue of the call. As we see, this call reformed him from strength to weakness, from persecutor of apostates to a persecuted apostate, from adherent to a religion licit under Roman rule (phariseeic Judaism) into one of an illicit religion (that would later be known as Christianity). 'But', as the British philosopher Simon Critchley writes, 'what is essential to Paul's calling is that he does not celebrate or even communicate directly the experience of being called'.[32] In his 'refusal of rapture', Paul insists 'that faith in the Messiah can only be experienced in weakness'.[33]

Critchley's point is not to add another reading of Paul to an already sizeable literature. Rather, in his *The Faith of the Faithless*, he pursues an inquiry into faith 'as the fidelity to an infinite demand'.[34] This makes him track a Pauline line in Heidegger's thought. As this conception of faith is 'not necessarily theistic', Critchley is well served by Heidegger's non-mystical and emphatically worldly Paul. And so am I, as my inquiry has reached a point where jurisdiction is no longer determined by a structurally theistic creator or redeemer, but by a human listening to a call.

Third, the step outside a theistic top-down structure means a lot of insecurity. I imagine this listening human to be without guidance. And so were the early Christians, as they had given over the law to live in faith alone. Faith is something that makes sense in an environment of insecurity. With Heidegger, Critchley explains that this insecurity is a consequence of the strange temporality in which the early Christian congregations lived. When would the world come to an end and redemption occur? How was one to behave in the time that remained until then? Before redemption, Paul warned, rebellion would come, and the Anti-Christ 'the man of lawlessness is revealed' (2 Thess 2:3, *Revised Standard Version*). For the time that remains, it is a major challenge to discern the voice in which I may have faith from the voice that leads astray—the voice of lawlessness. In Pauline thought, this insecurity is persistent and irreducible. Once we have realized that the conventional accounts of international law jurisdiction have become baseless and unreliable, we are jolted into an analogous insecurity.

This insecurity is not one that comes to humans from the outside alone. In an analogous process, insecurity emerges from inside those called. To them, the world is no longer familiar, and life is no longer routine. So the world has become *strange* to them, and their life has been filled with *anguish*. Both Paul's and Heidegger's addressees—the Early Christians and the Late Moderns—share these two conditions. This cuts short Critchley's detailed analysis, in which he has laid bare what

---

[32] S Critchley, *The Faith of the Faithless* (Verso London 2012) at 171.   [33] Ibid.
[34] Ibid 18.

we might call Pauline structures in Heidegger's *Being and Time*.[35] The world's strangeness translates into an externally imposed insecurity, and one's own self being threatened by the unresolvedness of existence is internally imposed insecurity. Without a foundational norm of jurisdiction, the world is strange to us, and without guidance by the law, we remain anxious for not knowing what we may do.

How will the individual handle the determination of authoritative *juris dictio*? By putting the question to her conscience, one might answer with Heidegger. His concept of conscience is different from its common understandings where we hear an internalized voice speaking for a superimposed agent ('God', 'the common good', 'morals'). Rather, conscience is something that intervenes into the worldly life of an individual (something that Heidegger literally terms as 'being there', or, in the German original, *Dasein*) *from within* that individual.[36] *Dasein* comprises both the trivial existence of the human as part of a mass and that which makes a particular human into a singular being. It internalizes a tension that was staged at least partially outside the individual in kerygmatic Christianity.

> If we analyse conscience more penetratingly, it is revealed as a call. Calling is a mode of *discourse*. The call of conscience has the character of an appeal to *Dasein* by calling it to its ownmost potentiality-for-Being-its-Self; and this is done by summoning it to its ownmost Being-guilty.[37]

Yet, Critchley reminds us, we must not imagine that this call has a particular content, a message ready to be implemented. Indeed, *nothing* is said in this call.[38] Put simply, when I am called to be myself by my conscience, this does not come along with a predetermined message on what to do in order to be myself. Heidegger emphasizes that we face a silent call. As I wrote earlier, neither does a norm of jurisdiction come along with a substantive content. The norm authorizing a judge is separated in time and in space from the norms that this judge enacts. A jurisdiction norm only tells me who my judge is, not what my judge is going to hand down. Indeed, the foundational norm that gives the idea of jurisdiction its meaning is silent, too, as we have seen in the earlier parts of this text. But if that is so, how can I then be summoned to my 'ownmost Being-guilty'?

'Guilt' evokes associations to the legal domain. Yet Heidegger takes care to distance himself from 'vulgar' conceptions of guilt as something owed to someone or

---

[35] *The Faith of the Faithless* (n 32) 155–206.

[36] Even English-language texts on Heidegger tend to use the term '*Dasein*' in its German original so as not to haphazardly eliminate its overtones.

[37] M Heidegger, *Being and Time* (J Macquarrie and E Robinson trans) (Blackwell Oxford 1962) at 269 (emphasis in original). The German original reads: 'Die eindringlichere Analyse des Gewissens enthüllt es als *Ruf*. Das Rufen ist ein Modus der *Rede*. Der Gewissensruf hat den Charakter des *Anrufs* des Daseins auf sein eigenstes Selbsteinkönnen und das in der Weise des *Aufrufs* zum eigenen Schuldigsein'. M Heidegger, *Sein und Zeit* (19th edn Niemeyer Tübingen 2006) at 269.

[38] *The Faith of the Faithless* (n 32) 185, explaining the significance of *Sein und Zeit* (n 37) 273.

something reprehensible caused by me.[39] Guilt emerges where I realize what I *can* be in this world. Conscience calling me is but a silent reminder that I owe myself in this world. *What* I owe myself it does not say. It seems that Heidegger's concept of guilt is an intensifying relation to the negative. '[O]nce I have heard the call, I look at everything as if it were not and I look at everything that is from the standpoint of that which is not.[40] This is, as Critchley emphasizes, an eminently Pauline figure of thought. He points back to Paul's exhortation to let 'those who deal with the world [live] as though they had no dealings with the world' (1 Corinthians 7.31, *Revised Standard Version*).[41]

With Paul, the place of the divine in the world has been completely taken over by an imperative to live in this negation. In addition to Paul's radical abandoning of past normative ties rooted in creationist divinity, Heidegger's rearticulation separates the faithful from the promise of redemption. The exhortation to consider that I owe myself, and to consider that which I owe myself is perhaps the most radical invitation to live out of a momentary normativity: momentary, because it marshals its entire prescriptive energy out of the moment just lived, and out of the individual living it. 'Being faithful' attains a quite different meaning under such agnostic conditions.

7 CONCLUSION

At the outset of this text, I sought to answer the question how the holder of jurisdictional entitlement is attached to its creator. I now realize how much my formulation of the question was tied up to a hierarchical creative-redemptive understanding of human history and the particular normative relations coming with it. At the end of my inquiry, the idea of a separate creator of jurisdictional entitlement and a holder of such entitlement seems to have evaporated. What I have is the individual, the one listening for and to *juris dictio*.

What were the necessary moves to arrive at this conclusion? I saw that general international law offered a terminology of jurisdiction, yet lacked a coherent conception underpinning it. Human rights law made me perceive two dominant and competing ideas working under the surface of concrete court cases. One is unity in law. It goes back to the divine mandate of *dominium terrae* and organizes

---

[39] *Sein und Zeit* (n 37) 281–2.   [40] *The Faith of the Faithless* (n 32) 187.

[41] This passage and Paul's preceding exhortations use the form of living 'as if…not'. In the Greek original, the negating expression '*hos me*' is used. Picking up the '*me*' (not), Critchley terms the emerging view of being as a 'meontology': ibid 177–81.

jurisdiction through the legal mandate over territory. Its roots are in divine creation. The concept of *kerygma* provided an entry point to illustrate how a particular idea of a divine calling is represented in the exercise of worldly power. The other idea is unity in fact. Its legitimacy is derived from the divine command of agape, and it organizes jurisdiction as a response to the actual exercise of power. Divine redemption is its end.

Should the discipline of international law work towards a concept of jurisdiction that does not reproduce Christian metaphysics to the same degree as the existing 'principles', 'categories', or 'entitlements'? That is no small question. What would be the consequences of an affirmative answer? An intense listening to *juris silentio* in the solitude of the individual. To relinquish the Christian structure of international law is not done cheaply. And not without a Pauline ladder, it seems.

CHAPTER 31

THEORIZING INTERNATIONAL ORGANIZATIONS

JAN KLABBERS

1 INTRODUCTION

THE law of international organizations is not particularly rich in overt theorizing. Partly this finds its cause in the fact that much of the law has been developed by practitioners, responding to practical challenges, often in piecemeal fashion and through mimicry and comparison: a solution that seems to work in organization A stands a good chance of being adopted in organizations B and C as well. It is no coincidence that some of the classic studies produced during the formative years of the discipline as it now stands (roughly, the 1950s and 1960s) have been written by practitioners.[1] Academics, in turn, have traditionally by and large limited themselves to inventorizing and systematizing such solutions.[2] Partly, the theoretical

---

[1] Classic examples include CW Jenks, *International Immunities* (Stevens & Sons London 1961); HJ Hahn, 'Continuity in the Law of International Organization' (1964) 13 *Österreichische Zeitschrift für öffentliches Recht* 167–239 or, more recently, CF Amerasinghe, *Principles of the Institutional Law of International Organizations* (2nd edn CUP Cambridge 2005).

[2] See perhaps most of all HG Schermers and NM Blokker, *International Institutional Law* (5th edn, Martinus Nijhoff Leiden 2011). The first edition, written by Schermers alone, was published in 1972.

paucity may also be due to international organizations being complex creatures inviting attention from a multitude of angles, involving different dynamics, different conceptions, and different levels of analysis. And all of these may be studied from the perspectives of different academic disciplines.

There are at least three different types of legal dynamics to be studied. There is, first, the relation between the organization and its member states. Second, the relations between the various organs of the organization *inter se* and the organization's internal functioning require study, as do, third, the relations between the organization and the world around it. Often, the acts of international organizations involve all three dynamics simultaneously: a decision by the North Atlantic Treaty Organization (NATO) to send troops to Afghanistan involves the relations between NATO and its member states; those between NATO's organs (in particular its political and military structure), and NATO's relations with the outside world as well—in particular with Afghanistan and its population. This holds true even with many universal organizations: activities of the World Bank or the World Health Organization (WHO) will come to affect the lives of many on the ground, and thus cannot solely be captured in terms of either the relations between the organization and its member states, or in terms of relations within the organization.

What complicates things further is that conceptions of organizations may widely differ, even within those three discrete dynamics. Thus, organizations are sometimes cast as vehicles for their member states, but sometimes also as actors in their own right. They may be seen as embodying some conception of the global good, but also as representatives of more particular interests, and they may be conceptualized as playing a largely managerial role, but also as being meeting places for states.[3]

Finally, there are different levels of analysis, if you will. One may look at the entire body of international institutional law, but also theorize about more specific issues—here doctrinal and theoretical work go hand in hand. Thus, lawyers have developed theories to explain law-making by organizations, to explain the non-binding nature of recommendations, or to explain the incidence of international legal personality.[4]

These different dynamics, conceptions, and levels of analysis may all be useful in their own right, but are bound to reveal only part of the phenomenon that is the international organization. And needless to say, answers to one set of questions may have little bearing on answers to other sets of questions. In other words, the phenomenon of international organization can hardly be captured in a single model or framework, and it is more than a little tempting to invoke Lindberg's

---

[3] See J Klabbers, 'Two Concepts of International Organization' (2005) 2 *International Organizations Law Review* 277–93.

[4] See generally J Klabbers, *An Introduction to International Institutional Law* (2nd edn CUP Cambridge 2009).

classic characterization of the European Union (EU) as a 'multidimensional phe-nomenon requiring multivariate measurement'.[5] And that statement referred only to the EU, and did so only from a neo-functionalist political scientist's perspective.

To the extent that international lawyers have engaged in theorizing about inter-national organization—a fairly limited extent[6]—they have occupied themselves predominantly with the first dynamic: the relations between the organization and its member states. Surprisingly perhaps, this has generated a strong theory, in terms of explanatory force as well as in terms of adherence by the relevant aca-demic community: the theory of functionalism. This has been so dominant as to invite comparisons with Molière's *bourgeois gentilhomme*: all international organ-ization lawyers have been speaking the language of functionalism, often without realizing it. It may be true, as Thomas Kuhn famously suggested, that the social sciences have resisted the creation of true paradigms (in his fairly narrow con-ception of the term),[7] but the theory of functionalism in the law of international organizations comes close enough.[8]

The first dynamic (relations between the organization and its members) has also been the main focus of international relations scholars but, understandably, they have asked different questions: while the lawyer is predominantly concerned with how the legal relationship between the organization and its member states is struc-tured, the international relations scholar tends to focus on the questions of why and how states come to cooperate, and under what conditions organizations op-erate effectively, questions which have also come to be asked by scholars working in the law and economics tradition.

By contrast, the other two dynamics have received far less academic atten-tion. The internal set of relationships within the organization has not been fertile ground for lawyers.[9] Even the law relating to the legal position of the international civil service is usually regarded as a rather esoteric specialization.[10] Instead, the in-ternal dynamic has been the province of sociologically inspired scholars, focusing

---

[5] See LN Lindberg, 'Political Integration as a Multidimensional Phenomenon Requiring Multivariate Measurement' (1970) 24 *International Organization* 648–731.

[6] Conceptual work is likewise rare. One recent example is CM Brölmann, *The Institutional Veil in Public International Law* (Hart Oxford 2007).

[7] See TM Kuhn, *The Structure of Scientific Revolutions* (2nd edn University of Chicago Press Chicago 1970) at 15.

[8] With one notable exception: Seyersted may well have been the only leading international organ-izations lawyer active during the formative years who did not succumb to functionalism. A syn-thesis of his main work was posthumously published as F Seyersted, *Common Law of International Organizations* (Martinus Nijhoff Leiden 2008).

[9] But see eg Y Beigbeder, *Management Problems in United Nations Organizations: Reform or Decline?* (Frances Pinter London 1987). See also J Klabbers, 'Checks and Balances in the Law of International Organizations' in M Sellers (ed), *Autonomy in the Law* (Springer Dordrecht 2007) 141–63.

[10] One of the very few writing systematically on the topic is CF Amerasinghe, *The Law of the International Civil Service* (2 vols, 2nd edn OUP Oxford 1994).

on the international bureaucracy and drawing on the sociology of organizations.[11] Moreover, this has also come to draw the attention of (legal) anthropologists, studying the culture of organizations such as the World Bank.[12]

Relations between the organization and its environment have only recently come to be discovered by international lawyers, and currently take the form, predominantly, of attempts to establish accountability or responsibility regimes for international organizations, be it in the traditional form of articles on responsibility, or the more adventurous form of developing a global administrative law or set of principles that can be applied to the exercise of public tasks by international organizations.[13]

This chapter will proceed as follows. I will first briefly outline a broad history of the development of thinking about the law of international organizations. I will then focus on the legal theory of functionalism, and discuss its considerable strengths and considerable weaknesses, before concluding with a discussion of recent attempts to paint a more nuanced picture. The final substantive section will be devoted to a brief discussion of scholarship in the broader academic landscape, while the concluding section will hint at a few challenges for both theory and practice.

2 A VERY BRIEF HISTORY

It is debated when the modern international organization first made its presence felt.[14] Some trace the development back to the creation of the early nineteenth-century river commissions, designed to manage common problems of navigation and shipping on international rivers, in particular in Europe, and usually between a limited number of riparian states.[15] Others place the beginning of the modern

[11] See eg TG Weiss, *International Bureaucracy* (Lexington Lanham 1975); M Barnett and M Finnemore, *Rules for the World: International Organizations in Global Politics* (Cornell University Press Ithaca 2004)

[12] See GA Sarfaty, *Values in Translation: Human Rights and the Culture of the World Bank* (Stanford University Press Stanford 2012).

[13] See eg B Kingsbury, N Krisch, and R Stewart, 'The Emergence of Global Administrative Law' (2005) 68 *Law & Contemporary Problems* 15–61; A von Bogdandy et al., (eds), *The Exercise of Public Authority by International Institutions* (Springer Dordrecht 2010).

[14] This builds, ever so loosely, on J Klabbers, 'The Life and Times of the Law of International Organizations' (2001) 70 *Nordic Journal of International Law* 287–317.

[15] A useful overview is B Reinalda, *Routledge History of International Organizations: From 1815 to the Present Day* (Routledge London 2009).

international organization a few decades later, in the 1860s and 1870s, when the first putatively universal organizations dealing with communication and standardization were established: entities such as the Universal Postal Union and the International Bureau of Weights and Measures. Yet others suggest that these years are the pre-history of the discipline by associating the 'move to institutions' with the creation of the League of Nations and the International Labour Organization by means of the Treaty of Versailles, after the First World War.[16]

Be that as it may, the first more or less systematic studies of the law of international organizations start to appear around the turn of the twentieth century. The Odessa-based international lawyer Pierre Kazansky published a large multivolume synthetic study in Russian in 1897, and extricated two relatively short general and reflective articles which were published in French.[17] More important still, a political science professor cum lawyer at the University of Wisconsin–Madison, Paul S Reinsch, published two detailed studies in the *American Journal of International Law*[18]—articles that would become the heart of a monograph published in 1911 and, it is fair to say, provided the basic outline for the theory of functionalism that would become so dominant.[19] I will return to this in Section 3 below.

The Permanent Court of International Justice, for its part, was confronted, through its advisory jurisdiction, with a number of requests concerning in particular the powers of international organizations, and after some hesitant beginnings started to systematically create the doctrines of attributed (or conferred) and implied powers.[20] Its successor, the International Court of Justice (ICJ), would continue to develop this, with the doctrine of implied powers in particular receiving much attention and refinement and, truth be told, a considerable expansion in the seminal *Reparation for Injuries* opinion: the powers of international organizations, so the Court suggested, include everything that is necessary in order for the organization to function effectively.[21]

---

[16] The seminal piece is D Kennedy, 'The Move to Institutions' (1987) 8 *Cardozo Law Review* 841–988.

[17] See P Kazansky, 'Les premiers éléments de l'organisation universelle' (1897) 29 *Revue de Droit International et de Législation Comparée* 238–47; P Kazansky, 'Théorie de l'Administration Internationale' (1902) 9 *Revue Générale de Droit International Public* 353–66.

[18] See PS Reinsch, 'International Unions and Their Administration' (1907) 1 *American Journal of International Law* 579–623; PS Reinsch, 'International Administrative Law and National Sovereignty' (1909) 3 *American Journal of International Law* 1–45.

[19] See PS Reinsch, *Public International Unions, Their Work and Organization: A Study in International Administrative Law* (McGinn & Co Boston 1911). See further J Klabbers, 'The *EJIL* Foreword: The Transformation of International Organizations Law' (2015) 26 *European Journal of International Law* 9–82.

[20] A fine discussion of these powers is V Engström, *Constructing the Powers of International Institutions* (Martinus Nijhoff Leiden 2012).

[21] See *Reparation for Injuries Suffered in the Service of the United Nations* (Advisory Opinion) [1949] ICJ Rep 174.

Following the Second World War, the number of international organizations mushroomed, both on the universal level and in various regions of the globe. This then provided the impetus for the development of something akin to a separate doctrinal branch of international law,[22] with scholars and practitioners alike starting to think about such questions as how international organizations are set up, whether international organizations can or should enjoy privileges and immunities, whether they can make law in any meaningful sense of the word, how their constitutions can be amended, whether they are capable and competent to conclude treaties with third states or even with each other, and whether they can dissolve or succeed one another. Much of the law as it currently stands was developed during the 1950s and 1960s, in response to the explosion in the number of organizations and the global reach of their activities and ambitions; hence, it is by no means eccentric to regard these two decades as the formative years, despite organizations having been around for roughly a century by then. It was also during this time that the first general textbooks were prepared, in the United Kingdom (UK) by Bowett,[23] and on the European continent by Schermers[24] and Seidl-Hohenveldern.[25]

The formative years did not herald a long period of stability. Already by the 1980s the insights of the 1950s and 1960s started to be questioned, again largely in response to practical developments. The most influential of these was, arguably, the collapse of the International Tin Council, leading to litigation in the British courts and raising awkward questions concerning the precise nature of the relationship between an organization and its member states: can member states be held responsible if and when their creation fails to deliver?[26] This in turn provoked an (almost) entirely new research question: that of the accountability, in law or

---

[22] I have argued elsewhere that it is an exaggeration to speak of a separate branch of international law dealing with international organizations; instead, organizations have their own law, and are embedded in international law generally. See J Klabbers, 'The Paradox of International Institutional Law' (2008) 5 *International Organizations Law Review* 151–73.

[23] See DW Bowett, *The Law of International Institutions* (Methuen London 1964). It currently goes through life as P Sands and P Klein, *Bowett's Law of International Institutions* (6th edn Sweet and Maxwell London 2009).

[24] See *International Institutional Law* (n 2). Incidentally, the law of international organizations has remained a rather European discipline, in that few non-European scholars have systematically and consistently written about it. Among the few exceptions in the US are José E Alvarez and Rick Kirgis, with the latter having authored the closest equivalent to a European-style textbook: see FL Kirgis, *International Organizations in their Legal Setting* (2nd edn West St Paul 1993), which first appeared in 1977. The leading non-western author is Amerasinghe (see *Principles of the Institutional Law of International Organizations* (n 1)) although it seems fair to say his approach is well-nigh indistinguishable from that of most western authors.

[25] See I Seidl-Hohenveldern, *Das Recht der internationalen Organisationen einschliesslich der supranationalen Gemeinschaften* (Heymann Cologne 1967).

[26] See *Australia and New Zealand Banking Group Ltd v Australia* (1990) 29 ILM 670 (UK House of Lords, 1989). For discussion, see *An Introduction to International Institutional Law* (n 4) ch 14.

otherwise, of international organizations. Until the mid-1980s, the topic had been anathema, subjected to few studies which invariably ended up focusing on the position of member states rather than the organization itself.[27] Thereafter though, it would become a staple of discussion on the work of international organizations, perhaps influenced by a move to accountability in both politics and international law more generally and culminating in the adoption, in 2011, of a set of articles on the responsibility of international organizations drafted by the International Law Commission. Either way, from the mid-1980s onwards international organizations started to lose some of their glamour.[28] Where earlier generations had characterized organizations as being devoted to the 'salvation of mankind'[29] and thus inherently good, the insight took hold that much like the states creating them, international organizations are political entities exercising public power. And much like the public power of states ought to be subject to legal controls under any conception of the rule of law, so too ought international organizations be subject to legal controls.

3 FUNCTIONALISM IN BRIEF

It is no exaggeration to state that the law of international organizations has been dominated by a functionalist approach. In basic outline, the idea is as follows. States, so functionalism holds, create international organizations to do things they are unable or reluctant to do on their own, yet consider inherently useful: organize postal relations, control the uses of atomic energy, regulate global health, etc. In order to do so, states create entities upon which they bestow these functions. These entities are given certain powers or competences in order to give effect to their functions, and a legal framework is created which should facilitate the work of these entities: after all, their functions are generally considered useful. Hence, the doctrine of implied powers makes sure that organizations can do their work even in the absence of a specifically granted competence, and privileges and immunities guarantee that organizations can perform their functions without interference by member states.

---

[27] See C Eagleton, 'International Organizations and the Law of Responsibility' (1959) 76 *Recueil des Cours* 319–426; K Ginther, *Die völkerrechtliche Verantwortlichkeit internationaler Organisationen gegenüber Drittstaaten* (Springer Dordrecht 1969).

[28] See J Klabbers, 'The Changing Image of International Organizations' in J-M Coicaud, and V Heiskanen (eds), *The Legitimacy of International Organizations* (UN University Press Tokyo 2001).

[29] This wonderful characterization was coined, without a trace of irony, by N Singh, *Termination of Membership of International Organisations* (Stevens & Sons London 1958) at vii.

Functionalism was never self-consciously developed, and no single manifesto outlining its main contours exists, but its development can be traced through the writings of certain key figures. Its main outline is already visible in the work of the abovementioned Paul Reinsch. Reinsch is often regarded as one of the pioneers of the discipline of international relations, teaching political science at the University of Wisconsin–Madison. He authored one of the first textbooks on international relations, as well as several studies on colonial government and administration.[30] These were to prove inspirational. Reinsch was not particularly keen on territorial expansion and the creation of colonial exploitative regimes so prevalent in his time,[31] but viewed colonial relations as a form of cooperation which could be mutually beneficial to both the administrator (for example, in the form of opening new markets) and the colonized, who would benefit from the civilizing influence and higher levels of welfare in the administering state.

Importantly, Reinsch held that the creation of international organizations could lead to similar results. For him, colonial administration and international organization were two sides of the same coin or, more accurately perhaps, two manifestation of the same drive to inter-state cooperation; what is more, they could be arranged in largely similar ways. That Reinsch came to this view is perhaps no coincidence: the situation in the Americas, ever since the proclamation of the Monroe Doctrine, was not all that different from the European colonial era, with a dominating USA surrounded by a number of smaller powers.[32] Indeed, Reinsch's work on international organizations was largely coloured by his practical experience as delegate to several of the Pan American conferences (the predecessor of today's Organization of American States).

Reinsch's writings already provided the outline of the functionalist theory that would come to dominate the field, complete with its recurring tensions. International organizations, so he strongly suggested, would merely exercise functional authority; they would not meddle with politics, except in the sense that they would contribute to world peace. They would provide a cost-effective way to help states achieve their goals, yet be independent from states.

This would become the dominant way of thinking: international organizations are apolitical and cost-effective, doing things states cannot do on their own (or are reluctant to do on their own) and, while apolitical, they nonetheless contribute

---

[30] For a useful study of Reinsch's impact on the study of international relations, see BC Schmidt, 'Paul S Reinsch and the Study of Imperialism and Internationalism' in D Long and BC Schmidt (eds), *Imperialism and Internationalism in the Study of International Relations* (State University of New York Press New York 2005) 43–70.

[31] The US officially became an imperial power following the war with Spain and the annexation of Hawaii in the late nineteenth century. See eg Walter LaFeber, *The New Empire: An Interpretation of American Expansion 1860–1898* (Cornell University Press Ithaca 1963).

[32] On Reinsch's influence, see J Klabbers, 'The Emergence of Functionalism in International Institutional Law: Colonial Inspirations' (2014) 25 *European Journal of International Law* 645–75.

to world peace or, at the very least, the 'salvation of mankind'. Hence, organizations are inherently good and benign, and their functioning should accordingly be facilitated—they form the benevolent alternatives to nasty states. If Louis Henkin could famously refer to state sovereignty as a 'bad word',[33] international lawyers had little problem referring to 'functional' and 'organization' as good words.

Perhaps because of its normative appeal, the theory was never self-consciously developed or considered. The closest to a theoretical statement was a short piece written by Michel Virally in the 1970s and focusing, inevitably, on the relationship between organizations and their member states.[34] Noteworthy is also Bekker's mid-1990s study of functionalism and immunities, which makes clear that the notion of function, in functionalism, serves not just for the benefit of organizations but also limits them: they can do or claim no more than their functions justify.[35] Problematically though, the very notion of 'function' is open-ended, and thus susceptible to a variety of interpretations.[36]

4 FUNCTIONALISM EVALUATED

The main appeal of functionalism resides, no doubt, in two circumstances. First, it taps into the self-image of internationalists and cosmopolitans: functionalism allows international organizations to prosper, and since those organizations are benign, it follows that functionalism too must be a force for good. Second, and more immanently academic perhaps, functionalism was always considered to have considerable explanatory force. Functionalism can help explain why international organizations exist to begin with: there are, after all, quite a few activities that states are incapable of doing on their own. Absent a global imperial power, no single state is in a position to control the uses of atomic energy, or make sure that letters sent from Rio de Janeiro are acceptable to postal services in Germany or Nigeria, or guarantee that one metre will equate to one hundred centimetres whether one is in Spain or in Botswana.

---

[33] See L Henkin, 'International Law: Politics, Values and Functions' (1989) 216 *Recueil des Cours* 9–416, at 24.

[34] See M Virally, 'La notion de fonction dans la théorie de l'organisation internationale' in S Bastid et al., (eds), *Mélanges offerts à Charles Rousseau: La communauté internationale* (Pédone Paris 1974).

[35] See PHF Bekker, *The Legal Position of Intergovernmental Organizations: A Functional Necessity Analysis of Their Legal Status and Immunities* (Martinus Nijhoff Leiden 1994).

[36] For a strong critique, see M Singer, 'Jurisdictional Immunity of International Organizations: Human Rights and Functional Necessity Concerns' (1995) 36 *Virginia Journal of International Law* 53–165.

Functionalism can also explain the incidence of powers of international organizations. The functions of organizations must be given concrete expression, and this happens through the powers or competences granted by member states, and can also explain why it is that organizations, their staff, and member states' representatives typically enjoy privileges and immunity.

On other points too, functionalism is able to offer helpful insights. Thus, it suggests that organizations can apply criteria for aspiring member states: if these cannot contribute to the organization's functions, such states can be refused.[37] Likewise, the existence of clauses on suspension or expulsion can be discussed in similar terms following a similar logic: not as punishment or sanction, but as the result of the member state behaving in such a way as to compromise the organization's functioning.[38] The fact that member states often have an obligation to pay a membership fee can also follow a functionalist logic: such compulsory fees may be necessary to enable the organization to function. Not all of this is ironclad though: some organizations rely on voluntary contributions by member states and others.

Functionalism is predominantly a theory about the relations between organizations and their member states; it has fairly little to say about other aspects of the law of international organizations, such as the relations between organs of the organization, or in particular the relations between the organization and the world around it, with the exception of treaty-making by the organization. But this involves, logically, the relation with the member states, as it is the member states that are deemed to have endowed the organization with its treaty-making powers.

It follows that functionalism has a number of blind spots: it has much to say about the first dynamic identified earlier (relations between organizations and member states) but little or nothing about the other two dynamics: the internal relations, and the external relations. Thus, functionalism has proved to be of little help in figuring out whether relations amongst the organs of international organizations add up to a system of checks and balances, and indeed, it may well be argued that the hold of functionalism has been so strong that the question has attracted little attention to begin with.[39] The ICJ suggested, in *Certain Expenses*, that it matters little how organs relate to one another as long as it is clear that activities of the organization are not *ultra vires*, and that each organ itself is responsible for the interpretation of its own powers, at least at first instance.[40] Likewise, the issue of judicial

---

[37] The leading study is TD Grant, *Admission to the United Nations: Charter Article 4 and the Rise of Universal Organization* (Martinus Nijhoff Leiden 2009).

[38] See generally K Magliveras, *Exclusion from Participation in International Organisations* (Kluwer Law International The Hague 1999); A Duxbury, *The Participation of States in International Organisations* (CUP Cambridge 2011).

[39] But see 'Checks and Balances' (n 9).

[40] See *Certain Expenses of the United Nations (Article 17, Paragraph 2, of the Charter)* (Advisory Opinion) [1962] ICJ Rep 151.

review over acts of the organization has remained largely unanswered: the ICJ may well have exercised such review on occasion, but without being very explicit about it, and without affirming that it actually holds a power of judicial review.[41] It is no accident that authors writing about judicial review within international organizations look for inspiration not to functionalism, but to domestic analogies and theories of constitutionalism and the rule of law.[42]

In a variation on the same theme, functionalism offers little or no insights into the functioning of the international bureaucracy, or the relations between the political organs of the organization and the organization's bureaucratic apparatus. International civil servants are supposed to be independent and work for the common good, and while interference by member states forms a legitimate subject of functionalist thought and can be responded to by means of the invocation of privileges and immunities, interference by the bureaucracy itself with decisions of the political organs remains firmly outside the reach of functionalism.

By the same token, functionalism is limited when it comes to issues of control. The main position is, not surprisingly, that control can be exercised by the member states,[43] because it is this relationship between organization and member states that functionalism addresses. Those members can control their creatures either by means of carefully delimiting the functions and powers of organizations, or by political mechanisms such as the withholding of contributions or the appointment— or ousting—of leading officials. This may be useful as far as things go, but ignores the fact that the relations between the organization and its member states are not the only relations of relevance. The more organizations act in the field, the more their actions also come to affect third parties, be these states, individuals, or others. In other words, there is an increasing recognition that the acts of international organizations create potential accountability relationships with those who are directly affected by those activities. The citizens of Timor Leste or Kosovo have a stake in the behaviour of the international administrations acting in their territories; refugees brought together in refugee camps have a stake in how the UN High Commissioner for Refugees (UNHCR) operates those camps; the poor and dispossessed in Bangladesh have a stake in World Bank sponsored projects that displace many of them, and individuals targeted by smart sanctions imposed by the Security Council of the UN have a stake in how those decisions are made.

Hence, alternative approaches have come up which may, for ease of reference, be grouped together under the label 'public law approaches'.[44] These comprise

---

[41] See *Legal Consequences for States of the Continued Presence of South Africa in Namibia (South West Africa) Notwithstanding Security Council Resolution 276 (1970)* (Advisory Opinion) [1971] ICJ Rep 16.

[42] For discussion, see J Klabbers, 'Constitutionalism Lite' (2004) 1 *International Organizations Law Review* 31–58.

[43] See, classically, 'La notion de fonction' (n 34).

[44] Elsewhere I have referred to these, loosely, as constitutional approaches. See J Klabbers, 'Contending Approaches to International Organizations: Between Functionalism and Constitutionalism' in J Klabbers

approaches insisting on the prevalence of human rights, or the applicability of procedural administrative law notions or, indeed, sometimes a rule of law inspired approach, in varying degrees of thickness.[45]

If functionalism suffers from some theoretical blind spots, its explanatory force has also become subject to some debate. Functionalism always had a problem with the EU: the structure and activities of the EU cannot plausibly be explained on the basis of functionalism. The discipline managed to solve this problem, for a while, by labelling the EU *sui generis*, but the paucity of this particular label has become better understood in recent years. Part of the problem is that the EU not merely exercises functions delegated by member states, but has come to replace the member states in various fields of activity[46] and even, importantly, as a source of domestic law. On minor points too, the EU catches functionalism by surprise: the EU has never, for example, enjoyed immunity from suit, contrary to what functionalism would make us expect.

Indeed, more generally functionalism has difficulties in clearly delimiting its reach. Many entities are created along functionalist lines but with their member states or observers insisting that the entity concerned is not an international organization, ranging from treaty bodies to international tribunals and including highly informal regular gatherings with a minimized institutional structure. Conversely, sometimes organizations are set up that may be little more than military alliances or interest groups for their member states, yet are generally treated as international organizations (the Organization of the Petroleum Exporting Countries (OPEC) may serve as an example). Functionalism has proved unable to help distinguish between entities here: where courts sometimes insist, in individual cases, on a public task as a defining characteristic of the concept of international organization, this is not reflected in a generally accepted definition.[47] Functionalism also has a hard time distinguishing between organizations and organizational programs enjoying a great degree of autonomy: such programs could, potentially, boast their own functional logic, yet remain subservient to the parent organization: UNHCR is perhaps the most prominent example. And the World Trade Organization (WTO) provides a challenge of yet a different nature: it is a fairly unique example of an international organization without competences, other than the competence to settle trade disputes or take a political decision to release a member state from its obligations.[48]

---

and Å Wallendahl (eds), *Research Handbook on the Law of International Organizations* (Edward Elgar Cheltenham 2011) 3–30.

[45] See eg J Farrall, *United Nations Sanctions and the Rule of Law* (CUP Cambridge 2007).

[46] Here the legal theory of functionalism is to be distinguished from its political science counterpart, which can claim to have predicted as much: see Section 5 below.

[47] See J Klabbers, 'Unity, Diversity, Accountability: The Ambivalent Concept of International Organization' (2013) 14 *Melbourne Journal of International Law* 149–70.

[48] On the latter, see I Feichtner, *The Law and Politics of WTO Waivers* (CUP Cambridge 2012).

5 THE BROADER ACADEMIC SETTING

International organization lawyers are, as a general rule, not terribly interested in matters of theory. As a result, whenever claims of a more or less theoretical nature are being made, such claims tend to draw on theories about international organizations that stem from neighbouring disciplines, carrying the risk that the specifically legal nature of the investigation gets lost.

The social sciences in general, and the discipline of international relations in particular, have tried to formulate answers to a number of important questions. First among these is the question why states set up international organizations to begin with. The second question is how they do this. A third group of questions addresses the effects of the existence of international organizations on both their own development and the world around them.

The standard answer to the first question chimes with functionalism: states set up international organizations out of self-interest. They are not able to engage in all activities on their own, and thus find themselves cooperating. And where the expectation is that problems keep recurring, inter-state cooperation can take the form of an international organization. This line of reasoning has one important qualification though through which it parts ways with (legal) functionalism: in this conception, the organization remains, by and large, a vehicle for its member states.

Over the years, this position has received several nuances. For instance, while self-interest is compatible with classic hard-nosed realism, the continued existence of international organizations capable of taking decisions against the wishes of member states challenges such hard-nosed realism. Hence, the explanation then shifts to more subtle forms of self-interest: organizations can help to create stability in international affairs and help lower transaction costs, as liberal institutionalists are wont to hold, and thus states may be enticed to join them, even at the cost of sometimes having to accept directives they might not otherwise have accepted. Even the very powerful may come to accept this logic,[49] though with the caveat that they might be able to exercise a disproportionate amount of influence on the organization.[50]

A second set of questions goes into more detail on how organizations are endowed with their functions and the precise parameters of the situation thus created, and the leading theory here is usually referred to as delegation theory.

---

[49] The seminal study is RO Keohane, *After Hegemony: Cooperation and Discord in the World Political Economy* (Princeton University Press Princeton 1984).

[50] See RW Stone, *Controlling Institutions: International Organizations and the Global Economy* (CUP Cambridge 2011).

Delegation theory thinks in terms of principals and agents, viewing organizations typically as the agents of their collective principals, the member states, and showing considerable interest in questions of institutional design. It is here perhaps that the links with the legal functionalists are most visible, if only because this theory is also a theory of the relations between organizations and their member states with little traction on other issues. Yet, its practitioners are mainly political scientists often working in the rational choice tradition,[51] with lawyers being more actively engaged in studying the precise legal conditions and the modalities of delegation.[52]

A different set of questions involves the effect of the existence of international organizations on both their own development and on the world around them. On the former question, writers developed theories of functionalism and neo-functionalism to account for the way organizations may develop—these theories must be distinguished from the legal functionalism described earlier. Functionalist integration theory held, in a nutshell, that once organizations exercised certain functions, they would naturally gather additional functions. Organizations and their member states would learn that outsourcing functions to organizations would not only be beneficial, but would naturally create incentives to cooperate or integrate further. This became known as the logic of ramification or, in more colloquial terms, a spillover effect. In a nutshell: cooperation on, say, management of fisheries would generate a need to cooperate also on conservation measures. These, in turn, would necessitate further cooperation on protection of the marine environment, and so on and so forth. The net result, so functionalist integration theory predicted, would inevitably be a worldwide web of institutions.[53] Neo-functionalism accepted the logic, but not its inevitability, and recognized that automatic spillover would be implausible. Instead, further cooperation would have to be the result of political decision-making, thus bringing politics back into the framework.[54]

Neo-functionalism often shades into constructivism, with constructivist international relations scholars typically holding that international organizations provide international society with a framework and vernacular to conduct relations and facilitate learning processes and socialization. In this way, international organizations reflect power relations between states, but also help to shape and transform those relations. More than realists and liberal institutionalists, therefore, constructivists ascribe to international organizations an independent, autonomous role as

---

[51] See eg DG Hawkins et al., (eds), *Delegation and Agency in International Organizations* (CUP Cambridge 2006); B Koremenos et al., (eds), *The Rational Design of International Institutions* (CUP 2004).

[52] See in particular D Sarooshi, *The United Nations and the Development of Collective Security* (OUP Oxford 1999) and D Sarooshi, *International Organizations and their Exercise of Sovereign Powers* (OUP Oxford 2005).

[53] See eg D Mitrany, 'The Functional Approach to World Organization' (1948) 24 *International Affairs* 350–63.

[54] See eg EB Haas, *Beyond the Nation-State* (Stanford University Press Stanford 1964).

actors in their own right.[55] This, in turn, sometimes shades into sociologically and anthropologically inspired bureaucracy studies, as mentioned earlier.[56]

Finally, in various branches of scholarship it is becoming increasingly common to view organizations no longer as the thing to be explained, but rather as the independent variable (so to speak). International lawyers have drawn attention to the fact that much of international law emerges from organizations and is managed by them,[57] while international relations scholars too have started to acknowledge that the relevant question is no longer why organizations are established or whether they matter, but how and to what extent they are actors in their own right in global politics.[58]

In the end, disciplinary divides remain deep. Despite occasional pleas to the contrary, there is little overlap or communication between scholars of international organizations coming from different academic backgrounds, and when such overlap occurs, it often aims at convincing one group of scholars that the methods and theories of another group are superior.[59] This comes with at least two obvious drawbacks. First, interdisciplinary scholarship still isolates itself from the methods and theories of yet other disciplines (and often enough, of course, disciplines are built in such diverse ways that they are incommensurate). Second, it presupposes that those disciplines themselves are monolithic—whereas often enough, academic disciplines tend to be characterized by serious internal rivalries. Perhaps then the better approach is not to adopt methodologies lock stock and barrel, but rather to carefully absorb such insights from other disciplines as can be meaningfully integrated into one's own discipline and approach, while always remaining alert to one's own blind spots.

6 To Conclude

Perhaps the main political challenge facing the law of international organizations is how to come to terms with issues of control. As noted, functionalism has little to

---

[55] See eg I Johnstone, *The Power of Deliberation: International Law, Politics and Organizations* (OUP Oxford 2011).

[56] See text accompanying nn 11 and 12.

[57] See eg M Ruffert and C Walter, *Institutionalisiertes Völkerrecht* (Beck Munich 2009). A related approach, albeit starting from different premises, underlies A Orford, *International Authority and the Responsibility to Protect* (CUP Cambridge 2011).

[58] Examples include I Hurd, *After Anarchy* (Princeton University Press Princeton 2007); JS Barkin, *International Organization: Theories and Institutions* (Palgrave MacMillan Basingstoke 2006).

[59] A recent example is DC Ellis, 'The Organizational Turn in International Organization Theory' (2010) 1 *Journal of International Organization Studies* 11–28. The journal's main aim appears to be to align international relations theory and the sociology of organizations.

offer here. Hence, either functionalism warrants a serious rethinking or ought to be replaced by a different theory. The latter will not be easy, partly because functionalism's explanatory force is considerable, and partly because functionalism is normatively attractive, and therefore difficult to abandon.

The need to work on issues of control becomes all the more clear in light of the popularity of the idea of organizations engaging in all sorts of joint ventures and partnerships, both with each other and with the private sector. The relationships between organizations (with one organization, for example, hosting another, or taking care of the other's administration) recently gave rise to an ICJ advisory opinion,[60] and partnerships with the private sector in particular will likewise raise all sorts of accountability concerns. Scholarship (from whatever academic background) has yet to catch up with these patterns of cooperation and the diffusion these patterns might generate in terms of accountability.[61]

Moreover, even without the accountability concerns, it is not clear that such activities can plausibly be explained by functionalism. If functionalism explains the existence, structure, and acts of organizations through a focus on their functions, then how can a sharing of functions be conceptualized? The only way to do so would be by pointing out that certain functions can better be exercised in partnership, perhaps because of efficiency gains or some other concern. But if that is the case, then international organizations lose some of their political attraction. After all, functionalism was never about more than, literally, functioning; it was never about functioning efficiently, or effectively—and if such adjectives come to dominate, it may well be the case that more efficient or effective alternatives can be conceived.

This gives rise to two foundational issues. First, the emergence of actors and partnerships in all kinds of forms raises fundamental issues about the subject of the discipline of the law of international organizations: what exactly is an international organization? Few would dispute that the WHO or Council of Europe qualify as such, but what about the Conferences or Meetings of the Parties (COPs or MOPs) established under environmental agreements, the Global Alliance for Vaccines and Immunizations (GAVI Alliance), or a loose network such as the Contact Group on Piracy off the Somali Coast?

Second, many would agree that global political authority is increasingly distributed or differentiated along functional rather than territorial lines, yet it would seem that the harbingers hereof—functionalist international organizations—are losing out. Having paved the way for functional differentiation, they are increasingly

---

[60] See *Judgment No 2867 of the Administrative Tribunal of the International Labour Organization upon a Complaint Filed against the International Fund for Agricultural Development* (Advisory Opinion) [2012] ICJ Rep 10.

[61] A recent overview is C Jönsson, 'The John Holmes Memorial Lecture: International Organizations at the Moving Public–Private Borderline' (2013) 19 *Global Governance* 1–18.

being accompanied, supplanted, or even replaced by other entities, and formal international organizations are well-nigh completely absent from two of the most salient functional domains usually identified as such: the environmental domain and the financial domain.

Whatever else this may suggest, it entails recognition of the fact that the functionalism in the law of international organizations always was a political project like any other, an ideology to help justify the shifting of authority to actors whose activities would, for a long time, go without scrutiny or control and would be justified by the idea of functionalism. This does not mean that functionalism ought to be discarded, but it does mean that it should no longer be taken as politically innocent.

CHAPTER 32

.....

THEORIZING
THE CORPORATION
IN INTERNATIONAL LAW

.....

FLEUR JOHNS

1 INTRODUCTION

.....

AT the signing of the Dutch–Spanish Peace of Münster in 1648—a critical moment in the modern international legal order's creation story—corporations were already on the international legal scene.[1] Negotiators may not have come to the table in Münster were it not for the '"glorious" deeds' of the Dutch East India Company (the VOC) and West India Company (the WIC) in challenging Iberian power globally during preceding decades.[2] These deeds had an explicit international legal

---

[1] The phrase 'creation story' is from S Pahuja, *Decolonising International Law: Development, Economic Growth and the Politics of Universality* (OUP Oxford 2011) at 111 ('...the myth of Westphalia...is habitually told as the creation story of a new world system of rule...'). However, the characterization of the Peace of Westphalia (the series of treaties signed at Osnabrück and Münster in 1648)—and its purported origination of the modern international legal order—as mythical has been developed across a body of literature spanning several disciplines: see eg S Beaulac, *The Power of Language in the Making of International Law: The Word Sovereignty in Bodin and Vattel and the Myth of Westphalia* (Martinus Nijhoff Leiden 2004); B Teschke, *The Myth of 1648: Class, Geopolitics, and the Making of Modern International Relations* (2nd edn Verso London 2009).

[2] C Schnurmann, '"Wherever Profit Leads Us, to Every Sea and Shore...": The VOC, the WIC, and Dutch Methods of Globalization in the Seventeenth Century' (2003) 17 *Renaissance Studies* 474–93.

dimension. The 1602 VOC Charter, for instance, empowered the corporation to 'enter into commitments and enter into contracts with princes and rulers...in order to build fortifications and strongholds'.[3] It charged the corporation with 'keep[ing] armed forces, install[ing] Judicial officers and officers...so to keep the establishments in good order, as well as jointly ensure enforcement of the law and justice, all combined so as to promote trade'.[4] The conduct of international legal affairs by or through such corporate entities was, nevertheless, already the subject of a 'lively public debate' in the seventeenth century.[5]

If the corporation has long been a feature of international legal practice and argument, it is nonetheless one upon which public international lawyers have tended to look askance. It is a stock observation of international legal writing that the corporation is addressed only indirectly by public international law.[6] International legal writings have often approached the corporate form on the basis of its similarity to, or influence upon, some other feature or agent of the international legal order (or vice versa). Relatively little by way of explicit theorization of the corporation has been done in international legal writing.[7] Rather, this theorization has tended to take place as a dimension of practice, en route to some other scholarly or regulatory objective.

Theorization as a dimension of practice may be a feature of international legal work more broadly, reflective of international lawyers' preoccupation with sustaining their discipline's 'move[ment] from theory to practice, from differentiation to

On the companies' accomplishments in countering Iberian power, see PC Emmer, 'The First Global War: The Dutch versus Iberia in Asia, Africa and the New World' (2003) 1 *E-Journal of Portuguese History* article 2, 1–14; J Glete, *Warfare at Sea 1500–1650: Maritime Conflicts and the Transformation of Europe* (Routledge London 2002) at 165–77.

[3] *A Translation of the Charter of the Dutch East India Company (Verenigde Oostindische Compagnie or VOC): Granted by the States General of the United Netherlands, 20 March 1602* (R Gerritson ed and P Reynders trans) (Australia on the Map Division of the Australasian Hydrographic Society Canberra 2009) at 6 <http://rupertgerritsen.tripod.com/pdf/published/VOC_Charter_1602.pdf> [accessed 27 February 2016]. Also available in E Gepken-Jager, G van Solinge, and L Timmerman (eds), *VOC 1602–2002: 400 Years of Company Law* (Kluwer Deventer 2005) at 17–38.

[4] See sources cited in *400 Years of Company Law* (n 3).

[5] '"Wherever Profit Leads Us"' (n 2) 476. See also E Thomson, 'The Dutch Miracle, Modified: Hugo Grotius's *Mare Liberum*, Commercial Governance and Imperial War in the Early-Seventeenth Century' (2009) 30 *Grotiana* 107–30 at 112–21; N De Marchi and P Harrison, 'Trading "in the Wind" and with Guile: The Troublesome Matter of the Short Selling of Shares in Seventeenth-Century Holland' in N De Marchi and M S Morgan (eds), *Higgling: Transactors and Their Markets in the History of Economics* (Duke University Press Durham 1994) 47–65.

[6] See eg CM Vázquez, 'Direct vs Indirect Obligations of Corporations under International Law' (2005) 43 *Columbia Journal of Transnational Law* 927–59, at 930.

[7] For important counter-examples, see D Danielsen, 'How Corporations Govern: Taking Corporate Power Seriously in Transnational Regulation and Governance' (2005) 46 *Harvard International Law Journal* 411–25; D Danielsen, 'Corporate Power and Global Order' in A Orford (ed), *International Law and Its Others* (CUP Cambridge 2006) at 85–99.

regulation'.[8] International lawyers' relative inattention to the corporate form might also be traceable to historical cleavages between public and private international law, and tendencies to distinguish the professional sensibilities of lawyer-diplomats from those of merchants, or to divorce politics from economics.[9] Whatever its provenance, in this instance, the tendency for theorization-while-focused-elsewhere appears to have had particular implications for the way that corporations have been characterized in international legal work. It has done so, especially, with regard to the power, autonomy, and coherence with which the corporation has been 'naturally' invested in much international legal writing, the promise the corporation is often deemed to hold for international legal renewal, and the influence that the corporate model has exerted as a benchmark for global decision-making across a range of settings.

This chapter will redescribe this oblique theorization of the corporation in public international law. It will begin by outlining some generic characterizations of the corporation in international legal writing, before turning to two areas of international legal doctrine, practice, and scholarly work: international investment law and international human rights. In both of these areas, the corporation has often been identified with potential dysfunction within, or subtraction from, the international legal order. International legal engagement of the corporation has, accordingly, been identified with the discipline's corrective realignment, rejuvenation or augmentation.[10] So figured, the corporation has been central to the maintenance of prospects of, and aspirations for, 'governance fusion' on the global plane.[11] Precisely because of the paragnostic way it has been known to international law, the corporation has been a pivotal figure in international legal knowledge practice.

---

[8] D Kennedy, 'A New Stream of International Law Scholarship' (1988) 7 *Wisconsin International Law Journal* 1–49, at 38.

[9] See generally JR Paul, 'The Isolation of Private International Law' (1988) 7 *Wisconsin International Law Journal* 149–78; A Mills, 'The Private History of International Law' (2006) 55 *International and Comparative Law Quarterly* 1–50. With respect to diplomats' traditional disaffiliation from (overt) commercial pursuits, Donna Lee and David Hudson observe that 'the dominant view of diplomacy found in the canon of diplomatic studies' includes 'structural inferences [as to] the separation of politics and economics'. Lee and Hudson emphasize, nevertheless, that widespread practices of commercial diplomacy have long coexisted with this disciplinary outlook: D Lee and D Hudson, 'The Old and New Significance of Political Economy in Diplomacy' (2004) 30 *Review of International Studies* 343–60, at 345. On international lawyers' inclination to divorce politics from economics, see D Kennedy, 'Law and the Political Economy of the World' (2013) 26 *Leiden Journal of International Law* 7–48.

[10] See eg D Kinley and J Tadaki, 'From Talk to Walk: The Emergence of Human Rights Responsibilities for Corporations at International Law' (2004) 44 *Virginia Journal of International Law* 931–1023, at 1021.

[11] LC Backer, 'Private Actors and Public Governance Beyond the State: The Multinational Corporation, the Financial Stability Board, and the Global Governance Order' (2011) 18 *Indiana Journal of Global Legal Studies* 751–802, at 757.

2 SOLICITING THE CORPORATION
IN INTERNATIONAL LAW

Global competencies attributed by law to the corporation over many centuries span a considerable range of hybrid combinations.[12] Nonetheless, public international lawyers tend to locate the corporation primarily in the context of relatively successful, large-scale, private commercial enterprise. Little attention has been paid to the role of municipal corporations in global legal affairs.[13] Scant ink has been spilled on the significance of small- and medium-sized business corporations in the international legal order.[14] Beyond doctrinal discussion in the field of investment and trade law and with regard to sovereign immunity, state-owned enterprises have not featured prominently in international legal analyses of global corporate power.[15] Corporations that are facing insolvency or are otherwise in a condition of frailty do not commonly appear on the public international legal radar.[16] Rather, when international law has turned its attention to global commercial activity, large, well-funded, non-state-owned multinational corporations and corporate groups have tended to fill its field of vision.

---

[12] P Muchlinski, 'Corporations in International Law' in R Wolfrum (ed), *Max Planck Encyclopaedia of International Law* (2010) <http://opil.ouplaw.com/home/epil> [accessed 27 February 2016].

[13] By way of exception, consider Y Blank, 'Localism in the New Global Legal Order' (2006) 47 *Harvard International Law Journal* 263–81; Y Blank, 'The City and the World' (2006) 44 *Columbia Journal of Transnational Law* 875–939.

[14] *Contra* NC Rougeux, 'Legal Legitimacy and the Promotion of Small Business in Sarajevo' (2002) 37 *Texas International Law Journal* 177–202. The work of the International Labour Organization's Small Enterprises Unit also represents an exception to this statement.

[15] For a counter-example, see PT Muchlinski, *Multinational Enterprises and the Law* (2nd edn OUP Oxford 2007) at 70–2. For illustrative discussion of state-owned enterprises in the investment and trade law contexts, see P Blyschak, 'State-Owned Enterprises and International Investment Treaties: When Are State-Owned Entities and Their Investments Protected?' (2011) 6 *Journal of International Law and International Relations* 1–52; LC Backer, 'Sovereign Investing in Times of Crisis: Global Regulation of Sovereign Wealth Funds, State-Owned Enterprises, and the Chinese Experience' (2010) 19 *Transnational Law & Contemporary Problems* 3–144; JY Qin, 'WTO Regulation of Subsidies to State-Owned Enterprises (SOEs)—A Critical Appraisal of the Chinese Accession Protocol' (2004) 7 *Journal of International Economic Law* 863–920. For an example of state-owned enterprises' discussion with respect to sovereign immunity, see A Dickinson, 'State Immunity and State-Owned Enterprises' (2009) 10 *Business Law International* 97–127.

[16] Richard Gitlin and Evan Flaschen identified, in 1987, a 'void' on the international plane in the regulation of multinational corporate bankruptcies: RA Gitlin and ED Flaschen 'The International Void in the Law of Multinational Bankruptcies' (1987) 42 *Business Lawyer* 307–26. This perceived 'void' is one which comparative legal scholars hastened to fill, but not in the register of public international law: see eg DT Trautman, JL Westbrook, and E Gaillard, 'Four Models for International Bankruptcy' (1993) 41 *American Journal of Comparative Law* 573–625; LM LoPucki, 'Cooperation in International Bankruptcy: A Post-Universalist Approach' (1998) 84 *Cornell Law Review* 696–762.

That this is the case may, itself, be unsurprising. The register of states commonly appearing in international legal debate is similarly selective, sovereign equality notwithstanding.[17] The fact that international legal understandings of the corporation exhibit presumed limits and loadings is not so much noteworthy as the lack of any articulation or defence of those limits and loadings. In international legal writing, it is more or less taken for granted that everyone knows what we are talking about when we invoke 'the corporation'. It is presumed, moreover, that the corporate form is power-laden. International legal language has tended to solicit the corporation as powerful and entitled relative to other figures of public international law.[18] This chapter will do likewise, in so far as it takes as given that vast concentrations of capital enjoy corporate safe harbour around the world, with international legal support. Nonetheless, this chapter's redescription is directed towards re-envisaging the corporation in international law in ways that do not necessarily elicit forbearance or submission.

3 PARAPHRASING THE CORPORATION IN INTERNATIONAL LAW

Across international legal fields of vision and work, the corporation has featured in three main ways: as a quasi-citizen or analogue to the individual, as a parastatal entity, and as a point of comparison or guidance for international institutions. In the first instance, the corporation is analogized to an individual and assimilated, for international legal purposes, to the legal order of one or more nation state(s). In the second, the corporation attracts international legal notice on the basis of its role in the re-routing or re-articulation of state power. In the third, the corporation registers as an archetype of international coordination. In particular, in this third instance, corporate conduct comes to serve as a powerful comparator and benchmark for the work and management of international organizations.

---

[17] G Simpson, *Great Powers and Outlaw States: Unequal Sovereigns in the International Legal Order* (CUP Cambridge 2004).

[18] This effect could be compared to the scripting of would-be rapists as powerful, and the 'commonplace sense of paralysis' induced by their threat, in linguistic practice surrounding rape: S Marcus, 'Fighting Bodies, Fighting Words: A Theory and Politics of Rape Prevention' in J Butler and J Scott (eds), *Feminists Theorize the Political* (Routledge New York 1992) 385–403, at 390. I am indebted to Anne Orford for drawing the connection to Sharon Marcus' argument.

3.1 Para-individualism

Individualistic representations of the corporation proceed from the attribution of legal personality to the corporate entity—that is, its capacity to bear rights and responsibilities in its own name. As a 'person', read in the singular, the corporation's primary hook into the international legal system is nationality. Through conferral of nationality, the task of both regulating and empowering the corporation is made to rest with the domestic legal order of one or more state(s). This is the corporation's designated touchstone or point of lift-off for international legal purposes.[19] Those who suffer from international legal wrongdoing committed by a corporate person must, accordingly, look to national legal orders for remedy.[20] Likewise, the corporation itself, and those who hold equity in it, must usually appeal to the state under the laws of which the corporation is organized to pursue international legal grievances on its or their behalf, by exercising a right of diplomatic protection.[21]

Where a corporation would opt in and out of national legal orders, for various reasons, it is in national laws governing contract, taxation, conflict of laws, and the like—harmonized, perhaps, by international agreement or international institutional influence—that the corporation is expected to seek and articulate that power of regulatory selectivity. Such 'housing' of global corporate activity in the legal order of one or more nation state(s) is acknowledged to be a matter of convenience or approximation, as is a corporation's treatment as being equivalent to other nationalized persons.[22] Nonetheless, the attribution of nationality to corporations has come to be seen by many as indispensable, for associated prospects of capital

---

[19] R Wai, 'Transnational Liftoff and Juridical Touchdown: The Regulatory Function of Private International Law in an Era of Globalization' (2002) 40 *Columbia Journal of Transnational Law* 209–74.

[20] Such a remedy may, nonetheless, be expressed in terms that transcend that legal order, as was the case in the United States jurisdiction afforded by the Alien Tort Claims Act (Alien Tort Statute 28 USC § 1350). See IB Wuerth, 'The Supreme Court and the Alien Tort Statute: *Kiobel v Royal Dutch Petroleum Co*' (2013) 107 *American Journal of International Law* 601–21.

[21] *Barcelona Traction, Light and Power Co Ltd (Belgium v Spain)* (Judgment) [1970] ICJ Rep 3, at [70] ('In allocating corporate entities to States for purposes of diplomatic protection, international law is based, but only to a limited extent, on an analogy with the rules governing the nationality of individuals. The traditional rule attributes the right of diplomatic protection of a corporate entity to the State under the laws of which it is incorporated and in whose territory it has its registered office. These two criteria have been confirmed by long practice and by numerous international instruments'). See also International Law Commission, 'Draft Articles on Diplomatic Protection' (2006) UN Doc A/61/10, annex 1, arts 9–12.

[22] The reference to nation states 'housing' corporations is drawn from E Engle, 'Extraterritorial Corporate Criminal Liability: A Remedy for Human Rights Violations?' (2006) 20 *St John's Journal of Legal Commentary* 287–337, at 300. For illustrative acknowledgement of the limits of any analogy of corporations to individual persons, see JE Alvarez, 'Are Corporations "Subjects" of International Law?' (2011) 9 *Santa Clara Journal of International Law* 1–36, at 4.

accumulation, regulatory competition, or claim, even as corporate nationality has remained controversial.[23]

This purposive, methodologically individualist approach to corporate characterization in international law may be linked to successive efforts, in Anglo–American corporate law doctrine, to theorize the corporation in ways consonant with individualism.[24] Like corporate law, public international law has been pressed to integrate the corporate unit 'with a wider legal fabric that assumes individual actors, makes them responsible, and seeks to facilitate their development'.[25] As in corporate law theory, however, the identification of corporations with individuals has always been problematic, not least because of 'the corporation's inability to replicate exactly [any] individual economic actor's profit-maximizing behaviour pattern'.[26] In corporate law, this difficulty contributed to the popularity of managerialist conceptions of corporate structure prevalent throughout much of the twentieth century.[27] In international law, individualist understandings of the corporation have persisted alongside continuing efforts to embed corporations in a state-centred governance structure.

3.2 Para-Statism

Para-statal characterizations of the corporation in international law focus on the corporation functioning more or less as a nation state on the international plane and thereby surpassing its legal subordination to nationality. Much is made of

---

[23] See eg S Sassen, *Globalization and Its Discontents: Essays on the New Mobility of People and Money* (New Press New York 1998) at 1–26 (discussing the embeddedness of globalization in a 'global grid of strategic sites' engaging the nation state); RS Avi-Yonah, 'International Tax as International Law' (2004) 57 *Tax Law Review* 483–502 (discussing the importance of nationality-based jurisdiction for tax law worldwide); JP Trachtman, 'Economic Analysis of Prescriptive Jurisdiction' (2001) 42 *Virginia Journal of International Law* 1–79, at 72 (discussing the conferral of nationality as a mechanism for promoting 'greater clarity of entitlement' and 'regulatory competition'). On controversies surrounding corporate nationality, see LA Mabry, 'Multinational Corporations and US Technology Policy: Rethinking the Concept of Corporate Nationality' (1999) 87 *Georgetown Law Journal* 563–674.

[24] WW Bratton 'The New Economic Theory of the Firm: Critical Perspectives from History' (1989) 41 *Stanford Law Review* 1471–527, at 1483–4 and 1502–6. This tendency in international law should be distinguished from any position-taking in debates surrounding the 'real' or 'fictional' nature of corporate personality, and the status of 'group-persons', ongoing in European, British, and American social and legal thought until the late 1920s: see J Dewey, 'The Historic Background of Corporate Legal Personality' (1926) 35 *Yale Law Journal* 655–73. These debates have nonetheless had an afterlife in international and comparative law: see eg K Iwai, 'Persons, Things and Corporations: The Corporate Personality Controversy and Comparative Corporate Governance' (1999) 47 *American Journal of Comparative Law* 583–632; RF Hansen, 'The International Legal Personality of Multinational Enterprises: Treaty, Custom and the Governance Gap' (2010) 10(1) *Global Jurist* article 1-128 at 9.

[25] 'New Economic Theory' (n 24) 1482.   [26] Ibid 1493.

[27] Ibid 1475–6 and 1487–98. One of the most influential accounts of the management corporation's rise and operation was written by institutional economists: AA Berle and GC Means, *The Modern Corporation and Private Property* (revised edn Harcourt, Brace & World New York 1968 [1933]).

the fact that the revenue or market capitalization of some corporations outstrips the gross domestic product of many individual nations.[28] Emphasis is placed, too, upon the corporate assumption of 'foreign affairs functions' or public powers traditionally identified with the state, through privatization and contracting-out.[29]

In light of their exercise of 'state-like' powers, multinational corporations are seen to merit direct international legal address. Even so, international legal account is taken of these phenomena primarily in terms of their distortion of the perceived normalcy of state-centred power (however embattled that normalcy might long have been).[30] Accordingly, public international law's policy responses to these phenomena are commonly framed around some re-affirmation of state power or state responsibility. Those policy responses presume clarity and consensus surrounding the state's role.[31]

Such understandings of the corporation, crafted with an eye to its para-statal role and affiliations, could perhaps be traced to historic notions—prominent in Anglo-American corporate law until the early nineteenth century—of the corporation as a creature of sovereign concession.[32] Broadly speaking, this understanding of a corporation shares a provenance with modern public international law: both are 'product[s] of the rise of the national state...its objection to *imperia in imperio* at a time when religious congregations and organizations of feudal origin (*communes* and guilds) were rivals of the claim of the national state to complete sovereignty'.[33] International law's quasi-statal theorization of the corporation might also be cross-referenced to later iterations of corporate law theory insistent on corporations' public character, sometimes by analogy to governments.[34] In both the international law and corporate law contexts, para-statal theorization of the

---

[28] See eg SM Hall, 'Multinational Corporations' Post-*Unocal* Liabilities for Violations of International Law' (2002) 34 *George Washington International Law Review* 401–34, at 405; K Greenfield, '*Ultra Vires* Lives! A Stakeholder Analysis of Corporate Illegality (With Notes on How Corporate Law Could Reinforce International Law Norms)' (2001) 87 *Virginia Law Review* 1279–379, at 1370 n 273.

[29] LA Dickinson, 'Government for Hire: Privatizing Foreign Affairs and the Problem of Accountability under International Law' (2005) 47 *William and Mary Law Review* 135–237, at 138; A McBeth, 'Privatising Human Rights: What Happens to the State's Human Rights Duties When Services Are Privatised?' (2004) 5 *Melbourne Journal of International Law* 133–54.

[30] On recurrent rejection of the logic of sovereignty in international legal scholarship, see DW Kennedy, 'A New World Order: Yesterday, Today, and Tomorrow' (1994) 4 *Transnational Law & Contemporary Problems* 329–75.

[31] See eg R McCorquodale and P Simons, 'Responsibility beyond Borders: State Responsibility for Extraterritorial Violations by Corporations of International Human Rights Law' (2007) 70 *Modern Law Review* 598–625; 'Privatising Human Rights' (n 29).

[32] 'Corporate Legal Personality' (n 24) 666–7; 'New Economic Theory' (n 24) 1483–84.

[33] 'Corporate Legal Personality' (n 24) 666.

[34] See eg E Freund, *The Legal Nature of Corporations* (University of Chicago Press Chicago 1897); D Millon, 'Theories of the Corporation' [1990] *Duke Law Journal* 201–62; 'New Economic Theory' (n 24) 1497–8; WW Bratton Jr, 'The "Nexus of Contracts" Corporation: A Critical Reappraisal' (1989) 74 *Cornell Law Review* 407–65, at 438–9.

corporation has been concerned with both taming and justifying corporate power. In international legal writing, the corporation is rendered state-like to justify its subjection to the constraints of public international law. The corporation's very state-likeness, however, simultaneously justifies its autonomy, as may be seen in the human rights setting discussed later in this chapter.

3.3 Para-institutionalism

Alongside these characterizations, the corporation also appears in international legal thought as competitor to, and comparator for, the practice of coordinating international endeavours through institutions. Drawing on traditions within social science or institutional economics of analysing corporations as organizational structures, or on conceptions of the corporation as a nexus of contracts, international legal writings have sometimes rendered the corporation as one among a number of possible expressions of 'integrative transaction' whereby common goals or 'efficiencies' may be pursued on a global scale.[35] The guiding analogy for the corporation in this context is not to a state or to an individual, but to an international organization.

This international legal theorization of corporations with reference to international institutions has mutually constitutive effects. For the organizations concerned, corporate comparators become a basis for exhortation and critique. International institutions such as the United Nations (UN) are urged to become more efficient and deliver better value for members and stakeholders by learning from corporate practice in the private sector.[36] International administrators may be encouraged, under the rubric of this comparison, to become better managers through mechanisms of indirect rule.[37] For corporations, the analogy to international institutions may offer countering pressure. Once pressed into the mould of global integration, alongside international institutions, the corporation may seem a readier target for activist or governmental appeals for corporate social responsibility, transparency, and the like, which corporations may or may not embrace.[38]

---

[35] JL Dunoff and JO Trachtman, 'Economic Analysis of International Law' (1999) 24 *Yale Journal of International Law* 1–60, at 41.

[36] See eg P Utting and A Zammit, 'United Nations–Business Partnerships: Good Intentions and Contradictory Agendas' (2009) 90 *Journal of Business Ethics* 39–56, at 44 ('it is often claimed that the UN can benefit by drawing on private sector resources, skills, and core competencies to achieve UN development objectives more effectively and efficiently').

[37] A Orford, *International Authority and the Responsibility to Protect* (CUP Cambridge 2011) at 199–205.

[38] See eg 'Private Actors and Public Governance' (n 11); P Muchlinski, 'The Changing Face of Transnational Business Governance: Private Corporate Law Liability and Accountability of Transnational Groups in a Post-Financial Crisis World' (2011) 18 *Indiana Journal of Global Legal Studies* 665–705.

Elsewhere, the comparison seems to ramp up the sense of global corporate ordering exerting autonomous, constitutionalizing force.[39]

I suggested earlier that analogies drawn between corporations or corporate groups, on one hand, and international organizations, on the other, might owe something to contractualist understandings of the corporation. Since the late twentieth century, corporate law scholarship has largely embraced an understanding of the corporation as a nexus of contracts (understood as voluntary relations among individual 'factors of production', directed towards exchange, delegation, and transaction-cost-minimization).[40] International legal writings that juxtapose international institutions with corporate firms, explicitly or otherwise, similarly approach international organizations as the outcome of voluntary participation for the maximization of members' net transactional gains.[41] Unlike writing surrounding the 'nexus of contracts' corporation, however, international legal work does not manifest a clear rejection of managerialist conceptions of ordering.[42] On the contrary, international law continues to place management at the strategic centre of international institutions and global ordering.[43]

3.4 Theorizing Corporate Analogues

In none of the modes of likening that I have just characterized has the predominance of analogical reasoning—or the distribution of particular analogies—in international legal theorization of the corporation been the subject of explicit debate.[44] A relative lack of reflexivity about corporate formations in international legal thought has allowed dissimilar configurations of these to flourish, without much by way of boundary patrolling or cross-referencing. Scholars have remarked on the importance of analogical reasoning to international law in general, and to

---

[39] G Teubner, 'Societal Constitutionalism: Alternatives to State-Centered Constitutional Theory?' in C Joerges, I-J Sand, and G Teubner (eds), *Transnational Governance and Constitutionalism* (2004) 3–28.

[40] See 'The "Nexus of Contracts" Corporation' (n 34). Such a theory of the corporation is typically traced to MC Jensen and WH Meckling, 'Theory of the Firm: Managerial Behavior, Agency Costs and Ownership Structure' (1976) 3 *Journal of Financial Economics* 305–60.

[41] See eg JP Trachtman, 'The Theory of the Firm and the Theory of the International Economic Organization: Towards Comparative Institutional Analysis' (1996–97) 17 *Northwestern Journal of International Law & Business* 470–555 at 473–4.

[42] For a discussion of the relationship between 'nexus of contracts' thinking and management-centred conceptions of the firm, see 'The "Nexus of Contracts" Corporation' (n 34) 415–17 and 451–7.

[43] *International Authority* (n 37).

[44] Contrast this with legal scholarly practice outside the international law field, as reflected in E Sherwin, 'A Defense of Analogical Reasoning in Law' (1999) 66 *University of Chicago Law Review* 1179–97; D Hunter, 'Reason is Too Large: Analogy and Precedent in Law' (2001) 50 *Emory Law Journal* 1197–264.

international investment law in particular.[45] However, the analogies so remarked upon have largely been drawn from among legal principles or legal regimes.[46] Analogizing a corporation to a state, as opposed to an international institution or an individual, may certainly lead to the drawing of further analogical relations between particular legal regimes or doctrines (by, for example, making international investment law seem more public law-like). Yet analogical understandings of the corporation also take effect non-doctrinally, as distinct trajectories for global political, social, and economic change and divergent ways of living a life with international law.

International legal choices of one or other analogical counterpart to the corporation are material for the distinct intuitions that these analogies tend to foster.[47] Likening the corporation to an individual may, for instance, favour an emphasis on activities of will-formation—both within the corporation and at other sites. The individualist analogy seems to predominate amid some international legal scholars' discussions of foreign investment, which often revolve around the enablement and conditioning of corporate and governmental decision.[48] Analogies between the corporation and the state might foster more of a focus on conduct and office or, in more conventional international legal terms, function. Consider, by way of illustration, international legal literature concerning private security firms, in which the corporation typically features as a 'quasi-state'. International legal analysis in this domain tends to fixate on the delineation of official duties and the ambit of governmental activities.[49] Recourse to an international institutional comparator for the corporation might, in contrast, direct attention towards matters of structure and system: towards, say, organizational cultures, orders, or markets cultivated and inhabited globally.[50]

---

[45] See eg M Paparinskis, 'Analogies and Other Regimes of International Law' in Z Douglas, J Pauwelyn, and JE Viñuales (eds), *The Foundations of International Investment Law: Bringing Theory into Practice* (OUP Oxford 2014) 73–108; A Roberts, 'Clash of Paradigms: Actors and Analogies Shaping the Investment Treaty System' (2013) 107 *American Journal of International Law* 45–94.

[46] See sources cited in 'Clash of Paradigms' (n 45).

[47] Anthea Roberts makes a similar point in relation to the drawing of analogies between legal disciplines: 'Clash of Paradigms' (n 45) 49.

[48] F Johns, 'Performing Party Autonomy' (2008) 71 *Law & Contemporary Problems* 243–71.

[49] See eg JC Zarate, 'The Emergence of a New Dog of War: Private International Security Companies, International Law, and the New World Disorder' (1998) 34 *Stanford Journal of International Law* 75–162; PW Singer, 'War, Profits, and the Vacuum of Law: Privatized Military Firms and International Law' (2004) 42 *Columbia Journal of Transnational Law* 521–49. See also International Law Commission, 'Draft Articles on Responsibility of States for Internationally Wrongful Acts with Commentaries' (2001) at 43 [5] (discussing Draft Article 5) <http://legal.un.org/ilc/texts/instruments/english/commentaries/9_6_2001.pdf> [accessed 27 February 2016].

[50] See eg 'Theory of the Firm' (n 41); G Teubner, 'The Corporate Codes of Multinationals: Company Constitutions beyond Corporate Governance and Co-Determination' in R Nickel (ed), *Conflict of Laws and Laws of Conflict in Europe and Beyond: Patterns of Supranational and Transnational Juridification* (ARENA Oslo 2009) 261–76.

Connections along these lines are, of course, not uniformly or consistently drawn. Theorization of the corporation in international law remains unsettled in respect of these associations, and in other respects as well. Nonetheless, if international legal language has tended to solicit the corporation as powerful and entitled relative to other subjects of public international law, as I suggested earlier, it has also paired corporations with different analogical partners, each of which has lent related legal analyses a distinct set of reflexes and orientations.

4 CONTENDING WITH CORPORATIONS IN TWO AREAS OF INTERNATIONAL LEGAL DOCTRINE

The analogies sketched earlier move through international legal doctrine and doctrinal scholarship with varying degrees of ease. As they do so, differences in emphasis emerge that have helped to shape the course of doctrinal development. Such divergence is apparent between corporations' theorization in international investment law and in the field of business and human rights.

International investment law writing often evokes the sort of scenes of productive alignment with which this chapter opened: recall the VOC and WIC breaking bread, as it were, with those seminal sovereigns of 1648.[51] Accounts of the corporation that predominate in the international investment law field stress corporations' plasticity, hybridity, and responsiveness; their capacity for 'moving with the times' in a pragmatic, need-meeting mode. This, in turn, has consequences for the range of doctrinal argument deemed tenable. Particular choices entrenched in investment treaties or otherwise tend to be cast as difference-splitting, moderate, almost inevitable. Doctrinal positions characterized as stark, inflexible, or too 'traditional' appear out of step with a pattern of argument so cast.

In contrast, international legal scholarship on business and human rights has often begun with a presumption of antagonism between corporations and international legal order. Characterizations of the corporation in this field have emphasized its likenesses to the state, its assumption of public functions, and its re-routing or sapping of governmental power. This, again, has implications for doctrinal

---

[51] This is not universally the case, however. Consider K Tienhara, 'Regulatory Chill and the Threat of Arbitration: A View from Political Science' in C Brown and K Miles (eds), *Evolution in Investment Treaty Law and Arbitration* (CUP Cambridge 2011) 606–27 (on the threat of arbitration by private investors as a disincentive to governments adopting regulatory measures).

argument. Corporate collaboration in international legal work, or adoption of international legal language, are often taken, in the human rights field, as indicators of international law incrementally taking hold on global corporate affairs. Often, the task for international law has been rendered as reconquering the space of authority from which the corporation has usurped the state. This approach has, in turn, been folded back into the line of thinking advanced in international investment law. The more scholars in the business and human rights field have pushed for some wholesale repositioning of lawful authority in relation to corporations, drawing on statist analogies, the more 'extreme'—and therefore untenable—their arguments have appeared to many with starting points outside that field.[52] For the time being, these two streams appear to have entered a choppy confluence in the work of John Ruggie, as explained later in this section.

4.1 International Investment Law

Writings on international investment law tend to put forward stories of maturation combining all three of the analogies outlined earlier.[53] In the first phase of the 'system' of international investment law, so one prevalent version of the story goes, the corporation was identified with the individual under a diplomatic protection model. Capital-exporting states sought to promote corporations bearing their nationality by entering into treaties with capital-importing states that would shield those corporations from the latter in respect of an investment. Enforcement powers were delegated, by this means, to tribunals authorized under a further array of standing or ad hoc agreements. Corporate coordination served as a benchmark for the international institutions so created, allowing analogies across organizational cultures to exert influence. Institutions such as the International Centre for Settlement of Investment Disputes were, for example, to be '"depoliticized" in the sense that they [would avoid]…confrontation between home state and host state' by following a transactional model of interaction.[54] Statist analogies also played a role: corporate investors operating through the international investment regime were understood to be discharging responsibilities that capital-importing states could not fully bear, such as developing public infrastructure and technological capacity.

---

[52] See eg John Ruggie's criticism of the 'central conceptual flaws' embedded in the draft Norms on the Responsibilities of Transnational Corporations and Other Business Enterprises with Regard to Human Rights developed under the auspices of the UN in 2003: JG Ruggie, 'Business and Human Rights: The Evolving International Agenda' (2007) 101 *American Journal of International Law* 819–40, at 822–7.

[53] See eg 'Clash of Paradigms' (n 45) 75–93.

[54] R Dolzer and C Schreuer, *Principles of International Investment Law* (2nd edn OUP 2012) at 9.

In the second (and now current) phase of this story, international investment law seems, at times, to prioritize the analogy of the corporation to the state. Emphasis is placed on the role that corporate investors play in allocating, developing or eroding public resources. Arguments are made, accordingly, for corporate investors' susceptibility to the sorts of public law standards to which state actors are routinely held.[55] At the same time, the benchmarking of international coordination to corporate comparators continues to exert influence: sustaining convictions that global policy development in the field can (and, in some accounts, should) take place through the more or less spontaneous efforts of managerial or entrepreneurial elites, trading in models, 'best practices' and voluntary principles.[56] Envisioning the corporation through an individualist lens remains, nonetheless, a widespread and influential practice as well. In much international investment law writing, the actions of a corporation tend to be 'read' through some attribution of the motives and interests of the individuals who form, invest, or work within it; the corporation becomes a 'portal' for individual strategic intent, primarily that identified with shareholders.[57]

International investment law has also moved beyond the realm of analogy to put forward quite 'thick' accounts of corporate structure. Doctrine surrounding the nationality of corporate investors and the protection of investments is illustrative. In these contexts, international investment jurisprudence makes available a number of different techniques for slicing and dicing the corporate form. Classically, if controversially, international investment law looked to a corporate entity—and that entity's nationality, determined largely according to formal criteria—to define the ambit of investors' rights on the international legal plane, absent special agreements between a state and private investors or other extenuating circumstances.[58]

---

[55] See eg B Kingsbury and SW Schill, 'Public Law Concepts to Balance Investors' Rights with State Regulatory Actions in the Public Interest—The Concept of Proportionality' in SW Schill (ed), *International Investment Law and Comparative Public Law* (OUP Oxford 2010) 75–104.

[56] See eg J Zhan, J Weber, and J Karl, 'International Investment Rulemaking at the Beginning of the Twenty-First Century: Stocktaking and Options for the Way Forward' in JE Alvarez and KP Sauvant (eds) *The Evolving International Investment Regime: Expectations, Realities, Options* (2011) 193–210. Note, however, that the ICJ has explicitly rejected the cogency of any analogy between a national entering into the service of an international organization and a national investing in a multinational corporation, for purposes of interpreting international legal doctrine on nationality: *Barcelona Traction* (n 21) at [53].

[57] See eg 'International Legal Personality' (n 24) 38; A Telesetsky, 'A New Investment Deal in Asia and Africa: Land Leases to Foreign Investors' in *Evolution in Investment Treaty Law* (n 51) 539–69. The identification of corporate intent with individual shareholder identity is mirrored in the attention paid to the allegiances and career trajectories of individual arbitrators for purposes of interpreting arbitral rulings: see eg 'Clash of Paradigms' (n 45) 87–8.

[58] *Principles of International Investment Law* (n 54) 47–52 and 56–60; *Barcelona Traction* (n 21) at [50]–[52] and [90]–[92]. For an indication of the contentiousness of this approach, see C McLachlan, 'Investment Treaties and General International Law' (2008) 57 *International & Comparative Law*

However, 'recent practice points towards the way of disregarding the corporate form and of looking for the true investor'.[59] International investment law also permits majority and minority shareholders to gain recognition as international legal claimants in respect of their 'investment'.[60] Taken together, these doctrinal renderings of corporate structure configure the firm as a multidivisional and shifting site of power on which management has no unilateral purchase. Viewed broadly, they may bear the imprint of a conception of business, prevalent since the 1980s, which casts 'the powerful business figure…not [as] the managerialist chief executive officer but [as] the capitalist deal maker—the financial entrepreneur or the investment banker'.[61]

Different configurations of the corporation, in dynamic relation, thus help to sustain the international investment law regime and accounts of its 'development'. Viewed through the lens of this analogical eclecticism, international investment law often appears to be surpassing, hybridizing, or blurring otherwise entrenched divisions of discipline, culture, or interest in the service of one or other 'business concept' and a multisectoral commitment to 'the increased flow of foreign investment'.[62] Typically, this overcoming has been rendered as difference-splitting, where the perceived starkness of an either/or helps to make the in-between that international investment law purports to occupy seem all the more palatable, indeed necessary.[63] The plasticity and restlessness with which the corporate form is invested in international investment law have been critical in sustaining a sense of that discipline's trajectory as less a matter of choice than one of necessary adaptation to contemporary global conditions.[64]

Quarterly 361–401, at 365–9 (setting international investment law's development against the backdrop of 'failure to reach multilateral agreement on an acceptable content of investors' rights').

[59] M Burgstaller, 'Nationality of Corporate Investors and International Claims against the Investor's Own State' (2006) 7 *Journal of World Investment & Trade* 857–81, at 859.

[60] U Kriebaum and C Schreuer, 'The Concept of Property in Human Rights Law and International Investment Law' in S Breitenmoser et al., (eds), *Human Rights, Democracy and the Rule of Law: Liber Amicorum Luzius Wildhaber* (2007) 743–62. See also SA Alexandrov, 'The "Baby Boom" of Treaty-Based Arbitrations and the Jurisdiction of ICSID Tribunals: Shareholders as "Investors" and Jurisdiction *Ratione Temporis*' (2005) 4 *Law and Practice of International Courts and Tribunals* 19–59.

[61] 'New Economic Theory' (n 24) 1523.

[62] *Principles of International Investment Law* (n 54) 12, 21, 27.

[63] See generally D Kennedy, 'Strategizing Strategic Behaviour in Legal Interpretation' [1996] *Utah Law Review* 785–825. See eg AF Lowenfeld, 'Investment Agreements and International Law' (2003) 42 *Columbia Journal of Transnational Law* 123–30, at 124 (situating the proliferation of bilateral investment treaties within a 'wide chasm—one would have said the unbridgeable chasm—between the developed countries on one side and the developing and socialist countries on the other').

[64] See eg 'Investment Agreements and International Law' (n 63) 130 (arguing that 'the [bilateral investment treaty] movement has grown to the point where one can speak of consensus' producing 'something like customary law' which—to the extent that it does not fit 'the traditional definition of customary law'—renders that 'traditional definition' either 'wrong' or 'incomplete').

4.2 Business and Human Rights

International legal literature in the 'business and human rights' vein also bears the imprint of the analogies described earlier. Theorizations of the corporation in this field, however, typically revolve around a statist comparison. This is the case notwithstanding a widespread commitment among human rights scholars to developing international legal principle 'that reflects the actual operations of business enterprises', as in Steven Ratner's oft-cited 2001 article.[65] In that article, corporate analogies to the state, and vice versa, nonetheless predominated. International legal recognition of corporations depended, in Ratner's account, on corporations' operation as agents of a state, corporate complicity with state wrongdoing, or the subordination of states or government personnel to corporate control. Operation 'under [colour] of corporate authority' was proposed as a basis for attribution of responsibility to a corporation, much as a state might bear legal responsibility for action under the colour of national law.[66] While corporations were noteworthy for their 'proximity…to individuals' in this account, the application of 'individual accountability standards' to corporate structures was deemed 'inappropriate'.[67] Comparisons between global corporate enterprises and the work of international organizations were little in evidence in Ratner's writing, although international human rights institutions have elsewhere been cast as 'norm entrepreneurs' under a business analogy.[68] Rather, Ratner showed a preference for an approach which 'views the business enterprise, *like the state*, as a unit engaged in a particular function, with its own internal structures'.[69]

Seeing the corporation like a state in the international legal order has been the preference of other scholars in the business and human rights field as well.[70] International human rights scholars and advocates have sought to generate something akin to international investment law's 'business concept' as an anchorage for corporate enterprise—a global 'business case' for human rights.[71] Yet the plasticity this would require has not been much in evidence in international legal understandings of the corporation in this field. Rather, in the human rights field, corporations have most often been envisioned as bearers of overweening rule in

---

[65] SR Ratner 'Corporations and Human Rights: A Theory of Legal Responsibility' (2001) 111 *Yale Law Journal* 443–545, at 496.

[66] Ibid 497–506 and 524.   [67] Ibid 508 and 523.

[68] HH Koh, 'How is International Human Rights Law Enforced?' (1998) 74 *Indiana Law Journal* 1397–417, at 1409; K Sikkink, 'Transnational Politics, International Relations Theory, and Human Rights' (1998) 31 *PS: Political Science and Politics* 517–23.

[69] 'Corporations and Human Rights' (n 65) 524 (emphasis added).

[70] See eg 'Direct vs Indirect Obligations' (n 6) 944 (emphasizing that 'corporations bear a stronger resemblance than individuals to the classic addressees of international law (states); like states, corporations are artificial "persons" comprising groups of natural persons').

[71] PT Muchlinski, 'Human Rights and Multinationals: Is There a Problem?' (2001) 77 *International Affairs* 31–47, at 38.

ways that mirror a state universalized under a 'brutally integrative vision of the republican tradition'.[72] This outlook has guided perceptions of corporate operation and regulatory opportunity. It has also enabled international lawyers to move from an expectation of corporate negation of international legal order to one of corporate involvement in—indeed, reinvigoration of—international law's traditional architecture.[73]

Just as a state is defined in international law with reference to governance of a population (both internally and in its external relations), so scholars in the human rights field have characterized the corporation with reference to governance: interest group representation, conflict resolution, and social protection.[74] In this mode, a corporation 'must consider the needs not only of internal stakeholders, such as the shareholders, managers and employees, but also the external stakeholders, such as customers, suppliers, competitors, and other special interest groups'.[75]

Under this governance-oriented account of corporate order, it seems natural that international regulatory initiative and responsibility should come to rest with corporations as such, more or less interchangeably with states. It seems natural, too, to emphasize generic structures of corporate order as a parallel to 'government', with an emphasis on more or less well-functioning versions of both.[76] Human rights scholars continue to encourage states to pursue 'control' over multinational corporations via bilateral, regional, and multilateral legal avenues.[77] Nonetheless, corporations are commonly vested with juridical authority over corporate conduct in the human rights field, typically through a management-centred and bounded sense of responsibility rendered as 'corporate social responsibility' or in other 'soft', voluntarist forms.[78]

---

[72] P Bourdieu, 'Rethinking the State: Genesis and Structure of the Bureaucratic Field' in G Steinmetz (ed), *State/Culture: State-Formation after the Cultural Turn* (Cornell University Press Ithaca 1999) 53–75, at 62.

[73] See eg 'Changing Face' (n 38) 666, 705 (moving from a depiction of 'transnational corporate groups [enjoying]...free choice of means in their global operations' to one of corporations having been 'resocializ[ed]...at the national and transnational levels').

[74] On the former, see the *Montevideo Convention on the Rights and Duties of States* (adopted 26 December 1933 entered into force 26 December 1934) 165 LNTS 19, art 1.

[75] 'Changing Face' (n 38) 700.

[76] *Contra* WW Bratton and JA McCahery, 'Comparative Corporate Governance and the Theory of the Firm: The Case against Global Cross Reference' (1999) 38 *Columbia Journal of Transnational Law* 213–97 (emphasizing the diversity of governance systems and the trade-offs they embody and arguing against accounts of global convergence or 'hybrid best practice').

[77] See eg *Multinational Enterprises* (n 15) 117–21.

[78] On the taking-for-granted of stockholder interests and objectives in corporate social responsibility debates, see IB Lee, 'Corporate Law, Profit Maximization, and the "Responsible" Shareholder' (2005) 10(2) *Stanford Journal of Law, Business & Finance* 31–72. For a representative survey of regulatory devices and opportunities in the business and human rights field, see *Multinational Enterprises* (n 15) 110–21.

The work of the United Nations Special Representative on the Issue of Human Rights, Transnational Corporations and Other Business Enterprises, John Ruggie, has signalled some ambivalence about statist analogies for corporations in the human rights field, perhaps in deference to the reflex disdain for such 'traditional' positions fostered by international investment law. Ruggie has counselled against viewing corporations as akin to 'democratic public interest institutions' or 'making them, in effect, co-equal duty bearers for...human rights'.[79] Nevertheless, the framework that Ruggie proposed in 2008 emphasized the 'entangle[ment]' of companies' responsibilities with those of states (albeit while acknowledging companies' 'unique' role).[80] Both this framework and the Guiding Principles which Ruggie presented in 2012 have been founded on the centrality of states' responsibility for the protection of individuals from human rights abuse and the parallel, yet distinguishable responsibility of business enterprises to respect human rights.[81] The state and state government remain central comparators for corporations in Ruggie's work, inspiring a focus on protective responsibility. Ultimately, however, the state analogy is downgraded to one among many: '[s]tate agencies are simply cast in a long line of other actors whose relationships with [transnational corporations] may create adverse human rights impacts'.[82]

Ruggie's work maintained a state analogue for corporate conduct, while relativizing that relation. In this respect, it fits quite well with a broader international legal project of 'consolidat[ing] and integrat[ing] the practices of executive rule' with appeals to protection as their grounds for authority.[83] It also affirms a widely held conviction, among human rights scholars and advocates, that 'corporations are controlling the rules of the game and will continue to do so'.[84] This is a conviction to which Ruggie's Principles offer an update, with an ethical loading presumed commensurate with international legal order: 'What I've said to the companies is...take the game over and stop being reactive, and become proactive, and drive the agenda'.[85]

---

[79]   Special Representative of the Secretary-General on the Issue of Human Rights and Transnational Corporations and Other Business Enterprises, 'Promotion and Protection of Human Rights: Interim Report' (22 February 2006) UN Doc E/CN.4/2006/97.

[80]   Special Representative of the Secretary-General on the Issue of Human Rights and Transnational Corporations and Other Business Enterprises, 'Protect, Respect and Remedy: A Framework for Business and Human Rights' (7 April 2008) UN Doc A/HRC/8/5, at para 6.

[81]   Special Representative of the Secretary-General on the Issue of Human Rights and Transnational Corporations and Other Business Enterprises, 'Guiding Principles on Business and Human Rights' (21 March 2011) UN Doc A/HRC/17/31, at 6–14.

[82]   JM Amerson, '"The End of the Beginning?": A Comprehensive Look at the UN's Business and Human Rights Agenda from a Bystander Perspective' (2012) 17 *Fordham Journal of Corporate & Financial Law* 871–941, at 926.

[83]   *International Authority* (n 37) 209, 212.

[84]   '"The End of the Beginning?"' (n 82) 933, noting that this is something that '[m]ost human rights activists believe'.

[85]   Ibid 933, quoting an interview by John Sherman with Professor John Ruggie.

Business and human rights scholarship ostensibly fixated on surpassing a statist model of global order thus proves utterly preoccupied with generic understandings of state politics and their analogues. International law's habitual relation to the 'prince'—or to embodiments of political and economic power cast as international law's touchstones—is restaged, in this context, as a relationship of counsel and guidance to corporate executives presumed to be effective rulers of a variegated set of relationships and constituents. By this means, international law is reframed in meaningful proximity to generic representations of dispersed or fragmented forms of power in and around the state system. Concerns about that system's 'relevance' are thereby assuaged and promises of effectiveness maintained; collaborative 'new governance' promises to succeed where public international law has failed.[86] Arguments which smack of the flexible, hybrid, demand-answering moderation with which the corporation has been invested by international investment law appear to fare best in contemporary scholarship on business and human rights. As in the seventeenth century, it is to 'glorious deeds' on the part of corporations that international lawyers look to reboot conventional understandings of international legal order.

5 Conclusion

Theorization of the corporation is typically presented as an incidental, sideline activity for international legal work. Far from undermining the resulting theorizations' potency, this routing has proven tremendously productive. Through an oblique, analogical approach to corporations, international legal writing has kept alive the prospect of the corporate form delivering some regenerative supplement to the international legal order. In the international investment law context, for example, corporations are understood to have bequeathed to international legal work the plasticity and sweep of a global 'business concept' to which states, international institutions, and individuals alike may submit. In the business and human rights setting, drawing in part on this 'business concept', corporations figure as bearers of newly cogent and legitimate practices of rule from which states, especially, are invited to learn.

---

[86] KW Abbott and D Snidal, 'Strengthening International Regulation through Transnational New Governance: Overcoming the Orchestration Deficit' (2009) 42 *Vanderbilt Journal of Transnational Law* 501–78.

In their haste to gain corporate succour for their professional projects, however, international lawyers may routinely overestimate the coherence, exceptionalism, and self-reliance of corporate power. Against this sense of corporate 'special[ness]', this chapter has emphasized the extent to which international legal impressions of the corporate form rest on analogies to forms of power located elsewhere and structured otherwise.[87] The variable analogies in which international legal writing regularly trades recall the dissimilar understandings, locales, techniques, and personas that corporations rarely if ever hold together in unalloyed consensus, either within multinational corporate structures or along corporate supply chains. Theorizations of the corporation in international law solicit figures of entitlement and might, but also figures of dependence, analogically and otherwise. It could be that international lawyers' payment of closer attention to those dependencies—and international law's role in structuring and sustaining them—might generate new routes for the actualization of lawful relations globally, through, within, around, or in spite of the corporate form.

---

[87] On the notion of corporations as 'special', see eg Ruggie's emphasis on their being 'specialized organs, performing specialized functions': 'Business and Human Rights' (n 52) 827.

CHAPTER 33

THEORIZING INTERNATIONAL LAW ON FORCE AND INTERVENTION

DINO KRITSIOTIS

...for if dumb beasts, which cannot make speeches and argue about the reasons for their anger, and which because of their innate ferocity are averse to peace and inclined to battle, yet live in peace; how much the more ought human beings ought to do this, unless they wish to seem more bestial than the very beasts.

(Gentili)[1]

Whoever entertains a true idea of war,—whoever considers its terrible effects, its destructive and unhappy consequences,—will readily agree that it should never be undertaken without the most cogent reasons. Humanity revolts against a sovereign, who, without necessity or without very powerful reasons, lavishes the blood of his most faithful subjects, and exposes his people to the calamities of war, when he has it in his power to maintain them in the enjoyment of an honourable and salutary peace. And if to this imprudence, this want of love for his people, he moreover adds injustice towards those he attacks,—of how great a crime,

---

[1] A Gentili, *De Iure Belli Libri Tres* (JC Rolfe trans) (2 vols Clarendon Press Oxford 1933 [1612]) bk I, ch V.

or rather, of what a frightful series of crimes, does he not become guilty! Responsible for all the misfortunes which he draws down on his own subjects, he is moreover loaded with the guilt of all those which he inflicts on an innocent nation. The slaughter of men, the pillage of cities, the devastation of provinces,—such is the black catalogue of his enormities.

(de Vattel)[2]

1 Introduction

ONE of the most striking—and, quite possibly, counter-intuitive—features to emerge from the practice of states in the period of the United Nations (UN) is not the extent to which states have had recourse to force in their international relations over the past six decades or so, but the fact that, on the occasions that they have done so and much more often than not, these actions have been accompanied by legal justifications for that force. This might seem a most anomalous turn for states to have taken,[3] given that while international law presents various rules for permissible force in international relations, at no point does it oblige states to provide either basic or elaborate accounts of the legal basis of their respective actions. It is true that article 51 of the *Charter of the United Nations* (1945) announces that measures undertaken by member states of the UN in the exercise of this right of self-defence 'shall be immediately reported to the Security Council',[4] but even this provision could be read to mean that it is the *facts* of force undertaken in individual or collective self-defence that need to be made known or reported to the Council—not a stipulation that states set out in engrossing detail the finer elements of the claim regarding each and every activation of that right.[5]

---

[2] E de Vattel, *The Law of Nations, or, the Principles of the Law of Nature Applied to the Conduct and Affairs of Nations and Sovereigns* (GG and J Robinson London 1797 [1758]) at bk III, ch III, §24.

[3] If turn it indeed be: for the depiction of a deeper historical current in this respect, see K Skubiszewski, 'Use of Force by States. Collective Security. Law of War and Neutrality' in M Sørensen (ed), *Manual of Public International Law* (Macmillan London 1968) 739–854, at 742. See also I Brownlie, *International Law and the Use of Force by States* (Clarendon Press Oxford 1963) at 40–50.

[4] Though the intended addressee of this requirement is not made explicit, it *is* clear that the reporting requirement is intended to facilitate the operation of the 'until clause' of article 51—whereby the right of self-defence obtains 'until the Security Council has taken the measures necessary to maintain international peace and security'. See H Kelsen, *The Law of the United Nations: A Critical Analysis of Its Fundamental Problems* (Stevens and Sons London 1950) at 801.

[5] In particular view of 'the authority and responsibility of the Security Council under the present *Charter* to take at any time such action as it deems necessary in order to maintain or restore international peace and security'—and the fact that, again according to article 51, the right of self-defence shall be exercised 'until the Security Council has taken measures necessary to maintain international peace and security': see N Benwitch and A Martin, *A Commentary on the Charter of the United Nations* (Routledge London 1950) at 108. Although, implicit in the ICJ's understanding of this requirement in *Military and Paramilitary Activities in and against Nicaragua (Nicaragua v United States of America)* (Merits) [1986] ICJ Rep 14, *both* of these factors seemed to be at stake, for the Court spoke of the Security Council as 'empowered to determine the conformity with international

In any event, it should be recalled that this provision of the *Charter* is confined to exercises of the right of self-defence in international law.[6] It does not purport to hold out lessons of general significance for recourses to force other than those involving the right of self-defence. Within this rubric, we would presumably include force that has been authorized by the Security Council under Chapter VII of the *Charter* or occurring within the framework for regional arrangements or agencies under Chapter VIII of the *Charter*,[7] as we would all force that amounts to an *intervention* within international law,[8] such as interventions undertaken at the behest of the target state by way of consent or intervention or in the name of the so-called rights of humanitarian intervention or of 'pro-democratic intervention'.[9] And yet, there is no question that this practice—that is, this *phenomenon* of justification—has very much become part of the repertoire of state action,[10] to the point where the prevailing expectation now is that states will indeed articulate some form of legal justification or set of justifications for force or intervention.[11]

law of the measures which the State is seeking to justify on the basis': at 105 [200]. Later in the same paragraph, the Court made reference to self-defence when 'advanced as a justification for measures which would otherwise be in breach both of the principle of customary international law and that contained in the *Charter*'.

[6] The Court was, however, quite clear in *Nicaragua* that 'in customary international law it is not a condition of the lawfulness of the use of force in self-defence that a procedure [such as the reporting requirement] so closely dependent on the content of a treaty commitment and of the institutions established by it': *Nicaragua* (n 5) 105 [200]. See also 'Resolution of the Institut de droit international' (8 September 2011) <http://www.idi-iil.org/idiE/resolutionsE/2011_rhodes_10_C_en.pdf> [accessed 28 February 2016] art 4(4): 'Any request that is followed by military assistance shall be notified to the Secretary-General of the United Nations'.

[7] See *UN Charter* art 53(1).

[8] Which, for the ICJ, involves an 'element of coercion': see *Nicaragua* (n 5) 108 [205]—though, as per the application made to the Court by Nicaragua in that case, the question of force was treated separately to the question of intervention.

[9] On the coincidence of force and intervention, in *Nicaragua* the Court considered that 'assistance to rebels in the form of the provision of weapons or logistical or other support' may be 'regarded as a threat or use of force, or amount to intervention in the internal or external affairs of other States'—even if it could not, as a matter of principle, rise to the level of an armed attack: ibid 104 [195]. This coheres with an earlier statement from the Court—that it is 'necessary' to 'distinguish the most grave forms of the use of force (those constituting an armed attack) from other less grave forms': at 101 [191].

[10] As Charlotte Peevers has maintained, we can observe 'the hailing of law through speech': C Peevers, *The Politics of Justifying Force: The Suez Crisis, the Iraq War, and International Law* (OUP Oxford 2013) at 4. The practice of justification is indeed remarked but not elaborated upon in LM Goodrich, E Hambro, and AP Simons, *Charter of the United Nations: Commentary and Documents* (3rd revised edn Columbia University Press New York 1969) at 345 and R Higgins, *The Development of International Law through the Political Organs of the United Nations* (OUP London 1963) at 197. Cf JH Westra, *International Law and the Use of Armed Force: The UN Charter and the Major Powers* (Routledge London and New York 2007) at 10–40.

[11] The failure to supply justifications is the exception rather than the norm: A Garwood-Gowers, 'Israel's Airstrike on Syria's Al-Kibar Facility: A Test Case for the Doctrine of Pre-Emptive Self-Defence' (2011) 16 *Journal of Conflict and Security Law* at 263–92.

That the overwhelming swathe of justifications for force and intervention occurs outside the rituals of litigation and the hallowed quarters of the courtroom—for immediate purposes, this would be the International Court of Justice (ICJ)[12]—is even more astonishing. In that context, the institutional rules of procedure make it difficult to avoid making a public profession of a legal kind in *defence* of state action: an application made for the initiation of contentious proceedings shall, according to the *Rules of Court*, 'specify as far as possible the legal grounds upon which the jurisdiction of the Court is to be based; it shall also specify the precise nature of the claim, together with a succinct statement of the facts and grounds on which the claim is based';[13] the subsequent memorial of the applicant state must contain 'a statement of the relevant facts, a statement of law, and the submissions' made before the Court,[14] whereas the counter-memorial of the respondent state must contain amongst other things 'observations concerning the statement of law in the memorial' as well as 'a statement of law in answer thereto'.[15] The instruction for advisory proceedings before the Court is set out in much less detail,[16] but even here we are able to make something of a start at discerning the elements and expectations that are in place for when the Court exercises its 'advisory functions'.[17]

Perhaps, then, this unmistakable practice of states has arisen from the current of social habit,[18] and perhaps it is due in part to the fact that force and intervention are—or can be—very public demonstrations of a state's power which will, in all likelihood, be met with an official account or justification by the respective state (or states) rather than a *denial* of such action.[19] It is through this lens—that is, the

---

[12] Although it of course need not be confined to the ICJ: see 'Eritrea-Ethiopia Claims Commission: Partial Award—*Jus Ad Bellum*: Ethiopia's Claims 1–8 between the Federal Democratic Republic of Ethiopia and the State of Eritrea, The Hague, December 19, 2005' reproduced in (2006) 45 *International Legal Materials* 430–5. See further SD Murphy, W Kidane, and TR Snider, *Litigating War: Mass Civil Injury and the Eritrea–Ethiopia Claims Commission* (OUP Oxford 2013) at 103–51 and C Gray, 'The Eritrea/Ethiopia Claims Commission Oversteps Its Boundaries: A Partial Award?' (2006) 17 *European Journal of International Law* 699–721.

[13] *Rules of Court* (1978) art 38(2).   [14] Ibid art 49(1).

[15] Ibid art 49(2). For an account of the recent turn to the ICJ, see C Gray, 'The Use and Abuse of the International Court of Justice: Cases Concerning the Use of Force after *Nicaragua*' (2003) 14 *European Journal of International Law* 867–905.

[16] See *Rules of Court* (1978) art 102(2) and art 105(1), and *Statute of the ICJ* (1945) art 68.

[17] Again, as it is put in *Statute of the ICJ* (1945) art 68.

[18] Or as a manifestation of 'well-established patterns of behaviour and expectations that, despite their consistency and clarity, are not regarded as manifestations of rules of law' as identified in V Lowe, *International Law* (OUP Oxford 2007) at 38.

[19] That said, at least as far as the compass of force is concerned, in October 1970, Thomas M Franck considered small-scale warfare as one of the central challenges to the prohibition of force: TM Franck, 'Who Killed Article 2(4)? or: Changing Norms Governing the Use of Force by States' (1970) 64 *American Journal of International Law* 809–37, at 812. The 'mysteriously well-armed professional gunmen' known as the 'green men' who seized Ukrainian government sites in town after town in February 2014 is a rare instance of denial: see A Higgins, MR Gordon, and AR Kramer, 'Photos Link Masked Men in East Ukraine to Russia' (21 April 2014) *New York Times* at A1. See further WM

art and craft of making legal justifications in the first place—that this chapter will concentrate its analysis of force and intervention. It will commence by asking why legal justifications are made at all, giving some sense of the circumstances in which these justifications take their essential shape and form. It is important to remind ourselves precisely what constitutes the subject of this specific set of enquiries; what is it that we are attempting to analyse?, what is it that is demanding theorization?, and what is the purpose of this theorization? Then, the chapter will move to consider how these justifications alert us to some of the unspoken assumptions about force and intervention in international law—what can be taken away from an analysis of the practice of justifications other than an engagement with the merits of their respective substance, which so consistently occupies much of the existing literature in this field. Finally, we shall attempt to connect these points to a broader set of issues theorizing the purpose or function of force in today's world.

2 THE PRACTICE OF MAKING LEGAL JUSTIFICATIONS

To commence with, it is important to get some handle on why legal justifications for force and for intervention might be devised by states at all: what logic or imperative explains the significance that attaches—or that might attach—to the emergence and making of such justifications? In particular view of the *context* in which most of the examples of justification for force and intervention occur—that is, outside the realm of regularized litigation at the international level—what considerations affect states to act in the way they do, going to such enormous lengths of endeavour and detail to explicate their positions or to set out their 'claims'[20] for action? In short, what explains the *simulation* of the experiences of the courtroom for broader audiences and much broader public consumption?[21] What illuminates the practice of this 'justificatory politics',[22] and the function of international law within this politics?[23]

Reisman and JE Baker, *Regulating Covert Action: Practices, Contexts, and Policies of Covert Coercion Abroad in International and American Law* (Yale University Press New Haven 1992).

[20] *Development of International Law* (n 10) 10; or 'an express claim': C Gray, *International Law and the Use of Force* (3rd edn OUP Oxford 2008) at 142.

[21] D Kritsiotis, 'Arguments of Mass Confusion' (2004) 15 *European Journal of International Law* 233–78.

[22] *The Politics of Justifying Force* (n 10) 17.

[23] Indeed, the notion of the 'international incident' was devised as against cases and judgments: '[b]ecause of the structure of the international political system, most international decision

On one account, we can imagine that a state engaged in force or intervention seeks to produce for the wider world the legal justification designed to persuade others of the case for action; *sans* this move by the state in question, the force or intervention cannot—will not—rationalize or validate itself by itself.[24] For the state to be deemed to have acted lawfully, it will need to discharge the associated argumentative and evidential burdens that attach to the laws or legal framework existing for force and intervention. Alberico Gentili's evocative metaphor of human beings as against 'dumb beasts' brings us into the realm of human choice, action, and reasoning.[25] As part of this process, the principal function of the claim or justification for action is to transform an action that would otherwise be regarded as *against* international law into something more meaningful and normatively coherent. We cannot make it across the line of legality—we cannot make it to acceptance and approval—without recourse to the *speech* of international law.[26]

It is possible, too, that legal justifications represent—or reframe—the legal advice that has been heard by a government at a much earlier stage of its deliberations or action,[27] which predate the moment or millisecond of the decision for force or intervention. So, here, all that a government is doing by making public its justification for action is to expand the circle of *cognoscenti* as to the precise basis that has structured its decisions for action,[28] as if the law carries with it an abiding power to choreograph each of the various elements of state behaviour. This affords a controlling—or causal—attribute to international law, such that, as Martti Koskenniemi has written in the context of potential responses to the Iraqi invasion of Kuwait on 2 August 1990, 'legal viewpoints [are] not only somewhat relevant, but in some respect central to devising a national position'.[29] Here, the

---

is found in incidents rather than cases and judgments': WM Reisman, and AR Willard, 'Preface and Acknowledgements' in WM Reisman and AR Willard (eds), *International Incidents: The Law that Counts in World Politics* (Princeton University Press Princeton 1988) vii–ix, at vii.

[24] Indeed, Higgins writes of a 'presumption of an unlawfulness' that *a fortiori* accompanies 'any massive-scale measure.... Violence of a less intense nature...may still prove a relevant factor when taken together with other circumstances': *Development of International Law* (n 10) 181. But see T Ruys, 'The Meaning of "Force" and the Boundaries of the *Jus ad Bellum*: Are "Minimal" Uses of Force Excluded from UN *Charter* Article 2(4)?' (2014) 108 *American Journal of International Law* 159–210; JHH Weiler, 'Armed Intervention in a Dichotomized World: The Case of Grenada' in A Cassese (ed), *The Current Legal Regulation of the Use of Force* (Martinus Nijhoff Dordrecht 1986) 241–68, at 246 (on 'the presumption of illegality').

[25] *De Iure Belli Libri Tres* (n 1) bk I, ch V.

[26] And where the 'language of international law...was also, at least in part, the language of just war': M Walzer, 'The Triumph of Just War Theory (and the Dangers of Success)' (2002) 69 *Social Research* 925–44, at 927.

[27] See eg G Marston, 'Armed Intervention in the 1956 Suez Canal Crisis: The Legal Advice Tendered to the British Government' (1988) 37 *International & Comparative Law Quarterly* 773–817.

[28] Note the distinction drawn between 'private sphere decision-making' and 'public justification': *The Politics of Justifying Force* (n 10) 69.

[29] M Koskenniemi, 'The Place of Law in Collective Security' (1996) 17 *Michigan Journal of International Law* 455–90, at 473–4.

law is then of sufficient clarity but also authority to channel state action in one direction as opposed to another; it is the law that determines or pre-determines state action and it is the law that is designed earliest and uppermost in sequence of the pathologies of power.[30]

Of course, this idealized portrait of the law in the service of its own ambitions can be (and very often is) complicated by several factors—including the fact that it is not always the case that the turn and speed of circumstance allow for legal advice to be sought let alone obtained before the decision for force or intervention is taken. We may wish to distinguish between, on the one hand, the example of the significant interval of time that preceded the intervention of Egypt in October 1956[31] or that against Iraq in March 2003,[32] from, on the other hand, the series of examples in which states have engaged *immediate* responses against approaching civilian aircraft thought to be aiming their wherewithal against that state—the problem of the 'intruding aircraft'.[33] So, when the USS *Vincennes* stationed in the Persian Gulf shot down Iranian Air Flight 655 in July 1988 with 290 fatalities, the United States (US) was to inform the Security Council that the action had been taken 'in self-defence at what [was] believed to be a hostile Iranian military aircraft, after sending repeated warnings (to which the aircraft did not respond)'.[34] The further problem then arises that the legal justification that ensues or that is ultimately offered occurs as an *ex post facto* rationalization of past actions, as if international law is no more and no less than an afterthought in shifting the levers of the ship of state.[35] Yet, truth be told, it is a common function of the law in its myriad manifestations in domestic settings throughout the world that it is invoked or pressed into service *after* facts have occurred, and is summoned in the cause of authoring its own narrative of that very same set of facts.[36]

---

[30] On this idealized portrait of 'the power of law', see 'Armed Intervention in a Dichotomized World (n 24) 242.

[31] As is foretold by Peevers: *The Politics of Justifying Force* (n 10) 66–128.

[32] See P Sands, *Lawless World: America and the Making and Breaking of Global Rules* (Allen Lane London 2005) at 174–203.

[33] See OJ Lissitzyn, 'The Treatment of Aerial Intruders in Recent Practice and International Law' (1953) 47 *American Journal of International Law* 559–89, at 565.

[34] 'Letter Dated 6 July 1988 from the Acting Permanent Representative of the United States of America to the United Nations Addressed to the President of the Security Council' (6 July 1988) UN Doc S/19989. See also 'Letter Dated 11 July 1988 from the Permanent Representative of the United States of America to the United Nations Addressed to the President of the Security Council' (11 July 1988) UN Doc S/20005; TM Franck, *The Power of Legitimacy among Nations* (OUP Oxford 1990) at 151–2.

[35] The metaphor is, of course, from Plato, *Republic* (2nd edn Penguin Classics London 2007) 488b–489d, though other metaphors—such as Philip Alston's notion of 'handmaidens'—might also be apposite in this context: see SV Scott, 'International Lawyers: Handmaidens, Chefs or Birth Attendants? A Response to Philip Alston' (1998) 9 *European Journal of International Law* 750–6, at 752–3.

[36] See especially AG Amsterdam and J Bruner, *Minding the Law* (Harvard University Press Cambridge MA 2000) at 110 (where 'the law is awash in storytelling').

Another complicating factor might be that the 'law' on a given matter—for example, the relevant categorization of an action as one of collective self-defence as opposed to one of collective security,[37] the scope of the right of anticipatory and actual self-defence,[38] the emergence of additional exceptions to the prohibitions of force and intervention,[39] the extent of a mandate produced by the Security Council[40]—lacks due precision, so that the law cannot be applied or imposed as if it were some neat jigsaw fit upon a set of recognized facts.[41] After all, the law—or a good share of the law anyway—is about contested scope and meaning, so that the advancement of a legal justification for action is in effect just another occasion for presenting a state's interpretations of the law, that is of sharing its *opinio juris sive necessitatis* with other states. And this very much stands to reason: notwithstanding the proclaimed purpose in its Preamble to 'save succeeding generations from the scourge of war', the *Charter* in fact establishes a framework or routine for distinguishing between lawful and unlawful threats and uses of force that is centred on the fulcrum of the prohibition of force as contained in article 2(4) of the *Charter*.[42]

That routine is not, of course, made fully explicit by the *Charter*, but the idea that the *Charter* is there to be interpreted—indeed, there to be interpreted time and time and time again—is affirmed by (amongst other things) the 'inherent' right of self-defence as declared by article 51: '[i]t does not follow from the character of the right of self-defence—conceived as an inherent, a natural, right—that the States resorting to it possess the legal faculty of remaining the ultimate judges of the justification of their action'.[43] This much is clear, for to allow states to become arbiters in their own cause on the settled or accepted meaning of points of

---

[37] As occurred with the Korean War between June 1950 and July 1953: see O Corten, *The Law against War: The Prohibition on the Use of Force in Contemporary International Law* (Hart Oxford 2010) at 331, and Operation Desert Storm following the adoption of UN Security Council, *Resolution 678* (29 November 1990) UN Doc S/RES/678. See also C Greenwood, 'New World Order or Old? The Invasion of Kuwait and the Rule of Law' (1992) 55 *Modern Law Review* 153–78, at 167–9.

[38] 'Actual' in the sense of against an existing rather than anticipated—or imminent—armed attack: see SD Murphy, 'The Doctrine of Pre-Emptive Self-Defense' (2005) 50 *Villanova Law Review* 699–748.

[39] V Lowe, 'The Principle of Non-Intervention: Use of Force' in C Warbrick and V Lowe (eds), *The United Nations and the Principles of International Law: Essays in Memory of Michael Akehurst* (Routledge London 1994) 66–84.

[40] *International Law and the Use of Force by States* (n 3) 335. This is most recently exemplified by the authorization given by the Security Council in UN Security Council, *Resolution 1973* (17 March 2011) UN Doc S/RES/1973, at para 4.

[41] Including legal facts: see 'Armed Intervention in a Dichotomized World (n 24) 247.

[42] See eg the exercise of treaty interpretation in G Distefano, 'Use of Force' in A Clapham and P Gaeta (eds), *The Oxford Handbook of International Law in Armed Conflict* (OUP Oxford 2014) 545–73.

[43] L Oppenheim, *International Law: A Treatise* (H Lauterpacht ed) (2 vols 7th edn Longmans, Green & Co London 1952) vol 2, at 159.

law would make a shaking mockery of the entire enterprise. 'They have the right to decide in the first instance', Lassa Oppenheim's treatise on international law maintains, 'when there is *periculim in mora*, whether they are in the presence of an armed attack calling for armed resistance'.[44] Any legal justification accounting for the exercise of that right therefore posits the evidence for this decision beyond the 'first instance' of the state, and this, in turn, might involve some appreciation of how the right of self-defence is to be configured within international law. In October 2001, the US elaborated before the Security Council how 'the ongoing threat to the US and its nationals posed by the Al-Qaeda organization have been made possible by the decision of the Taliban regime to allow the parts of Afghanistan that it controls to be used by this organization as a base of operation', but it also went on to explain in the same letter how it was responding to the attacks of 11 September 2001, 'in accordance with the inherent right of individual and collective self-defence'—and that its actions were 'designed to prevent and deter further attacks on the United States'.[45]

And interpretation does not come to an end with the *Charter* or its text, for we are as much immersed in the push or search for meaning when it comes to the iterations of international custom on force and intervention—that is, what the *interpretation* of a previous precedent or aspect of state practice might be, either as an instance of the formation or refinement of the position of international custom,[46] or as 'subsequent practice in the application of the treaty which establishes the agreement of the parties regarding its interpretation'.[47] As the ICJ observed in *Case Concerning Military and Paramilitary Activities in and Against Nicaragua* in June 1986, 'even if a treaty norm and a customary norm relevant to the present dispute were to have exactly the same content, this would not be a reason for the Court to take the view that the operation of the treaty process must necessarily deprive the customary norm of its separate applicability'.[48] And what applies to the law of force

---

[44] *International Law* (n 43). See also H Lauterpacht, *The Function of Law in the International Community* (revised edn OUP Oxford 2011 [1933]) at 187.

[45] 'Letter dated 7 October 2001 from the Permanent Representative of the United States of America to the United Nations Addressed to the President of the Security Council' (7 October 2001) UN Doc S/2001/946.

[46] As per the formulation in art 38(1)(b) of the *Statute of the ICJ* (1945). See also H Thirlway, *The Sources of International Law* (OUP Oxford 2014) at 56–7.

[47] *Vienna Convention on the Law of Treaties* (opened for signature 23 May 1969 entered into force 27 January 1980) art 31(3)(b), which provides that this consideration shall be 'taken into account together with the context' of the treaty for the purposes of the interpretation of the treaty. On 'context', see art 31(2).

[48] *Nicaragua* (n 5) 94 [175]. See also at 95 [177]. The extent of influence of convention on custom is not to be doubted however: in *Nicaragua*, the Court wrote of how the 'present content' of the right of self-defence in international custom 'has been confirmed and influenced by the Charter': at 94 [176]. See also *Continental Shelf (Libya v Malta)* (Judgment) [1985] ICJ Rep 13, at 29–30 [27].

applies even more so to the law on intervention, which is not presented as such in the *Charter*, at least as it applies to or is addressed to states:[49]

To insist that every international problem admits of an 'impartial' legal answer is essentially a dishonest position. All rules of international law are open to interpretation, and as many of the rules are fluid and unclearly stated, the interpretive element is very great. It is not possible always to choose between alternative interpretations purely on grounds of 'legal correctness'. It is necessary on some occasions to examine the political preferences involved in each alternative, and to decide accordingly.[50]

Essentially, this description of the law's 'interpretative element'[51] intimates the premise of an *audience* within international law, or, better, of the existence of an epistemic community involved in that set of interactions.[52] For Emer de Vattel, it is '[h]umanity' that constitutes this audience and 'revolts against a sovereign, who, without necessity or without powerful reasons, lavished the blood of his most faithful subjects, and exposes his people to the calamities of war, when he has it in his power to maintain them in the enjoyment of an honourable and salutary peace',[53] and it is these reasons that also serve the relationship between sovereign and subject ('so long as [the reasons] are only doubted, most men will be persuaded...to fight. Their routine habits of law-abidingness, their fear, their patriotism, their moral investment in the state, all favour that course').[54]

Finally, some attention should be given to the possibility that legal justifications are there as smokescreens for other (unknown) realities, that they serve as no more and no less than 'a mere façade for unfettered political power'.[55] Thus, they cannot instruct us further on what we do not (and may never) know. Be this as it may, the practice of justification for force and intervention has set itself apart from the law on genocide and torture (where, it has been said, 'we are not interest[ed] in explanation or justification'),[56] and it is essential to recall that each justification brings

---

[49] Unlike art 2(4) which is addressed to '[a]ll Members' of the organization, art 2(7) of the *Charter* is famously concerned with the organization *itself*—although the *chapeau* to art 2 does make clear that '[t]he Organization *and its Members*...shall act in accordance with the...Principles' set out in art 2 (emphasis added).

[50] *Development of International Law* (n 10) 9.

[51] In permanent search of its 'interlocutor': TM Franck, 'Humanitarian Intervention' in S Besson and J Tasioulas (eds), *The Philosophy of International Law* (OUP Oxford 2010) 531–48, at 548 ('law is useless, and may even be harmful, if its yardsticks are not wielded by a credible interlocutor').

[52] I Johnstone, 'Treaty Interpretation: The Authority of Interpretive Communities' (1991) 12 *Michigan Journal of International Law* 371–419.

[53] *The Law of Nations* (n 2) bk III, ch III, §24.

[54] M Walzer, *Just and Unjust Wars: A Moral Argument with Historical Illustrations* (4th edn Basic Books New York 2006 [1977]) at 39. On Walzer's 'reason of State' see 'The Triumph of Just War Theory (and the Dangers of Success)' (n 26) 927.

[55] As it is put by Higgins: *Development of International Law* (n 10) 9.

[56] TJ Farer, 'Political and Economic Coercion in Contemporary International Law' (1985) 79 *American Journal of International Law* 405–13.

with it not only a *principle* for action (in other words, whether a given action is either permitted or not permitted as a matter of principle) but also a *framework* of regulation (involving principles such as necessity and proportionality)[57] for governing how that principle is supposed to be applied in practice.

3 The Significance of Legal Justifications

Let us now consider what significance might be attached to the justification itself: what *becomes* of the justification when it has been announced—once a state has put into the public sphere what its legal argumentation is for the action (or actions) it has taken?

For the ICJ, '[i]f a State acts in a way *prima facie* incompatible with a recognized rule'—as was the case with both the prohibitions of force and intervention in the *Nicaragua* case—'but defends its conduct by appealing to exceptions or justifications contained within the rule itself, then whether or not the State's conduct is in fact justifiable on that basis, the significance of that attitude is to confirm rather than weaken the rule'.[58] The Court formed the view that actions that are '*prima facie* incompatible with a recognized rule'—whether concerning the prohibition of force or that of intervention—ultimately serve to strengthen ('to confirm') the rule in question.[59] It is noticeable that, at the outset of this remark, the Court restricts its logic to actions that are unlawful on initial approach ('*prima facie*'), but as it develops its thinking on the matter, it is clear that even if the action in question is indeed unlawful ('whether or not the State's conduct is *in fact* justifiable on that basis')[60] the Court maintains its view that the violated rule has nevertheless been 'confirm[ed] rather than weaken[ed]'.[61]

---

[57] On intervention by consent, to take another example, see the detailed study of L Doswald-Beck, 'The Legal Validity of Military Intervention by Consent' (1985) 56 *British Yearbook of International Law* 189–252.

[58] *Nicaragua* (n 5) 98 [186].

[59] Ibid. Notwithstanding the formulation of 'exceptions or justifications *contained within the rule itself*' (emphasis added), this prompts the question why the language of 'exceptions' or 'justifications' becomes at all necessary if the rule itself makes the relevant specifications. See also O Schachter, 'The Legality of Pro-Democratic Invasion' (1984) 78 *American Journal of International Law* 645–50, at 648.

[60] *Nicaragua* (n 5) 98 [186] (emphasis added).   [61] Ibid.

One can see the attraction of this line of thinking: that a state presents a legal justification for its actions to the outside world suggests that it has made a very particular choice—a decision against—cutting short the scope or general purport of the rule itself in practice, which would emphasize the qualification of the *Charter's* prohibition of force by its reference to the 'territorial integrity' or 'political independence' of any state, 'or in any other manner inconsistent with the Purposes of the United Nations'.[62] Evidently, this approach would constitute a separate and easier burden to that of developing exceptions or justifications to the rule in question— and, yet, it seems to be an approach that states have recoiled from in the main.[63] And the logic that goes for the courtroom does seem to yield significance further afield. Most classically, when Israel launched air strikes against the nuclear reactor based at Osiraq in Iraq in June 1981, its position was cast in the form of a legal justification as against the prohibition of force in the *Charter*, arguing before the Security Council that '[i]n destroying Osiraq, Israel performed an elementary act of self-preservation, both morally and legally. In so doing, Israel was exercising its inherent right of self-defence as understood in general international law and as preserved in Article 51 of the *Charter of the United Nations*'.[64] Setting aside the merits of this position, Israel's *choice* of its argument on this occasion was not to exploit possible shortcomings present *within* the prohibition of force;[65] the entire premise of its position was to argue that force had indeed been used, but that this force was made permissible— permissible in law—on the grounds of Israel's exercise of its right of self-defence.[66] More recently, in the context of a possible intervention against Syria by the US in August 2013, it seemed that President Barack Obama was prepared to argue for the enforcement of the prohibition of chemical weapons as a ground for permissible

---

[62] Article 2(4) of the *Charter*, and in particular view of the purposes of the UN—as set out in arts 1(1)–(4). This is done, eg, in WM Reisman, 'Coercion and Self-Determination: Construing *Charter* Article 2(4)' (1984) 78 *American Journal of International Law* 642–5.

[63] One of the first examples of this approach was in *Corfu Channel Case (United Kingdom v Albania)* (Judgment) [1949] ICJ Rep 4, where the UK had argued before the Court that its mine-sweeping operation of Operation Retail in Albanian territorial waters 'threatened neither the territorial integrity nor the political independence of Albania. Albania suffered thereby neither territorial loss nor any part of its political independence': 'Statement by Sir Eric Beckett (United Kingdom)' *Corfu Channel Case (United Kingdom v Albania)* (ICJ, 12 November 1948) 3 *ICJ Pleadings* 295–6. While this position 'was not specifically considered in the judgment, the Court's condemnation of Operation Retail [was] not in sympathy with it': DJ Harris, *Cases and Materials on International Law* (6th edn Sweet & Maxwell London 2004) at 892.

[64] '2280th Meeting' (11 June 1981) UN Doc S/PV.2280 at 8.

[65] As had been done in A D'Amato, 'Israel's Air Strike upon the Iraqi Nuclear Reactor' (1983) 77 *American Journal of International Law* 584–8, at 585.

[66] As against Iraq's accusation of 'a grave act of aggression committed by Israel against Iraq with far-reaching consequences for international peace and security': 'Letter Dated 8 June 1981 from the Charge d'Affaires of the Permanent Mission of Iraq to the United Nations Addressed to the President of the Security Council' (8 June 1981) UN Doc S/14509 at 2.

force in international law, rather than arguing that such force would not implicate the *Charter*'s prohibition of force.[67]

The purpose of this exercise, according to the Court, is therefore to detect the relevant legal justification advanced by a state, whether it is in the form of an invocation or emendation of an existing right (such as the right of self-defence) in international law or whether its platform is '[r]eliance by a State on a novel right or an unprecedented exception' which, the Court said, 'might, if shared in principle by other States, tend towards a modification of customary international law'.[68] The Court is eager to learn of the life of the legal justification once advanced—how, as a manifestation of *opinio juris sive necessitatis*, it finds traction if at all in the responses of other states, for '[e]ither the States taking such action or other States in a position to react to it, must have behaved so that their conduct is "evidence of a belief that this practice is rendered obligatory by the existence of a rule of law requiring it. The need for such a belief, that is, the existence of a subjective element, is implicit in the very notion of *opinio juris sive necessitatis*".'[69]

To be clear, that distinctions must be made between justifications posited on the 'political' and the 'legal' level was very much encouraged by the Court in its *Nicaragua* judgment.[70] The Court reflected there on how '[t]he United States authorities' had from time to time 'clearly stated their grounds for intervening in the affairs of a foreign State for reasons connected with, for example, the domestic policies of that country, its ideology, the level of its armaments, or the direction of its foreign policy'—but it did so in order to make the point that these were only 'statements of international policy, and not an assertion of rules of existing international law'.[71] By these words, the Court was therefore not only conveying its *own* innate sense of this distinction for analysing state practice—some pronouncements would go toward *opinio juris sive necessitatis*, others would not—but it suggested that the US[72] and Nicaragua[73] had done so as well in their practice. And it continued forward with the Vattelian notion that it had expressed earlier in the same judgment that at the core of the concerns of the Court was the issue of the legal justification invoked by the US and *not* any motive (or set of motives) for action:

In the Court's view...if Nicaragua has been giving support to the armed opposition in El Salvador, and if this constitutes an armed attack on El Salvador and the other appropriate conditions [for collective self-defence] are met, collective self-defence could be

---

[67] As would appear to have been argued in HH Koh, 'Syria and the Law of Humanitarian Intervention (Part II: International Law and the Way Forward)' on *Just Security* (2 October 2013) <http://justsecurity.org/1506/koh-syria-part2/> [accessed 28 February 2016].

[68] *Nicaragua* (n 5) 109 [207].

[69] Ibid, quoting *North Sea Continental Shelf Cases (Federal Republic of Germany v Denmark and Netherlands)* (Judgment) [1969] ICJ Rep 3, at 44 [77], although the formulation of 'practice that is rendered obligatory by the existence of a rule requiring it' does not sit happily in the same paragraph that suggests the possibility of 'a novel right or an unprecedented exception'.

[70] *Nicaragua* (n 5) 109 [208].   [71] Ibid 109 [207].   [72] Ibid 109 [208].   [73] Ibid.

legally invoked by the United States, even though there may be the possibility of an additional motive, one perhaps even more decisive for the United States, drawn from the political orientation of the present Nicaraguan Government. The existence of an additional motive, other than that officially proclaimed by the United States, could not deprive the latter of its right to resort to collective self-defence.[74]

It is for this reason that the Court emphasized throughout its judgment in *Nicaragua* that the justification of a state (or group of states) for force or intervention had to be consciously determined or established; it could not be taken for granted or conjured without more from thin air. The Court further remarked at one point that it does not possesses the 'authority' to 'ascribe to States legal views which they do not themselves advance'.[75] To do so would involve the Court in an intensely speculative (and quite possibly counter-productive) exercise of hypothesizing through the vast array of legal positions and strategies open to any state appearing before it,[76] which would invariably lead the Court into an ethical compromise regarding *its* task as compared to the responsibilities of all parties to whom it gives audience. It is important, therefore, to be clear on what the actual (rather than assumed) legal justification for force is, and this framework for analysis carries considerable appeal even in the absence of litigation. For example, Operation Iraqi Freedom was argued by the US and the United Kingdom (UK) (amongst others) in terms of the authorization of the Security Council under the *Charter*, and not in terms of the right of individual or collective self-defence as is so commonly assumed. The lawfulness of that intervention must therefore proceed—whether it succeeds or fails—on that basis, on that articulated prospectus.[77]

---

[74] Ibid 71 [127]. The reference to Vattel is to *The Law of Nations* (n 2) bk III, ch III, §25 (emphasis in original):

> Force is a wretched and melancholy expedient against those who spurn at justice, and refuse to listen to the remonstrances of reason: but, in short, it becomes necessary to adopt that mode, when every other proves ineffectual. It is only in extremities that a just and wise nation, or a good prince, has recourse to it... The reasons which may determine him to take such a step are of two classes. Those of the one class show that he has a right to make war,—that he has just grounds for undertaking it:—these are called *justificatory reasons*. The others, founded on fitness and utility, determine whether it be expedient for the sovereign to undertake a war:—these are called *motives*.

For Vattel, 'it is necessary that proper and commendable motives should concur with the justificatory reasons, to induce a determination to embark in a war'—though, he wrote, proper motives 'relate to prudence' whereas 'the justificatory reasons come under the head of justice': at bk III, ch III, §29.

[75] *Nicaragua* (n 5) 109 [207]. Hence, '[t]he significance for the Court of cases of State conduct prima facie inconsistent with the principle of non-intervention lies in the nature of the ground offered as justification': at 108 [207].

[76] Which the Court then—perhaps with a hidden sense of irony—proceeded to do in view of the predicament that had been delivered by the Court by the non-participation of the US in the merits phase of proceedings: ibid 106 [201]. See also at 117–18 [226].

[77] As I have argued elsewhere: see 'Arguments of Mass Confusion' (n 21).

As far as the Court's overall analysis in the *Nicaragua* case is concerned, there would seem to be two further points calling out for specific attention in respect of the making of legal justifications. The first is the relationship between the legal justification and any admission of facts occurring on the ground, for it might seem that the former entails or concedes the latter. In the *Nicaragua* case, the Court intimated that the legal justification 'itself'—that is, made on its own terms and without any form of qualification—can function as an admission of certain facts by a state, but it urged caution in too readily concluding an 'implicit overall admission' from that state as to what the full facts were. A legal justification for resort to force cannot therefore be taken as an acceptance of all of the allegations of fact levelled against a state,[78] presumably because the 'facts' are often not confined to the basic matter of the *initiation* of that force:[79] as far as the claim of self-defence is concerned, the facts remain essential for establishing both the 'necessity' of that defence and its *proportionality*. It therefore is appropriate for the Court to have concluded that 'the right of self-defence thus does not make possible a firm and complete definition of admitted facts'.[80]

The second point relates to the actual timing of the legal justification that is given. At what point does the 'invocation'[81] of a right under the *jus ad bellum* occur—at the time the justification is first made or first made public, or when it is made before the ICJ? What if proceedings before the Court never come to pass? In its judgment in *Case Concerning Oil Platforms* of November 2003, the Court focused on the 'contention' of the US *at the time* that it had used forced against the Reshadat as well as Salman and Nasr oil platforms in the Persian Gulf in October 1987 and then again in April 1988. In response to what it regarded as armed attacks against its targets (the US-flagged *Sea Isle City* and the USS *Samuel B Roberts*), the US 'gave notice of its action to the Security Council under Article 51 of the *Charter*'.[82] The Court then reflected on the path of this justification since given to the Security Council in October 1987 and April 1988, observing that the US 'has continued to maintain that it was justified in acting as it did in exercise of the right of self-defence'.[83] This assessment suggests that the Security Council forms one possible 'legal level' for justifications to be made by states, but that these can in fact change over time and in view of the prevailing context. For example,

---

[78] For this aspect of Nicaragua's claim, see *Nicaragua* (n 5) 18–19 [15] and 45 [75].

[79] Hence the Court's commitment to establishing the facts on the evidence before it: ibid at 48 [80].

[80] Ibid 45 [74].   [81] Ibid.

[82] Ibid 181 [37]. See also 'Letter Dated 19 October 1987 from the Permanent Representative of the United States of America to the United Nations Addressed to the President of the Security Council' (19 October 1987) UN Doc S/19219 and 'Letter Dated 18 April 1988 from the Acting Permanent Representative of the United States of America to the United Nations Addressed to the President of the Security Council' (18 April 1988) UN Doc S/19791.

[83] *Oil Platforms (Islamic Republic of Iran v United States of America)* (Judgment) [2003] ICJ Rep 161, at 181 [37].

justifications may undergo change because of the jurisdictional basis of any ensuing contentious proceedings before the Court,[84] or because a state has sought to
modify the substance of its original justification (or justifications) pleaded in public
or before the Court on account of shifting realities on the ground.[85] Importantly, in
the *Nicaragua* case, the Court concluded that 'for the purpose of enquiry into the
customary law position, the absence of a report [to the Security Council] may be
one of the factors indicating whether the state in question was itself convinced that
it was acting in self-defence',[86] indicating that this factor is relevant evidence in the
testing of justifications of self-defence.[87]

4 Assumptions for Force and Intervention

We shall now turn to some of the assumptions or background premises that belie
the legal regulation of force and intervention, at least as far as these have been
made more apparent from the justifications states have offered for their actions.
The first assumption concerns the concept of force itself, in other words what kind
of actions have brought justifications under the *jus ad bellum* into play?[88] A second
assumption arises in that the *jus ad bellum*, at times floated as a component of the
laws of war, in fact stands to be counted as part of the laws of peace: its position in

---

[84] The *Oil Platforms Case* proceeded on the basis of the *Treaty of Amity, Economic Relations and Consular Rights of August* (1955) between the US and Iran, which provided in art XX para 1(d) that it 'shall not preclude the applications of measures...necessary to fulfill the obligations of a High Contracting Party for the maintenance or restoration of international peace and security, or necessary to protect its essential security interests'—which is why, before the Court, the US argued its cases on the basis of this provision as well as the fact that its actions 'were not wrongful since they were necessary and appropriate actions in self-defence': *Oil Platforms* (n 83) 181 [37].

[85] The reason why I have argued elsewhere for provisional assessment.

[86] *Oil Platforms* (n 83) 105 [200].

[87] Hence Gray's observation of the tendency to 'over-report claims to individual self-defence, if anything' since the *Nicaragua* case: *International Law and the Use of Force* (n 20) 123.

[88] Outside the remit of these enquiries is, of course, the comparative study of force and intervention since the latter concept retains a broader sweep (covering as it does 'armed intervention and all
other forms of interference or attempted threats against the personality of the state or against its political, economic and cultural elements', as per UN General Assembly, 'Declaration on the Principles
of International Law concerning Friendly Relations and Co-Operation among States in accordance
with the Charter of the United Nations' GA Res 2625 (XXV) (24 October 1970) UN Doc A/RES/25/
2625). See DW Bowett, 'Economic Coercion and Reprisals by States' (1972) 13 *Virginia Journal of
International Law* 1–12, at 2.

the overall structure of international law suggests that, in matter of fact, its application predates the laws of war.[89] Finally, we shall turn to the *consequences* of legal justifications made in view of the fact that the lion's share of these are not (and do not appear) before the ICJ: what use are justifications if they are not subject to judicial determination? What is to be made of justifications that succeed and fail in their ambitions—and how, if at all, is this to be decided?

In the advisory opinion of the ICJ in *Legal Consequences of the Construction of a Wall in the Occupied Palestinian Territory* delivered in July 2004, the Court considered the lawfulness of 'the wall being built by Israel, the occupying Power, in the Occupied Palestinian Territory, including in and around East Jerusalem'—the terms put to it in the form of a request for an opinion from the General Assembly in December 2003.[90] Work on the wall, or 'complex construction',[91] had commenced following a decision of the Government of Israel to do so in April 2002.[92] In the course of its advisory opinion, the Court drew attention to Israel's defence of its construction as 'consistent with Article 51 of the *Charter of the United Nations*, its inherent right of self-defence and Security Council *Resolutions 1368 (2001)* and *1373 (2001)*'.[93] Furthermore, in October 2003, Israel's Permanent Representative to the UN had informed the General Assembly that the 'security fence':

has proven itself to be one of the most effective non-violent methods for preventing terrorism in the heart of civilian areas. The fence is a measure wholly consistent with the right of States to self-defence enshrined in Article 51 of the *Charter*. International law and Security Council resolutions, including *Resolutions 1368 (2001)* and *1373 (2001)*, have clearly recognized the right of States to use force in self-defence against terrorist attacks, and therefore surely recognize the right to use non-forcible measures to that end.[94]

The Court made reference to these positions—to this apparent justification—for the wall on behalf of Israel, only to conclude that article 51 (and presumably the right of self-defence more generally) 'has no relevance in this case'.[95] Its reasoning was grounded in the *lex specialis* of the right of self-defence (that article 51

---

[89] As appears to be the approach, eg, of A Roberts and R Guelff (eds), *Documents on the Laws of War* (3rd edn OUP Oxford 2000) at 1.

[90] UN General Assembly, 'Illegal Israeli Actions in Occupied East Jerusalem and the Rest of the Occupied Palestinian Territory' GA Res ES-10/14 (12 December 2003) UN Doc A/RES/ES-10/14; *Legal Consequences of the Construction of a Wall in the Occupied Palestinian Territory* (Advisory Opinion) [2004] ICJ Rep 136.

[91] As per the Court: *Wall Opinion* (n 90) 164 [67]. For further details of this construction, see at 170 [82].

[92] Details of this history are drawn from the judgment of the Supreme Court of Israel in *Beit Sourik Village Council v Israel* (High Court of Justice, Case No 2056/04, 30 June 2004) at 3 [3].

[93] At least as appearing in Annex I to the Report of the Secretary-General, recited by the Court: *Wall Opinion* (n 90) 194 [138].

[94] 'Emergency Special Session' (20 October 2003) UN Doc A/ES-10/PV.21, at 6. The Court adverted in part to this statement: *Wall Opinion* (n 90) 194 [138].

[95] *Wall Opinion* (n 90) 194 [139].

recognizes 'the existence of an inherent right of self-defence in the case of armed attack by one State against another State'),[96] but the Court also made mention of the fact that Israel regarded 'the threat which it regards as justifying the construction of the wall originates *within*, and not outside, that territory'.[97] In other words, according to the Court, there had been an inappropriate choice of legal provision as to the correct metric for measuring the lawfulness of the wall: this stood to be governed by the regime of belligerent occupation under the *jus in bello* rather than the right of self-defence under the *jus ad bellum* ('[t]he situation is thus different,' concluded the Court, 'from that contemplated by Security Council *Resolutions 1368 (2001)* and *1373 (2001)*, and therefore Israel could not in any event invoke these resolutions in support of its claim to be exercising a right of self-defence').[98]

What seemed to elide the Court on this occasion was that the measure in question—a 'non-violent' method of state action[99]—had been framed in terms of the right of self-defence, which (as we have seen) has been devised for the justification of force as understood under the *Charter*. The right of self-defence had been pleaded by Israel[100] in circumstances that would not ordinarily engage the prohibition of and framework for force contained in the *Charter*,[101] a matter picked up by Judge Rosalyn Higgins in her separate opinion where she remained 'unconvinced' that 'non-forcible measures (such as the building of a wall) fall within self-defence under article 51 of the *Charter* as that provision is normally understood'.[102] This was not an instance of self-defence 'properly so called' in her view.[103] Indeed, it seems apposite to remark at this point that, in one of the most classic iterations made of the right of self-defence in international law, the entire purpose of demonstrating the 'necessity' of self-defence is that it will 'authorize' a self-defending state 'to enter the territories' of the state against which it is seeking to defend itself.[104]

---

[96] *Wall Opinion* (n 90). For a detailed engagement of this position, see at 230 (Separate Opinion of Judge Kooijmans). See also SD Murphy, 'Self-Defense and the Israeli *Wall* Advisory Opinion: An *Ipse Dixit* from the ICJ?' (2005) 99 *American Journal of International Law* 62–76.

[97] *Wall Opinion* (n 90) 194 [139] (emphasis added).   [98] Ibid.

[99] Ibid. See, however, M Kearney, 'The Violence of Construction: Israel's Wall and International Law' on *The Electronic Intifada* (4 November 2003) <http://electronicintifada.net/content/violence-construction-israels-wall-and-international-law/4862> [accessed 28 February 2016].

[100] See 'Self-Defense and the Israeli *Wall* Advisory Opinion' (n 96) 63.

[101] Though Bowett suggests examples of 'economic measures' taken in self-defence: see 'Economic Coercion and Reprisals by States' (n 88) 7–8.

[102] *Wall Opinion* (n 90) 215–16 [35]. Cf 241–3 [4]–[6] and 244 [9] (Judge Buergenthal) and 215–16 [33]–[35] (Judge Higgins).

[103] Ibid 216 [35].

[104] As per the correspondence of US Secretary of State Daniel Webster of 24 April 1841, reproduced at The Avalon Project, Yale Law School, 'British–American Diplomacy: The Caroline Case' <http://avalon.law.yale.edu/19th_century/br-1842d.asp> [accessed 28 February 2016]. See further 'Self-Defense and the Israel *Wall* Advisory Opinion' (n 96) at 64–5 and 69.

There is, thus, a purity of meaning—a linguistic or normative integrity—that is at stake here,[105] and it is an integrity that is being defended against chance or erroneous interpretations of the right of self-defence that occur in the practice of states. The charged rhetoric and metaphorical possibilities of the right of self-defence aside,[106] the essential *meaning* of this right must surely emerge from *how* the right has been framed in the overall design of the *Charter*, as much as it derives from the accretion of precedent—from how it is that states have interacted and not interacted with this right in their practices. To be sure, the logic behind Israel's invocation of its right of self-defence as discussed here extends to that at work at the time the prohibition of force was conceived,[107] where Brazil famously fronted an effort to bring *economic* force within the strictures of the *Charter*.[108] For his part, in his study on *Self-Defense in International Law* published in 1958, Derek Bowett was not averse to accepting this latter proposition 'as a matter of fixed principle',[109] but, in the end, concluded that this was not represented within the *lex lata* of that time since 'there is no duty of non-intervention which, as a parallel to the duty of non-intervention relating to political independence or territorial integrity, generally prohibits action by [S]tates detrimental to the economy of another state'[110]—and, furthermore, that '[t]he context in which the right of self-defence has the most significance is that of force, and that context is not normally relevant to the defence of economic interests'.[111]

All of this said, it is instructive that in the first edition of the second volume of his treatise on international law—dealing with war and neutrality—Lassa Oppenheim itemized pacific blockades alongside retorsion, (armed) reprisals and intervention as '[c]ompulsive means of settlement of differences [involving] measures containing a certain amount of compulsion taken by a state for the purpose of making another State consent to such settlement of a difference as is required by

---

[105] Or, as put by Martti Koskenniemi, 'a shared normative code of meaning': 'The Place of Law in Collective Security' (n 29) 468. See also the notion of 'international normative expectations' as developed by CA Morgan, 'The Shooting of Korean Air Lines Flight 007: Responses to Unauthorized Aerial Incursions' in *International Incidents: The Law that Counts in World Politics* (n 23) 202–37 at 210.

[106] If this is indeed at all possible: see below n 177 and accompanying text. See also *Protocol Additional to the Geneva Conventions of 12 August 1949, and relating to the Protection of Victims of International Armed Conflicts* (adopted 8 June 1977 entered into force 7 December 1978) 1125 UNTS 3 art 54(5) ('*Additional Protocol I*').

[107] See DW Bowett, *Self-Defense in International Law* (Manchester University Press Manchester 1958) at 24.

[108] *Documents of the United Nations Conference on International Organization* (22 vols United Nations London 1945) vol 6, at 339–40. And, *prima facie*, there might be some merit to this given that the 'force' of article 2(4) is not qualified by the adjective of 'armed' as it is in the preamble to the *Charter* ('to ensure by the acceptance of principles and the institution of methods, that armed force shall not be used, save in the common interest') as well as arts 41 and 46. See also *Development of International Law* (n 10) 176–7.

[109] *Self-Defense in International Law* (n 107) 24, 107, and 111.

[110] Ibid 107. Accordingly, 'in the absence of conduct of a delictual character, there can be no violation of a state's legal rights which calls for the exercise of self-defence'.

[111] Ibid 109–10.

the former'.[112] Oppenheim recorded that, before the nineteenth century, the concept of blockade had been known to international law only 'as a measure between belligerents in time of war',[113] but that it was in the second quarter of the nineteenth century—with the blockade instituted in 1827 by Great Britain, France, and Russia against Turkey along the coast of Greece—that the notion of a pacific blockade came into its own, though he argued that 'all cases of pacific blockade are either cases of intervention or of reprisals'.[114]

Be this as it may, the quintessential aspect of the pacific blockade appears to have been that it constituted 'a violation of the territorial supremacy of the blockaded State';[115] more specifically, a pacific blockade entailed 'the seizure and sequestration of vessels' of those of the blockaded state 'for attempting to break [the] pacific blockade'.[116] Viewed in light of these characteristics, but also from the modern position of the *Charter*, it can be appreciated that force has been an inchoate or latent element of this enterprise—and that it is the *threat* of force that came to define the proposition in issue.[117] This perhaps explains why we find that Chapter VII of the *Charter* distinguishes between 'measures not involving the use of armed force [that] are to be employed to give effect to [the] decisions' of the Security Council[118] from 'action by air, sea, or land forces as may be necessary to maintain or restore international peace and security' should these earlier measures prove 'inadequate'.[119] It is in this latter context—in other words, measures beyond those 'not involving the use of armed force'—that Chapter VII mentions 'demonstrations, blockade, and other operations by air, sea, or land forces of Members of the United Nations'.[120] Indeed, President John F Kennedy found it fitting to provide a legal justification for the maritime interdiction he ordered against Cuba in October 1962, which combined an overall *threat* with particular *uses* of force. '[T]he blunt fact of the quarantine', wrote Abram Chayes, was that it *did* involve 'the use of naval force to interfere with shipping on the high seas',[121] but that, *in ultimo*, it was

---

[112] *International Law* (n 43) vol 2, 132 (and where 'the application of retorsion is confined to political, and that of reprisal to legal differences').

[113] Ibid 144. This might then be termed belligerent blockade as opposed to pacific blockade as discussed in AE Hogan, *Pacific Blockade* (Clarendon Press Oxford 1908).

[114] Ibid 145. See also J Westlake, 'Pacific Blockade' (1909) 25 *Law Quarterly Review* 13–23, at 16; SC Neff, *War and the Law of Nations: A General History* (CUP Cambridge 2005) at 234. For Brownlie, the pacific blockade 'was merely a special form of reprisal': *International Law and the Use of Force by States* (n 3) 223.

[115] *International Law* (n 43) vol 2, 148. See further the assessment of ND White, *The Cuban Embargo under International Law: El Bloqueo* (Routledge London 2015) at 7 and 140.

[116] Ibid 146 (as opposed to confiscation before a prize court, as applicable in belligerent blockages: *War and the Law of Nations* (n 114) 234).

[117] And *threats* of force outlawed as much as *uses* of force: *UN Charter* art 2(4).

[118] Ibid art 41.   [119] Ibid art 42.

[120] Ibid. See also UN Security Council, *Resolution 665* (25 August 1990) UN Doc S/RES/665, at para 1, and a recent instance of blockade under the authorization of the Security Council. See also Y Dinstein, *War, Aggression and Self-Defence* (5th edn CUP Cambridge 2011) at 299.

[121] A Chayes, 'Law and the Quarantine in Cuba' (1963) 41 *Foreign Affairs* 550–7.

in the *Inter-American Treaty of Reciprocal Assistance* (1947) that the justification for the action of the US came to be rooted.[122]

The experience of the Cuban Missile Crisis had suggested to some that the more appropriate and favourable 'fragment' of international law to be applied here was the laws of war—but, for this to have become active, the US would have had to have ensured the occurrence of 'declared war or of any other armed conflict' with Cuba.[123] In a similar vein, Yoram Dinstein has invited us to regard the Israeli action against Osiraq in June 1981 as part of 'the war between Iraq and Israel which started in 1948',[124] even though it was Israel's position—and, as we have discovered from the jurisprudence of the ICJ, it is Israel's position that matters most for defining any ensuing analysis[125]—that the action was qualified by reference to the *jus ad bellum* and not the *jus in bello*.[126] And it is for this reason that the ICJ in the *Wall Opinion* emphasized the importance of the 'applicable' international law—which it proceeded to examine on the basis of the right of self-defence as well as the state of necessity (amongst other things).[127] It was not convinced that 'the specific course Israel has chosen for the wall was necessary to attain its security objectives',[128] but, in its reckoning, it cast its eye on another fragment of international law—namely that which applies to 'the territory occupied by Israel' in the form of the international law of belligerent occupation.[129]

It is important to appreciate how each framework introduces separate terms of analysis and engagement: the *jus ad bellum* would require Israel in June 1981 to redeem each of the argumentative and evidential burdens for the right of self-defence in customary international law, including the requirement of 'imminence' given that Israel had sought to plead its right of *anticipatory* self-defence as against Iraq.[130] Under the *jus in bello*, however, the Osiraq nuclear reactor would count as a military objective and therefore a lawful target if it is one of 'those objects which by their nature, location, purpose or use make an effective contribution to military action and whose total or partial destruction, capture or neutralization, in the circumstances ruling at the time, offers a definite military advantage'.[131] To take another example: a state keen to deliver humanitarian assistance in the event of a non-international armed conflict might consider invoking the right of

---

[122] As opposed to making a claim under the right of self-defence—as explained in A Chayes, *The Cuban Missile Crisis: International Crises and the Role of Law* (OUP Oxford 1974). See also JS Campbell, 'The Cuban Crisis and the UN *Charter*: An Analysis of the United States Position' (1963) 14 *Stanford Law Review* 160–77, at 165.

[123] As per *Geneva Conventions* (opened for signature 12 August 1949 entered into force 21 Ocotber 1950) 75 UNTS 31 common art 2; 'Law and the Quarantine in Cuba' (n 121) 552, see also at 554.

[124] *War, Aggression and Self-Defence* (n 120) 49.   [125] *Wall Opinion* (n 90) 194 [139].

[126] Ibid.   [127] Ibid 195 [142].   [128] Ibid 193 [137].

[129] Ibid—presumably why the Court takes as its yardstick 'the requirements of national security *or public order*': ibid (emphasis added).

[130] Ibid.   [131] As per *Additional Protocol I* (n 106) art 52(2).

humanitarian intervention under the *jus ad bellum*, but to do this it would be faced with demonstrating that such a right had been 'shared in principle by other States' from previous practice.[132] This could be balanced against the arrangements of the *jus in bello* where

[i]f the civilian population is suffering undue hardship owing to a lack of the supplies essential for its survival, such as foodstuffs and medical supplies, relief actions for the civilian population which are of an exclusively humanitarian and impartial nature and which are conducted without any adverse distinction shall be undertaken *subject to the consent of the High Contracting Party concerned*.[133]

It therefore can make a great deal of difference as to which *framework* is adopted for argumentation and for analysis—whether this takes its cue from the law of peace, or whether states are *still* operating within the laws of war, including where they have not formally ended their hostilities by way of a treaty of peace. It is for this reason that relations between North and South Korea are still referred back to the *Panmunjom Agreement* of July 1953 which, as an armistice, did 'not produce peace in the full meaning of the term'.[134] If this assessment is correct, technically these two states remain within the framework of the laws of war—including the arrangements for armistices under the *Hague Regulations* of October 1907 ('[a]ny serious violation of the armistice by one of the parties gives the other party the right of denouncing it, and even, in cases of urgency, of recommencing hostilities immediately').[135] As will be appreciated, this sets an altogether separate benchmark to what is provided for under the *jus ad bellum*, and it is relevant to note that Operation Iraqi Freedom of March 2003 was actually argued on that latter prospectus when, on one legal reading of events, it was framed by a series of alleged violations committed by Iraq of the 'ceasefire resolution' of *Resolution 687* adopted by the Security Council in April 1991.[136]

Evidently, as has been pointed out already, the destination of legal justifications for force or for intervention might not ultimately be the ICJ, for this, as we know

---

[132] *Nicaragua* (n 5) 109 [207], assuming, of course, that the provision of humanitarian assistance comes with a forcible component and falls within the scope of the right as defined in international law: see at 124–5 [242]. In the alternative, the Security Council could authorize the 'use' of 'all necessary means to establish as soon as possible a secure environment for humanitarian relief operations' as it did in Somalia: *Resolution 794* (3 December 1992) UN Doc S/RES/794, at para 10.

[133] *Protocol Additional to the Geneva Conventions of 12 August 1949, and relating to the Protection of Victims of Non-International Armed Conflicts* (adopted 8 June 1977 entered into force 7 December 1978) 1125 UNTS 609 art 18(2) (emphasis added). See also J-M Henckaerts and L Doswald-Beck, *Customary International Humanitarian Law* (2 vols CUP Cambridge 2005) vol 1, 193–200 ('Rule 55').

[134] *War, Aggression and Self-Defence* (n 120) 43; see, generally, the *Armistice Agreement for the Restoration of the Korean State* (entry into force 27 July 1953). For Baxter an armistice 'creates a *de facto* state of peace': RR Baxter, 'The Legal Consequences of the Unlawful Use of Force under the Charter' (1968) 62 *Proceedings American Society of International Law* 68–75, at 74.

[135] *Hague Regulations respecting the Laws and Customs of War on Land No IV* (signed 18 October 1907 entered into force 26 January 1910) 205 Con TS 277, art 40.

[136] See C Gray, 'After the Ceasefire: Iraq, the Security Council and the Use of Force' (1994) 65 *British Yearbook of International Law* 135–74.

too well, decides on a bare fraction of the instances of state action.[137] Nevertheless, it would be a mistake to think that justifications for force and intervention expire the moment they are made; that they have no normative life beyond that moment or outside the ICJ. Thomas M Franck, for example, has turned our attention to the political organs of the UN—the Security Council, the General Assembly—in such circumstances as 'decision-makers' of claims or justifications made:

Pronouncing on the validity of claims advanced in mitigation of an unlawful but justifiable recourse to force is the task of these decision-makers. Some of this fact-and-context-specific calibration goes on in international tribunals, but most of it occurs in the political organs of the UN system, which constitutes something approximating a global jury; assessing the facts of a crisis, the motives of those reacting to the crises, and the *bona fides* of the pleas of extreme necessity. This jurying goes on not only in instances of humanitarian intervention but whenever there is a confrontation between the strict, literal text of the *Charter* and a plea of justice and extenuating moral necessity.[138]

This idea of the Security Council and General Assembly coming together as jury or as 'judges' has been contemplated before,[139] but the truth of the matter is that in addition to acting as bodies corporate as per their responsibilities under the *Charter*,[140] they also provide important arenas for states to share or make their legal positions known. And it is these verdicts coming forward from states—in something, too, 'approximating a global jury'[141]—that we are not only able to harness some sense of whether a particular force or intervention has been lawful or unlawful or whether some 'modification' has come of age for international law.

5 Purposes for Force and Intervention

The final section is devoted to the purpose of force and intervention, and the place of coercion within the international system more generally.[142] The rules as devised

---

[137] And even though this position is changing: 'The Use and Abuse of the International Court of Justice' (n 15).

[138] TM Franck, *Recourse to Force: State Action against Threats and Armed Attacks* (CUP Cambridge 2002) at 186.

[139] 'The Legal Consequences of the Unlawful Use of Force under the *Charter*' (n 134) 70.

[140] UN Security Council, *Resolution 248* (24 March 1968) UN Doc S/RES/248 on Jordan; UN General Assembly, *Resolution 1005 (ES-II)* (9 November 1956) UN Doc A/RES/1005(ES-II) on Hungary. Often, too, these political organs may be estopped from action due to exercise of the veto (eg, in relation to the US regarding Grenada in 1983).

[141] See also *The Function of Law in the International Community* (n 44) 188.

[142] For it might be that it is *coercion* that is the defining *specie* for analysis as against cooperative means of state interaction—rather than coercion distinguishing intervention (from the use of

and as set out here evidently reflect their own mechanics and functionality, but they do not seem capable of producing any deeper sense or set of introspections or critical enquiries on whether the rules are working to target or whether they are, as a matter of fact, exceeding ambitions: '[f]ar from enabling a more secure global environment, the knowledge produced by international lawyers about disorder and chaos contributes to the creation of a context in which oppressive military and economic actions in the name of the Security Council'—indeed, one can also add those taken outwith the *name* of the Security Council—'are rendered both plausible and possible'.[143] That knowledge somehow appears incapable of facilitating or informing this broader raft of investigations;[144] with this knowledge, we are scarcely found asking what good have force and intervention done over the decades of the *Charter*—what good, in the end, have force and intervention been *for*?[145]

For Vattel, war could assume one of two forms: either it could be defensive in character ('[h]e who takes up arms to repel the attack of an enemy, carries on a defensive war'),[146] or, '[h]e who is foremost in taking up arms, and attacks a nation that lived in peace with him, wages offensive war'.[147] Within this framework

[t]he object of a defensive war is very simple; it is no other than self defence: in that of offensive war, there is as great a variety as in the multifarious concerns of nations; but, in general, it relates either to the prosecution of some rights, or to safety. We attack a nation with a view either to obtain something to which we lay claim, to punish her for an injury she has done to us, or to prevent one which she is preparing to do, and thus avert a danger with which she seems to threaten us.[148]

Vattel's was thus an exercise in exposition, undertaken 'to indicate, in general, the various objects for which a nation takes up arms'.[149] That a war was offensive as opposed to defensive in kind would not, however, affect its lawfulness *ab initio* for Vattel was to write later in the same treatise that '[i]n order to estimate the justice of an offensive war, the nature of the subject for which a nation takes up arms must

---

force) in the *Nicaragua* case. On coercion, see also 'Friendly Relations Declaration' (n 88); 'Political and Economic Coercion in Contemporary International Law' (n 56) 406. See also *Development of International Law* (n 10) 169 especially at 178. On the concept of 'pressure' within the law of treaties, see I Sinclair, *The Vienna Convention on the Law of Treaties* (2nd edn Manchester University Press Manchester 1984) at 178.

[143] A Orford, 'The Politics of Collective Security' (1996) 17 *Michigan Journal of International Law* 373–409, at 376.

[144] For it is so enamoured of the 'crisis mode' of doing international law as discussed in H Charlesworth, 'International Law: A Discipline of Crisis' (2002) 65 *Modern Law Review* 377–92, at 377. See also *International Incidents* (n 23).

[145] See A Orford, 'Locating the International: Military and Monetary Interventions after the Cold War' (1997) 38 *Harvard International Law Journal* 443–85.

[146] *The Law of Nations* (n 2) bk III, ch I, §5—there '[t]o defend ourselves, or to protect ourselves from injury, by repelling unjust violence': at bk III, ch I, §28; or '[d]efensive war is just when made against an unjust aggressor': at bk III, ch I, §35.

[147] Ibid bk III, ch I, §5.   [148] Ibid.   [149] Ibid.

first be considered'.[150] The justice of offensive war was hence entirely possible in this worldview, though Vattel insisted that

[w]e should be thoroughly assured of our right before we proceed to assert it in so dreadful a manner. If, therefore, the question relates to a thing which is evidently just, as the recovery of our property, the assertion of a clear and incontestable right, or the attainment of satisfaction for a manifest injury,—and if we cannot obtain justice otherwise than by force or arms,—offensive war becomes lawful.[151]

The opportunities for war thus announced were decidedly more expansive and tolerant than those which exist (for force and for intervention) at present, especially if we consider Vattel's thesis that to 'deduce the just and lawful object of every war'— note, here, *every* war—there must be demonstration of that object 'to avenge or to prevent injury'.[152] And this Vattel went on to link to something he called '[t]he right to security',[153] or the 'care' or 'right' of 'self-preservation', a right that was 'nothing more than a *moral power of acting*, that is, the power of doing what is morally possible,—what is proper and comfortable to our duties'.[154] According to Vattel, such an overarching right produced at ground level the right of resistance,[155] the right of obtaining reparation,[156] and, finally, the right of punishing.[157]

The plenary significance accorded to war within the discipline of international law did not arrive with Vattel, however. Hugo Grotius had earlier advised us to consider war 'in a two-fold light', either (as he wrote) 'as a reparation for injuries, or as a punishment'.[158] Before that, Gentili formed the view that 'it has been shown that it is just to avenge wrongs, to punish the guilty, and to maintain one's rights'.[159]

---

[150] *The Law of Nations* (n 2) bk III, ch III, §37. Differences of procedure were nevertheless contemplated, for '[h]e who is attacked and only wages defensive war, needs not to make any hostile declaration': at bk III, ch I, §57. But see at bk III, ch I, §58 (on the possibility of 'omitting' the declaration in defensive wars).

[151] Ibid bk III, ch I, §37. See further N Maurer, *The Empire Trap: The Rise and Fall of US Intervention to Protect American Property Overseas, 1893–2013* (Princeton University Press Princeton 2013).

[152] Ibid bk III, ch I, §28. And 'to avenge', he wrote, is 'to prosecute the reparation of an injury, if it be of a nature to be repaired,—or, if the evil be irreparable, to obtain a just satisfaction,—and also to punish the offender, if requisite, with a view to providing for our future safety': at bk III, ch I, §28.

[153] Ibid bk III, ch I, §28. See also O Schachter, 'Self-Defense and the Rule of Law' (1989) 83 *American Journal of International Law* 259–77.

[154] *The Law of Nations* (n 2) bk II, ch IV, §49 (emphasis in original).

[155] Ibid bk II, ch IV, §50.   [156] Ibid bk II, ch IV, §51.

[157] Ibid bk II, ch IV, §52 (and, apparently, '[t]hey may even, if necessary, disable the aggressor from doing further injury').

[158] H Grotius, *De Jure Belli ac Pacis Libri Tres* (FW Kelsey trans) (2 vols Clarendon Press Oxford 1925 [1625]) vol 2, bk II, ch XX, §1.

[159] *De Iure Belli Libri Tres* (n 1) bk I, ch XX. See also at bk I, ch V: '[b]e it therefore established as a fact, that even a war of vengeance and an offensive war may be waged justly' and that in the case of the latter 'there is always a defensive aspect, if they are just'. See also A Blane and B Kingsbury, 'Punishment and the *ius post bellum*' in B Kingsbury and B Straumann (eds), *The Roman Foundations of the Law of Nations: Alberico Gentili and the Justice of Empire* (OUP Oxford 2010) 241–68, at 251 and L May, *Aggression and Crimes against Peace* (CUP Cambridge 2008) at 75–8.

Traces of this thinking continued to permeate through to the twentieth century where, at least in the first decades, international law distinguished between the purpose of self-defence and that of armed reprisal while admitting the permissibility of both. Whereas the right of self-defence exists 'for the purpose of protecting the security of the state and the essential rights...upon which that security depends',[160] armed reprisals, in contrast, have been said to be 'punitive in character' for 'they seek to impose reparation for the harm done'.[161] The lawfulness of the former remains assured under the *Charter* in the form of article 51; the latter commanded the support of the law at one point,[162] but have been frowned upon by the *Charter*.[163] Perhaps this development is one of the factors to explain the 'more general disappearance' that has been observed of the concept of punishment 'from the theories and vocabulary of contemporary legal theorists writing about war',[164] although complications attend the application of this distinction in practice.[165]

Still, it is somewhat curious[166] that while armed reprisals have traditionally been conceived as a method of ensuring the *enforcement* of international law—that, as a matter of principle, 'the target of the [armed] reprisal' must be preceded by 'the commission of a prior illegal act directed against the claimant state'[167]—the right of self-defence has somehow remained free of this choice of narrative. It is true that we are often caught referring to this right in the language of an 'exception' to the prohibition of force in international law, but it is much less frequently that we are found characterizing the exercise of this right as upholding the (violated) prohibition of force, of emphasizing the 'prior illegal act' that has given rise to the right of self-defence in the first place. Perhaps this is to do with the historical design of self-defence as 'the act of preventing the wrongdoing from being consummated',[168]

---

[160] DW Bowett, 'Reprisals Involving Recourse to Armed Force' (1972) 66 *American Journal of International Law* 1–36, at 3.

[161] Ibid. See also *Regulating Covert Action* (n 19) 90. To be distinguished from *belligerent* reprisals, for those occur in the context of an (international) armed conflict, even if they proceed from an identical logic: *The Law of Nations* (n 2) bk III, ch VIII, §142.

[162] As in the *Naulilaa Incident Arbitration (Portugal v Germany)* (Award) (1928) 2 RIAA 1012.

[163] At least as explicated in 'Friendly Relations Declaration' (n 88). See also *International Law and the Use of Force* (n 20) 150–1.

[164] See 'Punishment and the *ius post bellum*' (n 159) 241. However, Joseph Weiler has recently written of 'the seeming impossibility to definitively rid the system of the *Naulilaa* ethos'—of 'talk of punishment or reprisal, which is what *Naulilaa* really was about': J Weiler, 'Crime and Punishment: The Reification and Deification of the State (A Footnote to the Syria Debate)' on *EJIL: Talk!* (13 December 2013) <http://www.ejiltalk.org/crime-and-punishment-the-reification-and-deification-of-the-state-a-footnote-to-the-syria-debate/> [accessed 28 February 2016].

[165] *International Law and the Use of Force* (n 20) 151.

[166] Although here is Bowett: '[t]he essence of self-defence is a wrong done, a breach of a legal duty owed to the [S]tate acting in self-defence': 'Reprisals Involving Recourse to Armed Force' (n 160) 9.

[167] RA Falk, 'The Beirut Raid and the International Law of Retaliation' (1969) 63 *American Journal of International Law* 415–43, at 431.

[168] *War and the Law of Nations* (n 114) 61 ('[i]t must not be either preventive (prior to the attack) or punitive (subsequent to the attack)'). Note, however, that over four months lapsed before the 'defence' of Kuwait on 16 January 1991.

but, following the finding of the ICJ in the *Nicaragua* case on the importance of the occurrence of an armed attack for the right of self-defence,[169] it must also now be open to serious question whether it remains accurate to speak of this right in terms of an *exception* to the prohibition of force *ut totum*.

That the Court also found in the *Nicaragua* case that 'less grave forms' of force could not be met by the right of self-defence and 'could only have justified proportionate counter-measures on the part of the State which had been the victim of these acts'[170] might be taken to suggest that it is only *unarmed* reprisals that are now permitted as a matter of international law.[171] Equally, the Court could have been intimating a qualified return to armed reprisals through the discerning use of the idiom of 'counter-measures',[172] which would somehow be 'analogous' to the right of self-defence intended for responding to force falling short of an armed attack.[173] Though the Court briefly contemplated this possibility, it nevertheless issued a categorical rejection of the permissibility of *collective* counter-measures that joined its other substantive conclusions on that occasion—notably that, for example, 'the use of force could not be the appropriate method to ensure such respect [for human rights]'[174] and that 'in international law there are no rules, other than such rules as may be accepted by the State concerned, by treaty or otherwise, whereby the level of armaments of a sovereign State can be limited, and this principle is valid for all States without exception';[175] it did this, arguably, to demarcate a much-reduced provenance for unauthorized force and intervention in upholding the rules of international law.

As far as the right of self-defence itself is concerned, the Court has mapped its parameters with increasing detail and particularity, to the point where the Court concluded in its *Wall Opinion* in July 2004 that 'Article 51 of the *Charter* thus recognizes the existence of an inherent right of self-defence in the case of armed attack *by one State against another State*'.[176] That said, in its advisory opinion in *Legality of the Threat or Use of Nuclear Weapons* in July 1996, it was the position of

---

[169] See eg *Nicaragua* (n 5) 36 [51], which follows from the Court's distinction 'between the most grave forms of the use of force (those constituting an armed attack) from other less grave forms': at 101 [191].

[170] *Nicaragua* (n 5) 127 [249]; that is, individual counter-measures: the Court went on to conclude that these acts 'could not justify counter-measures taken by a third State...and particularly could not justify intervention involving the use of force'—what the Court called 'collective counter-measures': ibid.

[171] The interpretation in J Crawford, *Brownlie's Principles of Public International Law* (8th edn OUP Oxford 2012) at 586.

[172] See *Nicaragua* (n 5) 110 [210].

[173] Which it did seem to admit it was doing—albeit within the context of the collective counter-measures and right of collective self-defence: ibid 110 [210].

[174] Ibid 134 [268].   [175] Ibid 135 [269].

[176] *Wall Opinion* (n 90) 194 [139] (emphasis added). According to Judge Rosalyn Higgins in her separate opinion, this is a throwback to the earlier jurisprudence of the Court: at 215 [33].

the Court that 'in view of the current state of international law, and of the elements of fact at its disposal, the Court cannot conclude definitively whether the threat or use of nuclear weapons would be lawful or unlawful in an extreme circumstance of self-defence, *in which the very survival of a State would be at stake*'.[177] This accompanied the Court's earlier remark in the advisory opinion that it could not 'lose sight of the fundamental right of every State to survival, and thus its right to resort to self-defence, in accordance with Article 51 of the *Charter*, when its survival is at stake',[178] and, for some at least, this jurisprudence has presaged a possible return to the right of self-preservation.[179]

With these words, the Court did appear to suggest that every state possesses 'a right to survival', that this right is of a 'fundamental' kind within the legal order and that it might, in fact, even be separate to the right of self-defence.[180] Inescapably, the Court did not confine its analysis to the application of the right of self-defence pure and simple; the 'right to survival' has thus been understood to be deserving of its own 'particular treatment by law',[181] for the Court did not invest its faith in the principles of necessity and proportionality which govern (or should govern) each and every exercise of the right of self-defence, including the use of nuclear arsenal. We are therefore left pondering whether the right of self-defence is indeed connected or identical to that of self-preservation,[182] or whether it must take its place in the emerging constellation of propositions that constitute the modern *jus ad bellum*.[183]

Herein, then, lie the pressure-points for the law on force and intervention—the register of its activities is to calibrate how the swarming tides of practice refine or reshape the contours of existing rights (such as the right of self-defence) of the legal order or how they bring within their fold new 'rights' for state action (such as the right of humanitarian intervention) within that order. Jurisprudential

---

[177] By seven votes to seven, by the President's casting vote: *Legality of the Threat or Use of Nuclear Weapons* (Advisory Opinion) [1996] ICJ Rep 226, at 266 [105(e)] (emphasis added).

[178] Ibid 263 [96].

[179] For the notion of 'survival' is 'closely related to the idea of the existence or the preservation of the [S]tate': see MG Kohen, 'The Notion of "State Survival" in International Law', in L Boisson de Chazournes and P Sands (eds), *International Law, the International Court of Justice and Nuclear Weapons* (CUP Cambridge 1999) 293–314, at 294. See also WE Hall, *International Law* (Clarendon Press Oxford 1880) at 226; H Wheaton, *Elements of International Law* (RH Dana Jr ed) (8th edn Little Brown & Co Boston 1866 [1836]) at §61.

[180] If we proceed from the logic that a State's right to survival *thus* engages its right of self-defence.

[181] 'The Notion of "State Survival" in International Law' (n 179) 298.

[182] Bowett regards the view 'by which the while of the duties of [S]tate are subordinated to the "right" of self-preservation or the "right" of necessity' as 'destructive of the entire legal order': *Self-Defense in International Law* (n 107) 10. See also 'The Notion of "State Survival" in International Law' (n 179) 301 (on 'the negation of the legal system').

[183] For what it is worth, Henry Wheaton considered that the right of self-preservation 'necessarily involves all other incidental rights, which are essential as means to give effect to the principal end'—and that the right of self-defence is among these: *Elements of International Law* (n 179) §§61–2.

endeavour has further revealed that we should not make convenient assumptions or conclusions on this latter front, and that it matters a great deal what degree of empirical evidence is advanced to substantiate claims regarding change to the law. Subsequent to these arrangements, we have also learnt that the law is there to be applied, and to be applied in all of its infinitesimal detail, with a view to determining whether any given action by states acting alone or in concert is lawful or unlawful (or, as has become the theme of our times, whether it is far too close to call). It is these rituals—and these 'fundamentals'[184]—of law's practice that have come to sustain but also to corrode the possibilities of the discipline, for it is rare to probe whether force and intervention have in fact entailed 'a perpetuation of violence rather than a shift away from violence' in the general scheme of things,[185] or, equally, whether they have or should have some function in the realization of values held dear by international law (such as those involving personal or collective self-determination).[186]

[184] As used in J Crawford and J Watkins, 'International Responsibility' in S Besson and J Tasioulas (eds), *The Philosophy of International Law* (OUP Oxford 2010) 283–98, at 298.

[185] G Heathcote, *The Law on the Use of Force: A Feminist Analysis* (Routledge London 2012) at 141. But see the assessment in TM Franck and NS Rodley, 'After Bangladesh: The Law of Humanitarian Intervention by Military Force' (1973) 67 *American Journal of International Law* 275–305, at 277–8, and in 'Humanitarian Intervention' (n 51) 538.

[186] Though this is not far from the surface: consider Judge Stephen M Schwebel's interaction with the Court's reference to 'the process of decolonization' in *Nicaragua* (n 5) 108 [206].

CHAPTER 34

....

THEORIZING HUMAN RIGHTS

....

BEN GOLDER

Today, it seems, everyone is a human rights pragmatist[1]

1 Human Rights Pragmatism?

....

'Whereas recognition of the inherent dignity and of the equal and inalienable rights of all members of the human family is the foundation of freedom, justice and peace in the world,' commences the iconic Preamble to the *Universal Declaration of Human Rights* in 1948.[2] The Declaration, and similar official discourses on human rights, speaks *sub specie aeternitatis*, majestically uninflected by the vagaries of time and place. ('Everyone has the right to recognition everywhere as a person before the law,' declares article 6.) Human rights in this very familiar guise represent the preeminent universalist political credo of late modernity: idealist, foundationalist, metaphysical, irreducible to calculation. Indeed to call them a political credo is not quite to do them justice—human rights, according to this reckoning, are both pre- and supra-political, providing the moral foundation and limits to

----

[1] F Mégret, 'Where Does the Critique of International Human Rights Stand? An Exploration in 18 Vignettes' in JM Beneyto and D Kennedy (eds), *New Approaches to International Law: The European and American Experiences* 3–40, at 32.

[2] 'Universal Declaration on Human Rights' (10 December 1948) GA Res 217A(III) UN Doc A/810.

politics itself. But of course, such idealism is not the whole story, as numerous exceptions, derogations, and accommodations to these lofty principles in both juridical text and institutional practice attest. The universal has to be instantiated and in so doing a measure of calculation and pragmatic compromise is called for. It is with this latter, much less remarked upon, *pragmatic* element in human rights that the present chapter is occupied.

My focus is not so much on the particular institutional, legal, or political moves made in order to make human rights a reality but rather on the question of what it means to theorize them through the lens of pragmatism. According to several recent pragmatic theoretical accounts, human rights neither rest normatively upon any metaphysical claim about human nature, nor stand implausibly apart from politics (as their condition and limit). Rather, they are themselves merely a set of tools with which to address problems of global injustice, to begin to speak across cultural divides, to construct minimal juridical conditions protective of human agency, and so forth. Supposedly relieved of their metaphysical baggage, human rights emerge in this pragmatic vein as a more worldly wise, modest, flexible, pluralist, and (possibly) more appealing project (both to activists and institutional actors alike).

In what follows I begin to answer the question of what it means to think human rights *pragmatically* by tracking some different appeals to pragmatism in contemporary theoretical work on human rights (in the writings of Richard Rorty, Michael Ignatieff, David Kennedy, Martti Koskenniemi, and Florian Hoffmann). I do this neither in order to provide a comprehensive survey of pragmatism or of human rights nor indeed to assess the truth of these pragmatic theoretical accounts of human rights but rather, in line with the intentions of classical philosophical pragmatism, to pose the question of their utility. What difference does it make to think about human rights in pragmatic terms? What effects are thereby produced in the world? What kinds of political possibilities are enlivened and what kinds are foreclosed or rendered unintelligible? What *work*, that is, does the contemporary resort to pragmatism do in the hands of these theorists of human rights?

To briefly foreshadow the approach and argument pursued here, I hope in what follows to do two things. The chapter's first aim is to provide a conspectus of the way in which some recent and influential thinkers have theorized human rights through the lens of pragmatism. The second aim of the chapter is to problematize this very turn to pragmatism. In my argument, the critical potential of pragmatism too often ends up re-entrenching a conservative, liberal political vision of human rights (without the metaphysical trappings and false universalism) even as it licenses extraordinary militarism on behalf of powerful states and the international community. But if this chapter seeks to probe the limits of pragmatism, it also tries to think pragmatically about human rights. Hence, I want to argue that if we are encouraged by pragmatism to think in terms of the use or the outcome of our conceptions rather than their intrinsic truth value, then a pragmatic accounting of human rights compels recognition that human rights as a particular form of conducting global politics are not particularly useful for doing certain things (indeed *cannot* do them) and hence we should begin to think beyond them and to seek other political idioms and languages of global justice. But this is to anticipate the work of the next few sections. Let me start my discussion now with what is perhaps the most celebrated and influential engagement with human rights from a pragmatist philosopher: the work of Richard Rorty (and, in a related vein, Michael Ignatieff).

2 PRAGMATISM AS (POST-)FOUNDATIONALISM

Rorty's most important engagement with human rights is to be found in his Oxford Amnesty Lecture of 1993, entitled 'Human Rights, Rationality, and Sentimentality'. There he expands upon the claim of the Argentinean analytic philosopher, Eduardo Rabossi, that 'human rights foundationalism [is] outmoded and irrelevant' to the contemporary human rights project.[3] By 'human rights foundationalism' Rorty refers to those thinkers who seek to isolate ahistorical, context-transcendent characteristics of the human being (dignity and rationality, for example) which can serve as stable, knowable grounds for human rights. For Rorty, the kind of transcendental 'claims to knowledge about the nature of human beings'[4] that are advanced by foundationalist philosophers from Plato to Kant (and their contemporary followers) are inherently incapable of epistemic proof and, what is more, are not ultimately all that *useful* to the aims of the human rights project. We can sense already that Rorty's pragmatic post-foundationalism is not an attempt to displace or reject human rights but rather to insist that they need not rely upon metaphysics; indeed, they are arguably much better off without them. His real objection to the kind of ahistorical, essentialist knowledge claim about human beings and their inalienable rights is hence a pragmatic one which turns upon the assumption that '[s]ince no useful work seems to be done by insisting on a purportedly ahistorical human nature, there probably is no such nature, or at least nothing in that nature that is relevant to our moral choices'.[5]

Rorty's pragmatic rejoinder to the familiar foundationalist claims of human rights discourse (namely that we have human rights by virtue of our possessing

---

[3] E Rabossi, 'La teoría de los derechos humanos naturalizada' (1990) 5 *Revista del Centro de Estudios Constitucionales* 159–79, quoted in R Rorty, 'Human Rights, Rationality, and Sentimentality' in S Shute and S Hurley (eds), *On Human Rights: The Oxford Amnesty Lectures* (Basic Books New York 1993) 111–34, at 116.

[4] Ibid 117.   [5] Ibid 118–9.

reason, dignity, or simply 'humanity') is to insist that human rights are the contingent result of cultural and historical forces—a product of convention and agreement, of a transient 'redescription' of moral values and not their timeless legislation by the universe.[6] Such a position doubtless invites the charge of cultural relativism and the familiar spectre of illiberalism ('if human rights are not vouchsafed by context-transcending reasons and values, then by what means are they secured and how can we normatively oppose barbarism and cruelty in their name?').[7] But we shall see in a moment that if Rorty evacuates the metaphysical grounds of human rights he *is* quick to reassert their moral value (indeed, for him, their cultural 'superiority')[8] and to supply in place of metaphysics a new, more durable and pragmatic foundation for them.

But before doing so I want first to examine a related invocation of human rights pragmatism that also engages with the question of the foundation of human rights, and that is the work of the political philosopher Michael Ignatieff. In his celebrated 2001 Tanner Lectures entitled *Human Rights as Politics and Idolatry*, Ignatieff aims to develop an apologia for international human rights law, institutions, and activism in explicitly political, 'post-metaphysical' terms.[9] As the structural opposition embedded in the title of his two lectures makes clear, Ignatieff understands *politics* as being opposed to, and as taking its meaning from, *idolatry*, such that a politics of human rights cannot simply insist on the timeless and universal self-evidence of the human for its moral appeal. Human rights, Ignatieff argues, 'is not a creed; it is not a metaphysics. To make it so is to turn it into a species of idolatry: humanism worshipping itself'.[10] Ignatieff's worry here is, again, a tellingly pragmatic one, namely that 'metaphysical claims about human nature... are intrinsically contestable' and their dogmatic assertion or imposition, especially upon non-Western cultures, engenders a self-defeating and embarrassing resistance to what is, after all, supposed to be a universal regime.[11] What is needed instead is '[a] prudential—and historical—justification for human rights... [which chastened species of normativity] does not make appeal to any particular idea of human nature.... [n]or... seek[s] its ultimate validation in a particular idea of the human good'.[12] Rather, such a justification simply recalls 'what history tells us: that human beings are at risk of their lives if they lack a basic measure of free agency'.[13] Ignatieff's 'pragmatist rationale for human rights'[14] is a 'self-consciously minimalist'[15] one, and this in at

---

[6] On 'redescription', see R Rorty, *Contingency, Irony, and Solidarity* (CUP Cambridge 1989) at 9.

[7] Cf R Haule, 'Some Reflections on the Foundation of Human Rights—Are Human Rights an Alternative to Moral Values?' (2006) 10 *Max Planck Yearbook of United Nations Law* 367–95, at 380–1, 387.

[8] 'Human Rights, Rationality, and Sentimentality' (n 3) 116.

[9] M Ignatieff, *Human Rights as Politics and Idolatry* (Princeton University Press Princeton 2001).

[10] Ibid 53.   [11] Ibid 54.   [12] Ibid 56.   [13] Ibid 55.

[14] J Souter, 'Humanity, Suffering and Victimhood: A Defence of Human Rights Pragmatism' (2009) 29 *Politics* 45–52, at 45.

[15] *Human Rights as Politics and Idolatry* (n 9) 56.

least two senses.[16] It is *substantively* minimalist in the sense that it reduces human rights to a 'common denominator'[17] of negative liberty rights protective of bodily integrity and thus (supposedly) human agency. And it is *justificatorily* minimalist in the sense that it abjures a substantive vision of the human good or of the human being *as such* and hence 'minimizes theoretical aspirations in the statement of the conception of human rights with the aim of presenting a conception that is capable of winning broader public allegiance'.[18]

What conceptions of pragmatism are invoked by both thinkers here, and what work do they do? Both Rorty's and Ignatieff's pragmatic orientation towards human rights supposedly refute the need for, or doubt the very existence of, rationalist and transcendent grounds for human rights. In this sense they can both be understood as *post-foundationalists*. As we have already seen, Rorty specifies that for him this is more a matter of efficacy than epistemology, whilst Ignatieff's post-foundationalism manifests as a prudential worry about the alienating effect of 'thick' ethical conceptions of the good on the global stage. Yet despite their shared critique of foundationalism both thinkers are avowed *proponents* of human rights, and a very orthodox liberal conception of them at that. Their pragmatic refusal of foundationalism simply compels a different manner of advocating and justifying human rights. Or, if I can put it in a slightly different way, their pragmatic post-foundationalism actually functions by displacing one possible foundation of human rights (transcendent rationality) and replacing it with another, hence in both their cases what is at play is not so much a critique of foundationalism in human rights discourse as a pragmatic *refoundation* of human rights (along liberal lines).

For Rorty, the liberal values of contemporary human rights culture which he wholeheartedly endorses are not secured by an otherworldly guarantee, but are purely the result of a given community's historically, and transiently, agreeing to abide by a particular set of norms (that is, in Rorty's terms, its *solidarity*). The attitude that Rorty commends towards these values is that of the 'liberal ironist', a figure who simultaneously accepts and indeed self-consciously embraces their contingency (ironism) and yet resolutely defends their centrality nonetheless (liberalism), accepting all the time that even *these* fundamental values are not themselves vouchsafed from further redescription.[19] Rorty hence attempts pragmatically to displace the foundations of human rights from *reason* to *sentiment*. Recall that what is important in the fostering of these more contingent and yet durable bonds

---

[16] Here I follow J Cohen, 'Minimalism About Human Rights: The Most We Can Hope For?' (2004) 12 *Journal of Political Philosophy* 190–213, at 192.

[17] L Bacelli, 'Pragmatic Fundamentalism: Michael Ignatieff and Human Rights' (M Bellucci and S Benjamin trans) (2007) *Jura Gentium* <http://www.juragentium.org/forum/ignatief/en/baccelli.htm> [accessed 28 February 2016].

[18] 'Minimalism About Human Rights' (n 16) 192.

[19] *Contingency, Irony, and Solidarity* (n 6) xv.

of loyalty and normative obligation is the 'hearing of sad and sentimental sto-ries,'[20] which is why 'the novel, the movie, and the TV program have, gradually but steadily, replaced the sermon and the treatise as the principal vehicles of moral change and progress'.[21] Relinquishing the search for transcendent foundations allows more work to be done on establishing the *real* grounds of human rights, which seeks to 'expand the reference of the terms "our kind of people" and "people like us" through sentimental education'.[22]

For his part, Ignatieff replaces the normative and universal foundation of human rights with a world-weary invocation of the lessons of history (which sup-posedly teach us that without the protection of negative liberties the worst can always recur). And, at bottom, it is the prevention of the worst that animates the pragmatic anti-political projects of both these thinkers. By signalling that there is no necessary metaphysical human that provides a foundation for human rights, pragmatism as (post-)foundationalism initially suggests a more pluralist and ex-perimental recasting of the discourse (a suggestion I want to pick up upon in the penultimate section of this chapter) but we can see that the consequence of this appeal to pragmatism is ultimately the refoundation of human rights on disabused grounds. The result, for both thinkers, may be human rights without transcen-dental rationalist illusions but it is still very much a recognizably liberal endeavour which aims to winnow the human rights project to the prevention of state violence against individual human beings (as opposed, say, to the structural eradication or amelioration of poverty or material inequality).

Fear and suffering provide the affective and embodied foundations of this new-old 'postmodernist bourgeois liberalism'[23] and, for both Rorty and Ignatieff, the encounter with Judith Shklar's 'liberalism of fear' is a primary (dare I say it, foun-dational) one.[24] Their pragmatic reworking of the foundation of human rights thus departs from the disembodied Kantian subject only at the cost of reintroducing the wounded, sensate, suffering body of humanity beseeching protection from those sufficiently unlike 'us' to be motivated to inflict pain. This resort to pragmatism is hence not a radical attempt to displace foundationalism in the discourse of human rights and to open it to plural possibilities but rather a subtle attempt to rework and reimagine that foundation (from reason to sentiment, from abstract founda-tion to embodied fear) and in so doing to entrench a conservative liberal vision of human rights—conservative and mid-century modern, yet all the same one which, in the last decade of the twentieth century, licensed a radical interventionist

[20] 'Human Rights, Rationality, and Sentimentality' (n 3) 119.

[21] *Contingency, Irony, and Solidarity* (n 6) xvi.

[22] 'Human Rights, Rationality, and Sentimentality' (n 3) 122–3.

[23] R Rorty, 'Postmodernist Bourgeois Liberalism' (1983) 80 *Journal of Philosophy* 583–9.

[24] J Shklar, 'The Liberalism of Fear' in N Rosenblum (ed), *Liberalism and the Moral Life* (Harvard University Press Cambridge MA 1989) 21–38. See also *Contingency, Irony, and Solidarity* (n 6) xv; *Human Rights as Politics and Idolatry* (n 9) 173.

understanding of human rights and humanitarian action in the name of a suffering, victimized humanity.[25] I shall return to the afterlives of Rorty's pragmatism later in the chapter but let me now turn to the workings of a different form of human rights pragmatism, namely that of the critical international lawyer and theorist of global governance, David Kennedy.

3 PRAGMATISM AS EMPOWERMENT

If Rorty and Ignatieff's human rights pragmatism effects a slide from transcendental rationalism to a sensate, suffering, sentimental human body, then Kennedy's pragmatism, as we shall see, makes a similar shift. It commences life as a critical orientation towards human rights but ends up seeking to renew and reactivate them by embracing their potential for institutional and redistributive political power. Kennedy's best known work, *The Dark Sides of Virtue: Reassessing International Humanitarianism*, styles itself as a 'critical reflection' on the international human rights movement which, he provocatively suggests, has become 'part of the problem'.[26] The problems with the international human rights movement, it turns out, are multiple and complex, but each of them in some way can be referred back to the inability or refusal of human rights activists to think in properly pragmatic terms about the distributional consequences of their actions (specifically, their blindness to the titular 'dark sides' of the human rights project). Such familiar dark sides involve, for example, the displacement of alternative political and legal imaginaries, actors, and projects by the hegemonic discourse of international human rights; the siphoning of resources, support, and goodwill away from local projects to distant international actors; the often perverse framing of social, political, or ecological issues in the legal-juridical mould of a 'human rights violation'; and so forth.

According to Kennedy's persuasive account, the figure of the international humanitarian evinces a blind faith in the righteousness of her actions and is ill-equipped to think strategically about the effects of her practice in the real world. This naive devotion blinds the movement to the reality of its own dark sides, thus perpetuating and exacerbating those dark sides. Enter pragmatism. But what, exactly, does Kennedy mean by pragmatism in this context? Kennedy specifies his

---

[25] To historicize the two pragmatist contributions here, Rorty's Amnesty International Lecture (1993) and Ignatieff's Tanner Lectures (2000) can be located squarely in the post-Cold War shift regarding collective security and humanitarian intervention (and the run up to the second Iraq War).

[26] D Kennedy, *The Dark Sides of Virtue: Reassessing International Humanitarianism* (Princeton University Press Princeton 2004) at 3.

understanding of pragmatism early in the book. It is comprised of both a 'prag-matism of intentions' and a 'pragmatism of consequences'. The former he defines as 'a clear-eyed focus on the purposes of our work and a relentless effort to avoid being blown off course as we seek to make our humanitarian impulses real'.[27] Here Kennedy is critical of human rights practitioners who mistake means for ends, who 'pay more attention to compiling documents than developing solutions, to proclaiming rights than fashioning remedies', and so forth.[28] The pragmatism of intentions hence appears as a form of recalibrated idealism, of getting back on track. The latter sense of pragmatism is perhaps a more orthodox one, involving as it does a consequentialist focus on 'outcomes rather than good intentions'.[29] Kennedy writes: 'When activists think in instrumental or functional terms about their advocacy—when they make strategic choices about which rule or standard to invoke, which institution to engage—they focus on the consequences' and coolly assess 'who would win and who would lose from proposed government action'.[30] In this more socially scientific vein, human rights practitioners are eminently more comfortable with making distributional choices and identify themselves as part-ners in governance (which is where Kennedy would ultimately have them).

And yet for Kennedy pragmatism is itself insufficient and in need of a supple-ment, for he argues that pragmatism can in turn produce problems for the hu-manitarian. It can too easily ossify into a 'professional language and practice'[31] which obscures a very elusive and important human experience: the distinct and dangerous pleasure of exercising discretionary power unconstrained by rule or certainty. Kennedy hence worries that pragmatic evaluation merely substitutes calculative rules for faux humanist absolutes, allowing international human rights practitioners the better to see and to calculate, but not to feel and to be responsible for the awesome exercise of their power. He hints at this problem with the conclu-sion to *The Dark Sides of Virtue* when he enjoins humanitarians not simply to cal-culate but to exercise their 'will to power'[32] and to do so in the dark:

The darker sides of our nature and our world confronted, embraced, and accepted, rather than denied. I imagine this humanitarianism in the language of spirit and grace—at once uncomfortable and full of human promise.[33]

The problematic is more fully explored in Kennedy's subsequent work, *Of War and Law*, which discusses the merger of the humanitarian and military professions and their joint deployment of a shared legal vocabulary and expertise ('lawfare'). There he writes in a more directly existential vein of 'recapturing a politics of war [which] would mean feeling the weight and the lightness of killing or allowing to live'. 'The challenge for all of us,' he writes, 'is to recapture the freedom and the responsibility of exercising discretion in this common tongue'.[34]

---

[27] *The Dark Sides of Virtue* (n 26) xx.   [28] Ibid xxi.   [29] Ibid xxii.
[30] Ibid.   [31] Ibid xxiv.   [32] Ibid 346.   [33] Ibid 355.
[34] D Kennedy, *Of War and Law* (Princeton University Press Princeton 2006) at 171–2.

Kennedy's articulation of human rights pragmatism hence begins its life as a critique of the 'will to marginality'[35] of human rights actors (who disavow their investment in networks of global governmental power and hide behind a disingenuous and moralizing veil of anti-politics) but it ends as a renewalist call to arms (quite literally), which in the name of military humanitarianism sees its role not as opposing war and imperialist violence but as somehow ameliorating, civilizing, and ultimately legitimating them from within. Kennedy thus proposes a much more explicit avowal of the world-making power of human rights alongside advocating the civilizing integration (or collapse) of human rights language and standards into the operational idioms of the world's most powerful military. Humanitarians, on his account, need pragmatically (yet responsibly) to come out of the shadows and into the clear and powerful light of day.

There are evident dangers here which Kennedy's *pragmatism as empowerment* helps to produce, and I want now to sketch them through the work of a figure to whom I shall return in the next section. That figure is Martti Koskenniemi and the dangers are ones of institutional mainstreaming and cynicism/bad faith. To start with the former, Koskenniemi views the mainstreaming of human rights values within the policy mechanisms of the managerialist state (and international institutions) as a profoundly ambivalent move. In his view, the classical idiom of human rights, which arose precisely as an external and a critical limit to the instrumentalist weighing of interests (still best encapsulated by the Dworkinian metaphor of 'rights as trumps') becomes necessarily attenuated in the encounter with policy reasoning:

Human rights arose from revolution, not from a call for mainstreaming. One cannot be a revolutionary and participate in the regular management of things without some cost to both of those projects.[36]

This is not a call to return human rights to the position of principled ineffectiveness from which Kennedy sought pragmatically to retrieve them, but precisely a concern about the very *disempowering* loss of critical leverage that losing touch with the utopian tradition of human rights brings about. Moreover '[b]y remaining in the periphery,' writes Koskenniemi, 'human rights may be more able to retain their constraining hold on the way most people, and by extension most states, behave'.[37]

The other danger courted by Kennedy's pragmatic renewal of human rights as an institutional project is the danger of cynicism and bad faith. This is the bad faith of a political culture that professes a belief in universals whilst being constantly willing to undermine them in practice if the pragmatics of any given situation

[35] *The Dark Sides of Virtue* (n 26) 303.
[36] M Koskenniemi, 'Human Rights Mainstreaming as a Strategy for Institutional Power' (2010) 1 *Humanity* 47–58, at 55.
[37] M Koskenniemi, 'The Pull of the Mainstream' (1990) 88 *Michigan Law Review* 1946–62, at 1962.

demand it. 'A gap is [thereby] established', writes Koskenniemi, 'between political language and normative faith that encourages a strategic attitude as the proper political frame of mind as well as an ironic distance to politics by the general population'.[38] In such a setting the much-vaunted universality of human rights law and the foundational status of the liberties it seeks to protect for civil society are reduced to little more than a 'façade' for the technical-instrumental management of the economy and jurisdictional competition between competing governmental policy organs.[39] International lawyers and human rights activists who are disabused of human rights' false universality 'yet keep the truth secret, because revealing it might altogether undermine a structure of authority which otherwise is so beneficial [to them] and [to their] public identity as the technicians of an objective legal reason'[40] are complicit simultaneously in the hollowing out of the universal *and* of political contestation. Such are the possible wages of Kennedy's *pragmatism as empowerment*, and yet the final evocation of pragmatism which I discuss in the next section seeks to enliven the political possibilities of human rights, not by a return to (a discredited European) universal but by reactivating the possibility and promise of *universalization* (as dialogic and transformative process).

4 Pragmatism as Pluralist Possibility

Florian Hoffmann's recent appeal to a 'pragmatic theory of human rights' takes place 'after the epistemological critique' of their foundations. Once we expose the universal claims of human rights as having been structured by the contingent and the particular, he asks, '[c]an they still be considered a meaningful concept capable of achieving anything?…Or ought we simply discard the concept and withdraw into the vacuum of post-humanist amorality?[41] Hoffmann's answer to this endlessly recurring Nietzschean question is to insist, like Rorty, on the possibility of an affirmative and pragmatic human rights practice after the linguistic turn. Hoffmann's starting point is that human rights represent a *discourse* in which claims for justice are spoken by innumerable actors across the globe: 'they are…

---

[38] M Koskenniemi, 'The Effect of Rights on Political Culture' in P Alston (ed), *The EU and Human Rights* (OUP Oxford 2000) 99–116, at 100.

[39] Ibid.

[40] M Koskenniemi, 'Faith, Identity, and the Killing of the Innocent: International Lawyers and Nuclear Weapons' (1997) 10 *Leiden Journal of International Law* 137–62, at 160.

[41] F Hoffmann, '"Shooting into the Dark": Toward a Pragmatic Theory of Human Rights (Activism)' (2006) 41 *Texas International Law Journal* 403–14, at 406.

being discussed in virtually all places by virtually all kinds of people'.[42] And for Hoffmann it is precisely this discursive character of human rights (human rights 'talk') that 'secures' their democratic open-endedness and incipient plurality. In order to reach this conclusion, he makes an important conceptual distinction between human rights *discourse* ('all references to human rights, independent of context or speakers' intentions…a system or structure of signification which is taken to be analytically distinct from the subjective meaning constructed with it in specific contexts') and human rights *consciousness* ('the subjective perception of human rights as an ontological (re)description of personal identity').[43] Neither the 'objective' discursive meanings of human rights nor their unofficial 'subjective' articulations by individual speakers can ever finally be determined or delimited, and for him the very meaning of human rights only emerges fleetingly and from time to time when different discourses and subjective understandings of human rights encounter, affect and modify each other in 'a dynamic process of mutual feedback loops'.[44] For Hoffmann, this 'pragmatic perspective aims to comprehend human rights discourse, not in terms of what it could be, or ought to be, but in terms of what it arguably is, namely a plural, polycentric, and ultimately indeterminate discourse amenable to use by nearly everyone everywhere,' which is consequently 'beyond the control of those creating them, and is ultimately uncertain. There is no single correct signification and thus use of human rights'.[45]

The effect of Hoffmann's *improper* human rights pragmatism is thus potentially to democratize and pluralize the possibilities of human rights. His focus on what he calls the 'pragmatics' of human rights (understood as their concrete, situational, context-specific deployment in language; that is, their 'use')[46] wrests the meaning of human rights discourse away from the official, institutional language games of courts and committees and returns it, if not quite to 'the people' as a constituent or sovereign entity, nevertheless to a never-ending process of articulation between peoples and the institutional bodies which seek to determine their human rights. In a sense, what I have called Hoffmann's *pragmatism as pluralist possibility* is both indebted, and bears a superficial similarity, to Rorty's human rights pragmatism. Rorty famously describes the pragmatist conception of philosophy as a 'conversation' between fellow inquirers rather than as an attempt to isolate the objective truth of things.[47] For its part, Hoffmann's linguistic model of transnational human rights activism both moves within Rorty's epistemological insights *and* adopts the figure of a conversation (without end), yet in important ways Hoffmann's conversational

---

[42] '"Shooting into the Dark"' (n 41) 409.

[43] F Hoffmann, 'Human Rights, the Self and the Other: Reflections on a Pragmatic Theory of Human Rights' in A Orford (ed), *International Law and Its Others* (CUP Cambridge 2006) 221–44, at 229.

[44] '"Shooting into the Dark"' (n 41) 409.   [45] Ibid.   [46] Ibid 406.

[47] See R Rorty, 'Pragmatism, Relativism, and Irrationalism' (1980) 53 *Proceedings and Addresses of the American Philosophical Association* 717–38, at 726.

model of pragmatism pushes at the limits of Rorty's (ultimately quite insular) liberal chauvinism. For Rorty, the practices and values of a given social or cultural group can only be 'justified' from within that group's particular language games which go to compose its solidarity. Solidarity, whilst contingent, is nevertheless primarily an inward-looking process.[48] Rorty maintains that this does not cancel the possibility of dialogue between different cultural groups and insists that in the case of the transmission of a human rights culture the limits of a given 'we' or 'us' can be expanded to include others.[49] But on Rorty's understanding this process appears to be less one of groups mutually disturbing or transfiguring each others' immanent cultural conceptions of human rights than of the onward expansion of the liberal Euro-American understanding (in which cruelty is the constitutive *summum malum*) to encompass various benighted 'others'. As Hoffmann deftly puts it, 'a pro-active, cross-cultural human rights activism groundlessly founded on Rortyan ethnocentrism can ultimately only base itself on the exercise of at least discursive, if not political or military hegemony'.[50]

Hoffmann's more thoroughgoing anti-essentialist human rights pragmatism envisions a genuinely conversational cross-cultural practice which deconstructs the foundations of any given 'we' and opens it to alterity. Where Rorty stops short of interrogating the limits of 'his' own liberalism, Hoffmann pushes Rorty's own epistemological premises to their political limits. (Rightly) accusing Rorty of romanticizing and refusing to put into question the fictitious 'we' of the late twentieth-century American liberalism, Hoffmann proposes instead 'the logic of complexification...the "both", the hybrid, fluid and the contingently constructed'[51] which deconstructs any substantive identity.

For Hoffmann this global process of mutually contaminating human rights consciousnesses and cultures necessarily reintroduces a kind of (weak) universalism. Here a comparison with Rortyan pragmatism is again instructive. Rorty's ethnocentric refusal of the universal works to foreclose any genuine practice of cross-cultural fertilization or translation (for just as surely as any concrete claim to instantiate the universal must be exposed, so too must *universalization* be the condition of possibility for any possible act of *translation* between putatively self-enclosed particulars). Put differently, without an orienting horizon, there can be no Rortyan pragmatic dialogue between rival human rights cultures, only misrecognition, soliloquy, or imperial imposition. *Contra* Rorty, Hoffmann's 'chaotic'[52] and unpredictable human rights dialogue *does* invoke (and rely upon) a certain universalism, and here his work makes contact with Koskenniemi's. Koskenniemi (in)famously indicts public international law as *kitsch*, in the sense that it forgets

[48] R Rorty, 'Solidarity or Objectivity?' in M Krausz (ed), *Relativism: Interpretation and Confrontation* (University of Notre Dame Press Notre Dame 1989) 167–83, at 177.

[49] 'Human Rights, Rationality, and Sentimentality' (n 3) 122–3.

[50] 'Human Rights, the Self and the Other' (n 43) 241.   [51] Ibid.   [52] Ibid 244.

the particularity of its own tradition and nostalgically reimagines itself as (the) universal.[53] But this gesture (as if anything ever could) does not exhaust the possibilities of the universal. Koskenniemi swiftly proceeds to identity a different understanding of universalism and links it to what he calls (and commends) in *The Gentle Civilizer of Nations* a 'culture of formalism'. '[U]niversality (and universal community),' he writes there, 'is written into the culture of formalism as an idea (or horizon), unattainable but still necessary'.[54] (International legal) formalism in this sense provides an opening, an empty space for the articulation of competing hegemonic versions of the universal. It is precisely Rorty's refusal to elucidate an immanent/imminent orientation to the universal that handicaps his pragmatic dialogue. For both Koskenniemi and Hoffmann, on the other hand, the orientation to the universal performs important political work. '[R]ights,' explains the former, are 'valuable precisely because of the way they combine the particular with an attempt at the universal and thus provide resources for challenging existing hierarchies and exclusions... [for] to claim a right is...to claim in the name of universality: this belongs not only to me but to *everyone in my position*'.[55]

I have aligned Hoffmann's *pragmatism as pluralist possibility* with Koskenniemi's articulation of a culture of international legal formalism, emphasizing their shared attempt to leverage from human rights and from international law the possibility of emancipation and a democratic contestation. Hoffmann attests that Koskenniemi's position is 'not unlike [his own] pragmatics of human rights,' and indeed is 'quite close' to it,[56] but importantly signals a concern about the latter with which I want to conclude this conversational chapter (in the following section). That concern is with the understanding of *form* and *formalism*. Hoffmann observes that Koskenniemi's formalism 'allows for...universality, not because its inner logic would, in fact, be universal, but only because the particular language game of which it is made up allows its "speakers" to use it as a simulacrum of human rights'.[57] Hence the formality of international human rights law consists in articulating an empty semantic space in which competing versions of the 'human' are variously and successively inscribed. But Hoffmann queries whether 'all those within the formalist "dialect group" are aware that it is but a placeholder for an unattainable unity' and tend, forgetting this, to essentialize formalism itself and in so doing erect formalism as a 'hegemonic gatekeeperism' that works to contain the 'transgressive capacities' of Koskenniemi's universalism-as-lack.[58] If the form of international law, or of human rights, is after all a *particular* medium via which the

---

[53] M Koskenniemi, 'International Law in Europe: Between Tradition and Renewal' (2005) 16 *European Journal of International Law* 113–24, at 122–3.

[54] M Koskenniemi, *The Gentle Civilizer of Nations: The Rise and Fall of International Law 1870–1960* (CUP Cambridge 2001) at 507.

[55] M Koskenniemi, 'Human Rights, Politics, and Love' (2002) 13 *Finnish Yearbook of International Law* 79–94, at 93 (emphasis in original).

[56] 'Human Rights, the Self and the Other' (n 43) 243.   [57] Ibid.   [58] Ibid.

(impossible, but necessary) universal is sought to be instantiated, then it follows that it cannot be the only such medium, and moreover may not be the most emancipatory, or democratic, or transgressive one. In closing, it is to the limitations of the human rights form that I now want to turn, and to articulate another possible human rights pragmatism in response to those limitations—my own: *pragmatism as refusal.*

5 PRAGMATISM AS REFUSAL?

In 2000, Costas Douzinas concluded *The End of Human Rights* with the following lines:

When the apologists of pragmatism pronounce the end of ideology, of history or utopia, they do not mark the triumph of human rights; on the contrary, they bring human rights to an end.[59]

The three forms of human rights pragmatism I have been discussing are each, of course, not simply an ending of something, but also, simultaneously and unavoidably, a new beginning. Each invocation of pragmatism is an inauguration, a setting into motion of particular understandings of human rights, each with their particular political aims, investments, and limitations. Rorty and Ignatieff's *pragmatism as (post-)foundationalism* does not just evacuate the transcendental ground of human rights but also attempts to refound them upon sentiment and suffering (in a particular liberal form); Kennedy's *pragmatism as empowerment* marks a break with a certain disingenuous a-political presentation of human rights (as 'virtue') precisely to reintroduce a renovated human rights praxis based around institutional mainstreaming and accommodation to the imperatives of military power; and, finally, Hoffmann's *pragmatism as pluralist possibility* (echoing Koskenniemi's 'culture of formalism) works to generate democratic and transgressive possibilities for politics from within (a putatively empty) human rights form.

In closing I now want to spend some time on these questions of form and emptiness and, in so doing, to propose my own variant of human rights pragmatism. (At the same time, it is a variant of pragmatism which seeks to problematize the preceding examples of the pragmatist turn in human rights theorizing by, in a way, pushing beyond pragmatism.) To pick up on the concerns raised by Hoffmann

---

[59] C Douzinas, *The End of Human Rights: Critical Legal Thought at the Turn of the Century* (Hart Oxford 2000) at 380.

about the possible 'gatekeeping' function of legal form, it is important to empha-size that the conception of human rights as being an 'empty' form is of course a misleading one in many respects. Forms matter, in the dual sense that they are of crucial importance and that they directly materialize (and *dematerialize*) certain political possibilities. 'The forms of law', Anne Orford helpfully reminds us, 'are not apolitical and neutral', but rather work to inscribe particular political possi-bilities and to foreclose others.[60] To imagine the form of human rights as a space where the endless possibilities of 'the human' come to be juridically inscribed may well be true in principle, but likewise it is true in practice that not any con-tent can be given to that semantic term. The human of human rights is legally contoured and the question of form is an important part of that process. One can have any human one likes as long as it can be a rights holder, which, it turns out, means a particular thing; 'form' here goes to condition the possibilities for 'sub-stance' or 'content'. And, of course, the human rights form is still (despite limited jurisdictional exercises in horizontality and corporate social responsibility) an abidingly *liberal* one: the human rights holder emerges as an abstract, formally equal juridical subject confronting a state which is envisioned simultaneously as the guarantor and most likely infringer of those rights. Human rights arguments, in taking a primarily legal-juridical form, necessarily assume a certain aspect, a certain (ambivalent) relation to state power, and they envision certain forms of political activism, tactics, and strategy at the expense of others,[61] just as they im-agine and help to bring into being particular relations, forms of belonging, and community. Human rights, we might say, produce a particular form of political and legal subjectivity.[62] They represent a particular political project with a par-ticular history, entailment, and trajectory (albeit one characteristically oriented towards the universal). Because of this particularity they cannot possibly, despite the hopes invested in them by their idealist claims to universality, be 'all things to all people'.[63]

How does one respond *pragmatically* to this basic insight both about the ma-teriality and consequentiality of the juridical form of human rights, but also about the limitations that this form brings with it? The record of human rights, for ex-ample, in terms of combating and reversing some of the more egregious instances of global capitalism surely compels acknowledgement that human rights, as a matter of form, simply are not 'designed or equipped' to provide oppressed or

---

[60] A Orford, 'Beyond Harmonization: Trade, Human Rights and the Economy of Sacrifice' (2005) 18 *Leiden Journal of International Law* 179–213, at 180.

[61] See W Brown and J Halley, 'Introduction' in W Brown and J Halley (eds), *Left Legalism/Left Critique* (Duke University Press Durham 2002) 1–37.

[62] W Brown, '"The Most We Can Hope for"? Human Rights and the Politics of Fatalism' (2004) 103(2/3) *South Atlantic Quarterly* 451–63.

[63] S Moyn, *The Last Utopia: Human Rights in History* (Harvard University Press Cambridge MA 2010) at 231.

exploited social groups or classes with the political resources to halt the march of neoliberal accumulation (in its many and varied instantiations). And, moreover, that attempts to generate solutions from within (and *as*) human rights (the right to development, for example) 'risk reproducing the legitimacy of developmentalism as a set of institutional practices, a framework for understanding the world and as an alibi for exploitation'.[64] If pragmatism invites us not to ask after the enduring truth of our conceptions, but rather their use-values and their effectiveness in the world, then does not a sober reckoning with human rights compel the ultimate pragmatic conclusion that they should be dispensed with and that in their place we should seek to create other forms of politics to replace the stranglehold that human rights currently exerts on the global imaginary of emancipation? Each of the forms of pragmatism encountered here reframes or refounds human rights but what if, instead of trying pragmatically to rework and replenish the idioms of human rights, we attempted to 'take a break' from its language?[65] What new political possibilities would be opened up in and by this refusal? What new ways of approaching problems of global order and injustice would be disclosed or allowed to move into view? What would be lost and forgotten? Might it not be pragmatic to hazard *this* conversation?

The assumption undergirding each of the forms of pragmatism already discussed is that it is, on a certain basic level, *pragmatic* to attempt to work within the dominant political structures of the day, and to seek to leverage new possibilities from within their terms. Such a world-weary form of pragmatic thinking would seemingly oppose itself both to naive utopianism or discredited nostalgia. If human rights structure the present political possibilities, indeed structure the political possibilities of the present, so goes this argument, then we must surely work within that compass if we are to achieve anything. And yet by proposing the beginnings of my own kind of immanent critique-exhaustion of pragmatism I want to suggest that it is both too and too-little pragmatic of these pragmatists to make such an assumption. Surely there is a certain idealism that attaches to the subdued, profane faith of the human rights pragmatist in endlessly seeking to renovate and reframe existing political idioms in the face of their waning, exposure or demise? Or perhaps a kind of Benjaminian melancholic attachment to forms of thought and legal institutions once live, but now ossified in the historical present? (As Kennedy has argued in work subsequent to *The Dark Sides of Virtue*, the human rights 'moment' was 'a status quo project for a stable time'.[66] For him,

[64] A Orford, 'Globalization and the Right to Development' in P Alston (ed), *Peoples' Rights* (OUP New York 2001) 127–84, at 177, 180.

[65] Cf J Halley, *Split Decisions: How and Why to Take a Break from Feminism* (Princeton University Press Princeton 2006).

[66] D Kennedy, 'The International Human Rights Regime: Still Part of the Problem?' in R Dickinson et al., (eds), *Examining Critical Perspectives on Human Rights* (CUP Cambridge 2013) 19–34, at 34.

tellingly, '[h]uman rights is no longer the way forward—it focuses too longingly on the perfection of a politics already past its prime'.)[67]

Is mine, then, an argument for some pure form of politics unmediated by any (legal, juridical) form—or, at any rate, one not so fatally compromised as human rights today? Not at all; there is no outside to such political and legal forms. Political action requires mediation, which is necessarily impure and never without remainder. The pragmatic all-too-pragmatic critique of human rights broached here is hence not made on behalf of a newer and simplistically better political ideal (revolution, socialism, communism, self-determination, and so on) which would straightforwardly solve the problems of human rights once and for all. Rather, my critique is intended to be more modest, more historicist, more materialist (in a certain register) and far less stipulative than that. Political solutions (and they need not be temporally 'new', of course, but perhaps reworked versions of the 'old') need to emerge out of and respond to material conditions. It has been part of my critique of human rights pragmatism that in insisting on the endless reworkability of human rights it has not paid sufficient attention to the material limits of its own project, of what human rights can and cannot achieve in the world. It is but one project; there are others, old, new and as-yet-unthought, which for all *their* inevitable imperfections might work better for the people relying on them. However, the wager of my own pragmatism (the *pragmatism of refusal*) is that an initial step in beginning to weigh the costs and benefits of these other submerged political and legal possibilities is that we have to refuse human rights as the default framework through which we render global injustice intelligible. Only in that way will the possibility of something being not a human rights violation (demanding reporting, non-governmental organization censure, monitoring, and compliance mechanisms) but rather the occasion for a different epistemology and political response, emerge.

---

[67] 'The International Human Rights Regime' (n 66).

CHAPTER 35

....

THEORIZING
FREE TRADE

....

ANNE ORFORD

1 INTRODUCTION

....

THE idea that there is a free trade tradition that we might oppose to a mercantilist or protectionist tradition plays an important part in disciplinary histories of
international economics and of international trade law. The history of free trade is
remembered as a battle against protectionism and militant economic nationalism,
in which commercial sociability is equated with liberal government, cosmopolitanism, and a more peaceful world. That dominant account of trade liberalization
looks to history in order to root a contemporary set of doctrines and institutions in
the past, to provide a tradition that gives meaning to those doctrines and institutions as part of an unfolding story of progress, and to narrate the triumph of this
way of understanding the world over alternative ways of understanding the world.
According to this story, we can witness across the past two centuries a gradual
movement towards economic liberalization, hampered in certain areas by an in-
transigent commitment to protectionism, but furthered through the emergence of
new international institutions to oversee the commitment to liberalism. The story
usually begins with Adam Smith, moves towards a golden age of liberalization in
the late nineteenth century led by Britain, through a retreat to economic nationalism in response to the great depression and the two world wars, and on to the
slow attempt to rebuild a liberal world order after the Second World War. In this

story, the world is gradually improving, living standards are rising, and although the liberalization project is incomplete, it can still take credit for this gradual advance in the human situation.

The interrelated financial, food, energy, climate, and refugee crises of the early twenty-first century have given a new urgency to questions about the adequacy of this account, and reopened debates about what alternatives to the current global economic order are possible. While those crises have taken place in the context of an interdependent world economy, the vulnerability they have caused has been experienced in systematically uneven ways. Something in the routine operation of international economic life, organized around global value chains, free trade, border controls, freedom of navigation, investment protection, and open markets produces a system in which poorer countries continue to export vital resources even during periods of scarcity, investments are protected even during periods of civil war, and the people who labour to produce key commodities remain impoverished and undernourished. Many scholars and activists have turned their attention to international law in an attempt to grasp how this situation has come about.

This chapter joins that critical project by re-examining the history of free trade and its relationship to international law.[1] It locates contemporary trade agreements within a longer story about the relation between the state, the market, and the social; involving an intellectual community of economists, lawyers, and certain kinds of civil servants and diplomats; engaged in an ongoing process of interpretation and transmission of meaning. The institutionalization of free trade has been reliant upon control over land, labour, and resources; and accompanied by famine, riots, dispossession, and political volatility. Since the late eighteenth century, political economy has become the dominant discourse in which industrial and post-industrial society explains (to itself and to others) why forms of market relations should be preferred to other relations,[2] and thus why some people have entitlements to land, resources, and profits, and other people do not. International law, in the form of free trade agreements, has become a key vehicle for transmitting the economic doctrines, vocabularies, concepts, and practices that make sense of such relations on a global scale.

Section 2 explores why it is useful to place current trade agreements within a longer historical trajectory. Today's multilateral and regional trade agreements are justified according to an 'invented tradition' of free trade.[3] Any account of

---

[1] The chapter draws on and develops the arguments made in A Orford, 'Food Security, Free Trade, and the Battle for the State' (2015) 11(2) *Journal of International Law and International Relations* 1–67; A Orford, 'Law, Economics, and the History of Free Trade: A Response' (2015) 11(2) *Journal of International Law and International Relations* 155–80.

[2] TA Boylan and TP Foley, *Political Economy and Colonial Ireland* (Routledge London 1992) at 2.

[3] L Magnusson, *The Tradition of Free Trade* (Routledge London 2004). On invented traditions more generally, see E Hobsbawm and T Ranger (eds), *The Invention of Tradition* (CUP Cambridge 1983).

international trade law today involves engaging with that invented tradition. How the history of the free trade project is narrated already does a great deal of work in setting up the lessons that will be taken away about the inevitability and desirability of economic liberalism. In this sense, economic history *is* theory.[4] The theoretical work of this chapter thus lies in providing a different account of 'free trade' and its relationship to international law. The aim is to redescribe the free trade project, so that it is possible to perceive again the historical particularity of the contemporary relationship between that project and international law.[5]

Sections 3 and 4 offer a brief narrative of how the concept of free trade has moved across a 200-year period since the late eighteenth century.[6] Studying the transmission, juridification, and institutionalization of free trade involves considering how dominant meanings of free trade have been consolidated, contested, and transformed through interactions between institutions, norms, practices, networks, and powerful sponsors. This history shows that free trade is an expansive and contested concept, which has been invoked over the past 200 years to further a diverse range of political projects. Two things, however, have remained relatively constant over this period—first, that the argument for free trade has been located within a much broader debate about the proper relation between the state and the market, and second, that rationalizing who is entitled to basic resources such as food has been a recurring theme in struggles over what a commitment to free trade should mean in practice.

Section 5 concludes that this brief history can help us to rethink the conditions of the free trade project and its material limits. Concepts such as free trade (and related concepts such as discrimination, market distortion, protection, and subsidies) are the product of political struggles over particular ways of understanding the world, justifying entitlements to resources, explaining why some people should profit from the labour of others, and legitimizing the exercise of power. And the struggle over the meaning of free trade continues: as with other concepts that do a lot of political work, the concept of free trade is 'simultaneously unavoidable, ambiguous, and continuously contested'.[7]

---

[4] For two scholars with quite different political agendas arguing that economic history is theory, see J Banaji, *Theory as History: Essays on Modes of Production and Exploitation* (Haymarket Chicago 2010); PT Bauer, 'Economic History as Theory' (1971) 38 *Economica* 163–79.

[5] On the work of theory as involving the attempt to rearrange and redescribe what is already visible, see A Orford, 'In Praise of Description' (2012) 25 *Leiden Journal of International Law* 609–25.

[6] For the argument that legal scholarship engaging with the past cannot be governed by the Skinnerian prohibition against tracing the morphology of concepts across time, see A Orford, 'On International Legal Method' (2013) 1 *London Review of International Law* 166-97; A Orford, 'International Law and the Limits of History' in W Werner, A Galan, and M de Hoon (eds), *The Law of International Lawyers: Reading Martti Koskenniemi* (CUP Cambridge forthcoming).

[7] J-W Müller, 'On Conceptual History' in DM McMahon and S Moyn (eds), *Rethinking Modern European Intellectual History* (OUP Oxford 2014) 74–93, at 87.

2 WHY STUDY THE PAST?
HISTORY AS THEORY

So why revisit the received histories of the free trade project? The well-worn historical narrative that is reproduced as part of the invented tradition of international trade law makes it harder rather than easier to grasp how the global economy has come to take its current form, and the role of international law in that process. The dominant account renders the relation of international law and economic ordering opaque in four key ways.

2.1 Freedom, or the Lack of Conscious Attention to Economic Ordering

International law emerged as a profession committed to the spread of liberal ideas in the late nineteenth century.[8] It shares with liberalism a tendency to reflect upon itself within a language and framework organized around the notion of freedom, including free labour and a free market. Liberalism avoids consciously thinking about the way it institutes and regulates authority, labour, and goods,[9] while liberal legalism ignores both 'the legal ordering of economic policy' and the inherently political nature of that legal ordering.[10] The language of freedom of contract and free labour distracts our attention from the elements of compulsion involved in any system organized around the protection of property.[11] Those forms of compulsion are 'economic'—that is, they generally do not work through direct intervention in the relation between parties but rather through forms of law and regulation that sustain 'property (and propertylessness) and the operation of markets'.[12]

The conventional history of free trade makes it harder to see the coercion involved in institutionalizing liberalism. While liberals from Adam Smith onwards have been

---

[8] M Koskenniemi, *The Gentle Civilizer of Nations: The Rise and Fall of International Law 1870–1960* (CUP Cambridge 2002).

[9] AJ Treviño, 'Introduction' in K Renner, *The Institutions of Private Law and their Social Functions* (A Schwarzschild trans) (Transaction New Brunswick 2010 [1949]) ix–xxvi, at xvii–xviii.

[10] C Joerges, 'Europe's Economic Constitution in Crisis and the Emergence of a New Constitutional Constellation' (2014) 15 *German Law Journal* 985–1027, at 987.

[11] For a classic articulation, see RL Hale, 'Coercion and Distribution in a Supposedly Non-Coercive State' (1923) 38 *Political Science Quarterly* 470–94.

[12] E Meiksins Wood, *Empire of Capital* (Verso London 2003) at 4.

opposed to coercion that protects particular economic interests, creates monopolies, or leads to the acquisition of territory by force, they have nonetheless depended upon coercion in other ways: to sustain the liberal order against its opponents, to protect the right to property and the immunity of merchants from broader social obligations,[13] to compel workers to allow the profits of their labour to be transferred to others,[14] and to control the 'surplus' populations produced by land enclosures and capital-intensive development.[15] One aim in retelling this history is to reflect upon the forms of coercion that have enabled the project of liberal economic ordering. This chapter is in that sense overtly working against a liberal account by trying to reflect consciously upon these aspects of international law.

2.2 The Fragmentation of International Law

Second, conventional accounts of international law make it more difficult to study the constitution of the global economy because they treat international trade law as distinct from other areas of international law, and the history of international trade law as separate from the history of international law proper. This is in part an effect of a broader tendency towards what is now described in the field as 'fragmentation'.[16] Scholars increasingly specialize in a specific sub-field of international law such as trade law or human rights law, often organized around a particular treaty or institution, which is treated as distinct from the mainstream of the field.

The treatment of international trade law as separate from other areas of international law is evident in the approach that has been taken to writing histories of international law. While specialized histories of international trade and investment law have begun to appear,[17] broader international law histories have conventionally looked in earlier centuries for precursors to the international laws regulating war,

---

[13] On the immunity of merchants as the necessary complement of their liberty, see M Hill and W Montag, *The Other Adam Smith* (Stanford University Press Stanford 2015).

[14] For analyses of the role of humanitarian internationalists in embedding a distinction between (illiberal) forms of slavery and (liberal) forms of economic compulsion in international agreements, see A Ribi Forclaz, *Humanitarian Imperialism: The Politics of Anti-Slavery Activism, 1880–1940* (OUP Oxford 2015); V Stoyanova, *Human Trafficking and Slavery Reconsidered: Conceptual Limits and States' Positive Obligations* (Lund University Publications Lund 2015).

[15] See further 'Food Security, Free Trade, and the Battle for the State' (n 1) 37–48.

[16] International Law Commission, 'Fragmentation of International Law: Difficulties Arising from the Diversification and Expansion of International Law' (13 April 2006) UN Doc A/CN.4/L.682.

[17] For new histories of the trade regime, see G Marceau (ed), *A History of Law and Lawyers in the GATT/WTO: The Development of the Rule of Law in the Multilateral Trading System* (CUP Cambridge 2015); M Fakhri, *Sugar and the Making of International Trade Law* (CUP Cambridge 2014); A Lang, *World Trade Law after Neoliberalism: Re-Imagining the Global Economic Order* (OUP Oxford 2011); DA Irwin, PC Mavroidis, and AO Sykes, *The Genesis of the GATT* (CUP Cambridge 2008).

territory, and diplomacy, but not the precursors to the concepts embedded in current trade and investment agreements. Interwar debates about the ways in which access to colonial resources would be managed are not discussed as part of the discipline's practices of self-constitution, while debates over intervention or aggression are. The genesis of the UN is treated as part of mainstream international law history while struggles over the creation and role of the GATT or development agencies are not. Studies of international law and empire that link imperialism with political domination and territorial acquisition rather than economic exploitation and colonial administration reinforce an account in which liberalism and coercion remain separate.[18]

If the goal is to understand how a particular form of international law is being consolidated to order economic relations globally, the increasing specialist expertise of international lawyers is a barrier rather than an aid to comprehension. A historical approach makes it possible to trace how international law has participated in making economic, humanitarian, and security questions appear separate, and to challenge that representation. In addition, a focus on exploring the history of forms of law that have shaped the global economy directs us to a set of practices, concepts, laws, and actors that are often not included in the more conventional histories of international law. The material focus of a history of international law organized around the constitution of a global economy departs from the more traditional intellectual histories of international law, pointing in a different direction and to different collaborators. In order to understand the genealogy of that law, we need a new and different history, both in terms of our capacity to grasp the contemporary situation analytically and in terms of our capacity to understand the stakes of the twentieth-century mythologizing of international law.[19] In this view, international law does not derive purely from the genteel world of diplomats in European capitals, but also from the slightly dustier one of Poor Law reformers, colonial administrators, company civil servants, Treasury officials, political economists, and even theologians. Studying the development of modern international law requires attending to the ways that both state and empire were transformed over the course of the nineteenth century and into the twentieth. As territories were settled and colonial rulers were increasingly faced with rebellion, resistance, and demands for independence,[20] lawyers and colonial

---

[18] See further A Orford, *Reading Humanitarian Intervention: Human Rights and the Use of Force in International Law* (CUP Cambridge 2003) at 40–81 (analysing the continuity of imperialism as a system of exploitation rather than domination).

[19] A Orford, 'The Past as Law or History? The Relevance of Imperialism for Modern International Law' in M Toufayan, E Tourme-Jouannet, and H Ruiz Fabri (eds), *International Law and New Approaches To The Third World* (Société de Législation Comparée Paris 2013) 97–117; A Anghie, *Imperialism, Sovereignty and the Making of International Law* (CUP Cambridge 2005).

[20] K Mantena, *Alibis of Empire: Henry Maine and the Ends of Liberal Imperialism* (Princeton University Press Princeton 2010); D Armitage and S Subrahmanyam, *The Age of Revolutions in Global Context, c. 1760-1840* (Palgrave Macmillan New York 2010).

officials moved from developing doctrines justifying war to those explaining the principles of administration, policing, non-intervention, and free trade. The history of international law is thus not only to be found in the work of diplomats reflecting on their craft but also in the work of colonial administrators and trade officials reflecting on theirs.

2.3 Free Trade and the Battle for the State

Third, the conventional account narrates the free trade project as if it is aimed primarily at reshaping foreign relations. In this account, free trade is developed in opposition to protectionist trade barriers, typically the imposition of tariffs or quotas on imported goods. The dichotomy between free trade and protectionism, often presented as mapping onto an ethos of liberal commercial sociability versus one of nationalist economic militancy, continues to serve as a building block for disciplinary self-constitution in both international economics and international trade law. The free trade project is presented as a cosmopolitan response to mercantile strategies aimed at enhancing national power through the pursuit of economic strength and the protection of domestic producers, or more cynically as just another means for powerful states to make use of their comparative advantage to triumph over rivals. Either way, the focus of the narrative is on free trade as essentially part of a power play *between* states. In this account, the exponents of free trade are inherently agnostic about the internal ordering of economies and concerned with the external trade of states. While the latter half of the twentieth century has seen the focus of trade agreements shift from quotas and tariffs to 'behind the border' barriers to trade, this shift too is understood as part of a broader international power struggle, in which nation-states seek to entrench new commercial principles that can best promote their national interest as against their foreign competitors. Scholars focused primarily on the external relations of states treat all attempts to regulate economic matters, including 'behind the border' matters, as just more 'jealousy of trade' manoeuvring.[21]

Yet the philosophy of free trade has since the eighteenth century been concerned not only with regulating government controls over imports and exports, but also, and perhaps more importantly, with the attempt to shape the form of

---

[21] The phrase 'Jealousy of Trade' was famously used by David Hume in a 1758 essay, describing a world of competing commercial nations that understood success in international trade as essential to military and political survival and saw other trading states as rivals: D Hume, 'Of the Jealousy of Trade' in K Haakonssen (ed), *Hume: Political Essays* (CUP Cambridge 1994) 150–3. For the argument that the jealousy of trade transformed modern politics, see I Hont, *Jealousy of Trade: International Competition and the Nation-State in Historical Perspective* (Belknap Press Cambridge MA 2005).

the state and challenge certain forms of government intervention in the operation of the market. To put this in contemporary terms, the free trade project has always been as much concerned with 'behind the border' questions as with tariff barriers. This is not simply because 'behind the border' questions were linked to the competitiveness of foreign producers, however, but because the challenge to tariff barriers in the name of free trade has always been integrally tied up with a broader attempt to remake the state in a particular form. The emergence of the concepts of *la liberté du commerce* and of free trade in eighteenth- and nineteenth-century French and English political debates offered a language for arguing about the role of the state in relation to the market.[22] The attempt to create a science of legislation around the notion of free trade played a part in shaping the form of the state and colonial administration from the eighteenth century, and was furthered through international law and institutions from the twentieth century.

The tendency to understand the free trade project as one concerned with external relations between states is intensified when the project is taken up by international lawyers. International lawyers have developed an account of international law as a form of law directed to external aspects of the government of modern states. In this account, international law binds sovereigns in their dealings with other states—it sets out their rights and obligations and the way they conduct relations with each other through war, treaties, and diplomacy. This also shapes the way in which people narrate histories of international law. Yet modern international law is a project that is concerned as much with the regulation and administration of life *within* states, through international trade law, international law and development, and international human rights law, as it is with formal questions of relations *between* states. The genealogy of these forms of law lie not only in earlier attempts to constrain the foreign relations of states and the external aspects of government, but also in laws addressed to internal aspects of government and colonial administration.

2.4 International Law as Routine: Embedding Neoliberalism

Finally, international law renders opaque the political choices and struggles involved in institutionalizing liberalism because of the way in which law turns

---

[22] On the English debates, see further Section 3 below. On *la liberté du commerce*, see eg C-J Herbert, *Essai sur la police générale des grains* (A Berlin Paris 1755); LP Abeille, *Principes sur la liberté du commerce des grains* (Desaint Amsterdam 1768). For the relation between the French and British debates, see I Ross, 'The Physiocrats and Adam Smith' (1984) 7 *Journal for Eighteenth-Century Studies* 177–89; *The Other Adam Smith* (n 13) 267–96.

politics into routine. International law is not only a body of concepts, doctrines, and practices. It is also a way of going about things. In particular, law involves the transmission of concepts or ideas between legal actors, so that those concepts or ideas are worn smooth and cease to be politically volatile. Teaching students to be lawyers in part involves initiating them into the meaning of particular kinds of legal shorthand, so that they learn, for example, to treat certain legal fictions as if they were facts or to assimilate the complex set of political choices condensed into a legal concept.[23] While we might want to study the moment in which a text is first produced, whether through the writing of reasons for judgment, the drafting of legislation, or the negotiation of a treaty, what is more emblematic of legal knowledge production is the practice of repetition through which legal concepts, principles, and fictions come to seem—indeed come to be—real. Legal fictions and legal concepts are highly condensed forms of rhetorical material that allow often highly controversial political or philosophical propositions to be passed on as part of legal routine.

International law thus shares a tendency with other forms of law to create routines out of politics. And this is after all something for which we look to law. Rather than resort to force to achieve security or protect property, states look to law not only for particular outcomes but also for processes that will allow conflict to be avoided and channelled to more productive ends. Yet when we want to remember the politics that are embedded in the law, the successful operation of legal routines can make it harder to do so. This is particularly striking in the field of international law, where lawyers go to work within the kinds of functional specializations noted earlier, very swiftly taking up the language drafted by state officials and putting aside questions about the political viewpoints that language embodies, how conflicts are addressed by that language, what new ways of ordering the world are mandated, and what kinds of authority relations are needed to realize that way of ordering the world. Increasingly, international legal scholars are trained not to ask those questions if they are to be credible as experts.

International trade law, like other forms of law, is open to multiple interpretations. Yet while legal texts contain precedents, concepts, and arguments that can potentially be used to any end, that potential is also constrained through the ritualized processes of transmission and interpretation. Lawyers undertake the work of making particular meanings appear inevitable or acceptable.[24] In relation to international trade law, such work is shared with a broader interpretative community that at different periods has included diplomats, colonial administrators,

[23] A Riles, 'Is the Law Hopeful?' (Cornell Law Faculty Working Paper No 68, 2010) <http://scholarship.law.cornell.edu/clsops_papers/68> [accessed 28 February 2016] at 18–20.
[24] *Reading Humanitarian Intervention* (n 18) 35–6.

political economists, politicians, civil servants, and corporate executives. In recent decades, the process of securing the foundations of a liberal market economy through international law in the language of rational choice and efficiency 'has become a joint enterprise', carried out 'by economists, international lawyers, and rational-choice political scientists', with a particular focus upon informing doctrinal scholarship and institutional design through diagnosing 'substantive problems' and proposing legal solutions.[25] The field of international economic law was one of the first issue areas in which rational choice analysis was applied, with international economic lawyers and trade economists developing a detailed literature on international trade norms and their economic rationale.[26] Studying the history of international law as a practice of embedding neoliberalism thus involves studying the work of that broader interpretative community, and tracing an overlapping set of intellectual movements 'with shared concepts, theorists, and institutional support networks'.[27] While on the one hand such work can show that the currently dominant interpretation of the rules governing the global economy is not inevitable, predetermined, or unambiguous, it can also trace how and by whom alternative interpretations of legal concepts have been closed off.

3 TOWARDS A NEW HISTORY OF INTERNATIONAL LAW AND ECONOMIC ORDERING

In an attempt to address some of the barriers to comprehension that I have already described, this section takes a longer historical view of the free trade project and its relationship to international law. A historical approach makes it possible to consider the interrelated operation of legal practices and concepts before they were fragmented into separate fields. It can also make familiar concepts appear strange again, through attending to the debates that took place in order to secure their acceptance, the alternatives that they displaced, or the attempts to resist their adoption.

---

[25] See A van Aaken, 'Rational Choice Theory' in A Carty (ed), *Oxford Bibliographies Online: International Law* (OUP Oxford 2012).

[26] Ibid.

[27] SM Amadae, *Rationalizing Capitalist Democracy: The Cold War Origins of Rational Choice Liberalism* (University of Chicago Press Chicago 2003) at 251.

3.1 Around 1783: International Law and Revolution

Where this story begins is important. Different chronological periods 'throw up different interpretations'.[28] This history begins around 1783, the date on which the *Treaty of Paris* was signed recognizing the independence of the American colonies.[29] The choice to begin around 1783 highlights the significance of the dramatic changes to European thinking about internal government, empire, and foreign policy that followed the American, French, and Haitian revolutions of the late eighteenth century.[30] With the loss of the American colonies, British administrators turned their minds to new means of guaranteeing access to vital resources and securing the rights of merchants to trade, while the revolutions in France and Haiti placed questions of equality and freedom firmly on the political table. The issue of how to respond to the threat of revolution both in Europe and in European colonies began to occupy the thinking of elites. Out of that period of ferment emerged key concepts and techniques that continue to shape international law today.

This late eighteenth-century break also finds resonance in other work arguing for the significance of that moment as a turning point in political, social, and economic thought. Michel Foucault famously argued in *The Order of Things* that during the period between 1775 and 1825, a fundamental break occurred with the established ways of ordering knowledge, such that new disciplines including philology, biology, and economics could emerge and as a result of which 'History has become the unavoidable element in our thought'.[31] In German scholarship, Reinhart Koselleck used the term *Sattelzeit* to refer to the period roughly between 1750 and 1850, which saw 'the dissolution of the old world and the emergence of the new'.[32] Koselleck and his colleagues were interested in the historically oriented conceptual terms that developed to comprehend this revolutionary process of transformation and give expression to the new experience of the temporality of politics and the social world.[33] History was now perceived to open onto a new 'space of expectation',

[28] B Hilton, *A Mad, Bad, and Dangerous People? England 1783–1846* (Clarendon Press Oxford 2006) at 670.

[29] *Treaty of Paris* (signed 3 September 1783) 48 Con TS 487.

[30] *A Mad, Bad, and Dangerous People?* (n 28) 670; Y Benot, *La Révolution française et la fin des colonies* (La Découverte Paris 1988); D Geggus, 'The Caribbean in the Age of Revolution' in *The Age of Revolutions in Global Context* (n 20) 83–100. The Spanish colonial revolts of 1810 further contributed to this shift in imperial thinking: see further J Jobson de Andrade Arruda, 'Colonies as mercantile investments: The Luso-Brazilian empire, 1500-1808' in JD Tracy (ed), *The Political Economy of Merchant Empires* (CUP Cambridge 1991) 360–420.

[31] M Foucault, *The Order of Things: An Archaeology of the Human Sciences* (Routledge New York 2001 [1966]) at 238.

[32] K Tribe, 'Introduction' in R Koselleck, *Futures Past: On the Semantics of Historical Time* (Columbia University Press New York 2004 [1979]) vii–xx, at xiv, quoting R Koselleck, 'Richtlinien für das Lexikon politisch-sozialer Begriffe der Neuzeit' (1967) 11 *Archiv für Begriffsgeschichte* 81–97, at 81.

[33] *Futures Past* (n 32) 49–57, 59–60.

so that any study of the past became also a study of possibilities then imagined for the future.[34]

International law participates in the epistemological reconfiguration to which both Foucault and Koselleck draw our attention. It was one of the new forms of knowledge that emerged alongside political economy, and has been closely intertwined with it as a technology for implementing the science of human nature that economics sought to develop. International law carries with it the sense of historical time that emerged in this post-revolutionary period.[35] The vision of progress and human improvement conjured up by Enlightenment philosophers and articulated as a political program by the American and French revolutionaries has in turn been transformed into various projects of international law. International law emerged as a profession and an academic discipline carrying with it the sense of that liberalizing agenda in the latter half of the nineteenth century. The free trade project is one key vehicle through which that teleology plays out.

3.2 Free Trade and the Science of the Legislator

The philosophical origins of free trade are often traced back to the late eighteenth-century thinker Adam Smith. Smith had sought to promote and systematize the concept of free trade in *The Wealth of Nations* published in 1776, the year of the American Declaration of Independence.[36] Smith's overall argument concerned the need for economic reform within Britain and between Britain and its colonies. He considered political economy as 'a branch of the science of a statesman or legislator' and the principle of free trade as part of a much broader philosophy of government.[37] His systematic approach to government, strongly influenced by the French Physiocrats, criticized Britain's mercantilist regulation of its economic affairs and its colonial relations with America on the basis that this forced part of the country's industry 'into a channel less advantageous than that in which it would run of its own accord'.[38]

Smith's advocacy of a 'liberal system' of trade sought to address the tendency of economic policy-making to be influenced by the 'mean rapacity' and 'monopolising spirit' of merchants and manufacturers.[39] He commented that the monopoly that manufacturers had obtained as a result of mercantilist protectionism had 'so much increased the number of some particular tribes of them that, like

---

[34] *Futures Past* (n 32) 40–2.

[35] See also M Craven, 'Theorizing the Turn to History in International Law' and T Skouteris, 'The Idea of Progress' in this *Handbook*.

[36] A Smith, *The Wealth of Nations Books IV–V* (Penguin London 1999 [1776]).

[37] *The Wealth of Nations* (n 36) 5.   [38] Ibid 94.   [39] Ibid 72, 118.

an overgrown standing army, they have become formidable to the government, and upon many occasions intimidate the legislature'.[40] Smith opposed colonial rule for the same reason that he opposed mercantilism more generally—because it was conducted for the benefit of the 'rich and powerful' at the expense of 'the poor and the indigent'.[41] Colonial trade was enabled through government by unrepresentative assemblies under intimidation by powerful companies that had gained power and thus influence through commercial monopolies. The merchants who carried on colonial trade had become the principal advisors to the government on the regulation of that trade, with the result that the interests of the merchants were 'more considered than those of either the colonies or the mother country'.[42] Those companies were often granted formal monopolies over trade with particular colonies, and even companies that did not have a monopoly in law could nonetheless enjoy exclusive trade in fact due to the competitive advantages they gained through incorporation as joint stock companies with limited risk to the capital of those involved.[43]

While those trading companies effectively exercised the power of sovereigns over colonial territories, they did not consider it was in their interests to increase the profitability of the colony as a whole. Rather, their ambition was to profit by buying produce as cheaply as possible in the colonies and selling it at a higher price in Europe. In order to do so, they tried to keep all possible competitors from the colonial market, and thus keep the cost of colonial raw materials low. The result was that colonies were left with barely sufficient produce to meet the demands of their people, and did not have sufficient revenue to fund their own protection. This was in turn bad for the British people, who had to fund the protection of the colonies and of colonial trade without any revenue base on which to draw.

Smith's pragmatic call for a shift in British commercial policy from one of protecting colonial monopolies to engaging in free trade played a significant role in the terms of the government's eventual accommodation of the American demand for independence in the 1783 *Treaty of Paris*. The chief British negotiator of the *Treaty of Paris*, William Petty, Earl of Shelburne, considered himself Smith's disciple. He was an early supporter of Smith's free trade theories and of commercial liberty,[44] who had been known to present his friends with copies of Smith's *The Theory of Moral Sentiments*.[45] The *Treaty of Paris* effectively abolished the colonial system of monopoly between Britain and the former American colonies. When the result over the following decade proved to be an improvement of England's trading

---

[40] *The Wealth of Nations* (n 36) 48.   [41] Ibid 229.   [42] Ibid 165.   [43] Ibid 333, 343.

[44] B Semmel, *The Rise of Free Trade Imperialism: Classical Political Economy, the Empire of Free Trade and Imperialism 1750–1850* (CUP Cambridge 1970) at 27.

[45] R Whatmore, *Against War and Empire: Geneva, Britain, and France in the Eighteenth Century* (Yale University Press New Haven 2012) at 184.

position and economic strength rather than commercial ruin, 'the name of Adam Smith became a power in the land'.[46]

Whether Smith's solution was in the best interests of colonial subjects or the 'poor and indigent' of Britain is another question, as the implications of his arguments concerning free trade in subsistence foodstuffs illustrate. Smith was rare amongst political economists in his willingness to advocate liberal approaches to trade even during times of scarcity. This was an important topic in late eighteenth-century Britain. Food was a political flashpoint during this period of rapid transformation in the relations between landlords and tenants, forced enclosures of common lands, consolidation of larger holdings across England, clearances of rural land in Ireland, and growing commercial and military rivalry with France.[47] Food riots and the 'risings of the poor' that punctuated the 'great age of agricultural improvement' were a common form of direct action that represented the assertion by labouring people of traditional rights and customs.[48]

Few legislators or philosophers before Smith were willing to advocate complete freedom of trade during such periods of high food prices and hunger, fearing that if rulers were to deny their own duties in protecting the poor, they would devalue their authority to rule.[49] Many European states continued to control the trade in food throughout the eighteenth century, treating provisions as quite distinct from other commodities.[50] Smith challenged that 'ancient policy of Europe' and the restrictions it placed on agricultural trade.[51] In his famous 'Digression concerning the Corn Trade and Corn Laws', Smith argued that those ancient policies should be replaced by unrestrained freedom of trade in subsistence foodstuffs, even during times of poor harvest and high food prices. For Smith, to prevent 'the farmer from sending his goods at all times to the best market is evidently to sacrifice the ordinary laws of justice to an idea of public utility, to a sort of reason of state'.[52] While he did envisage that at times of 'most urgent necessity' government intervention might be justified, Smith otherwise expressed a steadfast commitment to free trade in food even in cases of famine. His arguments were taken up to justify limited governmental intervention during episodes of scarcity in England, Ireland, and India, as well as continued exports of foodstuffs out of areas suffering from famine.

---

[46] J Davidson, 'England's Commercial Policy towards Her Colonies since the Treaty of Paris' (1899) 14 *Political Science Quarterly* 39–68, at 40.

[47] K Polanyi, *The Great Transformation: The Political and Economic Origins of Our Time* (Beacon Press Boston 2001 [1944]).

[48] EP Thompson, 'The Moral Economy of the English Crowd in the Eighteenth Century' (1971) 50 *Past and Present* 76–136, at 79; G Rudé, *The Crowd in History: A Study of Popular Disturbances in France and England, 1730–1848* (Serif London 2005 [1964]); L Edgren, 'Livsmedelsprotesterna i Malmö 1799' [2014] (1–2) *Arbetarhistoria* 8–12.

[49] EP Thompson, *Customs in Common: Studies in Traditional Popular Culture* (New Press New York 1993) at 270.

[50] See further 'Free Trade, Food Security, and the Battle for the State' (n 1) 35.

[51] *The Wealth of Nations* (n 36) at 107.   [52] Ibid 119.

3.3 Malthus and the Principle of Population

The idea that hunger was an inevitable result of the laws of nature was the theme of another influential text of the age, *An Essay on the Principle of Population* published in 1798 by the Anglican cleric Thomas Robert Malthus.[53] The contribution of Malthus to the development of political economy was to focus attention on the government of the poor and dispossessed in England and the colonies, and the relation of that government to the question of scarcity. The late 1790s was a time of more than usually intense rioting around questions of food and labour in England, as well as a period of revolutionary unrest in Ireland leading to the Irish Rebellion of 1798.[54] In his *Essay*, Malthus sought to counter the effect that Francophone revolutionary thought was having upon politicians, intellectuals, and insurrectionary peasants in England and Ireland. He challenged the 'speculations' of radicals such as William Godwin and Nicolas de Condorcet, who considered that poverty, deprivation, and inequality could be alleviated by the perfection of human institutions.

According to Malthus, natural laws governing the relation between population and subsistence, rather than human institutions, were the cause of poverty, suffering, and famine. As population grew faster than the productive capacity of the earth, it was the 'unchecked' growth of population rather than any social, political or economic arrangements that produced 'the difficulty of subsistence'.[55] The limits to food security were natural, in the sense that natural laws were an expression of God's divine plan. As a result, '[n]o fancied equality, no agrarian regulations in their utmost extent', could remove the pressure of population growth upon food supply.[56] Malthus attacked attempts to ameliorate hunger and poverty, such as the English Poor Law that had since Elizabethan times mandated parish relief for the English poor, on the basis that such measures tended 'to create the poor which they maintain'.[57] By presenting the principle of population as a fixed law of nature, Malthus could defend the human institutions of property and government that shaped access to and use of land. His *Essay* offered 'an anti-Jacobin defence of property rights embedded in the religious world-view and theological framework of eighteenth century Anglican Christianity'.[58]

Malthus' essays and teaching about the causes of hunger and poverty were influential in reshaping the system of poor relief in England, and his appointment to the Chair of Political Economy at the East India College in 1805 ensured that his

---

[53] TR Malthus, *An Essay on the Principle of Population as it Affects the Future Improvement of Society: with Remarks on the Speculations of Mr Godwin, M Condorcet, and Other Writers* (OUP Oxford 1993 [1798]).

[54] RJ Mayhew, *Malthus: The Life and Legacies of an Untimely Prophet* (Belknap Press Cambridge MA 2014) at 64–5.

[55] *An Essay on the Principle of Population* (n 53) 13.   [56] Ibid 14.   [57] Ibid xv.

[58] AMC Waterman, *Revolution, Economics and Religion: Christian Political Economy 1798–1833* (CUP Cambridge 1991) at 7.

ideas would have an influence upon the conduct of colonial administration, first in Ireland and later in India.[59] Colonial administrators trained by Malthus developed programmes for responding to famine that focused either upon controlling population numbers or upon increasing the productivity of the earth, without questioning the practices of land clearances, enclosures, consolidation of large holdings by absentee landlords, and free trade that were then shaping access to and use of resources throughout the British Empire.[60] The dangerousness of government intervention in the market was impressed upon generations of civil servants taught at the East India College, where political economy was included in the curriculum from the inception of the College in 1805. Even after the abolition of the College in 1855, political economy continued to be a compulsory subject in Indian Civil Service examinations until 1892.[61]

Malthus' approach to government was informed by, and in turn informed, an evangelical vision of political economy that was central in shaping social and political thought in nineteenth-century Britain. That vision was premised upon the idea that Providence acts through general laws and that man should not intervene in the operation of those laws. God's Providence was responsible for everything that happens in this world, understood as an arena of moral trial.[62] Suffering was part of God's order, and would lead to contrition, reformation, redemption, and eventually grace. In its dominant 'moderate' form, the middle class piety represented by respectable groups such as the Clapham Sect had a major influence on thinking about domestic, colonial, and foreign policy.[63] Moderates believed that God did not miraculously intervene in earthly affairs to demonstrate special judgements. Rather, having instituted the laws of nature, God took a laissez-faire approach to the material world and did not interfere with the operation of the mechanism he had set in train. Society should operate as closely as possible to nature by repealing any laws considered to interfere with the unfolding of God's plan for the redemption of mankind. References to British faith in the 'sacred laws of political economy' or 'the Gospel of Free Trade' are thus not mere figures of speech.[64] Most evangelists in this moderate, natural law school 'were confident that *laissez-faire* policies would reveal a providential order', and moreover, that the order so revealed 'would be a *just* one'.[65] That mode of thought shaped British approaches to the government of the state, the conduct of colonial administration,

---

[59] P James, *Population Malthus: His Life and Times* (Routledge London 1979).

[60] EB Ross, *The Malthus Factor: Poverty, Politics and Population in Capitalist Development* (Zed London 1998).

[61] K Currie, 'British Colonial Policy and Famines: Some Effects and Implications of "Free Trade" in the Bombay, Bengal and Madras Presidencies, 1860–1900' (1991) 14(2) *South Asia* 23–56, at 25.

[62] B Hilton, *The Age of Atonement: The Influence of Evangelicalism on Social and Economic Thought, 1785–1865* (Clarendon Press Oxford 1986) at 8.

[63] See further 'Food Security, Free Trade, and the Battle for the State' (n 1) 37–8.

[64] *The Age of Atonement* (n 62) 6.   [65] Ibid 94.

and the direction of foreign policy, supplying the ideological underpinning for a liberal-conservative reaction to the forces behind the French Revolution and English Jacobinism and for governmental responses to poverty and famine in Britain and its colonies.[66]

3.4 The Corn Laws and the Free Trade State

By the mid-nineteenth century the political campaign for free trade had become one of the clearest articulations of English middle-class Providentialism. For its proponents free trade offered a principle for shaping domestic government, colonial administration, and foreign relations. Perhaps the most celebrated use of free trade as a tool of political campaigning in the nineteenth century was in debates over repeal of the Corn Laws.

The Corn Laws reintroduced protective tariffs on grain imports after the end of the Napoleonic wars, in an attempt to prevent a slump in grain prices following the resumption of continental trade. They were widely perceived and resented as a means of preserving aristocratic land-owning privileges at the expense of both the labouring poor who suffered from food shortages and high food prices, and the manufacturing class whose ability to export their products depended on healthy import trades generating sterling. The Corn Laws were part of the wider system of protectionist measures that had shaped English trade relations with Europe and with English colonies since the seventeenth century. Those measures included the Navigation Acts that restricted the use of foreign ships in trade between Britain and its colonies; widespread use of tariffs and import prohibitions; preferences for colonial products such as sugar, timber, and coffee; and the East India Company monopoly. All came under attack in the first decades of the nineteenth century, as advocates of free trade began to gain influence both within England and within the colonies.

The approach taken by free trade campaigners such as the cotton manufacturers Richard Cobden and John Bright illustrate the broad scope of the free trade principle during this period.[67] Cobden and Bright were influential in establishing the Anti-Corn Law League in 1836 to pressure members of parliament to repeal the Corn Laws.[68] The League largely represented industrialists and manufacturers based in the North of England whose profits depended upon free trade and who resented the ways in which Parliament both represented and privileged the landed interest. The eventual swing in Parliament in support of repeal of the Corn Laws in

---

[66] *Revolution, Economics and Religion* (n 58) 257.
[67] C Schonhardt-Bailey, *From the Corn Laws to Free Trade: Interests, Ideas, and Institutions in Historical Perspective* (MIT Press Cambridge MA 2006).
[68] Ibid 24–5.

1846 was driven by a combination of at least three, not necessarily compatible, sensibilities: the growing ideological and theological opposition to unnecessary state intervention in the market, the pragmatic sense even amongst those who largely represented the landed interest that without some concessions to giving up aristocratic privileges England could well go the way of revolutionary France, and a cosmopolitan and expansionist view of trade and industry as a vehicle for growth and progress.

Many of these interests were articulated in the support of 'free trade'.[69] For Cobden, the free trade principle represented a broad commitment to replacing the existing fiscal-military state with minimal government. Cobden and other like-minded reformers opposed government action that improperly interfered with the laws of the market both in the conduct of external relations and internal government. War expenditure, colonial acquisition, intervention, and import tariffs were denounced as infringements of free trade, alongside food taxes, the alienation of estates, restrictive land laws, factory legislation, and monopolies.[70] Free trade was as much a debate about the government of property, commerce, industry, finance, and the need for democratic reform in England as it was about import tariffs. Cobden saw in the free trade principle 'that which shall act on the moral world as the principle of gravitation in the universe, drawing men together'.[71] In one of his many speeches campaigning in favour of free trade, Cobden professed his belief 'that the speculative philosopher of a thousand years hence will date the greatest revolution that ever happened in the world's history from the triumph of the principle which we have met here to advocate'.[72]

As a result in part of the successful campaign to repeal the Corn Laws, free trade became one of the most commonly held values uniting manufacturing and working class reformists in England.[73] By the mid-nineteenth century, many of the core aspects of economic governance that had troubled Adam Smith were abandoned in England, with the Corn Laws and many other protectionist forms of regulation repealed, the East India Company monopolies in India and China abolished, the discretionary powers of the Bank of England curtailed, and the 'fiscal-military state' beginning its slow transformation towards the minimal state

---

[69] See further 'Food Security, Free Trade, and the Battle for the State' (n 1) 39–42.

[70] R Cobden, 'Foreign Policy, Rochdale, November 23, 1864' in J Bright and JE Thorold Rogers (eds), *Speeches on Questions of Public Policy by Richard Cobden, MP* (2 vols 3rd edn T Fisher Unwin London 1908 [1870]) vol 2, 479–96, at 493; FW Hirst, 'Introduction' in FW Hirst (ed), *Free Trade and Other Fundamental Doctrines of the Manchester School* (Harper London 1903) ix–xxv, at xii.

[71] R Cobden, 'Free Trade, Manchester, January 15, 1846' in *Speeches on Questions of Public Policy by Richard Cobden, MP* (n 70) vol 1, 181–7, at 187.

[72] Ibid.

[73] AC Howe, 'Free Trade and the City of London, c 1820–1870' (1992) 77 *History* 391–410, at 409; AC Howe, 'Free Trade and the Victorians' in A Marrison (ed), *Free Trade and Its Reception 1815–1960* (3 vols Routledge London 1998) vol 1, 164–83, at 164.

championed by free traders and political economists.[74] Yet while British advocates of free trade were committed to the dismantling of existing colonial relations, they also ushered in what was to become a new free trade imperialism.[75] The old mercantilist system of colonial relations was dismantled over the nineteenth century, yet this did not represent the end of the British Empire, if empire is understood to involve structured systems of exploitation. In place of the 'old colonial system' was erected a new system of free trade, premised upon an international division of labour and access to the resources of the colonies.[76] In that context, the 'issue of starvation' would remain the 'ultimate test' of the Victorian commitment to free trade and the principles of political economy.[77] It was a test that colonial administrators would pass with flying colours in Ireland and India.

3.5 Free Trade, Famine, and Colonial Administration

Free trade was the language in which the English governing classes debated the wisdom of government intervention to provide relief to the victims of famine in Ireland and India, while the science of political economy profoundly shaped the approach of English officials to the administration of Ireland and India more generally.

The influence of those ways of thinking about the role of the state was evident in official responses to the Irish famine of 1845–52. During what would become a seven-year period of mass starvation and emigration, the population of Ireland declined by over 20 per cent, with approximately one million people dying and more than one million people emigrating. Yet Ireland remained a major source of food for Britain during that period. From the beginning of the nineteenth century two sectors had developed in the Irish agricultural economy—the first a subsistence sector with potatoes as its primary product feeding the poor Catholic masses, and the second an export sector of wheat, grains, and live animal exports that met England's food shortfall. That export trade continued during the Irish famine. The language of free trade and Providentialist thinking were central to the way that officials justified that situation to themselves.

The Irish famine was characterized as a Malthusian crisis by the British government.[78] The role played by Malthus' student Charles Trevelyan in overseeing

---

[74] *A Mad, Bad, and Dangerous People* (n 28) 543.

[75] *The Rise of Free Trade Imperialism* (n 44) 3.

[76] On the 'old colonial system', see RL Schuyler, *The Fall of the Old Colonial System: A Study in British Free Trade, 1770–1870* (OUP New York 1945).

[77] D Hay, 'The State and the Market in 1800: Lord Kenyon and Mr Waddington' (1999) 162 *Past and Present* 101–62, at 159.

[78] See further 'Food Security, Free Trade, and the Battle for the State' (n 1) at 35–8.

famine relief was central to the approach that the British government adopted. Trevelyan had been a student of Malthus while at the East India Company College, and during the late 1820s and 1830s had served with the East India Company Civil Service in Bengal and the British Colonial Government in Calcutta. From 1840 to 1859 he was assistant secretary to Her Majesty's Treasury, and in that role administered the famine relief works in Ireland from 1845 to 1847. For Trevelyan, writing in 1848, the Irish famine was a 'great intervention of Providence', and history would trace to it 'the commencement of a salutary revolution in the habits of a nation long singularly unfortunate'.[79] Trevelyan and his fellow officials interpreted the Irish famine as a symptom of the overpopulation of Ireland by surplus rural labourers,[80] rather than an indictment of a British colonial system that continued to ship large quantities of grain, beef, and pork to England even at the height of the famine. The evangelical commitment to allowing God's plan to unfold through the unrestricted operation of natural laws shaped the approach taken by British officials both to the short-term provision of famine relief and to longer-term structural reform. The response of the government was overtly aimed at reshaping Ireland into a commercial society, enabling the clearances and consolidation of farming land, encouraging English and Scottish investment, and addressing the problem of 'surplus population' through promoting emigration to other colonies.[81]

The influence of political economy on thinking about the relation between famine and free trade was also evident in official responses to serial famines in India under British rule. Colonial administrators in India were some of the earliest officials to take up the principles of Adam Smith and Thomas Malthus as the basis for policy-making.[82] In part this was a result of their training at the East India College, and in part this was because many of the influential early administrators of newly conquered parts of British India in the early nineteenth century were Scottish, including Sir John Malcolm, Mountstuart Elphinstone, and Sir Thomas Munro.[83] They brought Scottish Enlightenment conceptions about forms of government, law, theology, and political economy to the problem of governing India. As administrators they self-consciously sought to act as Adam Smith's ideal legislators, building a science of government upon the principles of political economy.[84]

---

[79] CE Trevelyan, *The Irish Crisis* (Longman, Brown, Green & Longmans London 1848) at 1, 8.

[80] Ibid.

[81] See eg the proposals made in J Caird, *The Plantation Scheme; or, the West of Ireland as a field for investment* (W Blackwood & Sons Edinburgh 1850), discussed further in 'Food Security, Free Trade, and the Battle for the State' (n 1) at 44–5.

[82] S Ambirajan, 'Political Economy and Indian Famines' (1971) 1 *South Asia* 20–8, at 21.

[83] M McLaren, *British India and British Scotland, 1780–1830: Career Building, Empire Building, and a Scottish School of Thought on Indian Governance* (University of Akron Press Akron 2001).

[84] J Harrington, *Sir John Malcolm and the Creation of British India* (Palgrave Macmillan New York 2010).

The centrality of the free trade concept to British colonial administration in India is illustrated in the reports of the famine commissions that were established from the mid-nineteenth century onwards in an attempt to develop a generally applicable 'famine policy'.[85] Those reports stressed the centrality of the principle of free trade in determining the appropriate response to famine. Their studies of earlier examples of famines in India sought to show that when governments attempted to interfere with the principle of free trade, they made the situation worse.[86] Smith's *The Wealth of Nations* was cited to establish that 'in the natural laws of trade left to their free action, or if helped only by the removal of obstructions, one of the best and surest aids against Famines is to be found'.[87] The 1880 Report of the Commission of Inquiry on Indian Famines admitted that complying with the principle of free trade had often led to 'excess' deaths of a million or more people per famine, yet stressed that situations in which the government interfered with private trade often led to reserves of grain left in government storehouses that had to be 'disposed of at a loss'.[88] The Commission concluded that the 'principle of non-interference with trade' should provide the foundation for future British administration of famine relief in India, and recommended that the government should 'adopt as its general rule of conduct' to 'leave the business of the supply and distribution of food to private trade, taking care that every possible facility is given for its free action, and that all obstacles material or fiscal are, as far as practicable, removed'.[89] Measures to prevent famines, such as supplying grain during times of scarcity or stockpiling grains in the period between famines, should be abandoned.

The free trade philosophy of the political economists had lasting effects on principles of colonial administration, and contributed to the consolidation of imperial economic systems over the course of the nineteenth century and the early decades of the twentieth. Those systems succeeded in ending famine in much of Europe, and producing sufficient food to feed the workers of the continent's rapidly industrializing cities. Yet catastrophic famines never ceased to plague European colonies.[90] As Mike Davis has argued, the issue is 'not simply that tens of millions of rural people died appallingly', but that they did so while British administrators quoting Smithian dogma 'allowed huge grain exports to England in the midst of starvation'.[91]

---

[85] See further 'Food Security, Free Trade, and the Battle for the State' (n 1) at 46–8.

[86] See eg *The Special Commissioner's Final Report on the Famine of 1860–61 (14 August 1861)* (Englishman Office Calcutta 1861) Section II, 9.

[87] Ibid.

[88] *Report of the Indian Famine Commission: Part I, Famine Relief* (Her Majesty's Stationery Office London 1880) at 10, 16.

[89] Ibid 49.

[90] J Vernon, *Hunger: A Modern History* (Belknap Press Cambridge MA 2007) at 4.

[91] M Davis, *Late Victorian Holocausts: El Niño Famines and the Making of the Third World* (Verso London 2001) at 9, 11.

3.6 Force and Free Trade

Despite the advocacy of 'free' trade and the rhetorical arguments for the liberty of the merchant, the free trade project existed in a complex relationship with coercion. The realization of free trade in nineteenth-century Britain depended not only on 'commercial acumen and entrepreneurial dynamism, but also on the fiscal-military state'.[92] While the version of free trade associated with Adam Smith and Richard Cobden was pacifist in inclination and designed to challenge the development of a British fiscal-military state, many other proponents of free trade were more comfortable with the idea of using force in the interests of commerce. Perhaps the most infamous example of that muscular free trade policy is the so-called Opium War of 1839–42. While the immediate trigger for the war was the 1839 decision by the Chinese government to confiscate opium being smuggled into China from India by British merchants, the war was part of a longer clash between Britain and China designed to force China to open its economy to British trade and finance.[93] While the Cobdenite Tory opposition argued against the war, the government position, supported by many Liberal and Radical free traders, was that the use of force was necessary to protect British life and property.[94] The parliamentary free traders, like the mercantilists of an earlier era, were willing to urge the government to use force, this time in the interests of securing free trade, defending the lives and property of British subjects trading in foreign countries, and extending British markets.[95]

In addition, free trade was conditioned on the use of force to control the people who were dispossessed as a result of the enclosures and agrarian reforms carried out throughout the nineteenth century. While the account given by Malthus might have suggested that governments could simply abandon the poor to the designs of Providence, in fact the threat of rural riots and urban insurrection meant more active intervention was necessary. Emigration to the colonies (both voluntary and forced) emerged as a central strategy for controlling 'surplus' population during the nineteenth century. This 'more repressive type of interventionism' was vital to mitigating the revolutionary consequences that could have followed in Britain from rapid industrialization combined with the 'reforms' that limited access to poor relief.[96] The nineteenth century became 'a great machine for uprooting countrymen'.[97] There were significant movements of peoples from the

---

[92] M Daunton, *Wealth and Welfare: An Economic and Social History of Britain 1851–1951* (OUP Oxford 2007) at 4.

[93] M Lynn, 'British Policy, Trade, and Informal Empire in the Mid-Nineteenth Century' in A Porter (ed), *The Oxford History of the British Empire Volume III: The Nineteenth Century* (OUP Oxford 1999) 101–21, at 110, 116.

[94] See the debate recorded in Hansard: HC Deb 9 April 1840, vol 53, cols 844–950.

[95] *The Rise of Free Trade Imperialism* (n 44) 157, 206.

[96] *A Mad, Bad, and Dangerous People?* (n 28) 22.

[97] E Hobsbawm, *The Age of Capital: 1848–1875* (Abacus London 1975) at 231.

European countryside to the towns, from Europe to places of settlement in the United States (US), Canada, Australia, and New Zealand, and between Asian and African colonies.[98] This 'vast labour and social transformation' saw fifty million people—almost all peasants—leave Europe in the century to 1914, pushed out by the spread of industry and the commercialization of agriculture.[99] The success of European free trade was thus also conditioned on the continued dispossession of the indigenous inhabitants of colonies in Africa, Asia, and North America during the nineteenth and well into the twentieth centuries. The effect of the population movements required by European industrialization was that indigenous peoples become the bearers of the burden of global capitalism, as successive waves of peasants pushed out of Europe arrived in European colonies through to the end of the Second World War.

4 International Law and State Planning: The GATT in Context

4.1 International Economic Disintegration and 'Peaceful Change'

Today's trade lawyers often suggest that the world wars and depression of the early twentieth century interrupted a worldwide liberalization of trade, labour, and commerce.[100] Yet many European states maintained high tariff regimes and protectionist policies throughout the nineteenth century, and to the extent they liberalized tariffs it was as a result of bilateral trade agreements.[101] Trade in goods produced in the colonies still primarily moved according to patterns of imperial preference and monopoly, shaped by colonial business interests and investors who acquired land, managed plantations and mines, made use of slave or indentured labour, and built railways and ports to integrate imperial assets into European commercial networks. Nonetheless by the late nineteenth century the network of bilateral

---

[98] J Rosenberg, *The Empire of Civil Society: A Critique of the Realist Theory of International Relations* (Verso London 1994) at 163.

[99] Ibid; ER Wolf, *Europe and the People without History* (University of California Press Berkeley 1982) at 361–79.

[100] See eg *The Genesis of the GATT* (n 17) 5–7.

[101] *Wealth and Welfare* (n 92); G Cohn, 'Free Trade and Protection' (1904) 14 *Economic Journal* 188–95.

agreements between European states had led to the creation of a low-tariff zone throughout much of Europe, and there was a higher degree of international integration between wealthier nations prior to the First World War than afterwards.

The free trade concept suffered a blow when governments responded to the financial crisis of the 1920s with tariff barriers and other policies designed to stop the spread of economic depression. The challenge that absorbed liberal international lawyers and political economists was how best to confront the perceived 'disintegration' of international law and economic order.[102] For some, the international law and 'integrated world system' made possible by European liberalism had already disintegrated by the end of the nineteenth century.[103] For others the cause of the decline was protectionist responses to the First World War and the Great Depression.[104] For still others, the challenge to the social foundations of international law came from the foreign policies of fascist states and, to a lesser extent, Soviet Russia.[105] Nonetheless by the 1930s, liberal internationalists shared the sense that the disintegration of the international system was a real problem, that it coincided with the end of European liberalism, and that it meant the weakening of international law.[106]

In addition, the colonial question became a pressing issue for states during the interwar period. For many internationalists, it was apparent that collective security could not be guaranteed without a means for addressing disputes about the legitimacy of colonialism. 'Peaceful change' was the vocabulary in which the rights and privileges of colonial powers, specifically access to 'essential colonial raw materials' and to the space perceived as necessary for addressing problems of 'overpopulation', was debated.[107] The fascist expansionist policies that mirrored colonialism, whether in the form of the Italian invasion of Abyssinia or the expansionist German policy of *Volk ohne Raum*, were widely seen to represent a problem.

---

[102] See W Röpke, *International Economic Disintegration* (W Hodge London 1942); W Friedmann, 'The Disintegration of European Civilisation and the Future of International Law' (1938) 2 *Modern Law Review* 194–214; L von Mises, 'Economic Problems: The Disintegration of the International Division of Labour' in P Mantoux et al., *The World Crisis* (Longmans, Green London 1938) 245–74.

[103] A Rüstow, 'Appendix: General Sociological Causes of the Economic Disintegration and Possibilities of Reconstruction' in *International Economic Disintegration* (n 102) 267–83.

[104] *International Economic Disintegration* (n 102).

[105] 'The Disintegration of European Civilisation' (n 102).

[106] On the relation of liberal conditions of economic order to the existence of international law prior to the First World War, see ibid 194–5; 'Appendix' (n 103) 273–4; *International Economic Disintegration* (n 102).

[107] See eg JB Whitton, 'Problems of Markets and Raw Materials' (1936) 30 *American Society of International Law Proceedings* 104–111; FS Dunn, *Peaceful Change: A Study of International Procedures* (Council on Foreign Relations New York 1937); CAW Manning (ed), *Peaceful Change: An International Problem* (MacMillan New York 1937; International Institute of Intellectual Co-operation, *Peaceful Change: Procedures, Population, Raw Materials, Colonies: Proceedings of the Tenth International Studies Conference, Paris, June 28–July 3, 1937* (League of Nations Paris 1938); JB Whitton, 'Peaceful Change and Raw Materials' in *The World Crisis* (n 102) 293–323.

Yet perhaps surprisingly, many commentators expressed some sympathy with the position that fascist expansionism was in part a response to an unfair world order, in which colonial powers enjoyed a monopoly of access to 'essential colonial raw materials' and to the space perceived as necessary for addressing problems of metropolitan overpopulation.[108]

Thus, during the 1930s internationalists began to question the exceptional status and privileges of colonial powers and to link the resolution of the world crisis to the development of mechanisms for 'peaceful change' towards decolonization.[109] Ideas about international integration became central to considerations about the forms of spatial order suited to emerging economic arrangements, the need for states to access raw materials, new forms of energy and the infrastructure that supported those forms, and issues related to the distribution of population. Questions about how to secure access to raw materials, find space for 'redundant' populations, and maintain an open door for free trade, shifted from the domain of colonial law and policy to international law. Major international law figures such as Karl Strupp and Hersch Lauterpacht wrote treatises and took part in collaborative projects with economists, historians, and sociologists aimed at creating a new liberal order that could ensure peaceful change from an era of imperial states and economies to one of global economic integration.[110]

4.2 International Liberalism Versus State Planning

One view in particular that began to emerge during that period has since come to exert a strong influence over international approaches to economic integration. During the 1930s, an affiliation of liberal economists, lawyers, corporate leaders, publishers, and policy-makers began to express concerns about the collectivism and optimistic approaches to state planning that had begun gaining support. Through events such as the Colloque Walter Lippmann held in Paris in 1938, the creation of think tanks such as the Mont Pèlerin Society in 1947, and the academic networks associated with Freiburg University, the London School of Economics and Political Science, and the Chicago School of Economics, this group analysed what they saw as the emerging crisis of liberalism. They developed new proposals for constraining

[108] Moves in favour of 'doing something about raw materials' at an institutional level were partly fuelled by the speech of Sir Samuel Hoare to the League of Nations Assembly in September 1935, the aim of which was understood to be dissuading Mussolini from invading Abyssinia. See further AD McNair, 'Collective Security' (1937) 17 *British Year Book of International Law* 150–64; H Nicolson, 'The Colonial Problem' (1938) 17 *International Affairs* 32–50.

[109] See eg *Peaceful Change: A Study of International Procedures* (n 107); *Peaceful Change: An International Problem* (n 107).

[110] See K Strupp, *Legal Machinery for Peaceful Change* (Constable London 1937); H Lauterpacht, 'The Legal Aspect' in *Peaceful Change: An International Problem* (n 107) 135–65.

collectivism and sought to develop the foundations of a new liberalism, in part through approaching the question of how to create a competitive market economy as one of international order.[111] For these liberal thinkers, liberalism and parliamentary democracy were not necessarily compatible. They believed that democratic states too easily become the prey of organized special interests and unable to act for the collective good. International economic integration offered one means of freeing the market from special interests and enabling competition.[112]

The work of Friedrich Hayek provides an example of the link made between international economic integration and the defeat of state planning. Hayek sought to prevent what he perceived as the threats to liberty posed not only by communism and fascism, but also by the proposed post-war planned economies of the United Kingdom (UK), the US, and France.[113] Planning necessarily involved the 'deliberate discrimination between particular needs of different people' and thus 'the decline of the Rule of Law'.[114] For Hayek, one means of dismantling planned economies was through a systematic process of interstate economic integration. He argued that the removal of tariffs and other barriers to the movement of goods and capital had important consequences that were frequently overlooked.[115] In particular, the absence of such 'economic frontiers' made it much more difficult to 'create communities of interest on a regional basis' and of an 'intimate character'.[116] For Hayek, the destruction of any 'solidarity of interests' was the most important overlooked consequence of economic integration.[117] That in turn would limit the capacity of states to develop monetary policy, regulate methods of production, set minimum wages, limit working hours, prohibit child labour, and tax commodities.[118] Hayek considered it unlikely that 'restrictive or protective' forms of government regulation would be adopted by any newly created interstate government.[119] People would be less willing to make sacrifices or pay more for goods to help producers in other states—as a result, there would be little support for restrictive or protective measures aimed at helping foreign producers or workers within an internationalized market.[120]

---

[111] See S Audier, *Le colloque Lippmann: Aux origines du 'néo-libéralisme'* (BDL Editions Paris 2012); H Schulz-Forberg and N Olsen, *Re-Inventing Western Civilisation: Transnational Reconstructions of Liberalism in Europe in the Twentieth Century* (Cambridge Scholars Newcastle upon Tyne 2014); P Mirowski and D Plehwe (eds), *The Road from Mount Pèlerin: The Making of the Neoliberal Thought Collective* (Harvard University Press Cambridge MA 2009); K Tribe, *Strategies of Economic Order: German Economic Discourse 1750–1950* (CUP Cambridge 1995).

[112] See further A Orford, 'Hammarskjöld, Economic Thinking, and the United Nations' in H Melber and C Stahn (eds), *Peace, Diplomacy, Global Justice, and International Agency: Rethinking Human Security and Ethics in the Spirit of Dag Hammarskjöld* (CUP Cambridge 2014) 156–89.

[113] FA Hayek, *The Road to Serfdom* (University of Chicago Press Chicago 2007 [1944]).

[114] Ibid 82.

[115] FA Hayek, 'The Economic Conditions of Interstate Federalism (1939)' in *Individualism and Economic Order* (University of Chicago Press Chicago 1948) 255–72, at 258.

[116] Ibid 257.   [117] Ibid 258.   [118] Ibid 258–9.   [119] Ibid 261.   [120] Ibid 263.

Hayek thus specifically saw the removal of 'economic frontiers' and consequent dissolution of the sense of community and sympathy created by the nation state as a strategy to attack planning. Because planning or the 'central direction of economic activity' presupposed 'the existence of common ideals and common values', international economic integration would make planning much more difficult to carry out by limiting the extent to which 'agreement on such a common scale of values can be obtained or enforced'.[121] Economic integration was therefore not merely a means of attacking the capacity of the state to discriminate between national producers and foreign producers, but rather it was a means of attacking the capacity of the state to discriminate—that is, to plan—at all. Through establishing the Mont Pèlerin Society, Hayek sought to promote those ideas through 'a new liberal program which appeals to the imagination', and makes 'the building of a free society once more an intellectual adventure, a deed of courage'.[122] For Hayek, in this context 'free trade' was an ideal that 'still may arouse the imaginations of large numbers'.[123]

The vision of the relation between economic order and international law that emerged during this period is also well illustrated by the work of the economist and sociologist Wilhelm Röpke. In his 1942 book, *International Economic Disintegration*, Röpke argued that 'the real ultimate cause of the breakdown of international economic life as well as the functional disorders of the liberal economic system is to be found in the far-reaching disturbances, moral and material, caused by the collectivist principle'.[124] In a similar vein, Röpke's 1954 lectures at the Hague Academy of International Law took the demise of liberalism and 'international planning' as their target. According to Röpke, the 'international "open society" of the nineteenth century may be regarded…as a creation of the "liberal" spirit', meaning 'the widest possible separation of the two spheres of government and economy, of sovereignty and economic exploitation, of Imperium and Dominium'.[125] However the 'international "open society" of the nineteenth century' had been destroyed by the emergence of an 'interventionist-collectivist system' after the Second World War. As a result, international law had 'entered the phase of disintegration'.[126] The answer to the current impasse was not to 'turn the national system of collectivism, which has shown itself to be the villain in the piece, into an international one'.[127] Rather, the answer was to abolish that 'excessive sovereignty' upon which states drew to undertake 'collectivist economic control'.[128]

---

[121] 'The Economic Conditions of Interstate Federalism (1939)' (n 115) 264.

[122] FA Hayek, 'The Intellectuals and Socialism' (1949) 16 *University of Chicago Law Review* 417–33, at 432.

[123] Ibid.   [124] *International Economic Disintegration* (n 102) 260.

[125] W Röpke, 'Economic Order and International Law' (1954) 86 *Recueil des Cours* 203–73, at 223–4 (emphasis removed).

[126] Ibid 226.   [127] Ibid 241.   [128] Ibid 250.

To the extent there was a role for international law and institutions, then, it lay in constraining this excessive sovereignty: 'the alternative to order provided by the government (planning) is certainly not anarchy but another kind of order, provided by the market'.[129] Röpke vehemently opposed the 'economic nationalist or socialist policies followed by most post-colonial developing nations', and sought to counter the influence of economists like Gunnar Myrdal, who both offered prescriptions to newly independent governments and 'advocated welfare states, nationalization and inflationary investment policies in their own countries'.[130]

The UK economist Lionel Robbins, one of the principal negotiators of the GATT, was another major figure involved in the attempt to bring into being an international institutional architecture that could foster liberalism. Robbins was appointed to a chair at the LSE in 1929, and was responsible for bringing Hayek there, first in 1931 as a visiting professor and then as a permanent appointment.[131] Robbins remained a close collaborator of Hayek during the 1930s and 1940s.[132] He attended the first meeting of the Mont Pèlerin Society in 1947, and drafted its statement of aims, stressing the centrality of competitive markets to the preservation of individual liberty.[133] Robbins' 1937 book *Economic Planning and International Order* was an influential contribution to interwar debates about the future of international order. Robbins argued that the causes of war could be found in the emergence of 'planning', which had become 'the grand panacea of our age'.[134] Planning here meant 'collective control or supersession of private activities of production and exchange'.[135] Robbins examined the significance of planning 'from a specifically international point of view'.[136] He argued that the international consequences of national planning included the diversion of resources from productive uses, destructive attempts by labour to use democracy as a means to determine the conditions of their employment, and war.[137] It was necessary to reject socialist or state planning in favour of a liberal model of economic order premised on 'the free market and the institution of private property', and restrained within suitable limits by a framework of institutions'.[138] Robbins lauded the 'administration of the free-trade Empire' as an example of a form of international order based on 'the splendid principles of internationalism and freedom'.[139]

---

[129] 'Economic Order and International Law' (n 125) 248.
[130] S Gregg, *Wilhelm Röpke's Political Economy* (Edwar Elgar Cheltenham 2010) at 149.
[131] S Howson, *Lionel Robbins* (CUP Cambridge 2011) at 163–6, 196–241.
[132] H Schulz-Forberg, 'Laying the Groundwork: The Semantics of Neoliberalism in the 1930s' in *Re-Inventing Western Civilisation* (n 111) 13–39, at 28.
[133] K Tribe, 'Liberalism and Neoliberalism in Britain, 1930–1980' in *The Road from Mount Pèlerin* (n 111) 68–97, at 87.
[134] L Robbins, *Economic Planning and International Order* (Macmillan London 1937) at 3.
[135] Ibid 13.   [136] Ibid 9.   [137] Ibid 46, 61–2, 72–3, 96.   [138] Ibid 6, 222, 227.
[139] Ibid 126–7.

4.3 Negotiating the GATT

The growth of international institutions that followed the Second World War provided one site to which free trade advocates might look to address the 'disintegration' diagnosed by Röpke, Robbins, and Hayek. Of particular relevance to this chapter are the negotiations that led to the *General Agreement on Tariffs and Trade* (GATT) in 1947.[140] The turn to commercial diplomacy during the interwar period was largely driven by the US. Cordell Hull, Secretary of State from 1933 to 1944 in the administration of President Franklin Roosevelt, was the driving force in repositioning US foreign policy toward trade liberalization during the 1930s and in shaping planning for post-war reconstruction during the 1940s. Under his leadership the US negotiated trade agreements with twenty-two countries during the 1930s, many of them in Latin America. The provisions of those agreements formed the basis for much of the GATT.[141] The US took advantage of the UK's need for financial assistance during the Second World War to require as a condition for the Lend Lease aid program that the UK negotiate a reduction in imperial preferences and an agreement on principles for a liberal international commercial policy and free trade regime.[142] Pursuant to those negotiations, as stated in the Atlantic Charter issued by President Roosevelt and Prime Minister Winston Churchill in 1941, the two countries would 'endeavour, with due respect for their existing obligations, to further the enjoyment by all States, great or small, victor or vanquished, of access, on equal terms, to the trade and to the raw materials of the world'.[143]

A small number of 'internationally minded civil servants and economists' had 'enormous influence' over this process, amongst them the liberal economists Harry Hawkins and Clair Wilcox from the US State Department, and Lionel Robbins and James Meade from the Economic Section of the British War Cabinet Secretariat.[144] They were able to overcome the opposition to trade liberalization from the US Departments of Agriculture, Labor, and Commerce, and the British Treasury, the Ministry of Supply, the Ministry of Agriculture, the Ministry of Food, and the Board of Trade.[145] With the successful completion of the Anglo-American negotiations in 1945, the State Department moved to sponsor an international conference to negotiate a multilateral convention, which resulted in the GATT. Embedded within the GATT was a particular Anglo-American vision of a new international economic order premised upon open markets and guaranteed by the operation of a multilateral treaty that would provide a stable framework for the conduct of trade.

---

[140] *General Agreement on Tariffs and Trade* (signed 30 October 1947 entered into force 1 January 1948) 55 UNTS 194.
[141] *The Genesis of the GATT* (n 17) 12.   [142] Ibid 12–43.   [143] Ibid 17.
[144] Ibid 23–27.   [145] *Lionel Robbins* (n 134) 424–61.

4.4 The Haberler Report: Free Trade and the Trojan Horse of Development

The mid-1950s saw the intensification of a struggle between advocates of state-driven modernization models committed to planning, import substitution, and social reform, an emergent world systems theory that offered more radical critiques of the unequal integration of independent states into the global economy and their continued exploitation by foreign corporations and investors, and the consolidation of the liberal attack on state planning described earlier.[146] During this period, the argument that free trade would enable Third World development became a core plank of the moral argument for greater trade liberalization. The publication of the Haberler report played an important role in that linkage of trade liberalization, the dismantling of the social state in Europe, and development in the Third World that continues to structure the field.[147]

The Haberler report is often discussed as the moment when 'development' entered the GATT trade agenda. It is presented as a 'turning point' for the GATT regime's response to the 'development challenge', when growing 'agricultural protectionism' in the industrialized world 'prompted developing countries to make their voices heard more effectively within the GATT'.[148] Yet the report can better be understood as part of a major attempt to reconfigure relations between the state, finance, and labour played out through debates about development economics and the place of free trade in development. Three of the report's authors were committed liberal economists. Gottfried Haberler was an Austrian economist and one of the most active members of the Mont Pèlerin society, closely connected to Ludwig von Mises and Hayek.[149] Roberto de Oliveira Campos was a Brazilian economist, diplomat, bank president, and cabinet minister, described in his New York Times obituary as an 'apostle of free trade'.[150] He was on the Brazilian delegation to the conferences that created the International Monetary Fund, the World Bank, and the GATT, and was a supporter of the right-wing dictatorship that came to power after the military coup that ousted President João Goulart in 1964. Campos served as Minister for Planning in the first three years of the dictatorship, and was subsequently appointed as the military government's envoy to the UK. James Meade was

---

[146] K Fischer, 'The Influence of Neoliberals in Chile before, during, and after Pinochet' in *The Road from Mount Pèlerin* (n 111) 305–46, at 311.

[147] G Haberler et al., *Trends in International Trade: A Report by a Panel of Experts* (General Agreement on Tariffs and Trade Geneva 1958).

[148] *World Trade Law after Neoliberalism* (n 17) 45.

[149] J Bair, 'Taking Aim at the New International Economic Order' in *The Road from Mount Pèlerin* (n 111) 347–85, at 357–9.

[150] L Rohter, 'Roberto Campos, 84, Apostle for the Free Market in Brazil' (21 October 2001) *New York Times* <http://www.nytimes.com/2001/10/12/world/roberto-campos-84-apostle-for-the-free-market-in-brazil.html> [accessed 29 February 2016].

one of the initial negotiators of the Anglo-American loans agreement and a close colleague of Robbins at the LSE.

The Haberler report reflected the position developed by influential liberal economists who were concerned that the problems facing Third World countries, combined with the tendency to look to state planning in response, would lead to another Keynesian revolution.[151] In the view of these liberal thinkers, the postcolonial state threatened to become a vehicle for land reform, redistribution, and the pursuit of economic growth through import-replacement industrialization or command economies. Such a vision for the postcolonial state would require new social settlements involving the establishment of labour rights, redistribution, education, and land reform. The vision of development through trade liberalization was presented in the Haberler report and other Mont Pèlerin influenced literature in conscious opposition to those redistributive approaches. The neoliberal developmental strategy was premised on building export-oriented mining and industrial agriculture rather than manufacturing industries in developing states, with a focus on attracting funding from foreign investors. It was developed in connection with authoritarian governments and elites in Mexico, Chile, South Africa, and Brazil as a means of retaining the support of propertied classes and the US while not creating political opportunities for parties and unions associated with the industrial working class.[152] Thus rather than treating the 1958 Haberler report as the moment when a Third World challenge was posed to the free trade project, the report should instead be understood as reflecting the outcome of intense strategizing in neoliberal circles about the form that the postcolonial state should take.

4.5 Trade Rounds and the *Telos* of the Free Trade Project

One of the basic aims of the GATT was that all non-tariff barriers to trade should be eliminated and replaced by tariffs. That process of 'tariffication' is a technique for reconfiguring governmental actions into a quantified form, which can then be subjected to bargaining. Already through that initial 'commensuration' process of translating different governmental measures into the tariff form,[153] the new liberal understanding of economic ordering was embedded in institutional practice. The

[151] D Plehwe, 'The Origins of the Neoliberal Economic Development Discourse' in *The Road from Mount Pèlerin* (n 111) 238–79.

[152] R Connell and N Dados, 'Where in the World Does Neoliberalism Come From? The Market Agenda in Southern Perspective' (2014) 43 *Theory and Society* 117–38, at 122; JG Valdés, *Pinochet's Economists: The Chicago School in Chile* (CUP Cambridge 1995).

[153] On commensuration more generally, see WN Espeland and ML Stevens, 'Commensuration as a Social Process' (1988) 24 *Annual Review of Sociology* 313-43.

liberalization strategy was that those tariffs would then be reduced through negotiations between contracting parties conducted during trade rounds. In addition,
the inclusion of an unconditional most-favoured-nation clause as Article I of the
GATT meant that benefits extended to any contracting party would be multilater-
alized to all parties. GATT parties were thus committed to an ongoing process of
reform and movement towards a goal of greater liberalization. It was through the
process of successive negotiating rounds that new areas were brought within trade
'disciplines', particularly as a result of the Tokyo (1973–9), and Uruguay (1986–94)
Rounds. During the 1970s and 1980s, free trade advocates began to explore ways
to address 'the pressures put upon importing economies by a myriad of subtle
(and sometimes not so subtle) government aids to exports',[154] or in other words,
to find ways to counter the policies of states that provided support to industry and
agriculture.

To take one example, while most states viewed support for industry and agriculture as a 'fact of modern economic life',[155] American policy-makers sought to characterize such support as illegitimate and unfair. In the words of trade lawyer John
Jackson, while consumers in importing countries may benefit from the cheaper
prices of commodities produced with the support of foreign governments, 'the domestic producer feels outraged that while playing by the free enterprise rules he is
losing the game to producers not abiding by such rules'.[156] Disputes during negotiations over what counts as a subsidy, and whether and when subsidies should be
disciplined, have ever since reflected deep divisions over the proper role of the state
in relation to the market. As two US trade negotiators remarked in reflecting on
the Tokyo Round process:

The writing of new international rules governing the use of subsidies necessarily raised
fundamental questions concerning the nature and degree of government involvement in commercial affairs and the right of other governments to inquire into that
involvement.[157]

Yet with the conclusion of the Uruguay Round and the negotiation of the
World Trade Organization (WTO) *Agreement on Subsidies and Countervailing
Measures* (the SCM Agreement), subsidies and the practice of imposing countervailing duties as a remedy became the subject of a free-standing multilateral agreement.[158] The use of the language of subsidies to challenge state support remains an

---

[154] JH Jackson, 'The Crumbling Institutions of the Liberal Trade System' (1978) 12 *Journal of World
Trade Law* 93–105, at 95.

[155] RR Rivers and JD Greenwald, 'The Negotiation of a Code on Subsidies and Countervailing
Measures: Bridging Fundamental Policy Differences' (1979) 11 *Law and Policy in International
Business* 1447–95, at 1452.

[156] Ibid 1447.   [157] Ibid 1448.

[158] *Agreement on Subsidies and Countervailing Measures* (opened for signature 15 April 1994
entered into force 1 January 1995) 1869 UNTS 14.

agenda driven by the US, which is by far the predominant initiator of challenges to subsidies.[159] We can see some of the implications of this in the agricultural field, where the US and US corporations are leading the push to have the building of public food security stocks in developing countries treated as a form of subsidy with trade distorting effects.[160]

This was just one of a number of areas in which the creation of the WTO at the completion of the Uruguay Round led to a significant expansion in the range of activities brought within the scope of the international trade regime. The idea that international integration should ensure that trade was not only 'free' but also 'fair' became a central feature of WTO agreements. The Uruguay Round negotiations resulted in a raft of new trade agreements that took an ambitious approach to remaking the state in the interests of the market. The Uruguay Round outcomes significantly expanded the range of activities brought within the scope of the multilateral trade regime to include trade-related aspects of intellectual property, trade in services, product labelling, and the harmonization of public health and safety regulations, and greatly increased the enforcement powers of the regime through the establishment of a sophisticated dispute settlement process.

While a balance between the imperatives of trade liberalization and respect for state sovereignty is expressed in WTO agreements, there has been a strong tendency for interpreters of those agreements to read them in ways that expand the constraints on states to regulate in ways that are seen as trade-distorting and limit the scope for states to take 'exceptional' measures aimed at conserving exhaustible natural resources, responding to critical shortages of essential products, and implementing measures to protect human and animal health and safety. The end result is a form of 'neoliberalism without neoliberals'.[161] While few international trade lawyers would see themselves as card-carrying members of the Mont Pèlerin Society, it becomes harder and harder to distinguish much trade law jurisprudence from the core doctrines produced by neoliberals in earlier decades. The effect has been to make it increasingly costly in terms of time and resources for a government to introduce forms of regulation that do not comply with that vision of the relation between state and market.

---

[159] M Trebilcock, R Howse, and A Eliason, *The Regulation of International Trade* (4th edn Routledge London 2013) at 364.

[160] See the analysis prepared by a US law firm representing three major US farm industry groups presented to delegates at the WTO: DTB Associates LLP, *Agricultural Subsidies in Key Developing Countries* (November 2014) <http://www.dtbassociates.com/docs/DomesticSupportStudy11-2014.pdf> [accessed 29 February 2016]. On attempts by the US to challenge the public stockholding policies of developing countries, see E Diaz-Bonilla, 'On Food Security Stocks, Peace Clauses, and Permanent Solutions after Bali' (International Food Policy Research Institute Discussion Paper No 01388, November 2014) <http://papers.ssrn.com/sol3/papers.cfm?abstract_id=2539584> [accessed 29 February 2016].

[161] I borrow this phrase from Hagen Schulz-Forberg and Niklas Olsen, who use it to describe the history of neoliberalism in the Scandinavian countries: H Schulz-Forberg and N Olsen, 'Introduction' in *Re-Inventing Western Civilisation* (n 111) 1-10, at 7.

5 CONCLUSION

I opened this chapter by suggesting that the aim of offering a new history of free trade was a critical one: to render the current situation intelligible in ways that might make it more amenable to transformation and political action. I want to conclude by suggesting four ways in which rethinking the history of free trade opens up the field of international trade law to new questions and challenges.

First, this chapter has suggested that the championing of 'free trade' and the battle for the state have been closely related projects over the past 200 years. Since the emergence of international law in the nineteenth century, international lawyers have been deeply involved in a conversation with political economists and free trade advocates about the proper limits to state power in relation to the market. Where in the nineteenth century free trade advocates challenged feudalism, mercantilism, and the fiscal-military state, the twentieth century saw communism, the social state, and at times even democracy become the targets of free trade challenges. The project of state reconstruction to enable the market to operate without restraint has been entrenched quite consciously through transnational economic integration, both through the European integration project and through the negotiation of multilateral free trade agreements. International lawyers and economists have worked together for at least a century on the project of realizing the free trade state through the creation of an international legal order. The dominance of this approach constrains the capacity to think in new and imaginative ways about the possibilities that have been, and still are, available for using the state form more democratically and progressively.

Second, this history reminds us that the free trade project carries with it a moral charge. In order to understand the moral charge carried by criticisms of 'protectionism' today, the theological origins of this view of economic life need to be remembered. It is based upon an uncompromising and at times harsh morality, premised upon the idea that Providence acts through general laws and that man should not intervene in the operation of those laws. A sobering reminder of what this meant in practice can be found in the responses to famine in Ireland and India discussed in Section 3. That moral charge is still evident in attacks on the distorting effects of government intervention by contemporary free traders. In addition, the constant slippage in legal texts between protection as national economic militancy and protection as collectivist action against the vagaries of the market means that the latter is delegitimized as if it were the former. Similarly the constant slippage between discrimination as illegitimate privileging of domestic over foreign producers and discrimination as state planning means that the latter is treated with the same moral opprobrium as the former.

Third, attention to the history of free trade also reveals some of the significant ways in which current trade agreements depart from earlier forms of liberalism. The nineteenth-century free trade project was connected with campaigns to enfranchize the manufacturing and working classes and to tackle the entrenched privilege of the landed aristocracy and company monopolies. The ambition was to reform the state so that it would represent a broader range of interests. In contrast, modern free trade agreements are negotiated in secret, as if they were private contracts. The terms of those negotiations are not made available to the public, and democratic parliaments have limited opportunities to intervene in negotiations. Corporate leaders play a major role in shaping the conduct of trade negotiations and working with governments to enforce trade agreements.[162] Yet the central role of corporations in the negotiation of free trade agreements, and their innovative proposals for redescribing many forms of state action as 'foreign barriers to trade', are examples of the kinds of relationships between government and merchants about which Adam Smith was so scathing. The effect, as Smith might have predicted, is that free trade agreements increasingly represent the interests of specific monopolists.

Fourth, this history reminds us of the material limits to free trade. Famine and hunger haunt the commitment to political economy and free trade. That is no accident. The free trade debate over the Corn Laws in England, the economic response to famine in Ireland and India, the debate over the Common Agricultural Policy in Europe, and the riots and political instability that accompanied rising food prices in over thirty countries between 2006 and 2008 are all markers of something that liberal economic ordering cannot (yet) fully manage and control. While debates about free trade and investment often have an abstract and rationally persuasive quality to them, the schemes they propose are dependent upon controlling people and territory. The question of what to do with 'surplus', 'redundant', or displaced populations is a question that has haunted attempts to constitute a market-oriented agricultural order since the nineteenth century, as has the question of how to protect foreign investments and secure the free movement of goods and people necessary to enable profits to be made. Indeed many contemporary debates have an eerie resonance with those relating to the conduct of Irish and Indian famine policy during the nineteenth century.[163] So for example scholars have argued that existing WTO disciplines should be revisited or reinterpreted to limit the capacity of states to restrict the export of grains and other foodstuffs from their territory.[164] Similarly, the Doha Round of trade negotiations has replayed debates from

---

[162] J Braithwaite and P Drahos, *Global Business Regulation* (CUP Cambridge 2000).

[163] See further the discussion of these developments in 'Law, Economics, and the History of Free Trade: A Response' (n 1).

[164] See R Howse and T Josling, *Agricultural Export Restrictions and International Trade Law: A Way Forward* (International Food & Agricultural Trade Policy Council Position Paper, September 2012) <http://www.agritrade.org/Publications/ExportRestrictionsandTradeLaw.html> [accessed

nineteenth-century Indian famine reports about whether Indian administrators should be permitted to stockpile grain as a food security measure. Negotiators have struggled to overcome the impasse caused by the firm stance taken by the Indian government on the question of stockpiling food reserves, and the objections of the US to such policies.

In many ways, the older sense of the free trade project as involving a battle for the state was lost with the move into the WTO era. The language of non-discrimination and of 'barriers to trade' hides the relation of trade law to the project of remaking the state. Lawyers have adopted the ideologically loaded and morally charged language of protection to describe state attempts to regulate free trade as that language has become the stuff of relevant WTO treaties. The negotiation of those treaties has thus been an extremely effective means of embedding a particular way of thinking into international relations and legal practice. The successful negotiation of the WTO agreements during the 1980s and 1990s is a high point of success for a particular version of the free trade side of this battle. Yet even within the world of 'free trade', the WTO agreements represent an extreme version of a political position concerning the proper role of the state in relation to the market.

The discipline of international trade law has for the most part lost the sense it once had that the developments I have been describing represent a significant shift of world historical proportions. Writing in the *Journal of International Economic Law* in 2000, Donald McRae argued that the expansion of trade disciplines as interpreted and applied through the WTO dispute settlement processes 'raises questions about the nature of states as political and legal entities'.[165] He used the example of agriculture to make his point.

The field of agriculture provides a useful example. The ability of states to manage agricultural policy in order to avoid food scarcity, maintain employment, and preserve rural communities has historically been regarded as fundamental to a state's role. Food security has been a key part of a nation's perception of its security... Yet, today, under the Agreement on Agriculture, that exclusive domain has been whittled away.[166]

McRae concluded that the expansion of the trade liberalization project to include such issues as liberalization of trade in services and investment 'calls into question notions about traditional state functions, and hence calls into question some of the traditional assumptions on which international law is predicated'. He thus

29 February 2016]; R Sharma, *Food Export Restrictions: Review of the 2007-2010 Experience and Considerations for Disciplining Restrictive Measures* (FAO Commodity and Trade Policy Research Working Paper No 32, May 2011). <http://www.fao.org/fileadmin/templates/est/PUBLICATIONS/Comm_Working_Papers/EST-WP32.pdf> [accessed 29 February 2016].

[165] DM McRae, 'The WTO in International Law: Tradition Continued or New Frontier?' (2000) 3 *Journal of International Economic Law* 27–42, at 40.

[166] Ibid 40.

suggested that 'it is not just trade lawyers who should be following the work of the Appellate Body'. International lawyers, including international trade lawyers, needed to 'move beyond the easy assumption that the WTO is no more than the continuation of a tradition'.[167]

This chapter has argued that the changes over the past two centuries in the situation in which free trade projects operate do indeed render the idea of an ongoing tradition questionable. And as controversy continues to shadow the negotiation of trade agreements and economic partnerships within and beyond the WTO, the political vision of the role of the state and its relationship to the social that has been embedded in trade agreements is coming under increasing challenge. The ongoing food security crises, civil wars, riots, and mass movements of peoples that have accompanied the intensification of economic liberalization globally suggest that it is timely to explore alternatives to the forms of the state that have been pursued through the free trade project.

---

[167] 'The WTO in International Law' (n 165) 41 (citations omitted).

CHAPTER 36

....

INTERNATIONAL CRIMINAL LAW

THEORY ALL OVER THE PLACE

....

SARAH NOUWEN[*]

1 INTRODUCTION

....

EVALUATING the state of theory in international criminal law, one finds theory all over the place. Theory in international criminal law is almost irrelevant as well as highly influential; explicated and covered up; developed and immature. Theory is almost irrelevant in that the field owes its growth mostly to practice[1]—for a long time, the field's implicit maxim was *ago* (rather than *cogito*) *ergo sum*. Not theory, but historical events led to the creation of tribunals; the availability of evidence or the accused to the selection of cases; fact patterns to the production of case law. The practice of international criminal law—the investigation, prosecution, and trial of concrete cases—preceded the theorizing: the systematization, rationalization, and justification of this body of law. However, while in some ways almost irrelevant,

* I am grateful for valuable research assistance provided by Rose Cameron and Jessie Ingle. I thank Sara Kendall, Simon de Smet, and Darryl Robinson for constructive comments and ideas.

[1] See also F Mégret, 'Anxiety, Practices, and the Construction of the Field of International Criminal Justice' (Paper presented at the International Studies Association Conference, Toronto, March 2014) at 2.

theory is also highly influential: the practice of international criminal law is replete with theoretical assumptions:[2] about the potential of individual agency, the utility of punishment, and the relationship between criminal justice and peace. Theory is explicit where scholars have developed great narratives about international criminal law. Theory is developed in that many authors have written on criminal law concepts within international criminal law—libraries can be filled with literature and case law on theories of modes of liability.[3] But theory also remains covered up and immature: the theories of change implicit in the grand rationales for international criminal law are seldom spelled out and foundational questions such as 'what is an international crime' are often sidestepped.

It is not just that the state of theory is all over the place; there is no shared understanding of what 'theory' in, or of, international criminal law refers to. Theorizing theory in international criminal law, we can distinguish at least four types of theories. First, the word 'theory' is frequently used in the courtroom practice of international criminal law in the concept of the 'theory of a case'. During the trial, the prosecution and the defence each present their, usually opposing, case theories and ultimately the judges set forth their theory of what happened and how this should be legally qualified.[4] For instance, a defendant 'challenged the Prosecution's case by…alleging inconsistencies in the theory of the case',[5] and 'the Prosecution never put its theory to [a specific] Witness…that the…documents [in question] were forgeries…'.[6] We can call the case theories the *factual theories* in international criminal law.

However, both in proceedings and in scholarship on international criminal law, the word 'theory' is used more often in a second context, namely to refer to the mental schemes that the field employs in its operations, for instance for organizing modes of liability, systematizing crimes, and classifying sentences. These *operational theories* are referred to where, for example, 'the Defence…requests the Pre-Trial Chamber to set out the theory of liability as a co-perpetrator pursuant to Article 25(3)(a) of the…Statute [of the International Criminal Court (ICC)]',[7]

---

[2] See J Meierhenrich (ed), 'Special Issue: The Practices of the International Criminal Court' (2013) 76(3/4) *Law and Contemporary Problems* i–x, 1–339.

[3] See also JG Stewart, 'The End of "Modes of Liability" for International Crimes' (2012) 25 *Leiden Journal of International Law* 165–219, at 165.

[4] One case can have many case theories, each serving a different purpose at different stages of the proceedings: see B Miller, 'Teaching Case Theory' (2002) 9 *Clinical Law Review* 293–336, at 305–6.

[5] *Prosecutor v Muthaura et al.*, (Prosecution's Written Submissions following the Hearing on the Confirmation of Charges) (ICC, Pre-Trial Chamber II, Case No ICC-01/09-02/11-361, 28 October 2011) at [42].

[6] *Prosecutor v Gombo* (Defence Reply to the Prosecution Response to the Defence Motion to Admit Materials Pursuant to the Chamber's Third Order (ICC-01/05-01/08-2565)) (ICC, Trial Chamber III, Case No ICC-01/05-01/08-2636-Red, 15 November 2013) at [2].

[7] *Prosecutor v Katanga and Ngudjolo Chui* (Defence Written Observations Addressing Matters That Were Discussed at the Confirmation Hearing) (ICC, Pre-Trial Chamber I, Case No ICC-01/04-01/07-698, 28 July 2008) at [15].

or the Defence will 'set out reasons why the Trial Chamber should not adopt the Prosecution's suggested revisions to the joint control theory of criminal liability'.[8] When one scholar concludes that '[i]nternational criminal courts and tribunals work with unclear legal theory', she, too, uses the word 'theory' to refer to key concepts such as modes of liability, *mens rea* (the intent or knowledge of the accused), and defences.[9]

A third way in which the word theory is used in international criminal law is to refer to the premises on which the field of international criminal law has been constructed. We can call these *foundational theories*: systems of ideas about the origins, essence, and rationales of the field. For instance, when one author discusses 'four theoretical shortcomings of international criminal law' he discusses foundational issues such as the meaning of 'International Criminal Law', the overall function of international criminal law, the purposes of punishment in international criminal law, and whether and how punitive power can exist at the supranational level without a sovereign.[10] Identifying a 'theoretical gap' in international criminal law, another scholar points to the incorrect assumption that ordinary criminal law methodologies are a suitable response to international crimes.[11]

Fourthly, there are the theories that try to make sense of international criminal law as a phenomenon, and study the meaning and effects of the field as a whole beyond its stated objectives. We can call these *external theories* since they often emerge from an encounter of the field of international criminal law with an external perspective, for instance, that of political science, philosophy, political economy, or anthropology. A political scientist doing fieldwork in Uganda has theorized, for example, the 'deleterious effects that ICC intervention can have on the capacity for autonomous political organization and action among the civilian victims of violence, arguing that ICC intervention tends to lead to a depoliticization of those victims by promoting among them a political dependency mediated by international law'.[12] External theories treat international criminal law more as an object than as

---

[8] *Prosecutor v Katanga and Ngudjolo Chui* (Defence for Germain Katanga's Pre-Trial Brief on the Interpretation of Article 25(3)(a) of the *Rome Statute*) (ICC, Trial Chamber II, Case No ICC-01/04-01/07-1578, 30 October 2009) at [2].

[9] Faculty of Law University of Copenhagen, 'International Criminal Courts and Tribunals Work with Unclear Legal Theory' (2 September 2013) <http://news.ku.dk/all_news/2013/2013.9/international_criminal_courts_and_tribunals_work_with_unclear_legal_theory/> [accessed 29 February 2016].

[10] K Ambos, 'Punishment without a Sovereign? The *Ius Puniendi* Issue of International Criminal Law: A First Contribution towards a Consistent Theory of International Criminal Law' (2013) 33 *Oxford Journal of Legal Studies* 293–316.

[11] MA Drumbl, 'A Hard Look at the Soft Theory of International Criminal Law' in LN Sadat and MP Scharf (eds), *The Theory and Practice of International Criminal Law: Essays in Honor of M Cherif Bassiouni* (Martinus Nijhoff Leiden 2008) 1–18, at 7. Using the word theory in a similar context, David Luban discusses Hannah Arendt as a 'theorist' of international criminal law: D Luban, 'Hannah Arendt as a Theorist of International Criminal Law' (2011) 11 *International Criminal Law Review* 621–42.

[12] A Branch, 'Uganda's Civil War and the Politics of ICC Intervention' (2007) 21 *Ethics and International Affairs* 179–98, at 180 (emphasis omitted).

a system, as a phenomenon of which to make sense rather than a phenomenon that must make sense, and, potentially, as a question rather than a given.[13]

The taxonomy of factual, operational, foundational, and external theories is based on the theories themselves—the theories as speaking subjects—and not on the identity or identification of the people who theorize. These types of theorizing are not exclusive to, for instance, one profession or discipline. Thus, while most legal scholars focus on operational theories, and to a lesser extent, foundational theories, there is nothing that prevents a legal scholar or practitioner from adopting non-legal approaches and developing a theory based on that encounter with international criminal law. Similarly, a philosopher can apply her or his mind to factual, operational, foundational, and external theories.

Indeed, theorizing international criminal law is not exclusive to scholars or practitioners: international criminal law is also 'theorized' by millions of people who, without considering themselves a 'theorist' or ever using the word 'theory', try to make sense of international criminal law as they encounter it in their daily lives.[14] While some debates about the operational theories, for instance addressing the intricacies of a particular mode of liability, may be so specialized that only a few international criminal law experts can and will engage with them, there is also something inherently popular, in the sense of prevalent among the general public, about international criminal law. Some elements of international criminal law—the arrest warrant, the opening statement, judgment day—are sufficiently spectacular to make the media headlines, rendering international criminal law a subject for general discussion, for example, on the local radio in Gulu, in *amjads* (shared taxis) in Khartoum, at a tea seller's stand in a camp for displaced persons in Darfur and in hair dressing salons in Nairobi. International criminal law's 'commonness' thus gives rise to 'popular' or 'quotidian' theorizing: an attempt, on the basis of a daily-life encounter, to make sense of a phenomenon.

Whereas 'official' theories of international criminal law stem from the work of the practising and scholarly lawyers, philosophers, and scholars in other disciplines, popular theorizing is practised by people who try to make sense of international criminal law but do not have international criminal law or theorizing as their profession. The quotidian theorizer, unlike the professional theorist, may not cast their arguments in an explicitly theoretical mould, draw on disciplinary concepts or coin new ones, or make linkages with existing theories. But the quotidian theorizer is no less involved in 'theorizing', understood as trying to make sense of a phenomenon. Thus, the Darfurian who explains over tea that the ICC's warrant

---

[13] On the difference between internal and external theorizing, see also F Mégret, 'Theorizing the Laws of War' in this *Handbook*.

[14] On the importance of theorizing on the basis of lived practice that may occur anywhere and everywhere, see J Comaroff and JL Comaroff, 'Writing Theory from the South: The Global Order from an African Perspective' (September–October 2013) *World Financial Review* 17–20, at 20.

of arrest for the head of state transforms the president into an 'enemy' of the world may not make the link to the work of the theorist Carl Schmitt, but is still theorizing in some form. So is the international civil servant who is confronted with international criminal law when negotiating a peace agreement. In this way, theory is all over the place in a most literal sense.

In addition to the axis along which we find factual, operational, foundational, and external theories, we can thus also identify an axis with 'official' and 'popular' theories at its ends. This axis can cross-cut the axis of the factual, operational, foundational, and external theories at all points. In other words: factual, operational, foundational, and external theories are produced or engaged with by both 'official' and 'popular' theorists.

The categories of theories are not entirely discrete or mutually exclusive: their boundaries are porous. And so they should be: a strong field is built on axes that connect—a case theory tailored to the operational theory; an operational theory based on the foundational theories; an external theory that takes into account the factual, operational and foundational theories. Similarly, a strong field is based on official theories that are aware of the popular theories, with popular theories being informed of the official theories.

However, for a field in which theory is all over the place, some of the axes in international criminal law are relatively weak. Indeed, it is usually when the different types of theories are considered in light of each other that theoretical weaknesses are revealed and, on that ground, the field is labelled as being 'undertheorized'. Thus, operational theories, for instance on the modes of liability, continue to be applied even if the foundational theories, for example on the justifications for punishment, appear untenable. Similarly, the external theories, such as those on the political implications of the project, have little bearing on the foundational theories, for instance, those on the rationales of the field.

Perhaps the greatest disconnect at the theoretical level is between the official and the popular theories. More and more attention is being paid to ensuring that the official theories, particularly the foundational theories, inform the general public's views, especially in countries where international criminal tribunals intervene. Millions of dollars are spent on so-called 'outreach programmes'. Far less attention, however, is given to ensuring that popular theories feed back into the official theories. While using the language of 'communication' and 'dialogue', many 'outreach programmes' remain one-directional: their primary purpose is to inform the public about the courts; not for the public to inform these courts.[15] Those who are most affected by international criminal law and in that sense most 'proximate' thus remain remote from shaping the field's theories, irrespective of the quality

---

[15] See eg International Criminal Court, 'Outreach' <http://www.icc-cpi.int/en_menus/icc/structure%20of%20the%20court/outreach/Pages/outreach.aspx> [accessed 29 February 2016].

and relevance of their theorizing. However, as some external theories illustrate, factual, operational, and foundational theories have much to gain from connecting with the day-to-day experience of international criminal law. For that to happen though, official theories of international criminal law must first recognize popular theories as valuable.

2 Factual Theories
in International Criminal Law

Factual theories are the most practical of all the different types of theories in that they are part of the core business of international criminal law's practitioners: prosecutors, defence lawyers, and judges all develop and argue their theory of what happened in the case at hand and how it should be legally qualified. The prosecution's factual theory zooms in on the role of the defendant in the situation in which international crimes were committed. The defence's factual theory usually rejects that such crimes were committed, denies the involvement of the defendant in the commission of the crimes or argues that there are circumstances amounting to a ground for excluding criminal responsibility. On the basis of the evidence presented, the judges then set out their theory of the facts of the case, before legally qualifying those facts. Factual theories are also the most practical in that they are more products of the practice of international criminal law than pre-existing organizing principles developed by scholarship and then applied in practice. Indeed, there has been little scholarly attention to factual theories in international criminal law and, perhaps therefore, little theory on factual theories.

There is scope, however, for more theorizing of factual theories, for factual theories are theoretically interesting. First, many factual theories are based on assumptions about legal epistemology. Counsel and judges refer to concepts such as 'corroboration' or 'circumstantial evidence', but use these concepts in different meanings. Epistemological assumptions are seldom spelled out, let alone developed. Making explicit the underpinning epistemological theories could substantially improve the way in which case theories are formulated and evaluated.[16]

Secondly, factual theories are theoretically interesting because of their importance for, and their own importance being influenced by, other theories in international criminal law. For instance, it could be argued that because of the

---

[16] For more on epistemology in international law, see S de Smet, *Rethinking Fact-Finding by International Courts* (CUP Cambridge, forthcoming).

characteristics of international crimes and the ensuing operational theories in international criminal law, case theories play an even bigger role in proceedings concerning international crimes than in trials involving ordinary crimes. First, international crimes are often adjudicated by foreigners and before a partially foreign audience who know very little of the context in which the crimes were committed.[17] The case theory must therefore narrate that context: for instance, who was fighting whom, when, and why, in a conflict far removed in time, distance, and environment from the courtroom where the trial takes place? Secondly, many international crimes contain elements that require this complex context to be proved: war crimes require evidence of an armed conflict; crimes against humanity proof of a widespread or systematic attack against a civilian population. The case theory must therefore present facts to satisfy these elements of crime, which for their part have been systematized by operational theories on international crimes. Thirdly, that same complex context also usually involves a multiplicity of actors in the commission—more or less directly, actively, or passively, to a greater or lesser degree—of the offences, which has led to the development of several operational theories on modes of liability. The case theory must convincingly present a narrative that fits one of international criminal law's many modes of liability. Finally, international criminal law being criminal law, the accused must have had a 'guilty mind' for him or her to be convicted. Since it is impossible to read a mind, the *mens rea* is often established by inferences.[18] The persuasiveness of these inferences to a large extent depends on the case theory. Establishing intent is particularly challenging in case of a complex mode of liability, for instance aiding and abetting or joint criminal enterprise.[19] The complexity of the situation in which the crimes were committed must then be reflected in multifaceted case theories. Such theories have for their part, in an attempt to capture that complex reality, pushed the development of operational theories on crimes and modes of liability to reflect fact patterns characteristic of international crimes.[20]

Case theories are also theoretically interesting when considered in the light of foundational theories. For instance, some foundational theories argue that among the purposes of the criminal trial are to write history, counter revisionism, and

---

[17] This is not the case when international crimes are adjudicated in domestic courts in the country where the crimes took place.

[18] See eg *Prosecutor v Milutinovic, Sainovic, and Ojdanic* (General Ojdanic's Appeal of Decision on Motion for Additional Funds) (ICTY, Appeals Chamber, Case No IT-99-37-AR73, 23 July 2003) at [14]–[15].

[19] See eg *Prosecutor v Tadić* (Judgment) (ICTY, Appeals Chamber, Case No IT-94-1-A, 15 July 1999) at [203], [220], [228] and [232]; *Prosecutor v Vasiljevic* (Judgment) (ICTY, Appeals Chamber, Case No IT-98-32-A, 25 February 2004) at [131]; *Prosecutor v Brđanin* (Judgment) (ICTY, Trial Chamber, Case No IT-99-36-T, 1 September 2004) at [704] and [969]–[991].

[20] But arguably not far enough, as we will see when we turn to the foundational theories.

promote reconciliation by establishing 'the truth'.[21] However, the assumption that the 'judicial truth' as produced by the judgment, on the basis of the prosecution and defence theories, amounts to 'the historical truth' is challengeable, both theoretically and empirically.[22] Theoretically, it can be questioned whether the rules of procedure and evidence of a criminal trial are best tailored towards producing the truth: prosecutors select charges and sometimes engage in plea bargaining, witnesses may be reluctant to testify, and evidentiary thresholds must be met. Trials thus produce 'a' truth—a legal truth—but leave out other truths. Moreover, trials focus on the criminal guilt of individuals, thus ascribing events to their agency and downplaying the political, social, economic, and legal structures that fostered the criminality as mere 'context'.[23] Assumptions underpinning expectations of criminal trials producing the truth can also be contested on an empirical basis: international criminal tribunals have faced huge challenges in establishing the facts,[24] thus producing factual theories that fail to support foundational theories according to which criminal trials write authoritative history.

Finally, factual theories are interesting material for external theories about international criminal law. Consider factual theories, for instance, as a form of story-telling.[25] By choosing one factual theory over another, legal practitioners tell one story and leave out many others.[26] They will select stories on the basis of whether they matter for the law, not necessarily of whether they matter for individuals concerned, for instance those who have lived through international crimes. At the same time factual theories are a form of representation that shapes what has happened, as well as constructs the future.[27] A case theory shapes by serving as a lens, constructed by the law, through which to understand facts, relationships, and circumstances of the persons involved in the case.[28] A case theory constructs the future by influencing what will become established as the juridical truth—a truth that enjoys legal power, and in some circumstances can be enforced. International criminal trials are particularly interesting because of the various cultures involved

---

[21] See eg *Prosecutor v Erdemović* (Sentencing Judgment) (ICTY, Trial Chamber, Case No IT-96-22-Tbis, 5 March 1998) at [21]. See also, among many others, A Cassese, 'On the Current Trends Towards Criminal Prosecution and Punishment of Breaches of International Humanitarian Law' (1998) 9 *European Journal of International Law* 2–17, at 9–10. See, critically, on the role of trials of international crimes in writing history, H Arendt, *Eichmann in Jerusalem: A Report on the Banality of Evil* (Penguin Harmondsworth 1977 [1963]). For a nuanced analysis of the extent to which international criminal courts can write history, see RA Wilson, *Writing History in International Criminal Trials* (CUP Cambridge 2011).

[22] See also M Koskenniemi, 'Between Impunity and Show Trials' (2002) 6 *Max Planck Yearbook of United Nations Law* 1–36, at 11.

[23] See also ibid 14–15.

[24] See ibid 22 and NA Combs, *Fact-Finding without Facts: The Uncertain Evidentiary Foundations of International Criminal Convictions* (CUP Cambridge 2010).

[25] See also 'Teaching Case Theory' (n 4) 297.   [26] See also ibid 303.

[27] See also ibid.

[28] See also B Miller, 'Give Them Back Their Lives: Client Narrative and Case Theory' (1994) 93 *Michigan Law Journal* 485–576, at 487.

in the telling and interpretation of the story. In the case of international courts, foreign judges may understand concepts such as causation, agency, and truth differently from the witnesses of the crimes who give their testimony.[29] Questions then arise that could inspire external theories on the meaning of factual theories beyond their legal meaning: To which audience do the legal practitioners, judges included, direct their story? To whom should the story be comprehensible? How are the defendant, the victims, and the context represented? Which truth emerges out of this story? What impact do these stories have outside the legal process, which power relations do they reflect and constitute, what stories have they replaced?

In sum, while factual theories are primarily developed in the proceedings of international criminal law, they are worth theorization beyond the courtroom.

3 Operational Theories in International Criminal Law

Operational theories are the mental schemes with which the field of international criminal law works when investigating, prosecuting, and trying crimes. Some of these mental schemes are explicitly referred to as theories. For instance, in international criminal proceedings, the word theory is most frequently used in relation to modes of liability.[30] But other elements of the practice of international criminal law, such as the organization of crimes, defences, and sentences, are also based on theories, even if they are not explicitly called as such. Unlike factual theories, operational theories have developed as a result of a fruitful interaction between practice and scholarship: scholarship systematizes crimes, modes of liability and sentences, while drafters of statutes and case law rely on scholarship. That scholarship has often drawn heavily from theories of domestic criminal law.

---

[29] See T Kelsall, *Culture under Cross-Examination: International Justice and the Special Court for Sierra Leone* (CUP Cambridge 2009).

[30] Sometimes the mode of liability itself is called a 'theory' (the 'theory of joint criminal enterprise': see eg *Prosecutor v Limaj* (Judgment) (ICTY, Appeals Chamber, Case No IT-03-66-A, 27 September 2007) (Partially Dissenting Opinion of Judge Schomburg) at [10]). Other times, the word 'theory' refers to a particular interpretation of a legal provision setting forth a mode of liability (for instance, the 'control of the crime theory' as an interpretation of art 25(3)(a) of the *Rome Statute*: see eg *Prosecutor v Lubanga* (Judgment pursuant to Article 74 of the *Statute*) (ICC, Trial Chamber I, Case No ICC-01/04-01/06-2842, 14 March 2012) (Separate Opinion of Judge Fulford) at [10]. Still other times, the word 'theory' refers to the interpretation of the legal provision setting forth the mode of liability. (See, eg *Prosecutor v Ngudjolo Chui* (Judgment pursuant to Article 74 of the *Statute*) (ICC, Trial Chamber II, Case No ICC-01/04-02/12-4, 18 December 2012) (Concurring Opinion of Judge van den Wyngaert) at [4]–[5].

Operational theories are probably the most belaboured theories in the field of international criminal law. Although there continue to be calls for more 'debates among scholars about the correct interpretation of special offences as well as the general principles of liability',[31] there already exists an extensive body of literature on the crimes, modes of liability, and sentences applied in the practice of international criminal law—so much so that it is beyond the scope of this contribution even to begin summarizing it.

And yet, modes of liability and sentencing are also areas of international criminal law that have been explicitly labelled as 'undertheorized'.[32] That assessment often results from the observation that many of international criminal law's operational theories are based on those pertaining to domestic criminal law, while failing to take into account the unique features of international crimes.[33] Mark Drumbl has, for instance, argued that the sentences meted out for international crimes are remarkably similar to those for ordinary crimes, the 'extraordinary' character of international crimes notwithstanding.[34] Modes of liability derived from domestic law for their part fail to reflect the often complex collective ways in which international crimes are committed.[35] At the same time, tribunals have extended modes of liability that can capture commission by collective entities to such an extent that they have been criticized for effectively convicting on the basis of guilt by association:[36] some therefore dub the mode of liability abbreviated as 'JCE' (joint criminal enterprise) as 'just convict everyone'.[37] This outcome is in tension with what some foundational theories hold to be one of international criminal law's aims: the individualization of guilt.[38]

[31] GP Fletcher, 'The Theory of Criminal Liability and International Criminal Law' (2012) 10 *Journal of International Criminal Justice* 1029–44, 1031.

[32] In the context of modes of liability, see E van Sliedregt, *Individual Criminal Responsibility in International Law* (OUP Oxford 2012) at 12. On sentencing, see eg JD Ohlin, 'Towards a Unique Theory of International Criminal Sentencing' in G Sluiter and S Vasiliev (eds), *International Criminal Procedure: Towards a Coherent Body of Law* (Cameron May London 2009) 381–413, 381. For other operational theories that have been considered undertheorized, see eg K Ambos, *Treatise on International Criminal Law* (2 vols OUP Oxford 2014) vol 2, at 247ff (on the law of concours).

[33] See eg M Drumbl, 'Collective Violence and Individual Punishment: The Criminality of Mass Atrocity' (2005) 99 *Northwestern University Law Review* 539–610.

[34] See MA Drumbl, *Atrocity, Punishment, and International Law* (CUP Cambridge 2007). See also 'Towards a Unique Theory of International Criminal Sentencing' (n 32).

[35] On 'system criminality', see A Nollkaemper and H van der Wilt (eds), *System Criminality in International Law* (CUP Cambridge 2009).

[36] W Jordash and P Van Tuyl, 'Failure to Carry the Burden of Proof: How Joint Criminal Enterprise Lost Its Way at the Special Court for Sierra Leone' (2010) 8 *Journal of International Criminal Justice* 591–613; E van Sliedregt, 'System Criminality at the ICTY' in *System Criminality in International Law* (n 35) 183–200, at 197.

[37] ME Badar, '"Just Convict Everyone!"—Joint Perpetration: From *Tadić* to *Stakić* and Back Again' (2006) 6 *International Criminal Law Review* 293–302, at 302 n 47, attributing the term to Professor William Schabas.

[38] See eg A Cassese, 'Reflections on International Criminal Justice' (1998) 61 *Modern Law Review* 1–10, at 6. For other tensions between some of the modes of responsibility employed by international

The conclusion of such reflections may be that modes of liability and sentences are 'undertheorized', but that conclusion itself is based on rich theories that evaluate operational theories in light of foundational and external theories.[39] Areas of international criminal law that are often deemed 'undertheorized' are thus arguably at the same time among the better theorized.

4 FOUNDATIONAL THEORIES IN INTERNATIONAL CRIMINAL LAW

Foundational theories concern the origins, essence, and rationales of the field of international criminal law as a whole. Theories about origins concern not just the history of the field,[40] but also foundational questions about, for instance, the origins of jurisdiction: what are the philosophical reasons for the existence of jurisdiction by an international tribunal or jurisdiction by a foreign court? What are the 'linking points'? Who is prosecuting and judging, and in whose name?[41] Where does the *jus puniendi* lie?[42] Where do international crimes belong: in domestic, mixed, or international courts?[43]

criminal law and purported objectives of international criminal law, see S Darcy, 'Imputed Criminal Liability and the Goals of International Justice' (2007) 20 *Leiden Journal of International Law* 377–404.

[39] For modes of liability, see eg R Cryer et al., *An Introduction to International Criminal Law and Procedure* (3rd edn CUP Cambridge 2014) ch 15.

[40] For accounts of the dominant history of international criminal law, see eg G Werle and F Jessberger, *Principles of International Criminal Law* (3rd edn OUP Oxford 2014) 1–30; C Kreß, 'International Criminal Law' in *Max Planck Encyclopedia of Public International Law* (2009) paras 22–9. For often ignored parts of the history, see E Haslam, 'Redemption, Colonialism and International Criminal Law: The Nineteenth Century Slave-Trading Trials of Samo and Peters' in DE Kirkby (ed), *Past Law, Present Histories* (ANU E Press Canberra 2012) 7–22; E Haslam, 'Silences in International Criminal Legal Histories and the Construction of the Victim Subject of International Criminal Law: The Nineteenth-Century Slave Trading Trial of Joseph Peters' in C Schwöbel (ed), *Critical Approaches to International Criminal Law: An Introduction* (Routledge Abingdon 2014) 180–95; KJ Heller and G Simpson (eds), *The Hidden Histories of War Crimes Trials* (OUP Oxford 2013).

[41] See eg A Duff, 'Authority and Responsibility in International Criminal Law' in S Besson and J Tasioulas (eds), *The Philosophy of International Law* (OUP Oxford 2010) 589–604.

[42] See 'Punishment without a Sovereign?' (n 10); S Kendall and S Nouwen, 'Representational Practices at the International Criminal Court: The Gap between Juridified and Abstract Victimhood' (2013) 76(3) *Law & Contemporary Problems* 235–62.

[43] See eg 'Reflections on International Criminal Justice' (n 38) 6–8; LA Dickinson, 'The Promise of Hybrid Courts' (2003) 97 *American Journal of International Law* 295–310; F Mégret, 'In Defense of

Even more fundamentally, there is little agreement within the field as to what constitutes an international crime.[44] In technical language, 'crime' refers to a legal rule the violation of which results in the individual's liability to a penalty. But the field uses the word also to refer to the act of violating that rule, as in the expression 'committing a crime'.[45] In popular language, international crimes have an even broader connotation, also including human rights violations[46] or violations of international humanitarian law, even though technically not every violation of a right or a prohibition amounts to a crime[47] and violations of human rights law and humanitarian law as such lead to state responsibility rather than individual criminal responsibility.[48]

Within the field views diverge with respect to what needs to be international for a crime to amount to an 'international' crime. In some conceptions, international crimes are crimes that transcend boundaries;[49] in others, crimes are 'international' when they are within the jurisdiction of tribunals that are international;[50] in yet

Hybridity: Towards a Representational Theory of International Criminal Justice' (2005) 38 *Cornell International Law Journal* 725–51.

[44] For good discussions, see *An Introduction to International Criminal Law and Procedure* (n 39) ch 1; R O'Keefe, 'The Concept of an "International Crime"' on United Nations, 'Audiovisual Library of International Law' <http://legal.un.org/avl/ls/OKeefe_CLP.html> [accessed 29 February 2016]; B Broomhall, *International Justice and the International Criminal Court: Between Sovereignty and the Rule of Law* (OUP Oxford 2003) ch 1; MC Bassiouni, 'International Crimes: The Ratione Materiae of International Criminal Law' in MC Bassiouni (ed), *International Criminal Law* (3rd edn Martinus Nijhoff Leiden 2008) 129–203; 'International Criminal Law' (n 40); G Schwarzenberger, 'The Problem of an International Criminal Law' (1950) 3 *Current Legal Problems* 263–96.

[45] 'The Concept of an "International Crime"' (n 44).

[46] True, substantively human rights and international crimes, in particular crimes against humanity, may now be seen to protect the same values. But the way in which they do so is different: they have different addressees and different legal definitions. Moreover, international criminal law has not always been conceptualized as aiming to protect individual human rights; as David Luban argues, in Nuremberg the focus was on the protection of groups, rather than the individual: D Luban, 'Fairness to Rightness: Jurisdiction, Legality, and the Legitimacy of International Criminal Law' in *The Philosophy of International Law* (n 41) 569–88, at 574.

[47] Indeed, it is one thing to establish that certain conduct is prohibited under international law; it is another to find that there is individual criminal responsibility attached to that conduct.

[48] See also 'The Concept of an "International Crime"' (n 44).

[49] In this definition, it is the act, rather than the legal rule (the violation of which leads to the individual's liability to a punishment), that is international: there are many offences with trans-border components that are not governed by international law. The act would sometimes amount to an international crime and sometimes not, depending on whether or not in the specific case there is an international dimension to it. This does not make for a very coherent body of 'international crimes'. It is more common to refer to the body of law dealing with crimes with a trans border component as 'transnational criminal law'. Some of this law has its origins in domestic law (for instance, national rules on when courts may exercise jurisdiction over offences with an international component); other parts of that law have their origins in international law (for instance, treaties that aim to enhance inter-state cooperation in the suppression of such crimes).

[50] *An Introduction to International Criminal Law and Procedure* (n 39) 4–5. In this theory, the 'international' of 'international crime' refers to the legal character of the tribunal where the offence can be adjudicated. The problem of this concept of an international crime is that the character of the

again other theories crimes are international because of their gravity, scale, seriousness, atrociousness, or impact on the 'conscience of mankind' or 'humanity';[51] in still others a crime is international if it violates certain values of the international community, in particular that of peace and security.[52] The most convincing theory is that international crimes are those that are crimes under or pursuant to international law. For if a crime is a *rule*, the violation of which results in liability to punishment, the word 'international' in 'international crime' then refers to the source of that legal rule, namely international law. In the narrow version of this theory, international crimes are only those crimes which are criminal 'under' international law, in other words, where international law imposes individual criminal responsibility (irrespective of whether this has been done at the domestic level).[53] In this definition, individual acts of torture under the Convention against Torture, piracy, slavery, and terrorism in general, frequently referred to as international crimes pursuant to the other theories, may in fact not be international crimes: while there are treaties concerning these offences, allowing or even obliging states to exercise

tribunal need not say anything about the character of the legal rule: as the Special Court for Sierra Leone and the Special Tribunal for Lebanon illustrate, a court created by international law—and therefore an 'international' court—can have jurisdiction over crimes that are crimes only under the domestic law of a particular country. The category of international crimes is not coherent if the latter should suddenly be considered also 'international' crimes on account of their inclusion in the subject-matter jurisdiction of a specific international tribunal.

[51] See eg L May, 'Mass Rape and the Concept of International Crime' in CAL Prager and T Govier (eds), *Dilemmas of Reconciliation: Cases and Concepts* (Wilfrid Laurier University Press Waterloo 2003) 137–68, at 154 ('for truly international crimes something more than disrespect of the individual victim is required. There must be a clear sense in which humanity, for which an international tribunal stands in, is the victim of the crime.') The problem with this concept of international crimes is that while many international crimes may have such characteristics, they need not have them, and even if they do, it does not necessarily distinguish them from crimes under domestic law, which, in some cases, can be equally grave, widespread, serious, atrocious or shocking to the conscience of mankind. When a soldier unlawfully confines one civilian during an international armed conflict, this amounts to a war crime under international law. But when a father unlawfully confines his own daughter in a cellar and abuses her for decades, this does not amount to an international crime. It is difficult to understand why the former would be more shocking to the conscience of humanity than the latter.

[52] *International Justice and the International Criminal Court* (n 44) 44–51. The strength of this theory is that it actually focuses on the character of the crime in the sense of legal rule as opposed to the act. However, it is of little explanatory value: there are international community interests that are not protected by international criminal law (social and economic rights; free trade; the freedom of the high seas). Even if one focuses on the value of peace and security, the theory does not explain what amounts to international crimes and what does not: there are many acts that could undermine international peace and security (trading in arms; declaring independence; staging a coup) that are not subjected to international criminal law. States make international criminal law, but not necessarily on a principled basis. See R Cryer, 'The Doctrinal Foundations of International Criminalization' in MC Bassiouni (ed), *International Criminal Law* (3rd edn Martinus Nijhoff Leiden 2008) 107–28.

[53] See eg R Cryer, *Prosecuting International Crimes: Selectivity and the International Criminal Law Regime* (CUP Cambridge 2005) at 1; *Principles of International Criminal Law* (n 40) 31; 'The Problem of an International Criminal Law' (n 44).

their jurisdiction to prescribe and adjudicate at the domestic level, international law does not impose criminal responsibility directly on individuals committing these offences. In the broader version, however, these crimes are also international crimes because they are crimes 'pursuant to' international law.[54] That is, while they are criminalized only in domestic law, they are still international because they are defined by international law.[55]

The absence of a common definition of an essential concept—the international crime—stems from, and reveals, the reactive character of much of the field of international criminal law.[56] Rather than being first designed and then applied, international criminal law has grown out of ad hoc creation and application in response to specific crises. It is challenging to find subsequently in the concept of the international crime an essence that it may never have had. However, efforts to define an international crime are no longer a matter of theoretical interest only when far reaching consequences—for instance, allowing the exercise of universal jurisdiction or the denial of immunity or justifying humanitarian intervention—are attached to something being classified as such.

Whatever the essence of an international crime may be, international criminal law has boomed as a practice and rich theories have developed on the character of that practice. On the basis of its practice, it has been argued that the field suffers from an 'identity crisis'.[57] The crisis emerges because the field originates in traditions and philosophies that have at times contradictory assumptions and methods of reasoning.[58] For instance, international criminal law originates from both international law and criminal law. Whereas it is generally accepted that international law requires state consent, international criminal law is held against individuals even if it is not clear that their states have consented to the putative international criminal law. As Robert Cryer has pointed out, international tribunals have tried to bridge this gap by using naturalist thinking, while cloaking this reasoning in positivist arguments.[59] International criminal law is thus also in an ambiguous relationship with state sovereignty.[60] It is constituted by state sovereignty in that

[54] See 'The Concept of an "International Crime"' (n 44).

[55] See ibid and Y Dinstein, 'International Criminal Law' (1975) 5 *Israel Yearbook on Human Rights* 55–87, at 67.

[56] See also M Drumbl, '*Introduction to International Criminal Law* by M Cherif Bassiouni' (2005) 99 *American Journal of International Law* 287–90, at 289; MC Bassiouni, *Introduction to International Criminal Law* (2nd edn Brill Leiden 2013) at 27.

[57] D Robinson, 'The Identity Crisis of International Criminal Law' (2008) 21 *Leiden Journal of International Law* 925–63.

[58] See ibid with respect to one of the tensions, discussed below, namely between human rights liberalism and criminal law liberalism.

[59] See R Cryer, 'The Philosophy of International Criminal Law' in A Orakhelashvili (ed), *Research Handbook on the Theory and History of International Law* (Edward Elgar Cheltenham 2011) 232–67.

[60] See R Cryer, 'International Criminal Law vs State Sovereignty: Another Round?' (2005) 16 *European Journal of International Law* 979–1000; *International Justice and the International Criminal Court* (n 44) 2.

international criminal law, and international criminal courts, need state consent for them to exist. International criminal law depends on states for its funding and enforcement. But once established, international criminal law can be applied with respect to individuals even if some states object.[61]

Another identity crisis emerges from the fact that the field draws upon liberal principles of not only criminal law, but also human rights and humanitarian law.[62] As Darryl Robinson has theorized, characteristics of human rights and humanitarian law such as victim-focused teleological reasoning, the conviction that violations of human rights and humanitarian law must as such also amount to violations of international criminal law, and the ideological assumption that decisions that go against state sovereignty are in the interests of human rights and humanitarianism, work in opposite directions to the fundamental principles of criminal law.[63] It is thus that a field that aspires to comply with principles such as personal culpability, legality, and fair labelling has developed sweeping modes of liability, expanded definitions of crimes and been reluctant to accept defences.[64]

Perhaps the best known foundational theories of international criminal law concern the rationales and justifications for international criminal law. The theories rely heavily on theories justifying punishment in the domestic context, such as retribution, deterrence, incapacitation, rehabilitation of offenders, providing justice to victims, and communicating norms. However, the theories are often less convincing with respect to international crimes than with respect to ordinary crimes.[65] For instance, international crimes are often so egregious that, from the perspective of retribution, no accepted form of punishment can be considered 'proportionate'.[66] Whereas ordinary crimes are usually committed in times that crime is the exception, international crimes are sometimes committed in situations in which they are the rule—the problematic conduct of an offender of an international crime is therefore not necessarily deviant, but, on the contrary, too obedient.[67] In such circumstances it is questionable whether criminal law works

---

[61] The challenge to sovereignty derives not from the law itself, but from the creation of jurisdiction to adjudicate that law. That jurisdiction is granted by customary international law, by treaty, or on the basis of a binding resolution by the Security Council. Since all these grounds of jurisdiction are ultimately based on state consent, it can be argued that there is no tension with sovereignty. States' experience of the exercise of such jurisdiction against their wishes will be different though.

[62] See 'The Identity Crisis of International Criminal Law' (n 57).   [63] See ibid.

[64] See ibid.

[65] See eg MJ Aukerman, 'Extraordinary Evil, Ordinary Crime: A Framework for Understanding Transitional Justice' (2002) 15 *Harvard Human Rights Journal* 39–98; *Atrocity, Punishment, and International Law* (n 34) ch 6; M Koskenniemi, 'Hersch Lauterpacht and the Development of International Criminal Law' (2004) 2 *Journal of International Criminal Justice* 810–25, at 824; I Tallgren, 'The Sensibility and Sense of International Criminal Law' (2002) 13 *European Journal of International Law* 561–95.

[66] For this and other difficulties with retribution as a penological goal of international criminal law, see *Atrocity, Punishment, and International Law* (n 34) 165–9.

[67] *Eichmann in Jerusalem* (n 21); *Atrocity, Punishment, and International Law* (n 34) ch 2.

as a deterrent.[68] The communicative role of criminal law requires the offender, the prosecuting and adjudicating bodies, and the wider public to be part of the same moral community—a community that may exist at the domestic level, but is far less established or cohesive at the global plane.[69] If the aim of international criminal law is to help constitute that community, then international criminal proceedings easily become, as Martti Koskenniemi has argued, show trials.[70]

International criminal law has also been given its own unique rationales, for example, recording and authorizing history, preventing collective guilt, (re)establishing the rule of law, promoting peace and security, and enhancing reconciliation.[71] The assumptions as to how international criminal law generally, or aspects of international criminal law specifically (for instance: arrest warrants, trials or punishments) will produce the aspired outcomes (for instance: (re)establishing the rule of law, promoting peace and security, or enhancing reconciliation) are seldom made explicit. And without explicit theories of change it is difficult to assess the strength of the many assumptions—about individual agency, rationality, and the relationship between crime and conflict— upon which the theories are based.

Ultimately, however, the foundational justifying theories are of limited importance for the practice of international criminal law. The prevalence of teleological reasoning in judgments by international criminal tribunals may suggest that they are,[72] but the very same tribunal that in one case invokes an aim of international criminal law espoused in the preamble of the legal instrument by which it was created,

[68] For this and other difficulties with deterrence as a penological goal of international criminal law, see *Atrocity, Punishment, and International Law* (n 34) 169–73 and 'The Sensibility and Sense of International Criminal Law' (n 65).

[69] 'The Philosophy of International Criminal Law' (n 59) 266; A Branch, 'International Justice, Local Injustice: The International Criminal Court in Northern Uganda' (2004) 51(3) *Dissent* 22–6. On the implications of introducing international criminal law into an international society that is not fully developed as a society, see P Allott, *The Health of Nations: Society and Law Beyond the State* (CUP Cambridge 2002) at 62–9.

[70] 'Between Impunity and Show Trials' (n 22).

[71] See, for instance, 'Reflections on International Criminal Justice' (n 38) 6; 'On the Current Trends Towards Criminal Prosecution and Punishment of Breaches of International Humanitarian Law' (n 21) 9–10. On the overabundance of, and tensions among, objectives attributed to international criminal law, see MR Damaška, 'What Is the Point of International Criminal Justice?' (2008) 83 *Chicago-Kent Law Review* 329–65.

[72] See eg *Prosecutor v Tadić* (Judgment) (ICTY, Appeals Chamber, Case No IT-94-1-A, 15 July 1999). The prevalent practice of teleological reasoning by international criminal tribunals is remarkable. First, as a matter of principle, teleological reasoning to expand the scope of criminal law is difficult to reconcile with criminal law principles such as *lex certa* and *in dubio pro reo*. Secondly, as a matter of doctrinal law, it is remarkable that, contrary to what the *Vienna Convention on the Law of Treaties* prescribes, teleological reasoning is often applied even when there is no specific term that requires interpretation; see *Vienna Convention on the Law of Treaties* (opened for signature 23 May 1969 entered into force 27 January 1980) 1155 UNTS 331, art. 31. Thirdly, as a matter of epistemology, it is remarkable how lawyers make assertions about causal processes beyond the sphere of law, without invoking other authorities. For instance, see how in *Erdemović* ICTY judges made causal claims

sometimes in another case rejects responsibility for achieving that aim. And it is free to do so: the preamble reveals the aspirations of those who established the tribunal, but the tribunal itself is responsible only for that what it is mandated to do in the operative part of its Statute. It is the assumption of the states creating it that the tribunal, by acting in accordance with the operative provisions in the Statute, promotes the stated aims such as preventing crimes, enhancing reconciliation, recording history, establishing the rule of law, or promoting peace and security. However, for the tribunal itself, this consequentialist presumption is irrebuttable. It is only the states that have given the tribunal its mandate, that could be convinced by empirical evidence to revise the presumption, the theory, and the mandate.[73]

5 EXTERNAL THEORIES
IN INTERNATIONAL CRIMINAL LAW

Unlike the preceding types of theories, external theories do not emerge from within the field of international criminal law, but from an encounter of non-legal approaches—for instance political science, philosophy, economics, or anthropology—with that field.[74] These encounters have resulted in rich theories that take us far beyond the confines of law. To give just a few examples: international

---

about the psychologically complex phenomena of reconciliation and healing: 'Discovering the truth is…a fundamental step on the way to reconciliation: for it is the truth that cleanses the ethnic and religious hatreds and begins the healing process.': *Prosecutor v Erdemović* (Sentencing Judgment) (ICTY, Trial Chamber, IT-96-22-Tbis, 5 March 1998) at [21].

[73] See for instance the preambular considerations of the resolution establishing the ICTR: UN Doc S/RES/955 (8 November 1994). The Security Council is

> [d]etermined to put an end to such crimes [genocide and other systematic, widespread and flagrant violations of international humanitarian law] and to take effective measures to bring to justice the persons who are responsible for them, [c]onvinced that in the particular circumstances of Rwanda, the prosecution of persons responsible for serious violations of international humanitarian law would enable this aim to be achieved and would contribute to the process of national reconciliation and to the restoration and maintenance of peace, and [b]eliev[es] that the establishment of an international tribunal for the prosecution of persons responsible for genocide and the other above-mentioned violations of international humanitarian law will contribute to ensuring that such violations are halted and effectively redressed.

In other words, the Security Council establishes the Tribunal to prosecute those responsible for the mentioned international crimes because it believes that this will have certain consequences; the Tribunal is responsible only for the prosecution, not for the theory of change that the Security Council set out.

[74] As explained in the introduction, it is the approach, not necessarily the theorizer, that is external: there is nothing that prevents lawyers from also adopting non-legal approaches.

criminal law has been analysed through the lenses of cosmopolitanism,[75] realism, liberalism, and constructivism;[76] scrutinized from feminist perspectives;[77] studied as part and parcel of the political;[78] examined as instrument of global governance;[79] understood as accommodating the world's major powers;[80] accused of failing to understand local culture;[81] evaluated on the basis of the implications of its donor-driven logics;[82] critiqued for failing to prevent atrocities by prioritizing accountability over stability;[83] considered part of a movement that produces a global elite that works on naturalizing notions of good governance and the rule of law;[84] seen to obstruct truth seeking by exonerating the political, economic, and legal structures that have created the conditions for individual criminality;[85] found to jeopardize alternative conceptions of justice;[86] theorized from the perspective of diplomats participating in its development;[87] and criticized for being driven by Western states that, while remaining immune from prosecution themselves, have contributed to much of the violence that is subjected to international criminal law.[88]

External theories are often more interested in the effects of international criminal law than the foundational theories. And the empirical research upon which

[75] See, for instance, V Peskin, 'An Ideal Becoming Real? The International Criminal Court and the Limits of the Cosmopolitan Vision of Justice' in R Pierik and WG Werner (eds), *Cosmopolitanism in Context: Perspectives from International Law and Political Theory* (CUP Cambridge, 2010) 195–217.

[76] See, for instance, with respect to the International Criminal Court, BN Schiff, *Building the International Criminal Court* (CUP Cambridge 2008).

[77] L Chappell, 'Conflicting Institutions and the Search for Gender Justice at the International Criminal Court' (2014) 67 *Political Research Quarterly* 183–96.

[78] Hersch Lauterpacht and the Development of International Criminal Law' (n 65) 823–4; 'Between Impunity and Show Trials' (n 22) 32–3; GJ Simpson, *Law, War & Crime: War Crimes Trials and the Re-Invention of International Law* (Polity Press Cambridge 2007); SMH Nouwen and WG Werner, 'Doing Justice to the Political: The International Criminal Court in Uganda and Sudan' (2010) 21 *European Journal of International Law* 941–66.

[79] SC Roach, *Governance, Order, and the International Criminal Court: Between Realpolitik and a Cosmopolitan Court* (OUP Oxford 2009).

[80] DL Bosco, *Rough Justice: The International Criminal Court in a World of Power Politics* (OUP Oxford 2014).

[81] *Culture under Cross-Examination* (n 29).

[82] S Kendall, 'Donors' Justice: Recasting International Criminal Accountability' (2011) 24 *Leiden Journal of International Law* 585–606.

[83] J Snyder and L Vinjamuri, 'Trials and Errors: Principle and Pragmatism in Strategies of International Justice' (2003) 28 *International Security* 5–44.

[84] KM Clarke, *Fictions of Justice: The ICC and the Challenge of Legal Pluralism in Sub-Saharan Africa* (CUP Cambridge 2009).

[85] 'Between Impunity and Show Trials' (n 22) 14–15; 'The Sensibility and Sense of International Criminal Law' (n 65) 593–5.

[86] 'International Justice, Local Injustice' (n 69); *Atrocity, Punishment, and International Law* (n 34) 122, chs 5 and 7; S Nouwen and W Werner, 'Monopolizing Global Justice: International Criminal Law as Challenge to Human Diversity' (2015) 13 *Journal of International Criminal Justice* 157–76.

[87] I Tallgren, 'We Did It? The Vertigo of Law and Everyday Life at the Diplomatic Conference on the Establishment of an International Criminal Court' (1999) 12 *Leiden Journal of International Law* 683–707.

[88] A Anghie and BS Chimni, 'Third World Approaches to International Law and Individual Responsibility in Internal Conflicts' (2003) 2 *Chinese Journal of International Law* 77–103, 90.

some of them are based has proved many of the core assumptions of international criminal law's foundational theories to be problematic: international criminal law does not always promote peace—indeed, at times it does the opposite; victims do not always consider international tribunals to provide 'justice'; an intervention by an international tribunal need not promote the rule of law.

Yet, the external theories seldom feed back into the foundational theories. As with other grand social and political projects, international criminal law is more deeply embedded in philosophical arguments than in empirical evidence. First there was the practice; then the theory on the rationales and the justifications; and only then the empirical evidence.[89] The gap between expectations and evidence has been filled by a leap of faith—a faith that international criminal law contributes to its many stated objectives and that it is better than alternative responses to mass crimes.[90] This faith could end up as more than a temporary stopgap: when faith is strong enough, it turns into an independent foundation of a socio-political project, immune to contrary evidence.[91]

And yet, there are international criminal lawyers who, precisely in order to challenge the idées fixes, are reaching out to external theories in order to engage in what Mark Drumbl has called a 'second-generation dialogue': a dialogue that, now the field of international criminal law has established itself, engages in reappraisal, maturation, and self-improvement.[92] External theories are key to this. And so are the popular theories that we will now turn to.

6 POPULAR THEORIES IN INTERNATIONAL CRIMINAL LAW

ICC ni mono wun okelo ni pingo kaa?

[Why have you brought ICC? How is the ICC going to help us?]

Gamente we, wan openyo wu pingo?

[Our government, we ask you why? How is the ICC going to help us?][93]

---

[89] See D Koller, 'The Faith of the International Criminal Lawyer' (2008) 40 *New York University Journal of International Law and Politics* 1019–69.

[90] See also 'The Sensibility and Sense of International Criminal Law' (n 65).

[91] See SMH Nouwen, 'Justifying Justice' in J Crawford and M Koskenniemi (eds), *The Cambridge Companion to International Law* (CUP Cambridge 2012) 327–51, at 343–4.

[92] *Atrocity, Punishment, and International Law* (n 34) 22.

[93] For the song and lyrics, see ReverbNation, 'Jeff Korondo/Songs' <http://www.reverbnation.com/jeffkorondo/song/4282898-icc-jeff-korondo> [accessed 29 February 2016].

As the chorus from the song 'ICC' illustrates, international criminal law can become a 'popular' topic—popular in the sense of prevalent among the general public. The song, written by Ugandan musician Jeff Korondo, reflects some of the key questions that the Acholi community had about the intervention of the ICC in northern Uganda: 'How is the ICC going to help us?' and 'Do you think [the ICC is] the one bringing us peace or [is] it…the peace negotiation that will bring us peace?'[94]

Every day, people are confronted, more or less directly, through the media, in their discussions, or even through personal experiences, with international criminal law. They may not know about the factual, operational, foundational, or external theories. But they do see parts of the practice of international criminal law, and read this practice in a specific political, economic, social, and historical context. On the basis of this daily-life encounter, they try to make sense of the phenomenon of international criminal law. It is thus that they engage in quotidian theorizing.

When learning that the ICC would intervene in northern Uganda, some Acholi—the community most heavily affected by the conflict—were hopeful: 'The ICC will come and arrest Joseph Kony!'[95] But positions radically shifted when it was discovered that the ICC does not have its own enforcement powers and would rely on the Ugandan army, the very army that had failed to defeat the Lord's Resistance Army for more than twenty years. 'Does the ICC want to use *the UPDF* to arrest people? We are moving from the frying pan to the fire.'[96] People became even more critical of the ICC when it disclosed its arrest warrants for the LRA leadership. They feared that the arrest warrants would lead to more crimes, since the LRA would take revenge on the Acholi for perceived cooperation with the ICC. They also feared that the arrest warrants would impede peace negotiations, and thus perpetuate the conflict and their suffering. Moreover, they challenged the ICC's notion of justice, advancing instead a more community-based, reconciliatory, and restorative form of justice, at least with respect to alleged perpetrators from their own community. With respect to people from outside their community, in particular members of the government and army, they did want to see criminal justice done, but, much to their dislike, the ICC had not issued any arrest warrants for them. Hadn't the government failed to protect the Acholi, deprived them of their livelihoods, forsaken them in squalid camps for internally displaced people? A few Acholi community leaders argued that Ugandan President Museveni had referred the situation in northern Uganda to the ICC in

---

[94] 'Jeff Korondo/Songs' (n 93).

[95] This paragraph is based on SMH Nouwen, *Complementarity in the Line of Fire: The Catalysing Effect of the International Criminal Court in Uganda and Sudan* (CUP Cambridge 2013) ch 3.

[96] Interview with an attendant of a workshop on the ICC in Northern Uganda in 2004 (Kampala, November 2011).

order to gain more support for his military approach to the conflict and to defeat the Acholi initiatives for a peaceful resolution.

In Khartoum in 2008, *amjads*, privately run minibuses that pick up passengers along fixed routes, carried posters in support of Omar al Bashir in response to the ICC Prosecutor's request for an arrest warrant for the Sudanese President. 'An attack on our President is an attack on Sudan as a whole', says one of the drivers: 'The ICC is a tool of the West'.[97] At a tea seller's stand in Darfur, however, some men have great hopes that the ICC will bring peace: the ICC has made President Bashir an enemy of the world. They expect that the ICC arrest warrants will be enforced by international actors and help the armed movements win the conflict. Once the ICC has established peace, the Darfurian *ajaweed* (respected elders) will do justice on the basis of *judiya*, a mix of mediation and arbitration between groups, resulting in compensation and arrangements for future co-existence. Another man is more sceptical: 'we do not need the ICC—we need a political solution.'[98] Over lunch, international civil servants working for a UN-appointed peace broker lament the ICC Prosecutor's announcement of a request for an arrest warrant for the Sudanese president: since then, the armed movements are hoping that the ICC will remove their enemy and are thus no longer interested in peace talks, whereas the government has little to gain from those talks if the ICC arrest warrant is unaffected by the outcome.[99] Another UN diplomat argues that justice is a political objective, that should be achieved through a political rather than a legal process; the criminalization of politics leads to prisons, not peace.[100]

In a hairdressing salon in a suburb of Nairobi, people comment on international criminal law while watching the inauguration of President Uhuru Kenyatta and his Vice-President William Ruto. Kenyatta and Ruto had been in opposing camps during the previous elections and had both been accused by the ICC of having played leadership roles in the violence and crimes that followed those elections. One hairdresser argues that the ICC fostered the 'UhuRuto' alliance[101] and sets forth his factual theory: 'When they came together, there was no war...But when they were on two sides, there was war...That's how we know they were the cause.' But others in the hair dressing salon express their faith in democracy: 'If Kenyans had the confidence to vote for this guy, then he cannot have done anything bad.'[102] Yet another Kenyan regrets the monopolization of

---

[97] Conversation in the author's presence in an *Amjad* (Khartoum, October 2008).

[98] Conversation in the author's presence (Darfur, December 2008).

[99] Interview by the author (Khartoum, November 2008).

[100] Conversation in the author's presence, Ethiopia, July 2011.

[101] On which, see S Kendall, '"UhuRuto" and Other Leviathans: The International Criminal Court and the Kenyan Political Order' (2014) 7 *African Journal of Legal Studies* 399–427.

[102] J Hatcher, 'Controversy as Kenya Salutes Uhuru Kenyatta as New Leader: Ugandan Ruler Yoweri Museveni Astonishes Diplomats at Ceremony with Fierce Attack on Hague Court' *The Guardian* (9 April 2013).

the justice question by the ICC arrest warrants, arguing that it distracts from the causes of systematic injustice.[103]

The Acholi songwriter and leaders in northern Uganda, the *amjad* driver in Khartoum, the elders at the tea stand in Darfur, and the people in the hairdressing salon in Nairobi all theorized on the basis of their encounter with international criminal law. In doing so, they set forth or challenged factual, operational, foundational, or external theories, even though they never explicitly referred to these as 'theories'. The Acholi elders, for instance, challenged the foundational theory according to which international criminal justice leads to peace, setting forth an alternative theory of change in which international criminal justice obstructs peace. Indeed, some even challenged the idea that international criminal law could lead to a form of justice that would also be justice in the eyes of the Acholi. As regards other foundational theories, they took issue with the essence of international criminal law: why did the government's conduct, in particular its failure to protect the Acholi, merely amount to a human rights violation and not to an international crime? And they developed their own theories to make sense of the role of international criminal law, for instance by theorizing why President Museveni had referred the situation in northern Uganda to the ICC, namely to ostracize its domestic enemy internationally. The *amjad* driver espoused ideas on the relationship between international criminal law, politics, and sovereignty and the relationship between individual responsibility and collective stigmatization, even if he did not use these terms. The men drinking tea in Darfur engaged with the foundational theories on the rationales of international criminal law, the meaning of justice, and the relationship between law and politics. So did the international civil servants who contested the idea that international criminal law facilitates peace and who reflected on the relationship between international criminal law and enmity. Without mentioning the international relations scholar Hans Morgenthau or the international lawyer Hersch Lauterpacht, they were involved in a classic debate about the role that international law should play in the resolution of political conflict.[104] And in the hair salon in Nairobi, factual theories were set forth and challenged, while another Kenyan theorized how international criminal justice monopolizes the discussion of what amounts to injustice.

The increasingly prevalent practice of 'outreach' reveals that international criminal tribunals are aware of the importance of popular theorizing. These programmes are aimed at influencing such theorizing by informing the general

---

[103] Personal Correspondence (September 2013) (the quote is given in full in S Nouwen, '"As You Set out for Ithaka": Practical, Epistemological, Ethical, and Existential Questions About Socio-Legal Empirical Research in Conflict' (2014) 27 *Leiden Journal of International Law* 227–60, at 255–6.)

[104] M Koskenniemi, 'The Function of Law in the International Community: 75 Years After' (2009) 79 *British Yearbook of International Law* 353–66.

public, in particular in the countries where the tribunals intervene, about what the tribunal is doing and why, in other words, mostly about the operational and foundational theories of international criminal law. The aim of outreach is not just to promote understanding of, but also support for, international criminal justice.[105]

According to the definition on the ICC website, outreach aims at establishing two-way communication. Yet all the aims of that communication are focused on explaining the Court's theories; there is no process for adjusting those theories in light of the popular theories. For instance, confronted with questions and concerns from the Acholi leaders, the ICC Outreach Office in Uganda felt that it had to 'explain that our contribution to peace is justice',[106] even though the Acholi leaders challenged both the notion of justice promoted by the ICC and the theory of change according to which the Court's punitive justice leads to peace. Genuine two-way communication, in which not just the ICC's theories influence popular theorizing, but popular theorizing also the ICC's theories, is difficult for the same reason as to why the foundational theories are to a large extent immaterial to the Court: arguments that theories do not work are irrelevant if the theory is based on a principled rather than a causal idea, in other words, if the theory is based on how one thinks things should be, or would like them to be, rather than how they empirically prove to be.[107]

As discursive and lived theory, popular theory is seldom integrated into the other forms of theory, which favour the abstract and written. No matter the amount of 'outreach', those who are most affected by international criminal law and in that sense most 'proximate', thus remain remote from shaping the field's theories, irrespective of the quality and relevance of their theorizing.

Some external theories demonstrate, however, how literally 'meaningful' engagement with popular theories can be. Studies based on fieldwork and interviews reveal how discussions with those who encounter international criminal law or international crimes in their daily lives provide the basis for rich scholarly theories.[108] After all, while establishing effects empirically may generally be

---

[105] International Criminal Court, 'Outreach' <http://www.icc-cpi.int/en_menus/icc/structure%20of%20the%20court/outreach/Pages/outreach.aspx> [accessed 29 February 2016].

[106] Interview by the author (Kampala, October 2008).

[107] Whereas causal ideas can be influenced by evidence as they are ideas about cause and effect, principled ideas are primarily about right and wrong, in which evidence plays hardly any role. S Khagram, JV Riker, and K Sikkink, 'From Santiago to Seattle: Transnational Advocacy Groups Restructuring World Politics' in S Khagram, JV Riker, and K Sikkink (eds), *Restructuring World Politics: Transnational Social Movements, Networks and Norms* (University of Minnesota Press Minneapolis 2002) 3–23, at 14.

[108] See eg E Stover and HM Weinstein (eds), *My Neighbor, My Enemy: Justice and Community in the Aftermath of Mass Atrocity* (CUP Cambridge 2004); T Allen, *Trial Justice: The International Criminal Court and the Lord's Resistance Army* (Zed Books London 2006); *Culture under Cross-Examination* (n 29); *Fictions of Justice* (n 84); A Branch, *Displacing Human Rights: War and Intervention in Northern Uganda* (OUP New York 2011).

challenging, popular theories themselves are a clearly observable effect of the intervention of international criminal courts.

7 CONCLUSION

Theory in international criminal law has often come after the fact: case theories were developed after events had taken place; operational theories were produced to match complex facts; foundational theories were created to justify existing practices; external theories tried to make sense of the phenomenon of international criminal law as it had been observed; and so did the popular theories based on everyday encounters. *Ago*, rather than *cogito, ergo sum* was the field's implicit maxim. Against this background it is not surprising that the field is often considered to be 'undertheorized': theories have had difficulties in keeping up with the fact(s) of international criminal law.

That said, it has been argued that after a period of undertheorization, the field of international criminal law is now increasingly supported by theory.[109] And indeed, factual, operational, foundational, external, and popular theories are expanding and proliferating. However, while the pillars of the field are stronger and stronger, the axes among the pillars are still weak: factual, operational, foundational, external theories prove to be less coherent when they are considered in light of each other. Rich theories could thus emerge from more joint theorizing among those working on variably factual, operational, foundational, and external theories, between scholars and practitioners, and between scholar-theorists and quotidian theorists. The first step towards such activity is to recognize that there is not one theory, or indeed one type of theory, in international criminal law. Factual, operational, foundational, external theories, and 'official' and 'popular' theories, are *all* central to the field.

---

[109] 'The Philosophy of International Criminal Law' (n 59) 258; L May and Z Hoskins, *International Criminal Law and Philosophy* (CUP New York 2010) at 12.

CHAPTER 37

....

THEORIZING
THE LAWS OF WAR

....

FRÉDÉRIC MÉGRET

1 INTRODUCTION

....

ONE of the challenges of theorizing international humanitarian law may be that it is itself, in its modern juridical-technocratic version, a rather anti-theoretical, at times even anti-intellectual discipline. In short, the dominant understanding of international humanitarian law sees it as above all a pragmatic endeavour, one relatively unperturbed by foundational questions. As such, humanitarianism as an ideology is one that has traditionally foregrounded action, pragmatism, and empathy over ideas, abstraction, and theory.[1] One of the first tasks of theorizing about the laws of war may be to reflect on their undertheorization. Yet simultaneously the discipline is assuredly a strange mix and, alongside its dominant pragmatism, it is also heavily reliant on grand principles that betray a degree of at least implicit theory. The laws of war are inevitably tied to—even as they seek to dissociate themselves from—a pluri-secular philosophical tradition of thinking about the justness of war. Arguably, then, the laws of war occupy a very peculiar place; one devoted to the principled regulation of a thing—war—that is itself acknowledged pragmatically as existing and in a sense prior to attempts to regulate it.

[1] Interestingly and tellingly the only work that specifically bears the title 'Theory of the laws of war' is a relatively recent law and economics paper: EA Posner, 'A Theory of the Laws of War' (2003) 70 *University of Chicago Law Review* 297–317.

To make matters more complicated, not everything that calls itself theory is theory, and not everything that does not call itself theory is not theory. There is 'practical' work that is in fact highly theoretical (that is, in that it is submerged in all kinds of unacknowledged theoretical assumptions), and 'theoretical' work that is in fact highly practical (for example, in that the theory is instrumentalized to some particular practical end rather than merely being oriented at understanding).

In this context, the very fact of theorizing about the laws of war may be a critical move, one that seeks to move beyond the apparent evidence and simplicity of indignation ('this is horrible!'), action ('something must be done!'), and morality ('this concerns me!'). However, whether this is so also depends on what one understands by theory. At the very least, theorizing about international humanitarian law means abstracting some general meaning of the laws of war beyond specific rules. But this can be done with a view, for example, to understand how the laws of war *work* or, more deeply, what the laws of war *do* or stand for.

What, then, might be the nature of theorizing about the laws of war? I will suggest two predominant modes of theorizing, one 'internal', the other 'external'. Although this distinction is not foolproof it provides at least a useful shorthand for two relatively irreducible types of exercises. Internal theorizing is the sort of theorizing that devotes itself to making sense of the discipline among its practitioners and within bounds that are taken for granted. It is minimal in that its ambition is largely instrumental: providing the practitioners of the laws of war with the background necessary for them to function. One might describe it as a form of theorizing that is significantly invested in its object and takes for granted its existence as an object. It is a relatively hard type of theorizing to unearth because it typically does not present or understand itself as theorizing. External theorizing is a form of theorizing that is less interested in the laws of war as a system than as an object, less focused on explaining the operation of the laws of war than understanding what the laws of war mean generally and for international law specifically, and not particularly committed to the laws of war as a system and discipline. It is more explicitly theoretical precisely in that it seeks to highlight some of the ultimate functioning or purpose of the laws of war behind its dominant implicit theories.

2 INTERNAL THEORIES

2.1 Theories of Essence

The laws of war necessarily contain a theory of their essence, however little spelled out that theory may be. That essence is typically presented as a *telos*, namely the

ambition of humanizing war, notably by mitigating suffering and, in certain circumstances, loss of life. Indeed, what better project for the humanitarian sensitivity
than to demonstrate its ability to overcome the very denial of law and humanity?
War is seen as an unfortunate by-product of the existence of a society of states that
must be tolerated until it can eventually be done away with altogether, but which in
the meantime ought to be tamed in ways that conform to international law's broad
humanitarian project. The criticism that in humanizing war humanitarians make
it more palatable, such that it would be preferable to leave war in all its harshness
to dissuade powers from resorting to it, is dismissed by an appeal to the categorical
imperative to save lives whenever one can in the real circumstances that arise. In
fact, international humanitarian law is seen as conducive to peace in the long haul,
because of the way in which it ensures that bridges are not severed between parties
to a conflict.[2]

Second, the laws of war are understood as universal and as having, in fact, almost always existed in some way or other. Although other cultures or societies may
not have adopted quite the same rules, it is argued that over time all societies have
adopted some rules constraining warfare and this is presented as the key factor.
The implicit universalism of the laws of war makes them appear less as a mode
of cultural imposition and more as the distillation of various societies' time honoured wisdom. In that respect, the laws of war are properly *international* in that
they provide a common language that transcends international society's pluralism
(a pluralism that is never as obvious as in times of war). This universalism has in
the modern era been more than confirmed by the wide ratification of the *Geneva
Conventions* and the idea that humanitarian norms' wide customary status ensures
their global applicability. It is increasingly complemented by a cosmopolitan outlook that sees the laws of war as applying beyond the state directly to individuals
(notably soldiers).

A third key notion is that international humanitarian law is indeed law and
not simply humanitarianism or morality, and that war is susceptible to a specifically legal form of regulation. Although the tradition of restraint in war (humanitarianism) and international humanitarian law are often confused, it is
important to highlight the difference between the two and the extent to which
international humanitarian law is an essentially *legal* project. Humanitarianism
as a tradition had existed for centuries by the time Henry Dunant stumbled
upon the battlefield of Solferino and decided that an international treaty would
best safeguard soldiers wounded in combat. The late nineteenth-century project
of the laws of war, then, is very much the project of tying the humanitarian sensitivity to the project of regulating the relations between states through positive

---

[2] M Veuthey, 'International Humanitarian Law and the Restoration and Maintenance of Peace'
(1998) 7 *African Security Review* 26–35.

legal norms. That investment is widely seen as a source of strength and repeated at key junctions with a view to reaffirming the binding character of the laws of war. International humanitarian law is increasingly seen as an integral part of the constitution of international society and its norms regarded as having *jus cogens* and *erga omnes* status.

2.2 Theories of Possibility

Beyond this notion of its essence, the laws of war betray a more or less implicit worldview that makes them normatively possible. That 'normative space' is less evident than it seems, and its emergence is linked to a number of deep assumptions that structure the field. Perhaps the main assumption is that, contrary to the old Latin adage that '*inter armas enim silent leges*', there can be a degree of moderation in war and, as a result, a role for law amidst extreme violence. This means, crucially, that war is not or at least not necessarily the breakdown of all social bonds, but the emergence of conditions of enmity amongst actors that nonetheless remain bound by common norms. War operates very much in and as part of a society—a peculiar and polarized society no doubt, but a society nonetheless—even when all else has broken down. As a result, the system posits a lack of personal hostility between combatants on opposite sides of a conflict; combatants are adversaries rather than enemies. This is the Rousseauist premise on which the idea of a grudging respect for the opposite army seems to rest: 'War is not therefore a relationship between one man and another, but a relation between one state and another. In war private individuals are enemies only incidentally: not as men, or even as citizens, but as soldiers...'.[3]

Another assumption that international humanitarian lawyers are inevitably led to make is that the laws of war regulate only the conduct of war and not the fundamental legality or legitimacy of resort to it. This assumption is a marked departure from earlier religious doctrines that saw the two as deeply interrelated. The distinction between the *jus in bello* proper (the laws of war) and *jus ad bellum* (the law of resort to war), on the contrary, is a move characteristic of modernity and specifically of the late nineteenth century project to regulate war legally. In positing that these two are radically different normative registers, one merely emphasizes that the arguments in each registry are without incidence in the other. The theory of the laws of war, then, is constitutively reliant on this idea that *jus in bello* and *jus ad bellum* can be separated, and

---

[3] JJ Rousseau, *On the Social Contract* (DA Cress trans and ed) (Hackett Indianapolis 1987 [1762]) at 21.

considerable theoretical efforts are invested into preserving the irreducibility of the two.[4]

Finally, the laws of war accept that some violence in war is legitimate. This manifests itself in the acknowledgement of a 'privilege of belligerency' so that those allowed to participate in hostilities can never be faulted for the act of simply killing enemy combatants, as well as a certain tolerance for collateral harm. In exchange for this fundamental recognition of the possibility of war, as it were, the laws of war stipulate all kinds of violence-moderating conditions. As such international humanitarian law helps distinguish the particular use of violence known as war from other uses of violence that, as a result of not remotely abiding by any limitations, cannot possibly qualify as war: genocide, terrorism, crimes against humanity, and so on. Such is the distinguishing mark of 'war': there is a possibility of participating lawfully in it, whereas there is no 'proper' way of engaging in or conducting genocide or terrorism.

2.3 Theories of Operation

Once these major 'conditions of possibility' are validated, international humanitarian lawyers can turn to a theory of how the laws of war operate. This theory of practice is in a sense less theoretical, but it is theoretical to the extent that it requires some quite deep-seated assumptions about the normative mechanics of the laws of war. These assumptions then structure a whole prescriptive register of what ought to be done or not done in order to enhance respect for the laws of war.

First, the laws of war must be binding in a particular case. That is, they must exist not only as an idea but as actual, binding international law (in line with the system's founding legal hypothesis). Here the laws of war typically borrow heavily from general international law in order to determine their conditions of bindingness, and a range of theories about the conditions under which international actors become bound. Beyond treaties, much thinking goes into whether and which part of the laws of war have become customary and thus bind a range of actors that may not have formally agreed to be bound by them.[5] In that respect, the laws of war manifest their ability to transcend strict voluntarism, even as they can claim the solidity of convergent practice.

Second, the laws of war must be applicable in any given circumstance. An essential tool, perhaps the most important one, in the international humanitarian lawyer's tool kit, is the ability to detect when an 'armed conflict' exists, and what

---

[4] RD Sloane, 'The Cost of Conflation: Preserving the Dualism of Jus Ad Bellum and Jus in Bello in the Contemporary Law of War' (2009) 34 *Yale Journal of International Law* 47–112.

[5] T Meron, *Human Rights and Humanitarian Norms as Customary Law* (OUP New York 1989).

type of conflict it is. Alongside attempts to interpret the *Geneva Conventions'* understanding of international or non-international armed conflict, significant doctrinal theorizing has gone into distinguishing various shades of mixed or hybrid armed conflicts. Recent attempts to rebrand entire violent episodes as part of global wars (for example, the 'War on Terror') have elicited significant resistance to the 'normalization' of war as the default mode of inflicting violence globally.

Third, the laws of war are understood to function as a legal system in two principal ways. On the one hand, they regulate and prohibit a number of means and methods of combat. On the other hand, they protect certain persons. The notion of legitimate targets, in particular, is clearly central to the act of determining which targets are not legitimate. Moreover, the emphasis in policy and the literature is on the level of detail that the laws of war have achieved. At the same time, some of the most dire situations in war (for example, bombing) seem ultimately to rely less on detailed rules than on a number of principles such as discrimination, military necessity, or humanity. Broad principles are understood as having a role that is consonant with the project's largely positivistic ambitions, notably in infusing it with moral meaning that cannot be garnered from a purely technical approach.

2.4 Theories of Implementation

The discipline invests in particular theories of how the laws of war are implemented, complied with, and enforced. This is an area that lends itself relatively well to some theorizing because the conditions under which law will be respected are only partly contained in the dominant positivist model. The idea that the laws of war ought to be respected simply because they are the law seems to overlook the fact that their unmistakable existence as 'law' within the system authorized to label them as such, does not necessarily endow them with any intrinsic respect. Theories on the implementation of the laws of war vary tremendously.

One theory, which might be termed 'horizontal', is that the laws of war are best implemented when an impartial and neutral actor such as a third state or, more realistically, the International Committee of the Red Cross (ICRC), mediates between parties to armed conflicts. This understanding of how the laws of war ought to be primarily enforced dominated up to the end of the Second World War and even during the Cold War, and continues to have a significant role. It is based on a realist assessment of the possibilities of enforcement, and the priority given to assistance and protection over any form of condemnation as expressed by a sort of humanitarian *bons offices*. As humanitarian violations threaten international peace and security, the Security Council has also increasingly voiced concern about humanitarian violations and seen itself as an integral part of the effort to 'ensure respect' for the laws of war, a move sometimes resisted by the ICRC as dangerous for the notion of an impartial humanitarian space.

Another, more 'vertical' theory is that the laws of war require enforcement, particularly in the form of criminal repression of war crimes in order to be respected. The natural extension of the positivist model is a focus on the role of courts and punishment but also, perhaps more importantly, on the idea that respect for the laws of war ultimately lies in individual soldiers and their sense of responsibility. Hence perhaps no area of the laws of war has become more developed in recent decades than the idea of war crimes and the institutional machinery that comes with it (*aut dedere aut judicare*, universal jurisdiction, international criminal tribunals).[6] The theory of law enforcement on which such efforts are premised emphasizes the fact that soldiers act as rational actors who are likely to be deterred by the prospect of punishment or, failing that, at least international society's constitutive norms are reinforced by a process of guilt ascription. It typically leads to recommendations for reliance on centralized enforcement resources such as the state and, increasingly, the international community through its international tribunals.

Finally, there is a growing move to seek to diffuse the content of the laws of war in culturally appropriate ways. Moreover, there is by now a distinct effort to seek to bind non-state actors that cannot be parties to the relevant instruments, typically through unilateral acts (the Bulletin of the Secretary General of the United Nations on the applicability of international humanitarian law to peacekeeping troops, deeds of commitment by rebel movements under the supervision of the NGO Geneva Call).[7] All of these theories are not necessarily incompatible, but they can clearly be in tension, such as when a contradiction arises between denouncing crimes and discreetly mediating between parties, or insisting on confidentiality versus testifying before international criminal tribunals.

2.5 Theories of Evolution

At a somewhat more theoretical level, it is fair to say that the discipline has theories about 'where it is going'; in other words a general sense of provenance and destination that is an interesting guide to its practices. It is largely accepted that the laws of war are not static. In fact, they pride themselves on their unique

---

[6] See further S Nouwen, 'Theorizing International Criminal law: Theory all over the Place' in this *Handbook*.

[7] See United Nations Secretary General, 'Bulletin: Observance by United Nations Forces of International Humanitarian Law' (6 August 1999) UN Doc ST/SGB/1999/13; Geneva Call, 'Deed of Commitment' <http://www.genevacall.org/how-we-work/deed-of-commitment/> [accessed 29 February 2016].

adaptability to changing circumstances, and the various 'waves' of international instruments adopted throughout the twentieth century attest to their ability to update themselves. Typically, the laws of war are understood to adapt to some of the new challenges—practical, political, technological, and moral—raised or modified by a given conflict. Where some regularly proclaim the laws of war to be out-dated and some entirely new regime needed to take its place, the bulk of the profession is adamant that there is nothing in these new circumstances for which the law was not already in some way or other designed, or that cannot be remedied by ad hoc developments and further spelling out of the deep logic of the project.

The general direction towards which the laws of war evolve is typically presented as one of greater humanitarianism, as illustrated most notably by the move from a 'laws of war' to an 'international humanitarian law'. For example, amongst protected persons, the laws of war focus increasingly on non-combatants and particularly civilians: the taking of hostages is outlawed; the direct targeting of civilians is made into a crime; women and children are protected; some new weapons are prohibited; and so on. Moreover, the laws of war become more intrusive and less wedded to a classical Westphalian framework in which inter-state armed conflicts are paramount. Rather, they evolve towards a project to regulate all forms of conflictual violence, whether international or non-international. As such, they show themselves to be ultimately less wedded to a particular canonical view of the international legal system than to the need to protect victims of violence. The laws of war can at least claim to have won a decisive intellectual victory against the idea of 'total war' and its ambition to terrorize the civilian population, or the vulgar notion that military necessity justifies any attack even on civilians that is liable to reduce morale or coerce a nation into surrendering.

A particular motif in theories of the evolution of international humanitarian law is their increasing modification as a result of interaction with the idea of human rights.[8] This humanization thesis is understood to have induced structural changes in the law. For example, the emphasis has moved away from the reciprocal and synallagmatic character of the laws of war (despite the evident bilateralism or multilateralism of war), to the idea that the laws of war are owed to combatants and non-combatants as such. This has consequences in terms of the emergence of humanitarian norms or the response to their violation. The laws of war remain applicable in a conflict notwithstanding the fact that a participant is not a party to the relevant treaty, the 'tu quoque' defence is of little incidence, and reprisals are increasingly understood be have fallen into desuetude. This is seen as resulting

---

[8] T Meron, 'The Humanization of Humanitarian Law' (2000) 94 *American Journal of International Law* 239–78.

from the fact that humanitarian obligations are not owed primarily to other states but to humanity generally or enemy combatants and civilians directly as part of an implicit cosmopolitan bargain.

3 EXTERNAL THEORIES

Not all external theories are critical. An external theory, taking international humanitarian law as its object, might be concerned with what place it occupies more generally within international law. However, external theories are typically better suited to problematize the laws of war as a discipline.

3.1 Theorizing against the Laws of War

There has long been a distinct theoretical strand that can only be understood as hostile to the laws of war project and as, in fact, aiming at its denial. This effort can take three broad, somewhat related forms. First are largely discredited theories of *kriegsraison*, namely the idea that war should follow its own logic of destruction and override all other law. Such theories may have prepared the ground and share some affinity with various totalitarian, genocidal, or terroristic theories of war. They effectively destroy the humanitarian space by making necessity into a broadly permissive ('all that is necessary') rather than limitative concept ('only what is necessary'), and turning the exception (for example, the killing of civilians can be considered legal if it is indirect and proportional to the military advantage sought) into the rule (civilians can be targeted, except perhaps when this would serve no conceivable military purpose). In their more moderate version, they may simply translate into certain realist complaints that the laws of war are unduly constraining in particular circumstances in which military necessity should be granted a free hand.

Second, a distinct strand of theorizing against the laws of war takes a more sophisticated normative stance which argues that the project is at a deeper level self-defeating in a variety of ways. For example, making war more humane makes it more likely that states will resort to it, thus ultimately bringing about more human suffering; or making war seem—and even actually be—more moderate may simply prolong conflicts because no decisive advantage can be obtained; or assistance may be diverted by actors on the ground in ways that will only renew violence. In this view, painful and horrifying but short conflicts would make more sense from a humanitarian point of view. The insistence on the categorical imperative is more or less implicitly dismissed as short sighted and even hypocritical. Arguments for the possession and at least theoretical use of nuclear weapons make much of this sort of logic in that the possibility of widespread civilian destruction—un-humanitarian as it may be when and if it does occur—is widely understood, via deterrence, to act as a break on the very use of force. Evidently, such claims are based on a mixture of empirical and normative arguments that are beyond the scope of this chapter to examine, but it is undeniable that they remain influential.

Third are a group of theories that have long challenged the continued relevance of the 'war' model that seems to be at the source of the laws of war on the basis of the social evolution of war as a mode of violence. These theories emphasize the rise of technologies and political circumstances that make war 'total', the presence of new actors in warfare who are not socialized in the public international law model and are not committed to the values that undergird the system, and the decline of the spacio-temporal coordinates of warfare.[9] 'Total war', then, raises the spectre that international humanitarian lawyers will continue to seek to regulate armies whose actions have long ceased to be defined by their overwhelmingly military nature, and fundamentally miss the fact that what is going on is a form of crime against humanity (as in the famous case of the ICRC being manipulated in Theresienstadt). 'Unorthodox' participants in war (from '*francs tireurs*' to 'terrorists', rebel movements, and private military companies) challenge the equality of the parties to war and even their at least proto-public character, and thus threaten to corrode the structure of the laws of war as a regime focused originally on the application to equally situated parties.[10] Finally, whereas war between sovereigns and even between sovereigns and certain non-state actors traditionally occurred within fairly defined special and temporal boundaries, most typically associated with the conceit of the 'battlefield', war increasingly seems to occur globally (the 'war' on terror) or virtually (attacks on computer systems, and so on).

The consequence of these disruptions of the implicit social model informing the laws of war, then, is that 'war' is arguably vanishing and that the urge to continue to regulate violence as if war were still the model is fundamentally misconceived. Note however that these three modes of theorizing 'against' the laws of war have a tendency to telescope each other, some acting as a more respectable intellectual fig leaf for others. For example, the critique of the desuetude of 'war' may in practice be radicalized by realists whose real drive is to argue that it is illegitimate to rein

---

[9] F Mégret, 'War and the Vanishing Battlefield' (2011) 9 *Loyola University Chicago International Law Review* 131–55.

[10] ML Gross, *Moral Dilemmas of Modern War: Torture, Assassination, and Blackmail in an Age of Asymmetric Conflict* (CUP New York 2010).

in sovereigns fighting for their survival, and in turn make way for a deeper sub-version of war into torture, genocide, or terrorism.[11] Whilst the theory is typically presented as one of deploring, even nostalgically, the passing of 'war' as it is once imagined to have been, the agenda may very well be one to precipitate this desue-tude by jumping a little too quickly to the conclusion that the other party's faults justify one's own non-adherence.

3.2 Questioning the Legal in International Humanitarian Law

The laws of war, which Lauterpacht famously described as 'the vanishing point of international law', itself the 'vanishing point of law',[12] are a highly opportune avenue to think about international law more generally, its very possibility, and the nature of its ambition. Although the laws of war project is perhaps crucially shaped by its investment in positivism, it turns out to be a very interesting place to explore tensions inherent in that positivism. From the very beginning, the mass of positive norms designed to regulate warfare coexist with both grand appeals to some immanent morality, and, more importantly, seem to rely on naturalized principles (humanity, proportionality, and so on). Hence for all their commitment to positivism, the laws of war are in fact often a fairly typical mix of the positive and the natural. This is evident in contemporary develop-ments surrounding the question of customary international humanitarian law, in which adherence to a positivist methodology is in practice always conditioned by assumptions about the nature of the law that inevitably incorporate some of the very naturalist reasoning that positivism was supposed to have excluded.[13] Ultimately, the suspicion is that the laws of war rely dramatically on complex moral weighing exercises that are in practice almost always made by the military and very hard to second guess.

Scepticism about the specificity of the laws of war as law opens the way to alternative theories of the essence of the laws of war that either suggest that we should disinvest in the idea of law, or understand law in an altogether different way. Such theories also hope to explain why states and other actors sometimes abide by some laws of war limitations even in cases where there is little prospect of enforcement facing them. Essentially, international humanitarian lawyers are

---

[11] S Horton, 'Kriegsraison or Military Necessity: The Bush Administration's Wilhelmine Attitude towards the Conduct of War' (2006) 30 *Fordham International Law Journal* 576–98.

[12] H Lauterpacht, 'The Problem of the Revision of the Law of War' (1952) 29 *British Year Book of International Law* 360–82.

[13] M Koskenniemi, 'The Pull of the Mainstream' (1990) 88 *Michigan Law Review* 1946–62.

faulted for falling prey to a particular illusion that leads them to think that the laws are the cause of humane behaviour in war, where it is at best international humanitarian law that is the result of something else. One provocative view in this context focuses on the relevance of economic rationality and interest maximizing behaviour. Here the source of law's implementation is seen less as a sense of external sovereign compulsion or sheer respect for the 'humanitarianism' inherent to the law, than as the ability of the law to respond to and emulate the interest calculus of actors in the field.[14] Another more romantic view focuses on the laws of war as the locus of values that have long sustained a certain chivalry amongst men at arms.[15]

4 LAWS OF WAR OR WAR OF LAW?

The dominant theory of the laws of war is of them 'regulating' war; an alternative view is that they merely enable, constitute, and perpetuate it. Their deep structure is largely consonant with military logic of necessity and economy of means. Martti Koskenniemi's *From Apology to Utopia* can help us understand how this is so and how the laws of war risk never amounting to more than a ratification of the status quo of war.[16] If the laws of war become too utopian, for example by mandating that no civilian be killed even incidentally, they risk losing their claim to being law, that is, to being backed by sovereign authority and practice. The *jus in bello* must remain a reasonably bloody affair, a way to manage and regulate war and cannot be, indirectly, another way of effectively outlawing it. On the other hand, if the laws of war are too apologetic—for example by swaying too far in the direction of *kriegsraison*—they risk losing the element of utopia that is crucial to them being normative and not merely a license to do anything in war. This would be particularly wounding to a project that presents itself as at least reformist and often much more. Note that nor is this a purely a theoretical problem, in that what is at stake behind these equations is also the support of key constituencies (states, the military, civil society). Hence the tendency of the laws of war to navigate towards a sort of reformist *via media* that suggests a certain perpetuation of the war model.[17]

---

[14] 'A Theory of the Laws of War' (n 1).

[15] T Meron, *Bloody Constraint: War and Chivalry in Shakespeare* (OUP Oxford 1998).

[16] M Koskenniemi, *From Apology to Utopia: The Structure of International Legal Argument* (reissue CUP Cambridge 2005).

[17] M Koskenniemi, 'Occupied Zone: A Zone of Reasonableness?' (2008) 41 *Israel Law Review* 13–40.

Another way of looking at the role of law in reproducing war is by challenging the facile image of law 'coming to the battlefield' to regulate something that is 'already there'. Critical constructivists will typically argue, on the contrary, that the laws of war are less regulative than they are constitutive. There has never been such a thing as totally unregulated warfare in that the very idea of war as a contest between adversaries is already a heavily normative idea, rooted in particular understandings of sovereignty and public violence. The laws of war, therefore, are more generally part of the social construction and reproduction of war as a legitimate institution of international society.[18] In fact, some may argue that international humanitarian law only ever ratifies the accepted status quo, for example outlawing weapons that parties have by and large renounced as useless.[19] From there, it is perhaps only a small step to considering that the laws of war are also part of the reification and even fetishization of warfare. If anything this has become even more so, in an age that is characterized not so much by abuse of the law for combat purposes ('lawfare') than the very cosiness of law with military violence.[20]

Moreover, the laws of war delineate a highly peculiar, situated vision of warfare. First, they are deeply compromised with the evolving but always pertinent distinction between (a priori legitimate) public violence and (criminal) private violence.[21] Although the laws of war claim to have nothing to do with the *jus ad bellum*, they are at least the repositories of a notion of who is more fundamentally allowed to participate in war,[22] with states at the apex, state-mimicking non-state actors a relatively close second, and pure non-state actors that do not inscribe their action within a sovereign register as distant thirds. In addition, the laws of war's construction of individuals as mere instruments of state designs— humanitarian as they may be—reinforces the status of the state as fundamental security provider.[23]

Second, the laws of war seem devoted to the generalization of a model of violence first invented in Europe and which has been successfully exported to the rest of the world. In that respect, what constrains and limits also diffuses. It is very difficult not to engage in war against a party that is claiming to be engaging in war in a situation in which war has become another name for at least legitimate public

---

[18] N Berman, 'Privileging Combat: Contemporary Conflict and the Legal Construction of War' (2004) 43 *Columbia Journal of Transnational Law* 1–71.

[19] C Jochnick and R Normand, 'The Legitimation of Violence: A Critical History of the Laws of War' (1994) 35 *Harvard International Law Journal* 49–95.

[20] D Kennedy, *Of War and Law* (Princeton University Press Princeton 2006).

[21] P Owens, 'Distinctions, Distinctions: "Public" and "Private" Force?' (2008) 84 *International Affairs* 977–90.

[22] F Mégret, 'Jus In Bello as Jus Ad Bellum' (2006) 100 *American Society of International Law Proceedings* 121–3.

[23] I Clark, *The Vulnerable in International Society* (OUP Oxford 2013) at 59.

violence.[24] The laws of war thus act as a prime marker of the civilizational character of international law and those who partake in it. In that respect, the laws of war also serve a crucial function of distinguishing the (therefore) civilized world from the uncivilized. They do not simply regulate war as it exists in the abstract, but rather highlight war as humane when it occurs between civilized powers and inhumane when it occurs with or between barbarians. The 'universalism' of the laws of war, then, is relative; it is a universalism within a community of civilized nations that does not extend to all warring parties.

Third, the laws of war seem to be deeply embedded in certain gendered assumptions. Over the last two decades, the focus has been on how the laws of war ignored women's needs and in particular neglected the problem of sexual violence. Increasingly, this initial interest is both being challenged by some feminists in terms of its politics of representation,[25] and being complemented by a study of sexual violence as it applies to gender more generally.[26] More radically, scholarship is emerging that proposes a deeper gendered critique of the laws of war beyond the question of women's status in war and sexual violence.[27]

5 WHAT DO THE LAWS OF WAR DISPLACE?

In this context, one crucial question is what the laws of war do to the more general normative economy of international law. *Contra* a view that foregrounds the accomplishments of the laws of war within the overall narrative of international law, one might theorize about what the laws of war tend subtly to displace. A first element that the laws of war arguably displace, notwithstanding the influence that the discourse of human rights has had on them, is ordinary respect for human rights. This is *a fortiori* the case when the laws of war are over-applied, for example to justify targeted killings in situations that should really be considered to fall short of armed conflict.

---

[24] F Mégret, 'From "Savages" to "Unlawful Combatants": A Postcolonial Look at International Humanitarian Law's "Other"' in A Orford (ed), *International Law and Its Others* (CUP Cambridge 2006) 265–317.

[25] J Halley, 'Rape in Berlin: Reconsidering the Criminalisation of Rape in the International Law of Armed Conflict' (2008) 9 *Melbourne Journal of International Law* 78–124.

[26] S Sivakumaran, 'Sexual Violence against Men in Armed Conflict' (2007) 18 *European Journal of International Law* 253–76.

[27] HM Kinsella, *The Image before the Weapon: A Critical History of the Distinction between Combatant and Civilian* (Cornell University Press Ithaca 2011).

Although there is by now a veritable cottage industry of doctrinal writings on the relationship between international human rights and international humanitarian law, one basic conclusion seems inescapable; namely that the laws of war, as the *lex specialis* when it comes to killing in armed conflict, represent a considerable concession to the principles that normally protect human life.[28] This is evidently true of the tolerance exhibited by the laws of war for collateral civilian casualties, a tolerance that sounds like the right to life is being sacrificed on the altar of intergroup violence. It is also, more surprisingly, true of the laws of war's tolerance for the death of combatants, whose right to life ought also to be protected (the so-called 'internal *jus in bello*'). In this respect, the laws of war clearly appear more international than cosmopolitan and are in tension with what might be a more radical human rights view that would not consider war a fatality.

Secondly, the laws of war might be said subtly to displace what might be a resolutely *contra bellum* or even pacific sensitivity in international law. This is evident in the way war crimes have radically gained in prominence since the Second World War in relation to crimes against peace and aggression, as if the worst thing about war was the way it was fought rather than the fact that it was wrongly fought in the first place. It is also evident in the way in which despite being on the wrong end of the *jus ad bellum*, a state is 'recompensed' as it were with the notion of equality of belligerents. Interestingly and conversely, the focus on human rights might help reinforce the sense of even a 'clean' war of aggression being deeply problematic from a moral and legal point of view. Even though combatants and, to a lesser degree, non-combatants may be killed legally under international humanitarian law in conflict, their deaths should presumably be credited to the side waging an unjust war as part of the computation of the overall evil of aggression. Human rights might also in turn displace the operation of the laws of war in prolonged situations of occupation.[29]

6 A MORAL REINVENTION?

Finally, a new orientation in the theory of the laws of war that has gained ascendance in the last few decades seeks to revive the morale critique of the laws of war

[28] WA Schabas, 'Lex Specialis? Belt and Suspenders?: The Parallel Operation of Human Rights Law and the Law of Armed Conflict, and the Conundrum of Jus Ad Bellum' (2007) 40 *Israel Law Review* 592–613.
[29] A Roberts, 'Transformative Military Occupation: Applying the Laws of War and Human Rights' (2006) 100 *American Journal of International Law* 580–622.

and, increasingly, to invent different moral futures for it. Much of that critique is in fact less directly aimed at the positive laws of war, than an attempt to think through philosophically the elements of the 'just war' tradition as they apply to the *jus in bello*. Confusingly, moral concepts of limitation in war are often treated as if they were the actual laws of war but there is no doubt that at least implicitly this sort of normative critique has done much to rejuvenate theorizing on the conduct of war.

Moral theorizing on the laws of war was famously put back on the philosophical radar by Walzer's *Just and Unjust Wars*.[30] Walzer's main thesis ended up being more of a moral justification of the laws of war as they existed, a sophisticated attempt to provide a rationale embedded in deference to the institutions of international society rather than a critique of them. Post-Walzerian, 'revisionist' authors writing particularly in the 2000s have on the contrary struck at the core of some of the assumptions of the laws of war, in the process seeking to displace some of the basic building blocks of the international grammar of violence. Perhaps the most evident sacred cow to have been attacked in this context is the notion of the 'equality of belligerents'. For Jeff McMahan, for example, 'unjust warriors' (that is, those involved in an unjust war at the *jus ad bellum* level) should not be seen as having an equal right to kill combatants, and conversely 'just warriors' should not be seen as legitimate targets in war.[31] An even more radical critique challenges the notion that non-combatants on the unjust side of the war cannot be targeted because they are 'innocent'.

Some of these critiques merely serve to shape our theoretical understanding of the inherent morality or immorality of the laws of war. Some, however, have started receiving an echo amongst international lawyers.[32] For example, the possibility is increasingly entertained that actors in an armed conflict could be bound by different sets of normative obligations, without the laws of war falling apart, either on strategic, legally pluralistic or ethical grounds.[33] In other words, where some see in the growing asymmetry of warfare a risk of decay for the laws of war, others see a potential for renewal. This seems a further refinement of the idea that the laws of war do not express synallagmatic as much as a series of unilateral commitments anchored in deontology. Moreover, the possibility that combatants in non-international armed conflicts be granted a privilege of combatancy has been mooted, perhaps as part of a package of incentives.[34]

---

[30] M Walzer, *Just and Unjust Wars: A Moral Argument with Historical Illustrations* (revised edn Basic Books New York 2006 [1977]).

[31] J McMahan, 'The Morality of War and the Law of War' in D Rodin and H Shue (eds), *Just and Unjust Warriors: The Moral and Legal Status of Soldiers* (OUP Oxford 2008) 19–43.

[32] E Benvenisti, 'Rethinking the Divide between *Jus Ad Bellum* and *Jus in Bello* in Warfare against Nonstate Actors' (2009) 34 *Yale Journal of International Law* 541–8.

[33] G Blum, 'On a Differential Law of War' (2001) 52 *Harvard International Law Journal* 163–218.

[34] GS Corn, 'Thinking the Unthinkable: Has the Time Come to Offer Combatant Immunity to Non-State Actors?' (2011) 22 *Stanford Law & Policy Review* 253–94.

7 CONCLUSION

Theorizing about the laws of war is alive and well. The subject matter provides rich material. In a sense, the very project of civilizing war is nothing but one great theory about its plausibility, mode of functioning, and destination. Law, then, is just another name for a form of fossilized theory that no longer sees itself as a theory and claims some unchallengeable status as merely 'what is binding'. There is much, in fact a renewal of, theorizing on the outskirts of the laws of war that compensates for this lack of explicit theorizing within the mainstream of the discipline. This theorizing displaces the field's confidence that it is 'only law' and can shape our understanding of the laws of war as less immutable, progressive and benign than is typically accepted.

CHAPTER 38

THEORIES OF TRANSITIONAL JUSTICE

CASHING IN THE BLUE CHIPS

VASUKI NESIAH

1 INTRODUCTION

HUMAN rights discourse has gained remarkable traction in diverse arenas of the international public sphere, from courtrooms adjudicating war crimes in Liberia to snipers aiming at Bashir government convoys in Syria. Moreover, if the field of human rights is the ascendant sector in 'the political futures market', the subfield of transitional justice is a blue chip.[1] The Libyan transition from the Gaddafi era was accompanied by calls for transitional justice initiatives and International Criminal Court (ICC) indictments; Serbian membership in the European Union has been

---

[1] Ian Brownlie invoked the terminology of 'political futures market' in reference to human rights when writing about how agendas such as the New International Economic Order became reframed as the Right to Development in the 1970s, because it was already evident that policy agendas would have more traction if framed in terms of human rights: I Brownlie, 'The Human Right to Development' (Commonwealth Secretariat, Human Rights Unit, Occasional Paper, 1989) at 3. Brownlie was writing in 1989—this trend only intensified in the 1990s, with transitional justice (the subfield of human rights dealing with post conflict justice) taking centre stage in a decade that saw the inauguration of institutions such as the ad hoc tribunals in the Hague and Arusha and the truth commissions in Chile, El Salvador, South Africa, and Guatemala.

intertwined with the capture of Radovan Karadžić for trial at the International Criminal Tribunal for the Former Yugoslavia (ICTY). In all of these contexts transitional justice is invoked to reference the possibility of renewal and rebirth on a foundation of human rights—seeking to convey both an ethical departure from the past through accountability for past regime's atrocities, while also reaching forward into a future guided by human rights. Transitional justice is argued for in this way as both a matter of political ethics and as a matter of political pragmatics, the notion that it is only human rights that would provide a solid foundation for modernity.

This chapter seeks to examine the utopias called forth by this marriage of human rights accountability mechanisms on the one hand, and, on the other, arguments about the practical significance of these initiatives as preconditions for development, democracy, and political society as such. Transitional justice is seen to marry the ethical charge of the human rights field's march against impunity, with an instrumental potential facilitating transition from the rule of violence into the rule of law.[2] If the normative theories and agendas implicated by this marriage are advanced as being in the interests of justice, the accompanying instrumental theories and agendas are advanced in the interests of transition. Justice and transition operate here as allied and mutually reinforcing aspirations of and rationales for transitional justice institutions. This chapter will identify and analyse the stakes that attend this marriage of 'ethics' and 'expertise' in constituting the utopian political imagination of transitional justice.

In the following section, I first describe theories of transitional justice that foreground claims about the interests of justice and then move to theories that foreground claims about the interests of transition. The life histories of these two families of theories have been conjoined within the framework of transitional justice but they also emerge from and implicate intellectual and political stakes on different terrains and to that extent are valuably explored as two distinct if interrelated frames of argument. I flag questions regarding both sets of theories as I move forward with explicating them further. Subsequently, I briefly examine

---

[2] One striking dimension of transitional justice is that it has become consolidated not only as a framework of human rights norms and laws, but has also entrenched a discreet set of institutional models and policy frameworks (with prosecutions, truth commissions, and reparations at their core). In many ways this intertwined face of transitional justice achieved global visibility when concrete preparations for the South African Truth and Reconciliation Commission (TRC) got underway. The TRC itself captured the global imagination in ways worked on both normative and instrumental registers. This visibility is what propelled transitional justice into the blue chip currency it is today. That said, the groundwork of this merger of the normative and programmatic had been laid in arenas that include and extend from cold-war liberalism to post-cold war neoliberalism, from political science modelling of democracy to Weberian theorizing of the rule of law, from the Nuremberg and Tokyo war crimes tribunals to the birthing of the Office of the High Commission for Human Rights, from holocaust studies to trauma studies, from the invocation of human rights discourse in Eastern Europe and Latin America. Paige Arthur offers an important intellectual history of the field that foregrounds American social science literature on transitions and democratization: P Arthur, 'How "Transitions" Reshaped Human Rights: A Conceptual History of Transitional Justice' (2009) 31 *Human Rights Quarterly* 321–67.

these theories by looking at how they are elaborated in specific contexts. Such contexts include how terms such as the interests of justice have been debated in the context of the *Rome Statute* and how theories about the interests of transition have been discussed in the annual reports of the Secretary-General on 'The Rule of Law and Transitional Justice in Conflict and Post-Conflict Societies'.[3] I bring to bear the questions raised at the end of the previous section in relation to each of these specific contexts. For the most part this chapter seeks to offer an immanent critique through a reconstruction of dominant norms of transitional justice and an account of how the machinery of transitional justice practice unfolds. The aim of this reconstruction is to describe how hegemonic approaches get normalized, how distributive questions get displaced, and legitimacy performed. In other words, the aim is to track and trace the value chains that underpin transitional justice. In the concluding section, I take a different turn. I look at heterodox theories of transitional justice that did not accompany the field's historical march as anthems to the political futures market. I explore the possibility of mining the 'failed' theories of transitional justice as counterpoint to the 'successful' ones. This is not an effort to recuperate the field and redeem its future potential but an effort to explore the yield of the lost coinage of subaltern economies to interrogate the dominant currency.

2 THE INTERESTS OF JUSTICE

Theories of transitional justice are advanced at three different levels of theorizing—at the level of quotidian institutional performance or implementation, at the level of policy, and at the level of scholarly engagement, or what we may describe as, respectively, the micro-, meso- and meta-level of theorizing. There is an extraordinary degree of cohesion between these three levels but the different contexts of knowledge production also speak of transitional justice in different accents, thereby foregrounding different kinds of issues. In this section, I first describe these three levels and then focus on the interpretation of the 'in the interests of justice' clause in the *Rome Statute* as one particular context in which the theory of transitional justice has been debated and defined. This section aims to describe how the field presents itself, as well as the backstage assumptions and practices that frame the conditions within which the field reproduces itself and manages or deters challenge.

At the quotidian level, theories of transitional justice are immanent in the institutional rationality of the field and transmitted and accessed through notions of expertise, disciplinarity, and professionalism. These theories include

---

[3] Secretary General, 'The Rule of Law and Transitional Justice in Conflict and Post-Conflict Societies' (23 August 2004) UN Doc S/2004/616.

the normative common sense of human rights that is manifest in the routinized assumptions and practices of the transitional justice field. This everyday human rights common sense often includes ideas such as that individual prosecutions epitomize accountability, or that it is acts of bodily harm that constitute the gravest human rights violations, or that 'truth seeking' should be about a 'national' history of human rights abuse. While these theories of transitional justice may often be formulated and advanced at a certain level of abstraction, they are translated into concrete institutional practices as part of the entrenched background knowledge that informs different domains of the field, including national governments and United Nation (UN) agencies, the transitional justice funding loop (both the givers and receivers of aid), and the 'expert knowledge' of practitioners within transitional justice institutions (such as truth commission and courts). For instance, the 'justice cascade' that Kathryn Sikkink and Ellen Lutz have heralded references a sevenfold rise in individual criminal prosecutions from 1979 to 2004.[4] This conveys both a diffusion of ideas about the value of prosecution into the field of prosecutors and lawyers, as well as of expert observers such as Sikkink and Lutz who are both observers of a trend and contributors to it in employing a moral and political vocabulary that frames the meaning that attaches to individual criminal prosecutions. Most significantly this includes the idea that individual criminal prosecution is itself justice as if this were not a politically loaded equation that was already circumscribing the agenda in far reaching ways.[5] Rather, this equation becomes backgrounded as a sort of professional epistemic horizon that reflects the diffusion of theories of transitional justice at the quotidian level.

The background assumptions that shape these 'common sense' understandings of the theory of transitional justice may not always be explicit at the micro-level but they may be significant in structuring institutional practice, and constructing the meanings that attach to the notions of expertise and professionalism that have helped produce the field. Any research into the practice archive of the field evidences these assumptions in arenas such as funding applications, best practice protocols of transitional justice institutions, the coding categories of human rights violations in the information management systems (IMS), or the final reports of truth commissions.[6] Each of these could be arenas where those 'common sense

---

[4] E Lutz and K Sikkink, 'The Justice Cascade: The Evolution and Impact of Foreign Human Rights Trials in Latin America' (2001) 2 *Chicago Journal of International Law* 1–34.

[5] In the introduction to her book, Sikkink notes, 'I argue that these international, foreign, and domestic human rights prosecutions are all part of an interrelated trend in world politics towards greater accountability—a trend that Ellen Lutz and I have called the "justice cascade"': K Sikkink, *The Justice Cascade:* How Human Rights Prosecutions Are Changing World Politics. (WW Norton New York 2011).

[6] IMSs are employed by institutions that are working with thousands of complaints regarding human rights violations; the IMS is used to control and access the data, identify patterns, and

understandings' could be challenged, revisited, and defined differently but those assumptions are normalized and institutional practices routinized in ways that have consolidated rather than troubled the field. For instance, the South African Truth and Reconciliation Commission (TRC) followed the dominant approach of the human rights field and interpreted its mandate in ways that 'condensed suffering to traces on the body'[7] rather than to the larger atrocities of apartheid as a historical phenomenon. This interpretation was reproduced and entrenched in the course of the TRC's work through individual statement takers, researchers, investigators, lawyers, commissioners, and others discharging their duties on a daily basis. As their work was covered in the media, translated into non-governmental organization (NGO) best practice lists, referenced in workshops for truth commissions in other parts of the world, recorded in UN policy guidelines and so on, these quotidian actions gave ballast to how 'gross human rights' violations were interpreted in the field of transitional justice. Thus, cumulatively, we can understand the everyday work of truth commissions as part of the connective tissue of micro-practices that came to define justice in terms of bodily harm. Similarly, when the Peruvian Truth and Reconciliation Commission recommended the prosecution of specific individuals, it thereby underscored that individual prosecutions hold an apex role in how prominent strands of the transitional justice field interpret accountability. From the Special Court for Sierra Leone's prosecution of Charles Taylor to the ICC's prosecution of Thomas Lubanga Dyilo, this focus on individual accountability as central to the pursuit of justice is reproduced in the machinery of the prosecutor's office as the investigators develop evidence, the law clerks research precedents, human rights groups develop amicus briefs, and so on.

We could understand the relationship between the (often unstated) background assumptions and micro, everyday practices of the field through what Vivian Schmidt and others describe as 'discursive institutionalism' where theories of

---

develop a numerical picture of the human rights story. As a result the categories through which violations are coded and information transmitted become fairly significant. Truth commissions in Guatemala, Peru, South Africa, Sierra Leone, Timor Leste, Ghana, and so forth have used some form of IMS. The anthropologist Richard Wilson has written on the work of IMS and like mechanisms in the South African TRC process. See RA Wilson, *The Politics of Truth and Reconciliation in South Africa: Legitimizing the Post-Apartheid State* (CUP Cambridge 2001). Audrey Chapman and Patrick Ball have not only written about South Africa, Guatemala, and elsewhere, they have also helped develop the IMS programs and see them as a counter to the affective, subjective, and biased truth claims of truth commissions: AR Chapman and P Ball, 'The Truth of Truth Commissions: Comparative Lessons from Haiti, South Africa, and Guatemala' (2001) 23 *Human Rights Quarterly* 1–43.

[7] See F Ross, *Bearing Witness: Women and the Truth and Reconciliation Commission in South Africa* (Pluto Press London 2003) at 12. In addition, Lars Burr argues that the commission used a range of mechanisms to restructure the individual story and context of particular victims testimonies to produce 'a set of uniform entries' that could be described with a standard human rights vocabulary, shorn of ambiguity and complexity: L Burr, 'Monumental History: Visibility and Invisibility in the Work of the South African Truth Commission' (Paper presented at Wits University 11–14 June 1999) <http://wiredspace.wits.ac.za/bitstream/handle/10539/7736/HWS-42.pdf> [accessed 29 February 2016].

transitional justice (that may be visible in different ways at the meso- and meta-level) operate as the ideational underpinnings that legitimate and entrench fields of knowledge and their institutional norms and practices.[8] At the micro-level, theories of transitional justice are endogenous to the field and the institutional culture such that they are seldom articulated and are just part of the scaffolding within which everyday practices (such as the equation of accountability with individual prosecutions) thrive. In situating these micro-institutional moves within that larger ideational structure, we turn now to the meso-level of theorizing about transitional justice that offers theories of transitional justice as policy in building the bridge between micro-everyday practices of the field and the meta-philosophical foundations for the field.

The meso-level is articulated by both scholars and practitioners when they seek to define the field and impact background policy. Thus UN reports such as the Office for the High Commissioner of Human Rights' (OHCHR) 'Analytical Study on Human Rights and Transitional Justice',[9] and the Joinet-Orentlicher Principles,[10] or the United States Institute for Peace's (USIP) 'Information Handbook on Transitional Justice' offer typical venues for meso-level theorizing on transitional justice.[11] The meso-level is characterized by a framing discourse that rationalizes, integrates, and renders compatible diverse institutional practices (such as prosecutions policy and reparations policy) within a unitary agenda of transitional justice. Typically this entails the claim that a holistic approach was in the interests of justice. Accordingly, the field emphasizes legal accountability, alongside truth seeking, reparations, and institutional reform measures as critical and co-dependent dimensions of transitional justice, as well as emphasizing that institutional mechanisms advancing these goals operate in the interests of justice. For instance, the Secretary General's report on 'The Rule of Law and Transitional Justice' urged that 'where transitional justice is required, strategies must be holistic, incorporating integrated attention to individual prosecutions, reparations, truth-seeking, institutional reform, vetting and dismissals, or an appropriately conceived combination thereof'.[12] While prosecutions are seen to combat impunity, truth seeking is also seen to address the interests of society at large in developing a national account of

[8] VA Schmidt, 'Taking Ideas and Discourse Seriously: Explaining Change through Discursive Institutionalism as the Fourth "New Institutionalism"' (2010) 2 *European Political Science Review* 1–25.

[9] Human Rights Council, 'Annual Report of the United Nations High Commissioner for Human Rights and Reports of the Office of the High Commissioner and the Secretary-General' (6 August 2009) UN Doc A/HRC/12/18.

[10] 'Updated Set of Principles for the Protection and Promotion of Human Rights Through Action to Combat Impunity' (8 February 2005) UN Doc E/CN.4/2005/102/Add.1.

[11] United States Institute for Peace, 'Transitional Justice: Information Handbook' (September 2008) <http://www.usip.org/sites/default/files/ROL/Transitional_justice_final.pdf> [accessed 29 February 2016].

[12] 'The Rule of Law and Transitional Justice in Conflict and Post-Conflict Societies' (n 3) 9.

human rights abuse. Moreover, like reparations, truth seeking is represented as victim-centred: vindicating victims' right to justice, and providing an institutional forum for their voice. In a similar vein, institutional reform measures are similarly advanced as steps towards addressing victim's concerns and ensuring that human rights atrocities do not recur.

While the Secretary General's report on 'The Rule of Law and Transitional Justice' conveys the dominant approach to transitional justice, specific articulations of the vision admit some variation. For instance, David Crocker's discussion of truth commissions and transitional justice identifies eight related goals as being in the interests of justice: an accessible 'truth' or knowledge about the past; a public platform for victims; accountability and punishment of perpetrators; promotion of the rule of law; reparation for victims; institutional reform and development; reconciliation; and public deliberation about past abuses.[13] Some meso-level articulations of transitional justice may also emphasize memorials, while others may fold memorials into symbolic reparations or into avenues for public deliberation. Some (like Crocker) may include reconciliation, while others may find it ambitious, even problematic, to give reconciliation the same significance as prosecutions and approach reconciliation as primarily a long-term goal that may result from transitional justice, as opposed to something that is itself a constitutive element of transitional justice.

In general, however, there is a broad consensus about the elements of transitional justice within the mainstream of the human rights movement—from UN bodies such as the OHCHR, to international non-governmental organizations (INGOs) such as the International Center for Transitional Justice, to the work of scholars/ practitioners in the field such as Juan Méndez or José (Pepe) Zalaquett.[14] Thus while the theory that informs institutional practices may seldom be foregrounded in the quotidian workings of transitional justice institutions, that theory is explicitly invoked, often as settled truths, at the meso-level. Yet, while it is remarkable that on many different fronts there is, indeed, a settled consensus, there are also areas of robust debate within these parameters. Some of the contours of such debates come into focus when we turn to specific problems such as the interpretation of the *Rome Statute*'s 'in the interests of justice' clause where different actors may define justice by placing varying degrees of emphasis on issues such as combating

---

[13] See DA Crocker, 'Truth Commissions, Transitional Justice and Civil Society' in RI Rotberg and D Thompson (eds), *Truth v Justice: The Moral Efficacy of Truth Commissions: South Africa and Beyond* (Princeton University Press Princeton 2000) 99–121.

[14] For instance, the International Center for Transitional Justice also advocates 'a holistic approach' that takes 'into account the full range of factors that may have contributed to abuse' and elaborates on why anything less than a holistic approach may be problematic: International Center for Transitional Justice, 'What is Transitional Justice?' (2009) <https://www.ictj.org/sites/default/files/ICTJ-Global-Transitional-Justice-2009-English.pdf> [accessed 1 March 2016].

impunity, vindicating victims, affirming social values against gross human rights abuse, rebuilding trust, and so on.[15]

Meta engagements with the background conceptual underpinnings of the field of transitional justice treat the transitional moment as one where the agenda is the restatement of the foundational commitments of a post-conflict political community. In the conflict literature's evocation of the state of nature, meta-level transitional justice theorizing is also about political community as such. At the meta-level transitional justice theory is background to the field but is itself not backgrounded—rather its principles are developed and articulated explicitly. Typically agents at the meta-level are scholars of transitional justice; those who see themselves as spokespeople for the promise of the field. An important example is Pablo de Greiff, who is both an independent scholar (trained in analytical philosophy) and the UN Special Rapporteur on the Promotion of Truth, Justice, Reparation and Guarantees of Non-Recurrence. Greiff speaks of transitional justice as performing a social contract function—or, in his own words, realizing 'two mediate goals, namely recognition and civic trust, and two final goals, reconciliation and democracy'.[16]

At the meta-level transitional justice processes are described as a path back to first principles enabling a re-negotiation of the basic social contract through a condemnation of the abuse of power, a vindication of citizens' expectations of justice, and reparations to human rights victims for their loss. Thus it is not surprising that such settling of accounts is also, often, a constitutional moment and transitional justice processes are invested with the same utopian aspirations that also accompany constitutional drafting. Here, as Mark Osiel notes, liberal political morality's social contract tradition does much work in generating a philosophical framework that facilitates leaving behind the toxicity of past atrocities and the vicious cycles of grievance and vengeance that they generate. Indeed, he argues that 'the notion of a hypothetical social contract, for instance, forces one to start afresh, stripped of historical grievances and prejudices, to reason from a moral point of view, without appeal to prior status as (victimizing) power or (powerless) victim'.[17] To this end, even prosecutions or accountability processes are celebrated as efforts to individualize culpability and fight against notions of collective guilt. Thus, individual naming and shaming becomes the fabric with which the discourses of justice and truth weave a 'veil of ignorance' regarding collective or structural responsibility for past violations so that the 'interests of justice' can be defined anew. Here, transitional justice is meant to represent the values that knit society together across

[15] *Rome Statute of the International Criminal Court* (opened for signature 17 July 1998 entered into force 1 July 2002) 2187 UNTS 90, art 53.

[16] See P de Greiff, 'A Normative Conception of Transitional Justice' (2010) 50 *Politorbis* 17–29, at 18.

[17] M Osiel, *Mass Atrocity, Collective Memory, and the Law* (Transaction New Brunswick 1999) at 165.

different lines of social tension.[18] These are the values that provide the foundation for a renewed social contract within the terms of political liberalism—liberty and fairness, individualism and universalism, human rights and the rule of law. These values constitute the grammar of political vocabularies that are said to be in the interests of justice.

With transitional justice initiatives marshalling these political vocabularies, the state is also signalling its return; back-translating Carl Schmitt, we may say that the liberal state here is claiming its sovereignty by declaring a state of normalcy. Schmitt famously opened *Political Theology* with the line 'Sovereign is he who decides on the state of exception'.[19] Declaring 'a state of normalcy' in tumultuous times is a similarly audacious claim to sovereignty—however, perhaps by definition, the performance of normalcy requires that it does not announce itself as such. Accordingly, the micro-level theorizing of what is 'in the interests justice' are the unstated endogenous norms implicit in routinized institutional decisions. Concomitantly, the meta-level theorizing of justice renders those institutional details into the background and foregrounds contentious normative claims as if these were consensual founding values of political community. Significantly, transitional justice becomes a path then to overcoming political dissensus and deep social cleavage to produce post-conflict 'normalcy'.[20] Negotiating these poles on both ends, the meso-level theorizing of transitional justice builds from the meta-level and bleeds into the micro-engagement with the details of institutional procedure. Indeed much of the work of building the field of transitional justice takes place primarily at the meso-level. It is to this level that I turn next in describing how transitional justice has been defined and articulated as being in the interests of justice.

Theories of transitional justice framed in terms of 'the interests of justice' reflect, and are informed by, the dominant intellectual traditions of human rights in relation to ideas of moral universalism and the broader architecture of political liberalism. In turning now to theories of transitional justice that are framed in terms of the 'interests of transition', we foreground political liberalism in a different key: pragmatic and institutionalist.

---

[18] Reflecting what Osiel and others identify as Durkheimian conceptions of the role of criminal justice as a performance of the norms society privileges so that it can move forward even after there has been a violation of those norms or a rupture in the social fabric.

[19] C Schmitt, *Political Theology: Four Chapters on the Concept of Sovereignty* (G Schwab trans) (MIT Press Cambridge MA 1985 [1922]) at 5.

[20] In different but allied ways theorists such as Judith Butler, Jacques Rancière, and Chantal Mouffe theorized how unmarked exclusions are central to this notion of normalcy where post conflict becomes a synonym for pre-political. For instance, Rancière speaks of how theorists of consensus (one may translate the word consensus into 'recognition, trust, reconciliation, and democracy' to keep in play Greiff's vocabulary) aims to oust politics, which is by definition a space of dissensus: J Rancière, 'Who is the Subject of the Rights of Man?' (2004) 103 *South Atlantic Quarterly* 297–310.

3 THE INTERESTS OF TRANSITION

Within the field the 'transition' in transitional justice is taken to refer to transitions from authoritarianism to democracy, from war to peace, from impunity to accountability. The transitional context was critical to why transitional justice gained traction in a number of related domains, including peace building and nation building, prosecutions policy, and democracy promotion programs, the study of violence, and the study of the rule of law. Thus if transitional justice processes are theorized as being 'in the interests of justice', they are also theorized as being 'in the interests of transition'—or as one commentator puts it, as 'necessary to help a society move from a period of repression and/or conflict, where mass atrocities took place, to one in which human rights, democracy and the rule of law can prevail'.[21] Theories connecting the dots from transitional justice to the dynamics of transition can be framed in terms of two different categories of argument or rationales for why transitional justice processes may be in the interests of transition. These include, first, arguments that transitional justice initiatives entail processes that can remedy past violations, and secondly, that these processes themselves facilitate transition and advance political reconstruction by exemplifying the norms of liberal political morality, developing social capital, and building civic trust. The rest of this chapter elaborates on each of these branches of transitional justice theory sequentially. It brackets critique and simply describes the dominant theories through which the field presents itself. The following chapter, the conclusion, unpacks the stakes of this approach to 'transition' and develops a critical analysis of the dominant traditions of transitional justice before turning to heterodox approaches to the field.

Perhaps the most prominent theory of transitional justice is that it serves a remedial function with regard to past atrocities. In contrast, for instance, to amnesties, transitional justice is about creating channels for engagement with the past in ways that facilitate and consolidate transition. Rather than ignore history's demons, it is argued that national processes clarifying the truth produce 'usable knowledge' that lays the ground for institutional reform.[22] Similarly, by holding perpetrators accountable or by providing reparations to victims, transitional justice translates accountability questions into criminal justice processes and reparation programs with identifiable perpetrators and victims. Martha Minow

---

[21] C Sandoval Villaba, *Transitional Justice: Key Concepts, Processes and Challenges* (Institute for Democracy and Conflict Resolution Briefing Paper No 07/11, 2011) at 10 <http://www.idcr.org.uk/wp-content/uploads/2010/09/07_11.pdf> [accessed 1 March 2016].

[22] T Garton Ash, 'Preface' in PB Hayner, *Unspeakable Truths: Facing the Challenges of Truth Commissions* (Routledge New York 2002) xi–xii, at xii.

describes this translation work as collective efforts that aim to 'create armatures for pain and structure paths for individuals to move from grief and pain to renewal and hope'.[23]

Many initiatives associated with a turn to transitional justice (including anti-amnesty struggles) may be embedded in the meta-ethical commitments invoked 'in the interests of justice'. However, it is significant that these engagements with past atrocities are also accompanied with robust claims regarding their instrumental yield. Thus the focus of these theories is on political avenues which Minow describes as 'realistic options'[24] or which Charles Villa-Vicencio describes as a 'quest for a balance between the demand for both justice and peace'.[25] In other words, these are theories of transitional justice that are advanced as steps to confront a troubled past constructively to facilitate closure. In this vein, prosecutions, truth commissions, reparation programs, and like initiatives are represented as mechanisms for facilitating transition. They are described as institutional tools for drawing a symbolic line in the sand between the traumas of the past and the possibilities for the future. However, rather than amnesties and amnesia, the effectiveness of transitional justice programs is said to lie in a pragmatic process brokering structured remembering and managed accountability.[26] For instance, the push for transitional justice initiatives is at least partially premised on the theory that 'the resentment among victims who watched perpetrators escape justice may result in, and may foster, a notion of lawlessness, thus endangering the unconsolidated democracy'.[27] Yet alongside this interest in justice, limitations in material and human resources and an overriding interest in not disturbing a fragile peace are, frequently, also a concern; this, then, may entail policies to prosecute only a few people, to award reparations that have symbolic value but only a limited reparative effect, to highlight some truths but not those truths that may be seen to threaten the possibilities of moving forward. Thus transitional justice theory is often deployed for advocacy of complex policy initiatives situating human rights discourse within the framework of state building and democracy consolidation. As Juan Corradi has put it,

[t]ransitional justice is both more and less than ordinary justice. It is more because it aims beyond the simple ordering of human relations: it seeks to achieve moral and political

---

[23] M Minow, *Breaking the Cycles of Hatred: Memory, Law and Repair* (Princeton University Press Princeton 2002) at 19.

[24] Ibid 63.

[25] C Villa-Vicencio, 'Where the Old Meets the New: Transitional Justice, Peacebuilding and Traditional Reconciliation Practices in Africa' (Department of Peace and Conflict Research, Uppsala University and Nordic Africa Institute, Claude Ake Memorial Paper No 5, 2009) at 34 <http://www.pcr.uu.se/digitalAssets/65/65805_1camp5_charles.pdf> [accessed 1 March 2016].

[26] PJ Campbell, 'The Truth and Reconciliation Commission (TRC): Human Rights and State Transitions: The South Africa Model' (2000) 4 *Africa Studies Quarterly* 41–63.

[27] Ibid.

regeneration. It is less than ordinary justice because it is subject to serious irregularities, it is a political formula for the formal elimination of a scapegoat, it is imbued with problematic judgments by the power holders of the moment on the qualities and policies of their predecessors, and it is a constitutive act of a new regime.[28]

A second family of theories about how transitional justice processes can be 'in the interests of transition' are those that focus on the norms that guide transitional justice institutions during the course of implementing their mandate. If the set of theories of transitional justice discussed in the preceding paragraph are focused on how to deal with the past, the theories we want to highlight here may be seen as more future oriented. They look at the operation of transitional justice institutions in ways that uphold due process norms as exemplars of the rule of law and respect for human rights with important lessons for the future. From Barack Obama to Judge Jackson, many cite the Nuremberg trials as exemplifying this commitment to give the enemy 'their day in court' and that this served a pedagogical function as it 'taught the entire world about who we are but also the basic principles of rule of law'.[29] The UN has linked the everyday conduct of trials as having this future oriented capacity building function where observing the procedural norms of transitional justice processes contributes to the values of the post-transition society, such that these procedures themselves can constitute a 'lasting legacy in the countries concerned'.[30] Eric Brahms suggests that truth commission reports offer something of a reform blueprint for post-conflict societies.[31] Brahms and others also make the argument that when

[28] JE Corradi, 'Toward Societies without Fear' in JE Corradi, PW Fagen, and MA Garretón (eds), *Fear at the Edge: State Terror and Resistance in Latin America* (University of California Press Oakland 1992) 267–92, at 285–6 (citations omitted), quoted in 'How "Transitions" Reshaped Human Rights' (n 2) 330.

[29] President Barack Obama, quoted in J Goldsmith, 'The Shadow of Nuremberg' (22 January 2012) *New York Times* BR8. Aiming at precisely this historical legacy, in his opening address at Nuremberg, Jackson emphasized the importance of conducting trials with due process: '[T]he record on which we judge these defendants today is the record on which history will judge us tomorrow ... We must summon such detachment and intellectual integrity to our task that this trial will commend itself to posterity as fulfilling humanity's aspirations to do justice': RH Jackson, 'Opening Speech at the First Nuremberg Trial, 20 November 1945' in *The Trial of German Major War Criminals by the International Military Tribunal Sitting at Nuremberg Germany: Opening Speeches of the Chief Prosecutors* (His Majesty's Stationery Office London 1946) 3–46, at 5.

[30] 'The Rule of Law and Transitional Justice in Conflict and Post-Conflict Societies' (n 3). Indeed, a new research project and conference has focused on the 'impact of the design of transitional justice processes on the (re)emerging legal system'; the Transitional Justice and Rule of Law Interest Group of the American Society of International Law hosted a meeting on this subject titled 'The Relationship between the Rule of Law and Transitional Justice: Synergies and Tensions' (31 October 2013) <http://www.allianceforpeacebuilding.org/event/2013/10/the-relationship-between-the-rule-of-law-and-transitional-justice-synergies-and-tensions> [accessed 1 March 2016].

[31] E Brahm, 'Uncovering the Truth: Examining Truth Commission Success and Impact' (2007) 8 *International Studies Perspectives* 16–35, at 28.

truth commissions and trials function together they can enhance stability and contribute to human rights.[32]

Similarly, in designing the operational rules and procedures of the South African TRC, Alex Boraine, its deputy chair, stressed that commissioners were concerned that the truth commission exemplify the values of due process and fairness.[33] As the signature institution of the transition, they wanted the TRC to be the institutional embodiment of post-apartheid society: 'In uncovering the past and making perpetrators of abuse account for their actions, the TRC intends that South Africans should learn how to prevent future atrocities. Its recommendations are meant to help develop a human rights culture in South Africa.'[34] There are echoes of this vision in contemporary debates regarding the role of the ICC. For instance, Christian Rodriguez argues for the ICC's role is in midwifing a transition into a human rights friendly post-conflict society:

The ICC plays an important role in prosecuting individuals accused of human rights violations and in encouraging the development of domestic judiciaries so that states may try these individuals themselves. Therefore, the International Criminal Court is intrinsically linked with the uneasy work of transitioning a state from a repressive regime accused of gross human rights violations to one that upholds international democratic and human rights norms.[35]

This approach is allied with discussion about the legacies of the Special Court in Sierra Leone or of the ICTY, where scholars and practitioners have highlighted the performative dimension of these courts. In addition to the outcome of the cases they adjudicated or the physical buildings they leave behind (in the case of Sierra Leone), their legacy is seen to inhere in their embodiment of the rule of law in the course of delivering justice. By infusing the present with liberal values, transitional justice institutions appear to put the transition on a stronger footing. From the perspective of those who advocate transitional justice institutions as being 'in the interests of transition', prosecutions or investigations into the truth regarding past atrocities are one way of drawing a symbolic line between the past and the future and the upholding of liberal values in transitional justice institutions regarding politics and law presents another way of retracing that line.

The future oriented instrumental yield of transitional justice is partly linked to claims about their performative function in entrenching human rights and

---

[32] T Olsen et al., 'When Truth Commissions Improve Human Rights' (2010) 4 *International Journal of Transitional Justice* 457–76.

[33] Conversation with Author (New York, 2001).

[34] B Hamber and S Kibble, 'From Truth to Transformation: The Truth and Reconciliation Commission in South Africa' (Catholic Institute for International Relations, February 1999) <http://www.csvr.org.za/index.php/publications/1714-from-truth-to-transformation-the-truth-and-reconciliation-commission-in-south-africa.html> [accessed 1 March 2016].

[35] C Rodriguez, 'Libya and the International Criminal Court: A Case Study of Shared Responsibility' (2013) 4 *People Ideas and Things Journal* <http://pitjournal.unc.edu/article/libya-and-international-criminal-court-case-study-shared-responsibility> [accessed 1 March 2016].

rule of law values that we have discussed. Another related claim about their instrumental yield 'in the interests of transition' focuses on civic trust, social stability, and state legitimacy. Roger Duthie argues that 'transitional justice can make important contributions to processes of development' by bolstering civil society and helping build social capital that will be critical for development.[36] In a similar vein, Naomi Roht-Arriaza argues that by incorporating 'justice and human rights' oriented civil society groups, transitional justice initiatives are also recruiting those groups to work in the interests of transition: 'incorporating civil society groups, especially those concerned with justice and human rights issues, into a post-conflict accountability strategy can revitalize those groups and allow them to transition from a mission-centred response to conflict to one centred on post-transition peacetime issues.'[37] Valerie Arnould and Chandra Sriram argue that when situated in broader policies of institutional transformation, transitional justice measures can contribute to democratic institution building.[38] Some have argued that the value that transitional justice processes add to state legitimacy make it relevant even in contexts that are not immediately post-conflict. For instance, Stephen Winter makes the argument that the transitional justice process in New Zealand can perform this legitimation function for the New Zealand state vis-à-vis indigenous communities—that where the state has a legitimacy burden, 'transitional justice works to resolve that burden'.[39] Pablo Greiff not only sees transitional justice having a key role in consolidating transitions by strengthening institutions and building civic trust, he also describes the costs of not employing transitional justice institutions as dire, arguing that, 'left unaddressed, human rights violations can create a downward shift in people's expectations' and lead to 'a permanent state of defeated expectations'.[40]

This chapter has ventriloquized the field's self-representation of the 'interests of transition'. The following chapter develops a critical analysis of the field both by unpacking dominant traditions and surfacing marginalized approaches.

[36] R Duthie, *Building Trust and Capacity: Civil Society and Transitional Justice from a Development Perspective* (International Center for Transitional Justice, November 2009) at 4 <https://www.ictj.org/sites/default/files/ICTJ-Development-CivilSociety-FullPaper-2009-English.pdf> [accessed 1 March 2016].

[37] N Roht-Arriaza, 'Civil Society in Processes of Accountability' in MC Bassiouni (ed), *Post-Conflict Justice* (Transnational Ardsley 2002) 97–114, at 100, quoted in *Building Trust and Capacity* (n 36) 15.

[38] V Arnould and CL Sriram, 'Pathways of Impact: How Transitional Justice Affects Democratic Institution-Building' (Impact of Transitional Justice Measures on Democratic Institution-Building, Policy Paper No 1, October 2014) <http://www.tjdi.org/wp-content/uploads/2014/10/TJDI-Policy-Paper-Pathways-of-Impact-1.pdf> [accessed 1 March 2016].

[39] S Winter, 'Towards a Unified Theory of Transitional Justice' (2013) 7 *International Journal of Transitional Justice* 224–44.

[40] P de Greiff, 'Leaving Human Rights Unredressed Can Hamper Development: UN Expert' (UN Radio 28 October 2013) <http://www.unmultimedia.org/radio/english/2013/10/leaving-human-rights-unredressed-can-hamper-development-un-expert> [accessed 1 March 2016].

4 Conclusion: Critical Approaches to Transitional Justice

The field of transitional justice has consolidated and professionalized; it has developed a repertoire of settled practices and institutional forms and a vocabulary for normative justification. One characteristic of dominant approaches to the field of transitional justice is that in theorizing transitional justice they also promote it; they seek to legitimize the field in the dual registers of political ethics and political pragmatics. Thus the production of legitimacy also references a range of related claims, sometimes explicit and sometimes implicit, regarding conflict, the rule of law, human rights, and so on. For instance, as noted earlier, in theorizing transitional justice as both an embodiment of an emancipatory human rights foundation and a vehicle for stability and civic trust, theorists frame the normative and pragmatic stakes of transitional justice as an echo of the state of nature heuristic of liberal social contract theory. Liberal contract theory elides discussion of systemic fissures, inequities, and contradictions that shape and subject parties to the contract and circumscribe the contractual horizon. Contract or consensus oriented interventions are often premised on unmarked exclusions where political conflict is scripted as a problem that needs to be replaced by trust and reconciliation.[41] Thus like the metaphorical state of nature, conflict or violence becomes a critical back-story authorizing interventions framed as 'in the interests of justice' and/or 'in the interests of transition'. Against this backdrop, transitional justice processes are legitimized as overcoming political conflict to enable human rights and democracy promotion in the dual registers of ethics and pragmatics. This depoliticized and depoliticizing theorization of transitional justice cements it within the moral economies of intervention and the instrumentalist logics of state building.

The dominant theories of transitional justice discussed in the chapter are not the only approaches to the field. In this concluding section I want to highlight heterodox theories of the work, or potential work, of transitional justice processes. Shadowing the two-part description of dominant theories of transitional justice, I categorize critical approaches as exemplifying two allied stances, redefinition and interruption—redefinition of how the 'interests of justice' theories define the stakes of transitional justice processes, and interruption of how the 'interests of transition' theories describe the dynamics of transition. Both of these stances draw from the history of the field and the debates called forth by particular interventions.

First then, let me turn to critical traditions that stand in counterpoint to the dominant 'interests of justice' theorization discussed earlier; in particular, it is

[41] See 'Who is the Subject of the Rights of Man?' (n 19).

worth highlighting efforts that seek to fundamentally redefine justice. I want to flag two different registers for redefinition. One important category of interventions involves challenges to approaches to justice that are premised on the victim/ perpetrator dyad. For instance, Mahmud Mamdani has argued for a re-theorizing of transitional justice by foregrounding 'the beneficiary'—arguing that the dominant theorization of justice by the South African TRC was premised on the victim/ perpetrator dyad and that this theorization fundamentally misrepresented the architecture of apartheid and the political logics that sustained and reproduced its injustices.[42] Thus the South African TRC's focus on the culpability of the policeman who killed or the prison guard who tortured also distracted from the culpability of those who benefitted from the system even though they may not have dirty hands in the more proximate sense. Foregrounding beneficiaries would locate how the white population benefitted from the racial system that those policeman and prison guards helped maintain. This approach allows us to use transitional justice as an entry point to thinking through the systemic architecture of human rights abuse and the structural edifice that enables and reproduces oppressive arrangements. Mamdani's theorization never really gained traction but one can see gestures in that direction in measures such as the TRC final report's unimplemented recommendation that the government consider imposing a tax on all whites in acknowledgement of the racial structure that underpinned human rights abuses in South Africa. There was an understanding that restitution, and in that sense justice, was impossible; the primary significance of the tax would be symbolic but it would be significant to narrate the story of apartheid as a story not just of abusive police practices but as structural racism that was normalized into the everyday practices of democracy and the rule of law in apartheid South Africa. There are echoes here of Arendt's refusal to equate transition with the grievances of Jews and the sins of Eichmann; justice calls us to a more challenging and profound path than that captured by the identification of Eichmann as a perpetrator.[43]

A second register for the redefinition of justice has been theories of transitional justice that have challenged the relationship between justice and law. One of the most striking institutional manifestations of such theories has been the phenomenon of unofficial commission and tribunal process. From the Russell Tribunals catalyzed by the Vietnam War,[44] via the Indian/Independent People's Tribunals,[45] to the Women's International War Crimes Tribunal dealing with comfort women,[46]

---

[42] M Mamdani, 'A Diminished Truth' in W James and L Van de Vijver (eds), *After the TRC: Reflections on Truth and Reconciliation in South Africa* (David Phillips Cape Town 2000) 58–61.

[43] H Arendt, *Eichmann in Jerusalem* (Penguin New York 2010 [1963]).

[44] See eg P Limqueco and P Weiss (eds), *Prevent the Crime of Silence: Reports from the Sessions of the International War Crimes Tribunal Founded by Bertrand Russell* (Allen Lane London 1971).

[45] Indian/Independent People's Tribunals <http://www.iptindia.org> [accessed 1 March 2016].

[46] See eg C Chinkin, 'Women's International Tribunal on Japanese Military Sexual Slavery' (2001) 95 *American Journal of International Law* 335–41.

these processes have served to highlight issues and voices that have been excluded by the political and legal establishment. In this sense, 'Positioned as an alternative People's Court,'[47] they have also challenged definitions of justice that have fore-grounded legality, and (as noted earlier) the work of transitional justice institutions in performativity demonstrating the virtues of law and legal process. This is a theorization of transitional justice's potential to be politically counter-hegemonic and institutionally experimental, challenging the mainstream of human rights rather than being assimilated within it.

If the preceding examples have pointed to theories of transitional justice that seek to redefine justice, I want to now turn to theories of transitional justice that seek to interrupt the notion of transition. As noted earlier, a significant strand of transitional justice theory has sought to theorize how transitional justice facilitates and consolidates transition in ways that echo the metaphorical path from state of nature to social contract, from war to peace, from anarchy to order. Yet one significant critical strand of transitional justice theorizing has been efforts to contest the dots connecting the ends of transition to notions of social contract, peace, and political order. For instance, the mothers of the Plaza de Mayo in Argentina contested the Argentinean transition from dictatorship to democracy, arguing that the enduring reach of those disappearances challenged the virtues of social order and legal peace; in other words, closure engendered distrust, pain was pitted against transition, and enduring injustice called into question the terms of the contract. Ariel Dorfman's play *Death and the Maiden*[48] suggests something similar; Paulina, his protagonist, points to the truths elided in the commissions and procedures facilitating the transition to law and order. While her husband sees her determined attention to these elisions as anarchic, subversive, and lawless, Paulina sees law and order as premised on injustice and indeed the impossibility of transition for those who bare its costs—the past will always be with us. Like with Walter Benjamin's gloss on Paul Klee's 'Angelus Novus', even if we wish to 'make whole what has been smashed', the violent debris of history becomes inextricably intertwined with the wings of progress; there is no future that is clean of the past.[49]

Finally, in some cases long-term reparation claims have also functioned as a kind of proto-theorization of a counter-hegemonic approach to transitional justice. I am thinking here particularly of claims calling on the United States for reparations for slavery[50] and on the British for reparations for colonialism.[51] A few

---

[47] India Independent People's Tribunals (n 45).

[48] A Dorfman, *Death and the Maiden* (Penguin New York 1994).

[49] W Benjamin, 'Theses on the Philosophy of History (1940)' in *Illuminations* (H Arendt ed H Zohn trans) (Schocken Books New York 1968) 253–64, at 257–8.

[50] T-N Coates, 'The Case for Reparations' (21 May 2014) *The Atlantic*.

[51] See eg EK Yamamoto and SK Serrano, 'Reparations Theory and Practice Then and Now: Mau Mau Redress Litigation and the British High Court' (2013) 18 *UCLA Asian Pacific American Law Journal* 71–101.

years ago the Mau Mau claim against the United Kingdom for tactics used in suppressing anti-colonial uprisings achieved some success in the British High Court when translated into individual legal claims for torture; yet it evoked more collective claims for colonialism as such. Indeed, it spawned efforts by the Caribbean countries and others to advance claims that underscored colonial exploitation as the glue connecting the prosperity of some and the poverty of others. This was not about individual bad apples but about a criminal system. Yet the real radical thrust of these long-term reparations claims is to interrupt the progress narrative of 'established democracies'—rather than see human rights violations in these contexts as exceptional, the reparations claims suggest that 'progress' on its dark side; the destination of the transition cannot be extricated from the ongoing legacies of the path of slavery and colonialism. In this sense it is a critique of the policy conceits of state building, conflict reconciliation, and all the co-travellers of transitional justice theory's pragmatic promise.

It is significant that when exploring transitional justice theory, many of the critical approaches that we have highlighted in this concluding section emerge from projects that had little political traction. In this sense they are paths not taken, alive as theory and challenge rather than in institutional form and transitional justice practice. Nevertheless, these have had an impact in shaping the debate regarding what constitutes justice, be it through the scholarship of people such as Mahmud Mamdani, the social movements we identify with the mothers of the Plaza de Mayo, or the institutional experiments of peoples' tribunals and reparation claims. Thus mining the 'failed' theories of transitional justice as counterpoints to the 'successful' ones does offer significant profit. This is not an effort to recuperate the field and redeem its future potential, but an effort to explore the yield of the lost coinage of subaltern economies to interrogate the dominant currency.

CHAPTER 39

THEORIZING INTERNATIONAL ENVIRONMENTAL LAW

STEPHEN HUMPHREYS

AND YORIKO OTOMO

[T]he idea of nature contains, though often unnoticed, an extraordinary amount of human history[1]

1 INTRODUCTION

INTERNATIONAL environmental law raises a paradox. As the body of international law that regulates 'the environment', one might expect international environmental law to be a cornerstone of the international legal system. What, after all, is more fundamental to the constitution of the world than the human relation to nature? And yet it is striking how little international environmental law does, in fact, regulate. The global food regime, for example, mostly escapes it: agricultural practices and the slaughter of animals for food (or otherwise) are largely beyond its

---

[1] R Williams, 'Ideas of Nature (1972)' in *Problems in Materialism and Culture* (Verso London 1980) 67–85, at 67.

remit. Those phenomena referred to as 'natural resources' are generally managed under separate headers or, more often, private arrangements.

Instead we find international environmental law at the margins of these concerns, dealing with the 'conservation' of certain plants, certain animals, certain 'ecosystems'.[2] Marginalia complemented by effluvia: as a matter of treaty law, international environmental law also aims to curb certain forms of pollution.[3] In keeping with this general peripherality, the key environmental cases have arisen at the edges of other bodies of law.[4] International environmental law is generally characterized as quintessential 'soft law': general principles and aspirational treaties with weak or exhortatory compliance mechanisms, often dependent on other disciplines altogether—science and economics—for direction and legitimacy.[5] At the same time, the problems it is called upon to deal with are immense, frequently catastrophic, and global in nature: climate change, species extinction, increasing desert, disappearing rainforest.[6]

---

[2] See eg *Convention on International Trade in Endangered Species of Wild Flora and Fauna* (opened for signature 15 November 1973 entered into force 26 May 1976) 993 UNTS 243; *Convention on Biological Diversity* (opened for signature 5 June 1992 entered into force 29 December 1993) 1760 UNTS 79.

[3] See eg *Convention on Long-Range Transboundary Air Pollution* (opened for signature 13 November 1979 entered into force 16 March 1983) 1302 UNTS 217; *Convention on the Prevention of Marine Pollution by Dumping of Wastes and Other Matter* (opened for signature 29 December 1972 entered into force 30 August 1975) 1046 UNTS 120 (*London Convention*); *Convention on the Control of Transboundary Movements of Hazardous Wastes and their Disposal* (opened for signature 22 March 1989 entered into force 5 May 1992) 1673 UNTS 57 (*Basel Convention*); *United Nations Framework Convention on Climate Change* (opened for signature 9 May 1992 entered into force 21 March 1994) 1771 UNTS 107 (*UNFCCC*).

[4] See eg at the World Trade Organization: *European Communities—Measures Affecting Asbestos and Products Containing Asbestos* (12 March 2001) WTO Doc WT/DS135/AB/R; *United States— Standards for Reformulated and Conventional Gasoline* (29 April 1996) WTO Doc WT/DS2/AB/R; *United States—Import Prohibition of Certain Shrimp and Shrimp Products* (12 October 1998) WTO Doc WT/DS58/AB/R; *European Communities—Measures concerning Meat and Meat Products (Hormones)* (16 January 1998) WTO Doc WT/DS26/AB/R; *Canada—Certain Measures Affecting the Automotive Industry* (31 May 2000) WTO Doc WT/DS139/AB/R; *European Communities—Measures Affecting the Approval and Marketing of Biotech Products* (29 September 2006) WTO Docs WT/DS291/R, WT/DS292/R, WT/DS293/R; *Brazil—Retreaded Tyres* (3 December 2007) WTO Doc WT/DS332/AB/R; at the European Court of Human Rights: *López Ostra v Spain* (ECtHR, App No 16798/90, 9 December 1990); *Öneryıldız v Turkey* (ECtHR, App No 48939/99, 30 November 2004); *Budayeva v Russia* (ECtHR, App Nos 15339/02, 21166/02, 20058/02, 11673/02, 15343/02, 20 March 2008); *Fadeyeva v Russia* (ECtHR, App No 55723/00, 9 June 2005); and at the International Court of Justice: *Gabčíkovo-Nagymaros Project (Hungary v Slovakia)* (Judgment) [1997] ICJ Rep 7; *Pulp Mills on the River Uruguay (Argentina v Uruguay)* (Judgment) [2010] ICJ Rep 14.

[5] See eg P Sands and J Peel, *Principles of International Environmental Law* (3rd edn CUP Cambridge 2012) ch 5; P Birnie, A Boyle, and C Redgwell, *International Law and the Environment* (3rd edn OUP Oxford 2009) ch 4.

[6] *United Nations Convention to Combat Desertification in those Countries Experiencing Serious Drought and/or Desertification, Particularly in Africa* (opened for signature 14 October 1994 entered into force 26 December 1996) 1954 UNTS 3 (*UNCCD*); *International Tropical Timber Agreement* (adopted 27 January 2006 entered into force 7 December 2011) UN Doc TD/TIMBER.3/12.

Despite or because of all this, international environmental law, more than most bodies of law, has many of the trappings of a faith. It derives its effect largely from its affect: international environmental law stages a kind of global moral authority, premised on an aesthetic ideal and an ethical disquiet. For its acolytes, its essence lies in a series of general principles: the do-no-harm principle; the precautionary principle; the polluter pays principle; the principles of equity and 'common but differentiated responsibilities'; and of course the über-principle—'sustainable development'. Interposed into the practices of international commerce and diplomacy, as its advocates demand, these principles promise the radical reshaping of 'business-as-usual'. In vain, it seems: for, again more than most bodies of international law, this is law crying in the wilderness.

The little sustained theoretical attention this body of law has attracted to date has concentrated in the main on its relationship with property law—posited as one of mutual constraint.[7] While we touch on this important question, in this chapter we direct our principal focus elsewhere, situating international environmental law with regard to the constituent conceptual elements that generate its specific energy and propel its contradictions today. We find this energy and tension in two principal historical sources: first, the Romantic movement of the late eighteenth and early nineteenth centuries; second, the evolution of colonial governance practices through to the mid-twentieth century.

As to the first of these, it is through Romantic philosophy and poetry that contemporary ideas about 'nature' became firmly established. This influential movement, as political as it was artistic, implanted lasting notions of the beauty of 'unspoilt' wilderness, imbued with a profound moral significance, that have endured to the present and provide the ideational backdrop specific to this body of international law. In this venture, we will be aided by what is by now a significant body of work investigating the intellectual origins of modern environmentalism.[8]

As to the second source, from the outset, administrators in colonial territories found themselves grappling with concrete questions on the management of territorial, natural, and livestock resources. These included a demand for immediate returns on the significant investments of colonial enterprise, a belated preservationist impulse emerging from the burgeoning aestheticization of colonial landscapes, and a drive to ensure sustainable long-term access to the resources that

---

[7] See S Coyle and K Morrow, *Philosophical Foundations of Environmental Law: Property, Rights and Nature* (Hart Oxford 2004).

[8] J Bate, *Romantic Ecology: Wordsworth and the Environmental Tradition* (Routledge London 1991); L Buell, *The Environmental Imagination: Thoreau, Nature Writing and the Formation of American Culture* (Princeton University Press Princeton 1995); L Coupe (ed), *The Green Studies Reader: From Romanticism to Ecocriticism* (Routledge London 2000); G Garrard, *Ecocriticism* (Routledge London 2012); M Oelschlager, *The Idea of Wilderness: From Prehistory to the Age of Ecology* (Yale University Press New Haven 1993); K Thomas, *Man and the Natural World: Changing Attitudes in England 1500–1800* (Penguin Press London 1983); R Williams, *The Country and the City* (Spokesman Books Nottingham 2011 [1973]).

increasingly fuelled a global economy. In examining the competing discourses of colonial resource management, we will be drawing on a second literature that has recently flowered: that of environmental history.[9]

In this chapter, therefore, we will tentatively open up some new theoretical perspectives on a body of law that (perhaps surprisingly for such an epistemologically rich subject) has been subjected to little theoretical speculation.[10] After this introduction, we begin by posing a question of terminology—why 'international environmental law'? Then follow sections on the Romantic and colonial periods respectively, after which we return to the present in our conclusion to show how international environmental law's origins in the confluence of the Romantic and the colonial explains the apparent mismatch between its ambitious stated objectives and its muted regulatory provisions—and how this tension continues to inform its functioning today.

2 WHY 'INTERNATIONAL ENVIRONMENTAL' LAW?

'International environmental law' is not, at first glance, a body of law dealing with an 'international environment' (for what would this be?) but a branch of 'international law' dealing with 'the environment'. After all, an 'environment' presumes a specific locality, a *surround*.[11] 'Environmental law' would then be

[9] RH Grove, *Green Imperialism: Colonial Expansion, Tropical Island Edens and the Origins of Environmentalism, 1600–1800* (CUP Cambridge 1995); W Beinart and L Hughes (eds), *Environment and Empire* (OUP Oxford 2007); K Hutchings, *Romantic Ecologies and Colonial Cultures in the British–Atlantic World 1770–1850* (McGill-Queen's University Press Montreal 2009); A Walsham, *The Reformation of the Landscape: Religion, Identity and Memory in Early Modern Britain and Ireland* (CUP Cambridge 2011); P Thorsheim, *Inventing Pollution: Coal, Smoke, and Culture in Britain since 1800* (Ohio University Press Athens 2006); AW Crosby, *Ecological Imperialism: The Biological Expansion of Europe, 900–1900* (CUP Cambridge 1986).

[10] But see the contributions in A Philippopoulos-Mihalopoulos (ed), *Law and Ecology: New Environmental Foundations* (Routledge London 2011). Explicit theoretical engagement with aspects of international environmental law can also be found in: I Porras, 'Trading Places: Greening World Trade or Trading in the Environment' (1994) 88 *American Society of International Law Proceedings* 540–5; I Porras, 'The City and International Law: In Pursuit of Sustainable Development' (2009) 36 *Fordham Urban Law Journal* 537–602; K Mickelson, 'South, North, International Environmental Law, and International Environmental Lawyers' (2000) 11 *Yearbook of International Environmental Law* 52–81; and, in a different register, J Brunnée and S Toope, *Legitimacy and Legality in International Law: An Interactional Account* (CUP Cambridge 2010); D Bodansky, *The Art and Craft of International Environmental Law* (Harvard University Press Cambridge MA 2009).

[11] 'The traditional imaging of the environment [is] as a thing that turns (French *virer*) around a stable point (a distilled sense of pure humanity)': A Philippopoulos-Mihalopoulos, 'Introduction' in *Law and Ecology* (n 10) 1–17, at 7.

the law relevant to, in the words of the *Oxford English Dictionary*, '[t]he physical surroundings or conditions in which a person or other organism lives, develops, etc....',[12] that is, a *somewhere*. As such, it enters a context already steeped in law: at the margins of a property law whose excesses it potentially curtails and whose conflicts it mediates.[13] Abstracted to the international plane, however, 'environmental law' is unavoidably delocalized—the law now relates to '*the* environment' in a second sense provided by the *OED*: 'the *natural world* or physical surroundings *in general*...especially as affected by human activity'—the law of that which 'surrounds' *us*, humankind: our (shared/collective) surround.[14] This abstracted universal 'environment' is concretized in international legal instruments such as those dealing with climate change (the atmosphere as a global commons)[15] or biodiversity (the preservation of the world's species as a moral imperative):[16] the 'earthly environment', as the 1972 *Stockholm Declaration* puts it.[17]

International environmental law is, then, a body of law dealing with 'nature', as distinct from 'culture' or the 'human'. The sobriquet 'environment' is relatively new, dating from the 1960s or thereabouts. But what is altered, what is masked, in the substitution of 'environment' for 'nature'? The obvious answer—but not, we will suggest, the determinative one—is that the term 'nature' carries too much baggage. Whereas 'nature' presumably includes humankind, 'environment' apparently does not. And whereas nature (Latin: *natura*, 'essence') lends itself easily to contradictory doxa (both good and evil, creation and destruction, may be 'natural'), 'environment' is more muted, more technocratic. 'Nature' has, moreover, already been the site of countless battles—religious, political, scientific, economic—many of which are still unresolved today.

With this in view, a first—obvious but important—observation is that international environmental law articulates a regulatory interface with 'nature' not only in its material existence but also in its metaphysical insistence. A second observation is that with international environmental law we are not dealing with

[12] *Oxford English Dictionary* (OUP Oxford 2011) entry 63089. This usage dates to the 1830s, later popularized by Charles Darwin.

[13] *Philosophical Foundations of Environmental Law* (n 7) ch 1.

[14] *Oxford English Dictionary* (n 12) entry 63089 (emphasis added). This usage is dated to 1948.

[15] See eg the notion of the 'common heritage of mankind', which appears in multiple international treaty texts: the *Treaty on Principles of Governing the Activities of States in Exploration and Use of Outer Space, including the Moon and Other Celestial Bodies* (opened for signature 27 January 1967 entered into force 10 October 1967) 610 UNTS 205; *United Nations Convention on the Law of the Sea* (opened for signature 10 December 1982 entered into force 16 November 1994) 1833 UNTS 3; *Convention concerning the Protection of the World Cultural and Natural Heritage* (opened for signature 16 November 1972 entered into force 17 December 1975) 1037 UNTS 151.

[16] *Convention on Biological Diversity* (n 2).

[17] *Declaration of the United Nations Conference on the Human Environment* (16 June 1972) UN Doc A/CONF.48/14, preamble (*Stockholm Declaration*).

'natural law'. At first glance, these appear to be two far distant bodies of law. But clearly something significant is at work in the move from a law (extending to a law of nations) subject to something called 'nature' to a law that seems intended instead to subject 'nature'. Viewed from this angle, there is, in Europe at least, a historical turn (a *modern* turn, a hubristic turn), in which nature is dethroned or mastered.

The story of this 'turn' is familiar, and goes something like this. In Europe, Christianity implants itself within a richly pagan natural world, replete with spirits, gods, and demigods that are incrementally rolled and cajoled into Christ-compatible stories or purged altogether.[18] The human in the Christian universe was still part of nature, but a superior part. The natural world *tout court* was God's domain, unified and rational, and a natural or divine law—Right Reason, reflected in Man, immanent in Nature—was the in-principle source of human (positive) law well into the Reformation.[19] There is thus an emerging soft boundary between 'man' and nature, but plenty of scope for its transgression, for nature to act or react in sympathy with human affairs, for man to revert, return, or become subsumed into nature.[20]

It is possible to trace three broad articulations of the evolving human–natural relation across the subsequent early modern period. First there is the presumption of man's God-given *dominion* over plants and animals, as expounded in the Bible and relied upon by the Dominicans in the pre-Reformation era and, most pointedly, the Puritans afterwards.[21] This doctrine gave rise to the tenacious belief that there were few 'natural' bounds on human exploitation of the earth's resources—'the brute creation are [man's] property, subservient to his will and for him made'[22]— other than those imposed in civil society to avoid war. An ideology of ('natural') human dominion over the 'natural' world gains force during—indeed on some accounts actively underpins—the Reformation, appearing in a stronger form in, for example, Hugo Grotius's writing, weaker in Thomas Hobbes's—together with the cognate notion of sovereignty itself.[23]

---

[18] *The Reformation of the Landscape* (n 9) ch 1.

[19] S Humphreys, *Theatre of the Rule of Law* (CUP Cambridge 2010) ch 3; R Tuck, *Natural Rights Theories: Their Origin and Development* (CUP Cambridge 1979) especially at 17–31 and ch 3.

[20] *Man and the Natural World* (n 8) 75.

[21] Genesis i, 28; *Natural Rights Theories* (n 19) ch 1 (on the Dominicans); *Man and the Natural World* (n 8) 17–25 (on the Puritans).

[22] *Man and the Natural World* (n 8) 22, citing the poet-hunter William Somerville (1735).

[23] *Natural Rights Theories* (n 19) chs 3 and 6; H Grotius, *De Iure Belli ac Pacis* (R Tuck ed) (3 vols Liberty Fund Indianapolis 2005 [1625]) bk 2, ch 2. T Hobbes, *Leviathan* (JCA Gaskin ed) (OUP Oxford 1996 [1651]) ch 14: in the state of nature 'every man has a right to everything', albeit moderated (ch 15) by a right of equity and, therefore, usage 'proportionably to the number of them that have the right'; in civil society, however, there are no obvious restrictions on the right of the sovereign usage of natural resources (ch 18) except where the subject retains a right of resistance in cases of necessity (ch 21). See also *Philosophical Foundations of Environmental Law* (n 7) 11–35.

A second, somewhat countervailing, view of the human-natural relation, also derived from the bible, was the doctrine of usufruct, with which the pre-modern Franciscans resisted the predations and hubris of 'natural dominion'.[24] This doctrine reappears in diluted form in the post-Reformation era in the guise of *stewardship*, the admonition to act, as English Chief Justice Matthew Hale put it in 1677, as 'steward, villicus, bailiff or farmer over this goodly farm' of the earth.[25] It is an approach to the natural world that reaches us today in various configurations of the notion of trusteeship.[26]

With the enlightenment, however—comprising the third view—nature (Greek: *physis*) becomes an object of inquiry with empirically discoverable 'laws of nature' (*physics*), quite distinct from human laws. Around the same time, nature, or the 'state of nature', is counterposed to the human, the civilized—albeit with very different inflections in the principal exponents: Thomas Hobbes, John Locke, and Jean-Jacques Rousseau.[27] Not long afterwards, as a matter of historical fact, modernization (urbanization, secularization, the industrial revolution) alters the experience of nature: it becomes something 'out there', in the 'country'.[28] From within this new context a Romantic sensibility emerges that values nature intrinsically—as an object of aesthetic contemplation and site of an authentic human experience of the divine—to which we will turn presently.

'Man' and 'nature' are now, it seems, essentially distinct. Still, their relationship undergoes significant contortion and reconstruction, both as a historical and as a conceptual matter. Keith Thomas's *Man and the Natural World* (1982) is the outstanding account of the former; Raymond Williams's essay 'Ideas of Nature' (1972) is perhaps the most succinct inquiry into the latter. In his exhaustive account of the success of the early naturalists in removing the superstitions and beliefs attaching to plants and animals,[29] Thomas remarks:

[B]y eroding the old vocabulary, with its rich symbolic overtones, the naturalists completed their onslaught…In place of a natural world redolent with human analogy and symbolic

---

[24] *Natural Rights Theories* (n 19) 20–4.

[25] M Hale, *The Primitive Organisation of Mankind Considered and Examined according to the light of Nature* (William Godbid London 1677) at 370. In John Locke's work, these two approaches—nature as object of man's 'natural' dominion and of man's stewardship—reach a synthesis of sorts: see J Locke, *Two Treatises of Civil Government* (P Laslett ed) (revised edn CUP Cambridge 1988 [1689]) bk 2, ch 5, especially ss 26 and 31. For an insightful discussion, see CB Macpherson, *The Political Theory of Possessive Individualism* (OUP Oxford 2011) at 194–220 (especially at 204–10) and 238–46.

[26] For an influential example, see E Brown Weiss, *In Fairness to Future Generations: International Law, Common Patrimony and Intergenerational Equity* (UN University Press Tokyo 1989).

[27] 'Ideas of Nature' (n 1) 76; *Philosophical Foundations of Environmental Law* (n 7).

[28] *The Country and the City* (n 8) 1–2.

[29] This takes place, on Thomas's account, in part by replacing vernacular nicknames (such as 'Motherdee…so known because it would kill the parents of the child who picked it') with the Latin binomials introduced by the Swedish botanist Carl Linnaeus (so: *silene dioica*): *Man and the Natural World* (n 8) 75.

meaning, and sensitive to man's behaviour, they constructed a detached natural scene to be viewed and studied by the observer from the outside, as if peering through a window in the secure knowledge that the objects of contemplation inhabited a separate realm...[30]

Williams tells a similar story of a secular drive towards the separation between man and nature.[31] A 'problem' arises, Williams says, because 'nature' is effectively sliced up into very different entities depending on how it is used: part of it reappears in the form of products (coal), another part as by-products (slag; waste; pollution), while another part takes on the attraction of a pastoral scene (the pristine meadow aboveground).[32] For Williams, the accumulating 'interaction' necessitated a deepening ideological split between (an active) 'human nature' and (passive) 'nature'—and further, within nature itself: removing 'coal-bearing from heather-bearing, downwind from upwind'.[33] Williams concludes:

> As the exploitation of nature continued, on a vast scale...the people who drew the most profit from it went back...to an unspoilt nature, to the purchased estates and the country retreats. And since then there has always been this ambiguity in the defence of what is called nature and in its associated ideas of conservation...and the nature reserve.[34]

On this account, the destruction (exploitation/transformation) and 'conservation' of nature turn out to be mutually constitutive processes. The human and 'nature' separate conceptually in order to interact dialectically,[35] resulting in a split between economy (*oikos nomos*) and ecology (*oikos logos*):[36] the law that applies to our dwelling seems to exist in dynamic opposition to the reason we dwell there at all.[37]

Returning to our present theme, then, it seems right to find the culmination of this process in the turn to a vocabulary of 'environment' over 'nature'. The notion of 'environment' already presupposes the non-identity of the human and the natural, in a relational construct that renders the former (the human) active and the latter (their surroundings or 'environment') passive and acted upon. But 'international environmental law' forgets—or rather suppresses—the complex history

---

[30] *Man and the Natural World* (n 8) 89.   [31] 'Ideas of Nature' (n 1) 83.   [32] Ibid.

[33] Ibid 84: 'we cannot afford to go on saying that a car is a product but a scrapyard a by-product, any more than we can take the paint-fumes and petrol-fumes, the jams, the mobility, the motorway, the torn city centre, the assembly line...the strikes, as by-products rather than the real products they are'.

[34] Ibid 81.

[35] T Adorno and MW Horkheimer, *Dialectic of the Enlightenment: Philosophical Fragments* (GS Noerr ed E Jephcott trans) (Stanford University Press Stanford 2002 [1944]) at 1, citing F Bacon, 'In Praise of Knowledge' in *Francis Bacon* (A Johnston ed) (Batsford London 1965) 13–15, at 15: 'now we govern nature in opinions, but we are in thrall to her in necessity: but if we would be led by her in invention, we should command her by action'.

[36] 'Ideas of Nature' (n 1) 84: 'It will be ironic if one of the last forms of the separation between abstracted Man and abstracted Nature is an intellectual separation between economics and ecology.' See also 'Introduction' (n 11) 3.

[37] J-F Lyotard, *Political Writings* (University of Minnesota Press Minneapolis 1993), cited in *The Green Studies Reader* (n 8) 135–8.

of the changing human understanding of nature. One key effect is to dehistoricize the relationship (environmental law textbooks, with some exceptions, habitually trace the origins of this body of law to the 1960s and 1970s),[38] characterizing international environmental law as, instead, both novel and coextensive with an emerging environmental*ism* of (largely, by then) American provenance.[39] But this is to miss the key importance of the specific international context into which this body of law is summoned: decolonization.[40] For international environmental law must also be understood as a partial response to the vacuum, created by the recession of colonial power, in the international management of a flourishing global trade in natural resources.[41]

3 ROMANTIC ROOTS OF INTERNATIONAL ENVIRONMENTAL LAW

The Romantic era matters to international environmental law both because key concepts underpinning this body of law were expressed by Romantic writers during that period, and because the expression of those concepts was both novel and essential to the Romantic *ésprit* itself. Our aim here is not to track an early genealogy of specific environmental law formulae or principles appearing later on, but rather to trace an overarching shift in the approach to the natural world that finds its first, deeply influential, articulation during this period, one which continues to echo through legal texts today.

Conventionally, the Romantic movement refers to a loose grouping of artists, poets, and composers working in and around the revolutionary peaks of 1789 and 1848, united by a set of common themes and methodological presuppositions.[42] While we will focus in the main, here, on a subset of mainly English-language poets, the larger context is transcontinental and multidisciplinary, a movement in

---

[38] See eg *International Law and the Environment* (n 5) 1: 'The development of modern international environmental law start[s] essentially in the 1960s.' Cf *Principles of International Environmental Law* (n 5) 1. On this point, see 'South, North, International Environmental Law' (n 10) 54–5.

[39] Notably R Carson, *Silent Spring* (Penguin Classics London 2012 [1962]).

[40] 'South, North, International Environmental Law' (n 10) 56–60.

[41] See below text at n 107.

[42] See generally J Chandler, 'Introduction' in J Chandler (ed), *The Cambridge History of English Romantic Literature* (CUP Cambridge 2009) 1–18. The Romantic era may be dated back to 1770 and forward to the early twentieth century: at 1; C Siskin, 'The Problem of Periodization: Enlightenment, Romanticism, and the Fate of System' in *The Cambridge History of English Romantic Literature* 101–26.

which aesthetic compositions were conceived as political interventions at a time of social and ethical flux.[43] In this, the Romantics were profoundly successful, at least insofar as they provided the fundamental premises of much later thought on the relation between the 'human' and 'nature' and a platform for powerful critiques of scientific and industrial activity from both right and left.[44]

Three hallmarks of Romantic thought on nature have contributed to the contemporary constitution of international environmental law: the association of nature with the experience of: (i) the aesthetic, (ii) the authentic, and (iii) the divine.

3.1 The Aesthetic

Writing against the Enlightenment,[45] the Romantics pioneered the novel idea that 'nature' has intrinsic value in its own right. The Romantics sought to recharacterize the natural world primarily in aesthetic terms, infused with beauty and meaning and inaugurating a higher state of human possibility. True, the advancing art of landscaping in the mid-eighteenth century had, by then, displaced human-imposed symmetry and tree-lined avenues on the great estates with 'more natural' curves, clumps, lakes, and inclines.[46] However, even there the essential principle remained the desirability of 'improving' on that which is given—and it was just this point that the Romantics reversed. For the Romantics, nature was the improver: it could not be improved upon, though it could be spoiled.

This familiar Romantic love of *nature-in-itself* deserves a little scrutiny. Raymond Williams notes that it begins in awe-filled descriptions of the Alps shifting from (typically, in the 1600s) 'strange horrid and fearful crags and tracts' or 'ruins upon ruins in monstrous heaps'[47] to (Coleridge in 1802) 'motionless torrents…glorious as the Gates of Heaven beneath the keen full moon'.[48] So in addition to the revision of the 'pastoral'—the old literary form representing tranquil human coexistence with nature[49]—in the hands of these 'nature

---

[43] 'Introduction' (n 42) 1. (Proto-)Romantic figures from elsewhere (notably Germany) are also relevant to this story—such as Johann Wolfgang von Goethe and Friedrich Schiller.

[44] Compare the Marxian embrace of the Romantic analysis of human alienation in, for example, the Frankfurt School, with the deep conservatism of late Romantic figures such as WB Yeats, Paul de Man, and Martin Heidegger.

[45] As William Blake put it: 'May God us keep/From Single vision & Newton's sleep!': 'Letter to Thomas Butt (22 November 1802)', quoted in W Blake, *The Letters of William Blake* (G Keynes ed) (Macmillan New York 1956) 75–9, at 79.

[46] *The Country and the City* (n 8) 122.

[47] Ibid 128, citing C Hussey, *The Picturesque: Studies in a Point of View* (GP Putnam's Sons London 1927).

[48] *Ecocriticism* (n 8) 73.

[49] Such as John Clare's 'Pastoral Poesie' (undated) or William Wordsworth's 'Michael' (1800) subtitled 'a pastoral poem'.

poets' (itself a new term of art) and artists, there is the valorization of something new: 'wilderness':

> Lo! The dwindled woods and meadows
> What a vast abyss is there![50]

The admiration of nature in its own right was fundamental to the Romantic ethos. For as Williams notes,[51] what begins as a mere 'alteration of taste', an appreciation, among the discerning, for the 'picture-esque', was pushed in the hands of the Romantics to become an entirely new sensibility—in Wordsworth's words:

> ...some new sense
> Of exquisite regard for common things.
> And all the earth was budding with these gifts
> Of more refined humanity...[52]

This new sensibility became also a normative source for a radical politics. By 'more refined humanity', in this excerpt from the *Prelude*, is intended both a humanity more attuned to nature and one whose own wilder nature has been tamed through a closer contact with 'nature'. Wordsworth is representative of a pronounced strain among the Romantics foregrounding and lauding the lonely, solitary individual, whose self-understanding, arrived at through (purported) commune with nature, provides the basis for a broader and more egalitarian human community, individuals whose community, like their equality, is an effect not of their collectivity but of their common environment.[53] Romantic egalitarianism would come to inform nineteenth-century English radicalism (the push for greater social and civil rights culminating in an expanded franchise), which Wordsworth himself ultimately came to oppose.[54]

Meanwhile, 'wilderness' as an object of beauty and awe was to have a particularly vibrant life in the United States, becoming—notably in the hands of the American Romantic 'Transcendentalists' Henry David Thoreau and Ralph Waldo Emerson—a more rugged experience than that of the English lake poets. It was a friend and disciple of Thoreau's, the Scottish immigrant John Muir, who would go on to found the Sierra Club in 1893, arguably the first environmental non-governmental organization (NGO), and still among the most influential.[55] Ultimately the assertions and pleas of the Romantics and Transcendentalists would translate into a

---

[50] W Wordsworth, 'To ——, On Her First Assent of the Summit Helvellyn' (1816). See also *Ecocriticism* (n 8) 66–79.

[51] *The Country and the City* (n 8) 129.

[52] W Wordsworth, *The Prelude* (c 1798–1850) bk XIV (added much later to the first thirteen books of 1805).

[53] See *The Country and the City* (n 8) 130–3. Wordsworth's 'Michael' (1800), 'The Solitary Reaper' (1807), 'Lucy' (1798–1801).

[54] As an example of romantic radicalism, see ST Coleridge and R Southey, *Omniana* (Centaur Classics 1969 [1808]).

[55] *Ecocriticism* (n 8) 73–5.

language of legitimation that, in time, comes to underpin international environmental law—in, for example, textbooks on 'international wildlife law', in the 'principles' espoused in the major environmental declarations, and in the preambles to environmental treaties.[56]

3.2 The Authentic

The Romantics set themselves up against much that preceded them: eighteenth-century poetry and art, science, industry, and of course aristocracy. In Wordsworth's 1802 preface to his and Coleridge's poetic manifesto, *Lyrical Ballads*, he spoke of 'tracing...the primary laws of our nature', by relating 'incidents and situations from common life...in [the] language really used by men; and at the same time to throw over them a certain colouring of imagination'.[57] The 'Truth' (as he puts it elsewhere) is to be found in the ordinariness of 'low and rustic' subject matter.[58] The solitary figure silhouetted against the landscape in total harmony with the materials and processes of his or her own labour is the authentic human.[59] Wordsworth again:

> ...the sun and sky,
> The elements, and seasons as they change,
> Do find a worthy fellow-labourer there—
> Man free, man working for himself, with choice
> Of time, and place, and object...[60]

Implicit in the Romantics, in contrast to this authentic existence, is the experience of alienation in the emergent urbanism of the late eighteenth century.[61] One study on the sojourns of various Romantic writers in London—William Godwin, Wordsworth, and William Blake, as well as Mary Wollstonecraft—concludes that, 'London in the 1790s seems to produce, and be produced by, a new kind of metropolitan intellectual, marginalized by its economic and political divisions, alienated from its commercial values, wandering its chartered streets with a blank, or an appalled, sense of estrangement'.[62] Here are the seeds of the Romantic-inspired

---

[56] For example, M Bowman, P Davies, and C Redgwell, *Lyster's International Wildlife Law* (2nd edn CUP Cambridge 2010). See text below at n 72.

[57] W Wordsworth, *The Major Works* (Oxford World Classics Oxford 2000) at 596–7.

[58] Ibid 596.

[59] See above n 53. Also John Clare's rustic figures, and, in landscape painting, John Sell Cotman's 'The Shepherd on the Hill' (1831), Caspar David Friedrich's 'Wanderer Above the Sea of Mist' (1810).

[60] W Wordsworth, *The Prelude* (c 1798–1850) bk VIII.

[61] W Morris, 'Art and Socialism (1884)' in *The Works of William Morris* (M Morris ed) (24 vols Longman Green and Co London 1915) vol 23, 192–214 makes the point explicit.

[62] J Barrell, 'London in the 1790s' in *The Cambridge History of English Romantic Literature* (n 42) 129–58, at 158. See eg William Blake's 'Preface to Milton' also known as 'Jerusalem' (c 1804–8), contrasting London's 'dark satanic mills' to 'England's green and pleasant land'.

opposition to the industrial revolution, which continues as an 'environmentalist' undercurrent into the present. The anti-industrialism of environmental*ism* cannot, of course, translate, without dilution, into an international *law* that is itself premised on continuing 'development': hence, perhaps, the undertow of cautionary regret that provides the distinctively conflicted and compromised register of international environmental law.[63]

3.3 The Divine

In a related vein, the twentieth-century German philosopher Martin Heidegger too located the experience of the authentic in the Romantics, in his celebrated essay 'Poetically Man Dwells' (1953).[64] The essay takes a prose poem attributed to Friedrich Hölderlin, 'In Lovely Blue', as the starting point for a meditation on the human relation to 'home', combining a familiar Romantic brew of art, nature, and transcendence, to identify the 'basic character of human existence', dwelling 'poetically… on this earth'.[65] Hölderlin's poem is concerned with how the human may 'measure' itself against the divine: which becomes possible, he says, through our being rooted on earth yet capable of sizing up the heavens and stars. Indeed, a quasi-pantheism of this sort is common among the Romantics in response to the burgeoning atheism of the enlightenment. Wordsworth again provides a good example:

> But list! a voice is near;
> Great Pan himself low-whispering through the reeds,
> 'Be thankful, thou; for, if unholy deeds
> Ravage the world, tranquillity is here!'[66]

The poem is written during the Napoleonic wars, and Wordsworth finds an allegory for transcendent peace beyond human concerns. Nature is, as God had been, beyond the fray, timeless, still (that is, self-regulating, an idea that prefigures the contemporary notion of an 'ecosystem'). The same sentiment runs through John Clare's 'The Eternity of Nature' (1824).[67] Earthly peace is attainable through a deeper and more imaginative human engagement with the natural order. This is, of course, an ambition broadly associated with an international law that has its roots in a *ius naturale*.

But it is not merely that God *is* or resides *in* nature. It is rather that the experience of the divine is locatable only through imaginative immersion in the

---

[63] See Section 4 below.

[64] M Heidegger "'…Poetically Man Dwells…'" in *Poetry, Language, Thought* (A Hofstadter trans) (Perennial Classics New York 2001 [1953]) 211–27.

[65] Ibid 215.   [66] W Wordsworth, 'Composed by the Side of Grasmere Lake' (1806).

[67] J Clare, 'The Eternity of Nature' (1824).

natural world. The experience of divinity dwells in the imaginative creativity of the poet in correspondence with nature writ large. WB Yeats captured the point precisely in his musings on William Blake, who wrote a hundred years before him:

[Blake] had learned...that imagination was the first emanation of divinity...and that the sympathy with all living things [is what] the imaginative arts [must] awaken...He cried again and again that every thing that lives is holy, and that nothing is unholy except things that do not live—lethargies, and cruelties, and timidities, and denial of imagination.[68]

The enthronement of a certain kind of imagination was, for the Romantics, central to accessing the 'essential' truth behind superficial appearances. Fixed and mechanized, nature in enlightenment science was dead or asleep under the microscope. Observation informed by imagination yielded a truer, more authentic, experience of life: the 'primary' laws of nature, life infused with divinity. But wilfully investing 'nature' with 'imagination', as Blake recommended, is inherently problematic: the risk is that the self becomes sole arbiter of the 'authentic'. This is the essence of John Ruskin's famous charge of the Romantics' 'pathetic fallacy': that ultimately 'nature itself' is displaced by a symbolic and, paradoxically, anthropocentric will.[69]

This story of the Romantic imagination is relevant to our present inquiry for two reasons. First, it is a reminder that, despite regular rhetorical hewing to the 'real', to *nature itself*, the Romantics cultivated a decidedly shaky materialism. 'Nature itself' turns out to owe everything to the imaginative authorial voice pronouncing upon it. So where international environmental law prizes the 'intrinsic value of nature', the 'nature' in question will often turn out to be vague or unlocatable. The second point is that the Romantic imagination, from Wordsworth to Yeats, tends increasingly to fasten the lone authorial voice to an imaginative didacticism, itself centred on a community steeped in a landscape with nostalgic Volk-ish contours. The pronounced conservativism that marks the later Wordsworth develops into deliberate elitism in Yeats (the 'last Romantic') and flirts with full-blown authoritarianism in Heidegger—arch-philosopher of the 'authentic'. The imaginative dismissal of the human in much environmentalism may, in short, lend itself to dictatorial law.[70]

---

[68] WB Yeats, 'William Blake and the Imagination' in WB Yeats *Collected Works of WB Yeats, Vol IV: Early Essays* (RJ Finneran and G Bornstein eds) (Scribner New York 2007) 84–7, at 84.

[69] J Ruskin, 'Modern Painters' in *The Green Studies Reader* (n 8) at 26.

[70] A Giddens, *The Politics of Climate Change* (Polity Press Cambridge 2008) at 51–2; F-J Brüggemeier, M Cioc, and T Zeller (eds) *How Green Were the Nazis? Nature, Environment and the Nation in the Third Reich* (Ohio University Press Athens 2005). On Heidegger's place in modern environmentalism, see eg T Röhkramer, 'Martin Heidegger, National Socialism and Environmentalism' in *How Green Were the Nazis?* (n 70) 171–203; *Ecocriticism* (n 8) 34–6.

3.4 Romanticism in International Environmental Law

In the Romantics, then, there is a clearly dialectical move. The 'human', now quite apart from 'nature', adopts the position of audience or commentator, and—through a new appreciation and awe of this (wild, inspiring, motivating) nature—is reformed as a 'human' once again 'in touch' with the natural world.[71] This combination—of a human distinct from her surroundings, entailing a dynamic and politically transformative relationship with the natural world both for its intrinsic value and for the broader good it renders humanity—carries into the key documents of international environmental law in preambular language such as the following:

Stockholm Declaration (1971): Man is both *creature and moulder of his environment*, which gives him physical sustenance and affords him the opportunity for *intellectual, moral, social and spiritual growth*. …

World Heritage Convention (1972): [I]n view of the magnitude and gravity of the new dangers threatening them, it is incumbent on the international community as a whole to participate in the protection of the cultural and natural *heritage of outstanding universal value*.

Convention on Biological Diversity (1992): The Contracting Parties … Conscious of the *intrinsic value* of biological diversity … and of the … *educational, cultural, recreational and aesthetic values* of biological diversity and its components.

These invocations incorporate each of our earlier observations: the aesthetic and educational value of nature providing housing for an authentic human life, imbued with faith and spiritual growth.

4 THE COLONIAL ORIGINS
OF INTERNATIONAL ENVIRONMENTAL LAW

European colonialism was premised on the exploitation of natural resources and on the maintenance of conditions of global trade in raw materials. This was done in a context of tacit and at times explicit agreement between a small group of 'Powers'.[72] In fact, colonial era discoveries of 'new worlds' and new natural resources were reshaping thinking and writing on nature long before the Romantics. The rise of the botanical garden epitomized two colonial drives: a

---

[71] On the human as 'audience' for the natural world, see *Dialectic of Enlightenment* (n 35) 27.
[72] S Humphreys, 'Laboratories of Statehood' (2012) 75 *Modern Law Review* 475–510.

scient*ist* (naturalist) fascination with discovered 'paradises' and the pragmatic desire to capitalize on this novelty, by cultivating and commercializing seeds and species beyond their native lands.

There are many examples of international environmental law's colonial origins.[73] Take, for example, the *International Convention on the Conservation of Wild Animals, Birds and Fish in Africa* (1900)[74]—negotiated as the full consequences of the frenzied extermination of animal populations perpetrated by Europe's hunting classes throughout the nineteenth century became apparent.[75] The *Convention* was itself largely negotiated by hunters. It provides a set of rules categorizing animals into five schedules: some (the near extinct, such as white-tailed gnu) were no longer to be hunted; others were killable on sight ('dangerous' vermin, extending to lions and leopards); the remainder under certain conditions.[76] The *Convention* imagined immense nature 'reserves' or parks, parts of which would be off-bounds altogether, allowing animal stocks to replenish, other areas to be off-bounds to indigenous populations, allowing hunters to stalk animals 'in the wild'. The *Convention*'s most obvious descendent today is the *Convention on the International Trade in Endangered Species*, which mimics its aspirations, its schedules, and its calibration of killability.

In what follows, we confine ourselves to two representative moments of colonial activity, which we take from the eighteenth and twentieth centuries respectively. These provide examples of, in the first case, a policy response to observed environmental degradation, and, in the second, broad colonial economic policies in prototypical conformity with the contemporary notion of 'sustainable development'.

4.1 Environmental Degradation in the Early Colonial Period

In his seminal work, *Green Imperialism*, the first systematic account of the origins of environmentalism in the colonial experience, Richard Grove devotes

---

[73] This paragraph relies in the main on M Cioc, 'Hunting, Agriculture, and the Quest for International Wildlife Conservation during the Early Twentieth Century' (Paper presented at the Yale Agricultural Studies Program 3 October 2008) <http://www.yale.edu/agrarianstudies/colloqpapers/04cioc.pdf> [accessed 1 March 2016] at 9 and J MacKenzie, *The Empire of Nature* (Manchester University Press Manchester 1988) ch 8.

[74] *International Convention on the Conservation of Wild Animals, Birds and Fish in Africa* (signed 19 May 1900) 188 ConTS 418.

[75] *The Empire of Nature* (n 73) 123–8.

[76] The Convention never came into force although its principal terms were applied by Britain and Germany.

considerable space to island colonies such as Barbados, St Helena, and Mauritius.[77] Due to their relatively small size, he argues, the direct environmental impact of colonial-supported land practices became evident, and it was also possible to experiment with (legal) correctives. By the mid-1660s much of Europe was in the grip of a timber crisis, largely due to extensive shipbuilding, itself associated with colonial expansion and competition. One response was to attempt to limit deforestation at home, although in England these efforts often met with sufficient popular resistance to fail.[78] Another was to redirect supply abroad, treating 'countries yet barbarous as the right and proper nurseries' for the supply of timber.[79] Cutting down forests in the colonies brought other advantages too: land denuded of forests could be turned over to plantations and other uses, and, until the late 1700s (that is, until the Romantic period began), was considered both healthier and more sightly than untamed woods.[80]

Although the possibility that deforestation may affect the wider environment—by, for example, altering rainfall patterns—had been flagged as early as the fifteenth century, it was only in the eighteenth century that such effects were systematically observed and recorded on islands such as St Helena and Mauritius. In 1708, the then governor of St Helena, John Roberts of the East India Company, became worried that 'the island in 20 years time will be utterly ruined for want of wood'.[81] Over the next eighty years, successive governors raised concerns with the East India Company directors in London over increasingly evident environmental problems such as drought, floods, and soil erosion.[82] They attempted to slow the pace of deforestation, notably with the *St Helena Forest Act* (1731), mandating the 'destruction' of a portion of the island's many wild goats.[83] Their efforts were, however, frustrated by the Company's directors until 1794, when the directors, in a sudden *volte face*, directed the then governor, Rupert Brooke, to commence a reafforestation programme, since 'it is well known that trees have an attractive power on the clouds, especially when they pass over hills so high as those on your island'.[84] Otherwise, as the directors were later to warn, 'the present inhabitants will afford their posterity as just a reason for condemning their conduct as they have now to deplore that of their ancestors'.[85]

Of course, timber shortages and proprietary tussles over land use had underpinned forestry legislation and centrally organized tree-planting long before 1794.

---

[77] *Green Imperialism* (n 9).

[78] Ibid 57. For example, the *Dean Forest Act* (1657) and *New Forest Act* (1697).

[79] Dr Thomas Preston, quoted in *Green Imperialism* (n 9) 56.   [80] Ibid 65–7.

[81] Ibid 112, 109–15.   [82] Ibid 121–2.   [83] Ibid 120–4.

[84] Ibid 124, citing 'Council of Directors to Governor, 7 March 1794' in HR Janisch (ed) *Extracts from the St Helena Records and Chronicles of Cape Commanders* (Jamestown St Helena 1908).

[85] *Green Imperialism* (n 9) 124, citing 'Council of Directors to Governor, 25 March 1795' in *Extracts from the St Helena Records and Chronicles of Cape Commanders* (n 84).

The specific innovations captured here, however, are: the added cognizance of what we would today refer to as 'environmental degradation'; an acceptance of human impact upon the environment; and the appeal (with the Company directors echoing Roberts across the years) to 'posterity', a clear forebear of the regular invocation of 'future generations' that runs through much contemporary international environmental law.[86]

The Company's sudden reversal owed much to a 'sea-change' in climate science orthodoxy in the mid-eighteenth century—which Grove attributes in particular to the English scientist Stephen Hales, a leading figure in both the French Académie des Sciences and the English Society of Arts.[87] Key evidence for Hales's speculations on the human capacity to alter the atmosphere was found in small island colonies such as St Helena and Mauritius. A catalytic figure was Pierre Poivre, a naturalist, physiocrat, botanist, and administrator (for the French East India Company) of Mauritius, who, having developed a theory linking deforestation to rainfall patterns, introduced regulations on that basis in Mauritius in 1769.[88] On Grove's meticulously researched account, Poivre's work 'laid the foundation…for the forest protection policies [subsequently] set up in both French and British colonial island territories. These early policies became the direct forerunners and models for almost all later colonial forest-protection policies.'[89]

For reasons not dissimilar to the failure of seventeenth-century English forest laws, international agreement on forestry management remains elusive.[90] The essential point of this story is broader however: colonial forest-protection laws identify 'ecosystems'—loci of 'natural balance'—which, if overexploited, may be destroyed, contaminating a range of resources and ultimately damaging the wider economy.[91]

---

[86] See, eg, *Convention on Environmental Impact Assessment in a Transboundary Context* (opened for signature 25 February 1991 entered into force 10 September 1997) 1989 UNTS 309 (*Espoo Convention*); *Convention on Access to Information, Public Participation in Decision-Making and Access to Justice in Environmental Matters* (opened for signature 25 June 1998 entered into force 30 October 2001) 2161 UNTS 447 (*Aarhus Convention*); UNFCCC (n 3), *Convention on Biological Diversity* (n 2).

[87] *Green Imperialism* (n 9) 164.

[88] Grove provides a full account of deforestation and climatic change in Mauritius and Poivre's response: ibid 179–222.

[89] Ibid 166.

[90] See n 6; see also United Nations Framework Convention on Climate Change, 'Reducing Emissions from Deforestation and Forest Degradation and the Role of Conservation, Sustainable Management of Forests and Enhancement of Forest Carbon Stocks in Developing Countries (REDD-Plus)' <http://unfccc.int/land_use_and_climate_change/redd/items/7377.php> [accessed 1 March 2016].

[91] See eg *Convention for the Protection of the Marine Environment of the North-East Atlantic* (opened for signature 22 September 1992 entered into force 25 March 1998) 2354 UNTS 67 (*OSPAR Convention*), or the many conventions overseen by the International Maritime Organization (IMO): International Maritime Organization, 'List of Conventions' <www.imo.org/About/Conventions/ListOfConventions/> [accessed 1 March 2016].

4.2 Sustainable Development in the Late Colonial Period

For a second example, we have chosen the increasingly refined practices of species and crop management that developed across the British Empire from the late nineteenth century through decolonization. These amounted to de facto templates for 'sustainable development', perhaps the foremost principle of international environmental law today popularized by the 1987 Brundtland Commission.[92] According to this doctrine, 'development' should proceed so as to ensure that 'the needs of current generations are met without compromising the needs of future generations'—a desideratum already signalled at an earlier date, we will argue, in colonial resource management.

The case for early colonial practices of sustainable development builds on the evolution of practices over generations of colonial rule. Increasingly concerned with optimizing value in the colonies, by the late 1800s, annual reports to the Colonial Office followed a regimented template: finances, 'trade, agriculture and industry', climate, legislation, judicial statistics[93]—later extending also to: health, natural resources, labour, wages, banking.[94] The essential point (there were of course others) was to locate the comparative advantage of each territory—given climate, natural resources, conditions for production and trade—and to generate an enabling environment for effective specialization in export commodities. With few trade barriers across British governed spaces (though this was prone to vacillation), each territory could export to the Empire as a whole, at a minimum, and use the resulting income to buy imports from other colonial places.[95] In a virtuous circle, the Empire economy would grow as each territory developed.

This empire of free trade was not entirely, however, a free market. Especially after 1885, the metropolitan centre was not beyond giving the market firm guidance,[96] steering countries towards their comparative advantage and generating demand

---

[92] World Commission on Environment and Development, *Our Common Future* (OUP Oxford 1987).

[93] See eg Colonial Reports—Annual, Nos 260, 271, 346, 353, 381, 405, 409, 472, 633, 695, 773, 881, 1079, 1122, 1207, and 1410. Of these, Nos 260 and 346 (both written by Frederick Lugard and dealing with Northern Nigeria) do not follow the template. Elsewhere, however, by 1898, the template was already in use (see No 271 on the Gold Coast); universally by the early 1900s.

[94] Eg Colonial Reports—Annual, Nos 1657 and 1904.

[95] This assessment derives from a close reading of Colonial Office annual reports by territory from the late 1890s, through to the late 1930s (n 93 and n 94). On the related question of the British Empire approach to (international) free trade, see J Gallagher and R Robinson, 'The Imperialism of Free Trade' (1953) 6 *Economic History Review* 1–15; WR Louis (ed), *Imperialism: The Robinson and Gallagher Controversy* (New Viewpoints New York 1976); A Howe, 'Free Trade and Global Order: The Rise and Fall of a Victorian Vision' in D Bell (ed), *Victorian Visions of Global Order: Empire and International Relations in Nineteenth-Century Political Thought* (CUP Cambridge 2007) 26–46, at 41.

[96] 'Free Trade and Global Order' (n 95).

for territorial specialities (through an 'Empire Marketing Board'). From the early twentieth century, fact-finding missions were undertaken to determine whether individual colonies were optimally positioned within the wider economy, to recommend steps that might be taken to consolidate their position and, if needed, to reorient economies towards new products. The resulting reports evince a consistent interest in long-term sustainability: these were significant investments and they were intended to pay out over generations. However, once the prospect of decolonization appeared on the horizon, the need for establishing a lasting basis for colonial economies became even more pressing.

A series of Colonial Office reports appear from the 1920s through to the 1950s, the period when centrally dictated management of colonial economies reached its zenith and began its decline. For present purposes, what stands out in these reports is the degree to which they demonstrate a consistent concern for creating the conditions for long-term sustainability of the industries in question. A report on 'The Production of Fish in the Colonial Empire', which we will take as our example, proceeds territory by territory to document the kinds of fish produced (caught, processed, and readied for sale) in each one.[97] For each territory—from West Africa to Far East Asia—the report traces the proactive steps taken by colonial governments to place fish production on a stable footing and to expand it. Accounts are provided of: the numbers of fish caught; the amounts sold in local markets; exports; the sophistication of fishing and processing technologies; the existence or establishment of research centres monitoring fish stocks; the existence, mandate, and competence of authorities (Fisheries 'Departments', 'Officers', 'Surveys'); the training available to relevant officials; and—perhaps most intriguingly from the present perspective—the possibilities of investing in and sustaining fish farms.[98]

A follow-up 1953 report notes that, 'while the development of fisheries is a matter for each individual territory', 'fisheries research is organized on a regional basis, since groups of territories (for example, East Africa, West Africa, Malaysia) tend to have the same fundamental problems'.[99] Core-funded regional fish centres employed geneticists, 'in view of the importance of this work and its long-term character'.[100] In Kenya, a 'fish culture experimental farm' was started to 'obtain accurate data' of fish yields and to determine the 'life history' of the two 'most promising species' in order 'to control the breeding of mosquitoes and snails, which are responsible respectively for malaria and bilharzia'.[101] In Malaya, 'wherever new land has been brought under controlled irrigation for rice cultivation, provision for fish cultivation has been made'.[102] As a result of 'demonstrations, instructional pamphlets, and financial loans', more than 1,800 'new fish cultivators' had begun

---

[97] Colonial Office, *The Production of Fish in the Colonial Empire* (His Majesty's Stationery Office London 1949).

[98] Ibid 8–14.   [99] Colonial Office (1953) at 5.   [100] Ibid.   [101] Ibid 15.

[102] Ibid 19.

to reap a harvest and by 1952, there were '450,000 acres of irrigated padi [sic] land producing fish as a catch crop [sic]'. Moreover, 'a new form of fish farming, combined with pig raising, has been devised under the supervision and guidance of the Fisheries Department', such that 'the production of fruit, pigs and vegetables is integrated with the production of fish, resulting in economy of man-power, land and raw materials'.[103]

Sustainable development is not an easily applied principle—indeed, such is its inherent vagueness that some worry it may actually be unhelpful in determining policy.[104] Nevertheless, where sustainability is sought or claimed in practice to have been achieved, it is through systematic long-term anticipatory action—monitoring, substituting, and proactively replenishing stocks, and encouraging linkage between different kinds of food production (fish, rice) and other sectoral issues such as health (malaria, bilharzia). Of the many available examples of such practices in the colonial period, we choose fish, precisely because fisheries today generally exemplify unsustainable practice par excellence.[105]

5 CONCLUSION

This account identifies the historical forerunners of international environmental law in order to clarify two dominant and competing imperatives that drive it. In our sketch we have shown how the broad impetus underlying international environmental law—its principal motivating force—derives from a highly distinctive understanding of the human–nature relation that is directly traceable to European Romanticism. A newly aestheticized experience of the natural world gave rise to particular notions of an authentic human experience of nature. We have shown how a Romantic sensibility mobilized certain ideas that later find expression in international environmental law. We have indicated how the particularity of this vision underpins preambular language in core international environmental law texts. But its lasting power remains unarticulated, in the promise, hope, and faith invested in the leading principles of international environmental law: its implicit invocation of the divine. The Romantics present the non-human world as inherently

---

[103] Colonial Office (1953) (n 99).

[104] *The Politics of Climate Change* (n 70) 59–63. See RW Kates, TM Parris, and AA Leiserowitz, 'What is Sustainable Development: Goals, Indicators, Values and Practice' (2005) 47(3) *Environment: Science and Policy for Sustainable Development* 8–21.

[105] See eg World Bank, 'Global Program on Fisheries: PROFISH' <http://www.worldbank.org/en/topic/environment/brief/global-program-on-fisheries-profish> [accessed 1 March 2016].

valuable; essential to a version of human good life that conceives of well-being in a manner that may be described as 'ecological': responsive to and respectful of the *logos* of 'home'. This imperative reappears throughout environmental movements of the twentieth century in the direct action of Sea Shepherd, in 'deep ecology', and in 'pachamama' earth rights movements. And of course the vision driving these groups is also *romantic* in a second sense of the term, in that it brooks little or no compromise with competing imperatives.

International environmental law is clearly not exhausted by this Romantic vision, however. The second strong lineage we locate derives from practice—the long-standing management of natural resources developed through the colonial era. Colonial practices and conventions are not the only precursors of environmental management, of course—but they are arguably the most relevant to international environmental law precisely because they are constructed within a transnational context, viewing natural resources in terms of global production and demand, and managing them within a context of international trade. Our first example highlights how colonial rule inaugurated and consolidated an administrative capacity for observing and responding to environmental degradation, the threat of loss due to secondary effects (foreshadowing toxic pollution, climate change). Our second example shows colonial authorities positioned over time to understand resource production and consumption within the broadest global context and instituting long-term sustainable management practices for the replenishment and substitutability of stocks.[106]

On our reading, then, it is no accident that the rise of contemporary international environmental law coincides with the decolonization period of the 1960s and 1970s. The end of colonialism involved the dismantling of a key coordinating mechanism that had maintained and oiled the global movement of primary commodities and resources, and provided the rationale for a network of conservation areas. When global resource management moved into an 'international' domain, as the end of colonialism signalled, it is unsurprising that a body of law should have come into being to manage the exploitation of resources at the margins and their potential defilement through uncontrolled pollution.[107] In short, Romanticism and colonialism constitute two imperatives, each non-negotiable in its own way. Each can be seen at work through the key international environmental law principles and treaties. In each case, the promise to respect an inherent bound within 'nature itself' is destabilized by the necessity of exploiting, developing, and applying the

---

[106] 'Development' carries from the colonial into the postcolonial era and into international environmental law's constitutive developmentalism: see eg *Rio Declaration on Environment and Development* (14 June 1992) UN Doc A/CONF.151/26; *Stockholm Declaration* (n 17); UNCCD (n 6); UNFCCC (n 3).

[107] An important signal in this regard was the publication and widespread dissemination in 1972 of the Club of Rome's enormously influential *Limits to Growth*: DH Meadows et al., *Limits to Growth* (Potomac Associates Washington DC 1972).

non-human as a 'resource'. And whereas this body of law and principles is generally portrayed as mediating these competing demands, our analysis demonstrates the extraordinary difficulty of achieving any such mediation. For at bottom, these are not reconcilable views: what one holds sacred, the other profanes.

This is not to imply that international environmental law serves no function. Assuredly it does: it is the locus for the recognition of the sacred in the non-human world, and the occasion for its profanation, in full view, as it were. International environmental law publicly enacts the profanation of the thing it has designated as sacred. As a result, this body of law can appear improbably elastic, providing a framework for the ongoing (if occasionally attenuated) destruction and commodification of natural phenomena in a language of care and protection. International environmental law, then, is a principal locus for the dynamic that Raymond Williams remarked on forty years ago: a world split into an upwind of preservation and recreation and a downwind of waste and destruction, a pastoral idyll and a dump. International environmental law excoriates the dump, the waste, the loss of life and species—but it is not equipped to halt it, for—in Walter Benjamin's unparalleled image, 'a storm is blowing from Paradise [and] this storm is what we call progress'.[108]

---

[108] W Benjamin, 'Theses on the Philosophy of History' in *Illuminations* (H Arendt ed H Zohn trans) (Schocken Books 1967 [1955]) 253–64, at 257–8.

CHAPTER 40

....

THEORIZING INTERNATIONAL LAW AND DEVELOPMENT

....

KERRY RITTICH

1 INTRODUCTION

....

APPEARING as if from nowhere, development first emerged as part of the apparatus of modern international law in the postwar reconstruction of the international legal order. The mandates of the newly created Bretton Woods institutions (BWIs) spoke to issues such as poverty, employment creation, macroeconomic stability, and economic growth that had only recently come to be recognized as matters of peace and security and hence part of the province of international law.[1] In the intervening time, the field has undergone a massive expansion, both conceptual and institutional. Questions of law and governance have moved to the centre of development concerns; indeed, a well-governed state has itself become an essential

---

[1] JG Ruggie, 'International Regimes, Transactions, and Change: Embedded Liberalism in the Postwar Economic Order' (1982) 36 *International Organization* 379–415; R Howse, 'From Politics to Technocracy—and Back Again: The Fate of the Multilateral Trading Regime' (2002) 96 *American Journal of International Law* 94–117; B Rajagopal, *International Law from Below: Development, Social Movements, and Third World Resistance* (CUP Cambridge 2003).

marker of development. Not only is law increasingly relied upon to catalyse social and economic change: within mainstream development policy and practice, legal and judicial reform is often imagined simply *as* development.[2]

Law's relation to development—its expanding scope and the evolution in its methods and assumptions in particular—has tracked critically important and consequential changes to the international legal landscape as a whole. International financial and economic institutions have become important sources of normative authority and regulatory expertise on topics ranging from growth and productivity to human rights, democracy, and social inclusion, a development that has been part and parcel of the fragmentation of international law.[3] The itinerary of law and development is intimately connected to the intensified processes of economic and cultural integration conventionally styled 'globalization', as well as to the challenge to the regulatory authority of states and the rise of new forms of transnational law and governance that are such defining features of the contemporary legal landscape.[4] For all of these reasons, an inquiry into law and development provides an illuminating point of entry into some of the key normative preoccupations, ideational structures, and institutional underpinnings of contemporary global legal transformations writ large.

Rather than matters of peripheral or exceptional interest, shifting conceptions of the relationship between legal rules, norms, practices, and institutions lie at the heart of the enterprise. As a field, law and development might be understood as theoretical in its essence: it revolves around the rise, diffusion, transformation, and disintegration of ideas, theories, concepts, and paradigms concerning law and social change. Political agendas, institutional constraints as well as economic interests are all crucial to understanding the manner in which the law and development agenda has evolved. Nonetheless, politics are conducted, interests are furthered, institutions are built, and resistance is mounted in constant reference to ideas, theories, and models, both explicit and implicit. However paradoxical, even development understood simply as mastery of good technocratic practice represents development imbued with theory—and newly politicized. Thus, one way to approach the field is in terms of the varied and changing ideas *about* the nature of development and its possible or projected connections to law and legal institutions, both domestic and international.

---

[2] K Rittich, 'The Future of Law and Development: Second-Generation Reforms and the Incorporation of the Social' in DM Trubek and A Santos (eds), *The New Law and Economic Development: A Critical Appraisal* (CUP Cambridge 2006) 203–52.

[3] International Law Commission, 'Fragmentation of International Law: Difficulties Arising from the Diversification and Expansion of International Law' (13 April 2006) UN Doc A/CN.4/L.682; M Koskenniemi and P Leino, 'Fragmentation of International Law? Postmodern Anxieties' (2002) 15 *Leiden Journal of International Law* 553–79. See also A Peters, 'Fragmentation and Constitutionalization' in this *Handbook*.

[4] G de Búrca and J Scott (eds), *Law and New Governance in the EU and the US* (Hart Oxford 2006).

2 Historicizing International Law and Development

The field of law and development is informed by two clear and quite distinct historical antecedents: Weberian theories concerning the role of the state in modernization and earlier doctrines and institutions of international law, those that touch on relations between European and non-European peoples in particular. Viewed in retrospect, it also seems possible to locate law and development, the current moment in particular, within the more general economization of governance now visible across domestic as well as international law.[5]

Law and development can be understood as an outgrowth of the normalization of statecraft and bureaucratic administration as instruments of modernization and economic rationalization. A wide variety of reform proposals, directed primarily at the law and governance structures and practices of post-colonial and Third World states, have been advanced on the basis that they are necessary for successful transition to modernity and heightened economic growth, claims rooted in Max Weber's identification of the role of formal legal systems in capitalist economic development.[6] Development thought and practice also stands in direct lineage with the 'civilizing mission' that has organized the relationship between Europe and its others since the first colonial encounters.[7] Development first appeared as a term of art in international law within the powers conferred upon the mandatory states in the interwar period under the *Covenant of the League of Nations*, as part of the obligation to promote the well-being of the populations of territories under their administration and control.[8] These powers, in turn, had their headwaters in colonial governance practices of European states, from the 'dual mandate' to promote commerce as well as civilization[9] to the drive to

---

[5] M Foucault, *The Birth of Biopolitics: Lectures at the Collège de France, 1978–1979* (M Senellart ed G Burchell trans) (Palgrave Macmillan Basingstoke 2008); A Anghie, *Imperialism, Sovereignty, and the Making of International Law* (CUP Cambridge 2005); A Orford, *International Authority and the Responsibility to Protect* (CUP Cambridge 2011).

[6] DM Trubek, 'Max Weber on Law and the Rise of Capitalism' [1972] *Wisconsin Law Review* 720–53; D Kennedy, 'The Disenchantment of Logically Formal Legal Rationality, or Max Weber's Sociology in the Genealogy of the Contemporary Mode of Western Legal Thought' (2004) 55 *Hastings Law Journal* 1031–76; C Thomas, 'Max Weber, Talcott Parsons and the Sociology of Legal Reform: A Reassessment with Implications for Law and Development' (2006) 15 *Minnesota Journal of International Law* 383–424.

[7] *Imperialism, Sovereignty, and the Making of International Law* (n 5).

[8] *Covenant of the League of Nations* (adopted 28 April 1919 entered into force 10 January 1920) art 22(1); *Imperialism, Sovereignty, and the Making of International Law* (n 5).

[9] FJD Lugard, *The Dual Mandate in British Tropical Africa* (5th edn Cass London 1965).

discipline and transform native populations that preoccupied colonial states until well into the twentieth century.[10]

But resistance to colonial policies and practices and efforts on the part of postcolonial states to undo the colonial legacy and fundamentally reground international legal doctrines and obligations were also frequently articulated in the language of development. Development aspirations animated virtually every important international initiative emanating from the Third World in the postwar era, from the Bandung Conference and the creation of the United Nations Conference on Trade and Development to efforts to construct a New International Economic Order (NIEO) culminating in the *Charter of Economic Rights and Duties of States* that included both specific rights, such as recognition of permanent sovereignty over natural resources, and a general elaboration of the right and duties associated with development.[11]

Conflict between developed and developing states continues to the present day, most clearly in negotiations over multilateral trade agreements and the relative status of sovereign and investor rights in bilateral and regional trade agreements.[12] Yet the titanic struggles over the relationship between a just international legal order and the sovereignty and welfare of non-Western states have become increasingly peripheral in international debates. Within development policy and praxis, they have largely been displaced by depoliticized questions of governance focused primarily on the role of domestic legal rules, norms, and institutions in fostering economic growth and social, political, and cultural modernization.

Development was initially imagined as compatible with a range of political and economic orders, capitalist as well as socialist, a stance that reflected the centrality of sovereign autonomy and equality as organizing norms within the international order as well as the pragmatic necessity of a significant margin of policy and institutional variation in a world of highly diverse polities and economies.[13] Since the end of the Cold War, however, a wide range of issues formerly understood to be political, and thus fundamentally within the domestic control of states, have been reframed as matters of economic management and governance and thereby brought within the scope of development and the purview of institutions such as the BWIs.[14] At the same time, mainstream development policy has become securely tethered to the global integration of markets, with the private sector (as

---

[10] JS Furnivall, *Colonial Policy and Practice: A Comparative Study of Burma and Netherlands India* (New York University Press New York 1956).

[11] M Bedjaoui, *Towards a New International Economic Order* (Holmes and Meier New York 1979).

[12] M Sornarajah, *International Law on Foreign Investment* (3rd edn CUP Cambridge 2010).

[13] The *Articles of Agreement of the International Bank for Reconstruction and Development* (signed 22 July 1944 entered into force 27 December 1945) 2 UNTS 134, for example, compel the Bank to make lending decisions solely on economic criteria and simultaneously proscribe involvement in the political decisions of states.

[14] IFI Shihata, 'Issues of "Governance" in Borrowing Members—The Extent of Their Relevance under the Bank's *Articles of Agreement*' in IFI Shihata (ed), *The World Bank Legal Papers* (Martinus Nijhoff The Hague 2000) 245–82.

opposed to the state) now identified as the engine of growth and source of welfare gains. International financial and economic institutions, the World Bank in particular, have become important sites for the creation and dissemination of norms about 'good' law and policy in a market-centred world.[15] And as the problem of development has been transformed into a question of governance, the field of law and development has become more intertwined with a broader normative project around global governance.

This shift in focus, from the structure of the international order to the character of domestic law and institutions, from political questions of justice to technical matters of governance, occurred in conjunction with a fundamental paradigm shift in mainstream development thinking and practice concurrent with the monetarist revolution and the rejection of Keynesianism in the United States (US) and the United Kingdom. Known variously as neoliberalism, market fundamentalism and the Washington, now Post-Washington, Consensus,[16] this paradigm envisions law reform primarily as a post-political, technocratic project in the service of efficient market transactions. Informed in the first instance by the precepts of neoclassical and new institutional economic theory and the parallel discovery that 'institutions matter' to economic growth,[17] this paradigm shift has fuelled a multipronged effort to advance development through the adoption and diffusion of an idealized set of 'free' market rules and policies. It has also provided a means to reconceptualize the relationship between state, law, and markets in fundamental ways, and to rank the significance of legal rules and institutions to economic growth and other development goals. Thus, this move tracked a parallel shift in emphasis from the role of public law to that of private law in development, an impetus toward the comparative analysis of legal transplants and legal traditions, and the construction of benchmarks and indicators to both measure and promote legal and institutional reforms.[18] Because they are associated with optimally functioning markets, legal entitlements such

[15] World Bank, *Sub-Saharan Africa: From Crisis to Sustainable Growth: A Long-Term Perspective Study* (World Bank Washington DC 1989); World Bank, *World Development Report 1997: The State in a Changing World* (OUP New York 1997); K Rittich, *Recharacterizing Restructuring: Law, Distribution and Gender in Market Reform* (Kluwer Law International The Hague 2002); J Beard and A Orford, 'Making the State Safe for the Market: The World Bank's *World Development Report 1997*' (1998) 22 *Melbourne University Law Review* 195–216; World Bank Group, 'Doing Business: Measuring Business Regulations' <http://www.doingbusiness.org/> [accessed 1 March 2016].

[16] J Williamson, 'What Washington Means by Policy Reform' in J Williamson (ed), *Latin American Adjustment: How Much Has Happened?* (Institute for International Economics Washington DC 1990) 7–20; JE Stiglitz, 'Is There a Post-Washington Consensus Consensus?' in N Serra and JE Stiglitz (eds), *The Washington Consensus Reconsidered: Towards a New Global Governance* (OUP Oxford 2008) 41–54.

[17] DC North, *Institutions, Institutional Change, and Economic Performance* (CUP Cambridge 1990); OE Williamson, *The Economic Institutions of Capitalism: Firms, Markets, Relational Contracting* (Collier Macmillan London 1985); *World Development Report 1997* (n 15).

[18] 'Doing Business' (n 15).

as property, contract, and civil rights now have pride of place in mainstream development theory and practice, while a wide range of other rules, policies, and institutions are decried as 'interventions' in those rights that risk impairing the efficient operation of markets and, by extension, prospects for welfare gains through economic growth.

As international financial and economic institutions have become at once less agnostic and more prescriptive in respect of domestic law and policy and the perceived pathways to development in the international order have narrowed, the field of law and development has become more politically and theoretically contested. Three interrelated sources of contestation, all intimately related to the paradigm just described, have proved to be both enduring and productive.

One concern is whether there is 'one best way' or, by contrast, multiple institutional paths to development[19] and, relatedly, whether the history of the West represents the future of development or whether regions like East Asia and the new developmental states of the Global South now provide useful templates for institutional reform as well. It is well-recognized that the East Asian states industrialized using a range of policies that diverge from current development norms.[20] Many developing states, those in Latin America in particular, have now adopted, either directly or by default, a combination of state-led, dirigiste policies, incentives to private sector investment, and non-state forms of ordering to promote economic development as well.[21]

A second set of concerns, raised by Third World Approaches to International Law (TWAIL) scholars in particular, relate to the legitimacy and legality of constraints on sovereign and democratic control of national policy priorities through vehicles such as development aid and debt-related lending.[22] Closely related to these concerns about diminishing domestic policy space is the contentiously minimalist, 'low-intensity' approach to democracy that now prevails across the international economic order.[23]

Among the most active and intractable debates, however, are those that concern the relationship between technocratic development policy on the one hand and

[19] D Rodrik, *One Economics, Many Recipes: Globalization, Institutions, and Economic Growth* (Princeton University Press Princeton 2007); D Rodrik, *The Globalization Paradox: Democracy and the Future of the World Economy* (WW Norton & Co New York 2011).

[20] AH Amsden, *The Rise of 'The Rest': Challenges to the West from Late-Industrialization Economies* (OUP Oxford 2001); JKM Ohnesorge, 'Developing Development Theory: Law and Development Orthodoxies and the Northeast Asian Experience' (2007) 28 *University of Pennsylvania Journal of International Economic Law* 219–308.

[21] DM Trubek et al., (eds), *Law and the New Developmental State: The Brazilian Experience in Latin American Context* (CUP Cambridge 2013).

[22] BS Chimni, 'International Institutions Today: An Imperial Global State in the Making' (2004) 15 *European Journal of International Law* 1–37.

[23] S Marks, *The Riddle of All Constitutions: International Law, Democracy, and the Critique of Ideology* (OUP Oxford 2000) ch 3.

welfare gains and distributive justice on the other.[24] Non-governmental organizations (NGOs), activists, scholars, and states have all highlighted the extent to which groups such as women, workers, and tribal and indigenous peoples as well as populations in general might suffer harm, or simply fail to benefit, from reforms and interventions made in the name of enhanced economic growth and other development goals. Although such interventions are typically styled as neutral, objectively necessary to participation in liberalized global markets, and/or merely 'normal' elements of liberal market societies, two sets of concerns have repeatedly fuelled calls for reforms of the development agenda and greater attention to issues of social justice. The first concerns the extent to which it is safe to equate standard interventions with 'development' per se; the second concerns the distribution—more particularly, the maldistribution—of the gains that *do* accrue from resulting economic activity. The framing of many of these questions in the mid-1990s as matters of human rights both restaged the debate around law and development and intensified the fragmentation of international law, pitting human rights norms against norms of rational economic policy entrenched across the international order. It also generated a massive expansion of scholarly engagement in the field, engagement that has itself taken a wide range of forms.

3 What is Law and Development? Conceptualizing the Field

Like international law as a whole, law and development might be understood as both a tradition and a set of practices.[25] One complication of theorizing these traditions and practices, even a distinctive characteristic of the field itself, is the constant traversal and blurring of conceptual, institutional, and disciplinary distinctions and categories. The result is a 'field' with uncertain borders constituted by varied, often isolated, and sometimes incommensurable projects, preoccupations, and perspectives.

Perhaps the first thing to observe is that development is important to international law, while international institutions are central to the enterprise of

---

[24] In an early contribution, Cornia, Jolly, and Stewart identified the neglect of the 'human' side of development and debt-related interventions by international institutions: GA Cornia, R Jolly, and F Stewart (eds), *Adjustment with a Human Face* (2 vols OUP Oxford 1987–8).

[25] M Koskenniemi, 'The Fate of Public International Law: Between Technique and Politics' (2007) 70 *Modern Law Review* 1–30.

development. It is now a truism that development has driven the evolution and expansion of international law throughout the twentieth century, the postwar era in
particular. Scholars have repeatedly observed that development has played a constitutive role in the international legal order, generating institutional change and
programmatic innovation,[26] even framing the space of modern international law as
a whole.[27] At the same time, international institutions such as the World Bank and
the International Monetary Fund have been centrally involved in development-
and debt-related law reform initiatives, sometimes by intervening directly through
technical assistance in the drafting of laws and regulations or by making the provision of financial assistance contingent on regulatory and policy change. Equally
important is their role as producers of law and development knowledge, a position which gives them vast if indirect influence on normative and institutional
change through the dissemination of advice on 'best practices' in respect of law
and policy.[28]

But law and development is also located outside of international law. Research
and reform initiatives that are recognizably part of the field are now sponsored by
a wide range of institutions, national and transnational. Private actors such as the
Ford Foundation, along with hegemonic states such as the US, played key roles
as both funders and promoters of legal reform during the first wave of law and
development in Latin America;[29] since the post-Cold War revival of interest in
law and development, a broad array of other globally interlinked and interacting
institutions, funding agencies, states, civil society groups, and NGOs have become
involved too. The central role played by experts across these institutions in the design of governance norms and practices suggests that law and development should
also be situated within the rise of a post-Westphalian legal order in which private
actors, hybrid public/private institutions, and technocrats both compete and col-
laborate with states in the creation of global norms.

For related reasons, law and development might also be conceptualized as (international) law and development, a field that is, at least in theory, global in its reach and
application but one that owes no particular allegiance to international law as either
a discipline or a point of reference. Even within international institutions, much
law and development practice and policy-making is conducted with little attention
to either general or specific questions of international law. Indeed, *legal* analysis
has played a distinctly subordinate role within mainstream law and development

---

[26] B Rajagopal, *International Law from Below: Development, Social Movements, and Third World Resistance* (CUP Cambridge 2003).

[27] S Pahuja, *Decolonising International Law: Development, Economic Growth and the Politics of Universality* (CUP Cambridge 2011).

[28] 'Doing Business' (n 15); World Bank Group, 'Investing Across Borders: Indicators of Foreign Direct Investment Regulation' <http://iab.worldbank.org/> [accessed 1 March 2016].

[29] DM Trubek and M Galanter, 'Scholars in Self-Estrangement: Some Reflections on the Crisis in Law and Development Studies in the United States' [1974] *Wisconsin Law Review* 1062–1102.

in recent years; although questions of law and development would seem to engage legal knowledge and expertise in the most central of ways, it is economics that is the master discipline. Since the neoliberal revolution of the 1980s, development paradigms have been principally informed by or in conversation with theories and assumptions grounded in neoclassical and new institutional economics. At the same time, with the expansion of the development agenda to encompass general questions of governance, virtually every legal subject of any significance can now be found within the field, and domestic law, rather than international law, is likely to be the focus of interest. As an intellectual endeavour, the field of law and development broadens yet further. Legal scholars who work on questions of law and development come from widely varying disciplinary backgrounds—private law, corporate law, administrative law, intellectual property law, constitutional law, for example—and they bring equally varied methods and perspectives to the field: law and society, poverty law, comparative law, legal pluralism, legal history, and law and economics to list but the most common.

Law and development has been variously described as a movement[30] and a series of projects driven primarily by funding decisions.[31] Rule of law projects have been called a form of theatre, even the staging of a morality play.[32] If law and development is, in some sense, simply what law and development people and institutions *do*,[33] then it must be observed that scholars and practitioners inhabit a range of quite disparate roles: they are analysts, advocates, and activists; policy-makers and critics; model builders and historians; comparativists of difference and promulgators of best practices. For this reason, whether law and development should be conceived as a 'field' and, if so, what type of field are matters of uncertainty and dispute.[34]

At the most basic level, law and development is concerned with the relationship between legal norms and institutions and economic, social, cultural, and political transformation.[35] However, law and development analyses and initiatives are not concerned with such questions *in general*; rather, they are typically directed toward states that have already been designated as developing, emerging, in transition, or 'failed', and their perceived inability to either catch up or measure up when it comes to conventional benchmarks of economic and social performance.[36]

---

[30] 'Scholars in Self-Estrangement' (n 29).

[31] BZ Tamanaha, 'The Primacy of Society and the Failures of Law and Development' (2011) 44 *Cornell International Law Journal* 209–47.

[32] S Humphreys, *Theatre of the Rule of Law: Transnational Legal Intervention in Theory and Practice* (CUP Cambridge 2010).

[33] For a parallel observation in respect of international law, see D Kennedy, 'The Move to Institutions' (1987) 8 *Cardozo Law Review* 841–988.

[34] DM Trubek, 'Law and Development: 40 Years after Scholars in Self-Estrangement—A Preliminary Review' (University of Wisconsin Legal Studies Research Paper No 1255, 2014).

[35] See generally *The New Law and Economic Development* (n 2).

[36] D Acemoglu and JA Robinson, *Why Nations Fail: The Origins of Power, Prosperity and Poverty* (Crown New York 2012); *Decolonising International Law* (n 27).

Indeed the perception or representation of lack or failure is the essential condition for development interventions, legal and other. And if law and development represents an effort to capture, formalize, and systematize the relationship between legal transformation and social and economic 'progress', the field cannot be made intelligible in terms of their *actual* relationship. For one, the terms themselves are contested and unstable: to give but one example, rule of law promotion, despite the fact that it is a central preoccupation of development actors and institutions, contains enormous diversity at the level of concept and practice.[37] Causal connections between law reforms and development objectives remain notoriously elusive in any event. And despite immense amounts of research and scholarship devoted to elaborating the best institutional pathways for growth, accounting for recurring, quite obvious disjunctures between the claims and theories about the legal bases of development and the history of development outcomes remains a general puzzle in the field.

Attention to the evolution of the field suggests that it would be a mistake to think that law and development projects and agendas are centrally about the *effects* of legal structures and interventions in any event. Just as often, the process works in reverse: changes in ideas about development precede new development practices, and development projects may survive and even thrive quite apart from the facts or state of evidence on the ground. Even empirical studies of law and development, rather than disinterested inquiries into the *possible* relationships between law and social change, tend to be centrally informed, and constrained, *ex ante* by beliefs about what does—and does not—contribute to development outcomes.

On one level, law and development can be conceived as a series of discursive, material, and programmatic interventions, rooted in dominant norms and hegemonic theories and organized in conventional forms and practices, in the normative and institutional status quo of states. In general, these interventions are designed to catalyse or directly compel jurisprudential, administrative, regulatory, and/or professional change, under the claim that such reforms will contribute, if not directly lead, to development or progress as defined by the authors of those interventions.

While no effort to distinguish conclusively law and development initiatives from normal political processes can hope to succeed—after all, states routinely use law to promote economic and social transformation, and 'legal development' is a normal feature of every society[38]—'law and development' typically implies something beyond business as usual when it comes to legal and institutional change. True, references to the role of the 'developmental state' are common in regions such as Latin

---

[37] T Carothers (ed), *Promoting the Rule of Law Abroad: In Search of Knowledge* (Carnegie Endowment for International Peace Washington DC 2006); MJ Trebilcock and RJ Daniels, *Rule of Law Reform and Development: Charting the Fragile Path of Progress* (Edward Elgar Cheltenham 2008).
[38] 'The Primacy of Society' (n 31).

America and East Asia,[39] and development literature is replete with accounts of the varied paths that states have taken to economic success.[40] Yet what normally differentiates law and development from ordinary processes of law- and policy-making is the element of external engagement. Law and development initiatives are typically authored, funded, influenced, or aided in some way by outside actors, and they are often successors to, or continuous with, *other* external interventions such as rule of law projects, democracy promotion, or the fight against communism.[41] While some may be linked to the foreign relations, security, and economic interests of hegemonic states,[42] these initiatives may also reflect dominant conceptions about development in the international order, including ideas about the possible roles played by legal norms, rules and institutions in its advancement.

In light of this variegated history, law and development might be imagined in terms of a set of inter-related ideas, practices, and events. Law and development agendas and projects revolve around intersecting claims, grounded in dominant or hegemonic norms, theories and conventions *about* the relationship between legal change and social and economic development. As a field, law and development is both built and transformed as particular claims or conceptions of that relationship gain support within influential constituencies, become embedded as institutional commitments, take shape in particular practices, and are operationalized, either within particular states or regions or across the international order as a whole.[43] Law and development 'orthodoxy', then, simply represents the consolidation of a (provisional) consensus on what development is and what types of legal reform it requires or implies. The consensus is produced by, and itself produces, an epistemic community that participates in a set of beliefs about law's relation to development and constructs practices, institutions, and supporting narratives around those beliefs. The resulting development 'knowledge' is then diffused and sustained through the iterative power of officially generated or sanctioned policy reports, facts, and data sets. This process of knowledge construction also works in reverse, and old objectives frequently appear in new dress. The impulse towards reforming and improving 'backward' peoples and states, for example, remains a constant in development practice, if in continually evolving language and forms,[44]

---

[39] *Law and the New Developmental State* (n 21); Robert Wade, *Governing the Market: Economic Theory and the Role of Government in East Asian Industrialization* (Princeton University Press Princeton 1990).

[40] 'Developing Development Theory' (n 20).

[41] Y Dezalay and BG Garth (eds), *Global Prescriptions: The Production, Exportation, and Importation of a New Legal Orthodoxy* (University of Michigan Press Ann Arbor 2002).

[42] R Kleinfeld, *Advancing the Rule of Law Abroad: Next Generation Reform* (Carnegie Endowment for International Peace Washington DC 2012); W Easterly, *The Tyranny of Experts: Economists, Dictators, and the Forgotten Rights of the Poor* (Basic Books New York 2013).

[43] Sundhya Pahuja has advanced a related idea concerning the ideational/institutional complex organizing international law: see *Decolonising International Law* (n 27).

[44] A Anghie, 'Time Present and Time Past: Globalization, International Financial Institutions, and the Third World' (2000) 32 *New York University Journal of International Law & Politics* 243–90.

as does the related impulse toward salvation.[45] Rules and institutions once justified in the name of one value or objective may be rebranded in the service of another or infused with new theoretical or methodological justifications. Property rights, for example, a ubiquitous element of law and development policy, are now said to serve not simply economic growth but gender equality and the empowerment of the poor as well.

The field of law and development, however, is also constituted by responses to those interventions, norms, and governance projects. As the many scholars, states, and social movements engaged with questions of development have noted, the deliberate effort to use law to provoke development is an enterprise replete with failure and disappointment.[46] Interventions routinely generate unanticipated or even perverse results,[47] while outcomes that might well be judged as acceptable or even good not infrequently ensue from the use of heterodox or alternative approaches.[48] Indeed, whether and in what ways law and development interventions have failed or succeeded are matters that are themselves continually contested.[49] Like their predecessor practices in colonial administration, development projects and interventions are both normalizing and disciplinary.[50] Whether beneficial or not by any particular metric or calculus, they produce varied and complex outcomes, outcomes that are sometimes violently disruptive and/or deeply unpopular within some communities and constituencies. Because they are typically authored in the North and introduced in the South, because they advance particular, and thus unavoidably contentious, visions of social and economic progress, and because they tend to produce quite identifiable winners and losers, development interventions are also frequently received as both political and ideological as well.

It is hardly surprising, then, that there are continual calls for renewal and reform, both of development institutions and the projects and policies they sponsor.[51] The precise ways in which legal reforms might be linked to—or directly produce—these diverse experiences of development, however, is also a matter of

---

[45] J Beard, *The Political Economy of Desire: International Law, Development and the Nation State* (Routledge New York 2007).

[46] 'Scholars in Self-Estrangement' (n 29); FG Snyder, 'The Failure of "Law and Development"' [1982] *Wisconsin Law Review* 383–96; 'The Primacy of Society' (n 31).

[47] J Tendler, *Good Government in the Tropics* (Johns Hopkins University Press Baltimore 1997); *International Law from Below* (n 26).

[48] World Bank, *The East Asian Miracle: Economic Growth and Public Policy* (OUP New York 1993); JC Ramo, *The Beijing Consensus* (Foreign Policy Centre London 2004); S Halper, *The Beijing Consensus: How China's Authoritarian Model Will Dominate the Twenty-First Century* (Basic Books New York 2010).

[49] *International Law from Below* (n 26).

[50] *Imperialism, Sovereignty, and the Making of International Law* (n 5) 187.

[51] D Kennedy, 'When Renewal Repeats: Thinking against the Box' (2000) 32 *New York Journal of International Law & Politics* 335–500.

deep theoretical interest and contestation. These engagements *with* the interventions, practices, and reform projects conducted in the name of development must also be understood as an integral part of the field. Engagement comes in the form of both internal and external critique, with analysts and activists contesting the form of development projects while accepting their foundational premises; proposing alternative theories about the relationship of law to development goals and institutions and/or complicating the narrative of their effects; or, on a variety of theoretical and political bases, advancing alternative visions of development altogether. Although not all gain traction, some of these critiques and engagements enter the mainstream, affecting the form, content, and trajectory of development interventions or even becoming part of the orthodoxy itself. Whether particular claims and demands are recognized or not, they provide fuel for what is, by now, a predictable outcome: continued growth and expansion of the scope of development activities and institutions, as well as of the field itself. We might then think of law and development as built through normative and practical interventions that provoke further engagement, resistance, and critique at a variety of levels: theoretical, political, and institutional.

As even a brief sketch reveals, this process of theoretical engagement and progressive institutional expansion has been in play at every important turning point in recent development history. In the postwar era through the 1950s and 1960s—consistent with the embedded liberal compromise and the dominant development theory of the time, import-substitution industrialization—a large margin of manoeuvre was formally reserved to states in respect of domestic economic, social, and industrial policy.[52] Tariff barriers, import restrictions, and selective allocation of credit, for example, were all in common use as national development strategies. At the same time, US-based scholars and foundations—informed by American legal realist and legal process thought and theorizing in the Weberian tradition that reforms to legal education and the profession might provide a promising route to modernization—began modest attempts to turn the legal cultures and institutions of Latin America, then perceived to be excessively formalist in their orientation, in the direction of greater pragmatism.[53]

The neoliberal revolution of the early 1980s inaugurated a rejection of state-led development based on import substitution industrialization in favour of private-sector led growth. Animated by a commitment to the privatization of assets and industries and a belief in the virtues of economic liberalization and market 'deregulation', it also launched a second, much more ambitious, wave of law and

---

[52] Hegemonic states nonetheless sometimes imposed policy constraints on states within their respective spheres of influences. See J Faundez, 'Between Bandung and Doha: International Economic Law and Developing Countries' in L Eslava, M Fakhri, and V Nesiah (eds), *Bandung, Global History and International Law: Critical Pasts and Pending Futures* (CUP Cambridge forthcoming 2016).

[53] 'Scholars in Self-Estrangement' (n 29).

development, this time directed toward defining the role of the state in market-centred growth and specifying in ever greater detail its legal and institutional requirements.[54] It soon became clear, moreover, that market-led development involved legal and political reform as much as it did economic reform. In Latin America, human rights surfaced as part of the post-authoritarian transition to democracy, generating new interest in criminal law reform. 'Governance failure', a concept traceable to public choice theory that linked the problems of development to regulatory capture and the abuse of state resources and power by rent-seeking insiders,[55] was first identified in Sub-Saharan Africa in the wake of the lost decade of development of the 1980s.[56] But governance failure was soon identified as a general problem of development, and it fuelled what became an enduring preoccupation with corruption. In the early 1990s, during a moment of market triumphalism and as the international financial institutions became enmeshed in the transition of post-socialist states from plan to market economies, the pathologies of the 'interventionist' state emerged as a major theme. At this point, market-centred economic growth became fused with the promotion of liberal democratic reforms.[57] The case for property rights and minimal regulation, already canonical elements of market-centred development, was strengthened by the popularization of Hernando de Soto's theories linking over-regulation and the absence of property rights to poverty and impaired rates of growth.[58] The protection of property rights was soon linked to respect for civil and political rights, and even to the rule of law itself; in relatively short order, these elements came together to constitute an elite consensus on good governance.

Yet powerful counter-currents, theoretical and political, were evident throughout. Discontent and resistance were provoked by a generalised neglect of the 'social' side of development. But they also emerged from adverse events directly linked to neoliberal priorities and reforms. These events ranged from the displacement of peoples in the course of land reforms and large development projects to the disempowerment of workers through the global sourcing of products and labour enabled by economic liberalization. They also included increased risks and costs, including increased unpaid work for women that routinely followed from fiscal austerity measures implemented as part of conditional lending and structural

---

[54] 'Issues of "Governance"' (n 14).

[55] JM Buchanan and G Tullock, *The Calculus of Consent: Logical Foundations of Constitutional Democracy* (University of Michigan Press Ann Arbor 1962).

[56] *Sub-Saharan Africa* (n 15).

[57] European Bank for Reconstruction and Development, 'Agreement Establishing the European Bank for Reconstruction and Development' (September 2013) <http://www.ebrd.com/downloads/research/guides/basics.pdf> [accessed 1 March 2016].

[58] H de Soto, *The Other Path: The Invisible Revolution in the Third World* (J Abbott trans) (Harper & Row New York 1989); H de Soto, *The Mystery of Capital: Why Capitalism Triumphs in the West and Fails Everywhere Else* (Basic Books New York 2000).

adjustment policies. Much of this critique and resistance was cast as neglect of human rights, by now the universal language of social justice;[59] some was directed at the perverse distributional effects of market-centred rules and policies.

By the end of the 1990s, this discontent was powerful and organized sufficiently to produce a response, one which catalysed a further expansion of the development agenda. This transformation, too, was grounded in a theoretical break or innovation: Amartya Sen's influential reconceptualization of development as freedom identifying basic rights and the advancement of human capabilities as crucial means, as well as ends, of development.[60] Invoking Sen's definition, the World Bank soon incorporated a new complex of social, structural, and human goals into the development agenda.[61] These goals, in turn, licensed a massive expansion of legal and policy work in territory and subjects like gender equality, human rights, labour rights, and social policy that were newly designated as relevant to development.[62] Yet even as 'core' human rights and social concerns gained recognition within the field of development, the nature and status of human rights as a whole became, once again, a source of deep contestation on the international plane.[63] In what became a familiar dialogue, human rights scholars and institutions would assert the normative priority of human rights through a rights-based approach to development, while development technocrats, for their part, insisted on the necessity of market-centred reforms to the realization of human rights.[64] At the same time, a reciprocal economization of social concerns occurred with the emergence of market-centred social projects that were largely congruent, in legal and policy terms, with market reforms in the neoliberal style. Rather than mitigate the effects of market forces, these projects sought instead to mobilize the entrepreneurial capacities of citizens and workers and support their enhanced participation in markets.[65] Concerns such as poverty alleviation and gender equality were recast in the development lexicon as matters of empowerment and, in addition to targeted initiatives such as expanded microfinance and conditional cash transfers

---

[59] *International Law from Below* (n 26); ME Keck and K Sikkink, *Activists beyond Borders: Advocacy Networks in International Politics* (Cornell University Press Ithaca 1998).

[60] A Sen, *Development as Freedom* (OUP Oxford 1999).

[61] World Bank, 'Comprehensive Development Framework' (2013) <http://web.worldbank.org/WBSITE/EXTERNAL/PROJECTS/STRATEGIES/CDF/0,,pagePK:60447~theSitePK:140576,00.html> [accessed 1 March 2016]; World Bank, *World Development Report 2000/2001: Attacking Poverty* (OUP New York 2001).

[62] 'Second-Generation Reforms' (n 2).

[63] U Baxi, 'Voices of Suffering and the Future of Human Rights' (1998) 8 *Transnational Law & Contemporary Problems* 125–69; P Alston, 'The Myopia of the Handmaidens: International Lawyers and Globalization' (1997) 8 *European Journal of International Law* 435–48; JT Gathii, 'Good Governance as a Counter Insurgency Agenda to Oppositional and Transformative Social Projects in International Law' (1999) 5 *Buffalo Human Rights Law Review* 107–74.

[64] P Alston and M Robinson (eds), *Human Rights and Development: Towards Mutual Reinforcement* (OUP Oxford 2005).

[65] 'Second-Generation Reforms' (n 2); K Bedford, *Developing Partnerships: Gender, Sexuality, and the Reformed World Bank* (University of Minnesota Press Minneapolis 2009).

directed to low-income families, advanced through familiar strategies such as for-malization, the rule of law, and the protection of property rights.[66]

Since the turn of the millennium, there has been increasing investment in benchmarks and indicators as mechanisms to spur legal and policy reform. Two projects in particular exemplify this turn. The first is the Millennium Development Goals, a UN sponsored effort to address the social deficits of globalization and de-velopment through the adoption of benchmarks for progress in respect of widely endorsed goals, including eradicating extreme poverty and hunger and promoting gender equality and women's empowerment. The second is the World Bank's *Doing Business* indicator series, a project which purports to measure the quality of state regulation for the purposes of attracting investment and furthering economic ac-tivity. Relying upon the controversial 'legal origins' thesis from the law and finance literature holding that states with common law legal systems provide superior environments for the conduct of business,[67] these indicators measure the costs of doing business in eleven areas.[68] Both projects mark a new emphasis on empir-ical research,[69] a more general rise of the 'audit culture' across public and private institutions,[70] and a growing reliance on indicators as technologies of governance.[71]

Development thinking and practice is also now informed to some degree, par-ticularly in areas such as environmental regulation and labour standards, by the conventions of new governance and democratic experimentalism.[72] In a funda-mental shift of regulatory paradigms, new governance initiatives, in general, pursue normative and behavioural change not through conventional 'top-down' regulation promulgated and enforced by the state but through alternatives that involve the adoption of either 'soft' norms or of dynamic and revisable norms and standards developed in processes of 'learning by doing'. They typically rely for their efficacy on knowledge dissemination and peer uptake and benchmarking of standards and progress. They may be devised by private actors and 'stakeholders' as well as public officials and institutions and, like the Global Compact, may be

---

[66] Commission on Legal Empowerment of the Poor, *Making the Law Work for Everyone* (United Nations Development Program New York 2008); World Bank, *World Development Report 2012: Gender, Equality and Development* (World Bank Washington DC 2011); K Rittich, 'Engendering Development/Marketing Equality' (2003) 67 *Albany Law Review* 575–93.

[67] R la Porta et al., 'Law and Finance' (1998) 106 *Journal of Political Economy* 1113–55.

[68] 'Doing Business' (n 15).

[69] See AV Banerjee and E Duflo, *Poor Economics: A Radical Rethinking of the Way to Fight Global Poverty* (Public Affairs New York 2011).

[70] See eg M Strathern (ed), *Audit Cultures: Anthropological Studies in Accountability, Ethics, and the Academy* (Routledge New York 2000).

[71] See KE Davis, A Fisher, and B Kingsbury (eds), *Governance by Indicators: Global Power through Quantification and Rankings* (OUP Oxford 2012); K Rittich, 'Governing by Measuring: The Millenium Development Goals in Global Governance' in R Buchanan and P Zumbansen (eds), *Law in Transition: Human Rights, Development and Transitional Justice* (Hart Publishing Oxford 2014).

[72] KG Noonan, CF Sabel, and WH Simon, 'Legal Accountability in the Service-Based Welfare State: Lessons from Child Welfare Reform' (2009) 34 *Law and Social Inquiry* 523–68.

designed to establish either general standards or standards that reflect the specific character of the affected firm or sector.[73] At the same time, the commitment to reform of formal 'hard' law continues apace and in parallel, as is evident in the efforts of the international economic and financial institutions to advance a seamlessly integrated approach to matters of economic governance, in which states both implement and eliminate regulations across all sectors to stimulate competition and efficiency.[74]

All of these projects and interventions have provided fertile, indeed irresistible, terrain for both intellectual engagement and political resistance.

4 (DE)STABILIZING LAW; (DE)STABILIZING DEVELOPMENT: QUESTIONS OF METHOD

The field of law and development rests on the premise that it is both possible and useful to invoke two terms, 'law' and 'development', and to elaborate in general terms the normative and institutional relationships between them. This is a contestable premise, however, and not merely for the sceptics as opposed to the optimists.[75] Each term has multiple possible referents, descriptive as well as normative.

For example, what does it mean to speak about law as a cross-cultural phenomenon? Does it refer only to rules and standards promulgated by the state? Does it encompass informal, customary and social norms? Does it capture new forms of governance such as informal policy coordination by bureaucrats and technocrats, or codes, norms and practices developed by private actors and transnational firms? And how do we assess the significance of legal and normative transformation? Do we imagine that new normative pronouncements themselves instantiate change? Are we interested in the consequences of institutionalization? Do we measure the gap between the law in action and the law on the books? Do we approach legal rules as behavioural incentives? If so, (how far) do we account for the costs as well as their benefits? In short, nested within law and development is a thorny and complex set of questions about what we are talking about when we talk about law, as

---

[73] '40 Years after Scholars in Self-Estrangement' (n 34); *Law and the New Developmental State* (n 21).

[74] See eg Organisation for Economic Cooperation and Development, *Guiding Principles for Regulatory Quality and Performance* (2008) <http://www.oecd.org/fr/reformereg/34976533.pdf> [accessed 1 March 2016].

[75] KE Davis and MJ Trebilcock, 'The Relationship between Law and Development: Optimists versus Skeptics' (2008) 56 *American Journal of Comparative Law* 895–946.

well as equally varied and contestable ideas about what law does and how people use law as a normative/institutional complex.

Similar complexities beset the term 'development'. To what ends are we referring when we talk about 'development'? Do we mean sustainable growth and advances in welfare or merely expanded market activity? Do we include human rights and social and cultural development as well as economic growth? If so, by what means and metrics do we elaborate, order, and value development's constituent parts and what do we do where they compete or conflict? And how do we both account for and manage the role of culture in economic life?[76]

If each term is unstable, the relationship between law and development has proved to be equally elusive. Is law an instrument to provoke transformative social, economic, and cultural change? Or is development a vehicle by which to authorize reforms to legal norms and institutions? Does law merely regulate social and economic domains and processes? Or should we think of law as constituting those domains and processes at the same time?

If law and development as well as their relationship all require further specification, analysis, and defence, how are such concerns addressed and managed within the field? To put it simply, what makes law and development (somewhat) tractable, whether as a set of institutional practices or as an object of study? While there is no single way to manage these difficulties, the immense complexity, variability, and instability of law's possible relations to development require, first, that some things be held in view and in focus while others are eliminated from consideration. And whether at the programmatic or analytic level, this engagement compels, secondly, a series of methodological choices. These choices not only reflect different conceptions of law: different frameworks of analysis account for the relationship between law and social and economic processes in different ways, and they embed and prioritize different normative and political concerns and aspirations as well.

For example, the economic analysis of law typically foregrounds the efficient allocation of resources as the normative goal of development; it posits the autonomous individual as the central economic actor and assumes that s/he acts rationally in response to incentives to further a stable set of preferences over time. Such premises may co-exist with liberal legal assumptions that the state of development can be assessed by the presence of civil and political rights such as property and contract rights; periodic multiparty elections and parliamentary institutions; and restraints on the state's power over private actors. Both may be informed by administrative law norms and classic markers of the rule of law such as the independence of the judiciary and due process protections typically found in advanced bureaucratic states.[77]

[76] VA Zelizer, *Economic Lives: How Culture Shapes the Economy* (Princeton University Press Princeton 2011).

[77] B Kingsbury, N Krisch, and RB Stewart, 'The Emergence of Global Administrative Law' (2005) 68 *Law & Contemporary Problems* 15–61.

While mainstream approaches to law and development usually involve some fusion or amalgam of these assumptions, heterodox forms of analysis typically bring some range of other properties, operations, and possibilities of law into view; this, in turn, complicates the ways in which law and development arguments can be intelligibly made. Analyses in the tradition of American legal realism[78] typically underscore the range of legal rules, doctrines, and institutions that concepts of property and contract may underwrite, and hence the myriad institutional forms, or 'varieties of capitalism',[79] that market-centred development might take.[80] Following in this vein, post-realist and critical scholarship typically foregrounds the distributional consequences of legal rules; analysing entitlements not simply as norms or incentives but as bargaining endowments that differentially empower social groups and actors, thereby affecting the outcomes of contracts over market, familial, and other arrangements.[81] A central challenge to the field posed by these forms of analysis is the observation that legal rules and institutions are endogenous, rather than external, to social and economic spheres and processes: thus, all references to these spheres and processes themselves imply some baseline set of institutions that must, in turn, form part of the analysis of law's relation to development.

Other methodologies similarly complicate the analysis of law and development. Legal pluralists and legal anthropologists may investigate the range of normative orders in operation in different social fields, attending to the varied effects of legal transplants and interventions in their interaction with customary, religious, or other pre-existing norms[82] or their use (or non-use) by different social actors.[83] Analysing legal transplants, comparative legal scholars may attend to the range of ways that responses to common economic and social problems are structured and managed within different legal traditions and systems. Methodologically critical comparativists, however, may well highlight the limits of simple exercises in 'comparison by columns'[84] or, against conventional understandings within

[78] See D Kennedy and WW Fisher (eds), *The Canon of American Legal Thought* (Princeton University Press Princeton 2006).

[79] PA Hall and D Soskice (eds), *Varieties of Capitalism: The Institutional Foundations of Comparative Advantage* (OUP Oxford 2001).

[80] A Santos, 'Carving Out Policy Autonomy for Developing Countries in the World Trade Organization: The Experience of Brazil & Mexico' (2012) 52 *Virginia Journal of International Law* 551–632; RM Unger, *What Should Legal Analysis Become?* (Verso New York 1996).

[81] *Recharacterizing Restructuring* (n 15); 'Engendering Development/Marketing Equality' (n 66); JM Ngugi, 'Re-Examining the Role of Private Property in Market Democracies: Problematic Ideological Issues Raised by Land Registration' (2004) 25 *Michigan Journal of International Law* 467–527.

[82] SF Moore, 'Law and Social Change: The Semi-Autonomous Social Field as an Appropriate Subject of Study' (1973) 7 *Law and Society Review* 719–46.

[83] SE Merry, 'Legal Pluralism' (1988) 22 *Law and Society Review* 869–96; BZ Tamanaha, C Sage, and M Woolcock (eds), *Legal Pluralism and Development: Scholars and Practitioners in Dialogue* (CUP Cambridge 2012).

[84] G Frankenberg, 'Critical Comparisons: Re-Thinking Comparative Law' (1985) 26 *Harvard International Law Journal* 411–55.

development theory and practice, confound or complicate the narratives about the character and origins of the legal traditions associated with modernist development.[85] Feminist approaches to development are also internally differentiated in method and approach, but, in general, joined in their concern to foreground the status of women in the production of development norms and projects as well as their stakes in the outcomes of development interventions, their desires for different forms and conceptions of development, or both.[86] In a similar vein, TWAIL and post-colonial analyses typically note the adverse consequences of development projects and reforms for sub-altern groups, and mark the persistent disadvantage of post-colonial states within global economic norms and structures as well.[87] At this point, multiple hybrid analyses combining different methods and frameworks are to be found as well.

As this non-exhaustive list of approaches indicates, all analyses of law and development are unavoidably partial. At the same time, the significance of the chosen method or analytic framework is immense, for any choice will affect the range of policy, regulatory, and institutional choices under consideration and the vocabulary in which those choices are debated. But it will also operate in more fundamental ways. Different methods and approaches are oriented towards different questions; depending on the framework or starting point that is adopted, the focus may be on outcomes, processes, or relationships, and some facts or events will seem important while others will seem less significant or perhaps invisible entirely. To put it simply, different analytic and methodological frameworks do not merely operate *on* the problems of development in identifiably distinct ways; they cause different dimensions of development to both materialize and disappear as subjects of attention, framing and directing that attention in ways that shape development knowledge and projects at every level. Some pose challenges to the field itself. Take, for example, the insight that law helps constitute—and constitute in varied ways—the very entities and processes that law is often imagined to merely regulate: this disrupts in quite foundational ways the effort to generate general insights or best practices that apply across states with diverse legal structures and traditions.

Notwithstanding the significance of these choices and decisions to development endeavours, mainstream law and development institutions and practitioners typically represent development work as neither theoretical nor ideological, but rather

---

[85] PG Monateri, 'Black Gaius: A Quest for the Multicultural Origins of the "Western Legal Tradition"' (2000) 51 *Hastings Law Journal* 479–555.

[86] C Nyamu-Musembi, *For or Against Gender Equality? Evaluating the Post-Cold War 'Rule of Law' Reforms in Sub-Saharan Africa* (United Nations Research Institute for Social Development Geneva 2005); *Recharacterizing Restructuring* (n 15).

[87] 'Imperial Global State' (n 22); *International Law from Below* (n 26); JT Gathii 'TWAIL: A Brief History of Its Origins, Its Decentralized Network, and a Tentative Bibliography' (2011) 3 *Trade Law and Development* 26–64; 'Time Present and Time Past' (n 44); *Decolonising International Law* (n 27).

as the pragmatic exercise of solving 'real-world' problems.[88] Policy debates reflect an overwhelming preoccupation with 'what works' and the 'effectiveness' of legal reforms,[89] with consensus on both development goals and the methods and epistemic frameworks by which the 'effectiveness' of interventions is assessed simply asserted or assumed. As a result, development projects, practices, and analyses tend to be theoretically, politically, and methodologically laden, yet unconsciously so. Even when contentious assumptions are brought to the surface, for example through competing accounts of law's relation to economic and social phenomena and processes, they often remain embedded or inadequately addressed.

While development policy *in toto* might be described as both formalist and functionalist in its orientation to law,[90] the default approach is both instrumentalist and functionalist;[91] indeed, the idea that there are 'best practices' in respect of the law for development that obtain across different states and contexts is itself irreducibly functionalist. Yet functionalism provides less support for governance practices, whether mainstream or heterodox, than appears at first glance. For one, functionalism depends on a separation of law from society and economy that, although conventional in both liberal political thought and economic analysis, has long been collapsed in legal theory.[92] Neither liberalism nor neoclassical and institutional economic theories, on their own, compel support for the forms of law associated with orthodox approaches to law and governance.[93] Liberal societies have varied institutional histories. No single set of rules or institutions can be derived from the idea that legal regimes should enhance the efficient allocation of resources, secure the rights of investors, and reduce the costs of transactions to spur productivity and growth, even assuming development could be reduced to these objectives. De Soto's theories notwithstanding, crucially important questions as to how property rights should be allocated and institutionalized remain open;[94] even their relation to economic growth remains contingent.[95] And it is not necessary to resort to external critique to find theoretical support for diverse forms

---

[88] D Kennedy, 'Challenging Expert Rule: The Politics of Global Governance' (2005) 27 *Sydney Law Review* 5–28.

[89] *Rule of Law Reform and Development* (n 37); MJ Trebilcock and MM Prado, *What Makes Poor Countries Poor? Institutional Determinants of Development* (Edward Elgar Cheltenham 2011).

[90] K Rittich, 'Functionalism and Formalism: Their Latest Incarnations in Contemporary Development and Governance Debates' (2005) 55 *University of Toronto Law Journal* 853–68.

[91] For an illuminating discussion of functionalism in comparative law, see R Michaels, 'The Functional Method of Comparative Law' in M Reimann and R Zimmermann (eds), *The Oxford Handbook of Comparative Law* (OUP Oxford 2006) 339–82.

[92] RW Gordon, 'Critical Legal Histories' (1984) 36 *Stanford Law Review* 57–125.

[93] JE Stiglitz, *Globalization and Its Discontents* (Allen Lane London 2002).

[94] D Kennedy, 'Some Caution About Property Rights as a Recipe for Economic Development' in D Kennedy and JE Stiglitz (eds), *Law and Economics with Chinese Characteristics: Institutions for Promoting Development in the 21st Century* (OUP Oxford 2013) 187–212.

[95] M Trebilcock and P-E Veel, 'Property Rights and Development: The Contingent Case for Formalization' (2008) 30 *University of Pennsylvania Journal of International Law* 397–481.

of regulation within the field of economics either; it is already well-established in the discipline itself.[96]

When such methodological issues are acknowledged, there is rarely any attempt to engage in a systematic or inclusive way with the insights that might be generated through different analytical perspectives.[97] Instead, the typical result is an amalgam of responses and proposals that seems difficult to conceptualize in any coherent, non-arbitrary way. Yet neither are the forms of law thought conducive to development radically open. Because welfare gains, now social as well as economic, are represented as coterminous with private sector-led, globally integrated market activity, maximizing the possibilities of investment, transactions, and exchange remains at the centre of the legal reform agenda. Because the major institutions that generate development knowledge and practice are populated with economic technocrats, development is now associated with a characteristic set of preoccupations within the discipline of economics when it comes to law: the enforcement of private law rights to secure the micro-foundations of growth; scepticism about regulatory 'interference' with forces of supply and demand, except when it comes to rules and policies that demonstrably reduce transaction costs; and the application of cost/benefit analysis to questions like equality and social justice that elsewhere in the international order are more typically subject to normative pronouncements about rights. At the same time, the heavy investment in legal institutions thought to enhance efficiency and productivity produces characteristic forms of blindness: to questions of sovereign equality and autonomy; to the distributive consequences of legal rules; to the 'externalities' of efficiency-enhancing policies and reforms on non-market goods and services;[98] to the trade-offs between economic and non-economic values and objectives; and to the many informal but nonetheless effective modes of social and economic ordering.[99]

Yet if law is ineluctably 'for' development and often thought to further development aims and ends in predictable ways, legal rules and institutions now also serve as evidence 'of' development.[100] Recognition of the constitutive function of law reintroduces an element of legal formalism into the field, while the expansion of the development agenda to incorporate human rights and democracy promotion compels a degree of pragmatic balancing among rights and policies.[101]

---

[96] 'Is There a Post-Washington Consensus Consensus?' (n 16).

[97] A Perry-Kessaris, 'The Case for a Visualized Economic Sociology of Legal Development' (2014) 67 *Current Legal Problems* 167–98.

[98] M Waring, *If Women Counted: A New Feminist Economics* (Harper & Row New York 1988); JE Stiglitz, A Sen, and J-P Fitoussi, *Mismeasuring Our Lives: Why GDP Doesn't Add Up* (New Press New York 2010).

[99] *Institutions, Institutional Change, and Economic Performance* (n 17); E Ostrom, *Governing the Commons: Institutions for Common Pool Resources* (CUP Cambridge 1990).

[100] 'Second-Generation Reforms' (n 2).

[101] D Kennedy, 'Three Globalizations of Law and Legal Thought: 1850–2000' in *The New Law and Economic Development* (n 2) 19–73. See generally *The New Law and Economic Development* (n 2).

However, the commitment to market-centred development continues to exert a strong gravitational pull on the field, affecting the relative priorities among development aims as well as the modes and forms of law through which they are managed and advanced. Democracy promotion and social reform projects, for example, tend to be imagined in ways that are convergent rather than at odds with the preferred practices and institutions of economic life. The incorporation of human rights involves not simply the endorsement of established norms; instead, it requires continual decisions about what human rights to recognize and how they should be implemented. 'Basic' or 'core' civil and political rights may be distinguished from social and economic rights, for example, while the rejection of state-centred development makes it difficult to accommodate any concept of a collective right to development at all.

As a result, the theoretical basis of normative development practice can only be described as eclectic. Policy analyses will typically include both functionalist and formalist claims: sometimes legal rules are defended on the grounds that they are necessary to the health and flourishing of the economy; sometimes they are advanced as definitional to the normative commitments and institutions of liberal societies; increasingly often, they are both.

5 CONCLUDING THOUGHTS

As a field, law and development is both normatively and theoretically porous. Yet it also has a history, study of which reveals surprising continuity as well as novelty in both preoccupations and projects across time and space. And precisely because it is so open, at the level of practice, law and development is routinely—perhaps necessarily—informed by political, economic, and philosophical ideas and theories. In recent years, ideas about the centrality of market forces and market ordering to economic, social, and political processes have proved to be unusually productive, generating new institutional capacities and activities in myriad areas. They have also provided narratives and regulative ideals against which state practice, domestic as well as international, can be continuously measured.

The path of law and development has become inseparable from the main currents of legal, economic, and institutional change of our time. Development policy and practice have been crucially important to the generation of global governance norms, part of a vast edifice of knowledge production concerning the role of the state, the nature of democracy, the place of human rights, and the economic, social, and political possibilities of markets. In the aftermath of the global financial crises, it is evident that the reach of those norms and knowledge practices now extends well beyond developing and transitional states, at least to the peripheral states in the North. A collateral effect of this global diffusion is that law and development has become at once a source and repository of norms about the forms and functions of law, domestic as well as international, and a powerful counterweight to *other* sources of law in the international order.

All of these features ensure that the field of law and development will continue to be rich and contested in both scholarship and practice. Development actors and institutions have proved to be both responsive and resistant to external engagement, incorporating critique while deflecting and transforming it at the same time. The forms that this responsiveness and resistance take can themselves be telling, as are the routine 'failures' of law and development. Both suggest that consequences of law and development initiatives 'on the ground' are only one consideration. The doubled character of law and development—as global normative enterprise and as transformative intervention in particular states—serves as a reminder that at least some of the time, the point of law and development may be the intervention itself. Put simply, whatever their effects in particular locales or regions, the most significant and enduring consequence of law and development interventions may be the (re)structuring of norms and powers which they both provoke and authorize across the international legal order itself.

CHAPTER 41

THEORIZING
RESPONSIBILITY

OUTI KORHONEN
AND TONI SELKÄLÄ

1 INTRODUCTION

RESPONSIBILITY under international law is here divided into three main interpretants in theoretical terms.[1] The first is the hard core of responsibility doctrine,
namely the doctrine of state responsibility, a main topic of the United Nations
International Law Commission (ILC) since its early establishment. The second interpretant springs from the rise of human rights law discourse in the international
arena since the 1960s and 1970s: the never-quite-solidified semi-doctrine of humanitarian intervention that has warped into the (non-)doctrine of the responsibility to protect (R2P)—which has always been the most politically powerful or,
at least, the most prominently debated among international legal responsibility
concepts. All of the human rights responsibilities are, obviously, not subsumed
under this doctrine, while it has also enclosed other harbingers of liberalism, most

---

[1] The concept of interpretant as employed here is a loan from CS Peirce and his triadic sign theory.
Briefly, the interpretant can be understood as that which 'provides a translation of the sign, allowing
us a more complex understanding of the sign's object': A Atkin, 'Peirce's Theory of Signs' in EN Zalta
(ed), *The Stanford Encyclopedia of Philosophy* (2013) <http://plato.stanford.edu/archives/sum2013/
entries/peirce-semiotics/> [accessed 1 March 2016].

notably those of economic and environmental accountability. The third sort of international legal responsibility that will be discussed is a catch-all category for the remainder of the duties that imply responsibility and beyond; the responsibility of the United Nations Security Council or even, in exceptional circumstances, of the General Assembly and the entire global community for peace and security; the responsibility of international judicial organs to adjudicate cases in a manner that would provide effective solutions rather than mere formal replies; the issue of recognition of other subjectivities. We discuss this category as the response-ability of international law—a category that most obviously transcends, challenges, and pierces openings in the dogmatic and managerial conceptions of law and its responsibility. Notwithstanding the division into three for the purposes of the presentation here, the interpretants naturally overlap and coincide in various ways in practice, thus always challenging categorization.

2 RESPONSIBILITY FORMALISM: PRIMACY OF THE LAW

The responsibility doctrine is the necessary reciprocal element inherent in the doctrine of sovereign statehood according to a wide variety of formalist and dogmatic theories of law.[2] In these theories, law typically stands as an object of itself or as 'pure', in a Kelsenian sense, and separate from the sociologies, economies, power politics, and other contextual and subjectivism-beladen pollutants. Law is recognizable as law because of its essential law-ness, law-likeness, and justness, which entails equity and reciprocity—or, managerially speaking a kind of balance of costs and benefits[3]—among legal persons. In this theoretical vein, it is given that the rights, privileges, prerogatives, and powers of, for example, a state (as the main legal subject of international law) are counter-balanced by corresponding duties, responsibilities, obligations, checks, and so on.[4] This feature is the main

---

[2] The width and variety appears from the approaches to state responsibility discussed in the commentaries to the Draft Articles, see International Law Commission, 'Draft Articles on Responsibility of States for Internationally Wrongful Acts, with Commentaries' (2001) esp ch I, pt I.

[3] M Koskenniemi, 'Constitutionalism as Mindset: Reflections on Kantian Themes about International Law and Globalization' (2007) 8 *Theoretical Inquiries in Law* 9–36, at 22 and 29.

[4] Referring to analytical jurisprudence from Bentham to Hohfeld, see D Kennedy, 'The Stakes of Law, or Hale and Foucault!' in *Sexy Dressing Etc, Essays on the Power and Politics of Cultural Identity* (Harvard University Press Cambridge MA 1993) 83–125, at 90.

distinguishing or essential/izing element of law vis-à-vis, for example, politics in a variety of traditional (including cosmopolitan) formalist legal theories, while the same reciprocity, obviously, has no essential/ist claim in political theories of state sovereignty. Thus, state responsibility is the axiomatic reciprocal half of the concept of international law that stages the state as its principal legal subject with inherent sovereign rights and powers. The recognition of subjectivity is at the core of the different concepts of responsibility.

The formalist project in its many varieties and renaissances from Kant to Kelsen and Koskenniemi, also sets up the cosmopolitan peace project on the formal morality of law's equity and reciprocity, in which responsibility for one's transgressions is systemically given by virtue of the concept of law itself. In Zolo's words, Kelsenian formalism grounds a pacifist cosmopolitanism on

the rationalist presupposition that it is possible to abolish war, disarm states, attenuate political conflicts and overcome the immense economic and cultural disparities that cleave the planet, relying essentially on legal and institutional instruments; that is, giving rise to a supranational power which is supposed to be by definition impartial, rational and morally inspired.[5]

Sharing in the formalist project, the international legal community through the ILC has tasked itself with the codification of the essential difference-producing reciprocal side of states' sovereign power, that is, state responsibility, showing itself to be axiomatically deaf to the cynicism growing out of the problems that have impeded and drawn out the effort. If we identify the beginning of the project in the turn of the twentieth century, it has taken over a century to codify the rules that still remain draft rules though implying customary support.[6]

The duration and tenacity of the project seems ever more awesome to scholars from neighbouring disciplines while the aim is, put bluntly for example by Dunne,[7] to confirm a tautology that restates the formalist concept of law and that in the 2001 Draft Article 1 received the formulation:

Every internationally wrongful act of a State entails the international responsibility of that State.[8]

In other words, the very definition of law means that it is wrong to breach it and one is accountable for one's wrongs towards other subjects. In contrast to the

[5] D Zolo, 'Hans Kelsen: International Peace through International Law' (1998) 9 *European Journal of International Law* 306–24, at 324.

[6] See Crawford's edition of Brownlie's textbook of public international law: JR Crawford, *Brownlie's Principles of Public International Law* (OUP Oxford 2012) at 540 ('Part IX: The Law of Responsibility').

[7] T Dunne, 'The Diplomacy of Responsibility' (Lecture at POLSIS Research Seminar, University of Queensland, 1 November 2011).

[8] 'Draft Articles on the Responsibility of States for Internationally Wrongful Acts' (n 2) art 1.

responsibility in, for example, R2P, as will be discussed later in the section, the formal responsibility doctrine is individualistic and state-centric as it emphasizes state-to-state-relationships and foregrounds bilateralism as a main mode of international relations, notwithstanding its applicability to international organizations.[9]

The formal tradition often also attaches to an unproblematized concept of interpretation, which enters into the law of responsibility already at the concept of attribution, as in article 2(a) of the Draft Articles. The element of attribution is the 'subjective' if the breach is the 'objective' element in state responsibility. Formal legal doctrine uses the term 'subjective' to connote a judgement call and dependence on circumstances. As the ILC puts it, establishing attribution is 'a matter for the interpretation and application of the primary (that is, substantive) rules…in a given case'.[10] The interpretation in the formal sense follows the regressive analytical method of 'conservative hermeneutics'.[11] This is the method that, for example, the *Vienna Convention on the Law of the Treaties* codified in articles 31 and 32,[12] laying down the idea that there is a singular 'ordinary meaning' to every legally operational concept that can be ascertained through consulting the text in light of its instrumental ambit—including the object and purpose, original intent, the *travaux préparatoires*, and the authoritative languages. That method implies that deformalization, pluralism, and ambiguity of meanings, let alone in-built contestation over socio-economic stakes, in rich and changing global cultural contexts are non-issues that may only enter responsibility discourse in the more multilaterally inspired and deformalized modes of responsibility, as will be discussed later.

The difficulties with the traditional formalist concept are illustrated by a number of hard cases on interpreting attribution, such as cases in which attribution is based on effective or ultimate control over armed forces, for example *Behrami* (ECtHR) and *Nuhanovic* and *Mustafic* (The Netherlands).[13] It seems that judges do differ radically on whether attribution to only one or to multiple actors simultaneously is what the law and the world require. If multiple, overlapping controlling actors are accepted, it renders the interpretation exercise anything but a straightforward matter of regressive analytical hermeneutics and

---

[9] International Law Commission, 'Draft Articles on Responsibility of International Organizations' (2011).

[10] Ibid art 2(3).

[11] G Frankenberg, 'Comparing Constitutions: Ideas, Ideals, and Ideology—Toward a Layered Narrative' (2006) 4 *International Journal of Constitutional Law* 439–59.

[12] *Vienna Convention on the Law of Treaties* (opened for signature 23 May 1969 entered into force 26 January 1980) 1155 UNTS 331.

[13] *Behrami v France; Saramati v France, Germany and Norway* (2007) 45 EHRR SE10; *Netherlands v Nuhanović* (Supreme Court of the Netherlands, Case No 12/03324, 6 September 2013); *Netherlands v Mustafić-Mujić* (Supreme Court of the Netherlands, Case No 12/03329, 6 September 2013). These cases are briefly overviewed in *Brownlie's Principles of Public International Law* (n 6) 546.

frustrates the hope of ever disentangling one primary agent, original intent, and full responsibility-bearer from a tangled web of overt and covert power-yielding actors and agencies.[14] For this reason, contrary to certain domestic courts, international courts have not adopted the approach of attributing responsibility to multiple actors. Instead, as Crawford discusses with reference to the European Court of Human Rights:

> In making (the) formal distinction (on Security Council and non-Security Council mandated interventions), (the Court) stopped short of considering, as the Dutch court did, that multiple entities may have 'effective control' over forces, and that effective control by a state makes the conduct of these forces attributable to the state regardless of the form taken by the operation.[15]

Thus, it seems that the responsibility doctrine in its singularity, bilateral-modelling, essentialism, individualism, and conservative/textual hermeneutics is the backbone of the formalist concept of law as well as one of the formalistically oriented community's most important and centennially sustained projects—the codification of the law of responsibility of the main subjects (states and international organizations). The concept and the project have had a major significance in steering international law through the many storms of the twentieth century and beyond—not least, the challenges of 'fragmentation' and the 'fall of international law' that tend to receive cosmopolitan pacifism, reciprocity, equity, friendly relations, and the resulting systemic synergy as their typical responses.[16]

The emergence of state responsibility doctrine is symptomatic of mainstream formalism in international law. The way the international law community embarked on the quest to codify state responsibility and the many considerations and axioms taken into account are but impressive: everything is there from the enlightenment ethos to cosmopolitan pacifism, equity and balance between rights and duties, reciprocity, rationalism, the need to guard against egoistical subjectivism, and observance of the rules guiding how to backtrack to original consensus if and when disagreement arises. All this is beautifully rendered in the commentaries to the *Draft Articles*.[17] As such, it seems to have everything needed to arrive at world peace and codification—yet it does not quite do. The sections below will discuss other interpretants of responsibility that are more complex and messy in comparison to Kelsenian purity, open-ended, flexible, and continuously negotiable—in short, deformalized.

---

[14] *Brownlie's Principles of Public International Law* (n 6) 545–7.   [15] Ibid 547.

[16] As, for example, proclaimed and discussed by Koskenniemi in M Koskenniemi *The Gentle Civilizer of Nations: The Rise and Fall of International Law 1870–1960* (CUP Cambridge 2001); International Law Commission, 'Fragmentation of International Law: Difficulties Arising from the Diversification and Expansion of International Law' (13 April 2006) UN Doc A/CN.4/L.682.

[17] 'Draft Articles on the Responsibility of States for Internationally Wrongful Acts' (n 2) 31–9.

3 RESPONSIBILITY MANAGERIALISM: PRIMACY OF INTERNATIONAL AUTHORITY

'Unilateral military action by states to protect peoples or minorities—even with the blessing of the Security Council—should not be legalized', concludes Bothe in his 1993 article on the legitimacy of the use of force.[18] It is a curious conclusion for an article targeting legitimacy to end with legality, yet it is one in which international law is seen as harnessing hegemonic interests of the powerful, albeit at a cost to peoples and minorities. Campbell, writing the following year, posits the problem precisely at the core of legality condoned by Bothe—sovereign states. He finds '[t]he problem of responsibility…exacerbated by the way in which… sovereign states in an anarchic realm—are often the very object of violence'.[19] Campbell argues in favour of an ethical duty as central in defining the extent of responsibility that the global community must bear. The third position, of marrying legality and legitimacy, follows at the dawn of the new millennium, when the Independent International Commission on Kosovo in its report suggests that '[e]xperience from the NATO intervention in Kosovo suggests the need to close the gap between legality and legitimacy'.[20] Realism, pragmatism, moralism—all three converging under the aegis of responsibility; whether responsibility for state sovereignty, for peace and security, or for a complex weighing of interests.

Responsibility has undergone a veritable expansion in the two decades after Bothe. Notably, military action has been legalized when blessed by the Security Council to protect peoples and minorities from their government as in Libya and in the Central African Republic (CAR).[21] Further, the state is increasingly accountable not only for the sustenance of its population, but has to take care of the nature and resources within its territorial borders and also of good governance and prosperity of its citizens.[22] Alongside the expansion of the duties of the states in

---

[18] M Bothe, 'The Legitimacy of the Use of Force to Protect Peoples and Minorities' in C Brölmann, R Lefeber, and M Zieck (eds), *Peoples and Minorities in International Law* (Martinus Nijhoff Dordrecht 1993) 289–99, at 299.

[19] D Campbell, 'The Deterritorialization of Responsibility: Levinas, Derrida, and Ethics after the End of Philosophy' (1994) 19 *Alternatives* 455–84, at 456.

[20] Independent International Commission on Kosovo, *The Kosovo Report* (OUP Oxford 2000) at 10.

[21] *Resolution 1973* (17 March 2011) UN Doc S/RES/1973 and *Resolution 2127* (5 December 2013) UN Doc S/RES/2127 respectively.

[22] M Finnemore, 'Paradoxes in Humanitarian Intervention' in RM Price (ed), *Moral Limit and Possibility in World Politics* (CUP Cambridge 2008) 197–224, at 205; D Chandler, 'Resilience and the "Everyday": Beyond the Paradox of "Liberal Peace"' (2014) 40 *Review of International Studies* 1–20.

the international community, the traditional concepts of international crises have metamorphosed. A threat to peace and security—the veritable crisis of the international order—has in recent years materialized as much in acts of poaching as in acts of systematic destruction by a government of its subjects.[23] The importance of protecting security and peace has been a traditional theme in much of classical liberal political theory from Hobbes onwards. Therefore, it is no revelation for international legal scholarship to stand on the shoulders of these giants whilst trying to understand the transgression of international authority into the realm controlled by sovereign states in the past.

An active human rights agenda and the solidification of liberal democratic society as the ideal state intertwine in the most lauded formulation of novel responsibility. The responsibility to protect (R2P), first articulated in a report of the International Commission on Intervention and State Sovereignty (ICISS) in 2001,[24] and later unanimously endorsed by the UN World Summit of 2005,[25] has gained notable traction both in academia[26] and in the exercise of international authority.[27] The scope of R2P is limited to the gravest violations of the rights enshrined in the UN Charter, the main human rights conventions and the *Rome Statute of the International Criminal Court*,[28] for example genocide, war crimes, ethnic cleansing, and crimes against humanity. Even though the scope of R2P has been limited, there have been a number of critical voices against the renaissance of humanitarian intervention justified by the R2P doctrine. Like Bothe, they see in the R2P a sophisticated reformulation of the Westphalian just war doctrine and, thus,

---

[23] See *Resolution 2127* (n 21) at preamble and para 54 (on poaching as a violation of Central African Republic's international duties); Human Rights Council, 'Report of the Detailed Findings of the Commission of Inquiry on Human Rights in the Democratic People's Republic of Korea' (7 February 2014) UN Doc A/HRC/25/CRP.1 (on the North Korean regime's extensive violations of the international law as constituting a threat to peace and security).

[24] International Commission on Intervention and State Sovereignty, *The Responsibility to Protect* (Ottawa International Development Research Centre Ottawa 2001).

[25] '2005 World Summit Outcome' (14 September 2005) UN Doc A/60/355, at paras 138–9.

[26] See eg the journal *Global Responsibility to Protect* (Brill Leiden); F Egerton and AW Knight (eds), *The Routledge Handbook on the Responsibility to Protect* (Routledge New York 2012); A Orford, *International Authority and the Responsibility to Protect* (CUP Cambridge 2011); RC Thakur, *People vs the State: Reflections on UN Authority, US Power and the Responsibility to Protect* (UN University Press New York 2011); M Labonte, *Human Rights and Humanitarian Norms, Strategic Framing, and Intervention: Lessons for the Responsibility to Protect* (Routledge New York 2012); 'Symposium: The International Criminal Court and the Responsibility to Protect?' (2010) 21 *Finnish Yearbook of International Law* 1–105.

[27] See eg UN Secretary-General, 'Implementing the Responsibility to Protect' (12 January 2009) UN Doc A/63/677 and Permanent Representative of Brazil, 'Letter Dated 9 November 2011 from the Permanent Representative of Brazil to the United Nations Addressed to the Secretary-General' (11 November 2011) UN Docs A/66/551–S/2011/701.

[28] *Rome Statute of the International Criminal Court* (opened for signature 17 July 1998 entered into force 1 July 2002) UNTS.

demand its rejection.[29] For others, R2P fosters humanity, dignity, and/or global justice in international relations.[30] Their argument echoes much the same sentiments as those expressed by Campbell: the sovereign cannot be the sole guardian over its population since guardians also need guardians. A fuzzier third group argues for a complex multivariate calculus to explicate why certain crises necessitate an international response whilst others do not.[31]

The first two strands of R2P emanate from a notion of legality; their main difference lies in the meaningful context of law. Those considering R2P as a restatement of the just war doctrine recognize the sovereign state as the single most important contextual basis for international law. Violating sovereignty renders the international legal order subject to a rule of might whereby the rights and values behind that order are defined by those commanding the greatest power. Such a transgression vacates the very foundation of the UN system, established on 'the principle of the sovereign equality of all its Members' (*UN Charter* art 2). On the other hand, those supporting intervention in the name of humanity base their arguments equally on the *UN Charter*; yet prioritize its first article promoting peace and security in the international community. For them, the constituent element of international community is not the sovereign (state) but the individual. Thus, the meaningful context of inquiry is the well-being of individuals—human security, not merely security in terms of the sovereignty of a state. Thus, violence by a state cannot be justified based on its sovereign power and prerogative. The primary context for understanding rights and responsibilities is the normative human rights framework as accepted by the international community, not their interpretation by a state member of that community.

The third conception of the responsibility to protect transposes the focus of attention from the perceived legality of the rule to its legitimacy.[32] The acts of the international community vis-à-vis threats to peace and security are dictated not solely by legal considerations but also, to a large extent, by political and strategic interests. Both the sovereignty of the state and humanity as whole behind international order are to be considered in the exercise of international authority. Accordingly, the overlapping contexts of sovereignty and human rights are fused

---

[29] See eg M Mamdani, *Saviors and Survivors: Darfur, Politics, and the War on Terror* (Codesria Dakar 2010) at 323; E O'Shea, 'Responsibility to Protect (R2P) in Libya: Ghosts of the Past Haunting the Future' (2012) 1 *International Human Rights Law Review* 173–90.

[30] See eg R Teitel, *Humanity's Law* (OUP Oxford 2011) at 116–20; G Evans and R Thakur, 'Correspondence: Humanitarian Intervention and the Responsibility to Protect' (2013) 37 *International Security* 199–207.

[31] See eg AJ Bellamy, 'The Responsibility to Protect: Added Value or Hot Air?' (2013) 48 *Cooperation and Conflict* 333–57.

[32] Of such tactics, see eg J Vaughn and T Dunne, 'Leading from the Front: America, Libya, and the Localisation of R2P' (2015) 50 *Cooperation and Conflict* 29–49.

with an overall assessment of political feasibility functioning as a trump in deciding the outcome.[33] The authority of the international executive to interfere with
the state's primary duty to protect everyone in its territory emanates from the law
and legal commitments of the state, whilst the exercise of said authority is justified in the politicized setting of the Security Council. Interference based on international authority marks a state of exception to the general legal rule of peaceful
co-existence. Legalizing such an interference with pre-defined criteria would, indeed, mark a return to just war, whilst ignoring a grave violation of human rights
would be a negation of the entire UN project.

According to Agamben, the state of exception cannot be legalized. Rather,
the state of exception is a category *hors* legality.[34] It is within this no wo/man's
land that diluted responsibilities of states can equally amount to interference
as they can to non-interference, as keenly noted by Barnett with regard to the
Rwandan genocide.[35] The state of exception can be read as 'the political point
at which the juridical stops and a sovereign unaccountability begins', as de la
Durantaye explains it.[36] The authorization of the use of force against Libya to
protect civilians issued by the Security Council is illustrative of these aspects
of the state of exception. Security Council *Resolution 1973* authorized the use
of force to protect civilians and areas populated by civilians. What originally
emerged as an operation to protect civilians in the city of Benghazi, eventually
lead to the overthrow of the government with extensive support from NATO-
led air strikes. The civilian casualties from the maintenance of a no-fly zone and
an extensive interpretation of the mandate provided by the Security Council
would be difficult to accommodate under a dogmatic notion of international
law for they respect neither sovereignty nor humanity *stricto sensu*.[37] Thus, the
R2P interpretant seems a temporary abrogation of the rule of law in the international community, which is deemed as the only feasible alternative to solve an
unresolved dilemma.[38] A similar exceptionalism is traceable also in other fields

[33] An acute reminder of these political realities is provided by the reported remarks by the chair
of the committee reporting from the North Korean situation, Michael Kirby, drawing comparisons to responses to Nazi atrocities after the Second World War. 'Now the international community does know. There will be no excusing a failure of action because we didn't know. It's too long
now. The suffering and the tears of the people of North Korea demand action': P Walker, 'North
Korea Human Rights Abuses Resemble Those of the Nazis, Says UN Inquiry' (18 February 2014)
The Guardian.

[34] G Agamben, *State of Exception* (K Attell trans) (University of Chicago Press Chicago 2005).

[35] M Barnett, *Eyewitness to a Genocide: The United Nations and Rwanda* (Cornell University Press
Ithaca 2002) at 154.

[36] L de la Durantaye, *Giorgio Agamben: A Critical Introduction* (Stanford University Press
Stanford 2009) at 338.

[37] For this argument, see 'Responsibility to Protect (R2P) in Libya' (n 29).

[38] From the normalization of the state of exception, see G Frankenberg, *Staatstechnik: Perspektiven
auf Rechtsstaat und Ausnahmezustand* (Suhrkamp Berlin 2010).

of new state responsibility, most notably, in the decision-making on economic and environmental matters.

The economic state of exception and the concomitant state responsibility to alleviate the situation is dated by Agamben to France during the interwar period, where defence of the Franc emerged as a matter of urgency.[39] In the post-colonial social constellation, such economic imperatives were largely directed towards former colonies in Africa and Asia. Through extensive loan-giving and consequent insolvency of many of the former colonies, the International Monetary Fund (IMF) together with private investors gained an exceptional status whereby demands for serious cuts in spending and monetization schemes of natural property were privatized.[40] A similar economic crisis swept through a number of European countries in the aftermath of the 2007/08 financial crises; most notably Greece is subject to far-reaching limitations on its capacity to decide independently on matters of economy. Much as with R2P, the economic state of exception calls for external administration to correct the failing state for its violations towards the dictates of economy. Even outside the states of crisis, widely applied economic exceptionalism has caused a strain on parliamentarism and democracy as executives use such calls for a state of emergency to justify decisions.[41]

In its resolution providing authorization to foreign military forces to restore peace and security in the CAR, the Security Council noted that 'poaching and trafficking of wildlife are among the factors that fuel the crisis', and further, '[c]ondemns the illegal exploitation of natural resources in the CAR'.[42] Alongside people, also nature and its 'resources' were to be protected. Whilst natural resources are seen merely as tools for funding the war, the special value granted to poaching and nature in general is not merely happenstance. It seems, as Benvenisti argues, that states 'are...obligated toward humankind to use the resources under their control efficiently and sustainably'.[43] The global (Occidental) environmental consciousness and the realization of the limited amount of resources renders the question of elephants and tantalum a question of global concern—and, logically, demands responsibility and accountability for them. A careless use of these resources is a general loss for humankind, wherefore they are subject, in the final analysis, to enforcement measures and

---

[39] *State of Exception* (n 34) 13.

[40] See A Anghie, *Imperialism, Sovereignty and the Making of International Law* (CUP Cambridge 2005) at 211; N van de Walle, *African Economies and the Politics of Permanent Crisis, 1979–1999* (CUP Cambridge 2001).

[41] P Leino and J Salminen, 'Should the Economic and Monetary Union Be Democratic After All? Some Reflections on the Current Crisis' (2013) 14 *German Law Journal* 844–68, at 844 and 865.

[42] See UN Secretary-General, 'Report of the Secretary-General on the Central African Republic' (15 November 2013) UN Doc S/2013/677; J Humphreys and MLR Smith, 'War and Wildlife: The Clausewitz Connection' (2011) 87 *International Affairs* 121–42.

[43] E Benvenisti, 'Sovereigns as Trustees of Humanity: On the Accountability of States to Foreign Stakeholders' (2013) 107 *American Journal of International Law* 295–333, at 309.

international authority if breaches occur.[44] Even if climate change could not be contemplated as entailing responsibility, as Fitzmaurice suggests,[45] the more tangible resources have been and increasingly are matters of a state's 'humanitarian' responsibility under the indeterminate principles of sustainable and equitable use.

The expanded concern on the part of international authority ranging from peaceful co-existence of states to welfare of their citizens and sustenance of their resources has also transformed state responsibility from a geopolitical guardianship to a biopolitical actorship. Internalized ideas of common humanity with precise dictates of environmental and economic order are far-flung from minimal formalism emblematic of the world order still tractable in the 1990s and the draft articles on state responsibility (discussed earlier). The continuing rise of and appeal to international authority can be referenced back to the social democratic state of the interwar period. In his writings around the time of the First World War, Swedish state theorist Rudolf Kjellén, describing the state as a life form, comes close to the narrative of the R2P interpretant and the more general responsibility parlance. Kjellén concludes his study of 1916, with a vitalistic notion of the state and its population:

For one thing is certain: only through such a journey [of hardship] his [the stateman's] nation achieves that which for peoples as for individuals means more than happiness, the only thing that truly pays the cost of life, namely the improvement of personality to even greater perfection. Thus, to perfect the natural disposition of the people becomes at last the purpose of the state.[46]

Likewise, international authority has embraced its duty to guide its members towards ever greater perfection of their duties towards common humanity, whose definition remains elusive at best.[47]

In its calls for universalism and humanitarianism, state responsibility within the international setting has expanded to cover politics over life itself. Where early twentieth-century political scholarship attached the state's duty to promote prosperity and thriving to its territory and nation, international authority in the early twenty-first century, on account of permanent exceptionalism—terrorism, economic turmoil, global warming—requires a pastoral responsibility. Here the

---

[44] For a recent case study on states' financial resources in the context of state ownership policies, see M Rajavuori, 'How Should States Own? *Heinisch v. Germany* and the Emergence of Human Rights-Sensitive State Ownership Function' (2015) 26 *European Journal of International Law* 727–46.

[45] M Fitzmaurice, 'Responsibility and Climate Change' (2010) 53 *German Yearbook of International Law* 89–138.

[46] R Kjellén, *Staten som lifsform* (Hugo Gebers Förlag Stockholm 1916) at 183: 'Ty ett är visst: genom en sådan färd allena vinner hans nation det som för folk som för enskilda är förmer än lycka, det enda som i grunden betalar lifvets pris, nämligen personlighetens förbättring till allt större fullkomlighet. Att fullkomna folkanlaget blir sålunda till sist statens mål.'

[47] See D Kennedy, *The Dark Sides of Virtue: Reassessing International Humanitarianism* (Princeton University Press Princeton 2004).

pastoralism demanded by the international authority is akin to that traced by Nikolas Rose in biopolitics:

This is not the kind of pastoralism where a shepherd knows and directs the souls of confused or indecisive sheep. It entails a dynamic set of relations between the effects of those who council and those of the counseled.[48]

International authority is not replacing the sovereign as an absolutist ruler of the state of exception, but rather exercises control over the exceptions that are worthy of pastoral guidance; for example there are no qualitative differences in the outcomes whether people die through bombs, lack of medicine or destruction of the environment through careless industrial policy or mining of crisis minerals. In its pastoral duty to signal what marks a deviation, international authority has far-exceeded its former powers. This shift has taken place to the detriment of states that are no longer able to act in their collective role as shepherds. Authority has overshadowed the multilateral collective. '[A]s risk of the common becomes increasingly extensive, the response of the immune defense becomes increasingly intensive', proclaims Esposito as his immunization thesis.[49] The new interpretant of common managerial responsibility and its corollary—the rise of international authority at the expense of individual states—reflects similar developments as Esposito traces vis-à-vis life. And, consequently, any slipping from the common normative agenda of liberal internationalism intensifies the immune defence of international authority.

4 Response-Ability:
Primacy of Encounters

For the purposes of the present discussion we shall skip over the idea that international law would have a value independent of its meaning in the world. The practice of international law is a discussion on what to do here and now.[50] As Charlesworth and Kennedy write:

[international lawyers] have considerable power in shaping the way problems are identified, categorized and resolved at the international level. We are active participants in intensely

[48] N Rose, *The Politics of Life Itself: Biomedicine, Power, and Subjectivity in the Twenty-First Century* (Princeton University Press Princeton 2007) at 29.

[49] R Esposito, *Immunitas: The Protection and Negation of Life* (Z Hanafi trans) (Polity Cambridge 2011) at 5.

[50] M Koskenniemi, *From Apology to Utopia: The Structure of International Legal Argument* (Lakimiesliiton kustannus Helsinki 1989) at 482.

political and negotiable contexts and we must confront this responsibility without shelter-
ing behind the illusion of an impartial, objective, legal order.[51]

Analogically to Weber's postwar point on political decisions, all responsible governance decisions—including international legal—must account for the probable
and real consequences of the use or non-use of normative power.[52] Vertraeten
explains that 'responsibility conceived in this way...does not stand on its own,
rather it forms a triad together with clarity of insight and political passion', a statement that parallels Koskenniemi's view of international law as secular faith.[53]

In the praxis of such 'here and now' discussions international lawyers do not
confine themselves to interpretants one and two (discussed earlier): they reflect on
doctrine, strategy, management, feasibility, effects, and meanings as a package—
and the limits, borders, and potentials; the insides and the outsides of the system
of international law itself. The practical routines of international lawyering cross-
influence the context of international relations and vice versa; both affecting
change and changing themselves.

The third interpretant of responsibility is non-reductive, indeterminate, and dynamic. Its conceptual scope is open beyond the formal, dogmatic, or managerial
ideas and authorities; it encompasses the former but only together with the understanding that unforeseen, indeterminate claims will keep arising in the world as
the cross-influences, effects, and continuous changes described earlier manifest in
international affairs.[54] The third interpretant of responsibility proceeds from the
claim that its commands exist in an inter-relationship of law–world–lawyer, in a
situated conception of law that constantly defies systemic closures and totalities.[55]
Thus, law including responsibility cannot be isolated from practice in and effects
upon the world including the (re)creation of meaning, significance, and 'currency'
in the lives of their users and their subjects (lawyers, judges, and so on). Hence, responsibility is discussed through a dialogical analysis of the ability to respond to
'real-world' problems that present themselves to legal intervention and, on the other
hand, the occasional need to defer or encounter radical difference (otherness).[56]
Both the ability and the deference are implied by all three—the law, its users, and

[51] H Charlesworth and D Kennedy, 'Afterword: and Forward—There Remains So Much We Don't
Know' in A Orford (ed), *International Law and Its Others* (CUP Cambridge 2006) 401–8, at 408.

[52] M Weber, *Politik als Beruf* (4th edn Duncker & Humblot Berlin 1964) at 51.

[53] J Verstraeten, 'The Tension between "Gesinnungsethik" and "Verantwortungsethik": A Criti
cal Interpretation of the Position of Max Weber in "Politik als Beruf"' (1995) 2 *Ethical Perspectives*
180–7, at 182; M Koskenniemi, 'The Fate of Public International Law' (2007) 70 *Modern Law Review*
1–30, at 30.

[54] O Korhonen, *International Law Situated: The Lawyer's Stance towards Culture, History, and
Community* (Kluwer Law International The Hague 2000).

[55] Ibid.

[56] O Korhonen, 'On Strategizing Justiciability in International Law' (1999) 10 *Finnish Yearbook
of International Law* 91–101, at 99; O Korhonen, 'The Place of Ethics in International Law' (1998) 80
Reatfaerd 3–20.

the world. That is, none of the three elements is only either a master (actor) or ser-vant (target) vis-à-vis each other, and none of them should be taken as a mask or shelter for each other, as Charlesworth and Kennedy caution above.

To illustrate this by means of the *Nuclear Weapons* Advisory Opinion[57] and its questions of substance and strategy, one can ask whether the law has a response to the legality of the threat or use of nuclear weapons, which is a (theoretically) dif-ferent but related question to whether a court (lawyers and judges) can and should respond to it, a question in which justiciability strategy also plays a part.[58] The lat-ter is again different yet tied to the question of the significance of the threat and the use of nuclear weapons in the world—including the questions as to what legal consequences and what situational effects (to the law/lawyer/world) they entail.

The International Court of Justice took an unusual decision when responding to the legality of the nuclear weapons question by saying that 'the Court cannot conclude definitely whether the threat or use of nuclear weapons would be law-ful or unlawful in an extreme circumstance of self-defense'.[59] This decision has been characterized as a formalistic *non liquet* or as a management decision apply-ing the political question doctrine to international law.[60] Its *ratio decidendi* has been explained as strategic; once seen as politically impossible to persuade the nu-clear club to disarm, the Court must protect its (and the law's and common inter-national) authority by not rendering decisions that would be ignored.[61] Even if this reasoning does not seem to sit with many other hard cases—for example the *Wall Opinion* and the *Temple Case*[62]—it illustrates how formalistic legal responses may be fitted into a strategic, in other words, managing authority rationale when con-troversial cases hit. The shift of interpretant (from first to second, above) enables a bird's eye view of hard formal choices, and thus, makes these seem solvable on higher grounds (rationales). Thus, a proportionate nuclear first use in extreme self-defence cannot be said always to trigger formalist international legal responsibility according to the ICJ; and such indecision (inability to respond and allocate respon-sibility) can be explained as a defence of the Court's, the law's, and the common international authority vis-à-vis power politics that should be left outside law. And, therefore, it can be said to be responsible in a higher sense (second interpretant),

---

[57] *Legality of the Threat or Use of Nuclear Weapons* (Advisory Opinion) [1996] ICJ Rep 226.

[58] 'On Strategizing Justiciability' (n 56); K Kulovesi, 'Legality or Otherwise? Nuclear Weapons and the Strategy of Non Liquet' (1999) 10 *Finnish Yearbook of International Law* 55–89.

[59] *Nuclear Weapons* (n 57) para 105(2)(e), adopted by a vote of 7:7 with the President issuing the casting vote.

[60] 'Legality or Otherwise?' (n 58).   [61] Ibid.

[62] The *Wall Opinion* is an example of an advisory opinion delivered in a hard superpower-involving case, and the *Temple Case* an example of a dispute that reappeared on the docket for reasons of non-compliance: see *Legal Consequences of the Construction of a Wall in the Occupied Palestinian Territories* (Advisory Opinion) [2004] ICJ Rep 136; *Request for Interpretation of the Judgment of 15 June 1962 in the Case Concerning the Temple of Preah Vihear (Cambodia v Thailand)* (Judgment) [2013] ICJ Rep 281.

that is, demonstrating the ability to respond to strategic demands for law's (common) authority in the world. However, in the third interpretant of responsibility in international law, it is key to see that the most relevant questions do not end but rather start there.

In fact and as also recognized by the formal/strategic actors, demands grow from and alongside international legal practice, that is, the discussion of what to do here and now with burning problems. Hence, the Court recognized in the lead up to the decision (para 105(2)(e)) that it only applied 'in view of the current state of international law, and of the elements of fact at its disposal'.[63] Thus, the decision's closure (*non liquet*) provided by the Court was explicitly at best momentary, situational, tied to the current state of the law and elements of fact as discovered then. Since then, questions of law, elements of fact, and burning worldly concerns around nuclear matters have continued to arise: for example, what is the status of the nuclear club[64] vis-à-vis other sovereign states? How does one square sovereign equality and the responsibility for the maintenance of peace and security as the world changes and the Nuclear Non-Proliferation Treaty (NPT)[65] has frozen the nuclear weapons privilege to the situation and the power-rationale of 1968 (extended indefinitely in 1995), a move that cannot sustain self-evidence, necessity or any other sort of a priori legitimacy over time? Furthermore, the nuclear questions keep arising as both real and symbolic currency in, for example, the Middle East situation as well as in the China–Taiwan–Korea and India–Pakistan conundrums. The formalist *non liquet* indeterminacy and the strategic response of defending institutional and international authority (of the law, the Court, and the 'common') offer little if anything in the way of continuously demanded responses; the 'here and now' requires their reconsideration *ad infinitum*. Cosmopolitan pacifism or managerial reponsibilization and deference to international authority does not seem to bring about reassuring solutions to nuclear threats.

To rehearse a response-ability dialogue in international law's present-day practical challenges, one might ask what the international legal position on the decades of dance around the Iranian nuclear program would be. One would look beyond the formalist response and deferral on the basis of Iran not being among the NPT's nuclear club members any more than are Israel, India, Pakistan, or the Koreas; but also beyond the strategic, managerial response that may be equally meaningless and powerless in proposing to defer this political question to the P5+1[66]

---

[63] *Nuclear Weapons* (n 57).

[64] The NPT defines the five nuclear weapons states; they are the five permanent members of the UN Security Council: see *Treaty on the Non-Proliferation of Nuclear Weapons* (opened for signature 1 July 1968 entered into force 5 March 1970) 729 UNTS 161.

[65] Ibid.

[66] Since 2006 international negotiations with Iran on its nuclear program have been periodically conducted by a group of states including the five permanent members of the UN Security Council and Germany.

in order for them to strike a geopolitical balance in the Middle East that, idealistically, would manage a post-Arab Spring stabilization and establish human security without the need for much international legal process. It would take the political question 'doctrine' to justify deference away from law and legal minds, presuming that these are 'separate' from 'political' ones. In line with the second interpretant above, one may also argue the humanitarian rationales in order to ease the sanctions that cripple the health, nutrition, and other economic, social, and cultural rights of the Iranians—and 'our' authority implying responsibility to protect them even if a (an irresponsible) domestic government of a pre-defined rogue state fails this duty.

However, if the international legal response stops either at the apology for the frozen moment of the formal terms of the NPT and/or the utopia of transnational human rights protection, it manifests an inability to respond to the actual and practical terms of a deal with Iran and defers the relevance of law and its normative power. It falls short of bringing to the table the open international legal questions on nuclear weapons in the 'here and now' of Iran in the present regional and global context; and the abundance of international legal questions arising from the Middle East situation that a deal with Iran will necessarily cross-influence greatly. What are the costs and benefits of the terms of the deal for these questions? How are responsibilities for intended and unintended effects allocated? Surely, there is a long list of similar issues as, for instance, in the various rounds of the World Trade Organization deals or the long-negotiated codification of the law of the sea regime (in UNCLOS). Yet, to succumb to cynical reason in the shadow of the bomb,[67] to the irrelevance of international legal practice, and to the inability of international law to respond to such complex bundles of contested interests, accumulations of historical wrongs, and political hot rods as, for instance, the Middle East, excuses the potentials of international law and lawyers. And, thus, it fails the third sense of responsibility in international law; it fails, in Gadamer's terms, law's primary duty as a service (Dienst) to the world.[68] In the third interpretant, international law does not exist separated from its actual significance, which flows from its ability to recognize, encounter, and respond to real world problems.

The service can only be rendered after the recognition of the needs and demands, and their translation into legal questions as above. To defer something outside, that is, to deny its recognition, is an act of exclusion that always impacts the relevance of all three: the relevance of law, the worldly question, and the lawyer's practice and craft. Is international law relevant to nuclear weapons? Is international law relevant to the Middle East situation? The replies turn on which aspects are re/cognized

---

[67] P Sloterdijk, Critique of Cynical Reason (University of Minnesota Press Minneapolis 1997) at 131: Sloterdijk sees the bomb as the consummation of the Western 'subject'.

[68] HG Gadamer, Wahrheit und Methode (2nd edn Mohr Tübingen 1965) at 293 and 295.

and which potentials of wielding normative power on them are contemplated, referenced, and utilized. What emerges is the 'jurisprudence of the limit' as Orford explains, jurisprudential stances and reflections of the pros and cons of

[the] variety of ways to come to terms with the complicated and infinite process of constituting the self (law or lawyer) in relation to the other (worldly phenomena) through the institutions of law and language.[69]

Yet, the process at the 'limit' must recognize the risk that 'the other can only ever be represented by accommodating or assimilating it to existing economies, languages or practices'[70] except, perhaps, in strictly momentary encounters that respect the situationalist dictate for validity—in other words, that it is conditioned on a 'here and now' that remains open and diffuse at its borders. Parsley demonstrates the risks of totalizing assimilation in various encounters with indigenous peoples in Australia, in particular in the case of the taking of 'mixed race' indigenous children ('The Stolen Generation'), indigenous peoples in general, and the law including rights regimes. He observes that

attribution of subjectivity on the Western liberal model leads to the position where the relationship between an indigenous person or group and property is conceptualized as the same as that subsisting in (Western) law—ultimately enabling the treatment of indigenous property as alienable.[71]

Through formal recognition and fitting of an indigenous other to a pre-existing mould in a pre-existing systemic totality, the other while granted 'subjectivity' or rights is deprived of its non-systemic qualities, issues, demands; and, simultaneously, our ability to offer responses to them is radically handicapped if not lost.[72] There is a performance failure as to '"capturing anomie", or walking and transgressing a boundary between the inside and outside of the sovereign (systemic) order', as Parsley concludes.[73] In short, the 'here and now' of encountering, re/cognizing and responding—that is, response-ability in the triangle of law–lawyer–world—is foiled.

Kennedy's academic and practical intervention in 'Spring Break' against the violation of the prohibition of torture is a prime example of negotiating the wielding of normative power without assimilating the subjectivity of the 'other' reality and situation.[74]

---

[69] A Orford, 'A Jurisprudence of the Limit' in *International Law and Its Others* (n 51) 1–32, at 4.

[70] Ibid. The caution has also been prominent in the field of 'subaltern studies'.

[71] C Parsley, 'Seasons in the Abyss: Reading *Cubillo*' in *International Law and Its Others* (n 51) 100–28, at 121.

[72] Of similar effect of exclusion through category of persons in the West, see R Esposito, 'The Person and Human Life' in J Elliott and D Attridge (eds), *Theory after 'Theory'* (Routledge London 2011) 205–19.

[73] 'Seasons in the Abyss' (n 71) 127.

[74] D Kennedy, *The Rights of Spring: A Memoir of Innocence Abroad* (Princeton University Press Princeton 2009); D Kennedy 'Spring Break' (1985) 63 *Texas Law Review* 1377–1424.

Another example, provided originally by Badiou,[75] and later explored by Feltham vis-à-vis illegal immigrants[76] and their demands for rights in France illustrates the problem of borders. By accepting rights belonging to everyone—also to those not intimately connected to a nation through citizenship—the notion of citizen is transmuted at the core, as it does expand to cover those excluded from it. To provide rights to illegal immigrants is to make them part of a 'nation', and the law's ability to accommodate such rights signals its response-ability, even though the moment of recognition marks the moment of disappearance of the 'other' as perceived in the actual conflict at the border. The law is equally well capable of finding itself unable to respond by expanding its borders to cover that which is not.

Response-ability in international law is a complex but highly practical effort that sustains the inter-related relevance of law–lawyers–world to each other through the potential of systemic openness. Unlike interpretants one and two, its progress comes from continued (re)negotiation of the terms of the old, the new and the unknown, not from permanent closure, codification, and/or normalization.

[75] A Badiou, *Theory of the Subject* (B Bosteels trans) (Continuum London 2009 [1982]) at 262–4. Badiou concludes this chapter on illegal immigrants at 264 with the very problem: 'The subject *is* the splace, as that which has become, through the inexistent, from what has been destroyed.'

[76] O Feltham and A Badiou, *Live Theory* (Continuum London 2008) at 67–70.

CHAPTER 42

....

THEORIZING PRIVATE INTERNATIONAL LAW

....

HORATIA MUIR WATT

1 PART OF THE PROBLEM?

....

As a matter of epistemology, legal method and theory can sometimes be hard to differentiate.[1] This difficulty, which sets law apart from the (other?) social sciences, is well illustrated in the case of private international law, of which the hallmark has been, traditionally, its predominantly methodological content. Private international law is understood to operate at a remove from substantive rules on a procedural or jurisdictional plane or meta-level prior to any judicial enquiry into the merits of particular cases, which it assigns (at least metaphorically) to different (national) legal sub-systems. Indeed, broadly defined in technical terms, classical private international law[2] is generally understood by both courts and scholars to

---

[1] G Samuel, 'Taking Methods Seriously (Part Two)' (2007) 2 *Journal of Comparative Law* 210–36, at 214, explaining that any attempt to discover an epistemological meta-theory for legal method encounters the double difficulty of being sufficiently distanced from the *res* (legal method as object) and liberated enough from the legal norm that law is authority (and not to be questioned as a form of knowledge).

[2] There is much in a name. Part of the problem (to borrow from D Kennedy, 'The International Human Rights Movement: Part of the Problem?' (2001) 3 *European Human Rights Law Review* 254–67) may be traced to the inadequacies and uncertainties affecting the components of the name coined by Justice Joseph Story: J Story, *Commentaries on the Conflict of Laws, Foreign and Domestic* (Hilliard, Gray & Co Boston 1834). Its 'private' dimension was initially understood in opposition to

define the competent court, applicable law, and status of foreign judgments in transnational settings without regard for the final result in terms of individual rights and obligations or indeed of wider policy concerns.

This emphasis on method has eminently political consequences. The specifically 'allocative' stance (or distance) of private intentional law has nurtured the conventional view that it is normatively neutral, since it sets the field beyond domestic politics and above private interests. The regulatory dimension of this architectural function, along with the values that such an allocation may serve, has been hidden from view. And while the field has been shaken from time to time by contestation on this point (domestic policy analysis in the United States (US); current human rights jurisprudence in Europe), private international law nevertheless remains largely disconnected today from those issues of global governance on which it might have been specifically qualified to make a useful contribution. This is the case, in particular, where the rise of private transnational authority modifies the distributional consequences of legal institutions within the global economy, and where the emergence of communities beyond the state challenge conventional views of identity and membership.

At the same time, the overwhelming attention devoted to methodology, self-consciously unhampered by politics, has fostered a remarkable quantity of doctrinal speculation as to the foundations of this particular branch of the law, as distinct from both its public international and domestic law counterparts. The epistemological perspective from which this speculation has developed has remained consistently internal, however, meaning that it has elevated the specific methods of private international law to the rank of general theory. Thus, there is little search for an explanatory or normative framework among sources outside the discipline itself.

Nevertheless, the state of the conceptual art in this field tends to bear the imprint of the other departments of legal scholarship with which theorists of private international law tend most closely to associate their field. Thus, on the one hand, the dominant market-led approach to the regulation of global economic exchange owes much to the liberal theory of private law. This is perhaps most evident within the dominant, dogmatic strand of continental legal theory, which has its strongest philosophical underpinnings in Savigny's legacy of private law scholarship

'public' international law, and moreover by reference to the public/private legal divide foundational to legal epistemology in the nineteenth century. A hundred years later, across the Atlantic, private international law had been irrevocably and dogmatically linked to the domain of private law (within the civilian understanding of the category) where, like procedural law and in opposition to domestic policy, it was supposedly neutral or apolitical and could not transgress the divide (hence the 'public law taboo' excluding the justiciability of foreign public law claims). Moreover, its 'international' reach mirrored the representation carried by public international law of a world of multiple territorial states, so that it dealt exclusively with the consequences of contacts between state laws, ignoring forms of transnational normativity beyond the territorial community.

within the Roman tradition.[3] Here, method has traditionally been harnessed to further the perceived interests of the 'international legal order'—represented as a space devoted to inter-individual commerce beyond the state, and as such aspiring to both 'harmony' and 'legal certainty' (meaning that, in a bewildering world of conflicting regulations, status and personal relationships must be governed by the most reasonably predictable rules and thereafter recognized on the same terms everywhere). For example, the ideal of a permanent 'personal status' requires that issues of identity and family ties be regulated by the 'principle of nationality' (in the post-Napoleonic tradition), wherever the person is geographically located. Beneath the functional concern for cross-border consistency in private affairs, lies the assumption of the universal reach of the ecclesiastical canons of the Catholic Church as non-terrestrial sovereign.

While the link to liberal theories of private law is certainly emblematic of continental private international legal scholarship in the civilian tradition, the (English) common law tradition follows a more market-led orientation, which is in many respects the extension of domestic commercial law doctrine to transnational settings. Moreover, a combination of factors—the ancient legal fiction of local venue; extensive judicial discretion as to the exercise of jurisdiction in international cases; attachment to the law of the domicile of origin (that is, English law) for the regulation of personal status in the colonial setting; hypertrophy of issues characterized as procedural and subject as such to the rules of the forum; English influence in the field of seafaring trade and the law merchant, conducive to the predominance of English law in maritime transactions—has left little space for the application of foreign laws while accentuating the jurisdictional dimension of the field.

Today, English private international law is very largely a matter of contractual choice of law and forum. A similar expansion of contract is perceptible in more global trends, where traditional brands of theory seem to have been overtaken by the concerns of a market for legal products and arbitration. Across the Atlantic in the US, federalism concerns have led to an eclipse of the discipline, which signify that it has trouble surviving any deviation of its focus from method to policy, or from procedure to substantive values. On the European front, private international law may be faced with a similar challenge.

On the other hand, private international law has retained notions of justice developed within classical public international legal theory, at a time when the disciplines were still, if not indistinct, at least closely intertwined. Thus, while it is true that there has been some overflow more recently from various theoretical sites (such as regulatory federalism, comparative constitutionalism, fundamental rights, feminism, or theories of regulation) it is most common to find a formulation of private international legal theory which, expressed in terms of its ends and

---

[3] FC von Savigny, *Private International Law: A Treatise on the Conflict of Laws and the Limits of Their Operation in respect of Place and Time* (W Guthrie ed and trans) (T & T Clark Edinburgh 1869).

values, refers to a world viewed either from the perspective of interacting sovereign states or from that of mobile economic actors. Private international law, it is said, ensures predictability in an environment of legal pluralism, pursues a specific concept of transnational justice distinct from the purely domestic variety, and fulfils the interests of the community of states by providing harmony and mutual adjustment in jurisdictional concerns.

This does not mean that legal technique cannot be seen in some instances as a proxy for further theoretical considerations, such as lateral thinking or reflexivity.[4] Similarly, the purely allocatory or architectural function of private international law lends itself to a re-interpretation as a specific brand of transnational constitutionalism. In this view, it would be designed to bring issues linked to the extraterritorial exercise of power within the focus of domestic process, in order to protect the interests of foreign affected communities.[5] However, in the main, the predominantly technical focus of the discipline has diverted attention from the triple political issues of democracy, accountability, and identity in transnational society, and their theoretical counterparts. This means that it has not dealt with issues arising from the contractualization of public authority across borders; or from emerging private standard-setting beyond the state; or from new forms of community and status which do not fit within traditional state boundaries or social categories. It also suggests that there is little linkage between issues pertaining to new strategies and structures of 'global law' beyond the state and contemporary debates in other fields such as social and political theory. Correlatively, there is scarce regard within private international law for the urgent economic and social problems which haunt the transnational arena.

Contrasting with the discipline's internal methodological sophistication, the dearth of theory in this field is only apparently paradoxical. Indeed, the received account of its genealogy as a constant historical recurrence of two great methodological schemes serves to restrict the possible understandings of the goals which private international law is, or could be, pursuing, as well as the distributional consequences it serves and its conceptual links with connected areas such as transnational justice. Expressed as a series of open-textured philosophical considerations about the necessary balance to be struck between private justice and the public good, between the needs of national policy and the interests of international commerce, the theory of private international law tends to be reduced to a set of standard arguments and counter-arguments, intertwined with issues of

---

[4] R Michaels, 'Post-Critical Private International Law: From Politics to Technique—A Sketch' in H Muir Watt and DP Fernández Arroyo (eds), *Private International Law as Global Governance* (OUP Oxford 2014) 55–69.

[5] J Bomhoff, 'The Constitution of the Conflict of Laws' in *Private International Law as Global Governance* (n 4) 263–77; H Muir Watt, 'Private International Law beyond the Schism' (2011) 2 *Transnational Legal Theory* 347–427; C McLachlan, 'The Allocative Function of Foreign Relations Law' (2011) 82 *British Yearbook of International Law* 349–80, at 356.

method.[6] Familiar concerns oppose public policy and private interests, sovereignty and private autonomy, territory and extraterritoriality, substantive goals and the requirements of harmony or legal security at the transnational level. Today, as for the medieval jurists, these pairs are used to frame the question of whether and how a rule can be made to extend (metaphorically) beyond the sovereign territory of its author so as to bring a foreign subject to account under the rules of the forum.

This sense of ahistoricity or continuum cultivated within the discipline tends to accentuate the difficulty which legal theory in general encounters today in coming to terms with the various mutations of nationhood and statehood linked to global-ization and the correlative rise (or return) of non-state authority and normativity. The methods of contemporary private international law tend to hinge exclusively upon assumptions about the state, authority, and territory which emerged towards the latter half of the nineteenth century at the same time as the formation of public international law as a distinct discipline. Public international law has also had to tackle the hybridization of sovereignty through the emergence of transnational private authority (multinational firms, non-governmental organizations (NGOs), standard-setting bodies), but the conceptual apparatus of private international law has had paradoxically little to offer on this point. Moreover, its inadequate theor-etical foundations have prevented any contribution to the epistemological adjust-ments required by new understandings of law beyond the state which defy the schemes of intelligibility relevant to (domestic) normative ordering.

In order to better understand this paradox, the reflection that follows views the current state of the art through the prism of the three main explanatory models which might be said to represent the field cross-culturally—that is, in the (mainly Western) world which participated in modern international law and the schism between the public and the private. It also attempts, for each of these models, to pinpoint the reasons for their failure to address adequately the contemporary problems of the transnational sphere. Those problems are frequently linked to the profound transformations affecting the political foundations, structure, texture, and content of law beyond the state. The focus of this chapter is on the social and economic consequences of private international law as it stands, both for the dis-tribution of power in a transnational setting and for issues of identity and com-munity in a world in which new polities are emerging. However, it also attempts to highlight the potential insights provided by each of these existing models, which in some novel combination may help pave the way towards a renewed theoretical approach to private international law.

The three explanatory models considered in the following sections are based on conflict, cooperation, and competition. Each uses a distinct vocabulary: protection

---

[6] On the semiotics of private international law and inspired by Duncan Kennedy's structural analysis of private law argument, see H Muir Watt, 'A Semiotics of Private International Legal Argument' (2012–13) 14 *Yearbook of Private International Law* 51–70.

of sovereignty or state interests, conflicts of systems or, more recently, norm-collision; international harmony, comity, enlightened self-interest, or the mutual convenience of nations; and regulatory arbitrage and competition, a free market for legal products and judicial services, and the interests of the business community. Each proposes a vision which extends beyond the domestic legal sphere, and rests upon a specific combination of public and private interests, encompassing those of states and private economic actors, in addition to which there may or may not be a third component of concerns (the 'international legal order'). Moreover, each model entertains a complex, historically circular relationship with method, which within each paradigm takes on a variable, ideal form as a remedy or support to the particular problem or goal defined. Thus, the choice between available methods may be seen to serve, equally and alternatively, public or private interests, and can be made to fit a conflictual, cooperative, or competitive paradigm. Three main methodologies can be identified: unilateralism, multilateralism, and party choice. Each of these may serve, alternatively or successively, the different ends identified within a given teleological scheme.[7] Each can be made to express an enlightened view of the reasonable purport of jurisdiction in an ideal world, or the reflection of probable private expectations as to the laws and jurisdictions which may be relevant in a particular instance. Each, therefore, can be seen to suit a world-vision which sees multiple legal systems as concurrent, collaborative or colliding, with the significant distributional consequences that those visions entail.

2 CONFLICT

2.1 State of the Art

Historically, or at least according to the conventional genealogy of the discipline, the first main conceptual model was framed in terms of conflict between various

---

[7] Thus, for instance, as will be seen later in the chapter, the use of party choice in different forms (free choice of law or forum, options opened as among different fora, and so forth), may appear either as an extreme form of private convenience and predictability, or, alternatively, as a specifically regulatory tool designed to stimulate inter-jurisdictional competition. In turn, unilateralism can accommodate policy analysis and normative pluralism, and can be driven by tolerance and adaptability, as much as it can show closure, dogmatic rigidity, and chauvinism. And finally, the pattern which emerges under the aegis of the multilateralist model may be either an enlightened view of the reasonable thrust of sovereign will in an ideal world, or the reflection of probable private expectations as to the laws and jurisdictions which may be relevant in a particular instance.

systems of law, each claiming exclusive jurisdiction to regulate, according to its own views, a given person, thing or relationship. Such a model is considered to have originated with the largely medieval European doctrine known as 'statutism', which sought to define the spatial application of conflicting customs or written statutes of the various provinces and city-states that preceded the rise of the nation-state. According to this doctrine, each polity defines the reach of its own prescriptive jurisdiction and, correlatively, must refrain from imposing limits upon its peers. Generally the assumption here is that law operates territorially and does not (and should not) seek to regulate persons or things located outside that territory. However, when it is acknowledged that this is merely an assumption and that there will always be a discrepancy in the way overarching principles are perceived,[8] there needs to be some form of a mediating principle to solve overlaps and gaps. Indeed, a defining feature of unilateral methodology in all its forms is that the search for the latter—solutions to 'true' conflicts—is by necessity the methodological crux. At this point, the 'conflict of laws' (and in continental terminology, the 'conflict of jurisdictions') within this first paradigm may be viewed from two different perspectives.

The first perspective from which the unilateralist methodology may be seen is from the standpoint of sovereign actors in the exercise of their jurisdiction, which may be limited, countered, or frustrated by other sovereigns whenever a given object of regulation finds itself outside any clearly defined domestic sphere. Methodologically, therefore, this stance can be associated with the unilateral delineation of sovereignty. This perspective has prevailed most naturally in a (Westphalian) world of nation-states after the failure of religious, colonial, or cultural universalizing grand plans (which, as we shall see, are the hallmark of the multilateralist methodology).

The principal theoretical dilemma here is to explain how a sovereign can give effect on its own territory (that is, before its own courts) to the order of a foreign sovereign, since the power to define the reach of sovereign power in respect of private or domestic cases is perceived as an expression of sovereignty itself. The theory of 'vested rights' was invented to explain how a sovereign could obey or give effect to the authority of another within its own territory (before its own courts).[9] By virtue of this theory a foreign sovereign order was transformed into an individual pre-acquired right or downgraded to the status of fact. Recognition of rights privately vested avoided submitting formally to the direct authority of foreign sovereign laws—and honour, or sovereignty is saved.

---

[8] Marginally, the extraterritorial thrust of a legal rule or set of rules may then need to be justified by the 'personal' nature of such rules, meaning that they concern the individual's personal and family status and follow her wherever she is located.

[9] AV Dicey, *A Digest of the Law of England with Reference to the Conflict of Laws* (2nd edn Stevens London 1908) at 1–2. Inspired by the Dutch school and, particularly, the maxims of Ulrich Huber, vested rights doctrine is sometimes completed (Story) sometimes not (Dicey) by Huber's concept

However, this conceptual device contained an implicit but necessary methodological component. There can be no vested private right, first, if the forum has already created a conflicting right, and secondly, if a sovereign law has not operated beforehand, at least potentially, to ensure its protection. The device rests therefore on the implicit assumption that the scope of sovereign laws is pre-determined and exclusive. Given the political context in which the vested rights doctrine emerged and prospered, the key was certainly territory, perceived politically as the guarantee of the independence of the new Protestant (Dutch) state. In jurisprudential terms, that linkage of territory and sovereignty was also associated with the overthrowing of the universal reach of canon law and the disappearance of pre-Westphalian multiple overlapping legal (religious, professional, cultural) orders in a given territory.

Contemporary applications of public-orientated unilateralism tend to be carried by the language of state interests rather than sovereignty. At least as far as the thrust of prescription or regulation is concerned, they tend to relate to specific policies or rules rather than to abstract legal systems, and as such entail a functionalist analysis. The unilateralist approach requires identifying the purposes of the conflicting rules and assessing in that light whether it would further a particular policy to apply either or both of these rules to a given set of facts. Its most spectacular expression emerged in the US in the 1960s under the influence of Brainerd Currie, where it became known as the 'functionalist revolution'.[10] Its greatest contributions were issue-by-issue analysis and the distinction between true/false conflicts. This involved reasoning in terms of specific questions, rather than broad categories, and applying those questions to the substantive rule whose application made most sense in policy terms—in most cases, only one of the potentially colliding rules really claimed (or had an 'interest') in providing the solution. Such an approach was rejected at the time in Europe in no uncertain terms by private international legal scholarship on the grounds that private law rules were policy-neutral. Arguably, however, it was already present in medieval statutism, according to which given categories of rules were considered to have a given reach (personal or territorial) by reason of the assumed general (or pre-assigned) policies they pursued (such as protection of persons or security of territory).[11]

of comity: see U Huber, 'De conflictu legum diversarum in diversis imperiis' in *Praelectiones iuris Romani et hodierni* (1689).

[10] See SC Symeonides, 'The American Choice-of-Law Revolution in the Courts: Today and Tomorrow' (2002) 298 *Recueil des Cours* 9–448.

[11] More recently, in the European context, a similar phenomenon has emerged (as an exceptional methodology, however, designed to counterbalance contractual choice of law) known as '*lois de police*' or internationally mandatory rules, carrying imperious policies of which the fulfilment requires 'immediate' application, that is, they may not be contracted out of, or set aside under a non-policy-based method. Dethroning the more traditional public policy exception, they signal the incursion of policy considerations onto a scene where method still assumes the universality of private law. They will no doubt not be able to be channelled as exceptions for long (as their use extends outside

A further expression of public-interest based unilateralism can also be found today at the jurisdictional level, where a similar idea commands that each sovereign define the scope of its own (adjudicative) jurisdiction (in other words, the cases which it will decide and the cases in which it will give effect to other judgments). Except where it is synonymous with deliberate political closure to foreign interests, unilateralist methodology usually calls for a balancing or mediating principle. The doctrine of 'comity' plays this role. Historically, comity provided an explanatory principle grounded not in deference but in enlightened cooperation, for considering the laws of other sovereigns (with a view to reciprocity). By contrast, however, it is used today to justify non-intervention. In this respect, it can appear as a form of protectionism to the extent that it is a decision *not* to discipline national champions which might otherwise be subject to regulation. Thus, disputes over the demands of comity are at the heart of contemporary debates about the social responsibility or conduct regulation of multinational private actors.[12]

'Unilateralist' methodology also underlies a second, entirely different, private-orientated perspective, which turns its back on public international law and implicit or explicit public definitions of the reach of sovereignty, and purports to deal with the consequences of diverse legal orders from the standpoint of individual predictability in the transnational sphere. It draws attention to the obstacles that individuals encounter by reason of simultaneous, contradictory sovereign commands, and then puts into practice a generalized system of protection of legitimate expectations, purportedly outside any pre-defined plan as to the scope of jurisdiction. In the main, its practical applications have concerned foreign judgments or public acts: where an effective judgment (or public act) exists and generates a belief that it has disposed definitively of a given dispute (or relationship), it is considered fair to the individuals who have placed their faith in the authority of that act or judgment to give it effect within the forum, at least to the extent that such faith is reasonable in the circumstances given the links between the court (or public authority) and the subject matter of the dispute. This latter condition allows private international law of the recognizing forum to reintroduce its own requirements of geographical or personal connection. Today, however, the precept of recognition has been developed further in the field of family relationships under article 8 of the *European Convention on Human Rights*, which requires that effect be given to such relationships developed elsewhere, even if they are not compliant with the canons of reasonableness set by the forum.[13] The underlying idea is that expectations of continuity (or validity) of a particular legal relationship should not be upset for

---

instances of party choice, as illustrated by EC Regulation No 864/2007 on the Law Applicable to Non-Contractual Obligations (11 July 2007) OJEU L 199/40 (*Rome II*).

[12] *Kiobel v Royal Dutch Petroleum Co*, 133 SCt 1659 (2013).

[13] *Convention for the Protection of Human Rights and Fundamental Freedoms* (signed 4 November 1950 entered into force 3 September 1953) 213 UNTS 2889.

reasons that are only concerned with the accident of frontiers and the subsequent diversity of legal regimes.[14]

2.2 Potential Insights

From these various understandings of the foundations of unilateralist method-ology, several important insights can be garnered with a view to the elaboration of a contemporary theory of private international law in a complex world. First, either because of its pre-modern roots, or perhaps because it prospered initially in a common law setting, the conflict paradigm with its unilateralist method has paid very little attention to the distinction between public and private law. It 'works' as a heuristic regardless of the categorization of legal rules. This explains why its con-temporary applications (to ensure either the exceptional intervention of manda-tory public economic regulation or '*lois de police*', or the primacy of fundamental rights) are designed precisely to overcome the shortcomings of rival (multilat-eralist) methodologies. The adequate treatment of both these significant contem-porary phenomena requires ignoring the foundational public/private distinction within classical legal thought, which remains a mark of the European civilian tradition.[15] Furthermore, and perhaps most significantly, private international law might thereby relate to what has been defined as a new field of 'foreign relations law' with distinct public policy aspects, relating in particular to the extraterritorial reach of power in respect of foreign citizens and communities.[16] This might in turn allow it to reconnect with issues of the migration of populations and the status of aliens, which have steadily been wiped from the private international legal map.[17]

Secondly, unilateralist method is similarly indifferent to the law/fact divide which has proved equally foundational to the modern Western legal tradition

---

[14] The same idea finds expression *ex ante* in multilateralist methodology through the choice of nationality or domicile as (stable) connecting factors. Unilateralism, rejecting the grand plan that the latter suppose, imposes recognition *ex post*, once the relationship has been created in another legal system.

[15] All the various European private international law instruments adhere to this distinction, and exclude claims or disputes deemed to be public law (notably administrative and tax) from their scope of application (see EC Regulation No 44/2001 on Jurisdiction and Judgments (22 December 2001) OJEU L 12 (*Brussels I*) art 1-1; EC Regulation No 593/2008 on the Law Applicable to Contractual Obligations (17 June 2008) OJEU L 177/6 (*Rome I*); *Rome II* (n 11).

[16] 'The Allocative Function of Foreign Relations Law' (n 5). Were private international law to over-come its own taboos, however, it could plausibly be argued that there are not two fields here but one, involving the reach of rights to foreign citizens and a constitutional attention to the extraterritorial reach of forum law.

[17] On the (receding) inclusion of the status of aliens within private international law, particularly in the French tradition, see D Bureau and H Muir Watt, *Droit international privé* (2nd edn PUF Thémis Paris 2010).

and subsequently to dominant understandings of private international law. Here again, the influence of Kelsenian legal thought—largely associated with multilateralist method—induced a widespread perception that domestic legal systems are closed to normative phenomena outside of themselves (including foreign laws).[18] While this idea of closure has probably lost its theoretical bite and become an essentially practical or procedural problem relating to the ascertainment of the content of foreign law, it retains its vigour in respect of non-state norms, which are not considered as a legitimate source of the governing law in dominant accounts of contemporary private international law.[19] Unilateralism, on the other hand, does not operate on such a premise. Once—and on the condition that—the sovereign's own interests are protected, it makes no particular demands on the world (for better or worse)[20] and, in particular, does not subordinate the legitimacy of the normative claims of other law-makers to any requirement of identity or mirror-image of itself; it suffices that such claims are effective. This approach has the considerable advantage of opening a space for pluralism, in which non-state authority may find a place.[21] The latter must of course be subject to a mediating principle, since no allocative method can remain indifferent, if not to the issue of the legitimacy *ex ante* of the norms with which it deals, at least to its results *ex post*. But the quest for such a principle (whether through public policy, comity or some form of balancing) has always been at the heart of unilateralist thinking.

Thirdly, since unilateralism rests on a practice of tolerance for the Other, it can also accommodate the requirements of recognition as a political philosophy. Tolerance for alterity has developed within this method as a means of mediating differences, in the absence of a master-plan allocating or delineating authority.

---

[18] Even when not subscribing specifically to the methodological dimension of vested rights doctrines, many systems of private international law reduce foreign law to the status of fact (meaning that in many or all cases it has to be pleaded and proved like a fact, or is in some way specific as compared to the procedural status of local rules, particularly in respect of judicial knowledge).

[19] See *Rome I* (n 15) recitals 13 and 14.

[20] This lack of demand on the world can of course be framed as the fundamental weakness of pluralism: '[w]hat we now see is an international realm where law is everywhere—the law of this or that regime—but no politics at all...' : M Koskenniemi, 'The Fate of International Law: Between Technique and Politics' (2007) 70 *Modern Law Review* 1–30, at 29.

[21] As will be seen later in the chapter, this place is denied by dominant multilateralist methodology. The use of incidental application or '*prise en consideration*' is an important feature of unilateralist methodology: see D Boden, *L'ordre public: limite et condition de la tolerance. Recherches sur la pluralisme juridique* (PhD Thesis Paris I 2002) nn 54, 1105, 1112, and 1119. It has developed the idea—in the vacuum between law and fact—of 'taking account of' (or applying 'incidentally') the effects of other sovereigns' will. It has always kept at a (once unfashionable) distance from the rule-based vision of law (as a condition and an effect; a prescription and a sanction; as syllogistic reasoning). Like vested rights, incidental application is one way of expressing the relevance of one system for another, without running into the methodological difficulty of explaining how one sovereign can bend to the will of another. Unilateralism's aptitude for adapting to non-traditional models of normativity is important.

In this respect, such a methodology is in keeping with the requirements of proportionality analysis in human rights settings, and furthermore is open to the epistemological changes wrought in this field by 'standpoint' perspectives.[22] A deliberative approach to normative pluralism, which might seek to achieve a form of overlapping consensus between different axiological outlooks, can be said in this respect to be a feature of a new constitutionalism specific to private international law.[23] In other words, unilateralist methodology may have the potential to ensure recognition for individual identitarian claims for equal rights, or indeed for the voices of non-state communities which do not fit the formal legal criteria for the status of legal subjects in public international law.

3 COOPERATION

3.1 State of the Art

According to the received genealogy, unilateralism as developed by the medieval statutists and refined as the dominant method in continental Europe until the mid-nineteenth century gave way at that point, under the extraordinary influence of Savigny, to a cooperative model based on the coordination of legal systems.[24] Dominant for most of the twentieth century, the cooperative model has recently received extra impetus from the quasi-federal institutional framework of the European Union (EU). Multilateralism is currently favoured as a method in

---

[22] On the impact of standpoint jurisprudence on the conflict of laws, see H Muir Watt, 'Fundamental Rights and Recognition in Private International Law' [2013] *European Journal of Human Rights* 411–35. From this perspective, the law is seen not as a set or system of abstract rules but is perceived through its effects in individual situations. As Foucault remarked in *La Volonté de savoir*:

> ...la vie, comme objet politique, a été en quelque sorte prise au mot et retournée contre le système qui entreprenait de la contrôler. C'est la vie beaucoup plus que le droit qui est devenue l'enjeu de luttes politiques, même si celles-ci se formulent à travers des affirmations de droit. Le 'droit' à la vie, au corps, à la santé, au bonheur, à la satisfaction des besoins, le 'droit', par-delà toutes les oppressions ou 'aliénations', à retrouver ce qu'on est et tout ce qu'on peut être, ce 'droit', si incompréhensible pour le système juridique classique, a été la réplique politique à toutes ces procédures nouvelles de pouvoir qui, elles non plus, ne relèvent pas du droit traditionnel de la souveraineté.

M Foucault, *La Volonté de savoir* (Gallimard Paris 1976) at 191; M Foucault, *The History of Sexuality: Volume 1: An Introduction* (R Hurley trans) (Pantheon New York 1978) at 145.

[23] See 'The Constitution of the Conflict of Laws' (n 5).

[24] See eg H Batiffol, *Aspects philosophiques de droit international privé* (Dalloz-Sirey Paris 1956); H Batiffol, 'Réflexions sur la coordination des systèmes nationaux' (1967) 120 *Recueil des Cours*

the private international law of the EU, where it serves as a substitute—either as a second best or as a federalist alternative—for substantive unification of the law of member states. Such developments have served largely to put the whole discipline back on the map (in the form of a series of Regulations from Brussels or Rome) from which it had faded during the latter part of the twentieth century—either because it was swept away in the wake of legal realism (in the US), or because it had become synonymous with commercial dispute resolution (in the English common law tradition), or indeed because of the competition of international arbitration (worldwide).

The big multilateralist picture is that allocation of prescriptive and (although considered to a far lesser degree) adjudicative jurisdiction should take place according to a grand plan, in a spirit of cooperation, or at least to ensure against the gaps and overlaps perceived to be the fundamental shortcoming of unilateral method. A more contemporary, diluted version appeals to an analogous idea of (fictional or metaphorical) distribution of the scope of laws for the (functional rather than political) purpose of providing the court with the set of rules which are to constitute the applicable law. In either case, there has to be a grand plan based on universalizable criteria to allocate jurisdiction or distribute sets of rules. Other states may be taken to adhere to such criteria, either because this master plan is provided by a binding supranational (conventional, customary, or institutional) framework, or because those criteria issue from natural law, reason (or at least a shared sense of reasonableness), or from a narrower cultural 'community of laws'.

The most striking example of the latter is Savigny's doctrine of the conflict of laws based on Roman law categories.[25] That shift is presented as a swing from primitive (medieval) statutism to enlightened cooperative method. Savigny is famous for his demonstration that defining the scope of a set of rules (Roman law categories of private law) is equivalent to defining the reach of jurisdiction relating to those rules: whatever the starting point, the result is the same. However, the explicit assumption was that the participating systems all shared a common Roman–Christian culture and therefore defined their own scope similarly. Since definition of scope was in turn mandated by natural reason

---

165–90; H Batiffol, 'Le pluralisme des méthodes en droit international privé' (1973) 139 *Recueil des Cours* 75–148.

[25] The supposed 'naturality' of the principles of private international law owes an initial debt to von Savigny's great treatise of Roman Law *System des heutigen Römischen Rechts* (1849) whose famous chapter VIII is believed to be the fount of modern conflicts methodology: FC von Savigny, *System of the Modern Roman Law* (W Holloway trans) (J Higginbotham Madras 1867 [1849]) ch VIII. On the mythology involved in such a reading of the text, see P Gothot, 'Simples réflexions à propos du saga des conflits de lois' in M-N Jobard-Bachelier and P Mayer (eds), *Mélanges en l'honneur de Paul Lagarde: Le droit international privé: esprit et méthodes* (Dalloz Paris 2005) 343–54.

(informed by the same culture), this was a fairly credible assumption for traditions sharing a Roman law heritage, although it was discovered by the end of the next century that even here, differences and attendant methodological difficulties were unavoidable.[26]

At this point, arguably, it might have made sense to abandon any attempt to maintain the fiction of universality and return to unilateralism. The price of the refusal of twentieth-century mainstream doctrine to relinquish the claim to impose a grand plan was to condemn each national system of private international law to operate in a closed circle. Various techniques (*renvoi*, characterization) were developed so as to sustain the idea that the grand plan conceived by each for all—unilaterally!—was based on a spirit of cooperation and aspired to consistency in the treatment of individual relationships across the international board. The proliferation of such 'escape devices' led to the spectacular functionalist 'revolution' in the US in the later part of the twentieth century. In Europe, greater attachment to private law doctrine prevented a similar turn to policy based analysis. Moreover, today, the failure of multilateralism to achieve the international harmony it professed to pursue has become less significant due to the emergence of binding private international law instruments accompanied by the interpretative authority of the European Court of Justice, which leaves little margin for idiosyncratic characterizations. However, a new difficulty has arisen in this context since human rights standards require the recognition of foreign relationships, whether or not the outcome conforms to the allocative plan of the forum. The delineation between the rules of the conflict of laws (the grand plan) and the requirements for the recognition of foreign judgments (effective practice) therefore becomes somewhat fuzzy (as fuzzy as the foundational division between law and fact) and heralds, to a large extent, the theoretical breakdown and practical inadequacy of multilateralist methodology.

---

[26] On the conundrum of characterization in the absence of a community of laws, see *Droit international privé* (n 17). Should the 'nature' of a legal institution be determined by reference to the law of the forum or the law which is potentially applicable as a result? The latter option, formally rejected, is actually unilateralist. However, denial of the foreign law's standpoint returns under *renvoi*. According to this much theorized mechanism, a sovereign does not impose its allocative plan on other unwilling sovereigns, but makes an offer, which may be rejected and in turn followed by a counter-offer. In the common law tradition, 'foreign court theory' is a variant upon this idea. The discovery that each sovereign potentially defines the thrust of its laws differently marked the end of nineteenth-century 'universalism' in private international law and the failure of natural law or reason as a foundation for a general allocative system. This led in turn to faith in a 'harder' structure, setting off the process of the Hague Conference on Private International Law at the turn of the twentieth century. However, in the absence of an international convention, each legislator was considered to be fictionally all-powerful, since where else would a grand plan come from? The price to pay was to take a position on *renvoi*. If courtesy leads a sovereign to allow a voice to another (for how could one sovereign impose a plan on the other?), it leads, however, inevitably to *renvoi* and ultimately (at least logically) to unilateralism.

3.2 Potential Insights

Whatever the evident shortcomings of the ideal allocative model outside a supportive institutional framework, the idea—specific to the EU—that interstate commerce works better with uniform conflict rules, or, alternatively—as in the US—that state rules are subject to constitutional requirements, nevertheless provides significant food for thought. First, the federalist concern, which outside such a context could be expressed in terms of global constitutionalism or democracy, is to ensure that voice is given in the decision-making process to affected foreign communities. This might mean, for example, in the case of transnational environmental protection, that the conflict of laws should ensure that the interests of those affected by cross-border pollution should be ensured through the applicability of their laws,[27] and that this could be achieved politically by the choice of a suitable multilateral connecting factor: article 7 of the *Rome II* Regulation attains this objective by giving an option to the claimant. Interestingly, therefore, the place conceded here to individual choice is justified by policy considerations which cannot be reduced to private convenience. By giving expression to a principle of affectedness, so as to ensure the voice of local communities, multilateralism may therefore have the potential to embody a form of deliberative constitutionalism for the conflict of laws.[28]

Secondly, multilateralism suggests that the proper allocation of rules of domestic private law can enhance the regulatory function of the latter in a global setting. Notably, while public international law appears ready to support the development of principles of soft law concerning the accountability of private economic actors (the global compact, for example), at present it fails to ensure that home states assume any form of vicarious liability for the foreign conduct of private actors; by the same token horizontal effect cannot work similarly to create binding obligations on corporate actors with 'extraterritorial' effect. Efforts undertaken under the aegis of human rights tools (the *Alien Tort Statute* in the US; claims under the *European Convention on Human Rights* in Europe) have proved unsatisfactory to date. It is a significant governance problem that hard law standards applicable at home do not extend to govern the conduct of private actors in foreign countries, particularly in cases of delocalized production or extraction of natural resources.

---

[27] For a more complete analysis of the economic rationale and the distributional effects of this provision, see H Muir Watt, *Aspects économiques du droit international privé* (2004) 307 *Recueil des Cours* 25–383.

[28] As Jacco Bomhoff states, 'while it is widely recognized that *within* polities, democracy is incomplete without attention to constitutionalist concerns, such as those relating to the protection of minorities, the idea that, similarly, it is only reasonable to demand that the *external* projection of public authority pass through the constraints and exhortations of constitutionalism, is much less prominent': 'The Constitution of the Conflict of Laws' (n 5) at 274 (emphasis in original).

This is a situation which facilitates regulatory competition on a transnational scale and consolidates the global race to the bottom in respect of social, environmental, and human rights standards. Private international law has, however, the available tools to re-allocate domestic private laws so as to make home country standards applicable in tort cases. Indeed, nothing prevents it from adjusting its choice of law rules to the need for accountability generated by the unfettered exercise of transnational economic power. Private law would thereby regain the political 'teeth' of which the smooth, uncontested account of its action and function has tended to deprive it in a global setting.[29]

4 COMPETITION

4.1 State of the Art

The third and most contemporary paradigm, which might be termed competitive or neoliberal, is most closely linked to readings of the function of law within the globalized economy. Global law is often understood in this respect as supporting or indeed embodying a free market for legal products and services. While it draws much of its theoretical foundations from regulatory federalism, its key operative tool is the secular principle of 'party autonomy', which arose in the very different context of liberal contract law. What was to become a 'cornerstone' principle—the idea of a contractual choice of applicable law—can be traced back (at least) to the beginning of the twentieth century. Indeed, there was no reason why whatever could be done by tailored agreement between two private contractors could not be accomplished by reference to a pre-established set of rules created by national legislation.

This approach was supported by a battery of legal arguments about party convenience and predictability, and later taken up, within the EU, as an internal market concern. Of course, in a domestic scenario, tailored agreements can go only so far because national legislation does not impose mandatory limits in the name of the general interest; and as public economic regulation increased (antitrust, securities), certain legislative provisions appeared which were mandatory in the sense that they could not be contracted-out-of. However, subject to a much

---

[29] On the two (rough and smooth) accounts of (contested or consensual) private law, see R Wai, 'Private v Private: Transnational Private Law and Contestation in Global Economic Governance' in *Private International Law as Global Governance* (n 4) 34–54.

debated question of what made a contract international, it was also accepted, with the growth of cross-border trade flows, that for such transactions, no state had any overriding claim to regulate exclusively. International transactions were subject only to core mandatory constraints considered to be non-waivable by the forum. On the one hand, allowing for substitutability of legislation reflected the non-parochial cooperative spirit of international trade among liberal states (whatever the more ambivalent Cold War background which appeared through state immunities to allow socialist trading republics to be called to account like private actors). Party autonomy was a liberal, cooperative move in the interests of something like the 'international commercial legal order', which assumed a community of interests. On the other hand, the public law taboo showed that there was a limit to such a cooperative public mindset: no state would risk putting its organs to the service of foreign public law.

The 1960s saw the growth of legislative moves (statutes which were mandatory, '*lois de police*', blocking, claw-back, and so on) that contrasted remarkably with the free-for-all of party autonomy. Nevertheless, simultaneously, economic actors were able to sidestep such legislation through (quasi) unrestricted choice of forum (public or private), supported by free movement of judgments and arbitral awards. Party autonomy is still widely understood, and indeed still actively touted, as one of the fundamental principles of transnational legal ordering.[30] However, in its novel function as portal to a distinct, market-driven model of global law, it remains both under-theorized and politically problematic. To a large extent, the idea of free private choice of law is a mutant survival from a previous (liberal) paradigm of the law, which became invested with a novel function within the context of liberalized trade. Indeed, much of the current misunderstanding of its effects in heralding and facilitating a largely privatized regulatory world stems directly from an underestimation of the significance of the context in which the idea of party choice of law appeared on the comparative legal scene.

The move to 'regulatory lift-off' took place significantly after the Second World War, by promoting free choice of law in international contracts so as to liberate parties from local constraints (which were deemed parochial). Within a few decades, however, the free movement of judgments and awards obtained from a freely chosen forum under freely chosen law led to a generalized deactivation of those mandatory rules and principles of public policy which were designed to

---

[30] The principle of free choice expanded from choice of law to choice of forum. The most significant move, which came from the common law world, was to extend the principle equally to choice of forum and then to arbitration (including investment arbitration). Autonomy has also extended from contract law to procedural choice, to tort, and indeed to family law matters. Sometimes a link with the chosen law is required, sometimes not. Sometimes it takes the form of an option between different sets of legislation all with a reasonable connection to the subject matter of the dispute.

ensure that party freedom did not go beyond the bounds designed to protect the general interest. By allowing parties to opt out of mandatory rules, public law has become subject to private choice, compliant with neoliberal thought (and not the reverse, as within a liberal order). Meanwhile, when the publicly funded judicial system became overburdened, international arbitration came into being as a bright new idea. After establishing itself in the commercial space, it spread to investment disputes, where the need for liberation from local constraints set off a flurry of theorization of 'delocalized' state contracts which belonged to no legal order at all.[31] Public international law was brought in for the first time since the schism between public and private international law in order to reinforce the autonomy of state contracts, before providing the institutional support for the construction of the global network of investment agreements. And then there was no touchdown.

While the growth of a market for law and judicial services was more often than not presented either as a pragmatic step in the interests of the business community, or as a political move in the name of liberalized world trade, theorization was provided by economic accounts of inter-jurisdictional competition through free party choice, which could induce a globally optimal result across the board.[32] Indeed, the empowerment of economic actors to navigate various domestic laws through similar regulatory arbitrage is at the heart of global financial markets.[33] However, once the market becomes entirely autonomous, there is room for imbalance and abuse; unchecked regulatory arbitrage, or privatization through contractualization of public interests, is not necessarily salutary.[34] Weaker parties and affected stakeholders are likely to lose out. At the same time, there is an evident inconsistency in allowing private parties complete freedom to choose any positive domestic law (thereby excluding bygone regimes or out-of-date statutes) to govern their contractual relationships, while they do not have similar licence to choose private rules, or non-state laws, which are generally not acknowledged as governing law.[35] This restriction hardly makes sense if public policy concerns are explicitly reserved and offers little protection if they are not. Moreover, it deprives the global market of a dose of self-regulation which, if properly channelled, might possibly induce more private initiatives and a more reflexive governance.

[31] See eg P Mayer, 'The Trend towards Delocalization in the Last 100 Years' in M Hunter, A Marriott, and V V Veeder (eds), *The Internationalisation of International Arbitration: The LCIA Centenary Conference* (Kluwer Law International London) 37–46, at 46.

[32] H Hansmann and J Damman, 'Globalizing Commercial Litigation' (1998) 94 *Cornell Law Review* 1–71.

[33] K Pistor, 'A Legal Theory of Finance' (2013) 41 *Journal of Comparative Economics* 315–30.

[34] See M Waibel, 'Review of Expert Determinations of the International Swaps and Derivatives Association by Domestic Courts' on *EJIL: Talk!* (2 May 2012) <http://www.ejiltalk.org/review-of-isda-expert-determinations-by-domestic-courts/> [accessed 2 March 2016].

[35] See *Rome I* (n 15) recitals 13 and 14.

4.2 Potential Insights

The assumption behind the 'regulatory lift-off' which provided such a significant impetus to the global economy was that there was a set of legal safeguards in the background (public policy, mandatory rules, special access to justice for weaker parties, and so on) ensured by the presence of a benign community of states. Private autonomy or contractual freedom on the international level was therefore a sort of mutually beneficial prolongation of a space of domestic contractual freedom conferred so as to further the interests of international trade. As they stand, however, the regulatory checks and breaks that developed alongside party autonomy in a liberal context have become inadequate to provide a balanced protection of the interests of individual third parties and wider, affected communities of stakeholders. It is also difficult to imagine a return to the more protective pre-global area, where parochialism, protectionism, and nationalism were rife.[36] Rather than putting a break on self-regulation, one of the most promising tools for the regulation of the global economy, in its use of transnational value chains and multinational actors, would be to think in terms of network theory and reflexive regulation.[37] This would also allow room for further thought on the binding nature of private codes of conduct, on the inadequacies of the traditional distinction between contract and corporation to apprehend both transnational chains of supply and production, and the architecture of corporate groups. It would also ensure that non-state, private authority be treated as such in order to be able to associate it with correlative responsibility in the name of affected constituencies, whose interests and identities still fall through the international legal net.

5 CONCLUSION

Doctrinal speculation about method, which has tended to focus on the specific properties of one or other of the models described earlier within a given setting, seems to have taken the place of, or indeed inhibited, a wider theoretical reflection within the context of private international law on the governance of the globalized

---

[36] Regarding the European Court of Justice's attempts to rebuild firewalls, see eg *Eco Swiss China Time Ltd v Benetton International NV* [1999] ECR I-03055.

[37] On reflexive regulation and its potentially transnational impact, see the works of Gunther Teubner: G Teubner, '"And If I by Beelzebub Castout Devils…": An Essay on the Diabolics of Network Failure' in S Grundmann, F Cafaggi, and G Vettori (eds), *The Organizational Contract: From Exchange to Long-Term Network Cooperation in European Contract Law* (Ashgate Farnham 2013) 113–36.

economy and issues of membership and community beyond the state. Indeed, despite the contemporary turn to law in international politics, private international law has contributed very little to such debates, remaining remarkably silent before the increasingly unequal distribution of wealth and authority in the world, and the lack of recognition of the vagrant, the migrant, and the stateless. Under the aegis of the liberal divides between law and politics, and between the public and the private spheres, it has developed a form of epistemological tunnel vision, actively providing impunity to abusers of private sovereignty and consolidating exclusion.[38]

Such limits have detracted seriously from the usefulness of private international law doctrine and method as a starting point for understanding the role, nature, and content of law beyond the state, prior to rethinking the work that the discipline might be expected to do. As a technical matter, several significant blind-spots need to be tackled, including: the status of non-state norms insofar as they reflect the practice of transnational communities; the place of fundamental rights and their accompanying balancing methodology in the process of allocation of jurisdiction; and the public/private divide as far as it still interferes with the so-called extraterritorial reach of fundamental rights or mandatory economic law and shields contractual practices with widespread social consequences from public scrutiny. Relinquishing a focus on its own methods and internal concepts, private international legal theory needs the help of political philosophy and the social sciences to acknowledge and govern non-state authority, correlate responsibility to spheres of influence, and take account of affectedness in the decision-making process. It might then have the potential, in the absence of satisfactory expressions of democracy beyond the state, to make a significant step towards the improvement of global governance by constituting a site of deliberation,[39] contestation,[40] and recognition.[41]

---

[38] Paradoxically, on the other hand, public international law, on the tide of managerialism and fragmentation, is now increasingly confronted with conflicts articulated as collisions of jurisdiction and applicable law, among which private or hybrid authorities and regimes now occupy a significant place. Technically, this represents an inversion of roles as between the public and private branches of international law.

[39] See 'The Constitution of the Conflict of Laws' (n 5), conceptualizing private international law as a 'site of contestation and deliberation over questions of authority, responsibility and identity'.

[40] See 'Private v Private: Transnational Private Law and Contestation in Global Economic Governance' (n 29).

[41] See 'Private International Law beyond the Schism' (n 5).

CHAPTER 43

....

TRANSNATIONAL MIGRATION, GLOBALIZATION, AND GOVERNANCE

THEORIZING A CRISIS

....

CHANTAL THOMAS

1 INTRODUCTION

....

IN early June 2014, the United States (US) administration declared an 'urgent humanitarian situation' resulting from the surge in immigration of unaccompanied migrant children to its southern border from Central America, particularly the 'Northern Triangle'—El Salvador, Honduras, and Guatemala.[1] The United Nations High Commissioner for Refugees (UNHCR) had warned earlier in the year of the dire conditions accompanying the surge. Asylum applications from

---

[1] White House Office of the Press Secretary, 'Presidential Memorandum—Response to the Influx of Unaccompanied Alien Children across the Southwest Border' (2 June 2014).

adults who were nationals of those countries had increased 700% since 2009,[2] and the number of unaccompanied migrant children arriving at the border had doubled yearly since 2011.[3] The children had travelled to the border with overlapping motivations. Most were hoping for reunification with family members who had already entered the US—an estimated 40% of whom were undocumented.[4] The next most significant concern, motivating roughly half of the children, was to escape rampant violence by 'organized criminal actors'[5]—drug cartels, gangs, and, at times, overreaching state anti-gang enforcement.

The 2014 Central America–US immigration crisis (hereinafter the '2014 crisis', denoting the moment when the issue came to widespread public attention, though it began well before 2014 and continued afterwards) stoked the fires of a debate on immigration and immigration reform, roaring not just in the US but also in migration-receiving countries all over the world. This chapter theorizes the 2014 crisis as symptomatic of deeper systemic patterns visible across the global order. Despite the systematic liberalization of flows in goods and capital across borders through international economic agreements, such as the ones mentioned above between the US and Central America, few equivalents exist for governing flows of people. This asymmetry in policies towards globalization has not prevented immigration, but has contributed to its irregularity. This contradictory set of arrangements is mirrored by a concerted policy of global criminalization of certain markets, producing one form of globalization as legal and the other as illegal. The various distinctions drawn between categories of irregular migration under international law do not sit comfortably with the facts on the ground.

At a time when real growth in the global North continues to stagnate and income inequality continues to grow, conditions favour a certain kind of xenophobia that scapegoats immigrants for economic ills ('They take our jobs!').[6] Anti-immigrant political platforms see the influx of immigrants as a completely 'exogenous' phenomenon, that is, one due to factors entirely outside the receiving country. But in fact migration from the global South to the global North often operates in a kind of boomerang effect, reflecting reactions to previous political and economic interventions by the North in the home countries of the migrant populations.

Call it global karma: actors who attempt to manage world events to accommodate their perceived interests often set in motion dynamics that prove hard to predict or control. One need only contemplate that the term used to describe the gangs of Central

---

[2] United Nations High Commissioner for Refugees, *Children on the Run: Unaccompanied Children Leaving Central America and Mexico and the Need for International Protection* (2014) <http://www.unhcrwashington.org/sites/default/files/1_UAC_Children%20on%20the%20Run_Full%20Report.pdf> at 4 [accessed 2 March 2016].

[3] Ibid 16.   [4] Ibid 7.   [5] Ibid.

[6] For a discussion of these debates, see A Chomsky, *'They Take Our Jobs!' and 20 Other Myths about Immigration* (Beacon Press Boston 2007).

America, *maras*, comes from the streets of Los Angeles, and that the rise of Central American gangs was precipitated by US law enforcement policies that deported convicted gang members even when their lives and criminal histories had been shaped in the US.[7] It would seem that nothing, and nobody, can be disposed of or dismissed without triggering a chain reaction that eventually comes back to the source.

In the case of Latin America and the US, the link dates back at least to the early nineteenth-century's Monroe Doctrine, in which the US claimed the entire Western Hemisphere as its rightful sphere of influence and asserted its primacy over competing powers from Europe.[8] Certainly, even without this long history of interventionism, the existence of the US as a comparatively prosperous and stable destination that is also geographically relatively proximate to Central America would by itself exert a pull on populations desperate to leave their circumstances. But the point here is that much more is going on—the pull has been generated by concerted actions on the part of US policy-makers. What is happening now could be summed up as a relationship of cause and effect: aggressive ongoing intervention by the US in these countries has not only contributed to severe political instability, weakening governments' ability to control organized crime, but established—intentionally or not—webs of transnational connections that, once acute crises struck, helped draw displaced persons northwards.

In particular, this chapter will emphasize the role of political economy, and the ways in which global governance has affected (or failed to affect) it, in generating immigration crises. With respect to the 2014 crisis, commentary focused on military and political aspects of US intervention in Central America.[9] Going beyond politics towards *political economy* illuminates both the origins of US intervention in Central America, and the ways in which that intervention has shaped migration from the region. US involvement stemmed from global power struggles over the organization of economic production: namely, its concerns about the turn to socialism, particularly after the Cuban Revolution. If foreign policy origins stemmed from economics, often so did policy tools: post-Second World War strategies for political alliance building with Central America consistently included strengthening trade and investment ties, from the Kennedy Administration's Alliance for Progress, to the Reagan Administration's Caribbean Basin Initiative, to the Bush

---

[7] LM Harris and MM Weibel, 'Matter of S-E-G-: The Final Nail in the Coffin for Gang-Related Asylum Claims?' (2010) 20 *Berkeley La Raza Law Journal* 5–30, at 6.

[8] A Becker Lorca, 'Sovereignty beyond the West: The End of Classical International Law' (2011) 13 *Journal of the History of International Law* 7–73.

[9] Indeed, throughout contemporary times US involvement in Central American military and political affairs has remained substantial, from the civil wars of the 1970s, to US-backed military regimes and counterinsurgencies under the 'Reagan Doctrine' of the 1980s, through the countries' establishment of peace agreements in the 1990s, and up to and including the Obama Administration's 2009 acceptance of the results of a military coup in Honduras. See J North, 'How the US's Foreign Policy Created an Immigrant Refugee Crisis on Its Own Southern Border' (9 July 2014) *The Nation*.

Administration's Central American Free Trade Agreement. These measures oriented Central American economies towards the US as a destination for its exports, and increased the Central American presence of US investors and imports. They also engendered profound changes in Central American economic life: changes that each in their own way have reinforced patterns contributing to the current migration surge.

The influx into the US of Central American asylum seekers constitutes only one example of contemporary global surges in refugee movements, prompting media commentators to declaim 'the worst refugee crisis in generations'.[10] International lawyers have urged their 'invisible college'[11] to meet this challenge.[12] Their call to action arises out of a sense that international law should contain the resources necessary to address problems of this global scale, but also the sense on the part of international lawyers that our professional *raison d'être* requires attending to them.

How should international legal theory respond to acute social problems such as immigration crises? Hilary Charlesworth has observed that such crises often serve as catalysts for the development of international law, and actually 'dominate the imagination of international lawyers'.[13] This is not necessarily a good thing, however: Charlesworth argues, for example, that the impulse to respond to the Kosovo crisis caused some international lawyers to fashion a controversial theory of humanitarian intervention that, others charged, damaged the field's long-term integrity.

Charlesworth's critique echoes the adage that 'hard cases make bad law,' as the jurist Oliver Wendell Holmes surmised, 'because of some accident of immediate overwhelming interest which appeals to the feelings and distorts the judgment'.[14] Other lawyers have countered this axiom, however: the legal realist Arthur Corbin asserted on the contrary that 'it can be said with at least as much truth that hard cases make good law', since the refinement of judicial reasoning required to avoid '[w]hen a stated rule of law works injustice in a particular case' reflects not what is specious and sentimental, but what is noble and useful, about law.[15]

---

[10] P Boehler and S Peçanha, 'The Global Struggle to Respond to the Worst Refugee Crisis in Generations' (1 July 2015) *New York Times.*

[11] O Schachter, 'The Invisible College of International Lawyers' (1977) 72 *Northwestern University Law Review* 217–26.

[12] As an anecdotal example, at the last two professional association meetings of international lawyers that this author attended, keynote speakers urged those assembled to attend to the issue of irregular migration and refugee movements: R Barkett, 'Keynote Address' (American Society of International Law, Annual Meeting, 10 April 2015); D Turk, 'Keynote Address' (French Society for International Law, World Meeting of International Law Societies, 27 May 2015).

[13] H Charlesworth, 'International Law: A Discipline of Crisis' (2002) 65 *Modern Law Review* 377–92, at 382.

[14] *Northern Securities Co v United States* 193 US 197 (1904). See also *Winterbottom v Wright* (1842) 152 ER 402.

[15] AL Corbin, 'Hard Cases Make Good Law' (1923) 33 *Yale Law Journal* 78–82.

At the least, then, an effort to fashion new legal theory to respond to crises should remain mindful of the 'contentious' aspects that Charlesworth argues can lead to problematic outcomes: contested facts, isolation from past practice, and a failure to focus on larger context.[16] In other words, any effort to theorize a crisis must take into account the contestedness of facts, and study the crisis historically and systematically. This chapter seeks to theorize the 2014 crisis in precisely this way—pointing out the ambiguity of facts and the problematic implications of that ambiguity for legal categorization, and situating the crisis within the historical relationship between Central America and the US. More broadly, the chapter argues that this particular crisis is an instantiation of a systemic challenge for international law in addressing irregular migration. While much of the analysis is critical, the concluding section contemplates an alternative international legal imaginary.

2 A Framework for Critical Analysis of Irregular Migration and International Law

The treatment of migrants by states intensely expresses a central tension within international law between deference to sovereign states as autonomous, on the one hand, and emphasis on individual equality and rights, on the other. The structure of international law appears to constrain its ability to generate real solutions to the issue of global irregular migration, due to the presumed sovereign prerogative over territorial control and particularly over immigration. And yet, international law constrains that sovereign prerogative as well, establishing some limitations on states' treatment of migrants' entry, residence, work, and exit.

In particular, international law establishes a range of protections not only for refugees and asylum seekers, but also for other categories of vulnerable persons, such as victims of trafficking. More generally, the question of what rights are owed to irregular migrants—not by virtue of any special legal category but simply by virtue of their humanity—is emerging as an extraordinarily contested one. The problem is not as simple as a clash between formal international law, which respects the sovereign prerogative over borders and immigration, and a social reality in which irregular migrants are challenging that prerogative. The crisis is *internal* to international law, in at least two ways that this chapter will hope to demonstrate with

---

[16] 'International Law: A Discipline of Crisis' (n 13) 382–6.

respect to the 2014 crisis. These two ways can be thought of as '*legal production*' and '*legal fragmentation*'.

First, in terms of *legal production* the tension between sovereign territorial prerogative and the rights of irregular migrants is exacerbated by an era of globalization which is itself significantly produced by international law. Illegality and informality are 'legally produced through multiple layers of permission, omission, and prohibition'.[17] Clandestine and unauthorized migration can be seen as legally constructed not only through the direct categorization of some migrants as authorized and others as not, but also through the interaction of legal institutions and mechanisms with background social conditions; and through the formalization of some means of international economic regulation but not others.

International agreements for the liberalization and globalization of economic life create pathways and connections that facilitate unauthorized as well as authorized movement. Moreover, they can generate effects of dislocation and displacement that can further facilitate unauthorized migration. Section 3.1 explores this phenomenon with respect to Central America, both in the creation of legal transnational markets through instruments such as the Dominican-Republic Central American Free Trade Agreement (CAFTA-DR), and in the emergence of illegal markets such as the drug trade.

Moreover, a pronounced asymmetry exists between instruments for the liberalization of trade and investment, on the one hand, and liberalization of migration on the other.[18] CAFTA-DR, for example, explicitly renounces migration questions as a proper subject for liberalization, reserving them to the respective policies of the states parties.[19] In this, it resembles both other regional trade agreements the US has signed, such as the North American Free Trade Agreement (NAFTA),[20] and also the central international trade body, the World Trade Organization (WTO).[21] While there are means in these agreements for liberalizing migration connected to 'trade in services,' they are limited, both in terms of economic sectors covered and

---

[17] C Thomas, 'Migrant Domestic Workers in Egypt: A Case Study of the Economic Family in Global Context' (2010) 58 *American Journal of Comparative Law* 987–1022, at 990.

[18] I am indebted to Kerry Rittich for offering this pithy term during our shared panel: 'Anti-Trafficking Law: A Legal Realist Critique' (Workshop on Shaping the Definition of Trafficking in the *Palermo Protocol*, 7–8 May 2014, King's College London School of Law).

[19] CAFTA-DR includes a separate understanding which states: 'No provision of the Agreement shall be construed to impose any obligation on a Party regarding its immigration measures.' CAFTA-DR, 'Understanding on Immigration Measures' (5 August 2004).

[20] Both NAFTA and CAFTA make clear that the provision of visas and access to employment through immigration law are excluded as a general category: both state that they neither create 'any obligation on a Party with respect to a national of another Party seeking access to its employment market, or employed on a permanent basis in its territory,' nor 'confer any right on that national with respect to that access or employment.' *CAFTA-DR* art 11.1(5); *NAFTA* art 1201(3).

[21] *Marrakesh Agreement Establishing the World Trade Organization* (opened for signature 15 April 1994 entered into force 1 January 1995) 1869 UNTS 183, annex 1B, para 4 (*General Agreement on Trade in Services*).

in terms of skill level, for the most part excluding 'low-skilled' workers.[22] The international bodies that have emerged to address global migration are intentionally informal and non-binding, organizational choices that are made legible through a lens of 'managerialism'. Section 3.2 demonstrates this phenomenon in the context of the Latin American 'Pueblo Process' and its response to the crisis.

Second, as regards *legal fragmentation* the tension expresses itself in contemporary international law's fragmentation across treaty regimes, which Section 4 of this chapter demonstrates in the context of the Central American crisis. International law establishes varying levels of rights and privileges for migrants. A hierarchy exists not only among categories of regular migrants (permanent immigrants versus temporary migrants, who themselves will be subject to different constraints depending on their particular classification), but also among irregular migrants. Refugees receive greater protections than trafficking victims who receive greater protections than 'ordinary' irregular migrants. Far from a clearly sorted and operable framework, however, these legal hierarchies are subjects of considerable confusion.

The confusion arises in part out of the contrast between the legal demarcations and the blurriness of the facts surrounding much irregular migration. The facts of privation and desperation can make it difficult to distinguish between, for example, asylum seekers and ordinary irregular migrants. Where such clear distinctions do exist, it is far from certain that they should: a resounding critique of asylum law is that its classifications are too narrow to address contemporary displacement. An additional source of confusion then must be taken into account in the contrasts among even those treaties that deal with the same subject matter. The human rights of irregular migrants under the *International Covenant on Civil and Political Rights* may differ from those under the UN *Convention on the Rights of Migrant Workers and Their Families*.[23] The protections afforded to migrants who fear persecution in their home countries may differ among the *Refugee Convention* and the *Convention against Torture*.[24]

Third, in relation to *methodology* these analyses of legal production and legal fragmentation employ an interdisciplinary approach intended to show how socioeconomic background conditions interact with legal decision-making and vice versa. This approach opposes itself to a more classical and formalistic approach to law, on the argument that the effects and outcomes of legal decisions cannot be

---

[22] See C Thomas, *Globalization, Irregular Labor Migration and International Law* (manuscript on file).

[23] *International Covenant on Civil and Political Rights* (opened for signature 19 December 1966 entered into force 23 March 1976) 999 UNTS 171; *International Convention on the Protection of the Rights of All Migrant Workers and Members of Their Families* (opened for signature 18 December 1990 entered into force 1 July 2003) 2220 UNTS 3.

[24] *Convention relating to the Status of Refugees* (opened for signature 28 July 1951 entered into force 22 April 1954) 189 UNTS 137; *Convention against Torture and Other Cruel, Inhuman or Degrading Treatment or Punishment* (opened for signature 10 December 1984 entered into force 26 June 1987) 1465 UNTS 85.

understood without the broader view. A critical perspective attends to gaps, contradictions, and ambiguities within international law, not (or not only) as problems to be solved,[25] but as keys to sites of contingency, and therefore possibility. Such a perspective holds at bay the question whether, in the face of globalization and migration, 'sovereignty is increasing or decreasing'; rather, the question is 'how it is changing; how it mediates and is mediated by…legal discourse'.[26] As such, opposing and unstable tendencies to defer to sovereign prerogative or to resist it in the name of migrant rights can be read as expressions of a dichotomy between 'ascending' and 'descending' registers of international law.[27]

In the case of global migration governance, the argument against formalism should be self-evident. The sources of law are diffuse, and dramatically under-institutionalized. Hard law instruments are little-ratified. Much, but not all, is explicitly reserved to national prerogative. And yet it is indisputable that global migration is a product of global governance. The forces that set off migration flows arose significantly out of global law and policy decisions; the institutions that attempt to manage migration often rely at least in part on transnational norms; and the international documents that explicitly attempt to address migration are proliferating. An approach that can somehow synthesize and assess these complex dynamics is very much needed: this chapter hopes to contribute to an effort to develop one. Beyond critique, Section 5 calls for a reconceptualization of the foundational ethics of international law, from liberal atomism to interconnectedness.

3 PRODUCTION: IRREGULAR MIGRATION AS AN EFFECT OF INTERNATIONAL LAW

3.1 Migration and Global Political Economy

3.1.1 Legal and Illegal Markets: Background Conditions to Migration Crises

Many of the children who arrived on the Mexico–US border from Central American countries during 2014 were seeking asylum and international protection from the

---

[25] MS McDougal, HD Lasswell, and JC Miller, *The Interpretation of International Agreements and World Public Order* (Martinus Nijhoff Dordrecht 1994) at 41–77.

[26] C Thomas, 'What Does the Emerging International Law of Migration Mean for Sovereignty?' (2013) 14 *Melbourne Journal of International Law* 392–450, at 436.

[27] M Koskenniemi, *From Apology to Utopia: The Structure of International Legal Argument* (re-issue CUP Cambridge 2006).

scourge of violence related to illegal drug cartels. Others were seeking family re-unification with adults who had migrated earlier, themselves seeking asylum, or in search of work. The migration surge followed the deepening of an outward-looking, export-oriented, and globalized framework for economic growth and development. That framework contributed—intentionally or not—not only to the migration surge but also the growth of the illegal export economy, that is to say the illegal drug trade. The 2014 *Handbook on Central American Governance* asserts that the region had been characterized in the last quarter-century by first, the emergence of new exports in goods and services from Central America to the US; secondly, the increased importance of migrant remittances to Central American economies; and thirdly, the 'economy of crime' linked to drug trafficking.[28]

In fact the dynamics underlying these changes were mutually reinforcing. The emergence of a 'free trade' regime led to increased migration through a series of displacements in previous livelihoods, not only through the increased presence of imports but also through surrounding reforms that supported the implementation of trade liberalization, such as privatization. These displacements created vulnerable populations who were more likely to look to migrate to the US without authorization. They also helped to increase the relative appeal of recruitment to drug trafficking. The increase in legal trade across borders also created opportunities for illegal trade because the same channels of transportation and communication facilitated both. Finally, the imposition of heavy criminal sanctions policing the illegal drug trade paradoxically both entrenched organized crime and tended to increase its brutality. The brutality of the drug trade provided still further incentive for unauthorized immigration.

Before elucidating these factors, two qualifications are necessary. First, the decision to migrate in virtually every case is the result of multifactored agency and decision-making on the part of the migrant. Even those cases that can be described as forced migration or trafficking most often begin with an active decision on the part of the person who migrates.[29] A purely structural 'push–pull' analysis would deprive individuals of agency by mechanizing the causes of their migration and characterizing those causes as purely economic.[30] But the elucidation of structural factors need not be interpreted as an assertion of historical-materialist determinism. It is still the case, after all, that the majority of people often choose not to migrate but to stay at home, even in the most intolerable of situations. Consequently, the

---

[28] E Torres-Rivas, 'Prologue: Central America: Modernizing Backwardness' in D Sánchez-Ancochea and S Martí i Puig (eds), *Handbook of Central American Governance* (Routledge Abingdon 2014) 1–3, at 2.

[29] D Brennan, *Life Interrupted: Trafficking into Forced Labor in the United States* (Duke University Press Durham 2014).

[30] DS Massey et al., *Worlds in Motion: Understanding International Migration at the End of the Millennium* (OUP Oxford 2005). See also DS Massey et al., 'Theories of International Migration: A Review and Appraisal' (1993) 19 *Population and Development Review* 431–66.

decision to migrate must be viewed as a choice constrained by circumstances. It is those circumstances, and their relationship to international law and governance, that this chapter seeks to illuminate.

The second qualification relates to the question of power relations between the US and Central America. This chapter argues that the US supported a number of policies that both created profound transformations in Central America and established numerous linkages that helped to promote migration. Yet this should not be confused with an assertion that the US dictated these outcomes. Actors in Central America also sought to protect their interests, and to contribute to and engage with political and social discourse. For example, the landowners who supported the export economic model well predated the era of US influence, going back to the early conquest.[31] I offer no unidirectional theory of power here, but observe only that the precise balances and machinations of power that led to the implementation of the policies discussed necessarily were complex.[32]

3.1.2 *Structural Causes of Migration from the Growth in* Legal *Trade*

The modern history of Central American economies has been characterized by their increasing orientation towards export-based production focusing on the US market, with the active encouragement of the US and related actors. The export-led growth model has necessitated transformations of existing relationships of economic production, whether from subsistence-based small landholdings or feudalist large landholdings. Under the 1960s Alliance for Progress, traditional exports of coffee and bananas were supplemented with the establishment of new cotton and beef industries. The World Bank's regional affiliate, the Inter-American Development Bank, and USAID assisted with funding for roads to transport crops that resulted in a Pacific highway from the Mexican border at the northern end of the region through Costa Rica at the southern end.[33] Development agencies also assisted national governments to form the national banks necessary to provide credit to fund cash-heavy export production.

With the 1980s Caribbean Basin Initiative, the focus expanded to include trade preferences for Central American exports to the US. The 1980s also saw the emergence of a more focused neoclassical economic model for development, as opposed to the mixed bag that had characterized the previous era. Central American countries, like much of the developing world, had up to that point pursued both 'outward-looking' commodity export production and 'inward-looking' import substitution industrialization. The debt crisis of the 1980s and the rise of Anglo-American

---

[31] RG Williams, *Export Agriculture and the Crisis in Central America* (University of North Carolina Press Chapel Hill 1986).

[32] See M Foucault, *Power/Knowledge: Selected Interviews and Other Writings 1972–1977* (C Gordon ed C Gordon et al., trans) (Pantheon New York 1980).

[33] *Export Agriculture and the Crisis in Central America* (n 31).

conservative political movements ushered in a period of redoubled pressure on developing countries, leading to the infamous 'Washington Consensus' policies of structural adjustment.[34] With the end of the Cold War and the dawn of US unipolar hegemony in the 1990s, the liberal development model 'emerged as the only viable option'.[35]

It was in the 1990s that Central American countries began to undertake unilateral steps towards increasing openness to foreign trade and investment, in the hope of securing the trade agreement with the US that was ultimately finalized in 2005. The signing of peace accords in the 1990s set the stage for deeper liberal economic reform, as the World Bank and the International Monetary Fund (IMF) stepped in to provide assistance in advising and funding the new development strategies. Even before the CAFTA-DR was negotiated and finalized, Central American economies had slashed import barriers, carried out privatizations of state-owned firms, removed obstacles to foreign investment, and established export processing zones affording investors special tax breaks.[36] The result was a further diversification of exports to include manufacture assembly through *maquilas* established in these zones.

CAFTA-DR consolidated the duty-free access of Central American exports to the US market, and also provided for the elimination of remaining barriers to US imports in most sectors, although 'sensitive' agricultural products (staples such as rice, beans, onions, and potatoes) were given an extended period to phase out trade barriers, and maize (white corn) was excluded altogether.[37] CAFTA-DR also provided for liberalization of 'trade in services'. Effectively, this meant increased exports of US financial and professional services to Central America, and increased exports of Central American tourist services to the US (tourism is considered a service exported by the tourist destination country).[38] Both trends led to an increased US presence—whether US financial and professional service firms or US tourists—in Central America.

The focus on export commodities displaced the cultivation of local staples and often resulted in the eviction of previous residents from their traditional lands in order to allow for export agriculture or the building of related highways and other infrastructure. This displacement was sometimes conducted forcibly through the cooperation of large landowners with national governments and their military

---

[34] For a general exposition of the rise of neoclassical economic development policy, see C Thomas, 'Law and Neoclassical Economic Development: Toward an Institutionalist Critique of Institutionalism' (2011) 96 *Cornell Law Review* 967–1024.

[35] D Sánchez-Ancochea and S Martí i Puig, 'Introduction: Central America's Triple Transition and the Persistent Power of the Elite' in *Handbook of Central American Governance* (n 28) 4–22, at 9.

[36] A Schneider, 'The Great Transformation in Central America: Transnational Accumulation and the Evolution of Capital' in *Handbook of Central American Governance* (n 28) 25–44.

[37] CF Jaramillo and D Lederman, *Challenges of CAFTA: Maximizing the Benefits for Central America* (World Bank Washington DC 2006).

[38] Ibid.

and police forces.[39] The displacement steadily expanded the seasonal migrant and wage-labour workforce within these economies domestically. The creation of this newly mobile workforce also led to urbanization and the growth of large informal economies in urban centres.

The turn to export over subsistence production increased economic growth but also increased economic volatility. Export prices were linked to trends in global commodity markets and as such vulnerable to booms and busts in those markets. The replacement of staple crops with exports also meant that populations were now dependent on imports for subsistence foods. The growth of import-dependence accelerated in the 1990s: between 1990 and 2005, production in staple crops 'fell by half, substituted by exportable goods'.[40] CAFTA-DR furthered this process, increasing vulnerability to international price shocks and currency fluctuations that had been building for decades. The oil price shocks of the 1970s, the anti-inflationary interest hikes of the 1980s, and, most recently, the 2008 global financial crisis and the 2009 commodity food price crisis all generated deeply felt local effects in Central America.

Indeed, it was after 2009 that the UNHCR began to register a dramatic increase in asylum seekers from Central America.[41] This fact should not be taken as evidence that asylum seekers in fact were only 'mere' economic migrants. As the following section shows, the same shocks also exacerbated the illegal drug economy that in turn produced the violence from which many asylum seekers were fleeing. In addition, as Section 4 discusses, asylum law currently is profoundly limited and insufficient in its lack of recognition of the interrelatedness of economic and political factors that create asylum seekers. Profound economic destabilization leads to political disorder and collapse, and produces the conditions of extreme insecurity that cause people to undertake dangerous journeys abroad in search of refuge.

These developments created 'push' factors that displaced populations from previous livelihoods and rendered their economic environments more precarious—in short they helped to create the significantly migratory workforce that characterizes Central America today. But the same events also created 'pull' factors drawing migration towards the US, of which the early creation of the Pan American Highway to enable the transportation of crops is just one (particularly concrete) example. Increased trade meant increased communication with US firms and consumers and increased transportation between Central America and the US. Particularly with the growth of services, which by their nature necessitate

[39] *Export Agriculture and the Crisis in Central America* (n 31).

[40] C Aguilar, 'Free Markets and the Food Crisis in Central America' (Center for International Policy Americas Program, 21 November 2011) <http://www.cipamericas.org/archives/5726> [accessed 2 March 2016].

[41] United Nations High Commissioner for Refugees, '2009 Global Trends: Refugees, Asylum-Seekers, Returnees, Internally Displaced and Stateless Persons' (15 June 2010) <http://www.unhcr.org/4c11fobe9.html> [accessed 2 March 2016].

transnational interpersonal communication and transportation, the establishment of transnational networks was not only predictable but also inherent in the
process of trade facilitation. These networks would of course serve to facilitate
migration strategies.

This dynamic defies conventional economic wisdom that has tended to see
international trade and international migration as substitutes, and indeed this
conventional thinking was at times used to persuade sceptics in the US to accept
trade agreements. The idea was that trade between countries would forestall and
replace the need for labour migration because the workforces of each country
would remain in place to take advantage of new production opportunities servicing the other market. Observing how some US agreements, such as the North
American Free Trade Agreement (NAFTA) and CAFTA-DR, have played out in
fact suggests the contrary conclusion: trade and migration are not substitutes but
complements.

3.1.3 *Migration and Illegal Trade—Drug Trafficking as a Global Market*

Illegal globalization operates in *parallel* to legal globalization, benefiting from
the same dynamics of supply, demand, and efficiencies in communication and
transportation; and the ways in which it *mirrors* legal globalization, operating
under an oppositional trend of criminalization that has policed illegal markets
as assertively as liberalization has opened legal markets. The drug violence that
terrorizes Latin America must be seen as a product of the division of the global
economy between legal and illegal. The criminalization of drugs paradoxically
not only fails to reduce the incidence of production and distribution of drugs,
but also increases the likelihood of violence. Aggressive criminalization can create perverse consequences that contribute to irregular migration, whether in the
form of undocumented labour migration or in the form of refugees and asylum
seekers.

I am drawing an explicit link here between the specific policies of economic globalization enacted in Central America and the current refugee crisis, but, again,
in doing so I in no way seek to counter or undermine the asylum and protection
claims sought by the people who are on the border. Advocates emphatically distance the possible characterization of this population as composed of 'economic
migrants'.[42] The importance of this distinction results from the current content
of international refugee law—a subject taken up in Section 4. The centrality of
economic globalization policies as conceived and enacted in the region in contributing to the current disarray need not (and in my view should not) lead to

---

[42] 'How the US's Foreign Policy Created an Immigrant Refugee Crisis on Its Own Southern
Border' (n 9).

a recharacterization of asylum seekers as mere 'economic migrants'. Rather, the point is that the extremely real, 'non-economic', and terrorizing violence experienced by these claimants is in part a result of economic policies that were put in place. Even where the migration in question is deemed not to be merely 'economic', but rather a result of refugee flight, the dislocation resulting in that flight has often been significantly economic in nature.

In a 2003 article, 'Disciplining Globalization', I noted that illegal markets such as the drug trade were as much a product of globalization as legal goods and services.[43] First, the same effects of supply and demand operate to incentivize production and sale. It is well known that the US market for illegal drugs is vast. Though Latin America traditionally supplied mostly cocaine to this market, with opium coming from Asia, in recent years illegal export production has diversified much as legal export production has. Latin America has also become a major site of opium production, in part due to fluctuations in supply from more traditional sources such as Afghanistan, which experienced a major 'opium crop failure' in 2010.[44]

In recent years, 'farm-gate' prices for opiates and cocaine have continued to rise. The 'farm-gate' price for opium from Colombia rose from USD $200 per kilogram in 2004 to USD $500 in 2011.[45] The farm-gate price for coca rose from USD $650 per kilogram in 2005 to USD $784 in 2010.[46] Notably, this increase in price accompanied a decline in actual production levels for both opium and cocaine in Colombia, which was attributed in part to greater successes in law enforcement. The decline in supply only increased prices. Compare the average prices that farmers receive for cotton sales, according to the National Cotton Council of America: a little over *one* US dollar per kilogram in 2003 (USD $1.31) going up to almost *two* dollars per kilogram (USD $1.95) by 2011.[47] In other words, gross returns from coca and opium production amounted to between 150 and 400 times those from cotton.

Secondly, the same gains in technology, communication, and transportation that have facilitated the rise of legal global markets have also benefited illegal markets. This can be seen by examining the result of the decline in cocaine manufacture in Colombia between 2006 and 2010. According to the UN Office on Drugs and Crime, cocaine manufacture was able to reorganize in nearby countries Bolivia and Peru, which in turn have become 'increasingly important producers'.[48] Consequently,

[43] C Thomas, 'Disciplining Globalization: Law, Illegal Trade, and the Case of Narcotics' (2003) 24 *Michigan Journal of International Law* 549–75.

[44] United Nations Office on Drugs and Crime, *2012 World Drug Report* (United Nations Vienna 2012) at 30.

[45] Ibid.   [46] Ibid 40.

[47] This figure was calculated by looking at crop year average prices per pound (which are higher than calendar year prices) as reported by the National Cotton Council, 'Monthly Prices' <https://www.cotton.org/econ/prices/monthly.cfm> [accessed 2 March 2016]. The prices per pound were then converted to prices per kilogram by multiplying by 2.2.

[48] *2012 World Drug Report* (n 44) 12.

the decline in production in Colombia was partially offset by new production in neighbouring countries, motivated by corresponding price increases. Colombia remains the primary location for illegal drug production, though production has spread to other Andean countries. But the Colombian drug economy operates as a classic regional hub, establishing distribution networks in neighbouring countries in order to facilitate transportation of goods to the US market. These distribution networks account for the rise of drug trafficking and organized crime in Mexico and in the Northern Triangle countries closest to Mexico: Guatemala, Honduras, and El Salvador.

Thirdly, just as the particular dynamics of globalization of legal markets result from specific policy choices, so too do the dynamics of illegal markets. A mirror image operates here: whereas legal markets were aggressively liberalized over the past quarter-century, illegal markets have been aggressively criminalized. This criminalization has taken the form of the 'War on Drugs' in heavy criminal sentencing for drug convictions and heavy investment in anti-drug trafficking law enforcement. With increased sensitivity to the origin of illegal drugs from across the Mexico–US border, increased border patrol spending has also been justified in part as an anti-drug trafficking measure. And anti-drug trafficking efforts have been internationalized through the creation of multilateral treaties such as the UN *Convention against Transnational Organized Crime* and the establishment of global monitoring bodies such as the UN Office on Drugs and Crime.[49]

Perversely, these criminalization efforts have probably made drug trafficking more organized and more violent.[50] Whereas the logic of criminalization is that it will deter production of illegal drugs through the imposition of punishment, in fact what criminalization does is rearrange incentives and change the composition of supply, where demand remains relatively stable (or 'inelastic' in economic terms). Criminalization of markets means that producers cannot resort to legal means to structure contracts and settle disputes, and use violence instead. The heavier the criminalization and policing, the more organized and violent criminal producers become. The criminalization of drugs creates a 'black market premium' increasing their market prices, and criminal actors organize in order to be able to capture that premium.[51]

Successes in criminal law enforcement may only operate to increase this premium and exacerbate the very harms whose reduction is the stated goal of such enforcement in the first place. For example, in discussing the recent decline in illegal drug production in Colombia, the UN Office on Drugs and Crime noted

---

[49] *Convention against Transnational Organized Crime* (opened for signature 12 December 2000 entered into force 29 September 2003) 2225 UNTS 209.

[50] For a more extensive discussion, see 'Disciplining Globalization' (n 43).

[51] CJ Milhaupt and MD West, 'The Dark Side of Private Ordering: An Institutional and Empirical Analysis of Organized Crime' (2000) 67 *University of Chicago Law Review* 41–98.

that this decline did not prevent farm-gate prices from rising over the same period, and speculated that 'increasing prices at source may not reflect higher demand but rather an increased risk in cultivation and trafficking resulting from the intensification of law enforcement activities'.[52] In sum, increased criminal law enforcement against illegal drugs, against a backdrop of stable market demand for illegal drugs, may actually grow rather than shrink organized criminal activity in drug trafficking.

In addition to these parallel and mirror relationships, there is a final set of more dynamic interactions between legal and illegal markets. Legal trade and illegal trade sometimes happen simultaneously: the trucks, shipping containers, and travellers that cross borders under liberalized trade arrangements sometimes also are the sites for smuggled goods. In addition, the economic push and pull factors that displace existing livelihoods, and that render workforces mobile and vulnerable, have resulted from legal trade arrangements and have also at times helped to contribute to the rise of illegal trade. This division in turn creates perverse consequences that further contribute to irregular migration, whether in the creation of undocumented labour migration through economic desperation or in the form of refugees and asylum seekers fleeing the violence of the drug trade.

3.2 Migration and Global Governance

The border crisis came to broader public attention just as the US Administration's efforts to reform the immigration system was shifting course. Following President Obama's 2012 re-election and the decisive role that immigrant communities had played in bringing it about, a brief political consensus had seemed to emerge that a mandate existed to fix immigration, to which both Democrats and Republicans were behoved to pay attention. Despite the US Senate's passage of an immigration bill in the summer of 2013, the House of Representatives gradually dug its heels in further and further, and by June 2014 the House Republican Leader had flatly refused to consider immigration reform for the remainder of the year.[53] In turn, the President had declared an intention to pursue immigration reform through executive action.[54]

The border crisis unfolding over the same time period seemed only to fuel existing arguments on both sides: for immigration reformers, it underscored the humanitarian costs of inaction, but for opponents it exacerbated the siege mentality

---

[52] *2012 World Drug Report* (n 44) 30.

[53] J Kuhnhenn and E Werner, 'White House: Boehner Won't Seek Immigration Vote' (30 June 2014) *Associated Press.*

[54] White House Office of the Press Secretary, 'Remarks of the President on Border Security and Immigration Reform' (30 June 2014).

that viewed unauthorized migrants as law-breakers and security threats. The Obama Administration requested emergency funding to support the processing of asylum claims and detainment and deportation proceedings. Most detainees at the border enjoy few due process rights under US law, though an anti-trafficking measure enacted in 2008 gave children special rights in this regard.[55] The US has sought out consultations with Mexico and Central America, but also has warned those countries that the migrants' efforts to stay in the US were likely futile.[56] The US's counterparts in these talks have issued reciprocal warnings that such crises are unlikely to cease unless steps are taken to expand legal opportunities for work. In a meeting on 20 June 2014 in Guatemala City amongst the Presidents of El Salvador, Guatemala, Honduras, and Mexico and the Vice-President of the US, Guatemalan President Molina proposed the establishment of a formal guest-worker program.[57]

Where was international law in all of this? And, equally importantly, where *wasn't* it? The meetings among the government representatives took place under no formal international or regional framework on migration. Given the recent establishment of CAFTA-DR, the lack of a formal migration agreement is all the more glaring. If investment and trade in goods and services were on the table, why not also discuss migration? Instead, the services negotiations set aside the question of migration policy, deferring to the national legal systems of the parties.

The non-incorporation of migration into CAFTA-DR tracks a broader pattern in global economic governance, in which many international trade and investment agreements do not incorporate migration policy, or do so only to a limited degree that favours high-skilled professionals and excludes so-called low-skilled workers (as in the case of NAFTA). The exception comes from customs union arrangements, which seek a greater integration amongst members, and therefore allow for free movement of labour. The European Union, Southern Common Market (MERCOSUR), the Economic Community of West African States (ECOWAS), and the Southern African Development Community (SADC) all follow this model, though implementation in some member states remains incomplete.

Outside of these major integration efforts, however, migration is often dealt with separately, or not at all, or in the form of non-binding frameworks for co-operation. A number of multilateral fora have been established for the purpose of encouraging such cooperation, such as the International Agenda for Migration Management, and the Global Commission on International Migration. These frameworks are often established on a regional basis. In the European Union (EU)

---

[55] *William Wilberforce Trafficking Victims Protection Reauthorization Act 2008* s 237(d)(7). The important question of whether US practices on detainment and deportation comply with international law is not addressed here.

[56] RC Archibold, 'As Child Migrants Flood to Border, US Presses Latin America to Act' (20 June 2014) *New York Times*; D Boyer, 'Obama Talks Tough to Mexico: Illegal Immigrant Children Won't Get to Stay' (19 June 2014) *Washington Times*.

[57] M McDonald, 'Central America Presses Biden on Migrant Rights as US Vows Aid' (20 June 2014) *Reuters*.

context, such frameworks are often called 'partnerships,' as in the EU–Africa Partnership, the Strategic Partnership with Latin American Countries, and the Eastern Partnership.

Some regional frameworks, dubbed several 'Regional Consultative Processes', are managed by the International Organization for Migration (IOM), itself not a treaty-based organization (like the UN or World Trade Organization (WTO)), despite the name, but an agency established by governments for the purpose of managing migrant resettlement and return. For the Americas, the IOM forum is the 'Regional Conference on Migration' (RCM) or 'Puebla Process,' incorporating eleven member states and headquartered in Costa Rica. The Puebla Process has held annual meetings since 1996, rotating among the member states.

But the summit mentioned earlier was not sponsored by the Puebla Process— in fact, the Puebla Process held its own meeting in Nicaragua the very following week. At the Nicaragua meeting, the IOM's Director-General stated that the US border crisis should 'be seen as an opportunity to address disparities and vulnerabilities in [migrants'] home communities, which are the structural causes, and an opportunity to provide a coordinated regional response'. However, conspicuous non-coordination between the US-led summit in Guatemala on 20 June and the IOM's regional conference in Nicaragua on 28 June at the least suggests some way to go before such responses take hold.[58] In terms of the IOM's on-the-ground activity, the US imprint is clearly visible. IOM involvement has taken the form largely of attending to returnees, for example through the US-funded project 'Assistance to Returning Families and Unaccompanied Children in the Northern Triangle of Central America'.[59] Other involvement appears to have taken the form of US-funded education campaigns to deter migration by warning parents and guardians of the risks faced by unaccompanied children.[60]

The Puebla Process numbers just one of a host of such venues that have burgeoned over the past several years in the transnational space, that involve some combination of governmental and non-governmental actors and that operate in a key of 'managerialism' rather than legalism.[61] For example, the Global Forum on Migration and Development (GFMD), an intergovernmental working group, identifies itself as a 'voluntary, informal, non-binding and government-led process...

---

[58] IOM, 'IOM Director General Attends XIX Annual Meeting of the Regional Conference on Migration in Nicaragua' (28 June 2014) <https://www.iom.int/news/iom-director-general-attends-xix-annual-meeting-regional-conference-migration-nicaragua> [accessed 2 March 2016].

[59] IOM, 'US Supports IOM Aid to Returned Migrant Children, Families in Honduras' (20 February 2015) <http://www.iom.int/news/us-supports-iom-aid-returned-migrant-children-families- honduras> [accessed 2 March 2016].

[60] IOM, 'IOM Supports El Salvador Information Campaign Warning Parents of Risks Faced by Unaccompanied Children Traveling to USA' (18 July 2014) <http://www.iom.int/news/iom-supports-el-salvador-information-campaign-warning-parents-risks-faced-unaccompanied> [accessed 2 March 2016].

[61] F Johns, *Non-Legality in International Law* (CUP Cambridge 2013) at 14.

to foster practical and action-oriented outcomes'.[62] Despite having been founded as consequence of the United Nations' 2006 High-Level Dialogue on Migration and Development and open only to UN Members and Observers, the GFMD holds no formal ties to the UN and 'does not form part of the United Nations system'.[63]

All of these arrangements sit conspicuously against the rapidly proliferating and eminently enforceable hard-law trade and investment agreements that also characterize international space.[64] The new multilateral, regional, and bilateral trade and investment frameworks not only qualify as formally binding treaty law, but they also feature significant and toothy dispute settlement systems. CAFTA-DR, like many other recent agreements, established protections and a dispute settlement system for foreign investors. As with other investor-state systems, the resulting decisions have underscored the limited scope of the government's regulatory purview as against private interests. For example, Guatemala was held liable (in the amount of USD $11.3 million plus USD $2 million in interest and fees) for 'indirect expropriation' to an investor who had purchased privatized railroad assets in the 1990s, after the government initiated an investigation into voiding the investor's rights on the basis of contractual non-performance.[65] Though CAFTA-DR also established a basis for arbitrating labour disputes, to date no formal award has been issued, although some labour advocates maintain that the system may still provide some basis for improvement in leverage for labour issues. For example, in April 2013 the Guatemalan government agreed to a plan for improved labour enforcement in lieu of establishing an arbitral panel.[66]

The discussion so far in this chapter shows how how much of global migration sits outside formal international law. Instead, governance of global migration often exists in forms of 'non-legality',[67] ranging from illegality—that is, migration that is not condoned or organized by international law or by the national legal systems whose sovereignty is protected by international law—to informality, in which the forms of intergovernmental coordination that do exist eschew binding legal agreements and operate much more in the 'key of managerialism'.

The relative informality of migration governance has supported various theoretical explanations. Some see the chaotic array of frameworks, their fluidity and informality, as indicative of Habermasian communicative opportunity.[68] The

---

[62] Global Forum on Migration and Development, 'The GFMD Process' <http://www.gfmd.org/process> [accessed 2 March 2016].

[63] Global Forum on Migration and Development, 'Links with the United Nations' <http://www.gfmd.org/process/united-nations> [accessed 2 March 2016].

[64] A Roberts, 'Clash of Paradigms: Actors and Analogies Shaping the Investment Treaty System' (2013) 107 American Journal of International Law 45–94.

[65] Railroad Development Corporation v Guatemala (Award) (ICSID, Case No ARB/07/23, 29 June 2012).

[66] Office of the United States Trade Representative, 'Press Release, Fact Sheet: Guatemala Agrees to Comprehensive Labor Enforcement Plan' (11 April 2013).

[67] Non-Legality in International Law (n 61).

[68] N Piper and S Rother, 'Let's Argue about Migration: Advancing a Right(s) Discourse via Communicative Opportunities' (2012) 33 Third World Quarterly 1735–50.

optimistic view would be that the dialogues amongst all these actors will lead to 'democratic iterations' and a gradual opening up of rights for migrants.[69] The glaring question is whether the conditions of inclusion, non-coercion, and equality that are said to act as necessary prerequisites for validity in this kind of envisioned democratic discourse can be said to cohere, even in an imperfect way.[70] If instead the actors involved in political debate are seeking merely strategic ends, or are beset by deep structural biases, then the chances for democratic discourse to arrive at anything approaching justice become much more limited.

A more pessimistic view, one more attuned to strategic considerations, sees informality in migration governance as emblematic of the neoliberal style, in which sending country governments are encouraged to become self-regulating within a broader framework of governmentality and to indicate their responsibility by controlling their own migration flows.[71] Yet, as shown earlier, the neoliberal era in global economic governance was characterized at least as much by quite *formal* frameworks: the new trade and investment treaties substantially exceeded anything that had come before in international space in terms of their execution of formal enforcement mechanisms. One question here is whether there are strategic intentions and/or effects behind the adoption of formal legalism versus informal managerialism as a style for governance (acknowledging that this is an heuristic dichotomy and that most processes are a mixture of the two). The relegation of much of global migration governance to 'soft law' might suggest that the neoliberal framework has selectively accorded informality to lesser priorities. On this view the managerial operates at the peripheral, a zone where migration issues languish together with international human rights and environmental matters. Yet much of international financial regulation (which is anything but peripheral) also takes this 'soft law' form (albeit backed up by significant market pressure)—the fiscal adjustment and austerity that countries undergo at the behest of international financial institutions often takes place within a managerial context of policy advice and best practices.[72] Accordingly, some migration experts have advocated the development of a soft law framework as a practical way of providing helpful but non-binding clarification and institutional support to states.[73]

Will the border crisis create opportunities for Central America to formalize migration practices through a binding treaty framework? The opportunity for

[69] S Benhabib, *Another Cosmopolitanism* (OUP Oxford 2006).

[70] J Habermas, *The Future of Human Nature* (W Rehg, M Pensky, and H Beister trans) (Polity Press Cambridge 2003).

[71] R Kunz, 'Governing International Migration through Partnership' (2013) 34 *Third World Quarterly* 1227–46.

[72] For a classic discussion of hard law versus soft law, see DM Trubek and LG Trubek, 'Hard and Soft Law in the Construction of Social Europe' (2005) 11 *European Law Journal* 343–64.

[73] A Betts, 'Soft Law and the Protection of Vulnerable Migrants' (2010) 24 *Georgetown Immigration Law Journal* 533–52.

Central American governments to join forces with each other in negotiating with the US might provide them with greater leverage. And yet one must recall the background of global economic instability as a serious constraint on such negotiations. Where international labour migration agreements do exist, such economic pressures limit the rights and powers that can be granted to migrants or migrant-sending countries and can mean that such rights (where they do exist) are badly enforced. This is a rapidly shifting terrain with numerous strategic and institutional possibilities.

4 Fragmentation: Irregular Migration and International Legal Gaps, Contradictions, and Ambiguities

Section 3 of this chapter detailed the ways in which background conditions of political and economic instability in Central America operated to reinforce each other, each contributing to the current surge in asylum seekers. The point was to show how these dynamics resulted partially from interventions made by or on behalf of US interests. Consequently, migration surges to the US border have to be understood as at least partially a consequence of actions US interests took. This same interplay between economic and political crises also serves as the starting point for the observations in this section. The argument is that the various categories of irregular migration, and the accompanying differences in entitlements, have generated much confusion, both legal and political, about what kind of recognition and protection should be accorded to undocumented migrants.

Although much of global migration governance intentionally operates outside international law, looking to set and manage priorities in a non-legal way, there are also efforts to strengthen international legal rules on the rights of migrants. Here again, migration illustrates broader trends in the departure of contemporary international law-making from the classical ideal of international lawyers.[74] First, the international law of migration is highly fragmented through specialized instruments, each of which establish a particular set of rules whose relationship to all the other rules is left either entirely unspecified or only generally

---

[74] For examples of the extensive literature on this point, see A Boyle and C Chinkin, *The Making of International Law* (OUP Oxford 2007); A-M Slaughter, *A New World Order* (Princeton University Press Princeton 2005).

acknowledged. Second, decision-making and interpretation feature increasing participation by non-state actors. Very often, these two characteristics occur together and relate to each other.

For example, the UN system has established an interagency forum, the Global Migration Group, that states as its aim the promotion of 'wider application of all relevant international and regional instruments and norms relating to migration, and to encourage the adoption of more coherent, comprehensive, and better coordinated approaches to the issue of international migration'.[75] The UN's Global Migration Group currently coordinates among eighteen agencies, responsible for labour, human rights, refugees, health, development, and crime amongst other concerns.

The need for cooperation cited by these agencies on the development of norms might be seen as filling a void created by the lack of government action to establish coherent standards and interpretations. It is also a response to the proliferation of instruments addressing aspects of migration that exist under different treaty frameworks and different UN bodies. The state of formal international law on migrants' rights is highly patchworked. Some of the 'core' human rights instruments, such as the *International Covenant on Civil and Political Rights*, have established expansive interpretations of migrant rights.[76] Other more specialized instruments, such as the UN *Migrant Workers' Convention*, establish rights that are still extensive but less so.[77] On the subject of migrant workers' rights, the International Labour Organization (ILO) in turn has its own general and specialized instruments. Then there is the question of how the human rights of migrants as interpreted under these general and specialized treaties relate to the treatment of migrants under more specific scenarios, such as seeking asylum, which concerns the *Refugees Convention* and related instruments, or criminal law enforcement, which concerns the UN *Convention against Transnational Organized Crime* and its human trafficking and migrant smuggling protocols.[78]

Before continuing with this analysis it should be pointed out that the current body of migration law assumes a default legal rule that migrants should not enter without explicit authorization by the receiving state, and that the failure to gain such authorization is an act of law-breaking. But this rule has itself changed over time. Only in the late nineteenth century and early twentieth century was the presumptive authority of territorial exclusion formally accorded to the state in a systematic way. Rather, early modern international law established the presumptive

---

[75] Global Migration Group <http://www.globalmigrationgroup.org/> [accessed 2 March 2016].
[76] *ICCPR* (n 23).   [77] *Migrant Workers' Convention* (n 23).
[78] *Refugees Convention* (n 24); *Convention against Transnational Organized Crime* (n 49). For an extensive discussion of the relationship amongst all these treaties, see C Thomas, 'Convergences and Divergences in International Legal Norms on Migrant Labor' (2011) 32 *Comparative Labor Law & Policy Journal* 405–41.

admissibility of aliens, a 'qualified duty to admit aliens when they pose no danger to the public safety, security, general welfare, or essential institutions of a recipient state'.[79]

In part this was probably simply a function of administrative capacity. The state's ambition to manage populations in their entirety must be understood to co-emerge with the forms of knowledge and the techniques of governance that would allow them to do so.[80] Yet the emergence of the presumptively closed state cannot only be understood as a product of technology, but also as a product of shifts in the ways in which colonial power was asserted. The emergence of exclusion as a default rule also tracked with the change in directionality of migration between the centre and periphery. In early modernity and during colonial conquest and settlement, populations flowed from Europe outward; as formal colonialism wound towards its conclusion and the postcolonial world began to emerge, the vectors of migration reversed. Moreover, even after the default rule of exclusion of aliens emerged, the regulatory form for exclusion did not remain stable but rather changed over time. In the US, until recently an undocumented entrant into US territory had committed no crime, but rather committed an administrative infraction. Now, however, in the US as in many other receiving countries, unlawful entry constitutes a criminal offence.[81]

With undocumented migrants often described as 'illegal', one might assume that migration can be straightforwardly characterized as either lawful or unlawful. In fact, an undocumented person who arrives at the border or who is apprehended by border patrol might be placed into any number of legal categories each with its own rules: refugee/asylum seeker; trafficked person; smuggled migrant; or 'ordinary' labour migrant. A very distinct hierarchy accords differing rights and remedies across these categories. In this way, the phenomenon of 'illegal migration' is intensely regulated by law, but also internally differentiated through law.

4.1 Refugees versus Non-Refugees

For example, a shorthand distinction drawn between a refugee and an 'ordinary' undocumented migrant has often been that the former type of migration is political, whereas the latter is economic. Refugees are said to be fleeing political conflict whereas ordinary undocumented migrants are looking to better their economic opportunities. Refugees are also sometimes characterized as 'forced migrants,'

---

[79] JAR Nafziger, 'The General Admission of Aliens under International Law' (1983) 77 *American Journal of International Law* 804–47, at 805.

[80] See M Foucault, *The Birth of Biopolitics: Lectures at the Collège de France 1978–79* (M Senellart ed G Burchell trans) (Palgrave Macmillan Hampshire 2008).

[81] 8 USC §§ 1325, 1326.

compelled to leave their home countries. This description signifies the moral distinction being made between categories of migration, and accompanying legal consequences. Whereas ordinary labour migrants are seen voluntarily to be breaking the law of the receiving country by attempting undocumented entry, refugees are understood to be operating under a form of duress that should morally excuse any such unauthorized entry and provide a justification for compassionate treatment.

It was on the basis of this understanding that states have adopted the controlling international instrument on refugee law, the 1951 *Refugees Convention*. The *Refugees Convention* defines a refugee as a person with a 'well-founded fear of being persecuted for reasons of race, religion, nationality, membership of a particular social group or political opinion'.[82] The *Refugees Convention* addresses forms of political persecution, excluding ordinary labour migrants, of course. The idea was that one could divide undocumented migrants into refugees and non-refugees, according some protection and entitlement to the former category but leaving treatment of the latter to the prerogative of states (save for those that can establish a claim under complimentary obligations of protection discussed in the next section).

The current crisis points to what refugee advocates have criticized as the excessive narrowness of the categories under the *Refugees Convention*. Created to address the particular kinds of conflicts that had occurred during the Second World War, the *Refugees Convention* is ill equipped to address contemporary forms of displacement that would seem to be no less desperate. 'Climate change' or 'environmental' refugees are sometimes cited as an example of this.[83] Those who are fleeing violence from drug cartels present another example of this problem. The good news from the refugee advocates' perspective is that the text of the *Refugees Convention* can be interpreted expansively. Through the lens of 'progressive development of international law', the UNHCR has stated that those who are fleeing violence from 'organized criminal actors' (drug cartels, gangs, or state-sponsored anti-gang tactics) may qualify as refugees.[84] To do so, they must meet the two primary requirements of refugee status determination: first, whether the 'well-founded fear of persecution' exists; and second, whether the persecution is linked to one of the grounds of the *Refugees Convention* (race, religion, nationality, membership of a particular social group, or political opinion).

With respect to the first requirement, even where violence and intimidation are carried out by non-state rather than state actors, such activity will constitute cognizable persecution if the state is 'unwilling or unable to provide protection to victims'.[85] Either the persecution in question, or non-protection by the state, must occur on the basis of one of the grounds of the *Refugees Convention* (the

[82] *Refugees Convention* (n 24) art 1.

[83] J McAdam, *Climate Change, Forced Migration and International Law* (OUP Oxford 2014).

[84] UNHCR, 'Guidance Note on Refugee Claims relating to Victims of Organized Gangs' (March 2010).

[85] Ibid para 25.

second requirement).[86] The UNHCR has stated that the designation 'membership of a particular social group' may be met where the asylum seeker is clearly distinguished by young age (since gangs focus on recruiting young people). Similarly, if the asylum seeker resisted gang recruitment, this resistance may be interpreted to place him or her in a particular social group.[87]

The UNHCR's interpretive documents gesture towards still broader interpretations that would include, for example, for children, 'dependency, poverty and lack of parental guidance'[88] or other characteristics of 'origin, social background or class'.[89] However, these documents seem to imply that poverty by itself would not qualify as membership of a particular social group but rather would be viewed in combination with other more distinctive characteristics, such as age, gender, or religion. For example, the UNHCR suggests that 'age-based identification, combined with social status, could be relevant concerning applicants who have refused to join gangs'.[90] The UNHCR also cited approvingly Canadian immigration authorities that considered poverty a relevant characteristic when combined with HIV status, or with participation in a political anti-poverty collective.[91]

US immigration authorities—who are now obligated to address the asylum claims of those in the surge—have rejected most of this expansive reasoning, ignoring the UNHCR's criticisms of misapplication of the standard.[92] In an influential decision, the US Justice Department's Board of Immigration Appeals denied asylum to Salvadoran teenagers who had fled gang recruitment in 2008, stating lack of 'social visibility' and insufficient 'particularity' as bases for rejecting the 'membership of a social group' argument. In doing so, the Board narrowed the more open-ended potential of previous jurisprudence,[93] and, though some subsequent decisions have questioned the vagueness or inconsistency of the S-E-G- holding,[94] the decision has been widely followed.

But I would argue that the problem is not only that contemporary facts of displacement have outpaced the *Refugees Convention*. The problem is that the way in which the *Refugees Convention* is understood, which is to exclude ordinary labour migration, presumes a too-easy distinction between the economic and political that is belied by facts on the ground. In the case of Central America, economic crises contributed to political crises and vice versa: economic reforms that led to

---

[86] UNHCR, 'Guidelines on International Protection No 2: Membership of a Particular Social Group' (May 2002) para 23.

[87] 'Guidance Note on Refugee Claims relating to Victims of Organized Gangs' (n 84) para 41.

[88] Ibid para 36.   [89] Ibid para 41.   [90] Ibid para 36.

[91] Ibid para 41 n 69, citing *MA6-03043* (Immigration and Refugee Board, Canada, 29 February 2009) (Haitian women with HIV-AIDS) and *MA0-06253* (Immigration and Refugee Board, Canada, 18 January 2001) (participation in an agrarian reform collective).

[92] '*Matter of S-E-G-*: The Final Nail in the Coffin for Gang-Related Asylum Claims?' (n 7) 13.

[93] Ibid 5.

[94] *Henriquez-Rivas v Holder* (US Court of Appeals, 9th Cir, Case No 09-71571, 13 February 2013).

destabilization were the result of political crises. Economic destabilization displaced existing livelihoods and increased the population of potential migrants, as well as strengthened the drug cartels by swelling the rank and file. Strengthened drug cartels further contributed to ongoing political crisis.

4.2 The Effect of Migration Policing through Anti-Trafficking and Anti-Smuggling Efforts on Refugee Operations

Recognizing that asylum claims face steep odds in some cases, the UNHCR has called for 'international protection' under other instruments. Some of these instruments, such as the Organization of African Unity *Convention Governing the Specific Aspects of Refugee Problems in Africa* and the *Cartagena Declaration on Refugees*, broaden the definition of a refugee.[95] Others, such as the *Convention on the Rights of the Child* and the *Migrant Workers' Convention*, establish 'complimentary' obligations of protection.[96] However, the US is not a party to any of these instruments.[97] On the other hand, the US is a signatory to the *Convention against Torture* and has implemented immigration regulations that permit asylum where an applicant can establish that he or she will be tortured upon return to the home country. Unlike the *Refugees Convention*, persecution on the basis of specific grounds need not be shown; however, the grant rate for asylum in the US on both *Refugees Convention* and *Convention against Torture* grounds remains 'exceptionally low'.[98]

The question of the interrelationship between treaty frameworks more directly arises with respect to the two protocols dealing with irregular migration established under the *Convention against Transnational Organized Crime*—the *Protocol against Trafficking in Persons* and the *Protocol against Migrant Smuggling*.[99] The US has not

---

[95] *Convention Governing the Specific Aspects of Refugee Problems in Africa* (signed 10 September 1969, entered into force 20 June 1974) 1001 UNTS 45; UNHCR, 'Cartagena Declaration on Refugees' (adopted 22 November 1984) <http://www.unhcr.org/45dc19084.html> [accessed 2 March 2016].

[96] *Convention on the Rights of the Child* (opened for signature 20 November 1989, entered into force 2 September 1990) 1577 UNTS 3; *Migrant Workers' Convention* (n 23).

[97] The US did sign the *Convention on the Rights of the Child* in 1995, but failed to ratify it and so has not become a state party.

[98] S Rempell, 'Credible Fears, Unaccompanied Minors, and the Causes of the Southwestern Border Surge' (2015) 18 *Chapman Law Review* 337–86.

[99] *Protocol to Prevent, Suppress and Punish Trafficking in Persons, Especially Women and Children, Supplementing the United Nations Convention against Transnational Organized Crime* (opened for signature 15 November 2000, entered into force 25 December 2003) 2237 UNTS 319; *Protocol against the Smuggling of Migrants by Land, Sea and Air, Supplementing the United Nations Convention against Transnational Organized Crime* (opened for signature 15 November 2000 entered into force 28 January 2004) 2241 UNTS 507.

only ratified these instruments but also played an important leading role in their negotiation and adoption. The UNHCR has cited the *Trafficking Protocol* as a source of international protection for undocumented migrants who are apprehended by US authorities. Yet the actual level of protection afforded under the *Trafficking Protocol* probably falls far below that of the *Refugee Convention*. The *Trafficking Protocol* does establish as one of its purposes the protection of victims of trafficking and 'full respect for their human rights'.[100] Many commentators have pointed to the fact that this recognition translates into little in the way of clearly binding obligation: rather states are exhorted to 'give appropriate consideration to humanitarian and compassionate factors' in determining whether to afford protection or not;[101] and to provide law enforcement training that 'should also take into account the need to consider human rights and child- and gender-sensitive issues'.[102] By contrast to these 'soft-law' goals, the *Trafficking Protocol* does establish a hard obligation on the part of receiving states to accept repatriation of trafficked persons. Though the *Trafficking Protocol* requires that states 'shall' pay 'due regard to the safety' of trafficked persons,[103] it establishes no specific obligation on states to confer on trafficked persons any form of protection in the way of a visa or residential status.[104]

The specifics of such protection therefore arise under national law of member states. The US, for example, has established a visa for victims of trafficking, called the T visa. The shortcomings of this visa program have also been well documented. The number of visas in the program, amounting to 5,000 annually, falls far short of the magnitude of the problem as stated by US authorities (well over 12,000 annually, though this data is also disputed). Even this allotment has not been fully allocated, due to lack of capacity or implementation. Support services for trafficked persons are woefully underfunded. And, most importantly, all of this relief is generally dependent on the trafficked persons' cooperation with law enforcement, a condition that poses substantial potential dangers in the way of retaliation by those identified through cooperation.

Even these protections overshadow those afforded under the *Migrant Smuggling Protocol*. The *Migrant Smuggling Protocol* provides for the 'humane treatment' of apprehended migrants. It also recognizes the importance of protection of the migrant during repatriation, albeit with language that suffers even more from vagueness than does its counterpart in the *Trafficking Protocol*. (The *Trafficking Protocol* says that states 'shall' pay 'due regard for the safety of 'trafficked persons, whereas the *Migrant Smuggling Protocol* says that states 'shall take all appropriate measures to carry out the return…with due regard for the safety and dignity of the person'.)[105]

---

[100] *Trafficking Protocol* (n 99) art 2.   [101] Ibid art 7.   [102] Ibid art 10.
[103] Ibid art 8.
[104] For a discussion of this language and what obligations it may or may not generate, see A Gallagher, *The International Law of Human Trafficking* (CUP Cambridge 2010).
[105] *Trafficking Protocol* (n 99) art 8; *Migrant Smuggling Protocol* (n 99) art 18.

Importantly, both the *Trafficking Protocol* and the *Migrant Smuggling Protocol* contain 'saving' clauses that stipulate that their obligations are subject to existing rights and obligations under international law.[106] Together with the passing references to human rights elsewhere in these documents, one might conclude that the protocols may not be hugely sympathetic to unauthorized migrants, but they are not necessarily antagonistic. Yet these categories of international law do not sit well together.

One reason has to do with the messiness of facts on the ground as described in the previous section. These instruments set up a hierarchy of entitlements that seems to bear little relationship to the objective of compassionate and humane treatment. The violence, brutality, and fear of return experienced by a trafficked person might resemble that of a refugee, but only the latter can be assured of a right of protection in the receiving state. Moreover, a trafficked person and smuggled migrant might have started out on exactly the same journey, escaping the same circumstances at home, but differences in their treatment along the way or at their destination will result in different kinds of opportunities for continued residence.

The relationship between these protocols, on the one hand, and other sources of international protection for unauthorized migrants such as the *Refugees Convention*, on the other, not only risks arbitrariness in its hierarchical allocation of protection. It seems to arise out of a much more oppositional relationship. At bottom, the *Trafficking* and *Migrant Smuggling* Protocols come out of a criminalization framework. They require states parties to agree to enact and enforce criminal law systems to police unauthorized migration. In that sense, they mirror at the international level the trend within national legal systems, which has been to criminalize unauthorized migration. This criminalization is rendered against a national security policy backdrop. As such, its effects go beyond changes to substantive law, and include massive reallocations of administrative resources towards border security.

In the US, for example, the House of Representatives announced that its fiscal allocations for border patrolling in 2014 would allow for the 'highest operational force levels in history'.[107] The new 'border industrial complex' manifests itself in many interlocking ways. Expenditures have increased for policing at the geographical border, expansively defined as having a range of 100 miles into the interior, with minimal rights afforded to detainees by virtue of the 'border' designation. Significant resources are also devoted to apprehension in the interior, which include formal cooperation programs between federal and local law enforcement such that local law enforcement officers can act as deputies for immigration control.

---

[106] *Trafficking Protocol* (n 99) art 14; *Migrant Smuggling Protocol* (n 99) art 18.

[107] House Appropriations Committee 'FY 2014 Omnibus—Homeland Security Appropriations' (14 January 2014) <http://appropriations.house.gov/uploadedfiles/01.13.14_fy_2014_omnibus_-_homeland_security_-_summary.pdf>.

The dragnet approach to immigration control generates many problems, the foremost of which to many immigration advocates, is that it tends to result in the under-identification of detainees who stand to benefit from the generous protections offered under refugee law or even the minimal ones under anti-trafficking law. Advocates have complained repeatedly that immigration officers are not sufficiently trained or incentivized to examine the possibilities of such protection, railroading the apprehended into unfair detention and deportation. Notwithstanding the compassionate posture of anti-trafficking law, its few compassionate provisions operate within a larger framework that has generally tended to emphasize criminality and border security concerns.

The heavy emphasis on border security and the criminalization of migration creates an environment in which advocates charge that deportation proceedings are hasty and intake officers do not stop to determine whether an apprehended migrant might qualify for protection under asylum or anti-trafficking laws. The acknowledgement of this pressure is in the anti-trafficking provision that has operated most directly in the 2014 border crisis. The purpose of the provision is to guarantee minors a hearing on their potential asylum claims. The provision creates an affirmative obligation to inquire into the circumstances surrounding apprehension and whether an asylum claim exists. In the absence of such a guaranteed hearing, by implication, the sheer force of augmented border patrol might well jeopardize those claims.

The foregoing expresses a sceptical view of the overall humaneness of anti-trafficking efforts. They often seem to be as wolves in sheep's clothing: draped in the language of concern for victims' human rights, they install and legitimate increased policing and criminalization that at least arguably wind up hurting victims more than helping them. However, the jury is still very much out on anti-trafficking, and many advocates and experts have expressed a belief in the potential of the anti-trafficking framework to bring attention to victim's issues in a way that would never be possible with purely human rights or humanitarian efforts. An example of this certainly would be the particular provision in US legislation mentioned earlier, that establishes extraordinary (in the sense of more than ordinarily available) procedural rights for unaccompanied immigrant minors in the name of anti-trafficking. More diffusely, anti-trafficking discourse offers a vocabulary of exigency that can potentially be leveraged for progressive ends. For example, the Regional Conference on Migration's Extraordinary Declaration on the Central America border crisis prominently notes concerns regarding human trafficking and smuggling in urging an orderly and humane response that would focus on the best interests of the children involved.[108]

---

[108] Regional Conference on Migration, 'Managua Extraordinary Declaration' (10 July 2014) <http://mexico.usembassy.gov/press-releases/managua-extraordinary-declaration.html> [accessed 2 March 2016].

5 Crisis and Reconceptualization

The current crisis shows the interplay amongst areas of global law and policy that might at first glance seem quite separate—economic law, refugee law, and criminal law. It also exposes the dramatic shortcomings of refugee law in addressing conditions of global crisis today. The premise that seems to underlie the *Refugees Convention* is that countries should uphold humanitarian ideals by protecting individuals whose civil and political rights—formal equality under law, political or religious expression—have been threatened by other governments. The moral equation operating in the 2014 crisis, and in global migration today more generally, should be much different. First, a formalistic application of existing *Refugees Convention* categories in the face of today's crises, when the *Refugees Convention* is justified by an idea of compassion, which by its nature is unbounded, seems the very definition of arbitrariness and therefore injustice.

Second, the ethics of the situation seem to go beyond a unilateral notion of mercy or compassion. In fact the US holds partial responsibility for creating the forces that have led to this crisis. It may well be this alternative ethics of responsibility that helps shape unauthorized migration in the first place. Emily Ryo has conducted sociological work suggesting that undocumented migrants do not view themselves as immoral lawbreakers, but rather as fulfilling moral responsibilities such as provision for their families that overrides any sense of immorality that stems from breaking immigration law.[109] Considering Ryo's work in light of the foregoing, there may well be another moral consideration at work, which is the belief on the part of these migrants that the US holds some responsibility towards them on the basis of its past actions in their own countries. The US government consistently violated national and international laws in supporting military interventions in these migrants' countries. It sought out the establishment of export crops, trade agreements, and investment arrangements that eliminated preexisting livelihoods in agriculture and created dependency on US markets. And it at times promoted itself as a model of humanitarianism. The arrival of unauthorized migrants on the US's proverbial doorstep, in this calculation, may constitute no more than a richly deserved reward for decades of US involvement in Central America that has helped to lead to this moment.

Discussion of the immigration problem is often infused with a resigned sense of the impossibility of viable solutions. The reforms that are proposed are generally modest and deferential to presumed sovereign prerogative. This modesty is all the

---

[109] E Ryo, 'Deciding to Cross: Norms and Economics of Unauthorized Migration' (2013) 78 *American Sociological Review* 574–603.

more striking given the incredible boldness of current institution-making in other areas of international law, such as trade and investment. Clearly, international law is capable of metamorphosing in relatively short order.

So what kinds of solutions might be proposed to address the problems of irregular migration? Certainly, one can imagine amending existing provisions within international law to allow for more expansive interpretation of protected classes within the population of irregular migrants, and more expansive interpretation of the protections given. In the case of trafficking, the *Trafficking Protocol* might be amended to provide for concrete obligations to assist trafficked persons, including through the provision of immigration status relief. In the case of refugees, examples exist within positive international law, such as the Organization for African Unity's 1969 *Convention Governing the Specific Aspects of Refugee Problems in Africa*.[110] That convention expands the definition of refugee, from beyond the specific categories established by the *Refugees Convention* and towards a recognition of the broader dynamics of displacement, providing that a refugee is a 'person who, owing to external aggression, occupation, foreign domination or events seriously disturbing public order in either part or the whole of his country of origin or nationality, is compelled to leave his place of habitual residence in order to seek refuge in another place outside his country of origin or nationality'.[111]

One could also imagine a more consistent incorporation of free movement of labour into international trade and investment agreements, which would expand legal avenues of border entry even beyond the cases of duress and hardship required by international law on refugees and trafficked persons. Of course here too salient examples exist within positive international law: many regional economic integration agreements, such as the EU, MERCOSUR, and ECOWAS, have followed this path. Another possibility is the use of bilateral labour and migration agreements, though these tend to be hobbled in their effectiveness by an imbalance of bargaining power between sending and receiving countries, since concessions in the area of migration for sending countries cannot be traded against other concessions for receiving countries in such agreements.[112]

There have even been proposals for freestanding international organizations addressing migration. The economist Jagdish Bhagwati has long proposed a World Migration Organization that would provide a basis for negotiating concessions in immigration controls in much the same way that international economic organizations such as the General Agreement on Tariffs and Trade (GATT) and then the WTO, as well as international investment agreements, have provided the basis for

---

[110] *Convention Governing the Specific Aspects of Refugee Problems in Africa* (n 95).
[111] Ibid art 1(2).
[112] M Panizzon, 'Temporary Movement of Workers and Human Rights Protection' (2010) 104 *Proceedings of the American Society of International Law* 131–9.

negotiating concessions in trade and investment controls.[113] Such a framework need not entail an immediate 'open borders' prerogative—one could imagine piecemeal lists based on reciprocal negotiation along the lines of reciprocal tariff negotiations in the trade context.

The immediate counter with respect to all of the foregoing relates to political will, or rather the lack thereof. It is not the lack of imagination of alternatives to the status quo that has constrained the development of new international legal rules and institutions on migration, but the lack of any political imperative. The countries of the global South simply do not harbour enough influence to persuade countries of the global North to make concessions on migration.

One might then speculate as to the implications of the rise in stature of the large emerging markets—the so-called BRICS (Brazil, Russia, India, China, South Africa) and their like—on the political will calculus. As of the time of writing, it seems unclear: it is possible that the rise of the major players out-side the West will shift the balance of power in a way such as to place migration issues firmly on the table in multilateral negotiations. On the other hand, as countries in the developing world generate enough economic dynamism to become migration-receiving countries, they will ally themselves more with the receiving countries of the industrialized world against migrant rights. As it is, more refugees and asylum seekers reside in developing countries than developed ones. Migration issues, like trade and investment issues, might become another wedge differentiating those poor countries that seem to be moving towards con-vergence with the industrialized world and those that continue to struggle in the periphery.

Moreover, even where the political will might exist to expand migration rights as a formal matter, such formal action hardly resolves the matter. The EU serves as a potentially cautionary tale here: the rich countries of Western Europe have become wracked by spasms of anti-immigrant politics. The danger of domestic political backlash forms one of the primary lodestars for the 'apologist' or 'realist' view of international law: given that states are sovereign, after all, international lawyers must never charge them with greater responsibilities than they can will-ingly tolerate. The third rail of political legitimacy circumscribes the boundaries—figuratively and legally—to which international law can aspire.

What is needed, then, is an alternative legal imaginary.[114] As long as a concept of absolute sovereignty serves as the foundation for domestic and international law, migration rights must appear as a dramatic concession. A critical framework can do much to dismantle this preconception, by pointing out that both historically and currently the concept of sovereignty has been in many cases much more fluid

[113] J Bhagwati, 'A Champion for Migrating Peoples' (28 February 1992) *Christian Science Monitor.*
[114] This section draws from Thomas, 'What Does the Emerging International Law of Migration Mean for Sovereignty?' (n 26).

and open than the absolutist view would concede. This chapter has tried to demonstrate the ways in which this is so with respect to the 2014 crisis.

The issue of how migration should relate to sovereignty sharply expresses some of the paradoxes of this age of globalization.[115] A paradox can be defined as 'a statement or proposition that, despite sound (or apparently sound) reasoning from acceptable premises, leads to a conclusion that seems senseless, logically unacceptable or self-contradictory'. A defining paradox arises out of the conflict between the international community's universalistic aspirations, expressed in its founding and core documents, and the bounded states charged with realizing those aspirations. The former category constrains sovereignty; the latter category insists on it.

The classical way of resolving this apparent paradox or tension would be to see states as irreducible and fundamental components of the international legal system. Seen as such, there is no tension between migrant human rights and state sovereignty, because the construct of human rights *assumes* the idea of a state. In giving effect to the right (and duty) to admit its nationals to its territory, from this view, the state is not discriminating—it is taking into account a relevant difference. Modern thought provides ample reasoning from popular sovereignty, self-determination, and democratic legitimacy, to support a defined, and thereby exclusionary, community. There are both principled and pragmatic grounds for exclusion: the value of communal self-definition and self-determination, and the practical constraints of governance.[116] And, one might add, the primacy of states is encoded into international law. The limitation of the right to freedom of movement to those lawfully present within a state, as in the Civil and Political Rights Covenant,[117] expresses the supreme right of the state to determine who shall be territorially present and therefore designated as a rights beneficiary. Thus, any tension that exists between migrant rights and state sovereignty is at best a matter of speculation in uncodified moral discourse rather than international law properly so-called.

Yet the moral tension has found its way into positive law at both the international and national levels. The enforcement of rights claims on behalf of irregular migrants stands as incontrovertible proof of this. Were the state supremely in control of its ability to designate rights beneficiaries on the basis of granting or denying territorial entry, it would not be the case that it could be required to extend protections to unlawfully present migrants.[118] But such

---

[115] H Chang, 'Liberalized Immigration as Free Trade: Economic Welfare and the Optimal Immigration Policy' (1997) 145 *University of Pennsylvania Law Review* 1147–244.

[116] M Walzer, *Spheres of Justice: A Defense of Pluralism and Equality* (Basic Books New York 1983).

[117] *ICCPR* (n 23) art 12.

[118] See, eg, *Jamaa v Italy* (ECtHR Case No 27765/09, Grand Chamber, 23 February 2012); J Crawford, *Chance, Order, Change: The Course of International Law* (Brill Leiden 2014) at 275–82.

obligations have been articulated, on the basis of principles of universal human equality and liberty.[119]

If such principles are powerful enough to induce jurisprudential findings that states must be required to recognize the rights of irregular migrants in at least some instances, then it is not the case that international law can be seen as an orderly ecosystem neatly divisible into states. Rather, outgrowths and rifts in international law express competing principles—state sovereignty, and individual liberty and equality—each of which cannot be fully resolved into the other. An understanding of international law as composed by sovereign states charged with protecting universal human rights expresses these two foundational, but self-contradictory, premises: a paradox.

Political theorists have typically identified this paradox as arising out of the simultaneously interdependent and oppositional relationship between liberalism and democracy, or individual rights and majority rule.[120] The state in democratic theory is in fact a *nation*-state, with some notion of popular community undergirding the state's legitimacy. Whereas democratic theory considers the paradox from the perspective of the internal constitution of states through popular will, my focus here is on the exclusion of foreigners by states, and attends to society's external or outward-looking posture. These can be understood as complementary aspects of popular sovereignty: the state's exercise of sovereignty, including the power to exclude, is justified by this popular constitution. These two aspects influence each other, as in deliberations by constitutional and democratic theorists regarding the justifiability of a social contract or community that allocates benefits and exclusions on the basis of citizenship.[121] At the same time, they can, from the perspective outlined earlier, also expose a foundational paradox. Seyla Benhabib has termed this the 'paradox of democratic legitimacy'.[122] Benhabib centres the 'paradox of democratic legitimacy' on the 'tension between universal human rights claims and particularistic cultural and national identities'.[123]

This political or philosophical tension thus is also to a large extent a sociological one. Migrant identity is marginalized by definition in a state whose boundaries are intended to evoke and protect a membership community of political, cultural, and often ethnic mutual belonging.[124] Indeed, according to a famous sociological

---

[119] See eg interpretations of the *ICCPR* by the Human Rights Committee, and the texts of the ILO and UN conventions on migrant workers; see also US constitutional law holdings finding applicability of the Equal Protection Clause to undocumented migrants in some instances, eg *Plyler v Doe*, 457 US 202 (1982).

[120] C Mouffe, *The Democratic Paradox* (Verso New York 2000).

[121] L Bosniak, *The Citizen and the Alien: Dilemmas of Contemporary Membership* (Princeton University Press Princeton 2006).

[122] S Benhabib, *The Rights of Others: Aliens, Residents and Citizens* (CUP Cambridge 2004) at 43.

[123] S Benhabib, *Another Cosmopolitanism* (OUP Oxford 2006) at 32–3.

[124] *The Citizen and the Alien* (n 121) 23.

study, the migrant signifies simultaneously both the proximate and the remote. Translating in reverse from the equivalent French juridical term, '*l'étranger*'[125] allows for a contemplation of the sociologist Georg Simmel's influential 1908 analysis of 'the stranger'.[126]

The definition of 'alien' adopted by the International Law Commission ('ILC') reflects the precise qualities identified by Simmel: 'An alien is generally understood to be a natural person who is not a national of the State in which he or she is present.'[127] Both legally and epistemically then, the migrant embodies what is both present and distant and therefore what is strange, alien and outside—what is other.[128] Through this negation and affirmation, the figure of the migrant denotes the boundaries of the national self as a social body.[129] As such, the migrant as outsider is both excluded from and necessary to the nation-state. The existence of foreigners, being non-members, validates and gives value to the modern concept of a membership society: the social contract.[130]

It is through this disjuncture that the migrant inscribes the modern condition, traversing a global landscape bounded by national communities but also shaped by the ideals of universal human equality, and by the expansive and disruptive effects of unbounded markets. The presence of the migrant implies the existence of an extensive market—as Simmel notes that historically, migrants were commonly traders and vice versa[131]—the rise of both trade and migration are a product of, and produce, the powerfully disruptive and productive forces of a capitalist market economy.

Despite the migrant's juridical and epistemic marginality, the contemporary era of globalization is bringing the migrant more prominently into view. In the past, some advocates of economic globalization erroneously presumed that opening borders to trade in goods and capital would preclude the need for the movement of persons. In fact, migration of persons constitutes a predictable and profound complement to other dimensions of globalization.

---

[125] For example, the United Nations' Preliminary Report on the Expulsion of Aliens is published in French as the *Rapport prélimininaire sur l'expulsion des étrangers*: see Maurice Kamto, *Preliminary Report on the Expulsion of Aliens* (2 June 2005) UN Doc A/CN.4/554.

[126] G Simmel, 'The Stranger (1908)' in *Georg Simmel on Individuality and Social Forms* (DN Levine trans) (University of Chicago Press Chicago 1972) 143–9.

[127] International Law Commission, *Expulsion of Aliens—Memorandum by the Secretariat* (10 July 2006) UN Doc A/CN.4/565, at 23, 24 (citations omitted).

[128] EW Said, *Orientalism* (Random House London 1979).

[129] The denotation of the social body is taken from M Foucault, *Discipline and Punish: The Birth of the Prison* (A Sheridan trans) (2nd edn Random House London 1995).

[130] B Honig, *Democracy and the Foreigner* (Princeton University Press Princeton 2001). Thanks to Bernie Meyler for pointing me towards this work.

[131] 'The Stranger' (n 126) 144 ('In the whole history of economic activity the stranger makes his appearance as a trader, and the trader makes his as a stranger').

These paradoxes, or at least tensions, have manifested themselves in certain conundrums of state and social practice in this age of globalization: contradictory movements that express these opposing impulses. The increasing intensity of border control at a time of unprecedented liberalization emblematizes such conundrums. Accordingly Wendy Brown offers her own three paradoxes to describe the rise of border enclosures accompanying globalization, which entail 'simultaneous opening and blocking…universalization…and stratification, and…networked and virtual power met by physical barricades.'[132]

The complex of rules, institutions, and practices governing the international legal order is constantly subjected to 'ascending' and 'descending' structures of argument.[133] These institutions embody both political impulses: international law encompasses opposing positions of realpolitik apology for sovereign power on the one hand, and aspiration towards utopian universality on the other.[134] At the core of this theoretical framework lies a premise that our social worlds—our collective and individual selves—are riven by competing human impulses, the 'opposed rhetorical modes' of 'individualism and altruism.'[135] Through the particulars of legal history and social context, these impulses have created a jurisprudence that houses both dynamics. The interplay of rule and exception in the form and substance of legal doctrine, as a product of our making, can do no more than give effect to these conflicts.

As a consequence, the law contains within itself multiple avenues of interpretation. The diagnosis of indeterminacy has caused many to charge critical theory with nihilism, given that it not only endorses no grand narrative of progress, but resists the claims that correct legal answers can exist separately from questions of policy and politics, which are necessarily variable.[136] Yet it should be clear from the foregoing that critical theory does not espouse a vision of grand demise either. The contingency inherent in laws and institutions also provide opportunities for resistance to injustice.[137]

Given this, a critical legal understanding of the international law of migration might see sovereignty not as 'waning,' but rather 'fracturing,' as Brown herself ultimately concludes.[138] In any case, legal analysis should ask a different question: not whether sovereignty is increasing or decreasing, but how it is changing;[139] how it mediates and is mediated by 'opposed modes' in legal discourse.

---

[132] W Brown, *Walled States, Waning Sovereignty* (Zone Books New York 2010) at 20.
[133] See *From Apology to Utopia* (n 27).   [134] Ibid.
[135] DM Kennedy, 'Form and Substance in Private Law Adjudication' (1976) 89 *Harvard Law Review* 1685–1778.
[136] See eg OM Fiss, 'The Death of the Law?' (1986) 72 *Cornell Law Review* 1–16.
[137] L Eslava and S Pahuja, 'Between Resistance and Reform: TWAIL and the Universality of International Law' (2011) 3 *Trade, Law and Development*, 103–30.
[138] *Walled States, Waning Sovereignty* (n 132) 67.
[139] *Chance, Order, Change* (n 118) 108–12.

This chapter has briefly illustrated some of these instances of mediation with respect to the 2014 crisis, for example, the law of trafficking in persons seeks to aid victims of trafficking but also potentially to further criminal law enforcement at their expense. The treaties on the rights of migrant workers establish protections but also limitations;[140] they establish constraints on sovereign prerogative but also exhort its enhancement.[141] The ILC's *Draft Articles on the Expulsion of Aliens* establish minimum standards for the treatment of aliens, but in the service of assisting in their territorial expulsion as a consequence of state will. These instruments— after all products of interstate agreement—simultaneously express concern for the well-being of migrants and then reaffirm the importance of sovereignty.

Legal critique should also interest itself not only in detailing the particulars of these dynamics of mediation, but also in revealing the ways in which they amount to a legitimation of the status quo, stymying awareness of demands for and possibilities of social justice. Hence, the emerging international law of migration may legitimate broader practices of border control, despite or because of its establishment of limited rights against sovereignty.

Beyond critique, however, what of an alternative ethics? Modern lawyers have often gestured towards the idea of international federation, from Kant's perpetual peace to the McDougal and Lasswell's notion of world public order.[142] Typically, these have been perceived as unrealistic, but what defines even these aspirational theories is their foundational commitment to liberal legality, which at its core insists on the discreteness and autonomy of the individual. Yet foundational liberalism informs the political commitment not only to individual atomism but also to the atomism of states: in its historical formations, liberal philosophers reasoned the sovereign rights of individuals by analogy to states, and vice versa.[143] Against this worldview shaped by atomism, the project of universal federalism can only strain.

However, perhaps these foundational liberal commitments to autonomy and atomism reflect an outdated knowledge.[144] We can think of ourselves, in the late modern age, as embodying the remnants of a paradigm that no longer adequately explains our world.[145] Countless contributions of contemporary knowledge,

---

[140] Compare *Migrant Workers' Convention* (n 23) pt III (establishing rights for all migrant workers) with pt IV (establishing rights for 'regular' workers).

[141] See eg *Migrant Workers (Supplementary Provisions) Convention* (opened for signature 24 June 1975 entered into force 9 December 1978) 1120 UNTS 323 art 3 (obliging states parties to adopt 'all necessary and appropriate measures' to suppress illegal movement and employment of migrants).

[142] I Kant, 'Perpetual Peace: A Philosophical Sketch' in *Kant: Political Writings* (HS Reiss ed HB Nisbet trans) (2nd edn CUP Cambridge 1991) 93–130; MS McDougal et al., (eds), *Studies in World Public Order* (Yale University Press New Haven 1960).

[143] 'What Does the Emerging International Law of Migration Mean for Sovereignty?' (n 26) 448.

[144] Ibid 448–50.

[145] TS Kuhn, *The Structure of Scientific Revolutions* (3rd edn University of Chicago Press Chicago 1996 [1962]).

ranging from psychology to physics, suggest, against atomism, that our world is radically intra-connected. We depend on others for survival, let alone flourishing; our actions necessarily affect others as well as ourselves. Interconnectedness, not individualism, should be understood to define the human condition, and therefore form an alternative basis for moral and political possibility.

Recognition of interconnectedness does not require collectivism, or any of its horrors in antiquity or modernity. It can accept difference and even incommensurability. As such, interconnectedness may provide an ultimately thin basis for moral reasoning; but so too does liberalism, very often, and 'thinness' may be preferable in an international context.[146] Certainly, adopting interconnectedness as a starting point leaves a host of questions unanswered. What it also does, however, is potentially shift the ethical imperative: from the presumption that we are justified in defending our borders, the question becomes what implications arise, for ourselves and for others, when we do so.

---

[146] See SR Ratner, *The Thin Justice of International Law* (OUP Oxford 2015).

PART IV

DEBATES

CHAPTER 44

RELIGION, SECULARISM, AND INTERNATIONAL LAW

REUT YAEL PAZ

1 INTRODUCTION

RELIGION generates what is essential in society. In fact, the very idea of society is 'the soul of religion'.[1] Much 'unavowed theologeme' is therefore the result, even in the most secular societies.[2] The following contribution scrutinizes the tensions and fragilities between religiosity and secularism in international law. After all, whatever the conflicts between these 'supra-structures', the asymmetry is clear: religion precedes secularism which precedes but also pervades international law—one of secularism's many façades.[3] Understanding these delicate affinities remains

---

[1] É Durkheim, *The Elementary Forms of the Religious Life* (JW Swain trans) (G Allen & Unwin London 1915) at 314.

[2] The idea here is that regardless of how far one might think democracies have moved away from the ancient worlds' 'old ontologies'—patriarchal religions, monarchies, aristocracies, oligarchs, and so forth—reliance on the centrality of a sovereign God is still very existential, even if not admitted. See further JD Caputo, 'Without Sovereignty, without Being, Unconditionality, the Coming God and Derrida's Democracy to Come' in C Crockett (ed), *Religion and Violence in a Secular World: Toward a New Political Theology* (University of Virginia Press Virginia 2006) 137–56.

[3] The process of secularization is long, complex, and chaotic and can be explained in repeated collisions, distinctions, conflicts, shifting definitions, and alliances between the 'sacred' and 'profane'.

extremely important given both religion and law are resorted to interchangeably in the search for dictates of consciousness.[4] Christian monotheism, as discussed in more detail later in the chapter, had the largest impact on secularism and international law. Moreover, although a certain exchange between Christianity and secularism remains constant, whatever the interaction, it happens mostly through a profane image of Christianity. This raises difficulties, especially for international law. Not only is social homogeneity virtually absent in the international community, clear Christian bias in international law is still to be reconciled, if not overcome altogether.[5]

The focus here is the inseparable nature of the relationship between religion—more specifically, Christianity—secularism, and international law, because it remains in the hands of specific protagonist personae to 'replace' religion and, to a certain extent, morality in general with the 'order' of international law. As the history of international law itself reveals, its inauguration as a liberal profession depended on a group of men who shared a particular universal intuition and cultural agenda that mirrored their Western Christian European and cosmopolitan backgrounds at the end of the nineteenth century.[6] The main methodological premise here is that the reality of the international legal discipline (that is, its knowledge) is socially and historically constructed; the general lens here is that of the sociology of knowledge (*Wissenssoziologie*),

---

At the risk of over-simplification, the word secularism and secularization are used here interchangeably with reference to an incomplete *process* that assumes the lack of theological underpinnings of European thought. See further M Somos, *Secularisation and the Leiden Circle* (Brill Leiden 2011). However, Europe remains, as Christopher Dawson describes it, 'Christendom, though it was a Christendom secularized and divided,' at least until the eighteenth century, if not to this day: C Dawson, *Progress and Religion: An Historical Inquiry into the Causes and Development of the Idea of Progress and Its Relationship to Religion* (Sheed & Ward London 1929) at 169. For the purposes at hand, it is enough to keep in mind José Casanova's three distinctions: secularization can first be understood as the differentiation of the secular spheres from religious institutions and norms; secondly, it may denote the decline of religious belief and practices; and thirdly, secularization can refer to the marginalization of religion to a privatized sphere. Thus, the 'process of functional differentiation and emancipation of the secular spheres—primarily the modern state, the capitalist market economy, and modern science—[originates] from the religious sphere, and the concomitant differentiation and specialization of religion within its newly found religious sphere': J Casanova, 'Secularisation Revisited: A Reply to Talal Asad' in D Scott and C Hirschkind (eds), *Powers of the Secular Modern: Talal Asad and His Interlocutors* (Stanford University Press Stanford 2006) 12–30, at 12–13.

   [4] See more in RY Paz, *A Gateway between a Distant God and a Cruel World: The Contribution of Jewish German-Speaking Scholars to International Law* (Martinus Nijhoff Leiden 2012).

   [5] This might explain why for instance the United Nations has not pursued a covenant or any legally binding instrument on freedom of religion as it has done with issues such as the rights of minorities, women, and children. See further RF Drinan SJ, *Can God and Caesar Coexist? Balancing Religious Freedom and International Law* (Yale University Press New Haven 2005) at 3, 8.

   [6] For more on the formation of the international legal profession see M Koskenniemi, *The Gentle Civilizer of Nations: The Rise and Fall of International Law 1870–1960* (CUP Cambridge 2001).

which emphasizes that theories and ideas have homes and histories.[7] Otherwise stated, theories and ideas are not static nor do they depend on scholarly efforts alone: how such theories are received, echoed and/or recorded in history is of similar importance.[8] More precisely, this contribution begins with the a priori hypothesis that international law is not as unreligious as its practitioners argue it to be.[9] Secondly, the history of international law, just like the history of ideas in general, 'is not dead, it isn't even the past', as William Faulkner phrased it. That is to say, whatever the nineteenth-century developments are, they go back to previous generations of scholarly contributions and historical moments.[10]

Although there are numerous significant trajectories between international law and European Christianities, the need to remain in sync with the limitations of the present context necessarily constrains my approach to one very specific and signifi-cant time frame: namely, the sixteenth-century Renaissance in Spain. Considering the intention here is to scrutinize the relationship between Christian images and international law, the conditions that prompted the revival of twelfth-century Roman law by the Catholic School of Salamanca—more specifically, Francisco de Vitoria, Domingo de Soto, and their successors—ought to be recapitulated.[11] As Martti Koskenniemi phrased it: 'Modern international law was born as liberal

---

[7] 'The collective character of scientific work determines not only the elaboration of new ideas but also their genesis...a new idea, a new thought, can never be traced back to a particular individual [but] rather from collective cooperation whose medium is communication of thought': RS Cohen and T Schnelle, 'Introduction' in RS Cohen and T Schnelle (eds), *Cognition and Fact: Materials on Ludwik Fleck* (D Reidel Dordrecht 1986) ix–xxxiii, at xi.

[8] For more on this methodological angle, see *A Gateway between a Distant God and a Cruel World* (n 4) 32–6.

[9] David Kennedy sums up this desire:

[L]iberal ecumenicalism stands guard at the door of law's empire, insisting on a penitent and persistent pluralism. All who pass murmur Yes, we have no religion. Once inside, secular cosmo-politans recognize one another in declarations of faith, in progress, in the international, in the pragmatic, and worship together in the routines of bureaucratic power.... Everywhere there is ideology, politics, passion, but not here, among the reasonable men and women of the enlighten-ment, graced with infinite time, reason, and the modesty of the truly powerful.

D Kennedy, 'Losing Faith in the Secular: Law, Religion, and the Culture of International Governance' in MW Janis and C Evans (eds), *Religion and International Law* (Kluwer Law International The Hague 1999) 307–19, at 316.

[10] Tellingly, the story of international law usually begins with the Peace of Westphalia (1648) that ended the Thirty Years' War in Europe between Western Catholicism and Lutheranism. Apart from the Westphalian narrative, which, for all intents and purposes, created the present state system, the origin of international law can even be read in the Bible through, among others, the story of the Tower of Babel. See further *A Gateway between a Distant God and a Cruel World* (n 4) 86.

[11] The vast juristic/theologian scholarship by the School of Salamanca dedicated to the regulation by the Spanish Crown of its American colonies is usually divided into three eras: the first consists of the 'founders'—led by Francisco de Vitoria (1483/92–1546) and his younger colleague, Domingo de Soto (1494–1560); the second of those who represented the 'expansion' era, mainly led by Dominican professors; and lastly, the 'synthesis' era, ending with the Jesuit Francisco Suárez (1548–1617). See further M Koskenniemi, 'Empire and International Law: The Real Spanish Contribution' (2011) 61 *University of Toronto Law Journal* 1–36, at 7.

empires turned to formal annexation. But the ideological base lay in its religious critique of the Spanish empire.'[12] Jennifer Beard takes this even further and demonstrates thoroughly how these specific Christian practices continue to constitute the genealogy and practices of development and its subjects in the 'post-Imperialist world'.[13] Witnessing 'the discovery of the world and man', these Renaissance men evoked major transformations that transcended social, political, and geographical distances or barriers.[14] Crucially, it was *at least* since then that the public/private distinction—originally stemming from the Roman law *summa-divisio*—turned into religious, cultural, political, and legal facts in a universal manner.[15]

Thus, the following scrutinizes the Catholic School of Salamanca as a case study that mirrors how Christianity—Catholic missionarism more accurately—became an integral part of international law to date. It is important to underline that I refrain from examining all aspects of the School of Salamanca, given the recent attention the topic has received.[16] Instead, I focus on the leading and limiting questions of how and why the Salamancans' specific reconfiguration of the public/private has become a resilient and persistent formula to this day. After all, the brilliance of the Salamancan contribution lies in the manner in which it relied on a religious formula in order to link the general to the particular in an almost organic manner.

To do this, I begin by briefly setting the stage for the Salamancan protagonist personae in a twofold manner. I first unpack several theoretical and methodological concerns about Christianity, Europe, and international law. I then move to map several historical aspects that relate to the socio-economic conditions of the Salamancan legal contributions. This allows for a more general understanding of why and how the School of Salamanca succeeded in entrenching its scholarly products in their contemporaries as well as their succeeding schools, movements, and intellectual configurations. Furthermore, it sets the stage for a more specific link I make to Michel Foucault's approach to sixteenth-century Catholic religious practices that focuses on the relationship between knowledge, power, governance, and the Sacrament of Penance, which plays an extremely important role in the Salamancans' success.

---

[12] 'Empire and International Law' (n 11) 4.

[13] See J Beard, *The Political Economy of Desire: International Law, Development and the Nation State* (Routledge Abingdon 2007).

[14] 'The discovery of the world and man' is the title of part IV of Jacob Burckhardt's notorious 1860s book. See also J Burckhardt, *Die Kultur der Renaissance in Italien* (Phaidon Verlag Wien 1930 [1860]).

[15] Although Castile received the Roman law during the twelfth century, its relevance grew only during the sixteenth century together with the construction of the modern state, a definition that arguably typifies the Spanish Empire of the sixteenth century, particularly due to its 'new-world' conquests. See more in FV Caballero, 'The Public–Private Law Divide in Spanish Law' in M Ruffert (ed), *The Public–Private Law Divide: Potential for Transformation?* (British Institute of International and Comparative Law London 2009) 123–43, at 125.

[16] See eg B Sabahi, *Compensation and Restitution in Investor-State Arbitration: Principles and Practice* (OUP Oxford 2011); A Azevedo Alves and J Moreira, *The Salamanca School* (Bloomsbury New York 2009); M Koskenniemi, 'The Political Theology of Trade Law: The Scholastic Contribution' in U Fastenrath et al., (eds), *From Bilateralism to Community Interest: Essays in Honor of Judge Bruno Simma* (OUP Oxford 2011) 90–112; 'Empire and International Law' (n 11).

2 On Matters of Theory and Method: Christianity, Europe, and International Law

Examining how international law becomes infused with the (missionary) logic of Christianity demands a better understanding of how the very competition between Christianities facilitated the construction of the international legal project in a more general sense. The starting point here is the interesting nexus between the inauguration of international law as a profession during the end of the nineteenth century,[17] and the decline of overt religious contestations between Western European Christianities.[18]

In more than one way the tension lies between the imagination of how and what Europe was on the one hand, and its factual reality on the other hand. It is often forgotten for instance that the right to free exercise of religion granted *only* to Lutherans and Calvinists in the Holy Roman Empire—after the intra-Christian denominational war that ended with the Peace of Westphalia (1648)—was a rule of expediency. It cannot be stressed enough that religious tolerance—even within Western European Christendom, civilization, and/or culture—is nothing but a fragile and pragmatic acceptance that social stability has a price.[19] European international lawyers also exemplify this tension: Robert Ward's post-natural history of international law (1795) illustrates this too. For him 'CHRISTIANITY is the only *certain* foundation for that code [the law of nations] which is observed by Christian, in other words, by European nations'.[20] Ignoring the glaring differences

---

[17] The first professional association of international lawyers was established in Ghent, Belgium in 1873. It was in the first article of the statute of the *Institute de Droit International* there that eleven European men defined themselves as 'the juridical conscience of the civilized world': M Koskenniemi, 'International Law in Europe: Between Tradition and Renewal' (2005) 16 *European Journal of International Law* 113–24.

[18] Arguably, the last distinctly religious war between European Christianities was as late as the Crimean War (1853–6), which officially started in a conflict between European Empires over the Holy Places in Jerusalem. Significantly, alliances were made also according to which nations represented which Christianity. For instance the Greek Orthodox argued with the Armenians over division of the Virgin's Tomb; the Armenians struggled with the Syriac Jacobites over the cemetery of Mount Zion; the Orthodox fought with the Catholics over the ownership of the St Nicodemus Chapel in the Church, while the Armenians competed the Orthodox over the ownership of the Churches east of the main entrance staircases and the Copts disputed the Ethiopians over ownership of the rooftop monasteries. See further S Sebag Montefiore, *Jerusalem: A Biography* (Phoenix London 2012) at 315, 509.

[19] See further *A Gateway between a Distant God and a Cruel World* (n 4) 7.

[20] R Ward, *An Enquiry into the Foundation and History of the Law of Nations in Europe, from the Time of the Greeks and Romans, to the Age of Grotius* (2 vols Butterworth London 1795) vol 1 at xl (emphasis in original).

within Western European Christianities, Ward goes on to argue that 'there must be a different law of nations for different parts of the globe'.[21]

But matters do not necessarily get smoother once the fragmentation of Western Christianity is ignored. In fact, whatever the differences are, there is at least one essential aspect that is shared by all Christianities, namely, its profound mission-ary impulse.[22] Christianity is a universal, inclusive, and a 'sending' religion as the term missionarism itself indicates.[23] Especially since the eleventh and twelfth centuries, the ecclesiastical reformers of the Latin Church pushed for universal assent, 'for upon it depended God's favour for the Christian world'.[24] The religious command to share the revelation of God in Christ however does not mean it lacks the discriminatory element that, inter alia, establishes authority and subjugation.[25] Alas, focusing on that which Christianities share—their missionary element—is equally problematic for any real universal law that would respect all religious, pol-itical, social, and moral entities alike. Such law would have to deny all forms and shapes of missionarism, and by so doing, deny a central part of all Christianities.[26] It is hardly surprising therefore that Ward continues his argument by admitting that '[w]ith us in Europe, and the nations that spring from us, the Moral System is founded upon REVEALED RELIGION'.[27] Ward, similar to so many other international legal scholars, leaves clear ambiguities unresolved: building on that which unifies different Christianities while leaving open the question about what Europe exactly is, not to mention the ambiguities left by his reference to 'nations that spring from us'. The Christian and Eurocentric character of international law remains a tool of both subjugation and liberation of the 'Other' to date and

---

[21] *An Enquiry into the Foundation and History of the Law of Nations in Europe* (n 20) xiv.

[22] J Langan, 'Revelation in Christ: 1 John 1:1–4; Matthew 28:16–20; John 16:12–15' in D Marshall (ed), *Communicating the Word: Revelation, Translation, and Interpretation in Christianity and Islam* (Georgetown University Press Washington DC 2011) 37–43, at 42.

[23] The term 'mission' goes back to the Biblical Greek word for 'sending'.

[24] As Edward Peters continues to explain: 'Dissenting belief or behaviour not only threatened to corrupt Christian society, but it also entailed the danger of bringing down the wrath of God upon guilty and innocent alike': E Peters, *Inquisition* (University of California Press Berkeley 1989) at 41.

[25] While this is discussed further later, it suffices here to note that one of Christianity's funda-ments is what Mordechai Rotenberg terms 'hermeneutic missionarism': not only is its truth and revelation the only way for redemption (as written in John 14:6: 'I am the way, the truth, and the life: no man cometh unto the Father, except through me'), missionarism as institutionalized through the Christian methodology 'elucidates *how* the one, and presumably the only, "true" authentic ver-sion of a text or reality is disseminated, but also it determines who has the authority to impose that interpretation': M Rotenberg, *Rewriting the Self: Psychotherapy and Midrash* (Transactions New Brunswick 2004 [1987]) at 30–2 (emphasis in original).

[26] As indicated in Mathew 28:19–20: 'Go to the people of all nations and make them my disci-ples. Baptize them in the name of the Father, the Son, and the Holy Spirit, and teach them to do everything I have told you. I will be with you always, even until the end of the world.' See further 'Revelation in Christ' (n 22) 42. The Christian missionary movement began during the fourth cen-tury in Judea gradually expanding throughout the Roman Empire.

[27] *An Enquiry into the Foundations and History of the Law of Nations in Europe* (n 20) 128.

hence, albeit historical and circumstantial differences, continues to be the discipline's Achilles' heel.[28] In brief, it is impossible to scrutinize European secularism in general, and international law more specifically, without looking at Christian missionarism as well.

Dealing with Christianity, its secularization and international law by means of a sociological/historical approach is ideal as it impedes yet another iteration of the already over-determined stories about these supra-structures. Such repetitions are dangerous for they reproduce inaccuracies and biases about the way we think of the absent/present 'abstract ideal' that is at the centre of the three social phenomena: religion, secularism, and international law.[29] Instead, attention should be drawn to the fragilities and incompleteness of each of these social structures. These 'cracks', between the social ideal and social reality, are exactly what these supra-structures try—however competitively with one another—to complete. After all, social incompleteness, 'uncertainties', and 'failures' permit an exchange between diverging social domains such as religion and law in the first place.[30] Furthermore, these imperfections assist in distinguishing the ways in which such social structures shape and form our culture and society both directly and indirectly. Indeed, what the three phenomena share is their constant fluctuation from being established social structures, movements, and/or organizations on the one hand, and personal, psychologically, and emotional experiences and/or knowledge, on the other hand. Clearly, religious institutions—just like any civil or international legal organization—amount to very little without a living congregation as the reference point.

The upshot is that together, the universal and particular experiences of Christianity, its secularization and international law encapsulate a glimpse into the moral, epistemological, and spiritual reality of a particular being at a specific time. In short, a sociological/historical approach that contextualizes specific international legal contributions is especially beneficial because it avails a vantage point

[28] Unfortunately international lawyers—even the most critical ones—still use the definition of Christianity and Europe unquestioningly. For instance, Antony Anghie, one of the leading Third World Approaches to International Law (TWAIL) scholars, argues against European imperialism and colonialism without necessarily defining what is meant by 'Europe': see A Anghie, 'The Evolution of International Law: Colonial and Postcolonial Realities' (2006) 27 *Third World Quarterly* 739–53.

[29] For the religious person, the 'abstract ideal' can be the idealization of the divine, while for the secularist it is the belief in progress and development through science and knowledge. Consequently, for the international lawyer, the leitmotif is the looming but ever present scientification of global 'civilized consciousness'. For more on this binary opposition between absent/present abstract ideal see J Derrida, *Positions* (A Bass trans) (University of Chicago Press Chicago 1981 [1972]). For more on the way repetitions of such ideals work, see S Freud, *The Interpretation of Dreams* (J Strachey trans) (Harper Collins New York 1976 [1899]).

[30] As Harold Bloom argues, every idea begins with a powerful rebellion against the consciousness of the dying or death of another idea or the exhaustive position of being a latecomer: see H Bloom, *The Anxiety of Influence: A Theory of Poetry* (OUP New York 1997) at 12–15.

into the heart of the profession, namely the international legal *consciousness*, *intuition*, and/or *mentality* that is paradoxically both particular and universal.[31]

3 The School of Salamanca as a Case Study: On Its Socio-Economic Conditions

To fully appreciate the magnitude of the developments by the School of Salamanca, one ought to remember that the Renaissance remained mostly a cultural movement that spread slowly and involuntarily across Europe. That is to say, the atmospheric predisposition of the general public remained extremely religious. Even Christopher Columbus, the most famous explorer/trader, was a religiously motivated man.[32] Similarly to other *conquistadores*, he, too, could not avoid Christianity's original missionary impulse instructed from Rome. In fact, it was only after the consolidation of Spain, which took place with the marriage between Isabella I of Castile and Ferdinand III of Aragon, that the sturdier Spanish crown took advantage of the heightened corruption in Rome to negotiate an unprecedented centralized *coalition* with the papacy.[33] The mixture between national and religious sentiments reduced papal influences in temporal affairs. Moreover, Catholicism became tantamount to a new form of governing based on nationalism. As Robert C Padden phrased it:

In this unity of national and religious sentiment it was inevitable that the Church and the Holy Office should become quasi-political agencies of the Crown and so it came to pass that secular churchmen became recognized as civil servants.[34]

---

[31] Very similarly to monotheism, international law 'carries in itself enlightenment's major challenge, namely, to embody universalism but to remain the only particular that universalizes': see *A Gateway between a Distant God and a Cruel World* (n 4) 122.

[32] Carol Delaney argues, for instance, that it was Columbus' religiosity that drove him to seek for enough gold for the Spanish Crown to finance a new crusade to Jerusalem that needed to be under Christian control before the end of days. See further C Delaney, *Columbus and the Quest for Jerusalem* (Free Press New York 2011).

[33] Following Columbus' discoveries, the deal between the Crown and the Papacy was clear: as long as the Catholic kings accepted the perpetual obligation of evangelization—and assumed the financial responsibilities for it too—they were in control over both the spiritual welfare of the natives and the Spanish colonialists, as well as the riches and levies from the New World. See further RC Padden, 'The Ordenanza del Patronazgo of 1574: An Interpretive Essay' in JF Schwaller (ed), *The Church in Colonial Latin America* (Scholarly Resources Wilmington 2000) 27–48, at 27–30.

[34] See ibid 28.

By illustration, it was this form of government that gained, inter alia, the right to restructure and control the Spanish against European Jews, Muslims, and Morisco (Moorish convert) infidels. It was almost revolutionary that the Spanish Tribunal of the Holy Office of the Inquisition, a new institution that was governed by imperial civil servants, supplemented the earlier version that was led by the *Christian Church Inquisition* primarily against Catharism and Waldensian heretics.[35] Significantly, all forms of Christian inquisitions—that often worked simultaneously—adapted legal and political elements from the original *Roman Inquisitorial procedure*.[36] Be that as it may, the Spanish Inquisition—now an institution of the state/empire, which was significantly crueller than the Roman Inquisition[37]—altered the previous religious grounds for being classified as an infidel: that which previously was based on religion transformed into a civil or political accusation of being foreign, traders, or trespassing travellers.[38] Notably, only after this form of argument was successfully embraced in Europe against its own 'native Others' could this mechanism turn, very swiftly, against the native Others of the New World. This demonstrates not only the conversion of the vision of the Catholic religious and imperialist project into a universalist one, but also how Otherness morphed into nationalistic and thus more complex and segmented Otherness, that was nonetheless still premised on a religious template.

Whatever the political/economic desires and successes of this national project, the Spanish Crown now faced the greatest challenge in early modern history: namely the evangelical mission to the New World.[39] It did not help that the conquistadores returning from the Americas felt tangible fatigue and serious doubt about their role in this mission.[40] Self doubt, criticism, and moral questioning

---

[35] For more on the Medieval Inquisition, see JH Arnold, *Inquisition and Power: Catharism and the Confessing Subject in Medieval Languedoc* (University of Pennsylvania Press Philadelphia 2001).

[36] Edward Peters sums up the intricate relationship between the different inquisitions that eventually entrenched an undying myth in *Inquisition* (n 24), as follows, at 1:

> Between the twelfth and the sixteenth centuries in western Europe, the Latin Christian Church adapted certain elements of Roman legal procedure and charged papally appointed clergy to employ them in order to preserve orthodox religious beliefs from the attacks of heretics. Between the sixteenth and the nineteenth centuries, chiefly in Mediterranean Europe, these procedures and personnel were transformed into institutional tribunals called inquisitions charged with the protection of orthodox beliefs and the maintenance of ecclesiastical discipline in the Latin Christian community.

[37] While Spanish and Portuguese inquisitors operated according to the universal principles of the Latin Church, their structures remained specifically regional, centralized, and direct in jurisdiction. This was different than elsewhere in Catholic Europe because particularly in the north 'the offense of heresy fell largely under various regional secular or mixed secular-ecclesiastical jurisdiction': ibid 105.

[38] 'Empire and International Law' (n 11) 9.

[39] 'The Ordenanza del Patronazgo of 1574' (n 33) 30.

[40] See further 'Empire and International Law' (n 11) 12–13.

began to haunt even the most callous conquistadores. After all, they were mostly lay people, if not outright socially marginal figures,[41] who were made responsible for a paradoxical endeavour: guaranteeing an increase in economic gain as well as civilizing and evangelizing the native infidels.[42]

Upon their return to Spain, they sought redemption at the Convent of St Esteban in Salamanca, where Francisco de Vitoria and Domingo de Soto lived and worked. These priests and scholars were confronted with serious questions. Clearly, the conquistadores had done much wrong. But as Martti Koskenniemi puts it: 'what kind of sin was it to take infidel property, to kill an Indian, and to occupy their land?…Were the Spanish activities sinful, and if so, how grave were their sins?…[More specifically] were the conquistadors, the traders, or indeed the emperor himself living in sin?'[43] These questions brought the Salamancans to offer a very important and skilful twist to a possible solution.

4 FROM THE PRIVACY OF THE CONFESSION BOOTH TO PUBLIC INTERNATIONAL LAW

The intense anxieties and dilemmas facing both sides of the confession booth went deeper and further than a corrupt Crown. The role of the pastorate (shepherd in Latin) in Christianity is also to assume the responsibility for deeds done by the congregation as a whole.[44] In the words of Paul S Fiddes, '[t]he Christian idea of a personal God begins historically in pastoral experience, that is, in the experience of the congregation'.[45] The spirituality of the *conquistadores*, in this

---

[41] For instance, as if by inheritance, Diego Columbus—Christopher's son—was appointed governor in 1509 of the island of Hispaniola.

[42] Hernán Cortés (1485–1547), the Spanish conqueror of Mexico, was a failed law student who turned into a ruthless general and established Spanish hegemony in the new world. He and his men continued killing anyone and anything in their way even long after they accomplished their economic goals. They were driven by the belief in the revelation of St John, which necessitates the bloodshed of the native idolaters who represented the manifestations of Satan and his demons described in the Old Testament. See more in J Pohl and CM Robinson, *Aztecs & Conquistadores: The Spanish Invasion & the Collapse of the Aztec Empire* (Osprey Publishers Oxford 2005) at 9.

[43] 'Empire and International Law' (n 11) 13–4.

[44] As Alastair Campbell argues, 'pastoral theology' or 'practical theology' through 'religious belief, tradition and practice meets contemporary experiences, questions and actions…in an imaginative interplay between idea and action': A Campbell, 'The Nature of Practical Theology' in J Woodward and S Pattison (eds), *The Blackwell Reader in Pastoral and Practical Theology* (Blackwell Oxford 2000) 78–88, at 85.

[45] PS Fiddes, *Participating in God: A Pastoral Doctrine of the Trinity* (Westminster John Knox Press Louisville 2000) at 8.

world as well as their ability to reach eternal salvation, goes far beyond the complexities of personal liability. Indeed, the responsibility for their deeds reflects onto—and are shared with—the congregation as a whole. This, in turn, augments the importance of the pastoral Sacrament of Penance for the sake of everyone's souls. The Salamancans understood well the serious predicament the church was in: the troubles in the New World presented a contradiction to Christian theology's internal logic, and outer political factors were not making anything easier. Perhaps the papacy could continue to deny its loss of power to the Spanish Crown. The Spanish Church, however, knew better; it had a new order with which to reconcile.[46]

Arguably, the Salamancans were the right people at the right time to offer both the state and the church a 'bridging solution' that would strengthen the political society both in theory and in practice. Their theological and legal background provided them the key to declare and then negotiate a legal structure with a clear strategy and ideological goal in order to save their Christian congregation from loss of political power and moral deterioration. And the key was the Catholic confession lead by the pastorate.

Michel Foucault's scrutiny of sixteenth-century Christian religious practices is extremely revealing, offering an understanding of how the Salamancans' religiosity interacted with their legal intentions, approach, and even international accomplishments. Questions about the relation of knowledge, power, and the self brought Foucault's focus, rather similarly to the School of Salamanca, to the role of governance through 'the manner in which one is to be spiritually ruled and led on this earth to achieve eternal salvation'.[47] Through the formal regulation of religious confession, 'Christianity fashions a technology of the self that enables people to transform themselves because the principle product of this technology was a unique form of subjectivity'.[48] Importantly, such subjectivity is reached through a twofold process, notably the acceptance that the self possesses a truth-based value that can then be formally articulated.[49] This hermeneutical analysis is part and parcel of the Western critical tradition that accepts the assumption that the self can be known, which necessarily also means that self-knowledge can be incomplete and ruptured. The ingeniousness behind this technology is its enabling of the

---

[46] In 1493, the Pope still tried to send a nuncio to *Española* in an attempt to retaliate against the Crown's control of the colonial church despite being strongly advised against it by the Crown. This attempt, just as the ones following it, failed colossally. See further 'The Ordenanza del Patronazgo of 1574' (n 33) 29.

[47] M Foucault, 'On Governmentality' (1979) 6 *Ideology & Consciousness* 5–21, quoted in J Bernauer, 'Foucault and the Religious Question: A Manila Seminar' (1999) 3 *Budhi* 1–29, at 5.

[48] 'Foucault and the Religious Question' (n 47) 7.

[49] M Foucault, 'The Battle for Chastity' in *The Essential Works of Foucault 1954–1984, Volume 1 Ethics: Subjectivity and Truth* (P Rabinow ed R Hurley et al., trans) (New Press New York 1998) 185–97, at 195.

objectification and thus also of the renunciation of the self or parts of the self.[50] Here one need only evoke Christ's pledge 'Father, forgive them, for they do not know what they are doing' (Luke 23:4) that essentializes the power behind knowledge or ignorance on the one hand, but encourages a specific *methodology* of truth revelation that accommodates socially governed morality (that is, forgiveness and condemnation) on the other hand.

Crucially, the conditionality for this apparatus to work lies in obedience.[51] Christianity demands, as Foucault phrases it here:

obedience to a god who is conceived of as a despot, a master for whom one is slave and servant. It is obedience to his will which is in the form of law; and it is obedience to those who represent the despot, master and lord, and who retain an authority to which submission must be total.[52]

Decisively, the representation of such obedience depends on a binary representation: the individual's performance of asceticism is to be combined with 'obedience to the other in this world, the obedience to the other which is an obedience to God and to the men who represent him'.[53] Dangerously, such obedience often turns into an end in itself, particularly because it is socio-historically structured as the 'lesser evil' way of life, at least since Adam's Fall.[54]

It is almost impossible to deny the resemblance between the subjectification/objectification technology of the self through the Catholic confessional practices that work on the basis of the internalization of obedience to the social ideal, and the manner in which the Salamancans enshrined the binary opposition between the public and private in international law in order to discriminate among just/lawful and unjust/unlawful situations.[55] Just as commerce, which might discriminate

---

[50] Just as such abstract fragmentation of the self is reminiscent of the experienced body/mind split, it is also similar to the manner by which humanity accepts the de facto absent/presence of any abstract ideals discussed earlier. For more on the Christian process of subjectification/objectification, see 'Foucault and the Religious Question' (n 47) 5.

[51] After all, in Christianity, the very accessibility of the ascetic to the other world (that is both *autre monde* and *monde autre*) depends on the principle of obedience that is, for instance, neither found in Cynicism nor in Platonism: see 'Foucault and the Religious Question' (n 47) 15, citing M Foucault, 'Final Lecture' (Collège de France, 28 March 1984) 26–8.

[52] 'Foucault and the Religious Question' (n 47) 15, citing 'Final Lecture' (n 51) 26.

[53] 'Foucault and the Religious Question' (n 47) 15, citing 'Final Lecture' (n 51) 27–8.

[54] In James Bernauer's words in 'Foucault and the Religious Question' (n 47) 5–6:

With the Fall, the original subordination which human nature accorded to soul and will was lost, and the human being became a figure of revolt not only against God but also against himself. This situation was graphically illustrated in the lawlessness of sexual yearnings. Seditious sexuality signals the need for a struggle with one's self, and permanent obedience is essential to this struggle. The obedience that is intrinsic to the exercise and responsibilities of pastoral power involves specific forms of knowledge and subjectivity.

[55] To mention an archetypal example, one ought only look at how Vitoria relied on Aristotle in distinguishing between the 'two types of *ars mercatorum*, "natural" exchanges, the purpose of which was to see to the good of the household ("*ad usus necessarios hominum*") and those "artificial"

between the equal relationship of the buyer and seller, could nevertheless be justified if it served the greater good, so could *ius gentium*, for example, divide territories and properties for the sake of safe travels and trade internationally.[56] The way this functions remains as ambiguous as the confessional technology of the self. While the methodological requirements were highly convoluted and demanding, the management of both individual and communal violations of law could now be channelled through self-imposed suspicion, classifications, and fragmentation, so that when and if needed, certain particular objectified parts—of the individual/communal self—could be dismissed, silenced, and even pardoned through a god given right. Clearly, the efficacy of this method depends on a vague, but more importantly, subjectively determined intention. Given however that determining the benefits of one's intentions for the social good can never be straightforward, the leading principle remains the obedience to God and his will, but, most importantly, to His earthly representatives: namely, the Church clerics who now were, more than ever before, also national civil servants.

The Salamancans saw no real trouble in 'exporting' this technology of the self or the community into the New World. Thus, to start with, they accepted the indigenous populations' humanity and freedom, as well as their right to own property. That is to say, they dismissed the view that the Pope or Crown had rights over indigenous lands. Secondly, building on Thomism's intellectual realism, the School of Salamanca reshaped the Roman law of *ius gentium*. Understanding the need to limit and protect natural law's unchanging nature that lay with God, the intention was to create a schism between it and human-made law. Relying on earlier Roman terminologies was convenient: it was useful primarily because it could bear the stamp of tradition on the one hand, yet allow for enough historical ambiguities for the appropriation to bare the required difference, fragmentation, and thus, also objectification on the other hand. This allowed them to endorse natural law as both divine law and human-made law interchangeably, depending on the necessities of the situation.[57]

Similarly, the Salamancans adopted from Roman law's *summa-divisio* the three concepts—*dominium, ius gentium,* and the *bellum iustum*—which in time would

---

operations whose point was to produce profit ("*ad lucrum*"). The former were just and lawful but the latter, especially if practised systematically, involved great danger ("*est valde periculosum*") for the soul': 'Empire and International Law' (n 11) 19.

[56] See further ibid 15.

[57] For instance, the Roman *ius civile* that originally served to formalistically mediate transactions concluded with the peregrines, was made into a sub-division of *ius gentium*, itself initially only a sub-division of natural law (*ius naturale*). The reference to *ius naturale* indicates, on the one hand, Gaius' *naturalis ratio* that dictates the same law to all peoples. Although somewhat confusingly, this was adopted by Justinian in a manner that equated *ius gentium* with *ius civile*, on the other hand, it was used to regulate the economic and political growth experienced by the Roman state in the Mediterranean: see A Berger, 'Encyclopedic Dictionary of Roman Law' (1953) 43 *Transactions of the American Philosophical Society* 333–810, at 528.

delineate the imperial dimensions of international law. Their success can be discerned to date by the irreconcilable gap between the 'public', that deals with issues of territory, jurisdiction, regulating wars, and so on, and 'private', that covers matters of property, commercial, and contract law. Indeed, this was equally beneficial for governing Europe and the New World.[58] Despite the problematic consequences of this division, which are still experienced to date,[59] one should not assume the Salamancans were driven by malevolence: just as the Salamancans' approach was not linear, it was hardly meticulously premeditated. Yet their methodology that, inter alia, promoted authorized vagueness assisted to entrench the division between the legally binding and that which remains within the parameters of general recommendations 'only'.[60] This is decisive and destructive for public international law.[61]

In other words, together with the European conquests, the more organic experience of the public/private modes as a *distinction* that does not necessarily admit a *separation* axiomatically reconstitutes the public and private as categories that are susceptible to separation in both traditional and modern societies.[62] Granted that the very dichotomy between the public and private is synthetic and as such, socially and historically contingent,[63] its very impact stems from the authoritative way it constructed and still constructs our daily routines.[64] Indeed, the best

---

[58] The example of Spain's developments, discussed earlier, was not unusual. The very propagation of property law, natural law, and the just war theory relies on prevalent European transformations: centralized states; the global economic system that remains eternally hungry for profit; and constant warfare also between European rulers: 'Empire and International Law' (n 11) 14.

[59] As Nicola Lacey phrases it: '…the ideology of public/private dichotomy allows government to clean its hands of any *responsibility* for the state of the "private" world and *depoliticizes* the disadvantages which inevitably spill over the alleged divide by affecting the position of the "privately" disadvantaged in the "public" world': N Lacey, 'Theory into Practice: Pornography and the Public/Private Dichotomy' (1993) 20 *Journal of Law and Society* 93–113, at 97 (emphasis in original).

[60] See further 'Empire and International Law' (n 11).

[61] It is for these reasons and more that Martti Koskenniemi urges a thorough study that scrutinizes the Salamancans' open-ended universal policies—that exceeds any temporal empire—with both its public and private components together: 'Empire and International Law' (n 11) 3.

[62] See further M McKeon, *The Secret History of Domesticity: Public, Private, and the Division of Knowledge* (Johns Hopkins University Press Baltimore 2005) at xix.

[63] This is also why maintaining a mutually exclusive divide between the two concepts is virtually impossible: whatever is meant by 'public' or 'private' constantly collapse into each other and thus also mean very little standing alone. As Roberto M Unger argues, modern society is an artifact that is combined with the liberal goal of freeing society from structures of dependence and authority. Ergo, a modern society's aim is also to salvage a measure of subjectivity (privacy) and intersubjectivity (public) from rigid rules. For more on these dichotomies, see C Davis, 'Religion and the Making of Society' in RW Lovin and MJ Perry (eds), *Critique and Construction: A Symposium on Roberto Unger's Politics* (CUP Cambridge 1990) 242–55.

[64] Simply 'knowing' that the public/private realms are presumably separate spaces where the private covers the emotional, personal, sexual, familial, and subjective undertakings and the public refers to the objective, professional, social, and political reality, is mostly taken for granted. See B Mensch and A Freeman, 'Liberalism's Public/Private Split' (1988) 3 *Tikkun* 24–30, at 24.

example of how religion, secularization, and international law co-exist can be perceived through the over-determined, although imprecise, narratives about the public/private dichotomy, which are both integral to Christianity and the modern state's liberal legalism.[65]

While such complexities exceed the focus of this chapter, the religious basis of the Salamancans' approach that goes back to the confession booth should not be neglected. In fact, the very turning of a blind eye to this phenomenon is the reason Foucault characterized the Renaissance 'not by the beginning of a dechristianization but by the beginning of a Christianization-in-depth', which he terms, elsewhere, a 'new Christianization'.[66] À la Foucault, the religious missionary effort that keeps us all still locked in the dark ages came together with early modernity due to the 'vast interiorization' of the Christian experience. This took place through both the internal practice of the confession and its external expansion, especially since the Council of Trent (1545–63), to an ever larger number of relationships in the period after the crisis of the Reformation and Counter-Reformation.[67] Clearly, the Salamancans actively participated in the process of enshrining such Christianization-in-depth by elevating the process of confession onto a whole new and universal level. However consciously, they seized the moment to spread their word, the specific technology of the self, which now received unprecedented accessibility in the New World as well.

5 CONCLUSION

It is hardly surprising that in an attempt to find appropriate justification for the 'race for Africa', late nineteenth-century liberal jurists who established the international

---

[65] International law's demand to reconcile the public (and objective) with the private (that is, subjective) sphere is no exception: it too stems from the profession's insoluble 'ascending/descending' liberal dyad structured between theory and practice, concreteness and normativity, law and politics, apology and utopia, public and private, and so on. For more on how such structural dichotomies work within the law, see M Koskenniemi, *From Apology to Utopia: The Structure of International Legal Argument* (Finnish Lawyers Helsinki 1989) at 46–7; A Mills, *The Confluence of Public and Private International Law: Justice, Pluralism and Subsidiarity in the International Constitutional Ordering of Private Law* (CUP Cambridge 2009); D Kennedy, 'The Stages of the Decline of the Public/Private Distinction' (1982) 130 *University of Pennsylvania Law Review* 1349–57; SB Boyd (ed), *Challenging the Public/Private Divide: Feminism, Law, and Public Policy* (University of Toronto Press Toronto 1997).

[66] See M Foucault, '19 February 1975' in *Abnormal: Lectures at the Collège de France, 1974–75* (V Marchetti and A Salomoni eds G Burchell trans) (Verso London 2003) 167–99.

[67] M Foucault, *The History of Sexuality: An Introduction* (Pantheon New York 1978) at 61.

legal profession turned to history in search of a solid ideological basis. It is indicative that these modern men, who were mostly of a Protestant background and arguably possessed a liberal political international agenda, embraced the scholarship of a Catholic school rooted in the Spanish Renaissance. Evidently, Christian missionarism remained harmonious enough even after the Protestant Reformation. Not only were the Protestants missionaries themselves,[68] the Catholic missionary only intensified with the Reformation.[69] This suggests that the universalization of Christianity, which Foucault termed Christianization-in-depth, was mostly successful.

Even if it is accepted that religious dogma and Christian missionarism matters less since the secularization process was set in vogue until the end of the nineteenth century, the fact that in cases of emergency, ad hoc or otherwise, internationalists turn to a 'universal consciousness'—that is entrenched in Christian reasoning—demands questioning.[70]

Manifestly, all Christianities alike have done their best to colonize, internally as well as externally, not only the lives of their followers but also the lives of Others. Significantly, the modern period that contains the rise and arguably the decline of the international legal profession[71] remains a religious age, despite, but also due to, the lasting struggles among Western European Christianities.

---

[68] Although many questioned the Reformers' commitment to missions—particularly in comparison to the Roman Catholic Church's zeal for and success with missions—it is impossible to say that Protestants were indifferent to missionarism. Instead their smaller accomplishment was the result of specific circumstances: not only were Luther and Calvin occupied with doctrinal issues, they were also faced with significant opposition to their attempts to spread the Reformation across Europe (specifically, Calvin commissioned missionaries to work in France and on another (failed) mission to Brazil). Clearly, unlike Spain and Portugal, Germany and Switzerland were hardly imperial or dominant worldwide. See further Z Pratt, MD Sills, and JK Walters, *Introduction to Global Missions* (B&H Academic Nashville 2014) at 107.

[69] Almost expectedly, the outbreak of the Reformation—a new threat to the defenders of the Catholic orthodoxy—made the Inquisition turn its attention to these new heretics also through a tighter regime of different forms of expressions. See *Inquisition* (n 24).

[70] In the words of one of the Enlightenment thinkers, Blaise Pascal (1623–62):

Men despise religion; they hate it, and fear it is true. To remedy this, we must begin by showing that religion is not contrary to reason; that it is venerable, to inspire respect for it; then we must make it lovable, to make good men hope it is true; finally, we must prove it is true.

B Pascal, 'Of the Necessity of the Wager' in *Pensées* (WF Trotter trans) (Modern Library New York 1941 [1660]) 64–85, at 64.

[71] The putative decline discussed by international lawyers today is exemplified by Martti Koskenniemi's book entitled *The Gentle Civilizer of Nations: The Rise and Fall of International Law 1870–1960* (n 6).

CHAPTER 45

....

THE IDEA OF PROGRESS

....

THOMAS SKOUTERIS

1 INTRODUCTION

....

THE object of this chapter is to discuss the entwinement of the idea of progress with the theory of international law. Progress is one of these grand ideas that yield tectonic force and determine the way we speak to the world. Its meandering history implicates, give or take, every twist and turn of Western thought. It is also a term with pervasive use and variegated meaning in international law, especially during the past two centuries.[1] In professional language, it may feature in the uppercase, as the belief in the possibility of the improvement of the human condition as a whole over space and time by means of international law (for example, 'humanity has progressed from the cave to the computer and international law has been a progressive agent of this transformation'). It may also appear in the lowercase, as a prosaic mode of declaring measurable advance with doctrines, institutions, or policies (for example, 'monitoring compliance: a progress report'). One also finds numerous in-between modes, where it is not always plain whether

[1] See eg H Wheaton, *Histoire des progrès du droit des gens en Europe et en Amérique depuis la paix de Westphalie jusqu'à nos jours* (FA Brockhaus Leipzig 1865); L Renault, *Les Progrès récents du droit des gens* (JB Wolters Groningen 1912); JB Scott, *Le progrès du droit des gens* (Les Editions Internationales Paris 1930); MO Hudson, *Progress in International Organization* (Stanford University Press Stanford 1932); C Rousseau, *Scientific Progress and the Evolution of International Law* (UNESCO Paris 1954); IL Claude, *Swords into Plowshares: The Problems and Progress of International Organization* (Random House New York 1984); JI Charney, 'Progress in International Criminal Law?' (1999) 93 *American Journal of International Law* 452–64; RA Miller and RM Bratspies (eds), *Progress in International Law* (Martinus Nijhoff Leiden 2008).

the disciplinary advance is purported to have a social effect on a macro- or micro-level (for example, 'there is something inherently progressive in having more international tribunals').

The enormity of the topic in combination with space limitations leaves no hope of a systematic approach. This chapter is limited to two core points. The first is that the impact of the idea of progress in international law should be measured not only against the traction of paradigmatic progress narratives (for example, about perpetual peace, humanitarianism, civilization, liberty, democracy, and so on) which often constitute the object of critique; but also against the pervasiveness of more prosaic varieties of progress talk. Progress is not only a grand idea, but also a common trope of evaluation, in the form of 'progress reports', 'moving forward' with a certain issue, or as the *telos* of renewalism. In the shadow of postmodern critique and proverbial incredulity towards uppercase progress narratives, lower-case modes have proliferated. Assessing the impact of the idea of progress in the theory of international law may therefore require that we trade the lofty grounds of meta-narratives with the badlands of everyday language (Section 2). The second point is that any kind of progress talk, from the uppercase to the lowercase and back, is theoretical 'all the way down'. The idea of progress does not merely de-scribe directional change in an object *'an sich'* but imposes a frame over it. Move the frame, and the image becomes muddled. One's progress is another's regression, stagnation, or mere movement. As a consequence, any evaluative statement that uses progress as the benchmark of choice must be treated as a normative mode of speaking the world (Section 3). There is no better example of the resilience of the idea of progress than the prosaic varieties that continue to punctuate contem-porary arguments (Section 4). Ultimately, the call of this chapter is to point to the manner in which international law continues to construct/to be constructed by the idea of progress.

2 What is Progress? From the Uppercase to the Lowercase and Back

When looking up the term progress in contemporary dictionaries, two gen-res of definitions prevail. The first is about Progress in the uppercase. This is the name given in the history of ideas to the belief in the continuing improvement of the human condition throughout its history: the belief that improvement has occurred, that it continues to occur; and will continue to occur, even if under certain circumstances. This is how JB Bury, perhaps the most eminent of historians of progress, defines it in his 1920 classic: 'The idea of progress of humanity means that civilization has moved, is moving, and will move in a desirable direction'.[2] It is the mode of Francis Fukuyama when he uses 'end' to refer both to the final destination but also the *telos* of history.[3] It is a mode of reading the past, which ascribes significance to specific facts and events by reference to a general schema of historical development described as progressive. It is the mode of Voltaire and his aphorism that war and religion is the greatest obstacle to human progress: should they be abolished, the world would rapidly improve; the Physiocratic postulation that the end of society is the attainment of happiness for humanity, meaning abundance of objects and liberty to enjoy them; Condorcet's union between intellectual progress and liberty, virtue, and rights; Adam Smith's gradual economic progress through augmentation of wealth and well-being; Kant's realization of man's nature in a universal civil society; Hegel's final cause of the world as the self-consciousness of the Spirit of God; Darwin's natural selection; Spencer's universal law of socio-political development; and so forth. The agents of progress can be science, reason, technology, social institutions, education, self-consciousness, individual action and improvement. Progress can lead to an improved condition of human life, in the form of happiness, liberty, freedom, welfare, health, virtue, and so on. Progress in the uppercase operates on the register of grand narratives. It describes the evolutionary course of humankind and implicates in this assessment a unified human race, a unified time frame, a unified material space, a single *telos*, and a single greater good. It is based on an interpretation of the past and a prophecy about the future. Narratives don't get much grander than that.

The second genre is about progress in the lowercase. This is the meaning given to the term in everyday speech. Dictionaries define it, give or take, as gradual advancement by means of a process and towards a destination. It is a synonym for betterment and an antonym for deterioration, regression, or decline. This is the humdrum evaluative mode of 'I have made progress with my paper' or that 'nightfall did not impede the progress of my journey'. Here progress refers to directional change of a certain object, or class of objects, or a domain of reality, which receive a positive evaluation of standards imposed on them.[4] Progress in this second sense, on the face of it, eschews meta-narrative claims. It is not about a discerning purpose in human history. It is about describing forward movement.

When taking stock of the impact of the idea of progress in a given field (say, in international law) one is immediately drawn to progress in the uppercase as the obvious

---

[2] JB Bury, *The Idea of Progress: An Inquiry into Its Origin and Growth* (Echo Library Teddington 2006 [1920]).

[3] F Fukuyama, *The End of History and the Last Man* (Free Press New York 1993).

[4] S Nowak, 'Models of Directional Change and Human Values: The Theory of Progress as an Applied Social Science' in JC Alexander and P Sztompka (eds), *Rethinking Progress: Movements, Forces, and Ideas at the End of the Twentieth Century* (Unwin Hyman London 1990) 229–46, at 230.

starting point, and probably for good reason. Its palpability as a formal concept lends itself to scholarly enquiry. Progress, after all, is not a fringe notion in the history of thought. It is often described as the central organizing and animating principle of Modernity and the secular faith of the West. It is claimed to carry different significa-tion in ancient times, in the Renaissance, or in Modernity, and one could conditionally speak of an Ancient Greek, a French, a British, or a German conception. Exploring the historical evolution of the idea in the uppercase is the tenor of most histories in the field. The classical references in the literature are JB Bury's *Idea of Progress*[5] and Robert Nisbet's *History of the Idea of Progress*.[6] The reason for the popularity of these two works is, I suspect, twofold. The first is their wide scope, which covers sources in nat-ural and social sciences with a three-thousand-year backward gaze. The second is that they exemplify two opposite historical explanations. The former, which remains the dominant view, traces the formation of the idea to Modernity and to the beginnings of the eighteenth century in particular. The latter finds entelechies in ancient and medi-eval thought, especially in the recurrence of themes about growth and historical ne-cessity. Several other less-known treatises[7] have dotted the literature up until the 1990s. Characteristic of traditional enquiries[8] is their self-referencing character: they describe the evolution of the idea of progress in time and space by means of a progress narrative. Progress has 'progressed', that is, has incrementally taken shape through a slow and gradual evolution and the contribution of successive generations, like tributaries flow-ing into a river. Post-1990s the topic came back in vogue with a noticeable shift in tone, arguably due to the chiliastic and millenarian concerns that were prompted by Y2K on the one hand, and the mainstreaming of postmodern-styled enquiries in most fields of the social sciences and humanities on the other. The field was reinvented by means of contemporary assessments of the state of affairs at the end of the century.[9] Sub-genres[10]

---

[5] *The Idea of Progress* (n 2).

[6] RA Nisbet, *History of the Idea of Progress* (Transaction Publishers Piscataway 1980). For a related account focusing on theories of social change, see RA Nisbet, *Metaphor and History: The Western Idea of Social Development* (Transaction Publishers New Brunswick 2009).

[7] FS Marvin (ed), *Progress and History* (OUP Oxford 1916); B Sidis, *The Source and Aim of Human Progress* (RG Badger Boston 1919); SO Lodge, *Science and Human Progress* (Kessinger Publishing Whitefish 2005 [1927]); S Pollard, *The Idea of Progress: History and Society* (Watts London 1968); RA Tsanoff, *Civilization and Progress* (University Press of Kentucky Lexington 1971).

[8] See eg *The Idea of Progress* (n 2); *History of the Idea of Progress* (n 6).

[9] See eg JC Alexander and P Sztompka (eds), *Rethinking Progress: Movements, Forces and Ideas at the End of the Twentieth Century* (Routledge London 1990); L Marx and B Mazlish (eds), *Progress: Fact or Illusion?* (University of Michigan Press Ann Arbor 1996); A Burgen, P McLaughlin, and J Mittelstrass (eds), *The Idea of Progress* (De Gruyter Berlin 1997); J Willis, *The Paradox of Progress* (Radcliffe Oxford 1995); GA Almond, M Chodorow, and RH Pearce (eds), *Progress and Its Discontents* (University of California Press Oakland 1985).

[10] The theory of scientific progress is one of the most popular of sub-fields. See J Losee, *Theories of Scientific Progress: An Introduction* (Psychology Press Florence 2004); L Laudan, *Progress and Its Problems: Towards a Theory of Scientific Growth* (University of California Press Oakland 1978); TS Kuhn, *The Structure of Scientific Revolutions* (University of Chicago Press Chicago 1996);

and field-specific accounts[11] have also proliferated, including works in 'big history' that bring together under a single account natural and social sciences. Characteristic of contemporary accounts is their historicist perspective, with emphasis on different manifestations of the idea in time, its contextual signification, and cultural function.

Inasmuch as the impact of the idea of progress in the theory of international law is our concern, this essay could follow the standard route and attempt an intellectual history (dialectic, contextualist, historicist, or other) that links historically specific versions of progress with international law events, institutions, or approaches. Alternatively, one could focus on one form only, say Marx's historical materialism or Darwin's natural selection, and trace their respective legacy. One could even attempt an eidetic reduction and concoct an a-historical, formal version of the idea of progress as the basis of enquiry. All of the above would be helpful. While a genealogy of progress in international law is yet to be written, much of the work has already been done. Recent critical work has taken issue with the structural bias of the field's most influential meta-narratives, from sovereign equality and democracy[12] to the 'virtue' of humanitarianism,[13] the gender-neutrality[14] of technical rules and doctrines, and so on.[15] In its aftermath, intellectual projects that seek to reveal the bias of meta-narratives sound like yesterday's news. We have, after all, been there and done that already. Today it is indeed harder to defend the view that international law is automatically or necessarily an instrument of progress.[16] This is not to say that the view has been eclipsed.[17] It is however at least as common to argue that grand accounts of progress are empty forms that can be filled according to taste. All the same, faith in the possibility of progress remains

C Dilworth, *Scientific Progress: A Study Concerning the Nature of the Relation Between Successive Scientific Theories* (Springer New York 2008).

[11] CL Anderson and JW Looney (eds), *Making Progress: Essays in Progress and Public Policy* (Lexington Lanham 2002); C Elman and MF Elman (eds), *Progress in International Relations Theory: Appraising the Field* (MIT Press Cambridge MA 2003); RD Sack (ed), *Progress: Geographical Essays* (Johns Hopkins University Press Baltimore 2002).

[12] S Marks, *The Riddle of All Constitutions: International Law, Democracy, and the Critique of Ideology* (OUP Oxford 2000); G Simpson, *Great Powers and Outlaw States: Unequal Sovereigns in the International Legal Order* (CUP Cambridge 2004).

[13] D Kennedy, *Of War and Law* (Princeton University Press Princeton 2006); D Kennedy, *The Dark Sides of Virtue: Reassessing International Humanitarianism* (Princeton University Press Princeton 2011); A Orford, *Reading Humanitarian Intervention: Human Rights and the Use of Force in International Law* (CUP Cambridge 2003).

[14] H Charlesworth and C Chinkin, *The Boundaries of International Law: A Feminist Analysis* (Manchester University Press Manchester 2000).

[15] For an overview, see J Beckett, 'Critical International Legal Theory' in A Carty (ed), *Oxford Bibliographies in International Law* (Oxford Bibliographies Online 2014) <http://oxfordindex.oup.com/view/10.1093/obo/9780199796953-0007> [accessed 3 March 2016]. See also T Skouteris, *The Notion of Progress in International Law Discourse* (TMC Asser Press The Hague 2010).

[16] M Koskenniemi, *From Apology to Utopia: The Structure of International Legal Argument* (reissue CUP Cambridge 2005) at 513.

[17] See eg MN Shaw, *International Law* (5th edn CUP Cambridge 2003).

rooted in disciplinary practices and rumours of its demise are exaggerated. Even in this post-triumphalist juncture of betrayed End-of-History promises, the conviction remains salient that international law should nevertheless contribute to some sort of upward spiral of 'real' progress located in the not-so-distant future.

While critical rereadings of international law's history have debunked the progressivism of intellectual and regulatory projects, less has been said about the persistence of progress as an intuitive paradigm for the articulation of professional claims. The recent 'turn to history' in international law has taken little interest in progress as a self-standing concept with generative power of its own. Professional praxis continues to be measured against its contribution towards superior or inferior states of affairs. It somehow feels tricky to articulate a professional commitment that sidesteps the binary of progress/decline. The traditional route of intellectual history may therefore miss out on more prosaic progress tropes that punctuate academic and policy documents. The genres of 'progress reports', 'progress and challenges', 'rise and fall', or 'moving forward' are familiar examples of a widespread tendency to stake claims by reference to progress.[18] We speak of different institutional, doctrinal, methodological, or other milestones in international law's evolutionary march, as moments to be cherished or 'never again' repeated. Progress talk is a decisive discourse for policy-making.[19] It meets out resources, power, justice, and legitimacy.[20]

Accounts of progress in international law come in a dazzling variety. They differ in their plot, in the ways they imagine the relationship between progress and international law, in the desirable goal, or the manner in which the goal should be achieved. Two genres seem to dominate. The first is of international law *as* progress. Here the idea is that international law has an inherent progressive value for humankind, along the Kantian mantra that internationalism signifies a desirable move towards a superior state of social development. The second is of progress *within* international law. Here the idea is that international law has achieved and should continue to achieve progressive internal development as a working pure (a discipline, a technique, a system of rules). 'Better' international law has stood for a broad range of goals, such as more/less rules, standards, processes,

---

[18] For lowercase examples in the field of international criminal law, see L Arbour, 'Progress and Challenges in International Criminal Justice' (1997) 21 *Fordham International Law Journal* 531–40; 'Progress in International Criminal Law?' (n 1); IG Farlam, *The Establishment of an International Criminal Court and an African Court of Human Rights: A Progress Report* (World Jurist Association Kenwyn 1998); International Human Rights Law Institute, *Progress Report on the Ratification and National Implementing Legislation of the Statute for the Establishment of an International Criminal Court* (International Human Rights Law Institute Chicago 2000).

[19] See eg 'In Larger Freedom: Towards Development, Security and Human Rights for All: Report of the Secretary General' (21 March 2005) UN Doc A/59/2005. The Report makes no less than fifty references to the idea of progress in an equal number of pages.

[20] The *Charter of the United Nations* (1945) Preamble stakes out the promotion of 'social progress and better standards in larger freedom' as one of the primary commitments of the organization.

institutions, empiricism, radical critique, formalism, codification, and so on. In terms of the pattern in which progress occurs, it may occur in single revolutionary episodes (for example, the Treaty of Westphalia, The Hague Peace Conferences, the Nuremberg and Tokyo Trials) or by means of slow processes of incremental change (the accumulation of knowledge, professionalization, thickening of the fabric of the law, legalization, judicialization, creation of international institutions, and so forth). In terms of the goal to be achieved, the range of positions is wide—from approximation to truth (international law better reflecting the realities of international life), to efficiency (prevention, enforcement, compliance, accountability, justice, and so forth).

Most often, progress accounts flout the uppercase/lowercase typology and iterate between the two registers. Take for example a recent book on progress in international law.[21] In the opening essay, Professor Paust sets out to take stock of progress in international law during the past century.[22] This essay appears to be written in progress-in-the-lowercase mode, that is, evaluating change in a given object without linking, at least explicitly, directional change with wider normative questions about the *telos* of human society and its course. The author draws parallels between the interwar period and today and concludes that certain developments, such as increased human interdependence, the increased recognition of private and public individual roles, and the growth of international and regional institutions have brought the gradual effectuation of certain human values. These values include human dignity, tolerance, human rights, democratic values, and the cooperative use of armed force. For the author gradual effectuation of these values provides evidence and promise of 'progress in international organization'. The point here is not to take issue with whether Professor Paust is right or wrong, but, rather, to observe the way in which the relationship between law and progress is drawn. For example, the author's understanding of progress is not defined as such in the text, whereas attainment of the said values offers evidence and promise of its materialization. The precise relationship between values and forward movement is not explained, but taken as self-evident. One could legitimately ask about the meaning of 'more human dignity' or what are the costs or exclusions. Despite the absence of such ruminations, the argument does not alienate the reader. One reason is that the argument operates self-referentially against the background of a liberal-democratic narrative of progress, which is never spelled out but assumed as true throughout the text. This narrative adopts the said values as yardsticks of progressive internationalism over the past hundred years. The liberal-democratic narrative, however, is not questioned. Its various

---

[21] *Progress in International Law* (n 1).

[22] JJ Paust, 'Evidence and Promise of Progress: Increased Interdependence, Rights and Responsibilities, Arenas of Interaction, and the Need for More Cooperative Use of Armed Force' in *Progress in International Law* (n 1) 33–50.

failures, critiques, potential bias, or exclusions are not part of the account. As a consequence, the essay concludes that during the last hundred or so years a progress has been achieved.

Such iterations between the uppercase and the lowercase are hardly surprising. One reason is that progress is used with various degrees of commitment to grand normative claims. Another is that arguments, for stylistic or other reasons, choose not to fly full-mast their epistemic choices. Ultimately, postmodern critique is to blame. From the mid-twentieth century onwards, faith in Progress has understandably come under strain. The failure to prevent and ameliorate large-scale disasters (war, atrocity, poverty, inequality, and climate change), the dark sides of technological innovation, and the mainstreaming of post-modern critique, have all rendered belief in the continuous and necessary improvement of the human condition hard to defend. To survive, ideas of progress have become a more cautious, pragmatist, piecemeal business that trades myth for fact and faith for reason. While the inevitable progress of humanity is hard to defend, belief in gradual advance through human will and reason is hard to forsake. In historical studies, where questions of directionality and causality are at the heart of today's debates, the jury is still out on whether historiography is even possible without taking on the luggage of progress.[23] While salvation and the afterlife have lost their appeal as the yardstick for evaluating human action, it is common to assess acts of the present on the basis of their impact on future generations. As another historian writes, 'If the idea of progress does die in the West, so will a great deal else that we have long cherished in our civilization'.[24] Progress seems too intuitive and convenient a notion to throw away with the bathwater of 'everything goes' relativism. If it is passé to say that science, international law, or criminal justice have helped humanity edge closer to a Golden Age, it is still feasible to take stock of the current state of affairs on the basis of generally accepted criteria of betterment. Even if Progress is a myth, progress can be real. Or not?

3 THE STRUCTURE
OF PROGRESS ARGUMENTS

The previous section argued that scepticism towards uppercase progress narratives has not deterred the diffusion of lowercase, prosaic forms of progress talk as a standard

---

[23] B Mazlish, 'Progress in History' (2006) 7(5) *Historically Speaking* 18–21.
[24] *History of the Idea of Progress* (n 6) xvii.

mode of articulating evaluative claims in international law. This section argues that the uppercase/lowercase typology loses its analytical value once we turn to the structure of progress arguments. It claims that any kind of progress talk, from the uppercase to the lowercase and back, is in fact theoretical 'all the way down'. Far from describing directional change 'an sich', progress always frontloads change with positive ethical content. This act of frontloading consists of two separable elements.

The first is directionality. Progress is derived from the Latin word *progressus*, a moving or stepping forward, and implies that change depends on previous steps. In turn, the idea of progress refers to the existence of a rationally comprehensible directionality in human history: from the cave to the computer, from superstition to reason, from absolutism to democracy, from impunity to accountability, from interdependence to globalization, and so on. Discerning direction of a social object in its historical trajectory is the bread and butter of the social sciences. Despite the fact that this operation is always dependent on method (and therefore theoretical 'all the way down'), it is claimed that certain events and facts are indisputable. Indeed, most historians would agree that certain events have 'really' occurred. Relativists do, however warn that disputes about history, at least in their majority, do not concern the reality of facts, but the selection of facts included in the historical account on the one hand, and the relationships drawn between them on the other.[25] The historical narrative is impossible without a filter that identifies some facts as worth being mentioned and/or draws relationships between them. A conception of time is needed to situate advancement in a time frame with past, present, and future. A trope is used to recount the movement, in narrative form or another. It is historians who create the descriptive categories for reading and talking about the past. No historical narrative can fully recover the past because the past did not happen in the form of a story. As a consequence, directionality is not observed but constructed. The form of historical narrative is not the only way of doing history either. As Hayden White explains, notable masters of modern historiography have preferred non-narrative or anti-narrative modes of representation, such as the meditation, the epitome, or the anatomy.[26] Proper and rigorous historical method cannot recover the originality of the past because the problem remains as to what method to choose from. From the empiricists to the historicists and the postmoderns, there is a range of methods that stand the test of professional peer review but would lead to entirely different outcomes. Directionality becomes even more troubling when one turns to questions of etiology and teleology. A notion of causality is needed to account for the cause-and-effect relationships that result in advancement. An account of agency may be needed, that is to say a comprehensible sense of whether human or non-human action, will, contingency, or necessity, was causal. The advancement

---

[25] See eg K Jenkins, *Re-Thinking History* (Routledge London 2012 [1991]).
[26] H White, *The Content of the Form: Narrative Discourse and Historical Representation* (Johns Hopkins University Press Baltimore 2009 [1987]).

may have been predetermined, or due to superior forces in place, accident, natural selection, rational choice, and so on. The social significance of the development may be limited to the micro-level or it may be part of a macro-level transformation in human society. Speaking progress requires a theory of social change.

Let us for a moment entertain the hypothesis that, in spite of relativist caveats, certain glaring forms of directionality can be defended: the increased ecological influence of the human species during the last millennium; the increase in the number of judicial institutions on the international plane; the number of State parties to a given international instrument; and so on. On what basis can they be associated with progress? Here comes the second element of the progress, which can be called betterment. Ascertaining progress requires an evaluation that the new state of affairs is somehow superior to the previous one and an axiological criterion or standard on the basis of which the evaluation will be conducted. Take the relatively uncontroversial thesis that the mere accretion of knowledge constitutes progress in science. According to this thesis the accumulation of knowledge about a topic signifies advance. International law can be described as having progressed on account of the fact that, ever since its early years, it continues to amass in-depth knowledge by means of an increasing body of scientific work, legislation, case law, alternative approaches, and so on. We now know 'more' about international law and transnational legal relationships than we ever did before. But the accretion of knowledge thesis is meaningless without a meta-theory that demonstrates what constitutes a knowledge-fact and how the accumulation of information, data, evidence, teachings, doctrines, histories, make 'better' science. If this is correct, then declaring advancement is a question of identifying a decisive standard to be used for the assessment. For an account of progress to be persuasive, it ultimately needs to purge the possibility of relativity in this very evaluation. Should one demonstrate that the accretion of knowledge thesis has no stable meaning, the thesis is reduced to opinion. Progress must be evaluated on the basis of a standard that 'speaks itself' and trumps relativist criticism in a decisive manner. Otherwise, it would not be 'true' progress, but ideology. Progress can only be proclaimed if one axiomatically accepts a meta-narrative that declares closure or end to contestation. In that sense, it is always theoretical 'all the way down'.

4 PROGRESS IN INTERNATIONAL LAW ARGUMENT: AN EXAMPLE

The idea that the desirability of social change should be measured on the basis of its contribution to some sort of upward spiral of 'real' progress is the core of the debate on the judicialization of international law, an important concern for scholars during the previous decade.[27] Progress is the organizing principle of this debate. Even if Progress in the uppercase is rarely invoked as the goal to be achieved by proliferation, progress in the lowercase is the controlling vocabulary.

Tribunals-related literature is a heterogeneous body of texts produced in different parts of the world, notably on both sides of the Atlantic. Most of this work seems to be concerned with specific cases and procedural issues rather than with articulating an analytical framework for the study of the international judiciary. Nonetheless a sense of cohesion is forged by the certainty, sometimes stated explicitly, other times implicitly, that the turn to adjudication constitutes a moment of disciplinary progress: an institutional–professional development with benevolent systemic consequences. Proliferation is typically seen as progress in two different ways. First, as a process of internal maturation, marking the completion of international law's institutional structure (the missing 'third pillar' of the international division of powers),[28] thus leading to more cases resolved before the courts, more case law, more determinate rules, more certainty and predictability, more precedent, more thickening of the texture of the legal fabric. Second, as the hallmark of a new rule-oriented approach, widely regarded as an absolute and necessary condition for social progress.[29] Along these lines, the change in the social object as such, that is, the mere creation of more international judicial institutions, is said to have an immanent positive value.[30] It is to be noted that the understanding of proliferation 'in itself' as a moment of progress is already a radical shift compared to the past, when scepticism prevailed. But the new literature on tribunals raises the stakes further. It makes bold statements about a new paradigm of international lawyering that revolves around the development of judicial institutions. This new

[27] See eg C Brown, *A Common Law of International Adjudication* (OUP Oxford 2009); T Buergenthal, 'Proliferation of International Courts and Tribunals: Is It Good or Bad?' (2001) 14 *Leiden Journal of International Law* 267–75; B Kingsbury, 'Foreword: Is the Proliferation of International Courts and Tribunals a Systemic Problem?' (1998) 31 *New York University Journal of International Law and Politics* 679–96; JI Charney, 'The Impact on the International Legal System of the Growth of International Courts and Tribunals' (1998) 31 *New York University Journal of International Law and Politics* 697–708.

[28] Rosenne explains the necessity of the International Court of Justice on the grounds that '[since] the world organization already possessed executive, deliberative, and administrative organs, [it] would be incomplete unless it possessed a fully integrated judicial system of its own': S Rosenne, *The World Court: What It is and How It Works* (AW Sythoff Leiden 1962) at 36.

[29] This idea dates back to the Kantian claim about the importance of international dispute settlement. See I Kant, 'Perpetual Peace: A Philosophical Sketch' in *Kant: Political Writings* (H Reiss ed HB Nisbet trans) (2nd edn CUP Cambridge 1991) 93–130, at 102–5.

[30] H Thirlway, 'The Proliferation of International Judicial Organs: Institutional and Substantive Questions: The International Court of Justice and Other International Courts' in NM Blokker and HG Schermers (eds), *Proliferation of International Organizations: Legal Issues* (Kluwer Law International The Hague 2001) 251–78, at 255.

paradigm, the story goes, initiates a new rule-oriented approach to international governance, whose beneficiaries are the entire community of states and their citizens, as opposed to narrow (sovereign or other partial) interests. For some, proliferation is accompanied by an attitude shift: allegedly, and more than any other actor, courts are today willing to assume responsibility for social progress and apply international law in a manner beneficial for international community as a whole.[31] For others, the new professional community of 'dispute settlers' can forge a new culture of cooperation based on the respect for democratic values of pluralism, persuasive authority, positive conflict, comity, and so on.[32] Tribunals, along these lines, are able to serve justice in specific disputes without sacrificing the universality of international law.

In terms of directionality, authors refer to 'facts and trends' of proliferation. The post-1989 increase in the number of new judicial bodies, the increased number of cases decided by courts as opposed to the past, the diversification of the structural characteristics of tribunals, and a renewed faith in the capacity of tribunals as agents of transformative change are some among the relevant trends. These trends are metabolized in the form of historical narrative that sees proliferation as a natural stage in the evolution of the discipline signifying a 'growing sophistication' and a move from a power-oriented to a rule-oriented model of international affairs. Why did this legalization take place today and not in the past? The cause-and-effect relationship is found in the enabling concurrence of several factors. For some, the diversification of the ways in which states related to each other and the regulation of previously unregulated domains have led to the codification of new law and the creation of regulatory frameworks and corresponding international organizations.[33] For others, it is the increased interdependence of states, technological advances, globalization, and the progressive acceptance of compulsory jurisdiction clauses.[34] It can also be the gradual democratization of the world and the emergence of liberalism as the dominant socio-political paradigm. While the Cold War and its antagonistic nature encouraged 'discretionary behavior associated with the doctrine of national sovereignty',[35] following its end, obstacles were removed and conditions for a rule-oriented approach flourished. The trend is

---

[31] P Sands, 'Turtles and Torturers: The Transformation of International Law' (2000) 33 *New York University Journal of International Law and Politics* 527–60.

[32] A-M Slaughter, 'A Global Community of Courts' (2003) 44 *Harvard International Law Journal* 191–220.

[33] Y Shany, *The Competing Jurisdictions of International Courts and Tribunals* (OUP Oxford 2004); CPR Romano, 'The Proliferation of International Judicial Bodies: The Pieces of the Puzzle' (1998) 31 *New York University Journal of International Law and Politics* 709–52.

[34] CPR Romano, 'The Shift from the Consensual to the Compulsory Paradigm in International Adjudication: Elements for a Theory of Consent' (2006) 39 *New York University Journal of International Law and Politics* 791–872.

[35] RA Falk, 'Realistic Horizons for International Adjudication' (1970) 11 *Virginia Journal of International Law* 314–26.

presented either as a 'natural' development that hypostasizes the historical tele-ology of '*ubi societas, ibi jus, ibi curia*', or as the predictable consequence of the 'how nations behave' thesis. Progress is evolutionary with a direct correlation be-tween cause and effect: fact x brings systemic reaction y. One therefore speaks of progress that started in Versailles and culminated in the International Criminal Court (ICC).[36] Remarkably, the causes belong to a world external to the public international lawyer. Tribunals emerge, sprout, or spring out in a natural chain of cause and effect. The scholar adopts the posture of the observer whose mediation in the act of representation is unarticulated.

The invocation of directionality as an empirical fact has a crucial role in the feeling of progress. The historical account situates the reader within the context of an evolutionary narrative. Despite the seemingly incontrovertible evidence, such accounts are easy to de-centre. One only needs to ask whether a change occurred really and only in this direction; or whether the cause and effect relationship is over- or under-determined. Such questions are quite important: if tribunals are too different in their systemic function or morphology to constitute a homoge-neous object that 'moves' in a specific direction; or if the reasons behind the emer-gence of proliferation are other than those recounted; then our certainty about what is historically necessary should be different and other lessons would have to be derived from the observation of facts and trends. The capacity to envision a set of events as belonging to the same order of meaning requires a principle by which to translate difference into similarity. Along these lines, in recent years various authors have challenged the historical necessity of proliferation, with international criminal justice bearing the brunt of the criticism: proliferation may be not the apogee of historical determinism, but a savvy move of political redemp-tion, a fig leaf, the glorified by-product of collective unwillingness to engage in other forms of conflict resolution, a historical accident, and so on. Far from his-torically necessary development, tribunals can assuage guilt and convert atrocity into a humanist project that appropriates the suffering of the victims. In contrast to claims of jurists being mere witnesses to the phenomenon of proliferation, a cynical case could be made for a professional bias in 'reading too much' into the facts. Given the lucrative terms of employment and the creation of thousands of new posts for international lawyers in and around international tribunals, the invisible college is not the neutral third party in the rhetoric that resituates inter-national law in the driving seat of international post-conflict resolution efforts.

But even if the directionality of proliferation could be defended as 'true', what is the axiological standard on which it can be evaluated as progress? The answer comes in the form of the assumed systemic effects of judicialization. The long list varies from author to author but it often includes justice (higher proportion of disputes resolved

---

[36] MC Bassiouni, 'From Versailles to Rwanda in Seventy-Five Years: The Need to Establish a Permanent International Criminal Court' (1997) 10 *Harvard Human Rights Journal* 11–62.

by courts rather than forcible means);[37] limits to the power of the sovereign to determine the legality of their acts; peace (exposure of the truth, facilitate healing process); rule of law (recognition of the importance of law and strengthening of the legal fabric);[38] normalcy (routine subjection of disputes to courts);[39] increased quality of decisions through specialization (specialized tribunals possess expertise in particular areas which renders them more suitable for certain kinds of disputes);[40] renewed faith in international law.[41] In most cases statements are not supported by empirical evidence[42] and the question remains whether any of the above may be quantifiable or measurable at all.[43] Until the empirical results are conclusive 'the complacent and the critic alike will be at a disadvantage' as one author admits.[44] Should the empirical base be proven elusive, what is left is faith. The need for empirical research is both the promise and the defeat of the project of proliferation. The nature of the empirical work that is required is however never-ending. As long as the link between tribunals and their social effects remains unclear, presumed, or under review, directionality will continue to reside safely on the side of progress. Not as panacea but as a token of hope and as a pragmatist contribution to some sort of positively evaluated forward movement. In proliferation, progress trades myth for fact and faith for reason, but remains theoretical 'all the way down'.

5 In Conclusion

This chapter makes two points. The first is that the impact of the idea of progress in international law should be measured not only against the traction of grand

---

[37] *A Common Law of International Adjudication* (n 27) 257–8; P-M Dupuy, 'The Danger of Fragmentation or Unification of the International Legal System and the International Court of Justice' (1998) 31 *New York University Journal of International Law and Politics* 791–808, at 796.

[38] R Goldstone, 'Assessing the Work of the United Nations War Crimes Tribunal' (1997) 33 *Stanford Journal of International Law* 1–8.

[39] *The Competing Jurisdictions of International Courts and Tribunals* (n 33) 7; 'The Danger of Fragmentation or Unification of the International Legal System and the International Court of Justice' (n 37).

[40] 'The Proliferation of International Judicial Organs' (n 30) 255, 257.

[41] 'Assessing the Work of the United Nations War Crimes Tribunal' (n 38) 2; PS Rao, 'Multiple International Judicial Forums: A Reflection of the Growing Strength of International Law or Its Fragmentation?' (2003) 25 *Michigan Journal of International Law* 929–61.

[42] F Mégret, 'Three Dangers for the International Criminal Court: A Critical Look at a Consensual Project' (2001) 12 *Finnish Yearbook of International Law* 193–247, at 193.

[43] DS Koller, 'The Faith of the International Criminal Lawyer' (2007) 40 *New York University Journal of International Law and Politics* 1019–69.

[44] N Miller, 'An International Jurisprudence? The Operation of "Precedent" across International Tribunals' (2002) 15 *Leiden Journal of International Law* 483–526.

progress narratives but also against the pervasiveness of everyday, prosaic varieties of progress talk. The second is that all arguments that use the idea of progress as the evaluative standard of choice, from the uppercase to the lowercase, frontload directional change with ethical content. The proposal is not to do away with a grand idea that has displayed extraordinary resilience over the centuries and continues to be grafted in the general mental outlook of our time. Progress is likely to remain a standard trope of renewalism for years to come. Few would doubt that a 'progress kick', the zeal generated by being an agent of progressive politics, yields tremendous energy and can be a compelling source of institutional, disciplinary, and social transformation. It should therefore be studied as such. While one may choose to deploy progress as a convenient mode of evaluation, one should reckon with the difficulties in defending progress as a descriptive mode that 'speaks itself'. Progress is theoretical 'all the way down' and therefore a language of legitimation and de-legitimation.

CHAPTER 46

INTERNATIONAL LEGALISM AND INTERNATIONAL POLITICS

FLORIAN HOFFMANN

1 INTERNATIONAL LAW AND ITS 'ISM'

PERHAPS the most curious thing about the concept of 'international legalism' is the relative scarcity of its use. Rarely will one find an international judge, a legal advisor or even a teacher of international law who openly refers to it, nor is it the explicit subject of any of the great debates in doctrine or theory.[1] Indeed, there seems to be almost a refusal on the part of a majority of international lawyers to directly engage with the portrayal of their own practice as legalist. One reason for this is that the term is often used disparagingly to caricature the stereotypical international lawyer as either a rule-fetishizing utopian or as a conscience-free apologist. Neither description is particularly

---

[1] AL Paulus, 'Law and Politics in the Age of Globalization' (2000) 11 *European Journal of International Law* 465–72.

appealing to self-conscious professionals, not least as it tends to come either from critical scholars within the discipline or, 'worse', from outside, notably from 'functionalist' international relations scholars.[2]

It is, thus, not surprising that a recent treatise setting out to frame and denounce the international legal project as 'perilous' global legalism caused a good degree of uproar among those to whom it intended to attach the label. That treatise is, of course, Eric Posner's 2009 monograph, *The Perils of Global Legalism*, which in turn followed his and Jack Goldsmith's 2006 book *The Limits of International Law*.[3] In essence, both books argue that international law is ineffective in creating and maintaining international order—or, as Posner puts it, in solving global collective action problems—and that, as a consequence, all those international lawyers who claim otherwise are misguided and, indeed, perilous global legalists. Given that most international lawyers who self-consciously associate with that job description would, as a matter of course, fall into the latter category, Posner's (and Goldsmith's) argument unsurprisingly caused a distinct irritation in many quarters of the international legal academy.[4] This reaction was, arguably, not only due to the fact that both interventions seemed to simply recycle old style realist international law scepticism but also that they did this, polemically, in the wake of the (then) Bush administration's perceived pathological disrespect for international law, international institutions, and multilateralism in general. For many international lawyers, this was yet another gauntlet thrown down on behalf of the adherents of what Louis Henkin had previously called the 'cynic's formula'[5]—a *Feindbild* which, in the eyes of most international lawyers today, is comprised of international relations scholars, neoconservatives, neo-Schmittians and, generally, (American) exceptionalists, as well as those 'law and economics' rationalists that align with any of the former.

Yet, for all its apparent provocation, the response to *Perils* was similar to the one to *Limits*, which was, as one commentator observed, simply 'quarantined as

---

[2] M Koskenniemi, 'Law, Teleology and International Relations: An Essay in Counterdisciplinarity' (2012) 26 *International Relations* 3–34, at 5.

[3] EA Posner, *The Perils of Global Legalism* (University of Chicago Press Chicago 2009); EA Posner and JL Goldsmith, *The Limits of International Law* (OUP Oxford 2005).

[4] H Cohen, 'Book Review—Eric A Posner's *The Perils of Global Legalism*' (2012) 13 *German Law Journal* 67–75; S Kupi, 'Book Note—*The Perils of Global Legalism* by Eric A Posner' (2011) 49 *Osgoode Hall Law Journal* 43–4; A D'Amato, 'New Approaches to Customary International Law—EA Posner, *The Perils of Global Legalism*; AT Guzman, *How International Law Works: A Rational Choice Theory*; BD Lepard, *Customary International Law: A New Theory with Practical Applications*' (2011) 105 *American Journal of International Law* 163–7; R Hockett, 'Promise against Peril: Of Power, Purpose, and Principle in International Law' (2010) 17 *ILSA Journal of International and Comparative Law* 1–32; CJ Eby, 'Global Legalism: The Illusion of Effective International Law' (2010) 38 *Denver Journal of International Law and Policy* 687–99; and most recently JD Ohlin, *The Assault on International Law* (OUP Oxford 2015).

[5] L Henkin, *How Nations Behave* (Council on Foreign Relations New York 1979) at 49.

if it were a strange new variety of antigen in the body of international law schol-arship, with a fast-growing hedge of reviews and review essays playing the salu-tary role of antibodies'.[6] Hence, in the main, the immune reaction has consisted of simply turning the table on Posner's indictments, with the main line of defence being the attempt to rebut his presupposition that the assertion that international law was effective was founded on a tautology without empirical grounding.[7] Thus, where Posner endeavours to muster evidence for the ineffectiveness of customary and treaty law in solving global collective action problems ranging from climate change to the 'war on terror', his critics simply deny his pessimistic reading of the facticity of legalized inter-state relations.[8] Where he derives that ineffectiveness from the purported fact that 'states can [and will] depart from international law' because they are fundamentally interest-driven,[9] they counter-argue by pointing to the numerous examples of functioning inter-state cooperation underwritten by (international) law. And where, finally, Posner reveals his scepticism to be based on the absence of effective international institutions resulting from the inexistence of a world government, they argue that 'law without government' was a much more empirically realistic and normatively desirable proposition than he makes it out to be.[10]

However, typically for many an international lawyer's response to rule scepticism,[11] these refutations have tended to be casuistic in nature, seeking to get the better of Posner on empirical grounds while shying away from his argument's deeper tenets. In essence, these are, again, that international law's effectiveness is not em-pirically verifiable, that international law cannot, in any case, work in the absence of a real or presumed world state, and that promoting it is, therefore, misguided because it sets the wrong priorities and impedes effective problem solving in the international realm.

These positions echo three common variants of scepticism that have accompa-nied the international legal project since its inception. The first variant could be called epistemological scepticism and stems from a negative answer to the question of how international legality can be identified, notably that it cannot (be clearly iden-tified). It hits at the heart of a rather specific type of law which, for it to be applied to facts, needs always first to be found or, as contemporary legal positivism would have

---

[6] 'Promise against Peril' (n 4) 7.

[7] JP Trachtman, 'Eric A Posner, *The Perils of Global Legalism*' (2009) 20 *European Journal of International Law* 1263–70; 'New Approaches to Customary International Law' (n 4).

[8] *The Perils of Global Legalism* (n 3).

[9] EA Posner, 'The Rise of Global Legalism' (Max Weber Lecture No 2008/04 delivered at the European University Institute, 16 January 2008) <http://cadmus.eui.eu/bitstream/handle/1814/8206/MWP_LS_2008_04.pdf> [accessed 3 March 2016].

[10] Ibid.

[11] DC Gray, 'Rule-Skepticism, Strategy, and the Limits of International Law' (2006) 46 *Virginia Journal of International Law* 563–84.

it, ascertained.[12] If this cannot be done up to a certain standard, then, according to Posner, that project's foundational premise—notably that states *feel* and, thus, *are* factually bound by legal norms knowable and known by them—would turn out to be unfounded. Then there is what could be termed the ontological variant of scepticism that arises from the different interpretations of how international law *really* works when observed, as it were, from outside. Here the portfolio ranges from the canonical—and, according to its critics, therefore legalist—legal formalism that objectifies the internal perspective's norm-centric world view to Posner and company's realist anti-legalism that reduces international law to a form of (albeit ineffective) political discourse driven by rational state interest. Lastly, there is also an axiological dimension which, to Posner-like sceptics, inheres in the international legal project. It relates to the presumption, allegedly held by international lawyers of the legalist kind, that (international) law has a value of its own that bestows on it a fundamental legitimacy vis-à-vis other forms of (international) ordering, most notably (what Posner calls) politics. Indeed, by this line of argument, international law's legitimacy is even held to be capable of outpacing its own legality, or, rather, the ascertainment thereof. The intra-disciplinary fallout over the 'illegality but legitimacy' of the 1998 Kosovo bombings is the *cause célèbre* here, regurgitated by Posner to illustrate his point.[13]

The point behind the point is, of course, that law—or, rather, the rule of law—is here taken better to advance certain values, or valued objectives, such as peace, equity, or justice, than political process. The international legal project is, thus, essentially seen as a plot to spread the rule of law globally as a means to achieve a certain type of world order. It is, in other words, held out to be better than politics, or, indeed, the better politics, and it is this presupposition that is at the heart of Posner's critique. The latter's central tenet is that to counterfactually promote a law that is actually dysfunctional in terms of solving 'global collective action problems' risks advancing the wrong objectives. Such a law does not, in Posner's words, 'advance [people's] interests and respect their values';[14] it cannot, thus, be taken to be legitimate.

None of these scepticisms are particularly new, and the startled uproar following *Limits* and *Perils* was, arguably, due not so much to their originality but to the brash tone in which they were advanced. This has, however, made it easy for *Perils'* targets—virtually all self-professed international lawyers—to simply discard the argument as ideological propaganda, and to refrain from engaging with the concerns underlying the critique, even as questions surrounding international law's legality, legitimacy, and reality continue to haunt it, not least at a time when it

[12] J d'Aspremont, *Formalism and the Sources of International Law: A Theory of the Ascertainment of Legal Rules* (OUP Oxford 2011).
[13] 'The Rise of Global Legalism' (n 9) 29; 'New Approaches to Customary International Law' (n 4) 164.
[14] *The Perils of Global Legalism* (n 3).

seems, paradoxically, to be experiencing at once new heights of relevance and un-precedented challenges.[15]

At the heart of this reluctance to engage directly with such scepticism lies, arguably, a continuing unease about law's (most) significant other, notably pol-itics. To be sure, after half a century of critical legal scholarship, the 'p'-word is no longer taboo in the discipline and many an international lawyer has become confident enough to offer a political gloss on the margins of her scholarship, not least in order to talk back to those who have long claimed interpretive au-thority over (international) politics.[16] Yet, revealing the 'politics of international law' and rendering the discipline more overtly political is not the same thing.[17] Hence, the real *agent provocateur* is, arguably, not Posner and Goldsmith's em-piricist challenge to legal objectivism but their implicit attempt to move the terms of the debate onto the terrain of (realist) politics and to compel an an-swer within this remit. Most of the actual respondents did, indeed, refuse to take the bait by mounting a political defence of legalism but, instead, sought simply to undermine the realist interpretation of international legal practice. The question of the relationship between law and politics was, however, thereby left to be answered, as if a deeper and more direct engagement carried the risk of opening a Pandora's Box the contents of which might infect the lawyer's disciplinary high ground.

For inside that box lurks something that international lawyers, arguably, fear even more than the ritual provocations by political realists, and that is to find that their own discipline might, in fact, be something different from what it seems. What is, of course, hinted at here is the contention that international law is, in essence, an ideological framework; that its professional practice is, thus, ideological; and that its practitioners are, consequently, ideologues. Posner, of course, claims as much

---

[15] For instance, the recent expansion of international criminal law can be taken to point to a grow-ing tendency to assess complex political theatres by international legal standards and to base action on such an assessment: see SMH Nouwen and WG Werner, 'Monopolizing Global Justice: International Criminal Law as a Challenge to Human Diversity' (2015) 13 *Journal of International Criminal Justice* 157–76. On the other hand, such intractable issues as the proliferation of insurgent activities deemed terrorist or the consolidation of global migration streams seem to be capable of generating reactions by states that appear to be inconsiderate of even the most fundamental and established legal principles: see P Fargues and A Di Bartolomeo, 'Drowned Europe' (Migration Policy Centre, European University Institute, Policy Brief No 2015/05, April 2015) <http://cadmus.eui.eu/bitstream/handle/1814/35557/MPC_2015_05_PB.pdf> [accessed 3 March 2016]; T Basaran, 'The Saved and the Drowned: Governing Indifference in the Name of Security' (2015) 46 *Security Dialogue* 205–20.

[16] M Koskenniemi, 'Miserable Comforters: International Relations as New Natural Law' (2009) 15 *European Journal of International Relations* 395–422; 'Law, Teleology and International Relations' (n 2).

[17] M Koskenniemi, 'The Politics of International Law' (1990) 1 *European Journal of International Law* 4–32; M Koskenniemi, 'The Politics of International Law—20 Years Later' (2009) 20 *European Journal of International Law* 7–19.

when he defines global legalism as 'akin to an ideology or attitude or posture—a set of beliefs about how the world works',[18] except that to those charging others with being under the sway of ideology, it represents a wrong or at least distorted view of that world and the role of law in it. For at its (Marxian) most basic, an ideology is a function of the structural forces that shape social reality and, simultaneously, a cosmetic device to conceal their operation.[19] Hence, (international) lawyers-as-ideologues would, merely through their practice, be implicated in at once running and dissimulating, including to themselves, a particular 'scheme of things'. That 'scheme of things' would have an empirical grounding in factual power relations, though these would be continuously misrepresented in what amounts to a dialectical interlocking of reality and mystification.[20]

If, in other words, international law was an ideology, this would mean that international lawyers of the legalist kind would be both ignorant of the 'true' workings of the law, and, by militantly defending their 'false' view, complicit in a gigantic scam. Needless to say, this is not a representation likely to please those to which it is applied. Nor does it sit well with most lawyers' self-understanding as appliers, rather than defenders, of their particular type of knowledge (about rules), of being conveyors of the (objectively) given rather than crusaders for a cause, and of being mere servants of a (legal) Jupiter rather than shouldering the responsibility that comes with being a Hercules.[21]

It is that ideological attitude which the term 'legalism' is meant to express, with the 'scheme of things' it refers to being, of course, that grand meta-narrative of modernity, notably liberalism. In fact, if one follows a historical-critical reading of international law, the discipline was already born as an ideological framework to defend a liberal internationalist project.[22] However, after half a century of critical legal scholarship—more than a century if one adds the American legal realist tradition—none of this comes as much of a surprise any more.[23] That the Western legal tradition in general, and international law in particular, is implicated in the story of the unfolding of a liberal (capitalist) world and that it is, in that sense,

---

[18] 'The Rise of Global Legalism' (n 9) 11.
[19] S Marks, 'Big Brother Is Bleeping Us—With the Message That Ideology Doesn't Matter' (2001) 12 *European Journal of International Law* 109–23.
[20] Ibid 123.
[21] F Ost, 'Júpiter, Hércules, Hermes: Tres Modelos de Juez' (1993) 14 *Doxa—Cuadernos de Filosofía del Derecho* 169–74.
[22] See M Koskenniemi, *From Apology to Utopia: The Structure of International Legal Argument* (Finnish Lawyers' Publishing Helsinki 1989). Citations will, henceforth, be to the reissue: M Koskenniemi, *From Apology to Utopia: The Structure of International Legal Argument* (reissue CUP Cambridge 2005) at 71.
[23] A Hunt, 'The Theory of Critical Legal Studies' (1986) 6 *Oxford Journal of Legal Studies* 1–45; JA Beckett, 'Rebel without a Cause—Martti Koskenniemi and the Critical Legal Project' (2006) 7 *German Law Journal* 1045–88.

political, has been worked out in great detail and with increasing clarity since, at least, the (first) publication of Martti Koskenniemi's *From Apology to Utopia*.[24] That international legal practice is, therefore, marked by structural (political) bias and its substance by the historical legacies of colonialism and imperialism has by now been charted in its most intricate facets.[25] There is little, if anything, to add to this grand ideology critique of international law.

Yet, despite all this, those at whom it is primarily directed, the operators of that very ideological law, seem to remain largely undaunted by critique and solidly in the grip of liberal legalism. To them, legalism—denoting, again, the mindset that is produced by and, thereby, reproduces, that liberal ideology—is not, it would seem, an essentially contested concept at all. In fact, as was already hinted at, it is not even part of the day-to-day vocabulary. One reason for this may be the 'false consciousness' under which ideology critique postulates the legalists to be operating. However, such a purely epistemological conception of ideology in which those under its thrall would be but mindless automata incapable of self-reflective insight is highly implausible.[26] The reason why, after three decades of 'immanent critique',[27] contemporary international lawyers still tend not to engage in and act upon the critique of their own ideology is, arguably, that they choose not to do so. That choice results from the aforementioned deep reluctance to step outside of the box and to speak politics, whether it is an openly liberal or an anti-liberal one.

Legalism is the label that stands for this reluctance in the dual sense that it, on the one hand, represents international lawyers' professional preference for legal objectivism and political agnosticism and, on the other hand, their equally professional unwillingness to openly admit to this preference. It is, hence, everywhere and nowhere in international law, a paradox produced by the still empty space between the law and the political. For while the origins of this gap have largely been deciphered and its continued existence explained, bridging it has remained a tentative and marginal exercise, if, indeed, it has been deemed a worthwhile exercise at all. Is this because of some ontological property which renders law and politics fundamentally incommensurable, or is it because the gap, premised on particular (mis)conceptions of both law and politics, serves a specific function within the wider liberal 'scheme of things'? Thus, as a metaphor for this gap, legalism can still be meaningfully explored (even if only legalism with a small 'l'), in between the lines of the grand narratives of both liberalism and its critique.

---

[24] See *From Apology to Utopia* (n 22) ch 2.

[25] See ibid; A Anghie, *Imperialism, Sovereignty and the Making of International Law* (CUP Cambridge 2005); L Eslava and S Pahuja, 'Beyond the (Post)Colonial: TWAIL and the Everyday Life of International Law' (2012) 45 *Journal of Law and Politics in Africa, Asia and Latin America—Verfassung und Recht in Übersee (VRÜ)* 195–221.

[26] 'Big Brother Is Bleeping Us' (n 19).   [27] *From Apology to Utopia* (n 22) 600.

2 Liberal Legalism
as International Law's Ideology

The starting point for any attempt to measure the gap between law and politics is a recapitulation of where the liberal project of international law stands after the critique—where, in line with a post-Frankfurtian conception of *Ideologiekritik*, 'after' neither denotes a chronological order nor an end point, but simply the disposition of that critique 'out in the open'.[28] To attempt to do such a critique remotely any justice, a treatise the size of this *Handbook* would be necessary. Instead, the scene shall be drawn in a few rough strokes that merely aim to elucidate the basic question at hand, namely why (liberal) international lawyers continue to refuse to talk politics and whether there is any alternative at hand.

For these more limited purposes, an appropriate starting point might, arguably, be a quick glance back at two intellectual movements with which the term legalism is associated and which predate and prefigure its association with modern liberalism and liberal internationalism. The first concerns an ancient Chinese political theory, subsequently described as legalist, which accompanied the formation of a unified Chinese state during the so called Warring States period (475–221 BCE) and which extended into the first imperial dynastic period, the Qin Dynasty (221–206 BCE). Here the term legalism was employed to refer to the 'amoral science of statecraft' and it was developed in contrast to both Confucian moralism and Taoist naturalism. It expressed a position in which positive law was seen as the primary instrument to uphold the centralized rule of a unified sovereign.[29] As such, legalism (*fajia*) with its constituent elements of power (*shi*), method (*shu*), and law(s) (*fa*) broadly alludes both to Machiavellian (political) realism and to Hobbesian sovereigntism, with hints of legal positivism in its rule centrism and moral relativism. With its stress on the central role of positive law for the maintenance of effective control over people and territory it bears a certain likeness to the development of the Westphalian concept of statehood and sovereignty as well as to the empirical process of legalization that accompanied it. Hence Qin legalism stands for a particular conception of law and law's role in (political) society, as well as for a certain militancy towards the realization of this vision. As a doctrine, however, legalism came to be strongly repudiated for its alleged amorality and perceived cruelty in post-Qin times, even if it continued

---

[28] See S Žižek, 'Introduction: The Spectre of Ideology' in S Žižek (ed), *Mapping Ideology* (Verso New York 2012) 1–33.

[29] PR Goldin, 'Persistent Misconceptions about Chinese "Legalism"' (2011) 38 *Journal of Chinese Philosophy* 88–104.

to inform significant aspects of Chinese political thought under the cloak of Confucian(ist) rhetoric.[30]

The second semantic context with which legalism is frequently associated is Christian theology, where it is used to refer to the object of the Pauline critique of the 'salvation through (the) law' doctrine. Stylized as the Jewish Christian position that compliance with Mosaic Law (*Torah*)—for instance in the form of male circumcision—was a pre-requisite for salvation, it was contrasted by Paul with the notion that justification, that is, freedom from (original) sin, could only be attained through (God's) grace by means of faith.[31] While Paul's position on the Mosaic Law was actually ambivalent and may have been primarily concerned with finding a bridge between the (old) law and the (new) revelation, subsequent interpretation created a clear dichotomy between legalism and anti-legalism.[32] At its heart lie fundamentally different views on the role of individual agency in the quest for redemption. For legalists, it is the proactive compliance with preordained rules or other precepts, including 'good works', that contributes significantly to the redemptive process, whereas for anti-legalists, it is 'merely' the (albeit equally proactive) acceptance, through faith, of the gift of (God's) grace that delimits a human being's redemptive agency.

Ultimately, the difference between (theological) legalism and anti-legalism comes down to one between exteriority versus interiority, that is, between privileging either the collective adherence to a framework of rules external to individual conscience or, inversely, the primacy of that individual conscience, deemed to constitute the receptacle for grace, over any human-made or human-interpreted system of rules. Although, contrary to a commonly held view, this difference does not squarely map onto the Catholic–Protestant dichotomy, it does contrast, on an abstract level, a communitarian-multilateral approach with an individualist-unilateral one, even if a single unifying force, in this case God's will, remains in a more or less mediated form behind both conceptions.

What is significant about these two highly disparate historical debates is that they introduce many of the issues around which the contemporary discussion of legalism in international law is structured. Hence, the question of the meaning and role of (legal) sovereignty versus (real) power is prefigured, as is the related issue of the status of positive rules in (international) life. And in the background,

---

[30] K Hsiao, 'Legalism and Autocracy in Traditional China' (1976) 10 *Chinese Studies in History* 125–43.

[31] See, in particular, *Romans* 3:20 (KJV): 'Therefore by the deeds of the law there shall no flesh be justified...' and *Galatians* 2:16 (KJV): 'Knowing that a man is not justified by the works of the law, but by the faith of Jesus Christ, even we have believed in Jesus Christ, that we might be justified by the faith of Christ, and not by the works of the law: for by the works of the law shall no flesh be justified'. See TJ Shaw (ed), *The Shaw's Revised King James Holy Bible* (Trafford Bloomington 2010) at 567 and 587.

[32] T Schirrmacher, *Law or Spirit? An Alternative View of Galatians* (RVB International Hamburg 2008).

the (political) theological question of the nature of the international as a society of interests or a community of values, and of the primacy of law or politics in it, is articulated. What is, of course, at first sight puzzling are the more counter-intuitive associations of legalism in these two discourses. That law be seen as a mere instrument of power, as in Qin legalism, seems to contradict the contemporary narrative of it being an antidote to the latter. That the precedence of external rules over (political) judgement might be deemed negative seems to fly in the face of the dominant view that political will must be curtailed through externally binding rules. Yet, it is in this shift in the semantics of law, from it being an instrument *of* power to one *against* it, from it being a limitation of (political) freedom to it being its principal safeguard, that the work of liberal ideology can be discerned.

At the base of that ideology lies, arguably, the grandest of all meta-narratives, namely that of modernity itself. Of its many plotlines, one concerns the loss of a transcendental foundation for political authority and the consequent crisis that characterizes the modern predicament.[33] (Very) broadly speaking, that predicament poses the fundamental question of how order can be produced under conditions of plurality and from within the world. Its answer requires, amongst other things, some scheme to overcome the gap between the universal (abstract) and the particular (concrete) left open by the loss of transcendental-mythical authority. This gap threatens to pulverize social order and paves the conceptual way for the notorious *bellum omnium contra omnes*, with the modern history of (political) ideas, arguably, representing a continuous effort to overcome it.[34]

One scheme to this end has, of course, been liberalism which, in essence, operates by means of three ideological moves. First, it stylizes reason as a universal instrument for the articulation of (individual) self-interest, which, in turn, is deemed to be driven by the desire for self-preservation. Political freedom is, thus, simply the capacity to enact the precepts of reason with regard to one's self-interest. This is then deemed to 'naturally' introduce the need—as well as the individual insight into such need—for a political society which serves the (sole) purpose of enforcing order among its self-interested and, therefore, always potentially antagonistic members. Conceived of as a constraint on individual liberty, such ordering requires consent, which, in turn, is given by means of a hypothetical (social) contract. This, then, gives rise to liberalism's second ideological move, notably the postulate of a rigidly divided public and private sphere. For what liberal individuals ultimately consent to is a scheme for social order that is geared to ensuring that the

---

[33] See generally H Arendt, *Between Past and Future* (University of Chicago Press Chicago 1961). See also M Antaki, 'The Critical Modernism of Hannah Arendt' (2007) 8 *Theoretical Inquiries in Law* 251–75; F Hoffmann, 'Facing the Abyss: International Law before the Political' in M Goldoni and C McCorkindale (eds), *Hannah Arendt and the Law* (Hart Oxford 2012) 173–90, at 173.

[34] Q Skinner, 'The Ideological Context of Hobbes's Political Thought' (1966) 9 *Historical Journal* 286–317, at 298.

exercise of their liberty is not threatened by the inherent antagonism this implies. Liberalism purports to achieve this by separating off a private sphere, in which articulations of individual liberty are located, from a (much smaller) public sphere, in which the terms of basic collective survival are politically negotiated. However, this only works if politics is tightly enclosed in a girdle of fundamental rights and institutions representing a stylized *volonté general*—as well as, of course, a market-based, decentralized form of economic exchange and distribution—which radically reduces the space for political contestation and, thus, violence. In other words, the particular that gives rise to difference—in value or identity—is largely removed from the realm of politics in order to constitute a politically neutral public sphere which allows a universalized *homo oeconomicus* to (self-)interestedly pursue her individual well-being. The neutrality of this public sphere is, of course, not 'real', as the outcomes of the liberal scheme of politics are not universally equal but are distributed asymmetrically and linked to particular interests. This, however, impels the third ideological move of liberalism, notably the need to conceal the particularity of the value and identity positions that underwrite the liberal 'scheme' under a cloak of universality that makes them appear as necessary and 'natural'. Hence, liberalism's approach to avoiding the *bellum omnium* is to mythologize its own foundations—just as modernity itself does, namely by covering up its lack of foundation through a simulacrum of foundation.

Law, or rather, a particular conception of law, plays a crucial role in this scheme. It is the primary instrument through which the public–private divide is sustained and, hence, the means by which liberal politics is constituted. The particular conception that underlies liberal law is based on several premises which flow from the positivist ontology that derives from the instrumentalist conception of rationality that is privileged in (liberal) modernity. Hence, law is considered to be objective in the dual sense of being anchored in empirical social practice (termed, variously, as effectiveness, concreteness, or facticity) rather than in an ideal moral universe, as well as in its specific identity as a clearly delimited set of ought propositions endowed with the force to order or regulate their referent society (termed normativity or validity).[35] The empirical reality on which law's objectivity is premised does not, however, itself belong to the realm of law, but is, instead, represented through substantiations of a basic norm, a rule of recognition, or a 'first constitution'.[36]

Being an offspring of the neo-Kantian attempt to move philosophy into the age of scientific positivism, such legal positivism is concerned with defining a specifically legal category of cognition and with differentiating it against other cognitive

---

[35] *From Apology to Utopia* (n 22).

[36] See, respectively, H Kelsen, *The Pure Theory of Law* (M Knight trans) (2nd edn Lawbook Exchange Clark 2009 [1934]) and HLA Hart, *The Concept of Law* (PA Bulloch and J Raz eds) (3rd edn OUP Oxford 2012 [1961]). See also J Kammerhofer, 'Hans Kelsen in Today's International Legal Scholarship' in J Kammerhofer and J d'Aspremont (eds), *International Legal Positivism in a Post-Modern World* (CUP Cambridge 2014) 81–113.

categories.[37] Its central purpose is to bestow upon law an unmistakable identity that is autonomous in content and operation and can, thus, only be properly known and described in its own terms, that is, by an internal perspective which is non-reducible to other system logics—such as politics. Legal positivism aims both to explain that autonomy and to outline the conditions for understanding a particular type of normative language as law.[38] Hence, the ascertainment and application of such law must follow formalist lines, that is, the rules which make it up must be considered to be capable of being logically derived through their pedigree and to render determinate normative outcomes in adjudicatory contexts. As a performative language (game) structured by a uniform—yet, therefore, necessarily self-contained and closed—grammar, law must, in principle, be conceived of as being accessible to and useable by all members of its referent society on equal terms and, hence, universal. Liberal law is, thus, a jurisprudential amalgam of legal positivism, formalism, and objectivism.

These features evidently underwrite liberalism's ideological moves. For a law that is conceived as at once empirically objective and autonomous in operation is but an expression of the instrumentalist rationality which liberalism enshrines and which privileges function over purpose or, put differently, the 'how' over the 'why'. It thereby also feeds into the antagonistic individualism at the base of liberalism, geared towards the pursuit of self-interest in abstraction from the totality of social relations (and, indeed, from history itself). This, in turn, is only possible because, under positivist premises, law must be conceived as value free, and, thus, in strictly relativist terms,[39] a *conditio-sine-qua-non* for law to appear as a neutral procedural safeguard of individual liberties. Only thus can it maintain the smokescreen of a public sphere in which politics is stylized as a tightly regulated but, in principle, open-ended balancing of individual interests at the same time as it privileges, in the background, its own concrete order of (liberal) values. For the postulate of an objective and autonomous law that can be 'positively' ascertained makes it impossible to thematize from within its own premises the values which underlie it. The latter are, thus, (nearly) perfectly concealed behind a veil of formalism which makes their identification—and critique—an a priori *a-legal* act outside the remit of 'the law' and, hence, professionally irrelevant to (most) lawyers.[40]

---

[37] S Hammer, 'A Neo-Kantian Theory of Legal Knowledge in Kelsen's *Pure Theory of Law*' in SL Paulson and BL Paulson (ed), *Normativity and Norms: Critical Perspectives on Kelsenian Themes* (OUP Oxford 1999) 177–94.

[38] See eg T Huff, *Max Weber and the Methodology of the Social Sciences* (Transaction New Brunswick 1984); B Bix, 'Law as an Autonomous Discipline' in P Cane and M Tushnet (eds), *The Oxford Handbook of Legal Studies* (OUP Oxford 2003) 975–87; OM Fiss, 'The Autonomy of Law' (2001) 26 *Yale Journal of International Law* 517–26.

[39] J Raz, *Between Authority and Interpretation* (OUP Oxford 2009).

[40] See eg JE Alvarez, 'International Law 101: A Post-Mortem' *ILPost* (American Society of International Law, 12 February 2007). See also WP George, 'Grotius, Theology, and International Law: Overcoming Textbook Bias' (2000) 14 *Journal of Law and Religion* 605–31.

Historically, this liberal 'scheme of things' is linked both to the constitution-alization of political power in the domestic sphere and to the constitution of (Westphalian) statehood in the international sphere. Modern international law is, thus, quintessentially a liberal law, with all the strings that attach to this label. Through the concept of (state) sovereignty—and analogous to individuals in the domestic sphere—states are conceived as self-interested monads which acquire identity through antagonistic differentiation vis-à-vis one another.[41] State action is conceived as inherently strategic and utility-oriented, reducing international rela-tions to a network of 'private' economic and military engagements.[42] This private pursuit of survival comes to constitute the public sphere of states, while the public pursuit of freedom is relegated to the private sphere of civil society. It is inher-ently paradoxical in its 'structural coupling' of utopian legalism and the apology of sovereignty.[43] On one hand, international law's near exclusive focus on the state enshrines the idea of antagonistic sovereignty and creates a false *nomos* of politics; on the other hand, its articulation of universal features of humanity abstracts from concrete human beings and inverts cause and effect of (their) political action.[44] As such it serves to cover up any imbalance in the name of abstract humanity and substitutes political solutions with technical ones.

3 EMPIRE-BUILDING:
THE LIBERAL LEGALIZATION
OF (INTERNATIONAL) POLITICS

Anthony Carty has called this liberal 'scheme of things' a 'false ontology' based on a 'deuteronomistic' framing of both politics and law.[45] It derives, for him, from the Hobbesian conception of (international) order, built upon 'the opposition of the domestic and the foreign, and...a state system which rests upon the mutually exclusive suppositions that each is a self for itself and an other for all the others'.[46] It reduces politics to rational (self-)interest-driven *Realpolitik* which privileges the

---

[41] A Carty, *The Philosophy of International Law* (Edinburgh University Press Edinburgh 2007) at 161.
[42] H Arendt, *The Human Condition* (2nd edn Chicago University Press Chicago 1998).
[43] *From Apology to Utopia* (n 22) 570.
[44] L Keedus, '"Human and Nothing but Human": How Schmittian Is Hannah Arendt's Critique of Human Rights and International Law?' (2011) 37 *History of European Ideas* 190–6, at 195.
[45] *The Philosophy of International Law* (n 41) 143.   [46] Ibid 161.

'pure fact' of power and pits it against a (powerless) law enshrining the (value) ideals of justice and peace. Out of the former, the discipline of international relations would emerge as, initially, the realist venture to frame international life in strictly functional(ist) terms and thereby to kill off international law's pretence of objectivity and autonomy.[47] The latter, in turn, would linger on as a residue of naturalism and the permanent (bad) conscience of international society.

Yet, as was seen, this stylized antagonism is part of liberalism's plot, for only a clear-cut dichotomy between the apologism of power politics and the naïve utopian faith in the values of legal cosmopolitanism could compel the sort of compromise solution liberalism has on offer. It comes in the form of the Vattelian 'classical' system of international law, which has, arguably, been providing the basic blueprint for the way in which the international, its law and its politics are conceived in liberal modernity. In essence, that blueprint is based on the paradoxical combination of a strong concept of (state) sovereignty with the equally strong presumption of the rationality of state action. Hence, the narrow balance between the *bellum omnium*, on one hand, and hegemony (and subjection thereunder), on the other, is achieved by simultaneously attributing to each component of this 'society' free (political) will *and* the (rational) insight that free will must not be exercised discretionarily but in such a way as to be compatible with its (continued) exercise by all. In other words, political power and universal rationality are here deemed to relativize, and, indeed, neutralize one another.

In this scheme, law is not just an instrument to safeguard this balance but its very expression. It forms a new epistemic horizon which structures the way in which power-holders and their rationalizers (that is, international lawyers) communicate amongst themselves about the (international) world. To be sure, the history of modern international law has been nuanced on this count and there have been significant variations of emphasis in terms of the precise balance between apologism and utopianism. Hence, Vattel's 'classical' conception of international law has, notwithstanding his own differentiated position, been seen as coming out on sovereignty's (that is, apologism's) side, whereas the 'Grotian tradition', for instance, and its espousal of some form of legal cosmopolitanism has been deemed utopian.[48] In fact, what emerges from the ever more detailed picture of the development of modern (liberal) legal doctrine is not just its internal variety along a spectrum running from apologism to utopianism but also the inconsistency with which these labels are applied and the conceptual associations they carry. However, what all these different approaches share is a commitment to 'the law'—however it is

---

[47] BA Simmons and RH Steinberg, *International Law and International Relations* (CUP Cambridge 2006); G Simpson, 'The Situation on the International Legal Theory Front: The Power of Rules and the Rule of Power' (2000) 11 *European Journal of International Law* 439–64.

[48] See eg E Jouannet, 'The Critique of Classical Thought during the Interwar Period: Vattel and Van Vollenhoven' in this *Handbook*.

precisely defined—and a scepticism towards politics, seen in its realist guise as the (national) interest-driven will to power. Indeed, only if politics is, thus, styled as the 'bad cop' of international relations can (liberal) law emerge as its unequivocal 'good cop' who at once holds international society together and transforms it into a community of (liberal) values.

This double quarantining of politics—by first squeezing it into the straight-jacket of realism and then by legally ring-fencing it within a rump public sphere—corrodes the foundations for political authority, producing a vacuum into which 'the law' is drawn. Yet, law is, of course, not a real substitute for political authority. It can only mimic it in form but not in substance, and indeed, it must continuously expand its formal rule in order to cover up its inherent lack of political substance, leading to a process of legal hypertrophy. Liberal international law must, in other words, continuously expand and incrementally cover all the discursive space of international life in order to protect its (purely formal) authority and eliminate the possibility of uncovering its lack of (political) authority. As such, international law strives to rule, and the ideal of the international rule of law is a reflection of this imperialist discursivity.[49] Liberal legalism denotes, hence, not just a particular ontological position—or 'consciousness'—on what (international) politics is—namely *Realpolitik*—and what (international) law is, namely a liberal rule of law aimed at neutralizing the former, but also a militant stance towards (legal) empire-building.[50] Its empirical articulation is that of the gradual legalization of international life, a process underwritten by what legal sociologists have long identified as the modern phenomenon of juridification.[51] It springs from one of modernity's core characteristics, notably the rationalization of social relations that accompanies the rise of the 'spirit of capitalism'.[52] For, from a (post-)Weberian perspective, the complexities of a theologically 'disenchanted', pluralist, and capitalist world lead both to the rationalization of the cognitive horizon (in other words, lifeworld) through

[49] BZ Tamanaha, 'The Dark Side of the Relationship between the Rule of Law and Liberalism' (2008) 3 *New York University Journal of Law and Liberty* 516–47.

[50] JL Cohen, 'Whose Sovereignty? Empire versus International Law' (2004) 18 *Ethics and International Affairs* 1–24; JE Alvarez, 'Contemporary International Law: An "Empire of Law" or the "Law of Empire"' (2008) 24 *American University International Law Review* 811–42.

[51] R Kreide, 'Re-Embedding the Market through Law? The Ambivalence of Juridification in the International Context' in C Joerges and J Falke (eds), *Karl Polanyi, Globalisation and the Potential of Law in Transnational Markets* (Hart Oxford 2011) 41–64; D Loick, 'Juridification and Politics from the Dilemma of Juridification to the Paradoxes of Rights (2014) 40 *Philosophy and Social Criticism* 757–78.

[52] M Weber, *The Protestant Ethic and the Spirit of Capitalism* (G Baehr and GC Welsh eds and trans) (Penguin London 2002 [1905]). See also S Kalberg, 'Max Weber's Types of Rationality: Cornerstones for the Analysis of Rationalization Processes in History' (1980) 85 *American Journal of Sociology* 1145–79.

which individuals perceive themselves within society, and also to the emergence of functionally differentiated systems which are increasingly decoupled from that cognitive horizon. In particular, the economic and the political systems enable, through, respectively, the monetarization and the formalization of the allocation of power, continued societal coordination and integration under conditions of complexity and plurality.[53]

Law, in its modern conception as formalized, positive, and autonomous, is given a crucial, if paradoxical, role in this process, namely as both the medium through which the different functional systems are articulated, and as the primary mediator between the instrumentalist rationality of the latter and the communicative rationality of a lifeworld premised on mutual understanding. Yet, it plays this role to ambivalent effect: first, in the early modern state, it helps differentiate a rationalized and autonomous economic and administrative (functional) system out of a still largely traditional lifeworld, then, in the course of the 'bourgeois' revolutions of the seventeenth and eighteenth centuries, it is used to keep these systems and an increasingly rationalized lifeworld in reciprocal check by means of an institutionalized rule of law and a formalized popular sovereignty, only to subsequently 'colonize' the lifeworld by transforming ever more aspects of social life into legalized administrative acts in the wake of the rise of the welfare state.[54]

In other words, the ever increasing functional differentiation of late capitalist 'world society' is necessarily accompanied by an expansive juridification that unfolds as a dialectic of systemic imposition and emancipation. It is, of course, a dialectic that inheres in modernity itself, a 'dialectic of enlightenment' in which modern reason oscillates, Janus-faced, between empowerment and subjugation. Theodor Adorno and Max Horkheimer notoriously interpreted this inherent ambivalence of modern rationality in light of its apparent abnegation through the Holocaust and 'total war'.[55] To them, these very modern phenomena revealed modern reason's 'dark energy', notably the will to power, born out of the urge for self-preservation and, concurrently, for domination over nature, destiny and myth, which amalgamates (subjective) interest with (objective) knowledge, and power (*Macht*) with validity (*Geltung*) into instrumental rationality. If

---

[53] LC Blichner and A Molander, 'Mapping Juridification' (2008) 14 *European Law Journal* 36–54, at 39.

[54] J Habermas, *The Theory of Communicative Action* (T McCarthy trans) (2 vols Polity Press Cambridge 1989) vol 2, at 301. For a review of the phenomenon in the contemporary European Union, see D Kelemen, *Eurolegalism: The Transformation of Law and Regulation in the European Union* (Harvard University Press Cambridge MA 2011) and the review of the review in A Orford, 'Europe Reconstructed' (2012) 75 *Modern Law Review* 275–86.

[55] M Horkheimer and TW Adorno, *The Dialectic of Enlightenment* (G Schmid Noerr ed and E Jephcott trans) (Stanford University Press Stanford 2002).

Adorno, in particular, eventually resigns critical theory to the mere description of this 'negative dialectic', his student Jürgen Habermas purports to salvage the modern project by reconstructing the liberal constitutional state as a framework in which the imperatives of instrumental reason as they play out in public administration and the market economy can be balanced out through public deliberation based on non-instrumental ('communicative') rational argumentation.[56] Constitutionalization in this Habermasian sense is deemed capable of recharging the law with (political) legitimacy and thereby enabling it to resist its own systemic instrumentalization with a view to re-establishing the autonomy of the public sphere.

With the advent of globalization this modern predicament has transcended the black box of the state and has come to characterize the world at large. Hence, the much debated fragmentation of international law can essentially be seen as the increased juridification of international life which, in turn, is the consequence of an ever increasing functional differentiation lying at the heart of the globalization process itself.[57] Its normativity is linked to the multiple functional logics of a world society without a world government, and the identity of such governance is no longer exclusively determined by pedigree—notably (state) consent—but increasingly by normative output. Hence, a host of distinct international legal regimes—such as on trade, the environment, or armed conflict[58]—cater to specific functional imperatives, each with their own technical terminology and institutional edifice, not to mention professional career paths.[59] What connects them is not a common normative bracket but the shared cognitive horizon of being part of an ongoing process of functional differentiation— expressed through the conceptual artifice of (global) governance. International lawyers are, thus, transformed into expert managers who follow the precepts of a system-specific instrumental rationality and act as colonizing agents of their own lifeworld. As such, they are engaged in replacing substantive criteria to describe and manoeuvre the international with purely relational ones, such as efficiency, accountability, or transparency, and, thus, help produce a simulacrum of universality.

[56] J Habermas, *Between Facts and Norms* (W Rehg trans) (Polity Press Cambridge 1997).

[57] M Koskenniemi and P Leino, 'Fragmentation of International Law? Postmodern Anxieties' (2002) 15 *Leiden Journal of International Law* 553–79; G Teubner and A Fischer-Lescano, 'Regime-Collisions: The Vain Search for Legal Unity in the Fragmentation of Global Law' (2004) 25 *Michigan Journal of International Law* 999–1046; International Law Commission, 'Fragmentation of International Law: Difficulties Arising from the Diversification and Expansion of International Law' (13 April 2006) UN Doc A/CN.4/L.682.

[58] See T Skouteris, *The Notion of Progress in International Law Discourse* (TMC Asser Press The Hague 2010).

[59] PM Dupuy, 'The Danger of Fragmentation or Unification of the International Legal System and the International Court of Justice' (1998) 31 *New York University Journal of International Law and Politics* 791–807.

This is, of course, the process which Koskenniemi has tirelessly exposed as the turn to managerialism in international life, a move which, to him, is akin to a disciplinary take-over attempt—or, indeed, colonization—by the functionalist logic of 'international relations'.[60] In fact, he likens it to a new naturalism in international law which 'gives voice to special interests in functionally diversified regimes of global governance and control,'[61] and which, it may be added, is, like the old natural law, meant to stand against the uncertainties of political deliberation. In its stead, it purports to introduce a new objective normativity into international affairs, one that aspires to a paradigm of technically optimized self-regulation in which systemic functionality is isolated against disturbances from the lifeworld.

Yet, as critical scholarship has pointed out, the functionalist aesthetics of transparency, accountability, and participation is not neutral: it contains a normative agenda that serves the interests of, in particular, transnational markets. Cloaked by the universalist appeal to the (Weberian) values underlying modern statehood in abstraction from geography and historical trajectory, the (good) governance agenda is meant to make the state safe for a globalized market economy.[62] It aims to reshape public administration into an instrument of technocratic regulation and democracy into a strictly controlled mechanism for interest mediation. As such it transcribes the (neo)liberal paradigm into a legal notation geared to immunizing the state, and 'international society' against (re)distributional politics.[63] Hence, the less states govern through law the more governance there is by law—a state of affairs that the Posnerian realists claim to fear but in which they are just as implicated as their liberal legalist antagonists. Indeed, the apparent inescapability of the managerialist paradigm would seem to indicate the triumph of liberalism—and with it of liberal legalism—as the all-pervasive ideology of late modernity. Is this, then, the end of history and of international law (as we know it), or does the moment of liberal triumph carry the spark of hubris, as the dialectic of enlightenment would have it? And where should one look for an alternative, to a renaissance of an 'older' conception of international legality or, instead, to the genesis of a new politics?

[60] See eg M Koskenniemi, 'Constitutionalism, Managerialism and the Ethos of Legal Education' (2007) 1(1) *European Journal of Legal Studies* article 1; 'The Politics of International Law' (n 17); 'The Politics of International Law—20 Years Later' (n 17); 'Miserable Comforters' (n 16).

[61] 'Miserable Comforters' (n 16) 411.

[62] C Thomas, 'Re-Reading Weber in Law and Development: A Critical Intellectual History of "Good Governance" Reform' (Cornell Legal Studies Research Paper No 118, December 2008) <http://scholarship.law.cornell.edu/lsrp_papers/118> [accessed 3 March 2016].

[63] JT Gathii, 'Good Governance as a Counter Insurgency Agenda to Oppositional and Transformative Social Projects in International Law' (1999) 5 *Buffalo Human Rights Law Journal* 107–74.

4 SPEAKING POLITICS TO LAW: BACK TO THE ROOTS OR OUT INTO THE WILD?

An answer to this question requires, initially, a fundamental choice by all those wishing to think and do international law between engaging, or not engaging, this 'new obscurity'.[64] Choosing not to engage amounts to adhering to a culture of muddling-through, to take the language, the institutions, the professional community at face value, to uncritically adopt the latter's habits and world view, to dispense with trying to understand one's practice and to derive an ethical stance therefrom, to relinquish independent judgement; in short, to reject theorizing. Choosing to engage, by contrast, requires precisely that: namely the taking of a position in a spectrum of theoretical frameworks which respond to the predicament of international law in late (liberal) modernity. The defining feature of that spectrum is the dichotomy that lies at the heart of this reflection on legalism, notably the one between law and politics, or, put differently, between whether (international) law is seen as part of the solution or part of the problem when it comes to what Koskenniemi has termed 'questions of preference, of distribution, of good or less good choices'.[65]

Yet, politics and law are, of course, themselves ambivalent fields that look different in different spectral ranges. In fact, they can only be defined in relation to one another, that is, by the degree of autonomy with which each field is deemed to be invested vis-à-vis the other. For it is autonomy that is, arguably, at the heart of the debate about international law's role in international politics. Legalism implies a certain stance on the respective autonomies of law and politics in international affairs, anti-legalism another. Hence, the question Koskenniemi has put on the table is not so much what the equilibrium between absolute conceptions of law and politics is or should be, but how autonomy, or lack thereof, defines both fields relationally. This is, arguably, the question behind the question of politics (in international law) and the deeper reason for the ambivalent attitude of many contemporary international legal scholars—including Koskenniemi himself—when it comes to (their) politics. Hence, taking (a) position means not just to side with either law or politics as the solution for 'global collective action

---

[64] J Habermas, 'The New Obscurity: The Crisis of the Welfare State and the Exhaustion of Utopian Energies' (P Jacobs trans) (1986) 11 *Philosophy and Social Criticism* 1–18.

[65] M Koskenniemi, 'The Politics of International Law' (Lecture delivered at the Lauterpacht Centre for International Law, University of Cambridge, 26 January 2012) <https://www.youtube.com/watch?v=-E3AGVTHsq4> [accessed 3 March 2016].

problems', but to also come out on the 'nature' of either in terms of their respective autonomy or heteronomy.

What is more, there is a third colour in the spectrum which further complexifies the picture, notably the question of what a particular theory is meant to do, or rather, on which level of analysis it is situated and within which framework of reference it operates. It has, again, been Koskenniemi who has staked out the spectral range here, notably by working at once on a structural theory of modern international law and on a professional ethos for its practitioners. He has thereby picked up a question that has been exercising the social sciences since their inception, notably what the relationship between the macro-(structure) and micro-(agency) level of analysis is. Thus, positioning oneself on the theoretical spectrum also means to answer the question of what a particular structural theory of international law implies for one's individual professional *praxis* and, conversely, what a particular *praxis* entails for one's view of the law's structure and the concrete outcomes it produces.

These three spectral lines—the primary one alongside the law/politics dichotomy and the two ancillary ones on the autonomy/heteronomy and structure/agency ranges—are well illustrated in two statements (again by Koskenniemi) which highlight different aspects of the spectrum (at different points in his intellectual evolution). Hence, in 1990, two years before the triumph of liberalism and the end of history would be notoriously proclaimed by Francis Fukuyama,[66] Koskenniemi declared that

our inherited ideal of a World Order based on the Rule of Law thinly hides from sight the fact that social conflict must still be solved by political means and that even though there may exist a common legal rhetoric among international lawyers, that rhetoric must, *for reasons internal to the ideal itself*, rely on essentially contested—political—principles to justify outcomes to international disputes.[67]

Yet, twenty-three years later, he issued a '*jus cogens* prohibition' on politicization projects in general, and on the politicization of (international) law, in particular.[68] Drawing on Wittgenstein's rabbit–duck allegory, he claims that it is now meaningless to attempt to resolve the indeterminacy and structural bias of the law by making it more openly political. To be sure, one may—and some have—interpret(ed) these statements as simply contradictory, evidence of the maturation of Koskenniemi from insolent critic on the margins of the discipline to its veritable *praeceptor* at its centre,[69] who has simply come around to most international lawyers' core article of faith, namely

---

[66] F Fukuyama, *The End of History and the Last Man* (Free Press New York 1992).
[67] 'The Politics of International Law' (n 17) 7 (emphasis in original).
[68] See 'The Politics of International Law' (n 65).
[69] J Klabbers, 'Towards a Culture of Formalism? Martti Koskenniemi and the Virtues' (2013) 27 *Temple International and Comparative Law Journal* 417–35.

that the best—and only—professional way to advance a progressive political agenda is by letting the law—the very canonically hermetic, Eurocentric, conceptually limited, and biased international law which he and others have done so much to expose—do its job. Yet, if one looks carefully, there is not really any contradiction here, just different emphases on different aspects of the theoretical spectrum and what it entails to position oneself on it. The inescapability of politics and how one deals with it, as something other to the law or something of it, is one such aspect. The distinctiveness of the law (and the lawyer) and the consequences of this for political action is another.

Yet, which positions does the contemporary theoretical spectrum actually have on offer? At the risk of gross oversimplification and eclecticism, but for the sake of taxonomical clarity, one may broadly distinguish between those theoretical frameworks that conceive of (international) law as a remedy for the ills of international politics—here termed legalist—and those that see it as an impediment for the realization of a successful international politics—termed anti-legalist. Within this general divide, theories can then be further differentiated along an axis that depicts the degree of autonomy through which the relationship between law and politics is defined. This then yields a four-dimensional matrix within which the different positions can (very broadly) be charted: on the legalist side, the two principal positions are *international constitutionalism*, on one hand, and *legal pluralism*, on the other. The former can broadly be seen as an attempt to contain fragmentation and functionalist managerialism by recasting international law in terms of liberal constitutionalism.[70] To this end, it seeks to reconnect the dispersed legal regimes by means of higher-level constitutional principles geared to the realization of (individual) human dignity through 'the assurance of peace and freedom under the rule of law'.[71] In the absence of a global *pouvoir constituant*, these principles can however, only be derived inductively, notably by reconstructing from select legal regimes—human rights law, humanitarian law, and trade law are popular candidates here—a shared set of values which is then attributed to a (hypothetical) international community.[72] This introduces a hierarchically superior level in form of an imagined legislator whose stamp of legitimacy becomes a necessary requirement for international legality.[73] It is an axiological conception in which the law is deemed to be governed by a set of normative expectations that lie outside of (and above) it. As such constitutionalism essentially proposes to salvage liberal legalism by applying it to itself, that is, by purporting to reverse-colonize the fragmented functional regimes from the vantage point of a (presumed) global

---

[70] A von Bogdandy, 'Constitutionalism in International Law: Comment on a Proposal from Germany' (2006) 47 *Harvard International Law Journal* 223–42.

[71] M García-Salmones, 'On Carl Schmitt's Reading of Hobbes: Lessons for Constitutionalism in International Law' (2007) 4 *NoFo* 61–82.

[72] HG Cohen, 'Finding International Law, Part II: Our Fragmenting Legal Community' (2011) 44 *New York University Journal of International Law and Politics* 1049–1107.

[73] J von Bernstorff, 'Georg Jellinek and the Origins of Liberal Constitutionalism in International Law' (2012) 4 *Goettingen Journal of International Law* 659–75.

lifeworld—'humanity'[74]—constituted by the liberal value canon. International law would, thus, be shielded from the disintegrative force of functional differentiation and re-unified under the umbrella of an international community of values. The price for rescuing liberal legalism through constitutionalization is, however, a double surrender of autonomy because, on the one hand, the law is made a mere instrument for the realization of a specific value set—and the interests of those professing to hold it—and, on the other hand, it has to stake its empirical plausibility on the factual hegemony of particular regimes the essentialized normative substance of which it elevates to constitutional superiority.[75]

On the other side of legalism stand legal pluralist approaches which pretend to make a virtue out of the vice of fragmentation by redescribing international law as a transnational network of differentiated norm systems.[76] At their (autopoietic) extreme, legal pluralists take the legally polycentric world of fragmented 'regime rationalities' at face value.[77] It is a world in which law reigns supreme because the internal hierarchy tying it to (political) sovereignty has been replaced by a horizontalized web of private and transnational legal regimes that regulate 'world society'.[78] The latter has, as Niklas Luhmann already affirmed, 'no head or center',[79] state and non-state actors alike are turned into co-equal subjects of a global law that autopoietically reproduces itself.[80] Functional differentiation—in other words, fragmentation—is not the problem but rather the solution to system theory's principal normative concern, notably the old Hobbesian question of how (nowadays admittedly highly complex) societies can preserve themselves over time. Legal pluralism's particular answer is, of course, spontaneous order or, more precisely, the self-regulation of differentiated functional regimes which is deemed to generate some form of equilibrium over time. However, for this to work, the decoupling of law from political—in other words, lifeworld—concerns needs to be empirically accepted and normatively affirmed, each legal regime has to be able to follow its 'internal rationality' (*Eigenrationalität*), and interaction between legal regimes, in particular, and between law and other function systems, in general, has to be unconstrained by 'external' factors.[81] Indeed, radical legal pluralism can be said to

---

[74] R Teitel, 'Humanity Law: A New Interpretive Lens on the International Sphere' (2008) 77 *Fordham Law Review* 667–702.

[75] P Alston, 'Resisting the Merger and Acquisition of Human Rights by Trade Law: A Reply to Petersmann' (2002) 13 *European Journal of International Law* 815–44. For a recent critique, see A Orford, 'The Politics of Anti-Legalism in the Intervention Debate' (30 May 2014) *Global Policy* <http://www.globalpolicyjournal.com/blog/30/05/2014/politics-anti-legalism-intervention-debate> [accessed 3 March 2016].

[76] 'Regime-Collisions' (n 57) 999. See also G Teubner, '"Global Bukowina": Pluralism in the World Society' in G Teubner (ed), *Global Law without a State* (Dartmouth Aldershot 1997) 3–28.

[77] 'Constitutionalism, Managerialism and the Ethos of Legal Education' (n 60).

[78] G Teubner, 'The King's Many Bodies: The Self-Deconstruction of Law's Hierarchy' (1997) 31 *Law and Society Review* 763–87.

[79] N Luhmann, 'Die Weltgesellschaft' (1971) 57 *Archiv für Rechts- und Sozialphilosophie* 3–35.

[80] P Zumbansen, 'International Law as Glass Palace: Towards a Methodology of Legal Concepts in World Society' (unpublished manuscript on file with author).

[81] 'Regime-Collisions' (n 57).

transpose the liberal(ist) plotline onto the systemic level, so that it is not individuals or states, but function (or communication) systems that need to be surrounded by a ring of negative liberties. As a consequence, however, individuals and states are reduced to mere relay devices for different functional logics—if anything, a limited degree of state agency is still required to police recalcitrant actors and prevent them from making demands that may destabilize systemic functionality.[82]

A different and, arguably, less radical approach to legal pluralism is represented by the Global Administrative Law (GAL) school which aims to go back to the original purpose behind international law as a jurisprudential discipline, namely by identifying, collecting, and systematizing the 'real' rules that govern international life. As such it seeks to open up the black box of the (classical) sources doctrine and to shift law-ascertainment from its canonical focus on subjects and pedigree to normative output.[83] Like its systems theoretical (distant) relation, it (re)cognizes all forms of international and transnational, soft and hard, public and private normativity but unlike systems theory, it is primarily concerned with deriving from these the administrative legal principles that lurk behind global governance.[84] By, thus, postulating a higher-level structure that governs governance, GAL would appear to be closer to constitutionalism than to pluralism.[85] However, unlike the former, its focus is on the facticity of normative outcomes and not on their validity in terms of normative expectations. Its proposition is, hence, more that of a realist positivism than of a constitutional moralism. Moreover, the administrative principles distilled by GAL, including such liberal legalist staples as accountability, transparency, participation and, generally, due process and judicial review procedures, share with systems theory a penchant for (global governance) functionalism, notably as 'instrument[s] to uphold and secure the cohesion and sound functioning of an institutional order that is justified independently'.[86] What both approaches also share is an empirically justified commitment to the autonomy of a(n) (international) law the functional logic of which they deem to be irreducible to politics.

---

[82] K-H Ladeur, 'The Theory of Autopoiesis as an Approach to a Better Understanding of Postmodern Law: From the Hierarchy of Norms to the Heterarchy of Changing Patterns of Legal Inter-Relationships' (EUI Working Paper Law No 99/3, April 1999) at 16.

[83] J d'Aspremont, 'Cognitive Conflicts and the Making of International Law: From Empirical Concord to Conceptual Discord in Legal Scholarship' (2013) 46 *Vanderbilt Journal of Transnational Law* 1119–47; I Venzke, 'Contemporary Theories and International Law-Making' in C Bröllmann and Y Radi (eds), *Research Handbook on the Theory and Practice of International Law-Making* (Elgar Cheltenham 2016).

[84] B Kingsbury, 'The Concept of "Law" in Global Administrative Law' (2009) 20 *European Journal of International Law* 23–57; A Somek, 'The Concept of "Law" in Global Administrative Law: A Reply to Benedict Kingsbury' (2009) 20 *European Journal of International Law* 985–95.

[85] M-S Kuo, 'Taming Governance with Legality? Critical Reflections upon Global Administrative Law as Small-C Global Constitutionalism' (2011) 44 *New York University Journal of International Law and Politics* 55–102.

[86] B Kingsbury, N Krisch, and RB Stewart, 'The Emergence of Global Administrative Law' (2005) 68 *Law & Contemporary Problems* 15–61.

Indeed, both constitutionalism and legal pluralism not only presume that law and politics are distinct, but also that law is ultimately superior to politics in dealing with Posner's 'global collective action problems' (the equivalent of Koskenniemi's 'questions'), a claim based on the empirical presumption that there is neither a global polity nor a unified global legislator to which a global politics could be attributed. To these legalists, international *Realpolitik* is a pseudo-anarchical cacophony of (self-)interest-driven states the doings of which are either deemed illegitimate—lest they be governed by constitutional principles—or dysfunctional because of their inherent incapacity to live up to a functionally differentiated world society. As was seen earlier, the main type of anti-legalist challenge to this view, notably the *political realism* of Posner and others, draws on much the same argument only in an inverse key. For these scholars it is precisely the lack of a global sovereign that either seriously weakens or entirely invalidates the idea of an (empirically) hard international law. It is a tradition of thought that stretches from Hobbes to Carl Schmitt and from Hans Morgenthau to the 'law and economics' approach adopted by the author of *Perils*.[87] It pervades, in more or less direct ways, a substantial part of the international relations literature,[88] though it also underwrites the position of anti-legalist legal scholars of a rational choice or neo-Schmittian sovereigntist persuasion.[89] It is premised on two fundamental assumptions, namely that political authority is autonomous and indispensable and that actors are rational, with rationality in this context meaning 'choosing the best means to the chooser's ends'.[90] Political authority, in turn, is not a formal legal term but linked, ultimately, to the capacity to establish and maintain identity through differentiation, with rational action being defined as strictly instrumental to this objective. As was seen, such a deuteronomistic conception of politics is premised on the inherent antagonism of all actors and on the concomitant 'will to power' of each within a particular 'game'.[91] Such (identity) politics can only lead either to anarchy or to hegemony,

---

[87] See A Vermeule and EA Posner, 'Demystifying Schmitt' (University of Chicago Public Law Working Paper No. 333, 2011).

[88] JL Dunoff and MA Pollack, 'What Can International Relations Learn from International Law?' (Temple University Legal Studies Research Paper No 2012-14, 2012); MC Williams, *The Realist Tradition and the Limits of International Relations* (CUP Cambridge 2005); K Raustiala and A-M Slaughter, 'International Law, International Relations and Compliance' in W Carlsnaes, T Risse, BA Simmons (eds), *Handbook of International Relations* (1st edn Sage London 2002) 538–59.

[89] R Cristi, 'Carl Schmitt on Sovereignty and Constituent Power' (1997) 10 *Canadian Journal of Law and Jurisprudence* 189–201; C Burchard, 'Puzzles and Solutions: Appreciating Carl Schmitt's Work on International Law as Answers to the Dilemmas of His Weimar Political Theory' (2003) 14 *Finnish Yearbook of International Law* 89–128; R Howse, 'From Legitimacy to Dictatorship—and Back Again: Leo Strauss's Critique of the Anti-Liberalism of Carl Schmitt' (1997) 10 *Canadian Journal of Law and Jurisprudence* 77–103; M Koskenniemi, 'International Law as Political Theology: How to Read *Nomos der Erde*?' (2004) 11 *Constellations* 492–511.

[90] RA Posner, 'Rational Choice, Behavioral Economics, and the Law' (1998) 50 *Stanford Law Review* 1551–75.

[91] *The Philosophy of International Law* (n 41).

with the latter being the ontological power to determine the limits through which identity is defined, or, as Schmitt put it, to decide on the exception.[92]

From this perspective, norms and (sovereign) power are inherently inimical: they can only be brought together through strict hierarchization. Indeed, the realists' charge against liberal legalists is, in essence, that they make a category mistake when they assume the primacy of law over politics, when, to them, it is 'really' the other way around.[93] To them law is a function of politics, or rather of those who hold (hegemonic) political authority and if there is no such authority, as realists allege to be the case in international affairs, law is but another word for a passing coincidence of wills.[94] There is, of course, a strange disconnect amongst many adherents of this position between a hardcore instrumentalist and anti-objectivist stance vis-à-vis international law and a simultaneous acceptance of the liberal legal constitutionalist paradigm in relation to domestic law and politics.[95] It is strange because it seems to contradict realism's anti-liberal premises, though it may equally express the view that liberal hegemony has simply not yet been established in the international sphere. For, as was seen, the realist 'politics redux' is a prerequisite for legal liberalist intervention, a causal relationship Schmitt and his latter day followers have naturally tended to underexplore.[96]

The opposite side of the anti-legalist spectrum is occupied by structuralist readings of the law/politics divide, most notably positions inspired, in one way or another, by Marx. While only relatively few scholars now openly identify with Marxism, many more, not least within the critical legal fold, work with structuralist premises that derive from a (broadly) Marxian analysis. The, perhaps, crucial theoretical distinguishing marks of this line of thought are the Hegelian legacy in terms of a philosophy of history and the application of materialist premises to it. These moves translate into two fundamental hypotheses, namely that history is directional, that it has a *telos* and, therefore, an overall meaning which provides a measuring rod for its individual instances, and that it is driven by society's material basis, most notably, in Marx's case, the process of capital reproduction based on a materialist theory of labour. This historical materialism, however, implies a determinism which renders both law and politics epiphenomenal in the sense of being essentially functions of the material base at a particular historical stage.

[92] JP McCormick, 'The Dilemmas of Dictatorship: Carl Schmitt and Constitutional Emergency Powers' (1997) 10 *Canadian Journal of Law and Jurisprudence* 163–87; 'International Law as Political Theology' (n 89).

[93] D Dyzenhaus, 'Carl Schmitt's Challenge to Liberalism' (1997) 10 *Canadian Journal of Law and Jurisprudence* 3–4.

[94] *The Realist Tradition* (n 88) 19; *The Perils of Global Legalism* (n 3) x.

[95] *The Perils of Global Legalism* (n 3); L Vinx, 'Carl Schmitt and the Analogy between Constitutional and International Law: Are Constitutional and International Law Inherently Political?' (2013) 2 *Global Constitutionalism* 91–124.

[96] 'Demystifying Schmitt' (n 87).

Historical materialism, hence, redefines the relation between law and politics at least in their conventional-bourgeois (that is, realist-liberalist) connotation by denying them both autonomy and respective primacy. In their existing form, neither politics nor law have the capacity to problem-solve, in the Posnerian sense, or emancipate from the colonization of their respective other—only a fundamental change of socio-economic conditions can bring this about. Hence, *grosso modo*, a Marxian structuralist position is not only anti-legalist but also anti-political in the sense that it is bound to reject political agency from within 'the system'; indeed, some have critically argued that agency is here generally restricted to being the recognition of what is objectively necessary.[97] Yet, whatever the bounds of political agency in a structuralist perspective and however autonomous it is deemed to be in relation to wider social relations, (international) law is clearly seen as both lacking autonomous being and emancipatory (political) potential. As one of this perspective's primary exponents has plainly put it, in order to

fundamentally change the dynamics of the system it would be necessary not to reform the institutions but to *eradicate the forms of law*—which means the fundamental reformulation of the political-economic system of which they are expressions. The [political] project to achieve this is the best hope for global emancipation, and it would mean the end of law.[98]

This—in any case very roughly sketched—fourfold positional matrix does not, of course, exhaust the gamut of possibilities. There are, in particular, a number of positions that attempt to budge the choice between legalism and anti-legalism and between the full endorsement and the fundamental critique of the liberal (legalist) master narrative. They tend to combine a critical reading of liberalism—and liberal legalism—with an acknowledgement of its facticity, not least in legal and diplomatic practice, against the backdrop of the perennial challenge that the critical (legal) project allegedly fails to offer a tangible alternative to the current mindset of the majority of international actors (and their lawyers).[99] Hence, ironically though not surprisingly, international law's ontological position between apology and utopia also affects the (political) choices open to those who consider a direct engagement in and with the 'real existing' international legal project to be either desirable or inescapable.[100]

---

[97] WA Suchting, 'Marx and Hannah Arendt's *The Human Condition*' (1962) 73 *Ethics* 47–55; J Ring, 'On Needing Both Marx and Arendt: Alienation and the Flight from Inwardness' (1989) 17 *Political Theory* 432–48.

[98] C Miéville, *Between Equal Rights: A Marxist Theory of International Law* (Brill Leiden 2005) at 318 (emphasis in original). See also A Carty, 'Marxist International Law Theory as Hegelianism' (2008) 10 *International Studies Review* 122–5.

[99] JH Schlegel, 'CLS Wasn't Killed by a Question' (2006) 58 *Alabama Law Review* 967–77; WH Simon, 'Solving Problems vs Claiming Rights: The Pragmatist Challenge to Legal Liberalism' (2004) 46 *William and Mary Law Review* 127–210; SL Cummings, 'Critical Legal Consciousness in Action' (2007) 120 *Harvard Law Review Forum* 62–71.

[100] On the inescapability and yet futility of that engagement in terms of pinning down the project's 'true' social significance, by someone who has, herself, critically yet sympathetically engaged

The, arguably, foremost attempt at such synthesis between law and politics from a counter-(liberal)-hegemonic persuasion is, of course, Koskenniemi's own 'culture of formalism'. Although he has, by some accounts, abandoned the philosophical elaboration of this idea and has, by other accounts, transposed it into a political historiography of international law,[101] it still stands as the most elaborate proposal for both an alternative position and an alternative to positioning as such. In essence, the 'culture of formalism' seeks to reframe international legal discourse from within, notably by showing it to contain the elements necessary to move it back from managerialist deadlock to being a—indeed, perhaps, *the*— privileged language to advance such progressive utopias as global peace and social justice against the 'new natural law' of international relations.[102] To this end, Koskenniemi proposes to make a virtue out of (liberal) international law's vice of indeterminacy by drawing on the inherently open-ended nature of legal discourse, its innermost nature as an argumentative *praxis* that 'brings out into the open the contradictions of the society in which it operates and the competition of opposite interests that are the flesh and blood of the legal everyday'.[103] This clever theoretical move enables him to turn the inherent structural bias of (formalized) international legal practice, that is, the a priori 'shared understanding of how the rules and institutions should be applied',[104] into the very wedge by which it can be exposed and thereby undermined. For it is in the nature of that legal practice, by enabling an open-ended process of argumentation among nominal equals, to break down universalist claims into the particular positions and interests that drive them, while simultaneously enjoining the participants of that practice to make their particular claims (hypothetically) universalizable. In other words, as Jeffrey Dunoff has recently put it, Koskenniemi interlinks—what he sees as—international law's purpose with its promise, thereby opening up a navigable passageway 'between the Scylla of Empire and the Charybdis of fragmentation, [with] the culture of formalism resist[ing] reduction into substantive policy, whether imperial or particular'.[105] Hence, it is neither a new politics nor a different law that provides, for Koskenniemi, the most hopeful platform for transformative politics under current global conditions, but the vocabulary of formal (legal) norms and the judicial and quasi-judicial institutions within which it is performed.

---

with the 'culture of formalism', see A Orford, 'Scientific Reason and the Discipline of International Law' (2014) 25 *European Journal of International Law* 369–85.

[101] M Koskenniemi, 'Why History of International Law Today?' (2004) 4 *Rechtsgeschichte* 61–6; A Carty, 'Visions of the Past of International Society: Law, History or Politics?' (2006) 69 *Modern Law Review* 644–60.

[102] 'Miserable Comforters' (n 16).   [103] 'Law, Teleology and International Relations' (n 2).

[104] *From Apology to Utopia* (n 22) 608.

[105] JL Dunoff, 'From Interdisciplinarity to Counterdisciplinarity: Is There Madness in Martti's Method?' (2013) 27 *Temple International and Comparative Law Journal* 309–37.

This may seem like 'regulated madness',[106] but the inspiration for the argument is actually deeply embedded in the Western (liberal) canon, notably in the form of Kantian cosmopolitanism—interpreted, admittedly, in an anti-systemic and counter-hegemonic way. For unlike his nemeses, the 'miserable comforters' of international relations and liberal legalism, Koskenniemi refuses to weave Kant's reflection on the ontological pre-conditions of inter-state peace into a theoretical system and, instead, foregrounds its ethical dimension. Hence, international law as a practice is not about 'an end-state or party programme but the methodological use of critical reason that measures today's state of affairs from the perspective of an ideal of universality that cannot itself be reformulated into an institution, a technique of rule, without destroying it'.[107] Its politics, is thus, not substantive but procedural; it is a politics of redescription in which the language of the law becomes 'a place-holder for the languages of goodness and justice, solidarity and responsibility'.[108] Koskenniemi's cosmopolitan legalism is meant to strike at both realist politics and the liberal legalist response to it, though it does so at the cost of replacing political theory with professional ethos. For the 'virtue ethics' which Koskenniemi is, arguably, advancing in the 'culture of formalism' turns international law into a 'vocabulary to help evaluate political action', presumably by providing an independent discursive position from which to deconstruct political rhetoric and expose what lies behind it.[109] As such, international law would avoid representing any particular political position, and, thus, remain autonomous, while being deeply tied into the political system as a privileged language to render itself self-reflexive, or, as Anne Orford put it, to continuously engage with the question of 'how we may encounter, comprehend, and negotiate with other laws'.[110] In a recent essay on (anti)legalism in the debate on humanitarian intervention, she reinforced this (critical) legalist point, notably by arguing that, by appealing to diffuse legitimacy bestowing principles, anti-legalism, be it in its traditional realist or its liberal interventionist variant, seeks to pre-empt open and public debate about the grounds and justifications for intervention. Hence, by 'rejecting as morally suspect the public justifications that other governments give for their actions and the subsequent analysis of those justifications by international lawyers means that anti-legalists can present their interpretation of moral principles as universally valid and the practices they seek to champion as uncontroversial'.[111]

This is a strong point which, arguably, corresponds with many an international lawyer's view (on the subject and on their particular role). However, does the focus by such a 'culture of formalism' on what amounts to a critical

---

[106] 'From Interdisciplinarity to Counterdisciplinarity' (n 105) 334.
[107] 'Miserable Comforters' (n 16).   [108] Ibid 21.
[109] 'Towards a Culture of Formalism?' (n 69) 431.
[110] A Orford, 'Moral Internationalism and the Responsibility to Protect' (2013) 24 *European Journal of International Law* 83–108, at 108.
[111] 'Politics of Anti-Legalism' (n 75).

and non-essentialist ethics of legal practice represent a distinct (political) position or merely a variant of an overall still liberal scheme of things? After all, its
conceptual cornerstones resemble Habermas' social-theoretical reconstruction
of the Kantian ideal in modern liberal democracy, even if Koskenniemi, unlike
Habermas, refuses to substantialize Kant's normative model of a cosmopolitan
republic into a concrete historical form.[112] He remains, as Jan Klabbers has put it,
an 'iconoclast by temperament',[113] yet even that other great iconoclast, Richard
Rorty, could ultimately 'only' offer irony to temper the liberalism he felt compelled to endorse as the (only) framework within which a politics of redescription could take place.[114]

Is this the final position, then? The realization that both liberalism and legalism
are inescapable, that they prefigure and pre-empt their own critique, even when
that critique is nonetheless held to be the only way to instil political meaning into
a legalized notion of practice? A withdrawal into an—admittedly enlightened—
professional ethics, combined with a 'turn to history' that renders not just the liberal but all meta-narratives contingent? The ironic upshot of this (non-)position is,
of course, that the only tenable standpoint that seems to remain is that of Rorty's
liberal ironist for whom 'the demands of self-creation and of human solidarity [are]
equally valid, yet forever incommensurable'.[115] The bird's eye view of the ironist is,
hence, bought by splitting the space of politics into two: a private one in which political vocabularies are generated, and a public one in which they are mainstreamed
to the lowest common denominator consistent with a (reasonably) peaceful coexistence (that is, collective self-preservation). The law's role is to uphold this division
and to police the public sphere against potentially dangerous transgressions from
private political projects. Adherents of the culture of formalism nonetheless believe
that this liberal law—and *only* this liberal law—can be turned against itself; that
it can create pathways across the divide, and that it can thereby render the public
sphere open for progressive ends without the totalizing premises of either revolution or hegemony—though at the cost of legalizing political action. Politics is, thus,
made contingent upon the 'comfortable inauthenticity of [legal] formalism',[116] or,
as some would have it, on a legal iron cage in which complex issues are necessarily
reduced to a handful of legal categories, however much these may be open to continuous (re-)interpretation.

---

[112] P-A Hirsch, 'Legalization of International Politics: On the (Im)Possibility of a Constitutionalization
of International Law from a Kantian Point of View' (2012) 4 *Goettingen Journal of International Law*
479–518.

[113] 'Towards a Culture of Formalism?' (n 69) 424.

[114] M Funakoshi, 'Taking Duncan Kennedy Seriously: Ironical Liberal Legalism' (2009) 15
Widener Law Review 231–87.

[115] R Rorty, *Contingency, Irony, and Solidarity* (CUP Cambridge 1989) at xv.

[116] M Koskenniemi, 'Formalism, Fragmentation, Freedom: Kantian Themes in Today's
International Law' (2007) 4 *NoFo* 7–28.

Is law—and legalism—hence, the better politics? Yes, if one endorses liberal-ism's concept of politics. No, if one considers that concept to, be, in fact an anti-politics that obscures the 'real' meaning of politics. For the latter, one may turn to Hannah Arendt, who was, arguably, as inspired by Kant as Koskenniemi, but who drew the opposite conclusions from him. Her concern was to wrestle the political as a distinct and autonomous category back from the stranglehold both of liber-alism, by which she saw it reduced to the competition of conflicting interests, and of Marxism, in which it was a mere epiphenomenon of dialectical historical pro-cess. In both cases is the meaning of politics, notably the continuous exchange over the meaning of 'living in community', pre-determined and, thus, rendered literally meaningless. For, to pose the question of meaning means, for Arendt, to also con-tinuously question whatever system—of thought, political institutions, law and so on—is in place, a proposition which, she felt was acceptable neither to liberalism nor to Marxism. For Arendt, both are ideologies, systems of thought premised on foundational myths—human nature and historical structure—camouflaged as natural, that only work as long as their mythological foundation remains hid-den. For her, politics is, on the contrary, a continuous de-mythologizing exercise in ideology critique. At its centre lies her conception of political action as not an (instrumental) making of an object as in fabrication but the purposeless (*zweck-frei*) exchange among subjects who recognize one another in their subjectness.[117] The basis for this is difference: the plurality inherent in human existence, without which there would not be a public sphere in which an exchange over meaning could take place. Indeed, it is only by acting within that public sphere, that is, by acting politically, that human beings can articulate their humanity, in fact, they are thereby metaphorically (re)born unto their fellow human beings, a pro-cess which Arendt termed natality and which she considered definitive of human existence. Political action is, hence, at once the fulfilment of one's humanity and the concerted answering of the question of meaning. In accordance with this con-ception, Arendt also defines power in political terms, namely as the capacity 'not just to act or do something, but to combine with others and act in concert with them…it emerges among human beings when they act together, and it disappears when they scatter'.[118] This stands, of course, in contrast to conventional conceptions of power since Weber, which define it as the successful enforcement of one's will vis-à-vis others. For Arendt, however, this undue assimilation of power and force comes out of the logic of modernity and the prevalence of capitalism and imperi-alism it produces—they banish political action into the private sphere and thereby individualize and neutralize it, turning what she termed the *oikos*, that is, ques-tions of material survival (that is, 'the economy'), into the only legitimate topic of

---

[117] H Arendt, *The Human Condition* (University of Chicago Press Chicago 1999) at 188.
[118] Ibid at 200.

the public sphere. They, thus, substitute the purposelessness of political action with the instrumental rationality of (realist) politics.

It is not quite clear what role for law Arendt foresaw in her project of recovering the lost meaning of politics. She certainly was not a legalist, for law for her could never substitute genuine political action, yet neither was she an antinomian. Law accompanies politics but cannot not prevail over it, it is either a *nomos* which delimits and secures the space in which political action can take place, or a *lex* by which (temporary) linkages between political interlocutors are articulated.[119] After all, political action is, to her, essentially about 'promising, combining, and covenanting'[120] juridical terms within a political realm. Perhaps law was, to Arendt, a particular form of political action, not qualitatively distinct from it and without a logic of its own. It would express both the self-reflexive awareness by all (political) actors of their own actorness, as well as the heightened sense of responsibility that promises, combinations, and covenants imply. In contrast to Koskenniemi, law would, thus, also (but not only) be a wedge to enable (political) judgement, it would additionally be about naming things, insisting on argument, attempting to grasp people and things, as best as possible, in their complexity, resisting conclusion, facing up to contingency. It would, thus, be simultaneously within and outside of Koskenniemi's *jus cogens* prohibition, for it would be a means to give voice to an openly political militancy against the realist-liberalist politics redux that reigns (in) international relations. However, to go back to these roots of international legal discourse requires more than a comfortable walk around the paved roads of contemporary international law, it calls for a march out into the wild.

---

[119] C Volk, 'From *Nomos* to *Lex*: Hannah Arendt on Law, Politics, and Order' (2010) 23 *Leiden Journal of International Law* 759–79.
[120] H Arendt, *On Revolution* (Viking Press New York 1963) at 212.

CHAPTER 47

....

CREATING POVERTY

....

JASON BECKETT

1 THE FACTS OF POVERTY

....

POVERTY can be understood as a fact, and the facts of poverty are horrific. However, poverty is not a natural fact: extreme poverty is a man-made phenomenon, a thing produced, a choice. Poverty is a legal regime. Extreme poverty is a modern phenomenon, a product of industrialization, development, and the socio-economic polarization these entail. Poverty is a by-product of the creation of wealth. Wealth is the *concentration* of resources; poverty is the *absence* of resources. The conditions which create extreme poverty 'benefit some groups of people, even as they massively disadvantage others'.[1]

Destitution is a complex, and relative, phenomenon; easily given to misunderstandings, insincere sympathy, and complacent denial. As Thomas Pogge has noted,[2] few, if any, of us have neighbours in extreme poverty or have even first-hand *observations* of its devastating realities. It is hard accurately to describe, let alone empathize with,[3] the facts of global poverty; the lives of the billion or so human beings living on less than $1.25 per day.

At the last conclusive mortality measurement,[4] poverty was responsible for 50,000 easily avoidable human deaths every single day. That is 350,000 human deaths per

[1] S Marks, 'Human Rights and Root Causes' (2011) 74 *Modern Law Review* 57–78.
[2] TW Pogge, *World Poverty and Human Rights* (2nd edn Polity Press Cambridge 2008).
[3] See ibid; 'Human Rights and Root Causes' (n 1).
[4] See *World Poverty and Human Rights* (n 2). Current figures are disputed: as of 2011, UNICEF believed 21,000 children died daily of poverty related causes, see: UNICEF, '12,000 Fewer Children

week, *one million* human deaths every three weeks, 18,000,000 human deaths every single year. This figure has remained constant since at least the 1970s.[5] The *proportion* of human beings dying from poverty related causes has decreased as the world population has expanded; nonetheless, implication in a humanly constructed international order that kills 18,000,000 human beings per year is nothing short of abominable.

The Millennium Development Goals set the target of halving world poverty by 2015, but what does this mean? Halving the *number* of people who are in poverty, or halving the *proportion* of people in poverty? Halving against which baseline? The number of people poor on which date, according to which measure? Likewise, do we understand poverty as lack of food, lack of opportunity, lack of freedom, *or* as lack of 'purchasing power parity' (PPP—the World Bank's preferred understanding)? The way that a task is measured defines the task, and determines success—and the World Bank's focus on an ever changing PPP is designed to ensure success. PPP determines 'parity' by setting a series of currency baselines and representative 'baskets' of goods and services, drawn from each country's Consumer Price Index (CPI).[6] This creates an arbitrary and manipulable standard, which is presented as scientific and objective.[7] It also bears little reality to the consumption patterns of the extremely poor, whose expenditure is dominated by necessities, rather than luxuries; and for whom the prices of basic foodstuffs have an impact far in excess of their impact on national CPIs. A doubling in the price of rice and wheat can have a devastating effect on the extremely poor, but virtually no impact at all on CPI.[8]

The inclusion of services in PPP calculations offers another example. Services are not available to or consumed by the extremely poor, the destitute; yet services tend to manifest the greatest price differential between developed and developing countries. A 'hot towel shave' costs me $6 at a luxury salon in Cairo, $85 in Las Vegas, but this does not mean that the US$ generally has fourteen times more purchasing power (the 'parity' of the calculation) in Egypt than it does in the United States (US). The inclusion of services complements the low weighting of basic foodstuffs to ensure artificially high levels of 'parity' relevant to the actual consumption patterns of the extremely poor.

Perish Daily in 2010 than in 1990' (15 September 2011) <http://www.unicefusa.org/press/releases/ 12000-fewer-children-perish-daily-2010-1990/8070> [accessed 3 March 2016]. The World Food Programme attributes 3.1 million annual child deaths to malnutrition alone, see: World Food Programme, 'Hunger Statistics' (2015) <http://www.wfp.org/hunger/stats> [accessed 3 March 2016]. This figure is supported by research published as a special series by *The Lancet* in 2013: 'Series: Maternal and Child Nutrition' (6 June 2013) 382 *The Lancet* <http://www.thelancet.com/series/maternal-and-child-nutrition> [accessed 3 March 2016].

  [5] See *World Poverty and Human Rights* (n 2).
  [6] World Bank, 'PovcalNet: Data' <http://iresearch.worldbank.org/PovcalNet/index.htm?0,3/> [accessed 3 March 2016]; World Bank, 'Poverty & Equity Data' <http://povertydata.worldbank.org/ poverty/home/> [accessed 3 March 2016].
  [7] T Pogge, 'How World Poverty is Measured and Tracked' in E Mack et al., (eds), *Absolute Poverty and Global Justice: Empirical Data—Moral Theories—Initiatives* (Ashgate Burlington 2009) 51–65, at 58–62.
  [8] Ibid 60.

The purchasing power represented by PPP is not only arbitrary, but decreasing; consequently the International Poverty Line (IPL) itself represents an ever decreasing access to resources, *not* a fixed line against which decreases in poverty can be impartially determined. This means that less and less actual purchasing power is required to statistically 'escape' the poverty trap:

If we use the US Consumer Price Index to convert the Bank's four successive IPLs into 2005 dollars, we get:

$1.02 PPP 1985 = $1.85 (2005)
$1.00 PPP 1985 = $1.81 (2005)
$1.08 PPP 1993 = $1.45 (2005)
$1.25 PPP 2005 = $1.25 (2005)[9]

PPP-reliant measures of progress in combating poverty are inherently untrustworthy.[10] Revisions to the temporal baseline, and version of parity measuring the Millennium Development Goals

led UN Secretary General Kofi Annan tragicomically to report to the General Assembly that for the world's most populace region…the 2015 poverty target had been fully met already in 1999, a full year before this goal had even been adopted.[11]

This is a particularly egregious, but hardly isolated example, thus:

the turn to indicators is a manifestation of the anxiety of results, to shore up the project in the face of its failures, and to look for new ways to measure the project to 'prove' it is working.[12]

Beyond the statistical manipulations two points remain true: 950,000,000 people actually have access to currency equivalents of US $100 (or less) each *per year*;[13] and 18,000,000 of these people die annually as a result.

It might be objected that this data is old; specifically that it predates the recent financial crises. Although there is as yet no conclusive data for the prevalence of poverty intra- or post-financial crisis, history tells us that the poor and the extremely poor fare badly in global (or local) economic upheaval.[14] While the World Bank currently estimates that as of 2011 over 1 billion people still fell below their

---

[9] 'How World Poverty is Measured and Tracked' (n 7) 56.
[10] The tendency of PPP to produce 'distorted' assessments, radically understating poverty levels, is elaborated on in ibid 56–63.
[11] Ibid 52–3.
[12] S Pahuja, 'The Poverty of Development and the Development of Poverty in International Law' (2010) 3 *Select Proceedings of the European Society of International Law* 365–75; World Bank, 'PovcalNet: Data' <http://iresearch.worldbank.org/PovcalNet/index.htm?0,3> [accessed 3 March 2016]; World Bank, 'Poverty & Equity Data' <http://povertydata.worldbank.org/poverty/home/> [accessed 3 March 2016]. See also 'How World Poverty is Measured and Tracked' (n 7) 57–8.
[13] *World Poverty and Human Rights* (n 2) 103.
[14] World Bank, 'Financial Crisis Could Trap 53 Million More People in Poverty' (12 February 2009) <http://go.worldbank.org/1FWPZ7KCJ0> [accessed 3 March 2016].

PPP adjusted \$1.25 a day line,[15] the Office of the High Commissioner for Human Rights (OHCHR), using a different calculative method, noted:

The incidence of extreme poverty around the world is staggering. According to UNDP's *Human Development Report 2014*, over 2.2 billion people... 'are either near or living in multidimensional poverty'.[16]

Finally, Jason Hickel claims:

[I]f people are to achieve normal life expectancy, they need...a minimum of \$3.70 per day...at this more realistic level, we would see a total poverty headcount of about 3.5 billion people...We would also see that poverty is getting much worse, with around 500 million more people added to the ranks of the extremely poor since 1981.[17]

The stark facts of extreme poverty provide an important context in which to interrogate Collier's assertion: 'You don't have to try that hard to imagine this condition—our ancestors lived this way.'[18] This bizarre claim is questionable on at least two registers: scientifically it rests on an implied acceptance of 'genetic memory' theory; whilst historically it is simply false. As Susan Marks notes:

[P]overty of the kind experienced today is not a token of backwardness, but a modern phenomenon...linked to the destruction of traditional livelihoods and of the practices associated with them that once kept destitution at bay.[19]

As former World Bank chief economist Joseph Stiglitz has acknowledged, *if* any of our[20] ancestors lived in conditions of extreme poverty, this occurred only during the most exploitative phases of the industrial revolution.[21] What then is the purpose of Collier's assertion? It entrenches the comforting idea that poverty is a fact,

---

[15] See World Bank, 'PovcalNet: Regional Aggregation Using 2005 PPP and \$1.25/Day Poverty Line' <http://iresearch.worldbank.org/PovcalNet/index.htm?1> [accessed 3 March 2016]; World Bank, 'Global Monitoring Report: Poverty Forecasts' <http://www.worldbank.org/en/publication/global-monitoring-report/poverty-forecasts>.

[16] Office of the High Commissioner for Human Rights, 'Special Rapporteur on Extreme Poverty and Human Rights' <http://www.ohchr.org/EN/Issues/Poverty/Pages/SRExtremePovertyIndex.aspx> [accessed 3 March 2016].

[17] J Hickel, 'The Death of International Development' (February 2015) *Red Pepper* <http://www.redpepper.org.uk/essay-the-death-of-international-development/> [accessed 3 March 2016].

[18] P Collier, *The Bottom Billion: Why the Poorest Countries are Failing and What Can Be Done About It* (OUP Oxford 2007) at 5.

[19] S Marks, 'Human Rights and the Bottom Billion' (2009) 1 *European Human Rights Law Review* 37–49, at 46. See also M Davis, *Late Victorian Holocausts: El Niño Famines and the Making of the Third World* (Verso London 2001). The first, colonial, creation of extreme poverty prior to (but ultimately funding) the industrial revolution is depicted in heart-rending detail in E Galeano, *Open Veins of Latin America: Five Centuries of the Pillage of a Continent* (C Belfrage trans) (Monthly Review Press New York 1973).

[20] I am assuming Collier uses this collective noun to represent the white westerner for whom he is so obviously writing.

[21] J Stiglitz, 'Inequality is a Choice' (13 October 2013) *The New York Times*.

tragic, but uncaused; it also reinforces the progress narrative by which we 'escaped' poverty through our own ingenuity, development, and civilization.

This vision of poverty often appears in academic and activist literature. Poverty as a natural occurrence, inexplicable, and beyond human agency; 'free-floating bad events'[22] which strike like an earthquake, causing massive human suffering and death. This is a curiously comforting image: no one is to blame for the fact of poverty, just as no one is to blame for the occurrence of an earthquake. However, this comforting image is patently false. Poverty does not just happen: poverty is created, maintained, and regulated.

2 POVERTY AS A LEGAL REGIME

Poverty is created by socio-economic processes, and those processes are in turn effected through, and regulated by, international law; thus poverty is a 'legal regime'. As Pogge notes, poverty is deliberately, though not intentionally, inflicted upon certain people *by other people*. The intention is to create and concentrate wealth, but the production of poverty is a necessary and known by-product of the creation and consolidation of wealth.[23] The consolidation of extreme wealth entails the creation of extreme poverty; the latter is deliberate in the sense of being a known consequence of the pursuit of the former. Although the *intention* is solely to produce wealth, the production of poverty remains deliberate. The processes of wealth creation and concentration are managed through law; consequently, the corollary processes of poverty creation are also creatures of law.

There is a constant resource flow from South to North; from the 'Developing World' to the (Over-) 'Developed World'.[24] The average lifestyle in the developed world depends on this resource flow, which is materially unavailable to the majority of the planet's inhabitants; there are simply not enough resources to allow it: 'If all people adopted the American lifestyle…the world's population would need about five "Earths" to meet its needs.'[25] Even the more modest consumption patterns in the United Kingdom would require the resources of 3.1 Planet Earths to

---

[22] 'Human Rights and Root Causes' (n 1) 58, quoting *Report of an Amnesty International Mission to Argentina 6–15 November 1976* (Amnesty International Publications London 1977) at 120.

[23] *World Poverty and Human Rights* (n 2) 1–32 ('General Introduction'); 'Human Rights and the Bottom Billion' (n 19) especially at 46–8.

[24] U Mattei and L Nader, *Plunder: When the Rule of Law is Illegal* (Blackwell London 2008).

[25] M Hood, 'Humanity Falls Deeper into Ecological Debt: Study' (20 September 2011) *Phys. org* <http://phys.org/news/2011-09-humanity-falls-deeper-ecological-debt.html#jCp> [accessed 3 March 2016].

replicate universally.[26] The wealth of the North produces (and is produced by) the poverty of the South.

The management of poverty and exploitation have been the central functions of the international legal regime since the very foundation of international law. International law was forged in the heat of the colonial encounter with others,[27] in the need to justify the exploitation of those others, and the expropriation of their natural resources and wealth.[28] Contemporary international law serves the same functions, but under different rationalizations and justifications.[29]

The 'plunder'[30] of the Third World is written into the DNA of international law; it is its *raison d'être*. This can be seen in everything from the definitions of statehood and government (and the powers 'granted' to governments), to structural adjustment policies, bilateral investment treaties (BITs), international economic law, and debt peonage. The basic structure of international law incentivizes the creation of poverty. This flows from a combination of the focus on territoriality; the commitment to effectiveness (rather than legitimacy); the resource and borrowing privileges available to governments; and the rights of governments to buy and sell arms.[31]

In the *Island of Palmas* case, the arbitrator Max Huber confirmed that the sovereign state is a territorial concept. Under international law, whichever group is able to seize control of this territory (to impose its will as law) becomes the government of that state. Control can be imposed on the inhabitants of the territory; sovereignty need only be 'peaceful in relation to other States',[32] and is legally effective whether recognized or not.[33] The government then has the right to sell the state's resources, and to borrow in its name, as exemplified in the *Tinoco* arbitration;[34] where the arbitrator William Taft based his judgment on the priority of securing

---

[26] A Simms et al., 'The Consumption Explosion: The Third UK Interdependence Report' (New Economics Foundation 25 September 2009) <http://b.3cdn.net/nefoundation/41a473dfbe88oao742_ucm6i4n29.pdf> [accessed 3 March 2016] at 12.

[27] A Anghie, 'Finding the Peripheries: Sovereignty and Colonialism in Nineteenth-Century International Law' (1999) 40 *Harvard International Law Journal* 1–80. There was, of course, also a proliferation of treaties between the Imperial Powers.

[28] *Plunder* (n 24); C Douzinas, *Human Rights and Empire: The Political Philosophy of Cosmopolitanism* (Routledge-Cavendish Abingdon 2007).

[29] V Raina, 'Ecological Debt: An Enormous Debt the North Owes the South' (Paper presented at the International Tribunal on Debt, World Social Forum, January 2002) <http://www.enredeurope.org/docs/ecodebtpaper-18may.pdf> [accessed 3 March 2016].

[30] *Plunder* (n 24).

[31] *World Poverty and Human Rights* (n 2) 1–32 ('General Introduction'); T Pogge, 'Recognized and Violated by International Law: The Human Rights of the Global Poor' (2005) 18 *Leiden Journal of International Law* 717–45, at 738.

[32] *Island of Palmas Case (United States v The Netherlands)* (Award) (1928) 2 RIAA 829–71, at 839.

[33] Tinoco was not recognized.

[34] C Warbrick, 'Recognition of States' (1992) 41 *International and Comparative Law Quarterly* 473–82.

investor interests over the needs of the local population. The government also acquires the right to buy weapons, and legitimately exercise violence against its own population.[35] These powers are formally limited by that state's human rights commitments; but factually, they are limited only by the group's capacity to maintain effective control.

Beyond their resource, borrowing, arms, and violence privileges, governments also have the capacity to commit their states to treaties, investment agreements, and to the conditionalities imposed on loans they take out.[36] Since the 1980s, these commitments have shared a common core: neoliberalism provides the dogma of the international financial institutions, the World Trade Organization (WTO), and the bilateral investment treaty regimes alike. The imposition of this neoliberal agenda has been reinforced by the terms of trade agreements with the European Union (EU), US, and China. These have culminated in the imposition of a 'development policy' structured by the twin imperatives of attracting direct foreign investment, and expanding the export sector. The imposed reforms take on a predictable pattern: import tariffs and measures to protect local industry are decimated; the economy is opened to foreign investment, generally on preferential terms (low royalty mineral extraction, tax holidays, export-processing zones, and so on), and national industries are privatized.

Concurrently, labour rights are repealed or massively diluted, even as state welfare provisions are removed—forcing workers to accept ever deteriorating wages and working conditions. Fighting back is almost impossible. After a string of fatal incidents ranging from fires to building collapses, and a massive wave of strikes, 'Bangladesh's wage board has proposed raising the minimum salary for garment industry workers by 77% to 5,300 takas (US $68; £42) a *month*'.[37] This means present wages are *below £25 per month*, and employers are fighting to keep them that way. Likewise, under pressure from the American Government and corporations, attempts to raise Haiti's minimum wage to 61 cents per hour were defeated, and a minimum wage of 31 cents per hour was locked in instead.[38]

The competition for foreign investment becomes a race to the bottom:

The concentration of growth in export-oriented production…has contributed to the low levels of net job creation, as this sector tends to have weak links with the domestic economy, and to keep wages down…The lowest-income groups have tended to experience the largest increase in unemployment and the greatest deterioration in their wages…export sectors…have experienced growth through lower-cost labor.[39]

---

[35] H Kelsen, 'On the Pure Theory of Law' (1966) 1 *Israel Law Review* 1–7.

[36] *World Poverty and Human Rights* (n 2) 224–56.

[37] AJ Dipu, 'Bangladesh Seeks 77% Rise in Wage for Garment Workers' (5 November 2013) *BBC News* (emphasis added).

[38] Ibid.

[39] Structural Adjustment Participatory Review International Network, *Structural Adjustment: The SAPIR Report: The Policy Roots of Economic Crisis, Poverty and Inequality* (Zed Books New York 2004) at 86.

The supply of cheap resources to the world market is secured at the cost of decreasing wages and social support, and increasing exploitation. For example, a 2004 report on Structural Adjustment found that:

The Mexican minimum wage has lost 69 percent of its purchasing power since the beginning of adjustment in 1982, and the number of people living in extreme poverty…rose from 6 million to 30 million between 1994 and 2000. Salaries were restricted in order to maintain competitiveness.40

The imposition *by legal diktat* of an open, investor-friendly, economy also restricts governments' macro-economic discretion. With protectionist measures precluded, and external debts growing, there can only be minimal government investment—if this is allowed at all in the privatized economy—and minimal regulation:

[W]orkers experience a deterioration in working and living conditions and a loss of collective capacity to defend their rights…The result is greater poverty and social problems… [T]hese practices have also hindered the development of a quality-based competitiveness that would produce greater labor stability and directly improve the living standards of workers.[41]

As developing states are forced to open their markets, remove tariffs and other 'barriers to trade', deregulate and privatize their economies, 'integration' into the world market breeds poverty:

During the 1980s and 1990s, the policies that [the IFIs] foisted on the Global South… caused per capita income growth rates to collapse by almost 50 percent. [It is] estimated that during this period developing countries lost around $480 billion per year in potential GDP…Yet Western corporations have benefitted tremendously from this process, gaining access to new markets, cheaper labour and raw materials, and fresh avenues for capital flight.[42]

Given that any apparent 'growth' has been engineered through a combination of privatization, direct foreign investment, and the suppression of wages and working conditions, it is unsurprising that 'the benefits of export growth went primarily to the multinational corporations'.[43] The advantages of multinational corporations (MNCs) are compounded—through law—as the opening of markets is complemented by demands for low royalty payments, tax incentives, even tax holidays, and 'aggressive tax planning'.[44] All of this is legal, and legally regulated; but it sits alongside a zone of dubious legality: tax evasion.

---

[40] *Structural Adjustment* (n 39) 89–90.   [41] Ibid 83–4.

[42] J Hickel, 'Flipping the Corruption Myth' (1 February 2014) *Al Jazeera International*.

[43] *Structural Adjustment* (n 39).

[44] Africa Progress Panel, 'Equity in Extractives: Stewarding Africa's Natural Resources for All: African Progress Report 2013' (2013) <http://www.africaprogresspanel.org/publications/policy-papers/africa-progress-report-2013/> [accessed 3 March 2016].

At first blush, tax evasion is unlawful, yet it is also facilitated by law. Major banking and financial centres aggressively protect client confidentiality, relying on the imperatives of national law to do so. Revenue services in developing countries are usually understaffed (due to the neoliberal imperative to reduce government spending) and thus unable to track 'value-added through a maze of interconnected companies linked through shell companies, holding companies and other intermediaries registered in centres from the British Virgin Islands to Switzerland and London'.[45]

Regardless of which side of the blurred line between avoidance and evasion individual acts of 'tax planning' inhabit, the law remains consistently implicated in denying to the developing world hundreds of billions of dollars.[46] Developing countries are deprived of income as well as control. There is thus no scope to develop indigenous refining capacity, the developing states are fated to remain raw commodity producers:

African exporters typically capture only a small share of the final value of mineral exports. The Democratic Republic of the Congo is the world's largest exporter of cobalt, mostly in the form of unprocessed ore—but value is added elsewhere… Without processing industries that add value, mining creates fewer jobs, produces less revenue and contributes less to GDP growth.…The low level of value added in African mining is symptomatic of the low level of manufacturing activity in the region's economies.[47]

Riven with conflict, burdened with old loans and conditionalities, and bound by WTO membership to liberalize their economies, many developing countries are not in a position to develop indigenous refinement sectors. Nor under many trade and investment agreements would they be legally entitled to offer any such nascent sector the protection and subsidy needed to survive.

Augmenting the structural violences of international law, and loaded trade rules, are the conditionalities[48] tied to International Monetary Fund (IMF) or World Bank loans, making near identical demands. Indeed, World Bank president Jim Yong Kim's recent remark that 'developing world countries:…should undertake structural reform programmes to promote growth' prompted an Oxfam spokesperson to retort: 'Today we have seen a worrying glimpse of the old World Bank, focusing only on growth, structural reform and opening the gates to the private sector.'[49]

---

[45] 'Equity in Extractives' (n 44) 65.   [46] Ibid.   [47] Ibid 45.

[48] The former structural adjustment policies (SAPs), which have been repackaged, effectively unaltered, as poverty reduction strategy plans (PRSPs): see C Welch, 'Structural Adjustment Programs & Poverty Reduction Strategy' (12 October 2005) *Foreign Policy in Focus* <http://fpif.org/structural_adjustment_programs_poverty_reduction_strategy/> [accessed 3 March 2016].

[49] P Inman, 'World Bank's Jim Kim: Global Slowdown Will Harm Anti-Poverty Drive' (16 April 2015) *The Guardian*.

Together, these loans and conditionalities ensure that developing states are condemned to augment a permanent place at the bottom end of the supply chain with perpetual debt peonage:

Debt repayment has become an important mechanism for transferring wealth from the people of the South to financiers of the North. According to the United Nations, developing countries paid 1.662 trillion dollars in debt servicing between 1980 and 1992. *This amount is three times the original amount owed in 1980.*[50]

This trend continues, and the World Bank estimates that in 2012 developing countries made annual *interest* repayments of over $190 billion, on total debts which then exceeded $5 trillion, and continue to rise steadily.[51]

Mass exploitation is a product of law. Even where the conditions of exploitation appear lawless (for example, in the Democratic Republic of the Congo[52]), those conditions are encircled by law: sovereignty, borders, resource transfers, debt. Under the benevolent gaze of international law, the political, military, and economic elites of the 'developing countries' are encouraged to facilitate the mass exploitation of their people and resources. Patent laws are globalized, and antitrust measures universalized, but labour standards are rarely exported. Moreover, the first contact that the products of exploitation—for example, gold, diamonds, rare earth minerals, sweatshop clothes, or coffee—have with law is a cleansing one: the misery of their production washed away, they become legally absolved, legitimately transferable, commodities.

Demonstrating this is perilously close to attempting to prove a negative. However, a few observations are apt. First, at a general level no one appears to argue that worker exploitation and dangerous working conditions in Bangladesh,[53] Columbia,[54] or South Africa impact negatively on title to the clothes produced or minerals mined. Transferable title in the products of exploitation is simply assumed; and efforts instead focus on *persuading* intermediate buyers (for example, Walmart or GAP) to ameliorate the suffering in their supply chains.

In a similar vein, the 1980 *United Nations Convention on Contracts for the International Sale of Goods* (ratified by eighty states including much of the so-called First World), despite a preambular reference to 'the broad objectives in

---

[50] P Bond, *Elite Transition: From Apartheid to Neoliberalism in South Africa* (Pluto Press New York 2000) at 188 (emphasis added).

[51] World Bank, 'International Debt Statistics' <http://datatopics.worldbank.org/debt/ids/region/LMY> [accessed 3 March 2016].

[52] D Snow, 'DR Congo: Cursed by Its Natural Wealth' (10 October 2013) *BBC Magazine* <http://www.bbc.co.uk/news/magazine-24396390> [accessed 3 March 2016].

[53] See 'Bangladesh Seeks 77% Rise in Wage for Garment Workers' (n 37).

[54] R Needleman, 'Free Trade Agreements and Unfree Labor: The Case of Columbia' (2013) 22 *New Labor Forum* 51–8.

the resolutions adopted by the sixth special session of the General Assembly of the United Nations on the establishment of a New International Economic Order', has little to say about the generation of title.[55] Article 41 obligates the seller to 'deliver goods which are free from any right or claim of a third party' but there is no corresponding obligation of due diligence placed upon the buyer. Consequently, the buyer would appear to receive good title, whether the seller possessed such or not. Likewise, the Kimberley Process for restricting the circulation of conflict diamonds is purely voluntary. The very existence of this process highlights the absence of corresponding legal demands, and the optional nature of the process does little to fill this *lacuna*.[56] Finally, in the related area of 'conflict minerals':

Section 1502 of the US *Dodd-Frank Wall Street Reform and Consumer Protection Act*...passed in July 2010, is the first piece of legislation *in the world* that aims to break the links between eastern Congo's minerals trade and the abusive armed groups that prey upon it.[57]

Once again, such legislation would have been unnecessary had international law itself regulated the links between conflict, appropriation, exploitation, and marketable title. Moreover, as can be seen from Global Witness' decision to withdraw its support from the Kimberley Process,[58] and the utter ineffectiveness of the US–Columbian Labor Action Plan agreed in April 2011,[59] such piecemeal efforts are unlikely to preclude trade in exploitative or conflict commodities. The basic structures of international law incentivize exploitation whilst removing its dark shadow from the world of international commodity exchange, the realm of markets, trade, and regulated competition.

In these apparently free and cooperative spaces, primary producers are rarely able to set the prices of their commodities. The less processed a commodity is, the truer this becomes; so that exporters of raw natural resources have least control of all. As a fractured producer community, hobbled by antitrust and anti-cartel rules, faces a united consumer community, the latter set the terms of exchange. Developing countries—prohibited by the WTO and SAP/PRSPs alike from subsidizing or protecting domestic industry—are forced to sell unprocessed resources at

[55] *Convention on Contracts for the International Sale of Goods* (opened for signature 11 April 1980 entered into force 1 January 1988) 1489 UNTS 3.

[56] S Pickles, 'US "Conflict Minerals" Legislation: Opportunities and Obligations for Chinese Companies' (Global Witness, 12 November 2013) <https://www.globalwitness.org/archive/us-conflict-minerals-legislation-opportunities-and-obligations-chinese-companies/> [accessed 3 March 2016].

[57] Ibid (emphasis added).

[58] Global Witness, 'Conflict Diamonds' <http://www.globalwitness.org/campaigns/conflict/conflict-diamonds> [accessed 3 March 2016].

[59] 'Free Trade Agreements and Unfree Labor' (n 54).

that fraction of their worth termed 'going world market prices'. Extortion becomes the law:

A study by the Southern African Development Community of the value chain for a range of minerals in Africa found that the value of processed products was typically 400 times greater than the equivalent unit value (by weight) of the raw material.[60]

The advantages of MNCs are compounded—through law—as foreign investment is mediated through the BITs regime. This exempts MNCs from the vagaries of local laws, assigning dispute resolution almost exclusively to the International Centre for Settlement of Investment Disputes (ICSID) system, guaranteeing corporate profits, and leaving states alone subject to commercial risk.[61] In short, 'the property and investment rights of transnational capital are protected in "exquisite detail" under extensive NAFTA, GATT, and WTO regulations and articles'.[62]

So-called developing states are caught in a multipronged legal assault. They gained independence subject to colonial borders, and are obligated by colonial era treaties, contracts, and patterns of wealth distribution.[63] Moreover, the colonial era itself had destroyed traditional forms of livelihood and social solidarity,[64] and reduced colonial territories to deposits of natural and human resources.[65]

'Developing nations' are forced to sell their resources, including labour, cheaply to the developed nations; and to buy arms, processed commodities, and pharmaceuticals, at high prices, from those same developed nations.[66] Debt 'repayments' become a system of perpetual tribute, carefully calibrated to ensure continuing serfdom. The currency flows become circular,[67] while the resource flows are essentially unidirectional, from poor to rich.[68]

We turn full circle. The under-resourced governments of artificially (but deliberately) impoverished nations must maintain some form of social order, whilst also seeing off rivals to their power. Mass human rights abuses are a systemic response

---

[60] 'African Progress Report' (n 44).

[61] BS Chimni, 'Capitalism, Imperialism, and International Law in the Twenty-First Century' (2012) 14 *Oregon Review of International Law* 17–45.

[62] J Wills, 'The World Turned Upside Down? Neo-Liberalism, Socioeconomic Rights, and Hegemony' (2013) 27 *Leiden Journal of International Law* 1–23.

[63] The most egregious example would be the imposition by France onto Haiti of massive reparations for the loss of 'property' represented by the very same freed slaves forming the then Haitian population.

[64] *Late Victorian Holocausts* (n 19).   [65] 'Finding the Peripheries' (n 27).

[66] The luxuries ostentatiously enjoyed by the 'ruling kleptocracies', and ostentatiously reported by the international media, are in reality a footnote. It has been speculatively suggested that Hosni Mubarak and his 'cronies' may have stolen as much as $30 billion during his reign. Let us fantastically assume it was more, $80 billion! In an Egyptian nation of 80 million citizens, that amounts to $1000 per person—*over* 30 years. $33 per person, per year. In reality, then, probably $10 stolen from each citizen per year. A crime to be sure, but hardly an explanation for Egypt's widespread poverty.

[67] T Mitchell, *Carbon Democracy: Political Power in the Age of Oil* (Verso London 2013).

[68] See eg D Kar et al., 'Illicit Financial Flows and the Problem of Net Resource Transfers from Africa: 1980–2009' (Global Financial Integrity, 29 May 2013) <http://www.gfintegrity.org/report/report-net-resources-from-africa/> [accessed 3 March 2016].

to widespread dissatisfaction with, and protest against, a government's rule, its policies, or its authority.[69] Such protest must be suppressed because external factors preclude the demanded change in policy. The poor would like to be supported and treated with dignity, workers demand respect and living wages; if able, they organize and make their demands apparent.

However, economic conditions—engineered and imposed by international law—rule out making the necessary concessions. This is where the trouble erupts, and violence, repression, and 'mass human rights abuses' function as systemically rational responses.[70] A sad and uncomfortable truth then: it is cheaper to oppress a people than to appease them. The mooted subordination of WTO law to human rights demands has done little or nothing to ameliorate poverty.[71] Nor has the IMF and World Bank's adoption of a human rights friendly vocabulary.[72] On its face, this system is patently exploitative, unjust, and unethical. Consequently, it must be justified or, ideally, naturalized.[73]

The task of poverty apologism has necessitated two things—the turn to statistics outlined earlier; and a deployment of human rights analysis to obscure the systemic causes of poverty. The citizens of the developed world sit atop the human food-chain, the 'ultimate predator'.[74] Yet these same citizens are taught to conceive of themselves as enlightened and civilized, the bearers of humanity. This dissonance (the denial of the link between poverty and wealth) is managed through law. The naturalization of poverty allows us to believe in our development from—rather than implication in—the plight of the extremely poor.

Poverty-blindness is achieved by naturalizing our sense of entitlement to the spoils we enjoy as beneficiaries of a global order that perpetuates extreme poverty.[75] This in turn is achieved through an extremely partisan analysis of the causes of poverty.[76] Such analyses typically present poverty as caused by localized human rights abuses (themselves inexplicable), and imply that if human rights were respected, economic development would follow, and poverty would be eradicated. If only the Darker Nations[77] could learn to implement human rights, then they too could be like us. This is simply untrue.

---

[69] N Klein, *The Shock Doctrine: The Rise of Disaster Capitalism* (Knopf Toronto 2007).

[70] Ibid.

[71] J Beckett, 'Fragmentation, Openness, and Hegemony: Adjudication and the WTO' in MK Lewis and S Frankel (eds), *International Economic Law and National Autonomy* (CUP Cambridge 2010) 44–70.

[72] BS Chimni, 'International Institutions Today: An Imperial Global State in the Making' (2004) 15 *European Journal of International Law* 1–37; M Koskenniemi, 'What Use for Sovereignty Today?' (2011) 1 *Asian Journal of International Law* 61–70.

[73] SA Malik, 'As Natural as the Air We Breathe: Intellectual Property and the Naturalisation of Structural Violence' (Paper presented at Technologies of Imperialism: Law in Contemporary and Historical Perspective, School of Oriental and African Studies University of London, 16 March 2013).

[74] G Rose, *Mourning Becomes the Law: Philosophy and Representation* (CUP New York 1996).

[75] WEB DuBois, 'The African Roots of War' (1915) 115 *Atlantic Monthly* 707–14.

[76] 'Human Rights and the Bottom Billion' (n 19) especially at 48–9.

[77] 'The African Roots of War' (n 75).

3 HUMAN RIGHTS
AND GLOBAL POVERTY: A STORY
OF MISCONCEPTION AND EXONERATION

All of which brings us neatly to the thorny question of the relationship between human rights and global poverty. Of all the branches of international law, human rights has undoubtedly been the most vocal in its condemnation of global poverty—as a 'rights abuse' in itself, and as a cause of other rights abuses.[78] Nonetheless, the human rights regime has been resolutely blind to the 'root causes' of extreme global poverty.[79]

My basic contention here is that too much human rights analysis fails to engage with the causes of poverty, and has a habit of confusing causes and effects, the net result of which is to perpetuate and legitimate extreme global poverty. Human rights analysis functions not to ameliorate the conditions of the extremely poor, but to justify those of the affluent.[80]

Paul Farmer reminds us that we live in a world where affluence and deprivation are unevenly distributed, and that '[o]ne way to trace this geography of unequal risk is to consider how "structural violence" is meted out to the poor in myriad ways...by everyone who belongs to a certain social order'.[81] However, he also cautions that our epistemological and moral systems militate against recognition of 'how social arrangements create danger, disease, and death'[82] and emphasizes '*the discomfort these ideas provoke in a moral economy still geared to pinning praise or blame on individual actors*'.[83]

Thus, while Farmer's arguments—alongside Pogge's—have had some impact on the field, few have chosen to endure the discomfort of rejecting the individualist leaning of law and rights, or facing the self-implication to which structural analyses almost inexorably lead. A willingness to overcome this discomfort has, however, prompted Upendra Baxi, and then Obiora Okafor and Basil Ugochukwu, to outline 'a new human rights paradigm [which they] refer to as the trade-related market-friendly (TREMF) paradigm'.[84] This emphasizes the 'imperative that

---

[78] 'Human Rights and Root Causes' (n 1) 61–2.   [79] Ibid 65–7; *The Shock Doctrine* (n 69).

[80] JA Beckett, 'Faith and Resignation: A Journey through International Law' in M Stone, IR Wall, and C Douzinas (eds), *New Critical Legal Thinking: Law and the Political* (Routledge London 2012) 145–66.

[81] P Farmer, 'Never Again? Reflections on Human Values and Human Rights' (The Tanner Lectures on Human Values, delivered at University of Utah, 30 March 2005) 139–88, at 141.

[82] Ibid.   [83] Ibid (emphasis added).

[84] O Okafor and B Ugochukwu, 'Have the Norms and Jurisprudence of the African Human Rights System Been Pro-Poor?' (2011) 11 *African Human Rights Law Journal* 396–421, at 400. See also U Baxi, *The Future of Human Rights* (OUP Oxford 2002) at 132.

scholars and observers of governance systems and institutions…not assume that "pro-human rights" necessarily translates to "pro-poor"'.[85]

But even this imperative is not often accepted. Thus, despite their insightful analyses,[86] and impassioned advocacy,[87] Margot Salomon and Oliver De Schutter remain too accepting of human right's fundamental goodness and normative superiority; its pristine isolation, and its capacity to make demands of other systems:

Separate from any responsibility of the IMF qua the IMF, as above, the IMF Member States are required to comply with their existing human rights obligations, including when acting under the auspices of an international organisation.[88]

They refuse both Baxi's insights and Teubner's observation that (legal) systems are limited in their ability to make demands of one another.[89]

Instead of assuming that human rights can simply make demands of other legal and economic orders, we should begin to analyse the myriad and messy entanglements between human rights, economics, development, and international law: their relations of domination and subjugation; of complicity and compromise. However, this does not occur, and the same innocent superiority characterizes the human rights movement's institutional actors. Although poverty has been featured in the analysis, its specific logics remain unexplored: 'some mandate-holders put the issue to one side for reasons to do with time and information…Among those who did take it up, few took it into account in formulating their specific recommendations.'[90] Too often such recommendations focus on the idea that rights have simply been misunderstood and misapplied, which, as Marks notes, ignores the systematic and material bases through which the global economy generates poverty and hunger, 'not just contingently but necessarily, as part of its logic'.[91]

Finally, the widely heralded appointment of Jim Yong Kim as President of the World Bank in 2012, was expected to lead to a sea change in that institution's engagement with poverty and inequality, but three years later so little had changed,

---

[85] 'Have the Norms and Jurisprudence of the African Human Rights System Been Pro-Poor?' (n 84) 397.
[86] O De Schutter, 'Report of the Special Rapporteur on the Right to Food: Crisis into Opportunity: Reinforcing Multilateralism' (21 July 2009) UN Doc A/HRC/12/31; ME Salomon, *Global Responsibility for Human Rights: World Poverty and the Development of International Law* (OUP Oxford 2007).
[87] O De Schutter and ME Salomon, 'Economic Policy Conditionality, Socio-Economic Rights and International Legal Responsibility: The Case of Greece 2010–2015' (Legal Brief prepared for the Special Committee of the Hellenic Parliament on the Audit of the Greek Debt, 15 June 2015) <http://www.lse.ac.uk/humanRights/documents/2015/SalomonDeSchutterGreekDebtTruth.pdf> [accessed 3 March 2016]; ME Salomon, 'Of Austerity, Human Rights and International Institutions' (2015) 21 *European Law Journal* 521–45.
[88] 'Of Austerity, Human Rights, and International Institutions' (n 87) 538.
[89] G Teubner, *Law as an Autopoietic System* (A Bankowska and R Adler trans Z Bankowski ed) (Blackwell Oxford 1993).
[90] 'Human Rights and Root Causes' (n 1) 62.   [91] Ibid 69.

that the new UN Special Rapporteur on Extreme Poverty and Human Rights, Philip Alston, was moved to comment:

The World Bank…steadfastly refuses to use the language of economic and social rights…The IMF, for all of its enlightened concern about the consequences of inequality is every bit as resistant as the Bank to taking any account of human rights in its work.[92]

Nonetheless, it may be hoped that, with Alston's own appointment, change is afoot at the institutional level. His statement to the twenty-ninth session of the Human Rights Council certainly gives cause for optimism:

[I]t is instructive to move beyond the situation in these halls and look at what has been happening in the outside world.…we need to recognize that the concern is…with a range of extreme inequalities in relation to wealth, access to education, health care, housing and so on.…while a great many steps will need to be taken if extreme inequality is to be halted, the Council needs to do more than just adopt fine words.[93]

However, Alston himself expresses some doubt, continuing: '[f]or over 25 years, independent experts have been submitting reports warning of the consequences of inequality, but nothing has been done in response'.[94] This neatly reframes the question: how is it that all of the fine words and sentiments expressed in academic writings and UN reports have missed their mark, been co-opted, or ignored?

I suggest that there are structural reasons, inherent in human rights analysis, discourse, and demands which help to explain this apparent lack of impact. The movement's commitments to its internal purity and assumed hierarchical superiority preclude analysis of its messy entanglements with other aspects of international law. To demonstrate this, I sketch four different points of (dis)engagement between human rights and international law's project of facilitating and managing poverty.

Two important misunderstandings must be engaged as a prelude to analysis. First, good intentions are neither sufficient, nor a defence from negative consequences, and, secondly, intervention is never a question of doing 'something' or 'nothing', it is always active, and bears the possibility of negative as well as positive consequences. Thus we must reject the humanitarian myth that intervening is at worst neutral, and so always preferable to not intervening. Furthermore, following Anne Orford's analysis, we must also nuance our conceptions of intervention. Trade, investment, conditional loans, intellectual property regimes, and so on, are all forms of intervention of at least equal importance to the 'white knight' interventions on which we are encouraged to focus.[95]

---

[92] Office of the High Commissioner for Human Rights, 'Statement by the Special Rapporteur on Extreme Poverty and Human Rights at the 29th Session of the Human Rights Council' (22 June 2015) <http://www.ohchr.org/EN/NewsEvents/Pages/DisplayNews.aspx?NewsID=16131&LangID=E> [accessed 3 March 2016].

[93] Ibid.   [94] Ibid.

[95] A Orford, *Reading Humanitarian Intervention: Human Rights and the Use of Force in International Law* (CUP Cambridge 2003).

So, human rights critiques take place within a context of endemic intervention, of the enmeshing of First and Third World economies.[96] They are not neutral and nor is the terrain on which they act—they are political interventions with political consequences. These consequences present a predictable pattern: exoneration of the affluent, pathologization of the impoverished. This occurs on any of at least four registers:

1. Distraction: where attention focuses on the generation of ever more precise rights, rather than the amelioration of the plight of the poor.

2. Localization of pathology: where the poor, and their governments, are made to bear exclusive blame for their poverty.

3. Complicity: where human rights are co-opted by the WTO regime to provide an alibi, and thus legitimation.

4. Distortion: where human rights adopt and promote a false history of development.

These four registers exist complementarily, and function alongside what David Kennedy has identified as human rights' 'hegemony over the space of emancipatory politics'.[97] However, I wish to consider them in turn, and also to emphasize an important distinction between them: while the first 'engagement' distracts from the problem and any possible solutions; the latter three are *active* parts of the problem of extreme global poverty.

3.1 Human Rights as Distraction

Poverty, we are frequently informed, is a human rights issue. This is important, because human rights are important. If poverty breaches human rights, then poverty itself is wrong, and has no right to exist. And yet poverty continues, stubbornly, to exist. Attention then turns to two foci: proving that poverty is a human rights violation; and proliferating ever more precise rights to make it clear to poverty that it has no right to exist, and should vacate the premises.

Each strategy is completely detached from reality, and from the economic imperatives which preclude its realization. Focus turns to the ideal, the design of the normative web of the human rights project itself. It is precisely in constructing this fantasy world of legal perfection that advocates and acolytes fall foul of Kennedy's charge that it is more important to feel part of a good project than to effect positive change in the world.[98]

---

[96] 'Recognized and Violated by International Law' (n 31).

[97] D Kennedy, 'The International Human Rights Movement: Part of the Problem?' (2002) 15 *Harvard Human Rights Journal* 101–25.

[98] Ibid.

This is a project of good intentions and negative effects. Due to both the radical indeterminacy of international law and the largely 'unrealized' nature of human rights, progressive political demands can always be dressed in the garb of human rights: the right to life can be interpreted to include freedom from extreme want; the right to health to demand access to pharmaceuticals; rights to food, water, development, and so on, can be interpolated. New conventions can be pursued, final acts and declaratory statements proliferate; but facts on the ground do not change.

Human rights compensate for their lack of traction by growing ever more righteous and Messianic. Hegemonic as all functionally differentiated regimes are,[99] the human rights regime is also a mass producer of ever newer and more precise legal norms. Norms are brought declaratively into existence, designated as 'interpretations' (concretizations) of existing norms, new customary norms, or even general principles of law. Human rights norms are allowed to proliferate on the condition that they have no strong demands for realization in the actual world of distributions and outcomes. In other words, the increasingly dense web of human rights demands functions in a purely normative world, in which the only concern is to provide a point from which the real world can be assessed and critiqued.

This fantastical structure is central to understanding the functional economy of human rights: because they are largely deinstitutionalized—or promulgated only within weak institutional structures—human rights claims are hugely flexible. There are few courts to strike down such claims, and thus each practitioner can imagine their interpretations to be correct. Without having to confront the probability that their claims would not be institutionally endorsed, they can use them as a 'neutral' vantage point from which to castigate a recalcitrant reality.[100]

Presented in such a peremptory manner, the demands of human rights appear objective, impartial, and necessary: they fall precisely into the category Unger has termed 'false necessity'.[101] However, as Marks has noted, any understanding of false necessity must be complemented by an understanding of false contingency.[102] Although almost any political claim can be re-presented as a competent legal argument, not all have an equal chance of realization; indeed some have almost no chance of being actualized in the real world. This expansion of perspective also facilitates a change of focus: instead of analysing which human rights norms 'exist', or even the conditions for the proliferation of such norms, attention must turn

---

[99] 'Fragmentation, Openness, and Hegemony' (n 71).

[100] J Beckett, 'The Economics of Fantasy: Reflections on the Resurgence of Formalism in PIL' (2012) 1(3) *ESIL Reflections* <http://www.esil-sedi.eu/node/208> [accessed 3 March 2016]; 'Faith and Resignation' (n 80).

[101] RM Unger, *False Necessity: Anti-Necessitarian Social Theory in the Service of Radical Democracy* (Verso New York 2004).

[102] S Marks, 'False Contingency' (2009) 62 *Current Legal Problems* 1–21.

to which norms might be realized, which will not, and why this is so. Put differently, we should focus on when progressive political aims (such as the mitigation of poverty) might be advanced by advocating human rights claims, and when they will not. False contingency teaches us that there are reasons why some norms are actualized and others are not, and that these have little or nothing to do with any intrinsic legal or ethical quality of the claims advanced.

In trying to represent the law *either* positivistically 'as it is' (and as it is 'ignored') *or* through natural law, as 'the best it can be' (the international legal system 'in its best light')[103] the human rights movement (which, in reality oscillates between these strategies) structurally precludes itself from acknowledging or perceiving the dynamics, forces, and structures *causing* international law to do what it in fact does; as it is in fact *applied*, not ignored. The link between wealth and poverty is systematically obscured, and this leads to the 'breach' of these rights—the non-actualization of these interpretations, imaginations, and demands—being attributed exclusively to local causes.

3.2 Localizing Pathology

Analogous to what Pogge has termed 'explanatory nationalism',[104] this aspect of human rights engagement claims that a nation's economic development is an expression of its 'moral worth'.[105] The localization of pathology functions through both the analytic suppression of structural causes and the unconscious inversion of cause and effect.[106] This strategy begins with the unstated assumption that developing countries have *both* access to, *and* control over, sufficient resources to alleviate poverty within their borders; all that is lacking is the political will to do so. It further assumes that the developed world has no role, or interest, in the perpetuation of global poverty. All but one of these assumptions is false.

Many developing countries do have rich natural resource deposits; however few have much control over the disposition of those resources.[107] Generally, this control is ceded to foreign multinational companies, at the dictates of international financial institutions, the WTO, China, the US, or the EU.[108] Developed countries

---

[103] C Basak, 'On Interpretivism and International Law' (2009) 20 *European Journal of International Law* 805–22.

[104] 'World Poverty and Human Rights' (n 2).

[105] J Rawls, *The Law of Peoples, with the Idea of Public Reason Revisited* (Harvard University Press Cambridge MA 2001) at 108.

[106] 'Human Rights and the Bottom Billion' (n 19).

[107] 'Kofi Annan: Africa Plundered by Secret Mining Deals' (10 May 2013) *BBC News* <http://www.bbc.co.uk/news/world-africa-22478994> [accessed 3 March 2016].

[108] J Ferguson, *Global Shadows: Africa in the Neoliberal World Order* (Duke University Press Durham 2006).

require access to those resources at 'market rate',[109] and access to cheap labour to extract and ship, and even occasionally refine, those resources for export. The localization of pathology functions to disguise these external or international factors.

With haunting echoes of a colonial past, the discourse starts by portraying the peoples and political cultures of developing states as backward, primitive, even barbaric: in need of tutelage and correction.[110] Focus on rights violations, corruption, and the absence of democracy helps to construct an implicit image of the uncivilized other: savages and victims, awaiting our saviours.[111] The obsessive Western focus on female circumcision makes most sense within this political economy; as does the formal legal prohibition of 'harmful traditional practices',[112] pitting as it does 'tradition' against modernity, the backward peoples of Africa and Asia, whose 'traditional practices' compare poorly with their implied opposite, Western Civilization.[113]

Africa is plagued by poverty because it is backward and barbaric, corrupt and undemocratic, a continent which prefers bloodshed and the mutilation of its daughters to progress toward enlightenment, development, and freedom. This is the implicit message of the human rights critique, which neatly sidelines Anghie's query: just why do so many former colonies have a physical infrastructure connecting resource deposits in the centre to harbours on their shores?[114]

Running parallel to the construction of this blameworthy caricature is an equally implied, equally unanalysed reversal of cause and effect. The 'development-minded' British Prime Minister provides an excellent contemporary illustration:

> But I also think it is important we look at those things that keep countries poor. Conflict, corruption, lack of justice, lack of the rule of law.[115]

Even the UN has realized that poverty causes conflict more often than conflict causes poverty.[116] The same is true for the other 'causes' listed: why is it more likely

---

[109] See above nn 39–43 and 60–8 and accompanying text. See also *World Poverty and Human Rights* (n 2) 1–32 ('General Introduction').

[110] W Rasch, *Sovereignty and Its Discontents: On the Primacy of Conflict and the Structure of the Political* (Routledge London 2005) at 139–42.

[111] M Mutua, 'Savages, Victims, and Saviors: The Metaphor of Human Rights' (2001) 42 *Harvard International Law Journal* 201–45.

[112] *Convention on the Rights of the Child* (opened for signature 20 November 1989, entered into force 2 September 1990) 1577 UNTS 3; *Convention on the Elimination of All Forms of Discrimination against Women* (opened for signature 1 March 1980 entered into force 3 September 1981) 1249 UNTS 13.

[113] S Harris-Short, 'International Human Rights Law: Imperialist, Inept and Ineffective? Cultural Relativism and the UN *Convention on the Rights of the Child*' (2003) 25 *Human Rights Quarterly* 130–81.

[114] See 'Finding the Peripheries' (n 27).

[115] Patrick Wintour, 'David Cameron in Liberia: We Must Eradicate Extreme Poverty' (1 February 2013) *The Guardian* <http://www.theguardian.com/politics/2013/feb/01/david-cameron-liberia-poverty-talks> [accessed 3 March 2016].

[116] 'Human Rights and Root Causes' (n 1) 62.

that corruption causes poverty than that poverty causes corruption; or the absence of justice, or the rule of law? Conversely, would the presence of the rule of law eradicate poverty; or would the eradication of poverty enable the realization of the rule of law?

It is better to understand poverty, in Marks' striking phrase, as 'planned misery'; 'to suppose that the conditions which create vulnerability to hunger and malnutrition…exist at least in part because they benefit some groups of people, even as they massively disadvantage others'.[117] Poverty is not caused by corruption, lawlessness, or conflict, instead these are systemically explicable effects of poverty; a poverty which is itself explicable through the advantages to be drawn from exploitation of human and natural resources in the 'developing world'. Images of backwardness and barbarism are deployed to disguise this systemic logic; effects are presented as causes, and the pathologies of poverty conveniently localized.

3.3 Human Rights and International Economic Law

The efficacy of the first two encounters relies on the belief that human rights exist in an important normative reality, unaffected by their lack of actualization; and the plasticity this brings to human rights analysis.[118] The third engagement is altogether different, an effect of human rights' parallel attempt to gain traction in the realm of actualized or enforced law. The attempt 'to mainstream human rights into the work of the WTO'[119] begins thus: 'Although the WTO cannot mutate to a human rights organization, it must…acknowledge the human rights effects of its work in order to maintain credibility.'[120]

As it is the primary responsibility of states to protect human rights and pursue human rights principles, the challenge posed by globalization is to ensure that states liberalize trade in ways that are in harmony with their [human rights] obligations.[121]

However, this 'primacy' exists only in the minds of human rights advocates.[122] For trade lawyers, no rights could be realized without the benefits of exchange, thus trade law has primacy; for environmentalists, there can be neither trade nor rights without a living environment, and their concerns have primacy. There is no a priori reason to accept any particular one of these claims.

---

[117] 'Human Rights and Root Causes' (n 1).   [118] 'The Economics of Fantasy' (n 100).
[119] GM Zagel, 'WTO & Human Rights: Examining Linkages and Suggesting Convergence' (IDLO Voices of Development Jurists Paper Series Vol 2 No 2 2005).
[120] Ibid.   [121] Ibid.
[122] S Pahuja, 'Rights as Regulation: The Integration of Development and Human Rights' in B Morgan (ed), *The Intersection of Rights and Regulation: New Directions in Sociolegal Scholarship* (Ashgate Aldershot 2007) 167–91, at 170.

What is clear, however, is that WTO law has *institutional primacy* over other systems. This is, after all, the core incentive in seeking recognition by, or coherence with, the WTO system: access to its dispute resolution structure.[123] Engaging with the WTO is an attempt to *actualize* human rights norms. It is, however, a strategy doomed to failure, because the concerns of human rights lawyers with 'who has authority and jurisdiction to interpret and apply broadly defined human rights standards are [motivated by] the fear that human rights may be subjected to trade law, given the relatively powerful and unique position of the WTO and its dispute settlement mechanism.'[124]

As interpretative power must be traded for the possibility of actualization, human rights advocates lose the flexibility that non-institutionalization gave them. Rights are subject to fixed, restricted, meanings; and claims that a breach of the advocate's favoured interpretation equates with an objective breach of human rights lose credence. The WTO is able to 'maintain credibility' (and indeed gain legitimacy) by acknowledging human rights standards, even though it then subjects those standards to its own imperatives.[125] All that occurs is a change of vocabulary; unaccompanied by any emancipatory effect: '[h]uman rights become a means by which society is subordinated to the imperative of economic growth through markets.'[126] The effect of the human rights engagement here, like that of its earlier critique, is to legitimate the present system, and exonerate its beneficiaries.

3.4 Human Rights and the Imagined History of Development

The plasticity of human rights allows them to function as a hysterical distraction, fabricating an ideal normative world instead of engaging with the realities of this one. In localizing pathologies, they distract attention from the linkage between poverty and wealth, and in seeking actualization they help legitimate the WTO system, and the resource flows it enables. Each movement plays out within a white saviour dynamic: we provide the structure of our lives as a normative model for their salvation; we pathologize their leaders to open the route to salvation; and we 'mainstream human rights' into trade law as a mechanism to enable that salvation.

---

[123] 'Fragmentation, Openness, and Hegemony' (n 71).
[124] T Cottier, J Pauwelyn, and E Bürgi Bonanomi, 'Introduction' in T Cottier, J Pauwelyn, and E Bürgi (eds), *Human Rights and International Trade* (OUP Oxford 2005) 1–26, at 7.
[125] 'Fragmentation, Openness, and Hegemony' (n 71).
[126] 'Rights as Regulation' (n 122) 170.

What is missing is an analysis of our development, and an understanding of the relationship between our wealth and their poverty. The final aspect of the human rights 'critique' obscures even the recognition of this absence. Human rights discourse is implicated in a radically false history of development:

As a satisfactory human rights situation also improves the economic development and attractiveness of a state, human rights and economic development are not contradictory but mutually support each other.[127]

In this universalized reversal of the localization of pathology two new myths emerge: the myth of our ethical development; and the myth that by emulating our practices, the under-developed countries could access our lifestyles. This is, in short, the imaginary history that from respect for human rights and the rule of law flow democracy and material wealth; the standard, colonialism-free, hagiography of international law.

In this history the realization of rights preceded economic development, and neither had anything to do with colonial expansion or expropriation. That account is factually wrong,[128] and logically untenable. It is also ideologically very effective in maintaining the status quo by removing the ladder up which we climbed. Projected into the present it takes on a common-sensical (though implausible) form: developing countries need to implement human rights and respect democracy and the rule of law, then economic development will follow. Conversely, if these conditions are not met, then development cannot be expected.

This obscures the fact that in the developed countries, industrial development—financed by massive colonial exploitation[129]—financed the realization of rights and democracy. An understanding of the role and *scale* of colonial exploitation in European development is vital to any honest understanding of the history of development. The role of colonialism is elucidated by W E B Du Bois:

It is...a new democratic nation composed of united capital and labor...that is exploiting the world...the laborer's equity is recognized...Such nations it is that rule the modern world. Their national bond...is increased wealth, power, and luxury for all classes on a scale the world never saw before....Whence comes this new wealth and on what does its accumulation depend? It comes primarily from the darker nations of the world—Asia and Africa, South and Central America, the West Indies and the islands of the South Seas.[130]

For George Orwell, the key was:

[T]he prosperity of British capitalism [and]...the maintenance of the British Empire, for the wealth of England was drawn largely from Asia and Africa. The standard of

---

[127] 'WTO & Human Rights' (n 119).

[128] 'Finding the Peripheries' (n 27); J Newsinger, *The Blood Never Dried: A People's History of the British Empire* (Bookmarks London 2006); *Late Victorian Holocausts* (n 19); *Open Veins of Latin America* (n 19).

[129] *Open Veins of Latin America* (n 19).   [130] 'The African Roots of War' (n 75) 709.

living of the trade-union workers…depended indirectly on the sweating of Indian coolies.[131]

The issue of scale is also critical:

In 1947…Malayan rubber was the British Empire's biggest dollar earner, bringing in $200 million, compared with the $180 million earned by British manufacturing industry… Between 1946 and 1951 the colonial sterling balances held in London increased from £760 million to £920 million, a massive transfer of funds that gives lie to the pious rhetoric… regarding colonial development.[132]

Colonial expansion and exploitation *directly financed* European development. Without this the evolution of civil and political rights would not have been possible. The Vienna Human Rights Conference's famous indivisibility and interdependence of human rights[133] is true only in a counter-intuitive fashion: only if the material wants represented by 'second generation' rights are adequately satisfied can 'first generation' rights be realized or respected. Respect for any and all human rights requires material wealth; consequently such respect cannot be made a precondition for accessing wealth.

More importantly, the false history and modern myth also disguise the fact that the living standards currently enjoyed in the developed world are *subsidized by* the continuing exploitation of the developing world: there are not sufficient resources for everyone to enjoy our 'developed' lifestyle.[134] The promise of development cannot be realized, and human rights critiques function to disguise this fact by setting impossible conditions for the entitlement to develop.

4 CONCLUSION

Almost a century ago, Du Bois raised the central question of colonial poverty:

How can love of humanity appeal as a motive to nations whose love of luxury is built on the inhuman exploitation of human beings, and who…have been taught to regard these human beings as inhuman?[135]

---

[131] G Orwell, 'The Lion and the Unicorn (1941)' in *The Collected Essays, Journalism and Letters of George Orwell* (S Orwell and I Angus eds) (4 vols Secker and Warburg London 1968) vol 2, 74–133, at 113.

[132] *The Blood Never Dried* (n 128) 207.

[133] Office of the High Commissioner for Human Rights, 'Vienna Declaration and Programme of Action' (25 June 1993) UN Doc A/CONF.157/23 para 5.

[134] 'Humanity Falls Deeper into Ecological Debt' (n 25).

[135] 'The African Roots of War' (n 75) 712.

This remains apt in a decolonized world, in which love of humanity will not mo-tivate action on a sufficient scale.[136] Worse, now that we have been taught not to perceive the dehumanization of others, we are unlikely to link the luxuries of our lives with the deprivations of theirs.

The love of humanity—whether institutionalized as human rights or not—can however function very adequately to allow us to misunderstand the problem of world poverty, and thus to efface our implication therein. If poverty is under-stood as being caused by a combination of geography and localized human rights abuses, then any intervention on our part seems altruistic, an illustration of our humanity and charity. This has two important effects: our charity is always cur-tailed by our love of luxury; and the predicament of the world is fundamentally misrepresented.

Charity encourages us to believe in our entitlement to what we already have; and our generosity should we choose to share from this. In this para-digm, 'we' are normal—indeed we are the norm—and hence justified. We have no implication in 'their' problems. It is through goodwill that we inter-vene (charity) to help them overcome *misfortune* (not *injustice*),[137] to become more like us; to follow in the imaginary footsteps of our inverted history. In the sense developed by Marks, this creates a 'false' understanding of the world;[138] an understanding where much of importance is neglected or rel-egated to the shadows. Effects are perceived as causes and inappropriate solu-tions are imposed.

As a result, human rights are not only the wrong lens through which to ana-lyse the relationship of law and development, they are the worst possible lens. The comforting story of law identifying wrongs, categorizing them as rights abuses, codifying, and being implemented to effect their reduction, or eventual eradica-tion, is simply false. The progress narrative is prima facie falsified by the signal lack of 'progress'. The law has persevered with its original tasks: the production and perpetuation of poverty, and the direction and regulation of the resource flows this facilitates.

The standards by which the human rights movement 'neutrally' evaluates the world not only enshrine a very Western Eurocentric understanding of humanity and society, they also—more importantly—require our economic privilege for their practical realization. Human rights compliance does not make a society rich, quite the contrary; a society must already be rich in order to afford human rights compliance.

---

[136] L Abu-Lughod, *Do Muslim Women Need Saving?* (Harvard University Press Cambridge MA 2013).

[137] This key distinction is developed in JN Shklar, *The Faces of Injustice* (Yale University Press New Haven 1992).

[138] 'False Contingency' (n 102) 16.

However, by allowing themselves to become embroiled in an inverted history, human rights have degenerated into—or revealed their essence as[139]—instruments of stasis; techniques to ensure the stability of the *status quo*. By understanding rights as a cause, not an effect, of development, this discourse deprives the impoverished of even the moral right to develop. While international law denies the poor the conditions to attain material development, human rights analysis denies 'developing countries' the conditions to *deserve* material development or equality.

Global poverty occupies a unique position as both the 'blind spot' and *raison d'être* of an international legal system that has long attempted to secure a veneer of cooperation, justice, and legitimacy over a reality of competition, conquest, and exploitation. As such, it vividly illustrates the radical indeterminacy, and 'schizophrenia' that 'tear apart the fragile structure'[140] of international law. That this contradiction appears to be little analysed, that there is so little conversation to detail, is testament to the strategies deployed to naturalize, excuse, and obscure the 'fact' of poverty. It is time finally to confront our implication in, and subsidization by, the perpetuation of extreme global poverty.

---

[139] R Tuck, *The Rights of War and Peace: Political Thought and the International Order from Grotius to Kant* (OUP Oxford 2001) at 168–72.

[140] 'Faith and Resignation' (n 80); JA Beckett, 'Rebel Without a Cause? Martti Koskenniemi and the Critical Legal Project' (2006) 7 *German Law Journal* 1045–88.

CHAPTER 48

FRAGMENTATION AND CONSTITUTIONALIZATION

ANNE PETERS

1 INTRODUCTION

FRAGMENTATION and constitutionalization, understood as processes, seem to be two trends in the evolution of international law. Because both are a matter of degree and are not linear developments, the empirical claim that one or both phenomena are legally relevant beyond minimal or anecdotal episodes is contested. Moreover, each phenomenon is evaluated differently (for example, as constituting a risk or opportunity for international law as a whole) by different observers. The diverging assessments are to some extent pre-shaped by the fact that both fragmentation and constitutionalization are inevitably descriptive-evaluative—and thus loaded—terms. 'Fragmentation' has a negative connotation, and is used as a pejorative term (rather than diversity, specialization, or pluralism). 'Constitutionalization', in contrast, feeds on the positive ring of the concept of constitution. Finally, both constitutionalization and fragmentation are terms that describe not only legal processes in the real world of law but are also labels for the accompanying discourses (mostly among academics, less so among judges, and even less so among political law-making actors). The putative trends so far do not have a clearly definable end-result, such as a completely fragmented international legal order on the one hand, or a world constitution on the other. Rather, the state of the law resulting from these processes is in itself a matter of contestable conceptualization.

2 FRAGMENTATION

2.1 Evolution

The term 'fragmentation of international law' denotes both a process and the result of that process, namely a (relatively) fragmented state of the law. The diagnosis refers to the dynamic growth of new and specialized sub-fields of international law after 1989, to the rise of new actors beside states (international organizations, non-governmental organizations (NGOs), and multinational corporations) and to new types of international norms outside the acknowledged sources.

The evolution was triggered by the break-down of the communist bloc in 1989 which brought to an end the stable bipolar world order. In the wake of the post-Cold War 'new world order' (to use United States (US) President George HW Bush's term), a host of multilateral treaties were concluded: the *Rio Conventions* and numerous hard and soft environmental instruments were adopted in 1992, the membership of the *ICSID Convention* and the number of bilateral investment treaties exploded.[1] New organizations and other permanent international bodies were founded, such as the World Trade Organization (WTO) in 1994. New international courts and tribunals were established, in particular the Yugoslavia and other ad hoc international criminal tribunals (1992 onwards), the WTO dispute settlement body (1994), the International Criminal Court (ICC) (created by the *Rome Statute* in 1998 and functional since 2003),[2] and the International Tribunal for the Law of the Sea (1996). Investment arbitration increased dramatically, and the European Court of Human Rights (ECtHR) was transformed into a permanent Court with direct access for individuals in 1998.

By the end of the 1990s, the 'proliferation'[3] of these international dispute settlement institutions gave rise to a fear that specialized courts and tribunals bodies

---

[1] *Convention on the Settlement of Investment Disputes between States and Nationals of Other States* (opened for signature 18 March 1965, entered into force 14 October 1966) 575 UNTS 159.

[2] *Rome Statute of the International Criminal Court* (opened for signature 17 July 1998, entered into force 1 July 2002) 2187 UNTS 90.

[3] 'Symposium Issue: The Proliferation of International Tribunals: Piecing Together the Puzzle' (1999) 31 *New York University Journal of International Law and Politics* 679–933.

would 'develop greater variations in their determinations of general international law' and thereby 'damage the coherence of the international legal system'.[4] This concern was most prominently voiced by the then President of the International Court of Justice (ICJ), Judge Gilbert Guillaume, in his speech to the UN General Assembly in 2001.[5] The articulation of this 'problem' by that office-holder was later criticized as a hegemonic attempt of a professional to preserve the power of the World Court.[6]

Against this background, the International Law Commission tackled the topic in 2000,[7] and a study group was established that issued successive reports.[8] The heyday of the academic fragmentation debate was the first decade of the new millennium. Pierre-Marie Dupuy devoted his 2000 General Course in the Hague Summer Academy to the issue.[9] A symposium on 'diversity or cacophony' was held at Michigan Law School and resulted in a 500 page journal issue in 2004.[10] In 2007 still, fragmentation was 'le sujet à la mode'.[11] But by 2015, the constatation was: 'farewell to fragmentation'.[12]

2.2 Causes

The causes of fragmentation seem to be both functional and political. First of all, fragmentation is built into the decentralized structure of international law which results from the absence of a central world legislator. Secondly, and connected to the first cause, fragmentation originates in the domestic

---

[4] JI Charney, 'Is International Law Threatened by Multiple International Tribunals?' (1998) 271 *Recueil des Cours* 101–382, at 371.

[5] G Guillaume, 'Speech by HE Judge Gilbert Guillaume, President of the International Court of Justice, to the General Assembly of the United Nations' (30 October 2001) <http://www.icj-cij.org/court/index.php?pr=82&pt=3&p1=1&p2=3&p3=1> [accessed 3 March 2016].

[6] See eg M Prost, *The Concept of Unity in International Law* (Hart Oxford 2012) at 202–9.

[7] As a first text, see G Hafner, 'Risks Ensuing from Fragmentation of International Law' (2000) *Yearbook of the International Law Commission* vol 2, pt 2, annex, at 143–50.

[8] International Law Commission, 'Fragmentation of International Law: Difficulties arising from the Diversification and Expansion of International Law' (13 April 2006) UN Doc A/CN.4/L.682; International Law Commission, 'Draft Conclusion of the Work of the Study Group' (2 May 2006) UN Doc A/CN.4/L.682/Add.1; International Law Commission, 'Fragmentation of International Law: Difficulties arising from the Diversification and Expansion of International Law' (18 July 2006) UN Doc A/CN.4/L.702.

[9] P-M Dupuy, 'L'unité de l'ordre juridique international' (2002) 297 *Recueil des Cours* 9–490.

[10] 'Symposium: Diversity or Cacophony: New Sources of Norms in International Law' (2004) 25 *Michigan Journal of International Law* 845–1375.

[11] B Conforti, 'L'Unité et fragmentation du droit international: "Glissez, mortels, n'appuyez pas!"' (2007) 111 *Revue générale de droit international public* 5–18, at 5–10.

[12] M Andenas and E Bjorge (eds) *A Farewell to Fragmentation: Reassertion and Convergence in International Law* (CUP Cambridge 2015).

sphere: different issue areas are handled by different departments of government which negotiate different treaties, and different administrative authorities then apply them. Thirdly, fragmentation is a response to globalization. Global problems (ranging from climate deterioration to migration and terrorism to the financial crisis) have triggered a demand for more international—and also more specialized—regulation.

From the perspective of global constitutionalism, the political causes may be more interesting. Realist analyses have depicted fragmentation as the result of a deliberate agenda of powerful States. Benvenisti and Downs have argued that fragmentation serves the latters' interests because it limits the bargaining power of weaker states (which cannot group up within one forum but are isolated in a multitude of settings) and because only those states with a greater 'agenda-setting power' can easily create alternative regimes which suit their interests better.[13] While it is not clear whether Benvenisti and Downs have—beyond the anecdotal examples given—revealed a behavioural pattern that is strategically motivated and in fact has hegemonic effects,[14] their analysis has the merit of politicizing the seemingly technical fragmentation debate.

2.3 Risks and Opportunities

Fragmentation (and the pluralism that accompanies it) may enhance both the effectiveness and the legitimacy of international law and its application—but only when it is channelled by constitutional principles and procedures. On the other hand, the institutional, procedural, and substantive diversification called 'fragmentation' indeed bears risks. The most important one is a loss of coherence which in turn implies the loss of international law's quality as a legal order (or system). An agglomeration of isolated and diverse norms does not amount to a legal order.[15] A legal order is present only when norms refer to each other (ordered norms). But legal order means not only ordered law but also order through law. These two dimensions are mutually reinforcing: the normative pull of international law is fortified by its stringency and consistency. Understanding this interrelationship means understanding why consistency is particularly important for international law (more so than for domestic law): because its normative power is more precarious.

---

[13] E Benvenisti and GW Downs, 'The Empire's New Clothes: Political Economy and the Fragmentation of International Law' (2007) 60 *Stanford Law Review* 595–631, at 615.

[14] Critically M Zürn and B Faude, 'On Fragmentation, Differentiation and Coordination' (2013) 13 *Global Environmental Politics* 119–30, at 125–6.

[15] HLA Hart, *The Concept of Law* (PA Bullock and J Raz eds) (3rd edn Clarendon Press Oxford 2012 [1961]) at 234.

So what is at stake in fragmentation is unity, harmony, cohesion, order, and—concomitantly—the quality of international law as law. It is (too) easy to psychologize and thereby disparage these concerns as a 'postmodern anxiety' in a world which has lost stable values.[16] Rather, the justified concern is that international law could 'no longer be a singular endeavor,... but merely an empty rhetorical device that loosely describes the ambit of the various discourses in question'.[17] Without some glue holding together the 'special regimes' and 'institutional components', writes Georges Abi-Saab, 'the special regime becomes a legal order unto itself—a kind of legal Frankenstein' that 'no longer partakes in the same basis of legitimacy and formal standards of pertinence'.[18] So ultimately, at the bottom of the fragmentation debate lies, just as in the constitutionalization debate, a concern for a loss of legitimacy of international law, a loss which will ultimately threaten that law's very existence.

3 CONSTITUTIONALIZATION

3.1 Key Terms

The debate on constitutionalization suffers from the great variety of meanings assigned to its key terms. I will here use *constitutionalization* as the label for the evolution from an international order based on some organizing principles such as state sovereignty, territorial integrity, and consensualism to an international legal order which acknowledges and has creatively appropriated and—importantly—modified principles, institutions, and procedures of constitutionalism.

Global constitutionalism is an intellectual movement which both reconstructs some features and functions of international law (in the interplay with domestic law) as 'constitutional' and even 'constitutionalist' (positive analysis), and also seeks to provide arguments for their further development in a specific direction (normative analysis). The function of constitutional law normally is to found, to organize, to integrate and to stabilize a political community, to contain political

---

[16] See M Koskenniemi and P Leino, 'Fragmentation of International Law? Postmodern Anxieties' (2002) 15 *Leiden Journal of International Law* 533–79.

[17] M Craven, 'Unity, Diversity, and the Fragmentation of International Law' (2003) 14 *Finnish Yearbook of International Law* 3–34, at 5.

[18] G Abi-Saab, 'Fragmentation or Unification: Some Concluding Remarks' (1999) 31 *New York University Journal of International Law and Politics* 919–33, at 926.

power, to provide normative guidance, and to regulate the governance activities of law-making, law-application, and law-enforcement. The desired constitution-alist elements are notably the rule of law, containment of political (and possibly economic) power through checks and balances, fundamental rights protection, ac-countability, democracy (or proxies such as participation, inclusion, deliberation, and transparency), and solidarity.[19]

Importantly, the constitutionalization of international law is accompanied and co-constituted by the *internationalization* (or globalization) of state con-stitutions consisting in the (re-)importation of international precepts (such as human rights standards) into national constitutional texts and case law, which simultaneously brings about a 'horizontal' convergence of national constitutional law.[20]

The scattered legal texts and case law together might form a body of *global con-stitutional law*,[21] a specific subset of law, drawing both on international law and on domestic law, which has a particular normative 'constitutional' status, and the abovementioned specific 'constitutional' functions. This body is not united in one single document called 'world constitution'. Global constitutional law instead con-sists of fundamental norms which serve a constitutional function for the inter-national legal system at large or for specific international organizations or regimes, as well as norms that have taken over or reinforce constitutional functions of domestic law.[22]

3.2 Key Debates

Historically speaking, the constitutionalization debate is full of false friends. Although the concept of a 'constitution of the international legal community' had been spelled out in the interwar period by the Austrian Alfred Verdross,[23] that con-ceptualization is not at the roots of the contemporary debate.[24] In the 1990s, eminent German authors diagnosed an erosion of the consent principle (and hence an erosion

[19] Matthias Kumm and others have called the 'commitment to human rights, democracy, and the rule of law' the 'trinitarian mantra of the constitutionalist faith': M Kumm et al., 'How Large is the World of Global Constitutionalism?' (2014) 3 *Global Constitutionalism* 1–8, at 3.

[20] A Peters, 'The Globalisation of State Constitutions' in J Nijman and A Nollkaemper (eds), *New Perspectives on the Divide between National and International Law* (OUP Oxford 2007) 251–308.

[21] I use the term 'global' and 'international' interchangeably, although the former denotes better the multilevel quality of the body of constitutional law at stake.

[22] T Kleinlein and A Peters, 'International Constitutional Law' in A Carty (ed), *Oxford Bibliographies in International Law* (OUP Oxford 2014) <http://www.oxfordbibliographies.com/view/document/obo-9780199796953/obo-9780199796953-0039.xml> [accessed 3 March 2016].

[23] A Verdross, *Die Verfassung der Völkerrechtsgemeinschaft* (Springer Wien 1926).

[24] See E Lagrange, 'Retour sur un classique: A Verdross, *Die Verfassung der Völkerrechtsgemeinschaft* 1926' (2008) 112 *Revue générale de droit international public* 973–84.

of state sovereignty) and a rise of the 'international community'.[25] These writings are (maybe against the authors' intentions) in hindsight considered as the initiators of the contemporary debate. Ironically, the *topos* of constitutionalization at that time appeared in the law of international organizations whose founding documents have long been understood to be both treaties and constitutions[26]—and thus within sectoral, possibly fragmented regimes. The ICJ described the documents' hybridity as follows: '[f]rom a formal standpoint, the constituent instruments of international organizations are multilateral treaties...But the constituent instruments of international organizations are also treaties of a particular type'.[27] These debates referred to the United Nations (UN), the European Union (EU), and the WTO. But the structural features of those regimes which are pinpointed as being 'constitutional' actually differ dramatically from organization to organization, and accordingly the meaning of 'constitutionalization' of the respective regimes differs widely as well.

Some variants of constitutionalism beyond the state are extremely diluted, when constitutionalism is considered not as a matter of positive norms and 'doctrine', but (only) as a discourse and a vocabulary with a symbolic value, as a constitutionalist 'imagination'.[28] Other strands of the debate relate less to international law proper and rather more to the constitutional law of states, constitutional comparison, borrowing, and migration. Two journals, the *Journal of International Constitutional Law* or *ICON* (founded in 2002) and the *Journal of Global Constitutionalism* (founded in 2011) are forums for this strand. To the extent that constitutionalization covers both international law and domestic law, and is to that extent inevitably a multilevel phenomenon in which the various levels of law and governance may also compensate for each others' deficiencies ('compensatory constitutionalism'[29]

---

[25] B Simma, 'From Bilateralism to Community Interests in International Law' (1994) 250 *Recueil des Cours* 217–384; C Tomuschat, 'Obligations Arising for States without or against their Will' (1993) 241 *Recueil des Cours* 195–374, at 209–40. Simma is a 'disciple' of Verdross.

[26] A Peters, 'Das Gründungsdokument internationaler Organisationen als Verfassungsvertrag' (2013) 68 *Zeitschrift für öffentliches Recht* 1–57. See also A Peters, 'The Constitutionalisation of International Organisations' in N Walker, J Shaw, and S Tierney (eds), *Europe's Constitutional Mosaic* (Hart Oxford 2011) 253–85.

[27] *Legality of the Use by a State of Nuclear Weapons in Armed Conflict* (Advisory Opinion) [1996] ICJ Rep 66, at [19]. For the official terms, see *Constitution of the United Nations Educational, Scientific and Cultural Organization* (signed 16 November 1945, entered into force 4 November 1946) 4 UNTS 52; *Constitution of the World Health Organization* (signed 22 July 1946, entered into force 7 April 1948) 4 UNTS 221; *Constitution of the International Labour Organization* (signed 9 October 1946 entered into force 28 May 1947) 38 UNTS 583; *Constitution of the Food and Agricultural Organization of the United Nations* (signed 16 October 1945 adopted) [1946–7] *United Nations Yearbook* 693; *Constitution of the International Telecommunication Union* (signed 22 December 1992, entered into force 1 July 1994) 1825 UNTS 330. The aborted *Treaty Establishing a Constitution for Europe* (signed 29 October 2004) OJ 2004 C/310/1 had captured the hybridity in its official name.

[28] N Walker, 'Constitutionalism and Pluralism in Global Context' in M Avbelj and J Komárek (eds), *Constitutional Pluralism in the European Union and Beyond* (Hart Oxford 2011) 17–37.

[29] A Peters, 'Compensatory Constitutionalism: The Function and Potential of Fundamental International Norms and Structures' (2006) 19 *Leiden Journal of International Law* 579–610.

or 'supplementary constitutionalism'[30]), these discourses form part of the broader stream of constitutionalization too.

The constitutionalization debate has been initiated in continental Europe.[31] The early debate was strong among German public lawyers, not least due to their obsession with the state and initial doubts about severing the concept of the constitution from the state.[32] The discussion has meanwhile been picked up in the United Kingdom (UK),[33] in the US,[34] and in Japan.[35] The ideational background of the proponents of global constitutionalism may be a more or less openly Catholic (neo)jus-naturalism,[36] cosmopolitanism,[37] republicanism,[38] general systems theory,[39] discourse theory,[40] functionalism[41] and constitutional economics,[42] social constructivism,[43] social contract theory,[44] critical legal studies,[45] or agnostic. The co-existence of highly divergent

[30] J Dunoff and J Trachtman, 'A Functional Approach to International Constitutionalization' in J Dunoff and J Trachtman (eds), *Ruling the World? Constitutionalism, International Law, and Global Governance* (CUP Cambridge 2009) 3–35, at 14–18.

[31] J Klabbers, A Peters, and G Ulfstein, *The Constitutionalization of International Law* (expanded edn OUP Oxford 2011).

[32] See especially D Grimm, 'Does Europe Need a Constitution?' (1995) 1 *European Law Journal* 282–307.

[33] 'Constitutionalism and Pluralism in Global Context' (n 28).

[34] 'A Functional Approach to International Constitutionalization' (n 30).

[35] T Mogami, 'Towards *Jus Contra Oligarchiam*: A Note on Critical Constitutionalism' (2012) 55 *Japanese Yearbook of International Law* 371–402.

[36] AA Cançado Trindade, 'International Law for Humankind: Towards a New *Jus Gentium*: Part I' (2005) 316 *Recueil des Cours* 9–444; R Domingo, *The New Global Law* (CUP Cambridge 2010). Verdross would have to be counted here, too: see *Die Verfassung der Völkerrechtsgemeinschaft* (n 23).

[37] Habermas used Kant's concept of a 'cosmopolitan status' ('*weltbürgerlicher Zustand*') to demand the transformation of international law into a law of and for the global citizen: J Habermas, 'Does the Constitutionalization of International Law Still Have a Chance?' in *The Divided West* (C Cronin ed and trans) (Polity Press Cambridge 2006) 115–210; D Archibugi, *The Global Commonwealth of Citizens: Toward Cosmopolitan Democracy* (Princeton University Press Princeton 2008); M Kumm, 'The Cosmopolitan Turn in Constitutionalism: On the Relationship between Constitutionalism in and beyond the State' in *Ruling the World? Constitutionalism, International Law, and Global Governance* (n 30) 258–324; G Wallace Brown, 'The Constitutionalization of What?' (2012) 1 *Global Constitutionalism* 201–28.

[38] A Emmerich-Fritsche, *Vom Völkerrecht zum Weltrecht* (Duncker & Humblot Berlin 2007).

[39] G Teubner, *Constitutional Fragments: Societal Constitutionalism and Globalization* (OUP Oxford 2012).

[40] T Kleinlein, *Konstitutionalisierung im Völkerrecht: Konstruktion und Elemente einer idealistischen Völkerrechtslehre* (Springer Berlin 2012).

[41] 'A Functional Approach to International Constitutionalization' (n 30).

[42] JP Trachtman, *The Future of International Law: Global Government* (CUP Cambridge 2013) ch 11 ('International Legal Constitutionalization').

[43] O Diggelmann and T Altwicker, 'Is There Something Like a Constitution of International Law? A Critical Analysis of the Debate on World Constitutionalism' (2008) 68 *Zeitschrift für ausländisches öffentliches Recht und Völkerrecht* 623–50.

[44] M Rosenfeld, 'Is Global Constitutionalism Meaningful or Desirable?' (2014) 25 *European Journal of International Law* 177–99.

[45] CEJ Schwöbel, *Global Constitutionalism in International Legal Perspective* (Martinus Nijhoff Leiden 2011). The author propagates an 'organic constitutionalism' as a 'negative universal' based on Ernesto Laclau and Jacques Derrida: see especially at 158–65.

sources of inspiration on the one hand creates the danger of empty talk that is only seemingly a real discourse on an agreed topic. On the other hand, the pluralism of outlooks underlying the debate might be more positively assessed as demonstrating that global constitutionalism does not need a particular ideational foundation, but can build on an overlapping consensus.

3.3 Criticism

Sceptics of constitutionalization (as a phenomenon and as a label) often highlight the lack of 'politics' on the international plane (see also below Section 7).[46] For example, it is (correctly) pointed out that there 'is no political movement in sight that would move the international system in a constitutional direction', and that '[c]onstitutionalization talk is the denial of this situation'; it is just a vain attempt of 'talking up the system'.[47] '[T]he constitutionalization of international law, qua compensation for the absence of such political power, becomes hoisted by its own petard and, hence, part of the mess that it set out to clean up', writes Alexander Somek.[48]

A related stance is the insistence on an intrinsic link between popular sovereignty and constitutionalism, all the while pointing out that the former element is absent in the international sphere.[49] To the extent that these objections associate 'politics' with 'democracy', they all lead to the conclusion that the absence of a genuine global *pouvoir constituant* (and/or the absence of a global democratic process) renders constitutionalization talk meaningless.

Finally, a fundamental pluralist critique is that the political, economic, intellectual, and moral diversity of the world population makes constitutionalism both unachievable and illegitimate. Any constitutional arrangement would be imposed by one group on the others, and would thus be perceived as an imperial tool rather than as an expression of common self-government.[50] But this critique is effectively countered by the concept of pluralist constitutionalism (see below Section 5.2), however difficult this might be to realize on a global scale.

[46] Cf P Dobner and M Loughlin (eds), *The Twilight of Constitutionalism?* (OUP Oxford 2010).

[47] A Somek, 'From the Rule of Law to the Constitutionalist Makeover: Changing European Conceptions of Public International Law' (2011) 18 *Constellations* 567–88, at 578: constitutionalism is merely 're-description rather than reform'.

[48] Ibid 583.

[49] For Habermas, following Kant, a constitution deserving that name must be 'republican', established by the citizens to govern their affairs: 'Does the Constitutionalization of International Law Still Have a Chance?' (n 37) 133. Because this type of democratic foundation and a global political power to enforce the law are lacking on the international plane, international law as it stands is only a 'proto-constitution': ibid.

[50] N Krisch, *Beyond Constitutionalism: The Pluralist Structure of Postnational Law* (OUP Oxford 2010) ch 2.

4 THE RELATIONSHIP OF THE DEBATES

Often the scholarly diagnosis of constitutionalization and the academic or political quest for reinforcing the putative trend is depicted as a conscious or subconscious reaction against fragmentation; as a quest (formulated mainly by scholars) to counter that fragmentation (perceived as a threat) and to remedy its (presumably negative) consequences: 'constitutionalism as a means of solving fragmentation problems'.[51] For example, Joel Trachtman notes '[i]n the fragmentation context, constitutionalization … can be seen as a way of introducing hierarchy and order—or at least a set of coordinating mechanisms—into a chaotic system otherwise marked by proliferating institutions and norms'.[52]

Some observers framing the debate in that way chastise the idea of global constitutionalism as a naïve desire to recreate unity and harmony in international law.[53] From that perspective, an international constitution is (erroneously) hailed by its protagonists as a remedy against the threat of fragmentation, as a (vain) attempt to preserve order, stability and values, while in reality pluralism bordering on chaos reigns.

Contrary to that stance, this contribution does not depict global constitutionalism as holistic and thus naïve, but seeks to highlight that fragmentation and constitutionalization (both as legal processes and as accompanying discourses) stand in a more sophisticated inter-relationship and are mutually constitutive: On the one hand, constitutionalization phenomena within international law have exacerbated fragmentation, because they have from the outset taken place at multiple sites, and have produced only constitutional fragments. On the other hand, fragmentation in turn has triggered new forms of constitutionalization in international law; the processes of fragmentation are themselves being 'constitutionalized'. Put differently, constitutionalization (as a process) and global constitutionalism (as an intellectual framework) is profoundly shaping how law-appliers deal with fragmentation.

Moreover, both debates are largely motivated by a common root concern, namely the concern about the legitimacy[54] of international law. Both phenomena also share the merit of promoting contestation and politicization[55] within the

---

[51] A van Aaken, 'Defragmentation of Public International Law through Interpretation: A Methodological Proposal' (2009) 16 *Indiana Journal of Global Legal Studies* 483–512, at 487. See also JG van Mulligen, 'Global Constitutionalism and the Objective Purport of the International Legal Order' (2011) 24 *Leiden Journal of International Law* 277–304, at 284: 'Constitutionalism's anti-fragmentational virtue may indeed be said to represent its prime rationale, impetus, and driving force'.

[52] *The Future of International Law: Global Government* (n 42) 251–2.

[53] See eg J Klabbers, 'Constitutionalism Lite' (2004) 1 *International Organizations Law Review* 31–58, at 49.

[54] I will revert to this in Section 8.   [55] See on politicization below in Section 7.

international legal process; they are kindred spirits. The remainder of this chapter will explore the relationship between fragmentation and constitutionalization in more detail.

5 FRAGMENTED CONSTITUTIONALIZATION

5.1 Constitutional Fragments

The co-existence of diverse regimes within international law, the disrupted and sometimes reversed constitutionalization processes, the multilevel quality of global constitutional law, and sectoral constitutionalization (of the UN, the EU, the WTO, the ECtHR, and so on); all these phenomena preclude any conceptualization of constitutionalization as the emergence of a 'super-constitution' which would lie both 'above' domestic state constitutions and which would engulf the separate international regimes, too. Rather, constitutionalization (if we want to speak of it) is itself fragmented. We see *constitutional fragments* in different issue areas of law and governance (and on different 'levels' of governance), which interact with each other, sometimes converging but also conflicting.[56] Besides, the intellectual framework of constitutionalism is fragmented, too.

But is the notion of fragmentary constitutionalization and fragmentary constitutionalism not a contradiction in terms (or at least a dilution which renders the terms meaningless)? When different organizations have their own constitution, how can they still be members of a global constitutional order? Can constitutionalization and constitutionalism only be uniform and complete, or not be at all? Indeed, traditional Continental and US–American constitutionalism tended to be holistic in a dual sense, namely that one single constitutional document was supposed to provide a both *harmonious* and *complete* legal and political basis for societal life.

However, in the multilevel governance arrangements under conditions of globalization, both features have waned. First, even state constitutions do not govern or regulate all governance acts unfolding effects for their citizens and within their territorial borders. Secondly, within constitutional states' sub units, for example states within federal states, or local communities, often have their own constitutions. Thirdly, in culturally diverse societies the value-bases of shared, implicit norms carrying the legal constitution are crumbling too. So while it is true that the

---

[56] *Constitutional Fragments: Societal Constitutionalism and Globalization* (n 39) 52.

very idea of 'fragmented' (that is, multiple and multilevel) constitutionalism implicitly gives up the claim to totality, this idea better describes real-life phenomena (within and among states) than the more traditional holistic notion of constitution.

I submit that the abovementioned *multiple processes of constitutionalization* do not cancel each other out but are apt to co-exist, to reinforce each other and even mutually to compensate each others' deficiencies. Global constitutionalism relates to multilevel governance, implying nested constitutional orders, and covering various subfields of the law. Besides, members of a global constitutional order, notably nation states and international organizations, may have their own sectoral constitution. Finally, constitutional substance may be dispersed 'vertically' across different levels of the law and 'horizontally' across areas of the law. Overall, this means that the existence, growth, and sometimes regression of multiple constitutions and of fragmented constitutional law can still be reasonably qualified as manifestations of constitutionalism.

5.2 Pluralist Constitutionalism

In terms of normative substance, constitutionalism (within states and beyond states) is not and should no longer be, as James Tully put it, 'the empire of uniformity'.[57] Constitutionalism has been reconceptualized by Tully so as to 'recognize and accommodate cultural diversity'.[58] This recasting is relevant for global constitutionalism, because global constitutionalism is conceivable, if at all, only as pluralist constitutionalism.[59] Pluralism is used here as a label for a normative position which welcomes the multiplicity, diversity, and overlap of legal (sub-)orders, of rules and principles, of sources of authority, of norm-producing actors and institutions in various sectors and levels of governance that stand in a non-hierarchical relationship to each other (in the absence of a meta-norm, an overarching *Grundnorm*, or the like, to resolve the competing claims for validity, authority, supremacy), and which also welcomes the plurality of values and perspectives espoused by the multiple actors. This type of pluralism may go hand in hand with constitutionalism.

Pluralism does not require 'that each good should be pursued by an autonomous regime. It may well turn out that a relatively consolidated form of global constitutionalism, rather than unregulated global legal pluralism, is the best way to ensure

---

[57] J Tully, *Strange Multiplicity: Constitutionalism in an Age of Diversity* (CUP Cambridge 1995) ch 5.
[58] Ibid 1 and 58.
[59] A Peters, 'Rechtsordnungen und Konstitutionalisierung: Zur Neubestimmung der Verhältnisse' (2010) 65 *Zeitschrift für öffentliches Recht* 3–63. On 'constitutional pluralism', see also JL Cohen, *Globalization and Sovereignty: Rethinking Legality, Legitimacy, and Constitutionalism* (CUP Cambridge 2012) at ix, 45, 70.

a healthy pluralism of [human] values. Value fragmentation does not dictate institutional fragmentation'.[60]

Most importantly, 'pluralism' alone is not sufficient as a guideline for ordering a society, because it does not say anything about its own limits. Some additional principles, whether democracy, individual freedom, equality, mutual respect, and so forth, are needed, otherwise, 'global legal pluralism might end up consecrating a ruthless world governed…by "nothing other than the advantage of the stronger"' law-applying institution.[61] Therefore, constitutional principles and procedures are needed to constructively deal with pluralism (and fragmentation), notably to protect the weaker actors in international relations. To these we now turn.

6 CONSTITUTIONALIZING FRAGMENTATION

6.1 Processes and Techniques

The fragmentation of international law can be (better) managed, and its benefits can be harvested to the extent that it is constitutionalized. By 'constitutionalizing' fragmentation, we understand three processes. First, the substantive integration of some issue areas, inter alia, through accepting and applying common transversal ('constitutional') norms to accommodate multiplicity. Secondly, the strategy of developing and applying procedural techniques for creating compatibility of principles and rules stemming from different areas. Among these is the constitutional technique of balancing, which is applied to reconcile the competing spheres of autonomy of relevant actors (for example, states and international organizations). Thirdly and finally, the constitutionalization of fragmentation consists in the establishment (or reform) of bodies with a mandate to coordinate different treaties and regimes. This includes, importantly, a 'constitutional' 'framework of mutual recognition and contestation and of checks and balances between sites and their different claims to authority'.[62] The principles, techniques, and bodies that deal with discrepancy, collisions, and conflict may appropriately be called 'constitutional' elements of the international legal order because they seek to create compatibility, not only in a 'negative' sense of preventing legal

---

[60] T Isiksel, 'Global Legal Pluralism as Fact and Norm' (2013) 2 *Global Constitutionalism* 160–95, at 190 (emphasis added).

[61] Ibid 195 (citations omitted).

[62] 'Constitutionalism and Pluralism in Global Context' (n 28) 29. See also *Globalization and Sovereignty* (n 59) 70.

conflicts, but also in a supportive, 'positive' sense of seeking to achieve the objectives of other treaties.

Perhaps the modest plea for *internalizing an outside perspective* is more important than institutional fixes. Gunther Teubner observes that the differentiation and autonomization of 'systems' (which seems to include the various international treaty regimes) has resulted in a 'network architecture' of transnational regimes.[63] The important analytical and normative point is that 'each transnational regime needs to combine two contradictory requirements': all regimes spell out their own vision of a global public interest (from their own perspective), while all regimes 'at the same time take account of the whole by transcending their individual perspectives'.[64] 'Each regime must create the overarching *ordre public transnational* from its own perspective', a 'shared horizon of meaning' needs to be constructed, a 'counterfactual assumption of a *common normative core*'.[65] In international judicial practice, a companion to this approach is the 'systemic outlook' asked for by some judges.[66] It seems fair to say that the mentioned 'common core' is a kind of constitution.

6.2 Conflict Avoidance and Reconciliation

Beyond traditional conflict resolution maxims which lead to an 'either/or' application of norms, that is, those which constitute a relationship of mutual exclusiveness of treaties, a reconciliatory approach is now gaining ground. The clearest manifestation of this new approach is found in the three principles enounced in art 20 of the UNESCO *Convention on the Protection and Promotion of the Diversity of Cultural Expressions* (2005) whose heading is: 'Relationship to other treaties: mutual supportiveness, complementarity and non-subordination'.[67] These three principles seek to avoid the binary 'either/or' approach and instead favour the combined and cumulative application of international norms stemming from various treaties.

In the current legal process, law-applying bodies in fact first of all seek to avoid conflict by harmonizing the various international rules rooted in different

---

[63] *Constitutional Fragments: Societal Constitutionalism and Globalization* (n 39) ch 3 ('Transnational Constitutional Subjects: Regimes, Organizations, Networks').

[64] Ibid 161.   [65] Ibid (emphasis added).

[66] See *Whaling in the Antarctic (Australia v Japan)* (Merits) (ICJ, 31 March 2014) at [25] (Separate Opinion of Judge Cançado Trindade).

[67] *Convention on the Protection and Promotion of the Diversity of Cultural Expressions* (opened for signature 20 October 2005, entered into force 18 March 2007) 2440 UNTS 311. In this sense, see also *Cartagena Protocol on Biosafety to the Convention on Biological Diversity* (opened for signature 29 January 2000, entered into force 11 September 2003) 2226 UNTS 208 preamble indent

regimes. This can be done with the help of a presumption of non-deviation.[68] But this presumption faces the same objection that can be raised against the *lex posterior* rule: without an identity of law-makers, the presumption has no basis in their actual intentions.

The presumption of conformity can be reasonably combined with the principle of mutual recognition, based on the idea of functional equivalence of the norms originating from different sources.[69] But this approach fits only when the norms in question do not point in opposite directions (for example, the free importation of animal products versus import restrictions on the basis of animal cruelty concerns), but when they strive towards the same goal, if with different nuances (for example, the protection of property, but in different degrees). The idea of mutual acknowledgement of functional equivalence could be extended beyond the protection of fundamental rights to other constitutional standards, such as the standards of democracy and of the rule of law.

6.3 Principle and Practice of 'Systemic Integration'

Currently the most discussed 'de-fragmentation' technique is the systemic interpretation of international norms. International law-applying bodies have often practised harmonious interpretation, while not necessarily relying on art 31(3)(c) of the *Vienna Convention on the Law of Treaties*,[70] the 'master-key' to the house of international law.[71] Arguably, art 31 allows and even mandates treaty-interpreters to take into account all kinds of 'rules of international law': not only other treaty norms but also customary norms and possibly even soft law. 'Systemic integration' is adequate for the application of customary rules as well, for example for

---

9 (emphasis in original): '*Recognizing* that trade and environment agreements should be mutually supportive...'.

[68] *Al-Jedda v United Kingdom* (ECtHR, Grand Chamber, App No 27021/08, 7 July 2011) at [102]; *Nada v Switzerland* (ECtHR, Grand Chamber, App No 10593/08, 12 September 2012) at [169]–[172], [197]; *Stichting Mothers of Srebrenica v The Netherlands* (ECtHR, App No 65542/12, 11 June 2013) at [139].

[69] For this type of approach, see *Bosphorus v Ireland* (ECtHR, App No 45036/98, 30 June 2005) at [155]. On conflicts between EU law and national human rights protection, see *Solange II* (German Constitutional Court, BVerfGE 73, 22 October 1986) at 339 ff.

[70] *Oil Platforms (Islamic Republic of Iran v United States)* (Judgment) [2003] ICJ Rep 161, at [41]: art XX of the bilateral treaty on friendship between the US and Iran had to be interpreted (relying, inter alia, on art 31(3)(c) of the *Vienna Convention on the Law of Treaties* (opened for signature 23 May 1969, entered into force 27 January 1980) 1155 UNTS 331) in the light of general international law, to the effect that the 'measures' there precluded an unlawful use of force by one party against the other.

[71] This term was coined by now ICJ Judge Hanquin Shue when she still was an ILC member in debates in the ILC: see 'Draft Conclusion of the Work of the Study Group' (n 8) [420].

the identification of the scope of state immunity under due consideration for human rights.

The International Law Commission (ILC) qualifies the 'principle of systemic integration' as a constitutionalist device. That principle:

> articulates the legal-institutional environment in view of *substantive preferences, distributionary choices and political objectives*. This articulation is...important for the critical and constructive development of international institutions...To hold those institutions as fully isolated from each other...is to think of law only as an instrument for attaining regime-objectives. But law is also about protecting rights and enforcing obligations, above all rights and obligations that have a backing in something like a *general, public interest*. Without the principle of 'systemic integration' it would be impossible to give expression to and to keep alive, any *sense of the common good of humankind*, not reducible to the good of any particular institution or 'regime'.[72]

6.4 'Regime Interaction' as Constitutionalization Lite

A pragmatic approach to curb the negative effects and make the most productive use of the potential benefits of fragmentation lies in the practice of treaty bodies or organizations to entertain contacts all the while refusing to lay down guidelines for the resolution of potential conflicts. The only minimal prerequisite for coordination and possibly cooperation seems to be information exchange— potentially with a view to identifying possible common goals (or sub-goals) and shared principles. This phenomenon of institutional contact has been called 'regime interaction'.[73]

This interaction may shape and develop international norms beyond the consent of member states. That law-developing activity therefore requires an additional basis of legitimacy. That basis can be (and is in fact already) created through *participation* (state parties, stakeholder and experts) and *information/reason-giving*.[74] While this framework for regime interaction falls short of 'substantive' constitutionalism, it does amount to a *procedural constitutionalization*, based on procedural principles of inclusion and transparency. Again, the constitutionalist perspective helps to understand and possibly develop the interaction of regimes not as a managerial problem but as a political issue. These principles are precisely apt to counteract the dominance of that regime which is in political terms more powerful than the competing one.

---

[72] 'Draft Conclusion of the Work of the Study Group' (n 8) [480] (emphases added).
[73] MA Young (ed), *Regime Interaction in International Law: Facing Fragmentation* (CUP Cambridge 2012).
[74] MA Young, *Trading Fish, Saving Fish: The Interaction between Regimes in International Law* (CUP Cambridge 2011) at 255–6 and 279–80.

7 FRAGMENTATION, CONSTITUTIONALIZATION, AND POLITICIZATION

A common core concern in debates on both fragmentation and constitutionalization is 'politics', 'politicization', or the lack of both. In the context of fragmentation, 'politicization' is viewed, firstly, as the antidote to 'managerialism': 'the various regimes or boxes—European law, trade law, human rights law, environmental law, investment law and so on' pursue what Martti Koskenniemi has called 'managerialism':

Each regime understood as a purposive association and each institution with the task of realising it. ... *Differentiation does not take place under any single political society.* Instead it works though *a struggle in which every interest is hegemonic,* seeking to describe the social world through its own vocabulary so that its own expertise and its own structural bias will become the rule.[75]

A related, second theme is the insistence on the 'political' cause of fragmentation, namely its (again 'hegemonic') exploitation by powerful states (see above Section 2.2). Along this line it could be said that the specific lines of fragmentation and unity have '*ideological markings*'. Attempts to unify international law would only 'alter the terms by which difference is already expressed and articulated and refragment the terrain along different lines'[76] (and thus merely express different politics).

A third variant of the topic of 'politics' emerged in reaction to the initial focus of the fragmentation debate on international courts and their possibly diverging case law which highlighted the predominance of courts in the international legal process. This diagnosis has been met with the argument that deep normative conflicts arising from the fragmentation of international law could and should be resolved 'politically' (by the global law-makers which are still mainly states) and not 'technically' (by international courts and tribunals).[77] The concern that global constitutionalism is too apolitical, or pretends to be above politics, exactly mirrors that debate. The constitutionalization discourse (pushed by judges and stylized by academics) condones (according to its critics) an impoverished, legalist, and in that sense apolitical conception of constitution.

The call for de-fragmentation and constitutionalization *through global 'politics'* must be taken seriously. However, it suffers from the ambiguity of the terms 'politics' and 'political'. International law might be said to be 'too political' in

---

[75] M Koskenniemi, 'International Law: Between Fragmentation and Constitutionalism' (Paper presented at The Australian National University, Canberra, 27 November 2006) [13]–[14] (emphasis added) <http://www.helsinki.fi/eci/Publications/Koskenniemi/MCanberra_06c.pdf> [accessed 18 February 2016].

[76] 'Unity, Diversity, and the Fragmentation of International Law' (n 17) 34.

[77] 'Draft Conclusion of the Work of the Study Group (n 8) [484].

the sense that the law often just follows the power-relations between states and does not create any strong normativity against politics. From that perspective, a relative 'de-politicization' of international relations (through constitutionalization) is beneficial, because the introduction of constitutional principles contributes to the stability of expectations, legal certainty, and to equal treatment of the relevant actors.

Rather, what is properly meant by the 'lack of politics' both in dealing with fragmentation and in constitutionalization is the lack of an international political process that would be *democratic* in a much stronger sense than it is now. So the pertinent point is that global governance suffers from democratic deficits and—to some extent correspondingly—from too powerful courts.

Importantly, global constitutionalism unveils precisely those deficits by introducing the constitutional vocabulary. The constitutional paradigm also inspires and eventually facilitates the search for remedies. The remedy against a too 'legalist' and too 'judicial' process of constitutionalization is not to stop that process, but to democratize it. Overall, because constitutional law is a branch of law which is very close to politics, and because constitutionalism is (also) a political, not simply an apolitical, project (although it does suggest that there is a sphere 'above' everyday politics), the call for constitutionalization and global constitutionalism can trigger contestation and politics instead of just pre-empting it.

8 CONCLUSION

International law is in fact less fragmented than suggested by the discourse on fragmentation. Empirical findings on the scarcity of conflicts, the prevailing scheme of parallelism and reconciliation of norms from different regimes, and the migration of norms from one regime to another suggest that the problems of fragmentation have been overstated.[78] The diversification of international legal regimes should be welcomed as manifesting the political will of law entrepreneurs and the capacity of international law to address a list of very diverse global problems. The emergence of special fields within international law has been a necessary response to the complexity of global society (independently of the possibility of exploitation by states with huge resources to negotiate and manage the multiple regimes).

---

[78] See eg G Marceau, A Izguerri, and V Labonnovy, 'The WTO's Influence on Other Dispute Settlement Mechanisms: A Lighthouse in the Storm of Fragmentation' (2013) 47 *Journal of World Trade* 481–575.

Although the lack of a central law-maker has (inevitably) led to the existence of multiple legal regimes with overlapping but not identical memberships, whose main objectives often stand in tension, the law-appliers (both treaty bodies and court) are careful not to contradict each other. The actual instances of completely irreconcilable norms and case law or of divergent interpretations of cross-cutting norms by different courts and tribunals have been exceedingly rare.[79] This is due, last but not least, to the harmonizing approaches and techniques of international courts which have been careful not to contradict themselves (at the price of being extremely parsimonious). Several judges have portrayed the so-called fragmentation of the international judiciary in a positive light.[80] For example, ICJ Judge Greenwood declared in a recent case:

International law is not a series of fragmented specialist and self-contained bodies of law, each of which functions in isolation from the others; it is a single, unified system of law and each international court can, and should, draw on the jurisprudence of other international courts and tribunals, even though it is not bound necessarily to come to the same conclusions.[81]

The current state of international law is more appropriately described as 'ordered pluralism',[82] 'unitas multiplex',[83] or 'flexible diversity'.[84] As it is likely that the differenciation of international law will continue, the ongoing challenge for law-appliers and observers will be to refine principles, procedures, and institutions for coordinating, harmonizing, and integrating various international regimes.

Descriptively, the constitutional perspective usefully complements the fragmentation debate. It can well explain the international order as it stands *exactly because* of the international legal order's fragmented character:

[T]he time may have come when the concept of a constitution should be put at the forefront again, not because there was no constitution before—in fact...there has always been a constitution in international law—but because this concept is now more useful than ever in understanding and describing international law as it is today, that is a legal order which

---

[79] One example is the notion of 'control' in art 8 of the International Law Commission's Articles on State Responsibility: compare *Prosecutor v Tadić* (Judgment) (ICTY, Appeals Chamber, Case No IT-94-1-A, 15 July 1999) at [117] and *Application of the Convention on the Prevention and Punishment of the Crime of Genocide (Bosnia and Herzegovina v Serbia and Montenegro)* (Judgment) [2007] ICJ Rep 43, at [406].

[80] R Higgins, 'A Babel of Judicial Voices? Ruminations from the Bench' (2006) 55 *International and Comparative Law Quarterly* 791–804; B Simma, 'Fragmentation in a Positive Light' (2004) 25 *Michigan Journal of International Law* 845–7.

[81] *Ahmadou Sadio Diallo (Republic of Guinea v Democratic Republic of the Congo)* (Compensation Owed by the Democratic Republic of the Congo to the Republic of Guinea) (ICJ, 19 June 2012) at [8] (Declaration of Judge Greenwood).

[82] M Delmas-Marty, *Le pluralisme ordonné* (Seuil Paris 2006).

[83] *The Concept of Unity in International Law* (n 6) 191.

[84] R Hofmann, 'Concluding Remarks' in A Zimmermann and R Hofmann (eds), *Unity and Diversity in International Law* (Duncker and Humblot Berlin 2006) 491–4, at 491.

has become more complex, *fragmented*, and difficult to conceptualize with such elementary concepts such as sovereignty and consent.[85]

Put differently, global constitutionalism is a useful analytic lens for understanding how international law evolves and works, as long as it is understood as 'thin' (contending itself with procedures as opposed to substance), and multilevel (necessarily involving domestic constitutional law). Even if a global constitutionalism of this type stays (partly) outside the picture of international law proper, it will always be reproduced in the fragments of the international legal order.

Normatively, constitutionalism, just like other 'defragmentation' proposals, offers procedures and mechanisms to coordinate the working of specialized international legal bodies and to reconcile diverging rationales of the special branches of international law. It also offers some direction for resolving normative conflicts. However, traditional mechanisms of ordering (such as hierarchy) have been largely replaced by new mechanisms of stabilization. The quest for constitutionalization is, from that perspective, a call for improving the strategies of coordination of different legal fields and levels of law, for refining the techniques for the avoidance of conflict, and for designing clever mechanisms for resolving the unavoidable ones, in the absence of a clear normative hierarchy. In terms of a constitutional mindset, the relevant actors must be (at a minimum) willing 'to justify interpretations of regional, global, or relevant domestic law in general rather than parochial terms',[86] or to internalize specific outside perspectives. The constitutionalist paradigm also furnishes a yardstick for assessing the effectiveness and legitimacy of those mechanisms.

However, constitutionalism is currently in crisis, and the process of constitutionalization may be stagnating or retrogressing. That crisis affects both international and domestic constitutions. But far from rendering obsolete the discourse on global constitutionalism, the current constellation underscores its necessity. Importantly, the growing global welfare gap and the financial and economic crisis underscores the need for supplementing global constitutional law with more social, welfarist, or solidarity elements.

Fragmentation and constitutionalization debates can be viewed as two sides of the same coin. They have grown out of an overall concern for the legitimacy of the international legal system and its institutions, once the belief in state sovereignty as the necessary and sufficient basic principle had been lost. The constitutionalist approach seeks to regain that legitimacy by shifting the *Letztbegründung* from state sovereignty to human self-determination (rights, welfare, and democracy), by identifying and criticizing constitutional deficits of the international

---

[85] O de Frouville, 'On the Theory of International Constitution' in D Alland et al., (eds), *Unity and Diversity of International Law: Essays in Honour of Professor Pierre-Marie Dupuy* (Martinus Nijhoff Leiden 2014) 77–103, at 79 (emphasis added).

[86] *Globalization and Sovereignty* (n 59) 73.

order, and finally by reformulating constitutionalist principles and helping to implement them. From the other side, the fragmentation debate, notably in its second phase, has sought to tackle legitimacy deficits arising from internal contradictions and norm conflicts by suggesting coordinating devices. Overall, both debates turn around international law's legitimacy—in the sense of an external standard of propriety and fairness—while there are a broad range of views about the content of that standard, ranging from internal consistency (most clearly highlighted in the fragmentation debate) to democratic principles (often analysed in the constitutionalization debate).

The most important contribution of global constitutionalism (and of the fragmentation debate) is not to glosso ver, deny, or de-politicize conflicts over values, principles, and priorities among international actors and participants in the global legal discourse, or to impose certain legal concepts in a hegemonic fashion. Instead, global constitutionalism has precisely pinpointed the politics that are at stake. The lens of global constitutionalism, if conceived as a genuinely pluralist framework, allows us to accept and re-assess fragmentation as a positive condition which manifests and facilitates the realization of the constitutional values of critique and contestation.

INDEX

....